TEXT-BOOK

OF THE

HISTORY OF DOCTRINES

BY

REINHOLD SEEBERG

TRANSLATED BY

CHARLES E. HAY

COMPLETE IN TWO VOLUMES

VOL. I

HISTORY OF DOCTRINES IN THE ANCIENT CHURCH

BAKER BOOK HOUSE

Grand Rapids, Michigan

Paperback edition issued
September 1977

ISBN: 0-8010-8106-8

Library of Congress Catalog Card Number: 56-7584

PHOTOLITHOPRINTED BY CUSHING - MALLOY, INC.
ANN ARBOR, MICHIGAN, UNITED STATES OF AMERICA
1977

TRANSLATOR'S PREFACE.

THE appearance of the present work is in response to the expressed desire of the teachers of Dogmatic Theology in a number of institutions in various portions of the Church.

In a department which at so many points vitally affects the conceptions of fundamental truth, and which has to do with the entire historical development lying back of the Protestant Reformation, as well as with the formulations of doctrine then made, which have proved regulative in the sphere of dogmatics to the present day, it is imperative that our students of theology should enjoy the benefit of the very best modern scholarship, and that they should be led through the maze of conflicting views under the guidance of one who, while impartial as a historian, yet recognizes the validity of our ecclesiastical inheritance as embodying and expressing the essential results of both ancient and modern religious thought.

The "Lehrbuch" of Dr. Seeberg has since its appearance been constantly used as a book of reference in our theological seminaries. The unchallenged pre-eminence of the author in this his chosen field, the conservatism of his views, so well reflecting the spirit of our churches in America, and the condensation and lucidity of his style combine to commend his work as the most suitable for the purpose above indicated.

It is confidently expected that the Text-book will find a circulation far beyond the limits of the class-room. To the busy, working pastor it will prove a welcome companion as with ripened powers he reviews from time to time the field of his early studies, enabling also the intelligent layman to scan the field of ancient religious thought through the field-glass of a living historian of his own church.

The unusually full treatment of the doctrinal history of the Reformation will be found peculiarly helpful, displaying the lines of continuity connecting the theology of the Reformers with the central truths of the original Christian revelation, and indicating, at the same time, the sufficiency of the principles then enunciated to direct the religious activities of the present age.

It has been thought best, in order to facilitate the use of the work in wider circles, to translate the large number of citations

(iii)

from the Greek and Latin, but the pivotal words are in such cases also presented in the original form. The translation of citations has been made as literal as possible, sacrificing elegance of English idiom to exactness in reproducing the originals.

I desire gratefully to acknowledge the courtesy of the distinguished author in so cheerfully furnishing the large amount of valuable new material for this edition, thus anticipating future editions of the original.

CHARLES E. HAY.

AUTHOR'S PREFACE TO ENGLISH EDITION.

THE extracts from the prefaces to the German edition, appearing upon the succeeding pages, give a sufficient indication of the character of the present work. I have not endeavored to present to the reader historical constructions of doctrine, but I have sought to display the actual course of doctrinal development as objectively as possible and in strict harmony with the sources. The prevalent and controlling view-points have, however, in each case been kept steadily in mind and prominently indicated.

I have carefully revised the present English edition, amending and enlarging it at many points. This is true especially of the first volume, which has in various parts been very largely rewritten. I felt it to be particularly fitting to introduce a brief historical sketch of the development of the New Testament doctrine.

May the work in this English edition, by the blessing of God, prove a service to the church and to ecclesiastical science among my brethren in the faith in the distant West.

R. SEEBERG.

FROM AUTHOR'S PREFACES TO GERMAN EDITION.

PREFACE VOL. I., 1895, PP. 5, 6.

THE work whose first volume is herewith presented to the theological public claims to be but a text-book, and I have been at special pains to adapt it in all parts to the requirements of academic study. I have endeavored to condense the material as far as possible without allowing it to become obscure or unintelligible. I have, therefore, commonly contented myself with literal quotation of the original sources, and it is my hope that the most important passages from them will be found here collected. Historic and dogmatic criticisms are merely suggested. In my lectures upon the History of Doctrines I am accustomed to lay stress upon the ecclesiastico-historical setting of doctrinal development and to accompany its presentation with the appropriate biblico-dogmatic criticism. But in this work, with the exception of a few brief hints, I have refrained from such attempts. Many comments of this kind which I had at first included were stricken out in the last revision of the manuscript, in order that the work, which has nevertheless, despite the compact printing, somewhat exceeded the dimensions originally contemplated, might not become too large for its designed use. Such discussions, moreover, are not, strictly speaking, in place in a work of the present character. Perhaps an opportunity may be elsewhere found to offer some "Comments upon the History of Doctrines." That I do not entirely agree with Baur and Harnack, nor with Kliefoth-Thomasius, will be evident from occasional hints in the following pages. As the work owes its existence to my desire to secure relief from the burdensome task of dictation in the delivery of my lectures, it takes for granted that students, at least, will in the use of it have the assistance of academic lectures. But it is my further hope that, even for advanced theologians, the earnest study of the material here furnished may bring vividly before the mind the wealth of questions and problems embraced within the range of the formula, "Faith and Doctrine." It cannot be sufficiently emphasized in our day that a real answering of these questions and an inward emancipation from these problems can never be attained without thorough-going studies in dogmatic history. The revelations and "evidences" of that theological Dilettanteism, which selects the sphere of dogmatics as the field for its antics, must come to naught despite the favor or disfavor of parties. The History of Doctrines demands a hearing and requires an intelligent understanding.

The general plan and arrangement of the present work have been fixed in my mind since the preparation of my lectures upon the History of Doctrines in the year 1885-1886. That it is based upon a study of the original sources will be sufficiently evident to the reader. I would not fail to acknowledge with gratitude the frequent suggestions and enlarged fund of information which I have derived from the newer works upon the History of Doctrines, especially from Baur, Thomasius and Harnack, as also from the many faithfully executed Patristic monographs of the last decennia.

PREFACE VOL. II., 1898, PP. 3, 4.

It is manifest that the acquaintance of any single individual with the immense historical material embraced within the scope of the present volume must be far from exhaustive, especially since there is a great lack of preparatory monographs, such as exist in abundance for the earlier periods in the History of Doctrines. It may be readily understood also that the historian, in seeking to delineate the course of development, should endeavor, so far as his time and strength may permit, to fill up the existing gaps by original research. The delay in the appearance of the present volume is to be thus accounted for, as painstaking investigations were necessary in various fields, the results of which may, I trust, be recognized as constituting an enrichment of our Science. I mention, for example, the full presentation of the Scholastic theology, particularly that of the later Scholasticism, and the attempt to give to the teaching of Luther and the other Reformers its rightful place in the History of Doctrines. No one familiar with the subject can deny that it is amazing to find in the existing Histories of Doctrines very much about Anselm and Thomas, and but little, and that too often untrustworthy, about Duns Scotus and his followers—as though it were possible without a knowledge of this later development to understand the doctrinal construction in the Evangelical and Roman Catholic churches, either in its positive or in its negative aspects! It is just as clearly out of keeping with the fitness of things that we may in many Histories of Doctrines read much of Origen and the Damascene, and even of Osiander and Chemnitz, but only passing sketches of the four

great Reformers, and these marred by strong dogmatic preju-
dices.   I have here attempted to remedy this defect, although
the section upon Luther has thus grown almost to the dimensions of a small monograph, yet without exceeding the proper
limits of a History of Doctrines.

The reader will observe that the later portions of the work are
somewhat less condensed than the earlier sections.   I have thus
sought to meet the wants of the general reader as well as of the
technical student, without sacrificing the clearness and exactness
necessary in a text-book.   I have allowed myself also, as the
work advanced, somewhat more liberty in the critical estimate
of the positions reviewed.   I have not concealed my own doctrinal views, but have nowhere given prominence to them,
seeking only to make proper comment upon the actual historical
phenomena.   If the hand of the dogmatic theologian is more
evident in this than in the former volume, it is to be attributed
in part to the nature of the material under review.

R. SEEBERG.

CONTENTS.

GENERAL INTRODUCTION.

DEFINITION, OFFICE, AND METHODS OF THE HISTORY OF DOCTRINES.

HISTORICAL INTRODUCTION.

BOOK I.

DEVELOPMENT OF DOCTRINE IN THE ANCIENT CHURCH.

PART I.

CONCEPTION OF CHRISTIANITY IN THE POST-APOSTOLIC AND PRIMITIVE CATHOLIC AGES.

CHAPTER I.

THE CONCEPTION OF CHRISTIANITY IN THE POST-APOSTOLIC AGE.

(ix)

CHAPTER II.

PERVERSIONS OF THE GOSPEL AND REFORMATORY MOVEMENTS DIRECTED AGAINST CATHOLIC CHRISTIANITY.

CHAPTER III.

BEGINNINGS OF THE CHURCH'S THEOLOGY.

CHAPTER IV.

SEPARATE DOCTRINES AND GENERAL CONCEPTION OF CHRISTIANITY IN THE
THIRD CENTURY.

PART II.

DOCTRINAL CONSTRUCTION IN THE ANCIENT CHURCH.

CHAPTER I.

THE DOCTRINE OF THE TRINITY.

CHAPTER II.

DOCTRINE OF ONE PERSON AND TWO NATURES IN CHRIST.

CHAPTER III.

General Conception of Christianity. Completion of Doctrinal Construction on Greek Territory.

CHAPTER V.

AUGUSTINIANISM AS THE DOCTRINE OF THE CHURCH. COMPLETION OF
DOCTRINAL DEVELOPMENT IN THE ANCIENT CHURCH OF THE WEST.

2

GENERAL INTRODUCTION.

DEFINITION, OFFICE, AND METHODS OF THE HISTORY OF DOCTRINES.

§ 1 . *Definition and Office of the History of Doctrines.*

KLIEFOTH, Eine Einleitung in die Dogmengeschichte, 1839. R. SEE-BERG, Ein Gang durch die Dogmengeschichte, Neue kirchl. Zeitschr., 1890, 761 ff. G. KRÜGER, Was heisst u. zu welchem Ende studirt man Dogmengeschichte? 1895. STANGE, Das Dogma u. seine Beurteilung, 1898.

1. The theological term, Dogma,[1] designates either an ecclesiastical doctrine, or the entire structure of such doctrines, *i. e.*, the doctrinal system of the church. As Dogma is the formal expression of the truth held by the church at large, or by a particular church, the church expects the acknowledgment of it by her members, and, as legally organized, demands this of her recognized teachers. We apply the term, Dogma, not to every kind of theological propositions or formulas in which the general consciousness of the church may find utterance, but only to such propositions as have attained an ecclesiastical character, *i. e.*, such as have by a public declaration of the church at large, or some particular branch of it, been acknowledged as expressing Christian truth. Although the form of Dogma is the work of theology, its content is derived from the common faith of the Christian church.

2. Dogma is an exceedingly complicated historical structure. It has in its various constituent parts, constructed as they have been in the face of multifarious forms of opposition, and under the inspiration of many practical (ethical and devotional) impulses and external (political and canonical) occasions, received the impress of different theological tendencies. Thus dogmas have been "deepened," or "disintegrated" and super-

---

[1] Δόγμα is in ordinary Greek "commandment, precept" (Lk. 2. 1. Acts 17. 7; 16. 4. Eph. 2. 15. Col. 2. 14. Didache, ii. 3). The word is employed both in a political and in a philosophical sense. The theological conception accords most fully with the philosophical use of the term, as equivalent to "proposition, principle," *e. g.*, Cicero, Quaest. acad., iv. 9. Marc. Aurel., ii. 3. Ep. Barn., I. 6; x. 9. Ignat. ad Magnes, 13. 1. See fuller discussion in Münscher, DG., p. 1, and Hagenbach, DG., p 1 f.

ficialized—logically developed, or, under the influence of advancing views, transformed, restored, and again newly interpreted. To delineate these historical processes is the office of the History of Doctrines—to show how the Dogma as a whole and the separate dogmas have arisen and through what course of development they have been brought to the form and interpretation prevailing in the churches of any given period.

3. It is a historical fact, that the church gives her faith a fixed form in Dogma. The continuity of her development and the necessity of unity and purity in the proclamation of her message, as well as in her decisions upon questions of morality, afford a sufficient explanation of this fact. But, theologically considered, the fallibility of Dogma must, at least upon Protestant territory, be acknowledged as an axiom. The Scriptures and the religious faith of the church are the criteria by which Dogma must submit to be judged. But to prove the harmony or disharmony of Dogma with these courts of appeal is not the office of the History of Doctrines, but rather that of Dogmatics and Practical Theology.[1] The History of Doctrines can only be required to present the arguments which have been adduced by the original advocates of any given dogma. History is not historical criticism.

The necessity for a strict observance of the historical character of our Science excludes, first of all, the Roman Catholic view, that the Dogma of the church is as such infallible—a view which is proven to be without historical foundation by the mere fact of the conflicting dogmas of the various particular churches. There is no divine Dogma, just as there is no divine church discipline nor divine liturgy. And just as little can the History of Doctrines be influenced by a desire to establish the Dogma of the Confession to which the historian himself adheres. This might practically be a very desirable achievement, but theoretically it is an invasion of the proper sphere of dogmatic theology.[2] But it is, on the other hand, just as serious an offense against the strictly historical character of the History of Doctrines to represent the Dogma of the church as necessarily tinctured with error, either because it originated in ancient, unilluminated periods (Rationalism), or because it marks only a stage of transition to the spirit of modern times (Baur), or because it presents Christianity as apprehended by antiquity, *i. e.*, a

---

[1] This question has a place in the discussions of Homiletics, Catechetics, and Liturgics, as well as in (practical) Apologetics.

[2] *E. g.*, KLIEFOTH. Compare Thomasius, DG. Wolff, Die Entwicklung der christlichen Kirche durch Athanasius, Augustine, Luther, 1889. (See Theol. Litt.-bl., 1890, col. 156 ff.)

secularized or Hellenistic form of Christianity (Harnack). It is, of course, to be freely acknowledged, that the dogmas of the church have attained their present form through the use of the intellectual apparatus of the times in which they originated.[1] This circumstance suggests the possibility of perversion or adulteration of the content by means of the scientific form. The statement of the principles of the religious life of Christianity in the form of dogmas is accompanied also by the danger that the religious formula may assume the place of religion itself, or that faith may cease to be understood as obedience to God and trust (*fiducia*) in him, and become instead the mere acknowledgment of a doctrine concerning God (*assensus*). It cannot be denied that the History of Doctrines furnishes an abundance of examples of both these forms of error. But this acknowledgment does not by any means condemn the Dogma of the church as unchristian. It merely warns us to discriminate clearly between the substance of doctrine and its form—between that which the framers of the Dogma have sought to express and the form adopted for the expression of their thought. Upon this principle, it may be possible for one to recognize the Christian and Biblical character of the ideas maintained by the Councils of Nice and Chalcedon (and these form the chief subjects of dispute), while unable to approve all the terminology employed by them. At the same time, it must be constantly kept in mind, that the sense and content of a dogma are to be historically understood in the first instance as in contrast with some particular doctrinal view. Agreement with a dogma does not by any means indicate the acknowledgment of the technical and theoretical method of its presentation, but extends only to a similar rejection of the opposite position excluded by the dogma and to a sharing of the religious tendency which demands such exclusion.[2]

Nor is it to be forgotten, finally, that Dogma is perpetually subject to ecclesiastical and theological interpretation, which prepares the forms suitable to each age, which can and does express the ancient content in these new forms, and which furthermore seizes upon and preserves the religious experiences peculiar to its own age in the harmony of the ancient faith.[3]

---

[1] There is yet much to be done in the investigation of this terminology (a field upon which the general History of Doctrines cannot enter). Efforts in this direction have not seldom been marred by a too pronounced dogmatic bias.

[2] See fuller discussion of this principle in SEEBERG, Die Grundwahrheiten der christl. Religion, ed. 3, 1903, p. 60 ff.

[3] This is in some sense true of the valuable thoughts of nearly all the leading theologians of the last century, *e. g.*, Schleiermacher, Ritschl, Hofmann, Frank.

The History of Doctrines is therefore a department of Historical Theology, and its office is the historical presentation of the
origin and development of the dogmas which have been formulated up to the present time, and of the ecclesiastical Dogma in
its relation to the various doctrinal systems.

§ 2. *Method and Divisions of the History of Doctrines.*

1. The History of Doctrines, being a historical science, must
employ the strictly historical method.[1] What really occurred,
and how it came to pass, must be impartially related upon the
basis of original sources critically examined.[2] This requirement
is not met by the simple arraying of facts side by side—which is
not history at all—but by tracing the effective forces in their
origin and influence, as well as the interpenetration and co-
operation of the various forces. Only thus is it possible to
set forth truthfully *how it really was.* In doing this, we must
presume upon a general knowledge of the history of religion, of
the church, and of philosophy, as well as some practice and facility
in the sphere of historical criticism and objectivity. Every age,
furthermore, will preserve its own version of the History of
Doctrines, since our conception of the past is always conditioned
by the views, problems, and questions of the present age.

2. We thus at once exclude the formerly accepted division of
the science into the General and Special History of Doctrines,
as well as the subdivision of the latter (as in Baur and Hagenbach) according to the arrangement of topics in the systematic
theology of the day; for it is evident that this method of
treating the subject is not historical. Believers have not in the
various periods of history revised in turn all the separate topics
of theology, but they have in each case fixed their attention
upon some special vitalizing, fundamental thought, or some
peculiar point of view, and in this one great principle, or revolv-

[1] Warning cannot be too earnestly sounded in the interest of historical truth,
which must ever be one with Christian truth, against polemic, ecclesiastico-
political and dogmatic Dilettanteism in the History of Doctrines.

[2] The original sources of the History of Doctrines are, besides the respective resolutions, decrees, bulls, and confessions, the records of the transactions
of the bodies by which these were promulgated ; also the writings of the
theologians who participated positively or negatively, directly or indirectly, in
the origination of the respective doctrinal systems. Documents attesting the
faith of the church, such as sermons, hymns, and liturgies, and the literature
of church discipline must also be studied. The relation of the History of
Doctrines to the history of theology will always be a shifting one. The History
of Doctrines may be described as a branch of the history of theology, but must
nevertheless, on account of its great importance, be treated independently and
more exhaustively ; and it *can* be thus treated because its special material is
subdivided and held in cohesion by an organizing principle peculiar to itself.

ing around it as a centre, they have seen the whole sum and substance of Christianity, thus attaining new conceptions of the truth and deepening or transforming earlier conceptions. The historical presentation of the results must adapt itself to the course of this development. Along with the " central dogma " of every age there comes to view, not indeed a peripheral system of doctrine (Thomasius), but a general conception of Christianity dependent upon and involved in the central, dominating thought.

3. It would seem proper to begin the History of Doctrines with the adoption of the first Dogma, in the strict sense of the term, *i. e.*, that of the Council of Nice. Since, however, the Nicene, as well as the later formulation of doctrinal statements, rests upon the ideas and views of the Primitive Catholic age, the History of Doctrines must begin with the Post-Apostolic period. It closes with the last Dogmas which the churches have produced, *i. e.*, with the Second Council of Nice (787), the Vatican Council (1870), the Formula of Concord (1580), and the Synod of Dort (1619).[1] That these formal statements all have the character of Dogmas, or complete doctrinal systems, cannot be denied. It follows that, while it is not justifiable, with Thomasius, to make the Lutheran confession the goal, it must be a thorough perversion of historic verity to represent the History of Doctrines as closed before the Reformation, referring the later material to the sphere of Symbolics, or to close it with a portrayal of Romanism, Socinianism, and a general characterization of the Christianity of Luther—the last method being based upon the ground "that the entirely conservative attitude of the Reformation toward the ancient Dogma belongs not to the Foundation but to History ! " (HARNACK, DG., iii. 584). But we cannot recognize this fine distinction as valid,[2] in view of the clear facts in the case. Socinianism does not belong to the History of Doctrines at all, but to the history of theology (as the product of Nominalism). The view above taken of the limits of the period properly included within the range of the History of Doctrines may therefore be regarded as final. It is self-evident that it cannot be made to cover all

---

[1] So Hauck (Schmid, DG., ed. 4) ; Seeberg (Thomas. ii., ed. 2); Loofs.

[2] Ib. p. 585. " To present in detail a narration of historical events until the time of the Formula of Concord and the Decrees of Dort and then suddenly to drop the subject, I consider a serious error, inasmuch as countenance is thereby given to the prejudiced opinion that the dogmatic structures framed by the churches of the Reformation in the sixteenth century constituted the classical completion of the movement, whereas they can only be regarded as points of transition." Such an argument in a historical work must fill the unprejudiced reader with amazement.

the ecclesiastical and theological developments up to the present
time (*e. g.*, Baur, Hagenbach), since these movements have not
yet produced any dogmas, or authorized doctrinal statements.   On
the contrary, it has recently been demanded (see esp. G. KRÜGER,
in loco) that the distinction between the History of Doctrines
and the history of theology be entirely abandoned, since it is
based upon the Catholic estimate of the dogmas of the church, with
which Harnack and myself are supposed to treacherously sym-
pathize.   But, apart from purely practical considerations based
upon convenience in the study of the subject, it must be acknowledged that the products in the history of theology have not to
the same extent attained practical ecclesiastical significance.   If
Dogma is a tangible historical reality, it may very appropriately
be also historically depicted.   Catholic claims of infallibility
have nothing to do with the matter.

We note Three Chief Periods in the History of Doctrines
parallel with those of Church History :

1. *The Construction of Doctrine in the Ancient Church.*

In the study of this period we shall need to (*a*) Lay a secure
foundation by tracing the theological and ecclesiastical development of doctrine in the Post-Apostolic and Primitive Catholic
age.   (*b*) Describe the origination of the separate dogmas upon
the territory of Greek Christianity (Trinity, Christ, Images), in
connection with the prevalent type of piety, incidentally noting
the parallel lines of doctrinal opinion developing in the Eastern
Church.   (*c*) Depict the formulation of the doctrinal system
upon the territory of the Western Church (Augustine : Sin,
Grace, the Church).

2. *The Preservation, Transformation, and Development of
Doctrine in the Church of the Middle Ages.*

(*a*) Beginning with the emasculated Augustinianism of
Gregory the Great, we shall have occasion to describe the external conservation of Dogma until the eleventh century (with
the conquest of various concurrent misunderstandings), and
then (*b*) the abnormal refinement of Dogma by Scholasticism,
together with the genuine developments (Theology, the Atonement, the Sacraments, the Church) and the perversions (the
dissolution of Augustinianism, Hierarchism) of the doctrinal
system which fall within this period.

3. *The Development of the Doctrinal System through the Reformation, and the Opposing Crystallization of Doctrine by Roman
Catholicism.*

We shall here have to treat of (*a*) The reformatory ideas of Luther and Zwingle and the fixation of the same in symbolical form.
(*b*) The development of these reformatory ideas, together with

the doctrinal controversies, etc., up to the Formula of Concord and the Synod of Dort. (*c*) The conservation of the Doctrine of the Middle Ages by the Romish church (Trent, Jansenistic controversies, etc., Curialism, Episcopalism, the Vatican).

§ 3. *Literature of the History of Doctrines.*

S. BAUR, Lehrb. der DG., ed. 2, p. 19 ff., and Epochen der Kirchl. Geschichtsschreibung. HARNACK, DG., i. 23 ff. HAGENBACH, DG., p. 20 ff.

Neither the polemical works of the ancient church (Irenæus, Tertullian, Epiphanius, Philaster, Theodoret, etc.), nor Abelards' Sic et Non, Chemnitz' Examen Conc. Trid., nor Joh. Gerhard's Confessio Catholica (comp. Luther's Von den Concilien und Kirchen—a repetition of proofs drawn from the History of Doctrines [Weim. ed., vol. ii.], Melanchthon's tract, De eccl. et de autoritate verbi divini, C. R. xxiii.; also, the discourse upon bulls and the periods of church history, C. R. xi. 786), can be regarded as works upon the History of Doctrines. The first genuine attempt in this direction was made by the Jesuit, DIONYSIUS PETAVIUS : " De theologicis dogmatibus," 4 vols., Paris, 1644 ff. Before him may be mentioned CANUS, De locis theologicis, ll. 12. Salamanca, 1563. Beginnings were further made from different points of view by GOTTFRIED ARNOLD, Unparteiische Kirchen- u. Ketzer-historie ; J. W. ZIEROLD, Einleitung zur gründlichen Kirchenhistoria, Leipzig u. Stargardt, 1700, and Gründliche Kirchenhistoria von der wahren und falschen Theologie, Frankf. a. M., 1703 ; LAURENZ v. MOSHEIM (Dissert. ad hist. eccl. pertinent., 2 vols., 1731 ff.; De rebus christ. ante Const., 1753) ; CHARLES W. F. WALCH (Hist. der Ketzereien, etc., 11 vols., 1762 ff.; Gedanken von der Geschichte der Glaubenslehre, 1756), as also SEMLER (Einleitung zu Baumgartens Glaubenslehre und zu desselben Unters. theol. Streitigkeiten, 1762 ff.); comp. also PLANCK, Gesch. des prot. Lehrbegriffes, 6 parts, 1787 ff. All these attempts served to improve the traditional idea of doctrinal history, but in all of them there was lacking a generalized historical conception, and they did not get beyond monographical sketches and the gathering of materials. According to Semler, the causes for the constant modification of opinions are " of a purely subjective and accidental character, because one chooses to think this way, another that ; because the relations of things are now thus, now otherwise." It was from this point of view that the

first delineations in the sphere of our Science were undertaken.
It was then already quite generally recognized that the Christi-
anity of the church was permeated with Platonic ideas (Logos,
Trinity, etc.). To this result contributed in no small degree the
book of SOUVERAIN, Le platonisme devoilé (1700, translated by
Löffler, 1782). Historians as well as dogmaticians were influenced
by this thought (cf. the 17th book of HERDER, Ideen zu einer
Geschichte der Menschheit). We cite the separate works upon the
History of Doctrines. LANGE, Ausführliche Gesch. d. Dogmen,
1796. MÜNSCHER, Handb. d. christl. DG., 4 vols., 1797 ff. (the
first 6 Jahrbb.), and Lehrbuch d. DG., ed. 1, 1811; ed. 3, 1832 ff.
(excellent quotations from the sources). Comp. also AUGUSTI
(1805), BERTHOLDT (1822 f.), BAUMGARTEN-CRUSIUS (1832),
F. K. MEIER (1840; ed. 2, 1854), C. H. LENTZ (i. 1834), J.
G. V. ENGELHARDT (1839), et al.

The suggestive works of A. NEANDER and F. CHR. BAUR
marked an epoch in our Science. Both have incorporated in
their treatment the results of the great intellectual activity since
the end of the eighteenth century. The one possessed the
marks of personality; the other applied Hegel's conception of
development. The former's History of Doctrines was edited by
Jacobi (1857). Similar is Hagenbach, DG. (1850, ed. 6,
revised by BEURATH). Hegel's suggestions were soon followed
by MARHEINEKE (DG., edited by Matthies and Vatke, 1849),
then by BAUR, who handled the appalling mass of material in a
thorough and independent fashion, and presented it in the form
of a development (modified, however, by speculative considerations. See Lehrb. d. DG., 1847, ed. 3, 1867, and
especially Vorlesungen über. d. chr. DG., ed. F. Baur, 3
parts, 1895 ff. Also the large monographs: Lehre von d. Versöhnung, 1838, and Lehre von d. Dreieinigk. u. Menschwerdung, 3 parts, 1841 ff.). The labors of Baur were both positively and negatively of the greatest importance in the development of the History of Doctrines. TH. KLIEFOTH wrote his
Einleitung in d. DG. (1839) from the standpoint of revived
Lutheranism, and G. THOMASIUS furnished a careful presentation of the subject, prepared with methodical skill and a fine
perception of religious problems: Die chr. DG., als Entwicklungsgesch. d. kirchl. Lehrbegriffs, 2 vols., 1874, 1876
(Plitt edited vol. ii.); vol. i., ed. 2, published by BON-
WETSCH with many additions, 1886; vol. ii. revised by Seeberg, materially enlarged and extended in scope by including
the Reformed and Roman Catholic DG., 1889. Compare
with these, SCHMID, Lehrb. d. DG., 1860; ed. 4, revised
by HAUCK (an excellent collection of quotations from the

sources); also KAHNIS, Die luth. Dogmatik. (vol. ii., Der
Kirchenglaube, 1864). F. NITZSCH has in his Grundriss der
chr. DG., vol. i., 1870, given us a comprehensive and
careful exhibition of the material, attempting also a new arrangement of it. Finally, we mention A. HARNACK, Lehrb. d.
DG., 3 vols., 1886 ff., ed. 3, 1894, with which compare his
Grundriss der DG., ed. 2, 1893, and LOOFS, Leitfaden z.
Studium d. DG., 1889, ed. 3, 1894. In his great work
distinguished by richness of material (especially in vols. i. and
ii.), wide variety in the points of view, and vivacity in narration, Harnack attempts to present the History of Doctrines
in the light of the theory, that the process of their development
consisted in a Hellenizing of the Gospel, following the impulses
of RITSCHL'S work against Baur: Entstehung d. altkath.
Kirche, ed. 2, 1857, and of M. V. ENGELHARDT, in his Christentum Justins des Märtyrers, 1878. With this the History of
Doctrines turned back to an idea of the era of Illumination. The
criterion appeared to have been at the same time discovered for
the criticism of dogma—again in the line of the Illumination
theology. A Hellenizing influence upon dogma *was* a historical
necessity, but it furnishes at the same time the ground upon which
the church of the present is compelled to surrender the ancient
Dogma.

Finally, we have a long list of such monographs, undertaking to follow particular conceptions through the whole
course of history, but throwing light upon the ideas of entire
periods. In addition to the writings of BAUR already referred to,
we mention especially : F. A. DORNER, Entwicklungsgesch.
d. Lehre v. d. Person Christi, 3 parts, ed. 2, 1851 ff. A.
RITSCHL, Die Lehre v. d. Rechtfertig. und Versöhnung, vol. i.,
ed. 2, 1882. H. REUTER, Augustin. Studien, 1887 ; Gesch. d.
Aufklärung im MA., 2 vols., 1875 ff. R. SEEBERG, Die Theologie des Duns Scotus. KÖSTLIN, Luther's Theol., 2 vols., ed. 2,
1901. TH. HARNACK, Luth. Theol., 2 vols., 1862, 1866. G.
PLITT, Einleitung in die Augustana, 2 vols., 1867 f. F. FRANK,
Die Theol. der Conc. Form, 4 parts, 1858 ff. A. SCHWEIZER,
Centraldogmen, 2 parts, 1854, 1856. Excellent material is also
furnished in many articles in the PRE (Herzog's Real-Encyklo-
pädie für protest. Theologie und Kirche) and in the Dictionary
of Christian Biography, 4 vols., 1877 ff.

From Roman Catholic sources we mention : KLEE, Lehrb. d.
DG., 2 vols., 1837 f. SCHWANE, DG., 3 vols., 1862 ff. BACH,
Die DG. des Kath. MA. v. christolog. Standp., 2 vols., 1873 ff.
Also, the monographs of K. WERNER, Thomas v. Aq., 3 vols.,
1859, and Die Scholastik des späteren MA., 4 vols., 1881 ff.

HISTORICAL INTRODUCTION.

§ 4.   *Greek-Roman Heathenism in Its Relation to Christianity.*

Cf. CHANTEPIE DE LA SAUSSAYE, Lehrbuch der Religionsgesch., ii., ed. 2, 421 ff. CUMONT, Die Mysterien des Mithras (in German), 1903.   A. DIE-TERICH, Eine Mithrasliturgie, 1903.   FRIEDLÄNDER, Darstellungen aus der Sittengesch. Roms iii., ed. 6, 509 ff.   BOUSSIER, La religion romaine d'Auguste aux Antonins, 2 vols., 1874.   RÉVILLE, La religion à Rome sous les Sevères, 1886.   ZELLER, Die Philos. der Griechen, 3 parts, ed. 3, 1869 ff.   LUT-HARDT, Die antike Ethik, 1887.   BONHÖFER, Die Ethik Epiktets, 1894. MOMMSEN, Röm. Gesch., vol. v.   HATCH, Griechentum u. Christentum, translated by Preuschen, 1892.

But when the fullness of the time came, God sent forth his Son, born of a woman, born under the law (Gal. 4. 4 f.).   To make this declaration intelligible, and thus to secure a foundation for the History of Doctrines, is the purpose of the following paragraphs, which will present but a very rapid sketch, presuming upon the possession of the requisite biblical and historical knowledge upon the part of the reader.

We must first of all take a view of Greek-Roman Heathenism.

The religion of the period is exceedingly varied (see *e. g.*, Lucian, Deorum concil.), and it is from the time of Augustus an age of religious restoration.   Cosmopolitanism opens the door to strange gods, and these are in wonderful speculations amalgamated with indigenous ideas and forms.   Strange rites of worship, with their " wonderful tales and legends" (Strabo.; cf. Acts 14. 11 ff.), flourish.   The divinities of the Orient (Osiris, Isis, Mithras), with their strange, mysterious worship, find devotees; the mysteries of old are revived as means of salvation ($\sigma\omega\tau\eta\rho\iota\alpha$).   Above all, it was the worship of Mithras which now became rapidly diffused, so that from the end of the second century onward it met the wants of large sections and enlisted in serious conflict with Christianity.   Regeneration to a new life, or the counsel to live in heaven, became for multitudes a real religion imparted to them in many symbols and acts.   From the Orient was derived the worship of the Emperors as gods, which Augustus had already desired.   But the most ancient forms of worship are also again practiced (*" antiquity should be revered,"* Macrob. Saturn., iii. 4).   Interest in the highest problems of existence sustained the popular philosophy of Stoicism with its religious-ethical tendency among the great mass of the educated (see especially Seneca and Epictetus). God is the Spirit ($\pi\nu\epsilon\tilde{\nu}\mu\alpha$) which pervades the universe, the $\nu o\tilde{\nu}\varsigma$, $\lambda\acute{o}\gamma o\varsigma$, or world-sustaining Force ($\pi\rho\acute{o}\nu o\iota\alpha$)—hence the Stoic Determinism.   This Divinity, who was commonly conceived

with Plato as Being without attributes, but also as " Father," is
after all nothing more than Natural Law.   It is the office of the
knowledge of the truth to make men good.   He who desires to
become good must first learn to know that he is bad.   This
comes to pass through reflection, or reason, by the help of God (to
live agreeably to nature—ὁμολογουμένως τῇ φύσει ζῆν).   Man must
withdraw himself upon his inward life and die to the world, to
the state, to sense (καθῆκον and κατόρθωμα).   The world is our
state ; we are " brothers to nature."   The proper attitude is expressed in the familiar 'Ἀνέχου καὶ ἀπέχου, bear and forbear (Gel-
lius, Noctes att., xvii. 19. 5, and ff., following chiefly Epictetus).
Even the slave is free in soul.   All men are members of the
Greater Republic of this world.   Man is a sacred object to man.
All have God in themselves: " The sacred spirit has its seat
within us."   " What else is nature but God and divine reason implanted in the whole world and its parts."   With this combine :
" A happy life consists in this one thing, that reason be perfect
in us."   But between the reason (logos), or God within us,
and the flesh (caro) there is a conflict : " None of us is without
fault (culpa).   But let man do what is good."   Seneca's idea
was : " Trust thyself and make thyself happy."   To become
free from the flesh is the highest goal of man : the way of escape
stands open, and beyond it—great and eternal peace (Seneca).

In these conceptions of the philosophers, as in the great religious longings of the age, are embedded elements which prepared
the way for Christianity (the unity of God, the Logos of God
effectually working in the world, the emphasis upon the inner
man, the great longing to become God's by becoming free from
self and the world, the shattering of the ancient notions of state
and rank in the interest of a spiritual fellowship of all men).
But, freely as these conceptions were employed by the early
Christians, the difference between them and the sphere of
ancient Christian thought is no less clear (absence of the divine
Person and of personal intercourse with him, and the consequent
lack of the idea of moral guilt, resulting in the physical and
moralistic conception of morality).   The yearning after another
world is the great feature of the " fullness of time," but the means
by which this yearning might be made permanent and effectually
satisfied—this the world did not produce from within itself.
The moral life of even the better element seldom corresponded to
the lauded ideals, as history testifies.   It is, therefore, not difficult to understand the methods employed in the apologetic
writings of the ancient church (harsh combating of idolatry,
accommodation to the philosophical formulas, yet the constant
affirmation that Christians are " a new generation ").

§ 5. *Judaism.*

Comp. SCHÜRER, Gesch. des jüd. Volkes, 2 vols., 1890, 1886. WELL-
HAUSEN, Israelit. u. jüd. Gesch., 1894. WEBER, System der altsyragogalen
paläst. Theol., 1880. HILGENFELD, Die jüd. Apokalyptik, 1857. SACK,
Die altjüd. Rel. im Uebergang v. Bibeltum z. Talmudism. 1889. STAPFER,
Les idées religieuses en Palestine à l'époque de Jés. Christ, 1878. SIEGFRIED,
Philo, 1875. ZELLER, Philos. d. Griech., iii. 2. BOUSSET, Die Religion
des Judentums in neutest. Zeitalter, 1903.

1. It is only the ideas of the later Judaism which are here of
interest to us. The relation between God and man is a legal
relation. God commands, and man obeys in order thereby to
merit the reward : לְפוּם עָצְרָא אַגְרָא (Pirqe aboth 5. 23) and
הֱשֵׁבִּין וְדַע שֶׁהַכֹּל לְפִי (ib. 4. 22; cf. Tobit 4. 6; 2. 14; 12. 9;
14. 9; 13. 2). This connection of ideas explains the efficacy
attributed to the ordinances (הֲלָכָה tradition of the elders, Mk.
7.3), deduced by exegesis from (מִדְרָשׁ) the text of the Thorah and
constantly multiplied without restraint. There are so many commandments, in order that there may be great reward (Makkoth
3. 16). For this we wait in perpetual humility (עוֹלָם הַבָּא)

Hence the scrupulous observance of the specific laws (δικαιοσύνη
προσταγμάτων, Ps. Sol., 14. 1) and the insistence upon the
value of good works (fasting, prayers, alms. Tobit 2. 18 f.; cf.
Matt. 6. 16; 6. 2, 1; 5. 20. Sir., 3. 28. Ps. Sol., 3. 9. 4.
Esra 7. 7: thesaurus operum repositus apud altissimum; cf.
8. 36, and Tobit 4. 9; Weber, p. 273 ff.). This also in part
gave vitality to the Messianic hope of the nation, which looked
forward to the coming of Him who should deliver his people
from all the distress of the present time, bringing reward to the
pious and misery to the ungodly. This is the Christ of the
Lord (χριστὸς κυρίου, Ps. Sol., 18. 8, cf. 6; 17. 36), the Son of
David, the Son of Man (Par. of Enoch, *e. g.*, 46. 2; 63. 11;
69. 26; 62. 7, 14, cf. Son of a Woman, 62. 2, 3, 5; Son of a
Man, 71. 14; 65. 5; 69. 29), the Son of God (Enoch, 105. 2.
4. Esra 7. 28 f.; 13. 32; 37. 52; 14. 9). According to some,
the Messiah would come himself to bring the condition of
eternal blessedness (Sibyll., iii. 766. Ps. Sol., 17. 4. En., 62.
14 f. Jn. 12. 34). According to others, the Messiah but
prepares the way for the consummation. He was thought of as
a mighty king, who should rule Israel four hundred years and
then die (4. Esra, 7. 28, 29; cf. Apoc. Baruch, 39. 7; 40. 3);
only after this should follow the consummation of the world. He

is, therefore, a man of men (ἄνϑρωπος ἐξ ἀνϑρώπων—Trypho in Justin. Dial., 49).[1] The Messiah appears to have nothing in common with the spiritual beings who are the media of the divine presence in the world, with the angels who appear with increasing frequency, with the "great Scribe" of God, nor with the מֵיטַטְרוֹן (probably μετάϑρονος) and the מֵימְרָא (See Weber, p. 178.) But longing for the Messianic kingdom was awakened especially by the consciousness of sin, which oppresses the entire human race and from which man is absolutely unable to free himself. How can the law with its rewards bring help, if no man since Adam has fulfilled the law? Through the fall of Adam sin and guilt have come upon the human race (4. Esra; 3. 26; 4. 30; 7. 118 f.; 8. 35, 17. Apoc. Bar., 1703; 23. 4; 48. 42; 54. 15, 19. Cf. Weber, p. 216, 217). We have nothing without the Almighty and his law (Apoc. Baruch, 85. 3). Thus there is a continual advance, as well in pessimistic estimate of self and the universe, as in the vividness of the hope centering in the kingdom of the royal Messiah. We may mention also the rich development attained by cosmology, by a peculiar metaphysics (everything earthly pre-exists in heaven), and in eschatological conceptions.

2. It is of the highest importance to observe the combination formed by Judaism with Greek philosophy, in which are foreshadowed many of the developments of the earlier Christian theology. Here the chief sources are the Wisdom of Solomon and Philo; cf. also 4 Macc., the Jewish Sibylline books, and the didactic poem of Phocylides : (*a*) God is conceived (Platonically) as abstract Being, without attributes. (*b*) There accordingly yawns a great gulf between God and the ὕλη (matter). (*c*) This is bridged by the intermediate existences, angels, demons, δυνάμεις (powers), λόγοι (words), comprehended in the ἰδέα ἰδεῶν (forms of forms) or the σοφία (wisdom) or the λόγος, ὁ λόγος πρωτόγονος, δεύτερος ϑεός (word, first-born word, other God), neither ungenerated as God nor generated as are we, the

---

[1] The representation of the birth of the Messiah from the virgin is also foreign to Judaism, vid. Seeberg, Glaube und Glaube, p. 28 f., note 2. The announcement of the pre-existence of the Messiah occasionally met with is to be understood in the light of Enoch, 46. 3 : "Before the sun and the constellations were created his Name was mentioned before the Lord of spirits." The later rabbinical literature similarly describes the Name of the Messiah as pre-existent (vid. Weber, l. c., pp. 333, 339 f.), as also the Thorah is declared, being involved in the divine wisdom, to be pre-existent and the "daughter of God." (See Weber, p. 14 ff.) This is all but a part of the later Jewish metaphysics, according to which everything Judaic has its origin in heaven.

high-priest mediating between the creature (dem Gewordenen) and him who has begotten it, and representing man as his advocate, the bread from Heaven, the source of the water of knowledge. He is the instrumentality (ὄργανον) through which the world was created. But the Logos is neither conceived as a person, nor as bearing any relation to the Messiah. (*d*) The dualism of this system is seen in its anthropology, in which the body of man is regarded as a prison and the cause of evil: "From the way in which it came to birth, sinning is natural (συμφυὲς) to it." Vit. Mos. iii., 157 Mangey. (*e*) Salvation is therefore deliverance from sensuality. This is experienced through the fulfillment of the law, whose external forms must maintain their validity (de migr. Abr., i. 450 Mangey), but ultimately through enthusiastic ecstasy. (*f*) All this is deduced by allegorical interpretation, after the manner of the Haggadah, from the Old Testament. Philo presents it as authorized in the strictest sense by inspiration: "For the prophets are the interpreters, God using their organs for the proclamation of whatever things he wished (de monarch., ii. 222, and, especially, Quis div. rer. her. i. 511 Mangey; cf. also Sanday, Inspiration (Bampton Lectures), ed. 2, 1894, p. 74 ff.[1] Nägelsbach, Nachhomer. Theol., p. 173 ff. Homer. Theol., ed. 2, p. 187 ff. Pauly Realencycl., ii. 1117).

Among the Essenes also similar Hellenistic conceptions exercised a formative influence.

§ 6. *The Primitive Christian Proclamation.*

Cf. B. WEISS, Bibl. Theol., ed. 2, 1901. Die Religion des N. T., 1903. W. BEYSCHLAG, Neutest. Theologie, ed. 2, 1896. H. J. HOLZMANN, Lehrbuch der neutest. Theologie, ed. 2, 1897. HOFMANN, Bibl. Theol., ed. Volck, 1886. A. RITSCHL, Rechtf. u. Vers. ii. PFLEIDERER, Das Urchristentum, ed. 2, 1902. WEIZSÄCKER, Das ap. Zeitalter, ed. 2, 1892. NÖSGEN, Gesch. d. neutest. Offenb., 1891-93. P. WERNLE, Die Anfänge unserer Religion, 1901. H. H. WENDT, Die Lehre Jesu, ed. 2, 1901. H. CREMER, Die paulinische Rechtfertigungslehre, 1898. A. SCHLATTER, Der Glaube im N. T., ed. 2, 1895. R. SCHMIDT, Die paulinische Christologie, 1870. A. SEEBERG, Der Tod Christi in seiner Bedeutung für die Erlösung, 1895.

1. The prophecy of the Old Testament prophets culminates in the idea of the "new covenant" in Jeremiah (31. 31 ff.), and in the thought that God shall reign as king over his people and the whole world in righteousness and grace. Jesus Christ and his work constitute the realization of these ideas. He claimed for himself absolute authority. His words take a place of equal

---

[1] This Platonic theory of inspiration, which influenced Christian theology in many ways, leads us back to the Platonic conception of the inspired seer. See Phaedrus, c. 22, p. 244 a. Tim., c. 32, p. 71 e.

dignity by the side of the declarations of the law (Matt. 5. 7), and will outlast heaven and earth (Matt. 24. 25 f., 35). He announced himself as the promised Messiah. This is the meaning of the term which he applies to himself, the "Son of Man" (cf. Book of Enoch), and more than this is not in the first instance involved in his designation as the "Son of God." If the term "Son of man" describes the Messiah as of heavenly nature, origin, and goal (cf. Jn. 3. 12 f.), he is the "Son of God," as one who derives the content and motive of his inner life from God and therefore lives and works in the power of God (Matt. 11. 27; 3. 34 f.). Since now Christ as the Messiah lives, teaches, and works in God and by the power of God, he exercises divine dominion over men (Lk. 22. 29 f.; 17. 21, 23; 1. 33. Matt. 13; 12. 2, 8), and thereby establishes the blessed condition of men as a kingdom of God. Inasmuch as he exercises divine dominion, there belong to him the divine attributes of omnipotence and omniscience, the power to forgive sins—which did not according to Jewish teaching belong to the Messiah—absolute authority, power, over heaven and earth until the end of time. Although John often applies other terms, his ideas do not extend essentially beyond the synoptic representations. The conceptions of Christ as the light, the life, the truth and the way merely give fuller expression to the thought that he exercises the divine government of the world for the salvation of men.

2. Thus in Christ is the one expectation met. He rules with divine dominion for the salvation of men in the world, imparting to them life and righteousness, and gathering them into a kingdom of God. In this, one aspect of the new covenant is realized. But, according to Jeremiah, that covenant embraces a double purpose. The law is to be written by the power of the Spirit in the hearts of men, and their sins are to be forgiven. This second purpose was placed by Jesus in a peculiar relation to his death, the necessity for which he strongly emphasized ($\delta\varepsilon\tilde{\iota}$). Jesus came into the world to minister. This ministry embraces the surrender of his soul to death as a $\lambda\acute{\upsilon}\tau\rho o\nu$, so that many may be thereby delivered from death (Matt. 20. 28. Mk. 9. 35). Since now death may be regarded for us essentially as a penalty, Jesus has designated the giving of his life as a means of deliverance from the penalty of death, availing for many; or as a means of the forgiveness of sins (cf. Matt. 16. 26). The Gospel of John explains this by the illustration of a shepherd faithful unto death (Jn. 10. 11, 15, 17 f.; 12. 24 f.; 15. 13; 18. 11). His conception was, therefore, the same as that of Jesus himself, that the fidelity of Jesus even unto death and his obedi-

3

ence to the Father constitute the ground, or ransom, for the sake
of which God forgives the sins of many (Matt. 26. 28 ff.). The
declaration in 1 Cor. 11. 25 expressly represents the new
covenant established through the blood of Christ as embracing
the forgiveness of sins ; but the shedding of the blood of Christ
includes also the other aspect of the new covenant, *i. e.*,
the awakening of new life and the implanting of the law within
the heart. Each of these two cycles of thought—divine dominion and new covenant—thus of itself embraces the whole compass
of the work of Christ. He is the King, who bestows a new life
upon men ; and he does this by achieving for them, through his
death, the forgiveness of sins.

An analysis of the manifold particulars in which Jesus has
established the state of grace under his dominion, or in his
kingdom, would carry us beyond our limits. The chief categories
are as follows : (*a*) Repentance (μετάνοια), with faith, as the
consciousness of the divine authority and power of Christ (Matt.
8. 11, 13 ; 9. 2, 22 ; 15. 28. Lk. 17. 19 ; 7. 48, 50) ; as a
receiving (λαβεῖν) in relation to Christ and his gifts (Jn. 1. 16 ;
13. 20 ; 17. 18). (*b*) The following of Christ, and that which
it involves (Matt. 16. 16. Jn. 6. 68 f.; 8. 12). (*c*) The true
fulfilling of the law, or true righteousness, love (Matt. 22. 23 f.;
23. 23). (*d*) A prayerful life. According to Matt. 16. 18 ;
13. 9 ff., Jesus anticipated a historical unfolding of the kingdom
of God in the form of a congregation (ἐκκλησία). In this congregation he will be present (Matt. 28. 20. 1 Cor. 11. 24 f.;
16. 22. Matt. 26. 26 ff.). He will also take part as her Lord
in the last judgment. In the final days of his ministry he
indicated the tokens which should herald the latter (Matt. 24.
6-31). In various parables he combined the general tenor of
these prophecies. We should look for the return of him who
will soon come and summon to account, in order that the
eternal destiny of men may be determined (Matt. 24. 43 ff.;
25. 1 f., 14 ff., 31 ff.).

3. But, according to the Gospel narratives, the revelation of
Christ was NOT completed in these declarations uttered before his
death. And that which is said in the reports concerning the
words of the RISEN CHRIST we find fully confirmed in the other
New Testament writings. Everywhere we meet with the same
ideas and assertions, which are simply inexplicable in this their
absolute harmony if not derived from words of Christ himself ;
for they cannot be accounted for by anything contained in the
other sources accessible to the writers, *i. e.*, the Old Testament
and Judaism. The risen Christ, first of all, convinced his
disciples that he was really alive, and thus at the same time

awakened in them the conviction of his victory and his power over his enemies. He then instructed and exhorted them concerning his person and their mission. We unfortunately possess only very brief summarizing accounts of these instructions (Matt. 28. 18 ff. Lk. 24. 44 ff. Acts 1. 6 ff.). The task of their world-mission is revealed to the disciples. With it are combined preaching and baptism. At the same time there is imparted to them in the trinitarian formula a knowledge of the position of Christ and of the Spirit promised them in the life of the God-head. The term, "Son of God," received in consequence a new character. It no longer signifies merely, in the sense of the Old Testament usage, the man beloved and led by God, but the Son, who is in heaven with the Father, eternal and omnipresent as the Father. Thus the riddle of the person of Christ was solved for the disciples. His authority, claims, and promises during his earthly life now first attain for them their full significance and force. The Gospel of John in particular undertakes to present the human life of Christ in the light of the religious knowledge afterward attained. The last revelation of Christ serves to interpret his earlier revelations. This finds recognition when John discriminates between a state of divine glory (δόξα) belonging to the past, *i. e.*, to the pre-existence of Christ, and his present existence (Jn. 12. 16, 23; 17. 5), but in such a way that this glory is manifested in Christ's earthly life (1. 14; 2. 11; 11. 4; 17. 10, 6-9), and especially in his sufferings as the consummation of his earthly life (13. 31 f.; 17. 1). The glory of Christ is the unlimited power of divine activity. To the pre-existent Son of God (8. 58; 10. 35 f.) belongs as his peculiar nature the divine glory. This was the knowledge of Christ which the disciples received through their communion with the risen Jesus, and by which they became fitted to interpret his earthly life and actions. The immense historical significance of the Gospel of John consists in the fact, that it makes it possible for us to understand how the disciples of Jesus were enabled and compelled to associate the historical events which they witnessed with the religious experience of the eternal, omnipotent Lord: "The Word became flesh."

The Spirit, hitherto regarded, in harmony with the Old Testament conception, as a revelation of the presence of the divine power (Matt. 1. 18. Lk. 1. 35), as a creative source of religious knowledge and power (Lk. 1. 15, 41, 67; 24. 49. Acts 1. 8. Matt. 10. 19 f.; 13. 11. Jn. 3. 6; 20. 22), or of miraculous works (Matt. 12. 28, 32), is by the last declarations of Christ described as likewise a personal principle, as the ἄλλος παράκλητος, who, coming from the Father (Jn. 15. 26), sent by

Christ (16. 7), makes the revelation of Christ effectual in the disciples, and thus becomes the medium of the coming of Christ to them (14. 18 f.; 16. 12 ff.).

These were the chief features of the revelation of Jesus Christ. He exercised divine dominion, or actualized the new covenant. He thus revealed his divine nature, and he expressly based this nature upon the conception of the unity of the Father with the Son and the Spirit. He opened up to the disciples a great task, while at the same time he held out the prospect of his presence and co-operation for its accomplishment through the coming of the Spirit.

4. In accordance with the prophecy of Christ, the Spirit produced a great awakening. Wonderful words and wonderful deeds were given to those who believed on Jesus. A sphere of the miraculous (see Acts) surrounds the church. But the Spirit did not exert his power as a revolutionary principle. On the contrary, he manifested himself as the Spirit of Christ, establishing the authority of Christ as Lord in the church. But in connection with this element of stimulation there were other and stable elements which preserved the work of the Spirit from subjective exaltation and onesidedness. These were the Old Testament; the authority of the words of Jesus and of the apostles as his historical witnesses (Acts 1. 22; 3. 15; 4. 33; 5. 32; 8. 12; cf. also Matt. 16. 19); the ordinances of baptism and the Lord's Supper, established by Jesus; and, finally, a complex of traditions (παραδόσεις), embracing the ordinances just named. These traditions included a formula of belief, of which 1 Cor. 15. 3 f. has preserved a fragment easily recognizable. This formula of belief stood in a peculiar relation to the administration of baptism. It had a confessional character. There was accordingly a formulated basis of instruction for those desiring to receive the sacrament of baptism, i. e., a baptismal confession (cf. Rom. 6. 3 f. Acts 19. 2. Heb. 10. 22, 23; cf. 4. 14. Eph. 4. 5 f. 1 Pet. 3. 21 f. 1 Tim. 6. 12. 1 Jn. 2. 20). 1 Cor. 15. 3 gives an indication as to the age of this formula. It was made known to Paul already at the time of his baptism. Since in the New Testament we meet very frequently with a triadic arrangement and formulation of ideas (1 Cor. 12. 4; 6. 11. 2 Cor. 13. 13. Rom. 15. 16, 30. Eph. 2. 19-22; 5. 19; 4. 4-6; 1. 3-14. 2 Thes. 2. 13-15. Jude 20 f. 1 Pet. 1. 2; 2. 5; 4. 13 f. Heb. 10. 29-31. Jn. 14. 15-17, 26; 15. 26; 16. 13-16. Rev. 1. 4 f. With the last passage compare 1 Cor. 14. 12, 32; 12. 10. Rev. 22. 6), and since the command to baptize as given by Matthew contains the trinitarian formula, it is in the highest degree probable that the

formula of belief was arranged in a triad, *i. e.*, that it formed the basis from which at a later day our Apostles' Creed was derived. In favor of the triadic formulation is to be reckoned, first of all, the later form of the confession, and also the facts, that this confession is a baptismal confession, and that Matthew expressly combines baptism and the Trinity, as is the case also in Didache 7. 1, 3; cf. 1 Cor. 6. 11. Further, Acts 19. 2 appears to be most easily understood upon the supposition of a triadically divided baptismal formula of instruction.[1]

To this formula was then added a "tradition" concerning the Lord's Supper (1 Cor. 11. 23), which stands in connection with the custom of admitting the baptized at once to the celebration of the latter. But, besides this doctrinal material, tradition has preserved a great deal of an ethical character in the form of the enumeration of vices and virtues. Outlines of this character run through the entire New Testament and lie at the foundation of the "Two Ways" of the Didache. Compare the paradoxes of 1 Cor. 11. 2. To these two great chief elements may have been

---

[1] ALFRED SEEBERG in his important work, Der Catechismus der Urchristenheit, 1903, disputed the triadic form of this confession, as also its derivation from the tradition attested in Matt. 28. His arguments are essentially as follows: That the New Testament speaks of a baptism into the name of Christ, but never into the name of the Father and of the Spirit, which would be utterly incomprehensible if the formulation of Matthew 28. 19 had been already known to the writers. Further, that since the reception of the Spirit occurred only after baptism at the laying on of hands, a confession of the Spirit before baptism would not have been possible (7. 235 ff.). In response to this it may be said, that Matt. 28. 19 is not at all supposed to be a "formula" in the strict sense of the word, but only a summary of the last teachings of Christ parallel with the other summary in Lk. 24. 46-49, except that Matthew, in distinction from Luke, has given this summary a definite reference to baptism, recognizing that baptism in fact transports man into the sphere of the personal influence of the Father, Son, and Spirit. The apostles were taught what was involved in their commission to the whole world and in the revelation of God which was at the same time made to them. In this connection there was given to them, according to Luke, the idea of the Trinity, which Matthew has placed in a special relation to baptism. The triadic formula is thus in any case traceable to the tradition attested by both Matthew and Luke; but the particular formulation of this tradition, as Matthew has it, can scarcely have been generally known in the time of Paul. Baptism was administered commonly only into the name of Christ. It must then have been only through Matthew that the triadic formula came into general use. This does not, however, by any means exclude the view that instruction and confession during this period recognized the Father, the Son, and the Spirit (let the tradition preserved by Luke be borne in mind). If the baptized person looked forward at once to the reception of the Spirit, then must the instruction which he received and the faith which he was to confess also have had reference to the Spirit. It is my conviction that the triadic formula has its roots in the words of Jesus of which Matthew and Luke, each in his own way, have formed an epitome, and that the original basis for baptismal instruction and confession was triadically arranged.

later added instructions concerning ordination and congregational offices, as is suggested by various turns of expression in the pastoral epistles (*e. g.*, Tit. 1. 7 f.; 2. 1 ff.   1 Tim. 3. 1, 8, 10, 13, 15, 16.   2 Tim. 2. 2).   Heb. 6. 1, 2 offers a summary of these fixed elements of the instruction given by the church, which are now regarded as a " foundation ; " and the Didache, in perfect harmony with the latter, presents us a revision of the material in a later form.[1]

Thus the Spirit of Christ and certain definite forms of proclamation, or of doctrinal and moral instruction, stood from the very beginning side by side in the Christian Church. They worked together, although there were not wanting at a quite early day collisions between the two principles. Whatever heresies or disorderly elements appeared in the congregations seem to have appealed to the " Spirit."   Very early was heard the warning against " false prophets."   In opposition to them, the body of common ideas and representations in the church became constantly more fixed. Even with such a genius as Paul, the elements of the common Christianity outweigh the original elements of his own conceptions of truth.

5. This brings us to the gospel of Paul, or to the elements of a Pauline theology.   Natural endowments and talents, the culture which he had enjoyed, and the Christ whom he had been permitted to see, made this man the greatest of the apostles. The Pauline theology may be presented in the following categories : (1) Law and gospel, faith and works, atonement and justification.   (2) Spirit and flesh, the new life.   (3) The congregation of believers, or the church.   These categories have for their common basis the apostle's ideas of God and Christ. The extraordinarily vivid conception of God which distinguished Paul is concentrated in the thought that God is the omnipotent, spiritual Will.   To this Will are to be traced all events—whether it be the choice of the apostles and their mission, transformations in the religious and moral life, or the ordinary occurrences of daily life.   It is God who works in us to will and to do (Phil. 2. 13).   As everything comes to pass " according to the counsel of his will " (Eph. 1. 11), so revelation is a

---

[1] In a certain sense our Gospels might be also included in this category. If the Gospel of Mark, according to ancient tradition and reports, originated with Peter, and if Luke set himself the task of giving to Theophilus an orderly account of the things which he had been taught, the conclusion can scarcely be avoided that the synoptic Gospels have their common basis in collections of material which had been gradually formed in the missionary preaching of the apostles.   The problem as to the Gospels is not indeed thereby solved, but the peculiar, and in principle similar, grouping of the material in the synoptic writers is thus placed in a new light.

"making known to us the mystery of his will" (Eph. 1. 9)
and faith the "knowledge of his will" (Col. 1. 9), which however serves for the accomplishment of his "purpose according
to election" (Rom. 9. 11; 8. 2, 8 ff.; 9. 23. Eph. 2. 9 ff.).
This purpose includes an election made before all time (Eph.
1. 4. 2 Thes. 2. 13 f.), which, so far as individual men are
concerned, is actualized in the calling, which latter is always
conceived as being effectual (Rom. 8. 30; 9. 12, 23. 2 Thes.
2. 14). The absolute divine Will is therefore eternal and
rational will. It is characterized further as loving-will (Rom.
5. 5, 8) or grace (Rom. 3. 24; 5. 15. 2 Cor. 1. 3; 6. 1.
Col. 4. 18). At the same time God is represented as the Righteous One, in the double sense which this attribute bears in the Old
Testament, *i. e.*, as he who, because he is always consistent with
himself, is faithful toward the righteous but punishes the wicked
(Rom. 3. 26; 2. 5. 2 Thes. 1. 5, 6).

To this spiritual almighty Will, which rules in the world
in love and righteousness, all things which occur are therefore to
be traced. This point of view is constantly recurring in the
writings of Paul, and hence any presentation of his theology
must most strongly emphasize it. To this the Pauline Christology also leads. Christ is the Lord, to whom belongs the
fullness of the divine nature—the "Lord of Glory" (1 Cor.
2. 8 f. 2 Cor. 4. 4). In this designation of Christ as Lord the
same idea finds expression which was presented in the words
of Jesus when he spoke of the dominion (βασιλεία) which Christ
exercises (cf. esp. Rom. 4. 9; 10. 12 ff. 2 Cor. 4. 5. 1 Cor.
15. 24. Heb. 2. 11). But Paul now thought of Christ as the
ascended Lord, who from heaven, with divine omnipotence and
omnipresence, permeates the world and rules in his church.
Christ, "who is above all, God blessed forever" (Rom. 9. 5, cf.
Tit. 1. 3; 2. 13; 3. 4), is in us (2 Cor. 13. 3, 5), as we on the
other hand are in him (Rom. 8. 1. 1 Cor. 4. 16; 6. 17. Gal.
3. 27). He who fills all things, in whom all things exist,
is the head of the church (Eph. 1. 22 ff.; 2. 14 ff. Col. 1. 9,
18; 3. 11). All of these variations of thought rest upon the
conception, "the Lord is that Spirit" (2 Cor. 3. 17, cf. 1
Cor. 15. 45; 6. 17). The Christ of Paul is the spiritual
Energy which forms the world and shapes history. He is
related to the church as the governing head to the governed body.
As all-penetrating power, he is in us, as we on the other hand
are in him. In all these ideas we are to recognize, not highly
wrought similes, but assertions in regard to realities to be understood in the most literal sense. But this Lord-Spirit is one with
the Son of David, born of a woman (Gal. 4. 4), who came "in

the likeness of the flesh" (Rom. 1. 3 f.). Through the resurrection he has been transferred to the heavenly state of dominion (Eph. 1. 20 f.), which he at present exercises, and he will soon, at his Parousia, be manifest to all. This conception becomes comprehensible only when we remember that Paul speaks of a pre-existence of Christ "in the form of God" (Phil. 2. 6 ff. 2 Cor. 8. 9), as the "first-born of the whole creation," through whom all things were created (Col. 1. 15 ff. 1 Cor. 8. 6; 10. 4. 2 Cor. 4. 4). Christ, therefore, through the resurrection returned unto the state of the "form of God," which originally belonged to him, after having in obedience to the Father borne for a time the "form of a servant." Viewed theoretically, there yet remain here many questions unsolved. That the divinity of Christ, in the proper sense of the term, was firmly held by Paul is evident. The triadic formulas receive their interpretation from the principles above stated. Prayer to Christ (Rom. 10. 12, 14. Phil. 2. 10. 1 Cor. 1. 2; 16. 22. 2 Cor. 12. 8) is the practical consequence. The History of Doctrines, if it is to understand the further development of Christology, must keep this constantly before it as the starting-point. It is one of the most certain facts of history, that the thought and feeling of the apostolic age was based, not upon the man Jesus, but upon the Lord in heaven, who pervades and governs the universe, omnipotent and omniscient. It is simply absurd to attempt to explain this in a psychological way from the immense impression made by the man Jesus; for no imagination could mistake the most powerful man for God. Just as little can the resurrection in and of itself suffice for explanation; for even a resurrected man remains a man. A historical explanation is conceivable only upon the supposition that the disciples received from the Risen One impressions and evidences of his power and presence which compelled them to believe: He in us and we in him—as Paul also realized in his experience. Only from this point of view does the faith of the apostolic age become comprehensible. Every other explanation fails to explain anything historically, and ignores the simple facts of the case in the sources of our knowledge, not only in Paul and John, but also in the closing chapters of Matthew and Luke. But, despite all this, the question, how divinity and humanity are related to one another in Christ, finds no solution. The "fullness of the Godhead," the "spirit of holiness" (Heb. 2. 9. Rom. 1. 4), which constitute his divine nature, are something different from the existence "according to the flesh," but no definition is given of the relation of the one to the other.

Like the ascended Christ, the Spirit of Christ, or of God, is active, and that, too, in the hearts of believers, whether exciting within them the miraculous powers of the *charismata* (1 Cor. 12. 11; 14. 12. Col. 1. 29), or as the "demonstration and power of the Spirit" (1 Cor. 2. 4. 1 Thes. 1. 5 f.; 2. 13. Eph. 6. 17). And it was especially in the latter that Paul recognized the specific energy of the Spirit. Not outward miracles nor religious exaltation appeared to him as the peculiar domain of the Spirit; but the Word, which becomes effectual as a "power of God" (Rom. 1. 16). As Christ is for Paul divine energy, so too the Spirit. Thus Christ is the Spirit (2 Cor. 3. 17). The difference is, that Christ has the church at large as the object of his activity, whereas the Spirit is the divine energy, as apprehending and transforming individuals.

6. The first great group of ideas in the Pauline theology may be placed under the title : Spirit (πνεῦμα) and Flesh (σάρξ). Man is flesh—in the first place, according to his natural, visible substance; but also because the latter by virtue of its lust (ἐπιθυμία) determines the character of man's spirit, and thus the flesh becomes the instrument of sin. To be "after the flesh" (κατὰ σάρκα) denotes the immoral condition of the sinner; whereas to be "in the flesh" (ἐν σαρκὶ) belongs to human nature (2 Cor. 10. 3). Thus arises a "walking in the lusts of the flesh" (Eph. 2. 3), with a mind (φρόνημα) of the flesh (Rom. 8. 7) and a "minding earthly things" (Phil. 3. 19; 2. 4, 21), the "worldly lusts" (Tit. 3. 3; 2. 12), the "desires of the flesh" (Eph. 2. 3), and the "works of the flesh" (Gal. 5. 19 f.). It is not the idea of Paul, that the natural constitution of man produces sin in him; for sin came into the world by a particular act (Rom. 5. 12. 1 Cor. 15. 22). He means, on the contrary, that the historical power of sin (ἁμαρτία) gives a free rein to lust in man and thereby the flesh becomes the determining factor in his life. Sin, thus regarded, is for Paul a degradation of human nature, a perversity. From this condition, contrary to nature and unworthy of it, Christ as the Spirit sets free. His energy (ἐνέργεια) works with power (ἐν δυνάμει) within us (Col. 1. 29). We become in him a "new creature" (2 Cor. 5. 17. Gal. 6. 15). He lives in us (Phil. 1. 21. Rom. 8. 10. 2 Cor. 4. 10 f. Gal. 2. 20). Wisdom, righteousness, and sanctification proceed from him (1 Cor. 1. 30; 6. 11). He who puts on Christ ceases to obey the will (πρόνοια) of the flesh. But as through Christ a new life is begun in us, so will he also make us alive through the resurrection. It is only when we have received eternal life that the redemption of Christ is completed (Rom. 13. 11; 8. 23 f.). We have merely more precise and concrete delineations of this thought,

when Paul describes in many aspects the creative activity of the
divine Spirit in the soul of man (the Spirit reveals, teaches,
witnesses, confirms, inspires, impels, vivifies, renews, strengthens,
sanctifies, infuses love, fills us, sets us free, etc.). "As many
as are led by the Spirit of God, these are sons of God" (Rom.
8. 14). Christians live and walk "in the Spirit" and "according to the Spirit." They serve God in him and they lead
a new life through him (Gal. 5. 16, 22. Rom. 7. 6. Phil.
3. 3. Eph. 6. 18). They are spiritual ($\pi\nu\varepsilon\nu\mu\alpha\tau\iota\varkappa\omicron\iota$), whereas
other men are only natural ($\psi\nu\chi\iota\varkappa\omicron\iota$) (Gal. 6. 1. 1 Cor. 2. 14,
18). They expect at the resurrection, instead of the merely
natural body, a spiritual body $\sigma\tilde{\omega}\mu\alpha$ $\pi\nu\varepsilon\nu\mu\alpha\tau\iota\varkappa\acute{\omicron}\nu$ (1 Cor. 15. 44).

But the organ for the reception of the spiritual influences of
Christ, or of the Spirit, is faith (Eph. 3. 17 f.). Faith is also,
according to Paul, a taking and receiving. It is further characterized as a purely spiritual activity; as a knowledge of the will
of God (Col. 1. 9, 6. Eph. 1. 17. Phil. 3. 8. 1 Tim. 2. 4.
2 Tim. 2. 25); as an obedience of faith, or to the faith ($\dot{\upsilon}\pi\alpha\varkappa\omicron\dot{\eta}$
$\pi\acute{\iota}\sigma\tau\varepsilon\omega\varsigma$, Rom. 1. 5; 16. 26); as "the obedience ($\dot{\upsilon}\pi\alpha\varkappa\omicron\dot{\eta}$)
of your confession unto the Gospel of Christ" (2 Cor. 9. 13.
Rom. 6. 17; 10. 3 f., 16 f. 2 Thes. 1. 8. 2 Cor. 10. 4 f.); as
a personal conviction (Rom. 14. 23); as love for the truth
(2 Thes. 2. 10); as also a full persuasion, boldness, confidence
($\pi\lambda\eta\rho\omicron\varphi\omicron\rho\acute{\iota}\alpha, \pi\alpha\rho\rho\eta\sigma\acute{\iota}\alpha, \pi\varepsilon\pi\omicron\acute{\iota}\vartheta\eta\sigma\iota\varsigma$) (Rom. 4. 20, 21. Eph. 3. 12).
But as faith thus in manifold ways apprehends the spiritual gifts
and influences of God, it is, since God is efficient Will, essentially to be defined as subjection to God in obedience, or trust.
Even faith itself must according to Paul be received as an effect
of the Spirit; for it is a gift of God (Phil. 1. 29. 2 Cor. 4. 13)
and comes from the Gospel (Rom. 10. 17. 1 Cor. 15. 14.
Gal. 3. 2, 5), in which the effectual working of the Spirit is
exercised.

Thus there is awakened in man by the Spirit through faith a new
life: faith working by love (Gal. 5. 6). Inasmuch as the Spirit
makes the will of God effectual in man, man becomes free from
the authority of the law (2 Cor. 3. 17. Rom. 8. 2). Christian
morality culminates in liberty (Gal. 5. 1-13). The letter kills,
but the Spirit makes alive. Sin remains even in the believer.
Hence sanctification still proceeds in his life (1 Thes. 4. 3.
Rom. 6. 19, 22), as also conversion ($\mu\varepsilon\tau\acute{\alpha}\nu\omicron\iota\alpha$—2 Cor. 7. 9 f.;
12. 21. 2 Tim. 2. 25); grace is increased (2 Cor. 9. 8. Eph.
3. 16), and the moral life is a constant striving (Phil. 3. 13 ff.).
A process is begun in man through the Christ-Spirit, which finds
its consummation in eternal glory (Rom. 8. 18, 30. 2 Cor.
3. 8).

7. We pass now to the second combination of ideas found in the writings of Paul. Sin (ἁμαρτία), as we have seen, manifests itself in man as a carnal being. But it displays itself also as disobedience (παρακοή), and hence, as incurring personal guilt. This guilt is incurred by both Jews and Gentiles (Rom. 1. 3). The law cannot free from guilt. It only awakens a sense of sin. It kills, as Paul knew by experience (1 Cor. 15. 56. Rom. 7. 7 f.; 3. 19; 2. 13, 25; 5. 13). Nevertheless it comes from God, but has been imposed upon men only for pedagogical reasons and for a definite time (Gal. 3. 19, 21, 24. Rom. 5. 20). For the present time the Gospel (εὐαγγέλιον) holds sway, it being identical with the ancient gospels (εὐαγγελία) which preceded the law (Gal. 3. 17 f. Rom. 1. 2. Eph. 3. 6. Acts 13. 22. Tit. 1. 2 f.).

But since the entire race rests under guilt, and hence under penalty of death, and the law can only serve to make us sensible of our guilt, we need the forgiveness of sins upon the part of God. But deliverance from the guilt of sin occurs through the forensic justifying act (δικαιοῦν; cf. λογίζεσθαι εἰς δικαιοσύνην) of God (Rom. 2. 13, 26; 3. 4; 4. 4 f. Gal. 3. 6). Judaism also possessed the forensic conception of righteousness (זְכוֹת and הַעֲלוֹת): but whereas, according to Jewish ideas, the law is a living power and stimulates man to the good, which God then accepts as a basis for justification, according to Paul the law is incapable of making man good, and only faith justifies, and it does so simply because it accepts Christ. God pronounces righteous the ungodly man ἀσεβής (Rom. 4. 5), who has no righteousness of his own (Rom. 10. 3. Phil. 3. 9). The meaning of justification by faith and not by works is therefore, not that God recognizes faith as an ethical beginning, but that it is faith alone by virtue of which man apprehends the righteousness achieved by Christ (Gal. 2. 20; 3. 13. Rom. 5. 9; 4. 25; 3. 22 ff.). This is the sense in which we are to understand the "righteousness which is of God by (ἐπί) faith" (Phil. 3. 9). It is the righteousness of God, or his faithfulness (Rom. 1. 17; cf. 3. 3, 4, 26; 5. 21; 4. 16; 10. 3), which graciously accomplishes the non-attributing of guilt, or the pronouncing righteous (Rom. 4. 5 ff. 2 Cor. 5. 19. Col. 1. 14. Eph. 1. 7). The formula: Faith is accounted for righteousness (Rom. 4. 3 ff.; cf. Gen. 15. 6), in itself misleading—it is constructed in opposition to the Pharisaic idea: Works are accounted for righteousness—is therefore meant to indicate merely that the righteousness bestowed by God avails for man only upon condition of faith, because only faith can make it an inward possession of the man. "Of faith" (ἐκ πίστεως) is therefore (Rom. 4. 16) the same as "according to grace"

(κατὰ χάριν). Hence the thought of Paul is clear : The righteousness of God (θεοῦ) bestows upon man the righteousness which is
of (ἐκ) God ; but man possesses this as the righteousness of faith
(ἐκ πίστεως). But if faith itself is now a gift of God, there results a double connection with the line of thought developed
under item 6 : God works faith in us through the Spirit, and he
gives to faith righteousness as a conscious possession ; cf. also
Eph. 2. 8 ff. Tit. 3. 5-7. Phil. 3. 9 ff.

The justified man has peace with God (Rom. 5. 1 f.); sonship and right of inheritance (Rom. 8. 23, 15 f. Gal. 4. 5, 6 ;
3. 26 f., 29. Eph. 1. 5); freedom from the law (Gal. 2. 4 ; 4.
26 ff.; 5. 1), etc.

We are now, for Christ's sake, declared righteous. But is it
for the sake of his work of redemption ? On the one hand, Paul
defines the object of Christ, who, in obedience to God, gave himself to death on account of our sins, but was raised by God from
the dead, to have been deliverance from the world (Gal. 1. 4),
sanctification and purification (Eph. 5. 25. Tit. 2. 14), a life
dedicated to Christ (1 Thes. 5. 10); on the other hand, he
represents the death of Christ as the means through which we
receive forgiveness and are placed in a new relation to God.
The two conceptions stand side by side in 2 Cor. 5. 14 ff.: In
Christ we are a " new creature " and through him we have reconciliation (καταλλαγή), because God has dealt with Christ as per-
sonified sin. Thus in the one direction Christ's death and resurrection serve for the establishment of his redemptive dominion
(Rom. 14. 9) and for the awakening of zeal for good works (Tit.
2. 14), since the life of Christ in the flesh displays the divine condemnation of sin, and he, by his death, severed forever his relation to sin (Rom. 8. 3 ; 6. 10), and in death most fully attested
his obedience (Phil. 2. 8). Christ therefore died and rose again,
by his obedience condemning and abolishing sin. As he who has
done this, he acts in believers, enabling them to lead a new life
opposed to sin. Thus viewed, even Christ's sufferings serve for
the religious and moral regeneration of the race, of which we have
spoken under item 6.

This presupposes that Christ brings into a new relation with
God, or achieves for us the forgiveness of sins. But this has come
to pass, because God has made Christ in his blood a propitiator
(ἱλαστήριος), in order that those who believe on him may be for
his sake declared righteous (Rom. 3. 24 f.). His death,
acknowledged by God through the resurrection, brings to us forgiveness and justification (Rom. 4. 25), and Christ continually
represents us as our advocate before the Father (Rom. 8. 26 f.,
34 f.). By virtue of the death of Christ we are thus translated

into the state of reconciliation (2 Cor. 5. 18 f.), with the forgiveness of sins and justification.   We are thus again brought near to God (Eph. 2. 13, 18; 3. 12).   But if this has occurred, then at the same time we were made free from the law and its curse, under which Christ fell, in accordance with the declaration in Deut. 21. 23, since he bore the fate of the transgressor (Gal. 3. 13 f., 17; cf. also Col. 2. 14 f.).   What Paul thus means to assert is this: Since Christ attested to the utmost his obedience in the condition which sin had brought about for the race, he, in accordance with the appointment of God, covered the sins of men from the sight of God, or atoned for them, so that God now enters upon a new relation to the race, looking upon them for Christ's sake as righteous, and no longer permits the requirements of the law to determine his bearing toward mankind.   The one righteous man who preserved his righteousness to the utmost is the basis upon which God, for his sake—for he rules through his Spirit in the race—permits the race to enter into a new relation to himself.   These conceptions are not constructed upon the line of the sacrificial idea, but in accordance with the idea of the reconciling effect and the vicarious significance of the sufferings of the righteous one.

Even here Paul's teachings are not arranged as a "system." They are controlled by concrete aims, and the History of Doctrines proves how many interpretations may be placed upon them. Nevertheless they do not appear to lack a certain unity.   Since Christ as the Reconciler, by his obedience even unto death, appeared and continually appears for man as his advocate, he has brought the race into the new relation to God.   The law is abrogated, sin is forgiven, man is pronounced righteous.   But since this new relation has been established, the inner spiritual dominion of God in the race has also been made possible.   Thus the two lines of thought which we have traced here unite.   But at the same time it is clear that, for Paul also, the new covenant is actualized through Christ.   The reconciliation ($\varkappa\alpha\tau\alpha\lambda\lambda\alpha\gamma\acute{\eta}$) is the new covenant.

8. The idealism of Paul's faith beheld in the few Christian congregations of his time the beginning of a new epoch of history, and his practical sense saw in these congregations the means for actualizing this epoch.   In this, Paul adopted the conception of the church ($\dot{\varepsilon}\varkappa\lambda\eta\sigma\acute{\iota}\alpha$) held by Christ.   This, as viewed from the position of the History of Doctrines, is an idea of immense significance.   Christianity, accordingly, does not present the spectacle of a number of individuals accidentally associated, but it is the Christ present in the world.   The ancient idea of Menenius Agrippa, of a body of humanity organically

associated, was revived in many forms in that day. Paul gives
it a new aspect. Christ is the Head of this body, from whom
it derives its origin, its course, its life, its growth, and its goal
(Col. 1. 18 f., 24. Eph. 2. 20 ff.; 5. 23 ff.; 1. 22 f.). In this
community Christ works through the Spirit. All the gifts of
the Spirit are present in it. But, above all, is the power of the
Spirit actively exerted in the preaching of the Gospel. Among
other functions of the church are to be mentioned baptism and
the Lord's Supper. Paul in 2 Tim. 2. 20 testifies that there
are among the saints (ἅγιοι) in the church not only such as lead
a real Christian life, struggling and crucifying the flesh, but also
perverse members.

The Pauline eschatology cannot be here presented, further
than to note the suggestion in the sphere of the philosophy of
history, that the prophecies concerning Israel are yet to find
their fulfillment in the ingathering of the heathen into the church
in the present era and in the salvation of "all Israel" at the end
of the world (Rom. 11. 25, 26).

9. Having now noted the peculiar doctrinal points emphasized
by Paul, let us cast a brief glance upon the general views prevalent in the apostolic age. These laid the foundations upon
which the post-apostolic age carried forward the work of construction. The Old Testament, inspired by God (2 Tim. 3.
16. 2 Pet. 1. 20 f.), is the Holy Scripture of Christendom. It
serves for edification (Rom. 15. 4. 2 Tim. 3.16). From its
utterances doctrines are developed (see esp. Hebrews). Its
prophecies serve as the source of apostolic evidences (see esp.
the Gospel of St. Matthew). To the Old Testament are
added the historical sayings of Jesus (1 Thes. 4. 5. 1 Cor. 7.
12, 25; 9. 14. Acts 20. 35), but also the Spirit (πνεῦμα) and
the spirits (πνεύματα). But the spirits are to be tried (Matt. 7.
16 ff. 1 Thes. 5. 19-22. 1 Cor. 14. 34 f. 1 Jn. 4. 1). The
historical apostolate and the traditions (παραδόσεις) set a limit
to the working of the spirits (see above).

The vivid conception of God which we have found in Paul
is manifest also in other literature of the period. The loving-will
of God desires our salvation (2 Pet. 3. 9) and begets us into
a new life (Jas. 1. 18). The all-working God is also holy and
just (Rev. 15. 3 f.; 16. 5, 7; 19. 1 f. 2 Pet. 1. 1, 3. 1 Pet.
2. 23). Christ is the Lawgiver and Judge (Jas. 4. 12).
He is always thought of as now existing in the state
of exaltation. Rev. 1. 12-17 (cf. 11. 15; 17. 14; 19. 16;
22. 1) presents the popular conception. Having passed
through death, he has entered into glory (1 Pet. 1. 21).
He is the Lord of glory (Jas. 2. 1), our only Master and

Lord (δεσπότης και κύριος, Jude 4.), who is enthroned at the right hand of God (Heb. 8. 1 ; 10. 12 ; 12. 2), and to whom the angels are subject (2 Pet. 3. 18 ; 1. 14, 16). Interest centres, above all, in the power (δύναμις) and coming (παρουσία) of Christ (2 Pet. 1. 16). The latter is near at hand, but will occur unexpectedly (2 Pet. 3. 4, 10. Rev. 3. 11). Thus there will be a revelation (ἀποκάλυψις) of his glory (1 Pet. 4. 13 ; 1. 7). The present glory of Christ is in harmony with his pre-existent state (1 Pet. 1. 20, 11 ; 3. 19 f.).

That Christ died on account of our sin was the apostolic tradition (1 Cor. 15. 3) and the general belief (1 Pet. 3. 18). The death of Christ was universally regarded as the means by which we are transported into a new moral state of life, and this because Christ died the just for the unjust, in order that he, having died and risen again, might lead them to God and bring them into a new relation with God. The Epistle to the Hebrews follows a peculiar course. Its Christology recognizes Christ as pre-existent (Heb. 1. 2 f., 4 ff.) and locates his nature in the " power of an endless life " (7. 16, δύναμις ζωῆς ἀκαταλύτου), in his "eternal Spirit" (9. 14, πνεῦμα αἰώνιον). As such, he assumed flesh and blood (2. 14 ; 7. 14), in his earthly life experienced human emotions, and died in obedience (4. 15 ; 5. 7, 8). He is now at the right hand of God (1. 3 ; 8. 1 ; 10. 12 ; 12. 2). In the same way as in the writings of Paul, a discrimination is made also in this Christology between the human existence of Christ and a spiritual, eternal, divine element. The author has presented the exaltation of Christ in the light of his high-priesthood. The apologetic character of the work, which required this method of presentation, led him, first of all, to conceive of the death of Christ as a sacrifice. And this sacrifice is once for all and forever sufficient (5. 1 ff., 7 f.; 9. 12-14 ; 7. 27), as Christ also forever stands as our advocate before God (7. 25 ; 9. 24). The death of Christ, i. e., his blood, inaugurates the "new covenant" and purifies the heavenly sanctuary (9. 15 ff., 18 ff.). To this is added, as the object of his death, the purifying from sin (καθαρισμὸς ἁμαρτιῶν, 1. 3 ; 9. 14, 26), as also the expiatory covering over (ἱλάσκεσθαι) of sin and the despoiling of the power of the devil (2. 14 f.). If we leave out of account the emphasis laid upon the forms of the sacrificial ceremonies, the conceptions of the author do not carry us beyond the two-fold representation which we have already found in Paul, i. e., that God, by the death of Christ, establishes a new objective relation between himself and the human race, and that the death of Christ aids in establishing a subjectively new attitude of man toward God.

Christians are partakers (μέταχοι) of Christ and of the Holy
Spirit (Heb. 3. 14; 16.4). With this all the blessings of salvation are bestowed upon them, for God works in them what is
well-pleasing in his sight (Heb. 13. 21). The word is, however, the means through which the blessings of salvation are imparted to believers (Heb. 4. 2). It is a heavenly summons
(Heb. 3. 1. 1 Pet. 3. 21; 5. 10. 2 Pet. 1. 3) which penetrates to the ends of the earth (Heb. 4. 12), begetting a new
life (Jas. 1. 18. 1 Pet. 1. 3) and preserving us in it (1 Pet. 1.
23 ff.; 2. 2. Jas. 1. 21). This new life is to be conceived of,
first of all, as faith (Jas. 1. 3, 6, 8; 2. 1, 5. 1 Pet. 1. 7 f., 9,
21; 5. 9. Heb. 12. 7). This term is understood precisely as
by Jesus and Paul. Faith is called wisdom (σοφία, Jas. 3. 13;
cf. 2. 18); also knowledge (ἐπίγνωσις, 2 Pet. 1. 2, 3; 2. 20;
3. 18), and is exercised in "full assurance" (πληροφορία, Heb.
10. 22). But, above all, it possesses the trait of obedience (1
Pet. 1. 22. Heb. 11. 8; 5. 9). It is to be noted, however,
that faith constantly assumes more of the character of hope, and
directs its gaze upon the blessedness of the future (1 Pet. 1. 21.
Heb. 12. 1 f.; 10. 36; 6. 11, 12). Thus the spiritual attitude of
the Old Testament was revived. The well-known definition of
Heb. 11. 1 (cf. Rom. 8. 24) exhibits this tendency, and hence
does not express the New Testament conception with entire
fidelity. The modification which begins to appear at this point
appears contemporaneously with the constantly growing tendency to conceive of salvation (σωτηρία) as lying essentially in
the future. It is even designated "a salvation ready to be revealed in the last time" (1 Pet. 1. 4, 5; cf. Heb. 3. 1; 9. 15.
1 Pet. 5. 10; 1. 9, 13. 2 Pet. 1. 4).

The Pauline doctrine of justification is not found in any of
the other New Testament writers. Heb. 11. 7 furnishes a slight
reminder. The generally prevalent conception may be expressed
in the declaration of John : "He that doeth righteousness is
righteous" (1 Jn. 3. 7. Rev. 22. 11). God produces good
works in us (Heb. 13. 21). We are to become doers of the
word, or of the law (Jas. 1. 22; 4. 4). "A doer (ποιητής)
of the work, this man shall be blessed in his doing" (ποιήσει)
(Jas. 1. 25). Righteousness is the moral integrity which avails
before God, and which is recognized by him (Jas 1. 20. 1 Pet.
2. 24; 3. 14. 2 Pet. 3. 13). At the same time, the latter is
by no means to be accounted as constituting merit upon the part
of man. On the contrary, everything good is given by God, as
upon the other hand the law is meant only as a "law of liberty"
(νόμος ἐλευθερίας, Jas. 2. 12; cf. 1 Pet. 2. 16). From this
point of view, the theory of justification presented by James is by

no means to be considered particularly remarkable. James seeks to base the edict of justification, not exclusively upon faith, but upon the moral character which accompanies the latter. From Gen. 16. 5 it is directly inferred that "man is justified by works (ἐξ ἔργων) and not by faith alone" (ἐκ πίστεως μόνον) (Jas. 2. 17, 20 ff.). Distinctly as this view differs from the Pauline, we cannot see in it a falling back upon Judaism. But this must be the starting-point for anyone who desires to understand the history of the Pauline doctrine of justification in the following centuries.

The warnings to keep the life free from sin, to practice love, etc., are extraordinarily abundant, and attest the spiritual wealth of the period. The conception of the church as a "spiritual house" and a "chosen generation" (1 Pet. 2. 5, 9) embraces the assurance that it was in possession of all the gracious gifts of God, and was under obligation to discharge all the duties of love toward the members of the brotherhood. More and more the sanctified (ἡγούμενοι) take the place of the spiritual (πνευματικοί) as leaders of the church (Heb. 13. 7, 17, 24, 19). Office-bearers begin to exercise the ministry of the word (1 Tim. 3. 1 ff.; 5. 17. 2 Tim. 2. 2. Tit. 1. 7, 5). But these features of the period do not indicate any increasing worldliness. Eschatology, on the contrary, is a powerful factor of the religious life. Two characteristics meet and combine in mutual support in the Christianity of the apostolic age: upon the one hand, the powerful impulse to establish the dominion of Christ by serving him and in his power pressing out to the ends of the earth; and, upon the other hand, the conviction that only Christ himself can achieve this, and that he will soon do so. These two tendencies did not at first conflict, but aided one another. We may recall the vivid hope of Paul and his great labors in the service of this hope. In the Apocalypse is given in great pictures, with veiled imagery and many references to the great world-empires, a portrayal of the conflicts and the great victory of the last time, which was so varied in its forms that every period of history has been able to employ it as a mirror of its own age. The city of God, already prepared in heaven, will come down to the earth. It remains only for us to pray: "Come, Lord Jesus" (Rev. 22. 17, 20). Christ will soon be Lord alone (Rev. 11. 15, 17; 12. 9, 10; 14. 3 f.; 19. 2, 6, 16). This is the one controlling thought. But just because it is, the moral counsels and exhortations to conflict and devoted service gain the support of powerful motives. Of this, the letters to the churches, recorded in the Apocalypse, furnish an illustration.

10. At the end of the apostolic age we witness the active

4

ministry of John, which is of the greatest significance for the History of Doctrines. Standing between two eras, be impressed the message of the days of revelation deeply upon his generation. We may define his significance in three observations: (1) The Christ, of whose historical revelation he has been a witness, is the Lord of the world. The apocalyptic hopes of his youth, of which hitherto but few have been realized in their external form, yet remain. He sees in great visions the final victory of Christ. The apocalyptic traditions of his nation furnish for him the forms of these visions. (2) A separation begins to appear between the historical Jesus and the heavenly Logos-principle (Cerinthus). In response to this, the Gospel proves that the heavenly Lord was none other than the man Jesus. John expresses this as paradoxically and bluntly as possible · "The Word became flesh." From this resulted the peculiarity of his Gospel. The religious knowledge which he had gained in the course of a long life in communion with the exalted Christ enables him to interpret the life of Jesus, which he depicts in a thoroughly human way, with many minute human traits. He carries backward the knowledge gained at a later day. He seeks out the words which establish it and apprehends the words of Jesus in this higher sense. Profound contemplation characterizes this treatment of the life of Jesus. It saved to the church the history of Christ, since it made it possible to understand it religiously, as the Lord himself, when present, had been known to his disciples. (3) Vision and contemplation were in this remarkable man united with a practical, simple temper, averse to all foolish vaporings and pretense. To the watchwords of the age, such as "spirit" and "righteousness," he opposed this simple knowledge of the truth. Christianity is summarized in the "old commandment" (1 Jn. 2. 7) or the teaching (διδαχή) of Christ (2 Jn. 9 f.). This is the primitive Christian catechism, to which reference has been made above (item 4). Its contents are faith in God and love toward one another (1 Jn. 3. 23; 4. 15).

John does not mean, however, that faith and love are only an outward keeping of the commandments. On the contrary, they are given to man by the Spirit in the new birth, or regeneration. The Spirit does not, as once thought, produce separate states of excitement. John goes even beyond Paul, for whom the "power" of the word was, in the last analysis, the Spirit. The Spirit effects in man a permanent condition of fellowship (κοινωνία) with God (1 Thes. 4. 13). This communion with God is manifested in faith and love. But he who believes, believes in harmony with the commandment (ἐντολή), and he who loves, loves that which the commandment enjoins. Faith and love are awakened in the heart of man by the Spirit, and not by the commandment. But faith and love, if they be genuine and right, can never contain anything else than the commandment given by God. It is evident that John himself is far removed from the ancient Catholic conception of Christianity as a "new law," but that he yet helped to prepare the way for that conception.

But true faith is that which confesses that Jesus is really Christ. The Logos, or God only-begotten (Jn. 1. 14), the "true God and eternal life" (1 Jn. 5. 20), became the man Jesus. Unless all indications are at fault, John borrowed his conception of the Logos from Cerinthus, but he interpreted it in his own sense. The Logos is the revealing God—God, because he manifests himself not only in many words, uttered "in divers portions and in divers manners," as those of the prophets, but in an all-inclusive, complete revelation (cf. Rev. 19. 13 f. Heb. 1. 2. Ignat ad Magnes, 8. 2; 9. 2; ad Rom. 8. 2). This God became the man Jesus. He who denies this—*i. e.*, two principles, the divine and human, separate from one another (Cerinthus)—is the Antichrist (1 Jn. 2. 22; 4. 3, 15; 5. 1, 5. 2 Jn. 7; cf. Iren. i. 26. 1; iii. 11. 1).

And true love is the practical, active brotherly-love, which walks according to the commandments of God (2 Jn. 6. 1 Thes. 2. 3 f.). He who doeth righteousness is righteous. From this active righteousness may be known whether anyone has really been born of God (1 Jn. 2. 29; 4. 7; 5. 1, 4). The regenerated, as such, does not sin (1 Jn. 3. 9, 6; 1. 6; 2. 6). Nevertheless, John assumes sin in his readers, as well as a regularly observed confession of sin (1 Jn. 2. 1. f.; 1. 7 f.). This apparent contradiction may, if I am correct in my judgment, be solved by discriminating between a "sin unto death" and a "sin not unto death" (1 Jn. 5. 16, 17), *i. e.*, between the sinful state of ungodliness which forever prevents communion with God and the separate sinful acts which leave room for a restoration through repentance (1 Jn. 5. 16; 1. 7 f.). This conception also (cf. Heb. 6. 4, 8; 10. 26 f.; 12. 17) reminds us of ideas in the primitive Catholic period.

11. John subjected the traditional Christian conceptions to a noticeable redaction. In addition to him, only the Pauline type can be presented in distinct outlines. Between the two lie the conceptions of James, Peter, Jude, and Hebrews. These types of doctrine differ from one another in many particulars, but the elements common to all certainly outweigh the differences. And it was not really the peculiar features (*e. g.*, Paul's doctrine of justification, and the theories of the Epistle to the Hebrews),

but those which were common to all, which influenced the
future. The Apostolic Fathers, *e. g.*, presuppose a general
proclamation which embraced the common basis of the New
Testament doctrine.

These common ideas may be summarized as follows: The
acknowledgment of the Old Testament; the words of Christ,
together with the apostolic tradition and teaching, as of
binding authority; faith in the living God, who, in omnipotence and grace, directs the life of individuals as well as
the course of history; faith in Christ as the celestial and
omnipresent Lord, who became man, and, through the resurrection, entered again into glory; the conviction that God
and Christ, through the Spirit, renew and quicken man religiously and morally, granting him also the *charismata*, which
he needs for the upbuilding of the church. The work of Christ
embraces the efficacious atonement for sin as well as the transformation of man through the power of the Spirit. Forgiveness and
sonship with God, the filling with the Spirit, and eternal blessedness constitute the blessings of salvation, which are appropriated in faith and love. Love as an active disposition of soul
finds exercise in the congregational life, in which Christ and the
Spirit work through the word, baptism, and the Lord's Supper,
and through the *charismata*, and the miracles wrought through
the latter. The final goal of the church is the glory of the
divine kingdom, to be ushered in by the coming of Christ,
which is near at hand.

If we compare this with the teaching of Christ himself, it is
clear that it presupposes the resurrection of Christ and the manifestation of the risen Lord in his glory; and, further, that the
revelation made by Christ during his earthly life gives shape to
the whole structure. Christ exercises divine dominion, in that
he brings to man the forgiveness of sins and a new life, and ac-
tualizes the new covenant wherever these blessings are received.
Through the dominion of Christ, humanity is organized as the
church, or kingdom of God, and thus conducted to its appropriate goal. He accomplishes the salvation of men, forgiving
the evil and bestowing the good, and he brings the race to its
divinely appointed goal. In faith man bows to this beatifying
dominion and in love brings into active exercise his new attitude
in the kingdom of God. These ideas embrace the whole revelation of the New Testament. The redemptive dominion of
God and faith, the kingdom of God and love—this is the briefest
possible expression of the Essence of Christianity in the sense of
the New Testament.[1]

[1] Cf. Seeberg, Die Grundwahrheiten der christl. Religion, ed. 3, 1903;
lectures iii.-vi.

BOOK I.

DEVELOPMENT OF DOCTRINE IN THE ANCIENT CHURCH.

PART I.

CONCEPTION OF CHRISTIANITY IN THE POST-APOSTOLIC AND ANCIENT CATHOLIC AGES.

CHAPTER I.

THE CONCEPTION OF CHRISTIANITY IN THE POST-APOSTOLIC AGE.

§ 7. *The Apostolic Fathers.*

SOURCES : 1. From Clemens Romanus we possess a manuscript of the Roman congregation, addressed to the church at Corinth. It was written probably early in A. D. 97. WREDE, Untersuchungen zum 1. Klemensbrief, 1891.

2. In Rome appeared also the Pastor of Hermas, a call to repentance divided into 5 visions, 12 mandates, and 10 similitudes. Its composition is, with great probability, located in A. D. 97-100, while others, upon the testimony of the so-called Canon of Muratori, place it so late as A. D. 140-145. Cf. ZAHN, Der Hirte des H., 1868. HÜCKSTÄDT, Der Lehrbegriff des Hirten, 1889.

3. The documents which follow carry us to Asia Minor. First, the 7 genuine Epistles of IGNATIUS OF ANTIOCH (to the Ephesians, Magnesians, Trallians, Romans, Philadelphians, Smyrnans, and Polycarp), written about A. D. 110. Cf. ZAHN, Ign. v. Ant., 1874; Von der GOLTZ, Ign. v. Ant. als Christ u. Theologe, in Texte u. Unters., xii. 3 (1894).

4. In the same time appeared the Epistle of POLYCARP OF SMYRNA.

5. PAPIAS, Bishop of Hierapolis, wrote, about A. D. 125, 5 books : λογίων κυριακῶν ἐξήγησις. Of these, unfortunately, only a few fragments have been preserved to us in Irenæus, Eusebius, etc. Vid. in the small Leipzig edition of the Apostolic Fathers, p. 69 ff. Cf. also C. de BOOR in Texte u. Unters., v. 2, p. 170, and also p. 176 ff.

6. An Epistle ascribed to BARNABAS carries us to Alexandria. Chap. 16. 1 gives no aid in fixing the date of its appearance. According to Chap. 4. 3 f., it may have been composed under Nerva (A. D. 96-98). It is commonly assigned to the time of Hadrian. The unity of the composition is to be maintained.

7. It was also probably in Alexandria that the little liturgical handbook, Διδαχὴ τῶν ιβ᾽ ἀποστόλων, made its appearance. From a literary point of view, it is very closely related to the Epistle of Barnabas, as is especially manifest in the section upon "The Two Ways." It can be proved, however, that neither of the two made use of the other, but that an earlier document lay at the basis of both. The Didache most probably appeared in the first decennium of the second century. We refer to publications of it by HARNACK in Texten u. Unters., vol. ii., and FUNK, Patres apostolici, ii. ed. 2, 1901, and to the small edition : " Die Apostellehre u. die jüd. beiden Wege " (Leipzig, 1886), in which, p. 38 ff., is noted also the most important literature.

8. The so-called SECOND EPISTLE OF CLEMENT is in truth the most an-

cient church homily that has been preserved to us. It was probably delivered in Corinth (7. 1), hardly later than A. D. 140. Cf. ZAHN in Zeitschr. f. Prot. u. Kirche, 1876, no. 4. HARNACK, Zeitschr. f. Kirchengesch., 1877, p. 329 ff.
The best edition of the above-named documents, not including the Didache, is: Patrum apostolicorum opera rec. de GEBHARDT, HARNACK, ZAHN, 3 vols., Leipzig, 1876-1877; smaller edition, Leipzig, 1877; and FUNK, Patres Apostolici, 2 vols., ed. 2, Tübingen, 1901. LIGHTFOOT, The Apostolic Fathers (Clemens, 1890; Ignatius, 1885).
For estimates of their doctrinal contents, see RITSCHL, Die Entstehung der altkath. Kirche., 1857, p. 274 ff. LÜBKERT, Die Theol. d. ap. Väter, 1854. V. ENGELHARDT, Das Christenthum Justins, 1878, p. 375 ff. LECHLER, Das apostol. u. nachap. Zeitalter, ed. 3, 1885, p. 586 ff. PFLEIDERER, Das Urchristentum, 1887, p. 640 ff., 823 ff., 845 ff. HARNACK, DG., i. ed. 3, p. 140 ff. THOMASIUS, DG., i. ed. 2, p. 31 ff., with additions by Bonwetsch; cf. p. 141 ff. BEHM, Das christl. Gesetztum der ap. Vät. in Zeitschr. f. k. Wiss., 1886, p. 295 ff., 408 ff., 453 ff.

For the sake of clearness and in view of the importance of the matter, we deem it advisable to examine each of the above documents separately before attempting to present a summary account of their doctrinal contents.

1. CLEMENS ROMANUS.

(*a*) The leading thought is that of the One God, the Lord (δεσπότης; cf. 49. 6 and 47 fin. with 48 init.) of the world, the Creator, and, in this sense, the Father (*e. g.*, 35. 3; 19. 2). The conception of the latter term is different in 29. 1; 23. 1; 56. 16: the merciful and gracious Father by his holy discipline protects men and trains them for the reception of mercy. It is our duty to love him who elects us, and to draw near to him with a holy heart. God is θεὸς καὶ ὁ κύριος Ἰησοῦς Χριστὸς καὶ τὸ πνεῦμα το ἅγιον (58. 2; 46. 6).

(*b*) Christ is sent from God to deliver us (42. 1; 59. 2). In that God elected Christ, he elected us through him as his own people (64; 59. 3). As to his nature, he is the Son of God, exalted above the angels (36, following Heb. 1. 3 ff.); the Lord Jesus Christ; the sceptre of the majesty of God: and yet he came as the Humble One into the world (16. 2). Already in the Old Testament he spoke through the Holy Ghost (22. 1). In harmony with this, his descent from Abraham is by the term τὸ κατὰ σάρκα discriminated from another descent (32.2). The sufferings of Christ are described as the sufferings of God (2. 1), unless in this passage we are to read παθήματα αὐτοῦ, instead of παθήματα θεοῦ (Funk).

(*c*) Christ is the only mediator of our salvation. Through him we have become God's possession (vid. *b*). He is to us a helper in weakness and a high-priest in the offering of gifts (prayers; cf. 61. 3). Through his mediation we are made capable of seeing God and tasting immortal knowledge ; through it, faith, (godly) fear, peace, patience, temperance, and wisdom (σωφροσύνη) become the portion of the Christian (64). Out of love Christ gave his blood for us—his flesh for our flesh, his soul for our souls (49. 6 ; 21. 6). "By the blood of the Lord there is redemption (λύτρωσις) to all that believe and hope in God" (12. 7). This blood, which was shed for the sake of our salvation, is so precious to the Father of Christ, that it has obtained the grace of repentance for the whole world. The humility and patience which Christ maintained in his life's work are an example for us, who have through him come "beneath the yoke of grace" (16. 17).

To summarize : In Christ we have become the possession of God. Through him the knowledge of God, faith, and all virtues have become ours. His blood has redeemed us, since it brought us the grace of repentance. His life is for us a pattern of humility. It may be said, indeed, that Clement has not grasped the saving efficacy of the death of Christ in its full biblical significance ; but it is going too far to maintain that he believed nothing more to be accomplished by it than blotting out of past sins (Behm, l.c., p. 304. Vid. 7. 4).

(d) As to the personal standing of the believer, Clement teaches: "They were all (Old Testament saints) therefore glorified and magnified not through themselves nor their works, nor the righteousness which they wrought, but through his will. And we therefore, being called through his will in Christ Jesus, are not justified through ourselves, neither through our wisdom nor knowledge nor piety nor works which we have done in the holiness of our hearts, but through the faith through which God Almighty has justified all men from the beginning" (32. 3, 4). Such are the paths of blessedness (31. 1); faith in Christ brings us everything good (22. 1). Clement writes thus with a full conception of the wide scope of his words, for he follows them immediately with the remark, that good works are not thereby excluded, but on the contrary zeal in such works is required (33. 1, 7, 8). This is as truly Pauline as the definition of faith as confidence (πεποίθησις, 35. 2 ; 26. 1 ; cf. 2. 3 ; 58. 1). The humble temper of mind (16-19) and believing trust in God, obedience to God, and unreserved self-surrender to him (10. 1 ; 11) obtain salvation. But this line of thought is limited by another : "Blessed are we, beloved, if we shall have fulfilled the commandments of God in the unity of love, that so through love our sins may be forgiven us" (50. 5). No great weight is to be laid upon the mention of "hospitality" along with faith in the cases of Abraham and Rahab (10. 7 ; 12. 1 ; cf. also 10. 1 ;

31. 2); more upon the strong emphasis laid upon the laws (νόμοι) and commandments (προστάγματα) of God and Christ (1. 3; 2. 8; 3, 4; 13. 3; 37. 1; 49. 1; 40. 1). When Clement is thinking of the origin and nature of human salvation, he is controlled by Pauline conceptions; in view of the realities of life and the judgment, he lays great weight upon the moral activity of man in harmony with the law of God (but cf. also 26. 1).

(e) The church is, in Clement, the people of God, which he has chosen for his own possession (e.g., 59. 4; 30. 1; 6. 1; 64); those called to be saints (inscription; 65. 2); the flock of Christ (16. 1). It is of importance to note the legal argument based upon the Old Testament by which Clement supports the authority of the elders. Their duty is (40) accordingly, the conduct of worship (λειτουργία) and sacrifice (θυσία). The fixed office and its authority here took the place of the free activity of the Spirit in the church. Problems were thus created which were destined to occupy the best energies of the church of the future (cf. also Did. 15. 1; 14. 1, 2). In this fellowship reign discipline and order (2. 6; 4-6; 47. 6; 21. 6; 40), subjection to leaders and to one another (1. 3; 21. 6; 38. 1), piety and practical hospitality (1. 2 ff.; 2), firm fellowship one with another (46. 4 ff.; 30. 3; 15. 1). For Clement's ideal of Christian character, vid. Chapters I. and II.

(f) It may be mentioned, finally, that the author distinctly and intelligently maintains the resurrection of the body (24 and 25).

This document makes it clear that the ideas embraced in the apostolic proclamation have been preserved in the church, but that there may be already traced a lack of independent scrutiny of these ideas and of deeper penetration into their significance. One does not receive the impression that the biblical conception of Christ's work and the significance of faith are really understood and inwardly appropriated. However, in passing this judgment, we should bear in mind the particular object of Clement in the preparation of the work.

2. HERMAS.

To understand the peculiarities of the "Shepherd," we must remember its character as an exhortation to repentance.

(a) Hermas associates salvation directly with the Person of Christ (Sim. 9. 12. 4-6). His views in regard to this, however, furnish nothing really new. It is a perversion to make him a representative of an adoptionistic Christology, as though teaching that Christ was a man chosen of God, in whom the Spirit of God dwelt, and who, after having proved himself worthy, was

elevated to a position of lordship (Harnack, DG., ed. 3, p. 182
f.). Christ, the Son of God, is as well the ancient Rock, out
of which the tower of the church is hewn, as the new Door
through which we enter this tower. "The Son of God is, in-
deed, more ancient ($\pi\rho o\gamma\varepsilon\nu\acute{\varepsilon}\sigma\tau\varepsilon\rho\acute{o}\varsigma$) than any creature ; insomuch
that he was in counsel with his Father at the creation of all
things (Sim. 9. 12. 2, 3). He could very well have protected
his people through an angel (Sim. 5. 6. 2 ; cf. 2. 2) ; but he
did more, since he purified them by his own toil (Sim. 5. 6. 3).
The angels are his to command (Sim. 5. 5. 13 ; cf. 2. 2), and he
upholds the whole world (Sim. 9. 14. 5 ; cf. Heb. 1. 2). It
cannot therefore be doubted that Christ is for Hermas a pre-
existent Being, exalted above the angels.

It has been contended that, according to Hermas, Christ
is not a separate divine person, but that the Holy Spirit dwelt in
his flesh (BAUR, v. ENGELHARDT, p. 425 f. HARNACK, p. 185.
HÜCKSTÄDT, p. 26 ff.). But Sim. 5 distinctly discriminates between the lord of the farm, *i. e.*, the Father, the servant, *i. e.*,
the Son, and the son, *i. e.*, the Holy Ghost. The lord commits
to the servant the cultivation of the farm, and after this has been
done, he rejoices over it with the son, *i. e.*, the Holy Ghost
(5. 2. 6 ; 5. 2). If it is said immediately after this (6. 5) that
God caused the Holy Ghost to dwell in the flesh of Christ, and
that the latter served the Spirit without defiling it, the meaning
is not that the Holy Spirit constitutes the divine nature of Christ,
but that the pre-existent Christ is holy spirit ($\tau\grave{o}$ $\pi\nu\varepsilon\tilde{v}\mu\alpha$ $\tau\grave{o}$ $\H{\alpha}\gamma\iota o\nu$
$\tau\grave{o}$ $\pi\rho o\acute{o}\nu$, $\tau\grave{o}$ $\varkappa\tau\acute{\iota}\sigma\alpha\nu$ $\pi\tilde{\alpha}\sigma\alpha\nu$ $\tau\grave{\eta}\nu$ $\varkappa\tau\acute{\iota}\sigma\iota\nu$), and that this flesh, since it
did not defile the spirit, has been by God taken with the spirit
to himself (6 ff.). The other passage adduced in support of the
theory in question, Sim. 9. 1. 1 : "For that spirit is the Son of
God" means only to say that the holy spiritual being that spoke
with Hermas was the Son of God. The pre-existent Christ was
not "the Holy Spirit," but a pre-existent holy spiritual being.
It was not uncommon to speak in this way in the second cen-
tury. Christ is called Spirit of God ($\pi\nu\varepsilon\tilde{v}\mu\alpha$ $\vartheta\varepsilon o\tilde{v}$) in 2 Clem.
9. 5. Iren. adv. haer., v. 1. 2 ; cf. Arist. Apol., 2. 6. Celsus
in Orig. c. Cels., vi. 75. Theophil. ad Autol., ii. 10. Tertul.
Apol., 21 ; adv. Prax. 8. 26 ; de orat. 1. See already 1 Cor.
3. 17. The view of Hermas is, therefore, not essentially different from that of the New Testament. It would have been incomprehensible that he should, in view of the baptismal formula,
have fallen into such confusion. Vid. also Dorner, Christol.,
i., ed. 2, p. 200 ff., 194.

(*b*) Christ, the Son of God, placed men (evidently meaning
believers of Old Testament times) under the protection of

angels; then himself became man in order to purify men : " And he himself labored very much and suffered much that he might blot out their offenses . . . wherefore having himself blotted out the sins of the people, he showed to them the paths of life, giving them the law which he had received from the Father " (Sim. 5. 6. 2, 3). Thus Christ brought forgiveness for the sins of the past, and for the future gave to men his commandments. Cf. Link, Christi Person u. Werk im Hirten des Hermas (Marburg, 1886).

(c) As to the personal state of the believer, we are taught : In the hearts of men, which are in themselves weak and full of sin (e.g., Mand. 4. 3. 4. Sim. 9. 23. 4), which turn away from God, do not know him, and will not obey him (Vis. 3. 7. 2. Sim. 4. 4. 4, etc.), God causes his Spirit to take up its abode, or the powers of the Son of God are imparted to them. Only such as have obtained these are able to enter into the kingdom of God (Mand. 3. 1 ; 12. 4. 3 ; 6. 2, 1 ff. Sim. 9. 32.4 ; 13. 2 ; cf. 25. 4). But this good Spirit cannot live in man together with the evil spirits (Mand. 5. 1. 3 ; 2. 5 ff. Sim. 10. 3. 2). Sim. 8 explains how this gift is imparted. Branches from a willow-tree are given to believers. Some bring them back fresh and blooming : others, withering and withered (both classes in various degrees). The willow-tree is the law of God. " But this law is the Son of God, preached throughout the whole earth " (3. 2). It is therefore the preaching of Christ as a new code of moral life which accomplishes the above results in believers. We are futher told that life is given us through the water of baptism, and this is so necessary that it must in some way be applied even to Old Testament believers (Vis. 3. 3. 5. Sim. 9. 16. 2, 3, 5). Through baptism all the sins which a man has committed are forgiven (cf. below under d).

The fundamental subjective condition of the moral life in man is faith (Sim. 6. 12). This comes from above, and equips man with power ; whereas its opposite, double-mindedness, is of the earth and has no power (Mand. 9. 11). Since the latter, which leads to doubt, must be overcome, as well as care and trouble ($\lambda \acute{v} \pi \eta$), man turns in faith with his whole heart to God, praying and sure that his prayer is heard (Mand. 9. 1, 2, 5 ; cf. Vis. 4. 2. 4-6. Mand. 10). He who fears God becomes free from the fear of the devil (Mand. 7. 4). Although faith may be apparently presented as one among the Christian virtues (Mand. 8. 9 ; 12. 3, 1. Sim. 9. 15. 2), it is evident from the above that it is not so regarded. The elect are saved through faith. The other virtues are daughters of faith (Vis. 3. 8. 3, 4 ; cf. Mand. 5. 2. 3). The essential content of faith is presented in the passage quoted as Scripture by Irenæus, Origen and Athanasius, Mand. 1. 1 : " First of all, believe that there is one God, who created and framed all things, and made them from being nothing to be all things (cf. 2 Macc. 7. 28), and who comprehends all things, and who is alone incomprehensible (ἀχώρητος)." God created the world for the sake of men and the church (Mand. 12. 4. Vis. 2. 4. 2 ; 1. 4). That faith in Christ is not unknown to Hermas is of course to be taken for granted (vid. Sim. 8. 3. 2 extr.).

Faith is therefore not only a knowledge and acknowledgment of God as the Creator, but also an undivided turning of the heart to God, which makes man strong and is the root of all moral activity. It is "as truly fundamental duty as fundamental power" (ZAHN, p. 175. Cf. HÜCKSTÄDT, p. 59 f.).

But the relationship of faith and good works is not always observed by Hermas. "Take heed, therefore, ye that serve the Lord, and have him in your hearts : work the works of God, being mindful of his commandments and of the promises which he has given, and believe that he will perform these if his commandments are kept " (Sim. 1. 7). The moral activity commended is the fulfillment of the separate divine requirements. To such an observance of the commandments is attached the promise of life (Sim. 8. 11. 3 ; 6. 1. 1 ; 7. 6 ; 10. 1. 2 ; 2. 4 ; 4. 1. Mand. 4. 2. 4 ; 7. 5). Although this cannot be interpreted as equivalent to the later moralism, it yet distinctly prepares the way for it. Cf. also the designation of the preaching concerning Christ as law, νόμος (Sim. 8. 3. 2, 3).

The view of Hermas as to the possibility of fulfilling the divine commandments is not fairly represented in the assertion : "The power thereto is innate in man " (Schmid-Hauck, DG., p. 11). On the contrary, it is "the man having the Lord in his heart " (Mand. 12. 4. 3 ; cf. Sim. 10. 3. 1) who has this ability.

A certain narrowing of the moral horizon is manifest in Sim. 5. 3. 3 : "If thou shalt do some good thing not embraced in the commandment of God, thou shalt purchase to thyself the greater dignity, and thou shalt be more honored before God than thou shouldst otherwise have been " (cf. Mand. 4. 4. 2).

(d) Finally, for a proper understanding of the general view of Hermas, it is very important to note his conception of repentance, which is the dominating note in his discussions. His fundamental idea here is : " that there is no other repentance than this, that we go down into the water and receive the forgiveness of our past sins " (Mand. 4. 3. 1 ; cf. 4. 1. 8). It is a special favor of God, that now through the preaching of Hermas, in an exceptional way, a second repentance is granted the congrega-

tion of believers (Vis. 2. 2, 4, 5. Mand. 4. 4. 4. Sim. 8. 11.
1, etc.). He who from this time forward keeps the commandments shall find the forgiveness of his sins (Mand. 4. 4. 4) and
be saved. This idea of one repentance is based, indeed, upon
representations in the New Testament (1 Jn. 5. 16 ff. Heb.
6. 4. ff.). As Christianity was regarded as the consummation
upon which very shortly should follow the end of the world, there
seemed to be no further room for apostasy and repentance (cf.
Apoc. Baruch, 85. 12). Although Hermas in other connections
by no means regards sin as consisting merely in outward works, but
includes in it inward desire (ἐπιθυμία, Vis. 1. 1. 8; 3.
8. 4. Mand. 12. 1. 1; 2. 2; 4. 2. Sim. 5. 1. 5), yet of repentance he can say : " For he that hath sinned is conscious
that he hath done evil in the sight of the Lord, and his deed that
he has done comes into his heart, and he repents and no more
does evil, but does good most abundantly, and humbles his soul
and afflicts it, because he has sinned " (Mand. 4. 2. 2 ; cf. Sim.
7. 4). But it is not held that he whose sins have been forgiven
can thereafter live without sin. The " Shepherd " himself since
his conversion remains liable to many moral faults, and the
righteous as well as the wicked must, after every transgression,
take refuge to the Lord (Sim. 9. 31. 2 ; cf. ZAHN, p. 355).
Hermas does not venture to condemn to death the man who, after
hearing the call to repentance, shall sin under pressure of temptation (ὑπο χεῖρα, Mand. 4. 3. 6). He has in mind such sins
as effect a surrender of the moral power of the Gospel, a complete corruption : he is thinking of apostasy, which is to be
followed by a new conversion (Sim. 9. 14. 1 ff.; cf. Mand. 4.
1. 8. Sim. 9. 26. 6). Accordingly, repentance is like conversion : " If ye turn to the Lord with your whole heart, and work
righteousness the remaining days of your life, and serve him
strictly according to his will, he will heal your former sins "
(Mand. 12. 6. 2 ; cf. Sim. 8. 11. 3). This is the starting-point
of the Catholic discrimination between venial and mortal sins.
The error lies not really in the general idea of repentance, but
in an underestimate of minor sins. But the chief defection
from the biblical standard lies in the failure to understand grace
as the forgiveness of sins extending continuously throughout the
whole life. Hence the moralism of Hermas.

(e) In connection with the preaching of repentance, Hermas
gives great prominence to the conception of the church. The
church rests upon Christ, the ancient rock with the new door
(Sim. 9. 2. 2 ; cf. 12. 2. 3), i. e., the pre-existent Son of
God, who became manifest only in the last time. It is built
upon the waters of baptism (Vis. 3. 3. 5. Sim. 9, 16. 2), and

is extended through the preaching of Christ (Sim. 8. 3. 2).
The church is tne city of God with its own laws (Sim. 1. 1, 3,
9). But not all who receive branches from the great willow-tree,
or the word concerning Christ (cf. above, under *c*), preserve
them ; and not all who have been admitted to the tower of the
church stand the test when tried by Christ (Sim. 9. 6). Thus
the essence and the appearance of the church are often not in
harmony. The task of the preaching of Hermas is the purification of the church (Sim. 9. 18. 3). There is a pause in the
building of the church in order that sinners may be purified and
again admitted to the structure of the church (*e. g.*, Sim. 9. 7.
2 ; 10. 4. 4). It is necessary to turn quickly to repentance,
since the building of the church, and with it the time of the
world, will soon be ended (*e. g.*, Vis. 3. 8. 9. Sim. 9. 9. 4 ;
26. 6 ; 10. 4. 4, etc.). Thus by repentance the contradiction between the essence and the appearance of the church may
be overcome. In this way the ideal of the church would be attained : " After these (the wicked) are cast out, the church of God
shall become one body, one understanding, one mind, one faith,
one love : and then the Son of God shall exceedingly rejoice
among them and receive his pure people " (Sim. 9. 18. 4). It is
not hidden from Hermas, that this state shall never be attained
on earth. As in winter dead and living trees look alike, so it is
also in the church : " Neither the righteous nor the wicked are
recognized in this world, but they are alike (Sim. 3. 2, 3).
Only the future world will reveal the difference (Sim. 4. 2)."

We have thus attempted to translate the most important doctrinal views of Hermas from the prophetical form of speech into
the language of precise thought. Whatever stress may be laid
upon the prophetic-visionary elements which strike us so strangely,
upon the moralistic and legalistic elements, and the fateful limitation of forgiveness—the fact remains, that genuine Christian
ideas hold the central place in his faith and thought.

3. IGNATIUS.

The martyr bishop of Antioch furnishes in his seven genuine
epistles a portrayal of Christianity delightful in its religious fervor
and power. His general conception is closely related to the
Johannine doctrinal type.

(*a*) Christ is God, "our God," and " my God " (Eph.
inscr.; 18. 2. Rom. inscr.; 3. 3 ; 6. 3. Polycarp, 8. 3).
He is God, ὁ θεός (Smyrn. 1. 1), θεός (Trall. 7. 1), the only
Son of the Father, ὁ μόνος υἱὸς τοῦ πατρός, (Rom. inscr.), and the
Lord, ὁ κύριος (Polyc. 1. 2). Ignatius uses the formula "in
Son and Father and in Spirit" (Magn. 13. 1 ; in § 2 τὸ πνεῦμα

is doubtful ; cf. Lightf.).   He was with the Father before time began (Magn. 6. 1).   At the end of the days he became man —and this as a revelation of the One God, the Father, "who has manifested himself through his Son Jesus Christ, who is his word, λόγος, proceeding from silence" (Magn. 8. 2 ; cf. 9. 2 : "our only teacher," and Rom. 8. 2 : "the genuine mouth in whom the Father truly spake").[1]   Ignatius recognizes the reality of the earthly activity of Christ and confirms his presentation of its separate features by an emphatic "truly," ἀληθῶς (Smyrn. 1 and 2. Tral. 9. It is not allowable to say that he only seemed to suffer : Tral. 10. Smyrn. 2. Polyc. 3. 2 ; cf. Smyrn. 12. 2. Ephes. 7). But since Christ has completed his work on earth, he is now again with the Father (ἐν πατρὶ ὤν), but in consequence of this he may be but the better known (μᾶλλον φαίνεται, Rom. 3. 3) on earth.   Even after his resurrection, which he himself effected (truly raised himself, ἀνέστησεν ἑαυτόν, Smyrn. 2, in contrast with which, however, vid. 8. 1 : "The Father raised ; " cf. Trall. 9. 2), although spiritually united (πνευματικῶς ἡνωμένος) with the Father, he is yet "in the flesh" (Smyrn. 3. 1, 3).

Ignatius was fond of combining these two classes of utterances. Christ is at once God and man : "The one Healer is both fleshly and spiritual, born and unborn.   God became incarnate, true life in death, both from Mary and from God, first passible and then impassible, Jesus Christ our Lord" (Eph. 7. 2 ; cf. 18. 2.   Smyrn. 1. 1).   Upon the one hand he is, therefore, unborn, ἀγέννητος, but according to the flesh he is sprung from David's tribe, born of the Virgin according to the will of God (Eph. 19. 1), "conceived in the womb of Mary, according to the dispensation of God—on the one hand of the seed of David, on the other of the Holy Spirit" (Eph. 18. 2).   He is, therefore, perfect (τέλειος) man (Smyrn. 4. 2) and just as truly God (cf. supra).   It is impossible, in view of the above, to hold that Ignatius regarded Jesus as by nature a pre-existent spiritual being who, after completing his work on earth, returned again to heaven (the so-called "pneumatic" Christology, HARNACK i. 183 ff.).   How could he describe such a being as his God and the God of Christendom ?   We should observe further that the title, Son of God, in Ignatius designates Christ, not only as begotten in eternity, but also as the One sprung, according to the

---

[1] Thus the Johannine term, Logos, was authentically interpreted.   Christ is the Word, or the Mouth of God, i. e., the revelation of God.   Remarkable, further, is the combination of faith and love with the triadic formula (e. g., Magn. 13. 1.   Ep. 9. 1 ; cf. 1 Clem. 58. 2 ; 46. 6).   Were both formulas —they possess something of the character of formulas already in the New Testament—handed down together in the instruction preceding baptism ?

dispensation of God, at once "from Mary and God," "from David's tribe and the Holy Spirit," and entering upon a historical existence : "being truly of the tribe of David according to the flesh, the Son of God truly born of a virgin according to the will and power of God" (Smyrna 1. 1 ; cf. ZAHN, Ignat., p. 469 f.). By virtue of the double origin of his historical existence, he is "Son of man" and "Son of God." And, being this, he is "the new man" (ὁ καινὸς ἄνθρωπος, Eph. 20, a term further explained in 19. 3 : God appearing in the form of man unto newness, εἰς καινότητα, of eternal life).

(b) Christ became man in order that he might, as the Λόγος of God, reveal God to men (supra, and Eph. 3. 2 : the knowledge, γνώμη, of the Father; Eph. 17. 2 : the secret wisdom γνῶσις, of God ; Philad. 9. 1). His appearance itself is for us a revelation of God, inasmuch as he is God. This revelation is not nullified by the death of Christ, but is attested by it anew for the contemplation of faith (Magn. 9. 2). He who was himself impassible is for our sakes passible (Polyc. 3. 2). To the prince of this world, the virginity and motherhood of Mary and the death of Christ were alike incomprehensible (three mysteries). But faith knows that this all aims at the abolition of death (Eph. 19). Especially does our life now have its origin in the death of Christ (Magn. 9. 1); through this mystery we have obtained faith (ib. 2). Faith in his death enables us to escape death (Tral. 2. 1). Thus his suffering has in view and effects our salvation and peace (Smyrn. 2 ; 7. 1, cf. Tral. inscr. Philad. inscr. Smyrn. 6. 1).

Christ is our life, not only in that he will one day bestow immortality upon us, but in that he personally dwells in believers, working eternal life in them. This is the leading thought of Ignatius. Christ is our inseparable life (τὸ ἀδιάκριτον ἡμῶν ζῆν, Eph. 3. 2, cf. Magn. 15), our life forever (Magn 1. 2), our true life (Smyrn. 4. 1. Eph. 11. 1, cf. Tral. 9. 2). Christ now dwells in the hearts of believers, as does also the Father (e. g., Eph. 15. 3. Magn. 8 ; 12 ; 14 : "ye are full of God," θεοῦ γέμετε. Rom. 6. 3). In harmony with this, Ignatius calls himself a God-bearer (θεοφόρος); and Christians are God-bearers, temple-bearers, Christ-bearers, bearers of the Holy One (ναοφόροι, χριστοφόροι, ἁγιοφόροι, Eph. 9. 2), the temple in which God and Christ dwell (Eph. 15. 3. Philad. 7. 2). The expressions : being in Christ, living and acting in him, constantly recur ; "without whom we have no true life" (τὸ ἀληθινὸν ζῆν οὐκ ἔχομεν, Tral. 9. 2, cf. Eph. 8. 2 ; 10. 3. Magn. 9. 2).

(c) The Gospel has in it something peculiarly excellent, the appearing of the Saviour, our Lord Jesus Christ, his suffering

5

and his resurrection. For the beloved prophets prophesied of him, but the gospel is the perfection of incorruption. For all these things are together good, if ye believe with love (ἐν ἀγάπῃ, Philad. 9. 2). Man is, therefore, to apprehend the gospel in faith. He takes his refuge to the gospel as to the flesh of Jesus (Philad. 5. 1. Cf. also 8. 2), or the presentation of his sufferings and his resurrection (Smyrn. 7. 2), and in faith in the death of Jesus he escapes death (Tral. 2. 1. Cf. Smyrn. 5. 3). Faith leads to love : "Faith is the beginning, love the end. And these two in union are divine. But all other things relating to a holy life are consequences of these" (Eph. 14. 1). Faith and love are the entire sum (τὸ γὰρ ὅλον) of Christian life (Smyrn. 6. 1). The aim is the glory of God: "Let all things be done to the glory of God" (Pol. 5. 2). It is thus the theory of Ignatius that the new life, which has become man's through the indwelling of God, consists in faith in the gospel message and in love, and that this life is an eternal one, continuing after death. We may quote as summarizing his general view the passage, Eph. 9. 1 : "As being stones of the temple of the Father, prepared for a building of God the Father, drawn up on high by the engine of Jesus Christ, which is the cross, using for a rope the Holy Spirit. But your faith is the line and love the way drawing up to God."

When being led out to execution, Ignatius is filled with holy longing through death to reach God. He has only one passion, the Crucified (Rom. 7. 2 : my love, ὁ ἐμὸς ἔρως, was crucified), and desires to be united to him. "Let me go," he begs the Romans, "to find pure light. Arriving there, I shall be a man" (Rom. 6. 2 ; 5. 3 ; 2. 2).

(*d*) If the indwelling of God and Christ in us is for Ignatius the one focal point in Christianity, the other is his conception of church order. He is the first, so far as is known to us, to employ the term "catholic church" (χαθολιχὴ ἐχλησία): "Wherever the bishop appears, there let the people be ; " just as wherever Christ is, there is the catholic church (Symrn. 8. 2. Cf. Martyr. Polyc. 8. 1). It is certain that this does not at all involve the idea of the "binding of believers into an external unity " (ROTHE, D. Anfänge d. chr. Kirche u. ihrer Verfassung, 1837, i. 472 ff. Cf. RITSCHL, Entstehung d. altkath. Kirche, p. 459 f.). The ἐχλησία χαθολιχὴ is here the church universal in contrast with the single congregation.[1] This church universal has Christ

---

[1] For other applications of the term "catholic," vid. Justin. Dial. 81 : καθολικὴ ἀνάστασις ; 102 : καθολικαὶ και μερικαὶ κρίσεις. Cf. the Exposition of Cyril of Jerus.: "It is called catholic on account of being through the whole world from one end to the other "(Cat. 18. 23). Similarly Martyr. Polyc. 8. 1,

as its centre and the apostles as its presbytery (Philad. 5. 1).
But the episcopacy bears no relation to it. The idea of Ignatius
is, on the contrary, that as the universal church has its centre in
Christ, so the separate congregation should find its centre in its
bishop. What the apostles are to the church at large, that is the
presbytery to the individual congregation. Accordingly, the
bishop is a type of God or of Christ, the presbyters types of the
apostles (Tral. 2. 1 ; 3. 1. Magn. 2 ; 6. 1. Smyrn. 8. 1.
Eph. 6). Christ, the unseen Bishop, is contrasted with the
bishop who is seen (Magn. 3. 2, cf. Rom. 9. 1. Pol. inscr.).
The individual congregation subject to the bishop and presbytery
is a copy of the church universal, which is led by Christ and
the preaching of the apostles. Christ and the preaching of the
apostles, therefore, not the episcopacy, condition the unity of
the church universal.

Ignatius, it is true, attaches great importance to the episcopate, but in doing so he has in mind only the relation of the individual bishop to his congregation. He has, evidently, two
motives for thus emphasizing the authority of the bishops. First,
he wished to maintain the moral principle of authority and subjection in human society (he demands the same subjection and
reverence for the presbyters and deacons). Referring to the
three offices, he says : " Without these it is not called a church "
(Tral. 3. 1, cf. Eph. 2. 2 ; 20. 2. Polyc. 6. 1. Philad.
inscr. 4. 7. Tral. 2. 2 ; 13. 2. Magn. 13. 1 and 2 : " Be subject to the bishop and to one another "). Secondly, there was a
special reason for supporting the bishops at that time, as they
presented a fixed authority in opposition to the gnostic tendencies then spreading in Asia Minor (Tral. 7. Philad. 2. 3. 4.
Smyrn. 9. 1). The unity and harmony of the members of a congregation in prayer and in temper, in love and faith, in subjection to
one leader, the bishop, constitutes for him the ideal of congregational life (e. g., Philad. 7. 2 ; 8. 1. Polyc. 1. 2. Magn. 1. 2 ;
3. 2 ; 6. 2 ; 7. Eph. 4. 13). It is to be attained by attachment to the bishop and obedience to him. Cf. SEEBERG, Der
Begriff d. Kirche, i., 1885, p. 11 ff.[1]

The principle applies not only in matters of doctrine and life,

where the " catholic church " is the churches throughout the world (κατὰ τὴν
οἰκουμένην ἐκκλησίαι); but ibid. 16. 2 speaks of "the catholic church in
Smyrna." Cf. 19. 2.

[1] It is historically incorrect to find here—the case is somewhat different with
Clement—the beginning of the Catholic hierarchy or "divine church law,"
as does SOHM (Kirchenrecht i., 1893), a position to which he is led by his
erroneous principle, that every form of ecclesiastical law is in conflict with the
essential nature of the church and a source of all manner of evil. Cf. my
critique of the work of Sohm in Theol. Lit. bl., 1893, Nos. 25-27.

but particularly in baptism and the celebration of the eucharist, in the Agapæ and in the celebration of marriage : " It is not allowed without the bishop to baptize or hold the Agape, but whatsoever he shall approve, that is also well-pleasing to God, in order that whatsoever is done may be safe and secure " (Smyrn. 8. 2. Cf. Pol. 5. 2). Referring to baptism, Ignatius says that Christ in his own baptism designed to purify the water by his passion (Eph. 18. 2), and that baptism is for those who receive it, like faith, love, and patience, a part of the Christian panoply (Pol. 6. 2). It belongs to the defensive armor ($\ddot{o}\pi\lambda a$) of the Christian life, and has, therefore, a practical daily significance. Of the Lord's Supper it is said : "The eucharist is the flesh of our Saviour, Jesus Christ, which suffered for our sins, which the Father in his goodness raised from the dead." Of those who deny this, it is said : " It were profitable for them to commune ($\dot{a}\gamma a\pi\tilde{a}\nu=\dot{a}\gamma\dot{a}\pi\eta\nu$ $\pi o\iota\tilde{\epsilon}\iota\nu$, Smyrn. 8. 2. Apparently in the same sense we find $\dot{a}\gamma\dot{a}\pi\eta$ $\ddot{a}\varphi\vartheta a\rho\tau o\varsigma$, Rom. 3, cf. ZAHN. p. 348 f.), in order that they might rise again" (Smyrn. 7. 1. Cf. also Rom. 7. 3.). The effect of participating is thus described : " Breaking the one bread, which is the medicine of immortality, an antidote that we might not die, but live in Jesus Christ forever" (Eph. 20. 2). This view is based upon Jn. 6. 54-58. Considered in its connection, this asserts nothing especially new. It is the meaning of the author that the Lord's Supper is on earth already a means whereby we are made partakers of eternal life.

(e) Christianity is sharply opposed to Judaism as well as to heathenism. This also is a view closely related to the Johannine. " To live according to the law of Judaism " is to have not received grace (Magn. 8. 1). On the contrary, we must put away the old Jewish leaven in order that we may be salted in Christ ($\dot{a}\lambda\iota\sigma\vartheta\eta\tau\epsilon$ $\dot{\epsilon}\nu$ $\dot{a}\upsilon\tau\tilde{\omega}$, Magn. 10, 2). " It is absurd to name Jesus Christ and to Judaize ; for Christianity did not confess ($\dot{\epsilon}\pi\dot{\iota}\sigma\tau\epsilon\upsilon\sigma\epsilon\nu$ $\epsilon\dot{\iota}\varsigma$) Judaism, but Judaism Christianity, and every tongue confessing Christianity will be gathered together unto God " (ib. § 3, cf. Philad. 6. 1, 2). Judaism is thus only a positive, but now antiquated, stage of preparation for Christianity. Believers, whether Jews or heathen, belong to the one body of the church (Smyrn. 1. 2, cf. Paulus Eph. 2. 16). How impressive is this historic self-consciousness of Christianity, that Judaism is for Christianity simply a vanquished position.

Summarizing, we find that Ignatius in Christ worships God in person, who became man to reveal God to man, and through his passion and death to redeem men and make them partakers of eternal salvation. In the hearts of those who in faith receive the gospel message Christ henceforth dwells. The believer leads an eternal life, whose content is faith and love. Christ is his life, and death his gain ; and he who believes on Christ shall live though he die. The congregational life develops harmoniously, since believers are taught to be in subjection in life and doctrine to their bishops. Finally, we note a consciousness of living in the last times (ἔσχατοι καιροί, Eph. 11. 1. Cf. Magn. 6. 1).

4. POLYCARP.

(*a*) The epistle of Polycarp to the Philippians assumes that those to whom it is addressed acknowledge the divinity of Christ, the fulfillment of his mission on earth, and his subsequent glorification and exaltation above heaven and earth (1. 2 ; 2. 1 ; 9. 2). It is just as firmly held that Christ suffered on account of our sins for our redemption (1. 2 ; 8. 1). He knows also that we are saved by grace, not by our own works, through Jesus Christ (1. 3 extr.); and, further, that only upon the assumption that we now have faith can we attain the glory which should crown our earthly life ("if we walk worthily of him, we shall also reign with him, if we believe," 5. 2. Cf. 2. 1 ; 8. 2). Faith, love, and hope are the content of the Christian life (3. 3).

(*b*) But the practical force of his exhortations is laid upon the requirement that we walk in the commandment (ἐντολή) of the Lord (4. 1 ; 5. 1 ; 2. 2). Only he who possesses faith, love toward God and his neighbor, and hope fulfills the "commandment of righteousness." He who has love is far from all sin (3. 3). The righteousness (δικαιοσύνη) of the Christian consists in his moral activity, but the pledge (ἀρραβών) of our righteousness is Christ, who lifted up our sins in his body on the tree (8. 1. Cf. 1 Pet. 2. 24). Christians should follow Christ and suffer with him (8. 2 ; 9, 2, cf. 2. 2).

(*c*) These exhortations reach their culmination in the thought that God will raise from the dead all those who, following Christ, keep his commandments, and will permit them to share in the dominion of Christ. He that raised him up from the dead will raise us up also, if we do his will and walk in his commandments, and love what he loved, abstaining from all iniquity (2. 2, cf. 5. 1, 2).

The leading thoughts of Polycarp are thus seen to be thoroughly evangelical : The Christian, who has apprehended Christ in faith, will in love fulfill the law of Christ, following him with patience, in hope of being, like Christ, raised up by God to everlasting life and of enjoying eternal fellowship with Christ. The influence of Johannine ideas (especially from the Epistles) is in this

disciple of St. John just as apparent as is the different spirit
which animates him.

5. PAPIAS.

Among the fragments of Papias, only that preserved by Irenæus (v. 33. 3 sq.) is of special importance in the History of
Doctrines. It paints in glowing colors the wonderful fertility of
the earth during the millennial reign : " The kingdom of Christ
being established bodily upon this very earth" (Euseb. h. e. iii.
39. 12). The description is drawn from the Jewish apocalyptic
books (Enoch 10. 19. Apoc. Bar. 29), which accounts for
the vivid eschatological expectations and the conformity to Jewish
theology (Cf. Just. Dial. 80).

6. BARNABAS.

Despite the repulsive extravagances of Alexandrian exegesis
found in this author, he preserves the fundamental ideas of the
apostolic period in a relatively pure form.

(a) The pre-existence of Christ is affirmed, and with it his
divine creative activity (5. 5, 6). He will one day return again
as Judge in divine omnipotence (15. 5). He is not Son of man,
but Son of God (12. 10 ; 7. 9). He appeared in the flesh,
since men cannot look even upon the created and perishable sun
(5. 10, 11).

(b) The Son of God, who thus assumed human flesh, suffered
also upon the cross, according to the will of God. His sufferings are understood also as a sacrifice (5. 1 ; 7. 3 : and since he
would make the tabernacle of his Spirit [i. e., his body] a sacrifice for our sins, § 5 ; c. 8). The object and result of the
bodily sufferings are, first, the abolition of death and the demonstration of this in the resurrection (5. 6); but chiefly the forgiveness of sins and sanctifying of the heart, since we are thus made
new creatures (5. 1 : " For to this end the Lord endured, that he
might give his flesh to death, in order that we might be sanctified
by the remission of sins, that is, by his blood of sprinkling ;"
6. 11 : " Since, therefore, he has renewed us by the remission of
sins, he gave us another character, so that we might have the
spirit of children, as he had moulded us anew "). Accordingly,
the heralds of the gospel proclaim " the remission of sins and
the sanctification of the heart ". (8. 3). Through his suffering
for us Christ has bestowed upon us the covenant which Israel
(see below) forfeited, and has made us heirs of the inheritance
(14. 4). Although Barnabas has not made clear the necessity,
nature, and object of Christ's sacrifice, there is no ground for
attributing to him the idea that the Saviour's death has relation

only to sins of the past (BEHM, Ztschr. f. k. Wiss., 1886, p. 299 f.). His sufferings are represented as making death powerless and establishing in us the principle of a permanent renewal. Barnabas, it is true, has, like the other Church Fathers, failed to realize and teach distinctly that the forgiveness of sins remains a vital element of the Christian's entire life.

(*c*) The believer enters upon the possession of the blessings of redemption through baptism : "This he says in order that we may go down into the water bewailing our sins and uncleanness, and come up from it having fruit in our hearts, having reverence and hope in Jesus in our spirits" (11. 1, cf. § 8). Through baptism, therefore, we become free from sin. Our heart is thenceforth a dwelling of God (8. 15). As to the nature of this new state and the means (preaching) by which it is produced, we are taught in 16. 7-9 : "Before we believed in God, the abode of our hearts was perishable and weak . . . so that it was full of idolatry and the home of devils because we did the things which were against God. But it is to be builded up in the name of the Lord. . . How? Learn : Receiving the remission of sins and hoping in his name, we are become new creatures, created again from the beginning. Wherefore God truly dwells within us in the abode of our hearts. How? His word of faith, his proclamation of the Gospel, the wisdom of (his) pardons, the commandments of (his) doctrine, he himself speaking in us and dwelling in us, slaves to death as we are, opening to us the gate of the temple, which is his mouth [for the proclamation of the word], giving to us repentance, leads us into the imperishable temple." It will be observed that here also faith is presented as a fundamental act in the reception of grace (Cf. 2. 2; 4. 8; 6. 17; 9. 4; 11. 11). But faith is in Barnabas most intimately associated with hope. Faith and hope are but different aspects of the same inner possession (1. 4, 6; 4. 8 : "In the hope of his faith;" 6, 3 ; 11, 11, *i. e.,* of baptism · "having in our spirits reverence and hope in Christ;" 8. 5 ; 11. 8 ; 12. 2, 3, 7; 16. 8; 19. 7. Cf. Heb. 11. 1). The expectation that Barnabas will place a corresponding valuation upon justification (δικαιοσύνη and δικαιοῦν) is not gratified. With the above presentation of faith he combines a portrayal of moral integrity (1. 4; 4. 12 ; 5. 4; 20. 2 ; 4. 10 ; 15. 7. The passage 13. 7 is not decisive, nor is 1. 6, where the text is also fragmentary).

(*d*) He who has thus received with faith in Christ through baptism the forgiveness of his sins and the renewing indwelling of God will also seek to fulfill the "new law of our Lord Jesus Christ" (2. 6). Barnabas describes such an one as "being without the yoke of necessity" (ib., cf. Jas. 1. 5. Gal. 5. 1). This

assertion must not be overlooked amid the very strong emphasizing of the divine commandments (2. 1 ; 4. 11. Cf. 21. 1, 5, 8).
But that Barnabas was not free from moralistic overvaluation of good works in the Christian life is clearly evident from the language (not, indeed, original with him, but adopted with approval) of 19. 10 : "Or work with thy hands for the ransom (εἰς λύτρον) of thy sins." Christians should not bring outward but inward sacrifices (2. 9, 10); the insight which they have gained restrains them, as strangers, from observing the Jewish law (3. 6, cf. 4. 6).

We note, finally, as bearing upon the development of the moral life, the admonition : "Do not take it upon yourselves to live alone, as already justified ; but, assembling in one place, strive together for the common good " (4. 10, cf. 2).

(e) In one point Barnabas fails entirely to understand the connections of the traditional faith. He sees in Christianity the people of God, but does not recognize the historical relation of Israel in the development of the plan of salvation. According to his view, the covenant with Israel was never really concluded, since the tables of the law were broken by Moses (4. 8 ; 14).
Likewise, the assertion that the elder shall serve the younger (Gen. 25. 21 ff.; 48. 14 ff.) shows that the covenant was turned over to us (c. 13). Circumcision is accordingly without divine sanction (9. 6), and the entire conception of the law among the Jews, based upon a literal interpretation of it, is a colossal misconception (e. g., 10. 9). They rested in the allegorical exterior without penetrating to the real meaning. Γνῶσις furnishes Barnabas the proper and profound understanding of the law. As Philo interprets it in the interest of philosophy, so Barnabas in the interest of Christianity. For example, the prohibition of the eating of swine's flesh really forbids the association with men who are like swine. The prohibition of hyæna flesh warns us not to become seducers or adulterers, since that animal changes its sex every year (10. 3, 7). The 318 servants whom Abraham circumcised are thus interpreted : Learn that he first says the 18, and, after leaving a space, the 300. The 18 : I is ten, H is eight. There thou hast Jesus (᾽Ι Ησοῦς). But because the cross in the T would indicate grace, he says, "and 300." Thus he sets forth Jesus in the two letters and the cross in the third (9. 8), etc. This exegetical method, which soon became the prevalent one, prevented for 1500 years a historical interpretation of the Old Testament ; but it also forbade the acceptance of anything found in the Old Testament which was not thought to be in consonance with New Testament teaching.

(f) Barnabas, too, looks forward to the end of the world as

near at hand (4. 9 ; 21. 3). The last "offense" (σκάνδαλον τέλειον) of which Enoch speaks (4. 3—not found in our Book of Enoch) is near.   He calls attention to the signs of the end, as given in Daniel 7. 24, 7 f.   Cf. Barn. 4. 4 and § 9.   The ten kingdoms are the Roman emperors from Augustus to Domitian. The " little king " is Nerva, as the eleventh emperor.   The humiliating of the three kings together (ὑφ'ἕν) is fulfilled in the three Flavians, Vespasian, Titus, and Domitian, who are humbled together since their dynasty loses the throne.   There is need of watchfulness, lest the devil (ὁ μέλας, ὁ πονηρὸς ἄρχων) force his way and gain power (4. 9, 13).   To avoid this, Christians must keep the commandments and cling to (προσέχειν) the fellowship of the church (2. 1 ; 4. 10, 11 ; 21. 8).   Barnabas undertakes also to map out the future.   As there were six days of creation, so will God in six thousand years bring the present dispensation of the world to an end, since one day is with him as a thousand years.   Then follows a seventh millennium, corresponding to the Sabbath of creation, in which Christ renews the world and the righteous (δικαιωθέντες καὶ ἀπολαβόντες τὴν ἐπαγγελίαν, ἁγιασθέντες) hallow this last day of the world's week.   Then dawns the eighth day, the beginning of the other world (ἄλλου κόσμου ἀρχή).   The type of this is seen in the joyous celebration of Sunday, upon which day also Christ arose from the dead and ascended (!) to heaven (15. 5-9).

To summarize : Through his passion and death Christ brought us forgiveness of sins and deliverance from death.   Through baptism the forgiveness of sins is imparted to us, God dwells in us, and a new life begins.   In this new life we—with free will— fulfill the commandments of Christ.   The author is writing for those who are in danger of accepting the Jewish ordinances (3. 6 ; 4. 6.   Cf. his own description of the contents of his epistle, 17. 1), but he is free from any subjection to the Old Testament law.   The nearness of the end of all things and the severity of the account to be rendered should impel us to zeal.

7. The Didache.

This document can be employed in tracing the History of Doctrines only with the most extreme caution, since we know that it was not designed to present a statement of Christian teaching—not even of any particular doctrines.

(a) The designations of Christ as the Son of God (16. 4), as the God (or is υἱός the proper reading?) of David (10. 6), and as the Servant of God (9. 3 ; 10. 2, 3) are to be interpreted in the same sense as in the documents already examined.   We have also

already met the representation of God as Father, Son, and Holy
Ghost (7. 1, 3), preserved in the baptismal formula.

(*b*) Of the blessings of salvation bestowed upon us by God
through Christ are here mentioned life, the deeper knowledge
(γνῶσις), faith, and immortality (10. 2 ; 9. 3, cf. 16. 1 ; 4. 8),
and also the indwelling of the name of God in our hearts (10. 2).
Christians are those who hope in God (ἐπὶ τὸν θεόν, cf. Barnabas).
The Spirit of God prepares us for our Christian calling (4. 10).

(*c*) As means by which salvation is applied to the individual
may be mentioned baptism (7); the eucharist (9. 10), which is
spiritual food and drink (10. 3 : "upon us he has graciously bestowed spiritual food and drink and eternal life through his Son ")
and is received with consciousness of the personal presence of
the Lord (10. 6. Whether we read מרנא תא as in Rev. xxii.
10, "Come, Lord Jesus," or מרן אתא, "The Lord is here," does
not affect the question before us), through which presence there are
given to men the blessings which we have above (*b*) enumerated.
(It is, therefore, the Johannine conception of the Lord's Supper
which is presented here as well as in Ignatius); the proclamation
of salvation("for the imparting of righteousness and knowledge "
(11. 2) by traveling apostles (11. 1, 2), by prophets (speaking
in the Spirit. Cf. the description of prophets in Hermas, Mand.
11, and the labors of Hermas himself. Also Ignat. Eph. 20. 1.
Rom. 7. 2. Philad. 7. Vid. BONWETSCH, Die Prophetie im
apostol. u. nachap. Zeitalter in Ztschr. f. k. Wiss., 1884, p.
460 ff.), by special teachers inspired by the Spirit (13.2),
but also by bishops and deacons ("for these also minister
(λειτουργοῦσι) for you the ministry of the prophets and teachers,"
15. 1), and, as well, by brotherly admonition (4. 2).

(*d*) In this free exercise of spiritual functions there can be no
thought of hierarchical tendencies. Official positions stand upon
the same footing as the free agencies of the Spirit, and it is especially noted that the latter may fittingly render such service,
and are, therefore, to be accorded like honor (15). The church
(or the saints, 4. 2) is the body of believers scattered throughout the world, who are to be gathered into the (eschatological)
kingdom of God (9. 4, cf. 10. 5). This eschatological conception of the kingdom of God is a peculiarity of the apostolic fathers
(the view of Barnabas is different, 8. 6). Here, too, we find a
vivid expectation of the approaching end of the world. Cf. in
the communion-prayer : "Let grace come and this world pass
away" (11. 6).[1] The last chapter of the Didache treats of the

---

[1] It is possible, indeed, that these words have reference to the blessings bestowed in the Eucharist, in which case the petitioner expresses his desire that

Christian duty of watchfulness, of false prophets which shall come, of Antichrist (then shall appear the κοσμοπλάνος as the Son of God), of the final testing of the church, of the signs in heaven, the sound of the trumpets, the resurrection, and the coming of the Lord upon the clouds of heaven.

(*e*) In the introductory counsel to candidates for baptism ("The Two Ways," c. 1-6, cf. Barnab. 18-20) the Didache presents a formula which was frequently used, in which the chief features of the moral life of the believer are stated in a condensed form : (1) Love to God and one's neighbor, (2) avoiding gross sins, (3) opposing sins of physical and spiritual lust, (4) proper conduct toward teachers, the church, the needy, children and servants. The exhortation to the confession of sins in the congregation before prayer, and also before receiving the eucharist (4. 14 ; 14. 1, cf. 10. 6), indicates a vivid sense of sin. The Didache also quotes with approval the counsel which we have found adopted by Barnabas : "If thou hast by (the work of) thy hands, thou shalt give a ransom for thy sins" (4. 6). The moralism of the document is sufficiently indicated in the above.

God has through Christ bestowed upon Christians an immortal life, which is displayed in faith, hope, and knowledge. This is produced and preserved in man through baptism and the Lord's Supper, and through teaching and instruction given in many ways. He maintains this life in earnest moral striving and in perpetual penitence, and is thus prepared for the approaching judgment and its terrors.

8. THE HOMILY OF CLEMENT.

(*a*) The sermon opens with the demand : "It is necessary for us to think of Jesus Christ as of God, as of the Lord of the living and the dead" (1. 1). In proportion as we underestimate him will we also underestimate the salvation to come (1. 2). Of his person, it is said : "Christ the Lord who saves us, being first spirit, became flesh and thus called us" (9. 5). That is, he who was at first a spiritual being became flesh. But the author appears to regard this spiritual being, and likewise the Holy Ghost, as a creature of the Father. "Male" and "female" (Gen. 1. 27) are applied respectively to Christ and to the church as a spiritual entity (14. 2).

(*b*) God sent Christ to us as Saviour and author of immortality (ἀρχηγὸς τῆς ἀφθαρσίας) and through him reveals to us "the truth and the heavenly life" (20. 5). It is said, indeed, that

the world may fade from his view and the gifts of grace (χάρις used, as often, for χάρισμα) come to him.

Christ suffered for our sakes (1. 2), and that he had compassion upon the lost (2. 7). But these ideas are, for the author, mere formulas. The work of redemption means for him that Christ has abolished the darkness of foolish creature-worship (1. 6, 7) and brought us instead the knowledge of the Father of Truth (3. 1 ; 17. 1) and imparted to us his laws (3. 4). The promise of immortality is added as a reward for the keeping of his commandments (11. 1).

(c) The conception of the Christian life corresponds with the above. The controlling thought is : " that we give to him some recompense (ἀντιμισθίαν), or some fruit worthy of what he has given to us " (1. 3 ; 9. 7, cf. 15. 2). This consists herein : that we, in view of the magnitude of the work of Christ, confess him as the Saviour (3. 3), and that we thus confess him " by doing what he says and not disregarding his commandments " (3. 4), or " we confess him by our works " (ἐν τοῖς ἔργοις, 4. 3). Doing thus, we may live without fear of death (5. 1). The Christian should preserve his baptism without stain. It has publicly cleansed him from his sins (6. 9 ; 8. 6, here called a "seal"). He who in this way serves God is righteous (11. 1, 7 ; 12. 1), and he who does righteousness shall be saved (19. 3). But he who transgresses Christ's commandments incurs eternal punishment (6. 7). No person nor thing can then save him : " nor anyone be our comforter, if we shall not be found having holy and righteous works " (6, 9 and 7). For doing such works men must, it is true, have faith as a prerequisite ; but faith is nothing more (in contrast with doubt, διψυχία) than a believing of the divine promise of reward (11. 1, 5. 6).

But now, since men are sinful and full of evil lust (13. 1 ; 19. 2), this demand takes the form of a call to repentance. To this the preacher summons (8. 1 f. ; 9. 8 ; 13. 1 ; 16. 1 ; 17. 1 ; 19. 1). This embraces, first, the forsaking of the former sins (13. 1), and then at once the fulfilling of the Lord's commandments (8. 3, 4). Repentance is for the author not a change of mind, but a change of habits by good works. This repentance (μετάνοια) is the " recompense " which we owe to God and Christ (9. 8).

The externalizing of the moral life is further manifest in the fact that the orator (on the basis of Tobit 12. 8, 9) recommends certain particular works as peculiarly suited to repentance for sins : " Almsgiving is, therefore, excellent as a repentance for sins ; fasting is better than prayer ; but almsgiving better than either . . . for almsgiving becomes a lightening of the burden (κούφισμα) of sin " (16. 4).

If man has thus fulfilled the will of God, or Christ, striven against his evil passions, and done good, he receives from God eternal life in the kingdom of God (eschatologically conceived) as the reward for his works (8. 4 and 11. 7 ; 12. 1 ; 6. 7 ; 9. 6 ; 10. 4). The day of judgment is already approaching (16. 3). But the Christian receives his reward in the body in which he was called. The resurrection of the body dare not be called in question (9. 1-5, cf. also 9. 4). The kingdom of God will begin at the second coming of Jesus. Terrible tortures are impending over those who deny Jesus and do not keep his commandments (17. 4. 7).[1]

This last and latest book of the so-called "Apostolic Fathers" is beyond question the furthest removed from the Christianity of the apostolic age. What we have been able to detect in incipient form in the other "Fathers" here meets us in clear and undisguised form. Christ is essentially the Teacher of the knowledge of God and the new Lawgiver. Christianity is the reception of this teaching and this law into the heart and life. The motives prompting to the keeping of the law thus given are the consideration of the magnitude of the gift of God and faith in the promise of reward.

9. GENERAL ESTIMATE.

It has been necessary to examine the Apostolic Fathers at such length, both on account of the nature of the documents and because the material thus secured forms the starting-point for any proper presentation of the History of Doctrines. It places us in position to picture vividly to ourselves the faith of the Christian church at the close of the first and the beginning of the second century. The picture thus constructed can lay claim to fidelity, since its features have been drawn from the most diverse sections of the church and from writings of most various character—congregational epistles and hand-books, martyrs, teachers wandering widely in their conceptions of Christian truth, prophets, and preachers.

The common features thus elicited are :

(1) Faith in the One God, the Creator of the world,[2] the

[1] Incidentally we refer to the abstruse discussion of the church in c. 14. "The first spiritual church" is a creature of God, created like Christ before the creation of the world. It is the Holy Ghost. The rest of the text (especially § 4) is probably interpolated. The passage as it stands appears to identify Christ with the Holy Ghost (§ 4), but § 2 requires the recognition of a difference.

[2] Compare also the *Prædicatio Petri*, which probably dates from about the same time (in Clem. Al. Strom. vi. 5): "Know therefore that there is one God, who made the beginning of all things and who has the power of the

Father, the Governor of the earth and the church, who has chosen Christians as his people, who takes up his abode in their hearts and guides their lives. (2) Faith in Jesus Christ the Son of God, who was already actively engaged at the creation and under the old covenant ; who is God, and appeared in the flesh at the end of the days. We find, however, nothing doctrinally definite in regard to his pre-existence (according to 2 Clem., he is a creature), his relation to the Father, the method of the incarnation, or the relationship of the divine and the human in his person. The New Testament proclamation of salvation is reproduced, but no doctrinal conclusions are drawn from it. (3) The designation of God as Father, Son, and Holy Ghost is preserved in connection with the baptismal formula, and is occasionally employed, but not made (especially as to the Holy Ghost) a subject of particular study. (4) There is a general agreement also as to the sinfulness and misery (especially death) of the human race, which is, through its disobedience, lost to God and given over to the folly of idolatry, the power of devils, and eternal perdition. (5) Jesus Christ is the Redeemer. He revealed the Father and taught the new moral law ; but, above all, he by his passion and death freed mankind from sin and death. He brought to men a new life, forgiveness of sins, knowledge of God and confidence in him : he gave the impulse to true morality, the hope of immortality. Although this is made dependent upon his sufferings and death, we fail to find any distinctive conception, or original religious apprehension, of the latter. The death of Christ arouses and moves religious feeling, but it is not understood nor pursued to its consequences. Our authors miss entirely that interpretation of the Old Testament premises which is so prominent in the canonical Scriptures. (6) The salvation which Christ has obtained and brought to men is quite differently described : (a) Forgiveness of sins through baptism, new creation. In Hermas and 2 Clement, only the sins of the past are included. There is a great lack of clearness in conception ; it is particularly noticeable that the significance of the forgiveness of sins for the whole subsequent Christian life is greatly obscured. " Righteousness " is always merely an active, actual righteousness. Paul is not understood, but even the influence of his specific doctrinal ideas falls noticeably into the background. The type of doctrine which is followed corresponds generally— though in a cruder form—with that of the catholic epistles of

---

end ; the Unseen, who beholdeth all things ; the Unmoved, who moveth all things ; needing nothing, whom all things need and for whom they exist ; intangible, eternal, incorruptible, uncreated, who made all things by the word of his power."

the New Testament. (*b*) Communion with God, the indwelling of the Father, or Christ, or the Spirit in the heart (Ignatius, Hermas). (*c*) Knowledge of God as the One God, the Creator, Lord, Father, etc. (*d*) The new law. (*e*) Eternal life as the reward of moral living.

(7) The means by which these blessings of salvation are appropriated by the church, as the people of God, are particularly : (*a*) Baptism, for the begetting of a new life and for the forgiveness of sins. (*b*) The Word of God, as a message of salvation and as doctrine (Old Testment proverbs ; the works, cross, and commandments of Christ ; promises of life and threatenings of judgment), presented in many ways, as sermon or fraternal admonition, by teachers, apostles, prophets, ecclesiastical officials, etc. No theory is offered, however, as to the connection of the divine energy with this proclamation of the Word. But, since it is chiefly through these means that salvation is imparted to men, we must, of course, understand the divine working upon man as essentially an actual religious influence corresponding to man's moral nature. (*c*) The Lord's Supper, as a means to immortality. This is not connected by these authors with the forgiveness of sins, just as the proclamation of the Word is not clearly made subordinate to that end. (*d*) We may mention further the influence of good angels (Hermas), the providential dealings of God, the moral efforts of man himself, etc.

(8) The individual Christian apprehends God in faith, which is a knowledge of God, self-committal to him and confidence in him, *i. e.*, in his grace, nearness, readiness to help, and the sincerity of his promises and threatenings. These conceptions are also traceable to the New Testament, but, as the Pauline idea of justification was lost sight of, a moralistic element readily became interwoven with them. This faith is the first step. Upon it depends the moral development of the individual. But the knowledge of God is obscured. Sin, whose forgiveness has been effected in baptism, remains in man as a power, a difference being traceable between willful and accidental sins (Hermas). This sin man must conquer and overcome ; but he accomplishes this not through faith in the continuous forgiveness of sins, but through the sense of the nearness of God, through confidence in his help, and, above all, through love as the obedient fulfillment of the divine commandments. The connection with faith is by no means lost sight of, but it is not clearly apprehended, nor preserved in purity. After the forgiveness of sins has once been granted to man, he thereafter merits it by his good works. The latter take their place as a second and independent principle by the side of faith, since the fixed relation of faith to the for-

giveness of sins vanishes. Thus we note the second great defect in the doctrinal conceptions of the period. As the work of Christ is not understood as having directly in view the forgiveness of sins, so there is naturally a failure to retain this forgiveness as an essential object of faith. Good works are considered necessary in order to become sure of the forgiveness of sins. It is perfectly proper to speak of the " moralism " of such views. Faith is more and more robbed of its significance. Love assumes the leading place in the soul, but, having by the depreciation of faith lost the inner impulsive power, it turns to the fulfillment of the commandments and the performing of good works. Thus was lost, however, the attitude of soul which distinguished primitive Christianity, the sense of receiving everything from God and by his gift. Instead of this, man's own works now occupy the foreground. This moralistic modification of the primitive Christian position was, indeed, brought about by means of the popular Greek-Roman ideal of human freedom. It Hellenized, but at the same time it proved a doorway through which Judaic legalism forced its way into the church.

(9) The Christian lives in connection with a congregation, or church. (*a*) In this reign harmony of spirit (especially in the celebration of the eucharist), brotherly love, readiness to teach and admonish, to help the poor, etc. (*b*) It presents a sharp contrast to the heathen world, which is to be converted by the efforts of Christian love. (*c*) It affords just as sharp a contrast to Judaism, which represents an antiquated stage of development, led by national pride to imagine itself still in possession of its ancient prerogatives.[1] (*d*) The unity of the church at large is based upon Christ and the preaching of the apostles, to which is to be added the influence of a common history and a common destiny. The inner unity finds expression in letters and pilgrimages, admonitions and mutual intercessory prayers. The church polity, especially the episcopate, has only a local significance for each particular congregation. Whilst the clerical office is highly esteemed, there is the fullest recognition also of the free activity of all believers in spiritual things (Did., Herm.). But we may already observe the beginning of the conflict between tradition ($\pi\alpha\rho\acute{\alpha}\delta o\sigma\iota\varsigma$) and succession ($\delta\iota\alpha\delta o\chi\acute{\eta}$) on the one hand, and the Spirit and *charismata* upon the other (1 Clem., Did.).

(10) There is a vivid sense of the vanity and the perishable nature of this world, and of the glory of the eternal world, as

---

[1] Cf. the portraiture of Jewish piety in the *Prædicatio Petri* (in Clem. Al. Strom. 6. 5): " Do not worship after the manner of the Jews, for they, thinking to know God, do not really know him, worshiping angels and archangels, the moon, Selene, etc."

well as the terrible character of the torments of hell (see especially Apocal. Petri.). The end of all things is thought to be very near. Eschatology is moulded by the figures of Old Testament prophecy and the declarations of Christ. The kingdom of God, or the supreme good, is, in accord with the whole tendency of the prevailing religious conceptions, regarded as a purely future entity. The more ancient the document examined, the more fervent is the expression of longing for this kingdom. Before the end lies the millennial kingdom (Barnabas, Papias), which is, after the Jewish pattern, depicted in a fantastic way. It is going too far, however, to find in this expectation one of the leading impulses of the Christian propaganda of the first century (Harnack, i. ed. 3, 158, note). It is, on the other hand, perfectly proper to assert, with the same author (i. ed. 3, 165), that : " The chief thing remained the final judgment of the world, and the certainty that the holy shall go to heaven to God, and the unholy to hell." This was involved in the idea of reward for earthly conduct.

Such are the leading thoughts of the age discovered by candid dissection of the sources. The circuit of thought inherited from the apostolic age is preserved in outward form and in general content, but the connection of the component thoughts is destroyed ; and the apprehension of truth becomes at decisive points uncertain, when it does not entirely vanish. Faith, grace, and the forgiveness of sins fall into the background, and in their stead the new law and good works come into prominence. The thoughts which we have rapidly sketched are not always a real possession, but in some cases merely titles of possession, not understood by those who hold them.

A lack of comprehensive understanding and profound apprehension of the gospel itself (as related to its Old Testament antecedents) is here undeniable. And this defect certainly reaches far back into the apostolic age. But, as the most reliable result of the study of the period under review, it may be asserted that the variations of the range of Christian thought from the views of the apostles are not to be ascribed directly to Judaistic tendencies. The conclusion thus directly drawn from the general character of the prevalent conception is enforced by the fact, that in not a single point can any specific influence of Jewish-Christian thought or of the ceremonial law be detected. The legality which here appears is not of the Jewish sort, but it, nevertheless, without awakening suspicion, prepared the way for the intrusion of Judaic influences. The moralism is that of the heathen world, particularly in that age, and it has its origin in the state of the natural man as such. The misconceptions of the

6

gospel may be traced directly to the fact that the Gentile Christians did not understand the Old Testament ideas presupposed
in the apostolic proclamation of the gospel.   But moralism
always serves the interests of legalism.   Making much of man's
own works, the age accepted (*e. g.*, from the Book of Tobit) the
legalistic works of the later Jewish piety.

§ 8. *Rules of Faith.*

Already in the period of the Apostolic Fathers, the Holy
Scriptures and the baptismal formula began to be regarded as
presenting the norm of Christian faith.

We can here consider only the earliest traces of the recognition granted to these two sources of authority.   The problems
associated with them in the course of historical development will
demand our attention at a later period.

(1) Jesus himself describes and employs the Old Testament
as an infallible authority (*e. g.*, Matt. 5. 17.   Lk. 24. 44), and
the apostles also use it as such (*e. g.*, Rom. 1. 2.   Gal. 3. 8, 22 ;
4. 30, etc.).   But the Lord says of his own words also, that they
shall outlast heaven and earth, and asserts the same of the principles to be proclaimed by his apostles (Matt. 10. 40 ; 16. 19).
In harmony with this, the apostles appeal to Christ's words as of
binding authority (1 Thes. 4. 15.   Gal. 6. 2.   1 Cor. 7. 10 ;
9. 14.   Acts 20. 35), but claim also like authority for their
own utterances (*e. g.*, 2 Thes. 2. 15.   2 Cor. 2. 9 ; 7. 15).
There is, indeed, a manifest desire to have authoritative words
of Jesus himself (1 Cor. 7. 10, 12, 25).   The epistles of Paul
and the books of the Old Testament are λοιπαὶ γραφαί (2 Pet. 3.
15, 16).

The Apostolic Fathers still view the matter in the same light.
With them, too, the Old Testament is regarded as primarily the
absolute authority and norm of truth, however constantly it is
interpreted in a New Testament sense.   Quotations from it are
introduced with the traditional formulas, "the Scripture"
(ἡ γραφή) and "it is written" (γέγραπται).   If this formula,
which, in accordance with New Testament usage, was associated
peculiarly with the Old Testament, was very seldom applied to
the sayings of Christ (Barn. 4. 14.   2 Clem. 2. 4.   Cf. Polyc.
12. 1), yet the authority of the latter is just as fully recognized.
The words of Christ are appealed to in controversy as decisive.
"Of some who say : Unless I find it in the originals
(τοῖς ἀρχείοις) in the gospel, I do not believe, and when I
said to them, ' It is written,' they answered me, ' That settles
it ' " (Ign. Philad. 8. 2.   Cf. Smyrn. 7. 2).   The same is true
of the writings of the apostles, which are regarded as final au-

thorities for the church of all places and all ages (Ign. Tral. 2. 2 ;
3. 1, 3 ; 7. 1. Magn. 6. 1. Phil. 5. 1. Smyrn. 8. 1. Rom.
4. 3. The Didache announces itself as the "Teaching of the
Apostles"). The gospel is the flesh of Christ; the apostles
are the presbytery of the church (Ign. Philad. 5. 1). That
such was the esteem in which the writings of the apostles were
held is confirmed by the facts, that the documents which we have
just examined abound throughout in references to nearly all of
the New Testament books, and that the latter as well as the Gospels themselves were read in the assemblies for worship (cf.
1 Thes. 5. 27. Col. 4. 16. Jas. 1. 1. 1 Pet. 1. 1. Rev. 1.
3. 1 Clem. 47. 1. Cf. 2 Clem. 19. 1. Homily of Aristides,
vid. ed. Seeberg, 1894. Just. Apol. i. 67. Iren. adv. haer.
ii. 27. 2 ; iii. 21. 4. Can. Mur. l. 77 f.). The Antignostic
Fathers at the end of the second century regard this recognition
of the authority of the New Testament as having been always
prevalent in the church. Cf. below : Marcion's Canon and
Montanism.

The canon of Scripture was in this period by no means a
clearly defined whole, nor even a distinct dogmatic postulate.
As, on the one hand, not all of the New Testament books were
everywhere in use ; so, on the other hand, various other writings
soon came to be regarded with equal veneration, *i. e.*, Hermas,
Barnabas, the Didache, 1 and 2 Clement, the Apocalypse of Peter,
the Prædicatio of Peter. These were read in public as the other
books (*e. g.*, Herm. Vis. ii. 4. 3. Dionys. of Cor. in Euseb.
h. e., iv. 23. 11. Hegesip., ib. 22. 1). This was carried so
far that a like authority was thought to attach to every prophetic
utterance under the impulse of the Spirit (Hermas, Did. 11. 7).
Ignatius, in Philad. 7. 1, cites such a sentence uttered by himself :
"Crying out in the midst of them, I said with a loud voice, the
voice of God : Give heed to the bishop, and to the presbytery,
and to the deacons." (Cf. Eph. 20. 1. Rom. 7. 2 (?) and the
Montanistic prophetism.) Thus the author of the Epistle of
Barnabas regards himself as a pneumatic teacher (9. 9 ff.).
The conflict with Gnosticism, Marcion, and Montanism led to
the gradual development of the conception of the canon in the
dogmatic sense of the term. That which had always been held
in the church was thus distinctly recognized and expressed with
fixed design (see Irenæus).

Cf. CREDNER, Gesch. d. n. tl. Kanons, 1860. KIRCHHOFER, Quellen-
sammlung zur Gesch. d. n. tl. Kanons, 1844. OVERBECK, Zur Gesch. des
Kanons, 1880. WEISS, Einleitung in d. N. T., 1886, p. 21 ff. ZAHN,
Gesch. d. n. tl. Kanons, vols. i. and ii., 1888 ff. HARNACK, Das N. T.
um 200, 1889.

(2) The current text of the so-called Apostles' Creed may be traced in substantially the same form to the close of the fifth century. Its origin is located with great probability in Southern Gaul. But this form, as many others prevalent in the East, leads back to the old Roman symbol, from which it differs only in embracing a few additions. The latter was the common form in Rome in the fourth and fifth centuries (see the creed of Marcellus in Epiph. haer. 52 al. 72); but it may be traced back with certainty to the middle of the third century (cf. Novatian de trinitate). Since, moreover, the most ancient form is devoid of all theological, antignostic elements; since an Irenæus and a Tertullian declare that the rule of faith has been handed down from the time of the apostles; since not only the Western, but also very probably the various independently framed and theologically detailed rules of faith in the East, have all their prototype in a confession very similar to the ancient Roman one—it is to be concluded that this most ancient form still preserved and others similar to it were in common use at the beginning of the second and the end of the first century, and were then imported from the East, *i. e.*, Asia Minor, to Rome. About the middle of the second century a fixed form was in use in Rome. This view is confirmed by the fact that Ignatius and Justin employ various formulas which remind us of the Symbol (Ign. Magn. 11. Eph. 7. Trall. 9. Smyrn. 1. Just. Apol. 1. 13, 31, 46. Dial. 85).[1] Finally, we must bear in mind the suggestions above made (§ 6. 4), indicating the existence of a baptismal confession in the early apostolic age. In this we have, therefore, beyond doubt the basis of the so-called Apostles' Creed. But the form of this oldest confession can no more be reconstructed with certainty than can the actual wording be certainly established from the oldest patristic parallels. For us, the oldest form which is positively attested is the ancient Roman.

Since Greek was the ecclesiastical language at Rome until toward the middle of the third century, the most ancient text of the Roman creed within our reach is that employed by Marcellus (A. D. 337 or 338). We here reproduce this form, indicating emendations as seen in the traditional wording of the ancient Roman confession (the Psalterium of Rufinus):

Πιστεύω εἰς θεὸν [πατέρα] παντοχράτορα· καὶ εἰς Χριστὸν Ἰησοῦν τὸν υἱὸν αὐτοῦ τὸν μονογενῆ, τὸν κύριον ἡμῶν, τὸν γεννηθέντα ἐκ πνεύματος ἁγίου καὶ Μαρίας τῆς παρθένου, τὸν ἐπὶ Ποντίου Πιλάτου σταυρωθέντα καὶ ταφέντα, [καὶ] τῇ τρίτῃ ἡμέρᾳ ἀναστάντα ἐκ τῶν νεκρῶν, ἀναβάντα εἰς

---

[1] Fixed formulas appear to be found also in Aristides. Vid. SEEBERG in ZAHN'S Forsch., v. p. 270, note.

τοὺς οὐρανούς, [καὶ] καθήμενον ἐν δεξιᾷ τοῦ πατρὸς ὅθεν ἔρχεται κρῖναι ζῶντας καὶ νεκρούς· καὶ εἰς τὸ ἅγιον πνεῦμα, ἁγίαν ἐκκλησίαν, ἄφεσιν ἁμαρτιῶν, σαρκὸς ἀνάστασιν, [ζωὴν αἰώνιον].

Such is the usual wording,[1] from which there are slight variations in the churches of various countries.[2] It was explained and expanded with perfect freedom in theological argument. That this "rule of truth" (κανών τῆς ἀληθείας) has been identical, and everywhere employed in the church, since the time of the apostles, is maintained by Irenæus and Tertullian (Iren. adv. haer. i. 10. 1, 2 ; iii. 4. 1, 2. Tertul. de praescr. haeret. 37, 44, 42, 14, 26, 36; de virg. vel. 1). But this creed is nothing more than a historical development of the current baptismal formula (Matt. 28. 19. Did. 7. 1. Just. Apol. 1. 61; hence Tertul. de praescr. 9, 13, 37, 44, credits it to Christ himself). The "rule of truth," as it was afterward called, is thus in content only the primitive baptismal confession, no doubt variously interpreted.[3] "And he who thus holds inflexibly for himself the canon of truth which he received by his baptism,"—here

---

[1] The received text differs in one modification and several additions : (1) creatorem coeli et terrae, (2) qui conceptus est de spiritu sancto, (3) passus, mortuus, (4) descendit ad inferna, (5) catholicam, (6) sanctorum communionem, (7) vitam eternam. ZAHN, on the ground of reproductions of the rule of faith in Iren. and Tertul., concludes that the first clause originally stood : εἰς ἕνα θεὸν παντοκράτορα ; vid. also Eus. h. e., v. 28, p. 23 ff. But cf. HARNACK, Zur Gesch. der Entstehung des ap. Symb., in Ztschr. f. Th. u. K., 1894, p. 130 ff. In various ancient citations the term, μονογενής, is wanting (ZAHN, p. 45, note), and it is doubtful whether it was in the original formula.

[2] The majority of theologians of the present day hold, indeed, a view of the origin of the Apostles' Creed which is at variance with the account here given. According to HARNACK : (1) About A. D. 150 a confessional formula appeared at Rome, and was from that point spread through the churches of the West. (2) Simular formulas were also used in the East, but there was in that section of the church no commonly accepted confession. Against this it is to be said : (1) That Irenæus and Tertullian regard the confession as thoroughly ecumenical. (2) That they locate its origin in the apostolic age. (3) That the New Testament, as we have seen, testifies to the existence of such a confession. (4) That Ignatius and Justin appear to presuppose a fixed formula of this kind. Upon my hypothesis all the traditional facts in the case may be most simply explained.

[3] KUNZE has denied this (Glaubensregel, heil. Schrift u. Taufbekenntniss, 1899), as he does not regard the "canon of the truth" as limited to the baptismal confession, but as also including the Holy Scriptures. An anti-heretical character is thus given to the baptismal confession. In this there is the element of truth, that the "canon of the truth" at least represents the ecclesiastically interpreted baptismal confession ; but the Scriptures were by no means formally embraced in the "canon," for (1) This is said to be "apostolic," whereas the "Scriptures" of that age notoriously included non-apostolic elements, as e. g., Hermas. (2) In the Ante-nicene period the term "canon" is but very seldom used to designate the Scriptures (see JAHN, Grundriss der Geschichte des n. t. Kanons, p. 4 f.).

follows a short summary of the creed, which must, accordingly, be the content of the baptismal confession. (Iren. i. 9. 4, cf. 10. 1. Tert. de spectac. 4; de coron. 3; de bapt. 11; praescr. 14. See also Justin Apol. i. 61 extr. Clem. Al. Strom. viii. 15, p. 887. Potter. vi. 18, p. 826. Paed. i. 6, p. 116. Cf. Caspari : Hat die Alex. Kirche zur Zeit des Clem. ein Taufbek. besessen oder nicht, in Ztschr. f. k. Wiss., 1886, p. 352 ff. Also esp. Cyprian Ep. 69. 7 ; 70. 2 ; 75. 10 fin.)

This briefest and unbiased summary of the great realities of the Christian faith, which Irenæus rightly calls " the brief embodiment (σωμάτιον) of truth " (i. 9. 4), at once interprets and is interpreted by the creed of the Apostolic Fathers. They received from the time of the apostles the unquestioning conviction of the historical events thus related, and this has by means of the symbol remained as a possession of the church in all ages. As to the dogmatic use of the symbol by Irenæus, etc., see below. But even at this point of our investigation, it must be borne in mind that the historic significance of this brief summary of saving truth was very great. It preserved intact the consciousness that salvation is dependent upon the deeds of Christ ; it taught the church to construct Christian doctrine as the doctrine of the deeds of God ; and, finally, taught men to view the deeds of God under the three-fold conception of Father, Son, and Holy Spirit. How different—may we imagine—would have been the form assumed by dogmatics in the church without the fixed background of this formula, which the very first dogmatician known to us, Origen (de principiis), placed at the centre of his doctrinal system !

Cf. CASPARI, Ungedruckte, unbeachtete, u. wenig beachtete Quellen z. Gesch. d. Taufsymbols, Christiania, 1866, 1869, 1875, and Alte u. Neue Quellen z. Gesch. d. Taufsymbols, ib. 1879. V. ZESCHWITZ, Katechetik ii. ed. 1, § 19 ff. HAHN, Bibl. der Symbole u. Glaubensregeln, ed. 2, 1877. Patr. ap. opp., ed. Lips. i. ed. 2, 115 ff. A. HARNACK PRE. ed. 3, i. 41 ff. ZAHN, Glaubensregel u. Taufbek. in d. alt. K., in Ztschr. f. k. Wiss., 1881, p. 302 ff. ZAHN, Das ap. Symb., 1892. KATTENBUSCH, Das ap. Symb. i., ii. ff., 1894. SWETE, the Apostles' Creed, 1894. KUNZE, Glaubensregel, heil. Schrift u. Taufbekenntniss. A. SEEBERG, Der Katechismus der Urchristenheit, 1903.

CHAPTER II.

PERVERSIONS OF THE GOSPEL AND REFORMATORY MOVEMENTS DIRECTED AGAINST CATHOLIC CHRISTIANITY.

§ 9. *Judaic Christianity.*

CHIEF SOURCES. Justin. Dialogus c. Tryphone, c. 47. Iren. adv. haereses i. 26. 2. Origenes contra Celsum 2. 1, 3; v. 71. Hippolyt. Refut. vii. 34. Epiphan. Panarion haer. 29, 30. Euseb. hist. eccl., iii. 27. Jerome, esp. Ep. 112 (or 89) and occasionally. Upon the testimony of the Twelve Patriarchs and the Clementines, see below. Cf. HILGENFELD, Ketzergesch. d. Urhristent., 1884, p. 421 ff. Judent. u. Judenchristent., 1886. RITSCHL, Altkath. Kirche, ed. 2, p. 152 ff. HARNACK, DG., i. ed. 3, 271 ff. ZAHN, Gesch. d. n. tl. Kan. ii. 642 ff.

Inasmuch as Judaic Christianity, confined practically to the territory east of the Jordan and to Syria, exerted no more important influence upon the development of doctrinal views or tendencies in the church, it presents little material for the History of Doctrines, and a brief review must here suffice.[1]

The terms, " Ebionite " and " Nazarene," applied to different groups of Jewish Christians, cannot be sharply discriminated. We may note three general groups, indications of which may be traced as early as the apostolic period.

(*a*) Justin speaks of Jewish Christians who require of all believers a strict observance of the law, as well as of others who, while observing it strictly themselves, do not demand this of all Christians. He himself does not maintain that the latter class are excluded from salvation, but he knows that some Christians so believe (Dial. 47). Jerome still knows of these as a " heresy widely spread throughout all the synagogues of the Jews in the East, called Nazarenes, who believe Christ to be the Son of God, born of the Virgin Mary, and say that it was he who suffered under Pontius Pilate and arose from the dead, and in whom we also believe." But his opinion of them is : " While they wish to be both Jews and Christians, they are neither Jews nor Christians " (Ep. 112. 13 [or 89]. Cf. Epiph. h. 29. 7-9). It appears thus that for centuries a Jewish Christianity maintained itself in the East, whose confessors agreed in faith with the

---

[1] We may properly take account of the influence of the " Jewish " element upon the church, as is customary at the present day. But this influence is not exerted directly through Jewish Christianity, and just as little by Judaism itself, which has from the beginning, and especially since the Cochebean war, stood in opposition to Christianity. Its influence has, on the contrary, been exerted through the later Jewish literature, with its legalism and apocalypticism.

Catholic Church,[1] used only a Hebrew Gospel, acknowledged Paul and his work, but in their practice remained faithful to their national law, without demanding an observance of the latter by all Christians. They were really Jewish Christians, whereas the two following groups were only Christian Jews.

(*b*) The second group is represented by the Jewish-Christian opponents of St. Paul. They are Christian Pharisees. They held to circumcision and the law, demanding the practice of these by all Christians (Just. Dial. 47). They rejected Paul as an apostate from the law (apostata legis) and used only a recension of Matthew's Gospel, the Ebionite Gospel of the Hebrews (Iren. adv. haer. i. 26. 2. Cf. ZAHN, Gesch. d. Kanons, ii. 724ff.). Besides this, the divinity of Christ and his birth from the Virgin were denied (Iren. iii. 21. 1 ; v. 3). This is not to be understood as indicating a conservative tendency, but as a concession to Judaism. Origen classifies the "two kinds of Ebionites" according to their attitude toward the birth of Christ (c. Celsus, v. 61). The son of Joseph and Mary was through his baptism endued with the Spirit of God. He then assumed the prophetic office, and through his piety became the Son of God (Epiph. h. 30. 14, 18. Hipp. Ref. vii. 34. p. 406, ed. Duncker-Schneidewin).[2] In this path we should strive to follow after Christ,

---

[1] Eusebius (h. e. iii. 27. 3) says of these Christians, whom he discriminates sharply from the "Ebionites," that they held indeed to the birth of Christ from the Virgin, but did not acknowledge the pre-existence of the Logos : "And these likewise do not acknowledge that he pre-existed, being God, Logos, and Wisdom," etc. Cf. Orig. in Matth. tom. 16. 12 Delarue iii. 733. This cannot offset the above testimony of Jerome. It may be based upon a confusion with Ebionite views, or merely upon the lack of speculations in regard to the Logos, for which the Jewish Christians had little inclination. Origen testifies that the Jews know nothing of the identification of the Logos with the Son of God (Celsum ii. 31). Even the מִימְרָא of Jewish theology has no such reference (cf. Weber, System d. altsynag. paläst. Theolog., 1880, pp. 178, 339).

[2] Traces of this position are to be found in the Testamenta duodecim patriarcharum (ed. Sinker, also Migne gr. ii., 1037 ff.). I remark in passing that this originally Jewish document, after having perhaps been revised by a Jew, A. D. 70-130, was again interpolated by an Ebionite Jewish Christian in view of the destruction of Jerusalem. Brief additions were again made to it about the beginning of the third century by a patripassian Monarchist. The passage of chief interest for us is as follows : Test. Jud. 24 : "And there shall arise a man of my seed (*i. e.*, of a Jew) as the sun of righteousness, associating (συμπορευόμενος) with the sons of men in meekness and righteousness, and no sin shall be found in him. And the heavens shall be opened upon him, pouring out the Spirit, the blessing of the Holy Father (*i. e.*, at his baptism. Cf. Levi 18), and he shall pour out the spirit of grace upon you, and ye shall be to him sons in the truth, and ye shall walk in his commandments first and last " (cf. Zabul. 9. Naph. 3). This man "renewing (ἀνακαινοποιοῦντα) the law with power from on high," the Jews (specifically the descendants of Levi)

"confessing that we are justified according to the law" (Hippol.). With this are combined the crass conceptions of the millennium, derived, it is claimed, from the prophets of the Old Testament (Iren. i. 26. 2. Jerome, on Isa. l. 18, chap. 66. 20).

(*c*) As it has not been found possible always to draw the line accurately between the first and second groups, a similar difficulty is met in contrasting the second and third groups, the latter of which presents a type of Jewish Christianity marked by theosophic speculations and strict asceticism. The existence of this class is implied in the Epistle to the Collosians (cf. the Alexandrian Judaism and the Essenes). This tendency appears to have received a strong impulse during the reign of Trajan at the beginning of the second century through a man named Ἠλχασαί (according to Wellhausen, a man Alexius, Skizzen iii. p.

206, note, or הֵיל בְּסָי δύναμις κεκαλυμμένη, hidden power, Epiph.

haer. 19.2. Hippol. Ref. ix. 16, p. 468. Epiph., h. 30. 17, applies the same name to the book itself). An angel of terrible dimensions (Christ), accompanied by a female angel (the Holy Ghost), is said to have handed to Elkesai, in the land of the Seri, a book with new revelations. In this was enjoined a second baptism in the name of the Most High God and his Son, the great king, for the forgiveness (καινή ἄφεσις ἁμαρτιῶν) of all sins, even the greatest (adultery), and for the healing of wounds from the bite of mad dogs, and of severe diseases (in their clothing into the water with appeal to the heavens, the water, holy spirits, the angels of prayer, the olive tree, the salt, and the earth, accompanied with the promise to forsake evil). The doctrine to be accepted, and which must be kept secret, related to the observance of the law and the reception of circumcision. Christ was not born of the Virgin, but as other men. He had often appeared (an angel) at earlier periods. Paul was rejected, as were bloody sacrifices. The eucharist was celebrated with water (cf. Epiph. h. 30. 16 ; 19. 3). To this were added various astrological superstitions. In general, we must conclude that this Jewish-Christian movement is an attempt to aid Jewish Christianity to attain the ascendency by adapting it to the syncretistic tendency of the age. The whole movement falls, then, into a close parallel to Gnosticism. It is Gnosticism in the sphere of Jewish Christianity. (See Hippol. Ref. ix. 13 ff. Orig. in Euseb. h. e., 6. 38. Epiph. h. 19, cf. 53. 1 ; 30. 17.)

persecute and slay as a vagabond, not dreaming of his majesty (Levi 16). Israel is, therefore, cast off and Jerusalem destroyed (Levi 10. 14), until in the last time God will have compassion upon her (Zabul. 9. Asser 7. Joseph 19). Then the kingdom of the enemy will be destroyed (Dan. 6).

Alcibiades, of Apamea in Syria, attempted about A. D. 220, by employing the manner of a public crier, to establish a propaganda for this theory at Rome. The effect was but transient. But greater success attended its promulgation in the territory in which Jewish Christianity prevailed. Epiphanius, for example, in the second half of the fourth century, applies the term "Ebionite" to a tendency which, in all respects, manifests the closest relation to the teaching of Elkesai. For particulars, see haer. 30. 2, 3, 14, 15, 16, 17, 18. Cf. h. 53. 1, where his judgment is : "being neither Christians nor Jews nor Greeks, but being simply midway, they are nothing."

Here belongs also the complex of compositions known under the name, "Clementines."[1] It consists of a didactic romance preserved in various recensions, whose hero is the Roman, Clement. (1) The so-called TWENTY HOMILIES, introduced by a letter of Peter to James, the so-called διαμαρτυρία, edited by DRESSEL, Gœttingen, 1853, and DE LAGARDE, Leipzig, 1865. (2) The same material is worked over in the RECOGNITIONES, in which i. 27-74 is wrought in with the 'Αναβαθμοὶ 'Ιακώβου. We possess only the Latin translation of Rufinus, ed. GERSDORF, Bibl. patr. i., Leipzig, 1838. (3) Extracts from the material in the Epitomæ, of which DRESSEL edited two forms. (4) A Syrian recension compiled from the Homilies and Recognitiones, ed. de LAGARDE, 1861. Cf. SCHLIEMANN, Die Clementinen, etc. HILGENFELD, Die clem. Homil. u. Recogn., 1848. UHLHORN, Die Hom. u. Recogn., 1854. LEHMANN, Die clem. Schriften, 1869. LANGEN, Die Clemensromane, 1890. BIGG, The Clem. homilies, in Studia bibl. et ecclesiast. ii. 157 ff.

In these documents we find Popular-Catholic elements commingling with ideas of a gnosticizing Judaism. The world has emanated from God, who is the All (τὸ πᾶν). It moves dually and antagonistically. The devil as well as Christ is sprung from a change (τροπή) in God (Hom. 2. 15 ff., 33 ; 17. 7, 8, 9 ; 20. 8). God possesses, as in the Stoic conception, a body (σῶμα) and an outward form (σχῆμα) (Hom. 17. 7). In accordance

---

[1] In regard to the almost hopelessly complicated questions of literary and historical character clustering around the Clementine literature, I present but a few points in a tentative way. (1) Both the Homilies and the Recognitiones are dependent upon a comprehensive Jewish-Christian document. (2) This latter had a pronounced gnosticizing and Ebionite character. It had absorbed certain Jewish-Christian writings, such as the Περίοδοι Πέτρου (Epiph. h. 30. 15, 16), the 'Αναβαθμοὶ 'Ιακώβου (preserved in Recog. I. 27-74), etc. It was composed for the purpose of establishing a propaganda in the East (the Roman Clement, the mask of an Antimarcionite tendency), and in the latter half of the second century. (3) The document was, in the latter half of the third century, revised by two Catholic Christians (the time being estimated from the circumstances attending its composition). The Homilies were written first. The author of the Recognitiones made use of the primary document and of the revised Homilies. If this view be correct, we are justified in using—with caution—the Jewish-Christian primary document, which has, as a whole, been better conserved than the Homilies at large, for determining the character of the Jewish Christianity of about A. D. 200.

with the law of antagonism, there is a double line of prophets, male and female. The latter have a representative in Eve, the former in Adam. From the feminine line comes heathendom, and also false Judaism. From this false line of prophecy originate war and bloody sacrifices (parallel with menstruation), as well as idolatry (Hom. 3. 20-27. Cf. the double line in Recogn. 8. 52 ; 3. 61 ; 5. 9). On the other hand, the true prophet (Adam or Christ), "continually changing ever since the beginning of the world both his name and his form, proceeds through the world, until he shall have reached the times appointed, and, anointed by the mercy of God for his toil, shall find rest forever " (Hom. 3. 20. Cf. Recogn. 2. 22). This true prophet has, especially in Adam, Moses, and, above all, in Christ, taught the truth, that there is One God, who created the world, and is our righteous Judge. The idea that Christ is God is thus excluded (οὔτε ἑαυτὸν θεὸν εἶναι ανηγόρευσεν). Although he is son of God, he is not God ; since God is an unbegotten entity, he, a begotten (Hom. 16. 15, 16). Man has free will : "It has been enjoined what things it is proper to think and to do : choose therefore what lies in your power " (Hom. 11. 11 ; 10. 4 ff., cf. 2. 36 fin.; 3. 22, 23, cf. 8. 48). It is our duty now to fulfill the commandments of God. The Homilies do not mention circumcision (but see Diamart. Jak. 1); the Recognitiones (5. 34) distinctly discredit it. We have, however, frequent washings (Hom. 9. 23 ; 10. 26. Recog. 4. 3 ; 5. 36), vegetable diet (Hom. 12. 6 ; 15. 7 ; 8. 15 ; 14. 1), prohibition of marriage (Hom. 3. 68. Ep. ad. Jac. 7). A characteristic mode of dealing with the Old Testament led to the rejection of bloody sacrifices (Hom. 2. 52 f.; 3. 42).

The documents before us constitute a special foreshadowing of Elkesaism. Although their preparation appears to have been undertaken with a view of winning the West, and especially Rome, we have no evidence that such a result was in any measure attained. This form of Judaism exercised a historical influence only upon the genesis of Mohammedanism. (Cf. Wellhausen, Skizzen u. Vorarbeiten H. iii. 197 ff.) Out of the combination of the two great monotheistic religions of the Semitic race arose the third.

§ 10. *Gentile-Christian Gnosis.*

SOURCES. Of the abundant Gnostic literature there have been preserved for us in complete form only the Epistle of PTOLEMÄUS to Flora in Epiph. h. 33. 3 ff.—the PISTIS-SOPHIA (Copt.), ed. Schwartze-Petermann, 1853, from the latter half of the third century (cf. HARNACK, Texte u. Unters. 7. 2), and two other Gnostic works in the Coptic language, edited by Schmidt, Texte u. Unters. viii. 1. 2. Besides these we have only fragments. See the account

given by BONWETSCH in Thomasius DG. i. 153 f.; a comprehensive collection
in GRABE, Spicilegium ii.; HILGENFELD, Ketzergesch. des Urchristent., 1884.
Also, STIEREN, Irenæus i. 900 ff. (Ptol. Valent. Heracleon; fragments of
the last named were collected by BROOKE in Texts and Studies, i. 4. The
most ancient of the works directed against the heretics have been lost, *e. g.*,
AGRIPPA CASTOR (Eus. h. e. iv. 7. 5 ff.). JUSTIN'S Syntagma wider alle
Haeresien (cf. Apol. i. 26) and his writing against Marcion (Iren. adv. haer.
iv. 6. 2), etc. These have been preserved in Latin, and many Greek
fragments are found in Epiph., Eus., etc. In Irenæus we have Ἔλεγχος
καὶ ἀνατροπὴ τῆς ψευδωνύμου γνώσεως ll. 5 (edd. Massuet; Stieren; Harvey),
written about A. D. 180; in TERTULLIAN, de praescriptione haerticorum,
adv. Valentinianos, de carne Christi, de resurrectione carnis, de anima.
From HIPPOLYTUS we possess κατὰ πασῶν αἱρέσεων ἔλεγχος, ll. 10 ca. 230
(Refutatio oder Philosophumena, ed. Duncker-Schneidewin. Cf. STÄHELIN
in Texte u. Unters. vi. 3); his earlier Syntagma wider alle Häresien, Photius
Bibl. Cod. 121, written after A. D. 200 (to be reconstructed from Ps.-Tertul.
adv. omn. haeres., Philastrius and Epiphanius), has been lost. Further,
PHILASTRIUS, de haeresibus. ca. A. D. 380. EPIPH. Panarion, written A. D.
374-376 (both in Oehler, Corp. haeresiologie). ADAMANTIUS, de recta in deum
fide, Delarue Opp. Origen i. 803; Latin translation by Rufinus in CASPARI,
Kirchenhist. Anekdota, 1883. Cf. ZAHN, Ztschr. f. Kirch.-Gesch. ix. 193 ff.
ca. 310. Also the works of CLEMENS, ALEX., ORIGEN, EUSEBIUS, h. e.,
PLOTINUS, Ennead. ii. 9 (ed. Müller i. 133 ff.), Porphyr. Vita Plotin, 16.
    For Critical Estimates of the Sources, see VOLKMAR, Quellen d. Ketzer-
gesch., 1855. LIPSIUS, Zur Quellenkrit. d. Epiph., 1865. LIPSIUS, Die
Quellen der ältest. Ketzergesch., 1875. HARNACK, Zur Quellenkrit. der
Gesch. d. Gnostic., 1873; also in Ztschr. f. hist. Th., 1874, 143 ff. HILGEN-
FELD, Ketzergesch. des Urchristent., 1884. KUNZE, de historiæ gnosticismi
fontibus, 1894.
    Important works are: NEANDER, Entwickl. der vornehmst. gnost. Systeme,
1818. BAUR, die christl. Gnosis, 1835. LIPSIUS, Der Gnostic., sein Wesen,
Ursprung u. Entwicklungsgang, 1860. KOFFMANE, Die Gnosis nach Ten-
denz u. Organis., 1881. HILGENFELD, loc. cit. THOMASIUS, DG., i. ed. 2,
62 ff. HARNACK, DG., i. ed. 3, 211 ff. RENAN, Origines du christianisme
vi. 140 ff.; vii. 112 ff. ANRICH., Das antike Mysterienwesen in s. Einfluss
auf. d. Christent., 1894, p. 74. ff. WOBBERMIN, Religionsgeschichtl. Studien,
1896. ANZ, Ursprung des Gnosticismus, Texte u. Unters. 15. 4. LICHTENHAN,
Die Offenbarung im Gnosticismus, 1901. KRUEGER, PRE. vi. ed. 3, 723.

    1. Already in the apostolic age there arose, particularly in
Asia Minor and Antioch, heretical teachers, who drew their immediate impulse from Judaism. They were characterized by
speculations in regard to the realm of angels and spirits, a dualistically ascetic, ethical tendency, or immoral libertinism, a spiritualizing of the resurrection, and mockery of the church's hope
(Col. 2. 18 ff. 1 Tim. 1. 3-7; 4. 1-3; 6. 3 f. 2 Tim. 14-18.
Tit. 1. 10-16. 2 Pet. 2. 1-3, 4. Jud. 4-16. Rev. 2. 6, 15, 20 ff.
Cf. Acts 20. 29 f.). By the end of the apostolic period, about
the close of the first century, these views had taken a more fixed
form. This is the first type of Gnosticism : opposition to the
sensuous, freedom of the Spirit. John combats a theory which
discriminates between Christ and Jesus, denying that Jesus came
in the flesh as Christ (Ἰησοῦν Χριστὸν ἐν σαρκὶ ἐληλυθότα, 1 Jn. 4.

2; 2. 22; 4. 15; 5. 1, 5, 6. 2 Jn. 7. Jn. 1. 14). He refers
to the heresy of CERINTHUS (Iren. i. 26. 1 ; iii. 11. 1). This is
the second type : religious philosophical speculation. To the
apostolic period belongs also the Samaritan Pseudo-Messiah Simon
(Acts 8. 9 ff. Just. Ap. i. 26. 56. Iren. i. 23. Cf. perhaps
Joseph. Antiq. xviii. 4. 1), whose doctrine was transplanted to
Antioch by his disciple, MENANDER. He also practiced magic,
taught that the world was created by angels, which are sprung
from the divine intelligence (ἔννοια). He promised immortality
to those who should follow him (Just. Ap. i. 26. Iren. iii. 23, 5).
Similarly, SATORNIL, who, however, assigns a less important
position to the Jewish God (Iren. i. 24. 1 f.). This third type
bears the character of the magic of asceticism. The false
teachers cited by Ignatius do not deny their indebtedness to
Jewish ideas. As their chief error appears the theory that Christ
only seemed to suffer (τὸ δοχεῖν πεπονθέναι, Smyrn. 2-4. Tral.
10. Phil. 6-9. Cf. Magn. 8-11. Phil. 6. 1). But they are
themselves only in seeming (τὸ δοχεῖν), i. e., ascetics.

2. From the early part of the second century these errors were
openly proclaimed and immediately secured an amazingly wide
circulation (Hegesip. in Eus. h. e. iv. 22. 4 ; iii. 27. 7 f.).
This rapid growth is probably to be ascribed to wandering teachers (cf. 1 Jn. 4. 1. 2 Jn. 10. 3 Jn. 5 f. 10. Did. 11, 12.
Ign. Sm. 4. 1. Eph. 9. 1 ; 7. 1. Pist.-Soph., pp. 253, 372).
The particulars of its development are shrouded in uncertainty.
Only this much is clear—that within a few decades this mode of
thought had become very widespread among Gentile Christians,
and was still further developed in a specifically Gentile-Christian
way. The most important Gnostic "systems" are those of
BASILIDES, VALENTINE and his disciples (HERACLEON, PTOLE-
MÆUS, and THEODOTUS as the chief representatives of the Italian
school ; AXIONICUS and BARDESANES of the Eastern school), the
OPHITES, KAINITES, PERATES, SETHIANS, the Gnostic JUSTIN,
the NAASSENES. To these are to be added the ultras, such as
MARCION, CARPOCRATES, etc. (See a comprehensive classification in Möllers KG. i. 136 ff.)

The title, γνωστικοί, was assumed by some of these schools
themselves (e. g., Iren. i. 25. 6. Hippol. Ref. v. 11 ; 23).
Irenæus rightly applied it to all these tendencies exalting knowledge above faith (cf. Hilgenfeld, p. 343 f.).

3. In order to understand Gnosticism, it is necessary above all
to bear in mind the syncretism of that period in the church.
The religious unrest of the age eagerly absorbed all possible religious ideas and sought to generalize and harmonize them.
Preference was given in this process especially to the oriental

wisdom.   It was by no means the aim merely to satisfy the thirst
for knowledge, but it was sought to realize the upper world in
personal experience through religious revelation and through the
formulas and forms of the mysteries, and at the same time to secure
a sure path for the soul in its ascent to the upper world at death.
As the Gnostic religion addressed itself to this undertaking, so
Christianity seemed to be seeking—in parallel lines and success-
fully—to accomplish the same task.   And this tendency found
support in the universality of Christianity, in the idea that the
latter as the absolute religion was to be everything to all men and
bring all religions to their consummation.   This Gnosticism sought
to achieve.   It sought to elevate Christianity to the position of
the universal religion, by combining in it all the tendencies and
energies of the age, and thus adapting it to the comprehension
of all and satisfying the needs of all.   Thus revelation was to
be combined with the wisdom of the world, and Christianity
by this means become a modern religion.   It was the first attempt
in the history of the church to bring the world into subjection
to the church by interpreting Christianity in harmony with the
wisdom of the world.   Under the conditions then existing, this
attempt appeared to be assured of success, and it seemed to
oppose to the gospel of the church a tremendous combination of
forces.

Gnosis is characterized by the following features : (1) It does
not profess to be properly speculation or religious philosophy,
but it is divine revelation.   The "Spirit" lives in it, and it
brings revelations of the Spirit.   (2) It seeks to be the world-
religion, in that it combines in itself all truth and all the religious
revelation of the race.   (3) It seeks to save the soul by imparting the truth, but just as truly—this feature is universally prominent—to teach men the formulas of enchantment by means of
which they may find entrance through the various gates of the
upper world.   (4) It presents the truth in the form of mysteries,
and hence often combines its adherents in the form of mystery-
unions.

The religious questions which the heathenism of the second
century propounded, and whose solution it was very widely
thought was to be found in the religions of the Orient, Gnosticism thus undertakes to answer by the aid of a proper valuation
of Christian ideas.   It addresses itself to problems, not of
Christian, but of heathenish religious thought.   "Whence evil,
and in what does it consist?   Whence man and how, and what
is the highest thing?" asks Valentine—"Whence God?"
(Tertul. de praescr. 7).   "Baptism is not only the setting free
(pardon), but also the knowledge ($\gamma\nu\tilde{\omega}\sigma\iota\varsigma$) what we are and why

we were created, where we are or whither we shall be cast, what we are to understand by creation and regeneration " (Clem. Excerpta ex. Theod. 78).

This leads to a discussion of the origin of this world, and particularly of the mysterious commingling of spirit and matter in man, and to a pointing out of the way to deliverance from this condition, or to the attainment of immortality. To this end a phantastic cosmogony is devised, colored by a leaning toward oriental speculation, and with this is combined a corresponding "gospel history." The doctrine thus evolved is the content of Christianity. Following the pattern of the mysteries, and impelled by the same spirit which called them into being, the effort was made, by introducing a variety of symbolical ceremonies, magical miracles, and magical formulas, supposed to have significance for this life and for that which is to come, to secure the personal acceptance of these views.[1] They were attested as Christian by allegorical exegesis of the Old and New Testaments, and by appeals to the writings and secret traditions of the new teachers themselves. It was not philosophical knowledge which was thus offered to the individual, but intuitive, experimental knowledge, and experience of the divine life, and with these the inclination to view all things in a religious light.[2] "An astonishing spectre, this Gnosticism, begotten by the rising sun of Christianity in the evening shadows of departing heathendom ! " (Graul, D. chr. Kirche and Schwelle d. ir. Ztalters, p. 91).

Without entering into the details of the various systems, we must examine somewhat more closely their chief features.

4. (1) The world of spirit and that of matter stand dualistically opposed to each other, as above and below, as good and bad.

(2) From the spirit-world (profundity, βύθος, the self-father, αὐτοπάτωρ, pleroma, πλήρωμα), which is internally agitated by the aeons (αἰῶνες, sensations and emotions—movements of the primal spirit, or even personal entities, *substantiæ*, Tcrt. adv. Val. 4. Iren. ii. 13. 10; 28. 4), the present world appeared by emanation or evolution.

(3) The creator of this world was not the supreme God, but a subordinate being, the Demiurge, or God of the Jews (*e. g.*, Ep. Ptol. ad. Flor.: " And this Demiurge is hence also the creator of the whole world, being different from those other beings

---

[1] Cf. Hippol. Refut. i. proem : But the things esteemed by them had their origin in the σοφια of the Greeks, from their speculative teachings and attempted mysteries and warning astrologers.

[2] We may recall the opinion of Celsus : " Certain dancing syrens and sophistriennes, sealing up the ears (a Gnostic rite) and turning the heads of their victims, etc. Orig. contra Cels. v. 64.

[the supreme God and the devil], occupying properly a place between them''), or even an angel.

(4) In the world of matter there exists a remnant from the spirit-world, and the deliverance of this remnant is the aim of the soteriological process. According to the proportion of spirit in the matter in their composition, men are spiritual (πνευματικοί), psychical (ψυχικοί), and carnal (σωματικοί) (e. g., Iren. i. 7. 5. Tert. adv. Val. 29). This classification may be used to characterize Christianity, Judaism, and Heathenism.

(5) Sensuousness constitutes (in true heathen fashion) the evil in men. The spirit is imprisoned in the body : '' It explains the conflict in the body, that its structure (πλάσμα) is composed of warring elements (Hippol. Ref. v. 8, p. 154. Cf. the hymn of the Naasenes, ib. c. 10, p. 176 : '' From thy breath it wanders away—it seeks to flee from the black chaos—and does not know how to pass through,'' etc.). Demons of many kinds have their abode in the soul of man, and injure and defile it as travelers an inn (Valent. in Clem. Al. Str. ii. 20. 114). From this results the universality of sin, and the fact that it is so natural to man (Basilid. in Clem. Al. Str. iv. 12. 83, in Hilgenfeld, p. 208. Iren. iv. 27. 2).

(6) Redemption originates in the world of spirit. The Redeemer is Jesus Christ. There are many and greatly variant delineations of his person. He is a celestial aeon, which inhabits a body, practices self-restraint, and thus comes to be of the same nature as the latter : '' For we say of that which is seen, and of that which is unseen, that they are one nature '' (Valent. in Clem. Al. Str. iii. 7. 59, and in Photius Bibl. cod. 230. Vid. Hilgenf. 297, 302). Or he is an aeon which assumed a body formed of a psychic substance : being impassible, he did not suffer, but only his psychic body,—thus the school of Valentine (Iren. i. 6. 1 ; 7. 2. Otherwise, Tertul. adv. Val. 39. 1). Or the man Jesus, bearing the image of God, and by a special dispensation born through Mary, is chosen by God ; with him at his baptism the aeon Christ, also called '' Man '' or '' Son of man,'' unites himself,—thus Marcion in Iren. i. 15. 3. Cf. Cerinthus in Iren. i. 26. 1. Carpocrates, Iren. i. 25. 1, 2. Ps.-Tert. adv. omn. h. 15.—Satornil ('' He held '' that the unbegotten Saviour was both incorporeal and invisible, but he thought that he appeared a man,'' Iren. i. 24. 2) and Basilides ('' That Christ came in phantasm, was without substance of flesh, did not suffer at the hands of the Jews, but instead of him Simon was crucified ; whence we are not to believe in him who was crucified,'' Ps.-Tert. 4. Cf. Iren. i. 24. 4. Philaster 32, etc.) agree in discriminating sharply between the historical Jesus and

the celestial Christ, either considering the celestial aeon as
dwelling in an apparent body, or regarding the man Jesus as led
and prompted by the aeon.

(7) In regard to the object of Christ's coming, it is to be
said: "For the Father of all wished to dispel ignorance and
destroy death. But the recognition of himself became the dis-
pelling of ignorance" (Iren. i. 15. 2, Marcion). In the hymn
of the Naasenes, Christ says to the Father : " Having the seals I
shall affirm : I travel through all ages. I shall unfold all mysteries—I shall show the forms of the gods—the hidden things of
the holy way—I shall summon wisdom (γνῶσις) and teach "[1]
(Hipp. Ref. v. 10. Cf. also Pist.-Soph., p. 1 f. 182, 232 :
" Verily I say unto you, that ye shall know how the world,
κόσμος, was formed," vid. the enumeration, p. 206 ff.). The
gospel is the knowledge of supermundane things (ἡ τῶν ὑπερκοσμίων
γνῶσις, Hipp. Ref. vii. 27, p. 376). At the beginning of the
Jeû-books, p. 142, it is said: "This is the book of the
knowledges of the invisible God by means of the hidden mysteries which lead to the elect generation." "This is the doctrine in which the entire sum of knowledge dwells." Christ
thus brings knowledge to the world, and thereby the spiritual
elements are strengthened to release themselves from matter.
The self-consciousness of the human spirit begins, and it now
recognizes the means of grace and sacred formulas which aid it
to rise from this world into that above.

(8) Redemption has to do chiefly with the pneumatic. "They
teach that these are not only by practice, but by nature pneumatic, and will everywhere and absolutely be saved" (Iren. i. 6. 2.
Cf. Cl. Al. Str. v. 1. 3). The " only good Father " himself
looks upon the heart of man in Christ, and it is illuminated and
blessed in the vision of God. The man now lives bound to the
Saviour in mutual fellowship, and has become in himself immortal (Val. in Cl. Al. Str. ii. 20. 114; v. 6. 52 ; iv. 13. 91 in
Hilgenfeld, pp. 296, 301, 298). The knowledge (ἐπίγνωσις) of the
great Unutterable is redemption, but it has to do only with the
spirit, and not with the soul or body (Iren. i. 21. 4; 7. 5).
Thus the spirit by knowledge becomes free from the oppression
of the sensuous and mounts to God. The psychic, i. e., ordi-

---

[1] This hymn pictures the distress and anxiety of a soul which has fallen
under the " dense darkness," and seeks like a trembling hart to escape from
it, and yet does not know how to go in or out. Then comes Christ, the
Saviour. He brings knowledge and shows the way of escape, i. e., the
ascent of the soul to God through the realm of the planetary spirits—which
are the gods. The hymn furnishes a fine example of the practical religious
temper of the Gnostic circles.

7

nary Christians in the church, may be saved through faith and works, but the hylic will all be lost (Iren. i. 6. 2). In practical life the Gnostics regarded all their actual adherents as pneumatic (cf. Iren. i. 6. 1 fin.; iii. 15. 2. Hipp. Ref. v. 9, p. 174).

(9) The moral philosophy accompanying these views of redemption was dominated by the false estimate of sensuousness, and assumed a double form (Iren. iii. 15. 2), either a strict ascetic abstinence (Iren. i. 24. 2. Hipp. Ref. v. 9, p. 170. Pist.-Soph., pp. 250, 254 f.), or a lax carnality, confident that nothing could harm these favored ones, with scornful criticism of the strict morality of the church, as, for example, on the subject of martyrdom (Iren. i. 6. 2, 3; 25. 3; 28. 2; 31. 2. Cl. Al. Str. iv. 9. 73. Agrippa Cast., in Eus. h. e. iv. 7. 7. Isadore, in Cl. Al. Str. iii. 1. 1, assails the "theatric ascetics." Cf. also Plot. ii. 9. 15).

(10) In keeping with the whole trend of the system of Gnosticism, there is found in it no recognition of the resurrection of the dead, nor of the early Christian eschatology as a whole.[1] The return of the spirit freed from matter to the pleroma marks the end (cf. Iren. i. 7. 1, 5. Tert. c. Val. 32).

5. The attempt was made in various special associations to popularize this general cosmical theory by symbolic rites, mystic ceremonies, and the teaching of magic formularies, etc. Members of the orthodox church were particularly cultivated (Iren. iii. 15. 2. Tert. praescr. 42). The Gnostics either formed congregations outside the church or secret organizations within her pale (Iren. iii. 4. 3; 15. 2; i. 13. 7). At the reception of persons into these associations, and in their worship, strange forms and formulas played an important part. It was taught to have been the design of Christ to grant to his followers such " mysteries " as a means of protection and as powers to be effectually employed against sin, death, and the cosmic forces opposing in the state of death : "Jesus said . . . coming into the world I have brought nothing but this fire and this water, and this wine and this blood " (Pist.-Soph., pp. 372, 219. Cf. Jeû i. pp. 142,198). We note the principal rites observed :—
(1) The redemption (ἀπολύτρωσις), or leading into a bridal chamber, among the Marcosians (spiritual marriage) (Iren. i. 21. 2, 3). (2) Touching of the glove as a sign of recognition (Epiph. h. 26. 4). (3) Branding of the right ear (Iren. i. 25. 6. Cl. Al. Excerpt. ex proph., § 25. Celsus in Orig. c. Cels. v. 64). (4) Three-fold baptism with water, fire, and spirit (e. g., Jeû, pp. 195, 198, 200 ff. Pist.-Soph., 375 ff.). (5)

---

[1] What a difference is thus revealed between this system and the church !

Anointing with oil (Iren. i. 21. 3. Hippol. v. 7. Orig. c. Cels. vi. 27. Acta Thom. ed. Bonnet, pp. 20, 68, 73, 82). (6) The "mystery of the forgiveness of sins" (*e. g.*, Jeû, p. 206 f.): "Therefore must every man who would believe on the Son of Light receive the mystery of the forgiveness of sins, in order that he may become entirely perfect and complete in all mysteries . . . therefore now I also declare that, if ye have received the mystery of the forgiveness of sins, all the sins which ye have consciously or unconsciously committed, which ye have committed from the time of your childhood until the present day, and until the severing of the bond of the flesh of fate, are altogether blotted out, because ye have received the mystery of the forgiveness of sins." (Vid. Pist.-Soph., pp. 300, 375 f.) (7) The obscene rite (menstrual blood and male semen, Pist.-Soph., p. 386. Epiph. h. 26. 4. 2 Book Jeû, p. 194. Vid. Cyril. Catech. 6. 33; also August. de haeres. 46, de morib. Manich. 18. 66.) (8) Pictures (Iren. i. 25. 6). (9) Magic charms and sentences (Plot. Ennead. ii. 9. 14. Orig. c. Celsus vi. 31, Cels. ib. 39, 40. Cf. the various formulas preserved in the Coptic Gnostic works). (10) Hymns (Acta Joh. ed. Zahn, p. 220 f. Acta Thom. vid. Lips. Apokr. Apostelgesch. i. 292 ff. Hippol. v. 6. 10; vi. 37. Tertul. de carn. Chr. 17, 20, cf. Can. Mur. i. 81 ff. Pist.-Soph. 33 ff., 53-180). (11) Magic (Iren. ii. 32. 3). (12) Prophecy (Iren. i. 13. 3. Eus. h. e. iv. 7. 7).[1] (13) Miracles, such as the changing of wine into blood (Iren. i. 13. 2. Hipp. vi. 39, p. 296. Clem. Exc. ex Theodot. 82. Cf. the changing of wine into water, 2 Bk. Jeû, p. 200). (14) Anointing of the dying with oil (Iren. i. 21. 5. Cf. Orig. c. Cels. vi. 27. Epiph. h. 36. 2). The practical importance attached to all this ceremonial is evident from the original Gnostic works preserved in the Coptic language. It rested above all upon the belief that this was a means of gaining security in the world to come. It is at the same time very plain that this entire foolish trifling with symbols and formulas has an exact parallel in the heathen mysteries of the age. It is, really, only in view of this fact that we can estimate the true essential character of Gnosticism. It is an attempt to transform the gospel into a religious philosophy and

---

[1] In the unarticulated and senseless formulas of prayer and magic which are often met in the Pist.-Soph. and the Jeû books, we may be tempted to see an echo, *i. e.*, an imitation, of the speaking with tongues among the primitive Christians (cf. Harnack, T. u. U. vii. 2. 86 ff.). We are not compelled to so regard them, however, since similar formulas are very frequently found in the magic sentences of Jews and heathen nations. See *e. g.*, Dieterich, Abraxas, 1891, pp. 138, 139, etc. Also the Mithrasliturgie published by Dieterich, 1903.

into mystic wisdom—to make heathenism the Christianity of the enlightened.

6. Yet Gnosticism claimed to be Christian in character. The only way to establish this claim was that prevalent in the church, *i. e.*, by proving that the views held were based upon the Scriptures and the traditions of primitive Christianity. Appeal was made for this purpose wherever possible to the words of Jesus (Ep. Ptol. ad. Flor. fin.: "worthy of the apostolic tradition, which we also have in turn adopted, together with the establishing of all our words by the teaching of the Saviour "). To this end they employed freely the method of allegorical exegesis, then equally prevalent among heathen and Christian writers (*e. g.*, loc. cit. and Iren. i. 3. 8. Cf. Tert. de praescr. 38. 17. resur. carn. 63). Appeal was taken also to the professed secret tradition handed down from apostolic times (Iren. iii. 2. 1 ; i. 25. 5. Cl. Al. Str. vii. 17. Hipp. Ref. 7. 20 ; v. 7. Tert. de praescr. 25 f. Cf. in Pist.-Soph. and Jeû books). Upon this basis then arose a literature of sacred books ("an unutterable mass of apocryphal and spurious writings" (Iren. 20. 1 ; 25. 5. Gospels, see Zahn, Gesch. d. n. tl. Kan. i. 770 ff., 744 ff. See also the Sources of Hipp. Ref. whatever may be the opinion in regard to them). By thus treating the accepted writings of the church, it was not difficult to impose upon many of her members (to the amazement of the unthinking and those who do not understand the Scriptures of truth, Iren. i. 20. 1), and represent the Gnostic teachings as genuine Christianity.

Gnosticism is a coarse, anti-judaistic (cf. the condemnation of the demiurge) development upon the territory of Gentile Christianity. It is not merely Gentile Christian in character, but essentially heathenish. The fundamental problem to which it addresses itself originates in the religious thought of the heathen world, as well as the peculiar means employed for the solution of this problem. Its character is not altered by the fact that it applies the instruments of Christian and Jewish tradition to the problem in hand. Its claim to recognition as Christian is supported primarily by the high estimate which it places upon the person of Christ. His person marks the decisive turning-point in human history, and his teaching is the absolute truth. We may compare the attitude of Philo toward Judaism (there Moses, and here Christ), and the peculiar zeal of the age for oriental religious forms. It is misleading to designate Gnosis as "the acute Hellenizing of Christianity" (Harnack), or, with the same author, to call its leaders "the first Christian theologians."

Gnosticism is Hellenizing in so far as the problems of Greek and Roman culture influence its course, but the means by which it seeks to solve these problems are of essentially oriental origin. There were, indeed, systems—such as that of Valentine—in which the Hellenistic philosophical tendency was the controlling element; but, judged as a historical phenomenon, Gnosticism was the attempt to establish the universal religion, in which the religious problems of the educated world in that age should be answered by means of the ancient oriental mythology and magic, with the addition of the gospel of the church. We may, accordingly, instead of a Hellenizing, speak rather of an *Ethnicizing* of Christianity.

The historical significance of Gnosticism is very great. Christianity is here first conceived as "doctrine" and as a "mystery." Thus the church was compelled to determine positively what is Christian doctrine. And since the Gnostics used for their own purposes the standards of the church, the Scriptures, and tradition (which they were by no means the first to use in this way), the necessity of a clearer definition of the latter was early recognized. On the other hand, the positive influence of the Gnostics must not be overestimated.[1]

It is customary to count MARCION of Sinope also among the Gnostics; but it is better to treat separately of him. There were two

---

[1] We might here enter into many details, *e. g.*: the universality of sin. Of the Father of All it is said among the later Valentinians: It pleased him at one time that the most beautiful and perfect thing which he had in him should be born and proceed from him; for he was not a lover of solitude. For love, they say, was all; but love is not love unless there be something loved. Hence the begetting of the intelligence (νοῦς) and truth (ἀλήθεια) (Hipp. Ref. vi. 29, p. 272). Basilides used the formula: "That in consequence of the supermundane election, the cosmic faith of all nature has arisen (Cl. Al. Str. ii. 3, p. 434). But this election signifies only an advantage of nature" (ib. cf. Str. v. 1, p. 645). Cf. also the interesting formulas of Origen's Gnostic opponents: "To live virtuously is not our work, but entirely divine grace," or, "salvation (τὸ σώζεσθαι) is not from anything in us, but from the planning or choice of him who has mercy when he will." Cf. Rom. 9. 16 (Orig. de princ. iii. 1. 8 ff., 15, 18, ed. Redepenning, pp. 28, 33). But no one will think Augustine historically dependent upon these formulas, whose sense is so far different (cf. c. Cels. v. 61). Gnostic teachers were, perhaps, the first to use the term, ὁμοούσιος (*e.g.*, Ep. Ptol. ad Flor. in Epiph. h. 33. 7. Iren. i. 5. 1, 5, 6; 11. 3. Hipp. Ref. vii. 22. Cf. Clem. Hom. 20. 7. Iren. ii. 17. 2 ="of the same substance" (*ejusdam substantiæ*). Thus also Augustine translates it in Joh. tr. 97. 4. Cf. "*consubstantialis*" in Tert. adv. Hermog. 44. The Gnostic doctrine of the "two natures" has nothing in common with the teaching of the church, but the Gnostics (as early as Cerinthus) were the first to recognize the problem which is presented to the mind by the presence of the divine and the human in Christ. The relationship between the later Catholic doctrine of the sacraments and the Gnostic mysteries cannot, however, be denied. Both were influenced by the same models and the same necessities.

attempts at reform about the middle of the second century, that
of Marcion and that of MONTANISM. The former finds the justification of his undertaking in the writings of St. Paul ; the latter
draws its inspiration from St. John. The former takes up arms
against the increasing tendency to legality (cf. the Apostolic
Fathers and the Apologists); the latter points out a certain
spiritual torpidity in contrast with the spirituality of the primitive church and a decay of eschatological expectations. Such
was the condition of things about A. D. 150 (cf. supra, under
"Apologists").

§ 11. *Marcion's Attempt at Reform.*

. SOURCES. Iren. i. 27. 2-4 ; iii. 12. 12, fin. Celsus, in Orig. c. Cels. vi. 74.
53. Tert. adv. Marc. ll. 5. Ps.-Tert. 17. Philast. h. 44, 45. Epiph. h. 41,
42. Hippol. Ref. vii. 29-31. Adamantius, Dial. de orth. fid. i., ii. Esnik (Arm.
bishop of fifth century). Against the Sects, transl. by Schmid, Vienna, 1900.
Cf. also Rhodon, upon Marcion's disciple Apelles, in Eus. h. e. v. 13, and
fragments of the latter in Texte u. Unters. vi. 3. 111 ff. Cf. HARNACK, De
ap. gnosi monarch., 1874 ; DG., i. ed. 3. 254 ff. and Ztschr. f. wiss. Th.,
1876, p. 80 ff. BONWETSCH in Thomas. DG. i. 81 ff. ZAHN, Gesch. des
n. tl. Kan. i. 585 ff.; ii. 409 f. HILGENFELD, Ketzergesch., p. 316 ff.
MEYBOOM, Marcion en de Marcionieten, 1888.

About A. D. 140, Marcion came to Rome, apparently driven
from his home church in Sinope on account of adultery. He
became a member of the Roman congregation (Tert. iv. 4).
One question burns within him, *i. e.*, how can the new wine be
poured into the old bottles ? or, to put it in another form, the
conviction that no good tree can bring forth evil fruit, nor
evil tree good fruit (Matt. 9. 16 f. ; 7. 18). The replies
of the elders to his inquiries did not satisfy him. His eyes
were opened as he read the Epistle to the Galatians (Tert.
iv. 3 ; i. 20). He there finds Paul opposed by the Judaistic teachers, who corrupt the gospel through the law,
among whom are to be numbered the other apostles. In this
way is the preaching of the gospel corrupted, the latter being
commingled with the law (Iren. iii. 2. 2). "The separation
of the law and the gospel is the peculiar and principal work of
Marcion" (Tert. i. 19 ; iv. 1, 6). The Old Testament and
the New, the law and the gospel, he held, are absolutely distinct the one from the other. Perhaps he already felt the bold
contrast between the natural life and the kingdom of grace. His
doctrinal views assumed their final form when he learned of the
Gnostic teachings from the Syrian Gnostic CERDO (Iren. iv. 27.
1, 2. Tert. i. 2 ; iv. 17). His theory of opposites could be
best explained upon the supposition of a double God. The one
God is imperfect, full of wrath, a wild and warlike sovereign,

subject to error, mistakes, and regrets (Tert. i. 6; 2. 20-26.
Adam. i. 11). This is the creator of the world. Of grace he
knows nothing; he rules with rigor and justice only. All the
misery of human existence results from the character of this God
(*e. g.*, Tert. iii. 11, Cl. Al. Str. iv. 7, p. 584). The Old Testament comes from him : the Messiah whom it foretells has not
yet come, since the prophecies do not agree with the record of
Christ's life. (He was not called Immanuel, and did not rule in
Samaria and Damascus, Tert. iii. 12-23), and since he speaks
against the law of the God of the Jews, and died on the cross
which the latter had cursed (Adamant. i. 10 ff.; ii. 10. 15 ff.).
Over against this creator is the other God, who is good and
merciful (Tert. i. 6. 26, etc.). He was "the unknown God"
until the 15th year of Tiberius, when he revealed himself in
Christ (Iren. i. 27. 2. Tert. iii. 3; iv. 6; i. 19).

Christ is frequently called the "Saving Spirit" (*sp. salutaris*,
Tert. i. 19). He is the manifestation of God himself. As to
his relation to God, there are no plain deliverances. He is commonly spoken of as the good God himself (Tert. i. 11. 14; ii.
27; iii. 9; iv. 7). He did not defile himself with the body of
the demiurge, but—merely in order to make himself intelligible
—assumed an apparent body (Tert. iii. 8. 11). Thus his work
was a conflict with the ancient God. Because he revealed the
good God, and abrogated the law and all the works of the demiurge (Iren. i. 27. 2. Tert. iv. 25-27; i. 8. 19. Epiph. h.
42. 4), the latter secured his execution on the cross. Christ
thereupon went into the nether world and there liberated the
Gentiles, even the Sodomites and Egyptians, but not the pious
of the Old Testament (Iren. i. 27. 3). Paul has faithfully preserved the truth. It is to be received in faith (cf. Apelles in
Eus. h. e. v. 13. 5, 7. Adam. ii. 6: "he changed them
through faith, that, believing in him, they might become good").
Thus one attains the forgiveness of sins and becomes a child of
God (Adam. ii. 2. 19). An earnest spirit prevailed among the
adherents of Marcion, and the strictest asceticism was advocated,
particularly celibacy (Tert. i. 29. Cl. Al. Str. iii. 3, p. 515).
But the majority of men will finally be lost (Tert. i. 24), *i. e.*,
they will be consigned to the fire of the demiurge (Tert. i. 28).
The good God does not punish ; but he does not desire to have
the wicked. This is his judgment (Tert. i. 27, cf. Adam. ii.
4 f.). The bodily resurrection is denied (Iren i. 27. 3. Tert.
i. 29).

Such was the teaching of Marcion. The contrasts of law and
gospel, Judaism and Christianity, nature and grace, the just and
the good God, dominate all his utterances. He has presented

this distinctly in his "Antithesen" (Tert. i. 19 ; iv. 6. 9). His understanding of the Epistle to the Galatians led him to the idea that the apostolic writings in use in the church were partly interpolated and partly spurious. Inasmuch as he held firmly to the literal interpretation of Scripture, the only remedy lay in criticism of the texts of the accepted books. This led to the publication of Marcion's New Testament, which, besides a revised Gospel of Luke, contained ten similarly emended Pauline Epistles (Iren. i. 27. 2. Tert. iv. 2, 3, 5 ; v.). This undertaking is an evidence of the high place which the New Testament writings held at that time in the regard of the church.

Marcion was a practical genius. After leaving the church, he began to work. He proposed to reform the church and restore the pure gospel. "For they say that Marcion did not so much change the rule [of faith] by the separation of the law and the gospel, as restore it again to an unadulterated form" (Tert. i. 20). He established congregations (Tert. iv. 5, etc.), and as early as A. D. 150 his doctrine was spread "through the whole race of men" (Just. Apol. i. 26). In the sixth century, Marcionite congregations still existed in the East, their doctrinal views having been modified by either Gnostic or Catholic influences ($\mu\acute{\iota}a$ $\dot{a}\rho\chi\acute{\eta}$, Apelles in Rhodon, Eus. h. e. v. 13. Between $\dot{a}\gamma a\vartheta\acute{o}\nu$ and $\varkappa a\varkappa\acute{o}\nu$ as $\tau\rho\acute{\iota}\tau\eta$ $\dot{a}\rho\chi\acute{\eta}=\delta\acute{\iota}\varkappa a\iota o\nu$, Prepon. Hipp. Ref. vii. 31. The sufferings of Christ redeem men from the power of the demiurge. The Hyle as third principle, Adam. i. 27. Esnik, cf. Adam. i. 3. Cl. Al. Str. iii. 3, p. 515). The Marcionite controversy led the church to the clearer apprehension of two thoughts : that the Creator and the Redeemer are the same God, and that in God justice and mercy are combined.

§ 12. *The Montanist Reformation.*

LITERATURE. The Montanistic oracles have been collected by BONWETSCH, Gesch. d. Montan., p. 197 ff. and HILGENFELD, Ketzergesch., p. 591 ff. As to other documents, see BONWETSCH, l. c. p. 16, note. TERTULLIAN, de corona, de fuga, de exhort. castitatis, de virg. veland., de monogamia, de jejunio adv. psych., de pudicitia. The 7 books, DE ECSTASI (cf. Jerome, de vir. ill. 24, 40, 53), are lost. The most ancient replies have also been lost, *e. g.*, those, APOLINARIUS, MELITO, APOLLONIUS, MILTIADES, an ANONYMOUS WRITER from whom Eusebius gives large excerpts, SERAPION (vid. Eus. h. e. v. 16-19 ; iv. 26. 2). IREN. adv. haer. iii. 11. 9. Hippol. Ref. viii. 6. 19 ; x. 25. Ps.-Tert. 21. Philast. h. 49. Epiphan. h. 48, 49 (from ancient sources, cf. Voigt, Eine verschollene Urkunde des antimont. Kampfes, 1891). ORIGEN. de princ. ii. 7. 3 f. DIDYMUS, De trinitate iii. 41 (Migne Gr. 39. 984 ff.). Jerome, p. 41. Theodoret haer. fab. iii. 2.

Cf. RITSCHL, Altkath. K. 402 ff. BONWETSCH, l. c. 1881. HILGENFELD, 560 ff. Belck, Gesch. d. M. 1883. HARNACK, DG., i. ed. 3. 389 ff.

For Chronology, see ZAHN, Forschungen, v. p. 1 ff.

In A. D. 156 (Epiph. h. 48. 1. According to Eus. Chron. ed. Schoene ii. 172 f., not until January, 172. Cf. h. e. iv. 27 with v. 5. 4) Montanus appeared in Phrygia, and there first found a following. Hence the designation of his teaching as the Phrygian (κατὰ Φρύγας) heresy. He and the women, Prisca and Maximilla, announced themselves as prophets. The style of this prophecy is indicated by the claim of Montanus : " Behold man is as a lyre, and I play upon him as a plectron. Man is asleep, and I arouse him. It is the Lord who changes the hearts of men and gives a heart to men " (In Epiph. h. 48. 4, cf. 11, 12, 13 ; 49. 1. Anon. in Eus. h. e. v. 16. 7, 9, 8). On the basis of the writings of John, it was held that the last and highest stage of revelation had been reached. The age of the Paraclete had come, and he spoke in Montanus. The descent of the heavenly Jerusalem was near at hand. It would be located at Pepuza and Tymios (Epiph. h. 49. 1. Cf. Apollon. in Eus. v. 18. 2). In view of this, Christians should dissolve the bonds of wedlock, fast strictly, and assemble in Pepuza to await the descent of the New Jerusalem. Money was gathered for the support of the preachers of the new doctrine.

Such was probably the original form of Montanism. It soon spread through Asia Minor, and extended into Thrace, Rome, and North Africa, where Tertullian accepted its teachings. The fate of Montanism was that of all eschatological movements. When the end, whose imminence it had declared, failed to appear, the certainty of its coming became a mere dogma. The expectation of the immediate coming of the end was supplanted by a complex of statutory moral precepts. And instead of the Spirit which was to be imparted to all, men were obliged to content themselves with the belief that it has been manifested in certain persons. Instead of the original enthusiasm, the movement gained greater fixity in form and a theoretical determination of its essential character and significance, which may be thus summarized :

1. The last period of revelation has opened. It is the day of spiritual gifts. The recognition (*agnitio*) of spiritual *charismata* is a distinguishing trait of Montanism (Tert. monog. 1. adv. Prax. 1. Passio Perpetuae 1). This involves primarily the acknowledgment of the Paraclete. Maximilla said : " After me there will be prophecy no longer, but fulfillment " (Epiph. h. 48. 2). But there were visionary prophecies also at a later day. Prisca had prophesied this (Tert. de exh. cast. 10), and accordingly such actually appeared (Tert. de anima 9. Pas. Perp. 1, 14, 21, 4, 7 f., 10, 11 f.). Thus the possession of the charisms is a badge of Montanism. "It is necessary, say they, that we

also receive the charisms" (Epiph. h. 48. 1). These ideas
were propagated by collections of Montanistic writings (Hip.
Ref. viii. 19: βίβλοι ἄπειροι. Eus. h. e. v. 16. 17; 18. 5
[the Catholic Epistle of Themison]. Pas. Perp. 1).

2. The orthodoxy of the Montanists is acknowledged—their
acceptance of the rule of faith (Tert., cf. Epiph. h. 48. 1.
Philast. h. 49). The Monarchianism in utterances of Montanus
(Did. de tr. iii. 41. 1. Epiph. h. 48. 11) is due to lack of theo-
logical culture (cf. Tert. adv. Prax. 3. Orig. c. Cels. viii. 14),
but was here and there retained at a later day (Hip. viii. 19.
Ps.-Tert. 21. Theodoret h. f. iii. 2. Did. de tr. iii. 41. 1.
Jerome ep. 41. 3).

3. The nearness of the end of the world is strongly emphasized.

4. There are strict moral requirements. (a) Marriage to be
but once. (b) Fasting to be strictly observed (Tert. de jej. 1).
(c) Strict moral discipline. The Paraclete said: "The church
is able to pardon an offense, but I cannot prevent the commission
of other offenses" (Tert. de pud. 21). There is no pardon for
gross sins (especially fornication) committed after baptism. Another regulation, however, covers the "faults that daily beset"
(Tert. de pud. 6, 7, 19). In the West this conception led to a
conflict, as it was maintained that only the "church of the
Spirit through a spiritual man, and not the church as a number
of bishops," can forgive sins (Tert. pud. 21). Only martyrdom can atone for mortal sins (ib. 9. 22). (d) Martyrdom
is extraordinarily exalted (Anon. in Eus. v. 16. 20). Flight
from persecution (Tert.) is forbidden. A prophetic warning
urges: "Do not wish to die upon couches nor from mild
ailments and fevers, but in martyrdoms, in order that he may be
glorified who has suffered for you" (Tert. de fug. 9; de an. 55).

5. In the later period, the organization of separate congregations was effected. Pepuza was the central point, where
assemblies were annually held (Jerom. ep. 41. 3. Epiph. h.
49. 2).

The church was placed in a very embarrassing position (cf.
the attitude of the Roman bishop in Tert. adv. Prax. 1). The
Montanists were orthodox and opponents of Gnosticism. In the
days of Irenæus, the church still recognized special charisms
(Justin Dial. 39, 82, 87, 88; Ap. ii. 6. Iren. adv. h. i. 13.
4; ii. 31. 2; 32. 4; v. 6. 1. Eus. h. e. v. 1. 49; 3. 2, 3, 4.
Anon. in Eus. h. e. v. 17. 4). But such manifestations grew
less and less frequent: "But signs of the Holy Spirit were
shown at the beginning of the teaching of Jesus, more after his
ascension, and afterward fewer: except that there are yet traces

of this in a few whose souls have been purified by the word and
by their lives in accordance with it " (Orig. c. Cels. vii. 8, cf. ii.
8; i. 46; cf. also Iren. adv. h. iii. 11. 9: " They [the so-called
' Alogi '] at the same time reject both the gospel and the prophetic Spirit "). There was also a noticeable relaxation of
moral earnestness and of expectation of an early end of all
things (cf. Tert. Apol. 39: "we pray . . . for a delay of the
end." Hip. Com. on Dan. ed. Bratke, p. 18: "Tell me
if thou knowest the day of thy departure, that thou mayest be
so much concerned for the consummation of the whole world."
Just., Dial. 80, declares that even many orthodox Christians
take no interest in the millennial kingdom). It is not difficult,
therefore, to understand the favorable reception of the Montanistic prophecy. The Scriptures, they said, teach that the end
is at hand. Charisms are necessary for the church. Her life
on earth is but a pilgrimage, and she should hence keep her
members free from contamination with the natural secular life of
the world. It was thought to be in full accord with Scripture to
hold that with the prophetism of Montanus the age of the
promised Paraclete had come, and it was felt that through this
form of Christianity the secularized church (adherents of the
church were regarded as *psychic*, and the Montanists spiritual,
Tert. monog. 1) was being reformed. While Marcion based his
efforts at reform upon the teachings of the greatest apostle,
Montanus made similar appeal to the authority of the last apostle.
But this reformation was a revolution (cf. the Irvingites), as the
church gradually came to understand very fully.

From the eighth decade of the second century raged the conflict by which Montanism was driven out of the church. The
confessors of Lyons, A. D. 177, write in condemnation of it to
the Roman bishop (Eus. h. e. v. 3. 4. Cf. Voigt, l. c., p. 71 ff.).
The fanaticism involved in the new prophetism (νέα προφετεία),
as it was called, is easily seen. An attempt was made to re-
claim Maximilla by exorcism (Eus. v. 16. 16, 17, here a saying of Maximilla). Miltiades published a book : " That it is
not necessary for a prophet to speak in ecstasy " (Eus. v. 17. 1).
The prophets of the Old and New Testaments, it was said, as
those of the later church, were not in such a state when uttering
their prophecies. The new prophetism was pronounced a pseudo-
prophetism, inspired by the devil (Anon. in. Eus. v. 16. 4, 7,
8; 17. 2 ff. Apollon., ib. 18. 1. Epiph. h. 48. 1-8. Cf.
Orig. de princ. ii. 7. 3). It was also felt to be impossible that
this enthusiastic prophetism should usher in a new era of the
world (Eus. v. 16. 9. Epiph. h. 48. 8, 11, 12. Did. de tr.
iii. 41. 2). It is quite easy to understand that this opposition

should be carried too far, and that with the false prophetism the genuine gift of prophecy should be discredited (Iren. iii. 11. 9 : " they are imprudent who deny that pseudo-prophetism is anything, but reject prophetic grace from the church ").[1] The Muratori fragment says : " I consider the prophets a finished thing " (l. 79). And Tertullian writes : " And hence the offices have ceased, as also their benefits ; therefore thou mayest deny that he has continued the endowments until the present age, because this *law and the prophets* were also until John. It remains that ye put away from you whatever in you is so profitless " (de jej. 11 fin.). The church sees herself compelled to surrender one element of her former experience, the *charismata*. She in principle abandons her claim to the Spirit. Tradition triumphs over the Spirit. It was charged upon the Montanists that their teachings were unknown to tradition (Eus. h. e. v. 16. 7, 9). The Spirit expressed in the word and historical tradition triumphs over the Spirit which had become fanaticism. Synods—the first known to us—were held in Asia Minor, and the adherents of the new prophetism excluded from the church (Anon. in Eus. v. 16. 10. Thus also later in Iconium, Cypr. ep. 75. 19). Thus was Montanism expelled from the church. After the fourth century it began to feel the pressure of the civil power. With the sixth century it disappeared (Bonwetsch, l. c., p. 171 ff.).

The church rejected Montanism because she recognized these reformatory efforts as out of harmony with the principles of the gospel, her judgment being here entirely correct. She freed herself from responsibility for the charisms still claimed by a few, asserted more clearly the authority of biblical revelation (cf. the peculiar remark of the anonymous writer in Eus. h. e. v. 16. 3), and prepared the way for the forms of a compact organization. The conflict had, therefore, a most important influence upon the development of the church.

---

[1] This is " the heresy which rejects the books of John " (Hippol., vid. Epiph. h. 51. 3), whose adherents Epiphanius called the " Alogi " (cf. Epiph. h. 51. Phil. h. 60. Iren. iii. 11. 9). About A. D. 170 in Asia Minor they rejected the Gospel of John and the Apocalypse as spurious, and as composed by Cerinthus. As to their critical arguments, vid. Epiph. h. 51. 2, 18 f., 21 f., 32. 34. They are Catholic Christians, who sought in this way to undermine the foundations of Montanism. Cf. Zahn, Gesch. d. ntl. Kan. i. 237 ff.; ii. 967 ff. A similar attempt was made at Rome about A. D. 210 by Caius, who, however, rejected only the Apocalypse as Cerinthian. Of the writings of Hippolytus against him, Capitula adv. Caium, Gwynn has published five Syrian fragments, found in Zahn, l. c. ii. 974 ff.

CHAPTER III.

BEGINNINGS OF THE CHURCH'S THEOLOGY.

§ 13. *Christianity as Portrayed by the Apologists of the Ancient Church.*

SOURCES. The Greek WW. in Corpus apologetarum, ed. Otto, 9 vols., 1842 ff. Vols. 1-6 in 3d ed., 1876 ff. Tatian, Athenagoras and Aristides also in Texte u. Unters. iv. Cf. HARNACK, Die Ueberlieferung der griech. Apol., in Texte u. Unters. i. SEPARATELY : QUADRATUS ca. A. D. 125, a sentence in Eus. h. e. iv. 3. 2 ; cf. ZAHN in Neue kirchl. Ztschr., 1891, 281 ff. MARCIANUS ARISTIDES, his Apol. syr., edited by HARRIS, in Texts and Studies, i. 1. A Greek revision in Vita Barlaami et Joasaph. 26 fin. 27 (Migne, Gr. 96. 1108 ff.). A large Armenian fragment in S. Aristides philos. Atheniens. sermon. duo, ed. Mechitaristae, Venet., 1878, of which a good German translation by HIMPEL is found in Th. Quartalschr., 1880, p. 110 ff.—most correctly preserved in the Syrian text, ca. A. D. 140-145 ; vid. SEEBERG, Die Apol. d. Arist. untersucht u. wiederhergestellt, in Zahn's Forschungen, v., pp. 159-414, and SEEBERG, der Apol. Arist., 1894, where also the homily of Arist. and a fragment. The apologies of MELITO of Sardes (Eus. h. e., iv. 26—the Syrian apology bearing his name which has been preserved is not genuine), of APOLINARIUS of Hieropolis (ib. iv. 26. 1 ; 27), of MILTIADES (ib. v. 17. 5, cf. SEEBERG, l. c. 238 ff.) have been lost. They were all addressed to Marcus Aurelius (A. D. 161-180). The most important apologetic writer of the period is JUSTIN MARTYR, born ca. A. D. 100. About A. D. 150 he wrote his two apologies ; somewhat later, the Dialogus contra Tryphone. Of his book, περὶ ἀναστάσεως, two fragments appear in Otto, ii. 208 ff. His Σύνταγμα κατὰ πασῶν αἱρέσεων has been lost. Cf. ZAHN, Ztschr. f. KG., viii. 1 ff. VEIL, Just. Rechtfertigung des Christ., prefaced, translated into German and elucidated, 1894 ; vid. SEEBERG in Theol. Littbl. Febr., 1895. VON ENGELHARDT, D. Christent. Just. d. Märt., 1878. Also STÄHLIN, Just. d. Märt. u. s. neuester Beurtheiler, 1880. FLEMMING, Zur Beurtheilung d. Christent. Just., 1893. DUNCKER, Logoslehre Just., 1848. BOSSE, der präex. Christus d. Just., 1891. TATIAN, a pupil of Justin, wrote : λόγος πρὸς Ἕλληνας. Upon his "Diatessaron," vid. ZAHN, Forschungen, 1. ATHENAGORAS, about A. D. 170, addressed to Marcus Aurelius his Πρεσϐεία περὶ χριστιανῶν. He wrote also, περὶ ἀναστάσεως. THEOPHILUS of Antioch : ad Antolycum, ll. 3. Book iii. was not written until A. D. 181 (iii. 27). As to the commentary upon the gospels attributed to him, vid. ZAHN, Forsch. ii. HARNACK, Texte u. Unters., i. 4. HAUCK, Ztschr. f. k. Wiss., 1884, 561 ff. BORNEMANN, Ztschr. f. KG.,1889, p. 169 ff. The Epistle to Diognetus does not appear to belong to this period. We possess an apology of MINUCIUS FELIX, written in Latin and entitled, Octavius. It was written after A. D. 180 ; edited by Dombart, also by Halm in Corp. scr. eccl. lat., ii. Cf. KÜHN, Der Octav. d. Min. Fel., 1882. TERTULLIAN'S Apologeticum is dependent upon the latter (cf. EBERT, Gesch. d. chr. lat. Litt., i. 25 ff. SCHWENKE, in Jahrbb. f. prot. Th., 1883, 263 ff. RECK, in Th. Quartalschr., 1886, 64 ff. On the other hand, HARTEL, in Ztschr. f. österr. Gymn., 1869, 348 ff. WILHELM, De Minuc. Fel Octavii et Tert. apol., Breslau, 1887). Cf. also the apologetic material in the Martyrium of Apollonius in HARNACK in the reports of sessions of Berl. Acad., 1893, p. 721 ff., and SEEBERG, in the Neue kirchl. Ztschr., 1893, p. 836 ff. HILGENFELD, in his Ztschr., 1894, p. 58 ff.

1. We are now to note the beginnings of Christian theology. It was the pressure of practical necessity, no less than the force of inward development, which gave birth to theology. It was, on the one hand, necessary to assume a positive position against the assaults from without and the efforts of the age to produce a new Christianity. On the other hand, in proportion as Christianity became more widely diffused and permeated the thinking of the world, was it compelled to explain what it claimed to possess in its revelation. The Apologists undertook in their biblical writings to set forth Christianity in forms intelligible to the cultured classes of their age, while at the same time repelling all unjust accusations. The Antignostic Fathers displayed the unbiblical and unchristian character of Gnosticism, and in opposition to it gave form to an ecclesiastical and biblical Christianity. The Alexandrian theology first presented Christianity in the forms of science, and thus proved that the faith of the church is a Gnosis superior to the pretended Gnosis of their adversaries. We must first consider the Apologists.

2. To outline the Christianity of the early Apologists is a task to be undertaken with great caution. They defended Christianity after the traditional fashion against certain definite traditional charges.[1] In doing this, those features of Christianity which might most readily be comprehended and acknowledged by cultivated heathen (the unity of God, the Logos, virtue, immortality) were expounded. There was danger that in this process Christ might be almost entirely overlooked (Theoph. Minuc. Ath. 10. Cf. the apology, 11 init.). Christian doctrines were skillfully presented as similar to heathen teachings (Polytheism, Just. i. 6. Ath. 10 fin.; per contra, Ath. 24. The sons of Zeus, Just. i. 20 ff.; 24 init. Tert. 21 ; per contra, Just. i. 53 f. Lat. 21). A choice was made of doctrines suitable to the purpose in view, and the material was adapted to the conceptions of those for whom the documents were written. That the Christian beliefs of the writers were not exhaustively presented under such circumstances is evident, and finds confirmation from the comparison of the apologetic writings in question with other productions of the same authors (Just. Dial., Tert.

---

[1] ἀθεότης, ἀσέβεια, secret immorality, vid. ep. eccl. Lugd. in Eus. h. e. v. 1. 9: "that there is no atheistic nor impious person among us." Tert. Ap. 10: "We are assembled for the sake of sacrilege and sedition. This is the chief, yea, the whole charge." Athenag. 3 : "they prefer three charges against us : atheism, Thyestian feasts, and Oedipean intercourse" (cf. Plinii ep. 10. 79. Aristid. 17. Just. Ap. i. 6. 26 f.; ii. 12. Dial. 10. Theoph. iii. 4. 15. Eus. h. e. v. 1. 9, 14, 19, 26, 52. Minuc. 8 ff.; 28 ff. Tert. Apol. 27 f.; 7 ff., 39. Orig. c. Cels. vi. 27 ; viii. 39, 41, 65, 67, etc.

in other works, Aristid. Hom.). It may be said of the majority
of these writers that they had no clearer conceptions of the gospel than had the Apostolic Fathers ; but at the same time it
must be conceded that their views were no more defective. The
study of their works is instructive, not as adding anything to the
general faith of the church, but as furnishing the earliest attempts
of ecclesiastical theology. They have in common with the
Gnostics the attempt to make Christianity comprehensible to the
heathen, but they differ from them in that they do not admit the
syncretism of the age into their conception of Christianity. In
their view, Christianity stands in bold contrast with the religions
of the heathen world. Only in the case of philosophy is any
parallel conceded. The most important of their doctrinal views
may be classified as follows :

3. Christianity, Heathenism, and Judaism. Of Christianity
Justin Martyr declares: "I found that this philosophy only
is safe and useful" (Dial. 8, cf. Tatian. 31. Melito in Eus.
v. 26. 7, cf. Miltiades, ib. v. 17. 5). The "words of the
Saviour" should be observed, for they are full of power and
spirit (Dial. 8, 9). The attitude toward heathenism is one of
repulsion. When the purpose is to show the necessity for Christianity, the religious life of heathenism is characterized as folly
and immorality, and its gods as demons (cf. Just. Ap. i. 12, 14,
21. Dial. 79 fin., 83. Ath. 25 ff. 23. Minuc. 21 ff. Tert. 23.
For Scriptural proof, Ps. 95. 5 is quoted : "The gods of the
heathen are demons" (δαιμόνια), in connection with which the
different meanings of the term δαιμόνων in heathen and Christian
parlance must not be overlooked).[1] The philosophers and poets
are only promoters of idolatry (Arist. 13), inspired by demons
(Theoph. ii. 8); their productions are nothing but self-contradictory frivolity (Tat. passim, Theoph. ii. 8 ; iii. 2 f., 5 ff.
Min. Fel. 38. . Tert. 46). Whatever is undeniably good in
them has been borrowed from the Jewish prophets, who far excel
them in antiquity (Just. Ap. i. 44, 54, 59 f. Tat. 31, 40 f.
Theoph. i. 14 ; iii. 23 ; ii. 30, 37 fin. Minuc. 34. Tert. 47).
But, on the other hand, the Trinity, angels, and the Son of God
are represented as paralleled in Polytheism and in the heathen conception of "Sons of God" (vid. supra). In the philosophers
of Gentile nations the same Logos was supposed to have dwelt that
afterward appeared in Christ. "Our [doctrines] appear more
splendid than all human teaching because the Christ revealed
through us was the whole Logos-nature (τὸ λογικὸν τὸ ὅλον), body,

---

[1] Cf. e. g., the word as used by Celsus and by Origen in Orig. c. Celsus v.
2 ; viii. 24, 28, 33, 45, 58, etc. On the other hand, v. 5 ; vii. 67, 68 f.;
viii. 13, 25, etc.

intellect, and soul. For whatever things the philosophers and
lawgivers excellently uttered or invented were wrought out by
them through the co-operation of the Logos in discovery or contemplation'' (Just. Ap. ii. 10). Only germs (σπέρματα) of the
Logos dwelt in the prophets, whereas he revealed himself completely in Christ. Hence much is found in heathen authors
that is erroneous. Plato's teachings are thus related to the doctrines of Christ : ''not alien (ἀλλότρια) to Christ, but that they
are not everywhere the same'' (Just. Ap. ii. 13). Again, it is
said, '' Those living according to the Logos are Christians,''
such as Socrates, Heraclitus, Abraham, Elijah,'' etc. (Just. Ap. i.
46 ; cf. Minuc. 20 init.). The entire truth is contained in
the primitive writings of the Old Testament prophets, for they
were inspired ; the Logos himself spoke in them ; they correctly prophesied of future things (Just. Ap. i. 30 f., 36. Ath.
9 : '' Who, in the ecstasy of the thoughts within them, the
divine Spirit moving them, gave utterance to the things they
were impelled to utter, the Spirit using them as a flute-player
plays his flute. Cf. Just. Dial. 115). Their utterances are,
therefore, to be acknowledged even by the heathen as absolute
proof of the truth. Christianity, is, therefore, not a new religion, as Celsus charged (cf. Just. i. 53. Ath. 7, 9. Theoph.
ii. 9, cf. 36, the Sybils. As to this evidence from prophecy,
cf. also Celsus in Orig. c. Cels. iii. 26 ; viii. 12 ; vi. 2). The
prophets taught One God, true morality, and future rewards and
punishments (Theoph. ii. 34 fin.; iii. 9). Their writings contain the Christian truth (Just. Dial. 29). With their real
spiritual contents, however, was combined, on account of the
hardness of heart of the Jewish people, the ceremonial law
(Just. Dial. 19-22, 42, 44, 46, 67), which contains also veiled
references to Christ ('' I say that a certain law was ordained for
the cultivation of piety and right living, and a certain law and
ceremony was also announced as a mystery of Christ, or on account of the hardness of your hearts,'' Dial. 44). The Jews
have, by their doctrines (διδάγματα) supplanted those of God
(Just. Dial. 78). They are, consequently, no more the people of
God.[1] In accordance with the prophecies, Christians from the
heathen world are now the people of God and the true Israel
(Just. Dial. 25, 26, 123, 135 fin.).

What are then the true Christian '' doctrines? ''

4. There is One God, the Creator, Adorner, and Preserver of
the world (Just. i. 6. Ath. 8. Theop. iii. 9). The invisible
God is an unbegotten, nameless, eternal, incomprehensible, un-

---

[1] The judgment of Aristides is less severe. Cf. Seeberg, l. c. I, page 295 f.

changeable Being, without any needs and free from all passions
(Arist. 1. Just. i. 10, 13, 25, 49, 53 ; ii. 6. Dial. 127. Tat.
4. Ath. 10, 13, 16, 44, 21. Theoph. i. 4. 3 ; ii. 10, 3, 22).
He made everything for man's sake, and is therefore to be loved
(Arist. 2. Just. i. 10 ; ii. 4. Tat. 4. Theoph. i. 4 fin.; ii.
16). He created the world out of nothingness and gave form to
matter (Theoph. ii. 4, 13, 10 : "That in some way matter was
begotten, created by God, from which God made and formed the
world"). Yet, with all this, the true nature of the living God does
not find expression. There is no advance beyond the mere abstract
conception that the Divine Being is absolute attributeless Existence.

In both operations, God employed the Son as mediator. This
is not to be understood in a mythological sense (Ath. 10). He
is the Logos of God. This was a favorite term of the cultured
classes. Whenever it was mentioned, the interest of all was at
once secured. But that precisely this term was chosen proves
how entirely the thoughts of the church were centered in the
exalted Christ. If they had thought chiefly of the man Jesus,
they might have easily characterized him as a second Socrates.
But they thought of him as God, in God, and with God, and
hence selected a term such as "Logos," in order to make the
matter plain to the heathen. Originally God was alone, but by
virtue of the reasoning faculty (λογική δύναμις) belonging to him
he had in himself the Logos. By a simple exercise of his will,
the Logos sprang forth (προπηδᾷ). He is the first-born work of
the Father (Tat. 5 ; cf. Just. Ap. ii. 6. Dial. 100. Ath. 10 :
"The first begotten thing . . . not as coming into being, for
from the beginning God, being eternal intelligence, νοῦς, had
in himself the Logos, being eternally Logos-natured, λογικός).
Of the manner in which the Logos originated, it is said : "This
power was begotten from the power of the Father and his counsel ;
but not by a separation, as though the nature of the Father were
distributed," i. e., somewhat as a fire does not diminish another
by which it is enkindled, "and that which is taken away from
it appears to be also the same and does not diminish that from
which it was taken" (Just. Dial. 128, 61, 100. Tat. 5). He is
not an angel, but divine ; divine (θεός), but not God himself
(ὁ θεός) (Dial. 60 ; vid. per contra, Ap. i. 6). In respect to
the Father, he is something else (ἕτερόν τι) and another (ἄλλος
τις), and is such in number but not in mind, γνώμη (Just. Dial.
56, 50, 55, 62, 128, 129 : "And that which is begotten is
other in number than that which begets, as everyone must confess"). Thus the Logos is God together with the Father, and
to him alone, as to the Father, is worship due (Just. Dial. 68,
63 f. Ap. ii. 13).

8

Through the Logos, God has revealed himself. He it is who
in the Old Testament period appears to men (Just. Dial. 56 ff.,
60. Ap. i. 36). He is the messenger of God, " our teacher and
apostle," God revealed, γνωριζόμενος [1] (Just. Dial. 60, 127. Ap.
i. 12. Dial. 64 ; cf. Theoph. ii. 22). When God determined
to create the world, he begat the word which he had in himself
(λόγος ἐνδιάθετος) as the word uttering itself in speech (λόγος
προφορικός). For the use of the terms by the Stoics and Philo,
cf. HEINZE, Die Lehre vom Logos, p. 140 ff., 231 f.; Orig. c.
Cels. vi. 65 : " . . . the Logos always existing resident in the
heart of God. For before anything was created, he had this
counselor, which was his own reason (νοῦς) and purpose
(φρόνησις). But when God determined to make whatever he desired, he begat this Logos as the word (προφορικός), the first-
born of the whole creation, he himself not being emptied of the
Logos, but begetting the Logos, and always remaining associated
with his Logos " (Theoph. ii. 22 ; cf. 10. Ath. 10. Tert. adv.
Prax. 5 : *sermonalis* and *rationalis*). Christ is, therefore, the
Reason imminent in God, to which God granted a separate existence. As the divine Reason, he was not only operative at the
creation and in the Old Testament prophets, but also in the
wise men of the heathen world. The philosophical conception
of the Logos (cf. HEINZE in loco) here determines Christian
thought, although the important difference must not be overlooked, that the Logos of the Christian writers is an independent
personality. The divine person of Christ is acknowledged without any limitations ; and when the Johannine conception of the
Logos is presented as parallel with that of the Stoic philosophy,
it must be understood merely as an outward clothing of the
thought (momentous indeed in its consequences) in such garb as
to commend it to the heathen world.

Along with the " Word " is mentioned also the Wisdom of
God, or the holy prophetic Spirit ; but comparatively little
prominence is given to the latter (Just. Ap. i. 6. 60. Ath. 12.
24). But the Trinity is certainly an article of the common
faith. The term, Τριάς, occurs first in Theoph. ii. 15. Although
the Apologists find little occasion to speak of this mystery,
the apprehension of it constitutes for them the profoundest
problem and the supreme desire of their hearts : " carried away
with this desire only, to see God and the Logos with him.
What is the unity of the Son with the Father? what the fellowship of the Father with the Son? what the Spirit? what the

---

[1] We here note the influence of the Logos-conception in the sense of John
and Ignatius.

union and the difference of those who are thus united—the Spirit, the Son, and the Father?" (Ath. 12).

5. The Work of Christ. The Logos of God, who, before the incarnation, was only a holy spirit ($\pi\nu\varepsilon\tilde{\upsilon}\mu\alpha$ $\ddot{\alpha}\gamma\iota\omega\nu$), became man, born of the Virgin Mary (Arist. 2. 6. Just. Ap. i. 22, 31, 32 f. Dial. 43, 45, 48, 63, 66, 76, 78, 84 f., 100). The full reality of his bodily human nature is firmly held (Just. Ap. i. 21 ; ii. 10. Dial. 85, 99 : "He became a man, truly subject to suffering, made incarnate," $\sigma\varepsilon\sigma\omega\mu\alpha\tau\sigma\pi\sigma\iota\tilde{\eta}\sigma\vartheta\alpha\iota$, Dial. 70),[1] yet he was not by any means on that account only a man in the ordinary sense (Just. Dial. 54), but God and man (ib. 59); his divinity was concealed in his flesh ($\tau\dot{\eta}\nu$ $\alpha\dot{\upsilon}\tau\sigma\tilde{\upsilon}$ $\kappa\varepsilon\kappa\rho\upsilon\mu\mu\acute{\varepsilon}\nu\eta\nu$ $\dot{\varepsilon}\nu$ $\sigma\alpha\rho\kappa\dot{\iota}$ $\vartheta\varepsilon\acute{\sigma}\tau\eta\tau\alpha$) and he attested both in his life and work. "For, being alike both God and perfect man, he placed his two natures over us." It is said of him : "God suffered" (Melito, Corp. apol. ix. 415 f. Cf. Tat. 13 fin., $\dot{\sigma}$ $\pi\varepsilon\pi\sigma\nu\vartheta\dot{\omega}\varsigma$ $\vartheta\varepsilon\acute{\sigma}\varsigma$). Accordingly, he is now not a man executed upon the cross, but the Son of God, whom Christians honor next to the Father ($\dot{\varepsilon}\nu$ $\delta\varepsilon\upsilon\tau\acute{\varepsilon}\rho\alpha$ $\chi\acute{\omega}\rho\alpha$ $\ddot{\varepsilon}\chi\sigma\nu\tau\varepsilon\varsigma$), and together with the prophetic Spirit (Just. Ap. i. 13, 53). This view is supported by quotations from the prophets (Just. Ap. i. 30 ff.).

In defining the work of Christ, it is first of all emphasized that he became the teacher of the race ($\kappa\alpha\iota\nu\dot{\sigma}\varsigma$ $\nu\sigma\mu\sigma\vartheta\acute{\varepsilon}\tau\eta\varsigma$, Just. Dial. 18), as he had already shown himself before his incarnation. The content of his teaching is found in the ideas of the One God ; the new law, requiring a virtuous life ; and immortality ($\alpha\varphi\vartheta\alpha\rho\sigma\acute{\iota}\alpha$), more strictly speaking, the resurrection, bringing with it rewards and punishments (e. g., Just. Ap. i. 13-19). Aristides thus reports to the Emperor what is contained in the Christian Scriptures : "But you may learn from their writings, O King, to know their words and their commandments, and the glorious character of their service, and the expectation of compensating reward according to the deeds done by each of them, which they expect in the other world" (c. 16. 3. Cf. Just. Apol. i. 65 init.).

Man has the ability to keep these commandments, since God created him free (Just. Dial. 88, 102, 141. Apol. i. 28. Tat. 7). Although man, by disobeying the commandments of God, fell and became subject to death (Theoph. ii. 25. Tat. fin.), he is, nevertheless, still free to decide for God through faith and repentance (Just. Ap. i. 28, 43, 61 ; ii. 14 ; Dial. 141. Theoph. ii.

---

[1] Justin, according to a quotation attributed to Jeremiah, taught a preaching of Christ in the Lower World (cf. Marcion): "And he went to them to preach his salvation to them" (Dial. 72 fin.; also Iren. v. 31. 1. Cf. iv. 27. 2, 21. 1 ; iii. 20. 4. Cf. also Herm. Sim. ix. 16. 5. Barn. 5. 7. Ignat. Philad. ix. 1 ; Tral. ix. 1).

27): "For just as the man who refuses to hear brings death upon himself, so he who willingly submits to the will of God is able to secure for himself eternal life. For God has given us the law and the holy commandments, everyone who keeps which can be saved (δύναται σωθῆναι) and, experiencing the resurrection, inherit immortality." Freedom here appears, it will be observed, as an inamissible element of man's endowment. However deeply the fall and corruption of man is conceived, his freedom yet remains unquestioned. From this it may be understood also that Justin includes grace, in the sense of the effectual power of God, in his conception of Christian doctrine. Grace is no more than the revelation of doctrine and of the law.

Although it does not appear from such presentations of the subject why the sufferings and death of Christ were necessary (except as in fulfillment of Old Testament prophecy), yet the Apologists very positively testify that the belief in the significance of these experiences of the Lord formed an essential part of the common Christian faith. The sufferings of Christ deliver men because he thereby took upon himself the curse which rested upon them; they bring forgiveness of sins and set free from death and the devil (Just. Ap. i. 63, 50, 32; ii. 13. Dial. 40, 41, 45, 95, 54, 80, 88, 111, 134. Melito, Corp. ap. ix. 418). He who now believes in the Crucified is purified from his past sins, the Spirit of God stands by his side to help in all assaults of the devil, and Christ will deliver him from all trouble and receive him to his kingdom if he will but keep his commandments (Dial. 116). The wood of the cross, the water of baptism, faith, and repentance are the means by which to escape from condemnation on the day of judgment (Dial. 138).[1] There was no attempt to enlarge upon these ideas in the controversial writings of the period; but there can be no doubt that they held the same place in moulding the life of the church at large as in the post-apostolic age.

6. The Christian Church is the people of God, the true Israel, the high-priestly generation of God (Just. Dial. 116, 123, 135). The churches are islands of safety in the stormy sea of the world, where the truth is taught (there are, it is true, also desert islands inhabited by ravenous wild beasts, i. e., heresies, Theoph. ii. 14). In the Christian world prevail strict morality, holy love, and readiness to suffer with rejoicing. Its members belong to another world. They are a "new generation," "the generation of the pious," winged to fly like birds above the things of this

---

[1] It appears exceedingly doubtful to me whether Justin already employed the conception of the ἀνακεφαλαίωσις. The citation from him in Iren. adv. haer. iv. 6. 2 would prove more than is intended.

world ; but it is for their sake that the world is preserved (cf. Arist. 15 ff. Theoph. ii. 17. Just. Ap. ii. 7. Melito in Eus. h. e. iv. 26. 5, etc.).

7. Esoteric elements, which the Apology mentions only for the sake of completeness in its survey (vid. Just. Ap. i. 61 init.), are the means employed in public worship by which one becomes and remains a Christian. They consist of the reading of the prophets and the gospels, preaching and exhortation, united prayers (ib. 67), baptism, and the Lord's Supper. The candidate for baptism is washed in the name of the triune God, after having prayed for the forgiveness of his sins. Baptism brings repentance and the pardon (ἄφεσις) of sins, it transplants into a new existence, and without it there is no salvation (Just. Ap. i. 61 : being made new, καινοποιηθέντες ; 66 : the washing for the pardon of sins and unto regeneration, τὸ ὑπερ ἀφέσεως ἁμαρτιῶν καὶ εἰς ἀναγέννησιν λουτρόν cf. Dial. 19, 29, 44. Theoph. ii. 16 ; 61 : enlightenment, φωτισμός ; Dial. 8 : becoming perfect, τέλειον γίνεσθαι). Of the Eucharist, Justin (Ap. i. 66) says : " We have been taught that the food blessed by the word of prayer employed by him (Christ), from which our bodies and blood are by its transformation (κατὰ μεταβολήν) nourished, is also the body and blood of the same Jesus who was made flesh."[1]

8. The last article of the common faith of the church is the doctrine of the resurrection. Only upon the supposition of such an experience does the nature (φύσις) of man remain true to its essential character. As body and soul have become believing and done good, so shall both become participants in immortality (Just. Frag. de resur. 9, 10. Athenag. de resur. 15, 25, 21, cf. Theoph. ii. 13 f. Tat. 13. Tert. Ap. 48). As Christ promises immortality also to the body, he excels the philosophical representations upon the subject of the future life (Just. ib. 10).[2] The prophets foretold a first and a second coming

---

[1] These words, of course, do not teach transubstantiation. The meaning is only that the very same food, which, by virtue of its transformation, nourishes our bodies, is for faith the body and blood of Christ (see also Dial. 41. 70). The opinion of HARNACK, that " bread and water are the eucharistic elements in Justin" (Texte u. Unters. vii. 2. 117 ff.—Just. Ap. 65 fin. mentions "bread, wine, and water," as also 67. On the contrary, in 65, " ἄρτος καὶ ποτήριον ὕδατος καὶ κράματος"—the last two words being wanting in Cod. Ottob. Harnack declares that they, as well as the οἶνος, are later interpolations. Cf. especially Cypr. ep. 63), is refuted by critical textual examination, as well as by the unvarying historical tradition. Cf. ZAHN, in Neue Kirchl. Ztschr., 1892, 261 ff. JÜLICHER, in the Theol. Abhandlungen, dedicated to Weizsäcker, 1892, p. 215 ff.

[2] There was a wavering of opinion upon the question whether the soul is essentially immortal (Theoph. ii. 19 fin.). Justin (Dial. 6) and Tat. (13) deny

($\pi a\rho o v \sigma i a$) of Christ (Just. Ap. i. 52. Dial. 40, 49, 110 f.).
Christ will return again in glory and as judge; the world will
perish in fire; and after the resurrection, both the righteous
and the wicked shall receive their just reward (Just. Ap. i. 20,
52; ii. 7). For entire orthodoxy (and if any are in all respects
right-thinking Christians) Justin thinks necessary also an acknowledgment of the millennial kingdom in the restored,
adorned, and enlarged Jerusalem (Dial. 81 f.; also Ap. i. 11).

9. The Apologists are of importance to us from a double
point of view. In the first place, they make it evident that the
general conception of Christianity in their day labored under
the same defects and limitations as in the generation immediately preceding them (the work of Christ; moralism). In
the second place, we discover here the beginnings of theology in
the church. In order to bring the Christian religion within the
comprehension of the cultivated in heathen lands, it was forced
into a foreign framework (the religion of reason) and remoulded
after foreign patterns. The prominent ideas thus employed
were the abstract (Platonic) conception of God, the attempt to
make the divinity of Christ comprehensible by utilizing the
(Stoic) conception of the Logos, and the theory that man's fallen
state consisted essentially in his ignorance and subjection to
death, and redemption in instruction and the granting of immor-
tality ($\dot a\varphi\vartheta a\rho\sigma i a$). It is upon these attempts that the significance
of the Apologists for the History of Doctrines rests. That
back of their formulations lay a richer fund of religious belief,
of which we find only hints in the formal theological statements, has been already emphasized.

§ 14. *Theology of the Antignostic Fathers.*

SOURCES. IRENÆUS adv. haeres,, vid. supra, ¿ 10. Cf. ZIEGLER, Iren.
der Bisch. von Lyon, 1871. WERNER, der Paulinism. d. Ir., Texte u. Unters.
vi. 2. ZAHN, PRE. vii. 129 ff. TERTULLIAN, born ca. A D. 160; 197 at
the latest, a writer; 199 Montanist; died ca. 230. Cf. HAUCK, Tert. Leben
u. Schriften, 1877. BONWETSCH, die Schriften Tert., 1878. NÖLDECHEN,
Tert. 1890. Here esp., de praescriptione haereticorum; adv. Valentinianos;
adv. Marcionem ll. 5; adv. Hermogenem; de carne Christi; de resurrectione;
de anima, cf. adv. Praxeam, written 206-211. Opp. ed. Oehler, 3 vols., 1851
ff. HIPPOLYTUS, after ca. A. D. 190 active at Rome; 235, banished to Sar-
dinia. Upon the Refutatio and the Syntagma, vid. ¿ 10. Also parts of De
Anti-christo; comm. upon Dan. l. iv., after Georgiades, in the ᾽Εκκλησιαστικὴ
ἀλήθεια, 1885 f., reprinted by BRATKE, 1891 (cf. BARDENHEWER, des H.
Comm. z. Dan., 1877); c. Noëtum. Also perhaps the so-called "Small
Labyrinth" in Eus. h. e. v. 28. 6 (cf. Refut. X proem.). His writings
were edited by de LAGARDE, 1858, and recently by BONWETSCH and ACHELIS,

this, and Theoph. (ii. 24, 27) writes: "He made it, therefore, neither immortal nor mortal, but . . . capable of both."

1897. Cf. BUNSEN, H. u. seine. Zeit. DÖLLINGER, H. u. Kallist, 1853. VOLKMAR. H. u. die röm. Zeitgenossen, 1855. FICKER, Studien z. Hippolytfrage, 1893. Cf. esp., THOMASIUS DG., i. ed. 2, 88 ff. HARNACK DG., i. ed. 3, 507 ff.

For almost a century Gnosticism had extended its sway before the church met it with a harmonious formulation of her own doctrine.

From the writings of the Antignostic Fathers we are now made familiar with this formulation of the common faith of the church, and also the motives and means for the vanquishing of Gnosticism.[1] Here for the first time a churchly theology comes into conflict with a modern but unchurchly theology.

1. It was not deemed necessary to construct a new system in the church in imitation of the Gnostic method, but it was thought sufficient to establish more firmly the truth which the church had possessed from the beginning, and to gain a clearer understanding of it. The Christian is not to be forever searching. Seeking finds its end in faith. He seeks no more, who believes what he should believe (Tert. de praescr. 11, 10). The problems with which Gnosticism toils are of heathen origin (Ir. ii. 14. 1-6. Tert. praescr. 7). Christianity knows nothing of them: "What have Athens and Jerusalem in common, the Academy and the Church? What heretics and Christians? . . . They have produced a Stoic, and Platonic, and dialectic Christianity" (Tert. ib. 7; adv. Herm. 1. Cf. Plot. Ennead. ii. 9. 6, 17). Hence that which in their writings sounds like Christian truth has a different meaning (Ir. i. proem. 2 : "saying like things indeed, but thinking unlike things"). Over against this "gnosis falsely so called," the proper course is to believe what the church has always taught. Thus an ecclesiastical theology rises to confront the philosophical theology.

2. Doctrine of God (cf. KUNZE, die Gotteslehre d. Iren., 1891). The separation of God and the Creator appears as the fundamental error of the Gnostics. It was the guile of the devil which gave birth to the blasphemous conception of a Creator other than God himself (*blasphemia creatoris*, Iren. i. praef.; i. 22. 1; 31. 3; ii. 10. 2; iii. 24. 2; v. 26. 2; cf. already Just. Ap. i. 26, 58, 35. Dial. 80). The setting forth of the true faith must begin with the One God, the Creator (Ir. ii. 1. 1; cf. Hipp. Ref. x. 34).

(*a*) God is One, at once Creator, Preserver, and Redeemer. The supreme God is the Creator. This is testified by the crea-

---

[1] We must moreover bear in mind that the first Antignostic work was the Gospel of John.

tion itself, and even by the faith of the heathen (Ir. iii. 9-15 ; iv. 9. 3. Tert. de praescr. 13 ; adv. Jud. 2 init.). The definition of God demands his unity. "If God is not One, he does not exist" (Tert. adv. Marc. i. 3 ; cf. adv. Hermog. 17. 7). It is the same God who gave both the law and the gospel (Ir. iv. 9. 3 ; iii. 12. 11). (*b*) God is an intelligent spirit ; νοῦς, *spiritus*, and ἔννοια are accordingly not separate beings, but different aspects of his being (Ir. ii. 13. 3-6, 8 ; i. 12. 2. Tert. adv. Val. 4). Referring to the Stoic maxim, that everything real is corporeal (Tert. de carne Chr. 11 ; cf. ZELLER, Philos. der Griechen iii. 1. ed. 3, 124), Tertullian queries : " For who denies that God is a body (*corpus*), although God is a Spirit?" (adv. Prax. 7 ; also de bapt. 4 ; " but God is not flesh," *caro*, adv. Prax. 27). (*c*) God is not known through speculation, but from revelation. Hence we should not concern ourselves with idle questions as to what God did before the creation, how the Son was begotten, etc. (Ir. ii. 28. 3, 6 f.; cf. 25. 4 ; 26. 1 ; 28. 1). "Without God, God is not known" (Ir. iv. 6. 4). In his greatness God remains incomprehensible ; but in his love we learn to known him in Christ : " Who is unknown according to his greatness by all those who have been made by him . . . but according to his love he is always known through him through whom he formed all things. But this is his Word" (Ir. iv. 20. 4). " Just as those who look upon the light are within the light and partake of its brilliance, so those who look upon God are within God, partaking of his brilliance " (ib. § 5). We learn to know God by way of revelation and experience, not through speculation. (*d*) The justice and the goodness of God are not to be ascribed to two separate gods : " The Creator was from the beginning both good and just" (Tertul. adv. Marc. ii. 12). True goodness is controlled by justice. He who is good is an enemy of that which is evil : " Not otherwise is one fully good unless jealous of evil" (ib. i. 26. Cf. Ir. iii. 25. 1-3 ; ii. 30. 9 ; iv. 38. 3, adding wisdom). As against sin, justice becomes severity and wrath (Tert. adv. Marc. ii. 11 ; i. 26). Thus the moral character of the divine Person is preserved (Ir. iii. 25. 2). (*e*) The aim of the ways of God is the salvation of the human race : " Nothing is so worthy of God as the salvation of man " (Tert. adv. Marc. ii. 27 ; cf. de poenit. 2. Ir. iii. 20. 2). The world was created for man's sake (Ir. v. 29. 1 ; cf. supra, p. 113). The goodness, justice, and wisdom of God are all enlisted in the effort to make man capable of beholding God : " God determining all things in advance for the perfection of man and for the efficacy and manifestation of his own plans, so that his goodness might be displayed and his justice executed, and the church be assembled as a figure of the likeness of his Son, and that somehow at length man might become mature in such things, ripening to the capacity of seeing and apprehending God'' (Ir. iv. 37. 7). (*f*) God is the Creator and the Framer of the world. He created it by his Word and his will (Ir. ii. 30. 9; 2. 4; 3. 2. Hipp. c. Noët. 10); out of nothing (Tert. c. Hermog. 8, 45). The creation is not bad; all the contradictions which appear in it harmonize like the different tones of the cithara (Ir. ii. 25. 2). The same God provides redemption (*e. g.*, Ir. iv. 7. 2). In contrast with Gnosticism, this conception of God displays again concrete, living features, particularly in Irenæus. He is the active God, who accomplishes creation and redemption. He is the living God, who is just and merciful (contrast to Marcion), and he is the God historically revealed in Christ.

(*g*) The consciousness that God is a living God was also preserved intact by means of the triadic conception, which always compels the recognition of a spiritual life in God. The one God is the triune God (τριάς, Hipp. c. Noët. 14; *trinitas*, Tert. adv. Prax. 2, 3, 11, 12, etc.). Thus the church teaches (Ir. i. 10. 1). It is presupposed in the baptismal ceremony (Tert. adv. Prax. 26 extr.). The believer finds it in the Scriptures (Ir. iv. 33. 15). God, that is to say, was never alone: "but he, being the Only One, was many. For he was not wordless, nor wisdomless, nor powerless, nor counsel-less" (Hipp. c. Noët. 10; cf. Tert. adv. Prax. 5). "For God was not without his *Horae* (the angels) for doing the things which he had by himself pre-determined should be done, as though he had not his own hands. For there are always present to him the Word and Wisdom, the Son and the Spirit, through whom and in whom he made all things freely and spontaneously" (Ir. iv. 20. 1, 3; cf. v. 6. 1). These three are one God, because there belongs to them one power (δύναμις, Hipp. c. Noët. 8, 11). Tertullian expressed the thought more precisely in asserting that two *personae* partake of the one divine *substantia* in the second and third places, viz., the Son and the Spirit (*consortes substantiae patris*, adv. Prax. 3). "Everywhere I hold one substance in three cohering" (ib. 12). Thus in the one substance dwell three persons. Ib. 2: "Not as if the One were thus all things because all things are from the One, but through unity of substance; and yet there is preserved the mystery of the economy (οἰκονομίας) which disposes the unity in a trinity, placing in order the Father, the Son, and the Holy Ghost— three, not in condition but in order (*gradu*), not in substance but in form (*forma*), not in power but in aspect (*specie*), but of one substance, and of one condition, and of one

power, because one God, from whom are derived these orders
and forms and aspects in the name of the Father, and the Son,
and the Holy Ghost." By expressing the problem in these fixed
and simple formulas, Tertullian first presented it clearly to the
mind of the Western church; but, as always, so here the completed formula might serve to arrest the process of thought.

3. Doctrine of Man. (*a*) Good and evil in man are not
to be accounted for by different natural endowments. If evil
were in man's nature, it would be impossible to pass moral
judgment upon him (Ir. iv. 37. 2). On the contrary, sin is a
free act of man, who was endowed with independence (τὸ
αὐτεξούσιον) and "made free in his will and having power of
his own" (Ir. iv. 37. 1, 3; 4. 3). As to the original state, it
is held that man, as created, was not in a condition to receive
from God at the very beginning of his career perfection.
This consists in immortality : "For things just begotten
could not be unbegotten. But in so far as they are not unbegotten, in so far do they fall short of perfection" (Ir. iv.
38. 1). This is a Greek idea, not a Christian one. But
here, too, we must yet note the resemblance to the Johannine
conception of life. (*b*) Free but mortal man must be obedient
to God in order to become immortal. Since he was free, he must
learn to know evil. To be good, is to obey God ; to be evil, is
to be disobedient to him. Man could not become God (*i. e.*,
immortal) until he should first have become a proper man (Ir.
iv. 39. 1, 2; 38. 4). Sin is disobedience. But disobedience
brings death (Ir. v. 23. 1), whereas obedience is immortality
(iv. 38. 3). Sins are *carnal* or *spiritual* (*delicta voluntatis*),
but we dare not regard the latter as of small moment in comparison
with the former (Tertul. de poenit. 3, 7). (*c*) In Adam the
whole race was disobedient. In him it became subject to sin
and death (Ir. iii. 23. 3; v. 12. 3. Tert. de anima 40 ; de
carn. Chr. 16). As to the connection of our sin with that of
Adam, Tertullian makes some significant suggestions. Evil became, as it were, a natural element in man. "Evil has, therefore, the start of the soul . . . naturally, as it were, from the
blemish of origin ; for, as we have said, the corruption of nature
is a second nature." But to this it is added : "Yet so that good
pertains to the soul as the chief, the divine, and the real thing,
and in the proper sense natural ; for that which is from God is not
so much extinguished as obscured" (Tert. de an. 41, 16. Cf.
also de test. an. 2 ; de bapt. 18). This condition passes over
through generation upon the entire human race, "through whom
(*i. e.*, the devil) man, having been in the beginning enticed to
transgress the commandment of God, and having been in con-

sequence given over to death, made the whole race from that time onward, infected from his seed, the bearer also of his condemnation" (Tert. de test. an. 3). Tertullian speaks also of a "birth-mark of sin" (de carn. Chr. 16). These occasional hints are the incipient stages of the doctrine of original sin. They did not, however, prevent Tertullian from emphasizing in the strongest manner the freedom of man's will. "To us pertains a will and choice of selecting the opposite" (Sir. 15. 18) . . . "to will is in us alone" (Exh. cast. 2). "Therefore entire liberty of choosing either part has been granted to him" (c. Marc. ii. 6).

4. History of Redemption. God from motive of grace expelled fallen man from paradise and suffers him to die in order that the injury sustained may not remain forever (Ir. iii. 23. 6). God has from the beginning been deeply concerned for the salvation of the race, increasing from time to time the blessings bestowed upon it (Ir. iv. 9. 3). He has remained ever the same. The race, with its necessities, was constantly changing (Ir. iv. 16. 3; 38; 36. 2). God has by means of three covenants (διαθῆκαι, foedera. Ir. iii. 11. 8 fin. names four, corresponding to the four gospels) sought to win the race.

(a) The first covenant embraced the natural requirements of the law (naturalia legis, Ir. iv. 13. 1; 15. 1). This is the inherited, rational, natural law, as understood by the philosophers and jurists of the age. Its content, not differing from the Decalogue and the commandments of Christ, was love to God and one's neighbor. The patriarchs, who carried this law in their hearts, were through it righteous before God (Ir. iv. 16. 3, cf. Tert. adv. Jud. 2 ; also adv. Prax. 31). (b) As this covenant faded from the hearts of men, God renewed it through the Decalogue, or second covenant (l. c.). It was the covetous disposition of the nation of Israel, manifested in their sin in connection with the golden calf, and in their hankering after the bondage of Egypt, which gave occasion for the establishment of the ceremonial law : "They received another bondage suited to their concupiscence, not indeed severing them from God, but controlling them in his yoke of bondage" (Ir. iv. 15. 1). As the law prepares for the following of Christ and friendship with God (Ir. iv. 12. 5 ; 16. 3), so the prophets prophesy for the same purpose—the Spirit of God works through them in order to accustom men to bear the Spirit of God in their hearts (Ir. iv. 14. 2 ; 20. 5, 11 f.). But the law was diluted by the Pharisees and robbed of its chief content, love (Ir. iv. 12. 1, 4). (c) In the third covenant, Christ restored the original moral law —the law of love (Ir. iv. 12. 2, 5 ; cf. Tert. adv. Jud. 6). This

third covenant is related to the second as freedom to bondage
(iv. 13. 2); as the requirement of action to mere speech ; as
right disposition to the outward act (iv. 28. 2 ; 13. 1, 3); as
fulfillment to prophecy, or harvest to seed-sowing (iv. 34. 1 ;
11. 3, 4 ; 25. 3). Accordingly, it is our duty to believe, not
only on the Father, but also on the Son, who has now appeared
(iv. 13. 1 ; 28. 2). As the old covenant had validity for one
nation, so is the new valid for the whole race (iv. 9. 2). Christians have inherited a stricter law than did the Jews, and have
more to believe than they (iv. 28. 2 ; cf. Tert. de orat. 22 :
" our law is amplified and supplemented "); but they have also
received a greater donation of grace (iv. 11. 3) through the advent of Christ, who has brought to them life and salvation (iv.
34. 1). To this, Tertullian, in his Montanistic age, adds the era
of the Paraclete. This line of thought is important, first of all
on account of the historical significance of the whole movement
which it represents, and also because the attempt is here again
made to establish a positive relation between the religion of the
Old Testament and Christianity.

5. Person of Christ. (*a*) The Christology of IRENÆUS (cf.
DUNCKER, die Christol. d. h. Ir. 1843. ZAHN, Marcell v.
Ancyra, 1867, p. 235 ff.) is, in a marked degree, superior to
that of Tertullian and Hippolytus, upon whom it exerted great
influence. He does not begin with speculation as to the
origination of the Logos and his relation to the Father. As to
this, we know nothing, or have only probable guesses (ii. 28.
6 ; 13. 8). The starting-point in his study is the historically
revealed Son of God, who was actually born, lived and suffered as a man, and died.

(*a*) Nothing can be said, therefore, as to the mode of generation of the Logos. It is sufficient for us to know that he has
been from eternity with the Father, " the Son always co-existing
with the Father" (ii. 30. 9 ; 25. 3 ; iii. 18. 1). It has been
his nature from eternity to reveal the Father—to the angels and
archangels, and then to men, and to the latter from the beginning of the race (ii. 30. 9 ; iv. 6. 5 ff.; 20. 7). He is the
"measure (*mensura*) of the Father" (iv. 4. 2). He alone
knows the Father and reveals him : God (hence also the Son)
can be known only through God. The Son is God the Revealer.
Thus he acts in accordance with the Father's will, as well as in
accordance with his own (iv. 6. 3-7). The Logos has, therefore, been from all eternity God, as has the Father, by whose
determination and his own self-determination he acts as the revelation of the Father. All further questions are excluded. It is
to be observed in passing that Irenæus constantly maintained for

the Spirit, as the Wisdom of God, a special personal position by
the side of the Son (iv. 20. 1, 3 ; 33. 1). (β) The eternal
Logos became through the incarnation the historical Jesus.
Jesus was Christ, a fact emphasized in opposition to the Gnostics
(iii. 16-22). The Son of God is the Son of man (iv. 33. 11).
Jesus Christ is *vere homo, vere deus* (iv. 6. 7 ; cf. : "the Word
united to the flesh, iv. 34. 4). He became a real man, assuming not only the body but the soul" (iii. 22. 1 ; v. 1. 1). This
is maintained, not only as expressing a traditional conception,
but from practical religious interest, since the reality of the work
of redemption depends upon the real humanity of Christ and his
personal experience (*e. g.*, v. 21 ; 16. 3 ; 31, cf. under 6) of
human life in its entirety (ii. 22. 3, 5). Especially with respect
to his sufferings and death, the passible Jesus dare not be separated in Gnostic fashion from the impassible Christ : " (The
gospel) recognizes not that the Christ departing from Jesus before
the passion, but that he who was born Jesus Christ is the Son of
God, and that the same who suffered arose from the dead " (iii.
16. 5 ; cf. 18. 5). This union of God with the human nature is,
for Irenæus, of the greatest religious significance. Thus God himself has entered the race and become an active force in it. Inasmuch as the Logos assumed flesh of our flesh, he united all
flesh to God. From this point of view we must interpret the life
of the Lord : " For in what way could we have been able to be
partakers of this adoption as sons, unless through the Son we
had received from him that communion which brings us to him
—unless his Word,, made flesh, had communicated it to us ?
Wherefore he comes also to every age, restoring to all that communion which brings to God " (iii. 18. 7 ; 19. 1 ; v. 14. 2).

(*b*) TERTULLIAN starts with the Logos theory of the Apologists, but he develops it in a most remarkable and historically
significant way. (*a*) The Logos of Christians is, in distinction
from that of the philosophers, a real subsistence (*propria substantia*) to which belong word, reason, and power (*sermo, ratio,
virtus*, Ap. 21 ; cf. adv. Prax. 5, 6). He is an independent
person, who proceeded from God—was begotten by him. He had
a beginning : " There was a time when . . . the Son was not
. . . who made the Lord a Father " (adv. Hermog. 3, 18). In
his relation to the Father, emphasis is to be laid upon the unity
and identity of the divine existence and nature—the *substantia*
("other . . . in the designation of person, not of substance—
for distinction, not for division," adv. Prax. 12); but also upon
the separateness and difference of his peculiar existence and mode
of existence—the *persona* ("the *distinctio* of the two persons,"
adv. Prax. 21 ; " the *conjunctio* of the two persons," 24). Since

Father and Son are the same divine substance (*unitate substantiae*—Ap. 21 ; adv. Prax. 25, 26), they are to be discriminated not by *divisio* nor by *separatio*, but by *distinctio* and *dispositio* (οἰκονομία, adv. Prax. 8, 11, 12, 19 fin., 21, 22): "he proves two—as truly two as they are inseparate ; for a testimony of two individuals"). Hence : "'I and the Father are one '—as to *unity of substance*, not as to singularity of number" (adv. Prax. 25), and: "Father and Son are *two*, and this not from separation of substance, but from arrangement (*dispositio*), as we pronounce the Son an individual and separate from the Father ; other, not in condition (*statu*), but in order" (*gradu*) (ib. 19).

This relation is supposed to be made more plain by the idea that the Logos is only a part of the Father's substance ("For the Father is the whole substance, but the Son a derivation and portion of the whole," adv. Prax. 9, 26, adv. Marc. iii. 6), or by the illustrations of the sun and its rays, the root and the stalk, the fountain and the stream (Ap. 21. adv. Prax. 8 ; cf. Hipp. c. Noët. 11). If the Father is, so to speak, the God of the philosophers, the Son is the tangible revelation of the Father ; "the executive (*arbiter*) and minister of the Father" (c. Marc. ii. 27). Tertullian is a Subordinationist. (β) The pre-existent Logos became man when he was born of the Virgin Mary (de carn. Chr. 17, 18, 20 ff.). "How was 'the Word made flesh '— by transformation, so to speak, in the flesh, or by assuming flesh? Certainly by assuming." This reply is given in view of the immutability of the divine substance (adv. Prax. 27). Christ, in order that he might be able to die and to deliver man (de carn. Chr. 5, 6, 11, 14), assumed actual human flesh (ib. 6 ff.; 15, 18 f.), together with a human soul (ib. 12 f.; but cf. 18 fin.). He was, therefore, a real man. His flesh was sinless, since he made it his own (ib. 16). Its genuinely human character was concealed by his divinity (ib. 9). There are two substances, the divine and the human, the latter of which contains again two substances, the bodily and the spiritual, united in itself (ib. 13 extr.); but these two are combined in a unity in one person. "Thus a consideration of the two substances presents man and God—here born, there unborn ; here carnal, there spiritual ; here weak, there mighty ; here dying, there living" (ib. 5, 18). Now these two substances have not by a *mixtura* become a third, but "we behold a double condition (*status*), not confused, but combined *in one person*, Jesus, God and man" (adv. Prax. 27). Each nature here retains its peculiarity of substance (*proprietas substantiae*, ib.), and each acts for itself ("the two substances act separately, each in its own *status*," ib.). Accordingly, the sufferings and death pertain only to the human substance ("we say that he was mortal from the human substance," adv. Prax. 29); the divine is not capable of suffering (the Son is also impassible by virtue of that condition by which he is God," ib.). On the other hand, Tertullian can speak of the "sufferings of God," and declare that "God was truly crucified, truly dead" (de carn. Chr. 5). (γ) To the question as to the possibility of the humanity of Christ, Tertullian responded by referring to the inconceivableness, unsearchableness, and impossibility of the entire transaction: "The Son of God was crucified; he was not ashamed, because it was a thing to be ashamed of. And the Son of God died; it is credible, just because it is unfitting. And, having been buried, he rose again; it is certain, because it is impossible" (de carn. Chr. 5).

It cannot be said that Tertullian gave really greater depth to Christian thought upon these points, but he sketched a formula for it (see already Melito supra, p. 115), which was sufficiently capacious to receive the richer thought of a later age, *i. e.*: A divine substance, in which three persons subsist; and, again, the divine and human substances in Christ, which are combined in the unity of the person.[1] Tertullian established the Christology of the West.

(*c*) We notice briefly the Christology of HIPPOLYTUS. The Father begat the Logos out of his own substance, when he desired to create the world (c. Noët. 10. Refut. x. 33. De Chr. et Antichr. 26. Hom. in theoph. 2, 7). In distinction

---

[1] Harnack has endeavored to explain Tertullian's contrasting of *substantia* and *persona* by the latter's use of juristic language (DG., ii., ed. 3, 286 n.), *i. e.*, he supposes Tertullian to have used *substantia* in the sense of possession (*e. g.*, Cant. 8. 7), in which case he could, indeed, ascribe one possession to three persons, or also two possessions to one person. But this supposition cannot be established, as this sense cannot be proved in any passage that may be cited, while other passages make the meaning of Tertullian perfectly clear (adv. Hermog. 3 : "God is the name of his [Christ's] *substantia, i. e.*, of his divinity." Apol. 21 : "We have taught that he was produced from God and generated by production, and for that reason called the Son of God and God from the unity of substance;" adv. Marc. iii. 6, he calls Christ "the Son and the Spirit and the substance of the Creator;" de carn. Chr. 9 : "the human substance of his body;" adv. Prax. 2 : "but three, not in condition but in order; not in substance but in form; . . . but of one substance and of one condition, etc.;" de carn. Chr. 13 fin. : "If one flesh and one soul . . . the number of two substances is preserved." According to these citations, the meaning which Tertullian attaches to the term *substantia* is beyond question. To this we may add the usage of Melito : "his two natures;" see the passage cited, supra, p. 115. Tertullian had in mind, therefore, the divinity and the humanity of Christ. If now it was necessary to maintain the unity of these substances in one nature (cf. Iren. iii. 16. 5 : "They divide the Lord . . . saying that he is composed of one and another substance"), the origin of the formula in question is not hard to understand.

from all creatures, he shares the nature (*οὐσία*) of God (Ref. x. 33. Hom. 7: "the only-begotten according to the divine nature"). Here, too, the relation is conceived in the mode of Subordinationism (*e. g.*, c. Noët. 14: "For the Father is one, but the persons two; because there is also the Son and the third, the Holy Spirit. Here the Father is the Godhead"). The unincarnate Logos became man, in that he assumed flesh and a rational soul (*ψυχὴ λογική*, de Chr. et Antichr. 4. c. Noët. 4, 17, 12. 15: "the Logos incarnated and made man, made flesh, the incarnate Logos," *σεσαρκωμένου τοῦ λόγου καὶ ἐνανθρωπήσαντος, σαρκωθείς, λόγος ἔνσαρκος*). He assumed the actual nature of man. "God himself having for our sakes become man" (ib. 18), and: "And the impassible (*ἀπαθής*) Logos of God went under suffering" (*πάθος*, ib. 15). Having become man, he is the perfect Son; but his flesh is conditioned upon the Logos for its continued existence ("for the Logos unincarnate and of itself was not the perfect Son—although the Logos was perfect as the Only-begotten—nor was the flesh able to continue without the Logos, because it had its constitution in the Logos," ib. 15).

6. **Work of Redemption.** Irenæus described the work of Christ under various aspects. The premise is always the reality of the divinity and humanity of the Saviour. Only upon this basis could he furnish certain deliverance and deliver the particular race of man (Ir. iii. 18. 7). The leading ideas are: (1) That the Logos, entered into humanity, brought to the latter the sure knowledge of God, and by this vanquished it. (2) That he did and suffered for the whole race what it ought to do, and what it should have had to suffer, and that he thus became the source of a new estimate of man in the sight of God. (3) That he became a leaven through which humanity was purified, sanctified, and made immortal. The ideas which Irenæus here presents are Pauline and Johannine (cf. Methodius and Athanasius).

(*a*) The Son reveals the Father in his love, and teaches men to observe the primeval law of love (iv. 12. 5=of the *nova lex*, *e. g.*, Tert. praescr. 13). He shows God to men, and presents them before God (iv. 20. 7; v. 1. 1). United to God through him, we attain to the faith of Abraham and learn to know and properly honor God (iv. 7. 2; iii. 10. 2). But to this man could not attain unless freed from the forces of evil under whose dominion and bondage he had fallen. These are sin, alienation from God, and the devil. (*b*) Christ, therefore, became man in order to recapitulate (cf. Eph. 1. 10) the whole human race in himself. He thereby becomes a source of a new relation between God and man and the leaven of a new life in the latter (vid. supra, p. 125). He embraces in himself the entire human race and all human life: "When he became incarnate and was made man, he recapitulated in himself the long line of men, standing surety in compendium for our salvation, so that what we had lost in Adam, *i. e.*, our being in the image and likeness of God, this we might receive in Christ Jesus" (iii. 18. 1; cf. 21. 10; v. 23. 2). Jesus became nearly fifty years old, "sanctifying every age through that likeness which he bore to it" (ii. 22. 4; 3, 5 f.). As the human race was thus combined in him, he became a new progenitor like Adam (iii. 22. 4; 18. 1). He did what we and Adam should have done (v. 21. 1, 2). He, as the representative of the race, presented his obedience before God for our disobedience. By his blood Christ redeemed us from the unrighteous dominion of sin ("By his blood effectually redeeming us, he gave himself a ransom for those who have been led into captivity," v. 1. 1; 2. 1). Through this fellowship of Christ with the race, it becomes reconciled to God (v. 14. 3; 16. 3: "For in the first Adam we offended, not observing his commandment; in the second Adam we have been reconciled again, having become obedient unto death"). Through the fall, the race was brought under the dominion, though unlawful, of the devil. Christ has lawfully (*juste*) as a man, by the application and observance of the divine commandment (at his temptation), conquered the devil, and he has by his resurrection broken the power of death over the race (v. 21. 1-3; iii. 23. 1; 18. 7). Thus the race became free from the power of death and the devil and from condemnation (iii. 23. 1). In this way man became again the image of God (v. 16. 2) and the son of God (iii. 19. 1; 20. 1). And thus man became again precious in God's sight (v. 16. 2), and intercourse and fellowship between God and man was restored through the forgiveness of sins (*e.g.*, iv. 33. 2; v. 17. 1: "And having relieved (*consolatus*) our disobedience by his obedience, giving also to us that manner of life and subjection which is in accord with our Creator," v. 1. 1; iii. 18. 7; iv. 13. 1: "who leads man into the communion and unity of God;" iv. 14. 2: "communion with God;" iv. 20. 4: "through whom occurs a commingling and communion of God and man." (*c*) In Christ, who has become a member of our race, we are now united with God, and lead a new, eternal life: "For to this end the Logos became man . . . in order that man, having taken to himself the Logos and received sonship, might be the son of God." "For not otherwise could we have received incorruptibility and immortality, unless we had been united to incorruptibility and immortality" (iii. 19. 1). As fellowship with the first Adam brought death to us, so fellowship with the second

9

Adam brings life and perfection. "The Word, having been united to the substance of the ancient creation of Adam, made man alive and perfect, receiving the perfect God (v. 1. 1). In Christ we stand in fellowship with the God by whom we have been adopted as sons. We thus contend against our sins, and follow after Jesus in holy love " (iv. 12. 5 ; v. 1. 1 ; iv. 14. 1 ; 16. 5 : "generously granting to men through adoption to know the Father, and to love him with the whole heart . . . But he also increased fear (*timorem*), for it becomes sons to fear more than servants, and to have greater love for their father "). This union of God and man has its more immediate basis in the activity of the Holy Spirit, whom Christ gives to the race as its guiding Head (v. 20. 2, vid. under e). (*d*) But in all this the emphasis falls, not upon the forgiveness of sins, but upon the fact that man has through fellowship with Christ become *immortal.* This, primarily, is the result of the fellowship thus established (iii. 24. 1), of this union with God (iii. 187), of the overcoming of the devil (iii. 23. 7) and of sin (v. 12. 6). This is the consummation toward which Irenæus directs every thought, the real object of the redeeming work of Christ (cf. iii. 19. 1 ; 23. 7 : "for his (man's) salvation is the evacuation of death "). In that God became a member of our race, we have through fellowship with him become immortal (v. 1. 1 fin.). This is a perversion of the Johannine idea, that Christ is the life and gives life, resulting from the fact that the term life is understood by Irenæus in a one-sided way. But yet there is always thus preserved something of the important thought, that Christ gives us a new life and consummates our existence. Finally, as the curse of sin consisted in mortality, so salvation is immortality (iii. 20. 2). Thus men become gods ("first indeed men ; then at length gods ; " cf. Ps. 81. 6 f.), *i. e.*, like God the Creator (iii. 38. 4). (*e*) The union of man with God occurs through the Spirit of God, through whom God descends to us and we ascend to him. The Spirit has through Christ become the Head of the race (v. 1. 1 : "pouring out the Spirit of the Father for the uniting and communion of God and man, bringing down God to man through the Spirit, and again lifting up man to God through his incarnation." v. 20. 2 : "giving the Spirit to be the Head of man, for through him we have seen and heard and spoken."). The Spirit brings faith and produces fruits in man. He sanctifies a man's works and makes him a spiritual man (*homo spiritalis*). Only through the infusion (*infusio*) of the Spirit can we please God. But the Spirit in us is also a pledge of immortality (v. 10. 1, 2).

Irenæus accordingly means that Christ has taught us to know

God, and that he, by entering the race and becoming a member of the body of humanity, has, as the new Adam, made the latter acceptable to God and freed it from the devil, death, and the dominion of sin. Through fellowship with him the Spirit of God is brought to us, who begins in us a new life in holy works. But the aim in view is the immortality of man ; and thus the scope of apostolic teaching is, after the Greek fashion, contracted. Yet, as means to this end, biblical ideas find recognition as of fundamental importance.

TERTULLIAN does not give such a comprehensive and varied portraiture of the work of redemption (the death of Christ as the ground of salvation, and as a sacrifice, *e. g.*, c. Marc. iii. 8. adv. Jud. 13. scorp. 7. de bapt. 11 ; instruction and fellowship through the incarnation of Christ, c. Marc. 11. 27. praescr. 13. de orat. 4 ; the proposer of a new law and new sacrifices, adv. Jud. 6). HIPPOLYTUS represents the bestowal of immortality (c. Noët. 17) as the object of the incarnation. It is this which is effected by the impartation of the Spirit in baptism (hom. in theoph. 8). To this end Christ granted the gift of the Spirit in baptism, as well as his holy ordinances requiring obedience. Whoever obeys him will become a god, *i. e.*, immortal (Hipp. Ref. x. 34 : "deified, made immortal ; " cf. hom. 8, 10).

7. State of Grace. Through the redeeming work of Christ the believer is in baptism[1] endowed with the Holy Spirit and with the expectancy of eternal life (Ir. iv. 36. 4 ; iii. 17. 2). Sins are washed away and the man regenerated. He can now live in accordance with the word of Christ. For the attainment of this condition, faith in Christ is necessary (Ir. iv. 2. 7 ; cf. Hipp. hom. in theoph. 10 : " he confesses that Christ is God "). Faith is the acknowledgment of Christ and the Father, attachment to his person and doctrine (Ir. iv. 5. 4 f.; 7. 2 ; 13. 1). This recognition and acknowledgment, which, however, carry with them the observance of the primitive moral law, or the commandments of Christ (Ir. iv. 13. 1 : " because the Lord did not abrogate, but extended and completed . . . the natural requirements of the law, through which man is justified, which even before the giving of the law those who were justified by faith and pleased God observed ; " cf. 16. 3), are sufficient to make man righteous before God. Abraham knew Christ and the Father ; he believed on the Logos, and this was accounted to him for righteousness : " for faith, which reposes upon the Most High God, justifies man " (iv. 5. 5, 3, 4 ; cf. 34. 2 ; also 16. 3).

---

[1] As to infant baptism, vid. Ir. ii. 22. 4 ; also Tert. bapt. 18. Orig. in Lev. hom. 8. 3 ; in Rom. comm. 5. 9 : "The church received from the apostles the tradition to give baptism also to infants."

Faith itself falls under the category of the commandment (iv.
13. 1 ; cf. 16. 5), and justifying faith in Christ is defined as " to
believe him and do his will " (iv. 6. 5). It cannot, therefore,
be maintained that Irenæus understood the Pauline conception of
the righteousness of faith, as he held simply that God regards as
righteous everyone who acknowledges Christ and is ready to follow his teaching.

The Spirit of God fills the Christian with new life and elevates
him into the fellowship of God (v. 9. 1, 2). But yet the fundamental characteristic of this new life is that it brings the fruits
of righteousness in good works. " And thus men, if, indeed,
they have advanced to better things through faith, and have assumed the Spirit of God, and have allowed his fructifying power
to develop, will be spiritual " (v. 10. 1). " Man, implanted
by faith and assuming the Spirit of God, does not, indeed, lose
the substance of the flesh, but changes the quality of the fruits
of his works " (ib. 2). Irenæus compares true Christians to
clean beasts. They are beasts dividing the hoof, who with firm
step come to the Father and the Son in faith, and, like the animals that chew the cud, they meditate day and night upon God's
word in order to adorn themselves with good works (v. 8. 31).

The Soteriology of Tertullian is of special interest at this point,
since it became (through Cyprian) normative for the Western
church, and, like his doctrine of the Trinity and his Christology,
anticipates the later development in many particulars. He regards the relation of man to God from the legal point of view.
The gospel is the " law peculiarly ours " (monog. 7, 8. praes.
13); God is the Lawgiver and the Avenger of transgressions of
the law (exhort. cast. 2. c. Marc. i. 26). Hence the fundamental relation of man to God is that of fear : " but the fear of
man is the honor of God " (paenit. 7, 2, 4, 5, 6. ad ux. ii. 7).
But for the sinner remains, as a means of salvation, repentance, as a floating board for the shipwrecked (paen. 3). The
sinner by his repentance earns for himself salvation in baptism
(paen. 6 : " offers impunity to be purchased by this compensation
of repentance "). Hereby baptism gains a fixed position in the
order of salvation. The grace of God is necessarily connected with
this sacrament. By baptism, guilt and punishment are removed :
" death having been destroyed through the washing away of
sins, and guilt thus removed, punishment is also removed. Man
is restored to the likeness of God, as he receives again the breathing of the Spirit which was experienced in paradise, but since
lost " (bap. 5). We are born in the water, not otherwise than
we are saved by remaining in the water (ib. 1). Baptism brings
" remission of sins, abolition of death, regeneration of the man,

the obtaining of the Holy Spirit " (c. Marc. i. 28). Tertullian, in Stoic fashion, conceives of the Spirit as something material, which, on account of its tenuity, can enter the water and impart to it the power of sanctifying : " to penetrate and permeate easily on account of the subtility of its substance. Thus the nature of the waters, being sanctified by that which is holy, has itself received (power) to sanctify. The sanctified (waters) imbibe the power of sanctifying " (bapt. 4). The impartation of the Spirit can therefore scarcely be regarded otherwise than as the infusion of a spiritual substance, as, e. g., in de pat. 1 : " for the apprehending and performing of these (i. e., good) things, only the grace of the divine inspiration (inspirationis) is effectual " (cf. Loofs, DG., 104). We " remain " in baptismal grace if we do not sin, but fulfill the law of God (bapt. 15). If we, nevertheless, sin, we offend God (deum offendere, ad ux. ii. 7. exh. cast. v. dejejun. 3. c. Marc. i. 26 : "if he is offended, he ought to be angry ' '). Satisfaction must now be rendered in view of this wrath of God. This technical term also—derived from Roman law—was introduced into dogmatics by Tertullian. " Thou hast offended, but thou mayest yet be reconciled. Thou hast one to whom thou mayest render satisfaction, and he, too, is willing " (paen. 7 extr.). It is necessary " to satisfy the offended Lord " (ib. 10): " in order that I may reconcile to myself God, whom by sinning I have offended " (ib. 11). This is done by repentance : " by repentance God is appeased (mitigatur; ib. 9, 5 : " to satisfy the Lord through repentance of offenses "). But repentance consists of heartfelt sorrow (paenitere ex animo) and confession (confessio), which embraces a purpose of satisfaction (satisfactionis), ib. 9. The sinner humbles himself by the confession (confessio, ἐξομολόγησις); he sighs, weeps, fasts, and thus atones for his transgression. He makes satisfaction to God and earns for himself forgiveness (ib. 9 ; jejun. 3). He even brings a sin-offering to God (paen. 12. scorp. 7 ; resur. 8), and thus satisfaction is rendered to God. Since man thus punishes himself, he frees himself from eternal punishment. " By temporal affliction eternal punishments are —I will not say, frustrated—but expunged " (paen. 9).

The entire moral life is regarded from the same legal point of view. Man is to fulfill the law—not only its precepts (praecepta), but, if possible, also its counsels (consilia) (c. Marc. ii. 17. ad ux. ii. 1). Thus he becomes holy and righteous, and recompenses Christ for his redeeming work (resur. 8 ; patient. 16 fin.). " By continence thou shalt negotiate a great substance of sanctity ; by parsimony of the flesh thou shalt acquire the Spirit " (exh. cast. 10 in.). Let man acquire for himself merits before God.

"No one is advanced by practical indulgence, but by obeying his will ; the will of God is our sanctification" (ib. 1 ; cf. paen. 6. jej. 3 in.).   This is to be done in view of the divine recompense, especially from fear of the judgment ; for the reward will always be according to the merits.   "Good done has God as debtor, just as has evil also, because the Judge is a rewarder of every case" (paen. 2).   Why many mansions with the Father, if not on account of the variety of merits?   (scorp. 6 ; vid. also orat. 2, 4 ; resur. 8.   ad Scapul. 4 extr.).   Such is the program of the practical Christianity of the West !   Christianity, according to Tertullian, is salvation ; and it is such by the giving of *sacraments* and *laws*.   The sacraments (baptism and repentance) are the properly saving element.   The law points out to those who have been reconciled the way to meritorious works and holy life.   In the sacraments is concentrated the religious element in Christianity ; in the law and good works the moral element.   Thus there is, to a certain extent, a balance established between religion and morality, between the grace of God and man's deed, although there is wanting an inner connection between the two elements.   In all of this, Tertullian's view became normative.   Compare HARNACK, DG., iii. 13 ff.   WIRTH, Der Verdienstbegriff in d. chr. Kirche, i. (d. Verdienstbegr. in Tert), 1892.

8. Eschatology.   The resurrection of the flesh is, in harmony with the rule of faith, championed against the Gnostics. Irenæus adduces in its support the resurrection of Christ (v. 31. 2), the indwelling of the Spirit in our body (v. 13. 4), and also the Lord's Supper, since the latter, after God has been invoked upon it, is the body and blood of Christ (cf. in explanation : "the eucharist, consisting of two things, the earthly and the heavenly," iv. 18. 5), and as such nourishes our flesh (v. 2. 3 ; iv. 18. 5).[1]   The end will come when the devil shall have once more recapitulated the entire apostate throng in the Antichrist (v. 25. 1: "recapitulating in himself the diabolic apostasy . . . he will tyrannically attempt to prove himself God").   Then will Christ appear, and the six thousand years of the world will

---

[1] Irenæus, as is from the entire context of the passages cited beyond question, thinks of a real presence of the body of Christ in the eucharist.   The case appears to be the same, though not so evidently, with Tertullian.   De orat. 6 : "Thereby by praying for daily bread (4th petition) we ask for perpetuity and personal life from his body ; " c. Marc. 1. 14 : "bread, in which he presents (*repraesentat=praesentat*) his very body."   Ib. iv. 40 : "This is my body, *i. e.*, a figure of my body (*figura corporis mei*, vid. LEIMBACH, Beiträge zur Abendmahlslehre Tert. 1874.   Baptism and the Lord's Supper are often combined in such connections, *e. g.*, Tert. c. Marc. iv. 34 ; resur. 8 ; de virg. oel. 9 ; de exhort. cast. 7 ; de praescr. 40 ; de corona 3.

be followed by the first resurrection and the rest of the seventh
millennium (v. 28. 3 ; 33. 2). In Palestine believers will refresh themselves with the marvelously rich fruits of the land
(following Papias, cf. Matt. 26. 29 ; v. 33. 3 f. 1). Then follows the end, the new heavens and the new earth (v. 36. 1).
The blessed will live in graded order in the " many mansions "
in the Father's house, ascending from the Spirit to the Son, and
through the Son to the Father (as learned from pupils of the
apostles, v. 36. 2). Then will occur what is described in 1 Cor.
15. 26 ff. (ib.). Thus upon this subject also the teaching of
the church stands in sharp and conscious contrast with the
general Gnostic view (v. 36. 3).

9. Methods of Proof (cf., in addition to Irenæus, especially
Tert., de praescr. haeret.). (a) The church professes to teach
the truth concerning God, Christ, and salvation. This is attested
by the prophets, apostles, and all disciples of Christ (Ir. iii. 24.
1). Thus the decisive authority rests with the Scriptures of the
Old and New Testaments.[1] The idea that Gnosticism and Montanism forced the church to fix the canon of the New Testament
is erroneous. The limits of the New Testament were not more
positively fixed at the end of the second century than at its beginning (Jas. and Heb., e. g., were wanting in many national
churches ; others used Hermas [Ir. iv. 20. 2. Tert. de or. 16 ;
cf. de pud. 10. Can. Mur. l. 73 ff.], Barnabas [Cl. Strom. ii.
31, 35], and the Didache [Cl. ib. i. 100. Orig. de princ. iii. 2. 7 ;
cf. Clem. in Ir. iii. 33]—as canonical (cf. ZAHN i. 326 ff.). Appeal might be made to an established custom in citing the authority of these writings as conclusive. But the peculiar nature
of the opposition encountered in Gnosticism led to the attaching
of a special importance to the source of these documents—and
this, not so much as coming from the apostles, as because they
dated from the primitive period of the church, and hence contained the real gospel (Ir. iii. 1. Serap. in Eus. h. e. vi. 12.
3). Hence it is that Irenæus lays such stress upon the utterances of the " elders " (i. e., ad Florin. in Eus. h. e. v. 20.
4. adv. haer. iv. 27. 1 in.; 32. 1 ; v. 36. 2). It was but a natural consequence of this high estimation of the New Testament
writings, when inspiration ("Spirit-bearers," πνευματοφόροι ;
"spoken by the Word of God and his Spirit ; " " the Spirit

---

[1] In addition to the authority of Scripture, Tertullian appealed also to the
testimony of reason : " Reason is a thing of God . . . he has wished nothing
to be considered or known without reason " (paen. 1). Words have character,
not only by their sound, but by their sense, and they are heard not so much
by the ear as by the mind. " He who knows nothing believes that God is
cruel " (scorp. 7); vid. also corona 4 f. 10, and Cyprian, sub.

through the apostle," etc.; "God-inspired," ϑεόπνευστος) was expressly ascribed to them (Theophil. ad. Autol. ii. 22. 9 ; iii. 11, 12, 13, 14. Ir. 28. 2 ; iii. 16. 2, 9. Tert. de pat. 7 ; de orat. 20, 22 ; c. Marc. v. 7. Clem. Al. Protr. § 87). The conception of inspiration is found frequently in Judaism, as among the Greeks, but it received its specific meaning only when Christianity had adopted from Judaism the conception of the canon ; *i. e.*, that certain books are holy and every word in them is authoritative.[1] To this was, however, now added the Christian principle, that this authority attaches only to the original Christian documents. That from this time there should be also a constant tendency to greater definiteness in marking the limits of the canon may be easily understood. What was relatively new was really only the recognition of the canon, consciously and upon principle, as the legacy of primitive Christianity— as the norm and basis of the church's teaching (cf.: "in harmony with the Scriptures," σύμφωνα ταῖς γραφαῖς, Ir. in Eus. h. e., v. 20. 6). But since the heretics, apparently, in this particular followed the praxis of the primitive church, but introduced garbled writings, or misinterpreted those which were genuine, or appealed to private traditions of the apostolic circle, the appeal to the New Testament did not prove sufficient in controversy : "Therefore appeal is not to be taken to the Scriptures, nor a controversy instituted in those things in which there is either no victory, or a victory uncertain, or as good as uncertain" (Tert. de praescr. 19 ; cf. Ir. iii. 2. 2 fin.).

(*b*) A criterion must be found for the right understanding of the Scriptures, which will prove that the heretics have no right to them (Tert. de praescr. 15, 19, 37.   Ir. i. 9. 5 ; 10. 1 ; iv. 20. 2).   This criterion is the ancient baptismal confession, or the "canon of truth" (Tert. de praescr. 13, 16).   This was paraphrased and interpreted in the free way which had up to this time been customary. All the reproductions of this rule in Irenæus and Tertullian are free, expanded references. It is not this confession as such which is the criterion, but the confession as interpreted. But just on this account the church could not abide by the confession, but was driven to tradition and the episcopacy (see below under d).   (*c*) In regard to this confession, it was held that it could be traced back through the medium of the apostles to Christ (Ir. iii. praef.; v. praef.; i. 10. 1. Tert. praescr. 20 f. 37). It is not the formula itself, but its content, which is had in mind. It was thought that a histori-

---

[1] This idea of the canon appears nowhere, as far as I have observed, in the whole history of religion except in Judaism and Christianity.

cal support for this opinion could be deduced from the unbroken succession of bishops in the "mother-churches" since the days of the apostles (Iren. iii. 3 ; 4. 1 ; v. 20. 1). Tertullian (praescr. 21. 36, 32) says : "Let them [the heretics] therefore produce the origins of their churches ; let them display the order of their bishops, running through succession from the beginning in such a way that the first bishop had as his teacher and predecessor some one of the apostles or of the apostolic men who were closely associated with the apostles !" This applies most especially—and the praxis harmonized—to the church of Rome : "For it is necessary that the whole church, i. e., those from all places who are believers, should come, on account of its more potent headship, to that church in which has been preserved by believers from all places those things which are a tradition from the apostles" (Ir. iii. 3. 2).[1] The old doctrine is the true doctrine : "Wherefore it is to be henceforth equally urged in advance against all heresies, that whatever is the first is true, and whatever is later is adulterated" (Tert. adv. Prax. 2, 20). (*d*) If the bishops are the successors of the apostles, we must learn the apostolic truth at their hand, as they have received the apostolic doctrine, "the sure charisma of truth" through succession from the apostles. Their daily life, moreover, remains confessedly irreproachable (Ir. iv. 26. 2, 4, 5 ; 33. 8 ; 32. 1. Tert. 32. Hipp. Ref. prooem.). Where the gifts (*charismata*) of the Lord have been deposited, there we ought to learn the truth, among whom is that succession of the church which comes from the apostles, and among whom that is preserved which is wholesome and irreproachable in life and unadulterated and incorruptible in speech" (Ir. iv. 26. 5). In place of the ancient *charismata* comes the *charisma veritatis*, peculiar to the bishops. This consists in the possession of the traditional faith, and also in the ability to interpret it (iv. 26. 5). Thus not only the confession, but its interpretation also, became authoritative. It was a historically comprehensible and necessary, but an abnormal path into which these ideas conducted.

(*e*) But of this there was, as yet, no consciousness. Since the church is, as thus historically attested, the possessor of evangelical saving truth, it may be said : "For where the church is, there is the Spirit of God ; and where the Spirit of God is, there

---

[1] The meaning of this noted passage is evidently : Since two great apostles labored at Rome, there attaches to it a special pre-eminence. Accordingly, every church must be in harmony with Rome. In Rome, also, the apostolic tradition was known by people who had come from all parts of the world. The two apostles granted to Rome its primacy, and this is binding upon all, as people from all parts of the world have at Rome held fast the true tradition.

is the church and all grace.   But the Spirit is truth " (Ir. iii.
24. 1), and : "who are beyond the bounds of the truth, *i. e.*,
beyond the bounds of the church " (iv. 33. 7).   This conception of the church is, therefore, not as yet hierarchical, for the
episcopacy comes into consideration only as the bearer of the
historical truth.   The church is not " essentially the episcopacy "
(ROTHE, Anfänge der chr. K., 1837, p. 486.   RITSCHL,
Entstehung d. altkath. K. 442 ; per contra, SEEBERG, Begriff der
chr. K. i. 16 ff.), but the congregation of those who believe in
God and fear him, and who receive the Spirit of God (Ir. v. 32.
2 ; iv. 36. 2 ; iii. 3. 2).   They are all priests (Ir. v. 34. 3 ; iv.
8. 3 : "for all the righteous have sacerdotal rank."   Tert. de
orat. 28. exh. cast. 7 : "Are not we laymen also priests ? . . .
where there are three, though they be laymen, there is a church ").
But the Spirit and faith are imparted to man only through the
preaching of the church.   "For this gift of God has been entrusted to the church, just as that of breathing at the creation,
to the end that all the members receiving it should be vivified ;
and in it is included the communication of Christ, *i. e.*, the
Holy Spirit, the pledge of incorruptibility and confirmation of
our faith and the ladder of ascension to God " (Ir. iii. 24. 1.
Hipp., de Chr. et Antichr. 59, compares the church to a ship in
which Christ is the pilot ; the rudder, the two testaments ; the
cable, the love of Christ ; the accompanying boat, regeneration ;
the iron anchor, the commandments of Christ ; the ladder representing the sufferings of Christ and inviting us to ascend to heaven,
etc.   The church gives birth to the Logos, ib. 61 : "The church
does not cease from her heart to give birth to the Logos . . .
the Son of God . . . always bringing forth, the church teaches
all the nations ").   But the proclamation of this truth has been
committed to the successors of the apostles : it is found only where
their words are obeyed.

The unity of the church is not yet traced to the one episcopacy.   It is based upon the one Spirit, the one truth, the one confession.   "Our bodies have, through that washing, received that
union which makes for incorruption ; but our souls through the
Spirit" (Ir. iii. 17. 2).   Tertullian says : "Therefore such and
so many churches has become that one first from the apostles,
from which they all are derived.   Thus all are first, and all are
apostolic, since all are one.   The communication of peace and the
title of brotherhood, and the friendship of hospitality, which
laws no other rule controls than the one tradition of the same
sacrament, prove the unity " (praescr. 20 ; cf. de virg. vel. 2.
Apol. 39 init.—" sacrament " here refers to the rule of faith).

Let us now glance backward.   We have discovered the ele-

ments of the common faith of the church at the close of the
second century. The church found herself in a position to establish a positive doctrine (" I believed what it was proper for me to
believe") in opposition to Gnosticism. It traced the Gnostic
view to heathen influences. The fundamental features of the
church's doctrine were as follows: (1) One God, who is
righteous and good, the Creator, Preserver, Ruler, and Saviour
of the world. The one God is not a lonely God. In maintaining this, reference was had to the speculations of the Apologists
concerning the Logos, but, independently of these, it was regarded as fixed that we are to acknowledge a three-fold Ego in
God (Iren.). Tertullian endeavored to explain this relation by
introducing the conceptions of substance and person. (2) The
evil in man is not implied in the fact of his sensuous nature, but
is an act of his free will. The connection with the sin of Adam
is emphasized, but no way is found to consistently carry out the
idea. Even fallen man is free to choose "either part." (3)
The reality of the divinity and humanity of Christ is to be maintained unconditionally in the interest of redemption. His personal life is composed of two substances (Tert.). The salvation
which he brought consists, first, in the law of love which he
taught, and whose observance he made possible ; then, in immortality. Upon the latter the emphasis is laid. Together with
this, other scriptural ideas, especially of a Pauline and Johannine type, are still influential and of practical significance, e. g.:
Christ, as the second Adam, the source for us and the leaven in
us ; the Spirit, as making the fulfillment of the law possible and
bringing to us fellowship with God ; sonship to God ; the forgiveness of sins ; the weakening of the devil ; our reconciliation with
God, etc. (4) The preaching of the gospel imparts salvation,
and baptism applies it to the individual. It is apprehended in
faith. It is, indeed, a portentous turn of thought, when faith is
represented as the acceptance and acknowledgment of Christ, or
as obedience, and its object as " doctrine ; " but this position is,
after all, practically neutralized in part by the assertion that faith
cannot be awakened without the operation of the Spirit, and is
inconceivable without a life in union with God and holy love. If
it is said that faith justifies man, this is meant substantially in
the sense of an inciting to the fulfillment of the divine commandments. Tertullian, by treating the relation of God and
man in a legal scheme, prepared the way for the later development of doctrine in the Western church. (5) These ideas find
their consummation in the resurrection of the flesh, which the
teachers of the period seek not only to propagate as a doctrine,
but to understand in its relation to the practical religious life of

believers.   (6) In all of this, these men were conscious that they
represented the original Christianity, and were able to attest their
views as primitively Christian by the customary criteria of Scripture and the baptismal confession.   These positions were, indeed, further developed in the acknowledgment of the episcopacy
as the bearer and guarantor of the truth thus held, and in the
admission of ecclesiastical tradition to a place by the side of
scriptural authority.   It is a result of the great conflict with
Gnosticism, that the church first attained her unity as a
teaching church—in her doctrine.   The unity of the church embraces the elements absolutely essential if the church and Christianity are to continue in existence.   That this unity consists in
the pure doctrine is, leaving separate considerations out of view,
a result of the conflict with Gnosticism.

   The Antignostic Fathers were, broadly speaking, right in their
general conception, as against the position of their opponents.
They did not really present anything new, not even a distinctly
enlarged understanding of Christianity.   Their conception of
Christian truth and life is that which prevailed already at the
close of the first and the beginning of the second century.   The
only peculiarity is that the opposition encountered compelled
them to greater distinctness and lucidity, as well as to deliberate
utterances with respect to the canon and doctrinal tradition.
The essential content of Christianity is still held to be faith in
the Triune God and in Christ, the Son of God and man, observance of the new law, and the hope of immortality.   As formerly,
so now, religious life found nourishment in the reflections, that
Christ has delivered us and brought to us the forgiveness of sins ;
that grace saves us ; that the believer leads a life in Christ and
with Christ, etc.: but there was no certainty in the treatment of
these ideas.   In the last analysis, it is the chief thing that he who
observes the commandment of love becomes a child of God and
a partaker of immortality.   In reality, use was made for spiritual
edification of more material than was taken account of in the
books of the age—a fact which is of great importance in explaining the vigorous opposition to Gnosticism.

§ 15. The Theology of the Alexandrine Fathers.

LITERATURE : CLEMENS ALEXANDRINUS († ca. A. D. 215). Λόγος
προτρεπτικὸς πρὸς ῾Ελληνας ; Παιδαγωγός, ll. 3 ; Στρωματεῖς, ll. 8 ; ἐκ τῶν
προφητικῶν ἐκλογαί ; ἐκ τῶν Θεοδότου καὶ τῆς ανατολικῆς καλουμένης διδασκαλιας
κατὰ τοὺς Οὐαλεντίνου χρόνους ἐπιτομαί. Also the homily, Τίς ὁ σωζόμενος
πλούσιος. Finally, a large fragment from the ῾Υποτυπώσεις, preserved in Latin
(Adumbrationes); editions by Potter, 1715 (citations of chapter and page in
present work refer to this edition), and Dindorf, 1868, in Migne, t. 8, 9. ORIGEN
(† A. D. 254). We make use especially of his Περί ἀρχῶν, ll. 4, preserved

in the Latin translation of Rufinus, of which we have also large Greek fragments. Also κατὰ Κέλσον, ll. 8 ; editions by DE LA RUE, 1733, reprinted by
LOMMATZSCH, 1831 ff., in Migne, t. 11-17. Compare GUERIKE, de schola
quae Alex. floruit cat., 1824, 1825. BIGG, The christ. Platonists of Alex.,
1886. LUTHARDT, Gesch. d. chr. Ethik, i. 113 ff. ZAHN, Forschungen iii.
(Supplementum Clementinum), 1884. COGNAT, Clement d'Alexandrie,
1859. WINTER, Die Ethik d. Clem. v. Alex., 1882. MERK, Clem. Alex.
in s. Abh. v. d. griech. Philos., Leipz. Diss., 1879. HUETIUS, Origeniana,
1668. THOMASIUS, Orig., 1837. REDEPENNING, Orig., 2 vols., 1841, 1846.
H. SCHULTZ, Die Christol. d. Orig. in Zusammenh. s. Weltanschauung, in
Jahrb. f. prot. Theol., 1875, 193 ff., 369 ff. DENIS, La philosophie d'
Origène, 1884. Möller, PRE. xi. 92 ff. HOLL, Enthusiasmus u. Bussgewalt, p. 228 ff.

We have noted the league formed in Alexandria between the
Jewish spirit and the Hellenic philosophy, which produced the
type of thought represented by Philo. A similar compact
appears in the same locality toward the end of the second century. Hellenistic learning and gospel truth are associated in
the most astonishing way. The catechetical schools at Alexandria provided the basis for this movement, and it was promoted
by Pantaenus, Clement, and Origen (cf., as to the pedagogical
method of Origen, the Panegyricus of Greg. Thaum., c. 6-15).
It was sought to secure what had been attained by the most profound researches of the Gnostics, in the belief that this could be
done without surrendering the church's rule of faith. The Gnostics and Apologists were here excelled. Christianity became a
science in literary forms which assumed a place of equal rank by
the side of secular literature. This explains the unbounded veneration and admiration with which Origen was regarded. The
movement was of inestimable significance in the history of Greek
theology. It is associated distinctly with the name of Origen.
The teachings of Clement claim our attention only as preparatory
in their character.

The Greek spirit is in Clement combined with the faith of the
church in a way characteristically fresh and unsophisticated.
The difficulties encountered do not disturb him. He was a talented dilettante, with the virtues and the vices which belong to
such a character. He held that there is but one truth, in which
all lines eventually converge. God gave to the Jews the law,
and to the Greeks philosophy. " For it (philosophy) led the
Grecian world to Christ as did the law the Hebrews " (Str. i. 5. p.
331 ; vi. 17. 823 ; 5. 762). He spoke of the philosophers as
borrowing material from the Old Testament (Str. v. 14. 699 ff.
This was not the case, however, with their idolatry, Protr. 2).
Philosophy he regarded as still possessing a pedagogical signifi·
cance for every Christian who rises from bare faith (ψιλὴ πίστις)
to *Gnosis*. But this occurs according to the canon of the

church (κατὰ κάνονα ἐκκλησιαστικόν, Str. vii. 7. 855 ; vi. 15. 803).
Following Philo, Clement effects a compromise with the letter
of the Old and New Testaments by allegorical interpretation
(cf. Str. vi. 15. 806 f.).   Faith in revelation is necessary to
salvation.   Such faith is sufficient, but points beyond itself to
Gnosis (Str. ii. 2. 432 ; v. 1. 643 ; vii. 10. 864 f.: "to believe
is the foundation of gnosis ").   Hence, "to know is more than
to believe" (Str. vi. 14. 794).   Faith is the outward acceptance of God and of the doctrine of Christ in the literal sense,
from fear and respect for authority (*e. g.*, Str. ii. 12 ; v. 1. 643 ;
vii. 12. 873 f.).   The Gnostic, on the other hand, lives in
initiated vision (ἐποπτική θεωρία), apprehending salvation
inwardly and comprehending it (Str. vi. 10 ; i. 2. 327).   He
does not do that which is good for the sake of expected reward,
but for its own sake, in love to God (Str. iv. 18. 614 ; iv. 22.
625).   He avoids not only actual sin, but also every motion of
sinful desire (Str. ii. 11. 455; vi. 12. 789 f.).   He regards
himself, not as a servant, but as a child of God (Str. vii. 2. 831).
He prays always, for prayer is companionship with God (Str.
vii. 7. 851 ff., 854 ; vii. 12. 875).   If he who simply believes
(ἁπλῶς πεπιστευκώς) requires the purifications (καθάρσια), or
minor mysteries (μικρὰ μυστήρια) of the church, the Gnostic
needs the great (μεγάλα) mysteries, the ἐποπτεία (Protr. § 1, p.
9 ; § 12.   Str. v. 11. 689).   This is the royal way.   "By as
much as anyone loves God, by so much the more does he make
his way into God (Quis div. salv. 27 fin.).   Thus there result
two forms of Christianity.   In contrast with the barely believing, uncultivated beginner, inclined to externalities, stands the
Christian who beholds the mysteries of God, and who, with heart
and understanding, receives God to abiding fellowship.   The Stoic
discrimination between the wise and the advancing (προκόπτοντες)
is here transferred to Christianity.   There are now Christians of a
first and of a second class.   Thus the evacuation of the conception
of faith by means of the bare orthodoxy which is satisfied with
outward belief (Str. i. 9. 342 f.) is noted, but also granted
honorable recognition, while at the same time a way of escape,
although a dangerous one, from that error is discovered.   The
"Gnostic" of Clement really stands higher than his "believer."

    The separate doctrines in Clement—as the objects of faith and
knowledge—may be readily passed in review.   The One God,
who is Being beyond nature (ἐπέκεινα τῆς οὐσίας), and without
attributes (*e. g.*, Str. v. 12. 695 f.; v. 11. 689), is the Creator
of the world.   The formula and the conception of the Trinity
constantly recur (Str. v. 14. 710 ; cf. Exc. ex Theod. 80.   Protr.
12 init.   Paed. i. 6. 123 ; also iii. 12. 311.   Quis div. salv. 42

fin. Adumbr., p. 88, Zahn). Christ is the Logos of God (distinct from the paternal Logos, πατρικὸς λόγος, Hypot. in Photius Bibl. cod. 109). In him God is known. He has been from the beginning present and active in the world, giving it existence and offering the truth in prophets and philosophers. He has now become man. "Christ was, indeed, in ancient times this Logos and [the cause] of our being . . . and of our well-being ; but now this same Logos has appeared to men, the only One both God and man, the cause of all things good to us, by whom, having been thoroughly instructed in right living, we are conducted to eternal life" (Protr. 1, p. 6). He was a man with a human body and soul (cf., "impassible as to his soul," Paed. 1. 2, p. 99). Clement seeks, although without success, to avoid Docetism : "But in the case of the Saviour [to suppose] that the body, as a body, demanded the aids necessary for duration would be ridiculous. For he ate, not for the sake of the body sustained by holy power, but in order that those with him might not be induced to think otherwise concerning him, just as, indeed, afterward some thought that he was manifested in seeming (δοχήσει). But he was entirely impassible, upon whom no emotional impulse, whether of joy or grief, could manage to exert its power" (Str. vi. 9. 775; cf. iii. 7. 538. Adumbr., p. 87, Zahn). Christ surrendered his life to death for us, became a ransom (λύτρον) for us, and overcame the devil (Quis div., p. 37. Paed. iii. 12, p. 310 ; i. 5. 111 ; i. 11 fin. Protr. 11 init.). Not much importance is, however, attached to the conception of Christ as the propitiation (ἱλασμός; vid. e. g., Paed. iii. 6, p. 310). He grows eloquent, on the other hand, in extolling the Logos as a teacher beyond compare, as leader and lawgiver, and as the way to immortality (Protr. 11, p. 86 : "For if the Teacher who has filled all things with his holy powers, creation, salvation, goodness, legislation, prophecy, instruction, now as Teacher instructs us in all things, Athens and Greece also already knew everything in the Logos," ib. p. 88 f., § 12, p. 91. Paed. i. 3, p. 102 f.; i. 6. 113. Protr. i. p. 8 : "The Logos . . . having become man, just in order that thou also mightest learn from a man how at any time a man might become divine ; " cf. Paed. i. 12. 156. Str. iv. 23. 632 ; vii. 10. 865). Christ, as God, forgives sins, and his humanity serves the purposes of moral instruction : "As God, forgiving sins ; but as man, leading to avoid continuance in sin" (Paed. i. 3 init.).

Man, upon his part, is to render obedience to the teaching of Christ, and, with a view to reward, exercise love toward others, in accordance with the commandments (Protr. 11, p. 89 f. Paed. i. 3. 102). Clement knows full well that man lies bound

in the fetters of sin (Protr. ii. init. Paed. iii. 12. 307 : " For
to sin continually is natural and common to all ''), but this
does not prevent him from most strongly emphasizing his free-
will (αὐτεξούσιον) or the "in our power" (ἐφ' ἡμῖν, Str. vi.
12. 788). " But he desires that we may be saved from ourselves " (ib.). Thus man is free to do good and to exercise
faith (Str. iv. 24. 633 ; ii. 15. 462 ; iii. 9. 540). God offers
salvation, and man has power to grasp it : " Just as the physician furnishes health to those who labor with him for health, so
also does God furnish eternal salvation to those working with
him for knowledge and prosperity " (Str. vii. 7. 860). The
first right inclination (ἡ πρώτη πρὸς σωτηρίαν νεῦσις) is faith.
Then follow fear, hope, repentance (μετάνοια). The goal is
reached in love (ἀγάπη) and knowledge (γνῶσις) (Str. ii. 6. 445).
Faith is an " assent " (συγκατάθεσις) and a " perception of the
mind (πρόληψις διανοίας) concerning the things spoken " (Str. ii.
12. 458 ; 2. 437, 432). Inasmuch as faith is a necessary preliminary to salvation, our salvation may be ascribed to it (Str. ii.
12. 457 f.: " Faith is strength for salvation and power for eternal life ; " Paed. i. 6. 116 : " The one universal salvation of
the human race is faith ''). But this faith points beyond itself to
knowledge and love (vid. supra ; cf. Str. ii. 11. 454 : " reasonable," δοξαστικὴ, and " intelligent," ἐπιστημονική, faith). This
was a necessary inference when faith was regarded as merely an
assent, or a persuasion to comply with the commandments
(πείθεσθαι ταῖς ἐντολαῖς, ib.). With such an idea of faith, Paul's
doctrine of justification is untenable : " Righteousness is two-
fold : that produced by love and that produced by fear " (Str. vii.
12. 879). The " Gnostic " has complete righteousness. This is
illustrated in Abraham's faith and righteousness : " For example,
to Abraham, having become a believer, it was accounted for righteousness ; to him, having advanced to that which is greater and
more perfect than faith," etc. (Str. vi. 12. 791 ; cf. vii. 14. 885).
Thus, then, the believer of his free will decides for God and his
law, advancing from mere faith and the righteousness which
attaches to it to knowledge and love, to continual inward fellowship with God, to a life of faith and uninterrupted holy activity,
to genuine righteousness. Here the moral ideal is attained ; the
lust of the world has vanished : " He is not strenuous, but in a
state of calmness " (Str. iv. 22. 625). Yet, on the other hand,
it is maintained with all earnestness that " only the well-doing
which is for the sake of love, or for the sake of the beautiful
itself, is chosen by the Gnostic." He lives and labors in the
world without love for the world (e.g., Str. iii. 7. 537 ; vi.

12. 790; vii. 12. 874¹-878). He attains to right conduct (*κατόρθωμα*), whereas the simple believer (*ἁπλῶς πιστός*) reaches only median conduct (*μέση πρᾶξις*), according to the Stoic terminology (Str. vi. 14. 796).

The individual, however, secures his salvation only in connection with the church and its agency (Paed. iii. 12 fin.; i. 6. 123, 114: "His desire is the salvation of men; and this has been called the church"). Hierarchical aims are entirely foreign to Clement (cf. Str. vi. 13. 793). It is baptism which makes one a member of the church and a partaker of salvation. It brings the cleansing from sin, and thus the capability of apprehending the salvation which the teaching of the church offers. Thus one becomes through baptism a new man. Sonship, perfection, immortality have become his in faith (initially) through baptism (Paed. i. 6. 113: "Having been baptized, we are illuminated; having been illuminated, we are made sons; having been made sons, we are perfected; having been perfected, we are made superior to death." p. 114: "Thus nothing but believing and being born again is perfection in life." Ib.: "This doctrine, *μάθημα*, is the eternal salvation of the eternal Saviour. . . We, the baptized, having erased our beclouding sins, the condemnation of darkness, by the divine Spirit, have the free and unhindered and bright vision of the Spirit; by which alone we behold divine things, the Holy Spirit streaming in upon us from heaven." p. 116: "Therefore we have washed away all our sins, and are immediately no longer evil. This is the one grace of illumination, viz., to be no longer the same as before, or to have cleansed the way. But when knowledge, *γνῶσις*, appears, together with illumination . . . the unlearned are learned—whenever this learning may have been added; for thou hast not [power] to tell the time. For instruction indeed leads up to faith, but faith is taught together with baptism by the Holy

---

¹ A few sentences may be adduced in illustration: "Wherefore also he eats and drinks and marries, not from choice, but from necessity. As to marrying, if reason may speak, I say, also because it is proper. For he who has become perfect has the apostles as examples; and he does not really show himself a man who enters upon a single life, but he conquers men who, in marriage and the rearing of children and providing for his house, has exercised himself without pleasure and without pain in the care of the house, constant in his experience of the love of God, and escaping every temptation besetting him through children and wife, domestics, and property. 'But it falls to the lot of the houseless man to be in many things without experience. Hence, caring for himself alone, he is weakened for that which is still lacking with respect to his own salvation, and abounds in the management of affairs pertaining to [the present] life."

10

Spirit "). God cleanses sins committed after baptism by disciplinary sufferings (Str. iv. 24. 634).

The Eucharist, according to Clement, bestows participation in immortality. The communicant enters into fellowship with Christ and the divine Spirit. "On the one hand, the mixed wine nourishes to faith; on the other hand, the Spirit leads to immortality. The commingling anew in both of the potion and the Word is called the eucharist, a blessed and beautiful [gift of] grace, of which those who partake in faith are sanctified in both body and soul" (Paed. ii. 2. 177 f.; cf. i. 6. 125). These are the Christian mysteries (vid. Protr. 12, p. 91 ff.). But this all points beyond itself to the unshrouded knowledge of the "great mysteries" (vid. supra, p. 142). This is the Christian life: "right living, together with due appropriation of knowledge—for the perception of the truth and the fulfillment of the commandments" (Str. i. 1. 318; cf. vi. 12. 788 : "both in learning and in exercise").

Clement taught the resurrection of the body. He appears to have accepted the possibility of a conversion after death (Str. vii. 2 fin.; 16. 895), without giving prominence to the idea.[1]

ORIGEN is more positive than Clement, but Clement is more Christian than Origen. It was the age when Neoplatonism was beginning to control thought. Starting with God as the abstract Existence ($\tau\grave{o}\ \ddot{\varepsilon}\nu$), advance was made through the divine Thought ($\nu o\tilde{v}\varsigma$), the conceived order of things ($\varkappa\acute{o}\sigma\mu o\varsigma\ \nu o\eta\tau\acute{o}\varsigma$), the universal soul ($\acute{\eta}\ \tau o\tilde{v}\ \acute{o}\lambda o\nu\ \psi\nu\chi\acute{\eta}$), to this world, in which the souls of men live imprisoned in matter ($\ddot{v}\lambda\eta$). The task before them is escape from the sensuous by asceticism and ecstasy, through the medium of mystical symbolic rites. "The only salvation is a turning toward God" (Porphyr. ad Marcell, 24). In the great longing which broods over this conception lies its significance. There is a gradation of being, extending from God to the soul, which penetrates through all things and all religions with their forms. All things are but copies of the infinite. Again, the soul aspires to God through all possible suggestions, means, and symbols. All things draw it upward. A wonderful musical rhythm resounds through this structure of thought : from God to the soul, and from the soul to God.

1. This trend of thought was not unknown to Origen. His work, *De principiis*—the first attempt to construct a system of dogmatics—contains a philosophical system, although not consistently adhered to. But Origen is an orthodox Christian. The

---

[1] Clement expresses himself as against the theory of the pre-existence of souls (Eclog. 17). It is not taught in Str. v. 16. 808, nor in Quis div. salv. 33 fin.

Scriptures contain the truth ; and he sends forth in advance of his own doctrinal conclusions a completed rule of faith, the teaching of the church, *ecclesiastica praedicatio* (De princ. praef).[1] "It seems necessary before [treating of] these separate points to lay down a certain line and a plain rule." These "elements and fundaments" are to be brought together, with the application of the things which the Scripture teaches, or which result from the teaching as a necessary consequence (praef. 10).[2] But the Scriptures are to be interpreted "spiritually," or allegorically. Thus Origen was enabled to find his peculiar opinions in them. He developed the allegorical interpretation systematically (de princ. iv.). Passages which seem contradictory, or which have a crass external sense, conceal a "deeper thought." The Holy Spirit veiled the thought by means of a "cloak of spiritual things." Impossible things are asserted in order to call attention to the fact that the occurrences could not have taken place corporeally ($\sigma\omega\mu\alpha\tau\iota\varkappa\tilde{\omega}\varsigma$), as, *e. g.*, the visible paradise and the walking of God therein ; Lk. 10. 4 ; Matt. 5. 39, 29 f.; 1 Cor. 9. 9 ; many narrations of the Old Testament ; some features in the history of Jesus ; and in the Gospels other things which did not happen ($\check{\epsilon}\tau\epsilon\rho\alpha$ $\mu\grave{\eta}$ $\sigma\upsilon\mu\beta\epsilon\beta\eta\varkappa\acute{o}\tau\alpha$; cf. iv. § 9-18). Appealing to Prov. 22. 20 f., Origen teaches a three-fold sense of Scripture : the somatic, literal sense ; the psychical, moral sense ; and the pneumatic, speculative sense. Historical and doctrinal passages are alike subject to this rule. He finds his own doctrine everywhere. Christian language adorns ideas

---

[1] One God, the Creator, the God of the Old and New Testaments, who gave Christ ; Christ, born of the Father before all creatures, truly born a man, who suffered, died and rose again ; the Holy Spirit, partaking of equal honor, his nature not clearly defined in tradition. The human soul has substance and life of its own, but there is nothing taught concerning its origin. Man is rewarded according to his merit. He has free will. The existence of angels and devils, together with the frequent expression of the opinion that the devil was an angel. The world was created, but not what was before it, nor what shall be after it. Holy Scriptures, which have not only the sense which lies upon the surface (*qui in manifesto ist*). The whole law is spiritual. Whether God is corporeal, what is the nature of the soul, if the stars are living beings, is not decided (de princ. praef. 4. 9; cf. the summary in Joh. xxxii. 9). A wide scope is here left for scientific exposition. The first dogmatician of the church assumed in his labors a position of fundamental subordination to the Rule of Faith. This has remained the case with his successors. The Rule of Faith became normative in the arrangement of doctrinal systems, and is so to the present day. This is the significance which it secured in the history of the world through the Antignostic controversies.

[2] Origen treats in the 4 Books of his De principiis, (1) Of God, (2) Of the Word, (3) Of Free Will, (4) Of the Allegorical Interpretation of Scripture. The first three books present—when viewed in a certain light—almost the whole content of his teaching.

which are but slightly Christian. On the other hand, this method enables him to conceal the foolishness of the gospel and to glorify it as wisdom (*e. g.*, c. Cels. vi. 7; v. 60; iii. 19; cf. the estimate of Porphyry in Eus. h. e. vi. 19. 4, 7 f., and Cels. iv. 38). The simpler class and the multitude depend upon the *ipse dixit* (αὐτὸς ἔφα) and cling to the literal sense with their "bare and unreasoning faith" (c. Cels. iv. 9; i. 42. 13; iii. 53). They speak of God as the Creator, but think of him as a coarse and unjust man (de pr. iv. 8). They understand literally, and not in the sense of purifying, what the Scriptures say of judgment (c. Cels. vi. 26; v. 16), and it is nothing but the fear of the judgment which makes them Christians. This is a lower plane, above which the cultured believer rises, searching the Scriptures as Christ has commanded, and learning to understand their spiritual contents (c. Cels. ii. 5 f.; iii. 79; iv. 71; v. 31 f., 18). Thus, when contemplating the death of Christ, he reflects that he is crucified with Christ (c. Cels. ii. 69). He understands why Christ heals the sick upon the plain, but ascends the mountain with the disciples (ib. iii. 21). Christ is for him the teacher, and no longer the physician (ib. iii. 62: "Therefore the divine Logos was sent to be a physician to sinners, but to be a teacher of divine mysteries to those already pure and no longer sinning"). The Christian starts out with faith based upon authority (cf. c. Cels. i. 11) and with cleansing from sin in the fear of punishment; there follows the higher stage, of understanding and insight (cf. also de orat. 27). Origen thinks of this higher stage as essentially intellectual, taking thus a step backward toward Clement. He has, however, the acuteness to recognize it as a special advantage possessed by Christianity, compared with philosophy, that it is able to offer piety and salvation even to the mass of the common people (c. Cels. vii. 60; iii. 53 f.).

2. (*a*) "God is a Spirit," "God is light"—thus does Origen introduce his discussion of the doctrine of God. Yet he remains within the limitations of the Grecian idea. "God is Being, and beyond Being" (ἐπέκεινα οὐσίας; cf. c. Cels. vi. 64; in Joh. xix. 1 ad fin.: "in the Over-beyond of Being, in the power and nature of God"). He is an "intellectual nature" (de pr. i. 1. 1-6), free from everything material, not limited by space and time. Accordingly, he is "incomprehensible, inestimable, impassible, beyond want of anything," etc. (de pr. i. 1. 5; ii. 4. 4; iii. 5. 2. c. Cels. viii. 8, 21). "He is in every part solitary (μονάς) and, so to speak, a unit (ἑνάς), at once mind and the source whence is derived the beginning of all intellectual nature or mind" (de pr. i. 1. 6). But this Source of the world is, on the other hand, conceived of as a personality. He is

the Creator, Preserver, and Governor of the world (δημιουργήσας, συνέχων, κυβερνῶν; c. Cels. iii. 40; cf. vi. 79). In this government he is just and good: "This one and the same [God] is just and good, the God of the law and of the gospels; he does good with justice, and punishes with goodness" (de pr. ii. 5. 3). The spirit of man attains a relative knowledge of God, and this in proportion as he severs himself from matter (de pr. i. 1. 7). (*b*) The One God is primarily God the Father. We recognize him in the Son, who is his image, his radiant crown, his wisdom (*sapientia*) and his Logos (de princ. i. 2. 8, 2 f.). The Son proceeds from the Father, not by any kind of division, but in a spiritual way, somewhat as his will (de pr. i. 2. 6). Since everything in God is eternal, the begetting of the Son is also an eternal act: "The Father did not beget the Son and set him free after he was begotten, but he is always begetting him" (in Hierem. hom. ix. 4; de pr. i. 2. 4: *eterna ac sempiterna generatio*). Accordingly the Son has no temporal beginning. "There is not when he was not" (Orig. in Athanas. de decr. syn. Nic. 27; de pr. i. 2. 9. f.; iv. 28; in Rom. i. 5. Afterward, in Joh. i. 22: κτίσας; c. Cels. v. 37, fin.: "the eldest of all created things"). Upon the basis of this, the relation to the Father is that of unity of substance: "a vapor of the power, *virtus*, of God, an emanation of his glory . . . they show most clearly that there is in the Son a communion of substance with the Father. For an emanation (*aporrhoea*) is seen to be homousian,[1] *i. e.*, of one substance with the body of which it is an emanation, or vapor" (in Hebrew fragment, Lommatzsch, xxiv. 359). If the Son is thus one with the Father through possession of the same nature (οὐσία), he is yet, on the other hand, himself a being, a separate *hypostasis*, or complete in his own subsistence (*in propria subsistentia effectus*) (de pr. 1. 2. 2, 9).[2] There are two hypos-

---

[1] Upon the term, ὁμοούσιος, whose meaning is here rightly given, compare *supra*, p. 101, n., and especially ZAHN, Marcell v. Ancyra, p. 11 ff. HATCH, Griechentum u. Christentum, pp. 202, 204. The word stood also, perhaps, in the original text of Clem. Adumbr. (Zahn, Forsch. iii. 87): secundum aequalitatem substantiae unum cum patre consistit (cf., for its signification, Clement, Str. ii. 16, p. 467).

[2] The terms, οὐσία and ὑπόστασις, are, in themselves, identical, both signifying primarily "substance." The former is Platonic, the latter Stoic. But a discrimination begins to appear in Origen, according to which ὑπόστασις indicates the οὐσία ἰδία, or personal mode of existence (*e. g.*, in Joh. ii. 6; x. 21, it is held that "the Son does not differ from the Father in number, but the two are one, not only in nature, οὐσία, but also in attributes; that for certain purposes, κατά τινας ἐπινοίας, the Father and the Son are said to be different, not according to hypostasis, c. Cels. viii. 12. in cant., cant. iii.) and οὐσία the substance. Cf. BIGG, l. c., p. 163 f.; also HATCH, Griechentum u. Christentum, p. 203 ff., and the terms *substantia* and *persona* in Tertullian.

tases here, but One God (Origen cites Acts 4. 32). "Therefore we worship the Father of truth and the true Son, being two things in hypostasis, but one in sameness of thought and in harmony, and in sameness of will" (c. Cels. viii. 12). The two hypostases have the same will and the same activity (cf. de pr. i. 2. 12; in Joh. xiii. 36 : "to there being no longer two wills, but one will").

The ὁμοούσιος appears to require the complete equality of the divinity of the Son and the Father. None the less, we meet with Subordinationistic features in Origen. The Son is the "second God" (c. Cels. v. 39 ; cf. in Joh. vi. 23). He is God, but as the image of the Father. He is not the absolutely Good and True, but he is good and true as an emanation and image of the Father (de pr. i. 2. 13, a Greek fragment ; iv. 35 ; in Joh. xiii. 25 ; xxxii. 18 ; in Matt. xv. 10, etc. Compare, on the contrary, in Matt. xiv. 7 init.; c. Cels. iii. 41 ; vi. 47 fin.). The same is true of their activity. Christ is the executive officer (ὑπηρέτης) of the Father, carrying out his instructions, as, e. g., at the creation (c. Cels. vi. 60 ; ii. 9). This tendency in Origen appears also in his refusal to sanction unconditionally the addressing of prayer to Jesus. Petition is to be addressed to the Father, and is presented to him by Christ (de orat. 15, 16 fin., 14 fin.; c. Cels. viii. 13). Yet in other passages he maintains that we should pray only to the Father and to Christ, to the latter that he may bear it before the Father (c. Cels. v. 4, 11 ; 8, 26). The prayer to Christ which is widely prevalent in the church (e. g., Celsus in Origen viii. 12 : ὑπερθρησκεύουσι. Origen himself, ib. viii. 67. de orat. 16 init.) is not forbidden, but Origen has dogmatic objections to it. Thus Origen's doctrine of the Logos reflects the conception of his age. Christ is God as is the Father, like him eternal ; yet he is the "second God," and dependent upon the Father.

(c) Whilst some philosophers thus agree with Christian teaching in the doctrine concerning the Son, the doctrine concerning the Holy Ghost must be derived solely from revelation (de pr. 1. 3. 1-4). He is active, not like the Logos in all intelligent beings, but only in the souls of the saints. It is in harmony with this limitation that he is represented as inferior to the Logos : "The Son is less than the Father . . . for he is second to the Father ; yet the Holy Spirit is lower, extending to the saints alone" (de pr. i. 3. 5, 8). But he, too, is uncreated (de pr. i. 3. 3). As everything else, so he was brought into being through the Son : "all things having come into existence through the Son, the Holy Spirit is more honorable than all, and in the [front] rank of all those things created by the Father through the Son" (in

Joh. ii. 6). The hypostasis, as well as the divinity, of the Holy
Spirit, is firmly maintained. There is a lack, however, of clear
definition. The Father bestows existence, the Logos rationality,
the Holy Spirit holiness (de pr. i. 3. 5), and also the " substance
of the charismata which come from God " (in Joh. ii. 6).

Origen is, of course, familiar with the term, Trinity (in Joh.
v. 17; vi. 17; in Jes. hom. i. 4; iv. 1, etc.). In the Latin translation, and also in De principiis, the term is often of doubtful
genuineness.

3. God loved Jacob and hated Esau, and we constantly observe the most glaring contrasts in the fortunes of men. This is
to be explained, not by the arbitrary decree of God, but by the
freedom of the creature (de pr. ii. 9. 2, 5). Since everything
in God is eternal, his creative activity must be so (ib. i. 2. 10).
The Son serves him here as Mediator. A definite number of
incorporeal spiritual beings, originally all alike, was at first created (ib. ii. 9. 6). To these belonged, however, free-will
(αὐτεξούσιον), which is inseparable from their existence. But
their moral decisions were different. Man, who was intellect
(νοῦς), by reason of his fall from God, cooled down into soul
(ψυχή), since he lost his participation in the divine fire (de pr.
ii. 8. 3; Origen derives ψυχή from ψυχρός). The condition of
all creatures is regulated by their respective merits (meritum, ib.
i. 8. 2; ii. 9. 7). God has bestowed upon all creatures a material corporeity. Their bodies were framed to correspond with
their merit—those of divinities, thrones, and powers were light
and ethereal; those of the stars, which are also living beings
(cf. Plato and Philo), brilliant; those of Satan and the devils,
as being the creatures who fell first and more deeply than others,
coarse and dark. Between the two classes is the corporeal being
of men, " who, on account of the very great deficiencies of
their minds, needed bodies more crass and substantial " (de pr.
iii. 5. 4; ii. 1. 1-4). This accounts for the origination of the
world, which hence had a beginning in time (ib. iii. 5. 3).
This world itself is a judgment before the final judgment; thus
in the most literal sense, " the history of the world is the judgment of the world." The place and country, circumstances of
birth, etc., are appointed to everyone in accordance with his
condition in the pre-existent state (ib. ii. 9. 8). This explains
the infinite variety in the world, which is a result of the exercise
of free-will. But God thus attests his righteousness as well as
his goodness. To everyone was given that to which he was entitled; but God brought the countless contradictions "into the
harmony of one world " (ib. ii. 9. 6 f.). This world, accordingly, makes an impression of harmony, and God finds means to

make even the sins of the wicked—for which he is not responsible
—serviceable to the whole (c. Cels. iv. 54, 70 ; in Num. hom.
xiv. 2).

4. The Logos, from eternity active as the principle of reason
and as the demiurge (c. Cels. iv. 81 ; vi. 47, 60 ; vii. 70 :
" governing all things ; " cf. in Joh. vi. 23), became man for
our deliverance.   He took upon himself human nature (ἀνθρωπίνη
φύσις, c. Cels. iii. 28), and was God and man (c. Cels. vii. 17),
the God-man (θεάνθρωπος, de pr. ii. 6. 3).   The divinity remains unchanged, continuing upon the throne (c. Cels. iv. 5).
Thus also Christ is a real man, with body and soul (c. Cels. iii. 28,
41 ; ii. 31).   The soul of Jesus was, like all others, free in the
state of pre-existence.   It, from the beginning, surrendered itself to the Logos ("the entire receiving the entire").   Yea, it
grew into an indissoluble union with the Logos (following 1 Cor.
6. 17): "It was made essentially one spirit with it" (de pr. ii.
6. 3, 6. c. Cels. iii. 41 ; v. 39 ; vi. 47 f.).   This soul constituted the connecting link between the Logos and the flesh (de
pr. i. 1).   The flesh of Christ was produced in an unusual way
(c. Cels. 1. 69 f.), but was capable of suffering like any human
body (c. Cels. ii. 23 ; iii. 25 fin.).   It is a mystery beyond all
mysteries how we are to believe that the word and wisdom of
God were "within the limitations (intercircumscriptionem)
of that man who appeared in Judea . . . If one thinks him
God, he sees him to be mortal ; if one thinks him human, he
views him, having conquered the kingdom of death, returning
with spoils from the dead . . . thus is demonstrated the reality
of both natures in one and the same [person]" (de pr. ii. 6. 2).
After the incarnation, Logos, soul, and body constitute one
unity : " For the soul and the body of Jesus became, especially
after the incarnation (ὀικονομία), one with the Logos of God "
(c. Cels. ii. 9).   There was one person, which united in itself
divinity and humanity : " The one being was more than one in
mind " (ἐπινοίᾳ, c. Cels. ii. 64 init.).   He was a composite
being : "We say that he became something composite "
(σύνθετον τι χρῆμα; c. Cels. i. 66 ; cf. ib.: " Concerning the
composition, τοῦ συνθέτου, and of what [entities] the incarnate
Jesus was composed ").   Origen earnestly strives to maintain
intact the unity of the person and the integrity of the union of
the two natures.   In this he does not, indeed, succeed.   God
dwells in a man (c. Cels. i. 66, 68 ; de pr. iv. 3 : substantially
filled, substantialiter repletus, with God).   Divinity and humanity are yet not made one ; the divinity suffers nothing (c. Cels. iv.
15 : "Learn that the Logos remaining Logos in nature, τῇ ὀυσίᾳ,
does not suffer any of the things which the body or the soul

suffers . . . as though it had become flesh ; " cf. viii. 42).
" For the dying Jesus is a man " (in Joh. xxviii. 14. c. Cels.
vii. 16). As a man, he really suffered and really died (c. Cels.
ii. 16). His soul then preached in Hades (ib. ii. 43 ; cf. 16).
He really rose from the dead, and his body existed in a state
between the material and the psychic modes of existence (c.
Cels. ii. 62 ; cf. 64-66). After the ascension the human was
entirely absorbed in the divine. " But the exaltation of the
Son of man . . . this was the being no longer other than the
Logos, but the same with it " (in Joh. xxxii. 17 ; in Hierem.
hom. xv. 6 ; in Luc. hom. 29). The Lord now dwells omnipresent in the supramundane world : " Yet he is everywhere and
pervades the universe, but we cannot know him anywhere beyond that circumscribed body which, when located in our body
upon the earth, he possessed among men " (de pr. ii. 11. 6).
Cf. H. Schultz, loc. cit., 225 ff., 369 ff.

5. If we inquire for the work of Christ, we find the dominant thought to be, that Christ was physician, teacher, lawgiver,
and example. As he in olden time revealed the truth in philosophers and prophets, so he now brought to the world a new law,
which is designed for all and which has found acceptance from
all (e. g., c. Cels. iv. 4, 22, 32). Inasmuch as he brought the
saving doctrines ($\sigma\omega\tau\acute{\eta}\rho\iota\alpha$ $\delta\acute{o}\gamma\mu\alpha\tau\alpha$, de pr. iv. 2), the precepts of
the gospel (praecepta evangelii, ib. 24), he is the lawgiver of
Christians (c. Cels. iii. 7). He is to Christianity what
Moses was to Israel (c. Cels. ii. 52, 75 ; iv. 4 ; v. 51 ; vii. 26 ;
viii. 5, 53). This law was intelligible, since, as the necessities
of the case required, reward and punishment were attached to it
(c. Cels. iii. 79). He appeared as a physician for sinners, as a
teacher of those who had become pure (c. Cels. iii. 62). His
law is " the law of nature, i. e., of God," as contrasted with
" the law written upon tablets " (ib. v. 37). Its essential contents are : the knowledge and worship of the One God, the Creator ; faith in Jesus ; the fulfilling of his commandments in a
virtuous life ; the promise of salvation and threatening of eternal ruin (c. Cels. v. 51, 53 ; vii. 17, 48 f.; viii. 57, 51 : " The
whole foundation of the faith is God, with the promises through
Christ concerning the righteous and the announcements of punishment concerning the wicked "). To this is added the life of
Christ as the " model of a virtuous life " (c. Cels. i. 68 ; viii.
17, 56 ; de pr. iii. 5. 6), particularly as a pattern in the endurance of suffering (c. Cels. ii. 42). By this means we may become partakers, as far as possible, of the divine nature (de pr.
iv. 31). Origen gives expression already to the underlying
thought of the mysticism of the Middle Ages : " And, speaking

corporeally and as flesh delivering his message, he calls to himself those who are flesh, in order that he may first cause them to
be transformed into the likeness of the Logos made flesh, and
after this elevate them to the beholding of himself as he was before he became flesh " (c. Cels. vi. 68).

Prominent as these ideas are in the writings of Origen, he yet
recognizes the fact that the salvation of the believer is dependent upon the sufferings and death of Christ (*e. g.*, c. Cels. i. 54 ;
cf. 61 fin.; ii. 23, 44 ; vii. 57): "His death is not only presented as a model for [our] dying on account of piety, but also
effects the beginning and progress of our deliverance from the
evil one, the devil " (ib. vii. 17). The death of Christ is accordingly presented in the light of deliverance from the power
of the devil and the demons ; sacrifice for sin offered to God ;
the purification of man from sin ; and the advocacy of man's
cause before the Father (cf. THOMASIUS, Orig., p. 221 ff.). (*a*)
Through sin the souls of men have surrendered themselves to the
devil.   Jesus gave his soul (life) to death as an exchange
(ἀντάλλαγμα), or ransom (λύτρον), to redeem them from the
devil (in Ex. hom. vi. 9 ; cf. c. Cels. i. 31. ad mart. 12 fin.
in Matt. xii. 28 ; xvi. 8. LOMMATZSCH iv. 27 f. in Rom. iii.
7 ; iv. 11).   But the devil was not able to retain these souls
("For he controlled us until the ransom for us, the soul of Jesus,
was given to him, deceived as being able to rule over it, and not
observing that he does not possess the touchstone for maintaining possession of it," in Joh. xvi. 8).   Thus the souls of men
—even those in Hades—became free from the power of the
devil and his demons (vid. c. Cels. ii. 47 ; viii. 54, 27, 64 ; cf.
as to the exorcism of demons, ib. vii. 4, 69 ; viii. 58 ; i. 67,
etc.).   An idea is thus expressed which was destined to play an
important rôle in the History of Doctrines.   (*b*) Sin requires a
propitiatio before God, and this is effected by the bringing of a
sacrifice.   Christ is the high-priest, who offered to God in our
behalf his own blood as a spotless sacrifice, in order that God
might become gracious to us and forgive our sins (in Rom. iii.
8 ; in Num. hom. xxiv. 1).   He bore in our stead the penalty
belonging to us (in Joh. xxviii. 14, p. 355 : "And he assumed
our sins and was bruised for our iniquities, and the penalty which
was our due in order to our discipline and the reception of peace
came upon him ").   Since Christ thus, as the Head of the church,
intervenes for us, God is reconciled to us and we to God (in
Rom. iv. 8).   This work of reconciliation extends beyond the
world of men to the realm of the angels (in Joh. i. 40 ; in Matt.
xiii. 8 ; c. Cels. vii. 17).   Origen even seems to hint at a continuation of the sufferings of Christ in heaven (de pr. iv. 25, a

Greek fragment in Jerome). Thus the sufferings of Christ constitute a sacrifice which is offered to God as an atonement for sin,
while at the same time his soul was delivered to Satan as a ransom. (*c*) Christ continues through all ages his redeeming work.
The purification of the church is always a matter of deepest concern to him as its Head (in Lev. hom. vii. 2), although he binds
it together in unity in himself ("in himself embracing all who
are subject to the Father . . . and he is himself the Head of
all," de pr. iii. 5. 6). He works from heaven to purify his followers by his divine power and by his law (c. Cels. viii. 43 ; vii.
17). Thus the divine nature begins to unite itself again with
the human race : "From that time, the divine and the human
nature began to be associated, in order that the human nature
might in fellowship with that which is divine become divine, not
in Jesus alone, but in all those receiving with their faith (μετὰ τοῦ
πιστεύειν) the course of life which Jesus taught, which leads
to God in love and in fellowship with him everyone who lives
according to the foundations of Jesus" (c. Cels. iii. 28). In
these ideas we find the germs of the later conception of redemption as a ransom (Athanasius). Christ in himself again unites
human nature with the divine (cf. Irenæus); but, concretely expressed, he does this by teaching men divine truth. He imprints
upon the hearts of men a copy of his wounds ("an imprint of
the wounds appearing in the soul by virtue of the Logos, this is
the Christ in him," c. Cels. vi. 9). Thus effecting in us that
which is divine, he is, on the other hand, the mediator (μεταξὺ ὤν)
and high-priest who presents our prayers before God and leads
us to him (c. Cels. iii. 34 ; v. 4 ; vii. 46 ; viii. 4, 26, 34, 36 f.).
    We have here the conception of the work of Christ which was
characteristic of the second and third centuries. But we may
trace in it a commingling of the ancient and the modern. Christ
is, above all else, the teacher and lawgiver, the pattern, in whom
begins the deification of humanity. But he is this for us, after
all, only because he has snatched us from the power of the devil
and demoniac powers, has reconciled God to us and us to God,
and stands as mediator and high-priest between us and God.
    6. (*a*) The Logos is actively engaged in imparting this salva-
tion to men, as formerly through the moral law and the Mosaic
code, so now through the gospel (in Rom. iii. 7. 3 ; v. 1. c.
Cels. vi. 78 ; vii. 26). The latter, as has been shown, is conceived of as essentially a lawgiving and instruction. To the
doctrines are added, as further means of salvation, the mysteries.
He who has in faith accepted the teachings of Christianity is
baptized : "The washing by water, being a symbol of the
cleansing of a soul washed from every defilement (which comes)

from evil, is no less and precisely, to him who surrenders himself to the power of the names of the adorable Trinity, the beginning and fountain of divine charismata'' (in Joh. vi. 17).[1] Baptism is not a ''symbol'' in the modern sense, but as Christ's miracles of healing were symbols of the healing activity of the Logos. Yet, as these miracles nevertheless brought real healing to the individual in whose behalf they were performed, so baptism is for the recipient nothing less than the beginning and fountain of the divine blessings. It is a symbol of the purifying power of the Logos, but for the individual it is actual purification. Through its administration sins are forgiven and the Holy Spirit bestowed (in Luc. hom. xxi.; in Matt. xv. 23 ; ad mart. 30 init.). It is the ''first remission of sins'' (in Lev. ii. 4), which, in accordance with the custom (*observantiam*) of the church, is granted also to children (in Lev. viii.). Above water-baptism stands the fire-baptism of martyrdom. This washes away sins, and the sacerdotal intercessions of the martyrs are heard by God (ad mart. 30, 50, 34 ff.). But the mature Christian should partake of the solid intellectual food ($\sigma\tau\epsilon\rho\epsilon\alpha\iota\ \lambda o\gamma\iota\kappa\alpha\iota\ \tau\rho o\varphi\alpha\iota$) of the eucharist (c. Cels. iii. 60). He here receives the Logos and his words as the true food of the soul. ''That bread which God the Word declares to be his body is the nutritious word of souls, the word proceeding from God the Word . . . And that drink . . . is the word thirst-quenching and splendidly inebriating the hearts of those who drink it . . . For not that visible bread which he held in his hand, did God the Word call his body, but the word in whose sacrament (*mysterium*) that bread was to be broken. And not that visible drink did he call his blood, but the word in whose sacrament that drink was to be poured out. For the body or blood of God the Word, what else can it be than the word which nourishes and the word which delights the heart?'' (in Matt. com. ser. 85). The word of Christ, of which the elements are a symbol, is, therefore, the effectual thing in the eucharist. Primarily Christ's own word, and consequently the words of the apostles and their successors, are the body and blood of the Lord (in Lev. hom. vii. 5). According to this, the elements possess merely a symbolical significance. The word alone, which is spoken over them, brings benefit to him who approaches the eucharist with a pure heart and conscience (in Matt. xi. 14).[2]

[1] The text of Lommatzsch is here amended to agree with the citation in Basil. de spir. sanct. 29. 73.

[2] Origin himself occasionally employs another type of expression (*e. g.*, c. Cels. viii. 33 : ''We eat the bread which has, through the prayer, become the body, a thing holy and hallowing those who receive it with a proper pur-

(*b*) The New Testament proffer of salvation through doctrine is accepted by man in faith. (*a*) He is able to do this by virtue of the freedom of will which is inseparable from human nature. It is true, the soul of man at the fall before the creation of the world became disobedient to God, and sin is hence universal (cf. under 3, p. 151). " We are born to sinning" (c. Cels. iii. 66, 62 ; cf. Clem., supra, p. 141). " No one is pure even immediately after birth, not even though his life should be but a single day," Job 14. 4 f. (in Matt. xv. 23). What need would there otherwise be for infant baptism? (in Lev. hom. viii. 3 ; in Rom. v. 9). To the sin of the pre-natal existence is now added the further defilement involved in the union of the soul with the body (in Luc. hom. xiv.; in Lev. viii. 3, 4 ; c. Cels. vii. 50). Account must be made, still further, of the dominion of the devil and demons over the human soul, and the entrenchment of sin in the soul through the power of evil passions and under the influence of evil example (de pr. iii. 2. 2 ; c. Cels. iii. 69). However positively the sinfulness of man is thus maintained, it does not exclude his free-will (αὐτεξούσιον), the continuous and inamissible capacity for freely deciding for the good or the evil ; for the will has only the office, according to the Greek conception, of carrying out the decisions of the reason (de pr. iii. 1. 3). Only upon the recognition of human freedom can we understand the ethical exhortations of the Scriptures, and only thus is the moral character of man preserved (de pr. iii. 1. 20). There are, indeed, scriptural passages which appear to confirm the Gnostic doctrine of predestination (*e. g.*, Ex. 4. 21. Hos. 11. 19. Mk. 4. 12. Rom. 9. 16, 18 ff.), but these may be differently interpreted (de pr. iii. 1. 7 ff.). It remains, therefore, an indisputable fact, that free will is preserved in the salvation of man (ib. iii. 5. 8 ; 3. 4). Scripture varies in its representations of the subject : " It attributes everything to us," and " it seems to attribute everything to God" (de pr. iii. 1. 22). The truth is, that God endowed man, not with conquest (the *vincere*), but with the power of conquest (the *vincendi virtus;* ib. iii. 2. 3), *i. e.*, through the rational nature of man and the doctrine of Christ. As a teacher promises " to improve those who come to him, so the divine Logos promises to take away evil from those who come to him . . . not from those who are unwilling, but from those who, being sick, commit themselves to the physician " (de pr. iii. 1. 15). God offers salvation, but free man apprehends it, and is

pose ;" cf. in Ex. hom. xiii. 3). He is also aware that the more simple have " a commoner interpretation " of the eucharist (in Joh. xxxii. 16).

always himself active in its appropriation (ib. iii. 1. 18). He may, however, always rely upon the divine assistance (*adjutorium;* ib. iii. 2. 5, 2). Cf. MEHLHORN, Die Lehre von d. menschl. Freiheit, according to Origen's περὶ ἀρχῶν, Ztschr. f. KG., ii. 234 ff.   (β) In this sense, faith itself is an act of the free-will as well as an effect of divine grace (cf. c. Cels. viii. 43).   The object of faith is the doctrines (δόγματα) of the church (in Joh. xxxii. 9; c. Cels.i. 13). This faith is confidence (συγκατάθεσις), often dependent primarily upon outward motives, such as fear, or the recognition of authority.   It needs to be elevated to knowledge and understanding.   It is better to "assent to the dogmas with the reason and wisdom" (μετὰ λόγου καί σοφίας) than "with bare faith" (c. Cels. 1. 13; cf. also *supra*, under 1).   Many gradations may be traced in this process (in Matt. xii. 15).   Knowledge is the goal.   But the unfolding of faith is inconceivable without a corresponding moral conduct upon the part of the individual.   The Logos acts not only as teacher, but also as physician (cf. supra).   Threats of punishment and promise of reward are spurs to piety.   Thus faith is also the way to virtue (c. Cels. iii. 69).   A faith without works is impossible (*e. g.*, in Joh. xix. 6).   If with such a conception of faith (lacking the decisive element of an inward, obedient, and trustful acceptance), Paul's doctrine of justification does not receive an unqualified acknowledgment, this must be regarded as merely an evidence of religious tact and of real Christian temper.   Origen, in his commentary upon Romans, reproduced the Pauline doctrine of justification, but was not able to maintain himself at the altitude of that conception.   Faith is sufficient, indeed, for righteousness, but it finds its consummation in works, and suffices only because it has ever works in view.   "Righteousness cannot be imputed to an unrighteous man.   Christ justifies only those who have received new life from the example of his resurrection."   Accordingly, the forgiveness of sins and the salvation and eternal happiness of men depend, not only upon faith, but more upon their repentance and good works (cf. *e. g.*, in Lev. hom. xii. 3; ii. 4; c. Cels. iii. 71, 57; viii. 10).   "The salvation of believers is accomplished in two ways, through the acknowledgment (*agnitionem*) of faith and through the perfection of works" (in cant., p. 84; cf. *institutionibus ac disciplinis*, de pr. i. 6. 3).   Repentance consists primarily in the confession of one's sins to God, since he is the true physician of souls (in Ps. 36; hom. 1. 5); but also to one's fellowmen (ib.).   In the latter case it is necessary, however, to find a man, whether clerical or lay, who has the Spirit, who is devoted to the service of God, and who is like the merciful high-priest Christ, as were the apostles (de or. 28. 8; in Ps. 37; hom. 6). Repentance has here, it will be observed, an inward character, not a legal, as in the West. Origen's moral ideal embraces, first of all, the Gnostic contemplation of God, and also a strongly ascetic element (emphasis upon virginity and a corresponding depreciation of marriage; c. Cels. vii. 48; i. 26 fin.; viii. 55; commendation of those who, separate from the world, abstain from the cares of this life, in Lev. xi. 1; in different vein, Clem., supra, p. 145, n.).

(c) The church is the congregation of believers, the assembly of the righteous, the "city of God" (c. Cels. iii. 30; cf. vii. 31). Outside the church there is no salvation (in Jos. hom. iii. 5). Individual Christians are, indeed, also priests (in Lev. hom. iv. 6; vi. 5; ix. 1, 8; xiii. 5); but to the priests in the special sense of the term belong special prerogatives. It is theirs to announce the forgiveness of sins; but this may be done only by a pious priest (in Lev. hom. v. 3; cf. BIGG, p. 215 ff.). Further, Origen discriminates between the empirical church and the church properly so called (κυρίως, e. g., de or. 20; in Num. hom. xxvi. 7; in Jos. hom. xxi. 1. Cf. SEEBERG, Begriff d. chr. Kirche, i. 27 ff.).

7. The process of purification and instruction begun on earth is continued after death. The good, clothed in a refined spiritual body, enter "paradise," or "a certain place of education, an auditorium or school of souls." Now are solved for the spirit all the problems which have been presented here in nature, history, and faith (de pr. ii. 11. 4, 5). The wicked, on the other hand, experience the fire of judgment. This is a "flame of one's own fire" (proprii ignis), whose material is the individual's own sinfulness tortured by the conscience (de pr. ii. 10. 4). In this we are to see, not a permanent punishment, as imagined by the simple, but a process of purification: "The fire of God's vengeance avails for the purgation of souls" (ib. § 6). "It befits the good God to destroy wickedness by the fire of punishments" (c. Cels. vi. 72; cf. v. 15; vi. 26). It is a purifying fire (πῦρ καθάρσιον, c. Cels. v. 17).[1] While the wicked are thus purified, the good mount up from sphere to sphere to meet Christ (de pr. ii. 11. 5). But the former as well as the latter, although it be only after infinite ages, also attain the goal (de pr. iii. 6. 6). Then, with the day of the second coming of Christ, will come the end. Now occurs the resurrection of the

---

[1] This idea, which found recognition also in the West (Cypr. ep. 55. 20), reminds us of the ancient conception of the purifying power of the fire of Hades, e. g., Virgil Aen. vi. 742: Wickedness unconsummated is purged or consumed by fire; cf. Dieterich, Nekyia, 1893, p. 199 ff.; also, Rohde, Psyche, ii. ed. 2, 128 f.

bodies of men—glorified, pneumatic bodies (de pr. iii. 6. 4-9;
but cf. ii. 3. 7 ; iii. 6. 1, in Jerome's translation in Redepenning's
edition, p. 318 f., and also H. SCHULTZ, l. c., p. 220 f.). God
is now all in all, and all created things live in full vision of the
Godhead (iii. 6. 3). Here we shall understand the "everlasting gospel," which is related to the temporal gospel as is the
latter to the law (ib. iii. 6. 8 ; iv. 25). But, since there is even
yet the possibility of a change in the attitude of will of a free
agent, it always remains possible that this consummation of
earth's drama may prove to be but temporary, and that freedom
of will may call other worlds into existence (cf. de pr. iii. 6. 3,
in Jerome's translation ; also c. Cels. iv. 69 ; per contra, de pr.
iii. 6. 6 : "in which state they always and immutably remain ").

8. Tested by the original teachings of Christianity, the Alexandrine theology, as compared with the doctrinal development
of the second century, indicates in all points a progression, but
in very few particulars an actual advance. The Alexandrine
Fathers gave to Christian literature, in form as well as in scientific method, a position of equal rank with other literature of the
age, and prescribed for the future the method of theological
statement. They are the first dogmaticians. But they knew no
other way of accomplishing their task than by recasting the permanent elements of the church's doctrine in harmony with a religious philosophy of Grecian character (cf. the judgment of
Porphyry in Eus. h. e. vi. 19. 7 f.). What the Apologists were
compelled to do, these men willingly sought to accomplish. In
their philosophy the elements of the Christian tradition are commingled in an amazing way with ideas and problems of the
heathen world. It is easy to show the wavering character of the
movement and the illogical nature of the presentation. The traditional elements are retained *en masse* (by Origen in detail).
But in regard to these, nothing more was required than a simple
assent, which is the proper attitude toward *dogmas* and a *law*.
Beyond this lay knowledge and understanding, *i. e.*, of the philo-
sophically-framed doctrine. The curious fabric thus constructed
was glorified as the wisdom of the wise ; not, indeed, without
some perception of the real nature of Christianity, such as was
in danger of vanishing from the consciousness of the uniciated
(ἁπλούστεροι).

The significance of this theology for later times lay in the
fact that it preserved the traditional doctrines of the church in
a form which impressed its own generation (Trinity, divinity
and humanity of Christ, soteriological formulas, baptism and
its effect, elements in the appropriation of Christianity, resurrection). In Christology, inferences were drawn from the orthodox

view which were genuine logical deductions (cf. Origen). On the other hand, no little foreign material was given currency as Christian, and the foreign elements of the preceding age were carried to the most extreme conclusions (definition of God, conception of faith, moralism and asceticism in Christian life, limitation of the work of redemption to doctrine and example, definitions of sin and free-will). But it was just in this way that this theology succeeded in delivering the death-blow to Gnosticism. Whatever was influential in the latter, it also possessed, and possessed in connection with the faith of the church.

A general view of the historical development thus far traced leads to the conviction that the Christianity of the Apostolic Fathers was that which had characterized the church of the second century. Everywhere we note a consciousness of the sinner's lost condition, and the conviction that he can be saved only through grace, through Christ, through the sacred ordinances of the church; but everywhere also the heathen moralism —everywhere the zealous effort to hold fast to the ideas of primitive Christianity and surrender to the enemy not an iota of the sacred tradition. The more objective an asserted fact, and the more distinctly it pointed upward, the greater was the certainty attaching to it; the profounder its appeal downward to the heart of the believer, the more waveringly was it received. The former became an object of contemplation; the latter was more and more misunderstood. To the former, assent was given only in connection with suspicious heterogeneous material, and with a portentous employment of heathen ideas (Logos, faith); but the truths of the "Rule of Faith," however perverted may have been the relation of the individual to them, were, at least in general outline, preserved intact against the assaults of heathenism and a heathenized Christianity. This, together with the initial attempts at a scholarly interpretation of these truths, constitutes the significance of the theology developing during the present period.[1]

[1] What has been said applies also, with some modifications, to the faith of the common people. Cf. the discussion of Celsus, written probably not long after the middle of the second century, and occasional remarks of Origen, e. g., the sharp contrasting of the "Great Church" with the Gnostic parties (Cels. in Orig. c. Cels. v. 63); the faith in One God; the rude conception of his Person (de pr. iv. 8 fin.; Cels. c. Cels. iv. 71; vi. 61 ff.; the unique position assigned to the adorable Person of Christ ("your God," "they reverently worship," Cels. in Orig. c. Cels. viii. 41, 39, 12, 14; cf. iii. 41; vi. 10; vii. 36: Orig. de or. 16 init.); the hymns recognizing the divinity of Christ (Eus. h. e. v. 28. 5; vii. 30. 10; the hymn at the close of Clement's Paedag.; Tert. c. Jud. 7; Mart. Polyc. 17. 2; Lucian's de morte Peregrin. ii. 13; the Roman mock crucifix, etc.; the emphasis upon bare faith (Cels. l. c. i. 9, 12); the epitomizing of Christianity in the declaration, "the world is crucified to me,"

CHAPTER IV.

SEPARATE DOCTRINES AND GENERAL CONCEPTION OF CHRISTIANITY IN THE THIRD CENTURY.

The period under review had a decisive influence upon the construction of dogmatics. It was then that conditions and views asserted themselves in connection with the popular faith with which dogmatic theology was compelled to deal, which it could neither deny nor ignore. A method was inaugurated by which it was sought to harmonize these and explain their significance. There was now an ecclesiastical doctrine and a doctrinal church. Heresy had come to be definitely noted. Every new development of doctrine was so regarded. The great extension of the church produced new perils and new practical problems. A new outlook had been won, and new requirements must be met. The secularization of the church, which had been already deplored in the second century,[1] was greatly accelerated in the third, and with it there became manifest also a secularization of the religious sentiment. This explains both the general type of doctrine prevalent and the modifications in the views concerning repentance and the church, as also the strenuous opposition to all doctrinal differences, particularly to the attempts, reaching back into the second century, to reconcile the divinity of Christ with the principle of Monotheism. We begin with the latter.

§ 16. *Monarchianism.*

DYNAMISTIC Monarchians : Hippol. Refut. vii. 35. Ps.-Tert. adv. omn. haer. 23 (8). The small Labyrinth, Eus. h. e. v. 28. Epiph. h. 54. PAUL OF SAMOSATA : Eus. h. e. vii. 27-30. Epiph. h. 65. Fragments in ROUTH, Reliq. sacr. iii. ed. 2, 300 ff. MAI, Vet. scr. nova coll. vii. 68 f. PATRIPASSIANS : Tert. adv. Prax. Hippol. c. Noët. Refut. ix. 6-12. Epiph. h. 62. Eus. h. e. vi. 33. Compare HARNACK, PRE. x. 178 ff. HILGENFELD, Ketzergesch., p. 609 ff. THOMASIUS, DG. i. 168 ff.

The divinity of Christ is, in the second century, a recognized fact (cf. supra, pp. 63 f., 70, 75, 78, 113 f., 124 ff., 143, 149 f.,

etc. (Gal. 6. 4. Cels. l. c. v. 64); grace (Cels. l. c. iii. 71, 78); the vivid, sensuously-colored hopes of the future life (*e. g.*, Orig. de pr. ii. 11. 2 ; cf. in Method. de resur. 20. Cels. l. c., viii. 49 ; iv. 11 ; v. 14 ; vii. 28); the strong faith in the power of the devil and demons, who are to be overcome by Christian faith through the use of scriptural citations, etc. (Orig. c. Cels. i. 24, 25, 46, 67 ; ii. 8 ; iii. 24 ; v. 45 ; vii. 69 ; viii. 37, 58, 59, 61).

[1] Cf. the strictures of Irenæus upon those Christians who, for personal reasons and on account of false brethren, sever themselves from the church (iv. 33. 7 ; 30. 3 ; iii. 11. 9 ; iv. 26. 2 ; cf. Eus. h. e. v. 15, with 20. 1).

161, n.). The learned attempts to define the relation of Christ to the Father (Logos, second God) were, indeed, far from satisfactory. Christ was regarded as " a God," and his human nature was asserted. The Logos-christology was, in the main, framed in such a way as to guard the unity of God. But when the Logos, proceeding from the Father, assumes an independent existence, he is then regarded as " the second God," and thus Monotheism is endangered. Monarchianism made an effort to reconcile Monotheism, the most precious treasure of Christianity as contrasted with the heathen world, with the divinity of Christ without resort to the expedient of the " second God." In this consists its historical significance. It reminded the church that there is only One personal God. To this task it addressed itself, under the guidance of the two-fold principle : (1) making the man Jesus the bearer of the divine Spirit, (2) recognizing in Christ the person of the Father himself: " Since they reflected . . . that God is one, they thought it was not possible for them to maintain this opinion unless they should hold the belief, either that Christ was such a man, or that he was truly God the Father " (Novatian, de trin. 30; cf. Tert. adv. Prax. 3 : " Therefore they charge that two or three Gods are preached by us, but imagine that they are worshipers of the one God . . . they say, ' We hold a monarchy.' " Hippol. Refut. ix. 11 : Ditheists, δίθεοι, Epiph. h. 62. 2 ; Hilar. de Trin. i. 16).

1. *Dynamistic Monarchianism.* The " Alogi " are generally treated under this heading, but improperly so. Epiphanius, indeed, was disposed thus to classify them (h. 54. 1), but, following the authority before him, recognizes their orthodoxy (h. 51. 4 ; cf. Iren. and supra, p. 108, n.).

(a) THEODOTUS, the Fuller, brought this doctrine to Rome about A. D. 190 : " Maintaining in part the doctrines commonly held among those of the true church concerning the beginning of all things, confessing that all things were made by God, he yet holds . . . that Christ came into existence in some such way as this : that Jesus is, indeed, a man born of a virgin according to the counsel of the Father—living in common with all men, and most pious by birth ; and that afterward at his baptism in the Jordan, the Christ from above, having descended in the form of a dove, entered into him ; wherefore miraculous powers were not exerted by him before the Spirit, which he says is Christ, having descended, was manifested in him. Some think that he did not become God until the descent of the Spirit ; others, until after his resurrection from the dead " (Hipp. Ref. vii. 35 ; cf. Ps.-Tert. 8). Pope Victor excommunicated him (small Lab. in Eus. v. 28. 6). (b) In the time of Zephyrinus this view again appeared under the leadership of ASCLEPIODOTUS and THEODOTUS, the Money-changer (Eus. v. 28. 7 ; see also 17). Here again it was held : " He asserts that this man Christ (springs) only from the Holy Spirit and the Virgin Mary " (Ps.-Tert. 8). He was inferior to Melchizedek (see Epiph. h. 55. 8). But this " bare man " was at his baptism endowed with the Spirit of God (Hipp. vii. 36). The attempt was made to prove this doctrine exegetically, calling in the aid of textual criticism and subtle logical distinctions (Eus. v. 28. 13-18 ; cf., for examples, Epiph. h. 54). Nevertheless, these men claimed to teach the ancient confessional doctrine. " For they say that all the former teachers, and the apostles themselves, both received and taught these things which they now proclaim, and that the truth of the gospel message was preserved until the times of Victor . . . but that the truth was perverted by his successor, Zephyrinus " (small Lab. in Eus. v. 28. 3 ; cf. the charge brought against them by their orthodox opponent : " They have impiously slighted the divine Scriptures and repudiated the canon of the ancient faith, and have not known Christ," ib. § 13). It is beyond question that the claim of conformity to the teachings of the church was, speaking generally, without foundation. The Monarchian doctrine is not an attempt to reproduce the original Christian view, as is evident from a comparison of its tenets with the apostolic portrayal of Christ as the Lord of heaven and earth (per contra, HARNACK, DG.; ed. 3, 673 f.). The origin of this form of Monarchianism may be very easily traced to the Logos-idea—the Logos, or Spirit, being conceived not as a personal being, but as a divine energy. The attempt to establish a congregation of adherents to this view, although made at personal sacrifice, was not successful (small Lab. in Eus. v. 28. 8-12). (c) After the middle of the third century we find this view still advocated by ARTEMAS (or Artemon) at Rome, and he appears to have gathered about him a congregation of his own (Eus. h. e. vii. 30. 17).

(d) But its most important representative is PAUL OF SAMOSATA. This imperious and worldly-minded Bishop of Antioch (from about A. D. 260 ; cf. encycl. letter of Synod of Antioch, in Eus. h. e. vii. 30. 7-15) taught " Jesus Christ from below " (κάτωθεν, in contrast with ἄνωθεν, ib. vii. 30. 11). In the man Jesus, born of the virgin, dwelt the divine Wisdom. This is not a separate hypostasis, but exists in God as human reason exists in man : " That in God is always his Logos and his Spirit, as in the heart of man his own reason (logos); and that the Son of God is not in a hypostasis, but is in God himself . . . But that the Logos came and dwelt in Jesus, who was a man ; and thus, they say, God is one . . . one God the Father, and his Son in him, as the reason (*logos*) in a man " (Epiph. h. 65. 1). A parallel to this is seen in the indwelling of Wisdom in the prophets, except that this indwelling occurred in a unique way in Christ as the temple of God : " In order that neither might the anointed of David be a stranger to Wisdom, nor Wisdom dwell so largely in any other. For it was in the prophets, much more in Moses ; and in many leaders, but much more in Christ as in a temple." But also : "He who appeared was not Wisdom, for he was not susceptible of being found in an outward form . . . for he is greater than the things that are seen " (fragm. disput. c. Malchionem in Routh, Rel. sacr. iii. 301 ; in Leontius, ib. p. 311). As to the mode of this union, Paul teaches that the man Jesus was from his birth anointed with the Holy Ghost. Because he remained immovably steadfast in this relationship and kept himself pure, the power of working miracles became his, and, having been " born pure and righteous," he overcame the sin of Adam. It is a moral union (in the way of learning and fellowship, Routh iii. 312) in the will and in love, which here meets us, not a merely natural one : " Thou shculdst not wonder that the Saviour has one will with God. For just as nature shows us a substance becoming out of many one and the same, so the nature of love makes one and the same will out of many through one and the same manifested preference." (Also : "the things obtained by the natural reason have no praise, but the things obtained by the nature of love are exceedingly praiseworthy," frag. in Mai, Vet. scr. nov. coll. vii. 68 f.; cf. Athanas. c. Arian, or. iii. 10.) Thus Jesus in his moral development united himself intimately with God by the influence of the Spirit and unity of will, thus securing the power to perform miracles and fitness to become the Redeemer, and in addition attaining a permanent oneness with God. " The Saviour, born holy and righteous, having by his struggle and sufferings overcome the sin of our progenitor, succeeding in these things, was united in character ($\tau\tilde{\eta}$ $\dot{\alpha}\rho\varepsilon\tau\tilde{\eta}$) to God, having preserved one and the same aim and effort as he for the promotion of things that are good ; and he, having preserved this inviolate, his name is called that above every name, the prize of love having been freely bestowed upon him " (Mai, l. c.). Three synods were held at Antioch to consider the matter (264-269 ; Eus. h. e. vii. 30. 4, 5). Paul at first resorted to evasions and no conclusion was reached. Finally, the presbyter Malchion vanquished him at the third synod. " He did not formerly say this, that he would not grant that in the whole Saviour was existent the only-begotten Son, begotten before the foundation of the world " (frg. disp. adv. Paul. a Malch. hab. in Routh iii. 302 ; also Pitra, Analecta sacra iii. 600 f.; iv. 424. Eus.

h. e. vii. 28, 29). The decree of the synod proclaimed the heresy of Artemas and his exclusion from the fellowship of the church (Eus. h. e. vii. 30. 16, 17).[1] But Paul retained a following and his office until, in A. D. 272, the degree of Aurelian gave the church property to the control of the one who should be upon terms of epistolary correspondence with the bishops of Italy and Rome (Eus. vii. 30. 19). This was the first time that imperial politics carried into effect a condemnatory decree of the church.[2]

2. *Patripassian Monarchianism* is the more influential and more widely prevalent form of Monarchianism. It is this form chiefly which gives to the system the historical significance noted on p. 163. It is not accidental that Rome and Egypt were the breeding places of Sabellianism and the pillars of the *homousia*. The history of the separate representatives of this party is, to some extent, obscure, and it is, therefore, difficult to keep the peculiar tenets of each distinct in our minds. Here and there we may trace a connection with the primitive form of the doctrine. The prevalent term, "Patripassians," may be traced to Tertullian (adv. Prax.). Their fundamental idea is: "For thus it is proper to state Monarchianism, saying that he who is called Father and Son is one and the same, not one from the other, but he from himself, called by name Father and Son according to the figure of the times, but that this one appearing and born of a virgin remains one . . . confessing to those who behold him that he is a Son . . . and not concealing from those

---

[1] The synod rejected also the Origenistic term, ὁμοούσιος, according to the opinion of Athanasius, because Paul understood it as teaching an equality with the divine nature (οὐσία) and not with the Father, so that there would be three natures (οὐσίαι) to be acknowledged (de synodis 45 ff.), or because Paul himself expressed the relation of the impersonal Logos to the Father by this term (thus Hilar. de synod. 81, 86).

[2] In Pseudo-Cyprian, *De montibus Sina et Sion*, the fourth chapter (Opp. Cypr. ed. Hartel iii. 108) is by no means (as Harnack, DG., i. 676 holds) to be understood as presenting a Monarchian Christology. For when it is there said: "the Lord's flesh from God the Father is called Jesus; the Holy Spirit who descended from heaven is called Christ," this is but phraseology such as we find, *e. g.*, in Hermas, Sim. ix. 1. 1; Arist. Apol. 2. 6; Cyprian, quod idola dii non sint 11 ("the Holy Spirit assumes flesh; God is mingled with man"); Lactant. Instit. iv. 6. 1; 12. 1; Tertul. adv. Prax. 8, 26; Hippol. c. Noët. 4, 16; Celsus in Orig. c. Cels. vi. 69, 72, 73, 78, 79; Apollinar. in Greg. Nyss. Antirrh. 12. See my remarks upon Arist. 2. 6. The case is different with the Christology of the *Acta disputationis Archelai et Manetis* (ab. A. D. 300, in Routh, Reliq. sacr. v. ed. 2, 38-205). Here, c. 50, the Monarchian Christology really appears: "For he who was born the son of Mary, who resolved to undertake the whole conflict because it is great, is Jesus. This is the Christ of God who descended upon him who is sprung from Mary." But the author has at once brought this idea into connection with the teaching of the church: "For God alone is *his Father by nature*, who has deigned to manifest all things to us speedily by his *Word*" (c. 33).

who approach him that he is the Father" (Hipp. Ref. ix. 10).

(*a*) PRAXEAS, a martyr of Asia Minor, came with Victor to Rome, and gained an influence over this foe of Dynamistic Monarchianism by means of his Christology as well as by his anti-montanistic tendencies. His doctrine found acceptance also in Africa (Tert. c. Prax. 1). He taught: "After that time the Father was born and the Father suffered. Jesus Christ is proclaimed as the Father born, the Father suffering, God himself, the omnipotent Lord" (Tert. adv. Prax. 2 init.). Father and Son are therefore the same person(ib. 5 init.). In support of this the Scriptures were appealed to, particularly Isa. 45. 5 ; Jn. x. 30 ; xiv. 9, 10 (ib. 18, 20). It reveals a lean-ing toward the orthodox view, employing the term, Son of God, in the Biblical sense—but at the same time an inclination toward Dynamistic Monarchianism—when distinction is, after all, made between the Father and the Son : "And in like man-ner in the one person they distinguish the two, Father and Son, saying that the Son is the flesh, *i. e.*, the man ; *i. e.*, Jesus ; but that the Father is the Spirit, *i. e.*, God, *i. e.*, Christ" (ib. 27). In this way they avoided the assertion that the Father suffered ("Thus the Son indeed suffers (*patitur*), but the Father suffers with him" (*compatitur*); ib. 29 ; cf. Hipp. Ref. ix. 12).

(*b*) NOËTUS of Smyrna and the adherents of his theory, EPIGONUS and CLEOMENES, found again at Rome in the beginning of the third century an influential centre for the dissemination of their views (Hipp. Ref. i. 7), which were the same as those of Praxeas : "That when the Father had not yet been born, he was rightly called the Father ; but when it had pleased him to sub-mit to birth, having been born, he became the Son, he of him-self and not of another" (Hipp. Ref. ix. 10). "He said that Christ is himself the Father, and that the Father himself was born and suffered and died" (Hipp. c. Noët. 1). Thus the Father also called himself to life again (ib. 3). The Scriptures require us to believe this. Thus the Son is glorified (ib. 1) and thus salvation made possible : "For Christ was God and suffered for us, being the Father himself, in order that he might be able also to save us" (ib. 2). It was a religiously-inspired interest in the full divinity of Christ which led these men to insist upon their theory, and this accounts for their wide influence. They wished to maintain that Christ was God, and yet not waver in the asser-tion of the unity of God as confessed in the church's creed : "For some simple persons (not to say inconsiderate and ignor-ant, as is always the majority of believers) since the rule of faith itself leads us from the many gods of the world to the one and true God (cf. p. 85, n.), not understanding that he is to be believed as being one but with his own economy (οἰκονομία), are terrified at this economy. They think that the number and order of the Trinity implies a division of the unity" (Tert. adv. Prax. 3 init.).

(c) The final form of this doctrine appears in SABELLIUS of Pentapolis (?) at Rome (under Zephyrinus and Callistus). Father, Son, and Spirit are only different designations of the same person, corresponding to the degree and form of his revelation. God is, in his nature, the Father of the Son (υἱοπάτωρ, Athan. Expos. fid. 2): " He himself is the Father ; he himself is the Son ; he himself is the Holy Spirit—as I say that there are three names in one object (hypostasis), either as in man, body and soul and spirit . . . or as, if it be in the sun, being in one object (I say) that there are three, having the energies of light-giving and heat and the form of roundness" (Epiph. h. 62. 1 ; also Athanas. Orig. c. Arian. iii. 36; iv. 2, 3, 9, 13, 25, 17). Cf. ZAHN, Marcel. v. anc. 198-216.

(d) The Patripassian Christology had its adherents in the West as well as in the East. In Rome, the bishops VICTOR (Ps.-Tert. adv. omn. haer. 8 : " after all these a certain Praxeas introduced a heresy, which Victorinus sought to corroborate "), ZEPHYRINUS (Hipp. Ref. ix. 7, 11), and CALLISTUS (ib. ix. 11, 12) adopted it, with the assent of a large part of the local church. Hippolytus and his following, who opposed it, were charged with Ditheism. Callistus, indeed, as bishop, upon grounds of ecclesiastical prudence, denied his agreement with Sabellius ; but he felt himself compelled, for the sake of consistency, to advocate a somewhat modified Monarchianistic Christology. Father, Son, and Spirit are, of course, "one and the same," and the Spirit who became incarnate in the Virgin is identical with the Father, but the flesh of Jesus is to be designated as " the Son : " " For that which is seen, which is the man, this is the Son ; but the Spirit dwelling in the Son, this is the Father." Therefore we should not, indeed, speak of a suffering by the Father, but " the Father suffered with (συρπεπονθέναι) the Son " (Hipp. Ref. ix. 12, p. 458). But this is simply the doctrine of Praxeas (see p. 167) used by Callistus as a formula of compromise.[1]

---

[1] A representative of this Christology in the East may yet be mentioned, BERYL OF BOSTRA. As we have only one sentence of Eusebius setting forth his view, it is difficult to form a clear idea of it. " Beryl . . . attempted to introduce certain new articles of faith, daring to say that our Saviour and Lord did not pre-exist according to his own form of being before his coming among men, and that he did not possess a divinity of his own, but only that of

§ 17. *Ante-Nicene Christology.*

(*a*) But Monarchianism, even in the form last noted, failed in the East also to secure general acceptance. It meets us in the third century only in quite isolated cases (COMMODIAN, Carmen apol. 278 : "Neither was he called Father until he had become Son," 618, 94, 110 ff., 198, 358, 772, 257, 363 f., 634; but see also 340). CYPRIAN classed the Patripassians with the Valentinians and Marcionites, and designated them as "pests and swords, and poisons for the perverting of the truth" (Ep. 73. 4). That even in Rome the Tertullian view was triumphant as early as A. D. 250 is manifest from the tract of Novatian, *De trinitate:* Christ is the second person of the Trinity, the Son of God, preexistent and manifesting himself already under the old covenant, one with the Father by virtue of a communion of substance

the Father committed to him" (h. e. vi. 33. 1). Origen vanquished him at a synod at Bostra about A. D. 244. The synod took occasion, in refuting him, to lay emphasis upon the human soul of Jesus (Socrates h. e. iii. 7). According to this, Beryl (1) knew nothing of a personal divinity of his own inhering in Jesus; his divinity was that of the Father. (2) He taught that Christ became a separate personality only through his incarnation. (3) He does not appear to have been led to this conclusion by the study of the inner human life of Jesus during his incarnation (?). (4) He is not charged with teaching, as did the Dynamistic Monarchians, that Jesus was a "bare man." He, therefore, probably approximated the position of the Sabellians, that it was not until the incarnation that God assumed the special mode of existence as Son (cf. sub, Marcellus of Ancyra).

Of the Libyan Sabellians we shall have occasion to speak hereafter. It may be well at this point to call attention to the fact that the "Testaments of the Twelve Patriarchs" were, during this period, interpolated by a Patripassian writer. See Sim. 6. Levi 4 (πάθος τοῦ ὑψίστου); Cf. Zabul 9. Aser. 7. Benj. 9. Napht. 8). It is with mingled feelings that we turn from the acute attempts of the Monarchian theologians. They do not satisfy us, but their statement of the problem attracts and holds us. They endeavored to understand the divine-human nature of Christ from the point of view of his historical appearance without regard to the prevalent formulas. They did not, indeed, attain their object, for their theory does not give due prominence to the scriptural idea of redemption, nor does it make it possible to understand the historical significance of the person and words of Jesus. But, on the other hand, we must give them credit for certain profound intuitions which their contemporaries did not understand, and, under the prevalent system of theology, could not comprehend. Of these the most important were : (1) The strong emphasis laid upon the personal unity of God and the attempt to reconcile it with the divinity of Christ. The Sabellian position may have been at this point not without significance for Athanasius. (2) The attempt to establish the divine-human nature of Christ, not from the point of view of the two natures, but from that of the personal life, and thus of the will (especially Paul of Samosata). At this point the Antiochians joined them, but in such a way that they, by the orthodox coloring of their teaching, only enforced the chief weakness of the Monarchians—the impossibility involved in their conception of the appearance of Jesus in the flesh.

(*communio substantiae*, c. 31). He received his human bodily substance from Mary. He is "joined together from both, woven and grown together from both" (*ex utroque connexus, ex utroque contextus atque concretus*, c. 24). Monarchianism is energetically rejected (c. 12, 26, 27, 28, 30). He lays great stress upon the fact that Christ is not the Father, nor yet a mere man (c. 30). He is the Son of God, who has united with himself the "substance of flesh" ("*as it were betrothed*, sponsus, *to the flesh*"). The bodily human nature constitutes his humanity (c. 21, 25). At this point he falls short of the positions of Irenæus and Tertullian (supra, pp. 124, 126).

The occasional references to the person and work of Christ in the other Latin writers previous to A. D. 325 reveal no dogmatic interest in the doctrine and do not in any way modify the statement of it. It is a settled matter that Christ is God (ARNOBIUS adv. nationes, i. 53, 39, 42; ii. 11, 60: "Christ, or, if you object, God—I say the God Christ—for this must be often said, in order that the ears of infidels may burst and be destroyed." Cyprian ep. 63. 14: "our Lord and God"), although this is taught in a way that savors strongly of Subordination, as, *e. g.*, when LACTANTIUS declares, that God begat his energy (*virtus*), reason (*ratio*), speech (*sermo*) (cf. Cypr. ep. 73. 18: "God, the Creator of Christ"), and through this created the world: "finally, of all the angels whom this God formed from his spirits, he alone has been admitted to a partnership in supreme power, he alone is called God" (Epit. 36 [42], 3. Instit. iv. 6.2; 8. 7; 14 [20]: "On this account, because he was so faithful . . . that he fulfilled the commands of him who sent him . . . he also received the name of God;" cf. Cyprian, quod idola dii non sint 11). The incarnation is the assuming of human flesh. But this was necessary in order that he might be a mediator between God and man (Cypr. ib. 11), and in order that he might labor among men by word and example (Arnob. i. 62. Lactant. Epit. 38 [43], 8: "Therefore the supreme Father commanded him to descend to earth and assume a human body, in order that, being subject to the sufferings of the flesh, he might teach virtue and patience, not only by words but also by deeds." Just. iv. 12. 15). By virtue of his duplex origin—according to the Spirit from God, according to the flesh from the Virgin Mary—he is Son of God and of man (Lact. Epit. 38. 2. Instit. iv. 13. 6: "he was both God and man, compounded of both genera," *ex utroque genera permixtum*). Such are the essential ideas of this Christology. It is a reiteration of the faith professed in the baptismal confession, attempting, without great exertion, to in some measure justify the latter. But that the ideas of Tertullian were not without influence upon the Latin theologians is clearly seen in Novatian.

2. What Tertullian was for the Christology of the West, that was Origen for the East. His views upon the subject form the basis of the theories of the Greek theologians. Thus PIERIUS (Photius, Cod. 119), THEOGNOSTUS (Athanas. de decret. syn. Nic. 25, ad Serapion. ep. iv. 9, 11), GREGORY THAUMATUR-GUS : "One Lord, one of one, God of God, the impress and image of the Godhead, the effective Word . . . neither, there-fore, any created thing, nor a servant in the Trinity, nor brought in from without as though not having existed before but coming in afterward" (Conf. of faith in Caspari, Alte u. Neue Quellen, etc., p. 10). On the other hand, he also designates the Logos as created ($\varkappa\tau\iota\sigma\mu\alpha$) and formed ($\pi o\iota\eta\mu\alpha$) (Basil. ep. 210. 5). But his great earnestness in maintaining the divinity of Christ is attested by his discussions of "the susceptibility and unsuscepti-bility of God to suffering" (see RYSSEL, Greg. Thaum., p. 73 ff.), leading to the conclusion that the "divinity did, in-deed, suffer, but in an immortal and incapable-of-pain way, with-out experiencing pain" (c. 13 ff. 8 ff.).

Much light is thrown upon the views of the age by the mutual explanations of DIONYSIUS OF ALEXANDRIA and DIONYSIUS OF ROME (about A. D. 260).

Compare Athanasius, De sententia Dionysii and De decret. Syn. Nic. 25, 26; De Synodis 44 (fragments from Dionysius of Alex., Ep. ad Euphranorum et Ammonium, as also from the Elenchus et apol., in 4 books, and from the correspondence of Dionysius of Rome); see also DITTRICH, Dionys. d. Gr., 1867, p. 91 ff.

The doctrine of Sabellius had found very many adherents in the Libyan Pentapolis, even among the bishops (Ath. sent. Dion. 5). Dionysius felt himself, in consequence, impelled to make a literary demonstration against Sabellianism. He started with ideas of his master, Origen, and laid especial emphasis, in view of the nature of the doctrine which he was combating, upon the Subordinationist elements which he here found. He accordingly gave special prom-inence to the personal difference between the Father and the Son, and this seems to have been done also in the school of catechists at Alexandria (Athan. de decr. syn. Nic. 26). The Son is a creation of the Father, which has a different nature from the Father, somewhat as the vine differs from the husband-man, the ship from its builder, or children from their parents ("as a thing made was not existent before it was made," de sent. Dion. 4, 12, 13, 17, 18, 21). It was orthodox Alexan-drine Christians who regarded this teaching with suspicion and brought complaint against their bishop before DIONYSIUS OF

Rome (sent. Dion. 13). They accused the Alexandrine bishop of teaching that "he was not the Son before he was born, but there was a time when he was not, for he is not eternal" (sent. Dion. 14); and, further, that "when Dionysius says Father he does not name the Son; and, again, when he says Son he does not name the Father, but discriminates and puts apart, and divides the Son from the Father" (ib. 16); and "as saying that the Son is one of those who are born (τῶν γενητῶν) and not of the same substance (ὁμοούσιως) with the Father" (ib. 18; de decret. syn. Nic. 25). These charges were, no doubt, well founded.[1] They prove beyond question that the eternal existence of the Son (the eternal generation), as well as the ὁμοούσιως, was already firmly established in the consciousness of intelligent Christians, since they followed in the footsteps of Origen.

It is interesting in this connection to observe the nature of the teaching of the Roman Dionysius. He rejects the view of certain Alexandrine teachers which destroys the monarchy (μοναρχία), and substitutes for it "three powers" (δυνάμεις), and in the last analysis "three gods" (as Marcion). He opposes the designation of the Son as a created being (ποίημα), as also the ascription to him of a temporal beginning. On the contrary, we must, according to the Scriptures, connect the Son and the Spirit very closely with the Father: "I say now that it is fully necessary that the divine Trinity be brought together and summed up in one, as in a sort of consummation, the one God, the almighty Ruler of all things." Therefore the divine Unit (μονάς) dare not be split up into three gods, but we must believe: "in God the Father Almighty, and in Christ Jesus his Son, and in the Holy Ghost;" but the declaration must be unified (ἡνῶσθαι) in the God of all things. For thus the divine Trinity and the holy message of the Monarchy would be preserved (de decr. syn. Nic. 26). Regarded theologically, this discussion is non-committal (e. g., the ἡνῶσθαι); but it proves that the Roman bishop was in a position to approve and sanction the Origenistic formulas of the accusers of his Alexandrine colleague,[2] and that he was, on the other hand, accustomed to expound the baptismal formula in such a way as to give due prominence to the unity of God (cf. Tertullian, Novatian, and even Sabellius). The course of Dionysius is typical of the attitude of the Romish church in the Christological controver-

---

[1] That the Alexandrian bishop did not, as Athanasius suggests in his defense (e. g., de decr. syn. Nic. 25; sent. Dion. 21), think of the "economy (οἰκονομία) of the Saviour according to the flesh," is sufficiently evident from the situation. Cf. also Basil. ep. 9. 2.

[2] He appears (according to sent. Dion. 18, de decret. syn. Nic. 25) even to have laid emphasis upon the ὁμοούσιος.

sies : (1) The creed is regarded as a fixed quantity, and as expressing everything necessary upon all points, and hence upon the details of Christological statement.   (2) Tertullian's apparatus of formulas is considered as helpful.   (3) The subject itself is discussed as little as possible, as the final conclusion is supposed to have been reached.

It is particularly worthy of note how quickly Dionysius of Alexandria found his way back to the doctrine of Origen.   The charges of his opponents appeared to him in reality as a monstrous misunderstanding.   Influenced, indeed, by the opposition encountered, he had hitherto revealed only the half of his Origenistic soul.   He does not deny that there was a certain one-sidedness in his earlier expositions, and that his figures of speech were inappropriate.   There are not wanting attempts to help himself by strained interpretations of his former statements. But, beyond this, he expresses entire accord with his opponents : "For there was no time when God was not the Father.   Since Christ was the Logos and Wisdom and Power he always existed— being always the reflection of the eternal light, he himself also is eternal.   The Son always being with the Father " (sent. Dion. 15).   It is false that he denies the ὁμοούσιος, although, indeed, the expression is not biblical (ib. 18, 26).   "For as I do not think that the Logos is a creation, I also do not say that God is his Creator, but his Father " (21).   " We expand the Monity undivided into the Trinity, and again combine the Trinity undiminished into the Monity " (ib. 17).

Almost more instructive than the controversy itself is the readiness with which the opposing parties come to agreement. The Roman bishop agrees with the Alexandrine plaintiffs, and the bishop of Alexandria at once finds his way back to the standpoint of his opponents.   A certain uniformity is beginning to appear in the views entertained of the person of Christ and its relation to the Father.

3. A glance must yet be given to the Christology of METHODIUS OF OLYMPUS († A. D. 311.   Opp. ed. Jahn, 1865, in Migne Gr. 18 ; BONWETSCH, Meth. v. Ol. vol. i.   Writings, 1891). Christ is the Son of God " through whom all things became " (urchin, 7. 3), since he is the executive hand of the Father (de creatis 9, in Bonw., p. 343 f.), who stands beside the Father and the Spirit (who embraces in himself the knowledge of the Father and the Son), and of whom believers lay hold (conv. dec. virg. viii. 11, 9, 10 ; v. 2 ; iii. 8 ; cf. de resur. iii. 23. 8, 12 ; leprosy, 11, 4 ; distinction of meats, etc., 12. 3 f.).   He is the " pre-temporal Word " (leprosy, 11. 4 ; de resur. ii. 24. 5 ; cf. conv. vii. 4 ; viii. 9 ; pre-existing already before

the worlds), the first sprout (βλάστημα, conv. iii. 4), the "only-born Son " (de resur. iii. 23. 6), who is, however, "the begin-ning after his own unbegun beginning" (de creatis 11), the first of the archangels (the oldest of the aeons and the first of the archangels, conv. iii. 4 ; cf. urchin, 7. 3), the shepherd and leader of the angels (conv. iii. 6), who spoke to the prophets under the old covenant (ib. vii. 6), greater than all except the Father (conv. vii. 1). Prayers are addressed to him (de resur. iii. 23. 11 ; conv. 11. 2). According to the will of the Father he "truly" assumed the "unsuffering" yet "much suf-fering body" (cf. "he imitated the poor," vom Leben und vern. Handl. 6. 2), and truly died (de resur. ii. 18. 8 ; iii. 23. 4). " For this is Christ—a man filled with unadulterated and com-plete divinity, and God contained in man" (conv. iii. 4). But the Logos dwelt in Adam as well as in Jesus (ib.: but this same became Christ and this one [Adam]; cf. 8). The Lord had also the same "actual " body, consisting of the same substance, in his glorification (resur. iii. 7. 12 ; 12. 3 ff.). This Christology, imperfect as it is, represents the average faith of the age : the pre-temporal Son of God, conceived of in a Subordinationistic way, became a real man.

These are illy-defined ideas, falling considerably short of the position of Athanasius, and also of Origen. But it required only a concrete occasion—as shown by the controversy of the two Dionysius's—to produce a more definite and fixed formula-tion.[1]

§ 18. *Ordinance of Repentance and Advance in Conception of the Church.*

1. The church is the general body of men who believe the truth. The further development of the doctrine concerning the church by Irenæus and Tertullian started with this idea. The

---

[1] We may here notice briefly the Syrian, APHRAATES (A. D. 337-345), who was in time post-Nicene, but in principles ante-Nicene (WRIGHT, the homilies of Aphr., Lond., 1869, translated into German by BERT in Texte u. Unters. iii. 3, 4 ; we cite from the latter). Of Christ, it is said, "that he is Son of God, and that he is God, who came from God" (xvii. 2, p. 280), "and that through him we know his Father" (§ 6, p. 285). To the Jews it is pointed out that they have no occasion to regard this as anything "unusual" (§ 5), since the Old Testament also calls men gods and sons of God (§ 3). But the meaning here is not that Jesus was only a sort of prophet, etc. He "came from God," *i. e.*, the Father separated him from his own nature (ουσία) and sent him to men (xxiii. p. 402; also vi. 9, p. 102). It was a special act that he assumed a human body (ib. p. 378 f.), being born "of the Virgin Mary" and "of the Holy Spirit" (p. 388). Gabriel *took the Word from on high and came*, and *the Word became flesh* and *dwelt among us*. He is, there-fore, God by nature, "the first-born of all creatures" (xvii. 8 fin., p. 289),

bishops are the bearers of the truth. The Catholic church is the church of pure doctrines, guaranteed and represented by the bishops. But the church is also the holy people of God. The recognition of this truth led to consequences of historical importance. There were three possible interpretations of the holiness of the church, each of which found its advocates : (1) Every separate individual is holy (Novatian). (2) The bishops are holy (Cyprian). (3) The sacraments and ordinances of the church are holy (Rome).

2. Hermas had, in his day, in accordance with a special revelation (p. 61 f.), proclaimed the possibility of a "second repentance." The church did not lose sight of this idea, and it is almost certain that it was through the authority of this publication that the idea of the "second repentance" secured such general acceptance (cf. Tertul. de pud. 10, 20). The resulting praxis was at about the close of the second century the following : A discrimination was made between "sins of daily occurrence" (as anger, smiting, cursing, swearing, lies) and "sins more serious and destructive," "mortal" (1 Jn. v. 16), "capital" and "irremediable" (homicide, idolatry, fraud, denial or false testimony, blasphemy, adultery, fornication, "and if there be any other violation of the temple of God," Tert. de pud. 19 ; c. Marc. iv. 9). Sins of the first class might find at once forgiveness through the mediation of Christ, through prayer, good works and intercession, since the sinner by these means offered to the offended God sufficient satisfaction (see p. 133); but sins of the second group require an exclusion from the congregation of the "saints" (see Tert. de pud. 19). There was, however, a difference in the praxis of the church in regard to transgressors of the second class. To the greater number of these it granted the "second repentance," but only (Tert de poenit. 7, 12) upon condition that they felt bitter regret, manifesting this by their outward deportment, requested intercession in their behalf, and made the required confession (*exomologesis*) in the presence of the assembled congregation. The church granted this privilege through her presbyters and confessors (Tert. de poenit. 9, 12, 22 ; Apol. 39). Thus is suitable satisfaction made to God ("let him repent from the heart," *ex animo* . . . "confession of sins," *confessio delictorum* . . . "confession is the method of satisfaction," *satisfactionis consilium*, poen. 8 fin.). These are the elements of the Romish sacrament of penance. The worship of idols, murder, for-

"light of light" (ib. 2, the only Nicene turn in Aphraates). Trinitarian formulas are found, *e.g.*, xxiii., pp. 411, 412 ; cf. i. 15. These are ideas that fit easily into the line of thought traced in the present section. For the somewhat earlier "Acta Archelai," see p. 166.

nication, and adultery were absolutely excluded from this second repentance (Tert. pud. 5, 12, 22 ; cf. Orig. de orat. 28 fin.). Practically, the discussion centered about two offenses : in times of peace, especially fornication ; in times of persecution, denial of the faith and apostasy. The conflicts of the future naturally raged about these two centres. The opinions entertained concerning this "second repentance" were still for a time, indeed, quite fluctuating. Not to speak of the Montanists, Tertullian, even before joining their ranks, had only reluctantly accepted the theory ("I am afraid of the second, I should rather say, last hope," poen. 7). But others found fault with the strictness of the treatment (poen. 5, 10), and even thought that open sinners might be tolerated in the church, as the ark, which typifies the church, held unclean animals (Tert. de idololatr. 24 fin.; cf. remarks of Dionysius of Corinth in Eus. h. e. iv. 23. 6).

3. Such was about the situation when CALLISTUS of Rome (217-222), by the publication of a new penitential order, introduced a change of momentous import in the praxis of repentance, and thus also in the conception of the church.

LITERATURE. Hipp. Ref. ix. 12, p. 458 f. Tert. de pudic.; cf. HARNACK, Ztschr. f. Theol. u. K., 1891, p. 114 ff. PREUSCHEN, Tert. Schriften de paenit; et de pud. Giess. Diss. 1890. ROLFFS, Das Indulgenzedikt des röm. Bischof Callist, in Text. u. Unters. xi. 3.[1]

Callistus was the first to allow the second repentance in the case of fornication : "He first contrived to connive with men in matters pertaining to their lusts, saying that sins were forgiven to all men by him" (Hipp.), *i. e.*, he declared : "I remit by penitence to those who have committed them also sins of adultery and fornication" (Tert. 1). But this applied, as Tertullian's polemics prove, only to sins of. the flesh, and made provision for but *one* second repentance. In justification of this innovation, Callistus (or his adherents) presented a number of biblical arguments, *e. g.:* "God is merciful, and does not desire the death of the sinner," etc. (Ez. xxxiii. 11. Tert. ii. init.); it is not for us to judge our brethren (Rom. xiv. 4, ib.); the parables of the prodigal son and the lost sheep (7 f.); Christ's treatment of the woman taken in adultery (11); Paul's manner of dealing with such (2 Cor. ii. 5 ff. c. 13), etc. The aim of repentance is forgiveness (3); fellowship (*communicatio*) may be withdrawn

---

[1] The following analysis proceeds upon the supposition that the bishop whom Tertullian attacks in his *De pudicitia* was Callistus, and that we may, accordingly, from the work of Tertullian, fill out the portraiture given in Hippol. Ref. ix. 12. This was first done by ROSSI, Bulletino archeol. christ., 1866, p. 26. Extracts from the Edict of Callistus reveal the hand of Tertullian. ROLFFS attempted a reconstruction.

from the sinning, but only for the present (*ad presens*).   If he repent, let it be granted him again according to the mercy of God (18).   If the blood of Christ cleanses us from all sin (1 Jn. i. 7, c. 19), then it is also perfectly scriptural for Callistus to grant pardon to fornicators.   The church has the authority to do this ("but the church has, I say, the power of pardoning sins," c. 21); particularly the bishops.   "And, therefore, the church will indeed pardon sins, but the church as a spirit (*ecclesia spiritus*) through a spiritual man, not the church as a number of bishops" (c. 21).   Callistus here appeals to Matt. xvi. 18 (ib.), and appears to have attributed to himself, as the successor of Peter, peculiar authority (cf. the form of address, *apostolice*, c. 21, and the titles, *pontifex maximus, episcopus episcoporum*, c. 1).   A similar authority is also ascribed to the confessors (22).

The forgiveness of sins is thus practically given into the hand of the bishop, who exercises it as a divine right.   His own moral character is not taken into consideration.   He is not subject to removal : "If a bishop should commit some sin, even a mortal one, it is not permitted to remove him" (Hipp. ix. 12).   If the bishop tolerates sinners in the church, no objection can be made. He must allow the tares to stand among the wheat, and the ark contained many kinds of animals (Hipp. ix. 12, p. 460 ; Tert. de idol. 24).

The innovation of Callistus was certainly in harmony with the spirit of the age.   Many of his deliverances have an evangelical sound.   But that such is not really their character is evident from subsequent developments—from the fact that he did not advance a single new idea looking to the awakening of penitence, but only changed the praxis in regard to fornication upon practical grounds, and, above all, from his conception of the church, which gave direction to all his thought.   Callistus was evangelical— and even liberal—because he was the first conscious hierarch.[1] Henceforth the church is no longer the holy people of God, holding in common the faith of the apostles, *i. e.*, the faith of the bishops ; but it is an association of men, subject to the control of the bishop, whom he tolerates in the church, and this by virtue of the divine authority which has been given him to pardon or retain sins.   He whom the bishop recognizes belongs to the church. The bishop is lord over the faith and life of the Christian world by virtue of an absolute supremacy divinely bestowed upon him.

---

[1] Hipp. ix. 12 fin.: "Callistus . . . whose school remains, guarding morals and the tradition."   Perhaps these were watchwords among the Callistians. They sought to evangelize morals upon the basis of the misinterpreted tradition.

12

Callistus was the author of the Roman Catholic conception of the church.

4. The penitential praxis introduced by Callistus had become universal by about A. D. 250 (*e. g.*, Cypr. ep. 55. 20 ; 4. 4), although there were still lingering recollections of opposition to it (Cypr. ep. 55. 21). The circumstances of the congregations during the Decian persecution produced a further and logically consistent (cf. Tert. de pud. 22) step in advance. Even to such as had denied the Christian faith must now be extended the opportunity of return to the church. It was chiefly CYPRIAN († A. D. 258) who justified this step, and, in doing so, developed more fully the Catholic conception of the church.

Vid. collection of Cyprian's letters, his *De lapsis* and *De catholicae ecclesiae unitate* (Cypr. Opp. omn. ed. Hartel, 1868), and the letter of Cornelius of Rome to Fabius of Antioch, in Eus. h. e. vi. 43. Dionysius of Alexandria to Novatian, ib. vi. 45. Ambrose, de poen. ll. 2. Compare RETTBERG, Cyprianus, 1831. PETERS, Der heil. Cypr. v. Karthago, 1877. FECHTRUP, Der heil. Cypr. vol. i., 1878. O. RITSCHL, Cypr. v. K. u. die Verfassung der Kirche, 1885. GOETZ, Die Busslehre Cyprians, 1895. K. MILLER, Ztschr. f. KG., 1896, 1 ff., 187 ff. HARNACK, PRE. viii. 417 ff.; x. 652 ff.

During the Decian persecution it became evident that it would be impossible, in view of the number of backsliders (*lapsi*), to maintain the ancient praxis, *i. e.*, to exclude all such from the communion of the church (the eucharist, Cypr. ep. 57. 2), and to refuse to allow them to receive the benediction (*pax*) with the congregation. Those who had fallen applied to their " confessors " for letters of recommendation (*libelli*), which were freely granted (Cypr. ep. 20. 2 ; cf. 22. 2 ; 27. 1). Although these were primarily intended only as letters of recommendation (ep. 15. 1 ; 16. 3 ; 18. 1 ; 19. 2 ; 22. 2 fin.; cf. 36. 2), this recommendation (cf. the more ancient praxis, Tert. de pud. 22, and Dionys. of Alex. in Eus. h. e. vi. 42. 5 f.; ep. eccl. Lugd. in Eus. h. e. v. 1. 45, 46 ; 2. 6, 7) soon came to have the force of a command (see the letter of the confessor Lucian to Cyprian, ep. 23 ; cf. 21. 3). Cyprian did not dispute the right of the confessors, but he thought that an assembly of the bishops should first consider the matter and lay down the principles to govern such cases before any action was taken—particularly in the midst of the distractions caused by the persecution (ep. 19. 2 ; 20. 3 ; 20, cf. 31. 6). This was also the position of the church at Rome (ep. 30. 3, 5, 6 ; 21. 3 ; 36. 3). Meanwhile some presbyters at Carthage, during the absence of their bishop, Cyprian, admitted certain of the lapsed to the communion upon the basis of their *libelli*, without previous public confession (ep. 15. 1 ; 16. 2, 3 ; 17. 2 ; 20. 2), and in some cities the mass of the people (*multitudo*), relying upon the testimonials of the martyrs and confessors, compelled the bishops to pronounce the benediction upon them (ep. 27. 3). In contrast with those who, with the testimonial of the confessors in their hands, believed themselves authorized to demand the benediction, stood others, who declared their purpose to repent and to await the bishop's declaration (ep. 33. 1, 2; 35, cf. 36. 1). Cyprian instructed that the presbyters who would not submit to the episcopal decision should be excluded from fellowship (*communicatio*, ep. 34. 3; cf. 42). Thus the episcopal authority on the one hand, and on the other the pastoral office of the presbyters and the prerogative of the confessors, stand arrayed in opposition (cf. 16. 1). It is not in reality a discord in the praxis of repentance which here comes to view, but a discord between the bishop and the presbyters. As a result, an opposition party was formed under the leadership of five presbyters and a certain FELICISSIMUS (ep. 41. 2).) If the latter was the "standard-bearer of sedition," the presbyter, NOVATUS, was the soul of the insurrection, "a torch and fire for kindling the flames of sedition" (52. 2). FORTUNATUS became the bishop of this party (59. 9). Their motto was, "to restore and recall the lapsed" (43. 5), and they were opposed to an episcopal decision in the matter and to a more prolonged probation for penitence (43. 2). In accordance with the ancient privilege of confessors, they admitted at once to fellowship those who were recommended by the latter.

About the same time a schism arose also in Rome, occasioned by an election for bishop (ep. 44. 1. Euseb. h. e. vi. 43), in which CORNELIUS and NOVATIAN (about A. D. 251) were the candidates. Novatian, otherwise an orthodox man, established a party in opposition to Cornelius by retaining the ancient praxis in relation to the lapsed. He sought to build up a congregation of the pure (καθαροί, Eus. h. e. vi. 43. 1), since the idolatrous worship of some contaminates the remaining members of the church : "They say that one is corrupted by the sin of another, and in their zeal contend that the idolatry of an offender passes over to the non-offending" (Cypr. ep. 55. 27). He proposes to have a congregation of actually holy men. Hence he has those who come to him from the church at large re-baptized (Cypr. ep. 73. 2; Dionys. of Alex. in Eus. h. e. vii. 8; Ambros. de poenit. i. 7. 30). His adherents were compelled at the reception of the Lord's Supper to bind themselves by oath to adhere to his church (Cornel. in Eus. h. e. vi. 43. 18). There should thus be established a congregation of saints, such as Montanism had endeavored to form. But to what an extent church politics and personal motives were involved on both sides

is manifest from the league formed by Novatian—after his " confessors " had forsaken him (Cornel. to Cypr. ep. 49. 1, 3; cf.
53, 54)—with Novatus (see ep. 47. 50). Novatian appointed
opposition-bishops also in other places (ep. 55. 24; 68. 1), and
Novatianism ere long struck root also in the Orient (Eus. h. e.
vi. 46. 3; vii. 5). A Novatian counter-church, which afterward extended its rigor toward the lapsed to all guilty of mortal
sins (see *e. g.*, Athanas. ad Serap. ep. iv. 13; Socrat. h. e. i. 10),
had soon spread, variously combined with Montanism, over the
whole church (see HARNACK PRE. x. p. 667 ff.). But it never
gained a more than superficial influence. It was an essentially
powerless reaction in the interest of an archaistic idea, which
never was nor could be applied with real seriousness in practical
life.

In Carthage, after Cyprian's return, the proposed assembly of
bishops was held (A. D. 252). Its decrees present the actual
results of the agitation. In expectation of a new persecution, it
is here held to be proper " that to those who have not departed
from the church of the Lord, and from the first day of their
lapse have not ceased to exercise repentance and lament and
pray to the Lord, the *pax* should be given." Although this had
hitherto been granted only to those in immediate peril of death
(cf. Cypr. ep. 55. 13; 57. 1; de laps. 16), yet it is now, upon
the suggestion of the Holy Spirit and plain visions, extended to
all the lapsed (see Cypr. ep. 57; cf. 55. 6). To this Rome
also agreed (ep. 55. 6). This principle was not, indeed, at once
acted upon in all places (see ep. 55. 22; 59. 15), but as a principle it had carried the day. It is not in this fact, however,
that the real significance of the decision lay. In the question
concerning repentance, Cyprian accepted fully the position of
his opponents; but it was bishops who passed the final decree,
bishops were to decide in the case of individuals who had
lapsed, and from their authority the latter could not appeal. In
these controversies, therefore, Cyprian's conception of the church
was perfected. The whole heart of the great bishop was bound
up with this idea. In it concentred all the elements of his religious thought and feeling. He had the juristic, logical bent
of a Roman. Tertullian was his instructor. He had a warm
heart. He was fanatically devoted to the hierarchy, and he
loved Christ.

5. Cyprian's conception of the church embraces the following :

(*a*) The successors of the apostles are the bishops, who, like the
former, are chosen by the Lord himself and inducted into their
office (Cypr. ep. 3. 3; cf. Firmil. 75. 16) as leaders (*prae-*

positi) or pastors (*pastores*) (ep. 8. 1 ; 19. 2 ; 20. 3 ; 27. 3 ; 33. 1 ; 13. 1 ; 59. 14). This is to be understood not merely in the sense of an "ordinance of succession," but every individual bishop is inducted into his office by a "divine decree, for his own sake" (59. 5). He is a bishop, however, and his sacrifices and prayers are effectual, only so long as he remains faithful and leads a holy life.[1] He who criticises the bishops presumes thereby to pass judgment upon the judgment of God and Christ : "This is not to believe in God ; this is to be a rebel against Christ and his gospel, as, when he says : 'Are not two sparrows,' etc. (Matt. 10. 29) . . . thou wouldst think that priests of God are ordained in the church without his knowledge . . . For to believe that those who are ordained are unworthy or corrupt, what else is this but to contend that his priests are not appointed in the church by God nor through him?" (66. 1).[2] In harmony with this, the bishops are said to be guided in their decisions by divine suggestions and visions (*e. g.*, ep. 11. 3, 4 ; 57. 5 ; 68. 5 ; 66. 10 ; 63. 1 ; 73. 26, cf. 40 ; 81 ; see also de aleat. 3. 2).[3] The bishop, according to Cyprian, is, upon the one hand, a successor of the historical apostolate and hence the legitimate teacher of the apostolical tradition. But he is also an inspired prophet, endowed with the *charismata*—a claim not found in the teachings of Irenæus. Thus the bishop discharges the office of the ancient Spirit-endowed men, for he receives revelations from the Spirit. The place of the former πνευματικόι is filled by the bishop, as afterward by the monastic system. But if the bishops have the

---

[1] Ep. 65. 4 : "to separate the brothers from the folly and remove them from the contagion of these, since neither can a sacrifice be consecrated where there is not a holy spirit, nor does the Lord favor anyone on account of the addresses and prayers of one who has himself offended the Lord." And in ep. 67. 3 (circular letter of 37 bishops) it is announced as a fundamental principle : "All are completely bound to sin who have been contaminated [according to Hos. 9. 4] by the sacrifice of a profane and wicked priest," and "a people obedient to the Lord's commands and fearing God ought to separate themselves from a sinful leader, *praepositus*, and not participate in the sacrifice of a sacrilegious priest" (Numb. xvi. 26). These are statements to which the Donatists could afterward appeal. Cf. REUTER, Augustin. Studien, p. 254 ff.

[2] The divine decision at elections does not exclude "the vote of the people, the consensus of associated bishops" (ep. 59. 5 ; 55. 8 ; 67. 4, 5 ; 49. 2). It is even said of the populace (*plebs*): "Since it most fully possesses the power of electing worthy or rejecting unworthy priests" (ep. 67. 3).

[3] This is an archaistic feature. Visions are mentioned by Cyprian also in other connections (ep. 16. 4 ; 39. 1 ; de immortal. 19 ; ad Donat. 5 ; cf. Dionys. Alex. in Eus. h. e. vii. 7. 2, 3 ; Firmilian's letter, ep. 75. 10, and the criticism noted in ep. 66. 10 : "ridiculous dreams and absurd visions appear to some "). Cyprian has in mind, not a permanent official endowment, but illuminations granted from time to time. This patriarch was not far removed from superstitious fanaticism.

Spirit, it may be easily understood that all criticism must be forestalled by their deliverances, as formerly by those of the prophets (vid. Didache ; also supra, p. 181).

(*b*) According to Matt. xvi. 18 f., the church is founded upon the bishop and its direction devolves upon him : " Hence through the changes of times and dynasties the ordination of bishops and the order of the church moves on, so that the church is constituted of bishops, and every act of the church is controlled by these leaders '' (33. 1). " One in the church is for the time priest and for the time judge, in the stead of Christ '' (ep. 59. 5.). How seriously these principles were accepted is evident from the controversy above noted. The bishop decides who belongs to the church and who shall be restored to her fellowship (16. 1 ; 41. 2 ; de laps. 18, 22, 29). He conducts the worship as the priest of God, who offers the sacrifice upon the altar (67. 1 ; Cyprian is the first to assert an actual priesthood of the clergy, based upon the sacrifice offered by them, vid. sub, p. 196), and cares for the poor. He defends the pure tradition against errorists (ep. 63. 17, 19 ; 74. 10). Cf. O. RITSCHL, l. c., 216 ff. He is the leader (*praepositus*), whose office it is to rule the laity (*laici*, or *plebs*) by virtue of divine authority.

(*c*) The bishops constitute a college (*collegium*), the episcopate (*episcopatus*). The councils developed this conception. In them the bishops practically represented the unity of the church, as Cyprian now theoretically formulated it. Upon their unity rests the unity of the church. " The episcopate is one, a part of which taken separately is regarded as the whole: the church is one, which is ever more widely extended into a multitude by the increase of reproductive energy '' (de unit. eccl. 5). " The church, which is one and catholic, is in a manner connected and joined together by the glue of the mutually cohering priests '' (ep. 66. 8). In this connection it is said: " These are the church united (*adunata*) to the priest and the flock adhering to the pastor. Whence thou shouldst know that the bishop is in the church and the church in the bishop, and he who is not with the bishop is not in the church, and they flatter themselves in vain who, not having peace with the priests of God, deceive themselves and think that they may secretly hold fellowship with any persons whatsoever '' (ib.). This unity of the episcopate rests upon the divine election and endowment which the bishops have in common as successors of the apostles, and finds expression in the same sense (*e. g.*, 75. 3) in their united conferences and mutual recognition (cf. ep. 19. 2 ; 20. 3 ; 55. 1, 6, 7, 24, 30 ; cf. 75. 4, 45, etc.). The unity is manifest in the fact that the Lord in

the first instance bestowed apostolic authority upon Peter :
" Here the other apostles were also, to a certain extent, what
Peter was, endowed with an equal share of both honor and
power ; but the beginning proceeds from unity, in order that the
church of Christ may be shown to be one " (de un. eccl. 4).
Accordingly, the Roman church is the " mother and root of the
catholic church " (ep. 48. 3; cf. 59. 14, etc.). The Roman bishop
made practical application of these ideas (ep. 67. 5 ; esp. 68. 1-
3; cf. also ep. 8; 71. 3; 75. 17; de aleatoribus 1, as well
as the ideas of Callistus, supra, p. 177). As understood by
Cyprian, no higher significance was attached to them than
by Irenæus (supra, p. 137). In reality all the bishops—regarded
dogmatically —stand upon the same level, and hence he maintained, in opposition to Stephanus of Rome, his right of inde
pendent opinion and action, and flatly repelled the latter's appeal to his primacy (ep. 71. 3 ; 74 ; cf. Firmilian's keen criticism, ep. 75. 2, 3, 17, 24 f.; see also 59. 2, 14 ; 67. 5).
The bond which holds the church to unity is thus the episcopate.

(*a*) Rebellion against the bishop is, therefore, rebellion against
God. The schismatic is also a heretic (59. 5 ; 66. 5 ; 52. 1 ;
69. 1; de unit. eccl. 10). He who does not submit to the rightful
bishop forfeits thereby his fellowship with the church and his
salvation. " Whosoever he is, and whatever his character, he is
not a Christian who is not in the church of Christ " (55. 24,
referring to Novatian ! cf. 43. 5; de unit. 17, 19). The
possession of the same faith, to which such persons are wont to
appeal, benefits them as little as it did the family of Korah (ep.
69. 8). It is always chaff which is blown from the threshing-
floor (de un. eccl. 9 ; ep. 66. 8), even though the individuals
concerned were martyrs for the faith (ep. 73. 21): " because
there is no salvation outside the church." The true members of
the church will, therefore, above all, recognize the bishop and
obey him. Thus they remain in the one church, outside of
which there is no salvation : " It is not possible that he should
have God for his father who has not the church for his mother "
(de un. 6). The members of the church are related to the
bishop as children to their father (ep. 41. 1); members of the
fraternitas to one another as brothers, in that they give full sway
to peace and love, and avoid all discord and divisions, praying
with one another in brotherly accord, and even sharing with one
another their earthly goods (de un. 8, 9, 12, 13, 15, 24 f.; de
orat. dom. 8, 30 ; de op. et eleem. 25 fin.; de pat. 15 ; de zel.
et liv. 6).

(*e*) A logical result of this conception of the church is seen

in Cyprian's denial of the validity of *heretic baptism*. Tradition
was here divided. The bishops, assembled three times (A. D.
255-256) at Carthage under Cyprian, supported their opposition
by appeal to their predecessors (ep. 70. 1 ; 71. 4 ; 73. 3 ; cf.
Tert. de bapt. 15), and, as Firmilian reports (ep. 75. 19), the
synod at Iconium had taken the same view. The Roman usage
was, however, different, and Stephanus followed it ("let there
be no innovations, let nothing be done except what has been handed
down," 74. 1; cf. Ps.-Cypr. de rebaptismate 1; also Alexandrines,
Eus. vii. 7. 4), and appealed to the primacy of Peter (71. 3; cf.
sent. episcoporum, proem.). When confronted by tradition,[1]
Cyprian always appealed to the "decision (*consilium*) of a
sane mind" (68. 2 and 71. 3 ; 73. 13 ; 74. 2, 3, 9 ;
cf. 75. 19. Compare Tert., supra, 135, n.), *i. e.*, to the logical consequences of his conception of the church, according to
which, it was evident, no one who was himself outside of the
church could receive anyone into it. The baptism of heretics
is a "sordid and profane bath" (*tinctio*, 70. 1 ; 72. 1 ; 73. 6,
21, etc.). On the other hand : "the water is purified and sanctified through the priest of Christ " (70. 1). Only the leaders,
who receive the Spirit, have the power to impart the forgiveness
of sins, and it is only in the church that the Spirit of God is received (73. 7 ; 74. 5 ; cf. 75. 9); therefore, in receiving those
baptized by heretics, the term employed should be not re-baptism,
but baptism (73. 1). Stephanus severed fellowship with the
churches of Africa (75. 25 ; cf. FECHTRUP i., p. 236 ff.) and
threatened to pursue the same course with the Orientals (Dionys.
in Eus. h. e. vii. 5. 4). Thus Cyprian's conception of the
church was used as a weapon against himself. Cyprian held in
this controversy apparently the more logical position. But the
instinct of Rome was keener. Individuals are changeable and
open to assault. A principle is firmly established only when it
has become rooted in institutions, and when these bring individuals into subjection. Accordingly, the seemingly more liberal
praxis of Rome prevailed.

6. We have thus witnessed a momentous transformation in the
general conception of the Church. By the term is no longer
understood the holy people of God believing on Jesus Christ, but
a group of men belonging to the episcopacy. They obey it, not
because it advocates the truth proclaimed by the apostles, but
because the bishops have been endowed and appointed by God
to be the leaders of the congregations, ruling them in God's

---

[1] Hippolytus (Ref. ix. 12) says of Callistus : ἐπὶ τούτου πρώτως τετόλμηται
δεύτερον αὐτοῖς βάπτισμα.

name and by virtue of divine authority.   This subjection under
the episcopacy is the essential feature in the church, for it constitutes her unity.   Only he who obeys the bishop belongs to the
church and has relationship with God and salvation.   The ideas
of Irenæus must now receive a new interpretation and be brought
into harmony with this new conception, and the holiness of the
church is more and more distinctly associated with her sacraments.   The evangelical definition of the church was superseded
by the catholic.   The church is no longer essentially the assembly of believers and saints, nor an object of faith, but a visible
body, controlled by divinely authorized "ecclesiastical law."
Much is yet in a crude state, but the foundation has been laid.

§ 19.   *General Conception of Christianity.*

1. If the definition of the church is the church's own description of herself, defects in the definition must all find their counterpart in perverted views of Christian character, and the means
by which it may be secured and maintained.   We will find confirmation of this principle when we come to deal with the literature of the West, but we must first examine the writings of the
Eastern theologians.

2. Among these we mention : DIONYSIUS OF ALEXANDRIA († ca. A. D.
265.   Fragments in ROUTH, Reliq. sacr. iii., iv.   THEOGNOSTUS (ca. A. D.
280 ; cf. Phot. cod. 106).   PIERIUS (age of Diocletian, vid. Phot. Bibl. 118).
GREGORY THAUMATURGUS (vid. CASPARI, Quellen, etc., 1886, p. 1 ff.   Migne
gr. 10.   LAGARDE, Analecta syr., 1858.   RYSSEL, Greg. Thaum. Leben u.
Schriften.   PITRA, Analecta sacr. iii., iv.).   HIERACAS (Epiph. h. 67).   Above
all, METHODIUS of Olympus (Opp. edited by Bonwetsch, vid. supra, p. 173, and
cf. PANKAU, Meth. Bisch. v. Olymp.; in "Der Katholik," 1887, ii., p. 113 ff.,
225 ff.; BONWETSCH, Theologie des Meth., 1903.   With the latter, his contemporary, PETER († A. D. 311 ; fragments in ROUTH, Reliq. sacr. iv.   PITRA,
Analecta sacra, iv, 187 ff., 425 ff.   Cf. HARNACK, Gesch. d. altchr. Litt. i.,
p. 443 ff.).

The thought of Eastern theologians was largely moulded by
Origen, as may be clearly seen even in his most energetic opponents.   His dogmatic formulas and problems (creation, homousia
of the Son, spirit and body, freedom, resurrection, interpretation of Scripture, etc.) continue to exert a positive influence.
Compare, *e. g.*, the writings of DIONYSIUS OF ALEXANDRIA (his
Christology, supra, p. 130 ; his work, περὶ φύσεως, against the
atomic theory, frg. in Routh iv.; his exegetic method in
treatment of the Apocalypse, in Eus. h. e. vii. 25. 8, 21 ff.).
True, there was also energetic criticism (*e. g.*, NEPOS, who in his
work, ἔλεγχος ἀλληγοριστῶν, cf. Eus. h. vii. 24. 2, 5 ff., which
argues for a visible millennial kingdom and against the "lofty

and grand understanding '' of the parousia and the resurrection).
This opposition compelled orthodox theology to abandon the
"Gnostic" elements of Origen's teaching. At first, indeed,
the Alexandrine theologians reproduced his ideas quite faithfully.
THEOGNOSTUS and PIERIUS, *e. g.*, are said to have held his theories
of Subordinationism and the pre-existence of souls (vid. Photius
cod. 105; cf. Athanas. ad Serap. ep. 4. 11; de decr. syn. Nic.
25; Phot. cod. 119; cf. Hieracas in Epiph. 67. 1, 3).[1] But we
find PETER OF ALEXANDRIA already vigorously assailing the views
of Origen upon these topics (against the pre-existence of the
soul, see frg. from *de anima* in Routh iv. 49 f.; Pitra, anal.
sacr. iv. 193, 429. Defending the resurrection of a body substantially identical with the present body, frg. from *de resur.* in
Pitra, anal. sacr. iv. 189 ff.; esp. 427 ff.).[2] The wall of parti-
tion between the faith of the ignorant masses ($\dot{\alpha}\pi\lambda o\dot{v}\sigma\tau\varepsilon\rho o\iota$) and
that of the initiated ($\gamma\nu\omega\sigma\tau\iota\varkappa o\iota$) has been broken down. Only
thus have the ideas of Origen become common property, and
that not without the repression of his protests against the popular Christianity. This is, upon the one hand, a matter of inestimable significance; but, on the other hand, it diminished the
influence of Origen's justifiable antagonism to the type of Christianity prevalent among the masses in his day.

A remarkable character now meets us. In METHODIUS we find
a Greek theologian, under the general influence of Origen, yet
consciously in strong opposition to him, giving expression to
the Christian sentiment of the churches in Asia Minor. In
his opposition to Origen, whom he calls a "centaur" (de
creat. 2, 6), he is at one with Peter of Alexandria.

---

[1] Theognostus published 7 books entitled $\dot{v}\pi o\tau v\pi\dot{\omega}\sigma\varepsilon\iota\varsigma$, being the second to
attempt a scientific statement of the doctrines of Christianity. According to
Photius he treated: (1) Of God the Father, the Creator, antagonizing
those who hold that the universe is co-eternal with him. (2) Affirmed that it
was necessary for the Father to have a Son, describing the latter as created
($\varkappa\tau\iota\sigma\mu\alpha$), and as "presiding alone over rational beings," according to
Origen's teaching. (3) Of the Holy Ghost, endeavoring particularly to pre-
sent the proofs of his existence; in other respects following Origen. (4)
Also agreeing with Origen in his view of angels and demons, who have refined
($\lambda\varepsilon\pi\tau\dot{\alpha}$) bodies. (5 and 6) Concerning the incarnation ($\varepsilon\nu\alpha\nu\vartheta\rho\omega\pi\dot{\eta}\sigma\iota\varsigma$) of
the Saviour, "he undertakes, as is his custom, to show that the incarnation of
the Son was necessary," in this also following Origen. (7) "What he
writes about God, the Creator," made a more orthodox impression, especially
in the closing part referring to the Son. The personal Christian life and the
order of salvation are not, therefore, regarded as subjects of Christian knowledge. This is a characteristic omission.

[2] There are no doubts as to the genuineness of these fragments, but the
Armenian fragments (Pitra iv. 430) are exceedingly suspicious, *e. g.*, "Both
the God and the body (of Christ) are one nature and one person, from whose
will and ordering the Spirit comes."

He dislikes his method, and vigorously assails the allegorical exegesis (conv. iii. 2 ; resur. i. 39. 2 ; 54. 6 ; iii. 9. 4´ ff.), but he himself employs the latter heroically when it suits his purpose (see his rules, resur. iii. 8. 3, 7 ; cf. leprosy, 4. 5). He proposes to advocate a "theology of facts" as against the "theology of rhetoric:" "For there is nothing sound, whole, nor solid in them, but only a specious display of words merely for the amazement of the hearers, and an ornamented Pitho" (res. 1. 27. 2). Of the pre-existence of souls, the pre-temporal fall, and the spiritual interpretation of the resurrection, which is for him a "destruction of the resurrection" (ib. i. 27. 1), he will therefore know nothing (e. g., res. i. 55. 4 ; iii. 1. 1 ; 2. 2 f.; 3. 3 ; 5 ; 7. 12 ; 12).

We present a brief outline of his views in general. (1) The almighty God, out of love, for man's sake, created this world out of nothing, as well the essences (οὐσίαι) as the properties (ποιότητες) (de lib. arb. 7. 4-91 ; 22. 7, 8). The world is not eternal (de creat. 11. 2 ; de lib. arb. 22. 10, 11); but, as God was never inactive, the world existed in him potentially (δυνάμει), from eternity (de lib. arb. 22. 9). He created it through the Logos. As to the Logos and the Holy Spirit, see supra, p. 173. (2) The essential marks of man as created by God in time are freedom and immortality : "For man being free (αὐτεξούσιος) and independent (αὐτοκράτωρ), his will is both self-controlled (αὐτοδέσποτος) and self-determining in regard to choice" (res. i. 38. 3). "Made free in regard to the choice of the good, etc., . . . for God created man for immortality, and made him the image of his own eternity" (res. i. 36. 2 ; 34. 3 ; 51. 5). In this consists his godlikeness (θεοείδες and θεοείκελον, res. i. 35. 2). This freedom of choice has descended from the first man to his posterity. "From whom the subsequent members of the race also had allotted to them the like freedom" (lib. arb. 16. 2). This moral equipment of man involves that he was and is in position to fulfill the law of God : "For it belongs to him to be able to accept the commandment or not" (lib. arb. 16. 7). "For it lies with us to believe or not to believe . . . , with us to live aright or to sin, with us to do good or to do evil" (res. 57. 6 ; cf. conv. viii. 17). Since man was created for eternity, God sees to it that this becomes his portion (res. 1. 35. 2-4). This is the genuine Greek anthropology. (3) The devil's envy of man led to the fall (lib. arb. 17. 5 ; 18. 4 ff.), i. e., man employed his freedom in disobedience of God's command. "But wickedness is disobedience" (ib. 18. 8). The spirit of the world then gained control within him : "For thus first came about our condition ; we were filled with strifes and vain reasoning ; on the one hand, emptied of the indwelling of God ; on the other, filled with worldly lust, which the plotting serpent infused into us '' (res. ii. 6. 2). Thus man "chose evil from free choice '' (res. i. 45. 2). Thus it is not the flesh, but the soul, that is responsible for sin (res. i. 29. 8 ; 59. 3), but " every sin and every way of life attains its end through the flesh '' (res. ii. 4. 3). Henceforth evil lusts crowd in upon us, which we, indeed, ought to conquer : " For it does not lie wholly with us to desire or not to desire things improper, but to carry out or not carry out the desire '' (res. ii. 3. 1). But in order that the evil in man might not become immortal, God graciously appointed death (res. i. 39. 5 ; 38. 1 ; 45. 5 ; ii. 6. 3), which is a penalty intended, as are all penalties, to lead to amendment (res. i. 31. 4). As an artist breaks to pieces a statue which has been maliciously defaced, in order to recast it, so God deals with man in appointing him to death (res. i. 43. 2 ff.). We may here again clearly trace the influence of Origen, despite all the polemical assaults upon him.

(4) Wherein now consists the salvation which Christ has brought to the race? The answer assumes many forms. The souls of men are cleansed by the blood of Christ. He is our "Helper '' in the conflict (distinction of meats, 15 ; 11. 4 ; 2. 1). He is " helper, advocate, and physician,'' the "great Giver and great Helper '' (res. iii. 23. 11). Christ announced through the prophets of the old covenant that he would bring forgiveness of sins and the resurrection of the flesh (conv. vii. 6). Thus the "Word '' "directed us to the truth and brought us to immortality '' (res. iii. 23. 4, 6). He brings to men the redemption of the body (res. ii. 18. 8 ; 24. 4). But the controlling idea of Methodius is different from these, *i. e.*, Christ is born in those who are received by baptism into the church : " For since those illuminated (baptized) with the image of the Logos, impressed in figure upon them and begotten within them according to perfect knowledge and faith, receive also the marks and image and manhood of Christ, so, we may understand, is Christ born in everyone.'' Since they through the Holy Spirit enter into living fellowship with Christ, they themselves become, as it were, Christs : " As if having become Christs, being baptized according to their possession of the Spirit into Christ '' (conv. viii. 8 ; cf. Ephes. 3. 14-17). " For to proclaim the incarnation of the Son of God by the holy virgin, but not at the same time to confess that he also comes into his church as into his flesh, is not perfect. For everyone of us must confess, not alone his parousia in that holy flesh which came from the pure virgin, but also a similar parousia in the spirit

of everyone of us" (urchin, 8. 2, 3). "Be moulded by
Christ, who is within you" (ib. 1. 6 ; cf. distinction of meats,
4. 1). Christ becomes known to us, because he dwells in us
(cf. conv. viii. 9). But this fellowship in the Holy Ghost
produces in us a new life and energy, which lead to immortality (urchin, 4. 4, 6 ; 8. 3-5. Conv. iii. 8 : "It is impossible for anyone to be a partaker of the Holy Spirit and be
accounted a member of Christ, unless the Logos, having first
come to him, has fallen asleep and risen, in order that, having
arisen from sleep with him who for his sake fell asleep, he also
having been formed anew may be enabled to share in the renewal and restoration of the Spirit." Conv. viii. 10 : "He
chooses the thought of the restored"). Thus Christ has come to
take up his abode in men. When this is done through the Holy
Spirit, men are renewed, incited to choose the good and thus to
attain immortality. As the Logos once dwelt in Adam (supra,
p. 174), so now he dwells again in believers. (5) Man is introduced into this new life through the church, which is primarily "the whole assembly (ἄθροισμα) and mass (στίφος) of
those who have believed" (conv. iii. 8 ; vii. 3); but the more
perfect and morally mature properly constitute the church of
Christ, which has the power to prosecute his work (ib.). Further, in this "robe of the Lord," the church, are discriminated
the spiritual and the laity : " He calls the more powerful rank
of the church, *i. e.*, the bishops and teachers, the warp ; but the
subjects and laity of the pasture, the woof" (leprosy, 15. 4).
This is not yet understood in a hierarchical sense (see complaint
against bishops, ib. 17. 2). The church in which Christ dwells
now bears children to him. This occurs through teaching
(διδασκαλία, conv. iii. 8) and through baptism (ib. viii. 6 ; cf.
dist. of meats, 11. 6 : "as the mysteries have been ordained for
the illuminating and vivifying of that which has been learned").
Baptism introduces into the fellowship of the Spirit and bestows
immortality ("the illuminated [*i. e.*, baptized] have been duly
born again to immortality," conv. iii. 8). Thus the church increases and grows because it stands in living fellowship with the
Logos : "growing daily into loftiness and beauty and magnitude through the union and fellowship of the Logos" (ib.).
Thus she bears children to Christ—yea, even begets the Word
itself in the heart (ib. viii. 11 init.). (6) Evident as it is that man
has the ability to accept by the power of his will the salvation
proffered, it is just as certain that sin yet exerts its alluring and
stimulating power within him. " But now, even after believing
and going to the water of cleansing, we are often found yet in
sins." Faith only smothers sin, and does not root it out ; it cuts

off the suckers, but not the root itself (res. i. 41. 2-4). More than this man cannot accomplish (ib. i. 44. 4 ; only death can complete the work): but this much he must strive to do. He does so in the power of the Spirit working within him (*e. g.*, conv. viii. 10). Thus he represses the lusts that burn within him (res. ii. 3-5) and obeys not the world but God ("the law of God is self-control," res. i. 60. 3). In this conflict, Christ is helper and advocate (res. iii. 23. 11). God is called upon to grant "improvement of the heart," and "non-imputation and for-giveness of sins" (ib. iii. 23. 7-9). Thus, contending and re-penting (ib. iii. 21. 9), man struggles upward. Repentance has to do primarily with the lusts of the heart. These must be con-fessed to God. But if one is yet unable to overcome them, or if they issue in sinful acts, then one should entrust himself to the bishop and be by him subjected to the discipline of the church. This imposes upon the offender separation from church-fellowship and public confession. It is the duty of the bishop to note whether there be real penitence and a forsaking of sin, and, only in such case, to restore the offender to fellowship (leprosy, 5 ff.; cf. BONWETSCH, Theol. des Method., p. 103 ff.). It is important to observe how the point of view here as elsewhere differs from that of the West. The bishop is not a judge, and the aim in repentance is not to render satisfaction to God. The bishop is regarded as a spiritual adviser and official of the church, and the object of repentance is inward healing and amendment. The Christian's aim is : "that we may become strong and sound through faith to keep thy commandments" (ib. iii. 23. 11). All depends upon "the faith and the conduct," upon "orthodoxy,"[1] and "good works," and "an active and rational life" (leprosy, 15. 2 ; urchin, 8. 4 ; dist. of meats, 8. 2). At the same time there is running through the writings of Methodius a strong leaning toward asceticism and thoughts of the life to come. Suffering purifies (dist. of meats, 1-5). He esteems lightly "things present" ("a using, but no possession"), but he loves "things to come," which are eternal (life and rat. conduct, 5. 1 ; 6. 3). Of "lusts" the church will know nothing, for "they say that it is called ' church ' from having turned away from (ἐκκεκλικέναι) pleasures" (de creat. 8). But Methodius never tires of glorifying celibacy :[2] Virginity is nearness to God

---

[1] Cf. the value attached to orthodoxy, *e. g.*, res. i. 30. 2 : "For thou seest that the doctrines are not of small account to us, but in what way it is necessary to have believed ; for I think that nothing is so evil for a man as that of the nec-essary things he should believe anything false."

[2] The right to marry is not thereby curtailed, *e. g.*, conv. ii. 1. 2 ; iii. 11 ff.; lib. arb. 15. 1 f.

($\pi\alpha\rho\vartheta\varepsilon i\alpha$ $\gamma\dot{\alpha}\rho$ $\dot{\eta}$ $\pi\alpha\rho\vartheta\varepsilon\nu i\alpha$, conv. viii. 1). Christ is the chief Virgin
(ib. 1. 5). Virgins are the best portion of the church. "For,
although many are evidently daughters of the church, there is one
rank alone chosen and most precious in her eyes above all others,
the rank of the virgins (conv. vii. 3).

(7) The goal of the Christian life is immortality attained
through the resurrection. The latter term applies not to the
soul, but to the body, whose substance continues to exist, since
it was not the purpose of God to transform men into angels (res.
i. 50. 1 ; iii. 1 ff.). Immortality is, therefore, to be attained after
the final conflagration, which will result in a reconstruction
($\dot{\alpha}\nu\alpha\varkappa\tau\iota\sigma\vartheta\tilde{\eta}\nu\alpha\iota$) of the original creation ($\varkappa\tau i\sigma\iota\varsigma$) (ib. i. 48. 3). All
of this is in direct and designed opposition to Origen.

4. Such are the principles which constituted the "Christianity" of a cultivated Greek of about A. D. 300. It is a
unique mixture of ideas garnered from the popular philosophy of the Greeks, from the popular Christianity of the age,
from a glowing zeal for the ideals of asceticism, and from a
real interest in the problems which Origen had so forcibly stated.
Methodius has lost all conception of a righteousness to be attained
through faith. Faith is the acceptance of that which is to be
believed, and is accompanied by the moral application to the life
by means of self-control ($\sigma\omega\varphi\rho\upsilon\sigma\acute{\upsilon}\nu\eta$) and in obedience, through
good works and an ascetic life—with which is combined also the
hope of immortality. But throughout all these assertions is felt
the force of a great primitive Christian experience, "the Christ
in us," who is our strength, who renews us in our hearts, and
draws our hearts upward from this earth toward himself. "Up
to the heights of the regenerated who have been borne to the
throne of God . . . are lifted the hearts of the renewed, taught
there to see and be seen, in order that they may not be betrayed
into the depths of the mighty dragon" (conv. viii. 10). But
this *Sursum Corda !* rests upon the thought that he is the Vine
and we the branches—he in us and we in him. It is the legacy
of John and Ignatius which furnishes spiritual sustenance to this
theologian of Asia Minor. It is, perhaps, erroneous to characterize his theology as "the theology of the future" (Harnack);
but it reveals to us one of the factors which explain the bitter
conflicts of the future as to the person of Christ. We see here
the religious capital which was to bear the expenses of the long
campaign.

5. The *Western Theologians* now claim our attention.

SOURCES. The writings of Cyprian with the Pseudo-Cyprian works, De
montibus Sina et Sion, and the sermon, De aleatoribus (probably delivered at
Rome in the second half of the second century), ed. Hartel, vid. p. 178;

the best edition of De aleat. by Miodonski, 1889. Compare GÖTZ, Das Christentum Cyprians, 1896. COMMODIANUS, Instructionum ll. 2, and Carmen
apologeticum (ed. Dombart, 1887). ARNOBIUS, adv. nationes, ll. 7 (ed.
Reifferscheid, 1875). LACTANTIUS, divinarum institutionum, ll. 7. Epitome,
de ira dei (ed. Brandt and Laubmann, 1890).

"Christ . . . since he knew that the nature of mortals is
blind and not able to comprehend the reality of any things except
those placed before our eyes, . . . has commanded us to leave
and neglect all those things, and not to devote fruitless meditations to those things which are removed far from our knowledge,
but as far as possible to draw near with our whole mind and soul
to the Lord of all things . . . What is it to you, he says, to
investigate and search out who made man, what is the origin of
souls, who planned the schemes of the wicked, whether the sun
is larger than the earth . . . whether the moon shines with rays
from another luminary or with her own? Neither is it an advantage to know these things, nor any detriment to be ignorant
of them. Commit these things to God, and allow him to know
what, why, and whence they are, whether they ought to be, or
ought not to be, whether anything is without origin, or has its
primordial beginnings . . . it is not permitted to your faculties to
implicate you in such things and to be uselessly concerned about
things so remote. Your own interests are endangered, I say the
safety of your souls, and unless you apply yourselves to the
thought of the Lord God, evil death awaits you when freed from
the bonds of the flesh " (Arnobius, ii. 60, 61).

These remarkable words of a Western theologian direct the
interest of the Christian upon the salvation of souls, and deny
to him the consideration of physical and metaphysical problems.
There is here revealed a peculiar and growing tendency of Western Christianity, very clearly seen by a comparison of Tertullian
with Origen, or Cyprian with Methodius. Even the theological
interest of Cyprian did not extend further than the salvation
of souls (*salus animarum*) and immortality (*perpetuitas*, Arnob.
ii. 65). We note the same limitation in Commodian and Lactantius, in the naive heterodoxy of Arnobius and the correct
orthodoxy of Novatian. The practical Christianity of these men
—notably that of Cyprian, who so largely moulded the thought
of the succeeding ages—moves within the lines marked out by
Tertullian[1] (supra, p. 132 f.).

(*a*) By the Western theologians as well as by the Orientals

---

[1] Even the emphasis laid upon the *salus animarum* as the content of Christianity is an echo of Tertullian : " Of these blessings there is one superscription, the salvation of man " (paen. 2 ; cf., *e. g.*, ib. 10, 12 ; pud. 9 ; jej. 3 ;
bapt. 5 ; praescr. 14 ; c. Marc. ii. 27 ; res. 8, et supra).

the first and most important place is assigned to the doctrine of
the one almighty God, Creator of heaven and earth (*e. g.*, Commod. carm. ap. 90 ff.). Man is under obligation to obey him.
The relationship is viewed as a legal one (vid. sub : lex, satisfactio, meritum). (*b*) The sinner is one who has refused obedience. Sin and death passed from Adam upon his descendants
(Cypr. ep. 64. 5 ; Comm. carm. ap. 324 : " on account of whose
sin (*cujus de peccato*) we die." Cf. instr. i. 35. 3).[1] (*c*) God
now endeavors to deliver man from sin and death. This is first
attempted through the law, but finally through Christ, who as
teacher of the truth gives a " new law " and makes it impressive
by his example ; " by the grace of God we are incited to believe
the law " (Comm. carm. ap. 766 ; cf. instr. i. 35. 18 ; ii. 1. 6 ;
7. 5. Cypr. de op. et eleem. 1, 7, 23, 24 ; de laps. 21 ; unit.
eccl. 2, etc.). Lactantius scarcely gets beyond these ideas.
Both the incarnation and the death upon the cross find their purpose completely attained in instruction and example (vid. instr.
iv. 10. 1 ; 11. 14 : " When God had determined to send the
teacher of virtue to men, he then ordained that he should be re-
born in the flesh and become like to man himself, whose leader
and companion and teacher he was to be ; " iv. 13. 1 ; 14. 15 ;
16. 4 ; 26. 30 ; 24. 1, 5, 10, 7 : " God himself surely would
not be able to teach virtue, because outside of the body he cannot do the things which he shall teach, and on this account his
teaching will not be perfect ; " also epit. 38. 8 f.; 39. 7 ; 45 ;
46. 2 f.), if we except the peculiar power attributed to the cross
in the taking of an oath (epit. 46. 6-8. Inst. iv. 27 ; see also
iv. 20. 3). Cyprian and Commodian strike a deeper note.
Christ not only taught us the new law, but he suffered for our
sins (Cypr. laps. 17), and thereby made us children of God (ep.
58. 6). He has become our attorney and advocate, our mediator (ep. 11. 5 ; quod idola, 11), so that we find forgiveness of
our sins through him. His blood nullifies death (ep. 55. 22 ;
op. et al. 1). Thus Christ grants cleansing from sin (baptism),
forgiveness of sins (repentance), the new law and immortality.
He is the Saviour, because he establishes and imparts the grace
of the sacraments and of the church order.

(*d*) This salvation is imparted to man in baptism ; is preserved by faith, fear, and obedience ; and attested by repentance
and good works. Divine grace begins with baptism, " since thence

---

[1] " What he did of good or of evil, the leader of our nativity conferred upon
(*contulisset*) us ; we die likewise through him ; " cf. Instr. ii. 5. 8 : *genitalia*. Cypr. ad Donat. 3 : *genuinum*, op. et eleem. 1 : " He healed the
wounds which Adam had conveyed and cured the ancient poisons of the serpent," etc.

13

begins the whole origin (*origo*) of faith and the saving entrance (*ingressio*) upon the hope of eternal life and the divine regard (*dignatio*) for the purifying and vivifying of the servants of God " (Cypr. ep. 73. 12).[1] In baptism man experiences the second birth (*secunda nativitas*, Cypr. ad Donat. 4 ; orat. dom. 23). The recipient receives the Holy Ghost (ep. 63. 8 ; 73. 9), becomes free from the devil (ep. 69. 15), from death and hell (ep. 55. 22 ; op. et al. 2). The second birth secures for man health (*sanitas*, Cypr. hab. virg. 2); inborn sins are forgiven (Comm. instr. ii. 5. 8 : " in baptism *genitalia* are forgiven thee." Cypr. op. et al. 1); the subject really becomes another man (Cypr. ad Don. 3. 4). The new law now applies to him, by obeying which he is to preserve the purity attained : " he gives the law of innocence after he has conferred health . . . that pardon may no more be lacking after thou hast begun to know God " (Cypr. hab. virg. 2 ; cf. Commod. instr. ii. 5. 11 : " The conclusion for thee : Always avoid serious sins "). Christ, therefore, imparts a two-fold blessing to man. By baptism he makes him whole, and he grants to him as thus restored the law, by obeying which he may and should preserve himself in health. If he fails to do this, repentance is offered to him as a means of salvation. It is now a question of forgiving grace and the preservation of the good will which desires amendment. Man fulfills his duty toward God by faith and the fear of God : " the whole basis of religion and faith begins in obedience and fear " (Cypr. hab. virg. 2 init.; cf. op. et al. 8); by prayer (or. dom. 12); and by the reception through faith of the gifts of grace now richly granted (ad Don. 5 : " it flows continually ; it overflows abundantly ; it satisfies our utmost desire and yet flows on. As much of receptive faith as we bring thither, so much of the overflowing grace do we imbibe "). Although these words of Cyprian, which were written soon after his conversion, seem to reveal a vivid sense of the supreme significance of faith, yet the context leads us to a different conclusion. Faith is for him essentially the recognition of the divine law and belief in the veracity of the promises (*e. g.*, de mortalit. 6. 22 fin., 24 ; ad Demetr. 20 ; de patient. 1 ; cf. Commod. carm. ap. 311 ff., 615 ; Lactant. epit. 61. 3 ff.; inst. vi. 17. 23 ff.; also epit. 61. 1 : " faith

---

[1] As to the outward form of baptism, we note : It is administered in the name of the triune God, not merely in the name of Christ (ep. 73. 18 ; cf. 69. 7); the baptismal confession (ep. 70. 2 ; 69. 7 ; cf. 75. 10 f.); sprinkling or pouring, with the customary bath (*lavacrum*, ep. 69. 12); children to be baptized, not on the eighth day, but as soon as possible (ep. 64. 2 ; cf. laps. 10); they also receive the Holy Ghost (ep. 64. 3); anointing with the consecrated oil (*chrisma*, ep. 70. 2); cf. const. ap. vii. 40 ff.

is, therefore, a great part of righteousness."(!)   Hence we may thus summarize : Baptism brings forgiveness of sins and blots out sin in a man ; he is now equipped with the Spirit and fulfills the law of God, because he believes that God will reward this struggle to live virtuously and will bestow upon him eternal life.   By good works man really wins for himself a merit (*meritum*) before God (op. et al. 26 : " to our merits and works contributing promised rewards ").   He pays back what Christ has done for him (op. et al. 17. 23 ; cf. hab. virg. 2).   He who performs the works of the law is righteous before God.   It is the first concern of the Christian to be mindful of the law : " Nor let anything be considered in your hearts and minds except the divine precepts and the heavenly commandments " (ep. 6. 2).

(*e*) But the baptized also still commit sin.   For this, too, grace offers a way of escape : " He has given to the restored one a law and commanded that he should now sin no more . . . we would have been constrained and brought into a strait by the law, nor could the infirmity and imbecility of our human frailty have accomplished anything, had not the divine goodness, again intervening, opened out a certain way of preserving salvation by performing works of righteousness and mercy, so that we may *by alms wash away* whatever stains we have afterward contracted " (Cypr. op. et al. 1).   This is the idea entertained of repentance.   True, sincere penitence (in case of the lapsed, see p. 180) and confession before the church are prescribed, but, at least in the case of trifling daily sins, good works, and particularly alms, remain the principal thing.   By the giving of alms, the Christian repeats what was granted to him at his baptism : " just as in the bath of saving water the fire of hell is extinguished, so by alms and righteous works the flame of sin is quenched.   And because in baptism the forgiveness of sins is once bestowed, diligent and continual working, imitating the pattern of baptism, bestows again the favor of God " (op. et al. 2 ; orat. dom. 32).   By alms, the sinner renders to God suitable satisfaction (*satisfactio*, op. et al. 4, 5 ; cf. ep. 35 ; 43. 3 ; 55. 11 ; 59. 13 ; 64. 1 ; de laps. 17, 22, 34 ff.); reconciles God (*propitiando deo*) and merits (*mereri*) the mercy of God (op. et el. 5, cf. 13 fin.; 15, cf. Comm. instr. ii. 14. 14 ; de aleator. 11. 2).

If man thus by prayer and good works merits for himself the mercy of God in his battle with sin (*precibus et operibus suis satisfacere,* Cypr. 16.2), we find the Eucharist represented as a means of strengthening for the conflict.   It is a safeguard (*tutela*) in the conflict (ep. 57. 2.)   It elevates and inflames the spirit ("there is something lacking in the spirit which the reception of the eucharist does not uplift and inflame," ib. 4). It unites the church with Christ, and the sorrowing heart is by it filled with joy (ep. 63, 13, 11 : "Let there be a forgetting of the former worldly life, and let the sad and sorrowful heart, which was before oppressed by its increasing sins, be set free in the joy of the divine forgiveness"). These are genuinely Christian sentiments, which we are not at liberty to discredit because they give no direct answer to questions raised at a later period. But the eucharist is also viewed in another light. It is the *"sacrifice"* offered by the priest, and this can be done only in the church. Fellowship (*communicatio*) with the church really consists in the partaking of the eucharist. This sacrifice is offered (*offerre*) also for penitent sinners, and in their name (*e. g.*, ep. 16. 2 ; 17. 2). It is a repetition of the sacrifice of Christ : "This priest acts in the stead of Christ, imitating that which Christ did, and offering then a true and full sacrifice in the church to God the Father" (ep. 63. 14). "For the passion of the Lord is the sacrifice which we offer" (ib. 17). In earlier times, the virtues and prayers of believers had been called gifts (δῶρα, 1 Clem. 44. 4; 40. 2 ff.; 36. 1), particularly the eucharistic prayer (Did. 14. 1, 2 ; Just. Dial. 40, 70, 117). Thus also the presentation of the elements of the Lord's Supper before God (Iren. iv. 17. 5 ; 18. 1, 4), as well as the contributions brought at such times as on the anniversaries of the death of relatives, were looked upon as a sacrifice, and before long a peculiar significance began to be attached to them as such (*e. g.*, Tert. ad ux. ii. 8 ; de monog. 10 ; ex. cast. 11 ; de coron. 3 f.; de orat. 28 ; cf. Cypr. 1. 2). The Lord's Supper was called the "*sacrificium*."[1] Cyprian—since the clergy were, in his view, actual priests—adopted this idea with great earnestness. Through the priest the sinner is received into the church, and through the act of the priest the merit of Christ is applied to him. In this, a distinctive idea of Catholicism again comes to view. The history of the Lord's Supper is marked by two great modifications. The first transformed the fraternal Agape into the ecclesiastical sacrament ; the second designated as the chief thing in the transaction the bringing of the sacrifice before God as a repetition of the death of Christ, and not the gracious presence of God in our behalf. The second was effected by

---

[1] Tert. de cultu fem. ii. 11 : "Either the sacrifice is offered, or the word of God administered ;" cf. de orat. 19 ; ad uxor. 11. 8.   See the association of Word and Eucharist also in Ps.-Clem. de virg. ep. i. 5 ; cf. Abercius-title, lines 6, 9, 12 ff. (word, baptism, eucharist), and Method., supra, p. 189. For the sacrificial idea in ancient times, see HÖFLING, Die Lehre d. ältesten Kirche von Opfer, Erl. 1851.

Origen, and in it we have another illustration of the complete externalizing of religion.   Instead of the act and agency of God appears the work of man, the ordinance of a holy legal system.   It was thus in the eucharist, and most distinctly thus in the doctrine and praxis of repentance.   The Romish sacrament of penance was constructed by Tertullian and Cyprian.   In the attempt to make repentance difficult, it is made easy.   For that which is the hardest thing in religion—repentance and faith—is substituted good works :   "the salutary guardian of our security —a thing placed within our power to do—a thing both grand and easy " (op. et al. 26).[1]

(f) The inevitable consequence of the conception of the Christian life as an obedience rendered to the "new law" is a double morality.   The highest self-surrender to God cannot be *demanded* of all, but only *advised*.   The first precept commands to increase and multiply, and the second counsels continence (hab. virg. 23).   Virginity is the blossom of the ecclesiastical seed (ib. 3).   However beautifully Cyprian may depict the ideal of the Christian life (see esp. orat. dom. 15 ; zel. et liv. 16 ; cf. Comm. instr. ii. 17. 17 ff.), yet the best Christians are those alone who have chosen the heavenly Bridegroom (hab. virg. 20. 22)—and the language here is not meant, as in Origen, to indicate a really higher plane of Christian character.

(g) But, while thus accommodating the Christian life to the world, the desire was strongly felt to escape from the world, and there was much thought of the approaching end (Cypr. un. eccl. 16 ; de mortal. 25 f.; ad Demetr. 3 f.).   The resurrection was the chief object of faith, for from it was expected the reward for good works (e. g., hab. virg. 21, also supra).   Great delight was found in drawing portraitures of the last times and the conflicts under the reign of the Antichrist (Nero), with the consolation of the millennial kingdom (see esp. Comm. carm. ap. 791 ff.; instr. ii. 2-4 ; 39 ; i. 27, 28, 41, etc.   Lactant. ep. 66, 67).   The gulf between the church, as it was then conceived, and the kingdom of God lying wholly in the future, became but the wider :   "He declares that they shall be permitted to see the kingdom who have performed works in his church" (op. et el. 9, cf. de zel. et liv. 18).

---

[1] Cyprian, like Origen, believed in a purifying fire after death :   "It is one thing, tortured with prolonged misery for sins, to be cleansed and purged for a long time by fire, and another thing to have all sins purged in the passion " (*i. e.*, Lord's Supper).   Ep. 55. 20 ; cf. supra, p. 159, n.   Vid. also Tert. de monog., 10 : "'He prays for his (the deceased's) soul ; he implores for him meanwhile a cooling (in the flame)."   These are ideas borrowed from antiquity, *e. g.*, Plato, Phaed. 6, and the Orphic poems.

6. Such is Western Christianity in the third century.   Cyprian's work, *De catholicae ecclesiae unitate,* and, in at least equal degree, his *De opere et eleemosyne,* may be designated landmarks of the course of development.   But scarcely at a single point does he furnish more than a development of suggestions found in the father of Western Catholicism, Tertullian (cf. p. 132 f.).   There exists a legal relationship between God and man.   By baptism, God has in a magical way made man pure (the Stoic definition of spirit here influences the thought), and he is now under obligation to observe the new law of Christ.   Since he does not do this, he must render satisfaction to God by good works, by which he merits mercy for himself and secures as his reward the resurrection.   This is the chief content of the faith.   But it is only in the church, *i. e.,* in obedience to the bishops, who have been ordained by God and by him endowed with peculiar powers and authority (priests and judges of God's grace), that a man can become and continue a Christian.   This is the meaning of the "salvation of souls," which Christ has brought to man.

The Christianity of the West is thus marked by the following characteristics : (1) Sacramental grace. (2) The legal conception of the relationship between God and man. (3) The combination of the two ideas in the concentration of the whole energy of religion upon the salvation of souls (*salus animarum*).   (4) The subjugation of the soul, for the attainment of its salvation, to the control of the hierarchical church with its sacramental ordinances.   (5) But the sacraments in the hierarchy are held in balance by the merits (*merita*) of the individual.   (6) The formulas of Tertullian and the authority of the Apostles' Creed. The theology of the East, on the contrary, is distinguished by : (1) The adoption of the theology of Origen. (2) The emphasis laid upon "orthodoxy" and delight in metaphysical problems. (3) The fixing of immortality as the practical goal.   (4) The mystical conception of the work of Christ, as being born in us, dwelling in us, and permeating us with spiritual life.

The Christianity of the third century presents itself to us as a direct continuation of the doctrinal teaching of the second century.   The roots of the ideas here developed may in almost every instance be traced back to the Apostolic Fathers.   In fact, the departure of the teachers of this period from the views of the Apostolic Fathers was but small in comparison with that of the latter from the position of the Apostles.   Yet the development during the third century progressed with astonishing rapidity.   The original Christian ideas of a life with God in Christ and of an intercourse of the heart with God through repentance and faith, which in the second century still constantly assert themselves despite the general moralizing of the gospel, are now, particularly in the Western church, almost entirely forced into the background. The practical aims in view have become different from those prescribed by the spirit of Christ and the teachings of Paul. In the East, all stress is laid upon the acceptance of the pure doctrine, which is more and more reduced to abstract formulas and a life of celibacy—yet practical interest in the "Christ in us" does not altogether disappear. In the West, the controlling ideas are the preservation of a right relation to God and the Catholic church, the way in which man may come to God and remain in fellowship with him, and the ideal of celibacy—yet there persists a feeling that it is the highest duty of the church to care for the salvation of souls. The perversion, although differing in character, is common to the two branches of the church. The time will come when repentance will be held to consist only in good works, and yet, under the delusion of strange ideals, really good works will be neglected, and when an intellectual acceptance of doctrine shall take the place of faith. Nevertheless, "orthodoxy" will pursue its course in the East and the "hierarchy" in the West, and both will bring unutterable sorrow to the hearts of true believers. Yet it cannot be but that he who with a Christian's open heart seeks to realize and study the motives underlying the life of that age will stumble upon ideas and convictions which still attest the power of the ancient truth. In the one case it will be the "Up to the heights!" (p. 191), and in the other the "Salvation of souls." The Eastern church will endeavor to fathom the mysteries of the world above, and enjoy its raptures in mystic contemplation, while the salvation of the soul will remain the great problem in the West.

If we consider the course of development from the point of view of two prominent apostles, the East will be found following in the path marked out by John, while the West walks in the footsteps of Paul. These points of view were often much obscured in the course of the development, but a keen interest in the Divine Logos, who imparts new life to us, remains the central feature among the Greeks, while in the West the central problem continues to be "How may the sinner become righteous before God?" In the doctrines of the Trinity and in Christology the interest here centres in repentance and the church, and this continues to be the case in the last great religious agitation of the West, the Reformation of Luther (vid. vol. ii.). So far-reaching is the outlook which we may gain from the study of the Christianity of the third century.

For the grace of God hath appeared, bringing salvation to all men, instructing us, to the intent that, denying ungodliness and worldly lusts, we should live soberly and righteously and godly in this present world; looking for the blessed hope and appearing of the glory of the great God and our Saviour Jesus Christ; who gave himself for us, that he might redeem us from all iniquity, and purify unto himself a people for his own possession, zealous of good works.—*Titus ii. 11-14.*

PART II.

DOCTRINAL CONSTRUCTION IN THE ANCIENT CHURCH.

CHAPTER I.

THE DOCTRINE OF THE TRINITY.

§ 20. *Arianism and the Homousia of the Son (the First Council of Nice).*

1. We have had occasion to observe the diversity of views concerning the divinity of Christ which prevailed before the outbreak of the great controversy ; but we have also noted a certain unity of religious conviction at this point : "the church unanimously adoring the divinity of Christ." Although there was little attempt to fathom the procession of the Son from the Father, yet he, like the Father, was regarded as God, as the brightness of his glory and the image ($\chi\alpha\rho\alpha\kappa\tau\acute{\eta}\rho$) of his person ($\acute{\upsilon}\pi\acute{o}\sigma\tau\alpha\sigma\iota\varsigma$) (Heb. i. 3). These were regarded as the "apostolic dogmas of the church" (vid. Alex. ep. ad Alex. in Theodoret. h. e. i. 3). Opposite conceptions must now inevitably lead to conflict, as had become evident in the Monarchian and Dionysian controversies. After the unity of the church had become a theory of practical importance, and the conception of "heresy" had, in consequence of the fixation of the church's doctrine, become more definite, the ancient indefinite formulas became unsatisfactory, especially as they left room for such interpretations as that of Arius. But we shall utterly fail to understand the conflicts of the period before us if we shall interpret them as merely a result of the metaphysical tendency of Grecian thought. On the contrary, beneath these controversies lay most thoroughly practical and religious motives. Christ was the centre of Greek piety ; the new immortal life, the periphery ; the idea of salvation, the radius. The centre must be so located that all the radii may actually meet in it. Christ must be conceived of as in nature and character capable of bestowing the new divine life upon men.

Lucian of Antioch was an adherent of Paul of Samosata, and hence out of harmony with the church (ib. in Theod. i. 3, p. 739).

ARIUS was his pupil, as was also EUSEBIUS OF NICOMEDIA (ep. Arii ad Eus. in Theod. h. e. i. 4 fin. and Alex. ib. 4). Traces of relationship with Paul may be found in Arius (see Athanas. c. Arian. or. iii. 10, 51); but the views of Paul were developed by him in harmony with the later age. The impersonal energy (δύναμις) in the Father has become a special personality, which, however, does not—to the gratification of heathen and Jews (ep. Alex. in Theod. h. e. i. 3)—call the unity of God in question, and yet, in keeping with the consciousness of the church and the prevalent theory of the Logos, preserves the independence of the second divine person. It is thus that the doctrine of Arius, which, in its main features, Lucian may have already taught, is to be understood. It is merely the Christology of the third century theoretically carried to its logical conclusion. But it was this very fact of the logical consistency of the theory which opened the eyes of the church. The same process has been repeated in the case of most heresies. The controversies to which they gave rise have led to the construction of dogmas.

1. The Doctrine of ARIUS.

LITERATURE. Of the writings of Arius himself we possess : a letter to Alexander, bishop of Alexandria, in Athanas. de synodis Arim. et Seleuc. 16 and Epiph. h. 69. 7, 8 ; a letter of Eusebius of Nicomedia in Theodoret. h. e. i. 4 (opp. ed. SCHULZE, iii. 2), and Epiph. h. 69. 6. Fragments from his θάλεια in Athanas. c. Arian. or. i.; de synod. Arim. et Seleuc. 15).[1] For statements of his teaching, vid. especially the writings of Athanasius and the letter from Alexander of Alexandria to Alexander of Byzantium, in Theodoret. h. e. i. 3, and the Ep. encyclica in Socrat. h. e. i. 6. Compare GWATKIN, Studies of Arianism, 1882. KÖLLING, Gesch. d. arian. Häresie, 2 vols., 1874, 1883. MÖLLER, PRE. i. 620 ff.

(a) The dominant idea in the views of Arius is the monotheistic principle of the Monarchians (cf. Athanas. c. Ar. or. iii. 7, 28 ; iv. 10).[2] There is One unbegotten God : "We know only one God, unbegotten." This axiom led to a keen criticism of the prevalent representations of the relation of Christ to the Father. The Son dare not be represented as an emanation (προβολή), nor a part of the Father having the same nature (μέρος ὁμοούσιον), nor as alike uncreated (συναγέννητος). For if the Father were compound, divided, or mutable (σύνθετος, διαίρετος, τρεπτός), we should have to think of him as corporeal, and be compelled to accept two uncreated beings (δύο ἀγέννητοι). The Son would then be a brother of the Father (ep. ad Al. and ep. ad Eus.; Athanas. c. Arian. or. 1. 14 ; iii. 2, 62, 67 ; de

---

[1] Also, ᾄσματά τε ναυτικὰ καὶ ἐπιμύλια καὶ ὁδοιπορικὰ γράψαι . . . εἰς μελῳδίας ἐκτεῖναι, Philostorgius h. e. ii. 2.

[2] Appeal was made, among others, to Hermas, Mand. i. (Athanas. in Theod. h. e. i. 7).

decr. syn. Nic. 10). (*b*) God alone is unoriginated, or unbegotten, without beginning. The Son had a beginning, and was from a non-existent state created by the Father before the beginning of the world : "The Son is not unbegotten, nor a part of the unbegotten One . . . nor from something previously existing, but he existed with will and design before times and ages, the complete, only-begotten, unchangeable God ; and before he began to be, or was either created or founded, he was not. The Son has a beginning, but God is without beginning . . . He is, out of things not being (ep. ad Eus.). God was not always Father, but there was [a time] when God was alone, and was not yet Father, and afterward he became Father. The Son was not always. For, all things coming into being from not being, and all things created and made having begun to be, this Logos of God also came into being from things not existing ; and there was [a time] when he was not, and he was not before he was begotten, but he also had a beginning of being created " (Thal. in Athan. or. 1. 5). (*c*) The Son is the Logos and the Wisdom of the Father, but he is to be distinguished from the Logos immanent in God. The latter is a divine energy ($\delta\acute{v}\nu\alpha\mu\iota\varsigma$), the Son a created divine being, having participation in the immanent Logos (cf. the Dynamistic Monarchianism). He says thus that there are two *sophias;* the one peculiar to God and co-eternal with him, and the Son was born in the *sophia*, and, sharing in it, he is called simply *sophia* and *Logos* . . . and he says thus also that there is another Logos besides the Son in God, and that the Son, sharing in this, is again by grace called Logos and the Son himself" (Athan. l. c. i. 5). (*d*) The Logos is, therefore, a creature of the Father, created by him as the medium in the creation of the world (ib. and ii. 24 ; ep. encycl. Alex. in Socr. h. e. i. 6). Accordingly, he is not God in the full sense of the word, but through his enjoyment of the divine favor he receives the names, God and Son of God, as do also others (" and although he is called God, he is yet not the true God, but by sharing in grace, just as all others also, he is called by name simply God," Thal. ib. 1. 6 ; cf. ep. Al. ad Al. in Theod. i. 3. p. 732). It is, therefore, clear that " the Logos is different from and unlike the substance ($o\dot{v}\sigma\acute{\iota}\alpha$) and peculiar nature ($\iota\delta\iota\acute{o}\tau\eta\tau o\varsigma$) of the Father in all respects" (Thal. ib.). (*e*) In view of the significance of this unoriginated character ($\dot{\alpha}\gamma\epsilon\nu\nu\eta\sigma\acute{\iota}\alpha$) for the divine nature of the Son, a further consequence is unavoidable. The Logos is by nature mutable. But since God foresaw that he would remain good, he bestowed upon him in advance the glory which he afterward as man merited by his virtue (Thal. in Ath. i. 5 ; cf. i. 35 init.; ep. Al. ad Al. in Theod. i. 3, p. 732 ; cf. ep. encycl. Alex. in Socr. i. 6 : muta-

ble, τρεπτός, and variable, ἀλλοίωτος, by nature).[1] The Arians
held, with Paul of Samosata, that Christ is through unity of will
one with the Father (Athan. c. Arian. or. iii. 10). (*f*) By
the use of profane logic (Athan. c. Ar. or. ii. 68) and by the
citation of passages of Scripture treating of the humility of
Christ (Alex. in Theod. i. 3, p. 740), the Arians sought to establish their own view and disprove that which was becoming the
accepted doctrine of the church. It was the easier to carry out
this purpose, since Arianism did not attribute a human soul to
Christ (see Greg. Naz. ep. ad Cledon. i. 7. Epiphan. ancor.
33).

If we contemplate this theory as a whole, we at once observe
its relationship with Paul of Samosata and Dynamistic Monarchianism. But the earlier views referred to, in the process of accommodation, became much worse. What Paul taught concerning the man Jesus, Arius—and apparently Lucian before him—
transferred to a median being, the Logos. It is not the man
Jesus who is endowed with divine energy (δύναμις) and preserves
it in a moral life, but the Logos—the man Jesus does not even possess a human soul. The Logos is, therefore, a " creature of God "
and yet "complete God." The unity of God is preserved, but
only at the price of teaching "that there are three persons
(ὑποστάσεις), Father, Son, and Holy Ghost" (ep. ad Al. in
Epiph. h. 69. 8). Thus a mythological element is introduced
into Christianity, and bare Monotheism is transformed into the
Polytheism of heroes and demigods; cf. Athan. c. Ar. or. iii.
15, 16), or there is thought to be a necessity, with Philo, for a
median being between the world and God (cf. ib. ii. 24).
Arius reminds us at many points of the old Apologists (§ 13),
but what was in their case apologetic art and necessity is here a
deliberate theory, set up in opposition to other views.

There is also the further difference, that by the Apologists
Christ, as the Divine Logos, is regarded as truly God ; whereas
Arius makes him but a rational energy created by God. If we
look for the inspiring motive of this doctrine—which is the worst
Christology imaginable—Athanasius is probably not wholly
wrong in regarding it as Samosatianism modified by lack of courage (ib. iii. 51 ; i. 38). Arius interpreted Paul of Samosata in
the sense of the subordinationistic utterances of Origen and

---

[1] That this was the view of Arius is beyond question. He veiled it in correspondence with Eusebius (see the ἀναλλοίωτος above), just as the direct
declaration of the temporality of the Son was avoided (see citations above,
and cf. ep. ad Al. in Epiph. h. 69. 8 : being born achronously, and also
Athan. c. Arian. or i. 13), or, despite the utterances above cited, Christ was
described to Eusebius as "complete God."

pressed every point thus gained to its extreme logical conclusion.

With great activity, political sagacity, and tact, Arius made provision for the propagation of his theory. He not only gained a following in Egypt, among bishops and virgins (see ep. Al. ad Al. init.), but he succeeded in winning the schismatic Meletians (Alex. ep. encycl. Sozomen. h. e. i. 15), and also found comrades among the bishops in Palestine and Syria (Theod. h. e. i. 3; Sozomen. h. e. 1. 115. The mighty co-Lucianist, Eusebius of Nicomedia (see his letters to Paulinus of Tyre in Theod. i. 5), became the patron of this doctrine.

3. The first to oppose Arius was the Alexandrine bishop, ALEXANDER. He really understood the new doctrine (see his account of it in Theod. h. e. i. 3 and Socr. h. e. i. 6). He points out that the Word cannot itself have come into existence in time, since all things were made by it (Jn. i. 3). His person (ὑπόστασις) is beyond the comprehension of men (or angels, cf. Isa. liii. 8 ; xxiv. 16). If Christ is the effulgence of God (Heb. i. 3), then to deny his eternity is to deny the eternity of the Father's light. The sonship (υἱότης) is, therefore, different in kind from that of human beings. The theory of Arius is related to the heresies of Ebion, Paul, and Artemas. Against it, Alexander regards the claims of the "apostolic doctrines of the church," *i. e.*, of the Apostles' Creed, as vindicated by his defense of the eternal divinity of the Son, together with that of the Holy Ghost (Theod. 1. 3, p. 745 f., 742). Less certain is his positive teaching. He appears himself to have at an earlier period recognized an existence of the Father before that of Christ ("and he exists therefore before Christ, as we taught in harmony with your preaching in the church," says Arius of him, Ar. ad Al. in Epiph. h. 69. 8). But he now taught concerning the Son : "Always God, always Son. . . . The Son exists unbegottenly (ἀγεννήτως) in God, always begotten (ἀειγεννής), unbegottenly begotten " (ἀγεννητογενής) (Ar. ep. ad Eus. in Epiph. 69. 3). He does not deny the birth of the Saviour ("that his unbegottenness is a property having relation to the Father alone ") ; but it is a birth "without beginning so far as the Father is concerned," an always being from the Father (τὸ ἀεὶ εἶναι ἐκ τοῦ πατρός). He is thus immutable and unvariable, and is rightly worshiped as is the Father. When John locates the Son in the bosom of the Father, he means to indicate "that the Father and the Son are two entities (πράγματα), inseparable from one another." There are in the person (ὑπόστασις) two natures (φύσεις). When the Lord declares himself one with the Father (Jn. x. 30), he wishes to make himself known as the

absolute image of the Father. The Son is therefore a nature
(φύσις) separate from the Father ; but, since he is untemporally
begotten of the Father, he is God as is the Father. This view is
not clear.

The whole controversy appears in the first instance as a
repetition of the Dionysian dispute. Alexander attributed to
Dionysius of Rome an emphasizing of the "apostolic doctrines," but we have no intimation that the opposition became
more pronounced.

4. It seems proper at this point to present connectedly the
teaching of ATHANASIUS [born before A. D. 300 ; died A. D.
373], which he maintained unswervingly and unyieldingly in a
long life, subject to constant assault and persecution. Such a
study will reveal to us the profoundest motives underlying the
great controversy.

SOURCES. Apologia c. Arianos ; expositio fidei ; de decretis synodi
Nicaenae ; Ep. ad episc. Aeg. et Lib.; apol. ad Constant. imperat.; apol. de
fuga sua ; hist. Arianorum ad monach.; ep. ad Serapionem de morte Arii ; ad
Serapionem, ep. ii.; de synodis Arim. et Seleuc.; and especially his chief work,
Orationes iv. c. Arianos. Opp. ed. Montfaucon, in Migne ser. gr. 25-28 ;
the most important also in Thilo, Bibl. patr. graec. dogmat. i. Compare
MÖHLER, Athanas., ed. 2, 1844. VOIGT, Die Lehre des Athanas., 1861.
ATZBERGER, Die Logoslehre des Athanas., 1880. PELL, Die Lehre des
Athanas. von der Sünde u. Erlösung, 1888. LOOFS, PRE. ii., ed. 3, 194
ff. HARNACK DG. ii., ed. 3, 155 ff., 202 ff. STÜLCKEN, Athanasiana, 1899.
HOSS, Studien über das Christentum u. die Theologie des Athanasius.

The strength of Athanasius lay in the following particulars : (1)
In the very great stability and genuineness of his character. In a
long life, amid persecution and oppression, he remained immovable in his adherence to the truth which he had grasped, without
resorting to political expedients and without any waverings.
(2) He stood upon a secure foundation in his firm grasp upon
the conception of the unity of God, and this preserved him from
the subordinationism of the Logos-Christology. (3) He, with
an unerring tact, taught men to recognize the nature of the person of Christ and its importance. He was able therefore to
understand Christ as the Redeemer and to define his nature in
accordance with the logical requirements of his redeeming work.
Just here is located the peculiarity of his Christology, which
assures it a permanent place in the teachings of the church.
Since Christ effects in us the new supernatural life, therefore he
must be God in the sense of the *homousia*. To understand the
biblical character of Athanasius's statement of the problem, we
need but recall the representations of John and the κύριος-
πνεῦμα of Paul.

(*a*) We notice first the denunciation of Arianism. Athanasius clearly recognized the unchristian and irreligious conclusions to which this doctrine leads. If Arius is right, then the triune God is not eternal ; to the unity was added·in time the Son and the Spirit. The three-foldness has come into existence from the non-existent. Who can assure us that there may not be a further increase? (c. Ar. or. i. 17, 18). According to Arius, baptism would be administered in the name of a creature, which can after all render us no aid (ib. ii. 41 ; iv. 25). But not only is the Trinity thus dissolved by the Arians ; even the divinity of the Father is imperiled. The Father has not always been Father—some change has taken place in him in the course of time, and he did not always have within him the Word, Light, and Wisdom (ib. i. 20, 24, 25). Further, Arianism leads logically to the polytheism of the heathen world. Only if the Son partakes of the same nature and substance as the Father, can we speak of One God. The Arians, on the contrary, have two different Gods : " It is necessary for them to speak of two Gods, one the creator and the other the created, and to worship two Lords," which leads to Greek polytheism (ib. iii. 15, 16).[1] This is illustrated particularly in the worship rendered to Jesus in the church. It is heathenish to worship the creature instead of the Creator (ep. encycl. 4), and, according to Rev. xxii. 9, worship is not to be rendered even to the angels (c. Ar. or. ii. 23): " Who said to them that, having abandoned the worship of the created universe ($\dot{\eta}$ $\varkappa\tau\acute{\iota}\sigma\iota\varsigma$), they should proceed again to worship something created and made?" (ib. i. 8, 38, 42 ; de decr. 11 fin.). But, above all, the Arian view destroys the certainty of salvation. If the Logos is mutable, as the Arians consistently maintain, how can he reveal to us the Father, and how can we behold in him the Father? " How can he who beholds the mutable think that he is beholding the immutable?" (ib. i. 35 ; cf. Jn. 14. 9). In this way man can never reach the assurance of salvation, of fellowship with God, the forgiveness of his sins, and immortality : " For if, being a creature, he became man, he as man remained none the less such as he was, not partaking of God ; for how could a creature by a creature partake of God? . . And how, if the Logos was a creature, would he be able to dissolve a decree of God and forgive sin?" (ii. 67 ; iv. 20). " Again, the man partaking of a creature would not be deified, unless the Son was truly God ; and the man would not be equal with the Father, unless he who assumed the body was by nature also the true Logos of the

---

[1] Cf. Basil. ep. 243. 4 : " Polytheism has conquered—with them [there is] a great God and a small God." Also Greg. Nyss., in his funeral oration for Basil, Mi. 46. 796. Aug. de symbol., 1. 2.

Father" (ii. 70). Finally, this median being (μεσίτης) between God and the world is an utterly useless and senseless invention. Neither is God too proud to come himself as Creator into direct touch with a creature, nor in that case would the matter be made any better by the supposed Logos, since at his creation also some median creature would have been necessary, and so on *ad infinitum* (ii. 25, 26; de decr. 8). Hence, if Christ is not the true God and one substance with the Father, then it is all over with the Trinity and the baptismal-symbol; then polytheism and the worship of creatures are again introduced into the church; then the salvation of Christian believers comes to naught; and yet, after all, no logically tenable position has been reached. Thus the theory of Arius is just as impious as it is unscientific.

(*b*) What then is the doctrine of Athanasius himself touching the divinity of the Son? (*a*) "And since Christ is God of God and the Logos, Wisdom, Son, and Power of God, therefore, One God is proclaimed in the Holy Scriptures. For the Logos, being the Son of the one God, is referred back to him from whom he is, so that Father and Son are two, yet the monad of divinity is unseparated (ἀδιαίρετος) and undivided (ἄσχιστος). Thus it might be said also that there is one original source of divinity and not two original sources, and hence, also correctly, that there is a monarchy . . . the nature (οὐσία) and the person (ὑπόστασις) are one" (c. Ar. or. iv. 1). These theses voice the conviction that the divinity of the Son must be understood with a distinct and conscious effort to guard the divine monad. No basis is left for the "second God." Athanasius was led to recognize the importance of this position by the conclusions which Arius had drawn from his "second God." He may, perhaps, have been influenced also by the significant part played by Sabellianism in Egypt (vid. supra, p. 168). In this case we have another illustration of the historical recognition of the element of truth lurking in a false theory. But the circumstance should not be overlooked that Athanasius labored in the West, where the consciousness of the unity of God was always more vivid than in the East, which was so unquestionably controlled by the formulas of the Logos idea. (β) But Athanasius will not recognize a Son-Father (ὑιοπάτωρ) with the Sabellians, nor a sole-natured (μονοούσιος) God, for the existence of the Son would thus be excluded. On the contrary, the independent and eternally personal existence of the Son is a fixed premise, always bearing in mind that we are not to think of "three hypostases separated from one another," which would lead to Polytheism. The relationship between the Father and the Son is rather like that between a fountain and the stream that gushes from it: "Just as a river springing from a fountain is not separated from it, although there are two forms and two names, so neither is the Father the Son, nor the Son the Father " (expos. fid. 2 ; c. Ar. or. iii. 4). (γ) This distinction, as well as the unity, finds expression in the term " oneness of essence " (ἑνότης τῆς οὐσίας). The Logos is a production, or generation (γέννημα), from the nature (οὐσία) of the Father (de decr. 3, 22, 23 ; c. Ar. i. 29). As to his relation to created beings, it follows that "the Son is different in origin and different in nature from created beings, and, on the other hand, is the same and of the same nature (ὁμοφυής) as the nature of the Father " (ib. i. 58 ; de decr. 23, 12 ; de syn. 53). As he is thus other-natured (ἑτεροούσιος) than created beings, so he is same-natured (ὁμοούσιος)[1] with the Father, i. e., he shares with him the one divine substance (the Son is ὁμοούσιος and of the οὐσία of the Father, ad Serap. ep. ii. 5 ; de syn. 40). But if this is the case, then the Logos is immutable and eternal (de decr. 23. 12). (δ) The Son comes forth from the Father by a begetting, or birth. In view of the unique character of the divine nature, we cannot here think of any outflow from the Father, nor any dividing of his substance. " The begetting of men and that of the Son from the Father are different. For the things begotten of men are in some way parts of those who beget them . . . men in begetting pour forth from themselves. But God, being without parts, is without division and without passion the Father of the Son. For neither does there take place any outflowing of the incorporeal One, nor any inflowing upon him, as with men ; but, being simple in his nature, he is the Father of the one and only Son . . . This is the Logos of the Father, in whom it is possible to behold that which is of the Father without passion or division " (de decr. 11). Nor is it as though "the Son was begotten from the Father by purpose and will " (c. Ar. iii. 59), for thus the Son would be again degraded to the position of a creature created in time, one which the Father first determined to make and then made (iii. 60-63). All things were created by the will of God, but out of the Son it is to be said : " He is outside of the things created by the purpose [of God], and, on the other hand, he is himself the living purpose of the Father, in which all these things come into being " (64). " But the Son of God is himself the Logos and wisdom, himself the counsel and the living purpose, and in him is the will of the Father ; he himself is the truth and the light and the power of the Father "

---

[1] Athanasius himself never attached a particular significance to this word (see, e. g., de syn. 41).

14

(65). As the very image (τὸ ἴδιον) of the Father's person
(ὑπόστασις),[1] he did not originate in an arbitrary act of the
Father's will (ib.). But this does not imply that the Son was not
desired by the Father. " For it is one thing to say : he was begotten by desire (βουλήσει), and another thing to say that the
Father loves his Son, who is the same in nature as himself, and
desires him " (66). The Son is thus related to the Father as
radiance to the light : "the living Counsel and truly by nature
a production, as the radiance is a production of the light " (67).
Father and Son are, therefore, two persons (the Logos is not
impersonal, ἀνυπόστατος, as the word of man, de syn. 41 fin.),
the Begetting and the Begotten ; but they are again, by virtue of
this same relationship, one—a divine Being : " The Father is
Father and not himself Son, and the Son is Son and not himself
Father, but the nature (φύσις) is one. For that which is begotten is not unlike him who begets, for it is his likeness (εἰκών)
. . . therefore the Son is not another God. . . . For if, indeed,
the Son as a begotten being is another, yet as God he is the
same, and he and the Father are one in the peculiarity and
structure of their nature and in the identity of the one divinity "
(ib. iii. 4). But this relationship of the Begetting and the Begotten is an eternal one : " The Father was always by nature
generating " (γεννητικός) (iii. 66). " It is evident that the
Logos is both of himself and always existent with the Father "
(1. 27).

Athanasius starts with the conception of the One divine Being,
but this one God leads a double life (as to the triune feature, see
below, d). As Begotten and Begetting, Son and Father stand
opposed to one another as two persons, but not as two Gods.
They are one nature (μία οὐσία), of the same nature(ὁμοούσιος).
In these declarations is really expressed all that the church had
believed and taught concerning Christ since the days of the
apostles : the one Godhead and the divine " I " of the Son.
The elements of truth in Monarchianism and in the popular
Christology, with their conceptions of the " second God," the
" divine part," and the Logos of the Father, are all here combined and the errors of thought and expression carefully avoided.
The ancient formulas can never recur in the church in the same
shape. Athanasius really furnished something new. He reduced
the manifold representations of Christ to a simple formula, and
he established the necessity of this formula firmly by displaying

---

[1] A discrimination between the terms, ὑπόστασις and οὐσία, is yet unthought
of by Athanasius, as manifest from this passage and others already cited. Cf.
de decr. 27 ; de syn. 41 ; ad Afros 4. Cf. Harnack, DG., ii., p. 211. The
same remark applies to the Nicene Creed.

its relation to the doctrine of redemption. Imperfections, of course, still remain. The theologian of to-day will find fault, in addition to the defectiveness of the scriptural proof, chiefly with the indefiniteness of the term οὐσία; he will not fail to observe that the one personal God of Athanasius is, after all, to a certain degree, only the Father '' ('' and thus there will be proclaimed in the church one God, the Father of the Logos,'' ad Epict. 9 fin.; '' the Father as the source '' (ἀρχή) and fountain (πηγή), ad Serap. ep. i. 28); and he will demand a more distinct recognition of the divine personality, as well as a proper application of the principle of historical revelation in connection with the life of Christ. The problem which Athanasius endeavored to solve thus becomes more complicated. But it will not be denied that Athanasius made the best possible use of the materials then at hand. And we can in our day, with the New Testament in hand, scarcely do otherwise than acknowledge the problem of Athanasius as one well worthy of our study, and—perhaps from other points of view, in other terms, and with other methods of proof—hold fast to the ὁμοούσιος.

(*c*) It was not the demands of logical consistency, forced upon him alike by the assaults of his opponents and by the requirements of his own position, which inspired Athanasius. The arguments, both positive and negative, by which he justifies his discussions are primarily of a religious nature (see p. 207), and it is precisely this fact which constitutes the novelty and importance of his view. Only if Christ is God, in the full sense of the word and without qualification, has God entered humanity, and only then have fellowship with God, the forgiveness of sins, the truth of God, and immortality been certainly brought to men. (*a*) This will become clear, if we consider the soteriological ideas of Athanasius. The Logos assumed human flesh (σάρξ) and became man. He was true God and true man (ib. ii. 70; iii. 32, 41, 30; iv. 35, 36). '' He became man, and did not enter into man,'' as, for example, he visited the Old Testament believers (iii. 30; ad Epict. 11). ''He who was God by nature was born a man, in order that both might be one '' (c. Apollin. i. 7). But the union (ἕνωσις) between the flesh (σάρξ), *i. e.*, the entire human nature (ad Epict. 8; c. Ar. iii. 30) and the divinity (θεότης) exists '' from the womb '' (c. Apol. i. 4), and the union is indissoluble, but without leading to any mixture (c. Apol. i. 6: '' In order that the body might be according to its nature, and again, without division, might be according to the nature of the divinity of its Logos.'' He ascended in the body, c. Ar. i. 45; i. 10: '' Shall it not suffice thee that the body in the undivided physical union with the Logos has been made his own? '')

The Logos was not therefore in some way transformed into the flesh (ad Epict. 8), but he is so related to human nature as to use the latter as his instrument. Hence, the works of the divine nature are accomplished through the flesh. But, on the other hand, inasmuch as this impassible flesh belongs to the Logos, we may attribute to it that which, strictly speaking, applies only to the human nature, since the divine nature is not capable of suffering. "Being God, he had a body of his own, and, using this as an organ, he became man for our sakes; and, therefore, the things properly spoken of [the body] are said of him, when he was in it, such as hunger, thirst, suffering, . . . of which things the flesh is susceptible; but the works peculiar to the Logos himself, such as raising the dead and making the blind to see, . . . he did through his own body, and the Logos bore the infirmities of the flesh as though they were his own, for it was his flesh, and the flesh assisted in the works of the divine nature, because it was in the latter; for it was the body of God" (c. Ar. or. iii. 31, 32, 35, 41; ad Epict. 5, 10, 11). We may therefore, in a certain sense, speak of the sufferings of the Logos. "For the things which the human body of the Logos suffered, the Logos, being one with it, transferred to himself, in order that we might be enabled to become partakers of the divine nature of the Logos. And it was a paradox, that he was a sufferer and not a sufferer—a sufferer, because his own body suffered and he was in it as it suffered; and not a sufferer, because the Logos, being by nature God, cannot suffer" (ad Epict. 6; c. Ar. iii. 37, 35). Hence Athanasius designates even the human acts of Christ as good deeds (κατορθώματα) of God (c. Ar. or. iii. 41; cf. ad Serap. ep. iv. 14: All things were connectedly, συνημμένως, done . . . for he spat like men, and his spittle was full of God), and he could speak of the "crucified God" (ad Epict. 10; cf. c. Ar. iii. 34), of worshiping the man Jesus (c. Apol. i. 6), and of Mary as the Mother of God (θεοτόκος).

(β) The object of this whole method of regarding the subject is to establish a firm foundation for the salvation (σωτηρία) of men. Inasmuch as Christ was really God, he could deify the flesh which he assumed; and inasmuch as this was really human flesh (c. Epict. 7), human nature has thereby been deified. "Man could not have been deified, unless he who became flesh had been by nature of the Father and his true and peculiar Logos. Therefore such a conjunction was effected, in order that to that which was according to the nature of the divinity he might join that which was by nature man, and the salvation and deification of the latter might be secure" (c. Ar. ii. 70). "For as the Lord, having assumed the body, became man, so

we men are by the Logos deified, having been taken into partnership through his flesh, and, furthermore, we inherit eternal
life " (ib. iii. 34). Accordingly, since Christ assumed flesh, he
assumed human nature, and thereby deified and immortalized it :
" From the holy and God-bearing Virgin he raised up the new
form and creation of Adam, making it his own by union
(χαθ' ἕνωσιν), and thus appeared the man Christ, God from
eternity, and we are members of Christ." 1 Cor. vi. 15 (c.
Apol. i. 13, cf. c. Ar. i. 43 ; ii. 61 ; iii. 33 ; iv. 36). He is
thus the second Adam (c. Ar. i. 44 ; ii. 65). The life of the
Lord is to be interpreted in the light of this purpose. He was,
according to the flesh, without knowledge, in order that to
his flesh, and thus to humanity, might be given power to know
the Father (c. Ar. or. iii. 38 ; ad Serap. ii. 9). He feared
death, in order that we might become free from the fear of
death and partakers of immortality (ib. iii. 54 ff.; cf. ii. 70).
He was baptized, anointed with the Spirit of God, received
grace, and ascended to heaven, in order that we through his
flesh might secure the Spirit, grace, and immortality (ib. i.
43-48). To all assertions of this kind must be added, to insure
a proper understanding, the words : " And all such things in the
flesh wholly for our sakes " (ib. iii. 34, 38 ff.; cf. iv. 6 : "for on
this account he became incarnate, that the things thus given to
him might pass over to us "). But this all happens to the flesh of
Christ, and thus to the human race, because that flesh is joined
with true divinity (ib. ii. 70, 67 ; iv. 36). Thus sin is destroyed (ἀνήλωται) and humanity becomes free from sin and immortal (ib. iii. 32 ; 2. 56).[1] Thus, too, we become a temple
and sons of God (i. 43 ; ii. 59), the Spirit of Christ dwells in
us and we are thereby made one with the Father (ii. 25). We
must in all these discussions avoid the erroneous idea that in this
deification of man Athanasius sees a magical process by which
the seeds of immortality are physically implanted in man. The
deification embraces, on the contrary, all the spiritual and mystical processes in which Christ operates by his word and his example upon the hearts of men (ib. iii. 19 ff.). What Athanasius
means to assert is that Christ dwells in us, and, by the power of
his Spirit, gives us a new, eternal life. But now, since God was
in Christ, and from him a divine life flowed out upon men, the
man Jesus has become in all things the representative of the

---

[1] To this end it was necessary that the Logos should himself dwell in the
race, for although "many were indeed holy and pure from all sin " (e. g.,
Jeremiah and John the Baptist), yet death reigned from Adam to Moses also
over those who had not sinned, after the similitude of Adam's transgression.
Similarly, c. Ar. iii. 33.

race, or the second Adam. His death is, therefore, the death of all, or he has given his body to death for all, and thereby fulfilled the divine sentence against sin (ii. 69). This guiltless self-surrender to death is designated as a "ransom of the sin of men and an abolition of death" (i. 45). He presented this ransom, or sacrifice, to God the Father, and by his blood cleansed us all from sin (ii. 7). Athanasius here adopts traditional ideas. His own thought remains clear. Since we have become one body with Christ, his death is our death, and his victory over death is ours: "All men being ruined in accordance with the transgression of Adam, the flesh of this one was first of all saved and set free, as being the body of the Logos itself, and thereupon we, as being of one body (σύσσωμοι) with him, are saved. . . . Having endured death for us and abolished it, he was the first man to arise, having raised up his own body for us. Furthermore, he having arisen, we also in our order arise from the dead on account of and through him" (ib. ii. 61). As in all these positions we can trace the influence of the general point of view above noted, so too in the passages in which Christ is represented as the only mediator of the knowledge of the Father (i. 12, 16; ii. 81), as the pattern of unvarying righteousness (i. 51), as the dispenser of the forgiveness of sins (ii. 67), and as the bestower of the Holy Spirit (iii. 23-25, 33; de decr. 14). But it still remains the matter of chief importance that, through the incarnation of the Logos, God himself has entered into the human race for abiding fellowship, and the latter have thereby secured grace and righteousness, the Holy Spirit, a new life, and with it immortality: "Therefore the perfect Logos of God assumes the immortal body . . . in order that, having paid the debt for us (ανθ' ήμῶν τὴν ὀφειλὴν ἀποδιδοὺς), the things yet lacking to man might be perfected by him; but there was yet lacking immortality and the way to paradise" (ii. 66).

That these are really Christian ideas cannot be doubted. They follow the Johannine type of doctrine, and, at the same time, one of the lines of Pauline teaching (cf. Ignatius, Irenæus, Methodius). That the apostolic conception of the gospel is here reproduced, however, in a one-sided way, can as little be questioned. Yet it remains true, that it is a religious and Christian foundation from which the views of Athanasius are logically developed. Christ is God, or we cannot have God dwelling and operating in us and be sure of our salvation,[1] i. e., of the new eternal life and the forgiveness of our sins.

---

[1] Harnack's estimate is: "This absurdity (i. e., 'the Logos-ὁμοούσιος-formula') Athanasius endured; he thus unwittingly offered up to his faith a yet

(*d*) We mention here by anticipation that Athanasius at a later period employed the same means to prove the Homousia of the Holy Spirit (vid. ep. iv. ad Serap. and cf. tomi ad Antiochenos). As against the opinion that the Holy Spirit is a creature (κτίσμα) or an angelic being (ad Serap. i. 10. 12), it must be remembered that something of different nature (a ἑτεροούσιον) would thus be introduced into the Trinity, and the latter thereby be destroyed, or transformed into a Diad (δυάς, i. 29). Whatever is true of the Son must therefore be true also of the Holy Spirit (i. 9, 20, 21). He is of like nature (ὁμοούσιον, i. 27), immutable (ἄτρεπτον, i. 26), and ἀναλλοίωτον, ib.). And, as in the case of the Son, this is manifest also from the nature of his work as attested by our experience. He sanctifies us, and enables us to participate in the divine nature (θεία φύσις, i. 23). " When now we are called partakers of Christ and partakers of God, the anointing within us bears witness and the seal, which is not of the nature of things made, but of the nature of the Son through the Spirit who in him unites us to the Father (cf. 1 Jn. 4. 13) . . . But if in the fellowship of the Spirit we become partakers of the divine nature, he would be mad who should say that the Spirit is of created nature and not of the nature of God. Therefore, indeed, they into whom he enters are deified; and if he deifies, it is not doubtful that his nature is that of God " (i. 24).

Such is the doctrine of Athanasius. It, in his judgment, faithfully reproduces the teachings of the Scriptures, as well as of the Fathers (*e. g.*, Ignat. Ephes. 7, cited in de syn. 47), the " great councils," the baptismal command, and the baptismal confession (ad Serap. ep. i. 28, 30, 33; ii. 8; iii. 6; c. Apol. i. 2; ad Epict. i. 3). Its profound religious basis, as well as its simplicity and consistency, must be evident to all.

5. We turn back in our study to present the historical course of the controversy and the conclusions of the Council of Nice, A. D. 325.

SOURCES. The DECREES OF THE COUNCIL in Mansi, Acta concil. ii. 665 ff. Ep. CONSTANTINE ad Alex. et Ar. in Eus. Vita Const. ii. 64-72 and account there given (ib. iii. 6-22). EUSEBIUS ep. ad Caesareens. in Theodoret. h. e. i. 11. ATHANASIUS, de decretis syn. Nic. and epistle to Afros. EUSTATHIUS, in Theod. h. e. i. 7. Further, the accounts of the later church historians : Socrat. h. e. i. 7-10. Sozomen. h. e. i. 16-25. Theodoret. h. e. i. 6-13. Philostorgius h. e. i. 7 ff.; ii. 15. Also Gelasius (ca. A. D. 476); Σύνταγμα τῶν κατὰ τὴν ἐν Νικαίᾳ ἁγίαν σύνοδον πραχθέντων, l. ii. (in Mansi, Acta concil. ii. 759 ff. Cf. the collection of decrees in Mansi, l. c. NEANDER,

greater sacrifice—the historical Christ " (DG. ii. 221). But the peculiarity of Athanasius which made his teaching normative for the future lay precisely in the fact that he strictly guarded the unity of God, and yet without wavering maintained the divinity of Christ—and of the historical Christ at that.

KG. ii. 790 ff.). Möller-Schubert, KG. i., ed. 2, 424 ff. HEFELE, Concilien-
gesch. i., ed. 2, 282 ff. BRAUN, de synode Nic. (Kirchengeschichtl. Studien
by Knöpfler, iv. 3). SEECK, in Ztschr. f. KG. xvii. 105 ff. 319 ff.

Already in A. D. 320 or 321, Alexander of Alexandria had
directed two ecclesiastical assemblies in Egypt against Arianism,
and it was condemned by them (Hefele, l. c. i. 268 ff.). Arius
was compelled to leave Alexandria. But the agitation was thus
only increased, as a synod in Bithynia enlisted in his cause (Soz.
i. 15). The Emperor Constantine now found occasion to take
part in the affair. He at first endeavored to treat it as an unimportant strife of words, and exhorted to mutual reconciliation,
as, in any event, no "one of the chief commandments of our
law" was in question (Eus. vit. Const. ii. 70). The emperor,
indeed, changed his opinion upon this point (ib. ii. 69, 71 and
iii. 12); but he remained faithful to the political interest in the
preservation of the unity of the church's faith, which had from
the first been his controlling motive (cf. vita Const. ii. 65 init.,
with iii. 17, 21). As the agitation continued to grow and
threatened to spread through the entire East (ib. ii. 73. Socr.
i. 8), he summoned a general council of the church to meet at
Nicaea. About 300 bishops (as to the number, see Hefele i. 291),
chiefly Orientals, but also Thracians, Macedonians, Achaeans, and
the Spaniard, Hosius of Cordova (Rome being represented by tw
presbyters) responded to the call (vit. Const. iii. 7). The order
of business and the course of the debate are alike obscure for us.
There were in the council many elements lacking in independence
(Socr. 1. 8). We can note with some measure of certainty three
groups. An Arian section led by Eusebius of Nicomedia (see
his view in Theod. h. e. i. 5), small in numbers (Theod. i. 6.
Soz. i. 20), first presented its confession of faith. This was rejected with indignation, and even the partisans of Arius, with
the exception of two, did not dare to adhere to it (Eustath. in
Theod. i. 7). A compromising party now entered the field.
Eusebius of Caesarea presented an indefinite Origenistic confession : "We believe . . . in one Lord Jesus Christ, the Logos
of God, *God of God, light of light, life of life, the only-begotten
Son, the first-born of all creation, begotten of the Father before all
the ages;* through whom also all things were made ; who for the
sake of our salvation was made flesh and dwelt among men, and
suffered and rose on the third day and returned to the Father,
and shall come again in glory to judge the quick and the dead,"
etc. (Eus. in Theod. i. 11). This confession, as the italicized
words indicate, has all the advantages and defects incident to a
compromise formula. The Homousians could find their views
expressed in it as well as the Arians (see Ath. ad Afros). Taken

as it stood, it undoubtedly presented the view of the majority. The emperor approved it, but wished an acknowledgment of the ὁμοούσιος (ib.). It is very probable that he was under the influence of Hosius (cf. Socr. iii. 7. Philostorg. i. 17), who, in turn, was in sympathy with Alexander, and for whom, as a Western man, the term presented no difficulty (vid. Tert., Novat., Dionys. of Rome, supra, pp. 124 f., 169 f., 172). A basis was thus furnished and a program mapped out for the third group, that of Alexander and Athanasius : " Under the pretext of the addition of the ὁμοούσιον, they composed the writing," writes Eusebius, (ib.). With the professed purpose of cutting away the foundation beneath the Arians, the confession of Eusebius was changed, and finally read : " We believe in one God, the Father Almighty, maker of all things visible and invisible. And in one Lord Jesus Christ, the Son of God, *begotten of the Father, only begotten*, i. e., *of the nature of the Father*. God of God, Light of Light, very God of very God, begotten, not made, of one substance with the Father, by whom all things were made, both things in heaven and things on earth ; who for us men and for our salvation came down and was made flesh and assumed man's nature, suffered and rose the third day, ascended to heaven, [and] shall come again to judge the quick and the dead. And in the Holy Ghost. *But the holy and apostolic church anathematizes those who say that there was [a time, ποτὲ] when he was not, and that he was made from things not existing, or from another person (ὑποστάσεως) or being (οὐσίας), saying that the Son of God is mutable, or changeable* " (ib.). The words which we have italicized indicate in what spirit this modification was undertaken. This formula was accepted, also for the sake of peace, though not without some delay, by the median party (Eus. l. c.). It became the confession of the council. Besides Arius, only five persons refused to sign it (even Eusebius of Nicomedia, who, however, was unwilling to approve the condemnatory portion). These were banished by the emperor.

Thus the Homousia of the Son became a dogma. When, indeed, we consider the immediate circumstances under which this dogma was adopted, it was but natural that the real struggle should only then begin. Nevertheless, the assembled representatives of the church had accepted the Homousia, and the emperor deemed it his duty to give legal force to the decrees[1] of the coun-

---

[1] In addition to the decision as to the Houmosia, decrees were adopted upon the question of the Passover (Eus. vit. Const. iii. 18-20), upon the Meletian (Socr. h. e. i. 9 ; cf. Canon 6) and Novatian (Can. 8) schism and upon a number of questions of church order and discipline (cf. Hefele, CG. i. p. 320-431).

cil, demanding obedience to them and punishing those who opposed them. The state church comes into power. The emperor summons the councils; the state guarantees traveling expenses and entertainment; the emperor, or an imperial commissioner, opens the councils and regulates the proceedings; and an imperial edict gives legal force to the decrees. It is for Church History to point out the significance of all this. A historical parallel to Constantine is seen in Augustus' work of restoration. Both served God and politics, and both crowned their work by the introduction of imperialism.

§ 21. *Further Development Until the Council of Constantinople,*
A. D. 381.

1. The strife and contentions of this period belong in their details to the sphere of Church History and Patristics. We must, therefore, be content with a brief general view of them.

The Nicene Creed was really, after all, but the confession of a minority. The letter of Eusebius to his congregation at Caesarea (in Theod. h. e. i. 11) indicates what skill was required to make it appear acceptable. According to this explanation, the ὁμοούσιος means no more than that "the Son is of the Father," and that "the Son of God bears no likeness to begotten creatures, but is to be likened in every way alone to the Father who begat him, and that he is not from any other ὑπόστασις, or οὐσία, but from that of the Father." The rejection of the Arian formulas was interpreted to mean that "he was the Son of God also *before his birth according to the flesh,* . . . he was dynamically in the Father before he was actually born."

2. It may be easily understood from this why the adoption of the Nicene Creed did not bring peace, but became the signal for a violent renewal of the conflict. The inner dialectics of the conflicts of the ensuing years were as follows : (1) The decision of the matter lay in the hands of the Origenists, *i. e.,* of the larger middle party. (2) Upon these the Arians at first depended in their effort to secure the revocation of the Nicene Creed, and thus restore the *status quo ante.* To this end the Origenists cast their influence with the Arians. (3) When the Nicene Creed had been set aside, the Arians began to push their own positive dogmatic views to the front. (4) The Origenists now parted company with them, and the elements attached to the *homousios* were more strongly emphasized in their opposition to the Arians. (5) The middle party now joined Athanasius. It may be said that, in the development of the movement, the same inner legalism proved influential which had produced the

result attained at Nicaea itself.   Since now, instead of the anticipated peace, the Nicene Creed but provoked further controversy, it is not to be wondered at that Constantine himself undertook to change the aspect of affairs.   Eusebius of Nicomedia
was permitted to return ; Arius defended himself to the satisfaction of the emperor (Socr. i. 26); the leaders of the Nicene
party, Eustathius of Antioch and Athanasius (who had been
since A. D. 328 bishop of Alexandria) were removed from office
and banished upon the ground of slanderous treatment of their
opponents (the former A. D. 330 ; the latter by the Council of
Tyre, 335, being sent to Treves in 336).   Constantine died A.
D. 337, shortly after the death of Arius had prevented the
solemn restoration of the latter to the fellowship of the church.

After the death of Constantine, Athanasius was permitted to
return ; but Constantius carried out in the East the ecclesiastical
policy of the last years of his father's life.   Athanasius was
again, in A. D. 339, compelled to flee, and proceeded to Rome.
The Eusebians (Eus. of Nic. had meanwhile become bishop of
Constantinople) were now in control in the East.   It was necessary to find a form of doctrinal statement which would at the
same time establish firmly their own view, and, out of regard for
the Western theologians, avoid extreme Arianism.   This was
secured by the Council held at Antioch A. D. 341 in connection
with the dedication of the church, and that held in the same city
A. D. 344, at which the *formula macrostichos* was prepared.
The formulas of these two councils (see Athan. de syn. 22 ff.)
approach the Athanasian view as closely as possible (''complete
God of complete God, begotten of the Father before the
ages''), and reject the statement that the Son had a temporal
beginning, or is from any other hypostasis ; but the ὁμοούσιος is
avoided.   Athanasius is not indeed directly assailed, but in the
person of the like-minded Marcellus of Ancyra (see the three
formulas of the former of these councils and the *formula macrostichos* of the latter).

3. In the West, on the contrary, the doctrine of Athanasius,
as also that of Marcellus, was unconditionally endorsed at the
councils at *Rome*, A. D. 341 (see the letter of Pope Julius in
Ath. Apol. c. Ar. 20-35), and *Sardica*, A. D. 343 (ib. 36-50).

This brings us to the peculiar teaching of one of the most
zealous of the Nicene party, MARCELLUS, bishop of Ancyra (s.
Eus. c. Marcel., from which are taken the fragments in RETT-
BERG, Marcelliana, 1794; cf. ZAHN, Marc. v. Anc., 1867).
This man is professedly a scriptural theologian.   Not the
''dogmas'' (''for the name, dogma, has something of human
counsel and knowledge,'' p. 21 A), nor the authority of the

Fathers (p. 21), but the Scriptures are decisive.   In the Arian
doctrine, like Athanasius, he sees disguised polytheism (p.
25 D ; 26 A ; 27 C, D ; 28 A ; 29 C).   From this it appears
that he is interested, no less than Athanasius, in preserving
the unity of God.   If we insist upon investigating the eternal
nature of Christ and his relation to the Father, we should take
for the basis of our study such terms as : Christ, Jesus, Life,
Way, Day (cf. Just. Dial. 150), Resurrection, Door, Bread—for
" this starts with that which is new in him and with his new relationship according to the flesh " (p. 92).   The same may be said
of the names " Son of God " (p. 54 B), " image of God " (p. 47
D).   His eternal nature finds expression only in the term Logos
(in John i. 1 ff.).   As the Word of God, he is eternal (p. 35 D).
This term expresses his entire pretemporal experience (p. 35 B ;
40 C).   To speak of the " generation of the Logos " is not
scriptural (p. 37 B), but conception applies to him as incarnated.   John furnishes us three items of knowledge : " Where
he says, in the first place : ' In the beginning was the Word,'
he shows that the Word is *in power* ($\delta\upsilon\nu\acute{\alpha}\mu\epsilon\iota$) in the Father, for
in the beginning of all things created [is] God, of whom are all
things ; and in the second place : ' and the Word was with
God,' that the Word is *in energy* ($\dot{\epsilon}\nu\epsilon\rho\gamma\epsilon\acute{\iota}\alpha$) with God, for all
things were made by him . . . ; and, in the third place : ' the
Word is God,' he tells us *not to divide the divine Being*, since the
Word is in him and he in the Word ; for the Father, says he, is
in me and I in the Father " (p. 37 A.).   The terms $\delta\acute{\upsilon}\nu\alpha\mu\iota\varsigma$ and
$\dot{\epsilon}\nu\acute{\epsilon}\rho\gamma\epsilon\iota\alpha$ are here used to designate the Logos as power reposing in
God and power in action, the $\dot{\epsilon}\nu\acute{\epsilon}\rho\gamma\epsilon\iota\alpha$ $\delta\rho\alpha\sigma\tau\iota\varkappa\acute{\eta}$ (p. 41 D.) (see
Zahn, p. 123 ff.).   The Logos is, therefore, on the one hand, a
personal power immanent in God, and, on the other hand, in
the interest of his historical work, he proceeds ($\dot{\epsilon}\xi\epsilon\lambda\vartheta\acute{\omega}\nu$,
$\dot{\epsilon}\varkappa\pi o\rho\epsilon\acute{\upsilon}\epsilon\tau\alpha\iota$, p. 167 f.) from the Father, but without thereby
changing in any way the first relationship.   We dare not start
with three hypostases and then combine them into a divine
unity :   " For it is impossible that three, being hypostases, be
united in a monad, unless the triad has first originated from a
monad " (p. 167 D).   How is it to be accounted for, upon the
Arian theory of two separated persons ($\pi\rho\acute{o}\sigma\omega\pi\alpha$), that the Holy
Spirit proceeds from the Father and yet is bestowed by the Son?
(ib.).   We have not to do with three different beings, but
the inexpressible relationship is to be regarded somewhat as an
extension of the one God :   " Not distinctly and evidently then,
but in a mystic sense, the *monad* appears extended to a *triad*, but,
continuing to exist, is in no way divided " (ib. cf. Dionys. of
Rome in Ath. sent. Dion. 17 and Tert. Apol. 21).   These are

Nicene ideas : the one God leads a three-fold life ; only that
Marcellus, with greater exegetical prudence, refrains from applying directly to the prehistoric life of the divine nature the
knowledge of God which we have historically gained.   This is
evident also from the following statements : When God proposed
to establish the church and set apart the human race for sonship
(p. 12 D), the Logos proceeded from the Father as actively engaged in the creation, preservation, and redemption of the
world.   Less than 400 years ago he became the " Son of God,"
Christ and King (p. 50 D).   At the end of the days, since his
kingdom shall become the kingdom of God, he will return into
God (p. 41 C ; 42 A ; 52 C), ruling with the Father.   What
will then become of his body, Marcellus confesses that he does
not know (p. 53 A).

The significance of this theology lies in the fact that it gave
the Eusebians the opportunity of continually bringing the charge
of Sabellianism against their opponents ; but, on the other hand,
the fact that it was recognized by the Homousians as orthodox (in
Athan. Apol. 32, 47) indicates how sincere they were in their devotion to the strictly monotheistic conception of God, and that their
controlling interest centered in the three-fold historical self-revela-
tion of God.   But this theory itself made no impression historically.
It was too original and archaistic to secure wide acceptance
(cf. Iren., p. 124 f.).   Athanasius (or. c. Ar. iv.) also attacked
the views of Marcellus without naming him, and, after reviewing them, had only ridicule for the oddities of the "old man "
(Epiph. h. 72. 4).   It was further disastrous for them that they
were interpreted even by contemporaries in the sense of PHOTI-
NUS of Sirmium (Epiph. h. 71), according to whom Christ was
only a supernaturally (per contra, Marius Mercator, opp. ed.
Baluz., p. 164) begotten man, in whom the Logos dwelt.   This
was really the doctrine of Paul of Samosata.   The Eusebians as
well as the Nicene theologians rejected it.

4.   PHOTINUS fell under condemnation (Council at Milan, A. D.
345 (?) and 347).   In other points the Western theologians, with
Athanasius, adhered to their views.   Constantius, held in check
by the Persians, was driven to the determination to recall
Athanasius (A. D. 346), and two prominent Eusebians, Ursacius
and Valens, deemed it prudent to make peace with Rome and
Athanasius (see Athan. Apol. 51-58).   On the other hand,
the (first) Sirmian Council in A. D. 347 (?) condemned Photinus,
indicating Marcellus as the source of his heresy (Hilar. frg. 2. 21-
23).   The death of Constans (A. D. 350), who had inclined to
the Nicene orthodoxy, changed the situation.   Constantine at once
applied himself with energy to the suppression of the Nicene faith.

The Orientals had already, at the (second) Council at Sirmium (A. D. 351), again made themselves felt.   The Sirmian formula here adopted is in the positive portion identical with the Fourth Antiochian formula (p. 219), but a large number of Athanasianisms (see Ath. de syn. 27 ; Socr. h. e. ii. 30 ; Hilar. de syn. 38. ; cf. Hefele CG., i. 642 ff.) are appended.   The latter are in the line followed hitherto by the Eusebians.   The favorite phrases of the Arians were rejected (n. 1. 24), and also the views of Photinus and Marcellus.   Subordinationism appears in n. 18 : " For we do not co-ordinate the Son with the Father, but he is subordinate (ὑποτεταγμένον) to the Father."   At Arles, A. D. 353, at Milan, 355 (at Biterrae, 356), the Western men were compelled to recognize the condemnation of the " sacrilegious Athanasius " (Mansi, iii. p. 236).   It was politically prudent to demand no more than this.   Those who resisted this (Eusebius of Vercelli, Dionysius of Milan, Lucifer of Calaris, the deacon Hilarius of Poitiers, Hosius of Cordova, Liberius of Rome) were banished.   Athanasius, deposed, fled into the wilderness, A. D. 356.   In response to protests, the emperor asserted : " But what I desire, that is canon " (Athan. hist. Arian. ad mon. 33 fin.).   The orthodox now regarded him as the Antichrist and a monstrous wild beast (e. g., Ath. l. c. 67, 64 ; Lucif. Bibl. max. iv. p. 247, 244, 246).

But victory is a most dangerous thing for a bad cause ; and this victory led to the downfall of Arianism.   Who then were these victors and what would they do ?   Now that their common opponent no longer compelled them to harmony of action, it at once became evident how uncertain and how various were their positive ideas.   One party spoke of the pretemporal and eternal birth of the Son, and asserted that he is like the Father in all things.   This was " the royal path " between Arius and Sabellius (thus Cyrill of Jer. Catech. iv. 7 ; xi. 4, 7, 10, 14, 17). They, therefore, strenuously advocated the Antioch formulas, except that they could not reconcile themselves to the ὁμοούσιος. They thought to substitute for it ὁμοιούσιος (Sozom. h. e. iii. 18). In other words : they were willing to agree with Athanasius in the result attained by him, but they reached it by a different path.   Instead of starting as he did from the one divine nature, they, dreading Sabellianism,[1] followed Origen in beginning with two divine persons.   But the result itself might thus be brought into question, as these formulas could be approved also by elements more in sympathy with the left wing, i. e., Origenistic and

---

[1] This is plainly seen in the question of the Anomæan in Apollinaris dial. de trin. (Draeseke, p. 264): " What does ὁμοούσιον mean ?   I understand this to teach that the Son and Father are not the same."

Arianizing tendencies.   These formed the party of the Semi-arians or Homoiusians.   But the consistent Arians now came out in opposition to this party, as well as to the Homousians, under the leadership of AËTIUS of Antioch (vid. discussion by him, "concerning the unbegotten and the begotten God," in Epiph. h. 76. 11), and EUNOMIUS of Cyzicus (a confession of faith and an apolegetic discourse in Fabricius, Bibl. graec. viii., and in Thilo, Bibl. patr. gr. ii. pp. 580-629 ; cf. Philostorg. h. e. iii. 15 ff.; iv. 12 ; v. 2 ; ix. 6 ; x. 6 ; v. 1, etc.).   Of Eunomius, Theodoret says : " He presented theology as tech-nology" (haer. fab. iv. 3); and this is a just comment.   Al-though it was, indeed, deemed proper to appeal to the authority of the Scriptures and the ancients (Eunom. Ap. 4, 12, 15 ; see the citations in Greg. Naz. or. 29, 18 and the discussion, or. 30), yet the thinking of these men was dominated by the profane logic which Athanasius had rebuked in Arius (cf. Greg. Naz. or. 27. 2).   God is the unbegotten ($\dot{\alpha}\gamma\acute{\epsilon}\nu\nu\eta\tau o\nu$).   If this is his nature, then the view that we may fully know God (Socr. h. e. iv. 7 ; Theod. haer. fab. iv. 3 ; Basil. ep. 235) is quite intelligible.   If now it be proper to designate the Son as begotten ($\gamma\epsilon\nu\nu\eta\tau\acute{o}\nu$, Eunom. Ap. 11, 12), then it necessarily follows that he is not God as is the Father, not derived from the substance of the Father, but as his creature, from his will (ib. 12, 15, 28).   But if the Son is the first creature of the Father, then it follows : "that he is neither $\dot{o}\mu oo\acute{u}\sigma\iota o\varsigma$ nor $\dot{o}\mu o\iota o\acute{u}\sigma\iota o\varsigma$, since the one indi-cates a beginning and a division of the nature, and the other an identity " (Eunom. l. c. 26 ; cf. Aët. l. c. 4).   Even a similarity ($\ddot{o}\mu o\iota o\nu$) is, in regard to the nature, impossible between the Begot-ten and the Unbegotten (Eunom. 11. 26), although we may speak of an imitative moral similarity (Eunom. ib. 24 and conf. fid. 3 : " This only one like, $\ddot{o}\mu o\iota o\nu$, to the Begetter . . . is not an unbegotten like to the Unbegotten, for the Creator of all things is alone unbegotten . . . but as Son to the Father, as the image and seal [*i. e.*, impression made by seal] of the whole energy and power of the Creator of all things, he is the seal of the Father's works and words and councils;" cf. Philostorg. vi. 1 and iv. 12).   This is all merely consistent Arianism, and when Euzoius of Antioch (A. D. 361) proposes the formula : " In all things the Son is unlike the Father," he is also but consistent (see similar utterances at the Council of Seleucia, in Hilar. c. Const. imp. 12).   Thus had Arius himself taught.

Yet the Nicene Creed still remained the doctrinal basis, and it was necessary to secure its abrogation.   This was accomplished by the Third Council of Sirmium, under Ursacius and Valens, who had long before again become Arians, in the Second Sirmian

formula (A. D. 357): "But as to that which some or many
thought concerning the substance, which is called *usia* in Greek,
i. e., that it be understood very expressly as *homousion*, or what
is called *homoeusion*, it is proper that no mention at all be made
and that no one teach it, for this reason . . . that it is not contained in the divine Scriptures, and that it is beyond the knowledge of man (Isa. 53. 8)". Furthermore, according to Jn. 14.
28, "There is no doubt that the Father is greater" (Hilar. de
Syn. 11). Western men, among them Hosius, now almost a
hundred years old, accepted this formula, and it was approved
by a council at Antioch, A. D. 358 (Sozom. iv. 12). Thus the
Nicene Creed, and the terms ὁμοούσιος and ὁμοιούσιος as well,
appeared to be banished from the world.

5. But the development of ideas cannot be forced backward
by decrees. At the council of Ancyra, under the leadership of
Basil of Ancyra (A. D. 358, see the decree of the council in
Epiph. h. 73. 2-11), it became evident that Arianism was not
the faith of the Eastern church. As a son, the Son is not a
creation of the Father (creator and creature are one thing, father
and son another, c. 3). On the contrary, he is in his nature—
in another way than other children of God—like the Father, in
his οὐσία and not only in his ἐνέργεια ("certainly, as Only-one
from Only-one, like in nature, from the Father," c. 5; "of
likeness to the Father according to nature," c. 8; "He had
the attributes of divinity, being according to nature incorporeal
(ἀσώματος), and like (ὅμοιος) to the Father according to the
divinity and incorporeity and energy," c. 9. "And if anyone,
professing to believe upon the Father and the Son, say that the
Father is not his Father of like nature but of like energy . . .
thus taking away his being truly a son, let him be anathema," c.
11. But also: "If anyone, saying that the Father is in authority and nature the Father of the Son, should say also that the Son
is of like or of the same nature (ὁμοούσιον δὲ ἢ ταυτοούσιον) as the
Father, let him be anathema," 11 fin.[1] These formulas won the
ear of the emperor (Soz. iv. 13 f.). The fourth council of
Sirmium now made an attempt, by means of the third Sirmian
formula (A. D. 358), to establish peace by the revival of the
fourth Antioch formula. It was hoped to confirm this peace at
the double council at Ariminium and Seleucia (A. D. 359) by
the presentation of a formula previously prepared at the Court
at Sirmium (the fourth Sirmian), which was a compromise

---

[1] In the dual arrangement of these anathemas, placing the Arian extreme
side by side with the Sabellian, there is very clearly revealed the basis of the
mistrust of the term, ὁμοούσιος. They were afraid of being led into Sabellianism. Cf. Ath. de syn. 12; Socr. h. e. ii. 39.

between the second formula of Sirmium and that of Ancyra :
" The term, *οὐσία*, on account of its having been used only by
the Fathers, but being unknown among the common people, occasions scandal because the Scriptures do not contain it—request
that this be done away with . . . ; but we say that the Son is
like, *ὅμοιον*, the Father in all things, as the Holy Scriptures declare and teach " (Ath. de syn. 8.   Socr. ii. 37).   The Western
men were here aiming at the restoration of the Nicene Creed ;
the majority of the Eastern men were Homoiusians.   But the
emperor's will prevailed in the end.   The formula, conforming
thus to some extent to Nicene ideas, was finally adopted, but the
"in all things " was dropped [1] (Ath. de syn. 30).   Cf. HEFELE,
CG. i. 697-722.

The Arians under Acacius of Caesarea and Eudoxius of Antioch (later of Constantinople) now held sway at the court.
The council of Constantinople (A. D. 360) was under their
control.   The *ὅμοιος*, as well as the condemnation of the *οὐσία*,
was again proclaimed.   Aëtius was turned adrift (but Eunomius
honored with the bishopric of Cyzicus).   The leaders of the
Semi-arians were deposed (Socr. h. e. ii. 41, 42).

6. The Arians had carried the day and harmony was established, but it was only in appearance.   Over against the Arians
still stood the Homousians (council of Paris, A. D. 361; see
Hilar. frg. 11 and Mansi iii. 357-362), and also the old middle
party, or Homoiusians, who were constantly approaching the
right wing.   We may learn their position from a treatise of
Basil of Ancyra (in Epiph. h. 73. 12-22): "The Son is like
the Father in all things (*κατὰ πάντα*), *i. e.*, according to nature
(*κατ' οὐσίαν*) as being spirit (*πνεῦμα*), and not merely in will "
(*κατὰ βούλησιν*) (ib. 13, 17, 18, 22).   The term used by the
Orientals, *ὑπόστασις*, is only designed to indicate the separateness of Father, Son, and Spirit, but by no means to lead to the
introduction of three gods.   " And do not let the name subsistences, *ὑποστάσεις*, trouble any.   For the Orientals speak of
hypostases, in order to indicate the subsisting and existing attributes of the persons (*τὰς ἰδιότητας τῶν προσώπων ὑφεστώσας καὶ
ὑπαρχούσας*).   For if the Father is spirit and the Son is spirit
and the Holy Ghost is spirit, the Son is not thought to be the
Father ; there subsists also the Spirit, who is not thought to be,

---

[1] This brought the formula into entire harmony with the Arians, who could
now, as necessity might require, emphasize either the likeness or the un-
likeness, according as they referred to the nature or the attributes.   See supra,
p. 222, and especially Philostorg. h. e. iv. 12 ; cf. Basil of Anc. in Epiph. h.
73. 13, 15, 22.   The rejection of the *ἀνόμοιος* by Acacius at Seleucia was,
therefore, in reality only a pretense.   Cf. Hilar. c. Constant. 14.

15

and is not, the Son, etc., . . . not saying that the three hypostases are three sources or three gods . . . for they confess that
there is one Godhead (θεότητα) . . . and one kingship and one
source [of all things]. Likewise, they reverently indicate the
persons by the attributes of the hypostases, regarding the Father
as subsisting in the paternal dominion, and acknowledging the
Son not as being a part of the Father, but as begotten and subsisting from the Father, perfect from perfect, and designating the
Holy Spirit . . . as subsisting from the Father through the
Son" (c. 16, cf. c. 12). The parallel with the incarnation, according to Phil. 2. 6 ; Rom. 8. 3, leads to the result, that Christ
as Spirit is the same as the Father, and as flesh the same as
human flesh ; but that, as an acting personality, he is like the
Father and like the flesh : "According to the conception of
spirit, the same . . . yet not the same, but like, because the
Spirit which is the Son is not the Father" (18). Here the
Homousia is really acknowledged, the ὅμοιος applying only to
the different personages : "For whatever the Father does, that
does also the Son, not in the same way as the Father does it, but
in a like way" (ὁμοίως) (ib.).

Constantine died A. D. 361, and Julian the Apostate became
his successor. The banished bishops, including Athanasius, were
permitted to return. The latter at once arranged for a council
at Alexandria (A. D. 362, see esp. Tomi ad Antiochenos, ep. ad
Rufinianum ; also Socr. h. e. iii. 7. Rufin. h. e. x. 27-29). As
early as A. D. 359 Athanasius had, in his report of the councils
of Rimini and Seleucia, called the Homoiusians brethren (de syn.
41-43 ; cf. 12, 53). Inasmuch as they confess "that the Son is
of the nature (οὐσία) of the Father and not of another hypostasis,
that he is not a being created or made," he recognized that they
have something to rely upon and are not far from the *homoousios*
(41), although it is not distinct and clear to substitute *homoios*
or *homoiousios* for *homoousios* ("because that which is like
(*homoios*) is said to be like not on account of the natures
(οὐσιῶν) [of the objects], but on account of their forms and
properties. Thus a man is said to be like a man, not according
to nature, but according to form and character, for in nature he
is same-natured," ὁμοφυεῖς, c. 53). The great bishop was concerned not for his formula, nor for any formula,[1] but for the real
matter at issue. This was evident also at Alexandria. Here the
justification of the "three hypostases" was approved, provided
these be conceived, not as different in nature (ἀλλοτριούσιοι) nor
as separate natures (διαφόροι οὐσίαι) nor even as three sources and

---

[1] Cf. his ridicule of the making of formulas in these years—De syn. 32.

gods; but as of the same nature (ὁμοούσιοι) (tom. ad Ant. 5); but the "one hypostasis" ·was also justified, since many hold that "it is the same thing to say ὑπόστασις or οὐσία (6). The condemnation of Arius, Sabellius, Paul, Valentine, Basilides, and Manichaeus throws light upon the situation (ib.). The council taught also the *homousia* of the Spirit (3, 5) in opposition to MACEDONIUS of Constantinople, who had declared the Holy Ghost to be a servant and assistant, like the angels (Socr. ii. 45 ; Sozom. iv. 27) and the human soul of Christ (7). Leniency is urged toward those who have erred from the truth (3, 8, 9), the avoidance of strife about words, and contentment with the Nicene formulas (8).

Athanasius was finally banished again by Julian, but recalled by Jovian (A. D. 363). Immediately a council at Alexandria (A. D. 363) again endorsed the Nicene Creed (Ath. ep. ad Jovian), and also, although with some reserve (ὁμοούσιος=ὅμοιος κατ' οὐσίαν), a council at Antioch (A. D. 363 : see Socr. h. e. iii. 25).

These transactions were of epochal significance for the History of Doctrines. (1) The combination of the middle party with the Homousians assures the defeat of the Arians. (2) The Nicene interpretation of the nature of the Holy Spirit assigns to the third person of the Trinity a fixed position in the theological system. (3) The incipient discrimination between *hypostasis* and *usia* will give rise to new problems. (4) The interpretation of the ὁμοούσιος in the sense of ὁμοιούσιος and of ὅμοιος κατ' οὐσίαν will engender new ideas foreign to those of Athanasius and the Nicene Creed.

7. The *Three Cappadocians* wielded the controlling influence in the following period :

Zealous Christians, and equally zealous Hellenists,[1] these men

SOURCES. BASIL THE GREAT of Caesarea († A. D. 379 ; opp. ed. Garnier et Maran, 1721 ff., de Sinner 1839, 1840, Migne gr. 29-32). His brother, GREGORY OF NYSSA († after A. D. 394 ; opp. ed. Fronto Ducäus, 1615-1618, Migne gr. 44-46. Separate writings in Oehler, Greg. Nyss. opp. i., 1865, and Bibliothek d. Kirchenväter, i. 1858. Mai, Script. vet. nov. coll. viii. 2. 1 ff.). GREGORY OF NAZIANZEN († A. D. 389 or 390; opp. ed. Clemencet et Caillou, 1778, 1842, Migne gr. 35-38. See also the most important of the works of these Fathers in Thilo, Bibl. patr. gr. dogm. ii.). Here belongs also a part of the writings attributed by Draeseke, although upon insufficient grounds, to APOLLINARIS OF LAODICEA, especially the Antirrheticus c. Eunom. Dialogi de trinitate and De trinitate. On the other hand, κατὰ μέρος πίστις belongs beyond question, as Caspari has shown, to Apollinaris. Vid. these documents in Draeseke, Apollinaris v. Laod., in Texte u. Unters. vii. 3, 4. The citations below are from this edition.

[1] See, *e. g.*, the correspondence between Basil and Libanius (Basil ep. 335-359), the sermon 22 of Basil (de legendis libris gentilium) and the funeral sermon of Greg. Naz. upon Basil (or. 43, c. 17-22).

sympathized with the religious positions of Athanasius and had appreciation at the same time for the scientific dogmatics of Origen.[1] They understood and interpreted Athanasius in the sense of Origenistic theology. In this consists their significance for us; for it was by this means and in this form that the positions of Athanasius were victorious in the Orient. What Origen had sought to accomplish appears again in these men—Christianity and philosophy were to form a covenant with one another. These men stood actually in a Christianized world, which, it would seem, should furnish the new and necessary modes and forms of thought for the combination of the truth of antiquity and the truth of the gospel. With the gospel in hand, they thought themselves prepared to Christianize philosophy. The dream thus cherished was, however, never realized.

(*a*) Athanasius starts with the one divine nature (οὐσία, or ὑπόστασις); the three-fold personal life within which, being a self-evident presupposition, he does not at all attempt to prove. The Cappadocians begin with the three divine hypostases (cf. Basil of Anc.) and attempt to bring these under the conception of the one divine *usia*. The terms, *hypostasis* and *usia* are now carefully discriminated, the former being understood as indicating the individual separate existence, and the latter the substance common to all (*e. g.*, Basil, ep. 38. 1-3 ; 9. 2 ; 125. 1 ; 236. 6. Greg. Nyss. in Oehler. Bibl. ii. 218 f., 236, 234. Cat. magn. 1 in. Cf. Apollin. dialogi, p. 266 f., 271).

(*b*) There should be recognized three divine ὑποστάσεις, or πρόσωπα : Father, Son, and Holy Ghost. The different names applied to them correspond to real differences : "According to which the hypostases are to be clearly and without commingling discriminated from one another" (Greg. Nyss. öhl. ii. 162). Each hypostasis has its peculiarity (ἴδιον, ἰδιάζον), or its property (ἰδιότης) or attribute (ἰδίωμα). Thus, "the ἴδιον of the Father is unbegottenness ; that of the Son, birth ; that of the Spirit, procession (Greg. Naz. or. 25. 16 ; 29. 2 ; 31. 29. Basil. ep. 38. 4-6 ; 105 ; 125. 3 ; 210. 4 ; hom. 15. 2. Greg. Nyss. cat. mag. 3. Apollin. l. c., pp. 255, 258, 269, 354). This difference must be distinctly and clearly observed. There are three individual persons, as were Paul, Peter, and Barnabas. It is Marcellian or Sabellian to speak of *one hypostasis* or *one prosopon*, instead of *one usia* (Basil. ep. 125. 1 ; 69. 2).[2] (*c*) But it is not by any means the purpose to subordinate one of these three persons to

---

[1] See the Philocalia and compare Basil's estimate of Origen, in Basil. de spirit. s. pp. 29, 73.
[2] In this criticism of Marcellus, all the points of difference with Athanasius (compare the latter's judgment in regard to Marcellus) are clearly seen.

the others in respect of divine nature or dignity. Divinity ($\vartheta\epsilon\acute{o}\tau\eta\varsigma$) belongs to them all in the same way, for they possess the same energy ($\dot{\epsilon}\nu\acute{\epsilon}\rho\gamma\epsilon\iota a$) and power ($\delta\acute{u}\nu a\mu\iota\varsigma$) (Basil. ep. 189. 7, 8. Greg. Nyss. öhl. ii. 180, 196 f. 204 ff. 202 f. : "The Holy Trinity does not act apart according to the number of the hypostases, but every exercise of the good will is one, and an order is observed, from the Father through the Son to the Holy Ghost;" cf. Apollin. dialogi, pp. 272, 279, 277, 306, 313). But if there is an identical energy ($\dot{\epsilon}\nu\epsilon\rho\gamma\epsilon\acute{\iota}a\varsigma\ \tau a\upsilon\tau\acute{o}\tau\eta\varsigma$) of the three hypostases, this implies their equality in dignity and nature (Greg. Nyss. ib. 182; Basil. ep. 189. 7). This is Origen's way of thinking upon the subject (supra, p. 149 f.). That which is common (the $\kappa o\iota\nu\acute{o}\nu$) is brought into association with that which is peculiar (the $\iota\delta\iota\acute{a}\zeta o\nu$, Bas. ep. 38. 5). Accordingly, we may speak of the divinity ($\vartheta\epsilon\acute{o}\tau\eta\varsigma$) or nature ($\varphi\acute{u}\sigma\iota\varsigma$, $o\dot{u}\sigma\iota a$) common to the three hypostases. There is a sameness of nature ($\tau a\upsilon\tau\acute{o}\tau\eta\varsigma$ $\tau\tilde{\eta}\varsigma\ \varphi\acute{u}\sigma\epsilon\omega\varsigma$, Bas. ep. 8. 3, 5). The hypostases are the same as to nature ($\tau a\dot{u}\tau\grave{o}\nu\ \kappa a\tau'\ o\dot{u}\sigma\acute{\iota}a\nu$, Greg. Naz. or. 30. 20). With the peculiarity ($\iota\delta\iota\acute{a}\zeta o\nu$) of the hypostases stands contrasted the community ($\kappa o\iota\nu\acute{o}\nu$) of the usia (Bas. ep. 210. 5. Greg. Naz. or. 29. 2). This relationship finds expression in the *homousios*. "Confessing the sameness of the nature, we accept also the *homousios*. . . For he who is by nature ($\kappa a\tau'\ o\dot{u}\sigma\acute{\iota}a\nu$) God is *homousios* to him who is by nature God" (Bas. ep. 8. 3; cf. Apollin. Dial. pp. 264, 267 ff.). This, he declares, asserts no more than that they are "by nature exactly alike" ($\acute{o}\mu o\iota o\nu$, Bas. ep. 9. 3).[1] Now that the idea of the separate hypostases stands in the foreground, the predicate in question receives a new shade of meaning: "They rightly say $\acute{o}\mu o o\acute{u}\sigma\iota o\nu$, in order to set forth the equality of nature in honor ($\tau\grave{o}\ \tau\tilde{\eta}\varsigma\ \varphi\acute{u}\sigma\epsilon\omega\varsigma\ \acute{o}\mu\acute{o}\tau\iota\mu o\nu$, Bas. ep. 52. 2). It is the same nature ($\varphi\acute{u}\sigma\iota\varsigma$) and dignity of divinity ($\dot{a}\xi\acute{\iota}a\ \tau\tilde{\eta}\varsigma\ \vartheta\epsilon\acute{o}\tau\eta\tau o\varsigma$), an equality of nature in honor, which belongs to the three hypostases (Greg. Naz. or. 31. 9, 10, 28; 29. 2). The *homousia*, therefore, indicates the same divine substance or nature, but in consequence of this also the same dignity or glory, in the three hypostases.

(*d*) Thus arises the idea of the Triune God—three persons in

---

[1] The homousios originally sounded strangely to Basil, as is evident from a letter to Apollinaris (Draeseke, p. 102): "To such an idea, it seems to me that the meaning of the exactly equivalent *homoios* is even better fitted than that of the *homousios*. For light having no difference at all from light in being more or less, cannot, I think, be rightly said to be *the same*, because, in its own circuit of existence, it is different, but it may be accurately and exactly said to be *like in nature*." Starting with this understanding, Basil interpreted the *homousios* in this sense, as appears above.

one Godhead. "The three one in divinity, and the one three in individualities" (ἰδιότησιν) (Greg. Naz. or. 31. 9 ; 28. 31 ; 39. 11, 12). The point of view which forms the basis of this conclusion is : " In order that the unmingledness (τὸ ἀσύνχυτον) of the three hypostases in the one nature and dignity of the God-head may be saved " (ib.), and " for God is not the more and the less, nor the former and the latter, nor severed in will nor divided in power . . . but undivided in the divided . . . the Godhead" (ib. 14). Thus the hypostatic distinction is pre-served, as well as the substantial unity : " But an indescribable and inconceivable (One) is discovered in these two things, the community and the distinction—neither the difference of the hypostases rending the continuity of the nature, nor the commu-nity as to substance dissipating the peculiarity of the marks of distinction" (Bas. ep. 38. 4). "The doctrine of piety knows how to behold a certain distinction of hypostases in the unity of nature" (Greg. Nyss. cat. m. 1). Hereby, it is claimed, is established the proper medium between Paganism and Arianism, as between Judaism and Sabellianism. Due recognition is given both to the unity and the multiplicity, to the nature (φύσις), and the persons (πρόσωπα) : " Just as he who does not acknowledge the community of the essence falls into polytheism, so he who does not grant the peculiarity of hypostases is brought under Judaism " (Bas. ep. 210. 5 ; de spir. s. 30. 77. Greg. Nyss. cat. m. 1, 3 ; c. Eunom. iv.; Mig. 45. 644). But the formulas thus attained brought with them new problems. The Arians loudly proclaimed that this doctrine, and not theirs, was polytheism. If the three persons, Peter, James, and John, are three men, we must then speak here also of three gods (Greg. Nyss. öhl. ii. 188 ; Bas. ep. 189. 2 f. ; Apollin., κατὰ μερ, etc., p. 374 f.). But the increasing mystery was not regarded as a cause of offense (see above), and it was believed that the argument drawn from application of the number One to God was met by appeal to the quantitative nature of the conception of number (Bas. ep. 8. 2 ; de spir. s. 17, 18. Greg. Naz. or. 31. 18 f.). In reply to the objection made, appeal was taken to the authority of the Scrip-tures, which speak of one God (Greg. Nyss. ib. p. 192), but especially to the argument, that it is only by a misuse of terms that three persons are called three men. The word ἄνθρωπος designates the common element (τὸ κοινὸν) of the nature. Hence, in three persons there is one nature (φύσις), one essence (οὐσία); and hence it follows that, " in very accurate speech it would also properly be said, one man " (Greg. Nyss. l. c. pp. 192, 210, 222, 224, 226, 236). From this Platonic idea it was inferred concerning God : " We call the Creator of all things one God, although he is contemplated in three persons, or hypostases" (ib. p. 236). It is a relationship like that which existed between Adam and Eve and Seth : " Do not the clay (Adam) and that which is cut off from it (Eve) and the fruit from it (Seth) seem to you to be the same thing ? How can it be otherwise ? Are not things of the same nature (ὁμοούσια) the same ? But how can it be otherwise ? Let it then be confessed also that things subsisting differently are admitted to be of the same nature " (Greg. Naz. or. 31. 11, 14, 15, 32. Bas. ep. 210. 4). The three are one God, but : " It is plain that not the person (πρόσωπον) but the nature (οὐσία) is the God " (Greg. Nyss. l. c., p. 222; cf. Apollin. dial. de trin. p. 270 : " Is there therefore one hypostasis ? No ") ; and : " The monarchy is not one which one person circumscribes . . . but one which equal dignity of nature determines and unity of purpose and sameness of action and agreement extending to the oneness of the things proceeding from it . . . so that although it differs in number it is not divided in essence " (Greg. Naz. or. 29. 2).[1]

(e) It is to be observed, finally, that the theologians here named zealously maintained the Homousia of the Holy Spirit, in this, too, following in the footsteps of Athanasius (supra, pp. 215, 227). Vid. especially Bas. de spir. s.; c. Eunom. iii. Greg. Naz. or. 31. Apollin. antirrh. p. 223 ff. 248 ff.; dial. de tr. p. 307 ff. They found in the prevalent usage the most various statements in regard to the Spirit. Some regarded him as an energy (ἐνέργεια); others as a creature (κτίσμα); others as God ; while still others thought it scriptural to refrain from any definite statement as to his nature (Greg. Naz. or. 31. 5. See also Cyril of Jer. cat. 16. 23, and compare the Macedonian in Apollin. with his oft-repeated question : " Where is it written, ' the Spirit is God ' ? " pp. 307, 324 f., 321, 323, 317, 328 f., 330). The earlier state of this doctrine (except in Irenæus—see p. 120 f.) is here but reflected. In opposition to this uncertainty it was not difficult—pressing forward upon the path once chosen—to prove that he is an hypostasis such as the Father and the Son, according to the Scriptures and the baptismal confession ; that he shares with them the same *energy;* and that to him belong accordingly the same divine nature (οὐσία) and dignity (ἀξία); that he is accordingly ὁμοούσιος, and is to be worshiped with the

---

[1] The Dialogi de trin. of Apollinaris are instructive in revealing this tendency to Tritheism. Here the deity is compared to the one humanity (ἀνθρωπότης) which belongs to the two hypostases, Peter and Paul (p. 272; cf. 254, 271 f.), or p. 281 : " Bishop, presbyter, and deacon are *homoousioi.* Hast thou not then confessed that Father, Son, and Holy Spirit are a *homoousion ?* "

Father and the Son (e. g., Bas. hom. 15. 3; 125. 3; de sp. s. 1. 3; 10; 11; 16; 19. 49; 21; 25. C. Eunom. iii. 1, 3. Greg. Naz. or. 31. 4 f., 7. 9 f., 12. Greg. Nyss. öhl. ii. 160, 170 ff. Apollin. pp. 327, 333, 334).[1] The specific character of his activity was seen in the completion and execution of the work of redemption. He unites the human race with the Logos, and imparts to it the gifts of God (Basil de sp. s. 15. 36; 16. 38; hom. 15. 3.[2] Greg. Naz. or. 34). His relation to the Father is described, in contradistinction from that of the Son (otherwise there would be two Sons), not as a generation, but as a sending forth (ἔκπεμψις) and a procession (ἐκπορεύεσθαι) (supra, p. 228). The formula, "from the Father through the Son," is also found (Basil c. Eunom. iii. 6. Greg. Naz. Apollin. dial. p. 213; cf. THOMASIUS D.G. i. ed. 2, p. 270 f.).

The modification which has here been made in the ancient Nicene doctrine is very evident. Athanasius (and Marcellus) taught the one God, leading a three-fold personal life, who reveals himself as such. The Cappadocians think of three divine hypostases, which, as they manifest the same activity, are recognized as possessing one nature and the same dignity. The mystery for the former lay in the trinity; for the latter, in the unity. It was with labor and difficulty that the latter guarded themselves against polytheism. But it was only in this way that the Nicene doctrines were, for the Orientals, freed from the taint of Sabellianism, and that the personality of the Logos appeared to be sufficiently assured. The Cappadocians interpreted the doctrine of Athanasius in accordance with the conceptions and underlying principles of the Logos-Christology of Origen. They paid, however, for their achievement a high price, the magnitude of which they did not realize—the idea of the personal God. Three personalities and an abstract, impersonal essence are the resultant. In this form the οὐσία and φύσις are a heavy weight upon the doctrine concerning God, for they are in conflict with the personality of God. It was a partial corrective of this that they, after all—inconsistently—identified the Deity with the

---

[1] Appeal was made not only to the scriptural arguments, but to the Fathers, Irenæus, Clement of Rome, Dionysius of Rome, Dionysius of Alexandria, Origen, Gregory Thaum., Firmilian, Meletius (vid. Bas. de sp. s. 29, 72-74).

[2] He enlightens all for the knowing of God, inspires the prophets, makes legislators wise, perfects priests, strengthens kings, restores the righteous, exalts the prudent, exerts gifts of healing, revives the dead, sets free the bound, makes children of the estranged. Such things he does by virtue of his birth from above. . . . By him the weak are strong, the poor become rich, the unpracticed in learning are wiser than the wise. . . . He dwells entire in everyone and he is entire with God. He does not as a servant administer gifts, but autocratically distributes benefits.

Father, which was again a relic of the earlier Subordinationism. The Father is the Deity as the Source whence the Son and the Spirit proceed : "The nature in the three is one: God ; but the union is the Father, from whom and to whom they are in their turn referred" (Greg. Naz. or. 42. 15 ; 20. 8. And especially : "For one and the same person of the Father, from whom the Son was born and the Holy Spirit proceeded. Wherefore also certainly the one who is the cause of the things caused by him you call One God, since he is also in them." Greg. Nyss. öhl. ii. 226 ; Apollin. κατὰ μερ. etc., pp. 373, 273).[1] Thus, in place of the conception of the *one-natured, three-fold* God had come the doctrine of the *like-natured triune* God. That Athanasius was able to endure the latter, without ever zealously supporting it or condemning Marcellus, as he was urged to do (see Bas. ep. 125), may be understood from the foregoing.

Such was the teaching of the men who regarded themselves as the inheritors of the Nicene Creed (Bas. ep. 52. 1).[2] They believed that the God whom we worship as above the angels (Bas. hom. 15. 1) must be apprehended precisely in the terms of these formulas: "In regard to the doctrine of God, the different usage of terms is no longer so harmless, for what was a little thing then, is a little thing no longer" (Greg. Nyss. Öhl. ii. 192). The conflicts of the age and the toying with formulas produced an overstrained conception of orthodoxy. These Fathers—in league with the world—framed orthodoxy in the Grecian mould.

8. It was only through manifold reverses that the new orthodoxy pressed on to victory. JULIAN was really indifferent (persecuting Athanasius as "the enemy of the gods," Theod. h. e. iii. 5 ; Jul. ep. 6). JOVIAN reigned only ten months. VALENS persecuted Homousians and Homoiusians alike (Theod. h. e. iv. 11 ff.; Socr. iv. 16). The East inclined more and more toward the orthodoxy of the West (embassy to Liberius of Rome ; council at Tyana, A. D. 367 ; see Socr. h. e. iv. 12 ; council at Antioch, A. D. 379 ; Mansi iii. 461 ff.). Basil the Great had now come to the front as leader. In the West, the Nicene orthodoxy had been able meanwhile to establish itself securely

---

[1] Apollinaris, indeed, also writes : "It is necessary not only that what the Father desires the Son shall also desire, but it is necessary that what the Son desires the Father shall also desire. Wherefore, the Son is placed after the Father in regard to those things which he desires and which are also enjoined, but which, if they are only enjoined, he even though not desiring, being under necessity, performs," Draeseke, p. 209 ; cf. Augustine.

[2] Cf. Apollin. dial. de trin. p. 264: "For when thou didst confess that the Son is *homousian* with the Father, then didst thou become a Christian ; " similarly, pp. 276, 280.

under VALENTINIAN and GRATIAN, and under the Roman bishop
DAMASUS (his first Roman council, A. D. 369 or 370, confesses
that " Father and Son are of one essence or substance, *essentiae
sive substantiae*, and also the Holy Spirit," Mansi iii. 444. The
Macedonians are also, upon the urgent desire of the Orientals,
condemned at Rome, A. D. 374 ; see Mansi iii. 488, and also
the Marcellians, A. D. 380 ; Theod. h. e. v. 11 ; cf. Hefele
CG. i., ed. 2, 739 ff. Rade, Damasus). THEODOSIUS THE
GREAT, in A. D. 381, established the Roman-Alexandrian orthodoxy in the East as the law of the empire (Cod. Theod. xvi.
1. 2 : " We believe in one deity of Father, Son, and Spirit,
under equal majesty and under a holy trinity. We command
that all who honor this law shall bear the name of Catholic Christians ; deciding that others, mad and insane, shall bear the in-
famy of heretical doctrine, to be punished, first, by divine vengeance, and afterward also by the avenging of our intention which
we have derived from the heavenly will ;" cf. 1. 6). The Apostles'
Creed and the Codex Theodosianus make the doctrine of the
Trinity the chief and fundamental dogma. But Theodosius, with
a prudent forbearance, recognized the new Oriental orthodoxy,
as is proved especially by the attitude which he assumed in favor
of MELETIUS of Antioch. Here had existed since A. D. 360
the much-talked-of schism between the homoiusian, neo-orthodox
Meletius and the old-orthodox Paulinus (s. Möller, PRE. ix.
530 ff.; cf. Harnack, DG. ii. 260, n.). The emperor summoned the former as the leader of the great final COUNCIL OF CON-
STANTINOPLE in A. D. 381. It was an assemblage of Oriental
bishops (Theod. h. e. v. 6 ; cf. Hefele CG. ii., ed. 2, 3). A hundred and fifty Orthodox and fifty-six Macedonian bishops (esp.
from the vicinity of the Hellespont) participated. The attempt
of the latter to win the day failed (Socr. h. e. v. 8). The council prepared an exhaustive treatise (τόμος) upon the orthodox
doctrine of the Trinity,[1] but framed no separate confession, being content to rest in the Nicene Creed, which had become the
shibboleth.[2]

---

[1] Perhaps the anathematizing paragraphs handed down as the first canon of
the council belong to this treatise (Tillemont, Mémoires, etc., ix. 221). They
profess allegiance to the Nicene Creed, and condemn the Eunomians or
Anomoeans, the Arians or Eudoxians, the Semi-Arians or Pneumatomachians,
as well as the Sabellians, Marcellians, Photinians, and Apollinarians. The
doctrine of Marcellus, which Rome had also in the meantime abandoned, is
here classed with Sabellianism.

[2] The so-called Niceno-Constantinopolitan (or simply Nicene) Creed is
not the confession of this council ; for (1) It is not mentioned as such before
the council of Chalcedon, A. D. 451 (see Greg. Naz. ep. 102 ; the council of
Constantinople, A. D. 382 ; the council at Ephesus). (2) The section upon

With this, the doctrine of Athanasius was acknowledged also in the East, though only in the interpretation above given. The West was not entirely satisfied with the solution reached. A desire was felt for a council, to be held, perhaps, at Alexandria or Rome (Mansi iii. 623, 630). But Theodosius summoned a second council at Constantinople, A. D. 382. At the same time a council assembled at Rome. The former addressed a letter to the latter, professing adherence to the Nicene Creed, with reference also to the council at Antioch and the *Tomus* of the preceding year (Theod. h. e. v. 9). The Nicene Creed had now gained the ascendency both in the West and in the East. The attempt of Theodosius, at Constantinople, A. D. 383, to win the Arians and Macedonians was a failure. From this time forward, the State was upon the side of orthodoxy and opposed to the Arians (Socr. v. 10; Sozom. vii. 12). Thus the civil argument prevails at the close, as at the opening, of the great controversy. The church won its first dogma, in the stricter sense of the term, when the teaching-church became also a state-church, and ecclesiastical doctrine became a part of ecclesiastical law. But this dogma was an outgrowth of the faith of the church at large. Arianism continued for a little while, but its

the Holy Ghost does not suit the circumstances of that time. (3) It is cited as early as A. D. 374 by Epiphanius (Ancorat. 119). But this is really nothing else than the baptismal confession of the church at Jerusalem, prepared probably by Cyril of Jerusalem (Cyr. cat. 5. 12). How it came to be attributed to the council of A. D. 381 cannot now be certainly known. A. D. 500 it came into general use, displacing the Nicene Creed. Cf. CASPARI in Ztschr. f. luth. Theol., 1857, p. 634; Sources, etc., i. HORT, two dissertations, 1876, and esp. HARNACK PRE. viii., 212 ff.; KUNZE, Das nicänisch-constantinopolitanische Symbol (BONWETSCH-SEEBERG, Studien zur Gesch. der Theol. u. der Kirche, iii. 3), 1898. It reads as follows : " We believe in one God, the Father Almighty, Maker of heaven and earth, and of all things visible and invisible. And in one Lord Jesus Christ, the only-begotten Son of God, begotten of the Father before all worlds, light of light, very God of very God, begotten not made, being of one substance with the Father, by whom all things were made ; who for us men and for our salvation came down from heaven and was incarnate of the Holy Ghost and the Virgin Mary, and was made man ; and was crucified also for us under Pontius Pilate, and suffered, and was buried, and arose on the third day according to the Scriptures ; and ascended into heaven, and sitteth on the right hand of the Father, and cometh again with glory to judge the quick and the dead ; of whose kingdom there shall be no end. And in the Holy Ghost the Lord, the Giver of life, who proceedeth from the Father, who with the Father and the Son is worshiped and glorified, who spake by the prophets ; in one holy catholic and apostolic church ; we acknowledge one baptism for the remission of sins ; we look for the resurrection of the dead and the life of the world to come." Compared with the Nicene Creed, it lacks the " of the substance of the Father" and the anathemas ; compared with the more recent doctrinal development, it lacks the ascription of the $\delta\mu oo\acute{v}\sigma\iota o\varsigma$ to the Holy Spirit.

day was past (Philostorg. h. e. xii. 11 ; Sozom. h. e. viii. 1).
It still made a passing demonstration among the German nations.

§ 22. *The Completion of the Doctrine of the Trinity.*

1. Before entering upon the controversy concerning the two
natures in Christ, we must briefly note the final settlement of
the Trinitarian dogma. JOHN OF DAMASCUS († after A. D. 754)
marks the close of the controversy in the East, and AUGUSTINE
(† A. D. 430) in the West.

Later Monophysites, such as John ASCUSNAGES and John PHILO-
PONUS carried out the Cappadocian doctrine on the basis of the
Aristotelian philosophy (φύσις and ὑπόστασις=genus and individual) to the extreme of Tritheism (vid. Joh. Damasc. de haer. 83 ;
Leont. de sectis act. v. 6 ; Phot. Bibl. cod. 75 ; Joh. of Ephes. h. e.
v. 1-12, translated by SCHÖNFELDER, who discusses the doctrine
on page 275 ff.). To break the force of these deductions from
the system, JOHN OF DAMASCUS presented the orthodox doctrine
in his standard dogmatic work, *De fide orthodoxa,* following
especially the Cappadocians, but guarding the unity of God
more distinctly than they had done (opp. ed. Lequin, in Mign.
gr. 91 ff.; cf. LANGEN, Joh. of Dam., 1879).

2. The views of John of Damascus may be summarized as
follows : Father, Son, and Spirit are one God, or one substance
(οὐσία, fid. orth. i. 2), but not one person (ὑπόστασις or πρόσωπον):
" It is impossible to say that the three hypostases of the deity,
although they are united to one another, are one hypostasis "
(iii. 5 ; cf. iii. 15, p. 233). This one God is the Creator, Preserver, and Ruler of the world : " one substance, one deity, one
power, one will, one energy, one source, one authority, one dominion, one kingdom, in three complete hypostases, to be acknowledged and worshiped with one homage . . . united without mixture and continuously separated " (i. 8, pp. 132, 139,
140). Hence the Logos is the same in nature (αὐτὸς κατὰ τὴν
φύσιν) with the Father (1. 6). Accordingly, the three hypostases, although always to be thought of as realities, are yet not
related to one another as are three men (i. 8, p. 138). They
are one, but different in their mode of existence (τρόπος ὑπάρξεως):
" They are one in all respects . . . except those of non-genera-
tion, generation, and procession. The distinction is in thought ;
for we know one God, in the exclusive peculiarities of paternity
and sonship and procession " (i. 8, p. 139). This relationship
may be further defined as a mutual interpenetration of the three
hypostases without commingling (according to Jn. 14. 11):
" The hypostases are in one another. They are in . . . not so

as to be commingled with one another, but so as to be contained in one another ; and they move about within one another without any coalescing and without juncture " (i. 8, pp. 140, 138). " For the deity is, to speak concisely, undivided in the divided (ἀμέριστος ἐν μεμερισμένοις), just as also, in three suns contained in one another and unseparated, there is one blending and mutual connection of light " (ib.).   Despite his radical rejection of Subordinationism, John of Damascus describes the Father as the Source of the Godhead (i. 7. 8), and accordingly represents the Spirit as proceeding from the Father, although, indeed, "through the Logos " (i. 12 ; per contra, vid. i. 8 fin.).   This way of viewing the subject, which is simply a relic of the Greek Subordinationism, prepared the way for the controversy, long continued and never fully concluded,[1] between the Roman and the Greek churches, upon the procession of the Holy Spirit (*filioque*).   See LANGEN, Die trin. Lehrdifferenz, 1876.   GASS, Symbolik der griech. Kirche, p. 152 ff.   KATTENBUSCH, Confessionskunde i., p. 323 ff.

3. The Western conception of the Trinity reached its final statement in the extensive and magnificent work of Augustine, *De trinitate*, which clearly re-states the Latin view of the Trinity—in its divergence from the Grecian, and which, by virtue of its method and the problems discussed, exerted a commanding influence upon the dogmatics of the Western church.[2]   The Occident, as we have seen, stood unwaveringly upon the side of the Nicene theologians (Athanasius and Marcellus).   The formulas of Tertullian were the means of preserving the recognition of the strict unity of God as not prejudicing in any degree the personal distinctions in his nature.   The prevalent theory was not Sabellian, nor was there thought to be any reason for suspecting the Alexandrine theology of a Sabellianizing tendency.   The Neo-Nicene orthodoxy was therefore, though tardily, acknowledged.

In this respect, Augustine is thoroughly Western in his point of view.   It is not the Greek theology, nor even, in reality, the Council of Nice, which is decisive for him, but the " catholic faith," *e. g.*, ep. 120. 17 ; in Joh. tr. 74. 1 ; 98. 7 ; 18. 2 ; 37. 6 ; de doctr. chr. iii. 1 (cf. REUTER, Aug. Studien, p. 185 ff.).

As to Augustine's doctrine of the Trinity : BAUR, Lehre v. d. Dreieinigkeit, 1841, p. 828 ff.   NITZSCH DG., i. 305 ff.   THOMASIUS, DG. i., ed. 2, 281 ff. A. DORNER, Aug., 1873, p. 5 ff.   BINDEMANN, Der heil. Aug. iii. 709 ff. GANGAUF, Aug. spekulat. Lehre von Gott, 1865.

[1] Cf. the Russian Catechism (Schaff, Creeds of Christendom, ii. 481 f., 461) and the negotiations between Old Catholics and Greeks at Bonn, A. D. 1874, reported in REUSCH, p. 26 ff.
[2] See the brief outline of the contents in Book xv. 3, § 5.

The basis of Augustine's theology is the unity of God. The Trinity is the one and simple God, "not therefore not simple, because a Trinity " (de civ. dei xi. 10 ; de trin. v. 7. 9 ; viii. 1 ; de fid. et symb. 8. 20). "The Trinity itself is, indeed, the one God, and one God in the same sense as one Creator " (c. serm. Arian. 3). Accordingly, there belongs to the one triune God one substance, one nature, one energy, and one will : "The works of the Trinity are inseparable" (ib. 4; de trin. ii. 5. 9; Enchirid. 12. 38 ; de symb. 2 ; c. Maxim. ii. 10. 2 ; in Joh. tr. 18. 6 ; 20. 3, 7 ; 95. 1 ; 21. 11). These ideas are carried out to the fullest extent. Even the theophanies of the Old Testament are not referred exclusively to the Son (trin. ii. 15 ff.). The Son (and the Spirit) even takes an active part in his own *missio* into the world, since this was not accomplished otherwise than through "the Word of the Father :" "The incarnation . . . was effected by one and the same operation of the Father and the Son inseparably, the Spirit, indeed, not being separated from it ; " cf. Matt. 1. 18. "Since the Father sent him by his Word, it was brought about by the Father and his Word that he was sent. Therefore by the Father and the Son was sent the same Son, because the Son himself is the Word of the Father " (trin. ii. 5. 9). But the fact that it is just the Son (and Spirit), and not the Father, who is sent, is not because they are inferior to the Father, but because they proceed from him (ib. iv. 20. 27 ; c. serm. Ar. 4, cf. de symb. 9 and opp. viii. 1636). Father, Son, and Spirit are, therefore, not three persons different from one another in the sense in which three human persons differ although belonging to one genus (in Joh. tr. 39. 2 f.; 91. 4). On the contrary, each divine person is, in respect to the substance, identical with the others, or with the entire divine substance : "For Father, and Son, and Holy Spirit together are not a greater essence (*essentia*) than the Father alone or the Son alone, but these three substances, or persons, if they be so called, are together equal to each one alone " (de trin. vii. 6. 11 ; viii. 1 ; vi. 7. 9 ; 10. 12 : "Neither are two something more than one." In this sense, of the identity of substance, the term ὁμοούσιος is used in Joh. tr. 97. 4). It is plain that Augustine's entire conception of the unity of God leads inevitably to the recognition of his personal unity. Augustine felt this, but for him—and long afterward—a distinct enunciation of this truth was prevented by the triadic application of the term person (cf. de trin. vii. 4. 7 ; 6. 11).

The One (personal) God is thus for Augustine an established fact. No less certain is it, however, that there are three persons in the one God. Here lay for him, as for Athanasius, the greatest difficulty—the real problem. These are related to God, not as species to genus, nor as properties to a substance. Every quantitative or qualitative distinction is excluded (*e. g.*, trin. v. 5-6; vii. 3-6; v. 11; viii. 1). On the contrary, this terminology is designed to indicate the mutual inward relationship between the three: "They are so called, not with respect to substance, because they are thus called, not each one of them as related to himself, but as related mutually and the one to the other; nor with respect to property, because what is called Father and what is called Son is eternal and immutable in them. Wherefore, although to be Father and to be Son are two different things, yet there is not a different substance; for they are called thus, not with respect to substance, but with respect to that which is relative, which relativity is yet not a property, because it it is not mutable" (trin. v. 5, 6; 8-9; viii. 1 init.; cf. "Another, not other (*alius non aliud*)," civ. dei. xi. 10. 1). The one God is never either Father only nor Son only, but the three forms of existence of the one God, each requiring the others, are Father, Son, and Spirit. They are hence substantially identical—the relation of dependence between them is a mutual one. The Father, who commands the Son, is no less dependent upon him than is the latter upon the Father (c. serm. Ar. 3). Father, Son, and Spirit behold in themselves the entire undivided Deity, only that it belongs to each of them under a different point of view, as generating, generated, or existing through spiration. "Father and Son, therefore, know one another mutually, but the one in begetting, the other in being begotten" (trin. xv. 14-23). Between the three hypostases exists the relation of a mutual interpenetration and interdwelling (trin. vi. 7. 9). For the designation of this relationship, the term *persona* (or *substantia*) does not altogether satisfy Augustine. "Nevertheless, when it is asked, What are the three? human speech at once toils with great insufficiency. Yet we say, three persons, not in order to express it, but in order not to be silent" (trin. v. 9, 10).[1]

That, with this conception of the Trinity, the Holy Ghost is regarded as proceeding not only from the Father "but from both at once," follows as a matter of course (xv. 17. 29; in Joh. tr. 99. 6).

According to Augustine, then, the one personal God, from an inward necessity, leads a three-fold, mutually-related personal

---

[1] The whole passage is important in elucidating the terminology of Augustine. He translates μίαν οὐσίαν, τρεῖς ὑποστάσεις: *unam essentiam, tres substantias;* but decides for the formula: *Unam essentiam vel substantiam, tres autem personas.* Cf. vii. 5. 10, where, appealing to Ex. 3. 24, he prefers *essentia* to *substantia.*

life. The attempt is made to explain this view in a number of analogies, and thus prove the possibility of the three-fold life in the one God. These analogies are drawn from the human soul, because it was made in the image of God. Thus there is a trinity in sight (" thing seen, vision, intention of the will uniting the two" (trin. xi. 2. 2 ; cf. xv. 3. 5); in thought ("thus there is this trinity in memory, and inner vision, and the will which unites the two," ib. xi. 3. 6); in the human spirit (ix. and x.; xv. 3. 5 : "mind, and knowledge by which it knows itself, and love by which it esteems itself and its knowledge—memory, intelligence, will"); in love (ix. 22 : "that which loves, that which is loved, and love itself"). These analogies not only give expression to the idea that three are equivalent to one, which the ancient teachers sought to illustrate from nature (cf. in Aug. de fid. et symb. 9. 17), but they present the idea of a harmonious spiritual entity, impelled and controlled from a three-fold centre. In this there was a distinct advance upon the representations of the older theologians, which constantly wavered between the unity and the trinity. Augustine made it impossible for later ages to overlook the fact, that there can be no Christian doctrine of the Trinity which is not at the same time an unequivocal confession of the one personal God. "Thrice have I said God, but I have not said three Gods ; for God thrice is greater than three Gods, because Father, Son, and Holy Spirit are one God " (in Joh. tr. 6. 2 ; cf. serm. 2. 15. 8 ; *trina unitas*). Augustine did not conceal his deep realization of the inadequacy of all these attempted explanations. He closes his work with the words : " Lord, our God, we believe in Thee, the Father and the Son and the Spirit. For Truth would not have said, Go, baptize, etc. (Matt. 28. 20), unless Thou wast a Trinity. . . . I would remember Thee ; I would know Thee ; I would love Thee . . . Lord, Thou one God, divine Trinity, whatsoever I have written in these books by suggestion of Thee, the One, mayest Thou the Three accept, if anything of myself, mayest both Thou the One and Thou the Three overlook it" (xv. 21. 51).[1]

Such is Augustine's doctrine of the Trinity. In it is collected a wealth of psychological observations and profound speculations. Theorists have hence always returned to it anew. It is but the more noticeable on this account that it really exerted but a slight influence upon practical piety. This is accounted for by the fact that the Augustinian theory was concerned only with the *imma*-

---

[1] Ambrose represented the Trinity in a way more in harmony with the Cappadocian ideas : three persons who are one by virtue of their " one substance, divinity, will, law." See de fide ad Grat. i. 2. 17-19 ; iii. c. 12, 26 ; ii. 8. 73 ; 10. 86 ; iii. 14. 108 ; iv. 6. 68 ; 8. 83, etc.

nent Trinity, without deducing this from the view-point of the *economic* Trinity; whereas a practically religious conception of the Trinity can be secured only from a contemplation of the revealed Trinitarian activity of God. It was because Augustine did not start at this point, that he was compelled to confess that men in theory acknowledged allegiance to the absolutely One, Triune God, whereas their practical ideas were always tinctured with Tritheism. But, despite this, what a wealth of ideas and views has this doctrine of Augustine bequeathed to the church!

4. This Augustinian conception of the Trinity was—in its fundamental features—embodied for the Western church in the so-called Athanasian Creed, or *Symbolum Quicunque*:[1] "That we worship one God in Trinity and Trinity in Unity, neither confounding the persons nor dividing the substance. For there

[1] The mention of this symbol, which was not produced until a later period, at this point is justified by the fact that it contains the theology of Augustine.

Of the recent literature we cite: KÖLLNER, Symbolik i., 1837. FFOULKES, The Athan. Creed, London, ed. 3. LUMBY, History of the Creeds, ed. 3, 1887. SWAINSON, The Nicene and Apostles' Creeds, etc., 1875, p. 195 ff. OMMANNEY, The Athan. Creed, 1875, and Early History of the Athan. Creed, 1880. G. MORIN in La science catholique, 1891, 673 ff., and in the Revue bénédictine xii., 1895, p. 385 ff. BURN, The Athan. Creed and Its Early Commentaries (Texts and Studies, ed. Robinson, iv. 1, 1896). HARNACK DG., ii. 298 ff. LOOFS PRE. ii. ed. 3, 178 ff.

The origin of the symbol, despite the most diligent efforts of scholars in recent years to discover it, is still unknown. It is evident that it has no relation to Athanasius. The following relatively certain data throw some light upon the question: (1) The manuscript copies of the text carry us to the eighth century. (2) The ancient expositions would lead us still further back, if the *Expositio fidei Fortunati* (Burn, p. 28 ff.) can be attributed to Fortunatus († ca. A. D. 600), whom one manuscript represents as the author, while another manuscript names Euphronius the presbyter, who was bishop of Treves A. D. 555-572. But the crediting of this Expositio, which would otherwise come to us anonymously, to two men who were personal acquaintances is very remarkable, and the apparently probable solution, that Euphronius as presbyter (hence about A. D. 550) composed it, must still remain uncertain. (3) Parallels to the formula of the Creed appear in great numbers in Southern Gaul. Especially important is the Pseudo-Augustinian *Sermo 244*, which has from ancient times been attributed to Cæsarius († A. D. 542). But an *Expositio* discovered by Caspari in two Paris manuscripts (Anecdota i. 283 ff.) shows close relationship to *Sermo* 244, but does not contain the parallel to the Quicunque. On this account the originality of *Sermo* 244 is assailed. Caspari, Zahn, and Kattenbusch, however, zealously defend it. But if *Sermo* 244, in the form in which it appears in Pseudo-Augustine, was really composed by Caesarius, we then must here recognize, not only anticipations of the Quicunque, but an acquaintance at this early day with a completed formula. Such a formula must then have existed as early as about A. D. 500. (4) Vincent of Lerins, when he wrote his *Commonitorium* in A. D. 434, had no knowledge of the Creed (Loofs). (5) A council at Autun, at which Bishop Laodegar (A. D. 659 to ca. 683) presided, expressly mentions the "creed (*fidem*) of Saint Athanasius, the president." Thus at this time

16

is one person of the Father, another of the Son, another of the Holy Spirit; but the Godhead of the Father and of the Son and of the Holy Spirit is one, the glory equal, the majesty coëternal. Such as is the Father, such is the Son, and such the Holy Spirit. . . . And yet there are not three eternals, but one eternal; just as there are not three uncreated nor three unbounded, but one uncreated and one unbounded . . . not three omnipotents, but

already the Creed bore at Autun the name of Athanasius. (6) The codex Paris, 3836, dating from the eighth century, cites among canonical material a Christological rule of faith which is intimately related to §§ 28-40 of the Quicunque, but which varies considerably in the wording. But the writer of the Paris codex had before him a Treves manuscript. From the fact that the Christological part of the symbol stands by itself in this document, it has been inferred that this second part was added later to the above-cited trinitarian portion (Swainson, Lumby, Harnack). But Loofs (p. 186) has correctly surmised that the part of the Treves manuscript cited by the writer beginning: " Domini nostri, Jesu Christi fideliter credat," is merely a fragment torn from § 27 of the Quicunque. From this he infers that there was a page wanting in the Treves manuscript in the hands of the Paris writer, and that he (about A. D. 750) had no knowledge of the Quicunque, or he would not have copied this. This is supposed to disprove the so-called two-source theory. Yet this entire argumentation does not appear to be at all decisive. The very circumstance that the creed designated as Athanasian at Autun about A. D. 670 should have been unknown to this writer of A. D. 750 is sufficient to shake our confidence in the conclusion. Nevertheless, the suggestion with which Loofs starts is correct beyond question; but the inference drawn by him is false. The proper inference can only be : Since a librarian living about the middle of the eighth century would be familiar with the Athanasian Creed, and it was such a man who transcribed the Christological part, he must have been yet in ignorance of this portion of the document. This might be said already of the writer of the Treves Codex. Thus the two-source theory concerning the codex of Paris, 3836, receives, in my opinion, an important support. It commends itself also from the fact that the transition from the first to the second part (§ 27) plainly betrays the attempt to artfully unite two documents in hand. Compare also § 40. It is evident, for example, that, according to the first part, the *fides catholica* embraces nothing more than faith in the Trinity (§§ 1-3). To this § 27 adds that it is necessary to eternal salvation that one believe *also* in the incarnation ; while in § 28 the confession of the divinity and humanity of Christ is presented as the content of *fides recta*. This is evidently something new, which was not in view when § 3 was composed.

The history of the Quicunque must accordingly be somewhat as follows: The first part was composed from formulas of Augustinian theology for the elucidation of the Apostles' Creed. It may have attained a fixed form by about A. D. 500, and in South Gaul. But, in addition to this formula, there was also a second and Christological one, which was not much later in its appearance. It was probably bound up with the first named as early as the seventh century. Yet toward the middle of the eighth century there were scholarly people who knew nothing of the Christological formula. But, with this exception, the combination of the two formulas must be regarded as a fixed fact. Since the time of the Carlovingians, we find the Quicunque making its way into liturgies and then co-ordinated with the other two symbols as the Creed of Athanasius (Anselm, ep. ii. 41. Alex. of Hales, Summa iv. quest. 37, § 9, etc.). Thus the Reformers were also led to accept the symbol.

one omnipotent. . . . The Son is the only (son) of the Father ; not made, not created, but begotten. The Holy Spirit is of the Father and the Son, not made nor created nor begotten, but proceeding. . . . In this Trinity there is nothing before or after, nothing greater or less ; but the whole three persons are co-eternal together and coequal, so that in all things, as has been said above, both the unity in trinity and the trinity in unity is to be worshiped. Whoever, therefore, wishes to be saved, let him think thus concerning the Trinity '' (§§ 3-26).

CHAPTER II.

THE DOCTRINE OF ONE PERSON AND TWO NATURES IN CHRIST.

§ 23. *Origin of the Controversies Upon the Two Natures of Christ.*

1. Two things had been transmitted by tradition as fixed : the reality of the humanity of Christ, with his human activity and sufferings (recognized in conflict with Docetism in the second century), and the reality and Homousia of his divinity. Divinity and humanity are now combined in one person ; there is a synthesis (σύνθετον, Origen), but as to the question how this union was conceivable, especially how two personal natures can constitute one person, there was no further investigation, despite the propositions put forth by the Dynamistic Monarchians. Only the West possessed, in Tertullian's view of one person in two substances, a formula which appeared to adequately meet the situation, and which had been confirmed by the fuller development of the doctrine of the Trinity. Western theologians, with this theory in hand, felt themselves relieved from the necessity of further investigation, and in the conflicts of the succeeding era they presented it as an adequate solution of all the questions raised in the Orient.

2. This was the situation when APOLLINARIS OF LAODICEA (born about A. D. 310) carefully stated the Christological problem and, at the same time, presented a clear and challenging attempt at its solution. The learned bishop was prominent as a humorist as well as noted for his acquaintance with the Scriptures and his intellectual acuteness.

Of his writings, the following are here of interest : The treatise attributed to Gregory Thaum., κατὰ μέρος πιστις; de divina incarnatione, frg.; die pseudo-Athanasian, περὶ τῆς σαρκώσεως τοῦ θεοῦ λόγου, and a number of fragments, vid. DRÄSEKE, in Texte u. Unters. vii. 34. CASPARI, Alte und Neue Quellen, etc., p. 65 ff. Further, in opposition : Athan. c. Apol. (genuineness questioned); cf. in Epiphan. h. 77 ; Greg. Naz. ep. ad Nectarium, epistolae ad Cledonium; Greg. Nyss. Antirreheticus c. Apol.; Theodoret Eranistes dial. 5 ; haeret. fab. iv. 8.   Theodore of Mopsuestia, frg. from his c. Apol. et de Apollinari.   Compare DORNER, Entwicklungsgesch. d. Lehre v. d. Pers. Christi, i. pp. 975-1036. LOOFS PRE. ii. ed. 3, 177 ff. BURN, the Athan. Creed, Texts and Studies iv. I. G. KRUEGER, PRE. i., ed. 3, 671 ff.

(a) The Christology of this enthusiastic champion of the ὁμοούσιος took its form in opposition, both to the Arian doctrine of the mutability of the Logos and that of the external juxtaposition of the two natures of Christ, as taught by the Antiochian " Paulinizing" (Paul of Samosata) theologians, who " say that the man that is from heaven is one, confessing him to be God, and the man from earth is another, saying that the one is uncreated, the other created " (ad Dionys. ep. p. 348 ; cf. ep. ad Jov. p. 342 ; cf. p. 381). The idea of the God, Christ, held his thought in positive thralldom. On the one hand, it was his aim to so construct Christology that no shadow of mutability might fall upon Christ. But this appeared to be possible only if this man was really God—if there was in him no free human will (de incarn. pp. 383, 387, 388). Otherwise, he would be subject to sin (fid. conf. p. 393 and Athan. c. Apol. i. 2 ; ii. 6, 8 ; Greg. Nyss. Antirrh. 40. 51 ; Greg. Naz. ad Cled. i. 10) and the redeeming death of Christ would be only the death of a man (de inc. p. 391 ; in inc. adversar. p. 395). On the other hand, the outward juxtaposition of the two natures does not help to overcome the difficulties. It is impossible to make the divinity and the humanity combine in their entirety into one person (de inc. pp. 384, 388, 389, 400). Two persons (πρόσωπα) would be the necessary result (ib. 387, 392). "That two complete things should become one is not possible " (Athan. c. Apol. i. 2). We would thus be led to a fabulous being like the Minotaurs or Tragelaphs, or we would be compelled to introduce a quaternity instead of the trinity (Greg. Nyss. antirrh. 42). Only because the flesh (σάρξ) of Christ is one person (πρόσωπον) with his divinity is it possible to worship Jesus without, at the same time, worshiping a man (pp. 389, 349, 350). Only thus is redemption a work of God. (b) From this it follows that the immutable divinity of Christ and the unity of the Redeemer's person can be preserved only by yielding the integrity of his human nature. Arius and his followers had, with a purpose diametrically opposite to that of Apollinaris, maintained the same position (in order to make all evidences of mutability or infirmity in Jesus applicable to the Logos), *i. e.*, that Christ was not made man, but only became incarnate, and therefore assumed only a human body and not also a human soul (see Confes. of Eudoxius in CASPARI, l. c. iv. p. 180 ; Athan. c. Apol. ii. 4 ; Greg. Naz. ad Cled. ep. ii. 7 ; Epiph. ancor. 33 ; cf. supra, p. 203). This same inference Apollinaris now drew with a different purpose and in a different sense. He regarded the trichotomy of man's nature as established by 1 Thes. 5. 23 (de inc. pp. 382, 388, 390). The Logos assumed the body and soul of a man, but the divine Logos itself took the place of the spirit (νοῦς) or intellectual soul (ψυχὴ νοερά). " Christ, having, besides soul and body, a divine spirit, *i. e.*, mind, is with reason called the man from heaven " (de inc. pp. 382, 401). Hence it may be said : " Thus the one living being consists of a moved and a mover, and is not two, nor composed of two, complete and self-moving beings " (de inc. p. 384); and thus Christ is one person with one personal life in mind and will and energy, *i. e.*, the purely divine (pp. 349, 399, 400, 401). " For, saying that ' the Logos became flesh,' he does not add, ' and soul ; ' for it is impossible that two souls, a thinking and a willing, should dwell together in the same person, and the one not contend against the other by reason of its own will and energy. Therefore the Logos assumed not a human soul, but only the seed of Abraham " (de unione, frg. p. 401 ; cf. 396). The difficulties are thus overcome : " For God, having become incarnate, has in the human flesh simply his own energy, his mind being unsubject to sensual and carnal passions, and divinely and sinlessly guiding the flesh and controlling the fleshly emotions, and not alone unconquerable by death, but also destroying death. And he is true God, the unfleshly appearing in the flesh, the perfect one in genuine and divine perfection, *not two* persons (πρόσωπα), nor two natures (φύσεις). There is one Son ; both before the incarnation and after the incarnation the same, man and God, each as one. And the divine Logos is not one person and the man Jesus another " (κατὰ μερ. πιστ. pp. 377, 378). (*c*) But since Apollinaris in this way found in Christ one person, one harmonious being, he could also speak of his one nature (φύσις) and one substance (οὐσία) (*e. g.*, 341, 348, 349, 352, 363), the Logos being unseparated and undivided (ἀχώριστος καὶ ἀμέριστος) from his flesh (pp. 395, 396) and yet also distinguish two natures (de trin. pp. 358, 360): " For as man is one, but has in himself two different natures . . . so the Son, being one, has also two natures " (p. 358). Since this illustration from the nature of man is a proper one, it follows also that the relation of the two natures (συνάφεια, pp.

344, 346, 351, 367) is not to be conceived as a change (μεταβολή) nor as a mixing (σύγκρασις) and confounding (σύγχυσις) (c. Diodor. p. 366 sq.), for the Deity remains immutable (pp. 347, 393). (*d*) Apollinaris drew yet another notable inference from his premises, teaching, in a certain sense, a pre-existence of the σάρξ of Christ, appealing to Jn. 3. 13 and 1 Cor. 15. 47—not as though the Logos had the flesh already while in heaven and brought it with him to the earth (*e. g.*, Ath. c. Ap. i. 7 ; ii. 10 ; Greg. Naz. ep. ad Nect. 3, ad Cled. i. 6 ; Greg. Nyss. antirrh. 13 f.), for this Apollinaris expressly denied (ep. ad Dionys. pp. 348, 349).[1] But he wrote : " The man Christ pre-exists, not as though the spirit, *i. e.*, the divine Spirit, were that of another than himself, but in such a way that the divine Spirit in the nature of the divine man was the Lord " (de inc. p. 382 f.). Although this is obscure in some points, the meaning can scarcely be other than that the Logos was from all eternity predestined to become man, and was, in this sense, the pre-existent heavenly man.

Such was the teaching of this great bishop, which he, as an earnest exegete,[2] endeavored to establish upon biblical authority. "This man is certainly also God. If Christ had been only man, he could not have saved the world ; and if only God, he could not have saved it through suffering. . . . If Christ had been only man, or if only God, he could not have been a middle one between men and God. The flesh is, therefore, an organ of life adapted to sufferings according to the divine counsels, and neither are the words of the flesh its own nor its deeds, and, having been made subject to sufferings as is suitable for flesh, it prevailed over the sufferings through its being the flesh of God." He believed that he was not in reality in conflict with the "dogmas" of the church in his day,[3] but in this he was self-deceived.[4]

---

[1] Epiphanius, indeed, heard this view expressed by pupils of Apollinaris (h. 77. 2, 14).

[2] This (cf. Hieron. vir. ill. 104) is shown, *e. g.*, in the sensuous Chiliasm of Apollinaris (see Basil. ep. 263. 4 ; Greg. Naz. ad Cled. ii. 4).

[3] See ep. ad Dionys. p. 351 : " We are not divided on account of these expressions. For to pretend that the things in the expressions which differ from the dogmas agree with them would be wicked ; but to pretend that the things in the expressions which agree with the dogmas differ from them would be vain and foolish. But let those having this agreed upon, that Christ is God incarnate, and that he is from heaven and earth, in form a servant, and in power God, remain in unity, and neither be foolishly separated nor fall into the logomachy of the heretics, but rather esteem highly the simplicity of the church."

[4] Nor was Apollinaris able to free himself from the bonds of the Antiochian theology. Its statement of the problem remained regulative for him, and he could find no way to escape their solution of it except at the terrible price of the surrender of the human νοῦς of Christ. He substituted the human

From the decade A. D. 370-380, the Cappadocians assailed his views (see already Ath. c. Apol. and, perhaps, the Alexandrine Council of A. D. 362 ; tom. ad Antioch. 7). They were moved to opposition chiefly by their general sense of the integrity of the human nature of Jesus, as he is depicted in the Gospel narratives, and of its significance in the work of redemption. Only if Christ had a human mind ($\nu o \tilde{v} \varsigma$), could he redeem also the human mind—an idea which, from the standpoint of the deification theory of the Greek Soteriology, was not a mere phrase. On the contrary, the Athanasian Christology was against Apollinarianism : " If anyone imagines a man without a mind, such a one is really inconceivable and altogether not worthy to be saved. For that which cannot be added to cannot be cured ; but that which is united to God is already saved. If the half of Adam fell, it was the half also which was added to and saved ; but if the whole [Adam] fell, the addition was made to the whole that was born, and he was wholly saved " (Greg. Naz. ep. ad Cled. i. 7. Greg. Nyss. antirrh. 17). Apollinarianism was condemned at the councils of Rome, A. D. 374 and 376 ("If therefore the whole man was lost, it was necessary that that which was lost should be saved "), and also at Constantinople, A. D. 381.

3. But this did not answer the question raised by Apollinaris. It failed to explain how two personal natures could exist in one person. Apollinaris had stated the Christological problem for the ancient church. Its solution was attempted from two directions.

We must first note the view of the Antiochians, which had stirred Apollinaris to opposition. It was they who for some years manifested the deepest interest in the question (see Diodor. of Tarsus, † bef. 394, frg. in Marius Mercator in Gallandi Bibl. viii. 705. Theod. of Mopsuestia, † 428, dogmat. frgg. esp. from de incarn. and c. Apol. in Swete, Theod. comm. on ep. Pauli ii. 289-339 ; also Theodoret, see excerpts in Mar. Merc.). (a) A settled point is here the Homousia of the Logos. The Logos, by his birth from Mary, assumed a complete man as to nature, consisting of "soul and mind and flesh" ($\psi v \chi \dot{\eta}. \nu o \varepsilon \rho \dot{a}. \sigma \acute{a} \rho \xi$—Theod. expos. fid. p. 328). We are, therefore, to acknowledge in Christ two complete entities ($\tau \acute{\varepsilon} \lambda \varepsilon \iota a$). This applies to the nature ($\varphi \acute{v} \sigma \iota \varsigma$) as well as to the person ($\pi \rho \acute{o} \sigma \omega \pi o \nu$): "When we attempt to distinguish the natures, we say that the person of the man is complete and also the person

"flesh" for the complete human being controlled by the Logos, because he was as little able as the Antiochian theologians to understand the divine-human nature and life of Christ (cf. also Cyril. ad reginas ii. 55).

of the deity " (Theod. de incarn. viii., p. 300). We can speak
of the deity as becoming man, only in appearance : " For when
he says ' he took ' (Phil. 2. 7) . . . he speaks according to the
reality ; but when he says ' he became ' (Jn. 1. 14), he speaks
according to appearance ; for he was not transformed into flesh "
(ib. ix., p. 300). (*b*) Since, therefore, the integrity of the
two natures, especially that of the actual and developing human
nature, must be preserved (Diod. p. 705), the conclusion was
reached that the Son of God dwelt within the son of David.
This was illustrated by examples. The Logos dwells in Jesus,
somewhat as God dwells in a temple, or as he dwelt within the
Old Testament prophets, or even, as in all Christian believers, but
it is emphasized that this occurs in another but a uniquely complete and permanent way in the case of Jesus (Diod. p. 705.
Theod. de inc. xii. c. Apol. iii., pp. 303, 313). The Logos
dwelt in the man Jesus "from his very first formation " on
throughout his whole life, " conducting him to perfection "
(Theod. c. Ap. iii. 2, p. 314). It is hence, not a natural, but
a moral union which exists between the two—not "according to
essence " (οὐσία), but " according to good pleasure " (εὐδοχία).
The man Jesus desires what God desires. Through him the Deity
becomes efficient. There is one willing (θέλησις) and one
energy (Theod. ep. ad Domn. p. 339). " But the unity of the
person is to be seen in this, that he does all things through himself, which unity has been effected by inhabitation, which is according to good pleasure " (Theod. de incarn. vii., p. 297). This
unity has become an indissoluble one, and has attained its completion through the ascension of Jesus ("making him immutable
in the thoughts of his mind, but also in the flesh incorruptible
and indissoluble," Theod. p. 326 ; de incarn. xiv., p. 308).
(*c*) In view of this connection (συνάφεια) of the two personal
natures through their unity of will,[1] we may speak of the one person : " For the natures are discriminated, but the person made
complete in the union is one " (Theod. de inc. viii., p. 300).
"The manner of this union, according to good pleasure, preserving the natures unmingled, shows also that the nature of the
two is inseparably one, and the will one, and the energy one, in
consequence of the abiding of one control and sway (αὐθεντίας

---

[1] The lineal relationship of Paul of Samosata, Lucian—Arius, Diodorus—
Theodorus—is here plainly traceable ; Christ, a man united with God through
unity of will—a demi-god thus joined with God—a man, thus one person
with the personal Logos. The theory became step by step more orthodox,
but the difficulties in its fundamental structure were not thereby solved.
Theodorus, indeed, declares Paul to have been an "angelus diaboli" (pp.
332, 318).

καὶ δεσποτείας) in them" (Theod. ad Domn., p. 339). Thus
there are seen to be two different natures ("each of the natures
remaining indissolubly by itself—the natures being discriminated"—de inc. viii., p. 299), but in their combination they
are one person ("the natures combined into one person according to the completed union"—ib.; "difference of natures and
unity of person," ib., p. 302 ; "the reason of the natures unconfused, the person undivided," ib. p. 292). But, in further explanation, the union of man and wife as "one flesh" is cited
(ib. and p. 324); or, it is even said : "The one receives blessing, the other gives it!" (de inc. xi., p. 302).

(*d*) Upon this basis, the personal unity is little more than an
assertion. According to it, in the sufferings of Christ "the deity
was indeed separated from him who suffered (according to
Hebr. 2. 9, citra deum=χωρὶς θεοῦ), . . . yet it was not absent
according to love from him who suffered" (Theod. pp. 325,
310). The worship of Jesus is, therefore, possible only in so far
as the worshiper combines in his thought his humanity and his
divinity. "We adore the purple for the sake of him who wears
it, and the temple for the sake of him who dwells within it—the
form of a servant for the sake of the form of God" (Diodor. l. c.;
Theod. pp. 308, 309, 316, 329). Thus also Mary, the mother
of the man, can only in this metaphorical sense be called the
mother of God (Diod. ib.; Theod. de inc. xv., p. 310 : "for
she was mother of man by nature, since he who was in the womb
of Mary was man, . . . but mother of God, since God was in the
man who was being born ; not in him as circumscribed after the
manner of nature, but in him after the manner of the understanding," κατὰ τὴν σχέσιν τῆς γνώμης). In view of these statements,
we can understand the vigorous opposition of Apollinaris. The
unity of the person is endangered. The divine cannot be said
to have really become man, as there remains only the moral relative union (ἕνωσις σχετική) between two persons. The religious
significance of this union is that Christ, in prototype and
example, represented the union of man with God—in obedient
will. As did the man Jesus, so may we also attain sonship to
God "by grace, not naturally." His purpose was "to lead all
to imitation of himself" (Theod. de inc. xii. 7, p. 306 ; xiv.
2, p. 308 ; cat. 8, p. 331).[1]

(*e*) The church is indebted to this school of theologians for
the preservation of a precious treasure—the reality of the human
and personal career of Jesus. To what extreme the ideas of

---

[1] Cf. the saying attributed to Ibas : "I do not envy Christ," he says, "that
he was made God ; for what he has been made I have been made, because he
is of my nature" (Gallandi viii. 705).

Apollinaris lead may be seen in the later Monophysites. But it cannot be maintained that the "historical Jesus" would ever have received justice at the hands of those who were content with this theory. The abstract conception of God which lay at its basis prevented any real and historical understanding of the nature of the God-man. Two difficulties were felt : (1) The unity of the personal life of Jesus remained problematical, although this problem was perhaps soluble. (2) The tendency of Greek Soteriology toward a mystical deification of the humanity through the medium of the God-man did not appear to harmonize with the theory as proposed by the Antiochians. The only significance remaining to the work of redemption appeared to be instruction and imitation. This explains the often unjustifiable opposition to this Christology. The theology of the Antiochians at least prevented the acceptance of Apollinarianism as a solution of the problem of Apollinaris.

4. The other Greek theologians attempted to solve the problem in a different way, following upon the track of Athanasius : the God-man is a concrete unit, in whom, however, we discriminate in the abstract two natures (supra, p. 211). The Cappadocians maintained essentially the same position. But, in facing the problem of Apollinaris, they, like the Antiochians, could not get beyond mere allegations. They spoke of two natures ($\varphi \dot{\upsilon} \sigma \varepsilon \iota \varsigma$), but did not infer from this that there were "two Sons," although the two natures were to be conceived as each complete (Greg. Naz. ep. ad Cled. i. 7, 8). It was thought that the two natures coalesced in one. There is a miraculous commingling, the one deifying and the other being deified : "For both the taking and the taken are God, the two natures concurring in one ; not two Sons" (Greg. Naz. or. 37. 2); and "being that which deified and that which was deified. O, the new mixture ($\mu \dot{\iota} \xi \iota \varsigma$); O, the strange compound" ($\chi \rho \tilde{\alpha} \sigma \iota \varsigma$)! (or. 38. 13). It is, says Gregory of Nyssa, a relation like that between a drop of vinegar mingled with the sea and the sea itself. This simile indicates how utterly unlimited was the range of thought which these men allowed themselves. Since the Logos becomes flesh, the human is transformed into the divine ("changed, a mixing up, $\dot{\alpha} \nu \dot{\alpha} \chi \rho \alpha \sigma \iota \varsigma$, with the divine, a transformation, $\mu \varepsilon \tau \alpha \sigma \tau \upsilon \iota \chi \varepsilon \dot{\iota} \omega \sigma \iota \varsigma$, of the man into the Christ "). Thus the infirmity, mutability, and mortality of the human nature are consumed by the deity : "He mixed his life-giving power with the mortal and perishable nature. . . . The Immutable appears in the mutable, in order that, having changed and transformed from the worse into the better the evil commingled with the mutable subject, he might, having expended the evil in himself, cause it to disappear from the nature. For our God is a

consuming fire, in which all wood of evil is thoroughly burnt up"
(Greg. Nyss. c. Eunom. v., Mi. 45, pp. 700, 693, 697, 705,
708, also Antirrh. 42). It is also held, indeed, that "the beholding of the attributes of the flesh and of the deity remains
unconfused, so long as each of these is regarded by itself" (ib.
p. 706). Thus the humanity weeps at the grave of Lazarus, but
the deity calls him to life. But viewed concretely, the deity, by
virtue of the union, affects the human just as well as the humanity
the divine : "thus through the connection and union the (properties) of both become common to each, the Lord taking upon
himself the stripes of the servant, and the servant being glorified with the honor belonging to the Lord" (ib. 705, 697).
The relation of the two natures is thus a different one from that
existing between the persons of the Trinity : "God and man are,
it is true, two natures . . . but there are not two Sons nor two
Gods. . . . And if it is necessary to speak concisely : other
and other (ἄλλο καὶ ἄλλο) are the entities of which (τὰ ἐξ ὧν)
the Saviour . . . not another and another, ἄλλος καὶ ἄλλος. God
forbid. For both are one in the compound, God being human-
ized and man being deified . . . but I say 'other and other'
in a contrary sense from that in which it may be said of the
Trinity; for there it is 'another and another,' in order that
we may not commingle the hypostases, and not 'other and
other,' for the three are one and the same in their divinity"
(Greg. Naz. ep. ad Cled. i. 4).

Unfinished as is all this, we may yet clearly see the aim of
these writers. The historical character of Christ compels them
to maintain the two complete natures as well as the intimate
union of these two natures. But their conception of redemption
leads them to think of this union as a commingling of the natures, as a transformation of the human into the divine. They
maintained in their relation to the Antiochians a religious position, and in opposition to Apollinaris a historical standpoint.
In view of this tendency—though by no means in the importance or clearness of their ideas—they are superior to both (cf.
p. 246, n. 4).

5. This view received its final formulation at the hands of CYRIL
OF ALEXANDRIA (bishop from A. D. 412, † A. D. 444).

Opp. ed. Aubert, 1638. Mi. gr. 68-77. Especially : Quod unus sit Christ.
Dial. de incarn. unigeniti. De incarn. verbi. De incarn. domini. Adv.
Nestorii blasphemias, ll. 5. Quod s. virgo deipara sit. L. adv. nolentes con-
fiteri s. virgo esse deiparam. Explicatio duodecim capitum. Apologetic.
pro duodecim capitibus. Apologet. c. Theodoret. De recta fide ad reginas,
ll. 2. Frgg. ex libris c. Theodor. et Diodor. Ep. 1 ff.; ep. 17 ad Nestor.;
epp. 45, 46; ad Succensum, in Mi. t. 75-77. Cf. LOOFS, Leontius v. Byz. in
Texte u. Untersuch. iii. 1, p. 40 ff.

(*a*) Cyril starts with the person of the Logos. This person assumed complete human nature for our salvation. His formula is : "one nature of the divine Logos, made flesh." He does not speak of the one nature of the incarnated Logos, or Christ, but habitually of the one incarnated nature of the Logos. The Logos, as the subject contemplated, has thus the one incarnated nature. It may, however, also be said of the Logos that he was made man and incarnated (*e. g.,* c. Nest. v. 4, 7 ; ii. 10 ; ad regin. ii. 4, 33). In detail, Cyril teaches : Two natures are to be acknowledged, the divine and the human, both of them complete, so that the latter includes the reasoning soul (ψυχὴ λογικὴ) (ad reg. i. 13, Mi. 76. 1221 ; ii. 55 ; inc. unig., Mi. 75. 1208 f., 1220). Thus Christ is "of like nature (ὁμοούσιος) with his mother as with his Father" (dial. c. Nest., Mi. 76. 252 ; ep. 40, Mi. 77. 192). In consequence of his becoming man, there is a concurrence (συνδρομή) and union (ἕνωσις) of these two natures. How is this to be understood? Not as a conversion or change, since "the nature of the Logos is immutable and absolutely unchangeable" (ad reg. ii. 2, 22 ; inc. unig., Mi. 75. 1192 ff., 1200, 1253). "Neither as a mixture nor compound" (φυρμός, σύγκρασις, κρᾶσις); quod unus, Mi. 75. 1292 ; c. Nest. ii. 11 ; ep. 4, Mi. 77. 45); yet not as a mere connection (συνάφεια) or indwelling (ἐνοίκησις) (*e. g.,* c. Nest. ii. proem. quod b. virgo 8). On the contrary, both natures retain their own characteristics unmingled. The deity throughout all the changes of its earthly lot remains in its full glory what it was before (c. Nest. ii. 1 ; ad reg. i. 4 ; ii. 9, 16, 27, 33, 37 ; inc. unig., Mi. 75. 1216, 1220, 1221, 1229), and the humanity retains its complete Homousia with us (ep. 40, Mi. 77. 192 ; inc. unig., Mi. 75. 1216 : Christ's body mortal). Cyril can, therefore, speak of two natures (vid. esp. quod unus, Mi. 75. 1292), and he can compare the relation of the two to that between an emperor in his proper character, and as appearing in the garb of a consul (quod b. virg. 14); or to that of body and soul in man, which yet together compose one man (c. Nest. ii. 12 ; inc. unig., Mi. 75. 1224 ; ep. 17, Mi. 77. 116 ; ep. 45, p. 233, quod unus, Mi. 75. 1292). This illustration affords us a key to the interpretation of the above-cited formula of Cyril. The two natures are, indeed, after their union the same as they were before, but they are combined in indissoluble unity by means of the unity of the person—the Logos, as also by means of the consequent mutual communication of their respective attributes. Thus the two natures are kept distinct in abstract thought, although the concrete object of contemplation is the "one incarnate nature," which has the Logos as its controlling factor. The unity in this sense is, therefore, one of hypostases ($ἕνωσις καθ᾽ ὑπόστασιν$), as Cyril often describes it in his later writings, *i. e.*, it is the Logos-person which establishes the unity. Cyril, in opposing Theodoret, confesses the novelty of this formula, but maintains its importance in the combating of heresy. It asserts no more, in his view, than "simply that the nature ($φύσις$) or hypostasis of the Logos, *i. e.*, the Logos itself, is truly united ($ἑνωθείς$) with the human nature" (Apol. c. Theodoret, Mi. 76. 400). Inasmuch as the Logos-person of the God-man is for Cyril the self-evident postulate, he was not called upon to face the problem of Apollinaris, and hence, of course, furnished no solution of it.

(*b*) But Cyril's ideas lead us also upon a different path. We are to acknowledge "one Son, one Lord, one Christ," and him as "of two perfects:" "the two natures proceed together in unbroken union, unconfusedly and unchangeably . . . we do not at all detract from the concurrent unity when we say that it is (derived) from two natures. From two and different natures is the one and only Christ" (ep. 45, p. 232 f.). For, just as the Logos was God before his sojourn on earth, so also, having become man . . . he is again one. Therefore he has called himself a mediator between God and man (1 Tim. 2. 5), as being one from both natures" (quod b. virgo 12; cf. c. Nest. ii. 12; ep. 17, Mi. 77, 116; inc. unig., Mi. 75. 1220, 1221, 1233, 1253, 1208: "We are accustomed to guard absolutely the unbroken unity, believing him to be the Only-begotten and the First-born; the Only-begotten, as the Logos of God the Father . . . the First-born moreover in that he became man"). He is, therefore, one and the same before and after the incarnation: "for the Son according to nature from the Father, having taken to himself a physical and rational body, was carnally born . . . and, not turning into flesh, but rather taking it to himself, and ever mindful of his being God" (ad reg. ii. 2). "Being man, viewed outwardly; but inwardly true God" (quod b. virgo 4). Cyril denies the charge that in his conception Christ is two-personed ($διπρόσωπος$) (inc. unig., Mi. 75. 1221; inc. dom. 31; ep. 46, Mi. 77. 241); but without fully recognizing its force. (*c*) But all these speculations assume a practical shape when Cyril comes to speak of the concrete form of the God-man. Here he becomes really great. His conception of the historical Christ dominates his thought and lifts his ideas above their normal plane. "It is evident, therefore, that the mind beholds a certain difference of the natures" (inc. unig., Mi. 75. 1221), but: "the fact is, that the Logos, not dividing but combining both into one, and, as it were, commingling with one another the attributes ($ἰδιώματα$) of the natures, escapes us through whatever the multitude of our words" (ib. 1244, 1249), *i. e.*, "bestowing upon the proper flesh the glory of the divine energy ; but, on the other hand, appropriating the things of the flesh and, as though in some way according to the economic union, also conferring these upon its own proper nature" (ib. 1241). Accordingly, the expressions of the Evangelists, applicable now to the divinity and again to the humanity, are not to be referred to two *hypostases* or *prosopa* : "for the one and only Christ is not double, as though he were to be regarded as derived from two and different things" (ep. 17, Mi. 77. 116). Since there is here but one person, all the attributes may be ascribed to the one Christ. The Logos is visible and tangible. His sufferings are the sufferings of God. Hunger and thirst, learning and praying, were parts of his experience ; while, on the other hand, the body of Christ was a "divine body," and the Son of man comes from heaven, returns to it, is worshiped, etc. (*e. g.*, inc. unig., Mi. 75. 1224, 1244, 1249, 1228, 1233 f. ; ad regin. ii. 16, 36 f. ; c. Nest. i. 6 ; ii. 3 ; iv. 6 ; quod unus 75. 1309 ; inc. dom. 75. 1469 ; ep. 45, Mi. 77. 234 ; 46, p. 245 ; cf. THOMASIUS DG. i., ed. 2, 348 f.). Hence, also, the designation of Mary as the "mother of God" is dogmatically correct. But this *communicatio idiomatum* at once finds its limitation in the inflexible immutability and impassibility of the Logos : "suffering excepted, in so far as he is thought of as divine" (quod unus, Mi. 75. 1337, 1357 ; c. Nestor. v. 4). Suffering could as little affect him as strokes falling upon a piece of glowing iron permeated by fire affect the fire (quod unus, Mi. 75. 1357). It was, therefore, an "impassive passion" (ἀπαθῶς ἔπαθεν).

(*d*) It is very difficult to give a correct summary of Cyril's view. If we begin with his fundamental formula, "one nature of the divine Logos, made flesh," and keep in mind his own explanations, we reach the result : The Logos-person assumed the (impersonal) human nature, uniting it with the divine nature. The Logos is now no longer fleshless (ἄσαρκος), but is not on that account a duplex personality, "but has remained one" (ep. 46, Mi. 77. 241). If, on the other hand, we start with the community of attributes, we come to the formula : "from two natures the one Christ," and to the conception of a divine-human Christ-person. Our faith in Christ reposes not upon the man, "but upon the God by nature and truly in the person (προσώπῳ) of Christ" (inc. unig., Mi. 75. 1233). In the first case, Cyril starts with the one Logos-person, who has a divine human nature ; in the second, we have the two natures, constituting one divine human person. Cyril did not realize the dissonance of these ideas, as his views were developed in contrast

with those of Nestorius and not of Apollinaris. But a sound
historic[1] and religious instinct led him to emphasize, as against
the unhistoric tearing asunder of Christ, the unity of his person
and of his manifestation. In this lies the significance of his
teaching.

(*e*) Cyril's view, like that of Athanasius, grew upon religious
soil. Since the Logos assumed the entire human nature, the latter becomes partaker of God and immortality: "For Christ the
first man . . . the root, as it were, and the appointed first-fruit
of those transformed by the Spirit into newness of life, was to
effect the immortality of the body, and to make the human race
already, both by grace and in its entirety, secure and safe, as in
participation of the divine nature" (inc. unig., Mi. 75. 1213,
1216; also 1241 f.; c. Nestor. iv. 6; ad reg. ii. 55). Other
ideas connected with the Soteriology of Cyril demanded the
same basis, *c. g.*, the conception of Christ as the mediator between God and man (c. Nest. v. 1 ; inc. unig., Mi. 75. 1245 ;
quod b. virgo, 12), of redemption through his blood and the overcoming of the devil (ad reg. 7. 31, 36), of his life as an example
(ib. ii. 41 f.).

6. We must notice, finally, the Christology of the contemporaneous Western theologians (cf. REUTER, Augustin. Studien, p.
194 ff.). It is to be said in general that the leaders in the
Western church did not look upon the great question of the age
as a "problem." Since they firmly maintained the formulas of
Tertullian, they no more questioned the unity of the person than
the duplicity of the natures, only giving to the latter more prominence than did Cyril. As their formula gave some recognition
to the ideas of both parties in the East, it was the formula of the
future.

We can but glance briefly at the Christology of HILARY OF
POITIERS.

† A. D. 366. His chief work was De trinitate. Works edited by Maffei,
1730, in Mi. lat. 9. 10 ; cf. DORNER, Lehre v. d. Person Christi, i. 1037 ff.
LOOFS, PRE. viii., ed. 3, 57 ff. FÖRSTER, Zur Theol. d. Hilar. Stud. u.
Krit., 1888, p. 655 ff.).

Christ is God and man (trin. ix. 19). As One, he is God
just as he is man : "the whole in him is God the Word ; the
whole in him is the man Christ—retaining this one thing in the

---

[1] The widely prevalent opinion, that the Antiochians were inspired by historical and Cyril by dogmatic or "speculative" interests, is incorrect. Cyril
really came nearer than the Antiochians to the Christ of history, and he
manifests an extraordinary zeal for a true understanding of the historical facts
of the Saviour's life (*e. g.*, inc. unig.. Mi. 75. 1196 f., 1215 ; ad reg. ii. 36,
et pas).

sacrament of his confession, neither to believe that Christ is other than Jesus, nor to preach that Jesus is other than Christ '' (x. 52-71). Compare : " in him is the nature of man, just as the nature of God'' (in ps. 68. 25, or " person of both natures," trin. ix. 14). His strongly emphasized " evacuation '' of the Son of God in the interest of the incarnation arrests our attention : " For, remaining in the form of God, he assumed the form of a servant, not being changed, but emptying (*exinaniens*) himself and hiding within himself, and he himself being emptied within his power, while he adapts himself even to the form of human condition '' (xi. 48). But this asserts no more than that the Logos undertook a change of his condition. "The emptying (*evacuatio*) of form is not an abolition of nature '' (ix. 14). The power of omnipotence remains to him (xi. 48 fin.; xii. 6 ; x. 15 ; ix. 51 f.). The divine nature did not and could not feel the sufferings (x. 23, 48, 24 : " that which is customary to a body was endured in order to prove the reality of the body ''). Hence, the form of a servant implies a latency of the form of God.

AMBROSE († A. D. 397. See esp. de fide ad Gratianum, de incarnationis sacramento. Works edited by Ballerini, 1875 ff., Mi. lat. 14-17. Cf. FÖRSTER, Ambros., 1884) presented the genuine Western Christology of Tertullian : " the Son of God is said to be one in both natures, because both natures are in the same '' (de fid. ii. 9. 77): " a two-fold substance (*substantia*) . . . both of divinity and of flesh'' (ib. iii. 10. 65). The *distinctio* of the two natures or substances is to be sharply preserved (ib. ii. 9. 77 ; inc. 4. 23). The immutability and immunity from death of the divine nature (inc. 5. 37 ff.; 6. 55 ; fid. ii. 7. 57 ; 8. 60), as well as the completeness of the human nature, with the " rational soul'' (inc. 7. 64 ff., 76), are guarded.[1]

Around the " immutable wisdom'' has been thrown the " mantle of flesh '' (ib. 5. 41). He, too, speaks of an emptying (*exinanire*) and a hiding (*celare*) of the divinity (inc. 5. 41, de spir, s. i. 9. 107), without thereby attaining any greater lucidity, inasmuch as the form of God and the form of a servant are, nevertheless, alike regarded as belonging to the incarnate Being (ep. 46. 6 ff.; cf. REUTER, p. 210 ff.). But the two natures are now combined in one person : " The One is of two-formed and two-fold (*biformis et geminaeque*) nature, partaking of divinity and of the body. . . . Not divided, but one ; because

---

[1] Ambrose says, de fide ii. 8. 61, indeed : " from the person of man he called the Father greater ; '' but this must be interpreted in the light of the further remark, ib. 68 : " for it is not written from the person of the Jews . . . but the Evangelist speaks from his own person.''

one and the other are both in each, *i. e.*, either in the divinity
or in the body " (inc. 5. 35 ; fid. v. 8. 107 ; iii. 2. 8). " The
Lord of majesty is said to have been crucified, because, partaking of
both natures, *i. e.*, the human and the divine, he endured the sufferings in the nature of man " (fid. ii. 7. 58). This is the ancient theory of the Western church, which knew nothing of the
problem of the age.

7. AUGUSTINE follows in the same path. It is not our task to
present the Christology of Augustine in process of formation.
Our interest lies in its final form.   Yet a few remarks are necessary to a correct understanding of its appearance (cf. the
thorough discussion of O. SCHEEL, Die Anschauung Augustins
über Christi Person und Werk, 1901). Augustine had, as a
Manichæan, denied the true humanity of Christ. When he
found his way back to the church, the authority of the Scriptures
led him first to recognize this (cf. Confessions, vii. 19. 25). The
authority of the church's teaching then led him to accept also
the divinity of Christ. But since his speculative spirit was controlled by Neo-platonic conceptions, and had from his early days
been familiar with trinitarian ideas, his conception of the divinity
of Christ was moulded by the Neo-platonic ideas of the divine
νοῦς and the κοσμὸς νοητός.   The eternal Word is conceived primarily in his relation to the world, and not in a purely religious
way, in his relation to salvation and to human history. As, *e. g.*, all
things are but copies of eternal ideas, and these ideas are in God
(de oct. quaestionibus, q. 46. 2), so all things exist only in so far
as God gives to them a " continuing and unchangeable form "
(de lib. arb. ii. 17. 45). But the eternal ideas (*rationes*) of all
temporal things are present in the Logos (de genes. ad litt. iv.
24. 41), and the Logos is the " form of all real things," " the
unfashioned form " (*forma infabricata*), " without time . . .
and without local dimensions." Of him it is said : " For he is
a certain form, an unfashioned (*non formata*) form, but the form
of all fashioned forms, an unchangeable (*incommutabilis*) form
. . . controlling (*superans*) all things, existing in all things and
a kind of foundation in which they exist, and a roof under which
they exist. . . .   Therefore all things are in him, and yet, because he is God, all things are under him " (serm. 117. 2, 3).
These are clearly conceptions derived from Greek philosophy,
regarding the Logos as the cosmic principle of idea and form.
But, if we would rightly understand Augustine, we must also bear
in mind that he always thinks of this Logos as the second person
in the Trinity, as the Son of God immutably present with the
Father, who in time became man. All ideas of Subordinationism are utterly remote from his thought, however strongly the

17

Greek conception of the Logos might impel in that direction, as we have seen in the Apologists and in Origen. At this point, the church's doctrine of the divinity of the Son marked out for him an absolutely fixed path from which he never deviated. Nor did Augustine fail to draw from the divinity of Christ practical inferences in the sphere of Soteriology (vid. *sub*). But the starting-point of his doctrine, and hence its relation to other views, was always different from that of Athanasius.[1] Whilst the latter began really with the redeeming work of Christ, and upon this, as a basis, erected his homousian theory, Augustine started with an accepted ecclesiastical doctrine, which he interpreted for himself through speculative reflections, and from this drew his conclusions as to the redeeming work of Christ. Hence his Christology does not present the strikingly religious one-sidedness which marks the conception of Athanasius. Regarded as doctrine, its originality dare not at all events be too highly rated. Augustine maintained unconditionally the divinity of Christ, and he esteemed highly his humanity, as a fact of which he had gained knowledge in his personal experience. But in regard to the combination of the two natures, he did not advance beyond the views traditional in the West. The sources do not sustain the opinion of A. DORNER (Augustinus, p. 92) and HAR-NACK (DG. iii., ed. 3, 120), *i. e.*, that it was because of the susceptibility of the human soul of Jesus that the Logos appeared in it, nor justify the latter in declaring that "Augustine constructs the God-man from the standpoint of the human person (soul)," or that the chief interest of Augustine centres in the human soul of Jesus. We may, perhaps, characterize his fundamental tendency as in harmony with the positions taken in his *De civ. dei*, x. 23, 24. The oracular deliverance cited from Porphyry, "fountains can purify" (*principia posse purgare*), is correct, except that we can here speak of but One fountain. This fountain, the Logos, in entering humanity, purifies it : "Christ the Lord is the fountain, by whose incarnation we are purified. For neither the flesh nor the human soul (*i. e.*, of Christ) is the fountain, but the Word through which all things which were

---

[1] I mention here only the fact that this Christology, taking seriously as it does the idea of the divinity of Christ, cannot avoid questions concerning his activity before the incarnation. This is seen already in Paul and John. That is to say, since the work of Christ controls history to the attainment of the ends of the kingdom of God, and since there is a connection between the course of history before and after Christ, there must in some way be found a place for the direction of history by Christ also before the incarnation. We must, however, discriminate between such attempts and the purely cosmological discussions of the Greek philosophers, although the latter at a very early date influenced the structure of Christian thought.

made stand secure.   Therefore the flesh does not cleanse of
itself, but through the Word by which it has been assumed."
   We now address ourselves to the examination of the DOCTRINE
OF AUGUSTINE in detail.   It is for him an absolutely fixed fact that
in Christ two complete natures or substances (inclusive of the
rational human soul ; see in Joh. tr. 23. 6 ; 47. 9 ; conf. vii.
19 ; de agone christ. 19. 21) constitute one person : "Christ is
one person of two-fold substance, because he is both God and
man" (c. Maximin. Arian. ii. 10. 2).   "Now truly has thus
appeared the mediator between God and man, in order that, combining both natures in the unity of person, he might both exalt the
ordinary by means of the extraordinary, and temper the extraordinary by means of the ordinary" (ep. 137. 3, 9, 12).   "He
assumed the man, and from himself and the latter made the one
Jesus Christ, the mediator between God and men, equal to the
Father according to his divinity, but less than the Father according to the flesh," *i. e.*, according to the man.   But this unification in the man-God (*homo-deus*, enchir. 25. 108) is different in
kind from the indwelling of God in the saints, in whom the
Word does not become flesh : "it is evident that, by a certain
unique assumption, the person of this man has become one with
the Word" (ep. 137. 12, 40 ; in Joh. tr. 72. 1 ; de agone chr.
20. 22).   The idea is thus that the two natures are combined
in the unity of one person (cf. enchir. 10. 35 ; 12. 40, 41 ; in
Joh. tr. 27. 4).   But this is evidently the person of the Logos.
"The rational soul and the flesh entered into unity of person with
the Word."   "The Logos, who is the sole Son of God, and that
not by grace but by nature, was made also Son of man, and this
same, the One Christ, was both and from both."   He remained
that which he was.   "He assumed the form of a servant, not aban-
doning nor diminishing the form of God" (enchir. 10. 35).
There can here be no thought of any merit of the human nature
of Christ as leading to the union.   On the contrary, it is an exhibition of the same grace which justifies sinful men, that makes
it impossible for the man Jesus to sin, viz., inasmuch as his nature was "taken up in a unique way into the unity of the person
of the unique (unici) Son of God" (ib. ii. 36).   "The only-
begotten Son of God out of grace so united himself with his human
nature, that he became man.   The only-begotten Son of God, not
by grace by nature, by nature uniting himself in such unity of person, that he, the same, was also man.   This same "Jesus Christ,
the only-begotten Son of God, *i. e.*, the unique One, our Lord,
was born of the Holy Spirit and the Virgin Mary" (ib. ii. 36, 37).
But in all of this the Logos remains unchangeable (de agon. chr.
i. 1 ; x. 11. 23, 25).   But Augustine can also speak of the com-

bination of the natures as a "mixture : " "the man is joined to, and in some way mingled (*commixtus*) with, the Word into a unity of person" (trin. iv. 20. 30). It is such a mixture as is found in every human person : " In that person there is a mixture of soul and body ; in this person is a mixture of God and man" (ep. 137. 3, 11 ; serm. 174. 2). But at the same time the immutability of the divine nature is still carefully guarded, and we accordingly read also : "the same who is man is God, and the same who is God is man, not in confusion of nature, but in unity of person" (sermo 186. 1). The idea of a change of the divine nature, or a denuding it of power in the interest of redemption, is entirely foreign to Augustine. The divine nature remains as it was, except that the flesh is added to it, and becomes with it the same person. "The Word does not come into the flesh in order to perish, but the flesh comes to the Word in order that it may not perish" (sermo 186. 1 ; 121. 5 ; 264. 4 ; ep. 137. 7, 10 ; trin. i. 8. 15).[1]

But the religious interest of Augustine does not centre entirely in the divinity of Christ, rather in this no less than in his humanity. In Christ the divine nature reveals itself. Its wisdom is thus offered to us as milk to babes (sermo 117. 10. 16 ; 126. 4. 5 ; conf. vii. 18). The love of God manifest in him awakens us to a responsive love. His humility overcomes our pride (de catechiz. rudibus 4. 7, 8 ; conf. vii. 18). His whole

---

[1] Augustine has also the following modification (afterward employed by Abelard): "the Word of God having the man" (*habens hominem*, in Joh. tr. 19. 15), but also : "he assumed the man" (de agon. chr. 11. 12 ; 18. 20 ; 19. 21 ; 20. 22 ; cf. Hilar. de trin. x. 22). He also teaches a predestination of the man Jesus (de praedest. 15. 30, 31 ; cf. SCHEEL, l. c., p. 215 f.). These terms of expression are, indeed, of value in aiding to a proper understanding of Augustine, since they show to what an extent he was able to grasp independently the idea of the humanity of Christ (cf. also such expressions as : "The Son of God assumed man, and in that man (*in illo homine*) suffered," de agon. chr. ii. 12 ; ib.: "in which [*i. e.*, that man] the Son of God offered himself to us as an example ; " ib. 23. 25 : "Thus we say that the Son of God suffered and died in the man whom he carried, without any change or destruction of his divinity"). But when SCHEEL (p. 216) infers from the predestination of Jesus a fundamental departure from the doctrine of the two natures, since only a person and not a substance can be predestinated (HARNACK similarly speaks of a "profound relationship with the Christology of Paul of Samosata, and Photinus," p. 121), he is in so far correct, that the ideas and formulas cited testify that Augustine could conceive of the human life of Jesus as relatively independent and like our own (vid. with reference to the childhood of Jesus, Scheel, p. 230). Yet in this Augustine by no means abandons his controlling scheme of thought, for the predestinating of the man Jesus means exactly that that the Logos should absorb him "in order through him as the mediator to bring grace to the predestinated." At all events, there are here points of view at variance with Greek conceptions, which became significant in the theology of the West.

life and conduct, in both its human and its divine aspects, serves
as an example for believers (enchir. 14. 53; 25. 108). As man,
he is the mediator between us and God (conf. x. 43 : " For in
so far as he is man, in so far is he a mediator"); but only in so
far as he is also God.   As man he is the mediator (as Augustine
always states with emphasis), for thereby he stands near to men ;
but the nearness is the nearness of God.   The man becomes the
mediator, because he has God within him (enchir. 25. 108 ; conf.
x. 42).   Compare also in Joh. tr. 42. 8 : " His divinity whither
we journey, his humanity where we journey," similarly tr. 13. 5 ;
civ. dei xi. 2.

The West had, therefore—in independence of the East—its
own Christological theory.   It was more nearly in accord with the
Christology of Alexandria than with that of Antioch, although
not without points of agreement with the latter.

§ 24. *Nestorius and Cyril.   The Third Ecumenical Council
at Ephesus.*

Upon Nestorius, see Socr. h. e. vii. 29 ff., the letters of Coelestine ; his ora-
tions in Marius Mercator in Gallandi, bibl. viii. 629 ff., in Mi. lat. 48, cf.
HEFELE CG. ii. 149 ff. LOOFS, PRE. xiii. ed. 3, 736 ff.

1. The great controversy arose from the discussion of a liturgical formula.   Nestorius, who was called in A. D. 428 from
Antioch to Constantinople, desired to controvert the heretics.
He vigorously assailed the Arians, the Novatians, and the Macedonians, but joined hands with the western Pelagians.   The
designation of Mary as the mother of God, which was becoming
current, aroused his polemics.   He held the genuine Antiochian
view : The Logos, being as divine absolutely immutable, was not
born.   This can be said only of his garment, or temple, *i. e.*,
his human nature (or. 1. 2 ; 3. 2).   Hence Mary was not to be
called really the mother of God (θεοτόκος), God-bearing, but
God-receiving (θεοδόχος), and man-bearing (ἀνθρωποτόκος), or
Christ-bearing (χριστοτόκος) (or. 2. 8 ; 5. 2 ; cp. 1 ad Coelest.
3).   It is only to the man Christ, therefore, that birth, suffering,
and death can be ascribed (or. 2. 2 ; 3. 1).   The man Jesus
was the " organ of the divinity."   Hence the Logos as God is
strictly discriminated from the man, but without making two
Sons or Christs : " We call our Lord Christ in view of his nature
two-fold, in view of his sonship one (or. 3. 2); for to both natures belong, in consequence of their union, the same dignity
and a common reverence : for there are two, if you regard the
nature ; one, if you consider the dignity.   I divide the natures,

but I combine the reverence" (or. 1. 2 ; 2. 6, 8). And, above all, the Logos, after the incarnation, does not act except in union with the man Jesus (Cyril c. Nest. ii. 7). Of the worship of the human nature, he says: "I adore it as the animated mantle of the King" (2. 6). When vigorous opposition was at once manifested, Nestorius conceded the possibility of the θεοτόκος: "the genetrix of God . . . on account of the Word united with its temple," but he still thought that the term was calculated to give aid to the Arians and Apollinarians (or. 4. 3 ; 5. 2, cf. ep. 1 ad Coelest. 3 ; ep. 2. 2). In his Christology there is evidently nothing heterodox. It was only the usual doctrine of the Antioch school. Nothing was further from his thought than a denial of the divinity of Christ, or of the doctrine of the two natures.[1]

2. The controversy assumed larger proportions only when CYRIL OF ALEXANDRIA (supra, p. 251) entered the lists. "Without Cyril there would have been no Nestorian controversy," Loofs. A passionate correspondence arose between the two patriarchs. Cyril then thought it proper to inform Theodosius himself, as well as his wife and sister, of the existing doctrinal divergence. But the letters were very unfavorably received at the court. He held firmly to the incarnated nature of the Logos, as well as to the term θεοτόκος (supra, pp. 252, 254). He adduced an exhaustive array of testimonies for his view from the Scriptures and tradition. But he was, at this time and afterward, chiefly concerned in pointing out the irreligious consequences to which the doctrine of Nestorius would lead. According to Nestorius, we would be redeemed by the sufferings of a mere man (c. Nestor. iii. 2 ; iv. 4 ; v. 1); a man would have become to us "the way, the truth, and the life" (c. Nest. v. 1); we would worship a God-carrying (θεοφόρος) man (ib. i. 2 ; ii. 10, cf. inc. unig., Mi. 75, 1232); when we are baptized into Christ and by him, we would be baptized into a man (ad reg. ii. 52 ; c. Nestor. iii. 2 ; inc. unig., Mi. 75, 1240); we would in the Lord's Supper partake of the flesh and blood of a man (c. Nestor. iv. 5 ; inc. unig., Mi. 75, 1241). Compare THOMASIUS, DG. 341 ff. Thus the Christian world would be robbed by Nestorius of all the treasures which it possesses in the historical Christ. All these things have now only a human valuation ; and we no longer have in Christ God himself. The whole religious energy of Cyril's views is here

---

[1] Lechler has prepared the way for a juster estimate of Nestorius, proving that the latter taught the true divinity and humanity of Jesus, as well as the union of the two in one person, but did not draw the inference of the *communicatio idiomatum*. Further, he maintains that it was chiefly love of conflict and of debate which produced the controversy. Erl. Ed. 25, ed. 1, 304 ff.

revealed. The real point of controversy is, whether it was the man Jesus controlled by the Logos, or whether it was God himself, who was born, lived, taught, labored, and died among us. The positive teachings of Cyril have been already outlined. These writings of Cyril, viewed from the standpoint of church politics, are the works of a master hand. Theologically and morally, they make a different impression, giving evidence of a lack of capacity to understand and appreciate a theological opponent.

Rome was very soon drawn into the controversy. Nestorius wrote to Pope Coelestine as his colleague, and Cyril sought direction and instruction from the same source. Nestorius expressed his view in the charge which he brings against his opponents: "They confound, in the mutability of modification, both natures which, through the supreme and unconfused union, are adored in the one person of the only-begotten" (ep. 2 ad Coel. c. 2)—i. e., he expressed himself—in word—in harmony with Western ideas.[1] Nevertheless Rome, after some delay, decided against him at a synod, according to her traditional policy making common cause with Alexandria (A. D. 430). Coelestine could find nothing to say to Nestorius except that he was a ravening wolf and a hireling, and that he must within ten days subscribe to the teaching of the Romish and Alexandrine church, or, failing to do so, be excluded from the church (see Coelestine, ep. 11-14).

3. Cyril now drew the lines of opposition most sharply at the Council of Alexandria, A. D. 430. He addressed a communication to Nestorius, containing an exposition of his teaching, and closing with twelve anathemas (ep. 17, in HAHN, Bibl. d. Symbole, ed. 3, p. 312 ff.): Mary is the mother of God (1). The one Christ dare not be divided in accordance with the *hypostases*, and the latter are not bound together only by their conjunction in accordance with their dignity, *i.e.*, their sphere of dominion or power, but through a physical union (ἕνωσις φυσική) (3). The expressions of the Scriptures are not to be divided between the two persons, *i. e.*, hypostases (4). Christ is not a God-carrying (θεοφόρος) man (5). The man assumed is not to be called God and, as such, to be worshiped as "one in another" (8). The flesh of the Lord is life-giving (11). The Logos of God suffered in the flesh, was crucified in the flesh, and tasted death in the flesh (12). Nestorius at once replied with twelve counter-anathemas (in Marius Merc., Mi. 48. 909): Christ is Emmanuel, God with

---

[1] It should be borne in mind that Coelestine had received an account of the teaching of Nestorius from Cyril (M. iv. 548 and Cyril's first letter to Coelestine). The sermons of Nestorius had also been sent to Rome.

us; Mary is the mother, not of the Word of God, but of Emmanuel (1). If anyone should say that flesh is capable of (containing) the divine nature . . . and call the very same nature God and man, let him be anathema (2). Christ is one according to union, not according to nature (3). The words of Scripture are not to be referred to one nature, nor are sufferings to be attributed to the Logos (4). If anyone dare to say that, after the assumption of man, the Son of God is one in nature, since he is Emmanuel, let him be anathema (5). He who was made of the Virgin is not the Only-begotten, but has only through his union with the Only-begotten received a share in his name (7). The form of a servant is not to be worshiped on account of this union (8). The flesh united with the Logos is not "through the passibility of the nature the giver of life" (11). The sufferings of Christ are not to be attributed to the Logos "without discrimination of the dignity of the natures" (12).

4. The Antiochians now declared themselves (see the letter of John of Antioch in M. v. 756) for Nestorius, charging Cyril with Apollinarianism. The emperor, in a very harsh letter, accused Cyril of pride, love of strife and intrigue (on account of his letter to the women of the imperial household) (M. iv. 1109). A general council was called at EPHESUS on Whitsunday, A. D. 431, in the interest of the salutary union between civil welfare and religious harmony (M. iv. 1111). The invitation found Augustine († Aug. 28, 430) no longer among the living. Nestorius and Cyril appeared before the appointed time. Coelestine was represented by three legates, who were instructed to act in all things with Cyril, and, beyond this, not to dispute but pass judgment (M. iv. 556). The arrival of John of Antioch was unduly delayed (M. iv. 1121, 1229, 1329 f.; cf. 1225). Despite the protests of Nestorius, 68 Asiatic bishops and the imperial commissary (M. iv. 1129 ff.; v. 765 f., 770 f.), Cyril and Memnon of Ephesus opened the council. 159 bishops (M. iv. 1123 ff., 1170 ff.) participated, sanctioned the teaching of Cyril as in accordance with Nicene doctrine, and condemned the "godless Nestorius." Many patristic citations were then read, and passages from Nestorius. "With many tears" he was then declared to be deprived of episcopal rank and of priestly fellowship (M. iv. 1212). The decision was reported to the "new Judas," the city illuminated, and the decision announced to the populace by posters upon the walls, and to the church at large by letters. Nestorius protested. John of Antioch arrived at this juncture. He at once, in the presence of the imperial commissioner, opened the properly authorized

council, which must be so called,[1] although it numbered but 43 members. Cyril and Memnon were deposed because they had illegally opened the council, and their followers excommunicated until they should be converted to the " Nicene faith." Nothing was said of Nestorius, nor of his doctrine (M. iv. 1260 ff.). The Romish legates now, for the first time, came to the front. Since Peter is "the head of the entire faith," they requested the decrees for "confirmation" (M. iv. 1289). John was three times summoned, but declared that he would have "no intercourse with deposed and excommunicated persons." The papal decision in regard to the Pelagians was approved (M. iv. 1337).[2] It was then resolved to report the action of the council to the emperor and the pope (M. iv. 1325, 1329 ff.). Such was the course of the third ecumenical council. One of the participants (Theodoret, opp. iv. 1335) declares: " No writer of comedies ever composed such a ridiculous farce, no tragic author such a mournful tragedy." The only positive result was that it was known that Cyril had been able to win the majority of those who participated in the proceedings.

Both parties now addressed themselves to the emperor. The followers of Cyril were able to cultivate a sentiment in their favor (Dalmatius). Opinion was divided in Constantinople. The emperor, weakling that he was, approved the action of both parties, and the depositions on both sides were confirmed (M. iv. 1396). Both parties now turned to him again. Nestorius voluntarily entered a cloister. The emperor received deputations from both sides. He inclined to the Alexandrines.[3] Cyril and Memnon received their bishoprics again, and the council was adjourned (M. iv. 1465).

5. But peace was not yet restored. Efforts were, therefore, made to effect a union. They proved successful, as the Antiochians surrendered Nestorius, who was now abused as a heretic, the assemblages of Cyril's followers being recognized as the legal council (see John of Antioch in M. v. 285, 289), and as Cyril was willing to subscribe to a union-symbol, prepared apparently by THEODORET OF CYROS (A. D. 433), without, indeed, retracting any of his former utterances (for further particulars, see

---

[1] The designation of the Cyrillian assemblage as " the Council of Ephesus " is justifiable only because it was afterward so recognized in the course of ecclesiastical politics, and John himself, the leader of the Antiochians, agreed to so regard it.

[2] As to the inner relationship of Pelagianism and Nestorianism, see Cassian. de incarn. i. 3; v. 1 ff.; vi. 14; cf. Faust. de grat. i. 1.

[3] It was said that Cyril, through his nephew, bribed influential persons (M. v. 819). For accounts of such "presents" of Cyril, vid. M. v. 987 ff.

HEFELE ii. 247-288). The Creed of Antioch reads (HAHN, ed. 3, p. 215):

"We, therefore, acknowledge our Lord Jesus Christ, the Son of God, the Only-begotten, complete God and complete man, of a rational soul and a body; begotten of the Father before the ages according to (his) divinity, but in the last days . . . of Mary the Virgin according to (his) humanity; that he is of the same nature with the Father according to (his) divinity, and of the same nature with us according to (his) humanity. For a union of the two natures has taken place; wherefore, we confess one Christ, one Son, one Lord. In accordance with this conception of the unconfounded union, we acknowledge the holy Virgin to be the mother of God, because the divine Logos was made flesh and became man, and from her conception united with himself the temple received from her. We recognize the evangelical and apostolic utterances concerning the Lord, making the characters of the divine Logos and the man common as being in one person, but distinguishing them as in two natures, and teaching that the godlike traits are according to the divinity of Christ, and the humble traits according to his humanity."

The Antiochians had in this the rejection of Apollinarianism and the recognition of the two natures; Cyril, the one person,[1] the union of the two natures, and the ϑεοτόχος. Each party could read its own Christology into the symbol, and Cyril did this in a liberal way.[2] But inasmuch as the formula, which excluded both extremes, had been accepted, the submerging of the matter in the drawing of inferences was prevented. There was not lacking opposition upon both sides, but it was in part quelled by force. The Nestorians were persecuted, and were able to maintain themselves only in the Persian Empire (see HEFELE ii. 270 ff.).

---

[1] Whether the one person is that of the Logos or the divine-human person is not clear in the symbol.

[2] See the letters of Cyril in M. v., and, on the other hand, the attitude of Theodoret, who remained essentially in harmony with the Antiochian Christology. Yet he emphasized the unity of the person more strongly than his predecessors : see Eranistes u. haer. fab. v. Compare BERTRAM, Theodoreti doctrina christologica, 1883. His view is, in brief : "he showed in the one person the distinction of the two natures," i. e., Paul in Rom. 5. 9 (haer. fab. v. 14, opp. iv. 1. 433). Even after the incarnation there remain two natures : "that each nature remained also unmixed after the union" (Eranist. ii. opp. iv. 1, p. 101, also p. 99), and "we do not separate the flesh of the divine Logos, nor make the union a commingling" (ib. p. 102). The divine nature did not, indeed, depart from the human nature, either on the cross or at the grave, but "being immortal and immutable, it endured neither death nor suffering" (haer. fab. v. 15, p. 435 ; cf. ep. 113. 2).

§ 25. *Eutychian Controversy and Councils of Ephesus and Chalcedon.*[1]

1. Cyril may be designated either as a Dyophysite or as a Monophysite. This explains his historical position. The orthodox were trained under his influence, and he became the teacher of the Monophysites. The Greek theory of redemption more and more repressed interest in the man Jesus. Christ, in order to "deify" us, must be God, and practical Christianity constantly tended to find its entire expression in the doctrine and mysteries of the church. That these really were divine and possessed the power of deifying man appeared to be certain only if the man Jesus was deified—if he was absolutely God. The practical conception of Christ's personality demanded this view, and the administration of the mysteries in the ritual of the church gratified it. The tendency to sensualize the spiritual, which marked the age, was here also manifest. In this way arose a piety of Monophysite type. But in theology there still survived a part of the Antiochian Christology. We can understand it, therefore, that the energetic and shrewd successor of Cyril, DIOSCURUS (from A. D. 444 bishop of Alexandria), thought to best promote his own advancement by favoring the Monophysite conception. In February, A. D. 448, the emperor had renewed the anti-Nestorian edicts. The Alexandrine bishop zealously maintained intercourse with all Alexandrine territory, and thus, with a celebrated monk in Constantinople, EUTYCHES.

Opportunity for a decided stroke now appeared to be afforded him by the agitation aroused by this archimandrite. The latter, after A. D. 433, was in the habit of accusing the Unionists of Nestorianism (see Leo ep. 20). He was in consequence denounced by Eusebius of Dorylæum at a council at Constantinople, A. D. 448 (s. HEFELE ii. 320 ff.). After various refusals, he finally appeared before the council and declared : "I confess that our Lord was of two natures before the union, but after the union I confess one nature," and "until to-day I said that the body of our Lord and God was of the same nature with us" (M. vi. 744, 742).[2] He opposed the union symbol of A. D. 433, but did not by any means accurately reproduce the doctrine of Cyril. Eutyches can scarcely be said to have possessed a theory of his own upon the subject. He was deposed and excommunicated as a reviler of Christ, with the proper accompaniment of tears (M. vi. 748). But Eutyches did not rest quietly under condemna-

---

[1] LOOFS, PRE. v. ed. 3, 635 f.
[2] Exceedingly characteristic is his earlier utterance : "Which Father has declared that the God Logos has two natures?" (M. vi. 725).

tion. By the use of placards, he aroused the interest of the populace, and also of the emperor, in his cause and appealed to Pope
Leo of Rome (Leo ep. 21). But bishop Flavian of Constantinople also laid his " burden of grief and multitude of tears " at
the feet of Leo (Leo ep. 22), declaring that Eutyches had
revived the teachings of Valentine and Apollinaris, and demanding that the pope inform his bishops of the heresies of Eutyches.
The pope had meanwhile, of his own accord, requested an accurate account of the affair, in order that he might pass judgment
upon it (ep. 23, 14). Flavian complied with the request, and
implored the pope's approval of the "faith of the God-fearing
and Christ-loving emperor " (ep. 26). The pope now sent to
Flavian his "doctrinal letter" (ep. 28). He had thus definitely fixed the attitude of Rome, which is historically a fact of
the greatest importance, for it established a positive and powerful opposition to the Alexandrine doctrine. But, meanwhile,
Dioscurus of Alexandria had entered the lists and secured the
summoning of a general council at Ephesus. Theodoret was excluded from participation in the proceedings, and Dioscurus
presided. Everything seemed to assure a Monophysite victory.

2. This resulted in the Robber Synod of Ephesus. The
pope was here represented by three legates (ep. 31. 4), who
were informed that the Catholic doctrine was contained in the
"doctrinal letter" (ep. 29).[1] But Dioscurus dominated the
council by brutal terrorism and nearly all yielded to intimida-
tion. Discussion was not desired, but the faith of the Fathers
(i. e., of the councils of Nice and Ephesus) was to be acknowledged (M. vi. 625). Eutyches defended himself, and 114
of the 135 participants were of opinion that he was orthodox.
"Anathema to everyone who speaks of two natures still after the
incarnation " (M. vi. 737, 832 ff.). Leo's letter was not even
read. Eutyches was restored. Flavian, Eusebius of Dorylæum,
together with Theodoret, Domnus of Antioch, and others, were
deposed (M. vi. 908 ff. Theodoret ep. 113, 147).

3. The victory was thus with Dioscurus. Measured by the
standard of his age, and compared with the people who followed
his leadership, we can scarcely pass a severe judgment upon him.
He had the courage to discard the traditional policy of the Alexandrine church in its compact with Rome. He had vanquished
the New Rome without the aid of the Old Rome—had even
most seriously disabled the latter. For one moment the Bishop
of Alexandria was lord of the church. An Alexandrine priest

---

[1] As to the person of Eutyches, Leo expressed himself with remarkable forbearance. ep. 29; 31. 4; 32; 33. 2; 38.

under his control became bishop of Rome (Leo ep. 53), and
Leo was excommunicated by Dioscurus (M. vi. 1009). But Leo
was shrewd enough to be true to Flavian, himself, and his
"dogmatic epistle" (ep. 50, 51, 67, 68. 1, cf. 69. 1), since
the latter was in harmony with Cyril and the first council of
Ephesus. He became the refuge of the "humble and small,"
i. e., the opposite party, who sought "help at the apostolic
throne" (Theodoret ep. 113). His constant desire was to secure
the annulling of the decrees of the Robber Synod and the summoning of a new council to be held in Italy under his leadership (ep.
44, 54. 70, cf. 55-58). Thus, and only thus, could he recover
from the defeat experienced at the hands of the "Alexandrine
bishop who usurps all things to himself" (ep. 45. 2). But Theodosius held fast to the confession of the second council of Ephesus
as the "faith of the Fathers" (Leo ep. 62-64). Yet the pope's
waiting was not in vain. Theodosius died (A. D. 450). He
was succeeded by PULCHERIA, who was married to MARCIAN. It
was decided that the desired council should be held—although
in the Orient (ep. 73, 76, 77). It appeared to be a necessity,
for it is scarcely correct to say "that the council of A. D. 449
had really pacified the church in the East" (Harnack ii. 365).
If we consider the brevity of the period during which the second
confession of Ephesus was in force, it will be evident that Harnack's conclusion is merely a dogmatic one. It follows from his
assertion of the Monophysite-Apollinarian character of Greek
Christianity. But there were other tendencies opposed to this!
The Antiochian theology was not dead. The Union symbol had
had many adherents. Individuals and whole groups of theologians in the Orient accepted the second confession of Ephesus.
Neither the calling of the council of Chalcedon, nor its transactions, can be explained under Harnack's theory (vid. Liberatus
Breviarium 12 b, Gallandi xii. 140. Theodoret ep. 113, cf.
also the opinion of LOOFS, PRE. v. ed. 3, 647 f.). Leo, indeed,
no longer needed the council, and declared it now inopportune,
especially as it was to be held, not in Rome, but at Nicæa. And,
on the other hand, his *epistula dogmatica* was, without the aid of
a council, finding ever wider acceptance in the East (ep. 82. 2 ;
83. 2 ; 89; 90; 94). But the emperor clung to his purpose,
and the Council of Chalcedon (having been first summoned to
meet in Nicæa), was accordingly held A. D. 451 (cf. M. vi. vii.
HEFELE CG. ii. 410-544. Also, KRÜGER, Monophys. Streitigkeiten in Zusammenhang. m. d. Reichspolitik, Jena, 1884).
The pope claimed the right to preside—in the person of legates
—and considered his letter sufficient to decide the matters in
controversy (ep. 93. 1. 2).

4. The contents of this letter (ep. 28) may be thus summarized : Christ is God and man, born of Mary, *her virginity being preserved* (c. 1, cf. c. 4). The two substances remain what they were, but combine in one person : "The peculiarity of each nature and substance being therefore preserved and entering into the one person, humility is received by majesty," etc. This is necessary in the interest of redemption : "One and the same mediator of God and men, the man Jesus Christ, should from the one be able to die, and from the other be unable to die." But, inasmuch as each nature retains its own peculiarity, the "emptying (*exinanitio*, cf. p. 256) by which the invisible makes itself visible . . . is not a loss of power" (3). There is, therefore, after the incarnation only one person, but the natures of this one person act in alternating fellowship : "For each form performs what is peculiar to it in fellowship with the other, *i. e.*, the Word doing that which is peculiar to the Word, and the flesh accomplishing that which is peculiar to the flesh. The one of these shines forth in miracles, the other succumbs to injuries." The one nature bewails the death of Lazarus ; the other wakes him from the dead (4). In consequence of the unity of person ("on account of this unity of person in each nature"), it may be said that the Son of man came down from heaven (Jn. 3. 13), and that the Son of God was crucified and buried (1 Cor. 2. 8), etc. (5). The confession of Eutyches, "before the incarnation two natures, after it one nature," is in both its parts equally profane. He who regards the death of Christ as a real death cannot deny "that the man whom he sees to have been passible was of our body" (6). This much-lauded document is nothing more than a reproduction of the Western Christology (Tertullian, Ambrose ; cf. Augustine). It does not enter at all upon the consideration of the problem which perplexed the Greeks, and the dogmatic simplicity of the pope is most strikingly revealed in his opinion, that the twelve propositions of the Apostles in the Creed sufficed for the refutation of this and other heresies (vid. ep. 31. 4 ; 45. 2 ; 28. 1). As to the Christology of Leo, see also ep. 35. 2 ; 59. 3-5 ; 88. 1 ; 114. 1 ; 119. 1.

5. The council itself (21 sessions in 14 days, HEFELE ii., 411 f.), attended by about 600 bishops—all Greeks—makes an exceedingly unfavorable impression. Not only was it as boisterous[1] as the Robber Synod ; but worse than this was the cowardly and senseless abandonment of Dioscurus and of the position taken two years before ("we have all been wrong ; we all beg for

---

[1] At the very first session, as Theodoret appeared : "Cast out the Jew, the adversary of God, and do not call him bishop ; " to which the opposing party responded : "Cast out the murderer Dioscurus. Who does not know the

pardon," vid. M. vi. 637 ff., 674 ff., 690, 827 ff., cf. 973 f.,
1005). Dioscurus was self-consistent. With Athanasius, Gregory,
and Cyril he professed to agree in the "one incarnated nature of
the Logos." He did not question the "of two" (ἐκ δύο), but
"the two (τὸ δύο), I do not receive" (M. vi. 684, 689). He
was deserted by all, as his deposition had been a settled matter
already at the first session. At the later sessions he did not appear—not even when summoned at the third session. A number
of accusers of this "heretic and Origenist" now cried out that
Dioscurus was a reviler of the Trinity, a desecrator of relics, a
thief, an incendiary, a murderer, a licentious fellow, a traitor
(M. vi. 1005 ff., 1012 ff., 1021 ff., 1029 ff.). But he was at
length deposed for contempt of the "divine canons" and for
"disobedience toward the council" (M. vi. 1093). As to the
matters in dispute, the doctrine of the papal letter was approved :
"This is the faith of the Fathers, this the faith of the Apostles.
Thus we all believe. Anathema to him who does not so believe !
Through Leo, Peter has spoken . . . exactly thus taught Cyril !
Why was this not read at Ephesus? Dioscurus kept it hidden"
(M. vi. 971). It was thought that the harmony of Leo's teaching
with the confessions of Nice, Constantinople (supra, p. 235, n.),
and the First Council of Ephesus could be clearly established.
Only the 13 Egyptian bishops refused to subscribe to it, and they
were in earnest in their refusal : "We will be killed, we will be
killed if we do it. We would rather be slain here by you than
there (in Egypt). Have mercy on us ; we would rather die at
your hands and the emperor's than at home " (M. vii. 53 ff., cf.
the 30th canon of the council). Despite the opposition of the
Roman legates, the letter of Leo was not given dogmatic authority, but the council at its fifth session adopted a new formula
(M vii. 112 ff.). The synodical letters of Cyril against Nestorius were adopted in refutation of Nestorianism, the letter of
Leo to Flavian in refutation of Eutychianism. Those are condemned who teach a "dyad of sons," as well as those who dream
of "two natures before the union, but one after the union." On
the contrary : "We confess one and the same Son, our Lord
Jesus Christ . . . the same perfect in divinity and the same perfect in humanity . . . of a rational soul and a body, of the same
nature with the Father according to (his) divinity, and of the
same nature with us according to (his) humanity, and we recognize the same one Christ, Son, Lord, and Only-begotten, in two
natures (not, as the Greek text reads : of, ἐκ, two natures, cf.

---

crimes of Dioscurus?" M. vi. 589, cf. also the cry : "We shout for piety
and orthodoxy."

HEFELE ii. 470 f.[1]), unmingled, immutable, indivisible, inseparable; the difference of the natures being by no means obliterated by the union, but, on the contrary, the peculiarity of each
nature being preserved and entering into one person and one
hypostasis, not divided nor separated into two persons.'' It will be
observed that these definitions do not go beyond the statements
of Leo's letter. The Western Christology was forced upon the
Greeks, for the decree of the council marks a breach, not only
with Dioscurus and Eutyches, but also with the much-lauded
Cyril. The formula preserving the peculiarity (ἰδιότης) of the
two natures was contrary to Cyril's view, as also the terms, ''unmingled, immutable.'' The Christological contradictions of the
Orient found no solution, to say nothing of a solution of the general Christological problem. But in the course of the development an element was fortunately—we cannot regard it otherwise
—introduced, which, in the form now assumed by the contest and
the terminology of the day, fixed a barrier against extreme views
in either direction. It must be remembered, too, that it is not
the office of symbols to establish dogmatic theories. They
merely give expression to the religious convictions of their age.
Such convictions found expression in the Chalcedon creed—
essentially, in consequence of the peculiar circumstances of the
period, in a negative form. As the formula of the one person
and the two natures was adopted as a fixed dogma, the historical
Christ was gained, although only in faintest outline, as the norm
and corrective for the ideas of the dogmaticians. This may be
seen most clearly in Luther.[2]

§ 26. *Movements Growing Out of the Christological Conflict
(Monophysite and Monothelete Controversies) and the Result
of the Agitation.*

1. The emperor condemned Eutyches and Dioscurus to exile.
Strict measures were employed against their followers and the
Apollinarians (M. vii. 476, 498 f., 502 f.).

[1] Originally the overwhelming majority, despite the letter of Leo, demanded
the formula: '' ἐκ δύο φύσων.'' The reason for this is evident, as this formula
left open the possibility of speaking of *only one* nature even after the incarnation. Only after severe pressure had been brought to bear from above was the
victory gained for the ἐν δύο φύσεσι—thus saving the historic Christ.

[2] Leo endured the chagrin of having the council refuse to adopt his letter
as a dogma, increase the power of the bishop of Constantinople, and place
the bishop of New Rome, in view of the equal importance of the city as
an imperial city (nothing being said of Peter), by the side of the bishop of
Rome as second in dignity. Canon 28; cf. Leo ep. 104-107, 114, 119, 127,
135 f. At the opening of the council, the clerical delegates had requested

But peace was by no means restored. On the contrary, the history of the ensuing years is marked through its whole course by the records of wild excitement and horrible deeds of religious fanaticism. Within the limits of a general History of Doctrines the MONOPHYSITE CONTROVERSIES can be treated but briefly.

LITERATURE. Vid. the KG. of Zacharias Rhetor, syr. in LAND, Anecdota syr. iii. (Cerman by Ahrens and Krüger, Leipzig, 1899). Evagrius h. e. l. ii.-v. Johannes v. Ephesus h. e., translated from the Syrian by SCHÖNFELDER, 1862. M. vii.-ix. Cf. WALCH, hist. d. Ketzereien vi.-viii. SCHRÖCKH KG. xviii. GIESELER, Comment. qua Monophysitarum opin. illustr. i.-ii., Gott. 1835, 1838. HEFELE CG. ii. 564 ff. KRÜGER, PRE. xiii., ed. 3, 372 ff. KRÜGER, Monophys. Streitigkeiten, etc., p. 68 ff., Jena, 1884. LOOFS, Leontius oi Byzantium, 1888, p. 53 ff.

A strong party arose for the defense of Monophysitism, or the doctrine of Cyril—first in Palestine (Theodosius) and in Egypt (Timotheus Aelurus, Petrus Mongus), then in Antioch (Petrus Fullo), here in alliance with the Apollinarians. All the efforts of the emperor could gain but superficial control of the movement and secure but temporary recognition for the confession of Chalcedon. This was the situation under Leo I. (A. D. 457-474). The usurper, BASILISCUS, by his *Encyclion* (A. D. 476) rejected the Chalcedon Creed, and about 500 bishops agreed with him (Evagr. h. e. iii. 4; Zachar. v. 2). The emperor, ZENO, endeavored by his *Henoticon*, A. D. 482, to effect a union (Evagr. iii. 14; Zachar. v. 8). The definitions of the councils of Nicaea, Constantinople, and Ephesus, as well as the twelve anathemas of Cyril, were here recognized, and Nestorius and Eutyches condemned. Christ the true God and the true man is confessed to be of the same nature with the Father according to his divinity, and of the same nature with us according to his humanity, but "to be one and not two. For we say that the miracles and whatever sufferings he endured in the flesh are (those) of one." Whoever adopts another teaching ($\mu\acute{a}\vartheta\eta\mu a$) than this, whether taught now or heretofore, at Chalcedon or elsewhere, is anathematized. Nothing is plain except the authority of Cyril and the rejection of Nestorianism and Eutychianism. Beyond this, the disputed formulas are carefully avoided; the rejection of the Chalcedon confession is implied but not distinctly expressed. The agitation was not allayed by this formula. Neither the strict Monophysites nor the orthodox were satisfied. The former missed in the Henoticon the ex-

the exclusion of Dioscurus, because he had presumed to open an ecumenical council without the presence of Rome. For the further history of the question, see HEFELE ii. 562 f., 568 f. The foundation was thus laid for the schism between the East and the West.

press condemnation of the Chalcedon Creed and of the letter of
Pope Leo (Zachar. v. 7, 9 ; vi. 1). The latter, as in the days
of Chalcedon, took refuge in Rome. Pope FELIX III. turned to
the emperor in defense of the endangered Chalcedon creed and
excommunicated ACACIUS, the bishop of Constantinople, A. D.
484 (ep. 1-4, 6). The latter, in turn, struck the name of Felix
from the Diptychs. The breach with Rome had become complete. It was a necessity, as an agreement was not possible between the ancient Latin Christology and the Greek doctrine,
which inclined more and more toward Monophysitism. But
even in the East there were still elements which withstood the advance of the Monophysite views. The emperor, ANASTASIUS
(from A. D. 491), permitted the "Henoticon" to stand, but
favored the Monophysite interpretation of it. Nevertheless, there
were bitter controversies during the entire reign of Anastasius.
In Antioch, Severus, one of the Monophysite leaders, became
bishop, but the emperor yet labored to secure peace with the adherents of Chalcedon and the authorities of Rome. But it was
now evident that the situation had only become the more complicated, and that the Roman bishops were contending, not in the
interest of pure doctrine, but to secure the dominion of the entire church. Hence the transactions with Pope Hormisdas were
without result (cf. Krüger, PRE. xiii., 387 f.).

2. Anastasius was succeeded by JUSTIN I. (A. D. 518-527).
He was under the control of his nephew, JUSTINIAN, who succeeded him upon the imperial throne (A. D. 527-565). The
political plans of this great prince (cf. Krüger, PRE. ix., ed. 3,
650 ff.) required the pacification of the church. The ancient
universal empire was to be revived, and restraint put upon the
aggressions of the Germans. To this end there must be harmony in the government, the laws, and the church. He sought
for the formula of the universal empire and made everything
serviceable for his own purpose. "He still lives in the *Codex*
and the *Hagia Sophia*" (see delineation of his character in
RANKE, Weltgesch. iv. 2, p. 125 f.). No one before him had
attempted to carry out in so comprehensive and reckless a way
the idea of the state church. The ecclesiastical doctrines and
ordinances became state laws, and heresy and heathenism were
forbidden by the civil government. The power of the church
was thus vastly increased, but it at the same time lost every ves-
tige of independence and distinct character as contrasted with
the state. The emperor was unwearied in his efforts to
strengthen the power of the clergy, but he at the same time
ruled in the church with despotic power. Great as was his
power, however, he was confronted by immense difficulties in

the prosecution of his final plans. The old unity of the Greek and Roman churches had been dissolved. Rome and Constantinople were now independent centres, and it was sought to combine them in one. The church of the East was to be harmonized and again united with the church of the West. The restoration of the orthodoxy of Chalcedon was hence, from the start, the watchword. It was a difficult undertaking, as the power of the Monophysites was yet unbroken in the East, and they enjoyed the sympathies of the empress, Theodora, not to mention the favor of hosts of pious believers. The creed of Chalcedon must remain in force—that was now clearly seen— and an interpretation of it found which would be tolerable for the Monophysites. The ecclesiastical primacy of Rome must be recognized in principle (vid. Novella 131. 2 : " that the pope of Old Rome is the first of all priests, but that the most blessed archbishop of Constantinople, the New Rome, has the second seat after the holy apostolic seat of Old Rome "), but the power of the popes practically overcome. Such was the task, as complicated as the circumstances and the purpose which gave it birth. The first attempted policy, that of the forcible suppression the Monophysites (Zachar. h. e. viii. 5 f.), was soon abandoned by Justinian as fruitless.

3. The theology of Justinian's age accommodated itself to the tendencies of the emperor. This was particularly true in the case of the "Scythian" monk, a relative of Vitalian, LEONTIUS OF BYZANTIUM (about A. D. 485-543. See especially his publication in three " books " against the Nestorians and Eutychians in Mi. gr. 86. 1267 ff.; cf. LOOFS, L. v. B., 1888. RÜGAMER, L. v. B., 1894). The formulas of Chalcedon are here recast in accordance with Aristotelian categories (οὐσία, γένος, εἶδος, represented by the εἰδοποιοὶ διαφοραί, or ποιότητες οὐσιώδεις, ἄτομον, see LOOFS, p. 60 ff.): φύσις and ὑπόστασις are related to one another as εἶδος to ἄτομον. But now a nature (φύσις) exists only as a substance (ὑπόστασις), just as an image exists only as a body (Mi. 86. 1278, 1280). Therefore the acknowledgment of two natures would lead to two hypostases, or to Nestorianism (ib. 1276 f.). Leontius escapes this consequence by introducing the idea of a nature as being intrahypostatic (ἐνυπόστατος). That is, one nature may combine with another to form a unity in such a way that, although it retains the peculiar characteristic of its own existence, yet it has its substance (ὑπόστασις) in the second nature. It is then not without hypostases (ἀνυπόστατος), but (ἐνυπόστατος), e. g., a man composed of body and soul, or a burning torch ; indeed, " it has given of its attributes interchangeably, which continue in the abiding and uncommingled peculiarity of their own

natures " (ib. 1304, 1278 ff.). Thus the problem of the time
appears to be solved—two independent natures, and yet only
one hypostasis. The Chalcedon creed is justified, and Cyril is
justified, for the hypostasis of Christ is thus the hypostasis of the
Logos. "Our author stands for an orthodoxy leading back as
far as possible to the Alexandrine theology. This is the permanent impression left by all his discussions " (Loofs, p. 71).
This theology made it less difficult to approach the Monophysites, which was done by the recognition of the enlarged Trisagion first introduced in Antioch by Peter the Fuller : "Holy
God, holy Mighty, holy Immortal, crucified for us, have mercy
upon us.'' It was thus acknowledged that one person of the
Trinity had suffered, and the Scythian monks gave their approval. The same end was served by a religious conference held
with the Severians at Constantinople (A. D. 533 or 531, vid.
Loofs, p. 283), as also by the condemnation of the former leaders of the Antiochian theology, Theodore of Mopsuestia, Ibas.
Theodoret (vid. decrees in M. ix.),[1] which occurred in the
course of the Three-Chapter controversy (A. D. 544). The
East soon acquiesced, but the West resented this condemnation
of its honored teachers, who had died at peace with the Church
(s. esp. Facundus Hermian, pro defensione trium capitum, in Mi.
lat. 67). The part taken in all these controversies by the
Roman bishops was, on the other hand, but a pitiable exhibition
of their weakness—a wavering between the spirit of the West
and fear of the emperor, a kicking against the pricks and a half
or entire surrender (Hormisdas and the Trisagion, Johann II.,
Agapetus I., and the Theopaschite supplement, Vigilius and the
Three-Chapter controversy, the fifth ecumenical council).

4. The FIFTH ECUMENICAL COUNCIL, A. D. 553 (M. ix.
HEFELE CG. ii. 854 ff.) was called primarily to sanction the condemnation of the Three Chapters. The bishop of Constantinople presided. About 150 bishops participated. Pope Vigilius,
who was present, protested against the condemnation. He was
in consequence denounced as a liar in view of some of his earlier
utterances, and the council resolved to strike his name from the
Dyptichs. The Three Chapters were condemned : "A Theodore,
a Judas.'' "His defenders are Jews ; his adherents heathen.
Many years to the Emperor ! '' (cf. can. 12-14). The council
of Chalcedon was recognized, Origen condemned (can. 11), the

---

[1] The church politics of Justinian and the world-embracing church mark a
visible decadence of intellectual and spiritual energy. Heathenism was forbidden, Judaism repressed, the Manichæans destroyed. The ancient school of
Athens was closed A. D. 528, Origen condemned A. D. 544, and, finally, the
Antiochians surrendered.

doctrine of the Theopaschite supplement adopted (can. 10). Pope Vigilius subsequently acquiesced in the decisions of the council (HEFELE ii. 905 ff.), as also the African bishops (ib. 913).[1] The ecclesiastical politics of the emperor had proved successful.

5. But the emperor had not yet accomplished what he desired. The situation was made more hopeless by the dissensions which arose among the Monophysites themselves. Monophysitism was primarily but an opposition to the Chalcedonian and Cyrillian theology. Its adherents spoke of the "heresy of the Dyophysites" in opposition to the doctrine of "believers," who hold to the one nature ($\mu i\alpha$ $\varphi\acute{v}\sigma\iota\varsigma$). It was acknowledged in theory that Christ is $\acute{o}\mu oo\acute{v}\sigma\iota o\varsigma$ with the Father as well as with man. Apollinaris and Eutyches were rejected (Timoth. Ael. in Zachar. h. e. iv. 12 ; v. 7). Dioscurus was the "apostolic man" who would not worship the "idol image with two faces that was set up by Leo and the assembly at Chalcedon" (ib. iii. 1). But their temper became more pronounced, and the views of the Monophysites themselves became more and more divergent. There was also, from the beginning, a group of more strict partisans, who held about the position of Eutyches (vid. *e. g.*, Zachar. h. e. iii. 9. 10). The two chief parties were known as SEVERIANS and JULIANISTS, so named from their later leaders, Severus and Julian of Halicarnassus. Severus taught essentially the Christology of Cyril : "Of two natures one Christ." He expressly recognizes the reality of the two natures after the union, in which he accords with Nestorius. But there is an "unmixed union," in which, as Cyril says, the distinction can be noted "at a single glance." He appropriates the Areopagite formula of a "new theandric energy ($\grave{\varepsilon}\nu\acute{\varepsilon}\rho\gamma\varepsilon\iota\alpha$) of Christ." He is unable to accept the Chalcedon creed, because it leads to two persons, and even to a "duad of wills." This is all in the spirit of Cyril. It makes no real difference, that Cyril starts with the Logos without flesh ($\check{\alpha}\sigma\alpha\rho\varkappa o\varsigma$) and Severus with the Logos in the flesh ($\check{\varepsilon}\nu\sigma\alpha\rho\varkappa o\varsigma$), as the latter conception occurs also frequently in Cyril (despite Loofs, p. 206 f., frg. of Severus in antiquorum patr. doctr. de verbi inc., in Leont. Hierosolym. c. Monophysit., Eustathius. ad Timoth. de duab. nat., in Mai Scriptur. vet. nov. coll. vii.; vid. also Mi. gr. 86 and several letters in Zachar. h. e. ix. 11, 13, 16, 20, 22, 23. Cf. DORNER ii. 1. 166 ff., LOOFS, l. c. p. 54 ff.). The inference from this view is that the body of Christ

---

[1] A number of bishops of Upper Italy, indeed, renounced church fellowship with Pope Pelagius I. in consequence of the Three Chapter agitation (HEFELE ii. 914 f.). The downfall of the Lombards (A. D. 568) released the Roman pontiff from the critical situation. Subsequent bishops of Rome were compelled to exert themselves with energy for the healing of the Italian schism.

was, according to its nature, capable of suffering and corruptible. Hence its opponents spoke of it as *Phthartolatry*. Its advocates did not even shrink from the inference that the human soul of Christ was not omniscient (AGNOETAE). The JULIANISTS, on the contrary, taught that Christ assumed our flesh "in order that he might deliver it at once from corruption and from sin." His human nature, being sinless, is therefore not corruptible (Julian Anath. 6, 7, in GIESELER, comment. de Monoph., etc., ii. 6). On the contrary, the body of Christ is, from the moment of the union, glorified, incorruptible, and of the same character as after the resurrection (Gieseler ib. 11. 7). Hence, Christ's capability of suffering is not natural to him, but rests upon his free-will (octo quaesit. 4, in Gieseler ii. 7). Julian did not in this way by any means wish to deny the Homousia of Christ's human nature with our humanity. By the "incorruptibility" he understood, not a Docetic character, but the freedom of Christ's nature from all the human infirmities which have resulted from the entrance of sin. Christ assumed such a body and soul as Adam possessed before the fall (cf. KRÜGER, PRE. ix. ed. 3, 608). In the face of this position, the task of the Severians was a difficult one ; for, in the denial of the *Aphtharsia* of the human nature of Christ, his divine unity, which they asserted, appeared to be lost. Hence the Julianists accused them of Aphthartolatry. Yet the Severians maintained that there was a Docetic element in the theory of Julian, charged him with holding the doctrine of Eutyches, and reviled his followers as *Aphthartodocetes* or *Phantasiasts*.

(Upon Julian, vid. ZACHAR. h. e. ix. 9 ff. Leontius, de sectis, 10, Mi. gr. 86. 1. 1260 ff. Joh. Damasc. haer. 84. ASSEMANI, Bibl. oriental. ii. 168. WERNER, in Vien. Mus. lv. 321 ff. GIESELER, l. c. Krüger, PRE. ix. ed. 3, 606 ff.)

Other Monophysites (the GAIANITES) carried out their ideas to the absurdity, that the body of Christ, from the time of the union, was uncreated. They were called ACTISTETES. Stephen Niobes held that all distinction of the divine and human in Christ must be totally denied (ADIAPHORITES).[1]

6. Justinian tolerated the Monophysites (Joh. v. Eph. h. e. i. 4 f.). Even in the capital they had honored representatives (Theodosius, John of Ephesus); and the restlessly wandering

---

[1] We have here the germ of the later Syrian Monophysite pantheism, vid. FROTHINGHAM, Stephen ben Sudaili, 1886 ; his teachings, p. 28 ff. If the unity of the divine and human in Christ was granted as a natural characteristic, the inference might easily be drawn that the two natures are essentially one. Thus this form of Greek Christian philosophy reverts to the pantheism of Greek philosophy.

Jacob el Baradai was able to accomplish much for the unification and strengthening of the party. The emperor has held the church under his control, but he has not achieved his purpose. We can easily understand from this situation how he, at the close of his career, should conceive the idea of unifying at least the church of the Orient by the adoption of Aphthartodocetism. Death prevented the execution of the edict, which he fully purposed to enforce (Evagr. h. e. iv. 39). That which he failed to accomplish, his successors (Justin II., Tiberius, Mauricius) were equally unable to attain, although they spared neither the arts of persuasion nor force. Monophysitism steadily advanced to a permanent position in church life among the Syrian Jacobites and in the Coptic, Abyssinian, and Armenian churches.

7. The efforts to win the Monophysites gave occasion, further, to the MONOTHELETE CONTROVERSIES. Here, too, political aims furnished the controlling motive.

(Vid. Acta, in M. x., xi., cf. G. KRÜGER, PRE. xiii., ed. 3, 401 ff. WALCH, Hist. d. Ketzereien ix. SCHRÖCKH, KG. xx. 386 ff. HEFELE, CG. iii. 121 ff.; OWSEPIAN, Die Entstehungsgesch. des Monotheletismus, Leipz., 1897.)

The policy was to gain support for the empire, which was hardly pressed by the Persians and Saracens, by gaining over the numerous Monophysite elements in the Eastern church—preserving, of course, at the same time the Chalcedon creed. The patriarch SERGIUS of Constantinople advised HERACLIUS (A. D. 610-641) to employ for this purpose the formula, that the one Christ performs divine and human acts "by one theandric energy" (thus already Dionys. Areop. ep. 4 and Severus supra, p. 277). Although this formula served its purpose in Egypt and elsewhere, it was necessary to abandon it because of the opposition of SOPHRONIUS of Jerusalem. Whether there is one energy or two, is not a proper matter for investigation, thought Sergius. One will ($\xi\nu$ $\vartheta\epsilon\lambda\eta\mu\alpha$) was, however, postulated of Christ as self-evident. In this spirit Sergius wrote to HONORIUS OF ROME (M. xi. 529 ff.), and the latter responded approvingly, "that the question, whether there be one energy or two, is not biblical, and belongs only to the sphere of the grammarians. Among the uninstructed populace, one energy might be interpreted as having a Eutychian sound and two as savoring of Nestorianism." It follows, on the contrary, from the fact of the incarnation : "Wherefore also we confess one will of the Lord Jesus Christ" (M. xi. 537 ff.). In a second letter, the pope again rejected the question concerning the energies, and employed Leo's formula, that each of the two natures "works in fellowship with the other" (M. xi. 580). Sergius, therefore, secured the publication of his Ἔκθεσις πίστεως, A. D. 638): Two natures with their peculiarities, "but one hypostasis and one person of the divine Logos, together with rationally-animated flesh;" "we ascribe all divine and human energy to one and the same incarnated Logos . . . and do not by any means permit anyone to maintain or teach either one or two energies of the incarnate Lord." The two energies would work confusion, as they would give occasion for the inference : "And there preside two wills of those who are in opposition to one another," which even the impious Nestorius would not have dared to assert. It is thus impossible to accept "two, and these opposing, wills in the same (person)." Following the Fathers in all things, it is to be said : "We confess . . . one will of our Lord Jesus Christ" (M. x. 992 ff.). The Roman legates of Severinus, the successor of Honorius, declared themselves ready to adopt the Ecthesis; but as early as A. D. 641, JOHN IV. of Rome condemned Monotheletism (M. x. 607), while, at the same time, he endeavored to defend Pope Honorius from the suspicion of a Monothelete type of doctrine, maintaining that the latter had in mind only the human will of Christ, and denied that there were two contrary wills in Christ (vid. his Apol. pro papa Honor., M. x. 682 ff.). His successor, Theodore I., desired the rejection of the Ecthesis (M. x. 702, 705 f.). The Africans assumed the same attitude (Hefele iii. 205 ff.). The emperor, CONSTANS II., yielded in the τύπος of A. D. 648. The problem is to be banished from the world forever, as had been attempted in the Ecthesis. The latter is surrendered, and questions are to be decided in accordance with the five ecumenical councils, the utterances of the Fathers, and the doctrinal positions held before the controversy, just "as it would have been if no such controversy had ever arisen." "We decree that our subjects abiding in orthodoxy . . . shall, from the present time, not have permission to carry on any controversy whatsoever among themselves concerning one will or energy, or two energies and two wills," etc. Any who may disregard this decree are threatened with severe punishments (M. x. 1029 f.). It may be seen from this brutal composition to what tyranny the secularized church was compelled to submit.

8. But at Rome there were hopes of accomplishing something more. The monk, MAXIMUS, proved in writings and disputations that Dyotheletism is a necessary inference from the two natures of the Chalcedon creed (his writings were edited by Combesis, 2 vols., Paris, 1675 ; see esp. the interesting disputation with Pyrrhus in Combes. ii. 159-195 ; M. x. 709 ff.; cf. upon Maximus, Wagermann-Seeberg, PRE. xii., ed. 3,

457 ff.).[1] We must devote some attention to the Christology of Maximus. He was inspired by a keen interest in the
reality of the humanity of Christ. Without a human will, he
maintained, Christ would not have been a man (opp. ii. 105-
108). On the other hand, the doctrine of the Trinity demands
Dyotheletism ; for since, according to the Fathers, the Trinity
has a will, the theandric will of Christ must also be the will of
the Trinity (ii. 163). This is impossible. The real human nature of Christ requires a human will, and with this the divine
will united itself. The unity of the two is effected through the
one hypostasis which is common to both (ii. 164). Christ lived
as God and man (ii. 165). Since the Logos assumed human
nature, he received also a human will, which acts in a way corresponding with its natural psychological character. But this
will was not compelled, as is ours, to decide between opposites,
but, by virtue of its union with the Logos, it received a permanent, fixed moral inclination. In this way the true doctrine is distinguished from that of Nestorius (ii. 13, 14). The celebrated
formula of the Areopagite ($\vartheta\varepsilon\alpha\nu\delta\rho\iota\varkappa\grave{\eta}$ $\grave{\varepsilon}\nu\acute{\varepsilon}\rho\gamma\varepsilon\iota\alpha$) itself proves the
presence of two energies, but is merely the expression of the em-
pirical relationship (ii. 51). The opinion of Maximus is therefore : that the Logos appropriates to himself the human will of
Christ, since he by this union with it gives to it a fixed inclination, which, however, exerts itself in many separate free human
choices. The theology of Maximus rightly defined the nature of
the man Jesus, positing it in the spiritual will, and it exerted
itself with energy to maintain this nature intact within the lines
of the two-nature theory. This gives to it its historical significance. It is remarkable to observe how, toward the end of the
great controversies, ideas again came to the front which had at
the beginning been advanced by the Antiochians.

We return to the contemplation of the course of external events.
Pope MARTIN I., without waiting for the imperial approval, conducted a large synod (105 bishops) at Rome, A. D. 649. He here
declared himself opposed to the Ecthesis, as contradicting the
two natures, and also opposed to the Typos, which he dismissed
with the perfidious charge, that it denies to Christ will and
energy, and thus every kind of nature. The synod decided in
accordance with his wishes, adding to the Chalcedon creed :
" two natural wills, divine and human, and two natural operations " (M. x. 1150). With great energy the pope now sought
to interest the Frankish church and the two kings in his cause,

---

[1] Reversing the process, the Monotheletes from the one person inferred one
will, *e. g.*, M. x. 709.

and endeavored to gain influence in the Oriental churches among the Saracens. It was even charged that he gave money to the Saracens in Sicily. The emperor treated both the pope and Maximus as traitors. They died in exile, A. D. 655 and 662. EUGENE I. and VITALIAN of Rome adapted themselves to the situation, their scruples apparently met by the reflection that the two natural wills unite in one hypostatic will. We may, therefore, speak of one will as well as of two, accordingly as we use the term. Rome, on the other hand, would know nothing of this, as the doctrine of Maximus had there full sway.

9. Constans was murdered A. D. 668 and succeeded by CONSTANTINE POGONATUS (A. D. 668-685). The constantly obtruding antagonism between Rome and Constantinople induced the emperor to call a council and to yield, as far as possible, to the demands of Rome—the greater part of the Monophysites being in any event lost to the Byzantine empire. This resulted in the Sixth Ecumenical[1] Council, held at Constantinople, A. D. 680. There were about 170 participants (proceedings in M. xi.; cf. HEFELE iii. 249 ff.). The letter of Pope AGATHO here played an important part. It is presented as the doctrine of the Romish church, which has never departed from the way of truth, or the apostolic tradition, that—as an inference from the doctrine of two natures—the will of Christ is two-fold, having in it "two natural wills and energies just as two natures" (M. xi. 239). Accordingly, the council decided, after the reading of volumes of patristic excerpts—not, indeed, without opposition (Polychronius, a Monophysite, seeking by his formula to call a dead issue to life)—in accordance with the wishes of the emperor ("Thou hast established the completeness of the two natures of our God," M. xi. 656) and the pope ; but Honorius of Rome was anathematized as well as the Monothelete patriarch of Constantinople. The doctrinal decree recognizes the letter of Agatho and the five ecumenical councils. After citing the formulas of Chalcedon, it proceeds : "Two natural willings (θελήσεις) or wills (θελήματα) in Christ and two natural energies, inseparably, immutably, indivisibly, without mixture, according to the teaching of the holy Fathers. . . . It follows that his human will is not in opposition or conflict with, but, on the contrary, is subject to his divine and almighty will. . . . For just as his flesh is called and is the flesh of the divine Logos, so also his proper human will is called and is the will of the divine Logos. . . . His flesh deified is not divided . . . so also his human

---

[1] It was not the original purpose to summon an " ecumenical " council, s. HEFELE iii. 260.

will deified is not divided . . . for each form performs what
is peculiar to it with the fellowship of the other form '' (M. xi.
637).

The revival of Monotheletism at a later date (A. D. 711-713)
by the emperor, Philippicus Bardanes, and the Monotheletic
church of the MARONITES, which persisted in Lebanon until the
Crusades, are of no dogmatic significance.

The Council of Constantinople marks the termination of the
great intellectual movements which had agitated the church from
the days of Apollinaris, and of Nestorius and Cyril.   It did not
originate any new ideas nor intellectual tendencies, as the age did
not furnish the necessary inner religious force.   This was evident
from the fact that, as in all ages of deterioration, there was lacking the courage to undertake anything new.   Passages of the
''Fathers'' were anxiously sought after.   Citations were gathered by the volume, and it was not ventured to maintain any
position until some word of one of the great Fathers of the
earlier age could be found for support and protection.   Thus the
council did nothing more than draw an inference from the Chalcedon creed, and this was attached to the latter in a quite external way.   It was, however, a just inference.   It thus, in its
own way, gives evidence that the Chalcedon creed was not a
Trojan horse for the church of the Orient.   On the contrary, it
made it necessary for her theologians to pursue the doctrine of
the two natures to its profound depths.   The two natures must
be apprehended in their full significance, as extending not only
to the external φύσις, but also to the internal spiritual life with
its centre, the will.   In this way the problem became more and
more difficult : Two inner wills and yet only one inner person.
The council presented, not a solution, but an assertion.   Yet it
stated distinctly a fact, and one which summoned Christian
thought to a serious task.   There was, however, lacking in the
Greek Christianity of the age the energy necessary to a proper
discharge of this obligation, and the church of the West felt no
interest in the problem as such.

10. The historical development which we have reviewed in
the above paragraphs was a most remarkable one.   Forces which
appear to have everything in their favor succeed in making
their way but feebly, and their power is broken by cold formulas.
Intellectual forces which appear to have been entirely overcome
continue to exert a silent influence.   The formalism of Greek
philosophy comes to the assistance of the church's dogma.   External considerations of church policy become the decisive factors in the discussions of doctrine.   A reckless abandonment of
old and a compulsory adoption of new formulas alternate with

one another, and, as the result of it all, the recognition of a certain *inner* necessity!

We must note a few details of the process. The great Athanasius had, in the interest of practical religion, established the Homousia of the Son. The man Jesus served the divine Logos as the organ through which he acted. But this idea was capable of many interpretations, although the Homousia was the fixed premise for them all. One might adopt the bold course of Apollinaris, who treated the human nature of Christ as did Arius his divinity, *i. e.*, mutilated it. Or, one might conceive the problem in the sense of the first view of the Antiochians, and lay all stress upon the inner personal unity of the Logos with the man Jesus—a view which, as an intellectual formula, if not as an actual theory, continued to be influential even after it had been condemned in the person of Nestorius. Or, again, one might, with Cyril, centre his theory in the divine-human unity of Christ, his deified nature, and thus be led—under the increasing pressure of the mystical materialism of the age—to the Monophysite position. It is evident that the broad current of Greek piety flowed within this channel. Finally, one might face the problem with the formulas of Tertullian in hand, and constantly oppose these formulas, as a canon, to all assaults of the times. Rome possessed these formulas. But Rome was a political power. The desire to preserve intact the unity of the East and the West made the Greek emperors dependent upon the dogmatic teachings of Rome. They were compelled to give due recognition to the Roman formulas; and this became but the more necessary, as there were never lacking among Greek theologians and believers earnest opponents of Monophysitism. All who had any realization of the problem as stated by the Antiochians could adopt the Western formulas, but not the views of the Monophysites. It was political considerations, indeed, but not these alone, which compelled the emperors to join in league with the dogmatics of Rome. Thus was brought about the second decisive event in the history of Christology, ranking in importance with the adoption of the Nicene creed, *i. e.*, the construction and adoption of the creed of Chalcedon, marking the triumph of Western Christology in the East. That this was possible, and that the Chalcedon creed, despite the most bitter opposition, was not only able to maintain itself, but controlled the entire development of the future, proves very clearly that it is a great mistake to place the oriental Christology simply upon the plane of Monophysitism. But if the Chalcedon creed had really won a secure footing in the East, then the entire course of subsequent events is intelligible. Such theologians as Leontius and Maximus must labor to interpret the now accepted creed as far as possible in harmony with the teachings of Cyril. Monophysitism and Monotheletism must be driven from the church. The sixth ecumenical council was compelled to decide as it did, and John of Damascus could not tolerate any other doctrine. All this followed by necessity upon the adoption of the creed of Chalcedon.

It may be said, in view of the above : Thus it was the political scheming of the calculating demagogues at Rome and of the imperial advisers at Constantinople that framed the faith of the church ! This is not untrue, and yet it is not correct. It is not untrue, for without the political ambitions of the age, the creed of Chalcedon would not have been constructed, nor could it have secured the approval of Justinian, and the sixth ecumenical council would never have been held. On the other hand, the statement is not correct, for without the faith of the Greek church, Monophysitism and Monotheletism could never have been permanently banished. In order to realize this, it is only necessary to consider the Christology of Maximus, who was a thorough-going Greek and a fanatical Areopagite. Thus was formed the Christology of the Greek church. It is Chalcedonian, but limits the humanity as far as possible. It is Cyrillian, but also anti-Monophysite. Cyril and the Chalcedon Creed are the authorities by which it is determined. The two tendencies which, at the beginning of the controversy, struggled for the mastery—the Antiochian and the Alexandrine—were, as a result of the controversy, in a measure, united, having both found their secure unity in the Christological scheme of the West. Politics led to this result, but politics could never have chosen this way if the course of inward development in the church had not required it. The Western Christology was taken into account, not only in order to satisfy Rome, but also in order to gratify those in the East who were not in accord with the Monophysite doctrine.

The position recently taken, especially by Ritschl and Harnack, that Greek piety was Monophysite in type, and that, in consequence, the conception of Soteriology here dominant, can have represented only the Christology of Dioscurus or Julian, cannot be sustained in view of the actual facts. It generalizes upon an observation which is, in itself, correct. Generalizations of this character may be an effectual aid in the establishment of particular theories, but they cannot be permanently maintained. This is manifest from the account above given, but others also, as, *e. g.*, Loofs and Krüger, have begun to call attention to the one-sided nature of this modern interpretation of history.

11. John of Damascus gave the final form to Christology

also upon Grecian territory (see his Ἔχθεσις πίστεως, cf. supra,
p. 236). The dogmatics of this leader again mirror the character of the preceding centuries. Faith is the "not over-
curious assent" to the incomprehensible doctrine of the triune
God, the dogmas of the church, and the utterances of the
Fathers (iv. 9, 10, 11; i. 1), along with which many strange
things are advocated (adoration of the cross, the manger, the
socket of the cross, saints, relics, images, celibacy, iv. 11 f.,
15 f., 24).[1] (*a*) John is a thorough Chalcedonian and Dyothe-
lete in his Christology (vid. book iii. of *De fide orthodoxa :*
"One hypostasis in two natures"). From the latter it necessarily
follows that Christ also possessed two natural wills and energies
(iii. 13-15). We can no more accept the idea of one will (iii.
14) than we can speak of one composite nature (iii. 2). In the
Cyrillian formula : "One nature of the divine Logos, made
flesh" (μία φύσις τοῦ θεοῦ λόγου σεσαρκωμένη), the term "made
flesh" indicates "the essence (οὐσία) of the flesh" (iii. 7,
p. 215, c. 11, p. 221). (*b*) The union of the two natures is implied in the acknowledgment of one hypostasis. Here John
follows Leontius.[2] It is, indeed, true that no nature (φύσις) is
without hypostasis (ἀνυπόστατος), and no essence ; (οὐσία) is without person (ἀπρόσωπος); but it is possible for two natures to have
a common hypostasis. The flesh of Christ has no other hypostasis
than that which the Logos also has ; "but is, on the contrary, en-
hypostatic in the same hypostasis" (iii. 9). The Logos-hyposta-
sis, therefore, became the hypostasis of the formerly impersonal
flesh : "For he assumed a germ of our clay, not used before as
an actual hypostasis and atom and thus taken to himself, but
having its existence in the same hypostasis. For the hypostasis of
the divine Logos became an hypostasis in the flesh, and in this

---

[1] The divisions of this work are as follows (cf. Origen, Theognostos,
supra, p. 147, n. 2, 186, n. 1, and Gregory of Nyssa, Augustine, Peter Lombard, Melanchthon): Book I. treats of God, his incomprehensibility, revelation,
the Trinity, divine attributes, etc.   Book II. discusses the world, the devil,
heaven, the air, winds, paradise, man—including under the last-named heading the whole range of psychology, free-will, etc.   Book III. treats of Christ,
the two natures, the one hypostasis, the trisagion, the mother of God, the life,
energies, and will of Christ, his unblamable emotions, his fear, his prayers, his
sufferings, the descent to hell, etc.   Book IV. deals with the state of the risen
Saviour, redemption, baptism, faith, the cross, the mysteries, worship of
saints, images, the Scriptures, the Jews, celibacy, circumcision, Antichrist, the
resurrection, etc.   That this outline became—not to the advantage of dogmatic theology—a model for later discussions, cannot be denied.   We look in
it in vain for an answer to the question, What is Christianity ? or, What is the
Gospel?
[2] Whom he often uses and in iii. 11 expressly names (although Harnack,
DG. ii., ed. 3, 410, n., declares that Leontius is "never mentioned").

way 'the Logos became flesh' '' (iii. 11. pp. 220, 221 ; c. 2 :
"The Logos himself became an hypostasis in the flesh "). This
is the conception of Cyril and Leontius, and also of Apollinaris.
But, since the term "hypostasis" does not exactly correspond
with our term "personality," but indicates as well simply individual existence (iii. 7), the Damascene speaks of a "composite hypostasis" of Christ.   As Christ is God and man, there
belongs to him the separate divine-human existence, or hypostasis.
Hence John can say : "The hypostasis of the divine Logos before the incarnation was single and incomposite and non-corporate
and uncreate ; but it became incarnate and a hypostasis in the
flesh, and became compounded of divinity, of which it always
partook, and of flesh which it assumed, and it bears the properties
of the two natures, being seen in two natures, so that this one
hypostasis is uncreate in its divinity and create in its humanity,
visible and invisible" (iv. 5 ; similarly iii. 3, 4, 5, 7, 14).
(c) With this unity of the hypostasis is involved the mutual participation and interpenetration of the two natures : "The Logos
participates in the human (attributes) . . . and imparts of its
own to the flesh in the way of exchange through the mutual
revolution of parts and the hypostatic union, and because it was
one and the same performing both the divine and the human acts
in either form with the participation of the other" (iii. 3, the
closing part cited from Leo ; see also iv. 18).   But this interpenetration proceeds only from the side of the divine nature (iii.
7 fin.).   The human will of Christ is deified, so that he voluntarily wills what the divine will of Christ wills (iii. 17, 18).   His
humanity is also omniscient (iii. 21).   Christ does not know any
choice ($\pi\rho\omega\alpha\iota\rho\epsilon\sigma\iota\varsigma$, iii. 14).   The declaration of Lk. 2. 52
is to be understood as a revelation of the wisdom which dwells in
him, or as indicating that he assumes as his own the progress
made by the human nature (iii. 22).   The prayers referred to
in Matt. 26. 39 and 27. 46 are simply for our instruction, or designedly vicarious (iii. 24).   The divine nature has no direct
relation to the sufferings of Christ (iii. 15).   This is illustrated
by various similes.   If we strike a tree upon which the sunlight
is falling, the sun is not struck, but remains without suffering ;
and if we pour water upon glowing iron, the fire is extinguished,
but the iron remains, according to its nature, unconsumed (iii.
26).   From the hypostatic union is inferred, indeed, the propriety
of worshiping the flesh of Christ (iii. 8 ; iv. 2) and of employing
the term "mother of God" (iii. 12 : "For this name involves
the whole mystery of the economy "), and it is taught that Christ
effects our salvation according to his two natures (iii. 14); but this
does not overbalance the one-sided intoning of the divine nature

in the Christology of John. He is the diligent recorder of the
doctrinal development up to his own day, but there is no ground
for the extolling of the truthfulness and profundity of his view (as
is done by THOMASIUS DG. i. 391). His ideas followed the lines
of the Chalcedon creed and his spirit was Cyrillian ; but he did
not succeed in giving effectual prominence to the valuable
features of Cyril. He presents the result of Greek Christology—
i. e., the Chalcedon creed triumphed, but it triumphed in
alliance with Cyril.

CHAPTER III.

GENERAL CONCEPTION OF CHRISTIANITY.   COMPLETION OF DOC-
TRINAL CONSTRUCTION IN THE EAST (NICAEA, A. D. 787).

§ 27. *Greek Christianity.*

We can here make but a few general comments upon this
theme. The material is inexhaustible.

We shall depend chiefly—after the writings of ATHANASIUS ; those of the
three CAPPADOCIANS ; the homilies of CHRYSOSTOM († A. D. 407 ; opp. ed.
Montfaucon, 1718 ff. Mi. gr. t. 47-64); the 50 homilies of MACARIUS THE
GREAT († about A. D. 390, ed. Floss, 1850. Mi. gr. 34)—upon the comprehensive presentations of the subject by CYRIL OF JERUSALEM in his catechisms
(† after A. D. 381, ed. Touttée, 1720. Mi. gr. t. 33); the large catechism of
GREGORY OF NYSSA ; the De fide orthodoxa of JOHN OF DAMASCUS ; the works
of MAXIMUS THE CONFESSOR (ed. by Combesis, 1675), and of ANASTASIUS
SINAITA (Mi. gr. 89), etc.; and finally the writings of PSEUDODIONYSIUS AREO-
PAGITA (de coelesti hierarchia, de ecclesiastica hierarch., de divinis nominibus,
de mystica theologica, epistulae 10, ed. Corderius, 1634, also 1644 and 1755 in
Mi. gr. 4, translated and scrutinized by ENGELHARDT, 1823 ; cf. HIPLER,
Dionys. der Ar., 1861 ; STIGLMAYR, Das Aufkommen der ps.-Dionys.
Schriften, etc., 1895 ; H. KOCH, Das Aufkommen der pseudodionysian.
Schriften, in Theol. Quartelschr., 1895, 353 ff.; BONWETSCH, PRE. iv., ed
3, 687 ff.   BARDENHEWER, Patrologie, 1894, p. 284 ff.[1] Cf. further KUNZE,
Marcus Eremita, 1895 : HOLL, Enthusiasmus u. Bussgewalt beim griech.
Mönchtum, 1898. HARNACK DG. ii., ed. 3, 441 ff.).

[1] There is yet no general agreement as to the time when these writings appeared.   They are first mentioned at a synod at Tyre, which was held not later
than A. D. 513 (Zachar. rhet. h. e. vii.; 12 in Land, Anecdota Syr. iii. 228),
and by Severus (bishop of Antioch, A. D. 512-518, vid. Mai, Vet scriptor. nov
coll. vi. 1, p. 71); then at the religious colloquy at Constantinople, A. D. 533
(M. viii. 817 ff.; vid. also Liberat. breviar. 10 ; and BONWETSCH, l. c.
689).   It appears safe to place its appearance at the close of Cent. v. in Syria.
As the writings now stand (have they been revised ?) they appear (despite
the arguments of Hipler to the contrary) to be a designed forgery (cf. STIGL-
MAYR and KOCH).   Suspicion is aroused by the relationship of the eighth letter

1. " Orthodoxy " and "good works," according to Methodius, constitute Christianity (supra, p. 190, and Clem. Al., p. 146). Cyril of Jerusalem names " the teaching, μάθευμα, of the dogmas " and "good works " (cat. 4. 2 ; cf. Const. ap. iii. 12). But among the Greeks the emphasis was laid more and more upon the " orthodox " doctrine. The doctrine of the church as such, in its technical and detailed form, was regarded as an object of faith. This explains the acrimony in the conduct of controversies, and the bad habit of denying life and salvation to the adherents of another doctrinal formula. The " tradition of the Catholic church," *i.e.*, the dogmas of the Trinity and the two natures in Christ, is to be accepted and believed to be true (*e. g.*, Cyril. cat. 16. 24 fin.; 5. 12 ; 11. 20 init. Greg. Nyss. cat. m. 1-3 ; 39. Joh. Dam. iv. 10). It is only necessary to observe the style employed in the documents named in order to realize that the bread is here already beginning to turn into stone. The dogmas are state laws whose acknowledgment the state requires of its citizens. It therefore persecutes with its own weapons opposition to the doctrines of the church. But these same doctrines are also an expression of the most ancient convictions of Christian truth. It is only by their acceptance that a saving view of the truth can be obtained. But such a view is made dependent upon a merely intellectual apprehension of the truth. Here, then, appears the office of the mysteries. He who participates in these is lifted above the world in the experience of salvation. Here becomes manifest the life-giving fountain of religion. The doctrines are the theory of life : the mysteries bestow this life. But only he who accepts the theory can experience that which it contains. It is easy to understand that the conception of the inward nature of Christianity should thus be gradually lost. The Pauline doctrine of justification was never comprehended by the Greek church. The internal element which it contains did not become a motive for the regulation of piety. To believe means " simply to obey," *i. e.*, the traditional doctrine, and how this can bring salvation to a man, cannot be made plain to the inner consciousness (see, *e. g.*, Cyril. cat. 5. 5 ; the homilies of Chrys. upon Romans 1. 17 ; 4. 7 ; 3. 21 ; Gal. 2. 8, 16 f.; Heb. 11). Faith is nothing more than the acceptance of a doctrine, with its mysteries and with the injunctions to the performance of pious works. But when faith has been robbed of its true character, the church must find for herself a substitute. The church

---

(cf. eccl. hier. iii. 3. 7) to that which Dionysius of Alexandria wrote against Novatian (Eus. h. e. vii. 8 f.); and also by the relation of a passage of the letter (§ 5) to the *ep. ad Cononem* of Dionys. Al., § 3 (in Pitra, jur. eccl. Graecorum hist. et Monum. i. 547 ; cf. 549 f.).

of the West chose "good works;" that of the East, worship and its mysteries, mystic consecrations, relics and saints, amulets and images. Thus there is poured into the church the whole current of religious materialism, which seeks to realize the spiritual and eternal in sensuous, tangible and audible forms. Christianity *is* participating in worship, subjection to ecclesiastical ordinances. The sacred symbols are commended to the multitude, and the spirit of reverence for them cultivated—as in the "dreadful hour" when the "terrible mystery" of the eucharist is presented (cf. Chrysost. de sacerdot. iii. 4 ; ep. ad Olympiad. 2. 2 init.; the 9th homily upon repentance). This is represented as Christian piety. The same may be said of all parts of the "second order of Christianity," and even of the mystery of the dogmatic formulary itself. The interest of the populace in the dogmatic controversies was, after all, only that of veneration for a formula. There is nothing left to awaken devout longings and hold reverence in the "beholder" (Dionys. Ar.) but the venerated symbol. Thus visible sacred symbols were relied upon to lead the soul to the vision of the spiritual : "Since it is not possible for the spirit in our state to pass through to that immaterial imitation and contemplation of the heavenly hierarchies unless it makes use of the material guidance to it, we regard the visible beautiful things as reflections of the invisible loveliness, and the sensible odors as typifications of the spiritual largess, and the material lights as images of the immaterial glory, and the *sacred doctrines* as channels for the satisfying of the mind contemplatively. . . . In which way he would lead us through things sensible to things spiritual" (Dionys. coel. hier. 1. 3 ; eccl. hier. 1. 2, 4, 5 ; 3. 2 : "the multitude catching a glimpse only of the divine symbols;" 3. 3. 12 ; 4. 3. 1). It is the flourishing period of the *arcana disciplina*.

2. This reveals the fundamental thought of the work of DIONYSIUS AREOPAGITA, which became so influential in the East. (*a*) Christianity is the representation of the ladder of sacred symbols, mysteries, consecrations, which come down from God to men through the medium of divinely-enlightened hierarchs— and the persuading of men to climb upward upon the ladder of these mysteries to God. Grace reveals itself in a complex of purifying and consecrating mysteries. In this connection, the "hierarchy"—in a way peculiar to the Orient—finds its place. (*b*) God is the unpredicated, supersubstantial Existence. This "primeval source" (div. nom. 1. 3, 5), this "darkness above light" (theol. myst. 1. 1), this "unapproachable Light," and this "divine darkness" (ep. 5) is not approachable to man. But God allows himself to be known by man by means of the

hierarchical ladder. (c) The hierarchy is hence a sacred order and agency through which God, extending his energies from person to person, *purifies*, *illuminates*, and *perfects*—or actually *deifies*—those whom these energies reach (coel. hier. 3. 1, 2 ; 7. 2, 3 ; 9. 2 ; 10. 2; 12. 2 ; eccl. hier. 1. 1, 3 ; 5. 1. 4, 7 ; 6. 3. 6, 1, 3 : " For as one, in speaking of all taken together, calls the order of the priests a hierarchy, so evidently, when speaking of the chief priest (hierarch), he means the inspired and divine man who presides over all sacred knowledge. . . . The source of this hierarchy is the fountain of life . . . the one cause of existing things, the Triad, from whom come both existence and prosperity to existing things through his goodness. . . . And this is the common aim of the entire hierarchy, an intimate affection for God and divine things . . . the gnosis of existing things, in which all things exist . . . the vision and understanding of sacred truth, the inspired impartation of the unique perfection of this One as far as possible, the feast of contemplation spiritually nourishing and deifying him who attains to it"). (d) This hierarchy is primarily the heavenly hierarchy of angels, which in its three orders bears a graduated relation to the Deity (coel. hier. 4-9). Through it God revealed himself under the old covenant (ib. 4. 3). Then follows the earthly hierarchy, whose source, essence, and power is Jesus, the supremely-deified and supersubstantial mind (δ $\vartheta\varepsilon\alpha\rho\chi\iota\varkappa\omega\tau\alpha\tau\sigma\varsigma$ $\nu\sigma\tilde{\upsilon}\varsigma$ $\varkappa\alpha\grave{\iota}$ $\dot{\upsilon}\pi\varepsilon\rho\sigma\dot{\upsilon}\sigma\iota\sigma\varsigma$). Through him, or the Holy Trinity, according to the declarations of the sacred Scriptures, the hierarch is filled with divine knowledge and inducted into the "sacred and spiritual vision" (ib. 1. 2, 3 ; 3. 2. 1 fin.; 3. 3. 14). But there is here also a three-fold gradation (hierarch, priest, deacon), which is regarded as absorbing God, not in a local way, but according to capacity (ep. 8. 2), in which process purity becomes the portion of the deacons, illumination that of the priests, and perfection that of the hierarchs (cf. ib. 5. 1. 5, 6 ; 6. 3. 5). Furthermore, the incumbents of the higher orders possess also the endowments of the lower (ib. 5. 3. 7). (e) By means of the sacred mysteries, the hierarchs perform their official duties toward the people, purifying, enlightening, and perfecting them. These symbols are baptism (ib. 2), the eucharist (ib. 3), the holy oil (ib. 4), the consecration of the priesthood (ib. 5), monastic consecration (ib. 6 : "possessors of the most perfect philosophy"), consecrations and prayers for the dead (ib. 7). The aim of all these symbolical acts is union with God through the luxurious contemplation of his Being (coel. hier. 3. 2 ; eccl. hier. 1. 3): "Trinity more than nature, more than God, and more than good ! Thou guardian of the wisdom of Christians, lead us to the more than unknown and more than lofty and unapplauded summit of the mystic doctrines, where the simple and absolute and unchangeable mysteries of theology are veiled in the more-than-light darkness of the crypto-mystic science, shining with superlative brilliancy in the superlatively dark, and more than filling unfettered souls in the absolutely intangible and invisible (realm) of super-lovely glories'' (theol. myst. 1 init.).[1] Rightly did a philosopher term our author a "patricide" (ep. 7. 2). The Neo-Platonic premises of this opponent of heathenism are everywhere very apparent. "All transitory things are but a parable—the insufficient here is that which occurs." Such is the Neo-Platonism of the Areopagite. It is a distinct expression of the Greek Christianity of a later period. The Christianity of dogmatic formulas has been paralyzed by the devotional symbols, although the veneration of formulas finds in this very devotional tendency its strongest support. The great majority were satisfied with the formula, and the latter might easily become a mere formula of enchantment.

3. Recognizing this fact, we feel that less importance attaches to the separate doctrines presented by the Areopagite. We must constantly keep in mind his fundamental principle. Greek Christianity evolved no "dogmas," in the strict sense of the term, except those above discussed. We note particularly the lack of interest in matters pertaining to personal religious life. Men spoke of sin and grace with the same unsophisticated piety, or unsophisticated rationalism, in the centuries following as in those preceding the Nicene period. The problems which held the interest of Augustine leave no trace in the East. Yet it would be incorrect to regard the Oriental church as Pelagian, as the problem upon which Pelagius and Augustine joined issue does not even occur to their minds.

The state of man fallen into sin is, after as before the Nicene age, painted in the darkest colors. The devil has gained possession of the soul ; the serpent dwells as a second soul within our own (Macar. hom. 15. 35, 49): "Thus the evil prince clothed the soul and its whole substance with sin, and polluted it entire, and made it entire a prisoner to his kingdom, and did not release nor set free from him a single part, not the reasoning powers, nor the spirit, nor the body, but he clothed the soul in a garment of darkness. . . . The evil one put upon the whole soul, *i. e.*,

---

[1] Observe the transcendental character of the Neo-Platonic conception of God. Of God, as the Absolute Existence, everything existent must be affirmed and again denied (div. nom. i. 5-7 ; 7. 3 ; theol. myst. 3-5, cataphatic and apophatic theology). This accounts for the many combinations with ὑπέρ and α privitive in the Areopagite.

the essential member and part of man, its malady, *i. e.*, sin, and thus the body became passible and mortal" (Macar. h. 2. 1 ; Marcus Erem. c. Nestor. 18). Thus the whole man, with all his powers, is imbued with sin. He is separated from God. The devil holds sway over his soul. Sensuality overpowers the reason. Man, originally destined for immortality, becomes transitory and subject to death—in all things the very opposite of his original character and condition (Greg. Nyss. cat. 5. Athanas. c. gent. 3 f. Dionys. eccl. hier. 3. 3. 11). He has forfeited grace and boldness toward God, and has won for himself "mortality and the dullness of the flesh." He is "sentenced to death" and "subject to perdition" (Joh. Dam. iii. 1), the emphasis being laid finally upon the latter. Sin is at the same time regarded not so much in the aspect of guilt as in that of infirmity or weakness—of mortality and death. This is a different attitude from that of the West. It directs the thoughts not only upon the forgiveness of sins, but upon the contemplation of the state of sin and its conquest by means of a new inner life.

That the entire human race fell into this condition through the fall of Adam is acknowledged. But, although the idea of the inheritance of sin may at times appear to be advanced (Greg. Nyss. cat. 16 : "The pleasurable pain of human birth teaches . . . the beginning of death, having been made in one, has passed through upon the whole human nature" (de orat. 5): "to speak again of the common debts of human nature, in which each and everyone who shares the lot of nature bears a part" (Oehler iii. 300. Dionys. Ar. eccl. hier. 3. 3. 11 : "Having had its origin in corrupt births, it naturally pursues its course in a way conformable to its beginning"), yet it is only meant, after all, that since Adam the human race has been subject to corruption. In view of the conflict between the spiritual and the sensuous inclinations of man, it is difficult, or altogether impossible, to abstain entirely from sin (Greg. Nyss. l. c., p. 302). Hence we occasionally find new-born children referred to as "sinless" (Cyril. cat. 4. 19 init.); or we read of "many" who have kept themselves "free from sin" (as Jeremiah and John); or the opinion is expressed that this would have been possible if obedience had been rendered to the law (Athanas. c. Arianos serm. iii. 33 ; de incarn. 12). Commenting upon Rom. 5. 19, Chrysostom remarks that it is inconceivable that we should have become sinners through Adam's sin, but that we through Adam's sinning and becoming mortal have also become mortal. It is not meant that all are in Adam sinners, but that we have through him become mortal and thereby lost the power to give to the spirit dominion over sensuality. The terrible thing is not guilt, but subjection to death. " But whence did the evil spirit come and take up its abode with him ? It first assailed him from without through the hearing, then proceeded through his heart, and took possession of his whole being, and thus, he being subjugated, the whole creation beneath and above him was carried along with him" (the illustration of a chained nobleman with his vassals led after him has been used in the context). " For through him death gained dominion over every living soul and darkened the whole likeness of Adam on account of his sin, so that men were transformed and came to the worship of demons " (Macar. hom. 11. 5; cf. 12. 1). Marcus Eremita says likewise, that, since Adam had been given over to death on account of his sin, "we have all, whether sinners or righteous, fallen from eternal life" (adv. Nestor. 18). Only death and not sin, properly speaking, is inherited. The latter is expressly denied by Marcus (de baptism. Gallandi viii. 50 D; 54 B). Thus Adam is to blame for the wretchedness which has resulted, since it was through him that death gained the mastery and ruined the original image of Adam in us. There has, however, remained to man the *liberty* of deciding for God when grace is offered to him. This is the conclusion to which the view in question leads. The soul is free and lord of itself; the devil cannot drive it to do anything against its will, and God will not do so, since righteousness would otherwise not receive its merited crown (Cyril. cat. 4. 21. Macar. h. 15. 40 ; 27. 9, 11. Joh. Dam. ii. 25 ff.). There still remains something good, therefore, in every man. It is his inner nature, his reason, or free will. Only a stimulus is needed, and man can then decide in favor of the good. But the free will is always in such connections innocently embraced in the thought, as a " good co-operation ($\sigma u \nu \epsilon \rho \gamma \epsilon \iota a \ a \gamma a \vartheta \eta$) for the attainment of salvation " (Maxim. i. 414). But it is also often strongly insisted that no one can by his own strength overcome or drive out sin, and that to accomplish this divine help is always necessary (Macar. h. 2. 4; 3. 4. Greg. Naz. or. 37. 13). "And it is not the case, as some, misled by false doctrines, say, that man is totally dead and utterly unable to do anything good. For even a child, although it is not able to accomplish anything, nor to walk upon its feet to its mother, yet rolls upon the ground and calls and cries because it yearns for its mother. And this moves the mother's heart to pity, and she is pleased that her child, with struggle and outcry, seeks to come to her. And although the child cannot come to her, yet the mother, in view of this great yearning of the child, goes to it, constrained by love for the child, takes it up and cherishes and feeds it, with great love :

this does also the man-loving God for the soul that approaches and yearns for him" (Macar. h. 46. 3). It may be said, in brief, that the Fathers of this period remained throughout the entire range of their teaching upon the basis of the second and third centuries (vid. supra, p. 115 f., 139, 157). The fall of Adam made us mortal, giving free reign to sensuality. Since Adam, we are all sinners. Without his help there is no salvation. But we, by virtue of our liberty, may secure and accept his assistance.

4. The redemption achieved by Christ brings salvation. Here, too, the ideas of the past are adopted, without reduction or revision. In accordance with the conception of the primitive church, salvation is, first of all, dependent upon the death of Christ. The Damascene summarizes as follows : " For the whole activity and wonder-working of Christ is most great and divine and wonderful ; but his precious cross is the most wonderful of all. For by nothing else was death destroyed, the sin of our first parent atoned for, hell despoiled, resurrection bestowed, power given to us to disdain things present and death itself, the restoration to original blessedness accomplished, the gates of paradise opened, our nature seated at the right hand of God, we made children of God and heirs of heaven—but through the cross of our Lord Jesus Christ. For through the cross have all things been set right" (fid. orth. iv. 11 ; cf. iii. 20). This, of course, does not set forth all the ideas accepted in the period, as such summaries never do (Eusebius demonstr. ev. iv. 12 and esp. Epiphan. ancor. 65). The ancient ideas are developed more at length : the innocent Christ became a sacrifice, a ransom, which was brought to the Father that we might be made free from condemnation (Joh. Dam. iii. 27). It is also asserted that he intercedes with the Father for us (Greg. Naz. or. 30. 14). On the other hand, he has by his death freed us from the dominion of the devil (ib. iv. 4. Dionys. eccl. hier. 3. 3. 11). At the same time we find in its crassest form the idea, that he ransomed us from the devil by making satisfaction for Adam's guilt (Macar. h. 11. 10). The devil had a certain right to man, whom he had made his slave through lust. The justice of God prevented him from snatching us from the devil by force. Therefore Christ was offered to him as an object of exchange and ransom. In this is displayed the kindness of God toward us, and his justice toward the devil. But his wisdom also appears in the transaction. In order not to alarm the devil at the outset, the divinity of Christ is concealed in the flesh. With the bait of the flesh the devil swallows also the fishhook of the divinity. Since life now appears in death, death is brought to nought.

The devil is outwitted (thus Greg. Nyss. cat. 22-24; cf. Cyril. cat. 12. 15). Gregory of Nazianzum, indeed, rejected this offering of a ransom to the devil as outrageous (ὕβρις), as did also the Damascene (Greg. or. 45. 22 ; Joh. fid. orth. iii. 27): but they did not altogether break away from the idea (vid. Greg. or. 39. 13. Joh. fid. orth. iii. 1). In this, as in the sacrifice brought to God, is manifested the goodness, justice, and wisdom of God (Cyril. cat. 13. 33. Greg. cat. 23. Joh. Dam. iii. 1).[1]

But the real central thought of the Greeks in connection with the doctrine of redemption was, after all, a different one. The conceptions of sin which we have traced are based not so much upon the idea of deliverance from the torment of the devil and from the wrath of God, as upon the thought that we are to receive life and be freed from the power of the devil. The controlling conception here was that, since God himself entered the human race in Christ, humanity has been deified and made immortal—a conception which may be traced back through Athanasius, Methodius, Irenæus, and Ignatius to John. We have cited passages of this character from Athanasius, the Cappadocians, and Cyril of Alexandria (supra, pp. 212 ff., 251, 255). "For, since he has made us partakers of his own image and his own spirit, and we have not guarded it, he in exchange became partaker of our dull and weak nature, in order that he might purify and immortalize us, and make us again partakers of his divinity" (Joh. Dam. iv. 13). Since one member of the body of humanity (Christ's body) becomes immortal, the whole body of humanity becomes so : "just as when anyone of all the race is alive, the resurrection of the part, being communicated from the part to the whole, penetrates the whole in consequence of the continuity and unity of the nature" (Greg. Nyss. cat. 32). The Logos assumed a "man, who became a divine man (κυριακὸς ἄνθρωπος) in order that we might thereby become what he is. The Logos became flesh in order that the flesh might become Logos" (Marc. Er. ad Nicol. 9). The object of the creation, and likewise of the incarnation, is that we may secure a part in the divine nature and in eternity (Maxim.

---

[1] Also the power of God : That the almighty nature is even able to condescend to the humble things of humanity is a greater display of power than the great and supernatural features of the miracles. . . . What an overflow of the power that knows no restraint in things beyond nature is the condescension to humble things (Greg. Nyss. cat. 24 init.). Gregory denies the charge that his theory of the outwitting of the devil introduces a fraud, maintaining that justice demands that the deceiver be deceived, and, moreover, the latter will by this means be himself restored in the end (ib. 26 ; as to the restoration, see also 35 fin.).

i. 519, 525). God's will in regard to man is the deification (θέωσις) of the latter (ib. i. 345). The religious application of these ideas may be studied in Athanasius (vid. supra, p. 212 ff.). The deification of man is, on the one hand, a mystical conception. Man is drawn up into the Eternal Existence. In the symbols of worship the Eternal Existence comes near to him. He through them feels himself one with God, and has become a partaker of the divine nature, or of immortality. But these ideas are always capable of a spiritual interpretation. With them is intimately connected the thought, that Christ is the lawgiver, pattern, and example. Christ restores again in and through himself the original nobility of human nature together with immortality, but he imparts this to us by teaching us the knowledge of God and virtue. This idea is very distinctly expressed by John Damascenus (iv. 4): "In order that through and in himself he might restore that which was according to (his) image and likeness, and might teach us the excellent way, having through himself made it easy of ascent for us, and in order that, having become the first fruits of our resurrection, he might in the fellowship of life free us from corruption and restore the antiquated and shattered tabernacle, having called us to the knowledge of God in order that we might be ransomed from the tyranny of the devil . . . and that he might teach us to overthrow the tyrant by patience and humility." Good works are, therefore, by no means excluded by the deification of the believer. On the contrary, the path of deification is the path of virtue. Man attains the divine life of Christ by striving for the holy innocence preserved by him (Dionys. eccl. hier. 3. 3. 12. Joh. Dam. iv. 13 ; iii. 1. Greg. cat. 35).

It remains only to observe how this conception of Soteriology fits into the general view of Christianity presented by the Areopagite. The consciousness of being deified and immortal was to be awakened by the mystical worship in its intimate association with the imagination and the senses, and the demand for instruction and ethical inspiration was met by the symbolical acts. "How otherwise could the imitation of God be engendered in us than by our having the recollection of the most holy works of God constantly refreshed in the sacred benedictions and services?" (Dionys. eccl. hier. 3. 3. 12 init.; cf. 11). The symbol is the actual presence of that which is symbolized : "The sign of Christ (the cross) is, therefore, to be worshiped ; for wherever the sign is, there will he also be" (Joh. Dam. iv. 11, p. 265). We must, therefore, be careful not to understand the term, deification, which has a strange sound to our ears, in a one-sided, physical way, as do Ritschl and Harnack. There is not lacking in it, indeed, the hyperphysical hypnosis of natural mysticism, wrought by means of the holy symbols. But this does not exhaust its content. It always embraces also the inward, gracious, moralistically conceived influence of Christ. The worshiper becomes one with the immortal Christ, but this embraces as a means the keeping of his commandments and the imitation of his divine life.

5. This bring us to the means by which salvation is to be appropriated. With the increased importance attached to the forms of worship is intimately associated a comparative neglect of indoctrination looking to the moving of the will. Of course, there is still some effort to arouse the will by instruction and the Scriptures.[1] But the chief means relied upon were the formula and form of worship. Worship naturally centred about the ancient ecclesiastical sacraments (especially the eucharist). To these were added further mysteries (chrism, priestly and monastic consecration, prayers for the dead; see the Areopagite, p. 291). Then followed a whole array of mystic signs and consecrations. Thus there was a veneration of the cross, the nails, the lance, the clothes of Christ, the manger, the socket of the cross, etc. (Joh. Dam. iv. ii. Cyril. cat. 4. 10; 13. 6). The saints who intercede for us in heaven are to be adored (e. g., Greg. Naz. or. 43. 80), as also the "mother of God" (e. g., Greg. Naz. or. 24. 11. Joh. Dam. iv. 16) and the relics of the saints: "Christ the Lord gives us as fountains of salvation the relics of the saints, pouring forth blessings in many ways, distilling the oil of a sweet odor. Let no one neglect them" (Joh. Dam. iv. 15, p. 278). Amulets and images must be added to the list (e. g., Chrysost. ad cat. 2. 5. Joh. Dam. iv. 16). These were all means of salvation, "for where the sign is, there will he himself also be" (p. 297). But to what an extent this paganized Christianity, with its demoralizing faith in miracles and demons, had forced its way into the church, may be seen most strikingly in the biographies of the holy ascetics.[2]

---

[1] See e. g. Macar. hom. 39: The Holy Scriptures are letters of the King to us. Similarly Chrysost. in 2 Thes. hom. 3. 4. We meet very frequently in the homilies of Chrysostom discussions of the practical significance of the reading of the Scriptures and urgent exhortations to the practice of it; e. g., in Col. hom. 9. 1; in 1 Thes. hom. 7. 3; in 1 Tim. hom. 13. 1; in 2 Tim. hom. 8. 3. 4; 9. 1; de poenit. hom. 4. 1. Vid. also Cyril. catech. 4. 35; 9. 13; 16. 2; 17. 34. Athanasius, Festal Letter 39, in ZAHN, Gesch. d. Kanons ii. 212. Marc. Er. de leg. spirit. 4 ff., 24. 87. Upon the pedagogical significance of the Bible, see in Eph. hom. 21. 1 ff.; cf. Basil. serm. 22. 2 (de legendis libr. gentilium, ep. 2. 3). Also, Joh. Dam. iv. 17. In addition to this is the reading of the Scripture in religious services, see Dionys. eccl. hier. 3. 2; 3. 3. 4. and the liturgies.

[2] Harnack DG. ii. 442, n.: "It fell to the lot of monasticism, especially in

These life-portraits make a wonderful impression. Here the miracle still survives. Here visions and revelations are yet the order of the day. The old Grecianism appears to be unconquered; only all has become more crude and coarse. The entire range of Hellenic superstition finds covert in the manifestations of the Spirit. Yet, in the midst of all these strange phenomena, it must not be forgotten that there still remained, in the consciousness of the presence of God, an element of true religion; but it is, it must be confessed, a sensualized and externalized religion. In close relationship to these things stood also the sacraments. Under the circumstances, even the relatively small interest attaching to each of these must follow the lines of the general theory of the sacraments. Distinction is made between the metabolic and the symbolic view; but there is no good reason for ascribing credit to the advocates of the former, for it is commonly among them that the spiritual and religious character of Christianity is most seriously misunderstood. In addition to this, the distinction above noted is a modern one, and cannot be detected in the period under review. The symbol—as was in a Neo-Platonic way conceived—is the reality. In the symbolic act, the reality itself is received. "The things sensibly sacred are images of the things perceived in thought and a guide and way to them" (Dionys. hier. eccl. 2. 3. 2). In picture or cross, in water or in bread and wine, Christ himself is present and is imparted (cf. also HARNACK DG. ii. 429).

6. Of the separate sacraments, BAPTISM is effectual in laying the foundation of the Christian life. It brings to the individual regeneration and renewal, and makes him a member of the church (Basil. serm. 13. 4, 7). Hence, in contrast with the misguided custom of the fourth century, it was urged that its administration be not postponed (Basil. serm. 13. Greg. Naz. or. 40. Chrys. ad catechum. i. 1, cf. Joh. Dam. iv. 9 fin.). The requirements for its reception were faith, as a recognition of the doctrine of the Trinity (Basil. de spir. s. 12. 28. Greg. Nyss. cat. 39. Joh. Dam. iv. 9), and a penitent frame of mind (Cyril cat. 3. 15). It effects the blotting out of sins, which are "washed away as with a flood" (Chrys. in Rom. hom. 2. 6), and the new life in Christ; and it bestows immortality. "Baptism, release to the imprisoned, the pardon of debts, the death of sin, the new birth of the soul, a garment of light, an inviolable seal, a chariot to heaven, an ambassador of the kingdom, the chrism of sonship"

the East, to play the role of mediary between the Christianity of the first and that of the second type. It contributed, perhaps, more than any other influence, to introduce the watchwords of the former into the latter and the spirit of the latter into the former."

(Basil. ep. 189. 5. sermo 13. 5 closely following Cyril. procat.
16 init. Greg. Nyss. cat. 33, 35). There are references also to
the dying of the old and the arising of the new man, as set forth
in Rom. 6. If we meet the term "forgiveness of sins" frequently, the idea conveyed by it is that of a κάϑαρσις or καϑάρσιον,
i. e., the cleansing, or blotting out, of sin in the individual (Chrys.
ad catechum. 1. 3. Greg. Naz. or. 39. 1, 14. Cyril cat. 3.
4): although "not indeed completely banishing" (Greg. Nyss.
cat. 35). But baptism imparts to the individual the obligation
and impulse to "follow Christ by imitation." It is now his
duty, striving to walk in the footsteps of Christ, to contend
against sin, and thus, since God has healed the wounds of the
past, to guard against new offenses in the future, or to heal them
by repentance (Cyril. cat. 18. 20 ; cat. myst. 2. 5, 6. Basil. de
sp. s. 15. 35 ; sermo 13. 1 fin. Greg. Nyss. cat. 35, 40. Const.
ap. ii. 7. Chrys. ad catechum. 1. 4. Dionys. eccl. hier. 2.
3. 7. Joh. Dam. iv. 9, 13). With this, the sacrament assumes
a tangible and practical character. The mystery in some way
blots out sin, but its chief significance lies in its symbolic stimulus to the recipient himself to strive against sin and overcome it.
The question as to the relation between the visible symbol and
the divine agency is answered by "the divine being present with
the occurrences," or "by the ceremony being performed in accordance with divine directions" (Greg. Nyss. cat. 34). The
important point was, that the presence of God is not lacking in
the observance of the outward symbol : "for the things seen are
symbols of the things spiritually discerned" (Joh. Dam. iv. 9).
Essentially, it made but little difference whether it was said : "if
there is any grace in the water, it is not from the nature of the
water, but from the presence of the Spirit" (Basil. sp. s. 15.
35), or whether the "sanctifying power dwelling in the water"
(Cyril. cat. 3. 3 ; but see also cat. myst. 2. 5) was spoken of, or
it was said: "By the energy of the Spirit the visible water is
transmuted (ἀναστοιχειοῦται) into a certain divine and indescribable power, and it furthermore sanctifies those among whom
it may be found" (Cyril. Al. in Joh. under 3. 5, Mi. 73. 245).
Under all forms of expression, there is the conception of the
mystery which has been above outlined. But he who has now
become pure in baptism must contend against sin, and, if he is
overcome, repent, since repentance (μετάνοια) is the fulfillment
of the commands of Christ. In accordance with the Greek
conception of sin, the idea in repentance was not only the satisfaction rendered to God in order to secure forgiveness, as in the
West, but rather a discipline for amendment, an inward purification and sanctification. Thus Clement and Origen had regarded

the matter (vid. supra). Something of this idea long lingered, even in the presence of the ecclesiastical ordinance of penitential discipline. The duty of confessing all their sins—even their secret thoughts—which was imposed by Basil upon the monks, was not, indeed, extended to the laity (vid., *e. g.*, Chrysost. hom. 4 ; in Laz. 4); but the injunction to confess sin to God, in order thereby to deepen one's own conviction of sin, was often repeated in homiletic exhortations (ib.). Upon the history of the ordinance of public repentance in the Greek church the History of Doctrines has no occasion to enter (cf. HOLL, l. c., p. 240 ff.).

The EUCHARIST is, above all, enwrapped in the awe of mystery, as the chief symbol (ἀρχισύμβολον, Dionys. hier. eccl. iii. 1; 2. 1, cf. supra, p. 290), since all the angels hover around the priest as he offers the "awful sacrifice" (Chrys. de sacerd. vi. 4, and accounts by him of actual appearances of angels). Regarded from a dogmatic point of view (cf. STEITZ's discussions of the doctrine of the Greek church concerning the Lord's Supper, in Jarbb. f. d. Theol., vols. ix.-xiii.), we may distinguish a more scientific symbolic tendency from the practical metabolic view, a difference which did not, however, produce any actual conflict (cf. p. 299). Basil says, for example : " He called his whole mystic life (ἐπιδημία) flesh and blood, and taught a doctrine composed of practical and natural and theological elements, by which the soul is nourished and meanwhile prepared for the contemplation of things existing " (ep. 8. 4 fin.). Other teachers speak in a similar way of spiritual food, or spiritual reception of the flesh of Christ (Athan. ad Serap. iv. 19; in ps. 80. 17. Macar. hom. 27. 17). But it is not hereby intended to question a real presence of Christ. The difference between this and the metabolic view is, therefore, not so great. The latter regards Christ as himself miraculously dwelling in the elements. This is very plainly taught by Cyril of Jerusalem in his " mystagogical catechisms." By means of the invocation, the miracle of Cana is repeated ; the bread becomes body, and the wine blood (i. 7 ; iii. 3 ; iv. 1, 2). We are not to allow ourselves to be deceived by the sense of taste (iv. 6, 9). On the contrary, we call upon God " to send forth the Holy Spirit upon that which lies before us, in order that he may make the bread the body of Christ and the wine the blood of Christ. For, if the Holy Spirit should touch this at all, it would be sanctified and changed (μεταβέβληται)." But with this we must also keep in mind the declaration : " For in the type of bread is given to thee the body, and in the type of wine is given to thee the blood, in order that, partaking of the body and blood of Christ, thou mayest become of the same body and blood (σύσσωμος and σύναιμος) with him " (iv. 3). Now this body of Christ imparts itself to our body and makes it a partaker of the divine nature (iv. 3 ; v. 15), and thus the eucharist works for us immortality. The Origenist, Gregory of Nyssa, expresses himself in essentially the same way in his "large catechism " (c. 37). As the soul is purified in baptism through faith, so the eucharist bestows an antidote for the poison which has penetrated the body : " The body (of Christ) immortalized by God, being in ours, tranforms and changes the whole into that body itself." Bread and wine, as the natural means of nourishment, are the potency of every body, including that of Christ. Hence, it is said : " Well do we, therefore, now believe that the bread consecrated by the word of God is transformed into the body of the divine Logos." But the design of this is "in order that, by this union with the immortal, man might also become a partaker of incorruptibility." During the Christological controversies it became customary to regard the body of Christ, spoken of in connection with the Lord's Supper, as identical with the body which the Lord bore when on earth (thus Cyril. Al., supra, p. 262, cf. Chrys. in Tit. hom. 2. 4 ; in Eph. hom. 3. 3). Here again the Damascene summarizes the thought for us (orth. fid. iv. 13): He who framed for us a body from the blood of the Virgin, by the power of the Spirit also changes bread and wine into body and blood. The elements are now not "a type of the body and blood " (pp. 271, 273), nor are they the body come down from heaven ; but they are transformed : " The body is truly the body from the Holy Virgin united with divinity, not that the ascended body comes down from heaven, but that the bread and wine are transformed into the body and blood of God " (p. 269). A remarkable conclusion, which reveals how little of a religious character attaches to this system ! The purpose of the bestowal of the body and blood is the forgiveness of sins—but, above all, unification with Christ ; and this means deification, or the bestowal of immortality (pp. 271, 272). To this is added "communing, and being through this united with one another " (p. 273).

Side by side with this line of interpretation runs the other, which regards the eucharist in the light of the " unbloody, mystic, God-appeasing sacrifice," as a repetition of the sacrifice of Christ (Euseb. vit. Const. iv. 45. Joh. Dam. de imag. or. 2. 17. Chrysost. de poenit. hom. 9), which only a priest can administer (Chrysost. de sacerd. iii. 4, 5 ; vi. 4), and which is efficacious for the living and the dead (Eus. l. c. iv. 71. Chrysost. in 1 Cor. hom. 41. 5 init. Greg. Naz. ep. 240).

§ 28. *Iconoclastic Controversies. Final Dogma of the Greek Church.*

LITERATURE. Vid. the Byzantine chronographies in Corp. sacr. hist. Byz., esp. Theophanes Chronographia, edited by DE BOOR, 1883. For details of the proceedings, vid. M. Act. conc. xii., xiii. JOH. DAMASC. de imaginibus orat. tres. THEODOR. STUDITA, opp., in Mi. 99. Also the modern delineations of WALCH, Ketzerhist. vol. x. HEFELE CG. iii., ed. 2, 366 ff. HERGENRÖTHER, Kirchengesch. I. 528 ff. HARNACK DG. ii. 450 ff. SCHWARZLOSE, Der Bilderstreit ein Kampf der griech. Kirche um ihre Eigenart u. um ihre Freiheit, 1890. THOMAS, Theod. von Studion u. seine Zeitalter, Leipz., 1892. BONWETSCH, PRE. iii., ed. 3, 222 ff.

The 36th canon of the synod of Elvira (A. D. 306, or, perhaps, as early as A. D. 300) reads : " It seems good to us that there ought not to be pictures in the church, nor should that which is worshiped and adored be painted upon the walls." This principle was carried out also in decisions and in action (Eus. ep. ad Constantiam, Mi. 20. 1545, cf. h. e. vii. 18. Epiph. opp. ed. Dindorf iv. 2, p. 85). But it was not the view of the theologians which influenced public conviction in the matter, but the latter compelled the acquiescence of the teachers (*e. g.*, in Joh. Dam. or. i. 27 ; 2. 23 ; 3. 42). . It was an outgrowth of the exaggerated culture of mysteries (p. 290).[1]

That an assault upon images should cause a profound excitement, may be readily understood. It is not so easy to discern the motive which prompted it. Neither respect for the Jews nor regard for the Saracens can have been the stimulating force. The Emperor LEO THE ISAURIAN appears to have received the suggestion from Phrygia (Bishop Constantine of Nicolaea). To a man holding a legalistic conception of the Old Testament, the idea seemed self-evident (the imperial edict based its argument upon the Old Testament prohibition of images, Ex. 20. 4 ; 2 Ki. 18 4 ; cf. Joh. Dam. or. 1. 4 ff., and the first letter of Pope Gregory to the emperor); and it was as natural for the emperor to command the church in the matter as the limitation of the latter's power was desirable.[2] In A. D. 726 the emperor forbade the worship of images (HEFELE iii. 378 ff.), on the ground that they take the place of the idols of the heathen, and that the worship of them is forbidden in the Scriptures. We dare not worship "stones, walls, and boards." With the approval of the patriarch Anastasius, the agitation was renewed in A. D. 730.

Energetic opposition was at once aroused upon the part of the

---

[1] The controlling idea, that God is present in pictures of the Deity, is antique (see the Apologetes) and Neo-Platonic (see Zeller, Philos. der Griechen iii. 2, ed. 3, pp. 626, 697).

[2] The discussion by SCHWARZLOSE (p. 45 ff.) of the imperial "politics" is not satisfactory.

people as well as among the theologians, *e. g.*, GERMANUS of
Constantinople (in M. xiii. 100 ff.), GREGORY II. of Rome
(M. xii. 959 ff.), JOHN OF DAMASCUS (Mi. 94. 1227 ff.).
Appeal was made to tradition and custom, to the miracles
wrought through the images, to which at any rate only venera-
tion ($\pi\rho o\sigma\kappa\dot{v}\nu\eta\sigma\iota\varsigma$) and not worship ($\lambda\alpha\tau\rho\varepsilon\dot{\iota}\alpha$) was rendered, to
the cherubim, etc. The Roman bishop also reflected that " the
dogmas of the church are not an affair of the emperor, but of
the bishops," and pointed to the position of Peter " whom the
kingdoms of the West regard as the earthly God," at the same
time, in the most offensive manner, charging the emperor with
outrageous folly.[1]

John of Damascus published a comprehensive defense of the
images. The images of Christ and the saints may and must be
honored, not, indeed, by divine worship (or. 3. 29 ff.), but by
veneration. God himself is the originator of the use of images,
having sanctioned it by the method of Old Testament revelation,
the forms of Old Testament worship, and his own visible appearance in Christ (or. 3. 12, 18, 21 ff., 26; 1. 14, 20 ff.).
Everything on earth is a picture of God (1. 11). The spiritual,
and, therefore, the revelation of God, can be revealed to us only
through matter ($\ddot{v}\lambda\eta$). We honor the images just as we honor
the gospels, the eucharist, the cross, the spear and sponge, or
Golgotha (1. 16; 2. 14, 19)—not the materials composing
them as such (2. 19), but as being bearers of the divine.
The controlling idea of the age here finds expression : " Things
made by our hands are holy, leading us through matter
to the immaterial God (2. 23), through bodily vision to
spiritual vision " (3. 12, 25). We must either surrender
our veneration for the " parchments of the gospels " written with ink, and for the elements of the eucharist, or acknowledge " the veneration of images of God and of the precious things consecrated to the name of God, and thus overshadowed by the grace of the divine Spirit " (2. 14). Images
are, therefore, means of grace, since the material copy brings to
us God himself (" therefore I revere, $\sigma\dot{\varepsilon}\beta\omega$, and through the
unseen draw near and venerate, the material object through which
salvation comes to me. But I revere it not as divine, but as
filled with divine energy and grace," 2. 14). Such character is
possessed by them not only as the " books of the unlearned "
(3. 9). Hence, to deny them veneration is Manichæism (1. 16 ;

---

[1] SCHWARZLOSE'S attack upon the genuineness of the two letters of Gregory
has not convinced me. We may, at the most, acknowledge some alterations,
which may perhaps be charged to the account of a contemporary Byzantine
translator, who was familiar with the writings of the Damascene upon images.

2. 13). Not only does God himself, with his whole revelation to man, thus defend the veneration of images, but it is just as fully supported by the tradition of the church (1. 27, 23; 2. 23; 3. 42). To abandon the veneration of images is a worse offense than fornication (3. 13). At any rate, the emperor has nothing to do with the inner life of the church : "The emperor's sphere is the right conduct of political affairs; the management of ecclesiastical affairs is the province of pastors and teachers" (2. 12).

To the punctilious legality and Cæsaropapy of the emperor is here opposed the historically well-defined Greek Christianity, not without suggesting the idea—in spite of recent events—of the independence of the church. In so far the worshipers of images were right. But it is Christianity as represented in the lower form which magically sinks the spiritual in the material (*e. g.*, power of images against demons, 1. 27, p. 231; miracles performed by them, 1. 22; 3. 41—hence religious veneration). In this—impartially considered—lies the error of the image worshipers, and of the piety of the church which they represented.

It must be left to Church History to trace the outward course of the resulting controversies. CONSTANTINE V. (Copronymus, A. D. 741-775) proceeded against the images with the greatest energy, particularly after an insurrection of their defenders under his brother-in-law, Artabasdus, had most seriously endangered his throne. A general council was now planned to set the stamp of ecclesiastical authority upon the emperor's view. It met at Constantinople, A. D. 754 (see the *horos* of the council in M. xiii. 205 ff.). Since the devil could not tolerate the adornment of "glorious doctrines" in the church, he was constantly re-introducing idolatry. As God in ancient times equipped the apostles to contend against ancient idolatry, so now has he endowed the apostolic emperors with the spirit of wisdom for the conflict against images. The council realizes that the "iniquitous art of painting" reviles the incarnation of Christ, since Christ can be painted only by a Nestorian separation, or by a Eutychian confusion, of the divine and the human. Bread and wine in the Lord's Supper are the only authorized pictures of Christ. The Scriptures forbid images (Jn. 4. 24 ; Deut. 5. 8 ; Rom. 1. 23, 25, etc.). Accordingly, images dare neither be made, nor placed in churches or private houses, nor kept in secret. Any cleric who violates the prohibition shall be removed from office ; any layman or monk so transgressing anathematized, in which case he is amenable to the civil law as "an opponent of the commandments of God, and an enemy of the dogmas of

20

the Fathers.'' These decrees were executed with great energy.
The clergy yielded, but the monks resisted. Pictures were destroyed, plastered over, or replaced with landscape and hunting
views. The emperor pursued all who resisted with terrible
cruelty. The monks were treated with special severity. The
emperor went so far as to forbid the veneration of relics and
prayers to the Virgin Mary and the saints (Theophan., p. 439 ;
cf. Cedrenus, hist. compend. ed. Bekker ii., p. 3).

LEO IV. (Chazarus, A. D. 775-780) espoused the principles
of his father, but his cunning and ambitious wife, IRENE, was
friendly to the images. After the death of her consort, she felt
herself constrained, in order to retain her position as guardian of
her son, to depend upon the support of the image-venerating
party (cf. RANKE, Weltgesch. v. 89, 91 f.). Advancing by
slow stages, she crowned her efforts by securing the assembly of
the SEVENTH ECUMENICAL COUNCIL at Nicaea, A. D. 787. The
members of this council approved the veneration of images, supporting it by the Scriptures (ark of the covenant and cherubim,
Gen. 32. 24), and a great number of patristic citations, and refuting at length the *horos* of A. D. 754. The council's own
horos laid stress upon the assertion, that it held to the doctrines
of the first six ecumenical councils. With respect to images, it
was maintained, with appeal to tradition, that veneration is to be
shown, as to the cross, so also to images of Christ, of the stain-
less lady, the angels and saints, whether depicted in colors or on
stone, upon vessels, clothing, walls, or on the streets : '' for, as
often as they are seen from time to time in pictorial representation, so often are those who behold them incited to the recollection of and desire for the prototypes, and to render to them
affection and deep veneration ; not, indeed, true worship according to our faith, which is properly rendered only to the divine
nature, but in such a way as to the symbol of the precious and life-
giving cross and to the holy gospels, and to the other sacred objects, and to make a presentation of incense and lights for the honor
of such, as it was customary among the ancients piously to do.
For the honor rendered to the image passes over to the prototype.'' Clerics refusing to conform to these requirements are to
be deposed, laymen excommunicated. The decree was subscribed by those present. With loud salutations of the new
Helena and the new Constantine, and with abundant anathemas
against all heretics, especially such as refuse to venerate the
images and reject tradition, the seventh and chief session closed.
A feature of Greek Christianity was saved, but it is a peculiar
illustration of the irony of history, that the same city, Nicaea, in
which the first dogma was framed, was also the birthplace of this

last Greek dogma.   The two councils of Nicaea mark the course of Greek Christianity—from dogma to images.

The further history of the iconoclastic controversies does not belong to the sphere of the History of Doctrines.   The restitution of the images naturally followed, and was accomplished without bloodshed.   The superstitious practices in connection with images passed all bounds (see passages in THOMAS, Theod. v. Studion, p. 101).   The Armenian, LEO V., renewed the warfare against them.   MICHAEL II. (Balbus), and THEOPHILUS followed in his steps.   But the populace and the monks, led by the powerful abbot of Studion, THEODORE, resisted, despite all oppressive measures (THOMAS, p. 98 ff.).   THEODORA, the wife of Theophilus, restored the images, A. D. 842, and in celebration of this act it was appointed that the "festival of orthodoxy" should be annually celebrated.

With this, the dogma of the Greek church reaches its consummation ; for neither the separation between the Greek and Roman churches (Photius, Michael Cerularius, A. D. 1054) nor the later attempts to unite them (A. D. 1274, 1439) fall within the domain of the general History of Doctrines.   The same is to be said of the heretics in the Russian church and the great schism dating from the age of Nicon, A. D. 1654.   The study of these agitations furnishes nothing beyond what has been presented in the two preceding paragraphs.   As to the conditions of the present, see especially LE ROY BEAULIEU, das Reich der Zaren, vol. iii.

CHAPTER IV.

FOUNDATION OF ANTHROPOLOGICAL DOGMA (SIN AND GRACE). DEVELOPMENT OF THE CHURCH IN THE WEST. DOCTRINE OF AUGUSTINE.

§ 29. *The Fundamental Religious Ideas of Augustine and His Place in the History of Doctrines.*

LITERATURE.   The WORKS OF AUGUSTINE, Maurine ed., 11 vols., Paris, 1679 ff.   Reprint edit. tertia Veneta (from which we quote), Migne Lat. 32-46.   Cf. BINDEMANN, Der h. Aug., 3 vols., 1844 ff.   BÖHRINGER, Aurel. Aug., ed. 2, 1877 f.   DORNER, Aug., sein theol. System u. sein rel. phil. Anschauung, 1873.   REUTER, Augustin. Studien, 1887.   HARNACK DG. iii. 54 ff.   FEUERLEIN, Aug. Stellung in der Kirchen. u. Kulturgesch., Hist. Ztschr. xxii. 270 ff.   DILTHEY, Einleitung in die Geisteswissenschaft, 1. 335 ff.   EUCKEN, Die Lebensanschauungen d. grossen Denker, 1890, p. 258 ff.

CUNNINGHAM, Saint Aug. and his Place in the History of Christian Thought, 1881. BESTMANN, Qua rat. Aug. notiones phil. graec. adhib., 1877. LÖSCHE, De Aug. plotinizante, 1880. STORZ, Die Philos. d. h. Aug., 1882. SCIPIO, Des Aur. Aug. Metaphysik im Ramen s. Lehre v. Uebel, 1886. SIEBECK, Geschichte der Psychologie, 1. 2, p. 381 ff.

The general conception of Christianity which prevailed in the Western church in the third century has been seen (p. 198) to have been that of a legal relationship between God and man, whose result is the salvation of souls (*salus animarum*). "The whole foundation of religion and faith proceeds from obedience and the fear of God" (*observatione ac timore*, Cyprian, de hab. virg. ii.; cf. supra, p. 194 f.). We have seen, further, that in the Trinitarian and Christological controversies the West maintained its characteristic position (illustrated in Tertullian, p. 125 f.; also pp. 237, 255). Nevertheless, the Renaissance movement in the Eastern church made itself felt even here, as is manifest in the views of HILARY, and no less in the writings of AMBROSE, who was largely dependent upon the Cappadocians (especially Basil), and in the prevalence of the allegorical method of exegesis (cf. also Jerome). Such a man as the orator Victorinus, in a way which reminds us of Augustine, applied the Neo-Platonic theory of ideas in the interest of Trinitarianism and—which is of special interest to us—was able to reproduce Paul's doctrine of justification, although not, indeed, without exhibiting a naive Pelagianism (vid. Mi. viii., also Dict. of Christ. Biograph. iv. 1129 ff. R. SCHMIDT, M. Victorinus Rhetor, KIEL, 1895). At the same time, the chacteristic ideas of the West were not lost sight of, but even more fully developed. In the doctrines of original sin and grace (where Tertullian is still the controlling influence, vid. p. 122; cf. also Cyprian and Commodian, p. 192), Ambrose largely anticipated Augustine (vid. supra). The agitation which prevailed throughout the Western church from the days of Augustine was not without its forerunners. AMBROSE was an Augustine before Augustine, and remained for the latter the controlling authority. But such a man as the Docetic TYCONIUS likewise prepared the way for Augustine, not only in his views concerning the church, but also by his emphasizing of grace. At this point begin the labors of Augustine, who combined in himself all the elements of the culture and religion of his age, and yet produced something quite new. He is the dominating force for the History of Doctrines in the West during the following periods. The ideas which he expressed gave birth to the dogmatic history of the West; the form of piety which he represented remained as a model, and became one of the most powerful co-efficients in the intellectual and spiritual life of the race. The labors of scholasticism no less than the emotions of the mystics, Roman hierarchy as well as the antihierarchical parties of the Middle Ages, Rome and Wittenberg, alike leaned upon him and found support (cf. REU-TER, p. 479 ff.). His formulas, his statement of the perplexing problems of theology, and his religious temper, are constantly reappearing as we pursue the subsequent History of Doctrines. Even where an entirely different spirit is manifest, there is no escape from the masterful influence of his thoughts and terminology.

The history of his conversion is well known. AURELIUS AUGUSTINE (A. D. 354-430) was, despite his fervid sensuous temperament and the errors into which it led him, a noble soul, free from everything sordid. He was inspired with an intense yearning after truth and life. A disciple of the Manichæans, he was won by the glory of the Catholic church (conf. v. 14 ; vi. 1. 5, 11 ; vii. 19), the examples of her confessors (ib. viii. 2, 5, 6 f.), and the power of the grace of Christ (ib. vii. 5. 18 f.; viii. 8 ff.). The allegorical interpretations of Scripture in the preaching of the day (ib. vi. 5. 11 ; cf. vii. 1), the teaching of Paul (ib. vii. 21 init.; viii. 6), and the spirit of the Neo-platonic philosophy prepared the way for him into the communion of the church. The universal significance of Augustine results from his return to the original Christian temper of soul. He was from his youth distinguished by an insatiable longing for happiness, life, and wealth. Not quiet contemplation, but the utmost exertion of every power, was from the very beginning of his career the ideal of this daring genius. The will is the essential part of man. It turns away from God and toward nothingness. It is, accordingly, the cause of all misery. On the other hand, the new will, inspired by God, i. e., love, is the real blessing bestowed by divine grace. Only when God's will controls the will of man is man free (vid. conf. vii. 16. 22 ; viii. 5. 10 ; xiii. 10. 19 ; de civ. dei xxii. 22. 1 ; de sp. et lit. 30. 52). But God is the almighty Will, which controls and ordains all things. Over against and beneath the divine Will, stands the will of man. To be controlled and permeated by the will of God constitutes salvation and blessedness. Regarded from this point of view, religion is subjection to God in love. But from this same point all the positive and empirical ordinances of the church could appear to Augustine to exist rightfully, because designed and appointed by God. But to this principle of Augustine, which, in the last analysis, rested upon the primitive Christian recognition of the sovereignty of God and the subjection of the human will, was added the Neo-Platonic element in Augustine's sphere of thought. Fundamentally considered, it is the will which leads man to knowledge. That which is willed becomes a constituent part of the soul, since the latter knows it. "For certainly *a thing cannot be loved unless it is known*" (de trin. x. 1. 2). But knowledge arises not only from the perception of these heavenly truths. There is innate in the soul an "interior sense," which apprehends the nature of things through their intelligible forms (*per intelligibilem speciem*, de civ. dei, xi. 27. 2). This *species intelligibilis* is not attained, but innate. But here Augustine launches out into the "intelligible world" of the Platonic system—into the contemplation of the ancient fantasies of the original forms of all existing things. The contemplation of the eternal becomes for him—in genuinely Greek spirit—salvation (cf. de quaest. oct. 1. 46. 2).

These are the fundamental intellectual lines within which the thought of Augustine moved. First, voluntarism (God is Will and man is will; love is blessedness). Then, the Neo-Platonic intellectualism (the contemplation of the intelligible world is blessedness). Both are, in a marvelous way, interwoven, and over all lies the enchantment of inner and personal experience.

It was in the midst of earnest struggle that Augustine found salvation in the fellowship of the living God, of whom he could so impressively speak. All that he has written bears the marks of its origin in the depths of his personal life and earnest striving. There exist for him but two great realities: God and the Soul. God is light, truth, life; in the soul dwell darkness, misery, death. But where the soul lays hold upon God and God lays hold upon the soul, *there* is clearness of vision and the power to do good—*there* is blessedness. A few citations will best reveal this fundamental religious temper of the man: "What, therefore, dost thou desire to know? . . . State briefly. God and the soul I desire to know. And nothing more? Nothing at all." But this limitation of interest is a consequent upon the declaration: "*I love nothing else but God and the soul*" (soliloq. i. 2, 7; viii. 15; xv. 27). "Thou dost stir us up to find delight in praising Thee, because Thou hast made us for Thyself, and our heart is restless until it rests in Thee" (conf. i. 1). "For in this I sinned, that I sought pleasures, sublimities, truths, not in Himself but in his creatures, myself and others. And thus I rushed into griefs, confusions, errors" (ib. i. 20). "Who will give to me that I may find rest in Thee? Who will give to me that Thou mayest come into my heart and intoxicate it, so that I may forget my evil ways and embrace Thee as my only good? Say to my soul: I am thy salvation" (ib.

i. 5). "Too late I have learned to love Thee, Loveliness so ancient and so new—too late I have learned to love Thee. And behold, Thou wast within and I without, and there I sought Thee; and I, unshapely, rushed upon the shapely things which Thou hast made. Thou wast with me and I was not with Thee. Those things held me far from Thee, which would not be if they were not in Thee. Thou hast called and cried aloud, and broken through my deafness. Thou hast sparkled and shone and driven away my blindness. Thou hast broken and allured my spirit, and I pant for Thee. I have tasted, and I hunger and thirst. Thou hast touched me, and I have been consumed with Thy peace" (ib. x. 27). "And I sought a way of gaining the strength that would be capable of enjoying Thee, and I found it not until I embraced the Mediator between God and men, the man Christ Jesus" (ib. vii. 18). "His coming is his humanity; his remaining is his divinity. His divinity is the whither we are journeying; his humanity is the where we are journeying. Unless he had become for us the where we are journeying, we could never have come to him where he dwells (in Joh. tr. 42. 8). I have entered the depths under Thy guidance, and I have been able, since Thou hast become my helper. I have entered and have seen, as with a certain eye of my soul, above this same eye of my soul, above my mind, the unchangeable Light. . . . O eternal Truth and true Love, and lovable Eternity, Thou art my God. . . . And since I first have known Thee, Thou hast taken me to Thyself, that I might see that that exists which I should see, and which I who see am not yet . . . and I have trembled with love and terror" (conf. vii. 10). "For when I seek Thee, my God, I seek blessed life. I will seek Thee, that my soul may live. For my body lives from my soul, and my soul lives from Thee" (ib. x. 20). "For me, to cling to God is good; this is the whole good. Do you wish anything more? I grieve that you so wish. Brothers, for what more do you wish? There is nothing better than to cling to God" (in ps. 72. 34). "God is to be worshiped by faith, hope, love" (enchirid. iii.; cf. soliloq. i. 7. 14). "Give what Thou appointest, and appoint what Thou wilt" (conf. x. 37; cf. solil. i. 1. 5). "Do Thou suggest to me, do Thou show me, do Thou grant me help by the way . . . increase in me faith, increase hope, increase love" (solil. i. 1. 5). "But there is a delight which is not given to the wicked, but to those who willingly worship Thee, whose joy Thou Thyself art. And this is blessed life itself, to delight one's self toward Thee and on account of Thee; this it is, and there is no other" (conf. x. 22).

A new spirit breathes through these utterances, and they illustrate at the same time the enrapturing diction of Augustine. The very existence of man is sin and misery; but God is his salvation—not by virtue of fixed laws, not by way of reward or punishment, but in the direct personal fellowship of life and love. These are the ideas upon which rests Paul's view of sin and grace. But Augustine now proceeded, while maintaining as his central position that above indicated, to unfold his religious ideas within the lines of the traditional formulas and ideals of the church. He "deepened" and transformed the latter. But he had also from the start demanded submission to the authority of the church (vid. de utilitate credendi ix. ff.; c. ep. Manichaei 5. 6 : " But I would not believe the gospel, unless the authority of the Catholic church impelled me ''). This has been manifest in our study of his Trinitarian and Christological utterances (p. 238). It comes to view again in his doctrine of sin and grace, as developed in the conflict with Pelagianism, although here the characteristic religious elements of his theology assert themselves with peculiar force. In the same light are to be viewed his utterances touching the church and the sacraments during the anti-Donatistic controversy, as well as his acceptance and ennobling of nearly all the teachings of the popular Catholicism. He remains himself almost everywhere, but he is yet, at the same time, an orthodox Catholic teacher in the church of his age. He did not, like Origen, develop a theological system, but he furnished to his age a wealth of fruitful religious and speculative ideas, giving back to it in a purified and profounder form what he received from it. His " doctrine '' is deficient in unity, combining the most violent contradictions (gospel and philosophy, Catholic tradition and religion, voluntarism and intellectualism, etc.); but his writings proved stimulating in an unparalleled degree. He was a theologian and a philosopher ; but he was also more, a religious genius and a great man.

It will be necessary for us to examine : (1) His doctrine of the church and the sacraments, in opposition to Donatism. (2) His doctrine of sin and grace, in opposition to Pelagianism. (3) His general view of theology and the church, in tracing which we must follow the lines of his only comprehensive dogmatic work, the *Enchiridion ad Laurentium.*

§ 30. *Donatistic Controversy and Further Development of the Doctrines of the Church and the Sacraments by Augustine.*

LITERATURE. OPTATUS of Mileve, de schismate Donatistarum ll. 7 ed. Ziswa in Corp. scr. eccl. Lat. 26 (written perhaps A. D. 368, but see ii. 3). Synodal Acts and fragments of the same in M. iv. Original sources in Opp. Aug. xvii. 2446 ff. Also DEUTSCH, Drei Aktenstücke z. Gesch. d. Donat.

1875. VÖLTER, Der Ursprung d. Donat, 1883. SEECK, Quellen u. Urkunden über die Anfänge des. Donat., Ztschr. f. KG. x. 505 ff. RIBBECK, Donatus u. Aug., 1858. HEFELE, in Wetzer u. Welte's Kirchenlex. iii. ed. 2, 1969 ff. THÜMMEL, Zur Beurteilung des Donatism, 1893. F. HAHN, Tyconius-Studien (Bonwetsch-Seeberg, Studien zur Gesch. der Theol. u. der Kirche, vi. 2), 1900. BONWETSCH, PRE. iv., ed. 3, 788 ff. Of the works of Augustine : c. epistulam Parmeniani, ll. 3 (ca. A. D. 400); de baptismo c. Donatistas, ll. 7 ; c. litteras Petiliani, ll. 3 ; de unitate eccl. (after A. D. 400); c. Cresconium, ll. 4 (ca. A. D. 406); de unico baptismo c. Petilianum (ca. A. D. 410); breviculus collationes cum Donatistis (A. D. 411); ad Donatistas post collationem (A. D. 412); de gestis cum Emerito (A. D. 418); c. Gaudentium ll. 2 (ca. A. D. 420). Upon Aug's conception of the church, vid. KÖSTLIN, Die Cath. Auffassung v. d. Kirche in ihrer ersten Ausbildung, in Deutsche Ztschr. f. chr. Wiss. u. chr. Leben, 1856, p. 101 ff., 113 ff. H. SCHMIDT, Des Aug. Lehre v. d. Kirche, in Jarbb. f. deutsche Theol., 1861, p. 197 ff. REUTER, Aug. Studien, pp. 231 ff., 47 ff. SEEBERG, Begriff d. Kirche, i. p. 38 ff. SPECHT, Die Lehre v. d. Kirche nach dem. h. Aug., 1892. Upon his doctrine of the Sacraments, vid. HAHN, Die Lehre v. d. Sakr., 1864. DIECKHOFF, Theol. Ztschr., 1860, p. 524 ff.

1. THE DONATISTIC CONTROVERSY.

(a) The greatest schism in the ancient church arose from personal and local conditions in the congregation at Carthage. As in the case of the Novatian schism, a persecution furnished the occasion. Various courses of action were advocated in North Africa in response to the demand for the surrender of the Scriptures during the Diocletian persecution. Bishop MENSURIUS OF CARTHAGE represented the milder view (surrender of other writings of indifferent character permitted). He and his archdeacon CAECILIAN also opposed the exaggerated veneration of confessors and martyrs. SECUNDUS OF TIGISIS advocated a rigoristic view. After the death of Mensurius, Caecilian, who was hated by the strict party in Carthage, was chosen bishop and consecrated to the office by FELIX OF APTUNGA, whom the strict party regarded as a "traditor." This election awakened great indignation among the "pious" (Lucilla), which was encouraged by the foreign rigorists. The Numidian bishops had sent Docetus from Casae Nigrae to Carthage as vicar of the bishopric. An assemblage of 70 bishops in Carthage (A. D. 312) declared the ordination invalid. MAJORINUS was then elected Bishop of Carthage. His successor was DONATUS THE GREAT. Through a combination of many influences, this conflict led to the formation of two warring churches sharply opposing one another, the Catholic and the Donatistic. The pride of the martyrs, the spirit of piety quickened anew under the stress of persecution, the idea of the holiness of the church, archaistic religious reminiscences, the pressure soon brought to bear by the civil authorities, the league of the Catholic church with the state, social distress, perhaps also national motives, all

united to expand the personal dispute into the great schism
which distracted the church of Africa for a century. The African church was really split in two (in A. D. 330 there were 270
Donatistic bishops at a council, and in A. D. 311, at Carthage,
266). Outside of Africa, Donatism secured no following
worthy of mention (a bishop in Spain and another in Rome are
spoken of, gesta collationis i. 157), only Caecilian and his followers being recognized. The emperor, Constantine, after being
drawn into the matter by the Donatists, assumed a similar attitude. He ordered an investigation of the subject; then examined it himself, deciding that Caecilian and Felix were innocent, but that their assailants were contemptible slanderers.
Stringent laws were enacted against the latter, but, proving ineffectual, they were soon revoked. But the most important
measure was that adopted, under the influence of Constantine,
at the council of Arles (A. D. 316, according to Seeck, l. c., p.
508 f.; cf. Eus. v. C. 44, 45), $i. e.$, the establishment of the
milder view on the ground of principle. It was here decreed
that even the ordination administered by a " traditor " is valid,
provided only that the persons so ordained " remain reasonable "
(can. 13); also, that persons who had been baptized by heretics
should be questioned only upon the Creed, and that, if it be found
that they have been baptized in the name of the Triune God,
only the laying on of hands shall be further administered to
them (can. 8). According to this, ordination and baptism are
not dependent upon the worthiness of the administrant. Thus
a doctrinal difference runs parallel with the personal and historical conflict. The agitation spread with great rapidity, especially
among the lower ranks of society. Socialistic ideas as to property
and a reckless fanaticism, leading to a complete outward separation, to frightful deeds of violence, and to wanton and con-
temptuous surrender of life, became distinguishing marks of the
church of the saints (Circumcelliones, Agonistici, vid. Opt. ii.
18 f. 21 ; vi. 1 f.; iii. 4. Aug. unit. eccl. 19. 50 ; c. ep. Parm.
ii. 3. 6 ; c. Crescon. iii. 42. 46; brev. iii. 11). Against this,
church and state were alike powerless. Restrictive measures
under CONSTANS and CONSTANTIUS, as under JOVIAN, VALEN-
TINIAN, GRATIAN, and HONORIUS, were unable to suppress the
movement. The most serious obstacle encountered by the party
was its division into mutually antagonistic groups (Rogatus,
Tyconius, Maximian, and Primian)—the fate of all separatists.
Augustine, soon after entering upon the episcopacy, addressed
all his energy to the work of reconciling the opposing factions.
This resulted in the three-day conference at Carthage in June,
411 (vid. gesta collationis in M. iv. and Aug. brevic. coll.).

Both the historical and the doctrinal questions were here discussed. No reader of the proceedings of this assembly can
escape the impression that the Donatists here appear in the light
of embittered fanatics, incompetent but vain, adepts in the most
trifling legal quibbles, in questions of formality and in intrigue,
always seeking to impede the progress of the proceedings. The
imperial presiding officer (Marcellin) accorded the victory to
the Catholics upon both points of dispute. His decision was a
just one. Augustine continued to labor in the same spirit.
Strict imperial edicts forbade the assemblage of the Donatists
upon penalty of death, and their churches and church property
were given over to the Catholics. The power of Donatism was
broken, and it soon after disappears from church history.

(*b*) The doctrinal difference between Donatists and Catholics
may be briefly expressed. Donatism does not question the episcopal foundation of the church. It demands only that the
bishops be holy men, and maintains that only when they are
such are the sacraments administered by them effectual. In
this, as at other points, it could appeal to Cyprian. It was well
known that Cyprian denied the validity of heretic baptism (p.
184). He taught that there was no virtue in the sacrifices or
prayers of fallen priests (referring to Jn. 9. 31), and warned
against the contamination of their touch (p. 181, n. 1). When
the Donatists appealed to the miracles performed by their
bishops, to visions and dreams (Aug. unit. eccl. 19. 49),
they had in this also a precedent in Cyprian (p. 181, n. 3).
They maintained, further, that they were the only true and real
Catholic church (gesta coll. i. 148, 202; iii. 22, 91, 165), the
holy, persecuted church of the martyrs (ib. i. 45; iii. 116).
The Catholics are not a church, but adherents of Caecilian,
traditors, and blood-thirsty oppressors (Optat. ii. 14, 18; gest.
i. 148; iii. 14, 29, 258). The Donatist church is in reality the
holy bride of Christ, without spot or wrinkle, because it requires
holiness of its bishops and its members (ib. iii. 75, 249, 258.
Optat. ii. 20; vii. 2). They apply the term, Catholic, "not
to provinces or races," but : " the name Catholic is that which
is filled with the sacraments" (*sacramentis plenum*, gest. iii.
102, cf. Aug. brev. iii. 3), or, "thou shouldst interpret the
name Catholic, not from the fellowship of the whole world, but
from the observance of all the divine commandments and of all
the sacraments " (Aug. ep. 93. 7. 23). In accordance with the
holiness of this church, its members are to carefully avoid association with all who are not in its fellowship,[1] all such being re-

---

[1] Vid. Optat. i. 4; iv. 5; vi. 3. Aug. c. litt. Petil. ii. 83. 184. At the

garded as no better than heathen.[1] Any connection whatever
of the church with the civil government is regarded with abhor-
rence : " What have Christians to do with kings, bishops with
the palace?" (Opt. i. 22 ; Aug. c. litt. Petil. 92. 202).[2] The
dogmatic reason for this separateness lies in the invalidity of the
Catholic sacraments. The moral unworthiness of the bishops of
the traditor-church robs their sacraments of value : " How can
he give who has nothing to give?" (Opt. v. 6 ; cf. gest. iii.
258). Hence the repetition of the sacraments, the second baptism, and the repetition of extreme unction are necessary (Opt.
i. 5 ; iii. 2 ; iv. 4 ; v. 1. 3 f.; vii. 4). Yet it is going too far
to regard re-baptism as, without any modification, a characteristic mark of Donatism. The Donatist Tyconius advocated the
validity of the Catholic sacraments, and maintained that this was
the genuine Donatist view—a position that is supported by historical evidences from other sources (Aug. ep. 93. 43 ; cf.
HAHN, Tyconius-Studien, p. 102 ff.). But, since the Donatists
have the full observance of the sacraments, they are the Catholic
church. Hence, Christ and true baptism are to be found only
among them : " For how can it be, if the church is one and
Christ undivided, that anyone located without may obtain baptism (gest. iii. 258)?"

The Catholic position, on the contrary, is as follows :[3] The
orthodoxy of the Donatists is acknowledged, as well as the
validity of their sacraments, and they are regarded as Christian
brethren (gest. i. 16, 55, 62 ; ii. 50. Opt. i. 4 f.; iv. 2):
" Both among you and among us there is one ecclesiastical life
(*conversatio*), common texts, the same faith, the same sacraments
of the faith, the same mysteries" (Opt. v. 1). Even their baptism
is unassailable, for baptism is baptism, even though administered
by thieves and robbers (gest. i. 62); for it is not a man, but the
holy Trinity, which here bestows a gift (Opt. v. 7). The Trinity
is necessary in baptism, and also the faith of the recipient.
These elements are unchangeable ; but the administrant is a
variable element. "Administrants may be changed, but the
sacraments cannot be changed. If, therefore, you consider all

religious colloquy at Carthage, the Donatists could not be induced to sit with
the Catholics (gest. i. 45 ; ii. 3).

[1] Optat. iii. 11 (cf. vi. 8): You say even to the clergy, " Be Christians,"
and you dare to say to everyone : " *Gai sei Gaia seia : adhuc paganus es aut
pagana*" (translating the Punic words, vid. remarks in Ziswa's edition, p.
277).

[2] Yet the Donatists themselves called upon Constantine to act as umpire,
and, as it appears, did not at a later day disdain the assistance of the secular
arm (gest. iii. 194. Aug. brev. iii. 11).

[3] We take no account for the present of ideas specifically Augustinian.

who baptize, they are administrants, not lords ; and the sacraments are holy in themselves and not through men " (Opt. iv. 4, 1). Thus regarded, the Donatists are also a part of the church. But they are not so in the full sense of the word, since they lack catholicity and are only *quasi ecclesia*. They build a "ruinous wall" (Ez. 13. 10). There is no other house beside the house of God. What they build is only a wall, and that not even resting upon the corner-stone : " your part is a quasi-church, but is not Catholic" (Opt. iii. 10). They array " novelty against antiquity " (ib. iii. 2), and cut themselves off from the root (iii. 7). Among the Catholics, on the contrary, is found the house of God and the one Catholic church. It is the latter, because, according to the promise of Christ, it spreads abroad over all nations and is not confined " to a small part of Africa, to the corner of a little region " (Opt. ii. 1, 5 ; iii. 2, 3). But it is also the *holy* church, and this not because of the character of the men belonging to it, but because it has the " symbol of the Trinity, the chair of Peter, the faith of believers, the salutary precepts of Christ " (ib. ii. 9, 10 ; vii. 2), and, above all, the sacraments : " whose holiness is derived from the sacraments, not measured by the loftiness of persons " (ib. ii. 1). When the Donatists refuse to accord holiness to the church because some bishops at the time of the Diocletian persecution became traditors, they magnify what is irrelevant, if true, and what is, moreover, historically incorrect (gest. i. 16, 55. Aug. brev. iii. 19 ff.). There are, indeed, unholy persons in the church, but we are forbidden to cast these out before the time by the parables of the tares and of the net in which are gathered good and worthless fishes (gest. i. 18, 55. Opt. vii. 2). Those passages of Scripture which speak of a state of unmixed holiness in the church are to be understood as referring to her condition of final blessedness (Aug. brev. iii. 9. Opt. ii. 20). The church, therefore, as a whole, is holy in the present day by virtue of the divine agency exerted within its bounds in the sacraments, and it will one day be holy in all its members. The error of the Donatists consists in seeking to realize this final state before the time. It is certain that, viewed dogmatically, the Catholic position was the more correct, yet its victory was not a clear step in advance. The ancient idea, that the people of God should consist of holy children of God, was forced another step backward.

2. AUGUSTINE'S DOCTRINE OF THE CHURCH, THE SACRAMENTS, AND THE RELATION OF CHURCH AND STATE.

(*a*) Augustine's doctrine of the church is a complicated structure. Ideas evolved in the conflict with the Donatists, the popular conception of the church, his own doctrine of grace, and certain Donatistic tendencies are here brought into combination. Augustine was influenced especially by Tyconius' conception of the church. This Donatist maintained, indeed, that the church is composed of saints only, but he also taught that empirically the church for the present embraces evil as well as good persons, and that this is so by divine ordering. True, this mixed condition of the church is, according to his view, soon to be terminated, and to this end Donatism is a beginning (vid. HAHN, Tyconius-Studien, p. 80 ff.). As opposed to Donatism, Augustine thus formulates the point at issue : "The question is, indeed, discussed between us, Where is the church, whether among us or among them?" (de unit. eccl. 2. 2). With Optatus, Augustine holds that the great church is the *one Catholic* church by virtue of the distribution of the latter throughout the whole world (c. litt. Petil. ii. 38. 91 ; iii. 2. 3 ; de unit. eccl. 6. 11 ff.) and by virtue of its connection with the church of the apostles, whose successors the bishops are (c. Cresc. iii. 18. 21 ; de unit. eccl. 11. 30, cf. in Joh. tr. 37. 6). Outside of this one Catholic church, the body of Christ, there is no truth,[1] no salvation (ep. 141. 5 ; de unit. 2. 2). Separation from it is a *sacrilegium* (c. ep. Parm. i. 8. 14; 10. 16). Only chaff is blown off by the fan (bapt. v. 21. 29); only pride and lack of love can impel a Christian to split the unity of the church (c. Cresc. iv. 59. 71 ; c. litt. Petil. ii. 77. 172). The declaration of Augustine is not, however, inspired by hierarchial motive, but rests ultimately upon the thought that it is only in the Catholic church that the Spirit and love are bestowed upon man. But the saints are to be found only in the Catholic church. In this connection, Augustine championed the motto, *Extra ecclesiam nulla salus*, no less positively than Cyprian ; but, at the same time—as a result of the different character of the opposition—displayed less of hierarchical interest than the latter (cf. REUTER, l. c., p. 253 ff.).

(*b*) The idea of the ROMAN PRIMACY likewise receives no special elucidation at the hands of Augustine. We find a general acknowledgment of the " primacy of the apostolic chair " (*e. g,,* ep. 43. 7), but Augustine knows nothing of any special authority vested in Peter or his successors. Peter is a " figure of the church " or of the " good pastors," and represents the unity of the church (serm. 295. 2 ; 147. 2). In this consists the significance of his position and that of his successors (thus also Cyprian, p. 183). As all bishops (in contradistinction from the

---

[1] *E. g.,* it is manifest, faith admits it, the Catholic church approves it, it is true (serm. 117. 4. 6).

Scriptures) may err (unit. eccl. 11. 28), so also the Roman bishop. This view is plainly manifest from the bearing of Augustine and his colleagues in the Pelagian controversy (vid. p. 355 f., cf. ep. 177, 191 ; pecc. orig. 21. 24, cf. 8. 9). The infallible authority of the pope in the church at large was a dogma in which only the popes believed (vid. the letters of Innocent, p. 355 ; cf. as to Leo, p. 268, and Callistus, p. 177). Dogmatically, there had been no advance from the position of Cyprian. The Africans, in their relations with Rome, played somewhat the role of the Gallicanism of a later period (cf. REUTER, p. 291 ff.).

(c) The opposition between the Donatistic and Catholic churches was based upon their different conceptions of the sacraments. From the time of the Council of Arles (p. 314), the great point of discussion was whether baptism and ordination administered by an unworthy person retained their validity. Augustine's views concerning the sacraments, by an inner necessity, determined his attitude upon this question (cf. REUTER, p. 278). The sacraments are gifts of God, and the moral condition of the administrator cannot detract from the value of the gift conveyed : "What he gives is, nevertheless, real (*verum*), if he gives not what is his own, but God's" (c. litt. Pet. ii. 30. 69 ; unit. eccl. 21. 58). Only thus is the result certain, and salvation dependent upon God, not upon men. It is not the intercession of men, but that of Christ, which helps us (c. litt. Pet. i. 3. 4 ; c. ep. Parm. ii. 8. 16). "No reason is shown why he who cannot lose baptism itself can forfeit the right of administering it. For each is a sacrament, and each is given to man by the same consecration—the one when he is baptized, and the other when he is ordained : therefore, in the Catholic church neither dare be repeated" (c. ep. Parm. ii. 12. 28). This is explained by the fact that these sacraments impart to the recipient a permanent character : "just as baptism, so ordination *remains whole* in them" (ib.). Baptism and ordination impress upon man a fixed " *dominical character.*"[1] This military form of expression implies that, as there is a military brand (*nota militaris*) whose significance continues through the whole life, so also baptism and ordination have a perpetual and indelible (the term employed in the Middle Ages) force for the recipient (c. ep. Parm. ii. 13. 29). There remains in him something sacred, a *sanctum*. The spirit is preserved to him, not in a moral sense, but in the sense of an official equipment. He may have committed heinous

---

[1] Augustine introduced this term into theology. He was also the first to use the expression *obicem opponere* (ep. 98. 9).

crimes—may have severed himself from the church, yet this *character* once impressed upon him remains, and the sacraments administered by him retain their force. If he be converted, there is no need for a repetition of the sacrament (c. ep. Parm. ii. 11. 24; 13. 28 f.; bapt. iv. 12. 18; vi. 1. 1; de symbol. 8. 15; de bon. conjug. 24. 32: "in those ordained, the sacrament of ordination remains;" bapt. vi. 5. 7; in 1 Joh. tract. 5. 7). It is evident that this *character indelebilis* may be employed as the most telling argument against Donatism ; but it also brought Augustine into new difficulties. If the sacraments have bestowed such a character, how can objection be brought against the Donatistic church ? It was necessary, therefore, to maintain the validity of the Donatist sacraments, and yet to condemn them as seriously defective. This was accomplished by discriminating between the sacrament itself and the *effectus* or *usus sacramenti*. By failing to observe this distinction, Cyprian and others were led to the view " that the baptism of Christ cannot exist among heretics or schismatics." By observing it, we may say : " its effect or use, in liberation from sin and in rectitude of heart, could not be found among heretics " (bapt. vi. 1. 1). Baptism imparts to the recipient an abiding character, but if he do not live in the church, the " effect " in the forgiveness of sin does not follow. The baptism cannot, indeed, be repeated ; but only when the individual is converted to the *unity* of the true church does it become effectual : " He who has received the baptism of Christ, which they have not lost who have separated themselves . . . in any heresy or schism, in which sacrilegious crime his sins were not remitted, when he shall have reformed and come to the fellowship and unity of the church, is not to be again baptized, because in this very reconciliation and peace it is offered to him, that the sacrament which, when received in schism, could not benefit, shall now in the unity (of the church) begin to benefit him for the remission of his sins " (bapt. i. 12. 18 ; v. 8. 9 ; vi. 5. 7). In the case of ordination, it was held that the *character* remains, bringing, however, to the individual himself not blessing, but the contrary : "the Holy Spirit . . . fails, indeed, to effect his salvation . . . yet does not desert his ministry, by which he works through him the salvation of others " (c. Parm. ii. 11. 24 ; de bon. conjug. 24. 32). By this means the Donatist theory is discountenanced and, at the same time, the necessity of the return of its adherents to the Catholic church is made evident.

(*d*) The means by which the church is built up are the sacraments, especially baptism and the Lord's Supper, and also the Word. " Blood and water flowed (Jn. 19. 34), which we know

to be the sacraments by which the church is built up " (civ. dei,
xxii. 17). "God begets sons from the church . . . we are,
therefore, spiritually born, and we are born in the Spirit by word
and sacrament. The Spirit is present, that we may be born "
(in Joh. tract. 12. 5 ; serm. 88. 5 ; ep. 21. 3). The term,
sacramentum—corresponding exactly to μυστήριον—is applied
also to other ecclesiastical acts, such as confirmation (bapt. v. 20.
28 ; c. Faustum xix. 14), the presentation of the consecrated
salt to catechumens (de catechizandis rudibus, 26. 50), ordination (bon. conjug. 24. 32 ; c. ep. Parm. ii. 13. 28 ; cf. supra),
exorcism (serm. 27). But the proper sacraments are the two
which proceeded from the side of Christ (civ. dei, xv. 26. 1 ; in
Joh. tract. 15. 8 ; 120. 2 ; 50. 12 ; doctr. christ. iii. 9. 13), to
which is to be added ordination. The representation of the
divine agency exerted is essentially the same in the word and in
the sacraments.[1] The human transaction is accompanied by a
divine, inwardly effectual act. The word is read in the hearing
of others, preached, sung, and chanted by men : "we enjoy
the hearing of it, the truth speaking to us without sound inwardly " (in Joh. tr. 57. 3 ; 40. 5 ; 71. 1 ; 77. 2 ; bapt. v. 11.
24). Augustine is thus the first to formulate a doctrine of
the word as a means of grace. The problem is here presented,
how the spoken human word can be the medium through
which the divine Spirit operates. In the same way in the sacraments as in the word, men work outwardly, God inwardly (c.
ep. Parm. ii. 11 ; bapt. v. 21. 29 ; ep. 98. 2 : "the water,
therefore, presenting the sacrament of grace outwardly, and the
Spirit inwardly effecting the benefit of grace "). It is to be,
however, here noted that the outward observance of the sacrament
and the inner work of grace do not always correspond (bapt. iv.
25. 32 ; in Lev. iii., quaest. 84 ; enarr. in. ps. 77. 2).

We are now in position to define Augustine's conception of a sacrament. We must, first of all, discriminate carefully between the
outward sign and the inward power and efficacy : "the sacrament is one thing, the virtue of the sacrament another " (in Joh.
tr. 26. 11). Viewed in the first aspect, the sacrament is purely
symbolical. There are needed, says Augustine, in genuine Neo-
Platonic spirit, in religious associations "signs (*signacula*) or visible sacraments " (c. Faust. xix. 11). The visible signs are
symbols of an invisible content : "they are, indeed, visible
signs of divine things, but in them are to be honored the invisible things themselves " (de cat. rud. 26. 50). "They are
called sacraments, because in them one thing is seen, another thing

---

[1] Even the word is included among the signs (*signa*), doctr. christ. ii. 3.

21

understood " (serm. 272). The symbol has at the same time a
certain resemblance to that which it represents (ep. 98. 9). Accordingly, the visible symbols become what they are through the
interpreting word : " the word comes to (*accedit*) the element and
it becomes (*fit*) a sacrament—itself also, as it were, a visible
word." The "*fit*" is used here not in the objective, but purely
in the subjective sense : " Whence is there in the water such
virtue that it can touch the body and purify the heart, unless the
word effects this ?—*not because it is spoken, but because it is believed*" (in Joh. tr. 80. 3). In the light of this explanation,
Augustine would seem to have a purely symbolical view of the
sacrament ; and it is beyond doubt that the Neo-Platonic caste
of his thought at least inclined him in this direction. But we must
not overlook the fact, that an actual exertion of divine energy, as a
rule, accompanies the sacrament.   God really forgives sins in baptism, in it, as in ordination, imprinting a character upon the recipient.   In the Lord's Supper there is really an effectual refreshment
(*salubris refectio*) in the Lord's flesh and blood.   Thus to drink is
to live ; a spiritual eating and drinking accompanies the visible
reception (serm. 131. 1).   The two-fold aspect of the sacramental theory of the ancient church here comes into distinct prominence : The sacraments are purely symbols, but the reception of
the sacraments brings real, objective exertions of divine energy.
In Augustine, indeed, the whole conception is wavering, since
there is no fixed connection between the sacrament and the gracious divine energy.   Here, too, is felt the influence of his
theory of predestination. As to the sacramental *character*, see p.
319.

(*e*) The peculiarities of the separate sacraments may be briefly
stated. (*a*) Baptism, as the *sacramentum remissionis peccatorum*,
(bapt. v. 21. 29) works the forgiveness of sins, primarily the
forgiveness of the guilt of original concupiscence ; in this consists its chief efficacy (cf. p. 314). Augustine frequently speaks of
a blotting out of sins (*e. g.*, by baptism . . . sins are destroyed,
delentur, in ps. 106. 3).   Discrimination is to be made between
this forgiveness once granted and the recurring forgiveness of
daily sins in response to the fifth petition of the Lord's Prayer
(*e. g.*, serm. 58. 5. 6).   Augustine, however, made the latter
dependent upon the former : " by that which is given once it
comes to pass that pardon of any sins whatsoever, not only before but also afterward, is granted to believers."   Prayer, alms,
and good works would bring no forgiveness to the Christian if he
were not baptized (nupt. et conc. i. 33. 38).   But this idea was
obscured by the penitential discipline (vid. sub) and by the
relatively unimportant place of the forgiveness of sins in the

consciousness of Augustine (p. 346 f.). Compare Dieckhoff, l. c., p. 536 ff.). (β) In contradistinction from Ambrose (e. g., de fide iv. 10. 124 : " through the mystery of the sacred prayer they are transfigured into flesh and blood "), the symbolical character of the sacraments comes in Augustine into distinct prominence : " The Lord did not hesitate to say, ' This is my body,' when he gave the sign of his body " (c. Adimantum Manich. 12. 3 ; in ps. 3. 1). The blessing, or gift, of the sacrament is conceived in harmony with this. The body of the Lord is the mystic body, or the church : " hence he wishes the food and drink to be understood as the fellowship (societas) of his body and of his members, which is the holy church " (in Joh. tr. 26. 15, 14 ; serm. 272 ; civ. dei, xxi. 25. 2); or, " this is, therefore, to eat that food and to drink that drink—to remain in Christ and to have him remaining in us " (in Joh. tr. 26. 18 ; civ. dei, xxi. 25. 4). Augustine can even say that the eating of the body of the Lord is " delightfully and profitably to store away in memory that his flesh was wounded and crucified for us " (doctr. christ. iii. 16. 24).[1] It is true, there are not wanting passages in which Augustine expresses himself differently and more fully, speaking of the reception of the body of Christ, etc. (e. g., serm. 131. 1 ; bapt. v. 8. 9); but his real thought is even here not that which the words seem to convey, although he still has in mind the bestowal and reception of a real gift. Thus Augustine's theory of the Lord's Supper has more of a really religious character than his doctrines of baptism and grace, since the personal nature of fellowship with God here finds due recognition. It is to be observed, further, that in the view of Augustine, Christ is, indeed, omnipresent according to his divine nature, but according to his human nature he is in one place in heaven (ubique totum praesentem esse non dubites tanquam deum . . . et in loco aliquo caeli propter veri corporis modum, ep. 187. 12. 41). In this again we see the model after which the medieval theories were patterned. The genius of Augustine is manifest in his interpretation of the sacrifice of the mass : the congregatio sanctorum presents itself to God in good works under its head, Christ. " This is the sacrifice of Christians : Many one body in Christ "

---

[1] I purposely omit the famous passage which is usually cited in this connection (by Löscher already, in the Weimar edition, ii. 742): " Why preparest thou the teeth and the stomach ? Believe, and thou hast eaten " (in Joh. tr. 25. 12), for, in the context in which this occurs, the author has not the Lord's Supper in mind. The food to which he refers is the God-given commandment, to believe on Christ ; and in order to receive (eat) this, the teeth are not needed, but faith. Compare the similar statements (ib. 26. 1): " for to believe in him, this is to eat living bread ; " " he who believes eats ; " and 35. 3 : " with the mind, not with the stomach."

(civ. dei, x. 6). Of which thing [the sacrifice of Christ] he wished the sacrifice of the church (which, since it is the body of him, the Head, teaches that it offers itself through him) to be a daily sacrament [symbolical imitation] (ib. x. 20). (γ) As to the sacrament of ordination, see p. 319 f., and cf. REUTER l.c., 253, 264 ff.

(ƒ) But we have thus far seen but one side of Augustine's conception of the church. When we remember that the infusion of the Spirit and of love makes the Christian (p. 347 f.), we realize that we are brought to face another line of thought. (a) The good, who have the Spirit and love, constitute among themselves a communion (congregatio, compages). These saints are the unspotted bride of Christ, his dove, and the house of God, the rock upon which the Lord builds his church, the church which possesses the power to loose and bind (unit. eccl. 21. 60 ; c. litt. Pet. ii. 58. 246; bapt. vii. 51. 99). It is not being outwardly in the church, nor partaking of the sacraments, that decides, but belonging to the church in this sense : " Nor are they to be thought to be in the body of Christ, which is the church, because they become corporeally participants in its sacraments . . . they are not in the union (compages) of the church, which, in the members of Christ, grows through connection and contact to the increase of God " (c. litt. Pet. l. c.). It is this communion of the saints,[1] united by the Spirit and love, through whose intercession sins are forgiven, and through whose mediation the gifts of grace are bestowed. To it, and not to the officials of the church, are given these great promises. "God gives the sacrament of grace, indeed, through evil men, but not grace itself except through himself or through his saints. And, therefore, he effects remission of sins either through himself or through the members of that dove, to whom he says : If to anyone ye remit, they are remitted " (bapt. v. 21. 29). " Or does the sacrament and a secret dispensation of the mercy of God, perhaps, through the prayers of the spiritual saints who are in the church, as through the continuous cooing of the dove, accomplish the great thing, that even the sins of those who have been baptized, not by the

---

[1] The term, communio sanctorum, is found in the first canon of the Council at Nimes (A. D. 394. HEFELE, CG. ii., ed. 2, 62) and among the Donatists (Aug. in ps. 36 ; serm. 2. 20 and opp. xvii. 2532). In Augustine's own writings, serm. 52. 3. 6 ; cf. congregatio sanctorum (civ. dei, x. 6 ; bapt. i. 17. 26); communis unitatis corporis Christi (bapt. i. 4. 5); societas credentium (bapt. vii. 53. 102); christiana societas (c. litt. Petil. ii. 39. 94); bonorum societas (ib. ii. 77. 174); also communio malorum (bapt. vii. 25. 49). At a later date, as is well known, it appears in the Creed (Nicetas v. Romatiana in Caspari, Anecdota, 355. Faust. v. Riez, ib. 338. Ps. Aug. serm. 240, 241, 242 ; cf. vol. xvii. 1960).

dove but by the hawk, are remitted?" (ib. iii. 17. 22 ; 18. 23).
This is the essence of the communion of the good and pious:
They love God and one another, and they pray for the church.
This is the "invisible union (*compages*) of love" (bapt. iii. 19.
26; de unit. eccl. 21. 60) with the invisible anointing of love
(*unctio caritatis*, c. litt. Petil. ii. 104. 239). But this exists, and
is conceivable, only within the Catholic church, separation from
which is at once a renunciation of the Spirit and of love (ep.
141. 5, and citations on p. 318). Only in the Catholic church
is the spirit of love thus present. But Augustine here thinks not
only of the efficacious working of the sacrament, but also, and
particularly, of the working of the Spirit upon the spiritual life
through the personal fellowship of the believing and holy with
one another. He has not, therefore, yet reached the position of
medieval Catholicism.

(β) But is not the church then split into two churches,
the mixed church of the present and the pure church of the
future (Donatist criticism, brev. iii. 10. 19)? Augustine meets
this objection with a variety of illustrations. The question is
one solely of a present relationship. Good and evil are commingled in the church. According to the instructions of Christ,
the latter cannot be outwardly excluded, although they are inwardly entirely separated from the pious (c. ep. Parm. iii. 2. 12 ;
c. Cresc. iii. 65. 73 ; bapt. vi. 3. 5 ; vii. 51. 99), just as are
heretics : "Whether they seem to live within or are openly without, that which is flesh is flesh. . . . And even he who in carnal obduracy is mingled with the congregation of the saints is
always separated from the unity of that church which is without
spot or wrinkle" (bapt. i. 17. 26 ; also vii. 51. 99 extr.). But :
"he tolerates the wicked *in communione sanctorum*" (serm. 214.
11). It is a relationship like that between the wheat and the
tares upon the same threshing-floor (bapt. v. 21. 29); between
belonging to a house and being in the house (ib. vii. 51. 99);
between the outer and the inner man (brev. iii. 10. 20); or even :
"thus there are in the body of Christ in some way evil humors"
(in 1 Joh. tr. 3. 4). We may, therefore, speak of "the true and
the commingled, or counterfeited, body of the Lord," or of a
"commingled church." Hence, in the proper sense, the church
consists of only the good and holy : the wicked and heretics only
apparently belong to it by virtue of the temporal commingling
and the communion of the sacraments" (doctr. christ. iii. 32.
45). We can see that Augustine takes some account of the demand of the Donatists ; but he effects only in thought the separation which they sought to realize in fact. "We understand
the departure (*recessio*) spiritually, they corporeally" (serm. 88.

20. 23). From a critical point of view, the Donatistic objection is not without justification, for the church of the sacraments and the church of grace can only with the greatest difficulty be intellectually harmonized.

(γ) This difficulty is intimately connected with Augustine's definition of grace, and it becomes still more serious when the doctrine of predestination is taken into account. " The invisible union of love " is not identical with the " number of the predestinated." As the latter may extend beyond the bounds of the church (p. 351), so, on the contrary, some may belong to the church who are not in the number of the predestinated, and, therefore, do not have the " gift of perseverance " (corr. et grat. 9. 22 ; don. pers. 2. 2). Practically, indeed, Augustine did not realize this discrepancy any more than that between the inward and the outward church. That it nevertheless exists, cannot be denied, although Augustine only occasionally combines the conceptions, church and predestination.[1] We may, accordingly, speak of a two-fold, or even a three-fold, definition of the church in Augustine. Cf. REUTER, l. c., p. 47 ff. SEEBERG, l. c., 49 ff.

(g) It must be mentioned, finally, that Augustine applied the term, KINGDOM OF GOD, also to the church of the present, whereas the ancient church, as represented in other teachers, regarded the kingdom as the result and goal of the church's development,[2] looking to the future for the highest good. But Augustine says : "The church is even now the kingdom of Christ and the kingdom of heaven " (civ. dei, xx. 9. 1 ; cf. de fid. et op. 7. 10 ; serm. 213. 7 ; 214. 11). This utterance means primarily only that the saints are the kingdom of Christ and reign with him. But this dominion is at once attributed to the leaders (praepositi) "through whom the church is now governed " (ib. § 2). The kingdom of God is thus for Augustine essentially identical with the pious and holy ; but it is also the episcopally organized church. The contrast between the city of God (civitas dei) and the city[3] of

---

[1] We read, de bapt. v. 27. 28 : The church as an enclosed garden, paradise, etc., consists of the sancti and justi. Then appears as equivalent : " the certain predestinated number of saints," and from this again : "the number of the just." Yet many of the predestinati are now living carnally and unworthily—are heathen and heretics. And yet these are all to be considered as included in the enclosed garden, the church, which originally consisted of the holy and righteous. Cf. SEEBERG, p. 53.

[2] Vid., e. g., Did. 10. 5. Cypr. de op. et eleem. 9 ; de unit. eccl. 14. Hieron. adv. Iovin. ii. 19. Also Augustine himself, serm. 131. 6. 6 ; esp. brev. collat. iii. 10. 20 ; 9. 16.

[3] Civitas is here used as meaning "city" (civ. dei, xv. 1. 25), a signification which in general historical connections passes over into that of " state." Vid. REUTER, p. 131 f.

the world (*civitas mundi*), or of the devil, is for him that between Christanity and heathenism (in the first 10 books): between the good and the bad, including the devil and angels (civ. dei, xii. 1 ; 27. 2), or between the saints and the wicked even within the church; between the spiritual and the carnal, the love of God and self-love, grace and nature, those foreordained to glory or to torment (*e. g.*, xx. 9. 3 ; xiv. 1 ; 4. 2 ; 28 ; xv. 1. 2 ; 16. 3). The evil world is never represented, indeed, as itself equivalent to the state.   But since the *civitas dei* may be and is conceived as the empirical church, the reader very naturally thinks of the *civitas mundi* concretely as equivalent to the state (*e. g.*, xiv. 28 ; xv. 4 ; i. 35).   This is encouraged by the fact that, although Augustine recognizes the necessity of the (Christian) state and the civil law (xv. 4 in Joh. tr. 6. 25 f.), yet everything really and permanently good is found upon the side of the church.   From this it follows, that it is the duty of the state to execute the commandments of Christ, or of the church (xv. 2, ep. 138. 2. 14 ; 105. 3. 11). From this point of view, Augustine—in conflict with his earlier convictions (ep. 93. 5. 17)—desired the state to employ force against Donatists and heretics : " Compel them to come in " (Lk. 14. 23 ; vid. ep. 93 and 185 in Joh. tr. 11. 14).   Here, as so frequently, he falls into the current of the popular Christianity of the day.   The great work upon the " City of God "— capable of many interpretations (a double line of aims and means running through the work, just as through Plato's " State ") —became the criterion for the development of the church polity of the Middle Ages.   Cf. REUTER, p. 111 f.

Such, in outline, was Augustine's conception of the church. The power of the historic Catholic tradition, the opposition of the Donatists, the fundamental tendency of his doctrine of grace, the predestination theory, and a grandly broad view of the course of history—were the threads woven into the texture.   In it the best and the worst elements appear side by side.   It is Evangelical and Catholic ; superior to the world and compromising with the world ; at once, true and untrue.   Theoretically contemplated, it is a malformation without parallel : practically considered, a redundancy of large conceptions and impulses--not an organism, but a vessel full of fermenting elements.

Augustine prepared the way for the medieval ecclesiasticism ; but he also revived and gave practical efficacy to a central idea of primitive Christianity—the present kingdom of God.   He embraced the many treasures of Christianity in the one treasure— the kingdom of God, and thus made them concrete and historically visible.   He also, in his conception of the church, saved from the confusion of Donatistic ideas the primitive truth of the church as the communion of saints. In connection with this, he definitely asserted the natural character of the *charismata*. The Spirit, who creates new life, is the great gift of divine grace to the church. It may be said that Augustine was the first since Paul to renounce the grace of visions, dreams, and inner suggestions (cf. Cyprian and the Donatists), since he understood grace as consisting in the spirit of love animating the church. Not only could Rome appeal to Augustine, but the Evangelical theory of the church finds in him as well a champion.

§ 31. *Establishment of the Doctrine of Sin and Grace in the Conflict with Pelagianism.*

LITERATURE. WALCH, Ketzerhistorie iv. v. WIGGERS, Pragmat. Darstellung d. Augustinismus u. Pelagianismus, 2 vols., 1821, 1833. JACOBI, Die Lehre des Pelag., 1842. WÖRTER, Der Pelagianismus, 1866. KLASEN, Die innere Entwicklung d. Pelagianismus, 1882. DIECKHOFF, Aug. Lehre v. d. Gnade, in Theol. Ztschr. von Dieckhoff u. Kliefoth, 1860, p. 11 ff. LANDERER, Das Verhältniss v. Gnade u. Freiheit, Jarbb. f. deutsche Theol., 1857, p. 500 ff. LUTHARDT, Die Lehre vom fr. Willen u. sein Verh. zur Gnade, 1863. ROTTMANNER, Augustinismus, 1892. DORNER, Augustin, p. 113 ff. HEFELE, CG. ii., ed. 2, 104 ff. REUTER, Augustin. Studien, p. 4 ff.; THOMASIUS, DG. i., ed. 2, 456 ff. HARNACK, DG. iii. 151 ff. WÖRTER, Beiträge zur DG. des Pelagianismus, 1898.

1. DIVERGENCES OF THE EASTERN AND WESTERN CHURCHES.

We have had occasion to observe (§ 27) that the Eastern church laid great emphasis upon the freedom of the natural man. This is done especially in moral exhortations, while, at the same time, when treating of the work of redemption, the state of the natural man was often depicted in the darkest colors (*e. g.*, by Athanasius). We must bear in mind that the attitude of the Greeks toward the problem of free-will was fundamentally different from that of the Latins. They began with the intellect, to which the will was simply subordinate, as an organ through which it operates. Whatever a man thinks, that he is also able to will. The Romans, on the contrary, assign an independent position to the will. In the utterances of such a practical Greek teacher as Chrysostom, we find indeed both conceptions embodied, but that of human freedom holds the place of prominence : "For God created our nature self-controlling" (αὐτεξούσιος, in Genes. hom. 19). Accordingly, it is only the separate acts of man that are regarded as evil. There is no sinful *habitus :* "Thou shouldst not acknowledge any substantial (ἐνυπόστατος) power, but the evil deed, always coming into being and vanishing, not existing before it has occurred, and disappearing again after it has occurred" (in Rom. hom. 12). The result of the fall for us is that, as Adam thereby became mortal, so his descendants are also mortal (hom. in ps. 51). The conception of grace is in harmony with this view. Man makes the beginning in that which is good, and grace comes to his aid : "For it is necessary that we first choose the good, and when we have chosen it, then he also brings his part. He does not anticipate our wishes, in order that our freedom may not be destroyed. But when we have chosen, then he brings great help to us . . . it is ours to choose beforehand and to will, but it is God's to accomplish and lead to the result" (in Heb. h. 12 ; in Rom. h. 16 ; in Joh. h. 17). This expresses very fairly the position of the Eastern church, in which, moreover, the conception of grace itself becomes confused by its connection with the worship of the mysteries. Cf. Förster, Chrysostomus, 1869, pp. 63 ff., 139 ff. August. c. Jul. i. 6. 21 ff.

In contrast with the above, we may place the teaching of a Western theologian, AMBROSE († A. D. 397), the forerunner of Augustine upon the subject of sin and grace. In his conception of sin we can still trace the beginnings of a doctrine of original sin which we discovered in Tertullian, Cyprian, and Commodian (pp. 122 f., 193).[1] (a) In his practical addresses, Ambrose also occasionally used strong language in placing the responsibility for evil deeds upon the free will of man (e. g., enarr. in ps. 1, § 30 ; de Jac. et vit. beata i. 10). But his thought is dominated by the view, that through the fall of Adam we come into the world as sinners, that sin is an attribute which belongs to us from our conception, and that we, therefore, being from the outstart sinful, must sin even when for the time being we do not desire to sin : "Adam was, and in him we all were. Adam perished, and in him we all perished " (in Luc. vii. 234, 164). "I fell in Adam, I was in Adam ejected from paradise, I died in Adam " (de excessu fratr. sui Satyri ii. 6).[2] "No one at all who has been born under sin can be saved, whom that very inheritance of

---

[1] Hilary at this point betrays the influence of the Greeks, e. g., in ps. 118 lit. N. 20 : "There is, indeed, in faith a gift of continuance from God ; but the source of the beginning is from us, and our will ought to have this of itself as its own, that it wills. God will give an increase of the beginning, because our infirmity does not through itself attain the consummation ; nevertheless, the merit of reaching the consummation is, from the beginning, of the will." Yet he uses also the term, *vitium originis*, and says : "In the error of the one Adam, the whole race of men went astray" (in ps. 119 lit. N. 20 ; P. 6 ; in Matt. 18. 6). Cf. LANDERER, l. c., p. 591 f.

[2] Cf. also the so-called Ambrosiaster upon Rom. v. 12 : "It is manifest that in Adam all sinned, as it were, in the mass ; for all whom he who was himself corrupted through sin begat were born under sin ; from him, therefore all are sinners, because from him we all are." Vid. also the (apparently not Ambrosian) Apol. ii., David, § 71.

guilty condition has constrained to sin " (in ps. 38, § 29). " Before we are born we are defiled by contagion, and before we enjoy
the light we receive the injury of our very origin ; we are conceived in iniquity." In response to the question, whether this
last assertion relates to the mother or to the child, it is said :
" But see whether it may not be known which. The one conceived is not without sin, since the parents are not without fault.
And, if the infant of one day is not without sin, much more are
all the days of maternal conception not without sin. We are
conceived, therefore, in the sin (*peccato*) of our parents and in
their faults (*delictis*) we are born " (apol. David, 11. 56). Hence
also : " We are led unwilling and reluctant into guilt " (*culpam*),
and : " For our heart and our meditations are not in our power "
(de fuga seculi i. 1 ; ii. 9). According to these citations, Ambrose really taught the propagation of Adam's sin ; but we do
not find in his writings the idea of the imputation of Adam's
guilt to the race sprung from him. He recognizes a physical, but not a moral, original sin (cf. FÖRSTER, Ambr., p.
154 f.).

(*b*) As to his doctrine of grace, we note that Ambrose very
strongly emphasized the activity of grace, but yet knows nothing
of its alone-activity. " He who follows Christ, when asked why
he resolved to be a Christian, can respond : ' It seemed good to
me ' " (Lk. i. 3). " When he says this, he does not deny that it
seemed good to God, for *the will of men* is *prepared by God*.
For that God may be worshiped by a saint is from the grace of
God " (in Luc. i. 10). But also : " By free will we are either
disposed toward virtue or inclined toward vice. And, therefore,
either free affection draws us toward error, or the will, following
reason, recalls us " (Jac. et vit. beat. i. 1 ; de poenit. ii. 9. 80). It
is Christ, coming to us and into us, who effects this " (in Luc.
x. 7). But this occurs chiefly through baptism. The efficacy
of the latter is seen in the blotting out of iniquity (*iniquitas*, the
sinful *habitus*), the forgiveness of sins, and the bringing of the
gift of spiritual grace (*spiritualis gratiae munus*) (apol. Dav. 13.
62): " Thus perfect virtue destroys iniquity, and the remission
of sins every sin " (de myst. 4. 20 ; ep. 7. 20 ; 41. 7 ; in Luc.
ii. 79). If, indeed, after the manner of the ancient church,
room is here found for the blotting out of sins by the endowment with new spiritual power, yet Ambrose could, nevertheless,
write : " I will not glory because I am righteous, but I will
glory because I have been redeemed. I will glory, not because
I am empty of sins, but because my sins have been forgiven me "
(Jac. et vit.; b. i. 6. 21 ; cf. in ps. 44. 1 ; ep. 73. 10). It
is easily seen that this forerunner of Augustine was not unac-

quainted with Paul.[1] We find in him, it is true, a certain synergism. But while the Eastern theologians represent man as making the beginning for the attainment of salvation, and then
ascribe a *synergia* to God, here it is God who begins the work,
and the *synergia* is upon the part of man. The Eastern teachers
think of a divine, the Western of a human synergy.

Cf. FÖRSTER, Ambrosius, 1884, p. 139 ff. DEUTSCH, Des Ambros. Lehre
von der Sünde u. Sündentilgung, 1867 (Program of the Joachimsthal Gymn.
in Berlin). EWALD, Der Einfluss der stoisch-ciceron. Moral auf die Darstellung der Ethik bei Ambr., 1881.

2. PELAGIUS AND PELAGIANISM.

SOURCES. PELAGIUS, epistula ad Demetriadem in the Works of Jerome,
ed. Vallarsi, xi. 2. 1 ff. Ep. ad Livaniam, in fragments only in Augustine
and Jerome. Marius Mercator, in his Commonitorium super nomine Caelestii,
and in the Liber subnotationum in verba Juliani. Eulogiarum liber, fragments

---

[1] We must not fail to note also the remarkable teaching of the monk,
JOVINIAN (in Rome and Milan, about A. D. 390), although the sources do
not enable us to form a perfectly reliable opinion in regard to him. Jovinian
made a vigorous assault upon the low estimation of marriage, in which the influence of Manichæism and heathenism was so plainly seen ; maintained the
moral equality of marriage and celibacy, as also of fasting and the receiving
of food with thankfulness ; and asserted an equality of reward for all believers
(Jerome adv. Jovin. l. ii. 5 ff.). A difficulty meets us in his assertion (ib. i.
3): " That those who have been with full faith regenerated in baptism cannot
be subverted by the devil " (in ii. 1, "cannot be tempted," or, according to
Julian of Eclanum, who had read the work of Jovinian, "cannot sin ;" vid. Aug.
op. imperf. i. 98). It is beyond question that Jovinian expresses this view, but
it is also to be observed that he does so with appeal to Jn. iii. 9 ; v. 18 (ii. 1),
and that he did not deny to the baptized the possibility of repentance : "Although ye have fallen, repentance will restore you" (ii. 37). His real opinion
can scarcely be other than that expressed in ii. 27 : " But if the Father and the
Son make their abode with believers, where Christ is guest, *there* can be nothing
lacking." Hence, they in whom Christ dwells, who are baptized and believe,
are good, and fundamentally free from sin. They constitute the one true church
(ii. 18, 20, 27 ; i. 2). So far as their salvation is concerned, it matters not
whether they are married or unmarried, whether they fast or not; and every
sin is of equal guilt (11. 30 f.). They shall receive at last the same reward.
It must be noted, however, that he taught that "before baptism it is possible
to sin or *not to sin*" (Julian, l. c.), and : " But whoever shall yield to temptation (*tentati fuerint*) are proved to have been baptized by water only and not
by the Spirit, as we read of Simon Magus " (ii. 1). That the former of these
citations represents his view cannot well be doubted, and it proves that his
theory of sin was not as yet of the Ambrose-Augustinian type. It is surprising
that Jerome does not take more advantage from the second. Jovtinian probably means that baptism is of immediate (vid. ii. 37) benefit only when received
in faith (i. 3). The student of the History of Doctrines will note in Jovtinian
premonitions of the interest soon to be awakened in the great problems discussed by Augustine. Upon Jovinian, vid. NEANDER, KG. ii. 2, p. 574 ff.
GRÜTZMACHER, PRE. ix., ed. 3, 398 ff. HARNACK, Die Lehre v. d.
Seligk. allein durch den Gl. in d. alt. K., in Ztschr. f. Theol. u. K., 1891, p.
138 ff. W. HALLER, Jovinianus, 1897.

in Augustine, de gestis Pelagii, and in Jerome in his Dial. c. Pelag. Fragments of the work of Pelagius, De natura, in Augustine's De nat. et grat. Of
Pelagius, De libero arbitrio, ll. 4, also only fragments in Augustine. Commentary upon the Pauline epistles in the works of Jerome (Migne, 30. 645-
902). Libellus fidei ad Innocentium in Hahn, Bibl. der Symbole, ed. 3, p.
288 ff.

Of the many writings of CAELESTIUS only fragments remain, especially
from the Definitiones in Augustine's de perfectione justit. His confession of
faith is found in the Appendix to the works of Augustine, xvii. 2728 ff. Vid.
also citations in Marius Mercator (Migne, 48. 65 ff.).

Of JULIAN OF ECLANUM, who wrote Libri 4 and Libri 8 adversus Augus-
tinum, we have very many fragments in August. c. Julianum, ll. 6, and especially the Opus imperfectum. Vid. further the Confession, Hahn, ed. 3, p.
293 f., and Aug. opp. xvii. 272 ; also Marius Mercator (Migne, 48. 109 ff.).

Further, the Pseudo-Augustinian work, De vita christiana (opp. Aug. xvii.
1941), ascribed to Bishop FASTIDIUS, and other writings (letters and tractates) perhaps belonging to a Briton, AGRICOLA, in Caspari, Briefe, Abhandlungen u. Predigten, etc., 1890, pp. 1-167. Vid. especially Opp. August. and
Opp. Hieron. The Liber apologeticus of OROSIUS, ed. Zangemeister, p. 601 ff.
Collections may be seen in M., Acta conciliorum iv., and in the appendix to
the works of Augustine, xvii. 2649 ff.

PELAGIUS, a British monk of austere morality, began before
the close of the fourth century to preach repentance with great
earnestness. He seems to have been under Greek influence
(Marius Liber. subnot. praef. i. 2).[1] The starting-point of his
exhortations was the natural moral ability of man. When confronted, as he speedily was, with the Augustinian : "Grant
what Thou commandest, and command what Thou wilt" (Aug.
don. pers. 20), it but confirmed him in his theory and led him
to express himself the more positively. Two fundamentally different conceptions of Christianity were here brought into contact. The hitherto unharmonized doctrines of man's free will
and the influence of divine grace presented a serious problem.
Pelagius soon won, in the eloquent CAELESTIUS, a disciple who
stated the problems with keen discrimination and formulated
them in a most aggressive way. Contemporaries spoke not
without reason of the "Pelagian, or Caelestian, heresy." Their
adherents were not few nor insignificant. After A. D. 418, the
diplomatic and prudent Pelagius and the radical Caelestius were
reinforced by the young bishop of Eclanum, JULIAN, a keen-
witted but fundamentally rationalistic disputant, as champion of
the new views. That these three men present a progressive development cannot be denied. The practical ideas of Pelagius are
followed by the doctrinal formulation of Caelestius, and the con-

---

[1] In the theory of sin, following Theodore of Mopsuestia, through the medium of a Syrian, Rufinus, who, according to Jerome (in Hierem., lib. i. 1
praef.), appears to be identical with Aquileia. Vid. also Aug., De pecc. orig.
iii. 3.

ceptions of Julian, wrought out as component elements in his cosmogony, go beyond them both.

As we are in other connections to follow the course of the controversy, we shall here attempt merely to set forth clearly the Pelagian view of Sin, Liberty, and Grace. "Whenever I am called upon to speak upon moral training and the course of holy living, I am accustomed first to display the power and quality of human nature and show what it is able to accomplish, and then from this to incite the mind of the hearer to (some) forms of virtues, lest it profit nothing to summon to those things which it would have thought to be impossible for it." In these words of Pelagius (ad Demetr. 2 init.) we recognize distinctly his moral temperament. (*a*) God has commanded man to do that which is good ; he must, therefore, have the ability to do it. That is to say, man is free, *i. e.*, it is possible for him to decide for or against that which is good : "But we say that man is (always) able both to sin and not to sin, so that we confess ourselves to have always a free will" (Pel. in his confession). "Freedom of the will . . . consists in the possibility of committing sin or of abstaining from sin" (Jul. in Aug. op. imp. i. 78). This "possibility" has distinguished man ever since the creation : "For God, wishing to endow (his) rational creature with the gift of voluntary good and with the power of free will, by implanting in man the possibility of either part, made that to be his own which he may choose, in order that, being by nature capable of good and evil, he might choose either and bend his will to either the one or the other" (Pel. ad Dem. 3, cf. de lib. arb. i., ii., in Aug. de gr. Chr. 18. 19 ; 4. 5).[1] It, therefore, constitutes his essential nature, and is accordingly inamissible. Whether I will do good or do evil is a matter of my free will, but the freedom, "the possibility of this free will and of works," is from God : "By no means can I be without the possibility of good" (Pel. lib. arb. iii. in Aug. de gr. Chr. 4. 5). The ideas of Pelagius move within the limits of this scheme of freedom of the will, a scheme alike insufficient as seen from the religious or the moral point of view. It follows from it, that there is no such thing as a moral development of the individual. Good and evil are located in the separate acts of men. The separate works finally decide whether a man is good or evil. But it is possible for one, by a free use of the "possibility" of well-doing, to lead a holy life. This natural goodness (*bonum naturae*), historically regarded, made very many heathen philosophers capable of the most lofty

---

[1] In this and the following citations from Augustine, the first figure refers to the chapter and the second to the numbered paragraph in the parallel notation.

virtues; how much more, then, may Christians expect from it? (Pel. ad Dem. 3. 7). There is no shrinking back from the inference, that an entirely sinless life is possible : "I say that man is able to be without sin, . . . but I do not say that man is without sin" (Pel. in Aug. nat. et grat. 7-8 ; de gr. Chr. 4. 5). Despite the cautious statement of the passage cited, this declaration was very sincerely interpreted by the Pelagians; see Aug. de gest. Pel. 6. 16 ; ep. 156 (letter of Hilary from Syracuse to Augustine). Caelest. definitiones in Aug. de perfect. justit., and the Pelagian in Caspari, pp. 5. 114 ff. (ep. de possibilitate non peccandi).

(b) From this position we can understand the doctrinal teaching concerning sin. This consists, as a matter of course, only in the separate acts of the will. There is no such thing as a sinful character or a sinful nature. Otherwise, sin would not be sin—not something which can be avoided ; and God could not charge sin to our account as guilt and punish it (Caelest. in Aug. perf. grat. 2. 1 ; 6. 15). Since sin cannot have been created by God, it is not a thing (res), but an act (actus) (ib. 2. 4). It is a fault, not of nature, but of the will (in Aug. de pecc. orig. 6. 6 ; op. imp. i. 48). Man's peculiar nature, the justice of God, and the reality of sin, alike forbid us to speak of an "original sin." If such were the nature of sin, a deliverance from it would be impossible : "Even if we should wish not to be able not to sin, we are not able not to be able not to sin, because no will is able to free itself from that which is proved to be inseparably implanted in (its) nature" (Pel. in Aug. nat. et grat. 49, 50, 57, 58). "If original sin be contracted by the generation of original nativity . . . it cannot be taken away from infants, since that which is innate continues to the very end of him to whom it has adhered from the occasion of his ancestors" (Jul. op. imp. i. 61). Inasmuch as sin consists only in separate acts of the will, the idea of its propagation by the act of generation is absurd. Adam was certainly the first sinner, but such a connection between his sin and ours cannot be established. The sins and guilt of parents no more pass over to their children than do those of children to their parents (op. imp. iii. 14, 19 f.). "If their own sins do not harm parents after their conversion, much more can they not through the parents injure their children" (Pel. in Marius Com. 2. 10). The view of Augustine is habitually referred to by Julian as Manichæism (e. g., op. imp. vi. 10: "Your doctrine differs in nothing from the Manichæans"). In contravention of God's Word, it pronounces marriage and the desire for carnal intercourse sinful (de nupt. et concup. i. 1, 2 ; ii. 1. 2). Julian refuses to recognize Augustine's distinction between marriage (*nuptiae*) and concupiscence: "Natural sin within cannot be asserted without defamation of sexual intercourse" (op. imp. v. 5). Adam's little, childish sin (op. imp. vi. 21) is an act of disobedience which has only a temporary significance for him, *i. e.*, until his conversion (op. imp. vi. 11 f.), and none at all for us. Adam's death was not a punishment for sin, but only conformity to a law of nature (Aug. de gestis Pel. 11. 23 f.; op. imp. ii. 64, 93 f., but also vi. 30). Accordingly, new-born children are sinless, and baptism cannot in their case have any sin-remitting effect (vid. Caelest. in Aug. pecc. orig. 6. 6; Marius Lib. subnot. praef. v.; also Jul. op. imp. i. 53 : "He bestows his gifts according to the capacity of the recipients").[1] The passage, Rom. 5. 12, merely asserts "that sin has passed from the first man upon other men, not by propagation, but by imitation" (Aug. de peccator. meritis et remiss. i. 9. 9); or the term πάντες does not mean absolutely all (Aug. de nat. et grat. 41. 48).

(*c*) This brings us to the Pelagian explanation of the universality of sin, which all experience testifies. It is attributed to imitation, the "long practice (*longus usus*) of sinning and the long habit (*longa consuetudo*) of vices" (Pelag. ad Demetr. 8). "For no other cause occasions for us the difficulty of doing good than the long custom of vices, which has infected us from childhood, and gradually, through many years, corrupted us, and thus holds us afterward bound and addicted to itself, so that it seems in some way to have the force of nature" (ib. cf. 17 fin.). To this must be added the natural sensuous and worldly character of man (Pel. in Aug. de gr. Chr. 10. 11). This line of thought reveals the final conclusion reached by the naive Pelagianism of the Greeks: There are really no sinners, but only separate wicked acts. A religious conception of sin is hereby excluded, and nothing more is needed than the effort to perform separate good deeds. But just as truly is a religious conception of the history of the race impossible, since there are no sinful men, but only wicked acts of individual men.

(*d*) The religious and moral superficiality of this way of re-

---

[1] It is of dogmatico-historical interest to observe that the Pelagians were, on the one hand, charged with undermining infant baptism (Council of Carthage, vid. Aug. ep. 157. 3. 22. Innocent in Aug. c. duas epp. Pel. ii. 4. 7 : "They seem to me to wish to annihilate baptism itself"); and that they were, on the other hand, very anxious to free themselves from the charge (Aug. pecc. orig. 19. 21 ; c. duas epp. Pel. iv. 2. 2); the confession of faith of Pelagius and Julian, Caelestus, op. imp. iii. 146 ; i. 53 ; HAHN, Bibl. ed 3, 294, in reference to which Augustine indeed says : "You fear to say, Let them not be baptized, lest not only your faces be defiled by the spittle of men, but your heads softened by the sandals of women" (c. Jul. iii. 5. 11).

garding the subject is very plainly manifest in the doctrine of grace. The necessity of grace for the attainment of salvation is not denied. On the contrary, Pelagius has declared that grace is needed " not only for every hour or for every moment, but even for every separate act of ours " (Aug. de gr. Chr. 2. 2 ; 7. 8 ; 32. 36 ; de gest. Pel. 14. 31 ; Pel. ep. ad Dem. 3 fin.; Jul. in op. imp. iii. 106 ; i. 52).

Over against this affirmation of the "help of grace," or " divine assistance," Caelestius, indeed, declares in his fashion, " that the will is not free if it needs the aid of God," and that " our victory is not from the assistance of God, but from (our) free will" (Aug. de gest. Pel. 18. 42). This is but a blunt statement of the logical inference from the position of Pelagius. The latter wrote : "grace is given in order that what is commanded by God may be *more easily* fulfilled " (Aug. de gr. Chr. 26. 27), from which Augustine rightly infers : " that even without this, that which is divinely commanded can be done, although less easily." What do the Pelagians then understand by grace? Really nothing more than the " good of nature," or the endowment with free will, *i. e.*, the possibility of doing good or evil. So Pelagius distinctly expressed himself at the council at Diospolis : " this he calls the grace of God, that our nature, when it was created, received the possibility of not sinning, since it was created with a free will " (in Aug. de gest. Pel. 10. 22). The endowment with reason (Pel. ad Dem. 2) and free will is primarily grace. This was sufficient in the primitive age of the race (ib. 4 ff. 8). But when ignorance and the habit of sinning gained the upper hand among men, God gave the law (Pel. ad Dem. 8), and again, when the law proved too weak to break the power of evil habit, he gave the teachings and example of Christ (Aug. pecc. orig. 26. 30). Pelagius, indeed, writes : " We, who have been instructed through the grace of Christ and born again to better manhood, who have been expiated and purified by his blood,[1] and incited by his example to perfect righteousness, ought to be better than those who were before the law, and better also than those who were under the law " (ad Dem. 8); but the whole argument of this letter, where the topic is simply the knowledge of the law as a means for the promotion of virtue (9, 10, 13, 16, 20, 23), as well as the declaration, that God opens our eyes and reveals the future " when he illuminates us with the multiform and ineffable gift of celestial grace " (Aug. de gr. Chr. 7. 8), proves that for him that the " assistance of God " consists, after all, only in instruction. Augustine is correct

---

[1] The same idea occurs in Julian, op. imp. i. 171.

in maintaining that, in addition to nature and the law, it is only the teaching and example[1] of Christ which are thought of by Pelagius as embraced in the term, grace (de gr. Chr. 41. 45 ; c. duas epp. Pel. iv. 5. 11). "Briefly and summarily I reply to thee : ' He is a Christian in whom are to be found those three things which ought to be in all Christians : knowledge, faith, and obedience—knowledge, by which God is known ; faith, by which (our) acceptance is believed ; obedience, by which the compliance of servitude is rendered to the one believed ' " (ep. de possibil. non peccandi, 5. 1. Casp., p. 119). Christianity is law, and, as compared with the Old Testament, an enlarged law (ib. p. 71). It is, therefore, good works which decide whether anyone is good : " For the wicked are so called from their wicked works ; thus, on the contrary, the good are so named from their good works" (de vit. chr. 10). The Christian reads the "word of God" as a *law*, which requires to be not only known, but also fulfilled (Pel. ad Dem. 23). He acts, therefore, in accordance with it, and seeks to " extinguish habit by habit," since " it is habit which nourishes either vices or virtues " (ib. 17. 13). He abandons the " imitation of Adam," and lays hold upon the " imitation of the holiness of Christ " (op. imp. ii. 146). This doctrine of grace is in entire harmony with the theory of sin. Sin is overcome through free will enlightened by the reason, or by the giving of the law. This, properly speaking, is grace. That which is occasionally said of atonement through the blood of Christ, of the forgiveness of sins, and renewal through baptism, is inconsistent, and beyond the range of Pelagian ideas.

Instead of attempting a summary, I cite in conclusion the six propositions into which the first antagonist of Pelagianism, Paulinus of Milan, compressed the Pelagian doctrine : " Adam was born mortal, and would have died, whether he had sinned or not sinned. The sin of Adam injured only himself, and not

---

[1] For the Pelagian idea of following Christ (also de vita christ. 6, 14 ; Jul. in op. imp. ii. 146 ; ii. 223 ; Aug. de gr. Chr. 2. 2), vid. Caspari, pp. 5, 20, 40, 121. Julian emphasized the truth that we are by Christ incited to a responsive love toward God : " God, as is well known, did whatever he did toward us with inestimable love, in order that we might, though late, love him in return " (op. imp. i. 94). Pelagius could not clearly explain wherein consisted the unutterable impartation of grace which he maintained. He mentions, indeed, in reference to Rom. 4. 7, the forgiveness of sins (" in addition, faith is first imputed for righteousness in order that he may be absolved from the past and justified in the present, and prepared for future works of faith," Mi. 30. 688). But, under the Pelagian theory of sin, the significance of forgiveness is very slight, the more so since such forgiveness applies only to the sins committed before the renewal wrought in baptism (Aug. c. duas ep. Pel. iii. 8. 24 ; iv. 7. 17 ; de gr. Chr. 34. 39).

22

the human race.   Children who are now born are in the state in
which Adam was before the fall.   Neither does the whole human
race die through the death or fall of Adam, nor does the whole
human race arise from the dead through the resurrection of
Christ.   The law sends into the kingdom of heaven in the same
way as does the gospel.   Men were impeccable, *i. e.*, without
sin, even before the coming of the Lord " (in Marius Common.
I. I ; cf. I subnot. praef. 5).

3. AUGUSTINE'S DOCTRINE OF SIN AND GRACE.

Of the works of Augustine, the following are of chief importance for us :
Liber de 83 quaestionibus (about A. D. 388 to about A. D. 396), De libero
arbitrio (A. D. 388-395).   Quaestiones ad Simplicianum (397).   Confes-
siones, ll. 13 (400).   In connection with the Pelagian controversy : De peccatorum meritis et remissione, ll. 3 (412).   De spiritu et littera (412).   De
natura et gratia (415).   De perfectione justitiae hominis (415).   De gestis
Pelagii (417).   De gratia Christi et de peccato originali, ll. 2 (418).   De
nuptiis et concupiscentia, ll. 2 (419).   Contra duas epistulas Pelagianorum,
ll. 4 (420).   Contra Julianum, ll. 6 (421).   De gratia et libero arbitrio (427).
De correptione et gratia (427).   De praedestinatione sanctorum (428).   De
dono perseverantiae (429).   Opus imperfectum contra Julianum, ll. 6 (until
his death).   Also a number of letters, vid. Opp. xiv. 1705 ff.   Compare the
literature referred to at the beginning of the section.

A. The controlling factor in giving to Augustine's doctrine of
grace its peculiar form was not primarily the nature of his conversion, although this helped to mould his theory ; nor the Pelagian doctrine which he was compelled to face, although this gave
form to many details in the statement of the doctrine ; least of
all, the Augustinian conception of the church.   Historically
considered, Augustine, following Ambrose, gave recognition to
the religious common sense of the West, and was moulded by
the ideas of the Epistle to the Romans.   His doctrine was complete in its essential features before the beginning of the great
controversy (cf. the remarks, don. persev. 20. 52).

The first utterances of Augustine upon this subject remind us
of the view of Ambrose.   Indeed, they are even more moderate
than the latter.   The human race is a "mass of sin" (l. de 83
quaest. 68. 3, 4).   No one, not even new-born children, is free
from original sin (*peccatum originale*, conf. i. 7 ; v. 9 ; ix. 6).
Concupiscence or lust, ignorance, and death, reign in the human
race (qu. 66. 1; lib. arb. i. 4. 9 ff.; iii. 20. 55 : "lust comes from
a perverse will ; " conf. viii. 5. 10), "because it was just, that
after our nature had sinned . . . we should be born animal and
carnal " (qu. 66. 3).   But our nature sinned in Adam (66. 3-5 ;
lib. arb. iii. 20. 56).   Yet Adam sinned as a free man.   Evil
in the world is a result of freedom, as Augustine very frequently
reminds the Manichæans (vid. esp. de. lib. arb.).   The law

can accomplish nothing toward releasing from the state of sin, since it can only convince of sin (66. 1, 3). There is need of grace. "And since no one is able to will unless admonished and called, either internally where no man may see, or externally through the spoken sermon or some other visible signs, it comes to pass that God works in us even to will itself" (68. 5). But, although grace here produces the will (to do good), yet Augustine thinks: "But God would not have mercy . . . unless the will had preceded," and says the reason why God has mercy upon some and rejects others lies "in the most hidden merits" of the former, since God is not unrighteous (ib. 68. 5, 4). Of fallen man, it is said: "It was fitting that God should not only not hinder, but should even assist him in willing" (lib. arb. iii. 20. 55). The capacity for striving after salvation remained to his will (ib. iii. 22. 65). He is able of himself to believe and to will, but God must give him the power to do good (exposit. quarundam proposit. ex ep. ad Rom. 61; cf. retract. i. 23. 3; de praedest. 3. 7). The form of doctrinal conception may here be summarized as follows: Man has, through the fall of Adam, become subject to ignorance, lust, and death. In response to the call (*vocatio*) of God, he is indeed able to believe and to will that which is good, but it is only grace that works in him the power to perform it.

But, under renewed study of the Epistle to the Romans (vid. quaest. ad Simplician. i. quaest 2), Augustine revised this theory (vid. remarks, praed. sanct. 3. 8). The subject there under discussion is the election of Jacob, according to Rom. 9. Works can in this instance not be the ground of the election, nor can the divine prescience of the "merits of the faith" of Jacob (l. c. qu. 2. 2. ff.). According to Rom. 9. 16 and Phil. 2. 13, the resolution to save lies solely in the mercy and good pleasure of God. Hence salvation must be attributed solely to grace. It has its beginning in man in faith. Even this faith is a work wrought by grace—namely, through the divine call (10). But to this it might be objected, that grace of itself is not sufficient, but that the human will must be combined with it. To this Augustine replies: "But this is manifest, that we will in vain, unless God have mercy; but I do not know how it can be said, that God has mercy in vain unless we will. *For if God has mercy*, we also will; our willing belongs to the same mercy" (12). Therefore, it depends solely upon the omnipotent will of God, whether anyone shall will or not will. When this idea is combined with that of the divine call, it results in the discrimination of two classes: the elect (*electi*) who are suitably (*congruenter*) called, whom God calls "in whatever way was suitable for them;'' and the called (*vocati*), to whom the call indeed came, but ''because it was of such a character that they could not be moved by it and were not suitable (*apti !*) to accept it, they could be said to be called indeed, but not chosen'' (*electi*) (13). That Esau was not chosen is, therefore, because God did not have mercy upon him, and did not effectually call him (14). There can be no thought here of any unrighteousness in God, since no one has a right to be delivered from the '' mass of sin.'' But the judgments and ways of God are inscrutable (Rom. 11. 23). God ''therefore laments with justice and mercy'' (16). It is, hence, not the willing and the conduct of man which lead to salvation, but solely the grace of God, which has mercy upon some and effectually calls them, but leaves others to their merited fate. It is interesting to observe here that the peculiar effect of grace is held to be, not the awakening of faith, but an upright life : '' But grace justifies, in order that the justified man may be able to live justly (righteously): the first thing, therefore, is grace ; the second, good works'' (3, cf. 12 : '' the will of man alone does not suffice, that we may live righteously and rightly ''). This may be understood in the light of Augustine's personal Christian experience. He learned to lay hold upon the grace of God, not because it awakened in him, as in Luther, the assurance of faith, but because it overcame his unwillingness to lead a Christian life. He apprehended it as he read the exhortation to moral conduct in Rom. 13. 13 f.: '' Neither did I wish to read any further, nor was there any need; for immediately with the end of this sentence, the light of assurance being, as it were, poured into my heart, all the shades of doubt were dissipated '' (conf. viii. 12. 29, cf. 30 : ''Thou didst convert me to Thyself, that I might desire neither wife nor any other hope of this world ; '' also the prayer x. 1).

But we notice also in this connection the influence of the conception of God entertained by Augustine. Profoundly and fully as he recognizes the personal God holding intercourse with man, yet there is also a foreign element in his conception of the Deity. He thinks of God as pure Being, absolutely simple, immutable, and indestructible (*e. g.*, soliloq. i. 1. 4 init.; de trin. vi. 6. 8 ; in Joh. tr. 13. 5 ; 1. 8).[1] This absolute Subsistence (*substantia*) is the Good. All that exists either is this Subsistence or is derived from it. Hence it follows, that everything that exists is good. '' Therefore every subsistence is either God or from God, be-

[1] The last passage reads : '' What is formed in my heart when I say God ? A certain great and supreme Subsistence is thought of, which transcends every mutable carnal and animal creature.''

cause all good is either God or from God" (lib. arb. iii. 13. 36). Hence, the base and the evil are not subsistences. "And that evil of which I inquired whence it was, is not a subsistence, because if it were a subsistence it would be good" (conf. vii. 12. 18).[1] Evil bears a privitive character as a *privatio boni* (civ. dei, xi. 22). It has no "efficient cause," but only a "deficient cause" (civ. dei, xii. 7). It is a lack of existence, not a subsistence. Evil has its basis, not in God, but in free will: "And I inquired what iniquity was, and I found not a subsistence, but the perversity of a will turned away from God, the supreme Subsistence, to the depths (conf. vii. 16. 22). The evil will is the source of all evil (enchirid. 4. 15 ; civ. dei, xii. 7 ; op. imp. vi. 5).

But if evil be thought of in this (Neo-Platonic) scheme as a nonentity in man, then grace can be regarded only as a creative act of God, making of the nonentity an entity, by transforming the basis of the former, the *evil will*, through the *inbreathing of a good will*. It is only from this point of view that we can entirely understand Augustine's doctrine of grace. He has in view primarily, not the establishment of a personal communion, but a creative act. Grace is effectual as the almighty, creative Will, which infuses into man a new subsistence, the moral will.

B. These principles remained as normative for the exhaustive treatment given to the subject by Augustine in opposition to Pelagianism.

(*a*) God created man good and upright. He knew nothing of concupiscence. His will was positively good. Being thus good, he was in consequence truly free. "God made (man) therefore, as it is written, upright, and hence of a good will. . . . Therefore the decision of the will is truly free whenever it does not serve vices and sins " (civ. dei, xiv. 11. 1 ; 10 ; op. imp. v. 61). In this condition man served God, and found supreme satisfaction in doing so. The body meanwhile, with all its impulses, served the soul, and reason reigned in man (civ. dei, xiv. 24. 1 ; 26 init.; nupt. et conc. ii. 15. 30 ; pecc. merit. ii. 22. 36). But this condition was one of freedom : "It should be within his choice, either that he should always wish to be in this (good will) or that he should not always thus wish, but should change from it to an evil will without compulsion from any source " (op. imp. v. 61). The divine assistance (*adjutorium*) was within his reach, by means of which he was *able*, but *not compelled*, to persevere in the good. This was the "first grace " (corrept. et grat. 11. 31). There was a *posse non peccare*, but not a *non*

---

[1] Ib.: "Therefore whatever things exist are good."

posse peccare, and, in connection with this, a *posse non mori*, but
not a *non posse mori* (ib. 12. 33 ; op. imp. vi. 16), and hence :
" He had a possibility, but not a necessity, of sinning " (op.
imp. vi. 5). Man was, therefore, created with an inclination
of the will toward the good and was by God preserved in it, but
in such a way that, through his freedom, it was possible for his
inclination to be turned in another direction.

(*b*) All of this Adam lost in the fall. Since he transgressed
the commandment of God, which he might so easily have fulfilled, his will became evil. Pride was the cause of it. Man
was not willing to obey God, but wished to be his own master.
But, since man refuses obedience to God, God assigns it as his
punishment, that his flesh shall cease to serve the spirit, that
ignorance shall take possession of his soul, and the potential mortality of body and soul shall become a reality. "An evil will
preceded, by which credence was given to the wile of the serpent, and evil concupiscence followed, by which he stood gaping
before the forbidden food " (op. imp. i. 71 ; vid. also civ. dei,
xiv. 11 ff.; xiii. 3. 13 ; nat. et grat. 25. 28). Adam has not
merely done a single act, but has become a sinner.

(*c*) This character of Adam has now passed over to his posterity. Through the punitive decree of God, Adam has become
a different man, and human nature has thereby been changed :
" Nature (was) vitiated by sin : our nature, there transformed
for the worse, not only became a sinner, but also begets sinners ;
and yet that languor in which the power of living aright has
been lost is certainly not nature, but defect " (nupt. et conc. ii.
34. 57 ; 8. 20 ; c. Jul. iii. 24. 53 ; op. imp. iii. 11 ; ii. 163 ;
civ. dei, xiii. 3 ; cf. in Joh. tr. 44. 1 : "defect grew, *inolevit*, instead of nature "). But now all men were in Adam : "All men
were that one man " (pecc. mer. et rem. i. 10. 11); hence, according to Rom. 5. 12 (ἐφ᾽ ᾧ = in quo): " in Adam all then
sinned " (ib. iii. 17. 4 ; nupt. et conc. ii. 5. 15 ; op. imp. ii.
176). They were all, indeed, contained in him. From this it
follows : (1) That his moral character becomes theirs. (2)
That the penalty pronounced upon him (of being subject to concupiscence and death) passes over also upon them. We have his
sin, and are burdened with his guilt. "Wherefore condemnation in view of the magnitude of that sin has changed nature for
the worse, so that what preceded penally in the first sinning men,
follows naturally in other men in birth. . . . But what the
parent man is, that is also the offspring man. . . . To such an
extent was human nature vitiated and changed in him that it
should have to endure the disobedience of concupiscence warring
in its members, and be subject to the necessity of death, and

thus that which sprung from fault became penalty, *i. e.*, he should generate those subject to sin and death '' (civ. dei, xiii. 3, 13, 14; op. imp. iv. 104; vi. 22; i. 47). Thus, in Adam the whole human race has become a '' mass of perdition '' and is condemned in him. '' For all men were thus seminally in the loins of Adam when he was condemned, and, therefore, he was not condemned without them '' (op. imp. v. 12). From this no one is exempt, not even new-born children (c. Jul. i. 6. 22; op. imp. i. 56; iii. 154; cf. the scriptural proof in pecc. mer. et rem. 1. 27. 40 ff.). This is attested by the sufferings which the righteous God appoints for men, and especially by the sufferings of children (pecc. mer. et rem. iii. 10. 18) and by exorcism at baptism (c. Jul. vi. 5. 11). As original sin simply as such brings condemnation, it must have this effect even in the case of children, although there is meted out to them '' the lightest condemnation of all '' (pecc. mer. et rem. i. 12. 15; 16. 21). From all the above it follows, that there is in us a ''necessity of sinning '' (op. imp. i. 106; v. 61; perf. just. 4. 9). Of this life, it is said : '' whether mortal life or vital death, I know not '' (conf. i. 67; cf. civ. dei, xiii. 10 init.). But, above all else, the absolute unfitness of man for salvation must be emphasized. It is the energy with which Augustine maintains this idea, embracing all human activity under sin and guilt (the virtues of the heathen being but ''splendid vices ; '' cf. civ. dei, v. 12 ff.; xix. 25),[1] which marks his advance beyond Ambrose, and constitutes the religious significance of his theory. That nothing good and no salvation can be found except in Christ was the thought impressed upon the church by these discussions.

Original sin is regarded in the light of real sin, as well as of guilt. It is sin, and is a divine penalty. It is propagated among men, not in the way of imitation (c. Jul. vi. 24. 75), but by generation. ''Through one man it entered the world, and it passes through all men '' (pecc. mer. et rem. i. 12. 33). Although marriage is a moral good (pecc. orig. 37. 42; 33. 38; though celibacy is to be preferred, vid. op. imp. v. 17), yet generation never occurs without sinful concupiscence, as is proved clearly enough by the sense of shame associated with the act (nupt. et conc. ii. 5. 14), and the concupiscence passes over upon the children. This is the case even when the parents are regenerate, '' as from the seed of an olive springs nothing but a wild olive '' (ib. ii. 34. 58). '' Yet, when it shall come to the act of generation, it is not possible that allowable and honorable inter-

[1] This term does not itself occur in Augustine, but it admirably summarizes his view ; somewhat as the *credo quia absurdum* attributed to Tertullian ; cf. supra, p. 127.

course should occur without the burning of lust, so that what springs
from reason might be transmitted, and not what springs from lust.
. . . Of this concupiscence of the flesh, which I grant is in the regenerate not imputed as sin (previously described as ‘venial sins’),
but which is not found in nature except from sin—of this concupiscence of the flesh, I say . . . whatever offspring is born is
by virtue of its origin (*originaliter*) bound to sin” (nupt. et
conc. i. 24. 27). There is “a defect (*vitium*) of the seed”
(ib. ii. 8. 20). In the question of Traducianism or Creationism,
Augustine could reach no conclusion (de anima et ejus origine,
ii. 14. 20 ; 15. 21 ; retract. i. 1. 3). There is, consequently,
at this point a lack of clearness in his theory of sin. He certainly represents sin as propagated by lust in copulation, but this
is not to be understood as though he regarded the intercourse of
the sexes as in itself sinful or unworthy of man. His idea is
only, that man, being a sinner, can generate offspring only in a
sinful way. The sinful state, to his mind, logically precedes the
sinful act. It is, therefore, not correct to trace this idea to unvan-
quished Manichæan dualism (HARNACK, DG. iii. 191, note 3),
as was done already by Julian of Eclanum. It may be said that
the “monastic temper of Augustine favored” it (LOOFS, DG.,
ed. 3, p. 215), but beyond this we cannot go. In evidence
against the suggestion, we may recall that even yet there lies
in the background in Augustine’s mind the conviction that
sin has no subsistence, but is only a *privatio boni*, a μὴ ὄν (nat. et
grat. 20. 22 ; c. Jul. i. 8. 37 ; enchir. 11 ; cf. p. 341). From
original sin, which is thus a “ necessity,” proceed the individual
sins of man, which he adds to the former “ of his own free will,
not through Adam” (pecc. mer. et rem. i. 15. 20 ; conf. v. 9
init.). Yet, despite all this, we may speak of a free will
(*liberum arbitrium*) even in the case of the sinner, though not in
the sense of the Pelagian *possibilitas utriusque partis*, for a man
cannot be at the same time both a good and an evil tree (grat.
Chr. c. 18, 19, § 19 ff.). The *libertas* of paradise has been
lost, *i. e.*, “to have with righteousness full immortality ; ” for
this freedom (“ free to live well and uprightly”) now exists
only by virtue of the influence of “grace,” which is precisely
what is lacking in the sinner’s case. But the freedom to sin of
his own will has, however, remained to him. “ We do not say
that by the sin of Adam free will perished from the nature of
men, but that it is capable of sinning . . . but it is not capable
of living well and piously, unless the will of man has itself been
liberated by the grace of God ” (c. duas ep. Pel. ii. 5. 9 ; op.
imp. i. 94). Hence, “ we are not such against our will.”

(*d*) In harmony with what we have before observed, the

words of Augustine just cited indicate clearly that, in his view, righteousness is a "living well and rightly." This gives us a clue to his conception of the nature of original sin. It cannot be, as in Luther, unbelief. According to Augustine, it is above all, *evil* or *carnal concupiscence*, which finds its subject, indeed, in the soul : "for the flesh does not lust (*concupiscit*) without the soul, although the flesh is said to lust, because the soul lusts carnally" (perf. just. 8. 19). In this dominion of sensuality over the spirit we are to recognize the penal consequence of the first sin, but not its cause. "The corruption of the body which oppresses the soul is not the cause, but the penalty, of the first sin ; neither does the corruptible flesh make the soul a sinner, but the sinful soul makes the flesh corrupt" (civ. dei, xiv. 3 ; cf., as to the term, flesh, ib. c. 2). With this degradation of the spirit is intimately connected the "horrifying depth of ignorance." This enables us to understand why man surrenders himself to his passions and to vain things. "But these are all characteristics of wicked men, yet they come from that root of error and perverted affection with which every son of Adam is born" (civ. dei, xxii. 22. 1). Lust finds its explanation in ignorance. And both have their foundation in the perverted inclination of man. He turned away from God and toward himself, and in this fell a prey to the world. He wanted to love himself, and abandoned his love to God ; he is, in consequence, given over to the lust which loves and pursues the husks of the world. This "love of self" is the real essence of sin. That such is Augustine's conception is manifest from his magnificent presentation of the subject in *Sermo 96. 2. 2 :* "The first ruin of man was the *love of himself.* . . . That is, his making it his will that he should will to love himself. . . . For, having forsaken God, he begins to love himself and is driven away from himself to the loving of the things which are without. . . . Thou hast begun to love thyself : remain in thyself, if thou canst. What is without ? . . . Thou hast begun to love what is without thee ; thou hast destroyed thyself. Therefore, when a man's love passes from himself to the things which are without, he begins to lose himself (*evanescere*) in vain things and to squander his strength like the prodigal. He is emptied, poured out, rendered destitute, and feeds swine." Such is the nature of sin : love of self, ignorance, concupiscence. Man falls away from God, wishing to serve himself, and he is drawn into the whirlpool of worldliness. Henceforth his existence is but death. Of our first parents, it is said : "Therefore, although they lived many years afterward, yet they began to die in that day in which they received the law by which they should grow into the decay of old age" (pecc. mer. et rem. i. 16. 21). The whole host of evils now overwhelms man.

Thus life in the world was by sin transformed into a hell, from which only Christ was able to deliver (civ. dei, xxii. 22. 4). But, in discussing original evil, Augustine does not forget the *original good*. Men generate men,[1] and God permits the latter through his "efficacious power" to become men, with intellectual likeness to God. "In original evil there are two things, sin and penalty ; in original good, two other things, propagation and conformation. Yet there is not entirely extinct within man a certain spark of the character (*scintilla rationis*) in which he was created after the image of God" (civ. dei, xxii. 24. 1, 2, 3).

Such is Augustine's doctrine of sin. Here at length sin is treated from a purely religious point of view, as the absolute opposite of the good, and as the condition of the race, which can be changed only through Christ. But here, too, sin is regarded as the sin of *man* himself and of the *race*. The way is thus opened for the recognition of the spiritual character of man as in itself consistent, and for a proper conception of the historical development of the race. Augustine's doctrine of original sin is not only a matter of religious interest, but it is also a scientific advance in the realms of psychology and ethics, as well as a massive conception in the sphere of history.[2]

(*e*) In harmony with his doctrine of sin, Augustine attributes the salvation of men to grace alone. Grace begins the good in man, and it remains actively influential in him after it has liberated his will. "It goes before him when unwilling, that he may will ; it follows him when willing, that he may not will in vain" (enchir. 9. 32). God "prepares the will, and by co-operating completes what he begins by operating. Since he, in beginning, operates that we may will, who, in perfecting, co-operates with us when we will" (grat. et lib. arb. 17. 33). It is thus only under the gracious influence of God that man comes to the good and remains in it. We have already observed (p. 341) that Augustine conceives of grace as divine creative power in action. We understand, therefore, how it can be described as a "wonderful and ineffable power" which effects in man "not alone true revelations, but also good wills" (grat. Chr. 24. 25), and how its influence can be pronounced necessary even in the state of integrity in paradise (ep. 186. 11. 37 ; enchir. 25. 106). Grace is simply the resistless creative power of God, which ex-

---

[1] Observe the point of view under which Augustine could here regard the act of generation.

[2] I fail to find a proper recognition of this and other aspects in SEYREICH'S dissertation, Die Geschichtsphilosophie Augustins, Chemnitz, 1891.

erts its influence in the hearts of men as the power of the good.
This must be kept in view when we follow Augustine's delineation
of the work of grace. Not man himself, not doctrine, not example,
not the law, can help. The bare commandment is powerless
against concupiscence. Only through grace and faith can salvation be attained : " what the law of works demands with threatening, that the law of faith secures by believing." Here the
motto is : " Grant what Thou commandest ;" there, " Do what I
command" (sp. et lit. 13. 22). The first blessing is the *forgiveness of sins*, which man receives through baptism. With it
begins *renewal* (*renovatio*), which finds here its basis (pecc. mer.
et rem. ii. 7. 9 ; 27. 43 ; conf. i. 11). Sin is, therefore, forgiven
through baptism. Concupiscence, however, yet remains even in
the baptized ; but it is no longer sin, because God no longer so
accounts it (nupt. et conc. i. 25. 28 ; 31. 36 ; pecc. mer. et
rem. i. 37. 70). It is to be noted, however, that the forgiveness of sins is not brought into such unvarying connection with
faith as in Paul. The Christian life begins with faith, which is
wrought by God (supra, p. 339) as the "beginning of our religion
and life." Faith is described as " to agree that what is said is
true" (sp. et lit. 31. 54) or "to meditate upon with assent "
(praedest. sanct. 2. 5). Faith is, therefore, the *assensio* to the
preached truth (cf. enchir. 7. 20 ; conf. vi. 5 ; in Joh. tr. 40.
9 ; 79. 1). This explains why a higher stage is supposed to be
reached in knowledge (*cognitio*), according to Isa. 7. 9 : " unless you had believed, you would not know " (*e. g.*, sermo 43 ;
in Joh. tr. 27. 7 ; 22. 5 ; 29. 6 ; 48. 1 ; 112. 1 : " he can believe
before he can know ;" ep. 114. 7 ; 120. 3). We meet, indeed,
statements which appear to lead us beyond this definition, as, for
example, when the idea of "justification through faith " is occasionally reproduced (vid. sub), or when it is said that men would
not be free from sin, "unless united and joined by faith to his
body " (*i. e.*, Christ's, sermo 143. 1), or when a distinction is
drawn between " believing Christ" and " believing in Christ,"
and the latter is described as constituting Christian faith (sermo
144. 2). But just here the thought becomes clear, as Augustine explains : " For he believes in Christ who both hopes in
Christ and loves Christ . . . to him Christ comes, and in some
way is united to him and is made a member in his body ;
which cannot occur unless both hope and love are added " (cf.
in Joh. tr. 29. 6). Here, again, faith points beyond itself to a
higher stage. Instead of knowledge, this is now love.[1] The

---

[1] Through love there is effected also an advance in knowledge, in Joh. tr.
96. 4.

nature of faith is not that trustful attitude of heart which apprehends present grace, but it is the preparatory step toward a righteousness not yet attained. It is, therefore, also the ability to pray for this righteousness : "the spirit of grace brings it to pass that we have faith, so that through faith we may by praying secure the ability to do what we are commanded" (grat. et lib. arb. 14. 28 ; sermo 168. 5 ; enchir. 28. 117). Faith in itself is thus the belief of the truth of revelation. But it becomes Christian faith only when it is a "faith which works by love" (fid. et op. 16. 27 ; serm. 168. 2 ; cf. in Joh. tr. 6. 21).

(*f*) The chief work of grace is really the *infusion of love*,[1] or of a *new and good will*, by the Holy Spirit. "They who have love are born of God ; they who have not, are not born of God" (in Joh. tr. 5. 7). This is not effected by external commandments, nor by the example of Christ ; but "he gives an increase internally by shedding abroad love in our hearts by the Holy Spirit" (sp. et lit. 25. 42 ; pecc. mer. et rem. i. 9, 10), or there is even said to be an "*inspiratio* of good will and work" (corr. et grat. 2. 3). Thus evil desire is crowded out by desire for God and his will : "the Spirit inspiring good *concupiscentia* instead of evil—that is, shedding abroad love in our hearts" (sp. et lit. 4. 6 ; enchir. 32. 121). The endowing with new moral power, and thus the transforming of the man ("nature repaired by grace," sp. et lit. 27. 47), is for Augustine the proper meaning of the term, justification. Its essential nature consists in this, that man becomes actually righteous, and is, hence, able to perform righteous works. "For what else is it to be justified, than to be made righteous (just), *i. e.*, by him who justifies the ungodly man, that from being ungodly he may be made righteous" (ib. 26. 45 ; grat. et lib. arb. 6. 13). "Through the gift of the Spirit we work righteousness" (sp. et lit. 18. 31). Thus the individual becomes a new man—from being an ungodly, he becomes a righteous man ; from being a dead, becomes a living man. "He heals the sick in spirit and revives the dead, *i. e.*, he justifies the ungodly" (nat. et grat. 26. 29). "When the soul lives in sin, it is its death ; but when it becomes righteous, it becomes a participant in another life, which is not the same as before, for, by lifting itself to God and inbreathing God, it is justified by him" (in Joh. tr. 19. 11). This instilling of the good, justifying will by the Spirit is progressive and marks the entire Christian life, since concupiscence remains even in the regenerate (nupt. et conc. i. 25. 28): "We are justified (have been made righteous), but righteousness itself

---

[1] The expression is derived from Rom. 5. 5.

grows as we go forward " (serm. 158. 5). Although the essential nature of justification lies in the " inspiring of a good will,"
yet, in a wider sense, the forgiveness of sins may also be ascribed
to it ; in such a way, however, that the emphasis still rests upon
the inspiration.   " Nor is this grace only the remission of sins
. . . but it effects that the law is fulfilled and nature set free "
(grat. et lib. arb. 14. 27 ; cf. op. imp. ii. 165 ; civ. dei, xii.
22).   " For grace assists in both ways—by remitting the evil
things that we have done, and by aiding us to depart from the
evil and do the good " (op. imp. ii. 227 ; vi. 15).

We have thus secured a clear conception of Augustine's doctrine
of grace.   Grace is the action of divine omnipotence which makes
man's will good, or capable of doing good.   The view corresponds exactly with his doctrine of sin.   Ignorance is overcome
by the bestowal of faith ; the love of self, together with lust by
the imparting of the good will and of love to God and his law ; the
sinner's state of death, by the process of grace through which he
is made righteous and alive.[1]

Notable above all else in this doctrinal structure is the energy
with which everything is referred to the grace of God, to the exclusion of all human work.   But whoever scrutinizes carefully
the real character of the operation of grace as thus depicted will
observe how imperfectly this theory meets the requirements of
the fundamental religious impulse of Augustine.   The Pauline
character, which so largely distinguishes the latter, fails, after all,
to rise to the height of Paul's conception of the righteousness of faith.   Augustine cites the formula of Paul times
without number ; but he interprets it as meaning, that we
reach the conviction that righteousness is granted to us by
God without antecedent works upon our part, or that faith justifies because it works by love.   " This is the righteousness
of (ex) faith, by which we believe that we are justified ; that is,
made righteous by the grace of God through Jesus Christ our
Lord, so that we may be found in him, not having our own righteousness, which is of the law, but that which is through the faith
of Christ.   Which righteousness of (ex) God in faith, is in faith
in this way, that we by faith believe that righteousness is divinely
granted to us, not achieved by us by our own strength " (ep.

---

[1] Augustine's order of salvation (following Rom. 8. 29 f.) includes the following heads : " (Praescience) predestination, vocation, justification, glorification " (in Joh. tr. 26. 15 ; corr. et grat. 9. 23).   Or : " Remission of sins,
thine infirmities are healed, redemption from corruption, the crown of righteousness " (serm. 131. 6. 8).   Or : " Before the law, under the law, under
grace, in peace " (enchir. 31. 118).   " By the grace of God we are regenerated, purified, justified " (c. litt. Petil. iii. 50. 62).

186. 3. 8). " For we read that they are justified in Christ who believe in him, on account of a mysterious secret communication and inspiration of grace, by which whoever clings to the Lord is one spirit" (pecc. mer. et rem. i. 10. 11). Accordingly, it may be said that even this great disciple of Paul, powerfully as he was influenced by the apostle, yet misunderstood him at the crucial point.[1]

(g) Grace, as being irresistible, is characterized by Augustine as *predestinating* grace. Many lines of thought are concentrated in this term : the Platonic tincture of Augustine's doctrine of God, his personal religious experience, his recognition of the sole agency of grace, and exegetical considerations (p. 340). If grace lays hold of man, there can be no resistance, for God carries out his will in the human heart no less than in nature. " It cannot, therefore, be doubted that human wills are not able to resist the will of God, so that he may not do what he will, who has done all things which he has willed in heaven and in earth, and has done even those things which shall be, since, even with respect to the wills of men themselves, he does what he will when he will . . . who nevertheless does not do so except through the wills of men themselves ; having beyond doubt omnipotent power of inclining hearts whithersoever it may please him" (corr. et grat. 14. 45, 43 ; enchir. 21. 95). The difference between grace and the "primary grace," or "assistance," granted to Adam lies in the fact that the latter could be voluntarily relinquished, whereas the former produces the will (corr. et grat. 11. 31, 38). To the question, whether the freedom of man's will is hereby destroyed, Augustine replies in the negative. On the contrary, grace heals and restores the free will, so that it is able to freely choose the good (sp. et lit. 30. 52 ; enchir. 25. 105). Man does not, as the Pelagians would have us believe, attain grace by freedom, but freedom by grace (corr. et grat. 8. 17). But when we remember that a new will is in an irresistible way implanted in man, and this will then "indeclinably and insuperably" controlled by the divine power (*virtus*, corr. et grat. 12. 38), it cannot be open to question that the claim of freedom is here meant to be taken in a very peculiar sense. It can be understood only in the sense that God

---

[1] Yet Augustine—as many of the pious in the Middle Ages—was able to find his chief consolation in the forgiveness of sins, *e. g.*: " And this our righteousness, although it is a true righteousness on account of the end of real goodness at which it aims, yet is in this life of such a nature that it consists rather in the remission of sins than in the perfection of virtues. A witness to this is the prayer of the whole kingdom of God, ' Forgive us our debts ' " (civ. dei, xix. 27).

deals with man in a way consonant with his endowment with a will, so that man survives the transformation of his will as a creature still (formally) possessing the power of willing (see above citation). In this way man becomes free, *i. e.*, from the power of concupiscence. The state of spiritual subjection to God divinely wrought in him, by virtue of which he withdraws himself from the control of sensuous motives, is his freedom. The same result is reached if we consider the doctrine of perseverance in grace. This is a work of grace, the *donum perseverantiae* (don. pers. 1. 1). Here also applies the rule : "God effects that they may will" (corr. et grat. l. c.). A real freedom, in the metaphysical sense of the term, is thus excluded. This, again, is a consequence of Augustine's conception of grace as a creative energy (*virtus*) and not as a personal, spiritual relation.

But it is necessary to face the fact, that not all who are called (*vocati*) are subdued by grace. Augustine explains this on the ground of *predestination*. Before the creation of the world, God formed the resolution to redeem certain men in Christ and to apply to them his grace. "The predestination of God, which is in the good man, is a preparation . . . for grace, but grace is the effect of this predestination (praedest. 10. 19 ; don. persev. 9. 21). There is a "good-pleasure of his (God's) will," which has nothing to do with human merits, not even with such as were foreseen by God. On the contrary, the determination (*propositum*) of God is the ground upon which the good will is imparted to this or that one (praed. 18. 37). There is a strictly definite number (as maintained already in de bapt. v. 27. 38) whom God has thus foreordained to grace : "There is a number so fixed, that neither can anyone be added to them nor taken from them" (corr. et grat. 13. 39).[1] Predestination is the cause of salvation. All saving ordinances are means for realizing it, and therefore really serve and benefit only the predestinated. Only to the *elect* comes the effectual "peculiar calling of the elect" (praed. 18. 37), so that he may follow him who calls : others are not so (*non ita*) called (don. pers. 9. 21). The elect alone has the "gift of perseverance," whereas the foreknown (*praesciti*) may still fall away even in the last hour (corr. et grat. 9. 22 ; don. pers. 8. 19). All, therefore, rests in the hands of God, depends upon his choice : "Therefore whoever have in the most provident ordering of God been foreknown, predestinated, called, justified, and glorified, although yet, I will not say unregenerated but even yet unborn, are now the sons of God

[1] The fixity of the number is evident from Augustine's view that the elect are to form a substitution for the number of the fallen angels (enchir. 9. 29 ; 15. 62 ; civ. dei, xxii. 1).

and can by no means perish '' (corr. et grat. 9. 23). The predestinated is saved, commonly becoming a *called* and *justified*
member of the church.   But it must be held as possible that
such an one may not come into contact in any way with historical Christianity, and yet be saved—because he is predestinated
(ep. 102 quaest. 2, §§ 12, 14, 15 ; cf. with praedest. 9, §§ 17-
19 ; also REUTER, Aug. Stud., p. 90 ff.). The unpredestinated,
or *foreknown*, on the other hand, under all circumstances, fall
into ruin, as parts of the *massa perditionis*. Even if they appear
to be true Christians, called, justified, regenerated through baptism, renewed—they will not be saved, because they have not
been elected (don. pers. 9. 21).   No blame attaches to God ;
they are alone to blame, as they simply remain given over to
their just fate : '' He who falls, falls by his own will ; and he who
stands, stands by the will of God '' (don. pers. 8. 19).[1] In
such God reveals his justice, as in the elect his mercy (ib. 8.
16).   To the question, Why he chooses some and leaves others to
their fate, the only answer is : '' I so will,'' at which the creature
must humbly bow before his Creator (ib. 17).[2]

   In these conceptions, Augustine's doctrine of grace culminates.   Grace and nature, mercy and justice, are seen in direct
opposition to one another, as formerly in Marcion, and a solution is offered as paradoxical as was his, and as unsatisfactory to
the religious sense. The profoundly religious spirit of Augustine
is as manifest as is the fact that certain foreign and unevangelical
threads have found their way into the texture of his thought.
He had learned to present faithfully the *sola gratia*, but his doctrine suffered detriment from the fact that he did not understand
the *sola fide*—that the God whose fellowship his heart could so
wonderfully portray was yet for his intellect not the God of the
gospel. Assurance of salvation cannot—according to this theory
—be attained (corr. et grat. 13. 40 ; 9. 22 ; civ. dei, xi. 12).
'' Nevertheless, this is good : not to be too wise, but to fear ''
(don. pers. 8. 19), says the man who yet so well knew that religion is something more than the fear of breaking off a covenant
relationship.   But however deeply this mighty intellectual structure may be enshrouded beneath the shadows of the age, yet it
stated the problem for the doctrinal history of the future.   In

---

[1] Augustine commonly expresses himself in this way, but he also speaks of
those ''predestinated to eternal death '' (in Joh. tr. 43. 13, cf. 110. 2 ; civ.
dei, xv. 1. 1 ; enchir. 26. 100).
[2] Augustine escapes the force of opposing passages of Scripture, especially
Tim. 2. 4, by peculiar interpretations, as that no one is saved unless God wills
it (enchir. 24. 103), or that '' all '' means the predestinated, '' because the
whole race of men is in them '' (corr. et grat. 14. 44).

DOCTRINE OF SIN AND GRACE.

tones that can never be forgotten, it taught the church : There
is only one thing to be feared—rebellion against God, or evil in
the heart ; and there is only one thing good and great—the
effectual grace of the living God.

4. Historical Course of the Controversy.

The direct opposition between the positions of Pelagius and
Augustine is manifest. It was natural that a violent controversy
should ensue, in which the leadership should fall to the lot of Augustine. The ideas with which he confronts his opponents may be
readily inferred, *i. e.*, that Pelagianism knows nothing of grace,
and that it is not freedom of the will, but the grace of God, which
saves man. If man were free in the Pelagian sense, then would
Christ have come into the world in vain (nat. et grat. c. 19 ff.,
§ 21 ff.). If it was only a question of teaching and example,
then why did not the pious Abel long since become the chief of
the righteous ? (ib. 9. 10). Christian experience, no less than
the prayer of the whole church for the forgiveness of sins, testifies that man cannot by his own power avoid sin (serm. 181).
Further, the universality of the penalties imposed by a righteous
God, from which even children are not exempt, makes against
the Pelagian view (op. imp. iii. 154). In this connection,
Augustine strongly emphasizes infant baptism. Either new-born
children are sinful, or they are not. In the latter case, they
need no baptism (pecc. mer. et rem. i. 23. 33 ; 18. 23 ; op.
imp. ii. 222)—an inference, indeed, against which the Pelagians
protested (p. 335, note). Finally, Augustine appeals to a number of passages of Scripture (Rom. 5. 12 ; 7. 14-26 ; 8. 26.
Gen. 2. 7. Ps. 51 ; 143. 2. Eph. 2. 3. Joh. 8. 36). He
even endeavored to produce a proof from the history of the
church's doctrinal development (c. Jul. i. ii.). Thomasius
(i. ed. 2, 543 ff.) has treated exhaustively this critique of
Pelagianism.

The controversy was started when Caelestius was endeavoring
to secure an appointment as presbyter in Carthage. The first
offense appears to have been taken at the claim of the followers
of Caelestius, that infant baptism does not aim at the forgiveness
of sins (Aug. pecc. mer. et rem. iii. 6. 12).[1] Paulinus, a
deacon of Milan, brought charges against him (vid. the charges
in Marius Commonit. 1. 1, supra, p. 337 f.) at a council in Car-

---

[1] In the discussion, Caelestius laid emphasis upon the necessity of baptism
for infants. In the Relatio of the theses in Lib. subnot. praef. 5, Marius has
the declaration : "Since infants, although they are not baptized, have eternal
life." This is therefore, perhaps, original. All these instances give evidence
that the assertion of Caelestius in regard to baptism referred to in the text fixed
attention upon the subject.

23

thage (A. D. 411 or 412). Caelestius was excommunicated and went to Ephesus, where he secured—on Greek territory—appointment as a presbyter. Pelagius, who had also been in Carthage, had gone to Palestine. He, too, secured a following But Jerome wrote against him (ad Ctesiphontem [ep. 133] and dialogus c. Pelagianos ll. 3).[1] Reports from the West impelled John of Jerusalem to summon a council (Jerusalem A. D. 415, vid. account of Orosius in Liber apologeticus 3-6) to consider the case of Pelagius. But John unequivocally defended the thesis of Pelagius, that man may easily keep the commandments of God, *i. e.*, by divine help. Orosius, therefore, requested that, as Pelagius was a Latin, the matter be referred to Rome. Under the urgency of two exiled Gallic bishops, Heros and Lazarus, another council was called, A. D. 415, at Diospolis, or Lydda (cf. Aug. de gestis Pel.; also Mansi iv. 311 ff.). Pelagius adroitly satisfied the minds of the bishops, affirming that man can indeed do everything good, but only with the divine assistance (*adjutorium*). Assertions ascribed to him he pronounced apocryphal. He disclaimed responsibility for the positions of Caelestius, but with the remark : "But the things which I have declared to be not mine, I, in accordance with the opinion of the holy church, reprobate, pronouncing an anathema against everyone who opposes." This was a cowardly untruth. The council pronounced him orthodox.[2] But the Africans did not rest. A council at Carthage and another in Mileve (both A. D. 416) sent letters to his "Holiness," Pope Innocent I., at Rome. Then came an exhaustive and instructive private communication by five bishops (including Augustine—among his letters ep. 175-177), cautiously urging to energetic action. The situation is depicted, the doctrine of Pelagius described and confuted, the unique authority of the Roman bishop extolled (ep. 175. 2 f.; 176. 1 ; 177. 19), and the latter urged to take the matter in hand. Pelagius, who gloried in the decision of the Eastern

---

[1] This work, bitter and passionate in style (Jerome heaps upon the head of Pelagius the names of nearly all the heretics), proved that Jerome wished to please Augustine, but in the question itself stood not very far from Pelagius (*e. g.*, ep. ad Ct. 6. 10, dial. ii. 5 ff.; iii. 5. 6, cf. ZÖCKLER, Hieronymus, pp. 420 ff., 311 ff.).

[2] Pelagius shrewdly emphasized his orthodoxy upon the Trinity (Aug. gest. Pel. 19. 43), and also the fact that the question in dispute did not affect any "dogma." "I anathematize them as fools, not as heretics, if there is no dogma" (ib. 6. 16). This is to be explained not by a disinclination to enlarge "the sphere of the dogmatic" (HARNACK iii. 162, n. 1), but it is simply a means of defense, just as Caelestius declared at Carthage : "This is a matter of inquiry, not of heresy" (Aug. pecc. or. 3. 3, cf. the Roman confession of Caelestius in Aug. pecc. orig. c. 23. Julian's term, *quaestiones indisciplinatae*, in Marius l. subnot. 6. 12).

theologians (ep. 177. 2), was required to recall his statements or
to acknowledge the saving nature of infant baptism and the insufficiency of nature for the attainment of salvation (ep. 175. 6).[1]
The pope lost no time in answering the letters (vid. in the letters of Aug., ep. 181-183). In the labored style of the Curia,
there is, first of all, an acknowledgment of the praiseworthy and
proper observance of the discipline—now observed by the whole
world—in appealing, as all churches do, to the decision of
Rome (ep. 181. 1 ; 182. 2). But in the discussion of the doctrinal question, this pope, as some of his predecessors, showed
himself a poor theologian. The Africans have, indeed, spoken
rightly and said all. It is superfluous for any person of orthodox
views to dispute concerning grace and freedom (ep. 181. 7, 9 ;
183. 5), for it is clear that man needs the divine assistance for
his salvation (ep. 181. 4-6, 8 ; 182. 3 f.). In other words—
the Africans are of course in the right, because the doctrine of
their opponents is correct ! The dogmatic helplessness of the
pope in this instance, having no finished scheme at his command, is comical. As to other phases of the difficulty, speedy
help must be given against the pestilent poison (181. 2 f., 8).
The pope does not believe that Pelagius and Caelestius can be
converted (181. 8)—he doubts also if decision was really given
in favor of Pelagius at Diospolis—they are both to be excluded
from the church (ep. 181. 8 ; 182. 6).[2]

A strictly orthodox confession of Pelagius now found its way
to Rome. The questions at issue were but briefly touched upon,
infant baptism and the freedom of the will acknowledged (but
with the limitation "we are always in need of the help of
God"), and emphasis laid upon complete subjection to the
pope[3] (HAHN, ed. 3, p. 288 f.). Innocent had died (March,
417), and the confession fell into the hands of his successor,
ZOSIMUS. Caelestius, having in the meanwhile gone to Constantinople and been driven thence, had also appeared in Rome.
He acknowledged baptism for the remission of sins and the infallibility of the papal decision, but denied that "sin is born
with man" (HAHN, ed. 3, p. 292 f.). Zosimus was entirely satisfied, and in this he did not come into collision with the dogmatics of his predecessor. A council at Rome (A. D. 417)

[1] This practical inference in the letter from Carthage is interesting, as it
falls back upon the starting-point of the controversy.
[2] I do not interpret these letters in the customary way, nor as does HAR-
NACK (iii. 165). The pope did not leave "back-doors" open behind him—
but he simply did not understand anything about the matter.
[3] The words: "We execrate those who, with Manichæus, condemn first
marriage," are evidently a stab at Augustine.

certified to the orthodoxy of Caelestius. The confession of
Pelagius, which appeared soon afterward, to the support of
which the bishop of Jerusalem cast his influence, caused jubila-
tion. The pope was imprudent or honest enough to send a
report of this in two letters to the African bishops, and to re-
prove them sharply from the lofty station of the apostolic chair
for their lack of due consideration in the matter (vid. Zos. ep.
3, 4).[1] But a council at Carthage (A. D. 417, or early in 418)
explained to the pope that good reason had not yet been
shown for the various transactions, and that they would still
recognize as valid the condemnation pronounced by Innocent
(Mansi iv. 376, 378). The pope, alarmed, replied that Peter
received the authority to loose and bind, and that no one
dare oppose the pope, but that he would take counsel with
the Carthaginians in the matter, in which meanwhile no positive steps had been taken (ep. 15). At this point the great
African GENERAL COUNCIL, A. D. 418, was assembled at CAR-
THAGE, with 200 participants (Mansi iii. 810 ff.; iv. 377 ff.).
Condemnation was here pronounced against the doctrines : That
Adam was created mortal without respect to sin ; that children
are not subject to original sin inherited from Adam ; that grace
does not help with reference to future sins ; that grace consists
only in doctrines and commandments ; that grace only makes it
easier to do good ; that saints utter the fifth petition of the
Lord's Prayer not for themselves, or only from humility. But,
at the same time, the practice of appealing to Rome, "beyond
the sea," was placed under the ban. This interdict was repeated
A. D. 419 at Carthage (occasioned by the meddling of Zosimus
in African affairs). The emperor had (A. D. 418) issued an
edict against Pelagius, Caelestius, and their followers, which expelled them from Rome and threatened more serious measures
(Aug. opp. xvii. 2720 ff.). Zosimus now yielded and published
the *epistola tractoria* (frg. vid. Coustant-Schoenemann, pontiff.
Rom. epp. i. 709), which he requested all bishops to subscribe.
Eighteen bishops refused to accede to this request (Aug. c. duas
ep. Pel. i. 1. 3). The leader of the latter was JULIAN OF
ECLANUM, who in two letters to the pope (in Mar. l. subnot. 6.
10-13. Aug. opp. xvii. 2728 ff.) defended their course, upon
the ground that it was not right to condemn the absent without a
hearing, and announced the adherence of these men to a rather
mildly-expressed statement of Pelagianism (the paradoxes of
Caelestius being rejected). From this time, Julian (having lost

---

[1] The pope learned also from Caelestius that the quarrel was about en-
tangling questions and useless dissensions (s. ep. 3. 7).

his bishopric) assumed the offensive, and proved the most energetic, combative, and voluminous opponent of Augustine, charging Augustine and his adherents, for whom, as heretics, he invented the title· *Traduciani*, with Manichæism, contempt of marriage,[1] unscientific spirit, and unreasonableness (vid. frgg. in Aug. nupt. et conc. ii.; c. Jul.; op. imp.). He became more and more extreme, reaching at length the boldest rationalism : "What reason disputes authority cannot prove" (op. imp. ii. 16, 137, 144). Questions are to be decided, not by assemblies of clerics who have scarcely mastered the categories of Aristotle, nor by the uncouth populace, but by the small number of the cultured (c. Jul. ii. 10. 35-37, cf. KLASEN, Entwicklung des Pel., p. 98 ff.). He appealed to the testimony of reason and the Scriptures, neither of which recognizes original sin. Sin resides in the will. Infants have no will, and hence no sin (ii. 28). Imitation leads to sin (ii. 48. 209). The generating act is pure (iv. 6). Augustine's view leads to Manichæism. Christ redeems us, in that he brought to us our nature and his will, and thereby gave to us a mirror and a rule, namely, that our sin, as also our righteousness, consists in the will (iv. 84). Under his hands the teachings of Pelagianism became more and more secular and self-sufficient. But all of this exerted no influence upon doctrinal history. Pelagianism extended over considerable territory. We meet its adherents not only in Rome, Southern Italy, and Sicily, but also the district of Aquileia (Dalmatia), Brittany, and in the district of Arles. The council of Ephesus (A. D. 431), to the great gratification of the pope, confirmed the rejection of Pelagianism (vid. p. 264 f.).

§ 32. *Summary of Augustine's Theological and Ecclesiastical Views in the Enchiridion ad Laurentium.*

We are reminded of Origen (*de principiis*) and his school, Gregory of Nyssa (*catech. magna*), John of Damascus (*de fide orth.*), Lactantius (*Institut.*), as we undertake to review Augustine's brief general survey of Christianity, written about A. D. 421.

"God to be worshiped in faith, hope, and love," is the theme of the book. The question is : "What ought to be believed, what to be hoped, what to be loved?" Truths which may be learned by our natural intelligence are to be defended by reason. Those which lie beyond this province "are to be believed without any hesitation upon the testimony of the witnesses by whom was composed

---

[1] In connection with this point, Augustine was denounced by Pelagius before Comes Valerius (vid. nupt. et conc. i. 1, 2).

that Scripture which has hitherto been justly called divine, who, divinely assisted, were enabled, whether through the body or through the spirit, to see, or even to foresee, these things" (4). This is the " beginning of the faith which works by love," whose higher stage is attained in vision (5).   This is the Catholic conception of faith (cf. *assensio*, 7. 20, and supra, p. 347) and the scholastic division of Christian doctrine into natural and revealed truths.[1] Succinctly stated, faith has its object in the Creed ; hope and love find exercise in prayer (the Lord's Prayer, 2. 7). In discussing the question, " What is to be believed pertaining to religion?" we are not to think of insight into the physical laws of the universe :   " It is enough for the Christian to believe that the first cause of created things, whether celestial or terrestrial, . . . is nothing other than the goodness of the Creator . . . and that there is no nature which is not either the Creator himself, or from him " (3. 9).   This God is the God of the Trinity.   The world was made good, and even evil fits into its harmony (10).   Evil is the lack of good (*privatio boni*, 11). That which is, is good, since it comes from God.   Even evil, so far as it really is, is good: " corruption cannot consume the good except by consuming nature " (4. 12).   Evil, as a lack of existence, presupposes an existing good : " evil cannot be unless there be something good " (13 ff.).   The Christian must be acquainted, not with the general order of the universe, but with the causes of good and evil things, that he may be able to avoid error and misery (5. 16).   To err is to accept the false as true (17).   The worst error is for a man not to believe that which leads to eternal life, but to believe that which leads to eternal death (6. 18).   Not every error is sin, and the opinion of the Academy, that all assent must be held in suspense, is false.   There would then be no faith : "if assent be taken away, faith is taken away ; because without assent nothing is believed " (7. 21).   In matters not connected with the way which leads us to God, nor with the faith in Christ which works by love, error (faith being preserved) is no sin, or at all events only "the least and lightest sin ;" but even then it is to be counted among the " evils (*mala*) of this life " (21).   But every lie is a sin,

---

[1] It is to be noted that Augustine excluded from the objects of faith a series of physical and metaphysical speculations (3. 9; 5. 16; 7. 21; 15. 58 f., 66 ; 29. 86, 92).   Catholic truth is summarized in the Creed (in Joh. tr. 98. 7).   The content of "believing well " is the trinitarian God and the incarnation of the Word (ib. 18. 2 ; 74. 1 ; ep. 120. 2); but the true Catholic faith excludes also the teachings of Pelagianism (in Joh. tr. 67. 3).   The highest normative and only infallible authority is, for Augustine, the Holy Scriptures, *e. g.*, doctr. christ. ii. 8 ; ep. 82. 1. 3, unit.; eccl. 3. 5 ; 13. 33; 11. 28 ; bapt. ii. 3. 4 ; civ. dei, xi. 3 ; enchirid. 1. 4.

since "words were instituted, not that men might through them
deceive one another, but that each might through them bring
his thoughts to the knowledge of the other" (22). What we
need to know, therefore, in order that we may not fall into sin,
is the causes of good and evil, namely : "that the cause of good
. . . things is nothing else than the goodness of God, but that
of evil things is the will of a mutably good being—first of an angel,
afterward of a man—forsaking the immutably good" (8. 23).
The first evil (*primum malum*) of man is his unwillingness to do
(*nolle*) that which God wishes. From this results the "ignorance of things to be done, and the lust of things injurious ; "
hence "error, distress, fear, *i. e.*, the whole misery of men, as
well as the death of the body" (24 f.). Adam by his sin "vitiated his posterity . . . at the root, made them subject to the
penalty of death and damnation." All who are begotten
"through carnal concupiscence" have original sin (26). The
entire race is thus living in wickedness and subject to the "most
just wrath of God." This is evident both from the fact that the
wicked willingly indulge their concupiscence, and the further fact
that they are, against their will, visited with punishment. God
is, however, not only just, but also merciful,[1] and he, therefore,
does not abandon men to their merited fate (27). Inasmuch as
the angels are not bound together by natural descent, the fall of
the evil angels had no effect upon the good (9. 28). It is designed that men shall (in, perhaps, larger numbers) take the place
of the fallen angels (29). But that portion of the human race
to whom God has promised deliverance attains that end not
through the exercise of free will, for this has been lost, but only
through grace. As servants of God, they become truly free (30).
Faith itself is a gift of God (31). God alone works in us to will
and to do (Phil. 2. 13. Rom. 9. 16). "He precedes him who is
unwilling, that he may will ; he follows him who is willing, that he
may not will in vain." It is false to say : "the will of man
alone is not sufficient, if there be not also the mercy of God,"
for God works all things (32). "When men were, through
original sin, under this wrath, the more seriously and ruinously
they had added to this more and greater (offenses), the more
necessary was a mediator, that is, a reconciler, who *should pla-
cate this wrath by the offering of one sacrifice.*" The wrath of
God is not a "disturbance, such as that in the heart of an angry
man," but it is "his vengeance, which is nothing but just" (10.
33). The mediator became man (his divinity not being changed

---

[1] This contrast, which we have met before (pp. 120, 295, 340, and already
in Marcion, p. 102 f.), has been normative in dogmatics since the time of
Augustine.

into flesh), sinless, "not such as is born from the two sexes through
the concupiscence of the flesh with inevitable tendency to wrong-
doing," but of the Virgin, whose "integrity" was not impaired
at his birth (34). Christ was God and man (35). It was no
merit of the man Jesus which secured this combination, but only
the grace of God (11. 36). His human birth itself was a work
of the Holy Spirit (37). But Christ is not, therefore, according to his human nature a Son of the Spirit, as he is according
to his divine nature a Son of the Father (12. 38 f.). But the
grace of God is manifested in the incarnation "by which man,
no merits preceding . . . was joined with the Word of God in
such unity of person, that the very same who was the son of man
was the Son of God, and the very same who was the Son of God
was the son of man" (40). The absolutely sinless Christ has
now been pronounced "sin" (2 Cor. v.), since in the Old
Testament the sin-offering was thus designated. Christ is, therefore : "a sacrifice for sins, through which we might be able to be
reconciled." He became sin "in the likeness of the sin of the
flesh, in order that . . . he might thus, in a manner, die to sin,
when he dies to the flesh in which was the likeness of sin . . .
and might by his resurrection seal our new reviving life
from the old death in which we would have died in sin"
(13. 41). Hence, Christ died as a sacrifice for sin, as our representative, and he arose as an evidence of the new life brought
to us by him. We have a reflection of this in baptism, as we die
to sin and live through the washing of regeneration (42). All,
therefore, have need of baptism. Children thereby die to original sin, and adults also to the further sins actually committed (43).
The aim of baptism is the "remission of sins" (44 and 51 ; cf.
supra, pp. 322, 349). It is asserted, not without probability, that
children are bound also by the sins of their parents—not alone of
the first human beings, but also their own parents of whom they
were born" (cf. Ezek. 18. 2). But baptism has essentially to do
with deliverance from original sin, as individual sins may also be
atoned for through repentance (46). Original sin, as the root
of all sins, is removed and destroyed only through the one mediator, the man Jesus (14. 48). The baptism of Christ was significant, not for him, but for us : "in order that his great humility
might be commended." The same is to be said of his death :
"in order that the devil, overcome and vanquished by the
truth of justice, not by the violence of power, since he had
most unjustly slain him who was without any desert of sin,
might most justly lose those whom he for desert of sin held
in his power" (49). It is only as new-born in Christ that we
can become free from the condemnation which rests upon all

through Adam (51). As to the way in which this is accomplished : "just as true death has occurred in him, so true remission of sins in us ; and just as true resurrection in him, so true justification in us." The former takes place in baptism, which, however, has the latter as its goal (52, cf. supra, p. 322). As Christ is in this our pattern, so also in his whole history "in order that to these things, not only mystically spoken, but also done, the Christian life which is lived here might be conformed" (53). The coming of Christ to judgment is here excepted (54). That which we designate the doctrine of the Work of Christ is treated by Augustine under three aspects : as the sacrifice for sin, by virtue of which we receive the forgiveness of sins in baptism ; as deliverance from the devil ; and as a pattern and example for believers.[1]

[1] Sections 41, 42, 48, 51, 52, 53 reveal quite fully the aspects under which Augustine regards the work of Christ. We add a few remarks. The dominating thought is : Christ is the Head ; the church (the predestinated, in Joh. tr. iii. 1) is his body. All who are his and whom he has won belong to the church (pecc. mer. et rem. i. 26. 39 : civ. dei, xvii. 15 ; in Joh. tr. 21. 8 ; 108. 5 ; serm. 117. 10. 16). He who became man and yet remained God is, as man, the mediator or the way to God (often, following 1 Tim. 2-5, e. g., civ. dei, xi. 2 ; xxi. 16 ; ix. 15. 2 ; in Joh. tr. 82. 4 ; 105. 7). Hence, the rule is : From the man Jesus to God : "If thou wishest to live piously and christianly, cling to Christ according to that which he has done for us, in order that thou mayest come to him according to that which he is and according to that which he was" (in Joh. tr. 2. 3 ; 13. 14 ; cf. the passages cited on p. 261). The Head now reveals and secures salvation as a whole for his members (civ. dei, x. 32. 3). Regarded more closely, Christ (1) has by his blood brought us the forgiveness of sins ; by his sacrifice cleansed us from our sins, paid a ransom for us, taken away the wrath of God, bestowed upon us righteousness, reconciled us with God, and has become our advocate (e. g., in Joh. tr. 92. 1 ; 98. 2 ; 119. 4 ; 3. 13 ; 41. 6 ; 4. 2 ; 123. 4 ; 14. 13 ; civ. dei, vii. 31 ; x. 24 ; doctr. chr. i. 15, 17 ; serm. 134. 4, 5 ; 155. 8 ; 19. 3 ; conf. ix. 13 ; x. 43). (2) He has freed men from the power of the devil, who without any right seized upon the flesh of the righteous Christ, and to whom that flesh proved a *bait* (serm. 134. 3. 4 ; 5. 6 ; in Joh. 52. 6). (3) He has, as Mediator, in his person and work revealed to us God, his wisdom and love in : "That we have, therefore, been reconciled to God by the death of his Son, is not to be understood as though the Son had reconciled us to him, so that he should now begin to love what he had hated, as when an enemy is reconciled to an enemy, so that they are thereafter friends, and they who have mutually hated now mutually love ; but we are now reconciled to him who loves us, with whom we have been at enmity on account of sin" (in Joh. tr. 110. 6 ; cf. 2. 16 ; serm. 174 ; 126. 4. 6) ; by this love we are moved to love him in return (de cat. rud. 4. 7, 8). (4) He has given us an example and pattern of humility, patience, and trust in God (e. g., civ. dei, xviii. 49 ; in Joh. tr. 4. 13 ; 25. 16, 18 ; 51. 11 ; 58. 4 ff.; 113. 4 ; 116. 1 ; 119. 2); but "the animal man . . . does not perceive what the cross of Christ confers upon those who believe, and thinks that by this cross was accomplished *only* that an example for imitation should be given to us as we contend even to death for the truth" (in Joh. tr. 98. 3). (5) He has through his incarnation, and especially through his death and resurrection, brought to us immortality,

After thus treating of God, creation, sin, grace, and of Christ, Augustine, following the order of the Creed, comes to speak of the Holy Spirit. The church depends upon the Trinity : "The proper order of confession requires that the church be subordinated to the Trinity, just as to the tenant his house, to God his temple, and to the founder his city." In this we are to have in view, not only the Christians yet sojourning on earth, but also glorified saints and angels (15. 56). There is then a discussion of angels, in which the author confesses his ignorance as to the orders of celestial beings, and the propriety of numbering among them the sun and the moon (Orig., supra, p. 151), or the kind of corporeality involved in the appearances of angels on earth (58 f.). It is more important to discriminate when Satan transforms himself into an angel of light, in order that we may not follow him upon his paths of error[1] (60). The church is thus to be divided into the earthly and the heavenly. The redemption wrought by Christ extends also, in a certain measure, to the angels, inasmuch as by it the enmity between them and sinful men is removed, and the places vacated by the fallen angels are filled. Hence, as affirmed in Eph. 1. 10, the heavenly is by Christ united in peace with the earthly, and the earthly with the heavenly (61, 62). This peace shall be complete for us only in the full vision of the future world, but it exists here already through the forgiveness of sins. Hence, the next item in the Creed is the forgiveness of sins. Renewal begins (*incipit renovatio*) with the blotting out of original sin in baptism, yet everyone needs beyond this the forgiveness of sins, since he is, though perhaps without crime (*crimen*), not without sin (64). But even in regard to crimes, we dare not despair of the mercy of God. The church excommunicates the criminal ; but let him repent. In this, not the extent of time, but that of the sorrow, is important. Since now it is only in the church that sins are forgiven, there are fixed "times of repentance, in order that it may be exercised to the satisfaction of the church as well" (65). The regenerate are also subjected to temporal penalties, in order that their guilt may

in order thus to make us gods : "to make us gods who were men, he who was God was made man" (serm. 192. 1 ; 166. 4); but also : "by loving God we are made gods" (serm. 121. 1). Augustine presents not a consistent theory, but elements of religious truth which are genuinely Christian. In this he has again furnished dogmatic material to the church of the West. Cf. KÜHNER, Aug. Anschauung von der Erlösungsbedeutung Christi, 1890. SCHEEL, Aug. Anschauung über Christi Person und Werk, 1901.

[1] This is, indeed, difficult, but the very difficulty of this thing is beneficial in that no one may be hope for himself, nor one man for another, but God for all his own.

not be charged against them for eternity (66). But there are Catholic Christians[1] who hold that, if they have been baptized and believe, *i. e.*, do not renounce the name of Christ, they will be saved despite the most grievous sins, "which they neither wash away by repenting nor atone for by alms," that "they will be saved by fire—punished, doubtless, in proportion to the magnitude of their offenses and the duration of their shameful deeds, yet not with eternal fire" (cf. 1 Cor. 3. 11 ff.). Only faith manifesting itself in works saves: faith without works does not save (67). The fire in the scriptural passages under discussion refers to the pain endured in the giving up of that which is fervently desired (68). Augustine leaves it an open[2] question whether a purifying fire does not exist also after this life for such as through repentance, and especially through almsgiving, have secured for themselves forgiveness— whether "some believers are not saved more tardily or more speedily, through a certain purgatorial fire, in proportion as they have more or less loved the things that perish" (69). He adds, in explanation, that one cannot indeed daily atone by alms for sins which exclude from the kingdom of God, nor, forsooth, by them purchase for himself the right to sin in the future (16. 70).

Turning now to the practice of repentance, Augustine declares: "But for brief and light daily sins . . . the daily prayer of believers makes satisfaction" (*satisfacit*), *i. e.*, the fifth petition of the Lord's Prayer. But this prayer also blots out grave offenses, when the believer forsakes them—and when he also forgives those who trespass against him. For forgiveness is also an *alms*, just as are all good works done for those in need. "There are thus many kinds of alms, when we perform which we help to secure the remission of our own sins" (71, 72). Forgiveness of others and the love of enemies are the best alms (73). Only he who is ready to forgive receives forgiveness (74). Only he who also reforms his life becomes pure through alms (17. 75). Indeed, in a certain sense, everything is included in alms, if we give to ourselves the alms of charging guilt upon ourselves, *i. e.*, if we by the mercy of God seek

---

[1] As to the view of these "lay brethren," see retract. ii. 38; de fide et operibus; civ. dei, xxi. 19 ff. These people are in no kind of harmony with the evangelical view of justification by faith (despite HARNACK, Ztschr. f. Theol. u. K., 1891, p. 165 ff.). On the contrary, they anticipate the most extreme Catholicism: He who has accepted the teachings of the church, been baptized, received the Lord's Supper, and remains in the church, will be saved, without any regard to his moral character, the deficiencies of which will be re paired in purgatorial fire.

[2] Thus also civ. dei, xxi. 26. 4.

out ourselves in our misery (76; also serm. 87. 9. 10). The division of sins into *peccata levia* and *gravia* cannot be carried out fully by any means in our power; but it is established by such passages as 1 Cor. 7. 5 ff.; 6. 1 ff. (78). Some which seem light to us ("thou fool") are grievous according to the Scriptures (79), while many which are really grievous are from force of habit regarded by us as light (80). We cannot resist sins, whether arising from ignorance or from infirmity, "unless we are divinely assisted" (19. 81). The mercy of God also impels us to repentance (82). He who does not believe, or despises, the forgiveness of sins in the church is guilty of the unpardonable sin against the Holy Ghost (83).[1]

---

[1] Augustine's view of repentance is, in its essential features, fully presented in his *Enchiridion*. It is merely a continuation of the Ancient Catholic teaching upon the subjects (supra, p. 195). Although the East also possessed a penitential ordinance (vid. Greg. Thaum. ep. canon. and Basil. ep. 199, 217), yet the penitential discipline of the church never there attained so rigid a development as in the West (cf. the homilies of Chrysostom upon repentance, and *supra*). The antecedent of the Western view is the distinction drawn between venial, daily, petty sins, and damnable or great (*grandia*) sins, such as idolatry, the *constellations of the mathematicians*, heresy, schism, murder, adultery, fornication, robbery, theft, false witness (perf. just. 9. 20; in Joh. tr. 12. 14; op. imp. ii. 97; serm. 56. 8. 12). If we include repentance before baptism, there are three kinds of repentance : (1) Repentance for sins committed before baptism; in the case of children, "the faith of those by whom they are presented prevails" (serm. 351. 2. 2). (2) Repentance for the lighter daily sins, "whose committal runs through the whole of this life," the daily repentance, which brings to man a daily medicine of forgiveness (Augustine is fond of describing grace as *medicina*). This occurs through the daily use of the Lord's Prayer (fifth petition), as well as through alms and fasting (serm. 351. 3. 3 ff.; 352. 2. 7; 18. 5; 58. 5. 6; de symbolo ad cat. 7. 14; civ. dei, xxi. 27. 4; cf. Ambrose, de poenit. ii. 5. 35 : "He who exercises repentance, *agit poenitentiam*, ought not only to wash away his sin with tears, but also to hide and cover his greater offenses by better works, so that sin may not be imputed to him"). (3) Repentance in the proper sense of the term ("the more serious and painful repentance, in which they are properly called penitents, *poenitentes*, in the church") has to do with those who, on account of grave sins (forbidden by the Decalogue), have been excluded from the holy communion (*communio sacra*, Ambros. ib. i. 15. 78), or the Lord's Supper (Aug. serm. 355. 4. 7). Such must make confession to the bishop, who assigns to them an appropriate "satisfaction," and, if the matter has been publicly known, directs them to repeat the confession before the church (vid. 351. 4. 7-10; 352. 3. 8; ep. 265. 7. Also can. 30 of the council of Hippo, A. D. 393, HEFELE CG. ii., ed. 2, 58). This repentance is, like baptism, to be granted but once (ep. 152. 2; 153. 3. 7; cf. Ambrose, l. c. ii. 10. 95; the decretal letter of Pope Siricius to Himerius, A. D. 385, c. 5). Thus repentance becomes a continuation of baptism (ep. 56. 8. 12 init. Ambrose, l. c. ii. 11. 98 : "Repentance is therefore a good thing; for, if it did not exist, all would have to defer until old age the grace of cleansing"). But in this way repentance is externalized and set in opposition to grace, and thus was a new stone fitted into the hierarchical structure : "Let him come to the overseers (*antistites*), through whom the keys are administered for him in the church . . . let him receive from those placed over

Augustine treats, finally, of the Resurrection. After some remarks in regard to the resurrection body of the abortive fœtus (20. 85 f.) and of monstrosities (87), he declares that the material of the human body is for God not lost (88); that in the resurrection God will restore the entire body, it being not implied, however, that every particle of the matter shall become a portion of that member to which it once belonged (89). The bodies will not be all alike (*e. g.*, the notes of an anthem), nor will they be repulsive (wan or corpulent). They will be spiritual bodies, but in substance still flesh (*caro*), although serving the spirit in all things (90, 91; cf. civ. dei, xxii. 12 ff., 19 ff.). The lost have also a body; a continual dying and decaying is their fate (92). This is the second death. Condemnation (*damnatio*) is graded according to the measure of guilt, being lightest for children. "Certainly the lightest punishment of all will be that of those, who, beyond the sin which they have inherited from their ancestry, have superadded none" (93). It is only in the two-fold outcome of human life that we shall learn why one was saved and another left to condemnation. It will become clear how certain, immutable, and most efficacious is the will of God (21. 94, 95). Since God permits evil, its existence must be good; otherwise the almighty Will would not allow it (96). What God wills, that he does. But he wills that all men be saved (1 Tim. 2. 4; cf. 23. 27), and yet by far the greater number are not saved (97). God in mercy turns the evil will of some into a good will, without any regard to future works. To others he is simply just (22. 98 f.). The will of God rules in all, even in the wicked: "so that . . . even that which is contrary to his will does not occur without his will" (23. 100 f.). Therefore: "he does not do anything wicked, nor does he do anything unless he wills to do it, and he does all things whatsoever which he wills to do" (102). At this point Augustine takes up 1 Tim. 2. 4 (103) and endeavors by a forced interpretation to bring it into harmony with the above (supra, p. 352). The will of man is always free, even and particularly when it can no longer will to do evil (25, 105). But free will would not have sufficed even in paradise to merit immortality: even there the divine assistance (*adjutorium*) was needed—how much more since the fall! (106). Hence, strictly speaking, eternal life is a matter, not of reward, but of grace. "It is to be understood, therefore, that even the good merits of man themselves are gifts of God, to which when eternal life is given,

the sacraments (*praepositi sacramentorum*), the mode of his satisfaction" (sermo. 351. 4. 10). "Where, if ministers are wanting, how great ruin follows those who depart from this world either not regenerated or bound" (ep. 228. 8).

how is grace given except (in exchange) for grace?"[1]   God's
mercy is the ground of salvation; therefore let no one boast (107).
Even the Mediator through whom salvation is secured is not only
man but God.   In description of his work, it is declared : "it
was necessary for us to be reconciled to God in order to the
resurrection of the flesh unto eternal life."   Through him the
resurrection is set forth, the devil conquered.   Further, "an
example of obedience is by the divine man set before contumacious man."   He showed to men also in his person how far they
had departed from God (108).

   After death and before the resurrection, the souls of men are in
a secret retreat (*abdita receptacula*), where it goes well or ill with
them according to their deserts.   For the alleviation of their
condition, their friends may avail themselves of the sacrifice of
the mass and of alms.   But the latter avail as "*propitiationes*"
only for those who on earth have deserved that the benefits of
these things should now be enjoyed (those who were "not very
wicked," 20. 110 ; vid. also serm. 172. 2 ; civ. dei, xxi. 27. 6).
The *civitas dei* and the *civitas diaboli*, both of which include
men and angels, will continue to exist in eternity (111).   There
can be no doubt of the eternal duration of the punishments of
hell.   The most that could be deduced from Ps. 76. 10 would
be a temporary alleviation or interruption.   That condition itself is one of dreadful torment : "to depart from the kingdom
of God, to be an exile from the city of God, to be alienated
from the life of God, to be deprived, with so great a multitude,
of the delightful fellowship of God" (112 f.).

   These are the doctrines "which are to be faithfully believed."
Out of faith spring hope and love.   What we hope is shown by
the Lord's Prayer.   We hope only in God, not in men nor in
ourselves.   "Therefore only from the Lord God ought we to
seek whatever we hope either to do well or to receive (in exchange
for good works)" (27. 114).   Then follows a short exposition
of the Lord's Prayer, as given in Matthew and Luke (115 f.).

   Then comes Love.   "When it is asked whether anyone is a
good man, it is not asked what he believes or hopes, but what he
loves . . . he who does not love, believes in vain, even though
the things which he believes are true."   True faith is that which
works in love.   Love is shed abroad in us by the Holy Spirit ; it
annihilates concupiscence and fulfills the law" (28. 117 ; cf. supra,
p. 348).   The course of moral development is then sketched :

---

[1] For this strained interpretation of the term "merit," see further in Joh.
tr. 3. 10 : "he crowns his gifts, not thy merits ;" grat. et lib. arb. 7. 16.
Augustine, of course, uses the term also in the ordinary sense, *c. g.*, ep. 214.
4 ; grat. et lib. arb. 1 init.

(1) "Living according to the flesh, reason making no resistance—this is the first state (*haec sunt prima*) of man." (2) "Recognition of sin through the law," but "sinning knowingly . . . this is the second state of man." (3) Faith in the help of God: "and that the man has begun to be moved by the Spirit of God, he lusts against the flesh by the stronger power of love . . . his whole infirmity not yet being healed, pious perseverance—this is the third state of the man of good hope." (4) "Final peace remains—after this life. Of these four different stages, the first is before the law, the second under the law, the third under grace, the fourth in full and perfect peace." The history of salvation has followed the same course (118). But grace brings the forgiveness of sins and removal of guilt (*reatus*, 119). Every commandment of God has love as its aim. "Therefore, that which is done either from fear of punishment or with any carnal aim, so that it cannot be traced to that love which the Holy Spirit sheds abroad in our hearts, is not yet, although it may seem to be, done as it ought to be done" (121).

The treatise does not furnish the outlines of a doctrinal "system," but a connected presentation of that which Augustine regarded as essential in Christian teaching. The great underlying current of his thought runs through the composition. Into it he has interwoven his profoundest ideas upon sin, grace, and predestination. The metaphysical background is clearly traceable in his doctrine concerning God ; and the distinctively hierarchical elements are to a remarkable degree overshadowed. He skillfully arranged his ideas in harmony with the orderly statements of the Creed ; but, as in all his teaching, so even in this brief epitome, he has introduced nearly all the elements of the popular Catholicism of the day (ideas of merit, fastings, alms, together with hierarchism, sacramental magic, saint worship, veneration of relics, and the ascetic ideal of life). Wherever he stepped, the scene became one of verdure and flowers. He could attach the profoundest ideas to the most external things (*e. g.*, his exposition of merit and alms). Stones under his hand became bread. His influence upon the church is explained—in part, at least—by this wonderful power of assimilating and glorifying. But it may also be readily understood, in view of this same trait, that the loosely-connected elements of his general view, harmonized in him only by the power of his religious genius, were unable to exert a thoroughgoing reformatory influence upon the entire scope of ecclesiastical doctrine. He possessed the creative power of the reformer, but he lacked the talent required for tearing down. From this characteristic we may explain also the multitude of inconsistencies and self-contradictory tendencies in his teachings (*e. g.*, predestination and church, church and church, Christ and grace, grace and sacraments, the knowledge of God and the definition of God, faith and love, etc.). And yet the ideas of this man furnished the themes for the piety and theology of more than a thousand years. No one possessed the "whole" Augustine, but all lived upon the fragments of his spirit, from which each appropriated and understood what was "adapted" to his own wants.

CHAPTER V.

AUGUSTINIANISM AS THE DOCTRINE OF THE CHURCH.   COMPLE-
TION   OF   DOCTRINAL   DEVELOPMENT   IN   THE   ANCIENT
CHURCH OF THE WEST.

§ 33.   *The Semi-Pelagian Controversies.*

1. Augustine won the day in the conflict with Pelagianism, but his views were not by any means generally accepted in all their details (vid. p. 357). Offense was taken, especially at his doctrines of man's absolute inability to do good and of predestination, however for the time being his illustrious name and the charm of his writings may have smothered opposition. But, even before his death, doubts were openly expressed upon these points. In the cloister at Hadrumetum there were some, he reports, who "preached grace in such a way that they deny that the will of man is free," and all discipline and works were thus abolished (Aug. ep. 214. 1 ; cf. corr. et gr. 5. 8); while others held that "the free will is assisted by the grace of God, in order that we may know and do what is right" (ib.). Augustine agrees with the latter, for he was concerned above all else to counteract the ethically perilous consequences to which the view of the former group would lead. He thus formulates his position : "Both the will of man and the grace of God, without whose assistance it cannot be converted to God nor advance in God, are free" (ib. 7). This he sought to establish in his publications, *De gratia et libero arbitrio* and *De correptione et gratia* (cf. p. 350 f.). On the other hand, violent opposition arose in South Gaul, especially in Massilia. PROSPER of Aquitania and a layman named HILARY reported (Aug. ep. 225, 226) to Augustine that men in high positions and of lofty character, who were in other

points great admirers of Augustine (ep. 226. 9) were most strenuously opposing his doctrine of predestination, and, in doing so, were citing the latter against himself (ib. 3). That doctrine—it was claimed in the land of Irenæus—is new and of no value; it collides with the intuitions of the church (*ecclesiasticus sensus*), with antiquity, and the opinion of the Fathers (226. 2; 225. 2, 3); it is dangerous, because it cripples the force of preaching, reproof, and moral energy (226. 2, 5; 225. 3), and plunges men into despair (226. 6); finally, "under this name, predestination, there is introduced a certain fatal necessity, or the Lord the Creator is said to be of diverse natures" (225. 3). Pelagius may be refuted without resort to this theory (226. 8). All have sinned in Adam (225. 3), and no one can free himself by his own will (226. 2); but "everyone who is sick desires to be made well." Hence man wishes to have the Physician, *i. e.*, he believes on him (226. 2. 4). This believing (*credulitas*) is a deed of man, his merit (225. 6, 4). Grace now interests itself in behalf of the man through the "sacrament of regeneration" (225. 4). God assists the human will to do that which is good; but man, and not God, makes the beginning. "In order that he who has begun to will may be assisted, not that the power to will be also given (226. 2), they wish grace to be regarded as concomitant, and not prevenient to human merits" (225. 5). God wishes to save all (*indifferenter universos*) and the *propitiatio* of the blood of Christ avails for all (225. 4, 3). Predestination is therefore based upon fore-knowledge. The latter extends to the case of children dying in infancy, and to the historical diffusion of the gospel (226. 4;[1] 225. 5). Accordingly, there is not "a definite number of persons to be elected or rejected," "since he wishes all men to be saved, and yet not all men are saved" (226. 7). Hence, only the will of man is to blame. The motives, as well as the tendencies, of these Semiaugustinians are here plainly revealed. Augustine replied in the publications, *De praedestinatione sanctorum* and *De dono perseverantiae*, in which he maintained his position without modification.

2. But the struggles between the doctrine of Augustine and that of the Semipelagians were yet long continued. The name Semipelagians is not very appropriate; for the majority of that party might be more accurately described as Semiaugustinians, inasmuch as the influence of Augustine upon them was very marked, and they really found their starting-point in his teach-

---

[1] The appeal to Sap. 4. 11 is here rejected "as not canonical;" but see, on the contrary, the 36th canon of the council at Hippo (HEFELE CG. ii., ed. 2, 59) and also Aug. doctr. Christ. ii. 8; retract. ii. 4. 2.

24

ings.   The scene of these conflicts was the Gallic church.   For
almost two and a half centuries the African church held in its
hand the leadership of Western theology.   It was now, under the
pressure of political conditions, compelled to surrender this
leadership to the Gallic church.   The views of this Semiaugus-
tinian circle are clearly seen in the writings of JOHANNES CASSI-
ANUS (de coenobiorum institutis ll. 12. Collationum ll., 24 ed.
Petschenig in Corp. scr. eccl. lat. 13, 17, and in Migne lat.
49; cf. HOCH, Die Lehre des Joh. Cassianus von Natur u.
Gnade, 1894).   In the background is the monastic temper.   The
ideal of "evangelical perfection," as the fulfilling of the evangelical commandments and counsels, is to be attained by the
most severe ascetic discipline (coll. iii. 7; xi. 8, 10; xvi.
22; xix. 9; xxi. 5, 7 ff.).   The most painstaking carefulness is
made a duty.   But with the contemplations (*contemplationes*,
coll. i. 15; xiv. 8), flights (*excessus*, iii. 7), and profoundest
emotions (*secretissimi sensus*, iv. 2), alternate anxiety and
sadness (iv. 2; vi. 10).   Accordingly, human sinfulness, and
that in its sensuous aspects, is strongly emphasized,[1] and, on the
other hand, man's moral activity is made equally prominent.
The sin of Adam is a hereditary disease (inst. xii. 5);[2] since
the fall, there has been an *infirmitas liberi arbitrii* (coll.
iii. 12 fin.).   The Pelagian theory is very positively rejected
(coll. xiii. 16; cf. de incarn. i. 3; v. 1).   Two principles concerning divine grace are firmly held by Cassian : that we are unable to do anything good without the help of God (coll. xiii. 6),
and that the freedom of the will must be preserved : "For
through these things which we have presented we have not
wished to remove the free will of man, but to prove that the
assistance and grace of God are necessary for it every day and
moment" (coll. iii. 22).   From this it follows that grace and
free will *co-operate :* "And thus the grace of God always co-
operates for that which is good with our will and in all things
assists, protects, and defends it " (coll. xiii. 13; iii. 12, cf. inst.
xii. 14).   By grace Cassian understands illumination and instruction through the law, as well as the *illuminatio* of the spirit
for the spiritual understanding of the law, and *divina inspiratio :*
"To breathe into anyone the principles of salvation and to im-
plant the fervor of a good will" (vid. inst. xii. 18; coll. iii. 10, 14,

---

[1] The eight *principalia vitia* are : Gluttony, fornication, covetousness, anger,
melancholy, taedium, vainglory, and pride, coll. v. 2, also inst. v.-xii.   Upon
this list, which is found also in Evagrius and Nilus, vid. ZÖCKLER, Das Lehr-
stück von den 7 Hauptsünden, 1893, p. 16 ff. Upon the list of the seven chief
crimes, which may be traced to Gregory the Great, see ib., p. 40 ff.
[2] Original and actual sin, coll. xiii. 7.

15 ; xiii. 6, 18). Together with the imparting of the law, there is hence also an infusion (*infundere*) of grace (inst. xii. 16 fin.; cf. coll. vii. 1 : "The gift of chastity infused by a peculiar blessing "). Cassian occasionally attributes the willing, as well as the doing, of good to the working of grace ("the beginning of our conversion and faith," coll. iii. 15): Man cannot even preserve his own faith intact by the power of his will (ib. 16). Yet it is meant by this only that "he is not able to perform anything without the assistance of God, which produces industry," and that no one "may think that his work is the cause of the divine bounty " (coll. xiii. 3). Conversion is effected in this wise : "Who, when he has observed in us a certain beginning of a good will, immediately illuminates this and comforts and incites it toward salvation, bestowing an increase upon that which either he himself has implanted or which he has seen to arise from our own effort " (coll. xiii. 8, 7), and "the beginnings of good wills sometimes precede, which, nevertheless, unless they are directed by the Lord, cannot proceed to the attainment of virtues " (ib. 9, cf. inst. xii. 14). Man may, like Zacchæus, make the beginning; or God, as in the cases of Paul and Matthew (coll. xiii. 11, 12, 17, 18). The chief thing is the co-operation (ib. 13), and that "the consummation of our salvation be attributed, not to the merit of our works, but to celestial grace " (ib. 18); but, at the same time, the freedom of man must be preserved both at the beginning and through the various stages of the process (ib.). At this point, as in its assertion that God really desires to save all (ib. 7), this theory opposes Augustine. The idea of Cassian is, that the human will has indeed been crippled by sin, but that a certain freedom has yet remained to it. By virtue of this, it is able to turn to God, and, just as though God had first turned to it, it is able, with the assistance of divine grace, setting before it the law and infusing the needed power, to will and to do that which is good. Hence the sinner is not dead, but wounded. Grace comes to view, not as *operans*, but as *cooperans;* to it is to be attributed not alone activity, but synergy. This doctrine is theoretically as well as practically[1] untenable, but its appearance is a very severe arraign-

---

[1] The opinion has, indeed, been expressed that this doctrine of grace is "as a theory *entirely correct*, but as an expression of self-condemnation before God, *entirely* false " (HARNACK, iii. 223, n.); but, aside from the discrepancy between theory and praxis, which to my mind is not clear in this proposition, every doctrine of grace is "entirely false " which is not deduced from the idea of a personal intercourse of God with man or directly from "grace alone." That this is not the case in Cassian is evinced by the inconsistent double origin of conversion in his theory. This leads not to a life with God, but only to the idea of a parallel working of God and man.

ment of Augustinianism, as it proves that the doctrine of " infused grace," which Cassian had adopted from Augustine, was tolerable to the Christian consciousness only in combination with the conception of God as the Lawgiver and with man's relative freedom to obey the divine commandments.   It was an instructive attempt to preserve the personal and spiritual relationship of man to God.   But the attempt of necessity surrendered that which was the best in Augustine—the *sola gratia*.[1]   " For this it is to be under grace—to perform the things which grace commands " (coll. xxi. 34).   The effort thus led back again to about the ancient Latin position.

3. The controversy upon grace and freedom was protracted through the following decennia in the Gallic church.   The opponents of strict Augustinianism did not hesitate to draw the most appalling inferences.   They feared the annihilation of man's freedom, the introduction of fatalism and Manichæism.   Baptism and the divine call are robbed of their force and value.   God does not wish all men to be saved.   Christ did not die for all. Sin and the fall are to be attributed to God's planning.   God creates man and directly compels him to sin and crime.   This, they contended, is contrary to the teachings of the Scriptures (esp. 1 Tim. 2. 4), as well as to the intuitions of the church, and makes predestination coëxtensive with foreknowledge, etc. (vid. the separate propositions in Prosper's writings : *Pro Aug. responsiones ad capitula calumniantium Gallorum* and *Resp. ad objectiones Vincentianas*, Migne 51. 155 ff.; also, Aug. opp. xvii. 2887 ff.).   On the other hand, Prosper, in the writings named and in his *Liber contra collatorem* (Cassian, cf. his poem, *De ingratis*) defended the Augustinian position and made fierce assaults upon his opponents.   But he not infrequently ascribed to them Pelagian conclusions which they themselves did not draw, and in his positive statements he did not advance beyond a repetition of the ideas of Augustine (cf. WIGGERS, Augustinianism and Pelagianism, ii. 136 ff., 183 ff.).   His intemperate zeal can only have drawn the lines more sharply between the opposing parties.   And the attempt to bring the Augustinian doctrine into closer accord with the religious intuitions, made in the anonymous book, *De vocatione gentium* (Migne 51. 647 ff.), can hardly have produced any large results.   The ideas of Augustine are here reproduced, though in a diluted form.   By the fall of Adam, it is said,

---

[1] This is confirmed by the further soteriological views of Cassian. Vid., upon the definition of *merit*, WIGGERS, Augustinianism and Pelagianism ii., p. 81 f.; upon his theory of *repentance* as a satisfaction rendered by good works to an offended God, coll. xx. 3-8.

human nature has been depraved (*vitiata*, i. 6 f.): "the choice (*judicium*)) of the will has been depraved (*depravatum*), not abrograted. Therefore, what has not been slain by the wounder is not annihilated by the healer. He who is endowed with the power of willing is cured ; his nature is not removed. But that in the nature which has perished is not restored except by the author of the nature" (i. 8). Accordingly, it is not the human will by its merits that makes the beginning toward salvation (ii. 7), but the elective will of God (i. 18), who works everything good in us and upholds us in it (i. 23). "There is given to everyone without merit that by virtue of which he tends toward merit" (ii. 8). Christ died for all (ii. 16). Yet it is a fact, that not all are saved, as especially children dying unbaptized (i. 16, 22 ; ii. 20, 22) and the heathen world. This leads to the insoluble problem, "Why he who wishes all men to be saved does not save all men?" (ii. 1). Though utterly unable to solve this fundamental question, the author labors earnestly to make the course of God comprehensible. In the first place, he emphasizes the fact that the gracious working of God does not exclude the free exercise of the human will : "but the will of man is also subjoined to and conjoined with (*subjungitur et conjungitur*) it . . . so that it co-operates with the divine work within itself and begins to exercise for merit what it received for the awakening of energy (ii. 26) from the seed implanted from above," and also, "it does not take away from those who will persevere the mutability which can refuse to will" (ii. 28). He then presents the thought peculiar to himself, that God proclaims his desire that all men be saved, not in the first instance through grace, or a special call (*vocatio specialis*), but from the very beginning through general grace (*generalis gratia*) as a revelation made in nature (ii. 25. 4). The latter has always existed ; the former is now announced to the whole world ("no part of the world is now excluded from the gospel of Christ," ii. 33). But since this general assistance (*auxilium generale*) does not suffice for salvation, and since, on the other hand, from ancient times some, although indeed very few, from the heathen world, "have been separated by the Spirit to the grace of God" (ii. 5, 15 fin.), it is evident that this whole scheme does not solve the problem, but only complicates it. The author finds only the precarious ground of consolation, "the more difficult this is to understand, the more laudable is the faith that believes it. For he has great fortitude of faith (*consensionis*) for whom authority suffices to lead to acceptance of the truth, although reason remains dormant" (ii. 2). Augustine's conception of religious truth is thus supported by the medieval idea of

faith : the more unintelligible the matter in hand, the greater
the merit of the faith which accepts it !

4. Semipelagianism, or the old Western view, continued its
assaults upon the advocates of Augustinianism, and the latter·
may here and there have been betrayed into the extreme conclusions attributed to them.   The anonymous book, *Praedestinatus*
(Migne 53), written about A. D. 450, professes in its second
part to be the literary production of a Semipelagian, who, by
presenting the horrible doctrines said to be taught by a predestinarian sect, seeks to awaken in the pious a sense of alarm in
order that he may more effectually administer consolation.[1]   But
there were also doubtless Ultra-Augustinians, who allowed themselves to be led from grace to libertinism.   In consequence,
Augustinianism itself was charged with leading to immoral conclusions.   VINCENT of Lerinum, on the other hand, called attention to its novelty and its lack of support from the tradition of
the ancient church (*novitatis adinventores*, vid. Commonit. 32).[2]

But the Semipelagian view of grace found an especially zealous
champion in the highly-esteemed Bishop FAUSTUS of Riji († ab.
A. D. 495, vid. his writings in the corp. scr. eccl. lat. xxi. ed.
Engelbrecht, also Mi. 58 ; cf. WIGGERS, l. c. ii. 224 ff.   KOCH,
der h. Faust. 1895.   R. SEEBERG, PRE. v. ed. 3, 782 ff.).
Faustus contended (vid. esp. *De gratia*) sharply against Pelagius
and his denial of original sin, and of the necessity of grace
(i. 1).   He himself represented the Semipelagian view.   All
men have original sin, and that "from the carnal delight of
their progenitor" (i. 2, p. 12[3]), and are, in consequence, sub-

---

[1] Yet it is to be remarked that objections of no inconsiderable force may be
urged against this now prevalent solution of the historico-literary problem presented by this publication.   It is not impossible that there were libertines of
grace, and that the terrifying portraiture of predestinarian consequences, which
was continually drawn by their opponents, was utilized by them as a pillow for
their consciences (did not heretical tendencies influence these Augustinians?).
We cannot here go into details.   But let the polemical and not "symbolical"
character of the book (the publisher says it was used as a symbol, Mi. 53.
628) be observed, and also the statements of Lucidus (FAUST. ep. 1, p. 162,
ed. Engelbrecht).   But see recently VON SCHUBERT, Der so-genannte Praedestinatus, 1903.

[2] At this point should be considered the remarks of GENNADIUS upon
Augustine and Prosper, vid. De scriptoribus ecclesiast. 38, 84, as also Gennadius' own doctrine of grace, vid. De ecclesiastic. dogmatibus, c. 21, 56.   This
chapter may not be free from interpolation.   Chapters 22-51, which develop
the Augustinian doctrine of grace in exact harmony with the Council of
Orange, are also, upon the testimony of preserved manuscript, an interpolation
(vid. ELMENHORST in Mi. 58. 1023).

[3] Ib. p. 13 : " But whence comes that connection which produces posterity ?
. . . Through the impulsive ardor of accursed generation and through the
seductive embrace of both parents.   For since thou seest that he alone is

ject to death (i. 1, p. 11). But man has not lost his freedom
through sin. There is no "necessity of an ordained and imposed perdition," but a "power of choosing." The free will
has, indeed, been weakened, and freedom has lost the "bloom
and vigor of its grace" (i. 8, p. 24 f.). "The power of choice
of the human will has been attenuated . . . not abrogated" (i.
16, p. 50; ii. 10, p. 88). We are to speak, not of impossibility, but of infirmity and difficulty (ii. 8, p. 76). "We see,
therefore, that the consent of the human mind may pass over to
the good or to the contrary side" (i. 12, p. 41; i. 10, p. 32).
Hence, even fallen man possesses "the possibility of striving for
salvation" (ep. 1, p. 163). The appropriation of salvation by
man is effected in such a way that grace and the human will co-
operate : "we always associate grace with work" (i. 16, p. 51;
cf. 1. 6, p. 21 f.; ep. 1, p. 163). "And thus these two are
combined, the power to draw near, and the impulse to obey, just
as if a sick man should attempt to rise and his faculty should not
obey the mandate of his spirit, and he should, therefore, beg
that a right hand be extended to him" (i. 16, p. 52). From
this it follows, that man makes the beginning. He believes in
God, and God increases in him this faith and helps him to good
works (i. 6, p. 22). The word "assistance" implies equally two
(persons), one working and the other co-working, one seeking
and the other promising, one knocking and the other opening,
one asking and the other rewarding" (ii. 12, p. 91). Thus
also in baptism, the "desire of the will" comes first : "The
will of the applicant is first required in order that the grace of the
regenerator may follow" (ii. 10, p. 84). It appears sometimes
as though faith itself were regarded by Faustus as a gift of grace
(ii. 5, p. 67 f.), but in such cases the meaning is only that the
author regards the will itself as a gift of creative grace ("that I am
indebted to God for the will itself," ii. 10, p. 84; also ii. 12, p. 90;
cf. KOCH, l. c., p. 92 ff.). The matter can also be conceived in
this way : That God, as in the case of the prodigal son, by his
providential guidance gives to man the stimulus to serious reflection (i. 11, p. 38). But to comprehend fully the variance from
the Augustinian position, it is necessary to consider, further, that
Faustus understands by grace, not an inwardly illuminating and
renewing power, but, after the manner of Pelagius (p. 336), the
preaching, the comfort, the threatenings, and the promises of the

exempt from original contagion who was conceived not by flesh but by
spirit, and not with the passion that makes ashamed . . . behold the cause of
original sin, that one is born from the delight of conception and from the vice
of carnal pleasure." This is the monastic idea of original sin. Consider also
the reference to the origin of Jesus.

Scriptures.   Thus is the "drawing" of the Father (Jn. 6. 44)
explained (i. 16, p. 52), and the "divine assistance" is more
closely defined as the law and the prophets, the evangelical
oracles and divine laws (i. 10, p. 33[1]).   If this representation
of the view of Faustus be correct, he is yet further removed
from Augustine than Cassian (p. 371 f.) and nearer to Pelagius
(cf. WIGGERS, ii. 264 ff.).   In harmony with the general character of this theory, predestination and foreknowledge merge
into one.   " Foreknowledge foresees the things that will come
to pass ; predestination afterward defines the retributions to be
meted out.   The former foresees merits ; the latter foreordains
rewards.   And thus, until foreknowledge shall have explored,
predestination decrees nothing " (ii. 3, p. 63).   From this view-
point, the problem, why not all men are saved, may, so far as
human freedom is concerned, be easily solved (i. 16, p. 50 f.).
The question as to children dying unbaptized, man is not able
to answer (i. 13, p. 45 f.).   Thus, the Semipelagian doctrine,
as related to Cassian, had been further developed, i. e., had
approached nearer to Pelagianism.   Two councils were held, at
Arles about A. D. 473 (cf. Engelbrecht's prolog. to his edition,
p. 15), and soon after, at Lyons, in the spirit of Faustus, and against
the "error of predestination" (de grat. prolog., pp. 3, 4).   It
was under the instructions of these councils that Faustus wrote the
work above analyzed (vid. the prolog.).   The document, as
well as the letters exchanged by Faustus and the predestinarian
presbyter, LUCIDUS, give us some knowledge of the spirit of
these assemblages (ep. 1. 2, pp. 161-168).   Lucidus had championed certain ultra-predestinarian propositions (that the foreknowledge of God appoints men to death ; that a "vessel of
wrath" cannot become a vessel of glory ; that Christ did not die
for all, vid. ep. 1, p. 162).   He, under moral pressure, anathematized these propositions and, going still further, of his free
will acquiesced in the *praedicandi statuta* of the council (vid.
ep. 2, p. 165 f.).[2]

---

[1] In this very passage, indeed, side by side with the law, is mentioned a
working of grace : (he gave) "divine precepts ; to those observing them
through the duties of laborious servitude, grace co-operating, he has promised a
celestial kingdom."

[2] In his letter, addressed probably to the second council (at Lyons), Lucidus announces his agreement with the "council's recent statutes for preaching" (Fausti ep., p. 165 f.), and then cites a series of theses which do not
entirely correspond with those presented to him for his recantation.   We may
probably see in them the decrees of the council at Arles.   He condemns : (1)
Those who say that, after the fall of the first man, the choice of the will is
totally extinct.   (2) That Christ . . . did not undergo death for the salvation of all men.   (3) That the foreknowledge of God violently compels men

5. Various causes combined to check Semipelagianism. In the first place, its approach to Pelagianism, which was especially perilous while the latter was still in existence. Secondly, the literary assault upon the Traducianism of Faustus by the philosopher, Mamertus Claudianus (vid. Faust. ep. 3 and 5, also Mam. Cl. de statu animae), and the condemnation of Traducianism as heresy by Pope Anastasius II. (ep. 6, v. 23 ; Aug. 498).[1] But it must be emphasized, in the third place, that Rome clung to the Augustinian doctrine, though, indeed, only in the sense of Innocent I., *i. e.*, with an ignoring of predestination. The popes, maintaining this position, always pronounced Pelagianism heretical, and also expressed themselves against Semipelagianism. Vid. COELESTINE I., ep. 21. 2, where the Semipelagians are charged with "preaching things contrary to the truth." Hilary and Prosper are lauded, and the rule laid down : "let novelty cease to assault antiquity."[2] LEO opposes Pelagianism, appealing to the doctrinal instructions of Rome (vid. ep. 1, 2 of A. D. 442 ; so also GELASIUS I.; vid. ep. 4. 2, 3 ; 6. 1, 4, 5 f., 7, 8 f.). This pope from Africa expressed himself with exceptional thoroughness upon the subjects of original sin and grace (vid. also his Tractatus adv. Pelagian. haeresim, Thiel, epp. pontif., p. 571 ff.). The Romish position appears most fully in a dissertation upon grace preserved as a supplement to the 21st letter of Coelestine: In Adam all lost their natural power and innocence (5). Hence, no one, without the help of God, can, of himself

---

to death. (4) That whoever sins after baptism legitimately received dies in Adam. (5) That some are destined to death, others predestined to life. (6) That from Adam to Christ none of the Gentiles were saved through the primary grace of God, *i. e.*, through the law of nature, until the coming of Christ, because they had lost their free will entirely in our first parent. (7) That the patriarchs and prophets, or some most lofty saints, were living in the dwelling place of paradise even before the times of redemption. (8) That there are no fires nor infernal regions. Under the last thesis, vid. p. 167: "I confess, indeed, that eternal fires and infernal flames have been prepared for capital offenses, because divine judgment justly follows human faults persisting to the end." To this is added the positive assertion of the mere weakening of the will by the fall, and the proof from Scripture and tradition that Christ died for all.

[1] The pope was able to answer very easily, to his own satisfaction, the dogmatic question of whose solution Augustine despaired : According to Jn. 5. 17, the Father worketh always. He, therefore, gives souls also (c. 1. 4). It has been established that the child receives its spirit four weeks after conception (2. 5). Hence, Traducianism is heresy (3. 6). Nevertheless the sin of parents reproduces itself in the children (4. 7). The whole Scriptures teach Creationism, and, in view of Psalm 99. 3, it is said : "in this clearest trumpet tone all iniquity is silenced."

[2] That the force of these deliverances was felt in Gaul is evident from the perversion of the words by Vincent, comm. 32.

be good (6); even those who have been renewed through baptism attain steadfastness in the good only by the daily help of God (7). All merits are gifts received from God (9). God works the free will in man by giving him holy thoughts and the good will (10). This is also the end had in view in sacerdotal prayers (12). Hence: " By these ecclesiastical rules [utterances of Innocent, and Zosimus, and the African decrees], and by the documents received by divine authority . . . we are assured that we should acknowledge God as the author of all good emotions and works, and of all efforts and all virtues . . . and that we should not doubt that all the merits of man are preceded by the grace of him through whom it comes to pass that we begin to will and to do anything good—by which assistance and gift of God free will is not abolished, but liberated, so that instead of darkened it becomes light; instead of evil, right; instead of sick, well; instead of imprudent, provident. For such is the goodness of God toward all men that he wishes those things which are his gifts to be our merits. . . . Wherefore he effects in us that we will and do what he wills . . . so that we are also co-operators with the grace of God " (14). Finally, it is said : " We hold that as we dare not despise, so it is not necessary for us to affirm, the more profound and difficult parts of the questions before us, which those who opposed the heretics have fully treated, because we believe that, for confessing the grace of God, whatever, according to the proclaimed canons of the apostolic chair, the Scriptures have taught us, is sufficient, so that we simply do not regard as Catholic that which has appeared to be contrary to the universally accepted opinions " (15). Thus the non-Augustinian doctrine of grace is rejected as uncatholic, while predestination is, not indeed discountenanced, but yet not designated as an absolutely necessary element in the church's doctrine of grace. This important document plainly indicates the attitude of the Roman chair toward the doctrine of grace during the fifth and the early part of the sixth century.[1] It is Augustinian, but avoids committing itself to the extreme positions of Augustinianism. Pope HORMISDAS also, in his decision

---

[1] From the last section it is evident that Prosper cannot have been the author of the document. That it is not a part of the 21st letter of Coelestine is plain. The date of composition cannot be placed later than A. D. 431, since only utterances of Innocent I. and Zosimus are made use of (vid., however, expressions like those of Gelasius, ep. 4. 3), and no mention is made of the condemnation of Pelagianism at Ephesus (p. 264). On the other hand, Dionysius Exiguus found it so early as the days of Symmachus (A. D. 498-514) bound together with the letter of Coelestine (Mi. 67. 270). It may be included under the *capitula* of Hormisdas (ep. 124. 5); but it is, perhaps, already presupposed by Leo (ep. 1. 2) and Gelasius (ep. 4. 3 ; cf. 5. 2).

called forth by the assaults of the Scythian monks upon the orthodoxy of Faustus, pursues the same line. He goes even further, as
he describes the Catholic doctrine as being simply the Augustinian
("it may be seen in the various books of the blessed Augustine,
and chiefly in those addressed to Hilary and Prosper,"[1] ep. 124.
5). The same controversy called forth the (now lost) publication
of the Augustinian FULGENTIUS OF RUSPE, *Contra Faustum*, ll.
7 (vita Fulg. 28. 54). He, in a number of other writings,
championed the strict Augustinian doctrine of grace, including
the "double predestination, the one of the good to glory, the
other of the wicked to punishment" (vid. ad Minimum, ll. 3,
and especially vol. i. de veritate praedestinationis ; also ep. 15
in Mi. 65 ; cf. WIGGERS, ii. 370 ff., 419 ff.).

6. Thus Semipelagianism, as a theory, failed to secure acceptance in the most influential quarters. Then appeared a man in the
church of South Gaul, who was by personal religious conviction an
Augustinian, but who, nevertheless—or perhaps also therefore—
was able to look beyond the sacred paradoxes of predestination,
CAESARIUS OF ARLES († A. D. 542. Morin is preparing an
edition of his widely-distributed homilies. Portions in Mi. 67 ;
cf. ARNOLD, Caes. von Arel., 1894. As bearing upon our
question, see esp. 312 ff. and 533 ff.). But opposition arose
against the view of grace advocated by Caesarius,[2] which may
have been increased by political and practical considerations
(vid. ARNOLD, p. 344 ff.). His teaching, however, really con-
flicted with the legally binding decrees of Arles (p. 376).
The council at VALENTIA (A. D. 529) was accordingly summoned to oppose him. Caesarius was prevented from attendance, but sent representatives to conduct his cause, who argued
that no one can of himself make spiritual progress, unless
previously called by "prevenient grace," and that the will
of man becomes free only through Christ's redeeming work
(vita Caesar. i. 5. 46).[3] The decrees of this council have been

---

[1] *I. e.*, the strict predestinarian books, De predest. and De don. persev.,
vid. p. 368.

[2] Caesarius did *not* write the work attributed to him, *De gratia et libero
arbitrio.* The statement to that effect in Gennad. de scr. eccl. 86 is a rather
late interpolation (cf. ARNOLD, p. 498 f.).

[3] That the council of Valence was held before that of Orange is to-day
almost universally admitted (vid. HEFELE CG., ii, 739 f.). The passage cited
from the Vita Caes. permits no other conclusion. The council of Orange does
not, indeed, directly mention it, but indirectly in the statement that Caesarius
(after the council of Val.) presented the proof from apostolic tradition for the
view of his delegates (not of the council of Valence, as Hefele states, p.
738), and that Boniface II. confirmed this. Of course, Caesarius was not
"flatly accused of Semipelagianism" (KOCH, Faust. p. 53) at Valence. On
the contrary, his accusers were Semipelagians.

lost,[1] but that they bore a Semipelagian character does not admit of doubt.[2] Before the summoning of this council, Caesarius had appealed to Pope Felix IV., who sent to him "a few chapters." These, which have been preserved substantially in Can. 9-25 of the decrees of Orange, were taken from the Sentences of Prosper. When Caesarius, while in attendance at the dedication of a church at ARAUSIACUM (Orange, A. D. 529), learned of the Semipelagian decrees of Valence, he took advantage of the assemblage to reaffirm his views upon the doctrine of grace. He added to the Sentences sent by the pope, the introduction, the final confession, and decrees 1-8.[3] Thus originated the decrees

---

[1] But see further remarks below upon the decrees of Orange.

[2] Vid. ARNOLD, p. 349 f., especially, as otherwise the biographer of Caesarius would not have failed to mention the acceptance of the arguments of the latter's delegates at Valence.

[3] As to the origin of the Canons of Orange, ARNOLD is substantially correct (p. 534 ff.). We remark briefly : (1) N. 9-15 a, except n. 10, is derived from Prosper's Sentences (22-372, vid. the Maurine ed. of the works of Augustine, xvii. 2818 ff. HEFELE, ii. 730 ff.). These are the *capitula* sent by the pope. Caesarius inserted n. 10 and made some modifications (esp. n. 13, but not n. 18, where Arnold labored with a false LA. (2) The preface and the final confession, n. 25 b, are from Caesarius. (3) N. 1-8, in form and content different from the other sentences, are also the work of Caesarius, *i. e.*, of the synod. This is confirmed particularly by the fact that Caesarius has presented to the pope for his approval the proposition "that even faith is a gift of grace," and that the papal letter accordingly enlarges upon this proposition. But this is the leading thought in n. 3-6. (4) Caesarius framed the canon with a wise moderation and consideration for the opponents (avoidance of the double predestination, 25 b ; insertion of baptism, 13, 25 b ; the relation of grace to perseverance in good works, 10). (5) The question as to the motive for the construction of n. 1-8 is thus answered by Arnold : N. 1 and 2 are directed against Pelagianism ; 3-6, against Faustus ; 7, against the earlier Augustine ; 8, against Cassian (p. 557). But this does not harmonize with the concrete situation in which Caesarius was placed. It would be an astonishing thing if he had framed these sentences with a view to considerations of doctrinal history. Caesarius, as we know, sent with his own document to the pope the letter of a certain priest, Mansi viii. 737. This letter must have some reference to the Sentences of his opponent, the condemnation of which he was endeavoring to secure. It contained, in other words, the Sentences of the assembly at Valence. If Caesarius regarded the sending of these as necessary for the understanding of his canon, it then follows that n. 1-8 (but also the other comments and modifications of the documents received from Rome) were constructed in the light of the canons of Valence. And this is, in fact, in view of the entire situation, the only probable conclusion. This opens to us the possibility of reconstructing—in their fundamental features—the decrees of Valence. These began with a condemnation of strict Pelagianism. Not only death, but also sin, has come upon the race through Adam (according to n. 1, 2). Grace delivers man, if the latter calls upon God, desires to be pure, believes in God and the gospel message, and manifests an earnest longing and striving after grace and baptism (3 7). At the same time (according to Caesarius), there was left open the possibility that in some cases grace should make the beginning (8); while, on the other hand, as testified

of Orange, designed to put an end to the Semipelagian controversy. Pope Boniface II. (in Mansi viii. 735 ff.) confirmed
them, A. D. 530 or 531 (Hefele ii. 737 f.).

The leading ideas of this doctrinal decision[1] are as follows :
Both Pelagianism and Semipelagianism are in conflict with
the "rule of Catholic faith." By the sin of Adam, he himself and all his posterity were ruined in body and soul. Not
only death, but sin also, has through Adam come upon the whole
human race (1, 2, 8). "No one has of himself anything except
falsehood and sin" (22[2]). The free will has been inclined and
weakened in such a way that man of himself can neither believe
in God nor love him (25 b). If man even before the fall was
unable without the help of his Creator to maintain his original
integrity, "how shall he be able without the grace of God to recover what he has lost?" (19). The grace of God works in us
the impulse to call upon God and to strive after purification, as
also faith. Grace is an "infusio et operatio" of the Spirit (4).
That we believe, and that we will or are able to do these things as
we ought, is wrought in us through the infusion and inspiration of
the Holy Spirit (6. 5). Faith is "to consent to the preaching of the
gospel" (7, cf. ib.: "in consenting to and believing the truth").
The faith thus inspired by God impels us to baptism (25 H., p.
152). It is baptism which renews our will : "the choice of
the will, weakened in the first man, cannot be repaired except

by examples in the Old Testament, the natural goodness (the *bonum naturae*)
of man might stand at the beginning of the process (25 b). Finally, assault
is made upon the double predestination, and the evisceration of baptism and of
morality which it involves (cf. n. 10, 13, 25 b). This was the ancient Semipelagian position, which has close affinity with n. 3-7 of the Sentences of
Arles (supra, p. 376, n.). It was maintained with a certain moderation (the
preface of the Canons of Orange attributes the doctrine to the "simplicity" of
its adherents) and an energetic rejection of Pelagianism.

The origin of the Canons of Orange may accordingly be thus explained. But
if Caesarius was able to inform himself as to the canons of Orange only by
means of a letter, then it follows that the council of Orange was held immediately after that of Valence. This conclusion is demanded also by the
preface. It was only after assembling at Orange that information was secured
concerning the departure from the rule of faith (*esse aliquos*, etc.). But then
Caesarius had already, before the council of Arles, requested the papal advice,
and probably received it immediately before the council of Orange. Caesarius
did not summon the council for the purpose of conferring with them upon this
point, but merely embraced the opportunity afforded. The pope calls the
Canons a *collatio* (M. viii. 736). We may thus understand also the silence of
the *Vita* in regard to them.

[1] Vid. the decrees in HAHN, Bibl. d. Symb. 143 ff., and a revised text of
MAASSEN in Mon. Germ. Leg. sect. 3 ; concil. t. i. (1893), p. 44 ff.

[2] As to the solution of the problem bequeathed in this thesis to modern
Catholic theologians, vid. ERNST, Die Werke und Tugenden der Ungläubigen
n. Aug., 1871, p. 228 ff. (appendix).

through the grace of baptism" (13). God, therefore, works in us
to every good work. "The assistance of God must always be
implored even by the regenerated and restored (var. reading =
saints) in order that they may be able to attain to a good end, or
to persevere in the good" (10). Thus every good deed is to be
traced back to God (20, 23 f.). Accordingly, our worthiness
before God depends not upon our merit, but upon the gift of
God. "God loves us for what we are to be by his gift, not for
what we are by our merit" (12, cf. 18). The double predestination is expressly anathematized (25 b). We present as a
summary the leading sentences of the concluding confession :
"We ought to preach and believe, that the free will has been so
inclined and weakened by the sin of the first man, that no one
since would be able either to love God as he ought, or to believe
on God, or to work what is good before God, unless the grace of
the divine mercy had preceded him. We believe that, grace
having been received through baptism, all the baptized are able
and under obligation to perform by the assistance and co-operation of Christ the things which pertain to the salvation of the
soul, if they have resolved to labor faithfully. But that some
have by the divine power been predestinated to evil, we not only
do not believe, but even if there are any who are willing to believe such an evil thing, we with all detestation pronounce an
anathema upon them. He, no good merits preceding, inspires
in us faith and love of himself, so that we may both seek in
faith the sacraments of baptism, and may be able after baptism,
by his assistance, to perform those things which are pleasing to
him." Thus the doctrine of "grace alone" came off victorious ; but the Augustinian doctrine of predestination was abandoned. The irresistible grace of predestination was driven from
the field by the sacramental grace of baptism. The doctrine of
grace was hereby brought into a closer relationship with the
popular Catholicism, as also by the exaltation of good works as the
aim of the divine impartation of grace.[1]

§ 34. *Tradition and the Papacy.*

1. We have now traced the genesis of dogma in the ancient
church of the West. The doctrines of Anthropology and So-

---

[1] HARNACK says : "It is a fact which has not hitherto been duly considered, that the Catholic doctrine did not continue Semipelagian simply because it
declared the sexual passion sinful " (iii. 233). This is false, since it was just
Pelagianism (vid. Faust., supra, p. 374) which presented the strongest statements upon this point, and because the controversy between the Semipelagians
and the Augustinians really culminated elsewhere.

teriology were the most distinctly original products of Occidental Christianity. But even in the development of the doctrines of the Trinity and of Christology, the influence of the Western church was, as we have seen (supra, pp. 217, 272), of very great significance. Thus the Western theologians made themselves felt in the formation of both the Nicene and the Chalcedon creeds, and retained their peculiar conception of God and Christ in the forms of the Augustinian theology. The Trinitarian and Christological dogmas are hence common to the Eastern and Western churches, while the Greeks have given expression to their peculiar religious tendency in the doctrine of images, and the Occidentals in the doctrine of sin and grace. In the West, there was also a close and scrupulous adherence to the orthodox definitions and the heaping of condemnations upon heretics. This is clearly proved alike by the anti-heretical writings of the period (Augustine, Philaster) and by the efforts made to present a summary statement of Catholic truth (Vincent of Lerinum, Gennadius, Fulgentius of Ruspe[1]). But in close association with this regard for dogma stand the views and ideals, the superstition and cus-

---

[1] Vid. the writings of Faustus and Gennadius, cited by the latter, de vir. ill. 85, 100; the works attributed to Vigilius of Tapsus (in Mi. lat. 62); also the writings of Fulgentius (Mi. 65). As summaries, GENNADIUS, de ecclesiastic. dogmatibus (Mi. 58. 979 ff.), and FULGENTIUS, de fide (Mi. 65. 671 ff.) are of special interest. Gennadius treats of the Trinity and Christology, the resurrection, the creation, man and his soul, freedom (c. 21; as to c. 22-52, vid. supra, p. 374, n., and ARNOLD, Caesar., p. 535), then of baptism, the eucharist, repentance (54, 80), in condemnation of sensuous Chiliasm, upon angels, marriage, temperance, the Virgin Mary, relics, the necessity of baptism to salvation, the eucharist (c. 75: "pure water ought not to be offered in the sacrament in order to deceive some by the symbol of sobriety"), the resurrection, the influence of the death of Christ upon the dead, etc. Fulgentius, under the heading of Redemption (22 f.), gives a more exhaustive treatment of the Trinity and Christology in the spirit of Augustine. This constitutes the first part of the work, entitled by the author, De trinitate. The second part teaches: "What thou shouldst believe without doubt concerning created things" (24), viz.: creation from nothing (25, 29), the omnipresence of God, angels, freedom, and the possibility of falling, predestination and the leaving of some, especially of children dying unbaptized, to perdition (31); that original sin expresses itself primarily in unbelief (infidelitas) (34); eternal death and eternal life, wherein no "indulgence" follows repentance (36), whereas in repentance on earth: "if thou shalt have with the whole heart renounced past sins, and shalt have shed tears of the heart . . . for them, and shalt have been careful to wash away the stains of evil works by good works, thou shalt have at once indulgence for all thy sins" (37; cf. 82: "to wash away . . . thy sins by alms, fastings, prayer, or tears"); that baptism is not to be repeated; that "without association with the Catholic church neither can baptism profit anyone, nor works of mercy (42); that perpetual continence is better than a good marriage" (43); then follow forty rules which, for the most, are a repetition of what has preceded; § 84: "that the wicked are mingled with the good in the communion of the sacraments," i. e., in the church.

toms, of the popular Catholicism. In this also Augustine prepared the way for the later development (p. 367). We may,
accordingly, refrain at this point from a portrayal of the Christianity of the period, as this will form a fitting introduction to
Book II. (cf. p. 24).

At the beginning of the course of development, whose conclusion, relatively speaking, we have now reached, we met the
ideas of Irenæus and Tertullian upon Tradition (p. 136 f.). In the
present period VINCENT OF LERINUM, in his *Commonitorium*
(A. D. 434, in Mi. 50. 637 ff.), gave to this always influential
consideration a form in harmony with the views of his age, at
the same time recording some interesting remarks upon the development of doctrine. The Catholic faith is fundamentally distinct from heresy in the fact that it is based " primarily, of
course, upon the authority of the divine law ; then, likewise, upon
the tradition of the Catholic church." Although the canon of
Scripture is complete, "and of itself is sufficient and more than
sufficient for all things," yet tradition is needed for a proper
understanding of the Scriptures : " in the Catholic church itself
the greatest care must be exercised to hold that which has been
believed everywhere and always and by all."

Genuine tradition is, hence, that which has in its favor *universitas*, *antiquitas* and *consensio* (c. 2). Heresy is innovation :
"when well-established antiquity is subverted by wicked novelty" (14). This is confirmed by the study of the historical
heresies (*e. g.*, Apollinaris, Nestorius, Origen, Tertullian). Let
us, therefore, be on our guard against the darkness of heretical
illumination. "If novelty is to be avoided, antiquity is to be
cherished ; and if novelty is profane, age is hallowed" (21).
There is, indeed, progress in history, "but yet in such a way that
it advances truly in the faith, not a transformation." The
knowledge of the church grows, but "in its own kind (*genere*),
in the same doctrine, in the same sense (*sensu*), in the same
opinion" (*sententia*). There is a growth, just as the child becomes a man—a development, as the plant comes from the seed.
"Whatever, therefore, has in the agriculture of God been planted
in this church in the faith of the Fathers, this same flourishes
and matures, this same advances and is completed. For it is
right that these primal doctrines of celestial philosophy should,
in process of time, be carefully studied, refined, and polished ;
but it is nefarious that they should be changed, abbreviated,
mutilated" (23). Accordingly, the councils have only furnished more precise definitions of the ancient doctrine. "What
else has ever been produced by the decrees of councils, except
that what had before been believed in simplicity (*simpliciter*),

this same was afterward believed more heartily ; what had before been preached more moderately, this same was afterward preached more vigorously ; what had before been cherished in greater security, this same was afterward cultivated with greater solicitude? '' (ib.). That which was ''not a new doctrine (*sensum*) of the faith'' was now designated by the '' peculiarity of a new appelation.'' The heretics, on the contrary (*e. g.*, Pelagius, Sabellius, Novatian, Priscillian[1]), produce one innovation after another, and do not fail to adduce abundant proofs for their views from the Scriptures (Paul of Samosata, Priscillian, Eunomius, Jovinian), in this following Satan's example (24 ff.). The church must oppose to all heresies either the decisions of the councils or—if there be none applicable to the case in hand—the concensus of the ancient Fathers, *i. e.*, of those who remained until their death in the *communio catholica*, and, even in their case, not their obscure and private opinions upon minor points, but the fundamental views common to them all. Whatever has been plainly, frequently, and persistently accepted and handed down, either by all or by the majority, in one and the same sense, is to be regarded as true (28). Finally, as the letter of Pope Coelestine (p. 377) is quite evidently used as fully as possible *against* the Augustinians, this Semipelagian betrays his determination to apply his canon against the doctrine of Augustine. The doctrine of the ancient Fathers is, therefore, the truth, in comparison with which the authority of the Scriptures retreats into the background. Tradition was for Irenæus a tributary line of evidence for the establishment of the identity of the religious views of the church with the truth revealed in the Scriptures. Here tradition has become an independent entity, and really the chief consideration. From this time forward, side by side with the Scriptures—and in fact above them, runs the Catholic tradition. With this is combined the idea that the development of doctrine should and dare be nothing more than the formal restatement of the teachings of the Catholic Fathers —an idea which must stand or fall with the false presumption, that those Fathers had exhausted the contents of the gospel. The decreasing prominence of the episcopacy in this connection is worthy of note, but we dare not fail to observe also that the

---

[1] Upon Priscillian († A. D. 385) vid. Prisc. quae supersunt, ed. SCHEPSS, 1889 ; also PARET, Prisc. ein Reformator des 4. Jarh. 1891. HILGENFELD, in Ztschr. f. wiss. Theol., 1892, p. 1 ff. The solution of the historical problem presented by the theology of Priscillian (in which Gnosticizing, popular-Catholic, and archaistic elements are combined) does not lie within the province of the History of Doctrines. I regard PARET'S attempt as unsuccessful. Cf. also the instructive study of F. LEZIUS, Die Libra des Dictinnius (in Abhandlungen für Alex. von Oettingen, 1898).

episcopate is regarded as self-evidently the means for the preservation of the tradition.

3. When considering the evidence for the truth of the church's dogmas, mention must be made of the Papacy. It is the province of Church History to trace the extension of the temporal power of the popes; we can deal only with the dogmatic authority of the papal deliverances. The popes themselves with ever-increasing boldness referred to their doctrinal utterances as simply the truth (Callistus, p. 176; Stephan, p. 184; Leo, p. 271; Innocent I., p. 356); but they did so at first in the ancient sense (vid. Iren., p. 137, and also Tertul. praescr. 36, 20), that they were the representatives of the ancient doctrine—that, as the successors of Peter, they have the doctrine of Peter in their keeping (Stephan, p. 184; cf. Coelestine, p. 321). However lofty their utterances may sound, they are yet very far from asserting the " I am tradition " of a later age. The first traces of this theory may, indeed, be already noted, as at the council of Ephesus, A. D. 431, where the papal legates declare: "who (Peter) until the present and forever both lives and decides in his successors " (Mansi, iv. 1296). So also the ep. decret..Gelasii de recip. et non recip., libr. i. (Thiel, p. 455): " The Roman church has been exalted above other churches by no synodical decrees, but has obtained the primacy by the evangelical voice of the Lord and Saviour, Matt. 16. 18." But the councils by no means blindly acknowledge the papal claims, but subject them to scrutiny (e. g., at Chalcedon, p. 272, at the sixth ecumenical council, p. 282; cf. Mansi, xi. 331 ff.). This explains how a pope could be expressly condemned for error by a council and by another pope (Honorius, p. 282; also Jaffé Reg. pontif. Rom. i., ed. 2, n. 2118). The bishops always ascribed the highest value to the authority of the pope when that authority was enlisted, or thought to be enlisted, in favor of their own opinions (e. g., Aug., supra, pp. 354, 318; Caesar., vid. passages in ARNOLD, p. 298, n.). Where this was not the case, they were ready enough to set over against Matt. 16 the course of Paul, described in Gal. c. 2 (Cyprian, p. 183, Aug. and the Council of Carthage, p. 356 f.). Highly esteemed as was the papal authority—dogmatically, the views entertained scarcely went beyond the deliverance of Jerome: " But thou sayest that the church is founded upon Peter. Granted, that this same thing is in another place said with relation to all the apostles, and that they all received the keys of the kingdom of heaven . . . yet one was selected among the twelve in order that by the appointment of a head the liability to schism might be removed " (adv. Jovin. i. 26; cf. Cypr., p. 183; Aug., p. 318). Very similar

was the attitude of the emperors toward the popes. The actual power wielded by the latter forced from them expressions of the highest esteem, but they were never inclined to treat the papal teachings as infallible (cf. pp. 222, 235, 268 f., 272, n., 276 f., 281, 303, 356). In fact, the first decided interest was awakened by the edict of Valentinian III. (A. D. 445), which aimed to bring the Western church into complete subjection to Rome : " For then at length will the peace of the churches be everywhere preserved if the whole world (*universitas*) acknowledges its ruler ; " and " let this be law for them all, whatever the authority of the apostolic chair has sanctioned or shall have sanctioned " (Leon. ep. 11). The Justinian laws had only added emphasis to this. But that the papal utterances were even yet in the last analysis controlled by the traditional conception of the matter is best attested by the *Exemplum libelli* of Hormisdas : " Our chief safety is to guard the rule of the true faith, and by no means to deviate from the ordinances of the Fathers. And since the opinion of our Lord Jesus Christ when he said, ' Thou art Peter,' cannot be disregarded . . . these things which have been said are to be attested by the actual results, because in the apostolic chair the Catholic religion has always been preserved immaculate. Whence . . . following in all things the apostolic chair and preaching all its ordinances, I hope that I may merit to be with you in the one communion which the apostolic chair preaches, in which is the whole and true solidity of the Christian religion " (A. D. 515, ep. 7. 9 ; Thiel, ep. rom. pont., p. 754 f.). Cf. LANGEN, Das vatikan. Dogma vom Universalepiskopat u. der Unfehlbarkeit des Papstes, 4 parts, 1871-6. DÖLLINGER, Das Papsttum, 1892. Vid. Sources in MIRBT, Quellen zu Gesch. des Papsttums., ed. 2, 1901.

4. In the doctrine upon the subject of tradition there is again brought to view the harmony between the theological ideas of the later period of ancient dogmatic history and those of the second century, but none the less distinctly the departure of the former from the latter. The doctrines of the ancient church were constructed upon the basis of the primitive Catholic Christianity. In this process we may again remark (vid. p. 383) that the Trinitarian and Christological dogmas were a common product of the Orient and Occident, whereas the Soteriological dogma was an entirely Western construction.[1] This dogma, or these dogmas, became the basis of the entire doctrinal structure of the church and of the religious conceptions of the Chris-

---

[1] The condemnation of Pelagianism at Ephesus (p. 264) was merely an accident.

tian world. This explains the inestimable importance of a familiarity with the course of doctrinal development in the ancient
church in order to a correct understanding of the doctrines now
held in the church. But we are led, on the other hand, to the
conviction, that the established dogma of the ancient church does
not present the final truth, but is capable of and requires development, expansion, and continual recasting and progressive revision. For the evangelical believer, the Gospel of the Lord
and of the apostles is the norm for the criticism and revision of
the dogma of the ancient church. Inasmuch as the latter excludes certain conceptions, and, in their stead, formulates an
actual statement of religious principles in the philosophical forms
of antiquity, it has been a leaven modifying the course of further
development. It transmitted a gift to posterity which, like
every spiritual legacy, became of necessity for the recipient[1] a challenge to labor. The further course of dogmatic history must reveal
to what an extent the church of later times understood the
problem, and what progress was made toward its solution.

[1] Cf. FRANK, Syst. d. chr. Warh. i., ed. 3, 161 f.: "It is no less unjustifiable
to regard the fixed formulas of the church as of such a character that in them
is established a complete dogmatic conception of the topic under consideration,
whereas, in fact, they furnish, or attempt to furnish, nothing more than
the most suitable terms in which it is possible to define the realities of
faith as such;" and further, "that this is not to be so understood as though
the formula once established in consequence of the Arian controversy, and
since then handed down in the church, were in itself, and in this external form,
the basis for our dogmatic investigations. It is this only because, and in so far
as, in it finds expression a treasure of faith which . . . as an inherited legacy,
but one which, requiring, in order to its actual possession, to be appropriated
anew from generation to generation, leads us constantly forward." Vid. also
RITSCHL, Rechtfertigung u. Versöhnung, ii., ed. 2, 18 f.: "Even Philippi
(Kirchl. Dogm. ii. 150) attributes but a *negative* value for theology to the doctrinal formulas of the church. Yet this value is to be understood as *positive*
in character, in so far as these formulas keep within the range of view problems
whose solution has been attempted in the articles of faith, even though a more
careful scrutiny may have convinced us that the solution sought has not been
attained in them. Viewed in this light, both aspects of the doctrinal statements of the Lutheran church endure the test as a direct contribution toward
the derivation from the New Testament of the authentic content of the Christian religion."

INDEX.

A.

Ability, Human. In Judaism, 31; Hermas, 61; Barnabas, 71, 73; Apostolic fathers, 80; Ebionites, 91; Apologists, 115; Antignostic fathers, 122, 139; Tertullian, 123; Clement of Alexandria, 144; Origen, 147, 151, 157; Methodius, 187; John of Damascus, 286; Dionysius, 294; Eastern Church, 328; Western Church, 318; Chrysostom, 328; Ambrose, 329; Pelagius, 332 f., 337, 355; Cælestius, 332, 336; Augustine, 339, 341, 344, 350, 353, 359, 365; Pelagianism, 353; Cassian, 370 ff.; Faustus, 375; Lucidus, 376 n.; Council of Orange, 380, 381; Council of Valence, 379, 381 n.

Acacius of Caesarea, 225, 225 n.

Acacius of Constantinople, 274.

Actistites, 278.

Adam, sin of, 335, 337; original state of, 341.

Adiaphorites, 278.

Aelurus, 273.

Aeon, Christ as, 96.

Aëtius, 223, 225.

Agapetus I., 276.

Agatho, Pope, 282.

Agency, Divine. In Paul, 38; Apostolic age, 52; Apostolic fathers, 79; Augustine, 309 (see Will of God, Grace).

Agnoetae, 278.

Agonisti, 314.

Alcibiades, 90.

Alexander of Alexandria, 205, 216.

Alexandria, Council at (A. D. 362), 226; (A. D. 363), 227; A. D. 430), 263.

Alexandrine Fathers, works of, 140; aim of, 140; moralism of, 161; vs. Gnosticism, 161; estimate of, 160; on confession, 158; on divinity of Christ, 161; on rule of faith, 160, 161.

Almsgiving. In Clement, 76; Cyprian, 195; Augustine, 363, 367.

Alogi, 163.

Apollinarianism, condemned, 234; repressed, 272; and Antiochians, 246; and Cappadocians, 247; and Monophysites, 277; on Logos, 245.

Apollinaris, works of, 227, 244; problem of, 247, 250, 253, 255; and Cappadocians, 247, 250 ff.; on person of Christ, 233 n., 240, 284; on incarnation, 245; on Chiliasm, 246 n.

Apologists, The, 109-118; aim of, 110; vs. Judaism and heathenism, 111; estimate of, 110, 118; legalism of, 118; on God, 112; person of Christ, 113 f.; Trinity, 114; work of Christ, 115; human ability, 115; sufferings of Christ, 116; the church, 116; worship, baptism, eucharist, 117; resurrection, immortality, 117.

75; penalty of, 294; propagation of, 343, 344.

Sins, confession of (see Confession); forgiveness of (see Forgiveness); great and light, 364; purged by sufferings, 146; venal and mortal, 62, 175; willful and accidental, 79.

Sirmia, Council at (A. D. 347), 221; (A. D. 351), 222; (A. D. 357), 223; (A. D. 358), 224.

Son of God, Scriptural sense of the term, 35 (see Christ).

Sophronius, 279.

Spiritual believers, 42.

Subordination. In Tertullian, 126; Hippolytus, 128; Origen, 150; Arnobius, Cyprian, Lactantius, 170; Dionysius of Alexandria, 171; Theognostus, Pierius, 186; Sirmian formula, 222; Cappadocians, 233; John of Damascus, 237.

Substantia and persona. In Tertullian, 125 f.; Origen, 149.

Symbol, applied to sacraments, 322.

Symbols, sacred, 297.

Synergism, Ambrose, 331; Eastern and Western theologians, 331.

T.

Tertullian, works of, 118; legalism of, 132,133,139; influence of, on Latin theology, 171, 173, 237, 256, 270, 284, 308, 329; on Trinity, 122; original sin, 122; human ability, 123; person of Christ, 125 f., 243; work of Christ, communion with God, new law, obedience, 131; Soteriology, 132; baptism, 132; repentance, confession, satisfaction, 133; counsels and precepts, 133; Christianity, 134; authority of Scriptures, 135; universal priest-

hood, 138; second repentance, 176; salvation of souls, 192; papal infallibility, 386.

Testamenta duodecim patriarcharum, 88, 169.

Theandric energy, 277, 279, 281.

Theodora. In Monophysite controversy, 275; on images, 307.

Theodore I., on Monotheletism, 280.

Theodore of Mopsuestia, on problem of Apollinaris, 247; Paul of Samosata, 248; sin, 332 n.; condemned, 276.

Theodore of Studium, 307.

Theodoret, 207; views of, 266; formula of, 265; deposed, 268; at Chalcedon, 270; condemned, 276.

Theodosius of Palestine, 273, 278.

Theodosius the Great, patron of orthodoxy, 234; codex of, 234; at councils of Constantinople, 235; attempt of, to win Arians and Macedonians, 235; and Nestorian controversy, 262, 264; and Pope Leo, 269.

Theodotus, 93.

Theodotus the Fuller, 163; the money-changer, 164.

Theognostus, works of, 185; on person of Christ, 171; God, Holy Spirit, 186; Subordinationism, angels, incarnation, 186; system of theology, 186.

Theology, beginnings of Christian, 110, 118, 119; in Alexandrine fathers, 160, 161; in third century, 198; systematic, 186, 286 n., 331 n., 349, 357, 362, 383.

Theopaschite supplement, 276.

Theophilus, on images, 307.

Three-chapter controversy, 276, 277 n.

Tradition. On Gospels, 36 f.; Apostolic age, 46; Antignostic fathers, 136, 143; Greek Church, 289;

TEXT-BOOK

OF THE

HISTORY OF DOCTRINES

BY

REINHOLD SEEBERG

TRANSLATED BY

CHARLES E. HAY

COMPLETE IN TWO VOLUMES

VOL. II
HISTORY OF DOCTRINES IN THE ANCIENT CHURCH

BAKER BOOK HOUSE
Grand Rapids, Michigan

CONTENTS.

BOOK II.

THE PRESERVATION, TRANSFORMATION, AND FURTHER DEVELOPMENT OF DOCTRINE IN THE MIDDLE AGES.

PART I.

HISTORY OF DOCTRINES FROM THE SEVENTH TO THE TENTH CENTURY.

CHAPTER I.

INTRODUCTION. THEOLOGY OF GREGORY THE GREAT.

CHAPTER II.

DOCTRINAL CONFLICTS OF THE EARLIER MIDDLE AGES.

(i)

CHAPTER II.

DEVELOPMENT OF CHRISTIAN DOCTRINE DURING SECOND PERIOD OF SCHOLASTICISM.

BOOK III.

FURTHER DEVELOPMENT OF DOCTRINE THROUGH THE REFORMATION AND FIXATION OF THE DOCTRINES OF CATHOLICISM.

PART I.

GENESIS OF PROTESTANT DOCTRINE.

CHAPTER I.

THE VIEWS OF LUTHER.

CHAPTER II.

DOCTRINE OF ZWINGLI.   OPPOSITION OF LUTHER AND ZWINGLI UPON THE
DOCTRINE OF THE LORD'S SUPPER.

CHAPTER III.
THE NEW DOGMA.

PART II.

THE FURTHER DEVELOPMENT AND (PROVISIONAL) COMPLETION OF
PROTESTANT DOCTRINE.

CHAPTER I.

LUTHERAN DOCTRINE TO THE ADOPTION OF THE FORMULA OF CONCORD.

PART III.

COMPLETION OF DOCTRINAL CONSTRUCTION IN THE ROMAN CATHOLIC CHURCH.

BOOK II.

THE PRESERVATION, TRANSFORMATION, AND FUR-
THER DEVELOPMENT OF DOCTRINE IN THE
MIDDLE AGES.

PART I.

HISTORY OF DOCTRINES FROM THE SEVENTH TO THE TENTH
CENTURY.

CHAPTER I.

INTRODUCTION. THEOLOGY OF GREGORY THE GREAT.

§ 35. *Characteristics of this Period.*

1. Viewed historically, this period is characterized chiefly by
the disintegration of the ancient world. New nations and new
governments appear upon the scene. Yet the life of antiquity
is perpetuated among the barbarians by the church. Theology
becomes the bearer, not of doctrine alone, but of philosophy
and culture as well. For this task it was well fitted by the intimate connection of the fixed doctrines of the church with the
ancient modes of thought, and by the universal spirit of Augustine. Wisdom belonged to the past. "The first precept of
safety is to guard the rule of right faith and to deviate in nowise
from the ordinances of the fathers " (Vol. I., p. 387)—such is
the motto of the doctrinal history of the period. The only man
who indulged in independent speculations, the philosopher Scotus
Erigena, was misunderstood by his age. With Augustine, he
recognized two sources of knowledge, sound reason (*recta ratio*)
and proper authority (*vera auctoritas*). He endeavored from a
combination of the two to construct a speculative system. But
the speculative-pantheistic tendency prevailed, and the Scriptures
were subordinated by means of allegorical exegesis. His speculations had no influence worthy of mention upon the History of
Doctrines (cf. CHRISTLIEB, Leben und Lehre des Joh. Scotus
Erigena, 1860).

2. The German nations received Christianity from the church
in fixed forms and as a fixed formula. For them Christianity
became simply dogma, and faith the acceptance of tradition.[1]

---

[1] The only "dogmas," in the full sense of the term, in the Middle Ages
as for the preceding period, were those of the Trinity and the two natures of
Christ. Cf. *sub.* under Gregory the Great and also, *e. g.*, Agobard, de fid.
verit. 3 (Mi. 104, 269), and the Poenitentiale of Theodore of Canterbury (i. v.
6, p. 189, in WASSERSCHLEBEN, Penances): "from a heretic who should not

This, no less than the course of political events, served to confirm the hierarchical idea and the papal power.   Rome planted herself firmly in the new provinces of the Western church (cf. the Christianizing of the Anglo-Saxons, her relations with the Franks, Boniface), and, despite many rebuffs, secured power and maintained it.

3. Upon German territory Christianity was, it is true, conceived and publicly presented in a popular form (vid. the poetry of Cynewolf, Caedmon, the Heliand, the Crist of Otfrid.   Cf. SEEBERG, Die German. Auffassung d. Christentums in d. frueheren Mittelalter, Ztschr. f. k. Wiss., 1888, p. 91 ff., 148 ff. HAUCK, KG. Deutschlands, ii. 706 ff.).   The spirit of the theologians of the period was influenced by this (vid., *e. g.*, Hauck ii. 268, 589 ff.); but theology not so much as one should suppose.   The development of the practical life of the church produced, indeed, new forms which became influential in shaping doctrinal conceptions (the church, repentance, the Lord's Supper) and which the church could not ignore in her teaching ; but even here the old formulas were still the sacred material which lay at the basis of all theological labors.

4. The Greek church knew no Middle Age, for it never got beyond the range of the ancient problems of Origen, *i. e.*, the Greek church had no Augustine.   The dominant theological authority in the Middle Ages is Augustine.   The entire doctrinal history of the period may be treated as the history of Augustinianism.   His ideas controlled the leaders of the church and the unfolding of all ecclesiastical conceptions and institutions.   The worst features in this development may be traced back to him, as well as the best.   The piety of the age found in his teachings an unfailing source of inspiration.   They were not the Light, but they testified of the Light.   But while Augustine's formulas thus control the theology of the period, the theologians do not master the formulas.   They accomplished nothing more than the collection and arrangement of the Sentences of Augustine (ISIDORE of Seville, † 636 : Sententiarum sive de summo bono, ll. 3.   ALCUIN, † 804 : De fide sanctae trinitatis, ll. 3.   RABANUS MAURUS, † 856 : De clericorum institutione, ll. 3.   PASCHASIUS RADBERTUS, † 865 : De fide, spe et caritate, ll. 3.   Cf. Thomasius-Seeberg, DG. II. 13 f.).   But even this presentation did not faithfully reproduce true Augustinianism.   It was an Augustinianism misinterpreted in a Semipelagian spirit and degraded to a popular level.   Next to Augustine, the determining authority is Gregory the Great.

rightly believe the Trinity."   To these dogmas the later Middle Ages added only obedience to the church, the doctrine of the sacraments, and, particularly, repentance and the doctrine of the Lord's Supper.

The former was understood as interpreted by the latter. The History of Doctrines in the Middle Ages must, therefore, begin with an outline of the theology of Gregory.

5. It follows from the above that we cannot expect to find any real development of dogma in this period. The question in the disputes of the age concerns always the proper understanding or misunderstanding of the traditional formulas, not an actual development of them. Significant as is the period for the History of the Church, it furnishes very little material for the History of Doctrines. As in treating of the history of doctrines throughout the entire Middle Ages, so especially during this period the historian must constantly bear in mind the task immediately before him. He is not to embrace the whole field of theology, but only to portray the movements which prepare the way for and make possible the true doctrinal development of the Reformation period (Council of Trent and Protestant Confessions).[1] The great awakening of piety at the close of this period is to be studied in other connections.

§ 36. *Theology of Gregory the Great.*

The writings of Gregory († A. D. 604) which particularly concern us are the following :

Expositio in l. Iob sive Moralium, ll. 35 ; Homiliae in Ezech., ll. 2 ; Homiliae in evangelia, ll. 2 ; Dialogi, ll. 4 ; Regula pastoralis, ll. 3 ; Collection of letters in 14 volumes. Of the latter, the Liber sacramentorum and the Expositio in l. I regum are critically open to suspicion. *Editions.* The Maurine (Sainthe Marthe), Paris, 1705, in Migne Lat. 75-79. Die Briefe s. Greg. registr. epp. edd. Ewald et Hartmann (Mon. Germ. hist. epist. t. 1, 2). Cf. LAU, Greg. I. d. Gr., 1845. WOLFSGRUBER, Greg. d. Gr., 1890. CLAUSIER, St. Grégoire, Paris, 1886-91. Upon the doctrine of grace, vid. also WIGGERS, Schicksale d. aug. Anthropol., etc., in Ztschr. f. hist. Theol., 1854, p. 7 ff.

1. In theology Gregory is an Augustinian in his formulas, and something of the spirit of the great African is also traceable in his writings. But the ruder elements of the popular theology, which in Augustine are kept in the background, here come again into marked prominence. To this is added a crude superstition and mythological speculations touching angels, demons, etc., as found especially in the " Dialogues." Gregory is consciously orthodox. The Christian faith is for him *fides trinitatis* (mor. xxxiii., c. 10. n. 20 ; in Ezech. l. ii. hom. 4. 11), but includes also the incarnation (ep. l. vii. 15 ; ev. ii. h. 33. 6). The terminology, " trinity of persons" and " one substance " (*substan-*

---

[1] The History of Doctrines in the Middle Ages bears the same relation to that of the Reformation period as does the Ante-nicene to the Post-nicene. Cf. Vol. I., p. 23.

tia), occurs very frequently in his writings (Ez. ii. 4. 7 ; ev. i. 18. 3 ; 19. 7 fin.; mor. xxx. 4. 17).[1] His Christology is just as orthodox : Christ, the *deus homo* (Ez. ii. 1. 4), or the *homo deus* (mor. xxii. 17. 42), is true God and man : "of one (*unius*) with the Father and of the same nature" (mor. iii. 14. 26). But the divine and the human nature, united *inconfuse ac inseparabiliter*, constitute one person, *unus in utraque natura* (Ez. i. 8. 24 f.). "For we say that he exists, *of* (*ex*) two natures and *in* (in) two natures, but we avoid as impious the statement tnat he is to be considered as composed (*compositum*) of two persons" (ev. ii. 38. 3 ; mor. xviii. 52. 85 ; vid. also mor. i. 18, 26 ; xxiii. 19. 35 ; xxiv. 2. 2 ; xxix. 1. 1 f.; xxxiii. 16. 32 ; ev. ii. 22. 8, etc.).[2] The Holy Ghost is said to be : "of one substance (*substantia*), with the Father and the Son" (ev. ii. 30. 3).[3] Gregory knows himself to be upon these points in harmony with the doctrine of the church councils. He is orthodox, he holds, who accepts what *sanctae quatuor universales synodi* accepted, and rejects what they rejected (ep. vi. 66 ; opp. ii., p. 843). "I confess that I receive and venerate four councils, just as I receive and venerate four books of the holy gospel" (ep. i. 25, p. 515; also iii. 10 ; v. 51, 54 ; iv. 38).[4] Thus the authority of the church is recognized as on a par with that of the Holy Scriptures. Gregory, indeed, sustained by the strictest theory of inspiration,[5] sees in the Holy Scriptures the "foundation of divine authority" (*divinae auctoritatis fundamentum*, mor. xviii. 26. 39). God through them answers the "open or secret questionings of all men" (mor. xxiii. 19. 34). They must lie at the foundation of

---

[1] The divine activity is described, *e. g.*, in Dial. iv. 6: creantem et regentem, implentem et circumplectentem, transcendentem et sustinentem. Mor. xvi. 37. 45 ; vid. Ez. ii. 5. 10 ; mor. x. 6. 6.

[2] The birth from a virgin was necessary in order to avoid original sin. Vid. mor. xi. 52. 70 ; xviii. 52. 84 ; xxiv. 1. 3.

[3] Upon the procession of the Spirit, vid. mor. xxx. 4. 17 : "how the spirit of both proceeds co-eternal from both ; " mor. xxix. 31. 74 : "whose (*i. e.*, the Son's) spirit is the same spirit who proceeds from the Father." The symbol attributed to Gregory (opp. ii. 1283): "proceeding from the Father and the Son." Vid. further in LAU, p. 459 f.

[4] Gregory recognizes also the fifth council, *e.g.*, ep. i. 25, p. 515; ix. 52, p. 966. Cf. Vol. I., p. 276. The authority of the four councils was legally established by Justinian. See Novella 131 : "Therefore we decree that the holy ecclesiastical rules which have been announced or confirmed by the four holy councils shall prevail instead of laws. For we accept the doctrines of the aforesaid councils just as the Holy Scriptures, and the rules just as laws."

[5] Mor. praef. 1. 1, 2 : "Let it be faithfully believed that the Holy Spirit is the author of the book. He, therefore, wrote these things who dictated the things to be written." "The writers of sacred eloquence, because, filled with the Holy Spirit, they are drawn above themselves, become as it were (something) beyond themselves." The Scriptures are "words of the Holy Spirit" (Ez. ii. 10. 3).

all preaching ; by their study priests are to be prepared for their vocation ; the reading of them is most urgently commended to all.[1]   But the force of all this was broken by the introduction of allegorical exegesis as of fundamental authority (mor. i. 24, 33 ; xvi. 19. 24).   Thenceforth it became customary to laud the Holy Scriptures, but also to present as scriptural teaching the "ecclesiastical" doctrines.

2. In treating of the Work of Christ, Gregory employs the traditional mode of thought and expression (cf. Vol. I., p. 361 n.).   Christ is the *Redeemer* and *Mediator* of fallen humanity.   "The Lord appeared in the flesh in order that he might arouse human life by admonishing, stimulate it by furnishing models (*exempla*), redeem it by dying, and restore it (*repararet*) by arising from the dead" (mor. xxi. 6. 11).

(*a*) This involves the general conception that Christ surrendered Himself to sufferings and death for us and thereby delivered us from them (Ez. ii. 4. 20 ; i. 9 ; mor. xiii. 43. 48).   To speak more precisely, this occurs in the following way : God is angry with the sinner.   Hence there is need of a Mediator, who as a "mediator of God and man" must *be* God and man— "through flesh become *redemptor*, . . . *mediator dei et hominis*.[2] Because he appeared as the only righteous person among men, and, nevertheless, though without sin (*culpa*), faced the punishment of sin, both persuading man no more to sin and hindering God from smiting, he furnished an example of innocence and received the punishment of evil-doing.   By suffering, therefore, he who took away the sin of man by inspiring righteousness and tempered the wrath of the judge by dying, persuaded both and gave a hand to each, because he afforded man an example which might be followed and displayed to God deeds wrought upon himself by which he might be reconciled toward men" (mor. ix. 38. 61).   The appearing of Christ in our behalf thus appeases the divine wrath.   Upon this conception of the intercession of Christ Gregory laid great emphasis.   Christ,

---

[1] Gregory often and energetically advised the reading of the Scriptures, *e. g.*, mor. vi. 10. 12 ; xvi. 19, 24.   Ez. i. 10. 1 ff.; ii. 3. 20 ; ep. ii. 52 ; iv. 31, p. 712 : "The Lord of heaven has for (the good of) thy life transmitted to thee his epistles."   Cf. Vol. I., p. 298 n.   Ep. viii. 17 : "But I have inquired who of you belong to the *collegium* of sacred reading," points to conventicles for the reading of the Scriptures.   The Old and New Testaments differ essentially as presenting the lower (*minora*) and higher (*altiora*) precepts, inasmuch as the New Testament law addresses itself to the inner disposition.   Ez. ii. 4, 5, 9 ; 1. 10 ; mor. xviii. 4. 7.

[2] Instead of this exposition of the incarnation we find another : "Because there was no one among men who could appear before God as a righteous intercessor, I have made myself a man in order to make propitiation for men." Mor. xxiv. 3. 6.

as the Righteous One, makes his merit[1] available before the Father. "For to the Only-begotten Son, to plead for man is to demonstrate before the eternal Father that he is himself a man ; and to him, to have asked in behalf of human nature is to have taken upon himself that same nature in the altitude of his divinity " (mor. xxii. 17. 42). The effect of the merit of Christ is, therefore, that God abandons his wrath against sinners.[2]

(*b*) Another result of Christ's sufferings and death is our deliverance from the power of the devil. Man was in a state of guilt. The devil had a certain claim upon him ("held man, as it were, lawfully "). "This guilt must, therefore, be canceled ; but this cannot be done except through a sacrifice " (*sacrificium*). But beasts were not sufficient for such a sacrifice ; a man was required, and that a sinless man. Since there was none such, the Son of God became man in order to offer the sacrifice. Since the devil made a mistake in seizing the Innocent One, " he lawfully lost him whom he had, as it were, lawfully held " (mor. xvii. 30. 46 f.). The divinity veiled in humanity was thus the bait which God held out to the devil (mor. xxxiii. 7. 14 ff.).

(*c*) Of the Mediator it is said : "Who, although he could have striven in our behalf even without dying, nevertheless wished to aid men by dying, since he would certainly have loved us less if he had not taken upon himself our wounds, nor could he have shown us the power of his love if he had not himself borne for a time that which he took from us" (mor. xx. 36. 69). This shows plainly where the emphasis falls in Gregory's theory of the atonement. That Christ was a teacher and an example appears to him the principal feature of his work. He reveals to us the invisible God, instructs us in regard to our sinful state, and teaches us the will of God and his commandments (Ez. ii. 1. 15 f.; ev. ii. 32. 1 ; mor. vii. 2. 2 ; x. 6. 7 ; xvi. 30. 37 ; xxi. 6. 11 ; xxii. 17. 42 ; xxix. 1. 1). To the instruction thus given is

---

[1] Although the expression, "merit of Christ" (*meritum*), is not found, the conception appears very plainly : "For, interceding for sinners, he shows himself the just man who merited indulgence (*indulgentiam mereretur*) for others." Mor. xxiv. 2. 4, and ib. 3. 5. "But, because there was no one by whose merits (*meritis*) the Lord would have been bound to be reconciled with us, the Only-begotten . . . appeared as the only righteous (One), in order that he might intercede for sinners." Cf. ib. xvii. 30. 46. The term, "merit," thereby receives a new application. From ancient times the *merita* of men had been spoken of, but the term is now transferred to the work of Christ. The Reformation shattered the whole conception as applied to man, but allowed it to stand with reference to the work of Christ.

[2] It may be well here to note that Gregory speaks of the intercession of the saints and martyrs, as well as that of the church with its sacrifices (ep. ix. 52, p. 971 ; mor. xvi. 51. 64; xxxv. 8. 13); and also of an intervention (*intervenire*) of the Holy Ghost (ev. ii. 30. 3).

added the incitement by example. "For the incarnate Lord has displayed in himself everything which he has inspired in us, in order that he might commend by example what he had uttered in precept (mor. i. 13. 17). The life and active work of Christ, as well as his death, are regarded from this point of view (*e. g.*, dial. i. 9; ev. i. 18. 4; 16. 3; ii. 22. 7 f.; 32. 3; 21. 7; mor. xxi. 6. 11; xxviii. 18. 42). The purpose is: "That by presenting a form for imitation, he might change the life of previous evil-doing" (mor. xxiv. 2. 2).[1] Gregory's theory of redemption follows thus the Western type (Vol. I., pp. 193, 260, 361), since it understands Christ as essentially the historical power of goodness in the world, the teacher and exemplar. The idea of outwitting the devil also appears, it is true, in a terribly realistic form (cf. Vol. I., pp. 295, 361 n.). But it is a fateful phenomenon that Gregory seeks to combine the objective and subjective aspects of redemption : "Inasmuch as Christ dwelt among us, he both presented before the Father the new humanity and actually renewed humanity by his stimulating influence" (p. 5). All the Middle Age theories of the atonement find their prototype in Gregory—that of Anselm as well as Abelard's.[2]

3. In his doctrine of Sin and Grace, Gregory reveals himself as an Augustinian, or, at least, a Semi-Augustinian.

(*a*) The entrance of sin into the world is explained by the weakness of man (mor. iv. 3. 8).[3] The first sin was a free act of the first man (mor. iii. 14. 26). He surrendered his love to God, and hence was compelled to depend upon himself and his own flesh (mor. viii. 10. 19; 6. 8); he became afflicted with spiritual blindness (mor. viii. 30. 49; xi. 43. 59; ix. 33. 50) and spiritual death. "Man the sinner dies in sin, is deprived of righteousness, consumed in punishment" (mor. xii. 6. 9).[4] Through Adam all have become sinners (mor. iv. 27. 53; ep. vii. 14: "We come to this life with merit (*cum merito*) of our death" (mor. iv. 24. 45). This is effected through the medium of conception. "For conception itself is impurity on account of its

---

[1] Gregory often emphasizes the ideas of example and imitation in treating of the mutual relations among men, *e. g.*, Ez. ii. 3. 20; 10. 18; ev. ii. 31. 4; 38. 15; mor. x. 6. 9. Vid. especially xv. 51. 57, where the sin of children is explained as an imitation of the sin of the parents.

[2] Even the mystic view of Bernard is not foreign to him, *e. g.*, Ez. ii. 1. 16 : "Meditating upon his passion with anxious reflection;" mor. xxxi. 52. 104 : "Because the hearers are by no means able to understand the secrets of his divinity, they are content to recognize the blood of the crucified Lord."

[3] LAU, p. 376, has sought to find in mor. xii. 15. 19 and ix. 49. 73 the beginnings of the *donum superadditum;* but in this he is in error. Vid. mor. xxiv. 7. 13; viii. 6. 8.

[4] Vid. in mor. xxxi. 45. 87 ff. the seven principal vices : inanis gloria, invidia, ira, tristitia, ventris ingluvies, avaritia, luxuria. Cf. Vol. I., p. 313 n.

carnal delight '' (mor. xi. 52. 70 ; xviii. 52. 84). And : '' Because the human race became corrupt (*putruit*) in its first parent as in its root, it has carried out its barrenness (*ariditatem*) into its branches '' (ep. ix. 52, p. 970 ; cf. mor. xvii. 15. 21). As between Creationism and Traducianism, Gregory, like Augustine (Vol. I., pp. 344, 377), declines to decide (ep. ix. 52, p. 970). The consequence of Adam's sin as thus inherited is the damnation of unbaptized children dying in infancy (mor. ix. 21. 32 ; xv. 51. 57). This has an Augustinian sound,[1] but Gregory cannot make serious practical application of such ideas. For him sin is still always only weakness and disease. '' We are born with implanted defect of infirmity '' (mor. viii. 6. 8). Accordingly, he describes the human race in its natural state as : '' this one great and sick of very great infirmity—this is the human race lying languid throughout the whole world '' (mor. xviii. 45. 73 ; cf. xxi. 7. 12). Yet, with all this, freedom (but not goodness) of the will seems to remain for the natural man (Ez. i. 9. 2): '' prevenient grace had transformed the free will in him to a good will.'' Cf. mor. xxxiii. 21. 39 ; xvi. 25. 30.

(*b*) In the doctrine of grace also we find a similar emaciated Augustinianism. Gregory emphasizes the fact that without grace there can be no salvation, no human merits (mor. xxxiii. 21. 38 ; xviii. 40. 62 ; Ez. i. 10. 45). Only grace as *preveniens* and *subsequens* makes us capable of goodness. Grace, therefore, begins the work : '' Celestial piety in advance (*prius*) effects something in us without our agency (*sine nobis*), so that subsequently it may also effect with us by our free will the good which we now seek '' (mor. xvi. 25. 30). Prevenient grace works in us the willing of the good ; subsequent grace, that we are able to do the good (mor. xxii. 9. 20). In the latter, the will now becomes a good will, co-operates. '' For the good which we do is both of God and of ourselves, of God through prevenient grace, of ourselves through obedient free will '' (mor. xxxiii. 31. 40 ; xxiv. 10. 24 ; xviii. 40. 63). The first thing effected in man by grace is faith (mor. ii. 46. 71), as an acceptance of the doctrinal teaching of the church (dial. iv. 1 : '' that we should believe the things which we cannot yet know by experience ''). This beginning is effected through baptism, which works faith and forgives the guilt of antecedent sins, particularly of original sin (Ez. ii. 10. 7; ev. i. 10. 7; mor. ix. 34. 54; xvi. 51. 57; xviii. 53. 87). The next step in the process is the imparting of the good will, or love (*gratia spiritus infusi*, mor. xxx. 6. 22; *munus infusum*, ib.

---

[1] Augustinian, too, is the idea : '' Evil is without substance '' (Mal. xxvi. 37. 68 ; iii. 9. 15).

1. 5). This is accomplished by the preaching of the woid. A sharp discrimination is here observed between the outward, audible, and the inward, divine word (mor. xxix. 24. 49). Through this inward speaking of the word occurs the *inspiratio* or *aspiratio gratiae* (mor. xxx. 1. 4. 5; xi. 9. 12; xviii. 40. 63) and through it the good will (*bonum velle*), or love, is wrought (mor. xxii. 9. 20; Ez. i. 9. 2; 7. 16). "For to hear the voice of the Spirit is to mount up by the power of deep inward compunction to love of the invisible Creator" (mor. xxvii. 21. 41). Thus, after faith comes love (Ez. ii. 4. 13). This is thoroughly Augustinian (Vol. I., p. 347 ff.); but how wavering Gregory is upon this point is manifest from such assertions as the following : " For the commandments of the Lord are called justifications (Ps. 19. 92), in which he by correcting justifies us" (Ez. i. 7. 16 ; also ii. 10. 5).[1] According to this, grace would consist in the giving of the commandments ; and such is accordingly the view of Faustus. And it is to be observed that Gregory, in keeping with this, lays great stress upon man's co-operation. Thus place is found for the merit (*meritum*) of man in connection with the idea of reward. If we ourselves co-operate in striving after the good, then : "That which is a gift of the omniponent God becomes our merit" (Ez. i. 9. 2; ii. 4. 6; mor. xvi. 25. 30; xviii. 40. 63; xxxiii. 21. 40). In the same line is Gregory's assertion that man can do more than is commanded (mor. xv. 18. 20 ; xxvi. 27. 51).

(*c*) The doctrine of Predestination is retained only in form. The irresistibility of grace appears to be taught (mor. xi. 9. 13 ; cf. Ez. ii. 1. 13), but it is denied in mor. xxx. 1. 5. So, likewise, predestination is taught as a "secret counsel" (mor. xviii. 26. 43) in connection with the "certain and definite number of the elect" (mor. xxv. 8. 20 ; Ez. ii. 1. 11); but it is, after all, only a result of omniscience : "Whom he calls also elect (Matt. 24. 24), because he perceives that they will persist in faith and good works" (Ez. i. 9. 8; mor. xxv. 8. 19; xviii. 29. 46). The idea is, therefore, that there is a definite number of men whom God appoints to salvation, because he knows in advance that they will accept it. But no one is able to pronounce a certain judgment as to his own election or that of any other person (ev. ii. 38. 14; mor. xxv. 8. 19 ff.; xxiv. 11. 32).[2] Here, too, Gregory wavers, and it is evident that predestination has no important place in his religious convictions.

---

[1] I know of no other reference to *justification* in Gregory's writings.

[2] But *vid.* Ez. ii. 5. 22 : "but one sign of election is the firmness (*soliditas*) of love."

(*d*) Following the course of the Christian life,[1] as depicted by Gregory, we find it interrupted by many sins. God is thereby offended, but man must "abstain even from some things lawful, until by this he may make satisfaction to his Creator" in order that his sin may be forgiven him (ev. ii. 34. 15 ff.). This is repentance. It embraces first of all *compunctio*, or *contritio*, *i. e.*, contrition, mourning, penitence (mor. xxiii. 21. 40 ; xvi. 29, 36). This is effected either through fear of the merited punishment, or through the flame of love and longing for the heavenly fatherland (Ez. ii. 10. 20 f.; dial. iii. 34 ; mor. xxiv. 6. 10). Secret sins in the thoughts are washed away by the sinner's tears of penitence and his good works (mor. ix. 55. 83 f.). But in the case of public repentance, there follows a *confession* of sins (mor. viii. 21. 37 ; xxii. 15. 31 ; xxxi. 46. 93). When grace has accomplished this, *absolution* is granted : "Whom the omnipotent God visits through the grace of *compunctio*, them the declaration of the pastor absolves" (ev. ii. 26. 6). But the "pastors of the church" also lay a penalty (*poena*) upon those who thus publicly confess their guilt.[2] This is the *satisfactio*[3] which the sinner renders to God by abstaining from that which is otherwise allowable (vid. supra and reg. past. iii. 30; opp. ii. 87). Thus the sinner secures forgiveness from God, who takes the offering or gift (*munus*) for the offense (*culpa*) (dial. iv. 60). We have here essentially the fundamental elements of the Romish sacrament of repentance (cf. Vol. I., pp. 177 f., 195 f., 363 f.). "For there are three things to be considered in every one truly penitent, *i. e.*, the change of the mind, the confession of the mouth, and the punishments of the sin" (*conversio mentis, confessio oris, et vindicta peccati* (in 1 reg. vi. 2. 33).[4]

(*e*) In closest connection with the above stand Gregory's views upon the Sacrifice of the Mass and Purgatory. The whole significance of the Lord's Supper is found in the sacrifice of the mass. He maintains the real presence of the body of Christ (ev. i. 14. 1 ; 22. 7 ; also Libr. sacr. post. Theoph. dom. v. praef. opp. iii. 27). But the principal thing is that the appeas-

---

[1] Upon the division of Christian life into *active* and *contemplative*, vid., *e. g.*, mor. vi. 37. 57-61 ; xxxi. 25. 49 ; Ez. ii. 2. 2 ff. (=Martha and Mary); reg. past. i. 7. For a portrayal of the ideal of the Christian life, *e. g.*, Ez. i. 10. 9.

[2] The injunction is given : "But let those who preside show themselves to be such that those subject to them may not blush to make known to them even their secret" (sins) (reg. past. ii. 5. opp. ii. 19).

[3] The execution of the punishments (*vindicta*) constitutes the *satisfactio*, as is evident from ep. ix. 52, p. 968 f.

[4] Vid. also the compulsory penitence (*Zwangsbusse*) of clericals, monks, and nuns, *e. g.*, ep. i. 44, p. 537 f.; iv. 9.

ing wafer (*hostia placationis*) be so presented[1] that the sacrifice of Christ for us be repeated : " For as often as we offer to him the *hostia* of the passion,' so often do we renew (*reparamus*) his passion to ourselves for our absolution," and that the church may have in it a means of influencing God in addition to prayer and alms (ev. ii. 27. 7-9 ; dial. iv. 58). There has thereby been given to the church a means of enchantment, which may be of great service, *e. g.*, breaking chains and extending help to the shipwrecked (dial. iv. 57). But it is, above all, an effectual means of bringing help to the souls of the departed. " That for certain light offenses there is to be a *purgatorial fire* before the judgment," is to be believed, according to Matt. 12. 31 ; 1 Cor. 3. 12 ff. (cf. Vol. I., pp. 159, 197 n., 363). Some sins can, accordingly, be forgiven in that world (dial. iv. 39). The sacrifice of the mass is particularly efficacious for this purpose, freeing souls from purgatory (ib. iv. 55).[2]

4. We must yet glance at Gregory's conception of the Church. " The present church is called the kingdom of heaven—for the congregation of the saints is said to be the kingdom of heaven " (ev. ii. 38. 2 ; 32. 6 ; mor. xxxiii. 18. 34). The church is the kingdom, but primarily limited to the *ecclesia justorum, i. e.*, the elect (vid. mor. xxv. 8. 21). The " one, holy universal church " embraces angels and men—men from the time of Abel onward, all believers of the old covenant belonging to it (Ez. i. 8. 28; ii. 3. 17; ev. i. 19. 1).[3] In its concrete form, like its prototype, the ark, it embraces clean and unclean. " In this church, therefore, there can be neither the evil without the good, nor the good without the evil " (ev. ii. 38. 7 f.; Ez. ii. 4. 16 f.). But only in the church are truth and love to be found, only in it salvation

---

[1] Dial. iv. 58 : " Living in himself immortally and incorruptibly, he is for us again immolated in this mystery of sacred oblation. For there his body is taken, his flesh is broken for the salvation of the people, his blood is poured out, not now into the hands of unbelievers, but into the mouths of believers. Hence we consider what is the nature (*qualitas*) of this sacrifice for us, which always repeats (*imitatur*) for our absolution the passion of the Only-begotten. For who of the believing can have a doubt that in the very hour of the immolation the heavens are opened at the voice of the priest, that the choirs of angels are present in that mystery of Jesus Christ, that the lowest things are associated with the highest ? " . . . Also ev. ii. 37. 7. " The host offered with the tears and benignity of the sacred altar pleads in a peculiar way for our absolution, because he who, arising by his own power, now dies no more, through it in his mystery suffers again for us." Then follows the sentence above quoted.

[2] The fourth book of the Dialogue treats exhaustively of conditions in the other world. Vid. especially its conception of the bridge (iv. 36).

[3] Membership in the church is conditioned upon faith in the Trinity, and this the Old Testament believers possessed. Ez. ii. 4. 4, 7, 10 ; 3. 16 ; mor. xxix. 31. 70.

(mor. xxxv. 8. 13). The holy universal church proclaims that God cannot, except within it, be truly worshiped, asserting that all who are without its bounds will by no means be saved (mor. xiv. v. 5; ep. xi. 46). Only the church's sacrifice avails; only its members are in the valid bond (*compages*) of love; only is its martyrdom meritorious (mor. xxxv. 8. 12; xviii. 26. 40). Separation from the church proves lack of love (mor. xviii. 26. 41 f.). But everything upon which the necessity of the church to salvation depends lies in the hands of the "officers" (rulers, *regentes*, and subjects, *subditi*, mor. xxx. 6. 23; iv. 31. 61; reg. past. ii. 6; in reg. vi. 2. 21). Binding and loosing are prerogatives of the clericals. And "whether the pastor binds justly or unjustly, nevertheless the pastor's declaration (*sententia*) must be revered by the multitude" (ev. ii. 26. 5 f.). They watch over the lives of those under them (*subditi*), lead them to repentance, dispense absolution (mor. xi. 14. 22; xiii. 18. 21; dial. ii. 23), present the sacrifice, etc. For the accomplishment of her work, the church lays claim to the aid of the unchristianized state. "The holy church, because she is not sufficient in her own strength, seeks the assistance of that rhinoceros" (Job 39. 9), *i. e.*, the prince of this world (mor. xxxi. 5. 7).

5. If we compare the Christianity of Gregory with that of Augustine, we reach a remarkable result. Almost everything in Gregory has its roots in the teaching of Augustine, and yet scarcely anything is really Augustinian. That which was un-Augustinian in Augustine becomes the vital element of this Semi-augustinian. The fundamental spirit of Augustine has vanished, and superstition gained supremacy. Everything is coarser, more fixed, and ordinary.[1] The controlling motive is not the peace of the heart which finds rest in God; but the fear of uncertainty, which seeks to attain security through the institutions of the church. "For thus the holy church, in the course of her preaching to the faithful concerning the piety and righteousness of the Redeemer, *mingles hope and fear*, in order that they may neither incautiously trust in his mercy nor in despair fear his righteousness" (mor. xx. 5. 13). There are some rays of light in this dark picture (*e. g.*, the initiative of grace, the emphasis laid upon preaching, incidental remarks touching the nature of the church); but the crude Christianity, which is its characteristic, overshadows them with its sacramental magic, its ghostly miracles, its priestcraft, its superficial conception of sin, and its intoning of merit and reward. And even where Gre-

---

[1] Cf. the opinion of Melanchthon : "Gregory, whom they call the Great, I call the dancer and torch-bearer of the theology now passing away" (Corp. Ref. xi. 16).

gory's teaching was, in itself considered, more correct than that of Augustine, as upon predestination, the better was, as matters then stood, arrayed against the good. Such is the form in which the legacy of Augustine was preserved to the church—even thus a rich inheritance.

CHAPTER II.

DOCTRINAL CONFLICTS OF THE EARLIER MIDDLE AGES.

§ 37. *Adoptionist Controversy.*

SOURCES. The letters of ELIPANDUS, España sagrada v. 524 ff. Migne Lat. 96. Etherii et Beati adv. Elipandum, ll. 2. ALCUINUS adv. Elipandum; adv. Felicem (Opp. ed. Frobenius, 1777, and Migne 100, 101). PAULINUS, ll. 3, c. Felicem, Migne 99. BENEDICT OF ANIANE, Testimoniorum nubecula, Migne 103. AGOBARD, Liber adv. dogma Felicis, Migne 104. Cf. Mansi xii., xiii. GAMS, KG. Spaniens, ii. 2, p. 261 ff. HEFELE, CG. iii., ed. 2, 642 ff. WERNER, Alkuin, 1881, p. 54 ff. MÖLLER, PRE. i., ed. 3, 180 ff. GRÖSSLER, Ueber die Ausrottg. des Adopt. im Reich Karls des Gr., 1879 (Jahresbericht d. Gymn. zu Eisleben). HAUCK, KG. Deutschlands ii., 251 ff. BACH, DG. des MA. i., p. 103 ff. THOMASIUS-SEEBERG, DG. ii., 15 ff. HARNACK, DG. iii. 248 ff.

The great Renaissance of the Carlovingian age was of the profoundest significance for Church History. Its results for the History of Doctrines were comparatively small. So great dependence was placed upon antiquity that no advance was made in dogmatics beyond the interpretation of the Fathers. This is attested by all the controversies of the age, which were essentially disputes about misunderstandings of the accepted teachers of the church.

1. In Spain, a crude attempt was made by a certain MICETIUS to solve the problem of the Trinity. God, he affirmed, has revealed himself in a three-fold form : as the Father in David, as the Son in Christ, as the Holy Ghost in Paul (Elip. ad Miget. 3. Esp. sagr. v. 526). He was opposed by the aged bishop, ELIPANDUS OF TOLEDO. His Christological theory was championed especially by Bishop FELIX OF URGELLIS. The watchwords, *adoptio, filius adoptivus,* are taken from the Spanish so-called Mozarabic liturgy (*per adoptivi hominis passionem ; adoptivi hominis vestimentum carnis,* etc. Vid. HEFELE, iii. 651, and also HAUCK ii. 257 n.). The theory was that Christ, as the second person of the Trinity, was the " only-begotten of the Father without adoption ; " but that the Son of God assumed, or

adopted, the Son of man, who is thus *adoptivus* and *called God*
(Alcuini opp. ii. 568. Esp. sagr. v. 536. Gallandi xiii. 407.
Alc. adv. Fel. i. 1). The unity of person is thought to be preserved in this process, inasmuch as, from the time of his conception, the Son of man was taken up into the unity of the person
of the Son of God (Alc. l. c. v. 1). He suffered, indeed, only as
the adopted (*adoptivus*) man and was buried in his "adopted
flesh" only (Elip. iv. 16; Mi. xcvi. 879). The doctrinal
type of the Adoptionists is in the line of the Western Christology, which aimed to secure fuller recognition of the humanity
of Jesus.[1] They proved the necessity of this upon religious
grounds, adducing the resemblance of believers to Christ, their
relations to him as members of his body, and his human character (Alc. c. Fel. ii. 4. 14; v. 9; Paulin. iii. 3, 4). Only if an
actual man should, with his untainted blood, blot out the deadly
handwriting, could we become free from bondage (Elip. ep. 4.
14; Mi. 96. 878. As every man is according to the flesh
born from Adam, so everyone obtains the "grace of adoption,"
who receives it in Christ, the second Adam, born of the virgin
(Alc. adv. Fel. ii. 16, also Agob. adv. dogm. Fel. 37). This
theory was not really Nestorian, but it was possible to deduce
from it consequences which led in that direction. It is scarcely
justifiable, therefore, to attribute it to the influence of oriental
Nestorians (*e. g.*, GAMS, ii. 2, p. 264 f.). "Adoptionism is
to be accounted for by the continued influence of old religious
theories, the dependence upon ecclesiastical formulas, and the
defective theological culture" (HAUCK, ii., p. 258 n.).

2. This doctrine was vigorously assailed by the Asturians,
BEATUS and ETHERIUS; then particularly by the Frankish
church. Among its literary opponents the most prominent was
ALCUIN. The first charge against the Spaniards was that they
are led to teach a double person (*alter et alter*): "Just as the
Nestorian impiety divided Christ into two Persons on account of
the two natures, . . . so also your untaught temerity divides him
into two Sons, one a true and the other an adopted Son" (Alc.
adv. Fel. i. 11). Attention was then called to the inconsistency
of Adoptionism with the teaching of the Fathers and the church.[2]
These attempted refutations display a remarkably defective con-

---

[1] *Assumtio illius hominis; verbum habens hominem,* says Augustine (Vol.
I., pp. 260 n., 360. Cf. Hilar. upon Ps. 138. 2. To assume man (*hominem
suscipere*) is the standing formula in the Spanish Confession (vid. Hahn, Bibl.
d. Symbole, ed. 3, pp. 211, 236, 237, 245 f.). The Synod of Toledo, A. D.
675, says in regard to the Logos—not the Son of man—"He is a son by nature, not by adoption" (vid. Hahn, p. 243, also Hefele, iii. 115).
[2] For special instances, vid. BACH, i. 116 ff.

ception of the real problem at issue.   Their authors were content to rest in the simple thought : Christ was God, and as God he has delivered us.[1]   Yet they understood that : " In the assumption of the flesh by God, the person, not the nature, of the man perishes " (Alc. adv. Fel. ii. 12).   Adoptionism was condemned at Regensburg, A. D. 794 ; at Frankfurt, A. D. 794 ; at Aachen, A. D. 799.   Pope Hadrian I. had already rejected it as Nestorianism and blasphemy (Cod. Carol. 99, p. 294. Mansi, xiii. 865 ff.).   Under Leo III. it was again condemned by a Roman Council (Mansi, xiii. 1031, probably in A. D. 799). Nothing was gained as a result of the controversy.   The opponents of the Adoptionists could not refute them because they were themselves too orthodox to understand them.

§ 38. *Eastern Church and the Worship of Images.   Filioque Controversy.*

LIBRI CAROLINI, ed. Heumann, 1731 ; in Migne, 98. 999 ff. ALCUIN, de processione spiritus sancti, Migne, 101, 63 ff. HEFELE, CG. iii., ed. 2, 694 ff., 749 ff. HAUCK, KG., Deutschl. ii. 276 ff., 299 ff.

1. During the controversies concerning images, the popes arrayed themselves on the side of the image-worshipers (Vol. I., p. 304). The Frankish church had assumed the same position.   Delegates of Pope Hadrian had taken part in the Council at Nice, A. D. 787, and it had not been thought necessary to take special measures to protect the Frankish church.   But Charlemagne took hand in the controversy.   The LIBRI CAROLINI contain a keen criticism of the worship of images.   God alone, they declare, is to be adored and worshiped (*adorandus et colendus*); the saints are only to be venerated (*venerandi*).   Images, on the other hand, are only ornamental objects and reminders.   It is, therefore, folly to render them worship.   The Council of A. D. 754, which was hostile to image-worship, and the Council of Nice were both pronounced infamous and most incompetent (*ineptissimae*).   No attention whatever was given, it is true, to the distinction between veneration (προσκύνησις) and worship (λατρεία), the former word having been represented by the term *adoratio* in the Latin translation of the acts of the Council which was forwarded to Charlemagne.   Accordingly, the second canon of the Council of Frankfurt, A. D. 794, decided that all *adoratio* and *servitus* are to be withheld from images, and that the Nicene Council is to be condemned (Mansi, xiii. 909).

[1] It is possible that, as HAUCK maintains (ii., pp. 268, 271, 275), the Germanic conception of Christ as the rich God, our God, had something to do with this.

2. The Augustinian theology, as is well known, teaches the procession of the Holy Spirit from the Father and the Son (Vol. I., p. 239 f.). The formula, *a patre filioque procedens*, first meets us, excepting in the Athanasian Creed (Vol. I., p. 241), in Leo I. (ep. 15. 1 : *de utroque processit*, in opposition to Priscillian's Sabellianism, *e. g.*, tract 1); then in the confession of faith of a Council at Toledo (in HAHN, ed. 3, p. 210, probably about A. D. 444); also in the confession of Reccared and the Gothic bishops (A. D. 589, HAHN, p. 232 f.); in Gregory the Great (p. 4); and in A. D. 633, 638, and 675, in confessions of Toledo (HAHN, p. 236, 237, 243). From Spain the term reached the Franks. A council at Gentilly, so early as A. D. 767, appears to have pronounced in its favor (HEFELE, iii. 432). In the Confession of Reccared it already appears inserted in the Constantinopolitan Creed (HEFELE, iii. 48). In this enlarged form, the confession was used under Charlemagne in the Frankish church. Certain Frankish monks were called to account for this at Jerusalem. As Charlemagne had, at an earlier day, instructed his theologians to advocate the *filioque* (Alcuin, de processione spiritu sancto; Mi. 101. Libri Carol. iii. 3., p. 269 ff.), so THEODULF OF ORLEANS now wrote a defense of it (de spiritu sancto ; Mi. 105, 239 ff.), and the Council at Aachen, A. D. 809, adopted the doctrine and, most probably, also the term itself. But Pope Leo III. opposed, not indeed the doctrinal position, but the unauthorized enlargement of the symbol (Mansi, xiv. 19 ff.). The latter, however, despite the opposition, maintained its place even at Rome.

§ 39. *Controversy Upon Augustinian Doctrine of Predestination.*

SOURCES. GOTTSCHALK'S († A. D. 868) utterances upon the subject are collected in Migne, 121, 345 ff. Vid. further especially RABANUS, the letters to Noting, Eberard, and Hincmar in Migne, 112. HINCMAR, de praedest. dei et lib. arb., Migne, 125. JOH. SCOTUS ERIGENA, de div. praedest., Migne, 122. FLORUS, sermo de praed., Migne, 119. AMOLO in the Bibl. max. patr. xiv. For Gottschalk, REMIGIUS, de tribus epistolis and Libell. de tenenda immobiliter scripturae veritate, Migne, 121. PRUDENTIUS, ep. ad. Hincm., Migne, 115. SERVATUS LUPUS, libell. de tribus quaestionibus, Migne, 119. Ratramnus de praedest., Migne, 121. Mauguin published a collection : Vet. auctor. qui sec. ix. de praed. scrips. opera 1650; cf. HEFELE, CG., iv., ed. 2, 130 ff. BORRASCH, der Mönch Gottsch., 1868. SCHRÖRS, Hincmar, 1884. J. WEISZÄCKER in Jahrbb. f. deutsche Theol., 1859, p. 527 ff. BACH, DG. des MA. i. 220 ff. REUTER, Gesch. d. rel. Aufklärung im MA., 1875, i. 43 ff. THOMASIUS-SEEBERG, DG., ii. 24 ff. HARNACK, DG., iii. 261 ff.

1. Augustine had incidentally spoken of a double predestination (Vol. I., p. 352 n.). ISIDORE OF SEVILLE yet wrote : '' Pre-

destination is two-fold, either of the elect to (heavenly) rest, or
of the wicked to death'' (Sentent. ii. 6). But in this also the
Augustinians of the Carlovingian age understood their master in
the same sense as had Gregory the Great (cf. p. 22). Then arose
a man who, in a checkered career, had found peace for his soul
in the Augustinian doctrine of election (Mi. 121, 362 and
363). The monk, GOTTSCHALK of Orbais, had met with the
writings of Augustine, although he did not have the whole Augustine. His thought and emotions centered in the unchangeable God, who, of his own good will, elects men or rejects them.
This '' most salutary truth ''was his strength and stay. He paid
no attention to the ecclesiastical machinery, the system of good
works ('' not by merits, indeed, but by the gift of the Father,''
Mi. 121, 372). '' Just as the immutable God before the
foundation of the world through his gratuitous grace immutably
predestinated all his elect to eternal life ; so in like manner all the
reprobate who will in the day of judgment be condemned on
account of their evil deserts has this same immutable God
through his righteous judgment immutably predestinated to
death justly everlasting'' (in Hincm. de praed. 5). God has
not foreordained the evil, but the immutable God has ordained
salvation for the one class and them for salvation—a gift of
grace (*beneficium gratiae*)—and for others through a decision
of justice (*judicium justitiae*), the merited punishment, and
them for it (Mi. 121, 350). Each of these is a good act
(*bonum*, ib. 358). Hence it is said that God '' has predestinated only good things (*bona*, ib. 349). This cannot be based
upon the divine prescience, since God would then be mutable
and dependent upon the temporal (Mi. 121, 353). Prescience merely accompanies praedestination ; by it the justice of
the latter is attested. With Augustine, Gottschalk regarded the
redemptive work of Christ as having reference only to the pre
destinated (Hincm., de praed. 27, 29, 34, 35, and Mi. 121.
367, 372). That this is genuine Augustinian doctrine cannot be
questioned. It became the criterion for the '' Augustinianism ''
of the period.[1]

2. Gottschalk's opponents did not understand him. They
pressed home upon him, as the '' destroyer of the faith,'' the
familiar brutal consequence : '' God makes man sin against his
will,'' and is the author of evil, as, *e. g.*, RABANUS, to whose
attention the matter was first brought by Noting of Verona. At
Mayence, A.D. 848, Gottschalk's doctrine was condemned and he

---

[1] Even the expression, *trina unitas* (Mi. 121, 364) employed by Gottschalk, which harmonizes with the Augustinian conception, was assailed by
Hincmar : *de una et non trina deitate ;* cf. HEFELE, iv. 220 f.

himself delivered for punishment to Hincmar, in whose district his cloister lay. At Chiersy, A. D. 849, he was terribly scourged and condemned to life-long imprisonment.

3. But the matter now only assumed wider dimensions. Influential theologians, such as PRUDENTIUS of Troyes, REMIGIUS of Lyons, RATRAMNUS in Corbie, SERVATUS LUPUS in Ferrières, defended the theory of a two-fold (*gemina*) predestination as the Augustinian doctrine, while, on the other hand, RABANUS and HINCMAR further assailed it.[1] AMOLO and FLORUS MAGISTER pointed to its disastrous consequences. There was a possibility of reconciliation between these opponents, for they were contending more or less about words ; but the controversy between Gottschalk and his adversaries could not be compromised, for he was an Augustinian and they were Semi-augustinians. Such, indeed, were also Gottschalk's defenders at heart. Between them and his opponents the final contention was only in regard to formulas. The latter would apply the concept of predestination only to the election to life, and base reprobation upon prescience (Hincm., de praed. 16; Mi. 125. 424; Raban., Mi. 112, 155); the former spoke, with Augustine, of a double predestination, but likewise based reprobation upon prescience. But both agreed that the baptized and believers are predestinated, which Gottschalk denied. The controlling consideration for the former—but no less for the latter—was that of the dangerous consequences for the church involved in the strict theory of predestination. The sacraments would thus be robbed of their value, becoming a mere form and trifling ; the motive to good works, *i. e.*, the thought of rewards and punishment, would be removed, and thus the moral life, as they understood it, would be destroyed. The terrible bugbear of the predestination sect is exposed for the execration of the age (Amolo bibl. max. xiv. 333 f. Raban., Mi. 112. 1554, 1562. Hincm., de praed. 2. 15, 18 ff., 24 ff. The 5th Canon of Valence in HEFELE iv. 195 ; cf. BACH i., 235 ff.). Kurz says : " The spirit of Gregory for the first time joined issue with the spirit of Augustine, and it carried the day." The will of man has been wounded by sin. When grace heals it, it is free to perform good works. Hincmar asserts, with Gregory, that the good (which we do) is ours and God's : " God's, through prevenient grace ; ours, through obedient free will " (de praed. 37. 21).

---

[1] Scotus Erigena also, though in his own way, opposed Gottschalk : Sin and punishment are nonentities, and as such cannot be objects of the divine will, and hence there is only *one* predestination, *i. e.*, to life. His contemporaries do not seem to have fully understood him, but they suspected his criticism as an "invention of the devil" (Flor. Mag., Mi. 119, 101).

4. The decisions rendered at the two Councils of Chiersy and Valence, A. D. 853, were in harmony with these views. The four chapters of Chiersy accurately reproduce Hincmar's position. (1) The race became through the fall a *massa perditionis.* " But a good and just God elected from this same mass of perdition according to his prescience those whom he through grace predestinated to life, and predestinated eternal life to them. He foreknew that the others, whom by the judgment of righteousness he left in the mass of perdition, would perish ; but he did not predestinate that they should perish, but because he is just he predestinated to them eternal punishment. Hence, they acknowledge but *one* predestination. (2) Grace has made our will (*arbitrium*) free, " by grace set free and by grace healed from the corrupt state." (3) God wishes all men to be saved : " that some perish is the desert (*meritum*) of those who perish." (4) Christ died for all. That his death does not set all free " is the fault of those who are unbelieving, or who do not believe with the faith that works by love." The Augustinian party at Valence, on the other hand, adopted the following statement : " We confess a predestination of the elect to life, and a predestination of the wicked to death ; but that, in the election of those who are to be saved, the mercy of God precedes good merit (*meritum bonum*), and in the condemnation of those who will perish, evil merit (*meritum malum*) precedes the righteous judgment of God. But that in predestination God has determined only those things which he himself would do, either from gratuitous mercy or in righteous judgment . . . But that in the wicked he foreknew the wickedness because it comes from them ; and did not predestinate it, because it does not come from him." Those are condemned who think that " some are predestinated to evil by divine power, *i. e.*, so that, as it were, they cannot be anything else." The work of Christ is held to apply to all who believe on him.[1] At Toucy, A. D. 860, the controversy was abandoned without any decision having been reached (HEFELE, iv. 217 f.). No decision was needed after Gottschalk was removed from the field.

§ 40. *Divergent Views Upon Parturition of the Virgin Mary.*

SOURCES. RATRAMNUS, de eo quod Chr. ex virg. natus est, Migne, 121. RADBERTUS PASCHASIUS, de partu virginis, Migne, 120. Cf. BACH, DG. i., 152 ff. STEITZ, PRE. xii. 482 f.

Various views were expressed during this period in regard to the

---

[1] These declarations were repeated at Langres, A. D. 859, when they seem to have been confirmed by Nicholas I. Vid. Möller, PRE. v. 327.

partus virginis, which attest the growing disposition toward the worship of Mary. RATRAMNUS taught that the corporeal virginity was, indeed, preserved before, in, and after the birth of Christ ; but that he nevertheless entered the world by way of birth, through a being born (*nasci*), but not through a being brought forth (*erumpi*). RADBERT explained, in reply to the question of certain nuns, that it would be presumptuous to say that Christ was born according to the common law of nature. Such parturition rests under the curse of sin, and the "authority of the church," upon the contrary, teaches through the universal (*ubique ab omnibus*) worship of Mary that she remained free from sin in the womb, and, therefore, entered the world without sin (Mi. 120, p. 1371 f.).[1] Yet this was by no means a universally accepted doctrine. Anselm still spoke of the original sin of the Virgin (cur deus homo? ii. 16).

§ 41. *Controversies Upon the Lora's Supper.*

SOURCES. Of the writings of RADBERTUS PASCHASIUS, vid. Liber de corpore et sanguine domini (A. D. 831) and his commentary on Matt. xxvi. Mi. 120. RATRAMNUS, de corpore et sanguine domini, Mi. 121. Cf. STEITZ, PRE. xii. 474 ff., 535 ff. RÜCKERT, der abendmalsstreit des MA. in Ztschr. f. wiss. Theol. 1858, p. 22 ff. DIECKHOFF, Ev. Abendmalsl. im Ref. Ztalter, 1851, p. 13 ff. BACH, DG. i., 159 ff. THOMASIUS-SEEBERG, DG. ii., 33 ff. HARNACK, DG. iii., 275 ff. ERNST, d. Lehre d. h. Pasch. R. v. d. Eucharistie, 1896.

1. The Ancient Church produced no dogma of the Lord's Supper. Two methods of presenting the subject are found side by side without any attempt at discrimination. They are commonly spoken of as the *metabolic* and the *symbolic* views (Vol. I., pp. 196, 301, 323). Pope Gelasius I. taught that "the substance or nature of the bread and wine does not cease to exist, although the elements, the Holy Spirit perfecting them, pass over (*transeant*) into a divine substance, as was the case with Christ himself. And certainly the image and likeness (*imago et similitudo*) are honored (*celebrantur*) in the observance (*actione*) of the mysteries" (de duabus naturis in Christo, Thiel. Ep. pontif., p. 541 f.). The theologians of the Carlovingian period, as Augustinians, were fond of emphasizing the symbolic character of the ordinance, presenting it as a memorial and a symbol (vid. RÜCKERT, l. c., pp. 25, 53). On the other hand, as a result of the growing religious materialism, which found in visible miracles the characteristic trait of religion, and of the widening influence of the sacrificial idea, the conception of a transfor-

---

[1] Cf. already Augustine, de nat. et. grat. 36. 42.

mátion of the elements became more and more clearly defined. All manner of miraculous occurrences in connection with the celebration were related, as that the Christ-child had been seen at the consecration of the elements in the form of a lamb, and his appearance had led many a doubting Thomas to faith (Germanus in Martène Thes. anecdot. v. 96, 95. Radbert, c. 14. Cf. BACH, p. 166 ff.). And even the theologians in their technical discussions spoke of a " consecrating into (*consecrare in*) the substance of the body and blood of Christ " (Alcuin, ep. 41, 163, 90, in Mi. 100, 203, 423, 289).

2. A decisive step was taken in the first monograph upon the subject which we possess. It was written by a monk of Corbie, PASCHASIUS RADBERTUS. In his book, *De corpore et sanguine domini*, the attempt is made to combine the religious conceptions of the church at large with the theory of Augustine, as follows : (*a*) The omnipotent God does whatever he wishes to do. A miracle of divine omnipotence occurs in the Lord's Supper ; there is a creative act, a *creari* (4. 1 ; 15. 1, upon Matt. 26, Mi. 895). The God who created Jesus in the womb of the Virgin without seminal infusion, " to-day, through the consecration of his sacrament by his invisible power, effects (*operatur*) in the substance of the bread and wine the flesh and blood of Christ " (3. 4). Through this miracle the daily sacrifice for the benefit of the world is made possible (4. 1). The inference is : " so that, immediately after the consecration of Christ, the true body and blood are truly believed (8. 2). The body of Christ is, therefore, really present, and this body is in substance the same body in which Christ was born, suffered, rose from the dead, and which he still possesses in heaven (1. 2 ; 4. 3 ; 21. 9). The question as to the relation existing between the body now really and locally present in heaven (in this following Augustine)[1] and the body present at all places in the Lord's Supper, is not discussed by Radbertus. He speaks of the fruits of the flesh of Christ, and cites in illustration the multiplying of the loaves and increase of the meal, oil, etc., in scriptural miracles (7. 2). " From which wholesome field (*i. e.*, the body of Christ) the living bread of flesh and the drink of blood daily grow abundantly for believers, and are reaped by the faithful " (Ez. 21. 3. 2). According to this, the body is present, and yet there is present only a something effected by the body. To the objection, that as a fact that the bread and wine can be recognized as such by the senses (taste. color, form), Radbertus replies, that

---

[1] Vid. Vol. I., p. 323 ; also civ. dei xxii. 29. 4 ; in Joh. tr. 50. 4 ; de agone chr. 20. 28 ; serm. ad catech. 4. 11.

the actual eating of body and drinking of blood would be contrary to human custom, and that, just because of the difficulty in question, belief is meritorious (10. 1 ; 13. 1, 2 ; 1. 5 ; 8. 1, 2). The effect of participation consists in a deliverance "from daily faults and slight sins" (19. 3), in the testing and confirming of faith in the presence of the "visible sacrament" (4. 2 ; 1. 5), and in a bodily unification with Christ : "but even our flesh also is through it restored to immortality and incorruption" (19. 1 ; 21. 2). (*b*) Realistic as this sounds, Radbertus yet moves in Augustine's sphere of thought when treating of the reception of the sacrament. He pronounces it a "spiritual thing," which must be understood *in spiritu* (5. 1). Only those who have spiritually apprehended Christ receive the body and blood (8. 3 ; 6. 2). To the unbelieving they are only apparently offered. "Unless through faith and knowledge (*intelligentia*), of what does it taste but of bread and wine to those who eat?" (8. 2). (*c*) This line of thought seems quite out of harmony with the views noted under (*a*) above. Upon the one hand, we receive actually "nothing else" than the body and blood of Christ (20. 3 ; 1. 6 ; 4. 3); on the other hand, it is a spiritual participation of faith. But we have here to do with a "mystery." Hence *figura* and *veritas* must be side by side : "because the sacrament is mysterious (*mysticum*), we cannot deny that it is a figure ; but if it is a figure, we must inquire how it can be verity. For every figure is a figure of another thing and is always referred to that other thing as being the real thing of which it is a figure." In this case there is a *figure*, in so far as we have to do with the sacraments as evident to the senses ; and there is *verity* in so far as through the word of Christ "the body and blood of Christ are made (*efficitur*) from the substance of the bread and wine." This verity, however, only faith apprehends (*interius recte intelligitur aut creditur*). The relationship is like that between the outward appearance of Christ and his divine nature,—or like that between the letter and the word. The visible is present in order that we may through faith attain to the invisible (4. 1, 2). The idea of Radbertus is : In the Lord's Supper there is both a symbol and a reality. The outward visible and sensible forms, which remain despite the transformation, make it a *symbol;* the body of Christ, which is present, is the *verity*. But only he receives the body who believes that it is offered in these symbolic forms. It is, therefore, through (meritorious) faith, or the right understanding of this symbol, that the body is received. Subjectively considered, everything depends upon the merit of faith and the spiritual understanding of the ordinance. The latter may thus be considered the principal thing. We must not overlook, however, the re-enforcement of the idea of faith with that of merit, and the thoroughly un-evangelical conception of faith.

3. This book of Radbertus might have been written, in its principal parts at least, several centuries earlier ; for its leading ideas are those of the ancient church. It does not lead us be-yond the obscurity which marked the teaching of the earlier age. And yet it is of the greatest importance. It is the merit of Radbertus, that he preserved the eucharist from being entirely lost in the sacrifice of the mass, that he attached to its reception some sort of personal moral effect.[1] It is true, upon the other hand, that his statement of the problem proved portentous for the development of dogma. Without concerning himself about the historical circumstances connected with the institu-tion of the ordinance or about its religious effects, he understands the words of institution as a legal charter[2] (cf. in Matt., in Mi. 120, 890 f.). But the questions which he raised have never since ceased to agitate the church. We may find much in the doctrine to criticize, but we should not forget that the first at-tempt to formulate these problems might have proved different, and might easily have been worse.

4. The views of Radbertus met with opposition. Some thought, he reports (in Matt., p. 890 f.), that only the efficacy (*virtus*) of the flesh, and not the flesh—only the *figura*, and not the *veritas*—is present in the sacrament. Against these he maintains his position, appealing to the words of institution and the fact that the forgiveness of sins is (to be found) only in the very blood of Christ. A new turn of thought was given by RABANUS (vid. ep. ad Egilonem, Mi. 112, 1510 ff.). He too maintains that the true body of Christ is daily created by divine power (*potentialiter creatur*, p. 1512) out of the

---

[1] Apart from all other considerations, this is attested by his assigning to the eucharist a place by the side of baptism and the word : " For Christ has left to his church nothing greater in mystery than this and the sacrament of bap-tism, and also the sacred Scriptures, in all of which the Holy Spirit . . . in-wardly works the mysteries of our salvation unto immortality" (I. 4 ; cf. Vol. I., pp. 196 n., 189, 320 f.). Upon the number of the sacraments, vid. 3. 2 : " But the sacraments of Christ in the church are baptism and unction, and also the body and blood of the Lord." Cf. Agobard, De privil. et jur. sacerdotii, 15.

[2] The external conception of the miraculous element in the sacrament should not be overlooked. It is in keeping with the general conception of God, which was, no doubt, largely due to Germanic influences. The doing of wonders is the chief prerogative of God. Creation is, properly speaking, the only form of activity that is worthy of him. Everything connected with re-ligion is miraculous because brought about, or created, by God. God is power.

bread ; but he denies the absolute identity of the sacramental and the historical Christ. They differ not in nature, but in the form of their appearance : " Not indeed in nature (*naturaliter*) but in form (*specialiter*), that body of the Lord which is daily . . . consecrated from the substance of the bread and wine for the life of the world, and which is . . . offered by the priest, is one thing, and the body of Christ which was born of the Virgin Mary and into which the former is changed, is in form (*specialiter*) another thing " (p. 1514). Thus an idea of great importance for the future was injected into the new dogma.

5. Against the view of Radbertus appeared RATRAMNUS of Corbie in a publication addressed to Charles the Bold. He undertakes to answer two questions : Whether the Lord's Supper contains a mystery which only faith can recognize, and whether it is the historical body of Christ (5). (*a*) The bread, he maintains, remains externally what it is, but, inwardly considered, it is for faith something higher, heavenly and divine, which is seen, received, eaten, only by the believing soul (9). There occurs, indeed, a change into something better (*commutatio in melius*), but this is to be understood *spiritually* and *figuratively*. " Under the veil of the corporeal bread and the corporeal wine, the spiritual body and the spiritual blood of Christ exist." Outwardly considered, it is bread and wine ; for the eye of the spirit, it is body and blood (16. 21). " They are figures according to the visible form ; but according to the invisible substance, *i. e.*, the power of the divine word [the Logos], the true body and blood of Christ truly exist " (49). The Lord is spiritually present through the symbol. " The Lord is known to be present in some manner, and that manner is in figure and in image, in order that the verity may be felt to be the real thing " (84). This is evidently the view entertained, despite the occasional use of such terms as *converti, commutari, confici* (13, 15, 28, 30, 42, 43). (*b*) The second question Ratramnus answers in the negative. "In appearance (*specie*) it is bread, but in the sacrament the true body of Christ" (57). " What appears outwardly is therefore not the thing itself (*ipsa res*), but an image of the thing (*imago rei*); but what is felt and known by the mind is the reality of the thing " (*veritas rei*) (77. 88). Therefore bread and cup are memorial signs, likenesses of that which we spiritually receive (73 ff., 96, 98 ff., 86, 88). (*c*) What then does the sacrament bestow ? The answer can only be : The invisible bread, the spirit of Christ, the power of the Logos (22, 26, 44, 64, 83 f.). Christ, the Word, is therefore spiritually imparted to us through the mystic form of the sacrament. This is the Augustinian view, adapted to

meet the statement of the problem by Radbertus. The religious element which it contains, the spiritual fellowship of Christ, cannot be overlooked. Perhaps Ratramnus would have been able to furnish a more profound and lucid exposition if the problem had not been forced upon him from without and the direction of his thought thus determined for him. The question which he sought to answer was not, how we apprehend Christ in the Lord's Supper, but whether the historical body of Christ constitutes the Lord's Supper.

6. The future belonged to Radbertus, for he had the praxis of the church upon his side. His theory did not, indeed, as a theory secure general adoption ; but the Lord's Supper had become a subject of theological discussion, and the theologians of the age did not get beyond the obscure position of Radbertus. Some already distinctly taught the theory of transubstantiation, as HAIMO of Halberstadt († A. D. 853): "That the substance, *i. e.*, of bread and wine—that is, the nature of the bread and wine—is substantially changed into another substance (*substantialiter convertatur in aliam substantiam*), viz., into flesh and blood" (BACH, i. 213 n.). Others clung to the symbolic view of Ratramnus, *e. g.*, the author of an anonymous tract (BACH, i. 203 ff.): "Thou receivest the sacrament indeed in a similitude, but thou obtainest the grace and efficacy of the real nature " (ib. 205 n. Cf. the "some " who are said to deny the identity of the sacramental and the historical body, in a tract[1] attributed to Gerbert, *De corpore et sanguine domini*, Mi. 139, p. 179). Still others, as the author of the last named tract, called in question the distinction between *veritas* and *figura* (c. 4). Essentially (*naturaliter*) it is the one body of Christ ; in appearance (*specialiter*) we must discriminate it from the latter (5). It is a *figura*, in so far as we see the external bread and wine, but a *verity* when in truth the body and blood are inwardly believed (4). The effect of participation is a quickening of our flesh through the spiritual and bodily substance of Christ for the purpose of its resurrection (9 and 8). It is the position of RABANUS (supra, p. 38) which is here maintained, and it could be easily combined with that of Ratramnus. The discussion did not lead to the final adoption of any form of dogmatic statement.

---

[1] Upon the question of its authorship, vid. HAUCK, KG. Deutschlands, iii. 302 f.

CHAPTER III.

§ 42. *Papacy and Hierarchy.*

SOURCES. DECRETALES PSEUDOISIDORIANAE ed. Hinschius, 1863: cf.
WASSERSCHLEBEN, PRE. xii. 367 ff. DONATIO CONSTANTINI, especially
edited by ZEUMER in d. Festschrift für Gneist., 1888. Cf. FRIEDRICH, die
const. Schenkung, 1889, also KRUEGER in Theol. Litztg., 1889, nn. 17, 18.
SEEBERG in Theol. Littbl., 1890, n. 3-5.

1. To complete our review of the dogmatic history of the
period, we must (1) observe in what particular the hierarchical
conception of the Western church was extended and modified,
and (2) note the influence exerted upon the Christianity of the
world by the church through the ordinance of repentance, whose
history we must trace in outline, leaving details to the province
of Church History.

2. Charlemagne wielded supreme authority over the Western
church, and he recognized the primacy of the pope. These two
facts are the roots from which sprung the great conflict between
pope and emperor. This relation was not changed essentially in
principle, but it was changed in fact, under the immediate followers of Charlemagne. Especially did Pope Nicholas I. (A.
D. 858-67) assert in unheard-of fashion the claim of papal
power, of dominion over bishops and metropolitans, of authority
over princes and the imperial crown. Although his successors
did not always maintain his position ; although weak and unworthy popes, devoid of all political influence, sat after him in
the chair of Peter ; although powerful emperors enforced their
edicts upon the church and made popes prisoners—yet something
remained as a permanent gain to the church. The church in
general believed in the papal idea, and the popes themselves believed in it. The pope stood, in his sphere as sovereign, on an
equality with the emperor. The kingdom of God stands alongside
of and above the kingdom of the world. This was not changed
when, in A. D. 982, Otto the Great secured the rank of Roman
Emperor. Cf. HAUCK, KG. Deutschl. iii. 206 ff., 239 ff.

3. How high-strung were the papal claims is attested by the
Donatio Constantini, which appeared about A. D. 754. The
spiritual emperor is here presented in contrast with the secular
emperor, sharing the latter's glory and dominion, and even demanding and receiving service at his hands. To him, as the suc-

cessor of the prince of the apostles, belongs the primacy over the church of the whole world—and secular power as well (c. 11 ff.).

4. But the hierarchial ideals were carried out to their most extreme details in the Pseudo-Isidorian decretals. It will be necessary for us to note scattered utterances occurring in the document and gather a general impression from them taken as a whole. The priestly estate, particularly the bishops, is exalted in unmeasured terms above the laity. No one should venture to prosecute them before the law, for it is the prerogative of Christ alone to pass judgment upon them (Clem. ep. 1. 32 f., p. 40. Anaclet. ep. i. 3, p. 62 f. et pas.). Christ is the head of the church, "but the priests act by legation instead of Christ in the church." And, just as his church is joined to him, so are the churches joined to the bishops, to everyone according to his portion (Evarist. ep. 2. 4, p. 90). The bishops open and close the gates of heaven, and their decision is, therefore, to be accepted even if they be in error (Clem. ep. 1. 39, p. 43). This applies with especial force to the pope, for it is the Lord's will that the church at large shall be governed in doctrine and life by the Romish church (Anacl. ep. 3. 34, p. 84 ; ep. 2. 24, p. 79. Zephyrin. c. 10, p. 133, etc.). Accordingly, no one but God or the bishop of Rome can sit in judgment upon a bishop (Melchiad. ep. 1. 2 f., p. 243 et pas.).[1] For a fuller discussion see THOMAS.-SEEBERG, DG. ii., ed. 2., p. 187 ff. It was thus definitely settled that the popular catholic conception of the church should prevail, and not the higher ideal of Augustine, although the latter was still, as a definition, employed until even a later period. The church is the hierarchy, or the subjects (*subditi*), who obey the prelates (*praelati*). It is the province of the hierarchical state to direct the secular, since its rulers have the truth and the keys of the kingdom of heaven. There remained some elements of truth in these theories also, but the. falsehood in them was more potent than the truth.

§ 43. *Repentance in Earlier Middle Ages.*

LITERATURE. WASSERSCHLEBEN, Die Bussordnungen der abendl. Kirche, 1851. REGINO, De synodalibus causis et disciplinis ecclesiasticis, ll. 2. ed. Wasserschleben, 1840. Ps.-AUGUSTIN, de vera et falsa poenitentia, Aug. opp. xvii. 1849 ff.[2] SCHMITZ, Die Bussbuecher u. die Bussdisciplin d. K. 1883. HIL-

---

[1] The fraudulent tendency, afterward so prominent, is manifest in these claims (cf. the removal of the episcopacy from the jurisdiction of civil and metropolitan courts). But the chief gain was to the papacy. Nicholas I. accepted the new theory : " The decretal letters of the Roman pontiff are to be accepted, although they are not joined to (*compaginatae*) the codex of the canons." Mansi Coll. conc. xv. 695.

[2] As to the date of this document, which Gratian and the Lombard

DEFRAND, Unters. über d. germ. Poenitenzbb., 1851. MORINUS, Comment. hist. de disciplina in administr. sacr. poenit. Paris, 1651, and Venet. 1702. STEITZ, Das röm. Bussakr. 1854. V. Zezschwitz, System d. kirchl. christl. Katechetik i. 485 ff. K. MÜLLER, Der Umschwung in d. Lehre v. d. Busse, wärend d. 12 Jahrh., in den Abhandl. f. Weizsäcker, 1892, p. 289 ff. HAUCK, KG. Deutschlands, i. 212 ff., 252 f., ii. 223 ff., 664 ff. FUNK, in Kirchenlexikon ii. 1561 ff. LOOFS, DG., ed. 3, p. 258 ff. MOELLER, KG. ii. 105 ff., 206 ff.

1. The praxis connected with public repentance in the ancient church had already in the days of Augustine been to some extent abridged.[1] Upon Germanic territory it had been introduced, both in the episcopal courts established by Charlemagne and in a strict (*e. g.*, Regino ii. 1. ff.) ecclesiastical form (Morinus, l. vii. c. 2 ff.). But this public process was distasteful to the Germans. In England it could not be introduced at all (Theodor, Poenitentiale i. 13. 4, p. 197, Wassersch.), and even in the Frankish empire, despite various admonitions, it constantly lost ground (Hauck, ii. 224 f.). It became practically limited by the general adoption of the principle that " the repentance of those whose sins are in public (*in publico*) should be in public (Hraban. de clericor. instit. ii. 30 ; cf. decrees of the Councils of Rheims, Mainz, Chalons, A. D. 813. Hefele, iii. 758, 759, 765 ; De vera et fals. poen. 11. 26). It was accordingly only gross actual sins which were regarded as demanding public repentance.

2. The custom of Private Repentance now arose and soon largely usurped the place of the public ordinance. It was a form of cloister discipline originating in Ireland and England, and introduced into the Frankish empire chiefly through Columba (about A. D. 700), whence it spread to other countries. It was at first not required, but only urgently recommended (Counc. of Chalons, 813, c. 33. Hefele, iii. 765); but as it grew customary, it became also a positive requirement of the church. The penitential books gave directions to the clergy for interrogating the wrongdoer concerning his sins, and determining the appropriate works of satisfaction to be performed by him. The system was certainly not without beneficial results in that age. The sinner was compelled to scrutinize his whole life in search of his sins ; he was induced to look for and to recognize and

already cite as Augustinian, vid. Müller, p. 292 ff.   10. 25 seems to prove that the author was acquainted with the 33d canon of Chalons (A. D. 813). From various indications I would assign it to the end of the ninth or beginning of the tenth century.   Its spuriousness was detected already by the critical eye of Busch (Erl. ed., 27. 344. Letters i. 34).

[1] Vid. Vol. I., p. 364 n. Cf. Aug. serm. 82, 7, 10 f.: "Those sins are to be reproved before all which have been committed before all ; those are to be reproved more secretly which have been more secretly committed." For further details, vid. Morin. v. 9.

mourn as sins, not only gross outward offenses, but also the inward evil desire itself (Vinniaus, poen. 2 ff., 17. Columba, poen. 23, 35. Theod. poen. i. 2. 21 f. Halitgar, poen., in Morin. append., p. 8a. Reg. i. 304, p. 147), not only mortal sins, but their ramifications (Poen. Merseb. Wasserschl., p. 387 ff. Regino i. 292, 304, p. 146 f. Corrector Burchardi, c. 181, p. 665).[1] And the advice was given, that not only mortal sins, but every sin by which God is offended, be confessed to the priest (Reg. i. 292). If this involves a deepening of the religious life, it is, on the other hand, closely allied to a lamentable superficiality, as will appear if we examine in detail the practical application of the system.

3. The following outline of the theory, while keeping private repentance primarily in view, is applicable also, with such modifications as are involved in the nature of the case, to the public administration of the ordinance (vid. Morin. vii. 1. 21). (*a*) The benignant God is offended by sin (de ver. et fals. poen. 8. 20; 14. 29). Venial sins are absolved (gelöst) by the use of the Lord's Prayer (Vol. I., p. 364 n.); mortal sins, through the fruits of repentance (*fructus poenitentiae*, de ver. et fals. poen., v. 10). It is necessary now to make satisfaction (*satisfacere*) through suitable repentance (*condignam poententiam*, Reg. ii. 429; i. 303: *condigna satisfactio*). The satisfaction consists in bearing the penalty : "whatever of punishment I may be able to devise, that may suffice for thee" (de ver. et fals. poen. 2. 4). Hence, to do penance is to bear penalty (*poenitere est poenam tenere*, ib. xix. 35).[2] This penalty consists in sorrow (*dolor*) of heart on account of sin, which should continue throughout life (dolorem cum vita finiat, ib. 13. 28); then in the *confessio* before the priest (or even before a layman), which in itself brings a large measure of satisfaction (*multum satisfactionis*, ib. 10. 25); and, finally, in the performance of the appointed works of penance. He who has done, or endured, this is worthy of divine mercy, since he has rendered satisfaction to the divine righteousness (it is necessary (*oportet*) in order that the righteous One may righteously show mercy, ib. 10. 25). Reconciliation, therefore, cannot really occur until after the performance of the works of penance (vid. Vinn. poen. 1. 35. Benedikt Lev. c. i. 116. Hraban. de cler. inst. ii. 30 ; cf. de fals. et ver. poen. 15. 31).

---

[1] Vid., *e. g.*, the confessional formula in Reg. i. 304, p. 147 ; cf. Alcuin, de psalm. usu, pp. 2, 9 ; Mi. 101, p. 498 ff.

[2] In addition to this *vindicative* character, the works of penance have also a *medicinal* value. Vid., *e. g.*, Vinn. 28 : " So that it cures and corrects contraries by contraries." Reg. i. 292, 304, p. 148 : *remedia peccatorum ;* cf. Alcuin, de confess. peccator. 3.

But this rule was not observed. On the contrary, it became customary to admit penitents before the expiration of the penitential period to the "fellowship of prayer" (*communio orationis*), and also to full fellowship (*plena communio*) (Theod. poen. i. 12. 4, and many citations in Morin. ix. 16). It might even be granted immediately after the *confessio* and the assignment of the works of penance to be performed (Morin. ix. 17. 7 f.). In such cases, however, the subsequent performance of the required penances was taken for granted, for the sinner was not pardoned through his confession alone (de ver. et fals. poen. 18. 34). The motives for this hastening of the process were of a practical nature, *i. e.*, that the penitent might not be driven to despair or alienated from the church, etc. They are, of course, evident enough in the case of those who secured immediate release from the penalties imposed by the payment of money. He who thus experiences sorrow for sin and confesses the same to the priest has changed his *mortal* into a *venial* sin (de ver. et fals. poen. 10. 25), and is in consequence no longer subject to the punishments of hell. But if he do not now bring forth the "fruits of repentance" in works of penance, he will have to endure the fires of purgatory (*ignis purgatorius*) (ib. 18, 34). (*b*) The sinner applies to the priest; the latter examines him strictly in regard to his sins, assigns the atoning works to be performed, and wishes him forgiveness. The sinner confesses his sin and begs for the *intercessio* of the priest, as well as of Mary and the saints (Alcuin, de psalm. usu, p. 2. 9. Reg. i. 304, p. 147. Halitgar in Morin. app., p. 6b. Corrector Burchardi, 182, p. 666. Beichtanweisg. Othmars, Wasserschl., p. 437).[1] The priest prays to God ("Mayest thou deign to be appeased," *placatus esse digneris*) and pronounces the absolution: "God Omnipotent be thy helper and protector and grant indulgence for thy sins, past, present, and future" (Reg. i. 304, p. 148. Corr. Burch., 182, p. 667. Further particulars in Morin. viii. 8. 1 f., c. 10 f.). The absolution always bears this deprecatory character, partly in recognition of the traditional idea that God alone can forgive sin (August. serm. 99. 9), partly in view of the immediate situation, inasmuch as the pardon (*purgatio*) of sins could not really be secured until the works of penance should be actually performed (*e. g.*, Reg. i. 304 fin.). (*c*) An important feature of the system is seen in the *redemption of penances*. The works

---

[1] The way was prepared for later theories in the thesis: "It is to be believed . . . that all the alms and prayers and works of righteousness and mercy of the whole church combine (*succurrant*) . . . to effect conversion. Therefore, no one can worthily repent (*poenitere*) whom the unity of the church does not sustain" (de ver. et fals. poen. 12. 27; 11. 26).

of penance are chiefly : Fasting (bread and water on Monday, Wednesday, and Friday), discarding of linen clothing, going barefoot, pilgrimages (*peregrinatio*), entering a cloister, scourgings (introduced by Dominicus Loricatus, Petrus Damiani, vid. Morin. vii. 13 f.). It became customary at a very early period to substitute other good works for the required penances. These consisted commonly in prayers and alms, as also scourging, pilgrimages, striking the hands upon a pavement, etc. The German system of legal composition for crime opened the way for the adoption of a definite system for such "redemptions." There were tariffs fixing the character and amount of the works of substitution. It was considered a special advantage of the system that the penitential period could be thus shortened. For example, instead of one day's fasting, fifty psalms might be sung, or three denarii, or perhaps one, be given to a poor person ; for one year's fasting there must be twenty-two solidi given in alms, etc. (Corr. Burch., 187 ff., p. 671 ff.; poen. Merseburg, 41. Canones Hibern., p. 139 f. Beda, poen. 10. 229 f. Egbert poen. 15 f., p. 246). Worst of all, it was considered allowable to hire some righteous person to perform these works (Beda, 8, p. 230. Cummean. poen., p. 463 ; cf. especially Morin. x. 16 ff.). But the most convenient form of "redemption" was by the payment of money, which had a precedent in Germanic law (" Wergeld," vid. Schroeder, Lehrb. d. deutsch. Rechtsgesch., 1889, pp. 75 f., 330 ff., 707).[1] Fixed taxes were imposed, the payment of which exonerated from liability to penance, *e. g.:* " If anyone is not able to fast and does not know the psalms, let him give one denarius per day ; and if he has not the money, let him give as much food as he eats. For one year upon bread and water let him give twenty-six solidi " (Poen. Merseberg. 42 ; cf. 148. Columba, 25. Vinn. 35. Poen. Vindob. 43. Correct. Burch., 2 ff., 50, 190, 195, 198). The Council of Tribur, A. D. 895, first recognized redemption by money also for public penances (vid. Hefele, iv. 558). This praxis was extended through the Crusade movement. The journey to the holy sepulchre was regarded as the required work of penance (*iter illud pro omni poenitentia reputetur*, Council of Clermont, A. D. 1095, vid. Hefele, v. 222). But not only such as actually took the journey were credited with the performance of this penance, but also any person who furnished the necessary equipment for a crusader.[2] Since great multitudes now received

---

[1] On the other hand, it was, in any case, but a step from penance by almsgiving to redemption of penance by money.

[2] The comments of a contemporary, Leo Cassinensis in his chronicle (iv. 11), are worthy of note. He attributes the First Crusade directly to the "pen-

absolution immediately after confession, this became everywhere the usual praxis (Morin. 10. 20, 22). But inasmuch as, by the fixed rule of the church, the forgiveness of sins depended upon penitence and confession,[1] new problems arose leading to further doctrinal definitions. It was necessary particularly to clearly prove the legality of the works of penance as required after the forgiveness of sins had been already granted, as also the right of the church to substitute money for such works of penance and to insist upon confession to the priest as well as to God. To these problems Scholasticism turned its attention (vid. sub.).

4. Both the best and the worst elements in the Christianity of the Earlier Middle Ages come to view in the history of the ordinance of repentance : on the one hand, the vivid sense of sinfulness (cf. HAUCK, ii. 700 f.; iii. 289), which made the whole life of the believer a perpetual penitence (de ver. et fals. poen. 12. 28),[2] and the confidence reposed in the living God as the only One who is able to help ;[3] on the other, the complete externalizing of religion by the theory of the *opus operatum*. Compared with the ancient penitential praxis, there are here new features of great importance : (*a*) The substitution of private for public penance. (*b*) The extension of the sphere of penitential discipline to a wider range of outward conduct and into the realm of inner experience. (*c*) The consequent representation of man's relation to God as a legal one. (*d*) The introduction of " redemptions " for penalties prescribed. But just at this point the logical sequence of the theory was broken, inasmuch as (*e*) the reconciliation of the sinner was, in course of time, made more and more dependent solely upon penitential sorrow and confession. (*f*) This led to a transformation of the conception of repentance, the forgiveness of sins being associated with a

itents " of the age who were unwilling to forego the carrying of arms (Morin. x. 19. 7).

[1] Thus, for example, in Anselm, Meditat. 4 fin., "to be cleansed (*mundari*) by repentance and confession." But forgiveness is located in the *confessio*, since the latter embraces in itself the intention of the repentant one, *e. g.*, homil. 13 : " They are cleansed in the very confession on account of the repentance which they are about to exercise, . . . they begin to work righteousness, and the working of righteousness is their purification " (*mundatio*).

[2] This conception is frequently met with, as already in Eligius of Noyon : *omnis vita christiani semper in poenitentia et compunctione debet consistere* (in HAUCK, i. 289 n. 1).

[3] In contrast with the unevangelical conception of repentance, it may be well to call attention to the emphasis laid upon faith (*fiducia*) in the penitential praxis, *e. g.*, Otmar of St. Gall in Wasserschl., p. 437 : " swell (*surge*) with faith and true credulity ;" cf. de ver. et fals. poen. 5. 15 ; 7. 18. Sorrow for sin is attributed to a divine inspiration (ib. 17, 33 ; cf. Otmar, l. c., p. 437).

penitent frame of mind and confession, and the works of satisfaction with deliverance from purgatory. It was only after this idea had become prevalent that (*g*) repentance could become a sacrament in the strict sense of the term, for only then was there thought of a special divine gift imparted to the penitent, whereas repentance had hitherto consisted merely in a series of human transactions.

Such was the history of the ordinance of repentance from about A. D. 700 until about A. D. 1100. The History of Doctrines must present it with clearness, as an accurate knowledge of it is essential to a correct understanding of the dogmas formulated in the Reformation period. As the permission of the redemptions gave occasion in that age for a certain evangelizing of the conception of repentance, so, four hundred years later, opposition to them led to an evangelizing of the church.

PART II.

CHAPTER I.

FOUNDATIONS OF HIERARCHICAL AND RELIGIOUS IDEALS AND OF SCHOLASTIC THEOLOGY.

§ 44. *The Church and the World.*

1. The historical result of the movements and tendencies within the church from the end of the tenth to the close of the thirteenth century is found in the reformatory ideas which centered at Cluny, and which gradually brought the church under their control. It was an ethical reformation which was sought. A check was to be placed upon the secularizing of the cloisters, the rudeness and immorality of the clergy, and the anarchy which marked the social life, especially under the domination of the robber-nobility. It was a genuinely reformatory idea—the world was to adopt the principles of the church, and the church was to be free from the world. But both objects were sought in the spirit, and by the means, of the prevalent type of piety. The conception of the "City of God" (*civitas dei*) began to be regarded in a practical way, and the "State" of Charlemagne was abandoned. Many measures were employed, such as the revival of the religious practices of Mysticism, increased severity in cloister discipline, celibacy of the priesthood, repression of simony, *i. e.*, investiture by civil authorities, the complete independence of church property. But the movement was soon combined with the effort to realize the pseudo-Isidorian ideals (p. 41), which were interpreted entirely in the interest of the papal power. The mystical piety of the ancient Monasticism, the pseudo-Isidorian writings, and the church property were the ruling motives in the attempted Reformation. The church was actually reformed by it; but in the line, of course, of the motives indicated. It promoted the religious life of the individual, partly by giving a marked impulse to the worship of saints and relics, the craving for miracles, superstition, asceticism, pilgrimages, etc., but also by a real deepening of the religious sensibility.

(49)

Cf. SACKUR, Die Cluniacenser in ihrer kirchl. u. allgemeingesch.
Wirksamkeit, 2 vols., 1892-94 ; HAUCK, KG. Deutschl. iii.
445 ff., 459 ff.

2. The movement for reform opened and smoothed the path
to the realization of the pseudo-Isidorian ideals by the papacy.
This can be studied to advantage in the work of Cardinal Hum-
bert : *Libri tres adv. Simoniacos* (Mi. 143), in which the following line of progress is manifest : Independence of the civil
authority on the part of the church, its officials and property (iii.
3, 5, 10), and therefore of the investiture by secular rulers,
which is simony (iii. 6, 11 f.); denial of the efficacy of the sacraments when administered by simonists, since simony is heresy
and can bring only ruin (ii. 20 ff., 26 ff., 34); summons to insurrection against the civil government (iii. 16).[1] The life-work
of Gregory VII. aided in the attainment of these ideals.   His
ideas form the classical expression of the claims of the papacy in
the Middle Ages.   In the twenty-seven propositions of the
Dictatus attributed to him, they are presented with precision
(cf. especially Ep. ad Herimannum, Registrum viii. 21 ; Jaffé
Monum. Gregoriana, Mi. 148 ; also in Mirbt, Quellen zur Gesch.
d. Papsttums, 1895, pp. 47-64): The Roman church has never
erred and never will err.   Only he is catholic who agrees with it.
Accordingly, only the Roman bishop is *universalis ;* he has authority over all other bishops, whom he can appoint and remove; his
legates outrank all bishops.   The other bishops are only his substitutes (registr. i. 12, 60 ; iv. 11), and it is their duty to support him
even to the extent of furnishing soldiers when required (reg. vi. 17a ;
ep. collectae 13 fin.).   ''To him alone it is permissible to establish new laws according to the need of the time.'' All the graver
matters of dispute in any portion of the church are to be brought before his tribunal (cf. reg. i. 17; iv. 27). ''No section [of a law]
nor book may be regarded as canonical without his authority.''[2]
The pope alone decides matters at councils (reg. iii. 10).   Only
his foot is kissed by the princes.   He can remove emperors, but
can himself be judged by no one.   The canonical ordination
gives him sancity : ''by the merits of the blessed Peter he is infallibly made holy.''   He is not only the lord of the church,

[1] It is interesting to note the two conceptions of the relation of church and
state existing side by side. On the one hand : ''That the laity are forbidden to
take charge of ecclesiastical affairs just as they conduct secular affairs'' (iii.
9 in.); on the other hand : ''Just as the soul is higher than the body and
instructs it, so the sacerdotal dignity excels and instructs the regal, as, *e. g.*,
the celestial the terrestrial. . . . It is the duty of kings to obey ecclesiastics''
(iii. 21).   This is Augustinian, but Gregory VII. still holds the same position.
[2] In Gratian the inscription of Part I. dist. 19, c. 6 reads : '' The decretal
letters are counted among the canonical scriptures.''

but universal dominion (*universale regimen*) has been committed to him, and he is "prince (*princeps*) over the kingdoms of the world" (reg. ii. 51, 75 ; i. 63). Upon this is based the supremacy of the pope over civil governments and their princes. The latter are to receive their authority in trust from him (reg. viii. 26, 23 ; iv. 28). They stand related to him as the moon to the sun (reg. vii. 25 ; iv. 24). Independent dominion on their part is based on sinful pride. As they are notoriously dependent upon the priests in spiritual things, since they cannot administer (*conficere*) the communion, and do not have the power of the keys, so it is a valid maxim that in secular affairs they are subject to the pope alone. He who can bind and loose in heaven can surely do so on earth (reg. viii. 21). "But if the holy apostolic chair judicially determines spiritual things by the original authority divinely granted to it, why not also secular things?" (reg. iv. 2). The power of the keys is therefore the magic key which opens up to the pope all authority (cf. iii. 10a ; vii. 14). Gregory indeed allows to the state a relative independence (reg. i. 19 ; vii. 25 ; cf. MIRBT, Stellg. Aug. in der Publicist. des greg. Kirchenstreites, 1888, pp. 91, 94 f., 96), but it presupposes the willingness of the state to serve the church and obey the pope. Thus Gregory had given currency to an ideal of the papacy whose assumptions could not be surpassed. The infallible pope has authority over body and soul, the world and the church, time and eternity. To this extreme was the Augustinian idea of the *civitas dei* carried. He who opposes the pope is a heretic (*e. g.*, Henry IV. ; vid. reg. iv. 7, 12 ; viii. 21).[1] All these claims rested, in the last analysis, upon the objective effect of the sacrament of ordination. But the hierarchical idea was carried too far by Gregory (cf. Cyprian, Vol. I., p. 184) when, in his struggle against the marriage of priests and simony, he denied the efficacy of the consecration of schismatics and of the sacraments administered by them (vid. reg. vi. 5b ; v. 14a ; iv. 2 and 11).[2]

3. The reform, as Gregory regarded it, brought the church

---

[1] This is a new conception of heresy. In Irenæus, heresy was the denial of the ecclesiastical, biblical doctrine ; in Cyril, rebellion against the ecclesiastical organization (schism). Now it is opposition to the hierarchy.

[2] Vid. upon these conflicting views during the great conflict the exhaustive discussion of MIRBT, Publicistik in Ztalt. Greg. VII., pp. 378-446. The acceptance of the ecclesiastical or of the sacramental conception, alliance with the reformatory movement or adherence to the hierarchical tradition, determined the position taken in each case as to the efficacy of the simonistic sacraments. "In the later sects which rejected the sacraments administered by unworthy priests was reaped the harvest of the seed which the popes of the eleventh century had helped to sow." MIRBT, p. 445 f. As to Gregory's use of the ban and interdict, vid. ib. pp. 202 ff., 219 ff.

into the most intimate relations with secular life. He exalted
the hierarchical idea as no one before him had done, but at the
expense of reducing the church to the position of a political factor in worldly affairs. "The more completely the religious
spirit of the Middle Ages subdued the world, the more entirely
must the church become the world" (vid. EICKEN, Gesch. u.
Syst. d. mittellalt. Weltanschauung, 1887, p. 741). Well did
Bernard write to Eugene III.: "To evangelize is to pasture ; do
the work of an evangelist, and thou fulfillest the work of a pastor"
(de considerat. iv. 3. 6). Even he acknowledged : "Some are
called to the lot of care ; thou to plenitude of power" (ib. ii. 8.
16), and this *plenitudo potestatis* was the dominion over church
and world. Nowhere is the secularization of the church in this
age more clearly seen than in the impress given to the papal
canon law. The church is to be governed by the laws of the
papal decretals. They have binding authority. Collections of
them are made, and they constitute the law of the church. The
body of laws which had been historically developed was increased
by fraudulent additions. But, in the last resort, above this positive law stood the natural law of reason (vid. supra, Gregory's
argument for the authority of the pope over worldly affairs).[1]
The legal manuals (Gratian's Decretal, etc.) were the controlling authority for the theologians of the day upon the nature and
mission of the church. Since the church had become the world,
it was to be governed by the "divine ecclesiastical law." To
portray the struggles between the papal and the national conceptions of fundamental law, which continued until the Concordat
of Worms (A. D. 1122), is not the province of the History of
Doctrines.

Cf. upon paragraphs 2 and 3, MIRBT, Die Publicistik im Ztalt. Greg. VII.,
1894. MARTENS, Greg. VII., 2 vols., 1894. HAUCK, KG. Deutschl. iii.
752 ff., 844 ff. VON SCHULTE, Gesch. der Quellen d. Kirchenrechts i., 1875.
VON DOELLINGER, Das Pabsttum, 1892, p. 40 ff. MOELLER, KG. ii. 283 ff.
MUELLER, KG. i. 436 ff , 447 ff.

§ 45. *Christianity of St. Bernard.*

But the agitation for reform became the occasion also of an
actual revival and deepening of personal piety. The best
thoughts of Augustine were revitalized. Reverent speculation
(Anselm) drew inspiration from his writings, as well as that mystical absorption in Christ which Bernard of Clairvaux († A. D.
1153) so vividly portrayed to the piously inclined in the Middle

[1] Cyprian already appealed—when it suited his purpose—to the "sound
mind" in opposition to tradition (Vol. I., p. 184).

Ages. To gain a knowledge of the compass of his religious thought, we must study his homilies upon the Song of Solomon (Mi. 182). (*a*) The strongest feature of Bernard is the energy with which he leads the souls of his hearers and readers to immerse themselves in the contemplation of the humanity of Jesus, particularly his passion. " For what is so efficacious for the curing of the wounds of conscience, and for the clarifying of the vision of the mind as sedulous meditation upon the wounds of Christ ? " (sermo. 62. 7). We should allow the contemplation of his passion to lie upon our breast like a bundle of myrrh (43. 1 ff.). Thus God draws near to us in the man Jesus, and his love is revealed to us (61. 4 ; 20. 2 ; 11. 9). (*b*) This love now awakens a responsive affection in our hearts (20. 7 ; 11. 7). Devout contemplation of the man Jesus leads us, further, to a blessed union with his divinity. It is the " outgoing of a pure mind into God, or a pious descent of God into the soul. Let it receive him, gliding from heaven, with the deepest emotions and with the very marrow of the heart" (31. 6). Ecstatic contemplation is the personal experience (*proprium experimentum*) (3. 1.) of the soul. It is a blessed and delightful embrace between the loving soul and its beloved (7. 2 ; 73. 10 ; 75. 1 ; 74. 4.). The heavens are opened, new ideas flow down from above into the heart, which, like a fountain, pours forth from within the words of wisdom. There is the bridegroom present (74. 5 ; 69. 6). (*c*) But only he can obtain this goal who produces the fruits of repentance in pious works (3. 2-4 ; 18. 5 f.; 67. 8 ; 11. 2), who follows Jesus as his teacher, and seeks to follow his example beneath sufferings and the cross (22. 7 ; 21. 2 ; 61. 7 ; 47. 6 ; 20. 7). He himself gives the needful power to this end : " I thus receive examples for myself from the man and aid from the Mighty One" (15. 6). " If I with the name call to mind Jesus the man, meek and lowly of heart, kind, sober, chaste, merciful, and conspicuous for everything honorable and holy, and the same as the omnipotent God, who both restores me by his example and strengthens me by his aid." (*d*) But Bernard does not himself attain to a regular and constant life with Christ. The enchanting blessedness of pious contemplation gives place to hours of poverty, vacuity, and obtuseness of spirit (9. 3 ; 14. 6 ; 32. 2, 4 ; 74. 4). From this Bernard did not draw the inference of Quietism, but emphasizes the truth that, in addition to the contemplative life, the active life with the good works of love is also necessary (58. 3 ; 85. 13 ; cf. de diligendo deo 10): Martha is the sister of Mary (51. 2). This is all purely a gift of grace. " Grace restores me to myself, justified freely and thus liberated from the service of sin " (67. 10 ; cf. RITSCHL, Rechtf.

u. Vers. i. 111 ff.). But Christ has two feet, mercy and judgment. If we were to cling only to the first or the second, the result would be most injurious security or despair. We should, therefore, grasp both feet at once (6. 8, 9). (*e*) Bernard here follows a suggestion found in Augustine : " The humanity of Jesus is a way to (his) divinity " (vid. Vol. I., p. 361 n.); but when he, the preacher of Crusades, makes the entire practical knowledge of God dependent upon the contemplation of the good deeds of the historical Christ, he goes beyond Augustine. For him—and in this he fixes the type of piety for the Middle Ages— the whole of Christianity is an *imitation of Christ*. His Christ is not merely a dogmatic formula, not only the eternal judge of the world, but the actual historical Christ, the personal revelation of God, and he led the way in apprehending this Christ in a religious way. But these ideas were interspersed with the demands of the Areopagite Mysticism. Communion with Christ is at best attainable only in the ecstatic state. Hence, in the contemplation of the historical Christ, the soul does not after all experience a revelation of the living and present Lord, and such contemplation is only the bridge by which to reach the ecstatic union.

Cf. NEANDER, D. h. Bern. u. s. Ztalter ed. Deutsch, 1889-90. REUTER, Ztschr. f. KG., 1877, 36 ff. RITSCHL, Geschichte d. Pietism., p. 46 ff. SEEBERG-THOMAS., DG. ii. 2, p. 267 ff.

§ 46. *History of Theology from Anselm to Peter the Lombard.*

BULAEUS, hist. universit. Paris, 1655. DENIFLE, die Universitäten d. MA. i. 1885. KAUFMANN, Gesch. d. deutsch. Univ. i. 1888. HAURÉAU, Hist. de la philosophie scolastique, 2 parts in 3 vols., ed. 2, 1873. NITSCH, Art. Scholastik, PRE. xiii. REUTER, Gesch. d. rel. Aufklärung im MA., 2 vols., 1875-77. PRANTL, Gesch. d. Logik im Abendlande, 4 vols., 1855 ff. UEBER-WEG-HEINZE, Gesch. d. Philos. ii., ed. 7, 1883. RITTER, Gesch. d. Philos., vols. vii. and viii., 1844-45. ERDMANN, Gesch. d. Philos. 1, ed. 4, 1896. STOCKL, Gesch. d. Philos. d. MA., 2 vols., 1864 f. WILLMANN, Gesch. d. Idealism., vol. ii., 1896, p. 321 ff. LÖWE, der Kampf. z. d. Nominalism. u. Realism., 1876. SCHWANE, DG. d. mittleren Zeit, 1882. THOMASIUS-SEEBERG, DG. ii., ed. 2, 55 ff. HARNACK, DG. iii. 512 ff., 419 ff.

1. The term, Scholasticism, is used to designate the theology of the period from Anselm and Abelard to the Reformation, *i. e.*, the theology of the Later Middle Ages. Its peculiarity, briefly stated, consists in the logical and dialectical working over of the doctrine inherited from the earlier ages. The History of Doctrines cannot attempt to present an exhaustive history of the genesis and progress of the scholastic method, nor to note in detail all the doctrines espoused by the scholastics, as it would thus invade the domain of the History of Theology. It is our task simply to trace the scholastic theology in so far as it was influen-

tial in the creation of new dogmas (the sacraments) or in the modification of the traditional dogma (Augustinianism). The material to be selected must be such as will illustrate the influence exerted by the reformatory and anti-reformatory movements (Councils of Trent and the Vatican) in the moulding of dogmas.

As to the arrangement of the material, the question arises whether we shall present the scholastic doctrines as a whole in the various stages of their development (HARNACK, LOOFS), or trace each separate doctrine in its historical development throughout the entire scholastic period (SCHWANE, THOMASIUS). Much can be said in favor of either method ; but we decide upon the former, although in pursuing it we can scarcely avoid some repetitions, for the reason that the historical development can be thus so much more clearly seen. The method cannot, of course, be carried out to its full extent, as the result would be a history of scholastic theology.

2. The beginnings of Scholasticism were closely associated with the pedantic methods employed in the study of theology in the cloister schools (the schools of Tours and of Bec were of great importance) and in the universities, which began to appear in the early part of the thirteenth century. It received an impulse from the revival of interest in philosophy, and particularly in dialectics, which was enkindled and sustained by the study of Aristotle, as from the middle of the twelfth century onward, and especially since the thirteenth century, theologians became, partly through Arabian literature, better acquainted with all the works of Aristotle. But it was also in no small degree the natural logic of the situation which led to Scholasticism. If the traditional dogma was an inviolable legacy, the spirit of the age could be exercised upon it in no other way than in presenting by dialectic methods the evidence of its harmony with sound reason. This tendency first arrested the attention of the church at large in the controversy of BERENGER († A. D. 1088).[1] He appealed in arguing to the *ratio*, and denounced the senselessness (*vecordia*) of his opponents ; but the latter met him with arguments based likewise upon reason (*e. g.*, LANFRANC). There was an ever-widening circle of disputants who either depended solely upon rational arguments or held that faith should at least find confirmation in the deductions of reason.[2] And although there may have been some theologians who were content to simply ac-

---

[1] As to earlier instances, vid. HAUCK, KG. Deutschl. iii. 331 f., 935, 952 f.

[2] Anselm : cur deus homo? i. 2 fin.: "They ask the reason because they do not believe, but we because we believe ; yet that which we ask is one and the same thing."

cept the doctrines received by tradition, theirs was not the future
(vid. HAUCK, iii. 956 f., 963 f.).

Two theologians are to be considered as the founders of
Scholasticism, ANSELM of Canterbury († A. D. 1109) and PETER
ABELARD († A. D. 1142).

The contributions of Anselm to the general history of Scholasticism consist in the following particulars : (a) He possessed a great
talent for formulation, having the ability to express the traditional
ideas in forms which would arrest the attention of his own age.
His work, *Cur deus homo ?* is, *e. g.*, a masterpiece in this respect,
since Anselm here taught his contemporaries to apprehend the
meaning of redemption under the conceptions of the then prevalent penitential praxis (satisfaction). (b) He maintained the
realism of universals. Boëtius had, in the commentary accompanying his translation of the *Isagoge* of Porphyry,[1] left the objective existence of *universalia*, or genera and species, an open
question ; but in the commentary accompanying his translation of
Victorin he pronounced in its favor. The so-called Nominalistic view, according to which the general conceptions are not
realities (*res*), but only sounds (*voces*) and names (*nomina*),
was derived also from a passage in Boëtius, in which the latter
asserts that the reality (*res*) is apprehended by the mind (*intellectus*), and given expression by means of the voice (*vox*).
These problems were discussed at an early period.[2] Anselm
became involved in the controversy through ROSCELLIN of Com-
piegne, who applied the Nominalist theory, that universals are
merely subjective conceptions (breaths—*flatus voci*), to the
Trinity, and thus approached Tritheism (vid. Anselm, ep. ii. 35.
41 ; de fid. trin. 2. 3). This Anselm considered simply foolishness. To him universal conceptions appear as presenting truth
and reality, and the individual species as simply manifestations of
the *genera.* Thought is trustworthy only as it looks to the universal (vid. dial. et verit.). But Anselm did not further develop
these ideas. We have an evidence of his view in the Proslogium
(cf. c. Gannilanum), which presents the ontological proof of the
existence of God, *i. e.*, from the idea of God his real existence is
inferred. The highest can be thought of only as existent ; therefore
God cannot be imagined as non-existent. Existence belongs abso-

---

[1] The passage of Porphyry is as follows : Concerning genera and species I
decline to say, indeed, whether they subsist or are located in the bare intellect alone ; whether they are corporeal or incorporeal substances ; and whether
they are located apart from sensible things or insensible things, and existing in
connection with them.

[2] Vid. PRANTL, Gesch. d. Logik, ii. 118 ff., 41 ff. Barach, Zur Gesch. d.
Nominalism. vor Roscell., 1866 ; also Gunzo v. Novara, Mi. 136. 1294 ; cf.
HAUCK, iii. 331.

lutely to the highest being (c. Gannil. 3 ff.). (*c*) The object of theological research is faith, of which Anselm has a two-fold conception. He first interjects into subjective faith the idea of a striving after knowledge, which leads to the rule : " The Christian ought to advance through faith to knowledge, not to come through knowledge to faith, nor, if he cannot know, recede from faith. But when he is able to attain to knowledge he rejoices ; and when unable he reveres that which he is unable to grasp" (ep. ii. 41). Faith is always the necessary beginning of knowledge. We must always first of all grasp the object as such. Only then can an experience (*experientia*) of it be attained, and this then leads to a knowledge (*intelligere*) of it (de fide trinit. 2). This is the familiar " faith seeking knowledge : I believe, in order that I may know" (proslog. 1 ; meditat. 21 ; cur deus homo? 1. 2). It is a tending toward God (*tendere in deum*, monolog. 75 f.). Just what Anselm meant by this faith becomes evident when we consider the other requirement associated with the above, that the faith of the Catholic church, *i. e.*, the faith of the three symbols (Apostolic, Constantinopolitan, and Athanasian, vid. ep. ii. 41), is to be maintained (de fide trinit. 2 in.), and this even though knowledge (the *intelligere*) in the matter be denied to the intellect (monolog. 64). This faith, accordingly, which reaches a higher stage in knowledge, is the acceptance of the teachings of the church as true, which is at the same time a "tending toward God," and, just on this account, attains its summit in love (monolog. 76 f.). This is the Catholic conception. (*d*) With this conception of faith, it is easy to comprehend how Anselm could undertake (cur deus homo? i. 1 f., 10, 20, 25 ; ii. 9, 11, 15 ; de fide trinit. 4) to establish the faith of the church (incarnation, existence of God, Trinity) " by reason or necessity," and could believe that he had " by reason alone made manifest not only to Jews but even to pagans " (ib. ii. 23) the necessity for the incarnation. The speculative, rationalistic character of Scholasticism is here betrayed. The intellectual independence of the system, the energetic penetration into the nature of things which we observe, for example, in Duns Scotus, has its first great representative in Anselm. Cf. REUTER, Gesch. d. Aufkl. im MA. i. 297 ff. R. SEEBERG, Die Theologie des Duns Scotus, 1900, pp. 3 ff., 599 ff. Ans. Werke, ed. Gerberon, 1675, in Mi. 158-59 ; cf. HASSE, A. v. C., 2 vols., 1843-52. RULE, Life and Times of St. Ans., 2 vols., 1883.

3. Anselm is commonly called the father of Scholasticism, but if we regard the entire movement, the title of honor belongs rather more fully to Abelard. This wide-awake, richly endowed, and keen spirit furnished a wealth of suggestions, both positive

and negative, which continue to exert a marked influence upon
the development of Scholasticism, whereas Anselm's views upon
particular points, even his discussions of the atonement, seldom
find an echo in the subsequent periods.   At one time, indeed,
in the history of English theology, the spirit of Anselm exerted
an important influence.   (a) When Abelard in his *Sic et Non*
(ed. Henke et Lindenkohl, 1851) collected a number of mutually contradictory passages from the Bible and patristic literature, he introduced the method by which Scholastic dialectics
sought to reconcile these discrepancies (Sic et Non, prol., p.
1349, Mi.).   (b) He, too, placed *ratio* beside *fides*.   He opposes as well the "pseudo-dialecticians" who think that they
can prove everything (theol. christ. iii., p. 1226 f., 1212 f.,
1218) as the mere authority-faith, which makes faith rest only
in the mouth and not in the heart.   " Not because God said
anything is it believed, but because it has been proved to be so
it is accepted" (introductio ad theol. ii. 3, p. 1050).   Faith
is the foundation.   Faith, particularly the trinitarian faith, is,
according to Athanasius, necessary to salvation (ib. i. 4 ff.).
Faith is not to be, properly speaking, proved, but only made
clear and probable to reason (ib. ii. 2, p. 1040 ; theol. christ.
iii., p. 1227).   Yet there was in this thinker an independent attitude toward tradition which was foreign to his age.   The writings of the fathers are to be read " not with the necessity of believing, but with the liberty of judging."   Inquiry is the chief
key of knowledge, "for by doubting we come to inquiry, and
by inquiring we discover the truth."   He halts only when
brought face to face with " the excellency of the canonical authority of the Old and New Testaments."   Here no error is
possible.   If it appears so, either the codex or the interpretation
must be defective.   The opinions of later writers may be erroneous "unless it can be defended either by sure reason (*certa
ratione*) or that canonical authority "[1] (Sic et Non, prol. Mi., p.
1347).   These principles are not, however, always adhered to.
In his expositions of the Trinity, as well as in his theory of the
atonement, there is a very prominent rationalistic tendency, as
judged by the prevailing view of the age.[2]   An illustration of his

---

[1] Cf. Reuter, Aufklär, i. 224 ff., 326 ff.   His judgment of Abelard is, however, in keeping with the tendency of the book, one-sided.   He has no sympathy with the healthful tone in Abelard's theology, but sees him too largely
through the spectacles of Bernard.   Vid., on the other hand, DEUTSCH,
Pet. Ab., 1883, p. 173 ff.

[2] Vid. Abelard's tract, condemned at Soissons, A. D. 1121, De unitate et
trinitate dei, ed. STOLZLE, 1891, and also the Theologia christ.   The leading
proposition reads : "Thus it is, therefore, that God is three persons, . . . as
if we say that the divine *substantia* is powerful, wise, good ; or, rather, that it

intellectual independence is seen in his expositions of the Trinity. He maintains the unity of substance and the personal trinity. He teaches, in full harmony with Augustine, "each one of the three persons is the same substance" (de un. et trin. 32, 36, 76), and he rejects Sabellianism; but he thinks that, although the divine attributes and works belong without division to the entire Godhead, yet in a special and peculiar way (*specialiter et proprie*) power pertains to the Father, wisdom to the Son, goodness to the Spirit. That this attempt to interpret the Trinitarian idea was essentially inferior to the method inherited from Augustine will scarcely be affirmed.[1] (*c*) It is to be remarked, further, that Abelard proposed a new method of dividing systematic theology. In the *Introductio ad theologiam* has been preserved for us only a fragment of his dogmatic scheme. This great work was arranged under the headings: *fides*, *sacramentum*, *caritas* (introd. i. init.). Four works have been preserved whose intimate dependence upon Abelard is evident from the adoption of this scheme and from many internal indications: The *Epitome theol. christ.* (first edited by Rheinwald in 1835); the anonymous *Sentences of the Convent Library at St. Florian*, preserved only in manuscript; the *Sentences of Magister Omnebene*, likewise only in manuscript; and the *Sentences of Roland* (afterward Pope Alex. III., ed. GIETL, 1891; cf. DENIFLE, Ab. Sentenzen u. die Bearbeitungen seiner Theol. in Archiv f. Litt. u. KG. d. MA. i., 402 ff., 584 ff., especially 419 ff., 603 ff.). Among the disciples of Abelard was Peter the Lombard, of whom further notice must be taken. Abelard's arrangement of topics preserved in a very marked way for the doctrine of the sacraments the position which that doctrine held in the religious life of the Middle Ages. In correcting the scheme of Augustine's *Enchiridion* by substituting the sacraments for the second heading of the latter, *i. e.*, hope, he proves his dogmatic talent. It is this, too, which, to a great extent has

---

is power itself, wisdom itself, goodness itself" (de unit. et trin., pp. 3, 2, 62).

[1] At the basis of Abelard's theory lies the correct conviction that the interpretations of the Trinity must set forth the three-fold life as *personal*, which is not the case in the analogues of subject and object, appointer and appointed. But Abelard himself falls into the same error when he compares the Trinity with matter and object formed of matter (*materia et materiatum*), and with wax and waxen figure (theol. chr. iv., p. 1288, Mi.); whilst, on the other hand, the declarations that the persons of the Trinity are related to one another as different names for the same object, *e. g.*, *mucro* and *gladius* (de unit. et trin., pp. 51, 6), as attributes to the soul (p. 68), as the three grammatical persons when applied to the same individual (pp. 63, 70), lie very close to the Sabellian theory.

given him such an important influence upon the development of Christian doctrine. (*d*) We must note, finally, the place of Abelard in discussions of the theory of perception. His teacher, WILLIAM OF CHAMPEAUX, had advocated an extreme Realism, maintaining that universals are the true realities, which are present entire and undivided in all individuals, so that the latter do not differ essentially, but their differences are produced simply by the variety of their accidents (Abäl., hist. calamitatum, 2, Mi. 178, 119). Abelard forced his instructor to a modification of this view (vid. Deutsch, p. 103 f., n.). His own utterances upon the question are not entirely clear. On the one hand, general conceptions not only have a subjective existence, but they are called into being as thus subjective by virtue of the nature of things. They are thus objective in so far as begotten of objective things and subjective in so far as existing only in the subject (cf. Glossulae super Porphyr. opp. ed. Cousin ii. 761). Yet, on the other hand, Abelard deduces the species from the genus through the influence of the form, according to the common realistic theory (cf. Prantl, ii. 177 ff.). There are not wanting in his writings, however, utterances which betray a certain mistrust of the conception of universals (vid. Deutsch, p. 106 ff.). His view cannot now be reproduced with certainty, but his limitations of Realism were not lost upon succeeding ages. Works of Abelard, edited by Cousin, 1849-59, in Mi. 178. Cf. Deutsch, Pet. Abälard, 1883.

4. The first half of the twelfth century witnessed a remarkable intellectual activity. On the one hand were those *professores dialecticae*, whose arrogance was so great that, " despising the universal authorities," they thought themselves able to comprehend everything by their little reasonings (*ratiunculis*) (Ab. theol. christ. iii., pp. 1218, 1212 f.); on the other hand, the theology of Abelard and his widespread following (Denifle, Archiv. i. 613 f.). A storm of opposition now arose against the Master. It was charged that the faith of simple believers was ridiculed by him, the mysteries of God emptied of their meaning, the Fathers scorned—that "human genius was usurping all things to itself," that Abelard proclaimed a new "fifth Gospel" (Bernh. de erroribus, Abael. 5. 12; cf. Wilhelm v. St. Thierry in Mi. 180. 249 ff.). Dialectics was declared to be useless and foolish, ridiculous, and even Satanic (JOH. OF SALISBURY, WALTHER OF ST. VICTOR ; vid. Bulaeus, hist. univ. Paris. ii. 402, 629 ff. Reuter, l. c., ii. 16 f. Bach, DG. d. MA., ii. 384 ff.). Similarly spoke GERHOH and ARNO of Reichersberg. The former especially charges Nestorianism upon the dialectics of his time (vid. De investigatione Antichristi, ed. Scheibelberger, 1875, and Bach,

ii. 390-722).[1] Abelard was confessedly vanquished by his opponents at Soissons (A. D. 1121) and Sens (A. D. 1141). The agitation led to various attempts to present the "positive theology" in systematic form. The work of HONORIUS AUGUSTODUNENSIS (Augsburg or Autun), in which he undertakes to embrace in a short compass the entire Christian doctrine (vid. Elucidarium sive dialog. de summa totius christ. theol. in Mi. 172, 1109 ff.) seems to have appeared even before the outbreak of the controversy, *i. e.*, about A. D. 1120.[2] Then came HUGO OF ST. VICTOR († 1141) with his great work, *De sacramentis* and the *Summa sententiarum* (Mi. 176). The chief content of the Holy Scriptures consists of the the works of human restoration (*opera restaurationis humanae*), but for the proper understanding of these the work of the natural state (*opus conditionis*) must first be presented (de sacr. prolog. 2, 3). From this soteriological point of view are the doctrines of Christianity presented for the purpose of promoting a right understanding of the Scriptures. Having first treated of creation, the fall, original sin, etc. (lib. i. pars 1-7), he comes to *reparatio* (p. 8), and presents the work of redemption in harmony with the ideas of Anselm. The great Physician has appointed the sacraments as means of healing (c.12). These therefore constitute the chief part of the work. The principal sacraments are baptism and the Lord's Supper (6, 7). But since the sacraments are *sacramenta fidei*, and since *fides* belongs to salvation (8), part 10 treats of faith ; then part 11 of natural law, and part 12 of the written law. The Second Book begins with a discussion of Christology, followed by a section upon the church, the *ecclesiastici ordines*, etc. The author then turns to the sacraments, "baptism, confirmation, body and blood, and the minor sacraments and sacred things" (ii. 9), simony, marriage, vows, vices and virtues ; then treats of confession and repentance and remission of sins (ii. 14), and finally of the anointing of the sick and of eschatology. Hugo professes to be guided throughout only by the authority of the Scriptures (summ. praef.) Only the faith that has no experience (*experimentum*), and no reason (*ratio*),

---

[1] Vid. also Rocholl, Rupert of Deutz, 1886, p. 189 ff.

[2] He treats first of God, creation, the devil and the fall ; then of the necessity of satisfaction (here using Anselm, vid. I., 8, 16 f., 21), then of Christ's life and activity, the mission of the Spirit, the church as the mystical, and the eucharist as the actual body of Christ. The Second Book treats of sin, predestination (9), the origin of the soul, marriage, ranks, and orders (18), the forgiveness of sin through *confessio* and baptism (20), the prophets and the Holy Scriptures (27), guardian angels and demons, anointing of the sick (30) and death. In the Third Book he treats exhaustively of blessedness, perdition, and purgatory (3). Does i. 2 betray an acquaintance with Abelard ?

is meritorious (ib. i. 11, part 59).[1] However little we may be impressed with the systematic arrangement of this great work, it is very instructive to observe the subordination of the entire structure to the sacramental idea and the disregard of the *ratio*. But already in the Sentences of ROBERT PULLUS († ca. 1150, in Mi. 186), which were accepted by Bernard, the *ratio* asserts its claim along with the *auctoritas* (*e. g.*, i. 12 ; iii. 23), and dialectic investigation begins to appear in the midst of the positive presentation of traditional doctrine. The modern spirit carries the day, but it does so only by making concessions to the ancient spirit.

5. This is most plainly evident in the compendium of a disciple of Abelard, which became the manual of dogmatic study in the Middle Ages.[2] PETER THE LOMBARD († 1160 ; according to some authorities, 1164) in his *Quatuor libri sententiarum* furnished a work which, by virtue of its wealth of materials, its adaptation to the times, and the prudent withholding of the author's own opinions, was admirably fitted to become the basis of further dogmatic labors. The author proposes to set forth faith and the sacraments of the church. He rejects the . . . *garruli ratiocinatores* (i. dist. 4 B) and a "new dogma of their own desiring." He says in the prologue : "We have by the aid of God brought together this volume, in which thou wilt find examples and the doctrine of the greater teachers." His book is, accordingly, a great collection of citations from the Fathers. None the less, however, it is dominated by the *ratio* and the dialectic method. Reason is recognized along with authority (*e. g.*, iv. dist. 4 E ; 15 B). Questions are raised, authorities collected, and a result reached by dialectic treatment ; but in the end the author refrains from a positive solution of the problem in hand (*e. g.*, i. dist. 19 O ; iii. d. 7 N). He crosses swords with Abelard, yet constantly reveals the influence of his method and his teaching. In his positive presentations the Lombard frequently, often in the very terms employed, avails himself of the writings of Hugo of St. Victor and Gratian. Between the Sentences of a

---

[1] The genuineness of the Sentences ascribed to Hugo has been assailed by DENIFLE (vid. Arch. f. Litt. u. KG. d. MA. iii. 634 ff.); but see, on the contrary, GIETL, Die Sentenzen Rol. S. xxxiv. ff. A part of Hugo's Sentences have come down to us as the tract. theologic. of Hildebert of Lavardin (Mi. 171, 1067 ff. Col. 1150 closes with the passage found in Sent. iv. 3, Mi. 176, 121). Cf. HAURÉAU, Les oeuvres de Hug. de St. Vict., 1886, p. 71. As to the spuriousness of the seventh tractate (de coniug.), see GIETL, l. c., S. xl. f.

[2] GERHOH opposed the Lombard, and WALTHER OF ST. VICTOR counted him among the ruinous dialecticians. His orthodoxy was even assailed at Synods (Hefele, CG. v.. ed. 2, 616 ff., 719 f).

certain Master Gendulph and those of the Lombard, there is a manifest relationship. Already in the Middle Ages the Lombard was declared to be the borrower—whether justly or not, cannot be certainly known until the appearance of the work of Gendulph, which is still preserved in manuscript. The Lombard closes the first period of Scholasticism. His dogmatic system is that of the future, *i. e.*, Abelard's method combined with the traditional reverence for authorities.

The Lombard was familiar with the dogmatic works of the Damascene and made use of them.[1] The arrangement of the latter had great influence upon him (Vol. I., p. 285 f.), but he labored also with the Augustinian problems, and treated exhaustively the doctrine of the sacraments. His arrangement, briefly stated, was as follows: Book I. treats of God, his existence, trinity, and attributes; Book II., of the creation, man, sin, liberty, and grace; Book III., of Christology, the work of redemption—and, incidentally, whether Christ had faith and hope as well as love—of the cardinal virtues, the gifts of the Holy Ghost, and the commandments; Book IV., of the seven sacraments and eschatology. If we take a general view of this scheme, its similarity to that of the Damascene will be as evident as its variations from the latter are characteristic. Imperfect as is the plan, defective as its development, and loose its structure, there is yet a decided advance upon the dogmatic system of the Damascene. True, we will seek in vain in either for a real comprehension of the gospel. The Augustinian elements are presented with the Semipelagian interpretation of the Middle Ages. Really, the only feature which challenges our admiration is the consistent development of the doctrine of the sacraments, and here Gratian had already led the way. But it was not only the commendable features of the work, but in even greater degree its faults, that won for it the unique historical position which it came to occupy. It has been printed times without number. The Franciscans have furnished a critical edition in the publication of the works of Bonaventura, vid. vols. i., iv., Quarrachi, 1882 ff. Cf. R. SEEBERG, PRE. xi. 630 ff.; O. BALTZER, Die Sentenzen des Petrus Lombardus (in Bonwetsch-Seeberg, Studien zur Gesch. der Theol. u. der Kirche, viii., 1902. PROTOIS, Pierre Lombard, 1881. Vid. also the

---

[1] It is said of him in i. dist. 19 N : "The greatest among the teachers of the Greeks in the book which he wrote concerning the Trinity, and which Pope Eugene (iii. v. 1145-53) caused to be translated." Another translation is mentioned by Duns Scotus in Sent. iii. dist. 21. quaest. unica, § 4. Then follow citations from the De fide ortho, iii. 6, 4. As to the time of composition of the Sentences, we may accept the years between A. D. 1147 and 1150 (vid. Seeberg, PRE. xi., ed. 3, 631).

Sentences (5 books) of PETRUS PICTAVIENSIS († 1205) in Mi. 211).

The separate doctrines of the period under review must now be examined in so far as they exerted an influence in moulding the forms of doctrinal statement.   Such are the following : 1. Christology. 2. Doctrine of the Atonement. 3. Berenger's theory of the Lord's Supper and the fixing of the church's doctrine upon that subject. 4. Doctrine of the Sacraments. 5. Conception of the Church.   A few further doctrines will be reserved for treatment in another connection, *i. e.*, Sin, Grace, Liberty, Faith, Works.   It is proper for us at this point to call attention to the fact, that the real theological work of the church in the Middle Ages was not performed by the masters of dialectics who followed Thomas Aquinas, but was done in the present period by Anselm, Abelard, Hugo, and the Lombard.

§ 47. *Christology of Abelard and the Lombard.   Opposition of Gerhoh.*

BACH, DG. des Mittelalters, ii. 390 ff.   O. BALTZER, Beiträge zur Geschichte des christologischen Dogmas im 11th and 12th centuries (BONWETSCH-SEEBERG, Studien zur Gesch. der Theol. u. der Kirche, iii. 1, 1898).

1. The Christology of Abelard follows the Western, or Augustinian, type (vid. Vol. I., p. 259 f.). Its fixed premise is : One person in two substances, or natures (*una in duabus substantiis vel naturis persona*). In connection with this, it is maintained with special emphasis, that the immutability of God remains unimpaired.   The incarnation does not involve for God the introduction of a new element, "but we indicate a certain new effect of his eternal will " (introd. ad theol. iii. 6, p. 1104 f., Mi.).   So also the becoming, in his becoming man, is not to be understood in the strict sense of the word.   There is in the incarnation no *mutatio* of the divine nature, and the proposition, God is man, can be understood only in a unliteral sense : *nec homo esse proprie dicendus est* (ib., p. 1107 f., 1106).[1]   As to the mode of union of the divine and the human natures in Christ, Abelard reproduced the orthodox formulas, but yet gave a peculiar turn to the thought.   Christ is the man assumed by the Word (*assumptus a verbo*); this man now fulfills in all things the will of the divinity dwelling within him.   " That this assumed man never sought to do anything because he hoped that it would be agreeable to him-

---

[1] Abelard makes the remark that " transfers of names are often made from the whole to the parts, or from the parts to the whole, *e. g.*, when it is said of the Son of God that he is born (exposit. symb., p. 626, Migne); cf. DEUTSCH, Abelard, p. 302 n.

self, but because he believed that it would be pleasing to God (expos. of Rom. v. 15, p. 963).[1] Thus, at this point also, the keen-witted man indicated a needed modification of the church's teaching by locating the union of the divine and human natures in the sphere of the will or person.[2] Yet he might, not without reason, be charged with Nestorianism.

2. The Lombard, of course, adopts the formulas of the church. The second person of the Godhead assumed the impersonal human nature (sent. iii. dist. 5 C): " he assumed the flesh (*carnem*) and soul (*animam*), but not the person (*personam*), of a man." But he was greatly exercised over the question, whether the humanity of Jesus was not, after all, to be conceived of as a *persona*, deciding in the negative, because at the time of the assumption body and soul had not yet been combined into one person (*in unam personam*), (iii. d. 5, A, D, E; d. 10 C). "The intellectual development of Jesus was, accordingly, only apparent," not, indeed, in himself, but in others (*in aliis*) (iii. d. 13 B). In treating of the question, whether the Son in the incarnation *became* anything, the Lombard betrays his affiliation with Abelard, since he, though only by silence, indicates his preference for the view, that the Logos merely assumed human nature like a garment in order that he might be visible to human eyes. Thus the Logos-person remains " one and the same unchanged " (iii. d. 6 F; d. 10). God has become man, because he " has a human nature " (*est habens hominem*, iii. 7 K). Since, in this case, the human nature is not to be conceived as personal, it was inferred by some that " Christ, according to his human nature, is not a person nor anything " (iii. 10 A, see also GIETL, p. 179), but not a word can be cited from the Lombard in support of this absurd proposition. The view, which was called Nihilianism, was disapproved by Alexander III., A. D. 1163 and 1179.[3] As a consequence of the sharp discrimination between the divinity

---

[1] This way of regarding the relationship became current in the school of Abelard. Christ is " The Word possessing the man " and "the man possessing the Word" (*verbum habens hominem* and *homo habens verbum*), (epitome 24 extra Rol. sent., p. 171 f., 180. Omnebene in Denifle, Archiv. i. 466 f.). Roland here further appeals, and rightly, to Augustine (against Gietl, p. 175 n., vid. Aug. in Joh. tr. 19, 15; cf. Hilarius, de trin. x. 22, Mi. 10, 360, supra, p. 28). The view is clearly stated, Epit. 24, p. 1733, Mi.: "Thus that soul was subject to the Word, so that it could give no motion to the body except as far as the Word inspired." Vid. also c. 25, *de volunt. assumpti homin.*

[2] The problem of Christology is to be solved, not in the sphere of nature, nor of attributes, but of the person.

[3] Not condemned. Vid. REUTER, Gesch. Alex. iii., vol. iii. 703 ff. HEFELE, v. 618, 719.

5

and humanity, it was held that divine worship (*latria*) was not to be rendered to the human nature of Christ, but only servitude (*dulia*) (iii. d. 7), and that the sufferings of Christ were, as to substance, limited to his human nature (iii. d. 15 D). This formally orthodox conception of the subject receives its peculiar coloring on the one hand from the difficulty of a rational combination of the divine and the human, and on the other hand from the influence of the Augustinian Christology.

3. But contemporaries felt bound to condemn these views as Rationalism and Adoptionism. The most elaborate presentation of the subject in opposition was made by GERHOH of Reichersberg. He follows in the path of Cyril. He starts with the concrete God-man, in whom divinity and humanity are united, in nature as well as in person.[1] This union is not impossible, since the finite is capable of comprehending the infinite.[2] Gerhoh proves the importance of his view by its practical bearing upon the doctrine of salvation. Since God became man, human nature has been raised to the right hand of God, and a fire has entered human nature which destroys sin. The God-man is as man our way and example, and as God the truth and the life (*e. g.*, de investig., antichr. ii. 1, p. 190 f.). According to this view, the Nestorianism of the age is a curse. Christ, the one God-man, is "to be adored with one adoration" (de glor. et honore fil. hom. 12. 3, Mi. 194. 1114). Another inference relates to the presence of Christ in the Lord's Supper. Christ can at the same moment be in a thousand places at once. "And whence this unless because the same spiritual body has risen above all limitation of places and times . . . For neither is Christ, who, just as he wishes, is everywhere, to be thought of as corporeally in one place, however beautiful or desirable" (de invest. ii. 51, p. 299 f. Similarly, ARNO of Reichersberg, vid. Bach, ii. 685). Thus the balder Western theory was in the early stages of Scholasticism opposed by the ancient Alexandrian Christology. See the writings of Gerhoh cited p. 60, and Mi. 194. Cf. BACH, DG. ii. 390 ff.

§ 48. *Doctrine of Atonement. Anselm and Abelard.*

1. In his work, *Cur deus homo?* Anselm made the first attempt to present in a harmonious and consistent way the doctrine of

---

[1] The one and the same Christ is "at the same time a divine and a human person," in proof of which it is naively argued that, as when a person becomes good he is not thereby doubled, so also Christ did not duplicate his person when his divine person became the human person (de investig. antichr. ii. 40, p. 278).

[2] The perfectly pure humanity in Christ was, as a white cloud, capable of

the work of redemption (salvation). He seeks to prove upon rational grounds the necessity of the incarnation and redemption, although the omnipotence of God could have stood in no need of these (i. 6). Of any claim of the devil upon man, he knows nothing (i. 7 ; cf. medit. ii.). In addressing himself to the solution of the problem, he proceeds upon the assumption that man can attain salvation only through the forgiveness of sins (i. 10, extr.). Sin consists in the creature's withholding from God the honor which is his due. " He who does not render to God the honor due, robs God of that which is his and dishonors God, and this is to sin " (i. 11). Man has thus violated the obligation laid upon him as a rational being. The expectation sometimes cherished, that the divine mercy will remit sins, cannot be met, because the non-punishment of sin unatoned for would bring disorder into the kingdom of God, " but it is not proper that God should overlook anything disorderly in his kingdom " (i. 12). But order is preserved by righteousness. " Nothing is less to be tolerated in the order of things than that the creature should withhold the honor due to the Creator— should not render that which he withholds " . . . " God therefore preserves nothing with more just cause than the honor of his majesty." From the necessity of maintaining the order of the divine government and the honor of God is deduced the rule : " It is therefore necessary, either that the honor withheld be rendered, or that punishment follow " (i. 13). By either means the divine honor is vindicated—in the one case, since God thus displays himself as the Lord of the rebellious man (i. 14); in the other, in that the guilty one by a willing satisfaction for his offense re-establishes the violated order. Thus the above-cited rule assumes the form : It is necessary that satisfaction or punishment follow every sin (i. 15). But God has not pursued the way of punishment, or man would have gone to ruin and God would not have accomplished his purpose (ii. 4). God chose the way of satisfaction. Since men are to fill up the number of the angels who fell (i. 16 ff.), God cannot accept them as sinners (i. 19). Satisfaction must however be subject to the rule : " It does not suffice merely to restore that which was withheld ; but, for the contumely inflicted, he ought to restore more than he withheld " (i. 11). But since the most trifling sin, as an improper glance, weighs more than the whole world, a satisfaction must be rendered to God which is more than all things outside of God (i. 20 ; ii. 6). And since man dishonored God by sub-

receiving the divine light, and that light was capable of imparting itself to it. Bach, DG. ii. 425.

mitting to the devil, satisfaction in this case must include the conquest of the devil by man—under more trying circumstances (i. 22 f.; ii. 11). As, on the one hand, the satisfaction required is so great and comprehensive, so, on the other hand, man is absolutely incapable of rendering it, for whatever good he may do he is already under obligation to render to God, and it cannot therefore be taken into consideration as *satisfactio* (i. 20). Satisfaction of the character demanded only God can render. But a man must render it, one who is of the same race, in kindredship with humanity (ii. 8): (Unless there be a satisfaction), " which no one except God can render and no one but man owes : it is necessary that the God-man render it." The God-man must do for the honor of God something which he is not already under obligation to do. This cannot be the obedient fulfilling of the will of God, since this every rational creature is under obligation to render. But the free surrender of his infinitely precious life to death will suffice (ii. 11). The infinite value of this life is more than sufficient as a payment of all the sins of the whole world (ii. 14 fin.; 17). Thus the incarnation and sufferings of the God-man are necessary as a satisfaction rendered to the divine honor. Only incidentally does Anselm indicate a connection of Christ with humanity, speaking (ii. 11 fin.; 19 init.) of the instruction and example which Christ was able and desired to give to men ; but the two points of view are not expressly and clearly combined. This oversight explains why Anselm is so lacking in clearness when he attempts to show how the result of the work of Christ inures to the benefit of mankind. The Father cannot suffer the *meritum* of Christ to go unrewarded, or he would be either unjust or impotent. Since he cannot give anything to the Son, who needs nothing, the reward accrues to the advantage of those for whom the Son died. " To whom should he more appropriately attribute the fruit and reward of his death than to those for whose salvation . . . he made himself man and to whom by dying . . . he gave an example of dying for righteousness ; for in vain will they be imitators of him if they shall not be participants in his merit ? " (ii. 20). " Thus the sins of mankind are remitted " (ib.) In this way the divine justice is preserved as well as mercy (ii. 21). And thus also the doctrine of the Scriptures is proved " by reason alone " (*sola ratione*, ii. 23).

This discussion is of importance as the first attempt to present a connected view of the work of Christ.[1] It is a master-

---

[1] Gregory the Great is to be specially mentioned as a forerunner of Anselm (p. 19). As to Augustine, vid. Vol. I., p. 361 n.

piece, because the author really understands the subject under discussion and makes it intelligible to others. The cross of Christ, which was so often mentioned in pretentious phrases, was here recognized in clearly defined language as a means of salvation. Anselm anticipates the scholastic method, combining logical demonstration with juristic principles. The argument is based upon the (Germanic) legal maxim, which dominates the book : punishment or satisfaction (*poena aut satisfactio*).[1] Of special interest is the attempt of Anselm to deduce the divinity of Christ from his work. Whereas the ancient Greek theology, when speaking of the work of Christ in such connections, had in mind his "deifying" activities, Anselm sought to prove the necessity of his divinity from his sufferings and death. At all events, a proper recognition must be given to the effort of Anselm, not simply to accept the divinity of Christ in a merely external way as a dogma, but to understand it in its inner necessity, and none the less to his tact in bringing the matter home to the hearts of his generation by connecting it with the penitential practices of the day. On the other hand, the serious faults of the treatment of the subject are very apparent : (*a*) Anselm recognizes only a legal relationship between God and man—not, indeed, a personal legal relationship, but that of a subject to his legal ruler. (*b*) Redemption is based in a very one-sided way upon the death

---

[1] Cf. CREMER, Die Wurzeln d. anselm. Satisfactionsbegr., Stud. u. Krit., 1880, 7 ff., and ib. 1893, 316 ff. The attempt is here made to trace the dependence of Anselm's theory upon the fundamental principle of the Germanic legal system, *poena aut satisfactio*, showing that the principle of a substitution for penitential penalties was transferred from the penitential discipline (supra, p.45) to the doctrine of the atonement. Cf. BRUNNER, Deutsche Rechtsgesch. i. 163: "The right of challenge belonged only to the offended party or his blood relative. It depended upon the choice of the relative, whether the offender with his relatives should respond to the challenge (*die Feindschaft tragen*), or render the *compositio* fixed by law." The validity of this association of ideas has indeed been recently called in question from the juristic point of view (vid. Von Möller, Stud. u. Krit., 1899, p. 627 ff.). Möller shows that the Germanic penance through money has itself a primitive character, and that the idea of substitution is not embodied in German jurisprudence. According to this, the parallelism, "*aut poena aut satisfactio*," is not specifically German. Nevertheless, the general conception of the subject may be characterized as Germanic. It is only in the light of this system of procedure that we can understand the inner harmony of the transaction as viewed by Anselm, the emphasis laid upon the divine honor, the princely mildness in the conception of God (ii. 16), the substantial character of the service rendered by Christ (cf. WERGELD), the importance attached to the racial-relationship of Christ to mankind, since only a relative could perform specific works of satisfaction. The introduction of the idea of *meritum* is beset with difficulties (cf. Gregory, p. 20). In other connections also Anselm attributes to the sinner the obligation of rendering satisfaction (*debitum satisfaciendi*); vid. De conceptu virginal. 2.

of Christ, the latter being, under the influence of the juristic conception of the *satisfactio*, regarded as a material contribution. (*c*) The connection between the active life and the sufferings of Christ is not made clear. (*d*) The transfer of the benefits of the work of Christ to the church is not intelligibly stated. (*e*) Above all, the change in the attitude of God toward the sinner which Anselm maintains cannot be made intelligible from a religious point of view by the means which he employs, etc.

Cf. BAUR, D. chr. Lehre v. d. Versöng., p. 155 ff. HASSE, Ans. ii. 485 ff. CREMER, l. c. RITSCHL, Rechtfertigung, u. Versönung. i. ed. 2, 33 ff. HARNACK, iii. 341 ff., as also the presentation of the subject by Duns Scot. in Sent. iii. dist. 20 qu. un.

2. If we leave out of the account the theory of redemption as a ransoming from the devil, which Anselm rightly disowned, we will find in the theological contributions of the West, in addition to the soteriological construction of Anselm, especially that conception of the divinity of Christ in which he appears as revealing the love of God, and, by teaching and example, leading to responsive love and piety. It was perfectly natural that this view should soon assert itself in opposition to the theory of Anselm, as it did in the person of Abelard (vid. RITSCHL, l. c., i., ed. 2, 48 ff. SEEBERG, Die Versönungslehre Ab. u. ihre Bekämpfung durch Bernh. in Mitteil. u. Nachr. f. d. ev. K. in Russl. 1888, 121 ff.; also in Thomas. ii., ed. 2, 124 ff. MOURIER, Abél. et la rédemption, thèse Montaub. 1892). In his commentary upon Romans (under Rom. 3. 22 ff.), Abelard develops his doctrine of the atonement. He, too, rejects the theory of a meeting of the claims of the devil. Redemption has to do only with the elect, over whom the devil never had any power. Furthermore, the devil cannot by the wrong perpetrated upon mankind have gained any right over them. He can be regarded only a jailer and torturer, to whose power God commits men. God could before the death of Christ forgive the sins of men, as he did in the case of the Virgin Mary. To what end then did the Son of God take upon himself the burden of his sufferings? If Adam's slight offense required so great an atonement, what atonement will the slaying of Christ demand? Shall we think that God was pleased by the death of his Son, that he on account of this greater sin forgave the less? And to whom should the ransom of the blood of Christ be paid? Not to the devil; hence, to God. But is it not improper that the blood of the innocent should be demanded as a ransom? Can God have pleasure in the death of his Son, so that through it he should be reconciled to the whole world? (Mi. 178. 833-36). There-

fore the opinion of Anselm, that God is reconciled by the death of Christ, is disproved.

Abelard's positive statement of the doctrine is as follows: Through the works of the law no one could have become righteous. But in Christ the love of God was made manifest, in that he assumed our nature, and, as our teacher and example, remained faithful unto death. This love of God admonishes us to an answering love toward God and awakens it in us. By virtue of our faith in the love of God made manifest in Christ, we are united with Christ, as with our neighbor, by an indissoluble bond of love. The love thus awakened in our hearts is the ground of the forgiveness of sins, according to Lk. 7. 47. The phrase in Rom. 3. 25, "for the display of his righteousness," Abelard understands as referring to the righteousness imparted to men, that is, "of the love which justifies us before him" (p. 833). Thus we are redeemed from sin and from fear, since Christ works love in us. "Our redemption, therefore, is that supreme love in us, through the sufferings of Christ, which not only liberates from the servitude of sin, but acquires for us the true liberty of the sons of God, so that we fulfill all things from love rather than from fear of him who has shown to us such grace that, as he himself declares, no greater can be conceived" (pp. 836, 832 f.).[1] Side by side with this line of thought we find another. Under Rom. 5. 12 ff., Abelard declares that Christ, in becoming man, subjected himself to the commandment of love for others. This law he fulfilled "both by instructing us and by praying for us." It is in this way, since his prayers must on account of his righteousness be heard, that Christ "supplements from his merits what was lacking in ours" (p. 865). As instruction is still given by Christ (p. 859), so also his mediation through prayer in behalf of his followers continues (cf. serm. 10, p. 449). We are, therefore, redeemed through Christ, "dying once for us and very frequently praying and diligently instructing us" (p. 861).[2] The view of Abelard is thus evidently : God sent his Son to the sinful human race as a revelation of his love, and as a teacher

---

[1] Cf. 836 : But to us it seems that by this means we are justified in the blood of Christ and reconciled to God ; that through this particular favor manifested toward us, that his Son assumed our nature and persisted even until death in instructing us both by word and by example, he has very strongly drawn us to himself through love, so that, inflamed by this great benefaction of divine grace, true love now shrinks not from the endurance of anything whatsoever.

[2] The other passages which claim attention in this connection (serm. 5, p. 419 f.; serm. 12, p. 481 ; serm. 10, p. 452, in Com. to Romans, p. 860) all fall into place naturally in this line of thought, as shown in my comments, l. c., p. 131 ff.

and example.   By this means faith and love are aroused in sinful
men. This love becomes the ground of the forgiveness of their sins.
On the other hand, the love of Christ leads him to continue to
teach men and to intercede for them before God.   Thus their insufficient merits are completed.   But when Abelard now, in
response to the inquiry, why it was the Son and not the Father
who became man, declares that the Son, or the divine Wisdom
(supra, p. 59), became man, in order to instruct us by word
and example (theol. christ. iv. p. 1278 f.   Cf. serm. 5, p. 423),
it would seem that the former line of thought was the dominating one in his theology (cf. SEEBERG, l. c., p. 136 ff.).   This
theory derives from the treasures preserved in the traditional
theology of the church certain views which serve to counterbalance the one-sidedness of Anselm.   It was in harmony
with the medieval form of piety, since it represented the pious
walk of love as the aim of redemption.   There is lacking,
indeed, as in Anselm, the association of the work of Christ with
the institution of the sacraments.   If the latter were, in the
medieval conception, the vehicles of salvation for the regenerate,
then must they be expressly made intelligible as a product of the
work of salvation.   But as, in Abelard's expositions of the subject, no specific importance attached to the death of Christ, he
fell into the error of one-sidedness in the opposite direction.

3. Abelard's doctrine of the atonement was in turn assailed by
ST. BERNARD (vid. ep. 190, and SEEBERG, l. c., p. 143 ff.). Abelard, he contended, curtails Christianity, making Christ only a
teacher.   In reality, Christ brings the forgiveness of sins and
justification, and releases from the bonds of the devil (7. 17 ; 8.
20).   Just as little as the example of Adam made us sinners does
the example of Christ suffice for our redemption (8. 22 ; 9. 23).
No place, he holds, is reserved for the blood and the cross of
Christ in the system of Abelard, "who attributes everything
pertaining to salvation to devotion (*devotione*), nothing to regeneration, . . . he locates the glory of redemption, . . . not in
the value of the blood, but in its effects in our walk and conversation " (9. 24).   It is certain, indeed, that the example of the
love of Christ is great and important, "but they have no foundation, and hence no tenable position, if the foundation of redemption be wanting. . . . Therefore neither examples of humility
nor proofs of love are anything without the sacrament of redemption " (9. 25).   Instruction (*institutio*) or restoration (*resti-
tutio*), that is the question (9. 23). Bernard made practical use,
perhaps to a greater extent than Abelard himself, of the latter's
method, maintaining that we should meditate upon the love of
Christ in order to be incited to a responsive love toward him (in

Cant. serm. 16. 5 ; 43. 1-3). He is our teacher and example (ib. serm. 15. 6 ; 43. 4 ; 22. 7 ; 21. 2 ; 61. 7 ; 47. 6 ; 20. 7 ; 24. 8). But the other aspect of the doctrine is also made prominent. The blood of Christ is the " price of our redemption. Unless he had tenderly loved, his majesty would not have sought me in prison. But to affection he joined wisdom, by which he might ensnare the tyrant, and suffering, by which he might appease the offended God the Father" (vid. 20. 2). Bernard constructed no theory ; but the association of the two conceptions—the love of Christ begets love in response, he is teacher and example ; the blood of Christ redeems us from sin, death, and the devil, and effects the reconciliation of the Father—presents the general view of the subject which prevailed in the Middle Ages.

4. The central thought of Abelard was perpetuated in his followers. Thus, the author of the *Epitome* answers the question, *Cur deus homo ?* with a reference to true love and a good example (chap. 23, p. 1731, Mi.). And the Sentences of St. Florian assert that redemption was wrought " in the person of the Son " in order that, as often as we should recall the love which he has shown for us, we might abstain from sin. We have ourselves, " on account of the wonderful love which he has shown toward us," freed ourselves from our subjection to the devil (*Denifle*, archiv. i. 431). But the other contemporary theologians share the attitude of Bernard, *i. e.*, of Anselm. HONORIUS AUGUSTO-DUNENSIS repeats the thoughts of Anselm (elucidar. i. 8, 16, 17, 21). Hugo likewise reproduces him. It is necessary to "appease God," and this is accomplished by making good the damage (*damnum restaurare*) and making satisfaction for the insult (*de contemptu satisfacere*). This the God-man does. Even if this method of redemption cannot be shown to be necessary, yet it is the most appropriate, inasmuch as the magnitude of our guilt and of the future glory is thus set forth (de sacr. i. 8. 4, 6, 7, 10 ; ii. 1. 6). ROBERT presents both views. Christ has freed us by his sacrifice rendered to God, not to the devil (sent. iv. 14). This was the most appropriate, though not the only possible, way of effecting redemption (iv. 15). It is an appropriate way, because it makes known to us the magnitude of our sin and of the divine love (iv. 13). The work of redemption is, here too, presented under the aspect of instruction and example (iii. 28).

5. PETER LOMBARD, in his discussion of the problem in the 18th and 19th *Distinctions* of his third book, betrays as well his dependence upon Abelard as his correctness from the ecclesiastical point of view. His starting point is the *merit of Christ*. By his pious life Christ merited for himself glorification and free-

dom from suffering (18 A, B). His death occurred therefore
" for thee, not for himself " (18 E). And by it he merited for
us admittance to paradise and redemption from sin, punishment,
and the devil. " Christ the man was a sufficient and perfect
hostage," *i. e.*, for our *reconciliatio* (18 E). According to this,
it may be asked *how* this deliverance from the devil, sin, and
punishment is effected by his death. To this it is replied, first
of all, with Abelard, that the death of Christ reveals to us the
love of God. " But so great a pledge of love toward us being
displayed, we also are moved and inflamed to love God . . .
and through this we are justified, *i. e.*, being released from sins
are made righteous. *Therefore the death of Christ justifies us,
since through it love is excited in our hearts.*" But this occurs
also, according to Paul, through faith in the Crucified. When
we are thus freed from sin, we become free also from the devil.
But this thought is defaced by the reminiscence from an earlier
age, that the cross became a mousetrap and the blood a bait for
the devil (19 A). The fundamentally Abelardian tendency of the
author is revealed also in the remark (19 F), that we are reconciled
to God, who has *always* loved us, by the removal of our sins and
hostility toward God. Prominence is also given to the objective
aspects of redemption. God became man in order to overcome
the devil, because a man or an angel might easily have himself
fallen into sin (B). It is further held that Christ delivers us from
everlasting punishment by remitting our debt (*relaxando debitum*) (C), and also from temporal punishment, which is remitted in baptism and ameliorated in repentance : " For that
penalty could not suffice by which the church binds penitents,
unless the penalty of Christ, who absolves for us, co-operates "
(D). Thus, according to the Lombard : (*a*) Christ has merited
deliverance for us through the *meritum* of his death, since the
suffering endured by him works for our deliverance. (*b*) He
has overcome, *i. e.*, captured the devil. (*c*) His death has
awakened us to love and thereby made us righteous and delivered
us. Of especial interest for us is the prominent introduction of
the conception of the *merit of Christ* and of his endurance of
punishment, and we are particularly impressed by the lack of
clearness in the adjustment of the ideas presented in their mutual
relations. Thus the idea of redemption did not attain a fixed
or complete form in the present period, but the component elements were distinctly wrought out.

§ 49. *Berenger of Tours and Doctrine of Lord's Supper.*

SOURCES. BERENGER († 1088) wrote : Epistola ad Adelmannum and Liber
de sacra coena adv. Lanfrancum (ed. A. and F. Vischer, 1834). LANFRANC

(† 1089): De corp. et sang. domini adv. Ber. Tur., in Migne 150. 407 ff. Cf. Sudendorf, Berangarius Tur., 1850. SCHNITZER, Ber. v. Tours, 1890. DIECKHOFF, Abendmalslehre im Ref.-zeitalter, i. 44 ff. REUTER, Gesch. der rel. Aufklärung im MA. i. 91 ff. SCHWABE, Studien zur Gesch. des. 2. Abendmalsstreites, 1886. BACH, DG. i. 364 ff. THOMAS.-SEEBERG, DG. ii. 43 ff.

1. The doctrine of the Lord's Supper received its scholastic form as a result of the assaults which a forerunner of Scholasticism directed against the (Radbertian) theory which was at the time gaining general acceptance in the church. BERENGER taught as follows : Bread and wine become through consecration the body and blood of Christ, *i. e.*, they become a "sacrament of the body and blood of Christ." Bread and wine signify (*significant*) the body and blood of Christ ; they are a similitude (*similitudo*), sign (*signum*), figure (*figura*), pledge (*pignus*). The reality involved comes not into the hand nor into the mouth, but into the thought (*in cognitionem*, de s. coena, pp. 431, 223, ep. ad Adelm.). The elements therefore remain what they were; but something new is added to them through the consecration, *i. e.*, the spiritual significance, which is apprehended by the spirit of the communicant (*e. g.*, p. 125). We appropriate the sufferings and death of Christ, so that they become inwardly directive for us (p. 194). According to this conception, only believers receive Christ's body. In support of his view, Berenger appeals to the Scriptures (Jn. 6), and to the Fathers, especially Augustine. He regards the teaching of his opponents as silliness (*vecordia*) ; his own, as the only logical and reasonable view, required by the proposition : Bread and wine are body and blood—in which the former remains what it is in order that it may be the latter (pp. 50, 161). Since the body of Christ exists in heaven impassible and indivisible, how can the attempt be made to distribute particles of the flesh in the separate communions in various places (p. 199)? And did not Christ promise to give himself entire to believers, not only parts of himself? Finally, the doctrine of his opponents leads, as he acutely perceives, to two kinds of flesh (*duae carnes*, p. 200), a heavenly and a sacramental body (cf. DIECKHOFF, p. 50 ff.). To estimate Berenger correctly, it is necessary to bear constantly in mind the theory in opposition to which his views were developed, and to remember also that he had a deeper interest than his opponents in the religious bearing of the subject. He was concerned to maintain the idea of personal fellowship with Christ.[1]

[1] A group of the followers of Berenger taught that bread and wine indeed remain after consecration, but that "the body and blood of the Lord are there contained, truly but latently (*latenter*), and so that they may be understood in some such way as though I should say that they are impanated (impanari)"

2. The teaching of Berenger awakened opposition from many quarters. The keenness with which he expounded the Lord's Supper as a *figura*, and the rationalistic method of his argument (REUTER, i. 112, 293. BACH, i. 387 ff.) caused alarm. The "multitude of incompetents" were, as he declares, against him, and even Gregory VII. was unable to protect him. He was condemned at Rome and at Vercelli in A. D. 1050. Although the Papal legate, Hildebrand, at Tours (A. D. 1054), declared himself satisfied with the teaching of Berenger, he was still regarded with suspicion. At Rome, A. D. 1059, he was compelled to assent to a confession which presented transubstantiation in the crassest form : "That bread and wine . . . after consecration are not only a sacrament,[1] but also the true body and blood of our Lord Jesus Christ, and are not only in a sacrament, but in truth handled in the hands of priests, broken and torn by the teeth of the faithful " (HEFELE, iv. 826). Having at a later day again advocated his view in France, where he wrote his treatise, *De sacra coena*,[2] he was, in A. D. 1079, again compelled to recant at Rome.[3] But his views still remained unchanged. " In fact, Berenger was an acute theorizer of the Illumination, but a hero in its defense he was not " (REUTER, i. 126).

3. As a result of these controversies, the Lord's Supper became a favorite topic of theological discussion and the doctrine of Radbert—in a grosser form—the doctrine of the church. LANFRANC, HUGO of Langres (de corp. et sang. christi, c. Berenger, Mi. 142. 1325 ff.). ALGER, of Lüttich (de sacramentis corp. et sang. dom., Mi. 180. 743 ff.). DURAND of Troanne (de corp. et sang. dom., Mi. 149. 1375 ff.), and especially GUITMUND of Aversa (de corp. et sang. chr. veritate in euchar., Mi. 149. 1427 ff.) appeared in behalf of either the old or the new teaching. (Cf. Bach, i. 385 ff.). Guitmund (Mi. 149. 1469 ff.) maintains that there is a change (*mutatio*) in the elements, as is proved by the words of institution, which speak of the body of Christ, not figuratively, but substantively (*substantive*). Thus the church had taught from the earliest times (Lanfr. c. 18), and a whole series of miraculous appearances confirm it (Guitm., p.

(Guitmund, De corp. et sang. chr. i.; Mi. 149, 1430 ; cf. Alger, De sacr. i. 6 ; Lombard, sent. iv. dist. ii. D).

[1] Thus the word "sacrament" is no longer regarded as satisfactory ; and in reality the Lord's Supper was, according to this theory, not a sacrament in the ancient sense of the term. The conception of the mystery had become quite different.

[2] Written A. D. 1077-78. Vid. Bröcking, Ztschr. f. KG. 1892, p. 177 ff.

[3] Great prominence was here given to the identity of the sacramental body with that born of the virgin and dying on the cross. Vid. Lanfr., De corp. et sang. dom. c. 2.

1479 f.; Durand, Mi. 149. 1418). After the transformation, the properties of the elements (color, odor, taste) remain, in order that participants may not be horrified, and in order that believers may receive the fuller rewards of faith (Lanfr. 18). In every wafer the entire body of Christ—yea, more, the entire Christ— is, by virtue of his omnipotence, present (Guitm. 1434, 1480. Alger, i. 15). Anselm of Canterbury, ep. iv. 107, Mi. 159, 255. Believers and unbelievers alike receive him, the latter not with saving efficacy (*non salubri efficientia*) (Lanfr. 20. Alger i. 20). With reference to the question concerning the relation of the sacramental to the historical body, Lanfranc declares : " Both the same body which was received from the Virgin . . . and yet not the same—the former, so far as relates to essence ; the latter, if thou regardest the appearance (*speciem*) of bread and wine " (Lanfr. 18). Alger endeavored to meet the difficulty thus arising by maintaining that Christ can, by virtue of his omnipotence, be even bodily omnipresent : " In heaven and on earth he can be corporeally present everywhere, in whatsoever way it may please him—contrary to the nature of flesh—always the same and entire " (i. 15, Mi. 785). The term *transubstantio* is first found in Petrus Comester († 1179), in the sermons of Hildebert of Lavardin († 1134), sermo 93, Mi. 171. 776 ;[1] cf. PRE. viii., ed. 3, 69.

4. Even in the early days of Scholasticism the theory of transubstantiation was everywhere advocated. Thus in the school of Abelard,[2] we note especially Roland's Sentences, p. 223 ff.,[3] as also passages from the Florian Sentences and Omnebene, as presented by Gietl (in his edition of Roland, pp. 223, 227, 233, 234), and the Epitome, 29. Also in HONORIUS Augustod. (elucid. i. 28, 30). HUGO is particularly clear : " Through the words of consecration the true substance of the bread and the wine is changed (*convertitur*) into the true body and blood of Christ, the appearance only of bread and wine remaining, substance passing over into substance (*substantia in substantiam transeunte*), (de sacr. ii. 8, 9). Since the body of Christ is not

---

[1] But we find already in GERMANUS PARIS, in Martène Thes. v. 95 : "*transformatur.*" Haimo of Halberstadt, supra, p. 39. HONORIUS Augustod. Eucharistion, c. 3 : "*in substantiam translatum* " (5, 9, Mi. 172. 1252, 1255). STEPHAN Augustodunens. (ca. A. D. 1120), De sacr. altaris c. 16 : "*in corpus meum transsubstantiari* (Mi. 172. 1293). WILHELM of St. Thierry, De corp. et sang. dom. c. 3.

[2] We have no discussion of the Lord's Supper by Abelard himself, but the harmonious utterances of his followers reproduce his view.

[3] Roland here proceeds already in true scholastic fashion. He, like the other followers of Abelard, discusses the question whether a wafer eaten by a mouse is the body of the Lord (ed. Gietl, p. 234).

omnipresent (cf. ii. 2, 13), he is, therefore, only for the time
(*ad tempus*), so long as he will, now present in the Supper as
once on earth (ii. 8, 13; cf. summ. 6. 2).[1] As ROBERT PUL-
LUS (sent. viii. 5), so, too, PETER LOMBARD advocated the transformation theory : "It is certain that the true body and blood
of Christ are upon the altar; rather that the whole Christ is
there under both the forms, and that the substance of the bread
is converted into (his) body, and the substance of the wine into
(his) blood" (sent. iv. dist. 10 D). The accidents of the
earthly substance remain for the familiar reasons (dist. 11 A E).
But as to the manner of the *conversio*, he declines to attempt any
further explanation (11 C). He regarded the effect of the sacrament as consisting in the forgiveness of venial sins and in the
perfection of virtue (*perfectio virtutis*, dist. 12 G ; infusion of
grace, Hugo, sacr. ii. 8. 7). Finally, he considers the Lord's
Supper under the aspect of a *sacrifice*. It is a daily sacrifice :
"But he is daily immolated in the sacrament, because in the sacrament there is a commemoration of that which was once done."
The sacrifice is repeated on account of our daily sins. "Christ
was both once offered and is daily offered ; but then in one way,
now in another" (dist. 12 G). This sacrifice represents that
upon the cross only as a picture of the latter (Petr. Pictav. sent.
v. 13). Here, as often, theory tardily followed praxis.[2]

5. The doctrine thus elaborated by the theologians was exalted
to the position of a fixed dogma by Pope Innocent III. at the
Fourth Lateran council (A. D. 1215): "The body and blood are
truly contained in the sacrament of the altar under the forms
(*speciebus*) of bread and wine, the bread transubstantiated into
the body and the wine into the blood by divine power. . . . And
this sacrament no one can in any case administer except a priest who
has been properly ordained" (Mansi, xxii. 982.   Vid. already
Can. 6 of the Council of Piacenza, A. D. 1095, HEFELE, v. 216).

---

[1] But side by side with these fruitful ideas stands the barren suggestion
that, at the first celebration of the Supper, Christ for a time laid aside his mortal nature, and as mortal bore his immortal self in his hands : "In that
which gave he was mortal, and in that which was given he was immortal ;
and, nevertheless, he who as mortal gave, and he who as immortal was given,
were not two but one self" (de sacr. ii. 8, 3).

[2] Other theologians of the twelfth century also treated exhaustively of the
Lord's Supper. Vid. BACH, i. 392 ff.   Special mention may be made of the
theory of RUPERT of Deutz. If Radbert understood the transformation of
the elements as a creative act, Rupert conceived it as analogous to the incarnation. As the divine nature assumed the human without destroying it, "so
it does not change nor destroy the substance of the bread and wine according
to outward appearance subject to the five senses, but when by the same Word he
unites the latter in the unity (*in unitatem*) of the same body which hung
upon the cross" (in Exod. ii. c. 10, Mi. 167, 617 f.).

The "multitude of incompetents," the logic of the theologians, and the hierarchy combined in the production of this dogma. It was a corruption of the church's best possession (*corruptio optimi*); yet it served at least to preserve one article of religion to the Christian world.

§ 50. *Definition of Sacraments.   The Seven Sacraments.*

1. The significance of Scholasticism for the History of Doctrines consists chiefly in the establishment of the Catholic doctrine of the sacraments. The decisive steps in this direction also were taken during the present period. The divine efficiency is located in the sacraments, not in the word. Augustine, as we have seen, had a much more profound conception of the significance of the word. The definition of a sacrament was, to begin with, by no means clear, largely because of uncertainty as to the number to be recognized. Bernard still speaks of many, and enumerates ten (Mi. 183, 271 f.). Hugo of St. Victor recognizes among the sacraments the sign of the cross, the invocation of the Trinity (de sacr. i. 9. 6), and all manner of ecclesiastical symbols and formulas (ib. ii. 9). Roland thus designates the incarnation (p. 157). But in the twelfth century the constant tendency was to give prominence to certain definite sacraments. ROBERT (sent. v. 24) contrasts the unrepeatable (baptism, confirmation) and the repeatable (repentance, the Lord's Supper).[1] HUGO treats in his Summa of : baptism, confirmation, the eucharist, extreme unction, marriage, but also repentance (6. 10 ff.; cf. de sacr. ii. 14), and the power of the keys, which is conferred through ordination (6. 14). This is practically a recognition of the number seven. Here, too, the influence of the school of Abelard was felt. The *Epitome* has : baptism, confirmation, the Lord's Supper, extreme unction, marriage (similarly the sentences of ST. FLORIAN, Denifle, archiv. i. 432); repentance is treated of in the third section of the system under the heading of "love" (c. 35 ff.).[2] ROLAND and OMNEBENE, on the other hand (vid. DENIFLE, l. c., p. 467), have : baptism, confirmation, Lord's Supper, repentance, extreme unction, in connection with which the power of the keys and ordination (Rol., p. 267 f.) are spoken of, and marriage. Since Omnebene appears to have made use of Roland (vid. GIETL, Sent. Rol., p. 54), Hugo and Roland must be regarded as the

---

[1] It is not correct in view simply of the incidental utterance at vii. 14 to regard him as including ordination as a fifth sacrament.

[2] Abelard himself appears to have divided in the same way. Vid. Ethica, c. 23.

first to have placed the number of sacraments at seven.   But not
until we reach Peter Lombard do we find this number clearly
and definitely fixed (sent. iv. 2 A).[1] It was even then still customary to speak of baptism and the Lord's Supper as the chief
sacraments, which were said to have flowed from the side of
Christ (Lomb. sent. iv. 8 A ; Hugo, de sacr. i. 9. 7 ; ii. 2. 1).

2. The old (Angustinian) definition of a sacrament, as the
"sign of a sacred reality" (*sacrae rei signum*) or a "visible
sign of invisible grace," was still in vogue (Roland, p. 155 ;
epit. i.). But the conception was gradually becoming more
precise : " God instituted the remedies of the sacraments against
the wounds of original and actual sin " (Lomb. iv. 1 A; Hugo, de
sacr. i. 8. 12).   They are not merely signs, and were instituted
not only for the sake of signifying (*significandi gratia*), but for the
sake of sanctifying (*sanctificandi gratia*) (ib. B).   Faith and
repentance are mentioned as the subjective condition required
for a profitable reception (ib. iv. 4 B).   But no one so clearly
expressed the controlling thought as Hugo : "A sacrament is a
corporeal or material element, openly (and) sensibly presented,
representing by similitude and signifying by institution, and containing by consecration, some invisible and spiritual grace (de
sacr. i. 9. 2).   Thus, *e. g.*, it may be said of the water of baptism : " By consecration (*sanctificatione*) it contains spiritual
grace " (ib. ii. 6. 2).   This fully expresses the sacramental conception which dominates the Middle Ages.   The sensuous elements somehow contain grace ; with them grace is infused into
the recipients.   There are, indeed, differences between the various sacraments : " Some, as baptism, offer a remedy for sin and
confer assisting grace ; others, as marriage, are for remedy only ;
others, as the eucharist and ordination, strengthen us with grace
and virtue" (Lomb. iv. 2 A).   As we shall have occasion hereafter to discuss each sacrament separately, we here offer but a few
brief comments.

3. BAPTISM accomplishes man's renewal by a putting off of
vices (*depositio vitium*), and a contribution of virtues (*collatio
virtutum*) (Lombard iv. 3 L).   Original sin is remitted, because
(1) through the grace of baptism the vice of concupiscence is

---

[1] According to the above, my statement in Thomas. DG. ii., ed. 2, 216,
must be modified.   It is inaccurate to say that the Lombard was led to enumerate seven sacraments by combining those acknowledged by Hugo and Robert
(see note 1, p. 79).   It seems chronologically impossible that the Lombard
should have been influenced by Roland (vid. Gietl, l. c., p. 16 f.).   The
Lombard started out with the enumeration customary in the school of Abelard (vid. the Epitome), and, following Hugo, added to these repentance and
ordination.   But this was a natural result of the theological tendencies of the
age.

weakened (*debilitatur*), and (2) guilt (*reatus*) is abolished (*aboletur*) in baptism (ib. ii. 32 B).

4. CONFIRMATION works the bestowal of the Holy Spirit for strengthening (ib. iv. 7 A.; infusion of grace, Hugo, de sacr. ii. 7. 1). "Confirmation is as much worthier than baptism, as it is worthier to be made an athlete than to be cured of disease. . . . Wherefore confirmation is now granted only by a bishop" (Robert, sent. v. 23; Hugo, l. c., ii. 7. 4). Roland, on the other hand, declares that baptism is the worthier in its effect, and that confirmation can be called worthier only because it ought to be administered by a worthier person (p. 213).[1]

5. As to the LORD'S SUPPER, see Section 49, 3, 4.

6. We must examine the discussions of REPENTANCE somewhat more fully, since the theologians of the period attempted to justify upon theoretic grounds the advances made in the statement of this doctrine. Here, too, Abelard and his school exerted a great influence. He taught that (1) True repentance consists in contrition of the heart (*contritio cordis*).[2] Where this exists, God grants the forgiveness of sins (ethica 19). Also the Epitome (35) and Roland (sent., pp. 243, 245). Usually *confessio* will immediately follow contrition (eth. 24; epit. 36; cf. praxis, serm. 8 fin.); it is not, however, a condition required for the forgiveness of sins, but "a large part of satisfaction" (eth. 24). (2) But this forgiveness has reference only to the eternal punishments of sin : "For God, when he pardons sin to the penitent, does not remit all penalty to them, but only the eternal" (eth. 19; epit. 35). The "penalty of satisfaction," on the other hand, was held to release from all *temporal* punishment of sin, either in this life or in purgatory. If these works of repentance are not sufficient,[3] God will complete the punishment "by afflicting with purgatorial punishments either in this or in a future life" (expos. in Rom. 2. 4, p. 840; eth. 25; cf. epit. 37; Roland, p. 248). (3) Roland established the necessity of confession and works of satisfaction as follows : "We offend God by thinking wickedly, and we scandalize the church by acting perversely : and just as we offend both, we owe it to both to render satisfaction—to God through contrition of heart, to the church through confession of the mouth and satisfaction by works, if the nature

---

[1] Vid. also Petr. Pict. sent. v. 9 : "Baptism . . . is more useful . . . confirmation better and worthier and more precious, just as water is more useful than wine, but wine more worthy and excellent."

[2] According to the Epitome, 5, it arises "not from fear of punishment, but from love of righteousness."

[3] Observe the keen remarks of Abelard concerning "some of the priests . . . entrapping those under their care in order that for the oblation of coins they may condone or relax the penalties of the enjoined satisfaction" (eth. 35).

of the time demands'' (p. 249). Abelard thus deduced the propriety of works of satisfaction from the necessity of expiating
the temporal penalties of sin, and by this means solved a problem raised by the new penitential praxis. But, as he made the
remission of the eternal penalty dependent solely upon contrition, he increased the difficulty attaching to another problem of
the same praxis, *i. e.*, that absolution seems to be robbed of its
chief significance and the office of priest becomes merely to
give advice in reference to works of satisfaction for temporal
penalties.

(*b*) HUGO of St. Victor, controverting the views of Abelard,
becomes, upon the doctrine of repentance as elsewhere, the representative of the hierarchical orthodoxy. For him the *confession* is the chief thing in repentance, as was doubtless the case in
the prevalent praxis (cf. supra, p. 46). It presupposes contrition and the willingness to render satisfaction (de sacr. ii. 14.
1 ; summa 6. 10). He who will not make confession is a despiser of God (sacr. ii. 14. 8). But repentance is actually
secured only through confession *and* satisfaction : '' He confesses
his sin to the priest, who imposes upon him a just satisfaction,
for he is bound to make satisfaction, not according to his judgment, but according to the judgment of the priest, and *then* the
priest releases him from the debt of future damnation '' (summ.
6. 11).[1] Absolution accordingly follows confession, but it is
granted in view of the satisfaction imposed in connection with
the former (see foot-note). Hugo thus theoretically comes to
the support of the theory of the older penitential praxis (p. 43 f.).
Finally, he vigorously assails the opinion that priestly absolution
has only an ecclesiastical and declaratory signification. Against
this he argues : The sinner is bound in a two-fold way : ''by ob-
duration of the mind and by the debt of future damnation.'' The
former, God removes through the grace which works penitence in
us, ''so that . . . penitent we merit to be absolved from the
debt of damnation'' (sacr. ii. 4. 8, p. 565). As the resusci-
tated Lazarus was by the apostles ''loosed '' from his grave-
clothes, so the priests, by means of a power divinely conferred,
release the penitent sinner from eternal perdition (ib. p. 565 f.,

---

[1] It is necessary to observe that Hugo is aware that forgiveness depends
upon *contritio* and *confessio :* '' But there is this remedy, that he repent of his
fault in his heart and confess it with his mouth ; which, when he has done,
he will then no longer be a debtor of damnation'' (sacr. ii. 14. 8, p. 567).
The passage above cited does not exclude this view, as the ''then'' refers
only to the imposing of the satisfaction. Cf. somewhat later (p. 149).
'' The priest releases . . . from the debt of future punishment by absolving
through the satisfaction which he imposes.''

568, and summ. 6. 11).[1] In this idea lies the dogmatic significance of Hugo's teaching.

(*c*) ROBERT PULLUS, on the other hand, locates the essence
of the sacrament in absolution and confession. "Absolution,
which is, in confession, pronounced above the penitent by the
priest, is a sacrament, since it is the sign of a sacred reality"
(sent. vi. 61). But the priestly absolution is only the announcement of the forgiveness which God, upon the ground of penitence, imparts to the sinner (ib.; likewise Petr. Pict. sent. iii.
16). But after absolution it remains necessary to perform the
penitential works (vi. 52). If the latter be not rendered, they
will be completed by the penalties endured in purgatory (ib. and
vii. 1 ; vi. 59).

(*a*) The Lombard betrays also here the influence of Abelard.
Repentance embraces the usual three parts (sent. iv. 16 A). It
is a punishment, and, as such, of a satisfactory nature (*poena
satisfacit*, iv. 14 A, B, 15 C). The admission (iv. 17 C),
that forgiveness presupposes only contrition and confession before God, is supplemented by the declaration : "Confession
ought to be offered first to God and then to the priest, nor if
there be opportunity for this can entrance to paradise be otherwise attained (ib. D), since the latter is a kind of punishment
of sin" (ib. F). This does not involve any divergence from
Abelard. Confession is then followed by absolution (dist. 18).
The question, whether God or the priest forgives, is thus decided :
"That God only remits and retains sins, and nevertheless he has
conferred upon the church the power of binding and loosing ;
but he absolves in one way and the church in another" (18 E).[2]
The priests decide whether the sinner "is regarded as released
in the view of the church" (F). But the priests further bind
and loose by imposing and mitigating the *satisfaction*, and by
the admission to participation in the sacrament of those who
have been purified by rendering the required satisfaction. But
since this was, in fact, dependent upon absolution, the Lombard
further interprets his language : It is to be observed that, because they bind some with the satisfaction of repentance, by

---

[1] The practical frame of mind which harmonizes with this theory cannot be
better expressed than by Hugo : "How can I know when my repentance is
sufficient (*condigna*)? Because thou canst not know this, therefore thou hast need
always to repent. Thou canst make satisfaction ; thou canst not do too much. It
is better to do more than less . . . Nevertheless, in order that the conscience of
the sinner may sometimes find comfort, the mode and measure of external repentance has been appointed, so that when the latter has been completed and
perfected, thou mayest begin to have confidence" (de sacr. ii. 14. 2 fin.).

[2] Here, as often in the Lombard, we have the theology of "Yes and No."
In iv. 18 D the views of Hugo and Abelard are cited.

that very act they show such to be released from their sins, since
penitential satisfaction is not imposed upon anyone except such
as the priest judges to be truly penitent.   But upon any other
they do not impose it, and by that very act they adjudge that
his sin is retained by God (G).   A defective exercise of repentance results in the tortures of purgatory : "And they are
more severely punished than if they had fully completed their
repentance here " (20 B).[1]   The Lombard advanced the doctrine
of repentance by assuring to absolution, by virtue of its close connection with confession, a secure place in the sacrament, following in this in the footsteps of Hugo.   The dogmatic contribution of the present period lay in the fact that it began to establish a connection between confession and priestly absolution,
and to argue the necessity of satisfaction in view of the temporal, *i. e.*, purgatorial, punishment of sin.

7. The custom of EXTREME UNCTION, based on Jas. 5. 15,
was in, the present period included among the sacraments.   It
serves a double purpose : " for the remission of sins and for the
alleviation of bodily infirmity " (Lomb. iv. 23 B ; Hugo, de sacr.
ii. 15. 3).

8. The origin of the sacrament of ORDINATION has been
traced in Vol. I., p. 319 f.   A new motive was furnished
for the careful statement of the doctrine by the enlargement of
the penitential system and the sacramental conception of grace.
The priest receives through ordination the two keys, *discretio* and
potestas.   " In consecration these two are given to all, *i. e.*, the
office of exercising discretion and the office of exercising power."
Binding and loosing are thereby committed to them (Hugo,
summ. 6. 14 ; cf. Roland, p. 264 ff.; Lomb. sent. iv. 19 A-C).
Yet this is only one aspect of the matter.   Through ordination
is imparted a more abundant grace (*amplior gratia*, Lomb. iv.
24 A), as well as a spiritual power (*spiritualis potestas*) and spiritual
character (*character spiritualis*) (ib. K).   To it those are to be
admitted "who may be able worthily to administer the Lord's sacraments " (ib. B).   If this applies to all the seven orders (ostiarii,
lectores, exorcistae, acolythi, subdiaconi, diaconi, presbyteri),
it has yet special reference to the priesthood.   "The word priest
(*sacerdos*) is derived from the Greek and Latin, *i. e.*, *sacrum dans*,
or *sacer dux*.   For just as a king (*rex*) receives his title because he
reigns (*a regendo*), so a priest (*sacerdos*) receives his because he
consecrates (*sacrando*), for he consecrates and sanctifies " (ib. J).
In the conception of this sacrament, as elsewhere, no full and

---

[1] The Council at Aachen, A. D. 836, mentions it among the duties of the
spiritual adviser (Mansi, xiv. 681).   *Item*, at Pavia, A. D. 850 (Hefele, iii.
177).   The custom is first met with among the Gnostics (vid. Vol. I., p. 99).

clear conclusion was attained in the present period, but the controlling thought is clear enough. Ordination imparts the spiritual authority to administer the sacraments, and through them to sanctify the laity (cf. Greg. vii., supra, p. 51).

9. The sacrament of Marriage betrays the juristic origin by the form of statement.

It is clear from the evidence above adduced that the theologians of the twelfth century had already clearly wrought out the materializing of grace through the sacraments. The theologians of the thirteenth century inherited, indeed, a number of unsolved—and insoluble—problems, but also the firmly established fundamental conception which proved the regulating force of medieval Christianity, *i. e.*, Grace is the power efficaciously manifested in the sacraments, whose administration belongs by divine right to the priesthood.

§ 51. *Conception of the Church.*

1. The task of the present chapter would be imperfectly performed if we should fail to note the acceptance by the theologians of the day of the conception of the church which Gregory VII. introduced (supra, p. 50 ff.). The utterances of the Scholastics upon the subject are confessedly meagre. Neither the system of Abelard nor that of the Damascenes gave occasion for its discussion. The conception was a self-evident premise, whose application must be made practically by the canonical laws and theologically in the doctrine of the sacraments. It is, therefore, all the more significant that HUGO of St. Victor and ROBERT PULLUS should have expressed themselves plainly upon the subject. We have also discussions of the relation of church and state in the *Polycraticus* of JOHN of Salisbury († 1180, opp. ed. Giles, 5 vols., 1848. Cf. Gennrich, Die Staats- u. Kirchenlehre d. Joh. v. Sal., 1894).[1]

2. Augustine indicates the starting point in his query : "What is the church except the multitude of the believing, the whole number of Christians?" (*multitudo fidelium, universitas christianorum*). (Hugo, de sacr. ii. 2. 2). But inasmuch as, according to this, believers are simply Christians, this definition by no means brings us "to the true Christian idea of the church" (LIEBNER, Hugo v. St. Victor, p. 446); it only declares that the Christian world constitutes the church.[2] The correct

[1] Vid. also HONORIUS Augustod.: "The highest glory composed of the apostolic and the imperial." Mi. 172.

[2] Interesting is the definition of Alanus ab Insul.: "the church is the congregation of believers confessing Christ and the guardian (*subsidium*) of the sacraments" (de articul. cath. fid. iv. in., Mi. 210. 613).

conception is gained by the division of Christians into rulers and subjects (*praelati et subjecti*) (Hugo, ib. ii. 2. 5 ; cf. Robert, sent. vii. 19 : " prelates governing the church "). This formula, frequently occurring already in the writings of Cyprian (Vol. I., p. 180 ff.), signifies that the right side of the church consists of the clergy and the left side of the laity (Hugo, ii. 2. 3). There are, therefore, two lives or two nationalities, of which one ministers to temporal necessities, and the other administers what pertains to the spiritual life (ib. 3). Each of these nationalities is subject to a ruler, *i. e.*, the king and the pope (ib. 4). The nature of the church is in harmony with this idea, and there are discussions of its *orders, sacraments,* and *precepts.* The gradation of the orders is then treated of. The special privileges of bishops, as compared with priests, are placed upon the ground that otherwise the subjects might take advantage of their superiors and forget the obedience due the latter (ib. ii. 3. 12). The archbishops and the four patriarchs stand above the bishops, and over all is the pope (*papa*), *i. e.*, father of fathers, whom, presiding in place of Peter, the chief of the apostles, every ecclesiastical order is bound to obey, who alone has as prerogatives of his high rank the keys of binding and loosing all things upon earth (ii. 3. 5). No one but God may pass judgment upon him (Johann. Polycr. viii. 23 ; opp. iv. 363). According to the interpretation of the Augustinian conception of the two states which dominates Hugo, it is but a self-evident conclusion that the spiritual power stands far above the secular ; it is the older and has authority to institute the latter and sit in judgment upon it (ii. 2. 4 ; cf. Robert, vii. 7): " This sword, therefore, the prince receives from the hand of the church. . . . The prince is, therefore, a minister of the priesthood, and one who exercises that part of the duties of the priests which seems unworthy of the hands of the priesthood " (Polycr. iv. 3 in.).[1] Yet the state is also to be regarded as a divine institution (Polycr., l. c., iv. 1), but must be subject to spiritual (clerical) direction. Robert expresses the opinion that, according to Matt. 22. 21 : " The priesthood is superior to the kingdom in those things which it administers for God, and the kingdom to the priesthood in those things which pertain to the world " (vii. 7, p. 920 f. Cf. Hugo, ii. 2. 6, 7 ; Gregory VII., supra, p. 50). These utterances furnish a precise outline of the Gregorian conception of the

---

[1] John. says : " Therefore the prince is a minister of the public utility and a servant of equity " (Polycr. iii. 2). The gravest crime is tyranny, which is directed " against the very body of justice." From this is deducted the right of slaying tyrants : " To kill a tyrant is not only allowable, but right and just " (ib. iii. 15 ; viii. 17 in., 18 fin.).

church : (1) The clergy are related to the laity as a government to its subjects. (2) This exalted position of the clergy is explained by their authority to dispense the sacraments. (3) The clergy is a graded organism, whose summit is the pope. (4) The secular power is by divine right subject to the spiritual.

CHAPTER II.

DEVELOPMENT OF CHRISTIAN DOCTRINE DURING THE SECOND PERIOD OF SCHOLASTICISM.

§ 52. *Aims of the Church. Religious Life. Efforts at Reform.*

1. We are now standing upon the summit of the Middle Ages. The cornerstone and foundation of their theological structure were laid in the former period, its scope and tendency determined. The decisive work was not done by the leaders of the thirteenth century, but by their forerunners in the eleventh and twelfth centuries. This is true of the theologians no less than of the ecclesiastics and the reformers of the church's devotional life.

We must first of all trace the development of the hierarchical ideas and the religious ideals, whose introduction was noted in Sections 44 and 45. We recall the firm adherence of the later popes to the principles of Gregory VII. INNOCENT III. claims special attention. He held that " The pope is the vicar (*vicarius*) of Christ, placed midway between God and man, beneath God and beyond man, less than God and greater than man, who judges concerning all and is judged by none (Mi. 217. 658). Thus Aristotle once spoke of the genie as " O, thou to men divine ! " (Pol. iii. 13. 8). Not only the whole church, but the whole world, is subject to the sway of the pope : " James, the brother of the Lord . . . left to Peter not only the whole church, but the whole world, to be governed " (registr. ii. 209). Innocent accordingly sought to adminster the affairs of the church as its sole ruler (cf. the confirmation of bishops, their oath of obedience, their being called to the duty of *solicitudo*, appellation to Rome, the Roman land titles, etc. Vid. the bull of Eger., A. D. 1213, in MG. leg. ii. 224 f.; reg. i. 495, 496), and claimed also supremacy over states. As the moon receives its light from the sun, " so the royal power receives the splendor of its dignity

from the pontifical authority" (reg. i. 401, Mi. 217. 1180. Cf.
Döllinger, Papsttum, p. 401 f.).[1] These ideas were most abruptly
expressed in the bull "Unam Sanctam," issued by BONIFACE VIII.,
A. D. 1302, whose leading declarations are as follows: "We
are compelled by the faith to believe . . . one holy catholic
church . . . outside of which there is neither salvation nor the
remission of sins. . . . In which there is one Lord, one faith,
one baptism. . . . Therefore of this one and only church
there is one body and one head, not two bodies, as though it
were a monster, viz.: Christ and the vicar of Christ, Peter and
the successor of Peter. . . . That in this and in its power are
two swords, viz., the spiritual and the temporal. . . . Therefore both are in the power of the church, viz., the spiritual and
the material sword ; but the latter to be exercised for the church,
the former by the church. The one is in the hand of the priest ;
the other in the hands of kings and soldiers, but at the command
and permission (*ad nutum et patientiam*) of the priest. But it is
fitting that sword be under sword, and that the temporal authority be subject to the spiritual. . . . But that the spiritual power
excels both in dignity and nobility any earthly power whatsoever.
. . . For, truth being the witness, the spiritual power has (the
right) to establish the earthly, and, if it have not been good, to
judge it. . . . Whosoever, therefore, resists this power thus ordained of God resists the ordinance of God, unless, like Manichaeus, thou dreamest that there are two principles. . . . Moreover, to every human creature we declare, say, define and pronounce, that to be subject to the Roman pontiff is absolutely
necessary to salvation" (*de necessitate salutis*).

2. The writings of St. Bernard exerted a profound influence upon the devout speculation of the following period, but it
does not lie within the province of the History of Doctrines to
follow them in detail.[2] We must not, however, overlook the
protest against the secularization of the church which, at the
time when the hierarchy was at the summit of its power, and
when even ideas of reform had become merely a means for
further secularization, was raised by the Brethren of the Poor
Life of Christ. The power of love was revealed in Christ to

---

[1] Innocent maintained that the popes had in the time of Charlemagne
transplanted the Greek Empire to Germany, and that in consequence the
" right and authority of examining the person elected to be king" belonged
to them (de elect. 34, in Mirbt, Urkunden, p. 78).

[2] Vid. the mystical writings of HUGO († 1141) and RICHARD († 1173) of
St. Victor; also BONAVENTURA, Itenerarium mentis, as presented in detail in
THOMASIUS, DG. ii., ed. 2, 272 ff. Religious mysticism is here systematized
and developed into a philosophy. These writings may be described as the
beginnings of theological ethics.

FRANCIS OF ASSISI. The poor life of Christ overwhelmed his soul; the imitation of Christ became his ideal. He became the knight of "holy poverty." Poverty set him free from the world. As he, surfeited with the old life, shook off his relations with the world, he soon found something else and more than his ideal had promised—he found himself and individuality. He did not clothe his thoughts in doctrinal statements. The gospel frame of mind was everything to him. The love of Christ kept his tears of joy ever flowing and taught him to perform miracles of love. The whole creation testified to him of the love of God, and all living things demanded of him love. "Everything temporal" was to him "only an image," the image of the soul, which belongs to its God. Thus his life, and with it the whole creation, became a hymn of praise to God, for the service of free love. "Praise and bless the Lord, and render thanks, and serve him with grand humility" (Song of the Sun). "My God and all, who art thou, sweetest Lord, my God; and who am I, an insignificant worm, thy servant? Most Holy Lord, that I might love thee!" (opp. Franc. ed. v. d. Burg, 1849, p. 44). "May the glowing and mellifluous power of thy love absorb, I pray, O Lord, my mind from all things which are under heaven, that I may die from love of thy love, who hast deigned to die from love of my love" (ib. p. 43). Or, as Jacopone sings: "Make me truly to rejoice with—cling to Jesuline; then at length shall I have lived." Francis was made the founder of an order by the church of his age. But he sought and attained more than this. He discovered human individuality and opened to it an immediate intercourse with God. It may, perhaps, be correct to say that he wished to make all men monks; but he did certainly also teach the children of men to become Christians and men. As he found God and love in the Jesus of the gospels, and attained liberation from the world in the following of Jesus, he exerted a powerful stimulus upon his contemporaries. He taught the world the directly individual character and the present blessedness of the religious life, and he led men to look upon the world and mankind simply and without dogmatic spectacles. He glorified poverty and love, and taught men to realize in them the sense of personal *perfection*. His influence can be easily traced in the religious life, as well as in the art and literature, of the following period. This is especially true with reference to the direct and loving appreciation of the human life of Jesus which was manifested in the ensuing age. The one precious pearl of the church's tradition was thus found anew. How exhaustively and how lovingly have not BONAVENTURA (Meditationes vitae Chr. opp. vi.) and LUDOLF of Saxony

(Vita Christi; vid. also De vita et beneficiis salvatoris Jesu Chr. devotissimae meditationes) portrayed the human life of Jesus : " in order that in all places and deeds thou mayest be in mind, as though thou wast present in body " (Bonav. c. 88 fin.). Into the heart of him who thus regards the life of Jesus there comes a certain "familiarity, confidence and love " for the Lord (ib. proem.). He is, as is constantly emphasized, for us the good example : " Who to this end was sent from heaven to us in order that he might go before us in the path of virtues, and might give to us in his example a law of life and discipline " (Ludolf, pro- log.). This is the way " to behold him in spirit " (ib. ii. c. 89). Upon this point cf. SEEBERG, in Ztschr. f. K. Wiss., 1888, p. 163 ff. The lessons taught by St. Francis were, thanks to his monastic order and despite it, not lost upon the Christian world. He was a "pioneer of the reformers."

Cf. HASE, Fr. v. Ass. 1856. SABATIER, Leben d. h. Fr., German trans- lation, 1895. HEGLER, Ztschr. f. Theol. u. K. 1896. K. MÜLLER, Die Anfänge des Minoritenordens, etc., 1885. THODE, Fr. v. Ass. u. die Anfänge der Kunst d. Renaissance in Ital., 1885. EHRLE, in Archiv. f. Litt. u. Kirchengesch. d. MA. iii. 554 ff.

3. The reformatory agitations very naturally exerted a marked influence upon the piety of the laity. This was especially true in regard to the penitential brotherhoods attaching themselves to the third order of St. Francis. But it must be acknowledged, further, that among the great masses of the population an external eccle- siastical religious life was perpetuated. The people believed in God, Christ, the Virgin Mary, and the saints. They believed just " what the church believes."[1] " There is a certain body of the faith to which everyone is bound, and which is sufficient for the simple and, perhaps, for all laymen, i. e., that every adult be- lieve that God is, and that he is a rewarder of all the good. Likewise must all believe the other articles *implicitly*, i. e., that everything which the universal church believes is true." These words of Innocent IV.[2] justly represent the actual state of things.[3] Faith in God consists in the conviction that he guides the for-

---

[1] The "faith" is the Apostles' Creed, e. g., Schönbach, Altdeutsche Pre- digten i. 41, 46. Its essential content is the Trinity, ib. i. 4; ii. 115; iii. 114. It includes also the divinity of Christ and the seven sacraments (vid. Altdeutsch. Pred. ed. Wackernagel, p. 77 ff.). Vid. also i. 42 : "I believe all that which I as a Christian man ought to believe." Compare Tertullian's "credidi quod credere debui."

[2] Apparatus quinque libror. decretalium i. 1. Vid. RITSCHL, Fides impli- cita, 1890, p. 10.

[3] It was the law for inquisitors : They have power to excommunicate laymen disputing publicly or privately concerning the Catholic faith (Bernard. Guid. practica inquisit. iv., p. 207).

tunes of men, rewarding the good and punishing the wicked. Christ by his death overcame the devil (*e. g.*, Schönbach, Alt-deutsche Predigten, iii. 76, 174). He became for us an example of virtue, humility, and poverty (ib. iii. 7, 238, 252, 40). He is "the heavenly King" (ib. iii. 6). By faithful fulfillment of one's duties in the church the favor of God may be secured. Then comes the intercession of the saints, particularly of the Virgin Mary,[1] and the protective influence of relics, and, finally, almsgiving. Life should be spent in constant view of the future world. Every act of the Christian has reference to reward or punishment there.[2] And as he thus stands in constant touch with the other world, so its wonders are constantly injected into the present life.[3] The providence of God, implicit faith, Christ the vanquisher of the devil and the teacher of virtue, ecclesiasticism, alms, saints, relics, and the future world constitute the chief articles of practical Christianity.[4] But in the most culti-vated circles of the age even the utterance attributed to Frederick II. concerning the three deceivers (Moses, Jesus, and Moham-med) found currency (cf. REUTER, Gesch. d. rel. Aufklärung. ii. 276 ff.).

Vid. KNOBLER, Kathol. Leben. im MA., 4 vols., 1887 ff. (after Digby). FÖSTE, Zur Theol. d. Berthold v. Regensburg, Zwickauer Gymnasialpr., 1890. SOMMER, Deutsche Frömmigkeit in 13ten Jahrhundert, 1901. MICHAEL, Kulturzustände des deutschen Volkes während des 13ten Jahrhunderts, 1903.

4. The means by which the church influenced the religious life of the age were chiefly the following : (*a*) *Preaching*, which con-sisted mainly of admonitions to a moral life, in connection with which doctrine was presented only in general outlines, the liturgy explained, and the history of Christ and of the saints repeated.[5]

---

[1] Adoration of the virgin was rapidly gaining in popularity. So early as A. D. 1140 an attempt was made at Lyons to introduce a festival of the im-maculate conception of Mary, but Bernard expressed himself positively against the idea. Vid. ep. 174. For the position of St. Francis, vid. ep. 11, 12, and p. 40 opp. Konrad of Würzb. in the Gold. Schmiede (especially 210, 282, 488, 632 : Du bist ein êwic fundament—dar ûffe de geloube stât—diu Kristenheit gemûret hat—ir zuoversiht ûf dîne kraft, 1374, 1832, 1992. Altd. Predigten, ii. 79 : "Our Lord is the King and our lady the queen."

[2] Two brothers were expelled from that monastery. Unless these two shall have returned, its condition will never be good. One of these is called Give (*Date*); the other Take (*Dabitur*) (Caesar. Heisterb. dial. iv. 68).

[3] Vid. especially the Dialog. miraculorum of Caesar. v. Heisterbach (ed. Strange, 1851), and Peter Venerabil., De miraculis sui temporis, in Migne 189.

[4] There has, strangely enough, been as yet no systematic presentation of the religious ideas of medieval literature, although SCHÖNBACH has made a begin-ning : Uber Hartmann v. Aue, 1894.

[5] Cf. LINSENMAYER, Gesch. d. Predigt in Deutschl., 1886, p. 157 ff. Vid. SCHÖNBACH, Altdeutsche Predigten, 3 vols., 1886 ff. Honorius Augustodu-

Then came the *Sacrament of Repentance.* The transformation
of the church's teaching upon this point in the twelfth century
(supra, p. 45) gave rise to a number of new questions, as : Whether
contrition is sufficient in itself, or if it requires also confession
before a priest. Gratian still leaves it an open question, whether
" sins are remitted upon contrition of the heart, not upon confession of the mouth,'' or whether " without confession no pardon can be merited '' (decret. pars ii.; causa 33 ; quaest. 3
can. 30, 60, 89). The theologians finally decided for the latter
position (vid. sub). Inasmuch as confession before the priest
thus became the controlling factor of the sacrament,[1] the indicative form of absolution gradually supplanted the optative.[2] It is,
therefore, now the church which, through its representatives,
grants "absolution from penalty and guilt.'' Again, it was
asked whether all sins, or only mortal sins, were to be confessed.
In general, it was the rule that for a multitude of lighter sins the
" general repentance in the church, the Lord's Prayer, fasting,
and giving alms to the poor, and, at most, the salutary host of
the altar,'' were sufficient (Hugo, de sacr. ii. 14. 1 ; Lombard.
sent. iv. dist. 21 E ; an anoymous tract of the twelfth century,
de poenit., Migne 213. 880. Cf. Die taegeliche buoze, Schönb.
altd. pred. iii. 34). There was a constantly growing tendency
to substitute indulgences for the actual performance of works of
satisfaction, and for this purpose various occasions and forms
were devised (opposing heretics, jubilee celebrations, the building of churches, feasts of dedication, festivals of Corpus Christi
and the Virgin Mary, canonization of saints, brotherhoods, gar-
lands, crucifixes, etc. Vid. WILDT in Kirchenlex. i., ed. 2,
102 ff.).[3] Thus repentance came to be regarded as the chief
sacrament : " Where there is repentance (*poenitentia*) there is

nens., speculum ecclesiae (Mi. 172). ALANUS, ab Insulis, Summa de arte
praedicatoria (Mi. 210). GUIBERT, de Novigent., lib. quo ordine sermo fieri
debeat (Mi. 156), col. 26 : " But by the grace of God faith now becomes
known to the hearts of all, and although it has been necessary very often to
inculcate and discuss this anew, yet it is none the less proper to speak even
much more frequently of those things which may instruct their morals.''

[1] The new view appears with peculiar distinctness in Abelard, Serm. 8 fin.,
and later, *e. g.*, Schönbach, Altd. Pred. iii. 88.

[2] Honorius still differently, Specul. eccl., Mi. 172. 826. The Synod of
Treves, A. D. 1227, already employs the formula : *ego te absolvo* (HEFELE,
CG. v. 948). Cf. LEA, Hist. of conf. and indulg., i. 482 ff.

[3] Faith in the virtue of indulgences became a special criterion of orthodoxy.
The Council of Constance directed that those suspected of heresy should be
asked : " Whether they believe that the Roman pontiffs can grant indulgences
on reasonable grounds ? '' Later, pilgrimages were imposed upon those found
guilty of heresy. Vid. Bernard. Guid. practica inquis., ii. 5, 11 ; iii. 1, 8, 13,
45 fin. Meanwhile, the further custom of commutation arose (ib. ii. 11, 22),
and for money (ii. 23, 25 ; cf. iii. 45, p. 166 f.).

also indulgence. . . . As often, therefore, as God gives to a man repentance, so often does he give also indulgence " (Mi. 213. 873). The rule, that for public offenses there must be also public repentance, is still maintained in theory,[1] but, in point of fact, public repentance fell rapidly into disuse. Honorius Augustodunensis already speaks of those performing public penance as ridiculing God (*deum irridentes*, elucidar. ii. 18). In the fourteenth century it had been in many places entirely abandoned. " In such things, according to the course of the present age, there is seen rather a scandal than edification " .(Durand. sent. iv. dist. 14 qu. 4 a. 3). Innocent III. established the following rule at the Fourth Lateran council (A. D. 1215): " Let every believer of either sex, after arriving at years of discretion, faithfully confess all his sins alone at least once a year to his own priest, and endeavor with all his strength to observe the penance enjoined upon him, receiving at least at Easter the sacrament of the eucharist. . . . Let the priest be discreet and cautious . . . inquiring diligently as to the circumstances of both the sinner and the sin, from which he may prudently judge what counsel he ought to give to him, and what kind of remedy he ought to impose " (c. 21, Mansi xxii. 1007). This law was very often emphasized and observed (Councils of Narbonne, A. D. 1227, c. 7 ; Treves, A. D. 1227, c. 3 and 4 ; Canterbury, A. D. 1236, c. 18 ; Toulouse, A. D. 1229, c. 13, where confession three times annually is recommended. Vid. HEFELE, v. 943, 946, 1052, 982).

Cf. GOETZ, Revue internat. de theol., 1894, 300 ff., 431 ff., and Ztschr. f. KG. xv. 321 ff. LEA, A history of auric. conf. and indulgences, 3 vols., London, 1896.

(*c*) The other sacraments must also be mentioned. " And to them (the priests) the almighty God has committed the seven sacraments in order that they might with these sanctify Christians to the world, as they journey into the world, and as they journey through the world, and as they journey out of the world, with holy baptism, and with holy marriage, and with holy confirmation, and with holy confession and penance, and with the holy body of God, and with holy oil, and with the judgments " (Berthold of Regensb. ed. Pfeiffer, i. 142). We postpone for the present the further discussion of these, stopping at present

---

[1] *E. g.*, Schönbach, altd. pred. i. 36 : " A man does penance for his sin in two ways, public and private." A discrimination was made between *poenitentia publica* and *poenitentia solemnis*. The latter was appointed only by the bishop, was performed with peculiarly solemn ecclesiastical rights, and could not be repeated (Alex. Hal. summ. iv. quaest. 64 ; membr. 2. Thom. summ. iii. suppl. qu. 28, art. 3. Ricardus de Medievilla in sent. iv. dist. 14, princ. 11, quaest. 1 and 2. Cf. MORIN, de discipl. v. 25. 2 ff. HEFELE, vi. 183, 220, 502).

only to observe how closely the whole course of the Christian
life has been bound to the church, *i. e.*, the hierarchy.[1]

5. Finally, brief mention must be made of the heretical movements which assumed such large proportions after the eleventh
and twelfth centuries. The controlling aim of Western Christianity was the salvation of souls (*salus animarum*) through the
church (Vol. I., p. 192). It was in consistency with this that
the church of the Middle Ages expressed its characteristic
thought in its theory of the church and the sacraments, especially
the sacrament of repentance (penance). The same controlling
aim, however, gave impulse also to the heresies and schisms
(Novatianism and Donatism) which arose in the Eastern church.[2]
Even the great heretical groups of the Middle Ages display their
essential characteristics, not in their divergence from the accepted
theological views, but in the practical desire to secure liberation
from sin and, at least in the conception of their leaders, to rein-
state the holy apostolic church. We have to do with the two
great branches of medieval heresy—the *Cathari* and the *Waldenses*. The Cathari, indeed, in keeping with their Oriental
origin, revived, with various modifications, almost the entire
Gnostic system, *i. e.*, Manichaeism (two Gods, Gnostic Christology, Dualism, etc.). But even these agitations culminated
practically in the ideas that the Romish church was the whore
Babylon, her hierarchs Pharisees, and her sacraments invalid ;
whereas the Cathari were the only holy church, with the true and
holy hierarchy and effectual sacraments. The " good Christians "
and "the true imitators of Christ " are persecuted by the church
which is not a church ; but only they can actually release from
sin by their baptism and penance (*consolamentum, melioramen-
tum*).[3] Among the Waldenses the doctrinal divergence (denial
of purgatory, opposition to the worship of saints and images)
was given comparatively little prominence ; but practically these
preachers of apostolic poverty rejected finally Rome and its hierarchy (especially the Lombards), opposed their own hierarchy to
that of Rome, and offered the true sacrament of repentance to their

---

[1] This is the medieval conception of the relation of the individual believer
to the church. Vid. Greg. VII., supra, p. 51, and cf. HAGEN, Minnesinger,
iii. 11 a : " Wir waeren doch verirret gar, unt heten wir der pfaffen niht."
THOM.-SEEBERG, DG. ii., ed. 2, 214.

[2] The same is true of the Reformation.

[3] Vid., *e. g.*, REINER'S Summa de Catharis, etc. (Martene, Thes. anecd.
v.), p. 1764 ff., as well as in the original documents, published by DÖLLINGER
(Beiträge zur Sektengesch. d. MA., vol. ii.), *e. g.*, pp. 17, 286, 322, 372
(church); 188, 6, 39, 280, 295 (hierarchy); 197, 280, 198, 371, 115, 294
(sacraments); 280, 313, 323, 326, 370, 373 (repentance) ; and also BERNARD.
Guid. practica inq. iii. c. 32, 33 ; iv., p. 222 f.; v. i. 1. 2, 3, 4.

followers.[1] Neither of these parties overstepped the bounds of medieval Christianity. For them, as in the church at large, Christianity consisted in purification through the sacraments, obedience to the hierarchy, and good works in imitation of Christ. The church, from her point of view, rightly charged upon them : "they annulled the sacraments and made void the priesthood."[2] The immediate result of these agitations, constituting as they did the most energetic assault upon the church since the days of Gnosticism, was only a more distinct assertion of the ecclesiastical and sacramental character of Christianity (vid. especially chapters 1, 3, and 21 of the Fourth Lateran Council, HEFELE, v. 878 ff., 881 f., 888). More and more, for faith in God was substituted the summons to " obey the mandates of the Roman church."[3] On the other hand, the " free thinking "[4] heresy of the BEGARDS, which from the middle of the twelfth century was propagated in Germany, presents—with its pantheism, its ethical indifferentism, and its essentially anti-ecclesiastical spirit[5]— a symptom of the growing independence and discontent as against the church and her institutions. This is true of the radical Franciscanism[6] and of the apocalyptic speculations (the "everlasting gospel"), which from the time of Joachim of Floris († 1202) agitated and disturbed the church.

Vid. original documents in MÖLLER, KG. ii. 374 f., 383 ; Bernardi Guidonis practica inquisitionis haereticae pravitatis ed. Douais, 1886 ; cf. CH. SCHMIDT, Hist. et doctrines de la secte des Cathares ou Albigeois, 2 vols., 1849. DÖLLINGER, Beitr. z. Sektengesch d. MA., 2 vols., 1890. DIECKHOFF, Die Wald. im MA., 1851. K. MÜLLER, die Wald. u. ihre einzeln. Gruppen, 1886. PREGER, Abh. d. bayr. Akad. d. Wiss. xiii., xiv. PREGER, Gesch. d. deutschen Mystik, i. 207 ff., 461 ff. REUTER, Gesch. d. rel. Auf kl. ii. 240 ff. JUNDT, hist. du panthéisme populaire, 1875. DENIFLE, Das ev. aet. in Arch. f. Litt. u. KG. des MA. i. 49 ff. EHRLE, Die Spiritualen, iii. 553 ff.; i. 509 ff.; ii. 108 ff., 249 ff.; vi. 1 ff. HAUPT, Ztschr. f. KG. vii. 372 ff.

[1] In DÖLLINGER, ii., pp. 7, 287, 252, 306, 97, 288 f., 306, 332, 335 (Romish and Waldensian hierarchy); 256, 115 (sacraments); 288, 304, 332 (repentance). BERNARD. Guid. pract. inq. iii. 34, 35 ; v. 2, 3, 4, 5, 6.
[2] In addition to the above citations, see the collection of SEEBERG-THOMAS., DG. ii., p. 192 f.
[3] This is the ever-recurring formula in the renunciation of heresy. Vid., e. g., Bernard. pract. inq. iii. 10 f., 14, 46, p. 168; v. 6. 2, 4, 8, 11 ; 8. 7, 10.
[4] " Ein fry Geist " (Döllinger, ii. 386).
[5] Vid., e. g., Döllinger, ii. pp. 384, 390 (impeccabiles), 417, 384, 385 f., 390 (one with God, pares Christo); 390, 416 (omnia sunt deus. Omnia fiunt a deo); 386, 387, 403, 416 (ethics); 398, 416, 398 (Christology, purgatory), etc.
[6] The ideals of Francis are by this party exalted as a " fifth gospel," with the severest criticism of the church, which has become Babylon. Vid., e. g., Bernard. pract. inq. iii. 39; v. 4. 5 ; v. 3. 2, 3 ; 8. 1 ff. As they very often combined forces with the Begards, they were also designated by the latter term.

§ 53. *History and Characteristics of the Theology of the Thirteenth Century.*

See Literature cited under Section 46; also ETOLE in Archiv. f. Lit. u· KG. des MA. v. 603 ff. THOMAS.-SEEBERG, Die Theologie des Duns Scotus, 1900, p. 600 ff.

1. The history of the church's intellectual life from the middle of the eleventh to the end of the twelfth century may be depicted in the lives of three men—Pope Gregory VII., St. Bernard, and Abelard. The thirteenth century was likewise characterized by the activities of three great leaders—Pope Innocent III. (§ 52, 1), St. Francis (§ 52, 2), and Thomas of Aquino. The hierarchy had reached the zenith of its power, and maintained its position as against the world and the encroachments of heresy. But at the same time there was quietly inaugurated a process of liberation and refinement of the inner life, and, simultaneously, a fuller and more vigorous development of scientific study than had, been previously known in medieval history. Antiquity was again the teacher. Hitherto only the dialectic writings of Aristotle had been known, but to them were now added his metaphysics, physics, psychology, and ethics.[1] Their study was pursued with eager interest and enthusiasm. Men like Albert the Great and Thomas of Aquino wrote commentaries upon them. There was a larger conception of the universe, and the sphere of thought was refined and more accurately delineated. Aristotle, the *"praecursor Christi in naturalibus,"* became the regulating authority and the master of method. The effect of the knowledge of Arabic philosophy was also manifest. The materials and the problems of knowledge were rapidly multiplied. But all knowledge must in the end serve the church. Religion and secular learning are not yet separated. Thus the dogmatic systems continue to grow apace, being presented partly in commentaries upon the Sentences of the Lombard, and partly in independent works (summa theologiae).[2] The ancient dialectic method is still followed, and the wider the range of material becomes, the greater

---

[1] Vid. JOURDAIN, Recherches critiques sur l'âge et l'origine des traductions latines d'Aristotele, 1843. HAURÉAU, hist. de la philosophie scolastique, ii. 1. 124 ff. Upon the culture and learning of the age, vid. V. LILIENCRON, der Inhalt d. allg. Bildung in d. Zeit d. Schol. Munich, 1876. Cf. also PRANTL, in d. Sitzungsberichten d. Münch. Akad., 1867, ii., p. 173 ff. In the Chartularium universit. Paris (ed. Denifle), i., p. 644 ff., may be found a very interesting catalogue of the books which the booksellers of Paris had for sale in A. D. 1286, together with the prices.

[2] The title, "Summa," was employed before the times of the Lombard. Vid. DENIFLE, Gesch. d. Univ. i. 46.

becomes the number of proofs and authorities pro and con, the keener the logical distinctions, and the more complicated the lines of dialectical discussion. Dogmatics again became, as with the Alexandrines of the second and third centuries, a great system of the philosophy of religion, appropriating for itself all the learning of metaphysics and physics, with all the power of the church and her institutions, and which must never lose from beneath it the basis of the rule of faith and the accredited dogmas of the church. And yet it was evident that the structure thus reared must fall by its own weight, for during the very period of its construction it was discovered that the elements here joined together were mutually irreconcilable. The secularized church had a secular theology. Every church is secularized which strives toward any other goal than the kingdom of God and its gospel ; and every theology is secularized which seeks anything further than a true understanding of the gospel. And both alike must come to grief—missing the gospel, which they do not seek, and no less the world, which they seek. This was the sad experience of the medieval church. Boniface VIII. and Duns Scotus were contemporaries. The pope, who made the most audacious claims for papal supremacy (vid. § 52, 1),[1] aroused against that theory the opposition which has never since been allayed ; and the theologian who carried the dialectic presentation of the doctrines of the church to the greatest extreme himself fell into error as to the proper relation of faith and philosophy, and gave the final occasion for the severance of the two (vid. sub).

2. Taking a general view of the history of Scholasticism in the Second Period, we observe that nearly all the theologians claiming our attention belong to the Dominican or Franciscan orders. A few remarks may be necessary to insure a proper understanding of the historical course of events before entering upon the study of the leading theologians of the age. It is well known that there were sharp lines of contrast between the great leaders (as, e. g., Thomas and Duns). These find their explanation in the historical development. All received their inspiration from ARISTOTLE. But this was in the first instance mainly formal. In the general conceptions of truth, the predominant influence was chiefly that of Platonic-Augustinian Idealism. The reality of ideas was acknowledged, and they were regarded from a religious point of view. From Augustine was borrowed the view of the primacy of the will, in contrast

---

[1] The chief thesis of the bull : *Porro subesse*, etc., is taken from the *Opusc. c. error. Graec.* of Thomas.

with the reason. The symbolic concepticn of the sacraments
is also Augustinian. Thus, for example, taught both ALEX-
ANDER OF HALES and WILLIAM OF AUVERNE. But Aristotelianism gained ground. The reality of ideas began to be questioned.
The Greek primacy of the intellect was reässerted. Separate
doctrines were more and more subdivided and established upon
the basis of Aristotelian dialectics. It appeared to be a
"modern" theology which was advanced by ALBERT and
THOMAS OF AQUINO. The ecclesiastical authorities at first met
these "innovations" with severe censure (STEPHEN, bishop of
Paris, ROBERT KILWARDBY and JOHN PECKHAM, archbishops of
Canterbury, vid. Chartularium universit. Parisiensis, i. 543 ff.,
558 ff., 624 ff.). The Thomistic doctrine is charged with contradiction of Augustine. On the other hand, ALEXANDER and
BONAVENTURA are lauded (chart. univ. Paris. i. 634). This accounts in part for the attempt of the older theology to maintain
itself, not hesitating to employ to that end the scientific means
furnished by the age, i. e., Aristotelianism. In this attempt
Henry of Ghent and Bonaventura were most prominent. But
English theology brought important aid to this tendency. The
traditions of Anselm were still influential in England. To these
was added the stimulus of the important work of ROBERT
GROSSETESTE of Lincoln († 1253), who combined the Augustinian Realism with a Realism of the empirical philosophy as
applied to individuals. Such men as RICHARD of Middleton, and, above all, DUNS SCOTUS, as also ROGER BACON, continued to promote this tendency. Thus from various directions
the older Platonic-Augustinian theology antagonized the modern
Aristotelian dialectic theology, but in such a way as to turn the
entire scientific fabric of Aristotle against the Aristotelians.

It may be said that the two tendencies which were once represented by the schools of Tours and Bec, and which then in the
first period of Scholasticism found in Abelard and Anselm typical
representatives, i. e., the rational-critical and the speculative,
have been perpetuated to our own times. Upon one side stood
the Aristotelians, and upon the other the Platonizing Augustinians. Both parties were, indeed, dependent upon the scientific
method of Aristotle ; but the differences which separated them
may be rightly traced as above to their source.

We now, having gained a general view of the situation, turn
to note the individual theological leaders of the period.

At the head of the list we place ALEXANDER OF HALES (*doctor
irrefragabilis*, † 1245). He composed a *Summa universae theologiae*. He already betrays the influence of Aristotle. In his
great work, the problems and methods of the later Scholasticism

distinctly appear, and he exerted a controlling influence upon his successors, particularly in the doctrine of the sacraments. The new spirit is yet more plainly manifest in ALBERT THE GREAT (*doctor universalis,* † 1280). It was he who first employed the system of Aristotle in a comprehensive way in the construction of theology. His discussions upon metaphysics and the theory of knowledge moulded the thought of Thomas. Besides his *Paraphrases* upon Aristotle, special mention must be made of his *Commentary* upon the Sentences of the Lombard, a (not completed) *Summa,* and a *Summa de creaturis* (Opp. 21 vols., ed. Jammy, Lyons, 1651; cf. BACH, Alb. Mag. 1881). In the spirit of Albert, his greater disciple, THOMAS OF AQUINO (*angelus ecclesiae,* † 1274) toiled on. In him, with a comprehensive acquaintance with Aristotle and the ecclesiastical writers (the Areopagite now comes into prominence), were combined complete harmony with the teachings of the church and a genuinely religious spirit, together with pre-eminent dialectic talent. Thomas can scarcely be called a man of genius, but he was as great in systematizing as was Albert in collecting. Among his writings we may mention the *Commentary* on the Sentences of the Lombard, the *Summa totius theologiae,* the *Summa de veritate cath. fidei contra gentiles,* the *Expositio symboli,* and the *Compendium theologiae.*[1] The systematic talent of Thomas is at once manifest in the simple arrangement of the material in his *Summa:* (1) Concerning God. (2) Concerning the approach of the rational creature toward God, or of man. (3) Concerning Christ, who, on account of his being man, is for us the way of approach to God—under which he treats of Christ, redemption, and the sacraments. From God—to God—through Christ: this is the simple foundation thought. The work is confessedly unfinished, closing abruptly at the doctrine of repentance; but it was completed by the disciples of Thomas from his other writings. The scheme of the work is as follows: A question (*quaestio*) is stated, and then divided into a series of articles, each of which is presented in an interrogative form. Then, with the introductory formula, *videtur quod non,* a number of arguments, perhaps from the Bible, the Fathers, or Aristotle, are presented against the question. Then are given, introduced by a *sed contra est,* a number of other arguments on the affirmative

---

[1] They were often edited. Before me lies the Antwerp edition of 1612. I cite the Summa from the edition of Fretté and Maré (Paris, 1882 ff.), and the Compendium according to the edition of Albert, 1896. The literature connected with his name is also almost limitless. Vid. WERNER, d. h. Thom., 3 vols. WAGENMANN, PRE. xvi. 570 ff. PORTMANN, Das Syst. d. Summa d. h. Thom., 1894.

side.   Upon this follows the decision, beginning with *Respondeo dicendum*, and usually answering the question in the affirmative. The supposed counter-arguments are then answered under the captions :   *Ad primum, Ad secundum, etc., dicendum.*[1]   We cite an illustration.   In the First Part of the *Summa* the fourth article under the eighth question reads :   " Whether to be everywhere is an attribute of God ?   (1) It appears that to be everywhere is not an attribute of God."   Four philosophical arguments are adduced for this position, partly from Aristotle, and then are added two arguments from Augustine.   (2)   " But upon the opposite side is what Ambrose says."   (3) Here follows the answer :   " I reply : It is to be said, that to be everywhere is, from the beginning and essentially, an attribute of God."   Then we have the establishment of this proposition, and afterward a refutation of the six arguments for the negative :   " To the first, second, etc., it is to be said."

With Thomas, the Aristotelian, we here mention his friend, the Franciscan, BONAVENTURA (*doctor seraphicus*, † 1274), who, however, in theology maintained the old Augustinian-Platonic theories.   Bonaventura attached a greater importance to the mystic element in his theology than his predecessors.   It is not to be inferred, however, that he pursued with any the less energy the dogmatic and philosophical problems of his age.   He declared himself, in comparison with Alexander, a " poor and lean compiler" (in sent. ii. declaratio).   Of his writings, we mention his *Commentary* upon the Sentences, his dogmatic *Compendium breviloquium*, and also his *Compendium theol. veritatis*, the *Declaratio terminorum theologiae*, and the mystical *Compendium itinerarium mentis in deum.*[2]

3. Before scrutinizing the teachings of the age upon separate doctrines, it will be well for us to observe, in the case of Thomas, who was so influential in determining them, the method and aim of scholastic labors.   (*a*) The Object of faith, and therefore also of theology, is supernaturally revealed by God.   The necessity of revelation grows out of the fact that human reason cannot by the power of nature recognize the nature of God, *e. g.*, the Trinity.   But revelation extends also to such matters

---

[1] This is the treatment of material introduced by Abelard.   The *conclusio* printed in most editions at the end of the separate articles is not the work of Thomas himself.

[2] His works were often edited : At Rome, 1588 ff.; Lyons, 1668 ; Mayence, 1609; Venice, 1751 ; Paris, 1863 f.   The best edition is that of Quaracchi, 1882 ff.   HEFELE edited the Breviloquium in 1861 and Vicetia in 1881.   It is not to be imagined that Thomas held a monopoly of the theological ideas in the thirteenth century.   Bonaventura both as a Mystic and as a Scholastic followed to a large extent an independent course.

as reason might perhaps by itself discover, but only slowly and at a late period (c. gentil. i. 3 ff.; summ. i. qu. 1, art. 1). In this way man becomes absolutely certain in regard to his religious knowledge, since it comes "immediately from God through revelation" (summ. i. q. 1, art. 5). But revelation is contained in the Holy Scriptures. Their real author is God : *auctor sacrae scripturae est deus* (ib. i. q. 1, a. 10). By inspiration God imparted to the prophets definite items of knowledge by the way of transient impression (*impressionis transeuntis*). "Prophecy is a certain knowledge (*quaedam cognitio*) impressed upon the mind of a prophet by divine revelation through some manner of instruction (*per modum cujusdam doctrinae*) (cf. ii. ii. q. 171, a. 2, 6 ; q. 172, a. 3).[1] God has immediately confirmed this by the history of the diffusion of faith, as well as by miracles and signs. And thus he shows the teacher of the truth [to be] invisibly inspired (c. gent. i. 6). It must therefore be said : "The authority of those should be believed to whom revelation has been made" (summ. i. q. 1, a. 8). As the Scriptures must, on the one hand, be believed because of their origin, they are, on the other hand, the only sure and binding authority. "But one uses the authorities of the canonical scripture properly and in arguing from necessity ; the authorities of other teachers of the church in arguing, as it were, from one's own resources, but with probability. For our faith rests upon the revelation given to the apostles and prophets who wrote the canonical books, but not upon revelation, if such there were, given to other teachers" (ib.).[2] Thus did Thomas distinctly proclaim the Holy Scriptures as the revelation of God—as the source and absolute authority of Christian doctrine. Precisely so did Bonaventura also teach : "Authority resides primarily in the Holy Scriptures, which have been wholly established (*condita tota*) through the Holy Spirit for the directing of the catholic faith" (brevil. 5. 7). But revelation is a doctrine.[3] Its necessity is deduced, not from the ex-

---

[1] Vid. Bonaventura in hexaëm serm. 9 (opp. i. 35 f.), *e. g.*, it is proper that faith be confirmed, through the inspired word. Albert, summ. i. tract. 1, qu. 4 ; qu. 5, membr. 2. It will be observed how moderate is the view here taken of inspiration. In the earlier Middle Ages Agobard had rejected the view which so represented the matter as though "the Holy Spirit had not only breathed into them (*inspiraverit*) the sense of the preaching and the modes or arguments of their speeches, but had also himself from without formed in the mouths the corporeal words." Speech is not produced in the prophets as in Balaam's ass (vid. adv. Fredegis. 11, Mi. 104. 166).

[2] Cf. Quodlibeta xii. a. 26 : "The sayings of expositors do not carry with them necessity, that it should be necessary to believe them, but alone the canonical scripture which is in the Old and New Testaments."

[3] The proper object of revelation, *i. e.*, of faith, is the "first truth," or God. Everything else (as the divinity of Christ, the sacraments) is entitled to con-

istence of sin, but from the *debilitas* of the human intellect (summ. 1 q. 1, a. 5). The lines of thought presented in the Scriptures must, it was further held, be supplemented. It had been felt necessary in the church from the beginning, that what was contained in the Scriptures " diffusedly and in various forms and in some cases obscurely " should be plainly and briefly stated in a connected way, *i. e.*, "what should be proposed to all to be believed." This is furnished in the *symbolum apostolorum*, which contains the essence of the Christian faith (cf. also Bonav. breviloq. 5. 7). But since the heretics introduced false doctrines, it became necessary to enlarge and explain this symbol, which was done by the Nicene Creed, the deliverances of other councils, and the Fathers.[1] The confession is handed down, " as it were, by the personality of the entire church which is united through the faith." A "new edition of the symbol . . . for the shunning of rising errors" may yet be a necessity. Its preparation, in such case, is within the province of the pope. The counsel given in 1 Cor. i. 10 cannot be followed "unless a question of faith arising concerning the faith should be determined by him who presides over the whole church, so that thus his opinion may be firmly held by the whole church. And therefore a new edition of the symbol pertains to the sole authority of the supreme pontiff, just as do all other things which pertain to the whole church, as the assembling of a general council." Hence : "by whose authority a council is assembled and his opinion confirmed" (summ. ii. ii. q. 1, a. 9 and 10 ; cf. q. 11, a. 2). Accordingly, revelation is handed down to the Christian world in the symbols and the decrees of councils, and by means of the papal definitions of the faith. It is of course presumed that these are in harmony with the authority of Scripture ; but in reality, side by side with the *auctoritas scripturae*, and above it, stands the *sola auctoritas summi pontificis*.

siderati on "in so far as through these things we are directed toward God, and we assent to them also on account of the divine truth " (summa ii. ii. q. 1, a. 1).

[1] In the twelve, or as the Scholastics commonly enumerate, the fourteen articles, "are contained those things which are chiefly to be believed (Bonav. in sent. iii., d. 25, a. 1, q. 1). Three symbols are uniformly acknowledged : the first is for the teaching of the faith ; the second, for the explanation of the faith ; the third, for the defense of the faith " (Bonav. compend. theol. verit. v. 21 ; Centiloq., p. 3, sect. 38. Anselm, ep. ii. 41. Alex. Hales, summ. iv. q. 37, sect. 9, names four, but enumerates only three : Apostolic, Athanasian, Constantinopolitan, for which Bonaventura names the Nicene. So also Richard, sent. ii. d. 25, principale 2, q. 1 and 2. Duns, sent. i. d. 26, q. 1, 25. Durand, sent. iii. d. 36, q. 2. Biel, iii. 25, qu. un. Duns, sent. iv. d. 43, q. 1. 11). To the Scripture and the symbols are added the works of the teachers (*documenta doctorum*), of these, Bonaventura enumerates Dionysius, Gregory of Nazianzen, Gregory of Nyssa, John of Damascus, Basil, Athan-

(*b*) Since revelation cannot be comprehended by the reason, it follows that it must be acccepted *in faith*. This is necessary, if for no other reason, because otherwise the "merit of faith would be made void" (summ. ii. ii. q. 2, a. 9, 10). Thomas was the first to make a careful analysis of the conception of faith (vid. quaestio disputata de fide, opp. viii. 804 ff., and summ. ii. ii. qu. 1 ff.). He starts with the Augustinian formula : "To believe is to think with assent." The *intellectus possibilis*, or thinking faculty, reaches a conclusion in one of two ways, either that the object impresses itself upon this faculty in an intellectual way as true, or that the faculty is, by the will, inclined to assent.[1] "And thus also are we moved to believe things said, in so far as the reward of eternal life is promised to us if we shall believe, and the will is moved by this reward to assent to those things which are said, although the intellect be not moved by anything intellectual (de fide, art. 1, p. 805 b). That the intellect in this way responds to the impulse of the will is explained by the disposition (*habitus*) of faith divinely infused," *i. e.*, infused into the intellect (a. 4, p. 812 ; cf. Heinrich, quodlib. v. q. 21). Faith is thus incited by the will, but it has its seat in the intellect : "The act of faith consists essentially in cognition, and there is its perfection " (a. 2, p. 809). Faith is therefore an incipient knowledge of divine things, "which are above reason," dependent upon practical motives. It is because of the infirmity of human reason that faith alone is possible in this life. But the goal consists "in perfect knowledge (*cognitione*) of God " (a. 10, p. 820 ; c. gent. iii. 25, 8 ; 26 ; 50, 6 ; iv. 42, 1), and "eternal life will afford perfect knowledge of God" (a. 2, p. 807 b).[2] Upon these principles it can be understood, on the one hand, that faith should be regarded as reaching its consummation in knowledge. and, on the other hand, that faith, since it proceeds from the will, should be held to be meritorious (a. 3), and also that it should receive its moral character (*formatio*) from the will or from love : "faith is formed (*informatur*) by love " (a. 5, p. 813 a ; cf. summ. ii. ii. q. 4, a. 5 and 3 ; q. 2, a. 9). The ordinary layman, indeed, never attains an *explicit* faith (*fides explicita*) embracing all the articles of faith. Of him, it is ever to be said : "He believes *implicitly* the separate articles which

asius, Chrysostom, Hilary, Gregory, Augustine, Ambrose, Jerome (in Hexaëm. vid. 9, p. 36 a).

[1] Faith has to do not with the determination of the "simple natures" (*simplex quidditates*) of things, but with the decision. For we believe the true, and we disbelieve the false (de fide, art. 1).

[2] According to Thomas, the will is subordinate to the intellect, and is spiritual only in so far as it is dependent upon the latter (c. gent. iii. 26. 1).

are contained in the faith of the church."[1] But Thomas not only
expects of all teachers and spiritual advisers an *explicit faith*, but he
requires the same from the laity also in regard to the Trinity, the
incarnation, death, and resurrection of Christ, and "other
(articles) of this kind, concerning which the church appoints
festivals" (a. 11, p. 822). This demand is in harmony with
the fundamentally intellectualistic tendency of Thomas. If final
salvation consists in perfect knowledge, then a certain measure
of knowledge must be attained on earth as a preparation (p.
822 a). Faith is, therefore, an incipient knowledge of divine
revelation begotten of practical motives of the will. But the
first subjection of man to God is through faith (summ. ii. ii. q.
16, a. 1).

(*c*) This knowledge is just as little as revelation itself contrary
to reason ; it is above reason (de fid. art. 10 ad 7). It cannot,
therefore, be the province of theology to prove revelation by
human reason (*ratione humana*). This would be impossible,
since theology deals with super-reasonable articles of faith,
receiving its principles from God (summ. i. q. 1, a. 5 and 8 ;
cf. q. 32, a. 1). It can only elucidate somewhat by adducing
those things which the philosophers can also recognize. The
reasons (*rationes*) of theology are not really " *demonstrative*,
but a kind of persuasions, showing that the things which
presented in the faith are not impossible " (ii. ii. q. 1, a. 5).
They are useful also in refuting opponents (c. gent. i. 9).
But inasmuch as theology operates with the principles of revelation, its knowledge is more certain and more important than
that of all other sciences (i. q, 1, a. 2, 5). This is essentially
the position of Abelard. The great scholastics did not possess
the naive confidence of Anselm.[2]

(*d*) This was involved in their relation to the question of
Universals. Thomas here, in almost the same degree as Albert
before him, follows Aristotle or his Arabian interpreters. Man
by means of the senses perceives external things separately.
"Nothing is in the intellect which was not in the sense "
(summ. i. q. 85, a. 3 and 7). There thus arises from the
object a particular form (*forma particularis*). The active

[1] Vid. also Bonav. sent. iii., d. 25, a. 1, q. 3. Upon implicit faith, vid. G.
HOFFMAN, Die Lehre von der fides implicita, 1903.

[2] In the question, whether theology is a *scientia speculativa vel practica*,
Albert adopted the latter view (summ. i. tr. 1, q. 3, memb. 3), Thomas
rather the former (summ. i. q. 1, a. 4). Thomas argues that theology has to
do not so much with human actions as with the "divine affairs." There is
here no real contradiction, since this theology, which is no more than
advanced knowledge of the faith, is after all in the conception of Thomas
eminently practical.

intellect (*intellectus agens*) then transforms this in the intellectual faculty (*intellectus possibilis*) into an intelligible species (*species intelligibilis*) (ib. i. q. 79, a. 3 ; q. 85, a. 2). The intellect accordingly nas knowledge of the Universal, but by this it is by no means to be understood that it thereby directly cognizes ideas actually existent. The general conception, which we form for ourselves, is always merely derivative, a *universale post rem*. The universal does not exist as a general idea, but it is in the objects of sense under certain criteria (*universale in re*). Its original type is seen in the ideas of God (*universalia ante rem*), which eternally preëxist in him, as the artist's ideas exist in him before he executes his work. Thus Albert held, and before him Avicenna. Accordingly, the essential nature of things is dependent upon the divine idea, and in so far Plato was right (c. gent. iii. 24). Theoretically, this Aristotelian fully accepted the maxim : " For the present we cannot know (*cognoscere*) God except through material effects " (summ. i. q. 86, a. 2, ad. 1). But as revelation now supplies this defect, the knowledge of this world in its connection of causes and effects becomes a knowledge of God (c. gent. iii. 50). The ideas of God are made manifest in the order of the world.

4. Finally, it may be said that Scholasticism has two aspects. It is orthodoxy, maintaining that the teachings of the church, the declarations of the ecclesiastical canon, the customs and practices of the church, are absolutely and unassailably true. That which actually exists is true, if it be ecclesiastically sanctioned. On the other hand, Scholasticism has a rationalizing tendency. That which is unchurchly is condemned as being unreasonable, and that which is churchly proved to be reasonable, by the intricate methods of dialectics.

Here may be mentioned two great philosophic minds. ROGER BACON († 1294) emphasized the importance of experience and the knowledge derived from it.[1] RAYMUNDUS LULLUS († 1315) demanded, in opposition to the Averroistic illumination,[2] that the positions of the Christian faith be strictly proved : " We propose to prove the articles of faith by necessary reasons." The understanding must follow the faith, and thus they must mount together to the knowledge of the truth, even to the mysteries of revelation.[3] The joyous confidence in the omnipotence of logical demonstration, which marked the early days of Scholasticism, is here revived. But from the theological point of

---

[1] Vid. STÖCKL. ii. 916 ff.
[2] Vid. REUTER,.Gesch. d. Aufklärung, ii. 148 ff.
[3] Vid. his Ars magna and cf. NEANDER, Denkwürdigkeiten ii. (1846). STÖCKL. ii. 924 ff.

view, HENRY OF GHENT († 1293) is above all worthy of mention as a sturdy representative of the older theology (he wrote *Quodlibeta*, a *Commentary* upon the Sentences, and a *Summa theologiae*).[1] In his conception of universals, he varies from Thomas. He held that the patterns (*exemplaria*) of things exist as independent entities in God (quodl. vii. q. 1, 2). Only grace can secure for us a view of these (summ. i. q. 2). He also maintained an actual existence of matter, which Thomas, following Aristotle, regarded as a mere potency (quodl. i. q. 10). Body and soul have not one, but two forms (quodl. iii. q. 15). Everywhere we find the emphasis laid upon perception and the empirical, as well as upon the religiously-colored Realism of ideas. In this, as his exaltation of the will above the intellect, Henry betrays his Augustinian character, since the activity of the will is the dominating and controlling factor in life : " The will outranks the intellect " (quodl. i. q. 14 and 16). As DUNS SCOTUS establishes the transition to the last phase of the scholastic theology, we reserve notice of his position for our next chapter. We can here but refer also to his contemporary, RICHARD OF MIDDLETON, who likewise strongly emphasized the significance of the will in God and in man. (His commentary on the Sentences was printed, Brixen, 1591.) For the doctrine of Richard, vid. SEEBERG, Theologie des Duns Scotus, p. 16 ff.

§ 54. *Doctrine of God and Christology.*

BAUR, Die Lehre v. d. Dreieinigket u. Menschwerdung, ii. 1842. J. DE-LITZSCH, Die Gotteslehre d. Thom. v. Aq., 1870. RITSCHL, Geschichtl. Stud. z. chr. Lehre v. Gott, in Jarbb. f. deutsche Theol., 1865, 279 ff. WERNER, Thomas, ii. 619 ff. DORNER, Lehre v. d. Person Christi, ii. 399 ff. H. SCHULTZ, Lehre v. d. Gottheit Christi, 1881, p. 153 ff.

1. The doctrine of the Nature of God was not wrought out by the ancient church, as the entire interest of that age was absorbed by the Trinitarian problem. The term "person"[2] was restricted to the Trinitarian formulae, the divine nature being described as "substance" or "essense" (*substantia, essentia*). And even when this was embellished by the predicates of eternity or of superessentiality, it led no further than to

---

[1] Ed. Venet. 1613. Cf. STÖCKL. ii. 739 ff. WERNER, Heinr. v. Ghent in Denkschr. d. Wiener Akad. Phil.-hist. cl., vol. 28, p. 97 ff. SIEBECK, Ztschr. f. Philos. u. phil. Krit., vol. 93, p. 200 ff. For his biography, see EHRLE in Arch. f. Litt. u. KG. d. MA. i. 366 ff. For his theology, SEE-BERG, Theol. des Duns Scotus, p. 605-625.

[2] How persistent are such traditional usages is illustrated in the fact that Jacobi is the first who speaks of the "personal" God. Vid. EUCKEN, Grundbegriffe d. Gegenw, ed. 2, p. 269.

the unfruitful abstractions of the conception of God in Greek philosophy. Even Augustine defined God as Essence (*essentia*), and the conception of the Areopagite appeared to be in harmony with this (Vol. I., p. 290 f.). This theoretical deficiency was balanced practically by the doctrine of the divine attributes, and theoretically by the wealth of personal analogies, in the Augustinian doctrine of the Trinity, and, still more, by the recognition of God as energetic Will in the Augustinian doctrine of predestination. But it was a decided step in advance when Anselm expressly maintained that God is a thinking Spirit (monolog. 27. 7 ff.).[1] Here, too, the teaching of Thomas is very significant. He also spoke of God in the Grecian way, as the supremely Existent (*maxime ens*), the prime Mover (*primum movens*), and gave the maxim : " We cannot consider concerning God how he is, but rather how he is not " (summa i. q. 2, a. 3 ; q. 2 init.; compend. 3 ff.). But in such connections he yet always made it clear that the being of God is *thinking* and *willing* (summ. i. q. 19, a. 1). Since now God is the prime Mover, it follows that he is " pure Action (*actus purus*) and without any admixture of potentiality " (comp. 4, 11 ; summ. q. 3, a. 1, u. 7 ; 9, a. 1 ; q. 25, a. 1). Since this absolute Activity is *thinking* and *willing*, it realizes a goal ; and since God is goodness, His will is moved only by goodness or—it is *love* (ib. i. q. 19, a. 2; q. 20, a. 1). The final goal commensurate with God is He himself. Everything occurring in the world must therefore be referred to this goal, since God is the originator of the world. From this it is inferred that the fundamental relationship of God to the world is that of love for it. " When anyone loves another, he wishes good for him, and so treats him as he would treat himself, doing good to him as to himself " (ib. q. 20, a. 1, ad 3). The thought is clear : God always desires himself as the final goal. When he establishes the world, he desires it from eternity as a means to this end ; in other words, he is related to it as to himself, *i. e.*, he loves it. This relation of God to the world is manifested in that he gives to the world all things needful and preserves it in its course (this constituting his *justitia* and *veritas ;* q. 21, a. 1 and 2), and, further, in that he banishes misery. This is done when deficiencies are overcome " through the perfection of some good." This is the mercy of God (ib. a. 3). God therefore loves the world, since, in every action of his bearing upon it, righteousness and mercy are joined together. This classical argumentation leads to a religious conception of God which necessarily includes the idea

---

[1] Cf. the Germanic conception of God in *Cur deus homo ?* Esp. ii. 16.

of a personal loving will.   But instead of resting content in this positive conception, Thomas displays the influence of the Greek apprehension of God, *e. g.*, regarding redemption as merely the best adapted means "through which he better and more appropriately attains his end" (ib. iii. q. 1, a. 2).   Yet we cannot fail to note in Thomas a positive advance in the doctrine concerning God.

2. This cannot be said in regard to the doctrine of the Trinity.   When the Lombard, Alexander, and Thomas cite the spiritual functions of man as furnishing analogies, or when Richard of St. Victor (ll. 6 de. trin.) endeavors to find the solution of the problem in love, which requires a "mutual love" and a separateness (*alietas*) of the three persons,[1] they do not overstep the suggestions of Augustine.   Only one point calls for our attention here.   The Lombard (i. dist. 5) discusses the questions, whether the Father begat the divine *essentia*, or whether the latter begat the Son or himself.   He answers them all in the negative.   Since the divine essence, or nature, "is common to the three persons and entire in each," the Father would otherwise have begotten himself, *i. e.*, the essence by virtue of which he exists, which is impossible.   Furthermore, the divine essence would thus seem to be degraded to a mere relationship of the Godhead.   The Lombard decides that the divine essence, which is identical in the hypostases, neither begets nor is begotten ; accordingly, the intertrinitarian life is a relation subsisting between the hypostases.   These ideas, which were based upon the Augustinian premise of the strict unity of God, were assailed by JOACHIM OF FLORIS († 1202), who maintained that the discrimination of the divine substance from the persons leads to Sabellianism or Arianism.   He himself, like the Cappadocians, proceeds upon the supposition of the three persons, who together constitute one entity (*unum*), one substance (*una substantia*), or one God (*unus deus*), but not simply one individual (*unus*).   Collective terms, such as "one herd, one populace," are cited in illustration.[2]   The Fourth Lateran Council (A. D. 1215) made the following deliverance : "We believe and confess with Peter Lombard, that there is one certain supreme Entity (*una quaedam summa res*), incomprehensible indeed and ineffable, which truly is the Father, the

---

[1] Cf. MEIER, Die Lehre v. d. Trinit. i. 292 ff.   Rich. exclaims : "Behold, how easily reason demonstrates that there must be a plurality of persons in the Godhead ! "

[2] Vid. excerpts from Joachim in the Protocol of Anagni (A. D. 1255), DENIFLE, Archiv. i. 136 ff.; cf. also the citation in Duns Scotus, sent. i. d. 5, q. 1. 3.

Son, and the Holy Spirit, three persons at once, and separately either one of them.   And therefore in God there is a trinity alone, not a quaternity ; because anyone of the three persons is that Entity (*res*), viz., substance, essence, or divine nature, which alone is the source of all things, outside of which nothing can be found.   And that Entity is not begetting nor begotten, nor proceeding ; but is the Father who begets, the Son who is begotten, and the Holy Spirit who proceeds, that there may be distinctions in persons and unity in nature (Hefele, v. 880 f.).   The church of the Middle Ages thus explicitly adopted the Augustinian doctrine concerning God.[1]

3.   The Christological discussions of the twelfth century were not renewed in the thirteenth.   The great Scholastics present in their Christology merely a reproduction of the traditional dogma, in which we note however the failure to emphasize that contemplation of the Man Jesus which inspired the devotional ardor of the *Imitatio Christi*.   The fundamental ideas are as follows : The Logos-person, or the divine nature, takes the impersonal human nature into unity with itself.   There is not thus originated *one nature*, but the union is consummated in the person.   " The divine nature . . . united to itself human nature, although not to its very self, but in one person '' (Bonav. iii. d. 5, a. 1, q. 1).   " The union was made in the person, not in the nature '' (Thom. summ. iii. q. 2, a. 2).[2]   It is the entire human nature which is here involved.   But the result is, after all, not a real combination of the two natures.   The union consists in their common relation to the Logos-person.   The union . . . is a certain relation which may be considered between the divine nature and the human, according to which they meet in the one person of the Son of God.   The *unio* is real, not in the divine, but only in the human nature (ib. q. 2, a. 7).   Accordingly, the incarnation is to be understood only relatively :   " But God became man in this, that human nature began to be in the suppositum (ὑπόστασις) of the divine nature, which pre-existed from eternity'' (ib. q. 16, a. 6, ad 1).   It is the inherited

---

[1] The Lombard introduces into theology the Cappadocian terminology of the Damascene, and argues in its support (i. d. 19 NO).   But it is important to observe that, even in the sermons of the period, the Augustinian type of the doctrine is preserved.   *E. g.*, SCHÖNBACH, Altd. Pred. ii. 115, 110 ; iii. 115 f. (ein warer got in der heiligen drinüsse.   Der vater und sein wistum und sein minne ist neur ein got).

[2] Thomas accurately defined both terms.   "*Natura* signifies essence (*essentia*), or that which anything is, or the quiddity of a species (ib. q. 2, a. 1); *persona*, the rational, individual substance of a nature (*rationalis naturae individua substantia*) (a. 2, after Boethius); *hypostasis* is the same, with the omission of the term *rationalis*.''

defect of this Christology, that while divinity and humanity are
placed in opposition abstractly, as infinite and finite, the Christ
of the Gospels is only depicted in empty words.[1]   This drift is
clearly seen in the discussion by Thomas of the question, whether
there is only one being (*esse*) in Christ. He concludes that, as
there is no hypostatic being (*Sein*) in the human nature of
Christ, the question is to be answered in the affirmative (ib. q.
17, a. 2). Finally, the *communicatio idiomatum* is taught, as
existing between the concretes, God and man : " They are able
to impart to one another the attributes (*idiomata communicare*)
of that nature according to which they are spoken of in concrete," as though it should be said : God is man and man is
God (Bonav. iii. d. 6, a. 1, q. 1 ; Thom. iii. q. 16, a. 5). Upon
the two wills and two " operations," see Thom. iii. q. 18 and
19. The present period displayed no independent interest in
questions of Christology.[2] Theologians were content to demonstrate the logical consistency of the traditional teaching of the
church. They learned nothing—nor did they forget anything.[3]

§ 55. *The Work of Christ.*

1. The present period produced nothing new touching the work
of Christ. The attempt was made, as had been done by the
Lombard, to combine the objective view, in which the ideas of
Anselm were accepted, with Abelard's subjective interpretations.
Thus ALEXANDER OF HALES, following Anselm, teaches the
necessity of the satisfaction which Christ effects through his
"merit" (summ. iii. q. 1, memb. 4 ff.; q. 16, memb. 3 and 4).
BONAVENTURA states the doctrine with more precision. The
work of *reparatio* includes (1) That men through Christ,
especially through his innocent sufferings, learn to know, love,
and imitate God, and (2) that their sins be forgiven them
through a worthy (*condignam*) satisfaction. This makes the incarnation a necessity (breviloq. 4. 1. 9). "Since a simple
creature could not make satisfaction for the whole human race,
nor would it be proper that a creature of another race be taken
for the purpose, it was necessary that the person of the one

---

[1] How little the problem was understood may be gathered from the fact
that Thomas declared that it would have been possible for the Logos to
assume two human natures at the same time (ib. q. 3, a. 7).

[2] But note the attempt of Bonaventura in the Breviloq. to find for every
Christological proposition a ground in the theory of redemption.

[3] Luther charged upon the Scholastics, that they "make a wall between
the Son of God and the Son born of the Virgin Mary " (Erl. ed. 47. 362).
This charge cannot be brought against Bernard, but it is true as applied to the
scholastic method.

rendering satisfaction be God and man '' (sent. iii. d. 20, a. 1, q. 3). The satisfaction is effected through the merit of Christ (*pro nobis mereri et satisfacere*, iii. d. 18, a. 2, q. 2) which he won ''not only in action but also in suffering '' (*passione*) (ib. a. 1, q. 3. ; cf. brevil. 4. 7). Since in the acting and suffering of Christ there was a '' *concursus* of both natures '' (brevil. 4. 2), there belongs to the '' merit of the God-man—the perfection and plenitude of merit '' (ib. 4. 7). '' But to make satisfaction is to repay the honor due to God '' (4. 9). This was done by the sufferings of Christ as the most appropriate means '' for placating God '' (iii. d. 20, a. 1, q. 5). Herein is displayed the mercy as well as the righteousness of God (ib. a. 1, q. 2). But with this Anselmian view is combined also the Abelardian idea, that the passion commended itself also as the most appropriate means, because suited to arouse men to a responsive love toward God (ib. a. 1, q. 5). It is to be noted, finally, that Bonaventura, by developing the thought of Christ's relation to the church as the Head to the members, brought into view the connection between the work of redemption and the redeemed, as Anselm was never able to do.[1] Reparation is accomplished, accordingly, by remedying, satisfying, and reconciling (*remediando, satisfaciendo, et reconciliando*, brevil. 4. 2).

2. The noteworthy discussion of the subject by Thomas follows the same line. In Christ as the Redeemer, the human nature comes into prominence ; but to it belongs, in consequence of its union with God, a certain divine efficacy (*virtus*) (summ. iii. q. 48, a. 5, ad 1 ; q. 49, a. 1, ad 1 and 2). This is not incomprehensible, when we remember that the human nature exists only in the divine hypostasis (vid. supra). The work of redemption is thus presented : '' Inasmuch as he is also man, it is competent for him to unite men to God by exhibiting the precepts and gifts (of God) to men and by making satisfaction and intercession for men to God '' (q. 26, a. 2). In this summary the leading ideas of the discussion are clearly expressed. (*a*) In the human nature of Christ dwells the fullness of all grace (ib. q. 7, a. 1). He is now the Head of the human race, or of the church. From the Head, rank (*ordo*), perfection and virtue overflow upon the members (q. 8, a. 1, 3, 4).[2] On the other hand, the *merit* of the Head inures to the good of the members (q. 48, a. 1 ; q. 49, a. 1) in so far as the latter are willing to belong to the Head. '' But the members ought to be con-

---

[1] But see Bernard, De erroribus Abael., 6, 15 : ''Therefore the Head made satisfaction for the members.''

[2] Thus even the sacraments, ''which have their virtue from the passion of of Christ '' (q. 49, a. 1 ad 4).

formed to the Head " (q. 49, a. 3, ad 3). This great conception establishes the proposition, that Christ is the new man, who
is the leaven and principle of the new humanity. (*b*) The
work of redemption is accordingly to be considered primarily
from the point of view, that Christ by his teaching, his acts, and
his sufferings became the teacher and pattern of our race. This
applies to his circumcision (q. 37, a. 1), baptism (q. 39, a. 1),
temptation (q. 4, a. 1, 3), teaching : " By associating with men
. . . he manifested to all his divinity by preaching and performing miracles and by dealing innocently and justly among
men" (q. 40, a. 1, ad 1),[1] and miracles (q. 44, a. 3). It can
neither surprise nor give offense to observe that Thomas applies
this thought even to the passion of Christ : " Through this, man
recognizes how much God loves man, and through this he
is provoked to the loving of God, in which the perfection of
human salvation consists," and " through this he has given to
us an example of obedience, humility, constancy, righteousness,
and other virtues" (q. 46, a. 3 ; q. 47, a. 4, ad 2). The love
(*caritas*) to which we thus attain serves also (according to Lk.
7. 47) to secure the forgiveness of sins (q. 49, a. 1). Even
the resurrection, the ascension, and the session at the right hand
of God serve this end of instruction and suggestion, the last-
named particularly because the exalted Saviour " sends forth
thence divine gifts to men " (q. 53, a. 1 ; q. 55, a. 3 ; q.
57, a. 6). This is the first train of thought : The Head of the
church reveals God to his followers, teaches them, incites them
to good, and bestows his gifts upon them. (*c*) Then comes the
question of satisfaction. The absolute necessity of this Thomas
denies. Since there is no one above God, and he is himself the
" supreme and common Good of the whole universe," he could
even without satisfaction forgive sin (q. 46, a. 2, ad 3). But the
method of satisfaction would most clearly give expression to his
righteousness and mercy, and he therefore chose it (ib. a.
1, ad 3). At this point Thomas parts company with the juristic
conception of Anselm, a departure which is further emphasized
by his view that, on account of the greatness of Christ's love and
the value of his life, " the passion of Christ was not only a sufficient, but also a superabundant satisfaction " (q. 48, a. 2 and 4).
Thus both the necessity and the equivalence of the satisfaction
are surrendered. The satisfaction consists in the passion of
Christ. He bore all sufferings "according to genus " (q. 46,
a. 5), and the greatest possible grief (*dolor maximus*, ib. a. 6).

---

[1] Cf. q. 42, a. 2, an intelligent response to the inquiry why Christ did not
become a writer.

But the passion of Christ is now to be regarded, not from a material, but from a personal and ethical point of view. It was an act of obedience and love : " He suffered out of love and obedience " (q. 47, a. 2), since God " inspired in him the will to suffer for us by infusing love into him " (ib. a. 3). His death was also a sacrifice only in so far as it was an act of free will (q. 47, a. 2, ad 2 ; a. 4, ad 2 ; q. 48, a. 3). If the conception of "merit" forms the basis of man's ethical conduct, according to the theory of the Middle Ages, it is but consistent that Thomas should regard the passion also from this point of view : "Through his passion he *merited* salvation, not only for himself but also for his members " (q. 48, a. 1); for suffering is meritorious "only in proportion as anyone voluntarily endures it " (ib. ad. 1). The expiatory sufferings of Christ are the fundamental basis of our salvation. But that the aim of these is for our justification and the imparting of grace, is not clearly set forth by Thomas. As the stimulating influence of Christ continues in his state of exaltation, "his representation from human nature," in heaven is "a kind of intercession (*interpellatio*) for us " (q. 57, a. 6).

(*d*) The Result of the work of redemption, according to Thomas, embraces the following : (1) The forgiveness of sins, and this through the love begotten in us (vid. under (*a*)), as also through *redemtio* (cf. q. 48, a. 4), since the church is " regarded as one person with its Head " (q. 49, a. 1). This applies not only to original, but also to actual sins (ib. a. 5). (2) The releasing from sin releases also from the devil (a. 2). (3) Releasing from the punishment of sin (a. 3.). (4) The sacrifice of Christ has the effect " that on account of this good found in human nature *God is placated* with respect to every offense of the human race " (a. 4). (5) The opening of the door of heaven on account of the release from sin (a. 5). This genuinely scholastic analysis of the material obstructs a clear perception of the view of Thomas. But we may, in harmony with his spirit, condense the statement of his view as follows : Christ, the Head of the church, is by virtue of this position our Redeemer. (1) Because he reveals God to us, and by love overpowers us and incites us to good, and thereby makes us capable of securing the forgiveness of sins. (2) Because he through his passion reconciles God and renders satisfaction to him, and thereby effects for us salvation and immunity from punishment. (3) Because he by both these achievements delivers us from the power of the devil and opens for us the door of heaven. In this classical presentation of the subject are combined the views of Anselm (in a fragmentary way indeed) and

8

of Abelard.[1]   The result is evidently that forgiveness is accomplished and secured in a two-fold way.   The theory before us is the positive resultant of the discussion concerning the nature of redemption.

§ 56. *Doctrines of the Original State and of Sin.*

Cf. SCHWANE, DG. d. mittl. Zeit, p. 334 ff.

1. The doctrine of the original state stands in most intimate relations with that of sin and with the ethical ideal, and hence requires attention at this point.   It receives its peculiar scholastic form from ALEXANDER OF HALES, whose ideas were perpetuated and modified by Bonaventura, Albert, and Thomas. Its chief peculiarity consists in the strict line of discrimination between the original state of the first man and the additional endowment bestowed upon him by grace (Thom. sent. ii. d. 20, q. 2, a. 3).   (*a*) The inborn, natural ethical state (*habitus*) of man is by some described as original righteousness (*justitia originalis*), by which is meant the harmony of the natural powers and the absence of the concupiscence which now hinders their normal exercise (Bonav. sent. ii. d. 19, a. 3, q. 1. Thom. l. c.).[2]   (*b*) To this is added the *donum superadditum*, or

---

[1] This varies from the usual presentation of the case.   The observant reader will be disposed to make an attempt to reduce to one the two chief lines of thought—somewhat perhaps in this way : In becoming man, Christ opened to the human race through his life communion with God, and in his passion attested that the men who should follow him should, despite all the sufferings of the world, remain with God ; and by this means he became the ground of the forgiveness of sins, inasmuch as God looks upon the men who follow him and who have begun in the Christian life in the light of Christ's perfection, and, on the ground of his guarantee, passes upon them a different judgment than he has previously done.   I find some approaches to this in Thomas, *e. g.*, q. 49, a. 3, ad 3 : "That the satisfaction of Christ has effect in us *in so far as we are incorporated in him*," and ib. a. 4 : "That on account of this good found in human nature (*i. e.*, the work of Christ) God is placated . . . *in so far as pertains to those who are united* to the *suffering Christ*." Not the fact that this good is in Christ, but that it is through him in human nature, serves to reconcile God.   But Thomas did not plainly teach this.

[2] Among the natural ethical powers, especial prominence is given to the *synderesis*, or *synteresis*.   According to Alexander, who first treats the conception exhaustively, the Synteresis is the habitual inclination toward the good which, infallible and inalienable, dwells in man, as well in the reason as in the will (ii. q. 76, m. 1, 2, 3).   Similarly, Bonav. ii. d. 39, a. 2, q. 1 ff.; vid. also Heinrich, quodl. i. q. 18.   According to Thomas, this has its seat exclusively in the reason : "A natural *habitus* of first principles of action, which are natural principles of natural law.   Which has an immutable rectitude . . . whose office it is to object to evil and incline to good" (Quaest. disp. de synder. a. 1, 2, opp. viii. 836-838. ; cf. sent. i. q. 79, a. 12, 13, and Alb., De homin. tr. 1, q. 69, a. 1).   But the conscience (*conscientia*) embraces the acts which

added gift of grace. According to some theologians, as, *c. g.*, Henry (Quod. lib. ii. q. ii.; vi. q. ii.) this *donum super-additum* is the first ground of the original righteousness of man. It embraces, in the first instance, the separate "graces gratuit-ously given," such as the bestowal of the sciences, contem-plation, and the immortality of the body. Especially was there given to Adam, as the head of the race, such a measure of knowledge, "that he might always be able to instruct and gov-ern others" (Thom. summ. i. q. 94, a. 3). It was a "knowl-edge (*scientia*) illuminating the intellect for the recognition of itself and its God and this world" (Bonav. brevil. 2. 11).[1] (*c*) Yet the thing of chief importance is other than this, *i. e.*, the gift of "the grace which makes acceptable" (*gratia gratum faciens*). This *supernaturale complementum* (Alex. ii. q. 96, iii. 1. Bonav. in sent. ii. d. 29, a. 1, q. 1) consists essentially in an indwelling of God, or an infused love, adapting the feeling (*caritas habilitans affectum*) to the loving of God (Bonav. ii. d. 29, a. 1, q. 1; brevil. 2. 11). This grace which sanctifies man is a "universal habitus, moulding (*informans*) both the subject and all his powers and works, through which God, dwelling in all his saints, infuses the power of meriting eternal life" (Alb. summ. ii. tr. 16, q. 98, m. 4). This habitus of grace has its seat in the "essence of the soul," not in the separate powers (Thom. i. ii. q. 110, a. 4). According to some, this grace is not imparted to man at the moment of his creation, but at some later point of time; and hence man may and should earn it for himself by a merit of fitness (*meritum congrui*) (Alex. summ. ii. q. 96, m. 1. Bonav. sent. ii. d. 29, a. 2, q. 2. Alb. l. c., tr. 14,

---

in any given instance impel to or restrain from action, or pass judgment upon deeds performed, in either case in accordance with the principles contained in the *Synteresis* (Quaest. de consc. a. 1, ib., p. 840). According to Duns, the Synteresis is the "habitus of principles which is always right," resident in the intellect; whereas the conscience is the "personal (*proprius*) habitus of practical decision." If the former, therefore, contains the principles of ethical conduct, the latter applies these principles in any given case to the con-duct (Sent. ii. d. 39, q. 2. 4). The conception of the συντήρησις dates back to Jerome (opp. ed. Vallarsi v. 10) and is further defined by him as *scintilla conscientiae*. NITZSCH (Jarbb. f. prot. Theol. 1879, 500 ff.) makes it appear probable that simply συνείδησις stood originally in the passages in Jerome. E. KLOSTERMANN found manuscript evidence of this (Theol. Littztg. 1896, 637. Cf. APPEL, Die Lehre d. Scholastiker v. d. synt. 1891 and Ztschr. f. KG. xiii. 535 ff. SIEBECK, Gesch. d. Psychol. i. 2, p. 445 ff. SEEBERG, Gewissen u. Gewissensbildung, 1896, p. 69 f.).

[1] This *gratia gratis data* is, according to Thomas, given "in order that another may co-operate in securing justification;" the *gratia gratum faciens*, that through it "man may be united to God." The former is there-fore a kind of charismatic endowment. Vid. quaest. de grat. a. 5, p. 988; quodlibeta xii. a. 96, ad 1.

q. 90, m. 1). According to others, it is bestowed upon man together with original righteousness at his creation (Thom. in sent. ii. d. 29, q. 1, a. 2). If the motive of this new doctrine be sought, it is not to be found in the desire to minimize the distance separating the natural state from the state of sin. Such was an incidental result, but not the ground upon which the doctrine was based. The motive lay in a certain Augustinian tendency. An end can be attained only by the exercise of powers commensurate. "But eternal life is an end exceeding the proportion of human nature." There is therefore granted to man the supernatural power (*virtus*) commensurate with that high end. The moral life, however, is conceived under the dominating idea of "merit." And, as acts of merit are to be valid before God, they must be wrought by him (vid. Thom. i. ii. q. 109, a. 5 and 6. Bonav. in sent. iii. d. 29, a. 1, q. 1. Alb. ii. tr. 16, q. 98, m. 4). Therefore, man has need of the impelling power of grace before as well as after the fall (Thom. ib. a. 2).

2. Anselm already reproduces the Augustinian conception of sin as a nonentity (*Nichtsein*). Evil is an "absence of good" (dial. de casu diabol. 11). Original sin he defined as "the lack (*nuditas*) of original righteousness, caused by the disobedience of Adam, through which we are all the children of wrath" (de conceptu virginal. 27). The Lombard saw in original sin a tinder (*fomes*) of sin and an infirmity (*languor*) of nature, its essence consisting in concupiscence (ii. d. 30 F, G). The great Scholastics were the first to discuss the subject with thoroughness, and they agreed substantially in their views. Here, as usual, Alexander marked out the path, and Thomas drew the final formulas. (*a*) Alexander presents original sin under the two aspects of guilt (*culpa*) and penalty (*poena*). In the former aspect, it is a lack (*carentia*) of original righteousness; in the latter, concupiscence (ii. q. 122, m. 2, a. 1). This *carentia* embraces the loss both of grace and of the natural original righteousness, or order of nature, since nature has been sorely wounded by sin. "The natural powers in us and in the first man . . . are weakened and wounded and deteriorated" (Bonav. in sent. ii. d. 24, p. 1, a. 1, q. 2). Accordingly, Thomas defines: "Original sin is materially indeed concupiscence; but formally also a defect (*defectus*) of original righteousness" (i. ii. q. 82, a. 3). (*b*) The possibility of the fall lay in the fact that the creature, "made from nothing and defective, was capable of deficiency in acting according to God" (Bonav. brev. 3. 1); its cause was pride (ib. 3. 9). (*c*) Thomas carefully defines the nature of original sin. It is, as sickness in the body,

a state or condition (*habitus*) attaching itself to the soul in its essence (*essentia*), and hence a *languor naturae*. From this follows both that it is a negation and that it is something positive, *i. e.*, the lack of the original righteousness and the "unregulated disposition of parts of the soul" (i. ii. q. 82, a. 1 ; q. 83, a. 2). The powers of the soul are robbed of their original order and wounded, since "ignorance, malice, infirmity, and concupiscence" now rule in it (ib. q. 85, a. 3). But it is not entirely deprived of "the good of nature," for in that case it would have forfeited reason, and would then be no longer capable of sin (ib. a. 2). Man's natural endowment therefore remains, but it has no more the original inclination toward the good (a. 1). But the latter was, properly speaking, not natural. The conflict of the powers was involved from the beginning in their multiplicity (in sent. ii. d. 32, q. 2, a. 1). (*a*) Finally, the question as to the manner in which the sin of Adam and of parents is transferred to their children is answered, on the one hand, by a reference to the peculiar position of Adam as the head of the race (Alex. ii. q. 122, m. 3, a. 3. Thom. ib. q. 81, a. 1), and, further, by dwelling upon the corruption of carnal conception (Alex. ib. m. 4). Here, however, arises the difficulty, that, as the Scholastics regarded Creationism as the only orthodox theory as to the origin of the soul (Lomb. ii. d. 17 C, H. Bonav. sent. ii. d. 18, a. 2, q. 3. Thom. c. gent. ii. 86. Duns, sent. iv. d. 43, q. 3, 21), the connection between the nature corporeally propagated and the soul infused by an immediate creative act of God is not clear. Bonav. finds a medium in an inclination of the soul toward union with the corrupted flesh (ii. d. 31, a. 2, q. 3). According to Thomas, the propagated bodily nature is impure (i. ii. 81, a. 1 ; c. gent. iv. 50. 4). But the nature is propagated by generation, and the existence of the soul begins only in that act ; therefore the soul also becomes sinful (i. ii. q. 83, a. 1). But this does not make the matter clear. (*e*) The results of sin are sin as an evil, *i. e.*, the disordered nature (*natura inordinata*) and the evil itself—above all, the liability to punishment (*reatus poenae*), or eternal death (ib. q. 87 ; q. 109, a. 7). The punishment of children dying unbaptized is light—they are deprived of the vision of God (*visio dei*, Lomb. ii. 33 E). There is, in their case, not a punishment, but a "defect of nature" (Heinr. quodlib. vi. q. 12). Thus they occupy a median position : "They are without any outward or inward affliction," but "are deprived of the vision of God and of corporeal light" (Bonav. ii. d. 33, a. 3, q. 2. Thom. in sent. ii. d. 33, q. 2, a. 2).

If we now review the course of thought thus developed,

we can find no reason to designate it as un-Augustinian. The Scholastics teach, with Augustine, that through sin man has become subject to ignorance, lust, and death. And that they regard the natural endowments of man as only wounded and distorted, not destroyed, by sin, is also not an un-Augustinian idea. Their Semipelagianism first appears when they attempt to describe the state of the natural man in its relation to the workings of grace. We must therefore suspend judgment until we shall have examined their expositions of grace and human freedom.

§ 57. *Doctrine of Grace and Human Freedom.*

1. "Nevertheless, because human nature has not been totally corrupted by sin, *i. e.*, so as to be deprived of the whole good of nature, but is able even in the natural state of corruption by virtue of its nature to do some particular good thing, as to build houses, to plant vineyards, and other things of such sort, it does not follow that everything good is connatural to it so that it is deficient in nothing—just as a sick man may of himself have some motion, but cannot be perfectly moved with the motion of a whole man unless he be made whole by the aid of medicine" (Thom. i. ii. q. 109, a. 2). By this, every thought of self-redemption is excluded. Salvation must be traced back simply to God, for the attainment of the final goal can be secured only through the Prime Mover—in which aspect God is constantly regarded in Thomas's doctrine of grace : " It is necessary that man be turned (*convertatur*) toward the final goal through a motion of the Prime Mover" (ib. q. 109, a. 6 and 9). If this rule prevailed before the fall, it is thoroughly applied only after the fall (ib. a. 2). This metaphysical rule dominates the doctrine of grace as held by Thomas. Christ is mentioned in this connection only incidentally, as the Head of the church, who was alone in a position to merit the " first grace " for others (q. 114, a. 6 ; cf. Bonav. brevil. 5. 1 init.). Thus grace, and with it everything good in man, is referred to the divine agency, as indeed everything is the result of his agency as the Prime Mover.

2. But what is Grace ? The teachers of this period did not, like Abelard and the Lombard (sent. ii. 27 C, F.; iii. 4 a.) understand grace, or love, as being the Holy Ghost himself (*e. g.*, Thom. in sent. i. d. 17, a. 1). The term grace designates, according to Thomas, on the one hand, the gratuitous motion (*motio*) of God (ib. q. 111, a. 2 ; q. 110, a. 2 ; q. 109, a. 9, ad 2); on the other hand—and this is the vitally important signification—the effect of this divine act (*gratia increata* and

creata). "The motion of the moving God is itself an infusion of grace" (q. 113, a. 8).   Grace, it is expressly declared, is not only God's "eternal love" and the "remission of sins" (q. 110, a. 1, ad 1 and 3). It is, in essence, "a certain supernatural thing in man, coming into existence from God" (q. 110, a. 1), an infused condition (*habitus infusus*), which is "in the essence of the soul" (q. 109, a. 9; q. 110, a. 4; cf. Bonav. sent. ii. d. 26, a. 1, q. 5).   "A certain gift of inward condition (*habituale donum*) is infused into the soul by God" (q. 110, a. 2).   It is "supernatural qualities," which are infused into the soul, a "higher nature," which pours forth from God as multifarious force into the "powers of the soul" and renews them (q. 110, a. 2, 3, 4, ad 1; cf. Bonav. brevil. 5. 3: *recreare;* and 5. 4, upon the *ramification of grace*).   This is the grace which makes acceptable (*gratia gratum faciens*) as a divine inflowing, which makes man like God and pleasing to him (Bonav. ii. d. 26, a. 1, q. 2). This supernatural, ethical nature inborn in man embraces in itself all virtues, including faith, but above all love, which alone, as Bonaventura says, infuses life into "the whole spiritual machine" (i. d. 14, dub. 6. Thom. q. 3, a. 4, ad 3). Such is the conception of grace—the new nature created by God in the depths of the soul, which makes man capable of good.   This idea may find support in Augustine, but it has no footing in the gospel nor in the moral conception of religion.   Here, on the contrary, lies—the doctrine of the sacraments being most intimately associated with it—the deepest source of the process by which a mechanical character was impressed upon the religious life of the Middle Ages.

3. Since man is involved in this process, however, the old question of the relation of human freedom to grace again comes to view.   Thomas maintains that "conversion," it is true, occurs "through the free will (*liberum arbitrium*), but the free will cannot be converted to (turned toward) God, except when God himself converts it to himself (q. 109, a. 6, ad 11).   The will is moved by God.   Every supposed preparation for the reception of grace rests upon this "free will moved by God" (ib. a. 7; q. 112, a. 2, 3, 4).   God himself establishes in us the disposition toward the reception of grace (q. 113, a. 7). The divine causality alone effects moral impulses of the will (q. 111, a. 3).   If we regard grace from the point of view of God as its cause, we must speak of *operating grace;* but if we think concretely of the resultant movements of the will, of the consent of man, the term *co-operating grace* will find its place (q. 111, a. 2). Thomas is strictly Augustinian in his ideas; but, since he assigns the chief place to the infused substantial gift of grace instead of to

the personal divine working, it is necessary—in order not to lose the personal element entirely—to lay the greater emphasis upon human freedom, especially in connection with the conception of merit.   This is seen in Bonaventura, who represents the impartation of grace as having for its end to make men capable of merit (brevil. 5. 2), which can be attained however only through the free will (sent. ii. d. 26, a. 1, q. 5).   Under this practical view of the matter, despite all emphasizing of the agency of grace, the personal agency of man himself constantly presses to the front, as will hereafter plainly appear.

4. We now turn to the conception of Justification, which in the thought of the period embraces the following points : " Four things are required for the justification of the wicked, *i. e.*, infusion of grace, a movement of the free will toward God through faith, a movement of the free will toward sin, and remission of guilt " (Thom. q. 113, a. 6 ; cf. Bonav. brevil. 5. 3 : " infusion of grace, expulsion of guilt, contrition, and a movement of free will ").   It must be clearly understood, first of all, what is the object in view in justification.   But this is " a certain transmutation of the human soul " (Thom. q. 113, a. 3, ad 3), or, " the reparation (*reparatio*) of the soul is called justification " (Bonav. iv. d. 17, p. 1, dub. 1).   It is therefore not justification in the Pauline sense, which is here altogether excluded by the conception of grace ; but the making of man righteous by virtue of the supernatural power infused.   A more precise analysis yields the following : (*a*) If we start with the conception of grace as a divine agency, the basis of justification is the " love with which God loves us " and the " not imputing sin to man," but this presupposes upon his part the infusion of grace (q. 113, a. 2, resp. u., ad 2).   But it is the other conception of grace which dominates, *i. e.*, a divine agency " by which man is made worthy of eternal life " (ib.), and it is in accordance with this that justification is to be understood.   Forgiveness is therefore the object which is attained through this means. Thomas has indeed also designated forgiveness as the means of renewal (*transformation*, q. 113, a. 1), but in this case he evidently uses the former term as expressing the purpose of the divine will which precedes the entire process (vid. SEEBERG, Duns Scotus, p. 328, n. 1).   (*b*) The chief thing practically is the infusion of grace.   Simultaneously with this, the will is moved to its acceptance.   He so infuses the gift of justifying grace, that he also, at the same time with this, moves the free will to the accepting of the gift of grace (ib. a. 3).   (*c*) The soul thus incited by grace attains first to faith : " The first conversion to God occurs through faith."   This faith (vid. § 53, 3 *b*) would

be incomplete unless it were given form (*informatus*) by love
(ib. a. 4). But faith is necessary to justification, because man
must by it be convinced that "God is the justifier of men
through the mystery of Christ." (*d*) Since, moreover, "justification is a certain movement (*motus*) by which the human mind
is moved by God from the state of sin into the state of righteousness," the will must in justification turn away from sin and toward
God (a. 5). (*e*) The end in view is the forgiveness of sins, but
in such a way that it is dependent upon the infused grace: "For
by the selfsame act God both grants grace and remits guilt" (a.
6, ad 2)—for by far the most important thing is the infusion of
grace (a. 7). (*f*) Thomas conceives, too, of this act of justification as occurring in a moment, and not as a continuous
process. "The infusion of grace occurs in an instant without
progression," and hence also: "the justification of the wicked
by God occurs in an instant" (a. 7).[1] Accordingly, the succession noted in the various stages of the process is to be regarded,
not as temporal, but as logical. (*g*) An actual certainty of
salvation is thus not attainable, since the grace of God lies
beyond the sphere of human perception, and hence the possession
of grace can only be inferred *conjecturaliter* from good works
(q. 112, a. 5). Justification is therefore the making of a sinner
righteous. Since sin in him has been in principle destroyed,
God regards it as remitted.

5. This view of righteousness makes its aim not a personal intercourse with God, but the making of man capable of performing good works. Hence it is not faith which holds the central
place in the religious life, but love and good works. Perfect
faith, or the *fides formata*, is bound up with love in one: "An
act of faith is perfected and given form (*perficitur ac formatur*)
through love" (summ. ii. ii. q. 4, a. 3). But love tests itself in
good works, which are good in so far as they are in accordance
with the divine commandments. Thus man becomes righteous.
"But righteousness consists in conforming one's self to the rules
of the law." For this purpose God gave the law, that we might
obey it (Bonav. brevil. 5. 9). But, at the same time, there is
assured to man by the obligatory law the possibility of meritorious conduct (Bonav. sent. iii. d. 37, a. 1, q. 1). This brings us
to the important conception of "merit." As it was the aim of
the bestowal of grace upon our first parents in paradise to enable

---

[1] This is established by careful argumentation in the Quaest. disp. de justif.
a. 9: Whenever between "the two termini of a change" there is neither a
local movement nor a quantitative decrease and increase, "then the transition from one terminus to the other is not (accomplished) in time, but in an
instant."

them to perform meritorious deeds, this is likewise the chief
object of the grace infused into the sinner. "But grace is properly called an assistance divinely given toward meriting, . . .
for it, as the root of meriting, antedates all merits" (Brevil. 5.
2). Grace is, therefore, "the source (*principium*) of a meritorious work" (Thom. i. ii. q. 109, a. 6). The idea of merit
is not to be regarded as really applicable between God and man,
but only upon the ground of a divine appointment, that God will
reward the deeds for the performance of which he has himself
given the needed power (ib. q. 114, a. 1). But, since no merit
is conceivable without a co-operation of the free will (ib. a. 4),
there is, after all, a merit on the part of man. Therefore, all
human works originating in the grace of God are merits in the
sight of God. By them man merits for himself eternal life and
an increase of grace (q. 114, a. 2, 8, 9. Bonav. ii. d. 27, a. 2, q.
3). But he can never, according to Thomas, merit the first
grace (*prima gratia*, ib. a. 5); for conduct is at any time meritorious only as proceeding from grace (q. 109, a. 6 ; q. 112, a.
2, ad 1). Discrimination is made between the merit of worthiness (*meritum condigni* or *de condigno*) and the merit of fitness
(*meritum congrui* or *de congruo*). The former term describes
the conduct in so far as it is purely a product of grace ; the
second, in so far as it results from the exercise of free-will.
Under the former aspect the conduct is, indeed, worthy of eternal life ; whilst, regarded under the latter, it is to be said of it :
"For it seems fitting that to the man acting according to his
virtue God should give recompense according to the excellence
of his virtue" (q. 114, a. 3. Bonav. ii. d. 27, a. 2, q. 3). But
this discrimination is, in reality, a mere abstraction ; concretely,
merits exist only in the form of free actions (Thom. a. 4). The
Augustinian idealization of the conception of merit (Vol. I., p.
365), which Thomas follows, can scarcely be maintained in
practice. This may be strikingly observed in Bonaventura. According to Thomas, as we have seen, a merit before justification
is inconceivable, but afterward man may by worthiness (*de condigno*) merit eternal life. According to Bonaventura, a "grace
gratuitously given" constitutes the beginning of the process of
salvation, forming a connecting link between the "grace which
makes acceptable" and the free will (*e. g.*, servile fear, the piety
instilled by education, accidental impressions or words).[1] This
is, therefore, the influencing of the man through the word, or,
as Heinrich says, the calling (*vocatio*) through the external or

---

[1] Bonav. here uses the term in a general way. His specific conception of
it is the same as that of Thomas. Vid. p. 115 n. Also, iv. d. 7, a. 1, q. 3,
ad 2.

internal word (quodlib. viii. q. 5). So small, in comparison with the sacrament, is the significance of the word.[1] This general influence makes man capable of meriting by fitness the grace which makes acceptable (*gratia gratum faciens*) (ii. dist. 28, a. 2, q. 1; d. 27, a. 2, q. 2). Only after the infusion of the latter is a merit of worthiness (*condigni*) possible (ii. d. 27, a. 2, q. 3; brevil. 5. 2); but further grace can be merited only by fitness (*de congruo*) (ib. q. 2). Without any grace, no merit at all is possible (d. 27, a. 2, q. 1, concl.), but to the attainment of justification man can, nevertheless, dispose himself by fitness. This, however, points already toward the later apprehension of the matter, according to which man merits the grace which makes acceptable even by fitness, in so far as he does what he should do, and, after its reception, merits salvation by worthiness (Biel, in sent. iv. d. 16, q. 2, a. 3, dub. 4 : " Good works morally performed without love merit by fitness many spiritual good things ; which is evident, because they merit the grace of justification." Also, ib. dub. 6 : "Every act proceeding from love and grace in the pilgrim merits some grade of essential happiness. . . . He who works, merits such a reward by worthiness"). There are thus two dominant elements in the scholastic conception of grace : infused grace and merit. The Augustinian metaphysics and religion here woven together with the ancient Western moralism, when strictly interpreted, destroy one another (vid. the *meritum condigni* in Thomas); in reality, they restrained and thereby supplemented one another. The idea of merit was made tolerable by the pious interpretation given to it in the appeal to grace, and into the conception of grace was introduced through the scheme of merits the element which it lacked, *i. e.*, that of personal relation to God. We can scarcely avoid the conclusion that this vulgar conception of merit furnished a kind of corrective of the scholastic Augustinian conception of grace.[2] Cf. H. SCHULTZ, d. sittl. Begr. d. Verdienstes, Stud. u. Krit. 1894, 273 ff.

[1] The development of the mendicant orders increased the dogmatic significance of the word. In his writing, *De perfectione statuum*, Duns assigns to the clergy the administration of the sacraments, and to the mendicant friars the proclamation of the word, exalting the latter far above the former. Vid. SEEBERG, Duns Scotus, p. 474 ff.

[2] That in such a scheme justification, as connected with faith, could be brought only formally into consideration (as was the case already with Augustine) is self-evident (*e. g.*, Lomb. iii. d. 23 D : "Through this faith the wicked is justified, so that then faith itself begins to work through love." Cf. Robert, sent. iv. 14, and my remarks in Thomasius ii., ed. 2, 179). Instead of being scandalized at this, we should rather note it as an evidence of religious tact, for to what perversions would not a theory of justification by faith have led when the latter was regarded as merely an intellectual assent (*cum assensione cogitare*) ?

6. Merit must in the above system logically have for its correlate the gaining of eternal life as a reward. But as Thomas held it to be possible that one person might by fitness merit eternal life for another (i. ii. q. 114, a. 6), it was also regarded as possible for a man to earn more merit than is necessary to the attainment of salvation. The Christian may not only obey all the commandments of the gospel, but also observe its counsels (consilia evangelica). This occurs when he entirely renounces the good things of this world, i. e., property, sensual pleasure and honor, and becomes a monk: "in which three things is founded the whole religion[1] which professes the state of perfection " (i. ii. q. 108, a. 4. Bon. brev. 5. 9). Evangelical perfection, or the ideal Christian life, is thus realized in a monastic life, or one of similar character (ii. ii. q. 184, a. 2, 5 and 4; cf. Bonav. apol. pauper. resp. 1, c. 3). This is the *perfectio supererogationis* (Bon., l. c.), the *justitia superabundans* (brev. 5. 9 fin.). By this means the treasure of superabundant works is created (vid. sub.), the multitude of saints placed beside Christ as *intercessores* and *mediatores* (Thom. iii. suppl. q. 72, a. 2), and the monastic ideal of life brought within the comprehension of the common people.

It is, however, only the one side of the medieval ideal of Christian life which finds explanation in the light of the conception of merit then prevalent. Starting with the conception of grace, we discover another ideal, that of a supernatural "heavenly" life. If the new disposition (*habitus*) of grace in the soul is the true life, it is incumbent to root out and destroy the old soul (heart) with all its powers. It is by the path of an ascetic "imitation of Christ" that we are to reach the enjoyment of partnership in his divinity. The active life (*vita activa*) is followed by the contemplative (*vita contemplativa*). To give vivid expression to this conception was the task of German Mysticism. We therefore postpone its consideration to the following period. We desire, however, at this point to direct special attention to the connection of this ideal of life with the medieval conception of grace.

§ 58. *The Sacraments and the Church. Fixing of Dogma of Seven Sacraments.*

Cf. SCHWANE, DG. der mittl. Zt., p. 579 ff. HAHN, Die Lehre von den Sacramenten, 1864. SCHANZ, Die Lehre von den Sacramenten, 1893.

The doctrine of the sacraments received during this period the form in which it was afterward dogmatically fixed by Pope

---

[1] In the medieval sense, i. e., Monasticism, Order.

Eugene IV. at the Florentine Council of A. D. 1439 (vid. the Bull, Exultate deo, in Mansi xxxi. 1055 ff.; also Mirbt, Quellen z. Gesch. d. Papstt., p. 100 ff.). We shall be compelled, therefore, to follow the development of the doctrine somewhat beyond the limits of our period, citing at once from the definitions of the bull.

1. (*a*) The sacraments constitute the positive product of the work of Christ. Since the salvation of mankind is dependent upon the passion of Christ, and that of the individual upon the sacraments, it is clear "that the sacraments of the new law must have their whole efficacy from the passion of Christ" (Thom. summ. iii. q. 62, a. 5. Alex. summ. th. iv. q. 8, membr. 3, a. 5, § 7. Cf. Biel, sent. iv. dist. 2, q. 1, a. 3). That the number of the sacraments is seven is considered self-evident.[1] The necessity of this is argued in various ways. The Christian life, it is said, is allied in character to the development of the body, and, therefore, needs a sacrament of generation (baptism), one of growth (confirmation), one of nourishment (the eucharist). Then come the healing of daily sins (repentance) and the removal of the remains of sin (unction). From the social nature of men is deduced the necessity for marriage as a means of sanctifying the process of propagation, and for ordination as empowering those who receive it to lead the people (vid. Thom. ib. q. 65, a. 1 ; and, further, in Bon. brev. 6. 3. Cf. Duns, sent. iv. d. 2, q. 1, § 3. Biel, iv. d. 2, q. 1, a. 1). But baptism and the eucharist are the "most powerful sacraments" (Thom. q. 62, a. 5). According to some, they alone were instituted immediately by Christ (Alex. iv. q. 8, membr. 3, a. 2, § 3. Bon. iv. d. 23, a. 1, q. 2), while, at a later period, all the seven were traced back to a direct institution by Christ (*e. g.*, Albert, sent. iv. d. 23, a. 13. Thom. q. 64, a. 2. Duns, iv. d. 2, q. 1, § 4, 5. Biel, iv. d. 2, q. 1, concl. 2).

(*b*) Thomas defines the sacrament as "the sign of a sacred thing, since it is (a means of) sanctifying men" (q. 60, a. 2); Bonaventura, as "sensible signs divinely instituted as medicaments, in which, under cover of things sensible, divine power very mysteriously (*secretius*) acts" (brev. 6. 1; cf. Augustine, doctr. christ. ii. 1). The sensible sign becomes a real sacrament, however, only when it is administered with the *intentio* of producing by it a supramundane effect, or at least " to do what the church does, or, at all events, what Christ has

---

[1] The Third Lateran Council, A. D. 1179, still speaks of burial, the installation of bishops, and "other sacraments," Hefele, v. 713. A Council at London, A. D. 1237, enumerates the seven as the " principal sacraments," Hefele, v. 1056.

appointed'' (Bon. sent. iv. d. 6, p. 2, a. 2, q. 1).[1]   The sensible elements (*res sensibiles*) constitute the *materia* of the sacrament ; the words of institution, its *forma ; i. e.*, through the recitation of the words the sacrament is observed (*perficitur*) (Thom. q. 60, a. 7.   Alex. iv. q. 8, m. 3, a. 2).   Accordingly, Eugene IV. defines : ''All these sacraments are observed by three things, viz., by the elements as the *materia,* the words as the *forma,* and the person of the minister administering the sacrament with the *intentio* of doing what the church does—of which, if anyone be wanting, the sacrament is not observed.''

(*c*) There are therefore together in the sacrament an external sign and grace.   How are these two related ?   Hugo had framed the formula which practically gave direction to the solution of the problem : '' The sign contains the grace '' (supra, p. 80). This Thomas recognizes as '' not unsuitably '' expressed (q. 62, a. 3, ad 3).   He is also of the opinion that a causation of grace (*gratiam causare*) may be predicated of the sacrament (ib. a. 1), but he feels too the difficulty.   If grace originated from God, how can it be effected through created objects?   He sought to overcome the difficulty by discriminating between the *principal* and the *instrumental* cause, the latter (and thus the sacraments) being efficacious as set in motion by the former.   '' And in this manner is there spiritual power in the sacraments, in so far as they are appointed by God for (producing) spiritual effect.'' The words of institution effect a spiritual efficacy (*virtus*) in the external sign, which resides in the latter until this *virtus* has accomplished its end (ib. a. 1 and 4).[2]   But over against this view stands another throughout the whole period of the Middle Ages.   It appears plainly in Bonaventura (also in Richard). We dare not say that the sacraments contain grace.   This dwells only in the human soul.   The sacrament is in itself a symbol, somewhat like a letter with the royal seal.   There exists however a covenant (*pactio*) of God, that he will accompany the use of this sacrament with his own working upon the soul of the recipient.   Thus regarded, it can be positively said of the sacrament only that it, by inciting faith, prepares for the reception of grace ('' the motion of faith is excited through the exhibition of the sign '').   The infusion of grace results through

---

[1] Duns discusses this point exhaustively.   Report. Paris. iv. d. 6, q. 6. Cf. Biel, iv. d. 6, a. 2, concl. 5.

[2] Cf. Alex. iv. q. 8, m. 3, a. 5, § 1 : '' Power (*virtus*) wonderfully associated with (*collata*) the corporal agent itself.''   § 5 : ''Consecration (*sanctificatio*) is something coming to the water or oil, and it does not give substantial existence (*esse substantiale*) to the oil or water, but it gives accidental existence '' (*esse accidentale*).

a directly creative act of God in the soul, *i. e.* : " By such covenant the Lord has obligated himself to, in some way, give grace to him who receives the sacrament " (Bon. sent. iv. d. 1, p. 1, a. 1, q. 2, 3, 4; brev. 6. 1). This view, through its advocacy by Duns Scotus, became the dominant one in the later Middle Ages. Since God alone has power to create, grace can have only an act of God as its direct cause. The sacraments are "sure signs," since the divine covenant with the church makes a *concomitance* of the divine working certain. "The divine will alone is the invisible cause of the effect which the sacrament seals and accompanies. God therefore is the immediate cause of such effect of the sacrament through his assistance to the sacrament, upon which he has arranged always to bestow assistance and confer grace . . . and thus his will alone is the prime and principal invisible cause of this effect" (report. iv. d. 2, q. 1, § 2). We cannot say "that he binds his power to the sacraments" (sent. iv. d. 14, q. 4, 6). Accordingly, the external sign "signifies" that which the accompanying grace inwardly effects in the recipient, as, *e. g.*, in the case of baptism, purification : " But the cleansing of the soul from sin which it certainly signifies, it represents by divine appointment ; from which (it follows that) God, who instituted baptism, assists his sign to the producing of the represented effect " (Biel, iv. d. 1, q. 1, a. 1 ; cf. Durand. iv. d. 1, q. 4, a. 1). This view reminds us distinctly of the Augustinian origin of the definition of a sacrament, being in reality a remnant of Augustinianism in the Franciscan dogmatics : the external sacrament is in and of itself only an image of that which God works in the soul.[1] It was certainly only by artifice that transubstantiation could be maintained under such a definition. Of the two views noted, the church naturally chose the coarser. Eugene IV. writes : " They (the ancient sacraments) did not cause grace . . . but these of ours both *contain* grace and *confer* it upon those worthily receiving them."

(*d*) The sacraments bring to man justifying grace (*gratia justificans*, Thom. q. 62, a. 6). " By sacramental effect I understand the grace making acceptable, which he secures who receives the sacrament not unworthily " (Biel, iv. d. 1, q. 1, a. 2). Thomas here discriminated between the " grace of powers and gifts " and " sacramental grace," inasmuch as the former

---

[1] Thomas had already pointed out the possible consequence of this view : "According to this, the sacraments of the New Testament would be nothing more than signs of grace, although it is held by many authorities of the saints that the sacraments of the New Testament not only signify but cause (*causant*) grace " (iii. q. 62, a. 1).

complete in a general way the nature and powers of the soul, while the separate sacraments produce special effects (q. 62, a. 2 ; q. 89, a. 1 ; vid. also Bonav. iv. d. 1, p. 1, a. 1, q. 6). Later theologians acknowledged the essential identity of all *gratia gratum faciens* : " That there is one and the same grace in kind in all who have grace, whether this be infused through participation in the sacraments, or through merits acquired, or, even without either, gratuitously infused." The difference existing is " only in the mind (*ratione*) and not in reality nor in essence " (Biel, iv. d. 2, q. 1, a. 3, dub. 2 ; vid. already Alex. iv. q. 8, m. 4, a. 2, § 1). But the sacraments impart not only justifying grace. To those which are administered but once is attributed as a " secondary effect " the impartation of spiritual character (*character spiritualis*) which makes man continuously capable of honoring God according to the manner of the Christian religion (Thom. q. 63, a. 1, 2). And, inasmuch as this involves a certain participation in the priesthood of Christ, which is eternal, this " character " attaches to the soul " indelibly " (ib. a. 5). The " character " is therefore the indestructible habitual disposition of the Christian soul—and that " according to the intellectual part—toward those things which are for the promotion of divine worship " (a. 4, 5. Alex. iv. q. 8, m. 3, 4. Bonav. iv. d. 6, p. 1, a. 1, q. 3, 5). Duns located the character in the will (iv. d. 6, q. 11, § 4). But the conception is so lacking in clearness that we are led to infer that Duns (iv. d. 6, q. 9, § 13), as well as Biel, still entertains serious doubts upon the point. Neither reason nor the authorities demand it, and only one passage of Innocent III.[1] can be cited in its favor, and even this Biel thinks can be differently interpreted (Duns, iv. d. 6, q. 9, § 13 f. Biel, iv. d. 6, q. 2, a. 1, concl. 2). But Eugene IV. elevated this point also to the dignity of a dogma of the church : " Among these sacraments there are three which imprint a *character, i. e.*, a certain spiritual mark (*signum*) distinctive from others, indelibly upon the soul. Whence, they are not repeated in the same person."

(*e*) Only one further question concerning the sacraments in general remains to be considered—touching the worthy or unworthy reception of them. It is involved in the conception of the New Testament sacraments, that they are effectual *ex opere operato, i. e.*, through their objective administration. Thus teaches Alexander (iv. q. 8, m. 4, a. 1) and especially Albert (sent. iv. d. 1, a. 1) and all the later writers, *e. g.*, Bonaven-

---

[1] Vid. the passage in Denzinger, Enchiridion symbolor. et definit. n. 341, 342 ; cf. Duns, l. c. : " Therefore solely upon the authority of the church, running up to the present time, it is to be held that character is imprinted."

tura : "The sacraments of the New Testament justify and confer grace of themselves *ex opere operato*" (iv. d. 1, p. 1, a. 1, q. 5). A certain disposition is indeed desired in the recipient, perhaps faith (Lombard, iv. d. 4, B. Bonav. iv. d. 1, p. 1, a. 1, q. 2); but the later writers especially confined themselves to the requirement, that there be no obstacle (*obex*) nor mortal sin. As an *opus operatum*, the sacrament did not presuppose a good inner motive (*bonus motus interior*) as necessary to a profitable reception. Precisely this was one mark of distinction from the Old Testament sacraments (Duns, iv. d. 1, q. 6, § 10). With this efficacy *ex opere operato* is contrasted that based upon the personality or action of the participant (*ex opere operante*). That is to say, if the recipient prepares himself for the reception of the sacrament, he receives also as a reward, upon the ground of this merit, a further gracious influence. "Any sign may be understood to confer grace in a two-fold way. This occurs in one way by the sign itself or the sacrament, or, as some say, by the deed performed, *ex opere operato*. Thus by the very fact that the work (*opus*), *i. e.*, sign or sacrament, is celebrated (*exhibetur*), grace is conferred unless an obstacle of mortal sin hinder ; because, besides the celebration (*exhibitio*) of the sign externally celebrated, a good inner motive is not required in the recipient by which he may merit grace by worthiness or fitness, but it suffices that the recipient interpose no obstacle. . . . In another way, signs or sacraments are understood to confer grace by the one performing the work (*ex opere operante*) and by the way of merit, *i. e.*, that the sacrament externally celebrated does not suffice for the conferring of grace, but beyond this is required a good motive, or inner devotion, of the one receiving the sacrament, according to whose intention grace is conferred corresponding to the merit of worthiness or fitness, precisely, and not more, according to the celebration of the sacrament " (Biel, iv. d. 1, q. 3, a. 1, n. 2).

2. Turning to the separate sacraments, we begin with Baptism. The material (*materia*) of this sacrament is water, or, more precisely speaking, washing with water.[1] The form (*forma*) consists in the words : " I baptize thee in the name of the Father, and of the Son, and of the Holy Ghost." From the time of Alexander the effects of baptism were more precisely stated than had been done by the Lombard. It is said to impart the grace making acceptable (*gratia gratum faciens*), and this impartation effects both a capacitating of the soul for the doing of good and the

---

[1] Duns, iv. d. 3, q. 3, § 2 : " The first thing is the visible washing itself, for this, together with the words as a sign, signifies the first effect of baptism."

9

forgiveness of guilt and penalty.[1] " He who is baptized is freed
from the guilt (liability, *reatus*) of the entire penalty owed by
him for his sins" (Thom. summ. iii. q. 69, a. 2), and "through
baptism one secures grace and powers" (*virtutes*, ib. a. 4).
" From all eternal (penalty) baptism absolves by destroying all
sin (*culpa*)" and " grace has a two-fold action, viz., to destroy sin
(*peccatum*) and to make apt for good " (Bonav. sent. iv. d. 4, p.
1, a. 1, q. 2 and 3).   By it there is effected at the same time a
restraint of concupiscence (Lomb. iv. d. 4 F; ii. d. 32 A.
Duns, iv. d. 4, q. 7, § 1).   Finally, baptism imparts the spiritual
" character," which is to be thought of as an infused disposition
(*habitus infusus*).   According to this theory, in baptism grace
is infused into the sinner, and this grace blots out the sins of the
past and weakens the sinful impulses of the recipient.   But as
these impulses still remain active, there remain also for the baptized the punishments (*poenalitates*) of the present life (Thom.
q. 69, a. 3).   Both serve for testing and attesting.   Precisely
the same gifts are granted in infant baptism, any difficulties suggesting themselves in this case being met by the consideration,
that baptism confers not separate virtues, but the *habitus virtutum* (Thom. q. 69, a. 6).   To secure the benefits of baptism,
faith is required in the recipient.   In the case of unbelievers
(*fictio*), the benefit is secured when they have done penance for
their unbelief (Thom. q. 69, a. 10.   Bonav. iv. d. 4, p. 1, a.
2, q. 2 f.).   In the case of children, an obligation imposed
upon the sponsors to see to their instruction in the Christian
faith takes the place of the yet lacking confession of faith
(Lomb. iv. d. 6 G.   Bonav. iv. d. 6, p. 2, a. 3, q. 1).[2]
Eugene IV. defines as the effect of the sacrament : " the remission of all original and actual sin, also of every penalty which is
due for that sin."

3. There is no advance in the doctrine of later Scholastics
upon the sacrament of Confirmation ; for the assertion that it
was instituted by Christ (*e. g.*, Albert, iv. d. 7, a. 2), and the
attempt to justify the restriction of the right of administering
this sacrament to the bishop by all manner of fanciful reasons, do

[1] Duns, iv. d. 3, q. 2, ¾ 3 : " God . . . remits the sin of no one except of
him to whom he gives grace, for he frees no one from perdition except him
whom he ordains to be a son of the kingdom."   Also, ib. iv. d. 4, q. 5, ¾ 4 :
(God) "is prepared always after the reception of this sign to assist him who
has received it for the causing of its effect."

[2] Baptism is preceded by catechisation and exorcism (Lomb. iv. d. 6 H.
Thom. iii. q. 71, a. 1, 2).   The baptism of the children of non-Christian
parents, without or against the will of the latter, was disapproved by Thomas
(q. 68, a. 10), approved by Duns (iv. d. 4, q. 9), and declared of doubtful
propriety by Biel (iv. d. 4, q. 2, a. 3, dub. 5).

not constitute an advance. Eugene IV. designates the chrism as the *material*, and as the *form* of the sacrament, the words : " I sign thee with the sign of the cross, and confirm thee in the chrism of salvation in the name of the Father," etc. The proper administrator (*ordinarius minister*) is the bishop. "But the effect of this sacrament is, that in it is given the Holy Spirit and strength."

4. "All worship in the church is, as it were, in line (*in ordine*) toward this sacrament." These words of Duns (iv. d. 8, q. 1, 3) spoken in reference to the Lord's Supper, express the practical significance of this sacrament. The doctrine was received in completed form from the great Scholastics. The only task remaining for the present period was to make the traditional dogma somewhat more acceptable to reason by the arts of logic, and more conformable to the spiritual tastes of the age. Here also, Alexander suggested essentially the ideas and problems which later writers accepted. The fixed basis of all discussion was transubstantiation. When the priest utters the form-giving words of institution above the *materia*, or elements, the latter are in their entirety transformed into the entire body of Christ. "The whole wafer (*hostia*) is actually changed into the whole body of Christ" (Alex. iv. q. 40, m. 3, a. 5). This conception may be analyzed as follows :

(*a*) The words of institution, as they are spoken by the priest, effect the transformation : " Whence also the consecrating power (*virtus consecrativa*) consists not only in the words themselves, but also in the power conferred upon the priest at his consecration and ordination " (Thom. summ. iii. q. 82, a. 1, ad 1). Thomas is of the opinion " that in the formal words of this sacrament a certain power (*virtus*) is created for effecting the conversion of this sacrament " (q. 78, a. 4). According to Duns, it is, in reality, only the divine omnipotence which can effect the change. But God has appointed the priest as the administrator (Duns, iv. d. 13, q. 2, 3). " This is according to gospel law, and not only according to positive law " (Duns, report. iv. d. 13, q. 2).[1]

---

[1] It is only with great difficulty that a place can be made for transubstantiation in the Scotist view of the sacraments. The "sensible signs " testify that the things signified are really " contained under them." Further : " God has so established these elements that after their consecration he may assist them to (the securing of) this presence of Christ" (iv. d. 8, q. 1, 2 ff.). But for what purpose then the transubstantiation ? Would it not be in keeping with the general conception of a sacrament to maintain only an accompanying of the symbol with an exercise of divine power, either in such a way that a divine influence be exerted directly upon the soul, or in such a way that Christ be bodily present without affecting the continued existence of the substance of the bread ? It was an *adductive* instead of a *productive* transubstantiation, as

(*b*) The transformation occurs in the moment when the words
are spoken : " At the end of the utterance of the words the sacrament begins to be " (Duns, iv. d. 8, q. 1, 5). It is a peculiar advantage of this sacrament that it is realized not only in
the administration (*in usu*), but already in the consecration of
the elements (Thom. q. 78, a. 1).

(*c*) The resultant of the transformation is the presence of the
true body and blood of Christ (Thom. q. 75, a. 1), the soul of
Christ and his divinity being present, not by way of sacramental
power (*ex vi sacramentali*), but by way of real concomitance
(*ex reali concomitantia*) (ib. q. 76, a. 1. Alex. iv. d. 38, m.
5). On the basis of this, justification was found for the constantly extending custom of withholding the cup from the laity
(vid. Thom. q. 80, a. 12. Alex. iv. q. 32, m. 1, a. 2).

(*d*) The accidents of the substance of the bread and wine
still remain, which is, indeed, a new miracle (Alex. iv. q. 40,
m. 1, a. 2. Thom. q. 75, a. 5).[1] So long as the form (*species*) of
the bread and wine is retained, the sacrament continues. Hence
the advocates of this theory did not even shrink from the conclusion, that even if a dog or a mouse should eat the *hostia*, the substance of Christ would remain in it (Abelard. Thom. q. 8, a. 3,
ad. 3. Cf., as to the course pursued in distributing, HEFELE, CG.
vi. 203).

(*e*) The body which Christ gave to his disciples was the immortal glorified body, and of this he himself partook as an example for his disciples. " And, nevertheless, he who as mortal
gave, and as immortal was given, was not himself two, but one "
(thus Hugo. Vid. especially Alex. iv. q. 44, m. 1 and 3. Thom.
q. 81, a. 1 and 3).[2]

Duns Scotus says. Alexander already suggests the latter theory (" That in this
sacrament there is not any transformation, but, upon the utterance of the words,
without any transformation, it comes to pass by divine power that the body of
Christ is there "). He suggests as an objection, that this view might lead to a
worship of the bread, iv. q. 38, m. 1. Such was the view also of some followers
of Berenger (vid. p. 75 n. Cf. also Petr. Pictav. sent. v. 12), and Duns (iv. d.
11, q. 3, 3 f.), who presents this explanation as a possible one, and merely
says in comment : " Therefore the other way is more suitable than this."
But to this theory belongs the future, as we shall see. Duns continued to
maintain transubstantiation only because it was a dogma of the church. SEE-
BERG, Duns Scotus, p. 382 ff.

[1] Although it is said that the substance of the bread and wine do not remain (*non manere*), the term *annihilatio* was avoided, inasmuch as the resultant
is the body of Christ. Vid. Thom. q. 75, a. 2, 3. Duns, iv. d. 11, q. 4, 14.
Biel, iv. d. 11, q. 1, a. 2, dub. 6. Occam. iv. q. 6, ad dub. 7.

[2] Biel says that Christ gave to his disciples a " body such as he had, *i. e.*,
mortal and passible," without feeling the " teeth of those eating it " (iv. d.
9, q. 1, a. 3, dub. 3). From the other view it would follow, that if the *hostia*
of the first celebration had been preserved, Christ would have been, during the

(*f*) But at this point a difficulty emerges whose solution exercised the Scholastics beyond all others : If the body of Christ is, as is confessed, present in heaven at a particular place, how can it be received at the same time in the sacrament at various places? ALEXANDER'S opinion was that " Christ is circumscriptively, or locally, contained in heaven, but not contained circumscriptively, or locally, under the sacrament " (iv. q. 40, m. 3, a. 7). THOMAS similarly taught " that the body of Christ is in this sacrament in the manner of substance (*per modum substantia*), and not in the manner of quantity (*per modum quantitatis*) " (q. 76, a. 1, ad 3). The Christ who is locally present in heaven is, therefore, not present in a local manner in the sacrament, but only substantially (q. 75, a. 1, ad 3 ; q. 76, a. 4, 5 ; cf. Richard, iv. d. 10, princ. 2, q. 1. Durand, iv. d. 10, q. 10 fin.; vid. also Carthusian. iv. d. 10, q. 1 ff.). Duns rightly rejected this, since a thing without its properties is not conceivable (iv. d. 10, q. 1. 12). Duns himself thinks that God, by virtue of his omnipotence, which is limited only by the logically impossible, can very well cause a body to exist at different places at the same time. We cannot see, he argues, why the relations of a thing to space may not be multiplied (ib. q. 2. 11 ; q. 3. 5). Accordingly, Christ can be at the same time in heaven and at any number of places. The later writers disputed this, for its (realistic) premise is the independent existence of space, while to the Nominalists space is only the object presented as occupying space, upon which theory a spacial existence of Christ in the Lord's Supper is inconceivable. It is rather to be said, that quantity and the property of occupying space are accidental properties of a thing. If the thing be reduced to a point, it yet remains what it was, and, therefore, still possesses the property of occupying space, although it no longer exists in space. It is, therefore, to be said that the body of Christ is present in the Lord's Supper with the property of quantity, but without existing therein as a quantity (vid. especially Occam, tract. de sacr. altar. c. 16 ff. Biel, iv. d. 10, q. 1, a 1 and 2. Cf. fuller discussion at a later point). But these empty speculations, all combined, do not prove the impossible. The body of Christ is local in heaven, and it is in its entirety present in its substance at every celebration of the Lord's Supper. Dogma stands over against dogma, and all the efforts of logic cannot bridge the gulf.

(*g*) Finally, the effect of this sacrament claims attention. In general, it is to be said : " The effect which the passion of Christ

---

three days after his crucifixion, both dead and alive at once ! (Biel. exposit. canonis miss. lect. 46 L).

has produced in the world, this sacrament produces in man"
(Thom. q. 79, a. 1). Regarding it more closely, we may say
"that the eucharist was instituted to be a *sacrifice* and to be a
sacrament, or food" (Biel, exposit. can. miss. lect. 85 D). As
the latter, it signifies a strengthening of the spiritual life, the imparting of grace, and the forgiveness of venial sins (Thom., l. c.).
The later writers are but logically consistent when, in accordance
with their interpretation of the work of Christ, they make this
impartation of grace to consist in a reminding of the love of
Christ and his pious example, and in the awakening of a responsive affection and inciting to good works. The Supper is a
memoriale divinae passionis. This view is instructively presented
in Biel, exposit. can. miss. lect. 85 B, O, V, X, Y.[1] But, side
by side with this effect of the sacrament, stands its sacrificial
character. The body of Christ is really offered up : "There is
not only a representative (*repraesentativa*), but a real immolation (*immolatio vera*), (Albert, sent. iv. d. 13, a. 23). The sacrifice benefits first of all the participants in the sacrament, but
then also others " in so far as it is offered for their salvation,"
and in so far as they have faith in the sacrament (Thom. q. 79,
a. 7, q. 83, a. 1). The sacrifice is also effectual for souls in
purgatory.[2] The reality of the sacrifice does not interfere with
its being at the same time a representation and reminder of the
passion (Biel, l. c., lect. 85 F). But the principal thing is still :
"And this sacrifice is of operative effects similar to those which
the sacrifice upon the cross itself produced" (Biel, ib. K). This
formed the basis of the worst perversions of the practical life of the
church (meritoriousness of the mass; private masses; after A. D.
1264, the festival of Corpus Christi). Here also, theology made
no advance.

We cite from the definitions of Eugene IV. the following :
" For the priest, speaking in the person of Christ, makes (*conficit*)

---

[1] Biel enumerates the following effects : "vivificare, relaxare, inflammare,
patientiam dare, nutrire, restaurare, unire, copulare, sanare, conservare, robor-
are, perducere." Vid. also sermo 46 of Biel's Festival Sermons.

[2] Vid. Biel, sermo 46 R : "It is granted that the fruit of the eucharist is
more efficacious as a sacrament, but it is more general as a sacrifice, . . .
because as a sacrament it operates only in those who take it, but as a sacrifice it
has effect in all those for whom it is offered. But it is offered, not only for
those who participate by taking it, but also for all who are standing by, yea,
even for the absent, the living and the dead. . . . Although it is granted that
sinners are inflamed by partaking (*perceptione*) of the eucharist, but not by
the hearing of the mass. . . . Yet even to sinners not contrite nor . . . regarding with displeasure their continuing sins, it is useful to frequently give
help (*assistere*) by the office of the mass, and to procure that it be offered for
them in order that they may thus merit to be regarded by the Lord with pity,
and may be inspired to displeasure in their sins which they yet have."

this sacrament ; for, by virtue of the very words, the substance of the bread is converted into the body of Christ, and the substance of the wine into his blood, yet in such a way that Christ is contained entire under the form of the bread, and entire under the form of the wine, and under any part whatever of the consecrated wafer and consecrated wine, when separated, is the entire Christ.''

5. As the Lord's Supper blots out venial sins, and baptism original sin, so Repentance has been instituted to dispel mortal sins. It is with mortal sins alone that confession and absolution have to do, not with so-called venial sins. A certain displeasure in view of the failing, the repetition of the Lord's Prayer, sprinkling with consecrated water, the blessing of a bishop, are sufficient for the latter, which are not regarded as requiring an infusion of grace (Alex. iv. q. 77, m. 2, a. 5. Bonav. iv. d. 17, p. 3, a. 2. Thom. summ. iii. q. 87, a. 1.; a. 2, ad 2 ; a. 3).[1] Thus the disastrous discrimination between greater and smaller sins,[2] the latter of which were scarcely regarded any longer as actual sins, was justified. This discrimination was necessary, as only by this means could the petition for the forgiveness of sin have any meaning after the sacrament of repentance had been observed.

Turning now to the sacrament of Repentance, we recall the problem which the school of Abelard had left unsolved, *i. e.*, If divine forgiveness follows *contrition*, what need is there of *confession and absolution ?* This question was answered, as we shall see, by the Scholastics. In this sacrament also *materia* and *forma* are discriminated. The former consists in acts of the penitent (*actus poenitentis*); the latter, in the words of the priest : I absolve thee (Thom. q. 84, a. 2, 3. Bonav. iv. d. 22, a. 2, q. 2. Biel, iv. d. 14, q. 2, a. 1). The remark, ''that in anything whatsoever perfection is attributed to the form'' (Thom. ib. a. 3), fixes at once in advance the position of Absolution, as constituting the essential element of the sacrament.

(*a*) According to traditional teaching, the first element of the sacrament is *contritio*. To understand the course of development here we must constantly bear in mind that repentance, and particularly its first part, contrition, is already, as an act

---

[1] According to Duns not even *attritio* is here necessary (iv. d. 17, q. 1, 25).

[2] Thomas (q. 86, a. 4 ; q. 87, a. 2) thus discriminates : '' In mortal sin there are two things, *i. e.*, a turning away (*aversio*) from immutable good, and a turning (*conversio*) toward mutable good ;'' in venial sins, on the contrary, there is present only ''an inordinate turning to mutable good without turning away from God. Eternal punishment, therefore, befits the former, and only temporal punishment the latter.'' Upon this question, see also Biel, iv. d. 17, q. 1, a. 2, concl. 3. Cf. Melanchthon apol., p. 168, 6.

"formed" by love or as a Christian virtue, a product of grace. From this it follows, that contrition in itself merits and effects the full annihilation of guilt and punishment (Thom. suppl. q. 5, a. 2. Cf. Wilhelm v. Paris, de sacr. opp. Nürnberg, 1496, ii. fol. 41 v, 44 v, 46 r). On the other hand, in the sacrament of repentance, *contritio* is represented as an "inclination (*dispositio*) toward the receiving of grace" (Thom. ib. q. 5, a. 1, and iii. q. 89, a. 1, ad 2). But there is no need of any such *dispositio;* in fact, it makes the sacrament entirely unnecessary. Quite forced appears, therefore, the argument of Thomas, that, since no one can know whether he has a degree of sorrow sufficient to secure forgiveness, it is necessary for us to continually avail ourselves of the opportunity of confession and absolution (suppl. q. 5, a. 2, ad 1). And it is no more than an opinion, that the resolution to confess is always combined with contrition (ib.). When we consider, further, that the individual concerned is always one who has fallen into a mortal sin, it is evident that he cannot, without the influence of the sacrament of repentance, even produce contrition in himself. To meet this difficulty a new idea, that of an *attritio*, or purely human inclination toward the reception of grace, is introduced as being sufficient. This furnishes a key for the solution of the above problem, for this half-penitence does not fully merit the forgiveness of sins, and hence room is left for confession and absolution. The word, *attritio,* occurs first in *Alanus of Insulis,*[1] then in Alexander of Hales (iv. q. 74) and *William of Paris* (opp. 11. 45 v), but it is used by them in such a way as to indicate that it was already an accepted term in the language of the schoolmen. Thomas defines it: "Attritio signifies a certain, but not perfect, displeasure concerning sins committed" (suppl. q. 1, a. 2).[2] Its motive is commonly fear: "Servile fear is the source (*principium*) of attrition" (Alex. iv. q. 74, m. 1. Durand, iv. d. 17, q. 1, a. 3).[3] If now anyone has a certain displeasure toward his sin, he is in suitable condi-

---

[1] Vid. Regul. theol. 85 (Migne, 210. 665 C): "is either remitted by attrition . . . although he have not perfectly repented, or dismissed by contrition when he is fully converted from sin."

[2] Upon the two terms, vid. Biel, iv. d. 16, q. 1, a. 1, n. 3.

[3] Cf. Thomas (iii. q. 85, a. 5), who, in answer to the question, "Whether the source of penitence is from fear," replies that the acts of the soul in repentance are the following: "Faith, servile fear, by which one is restrained from sin by fear of punishments, hope, love, filial fear." Accordingly: "It is evident that the act of penitence proceeds from servile fear, as from the first motion of the affection inclining toward it." Cf. also Biel, iv. d. 14, q. 1, a. 3, dub. 6: "In beginners not yet perfect . . . it frequently arises from fear of punishment, which arises from love of self, but in the perfect it arises from the love of God and of righteousness." Durand (vid. supra): "For penitence is conceived in fear."

tion to make confessson.   " But if a penitent, prepared as far as in him lies, comes to confession, attrite but not contrite, I say that *confession*, with subjection to the will of the priest and *satisfaction* of the penance enjoined by the priest, is a sign and cause of the blotting out of guilt and penalty " (Alex. iv. q. 60, m. 1, a. 3).   Confession is made before the priest, because he only who can consecrate the eucharist has authority over the powers of grace (Thom. suppl. q. 8, a. 1 ; q. 10, a. 1.   Alex. q. 76, m. 3, a. 1).   Then follows absolution, which brings the divine forgiveness.   But it is impossible " that God should remit an offense to anyone without any change of the latter's will " (Thom. q. 86, a. 2).   Hence : " There can be no remission of sins except through infusion of grace " (ib. q. 89, a. 1).   Absolution, therefore, brings divine forgiveness by effecting at the same time the abolition of the mortal sin by an infusion of grace (cf. supra, p. 120).   If the *attrite* person do not now himself interpose an obstacle, he receives grace through confession and absolution (Thom. suppl. q. 18, a. 1).[1] This effects the forgiveness of the liability (*reatus*) to eternal punishment, as well as " something of (*aliquid de*) the temporal punishment."   This latter expression, which somewhat modifies the conception of Abelard, is to be attributed to a regard for the " satisfaction," which would otherwise be useless (ib. q. 18, a. 2).   Such is the teaching of Thomas.[2] Duns gives a different turn to the doctrine. *Attritio*, according to his view, when it has lasted for a definite time, establishes a merit of fitness (*de congruo*), a claim to the favorable regard of God.   The penitent must now make his confession, whereupon grace is infused, or sin is destroyed by the conversion of *attritio* into *contritio*, *i.e.*, since love is imparted, and thereby the *informa attritio* is transformed into the *formirta contritio* (sent. iv. d. 14, q. 2, 14 to 16).   The outcome of this is essentially the same as in Thomas, for since absolution infuses grace, it creates love, and by this means transforms the *attritio* into *contritio*. The infusion of grace takes place through absolution.   For the *attrite*, the process takes the following course : " For it is sufficient that some displeasure, although imperfect (*informis*), precedes, and then he is capable of sacramental absolution, and through it contrition is awakened " (iv. d. 16, q. 1. 7).   And

---

[1] If the confessing person is sufficiently *contrite*, absolution brings an increase of grace.

[2] It became afterward the general scholastic doctrine.   Alexander taught differently, *i. e.*, that " absolution from sin (*culpa*) belongs to God alone (iv. q. 80, m. 1), and that the priest can only remit a part of the penalty (m. 2, a. 1), and that temporal and not eternal " (ib. a. 2).   Similarly Bonaventura, iv. d. 18, p. 1, a. 2, q. 1.

further : " Thus the priest absolves what he yet binds. For he absolves from the debt of eternal penalty and binds to the discharge of temporal penalty " (ib.). It may, therefore, be said that absolution *transforms* eternal into temporal penalty (ib. d. 17, q. 1. 23. Cf. Durand. iv. d. 16, q. 1, a. 3), and thus that it *forgives* eternal penalty (ib. d. 19, q. 1. 32).[1] We present a brief summary of the theory of Biel, as a representative of the later writers : Forgiveness takes place through the destruction of sin by means of an infusion of grace (iv. d. 14, q. 1, a. 1, n. 2, 4). But for this there is necessary some preparation on the part of the sinner. And although this could be done by God without us, yet he requires also something from us " (ib. q. 2, a. 1); man can and should do " what in him is " (ib. q. 1, a. 2, concl. 2, 3). He should have a detestation of his crime (*detestatio criminis*) and a displeasure with his sin (*displicentia peccati*) (ib. concl. 5). Usually, repentance has its beginning in *servile fear ;* " for he who fears hell guards against evil things " (*mala cavet*) (ib. q. 2, a 3, dub. 3). Everything depends upon the " vow to be contrite " (*votum conterendi*). " Where the *votum conterendi* is, there is *contritio*." To refuse to have detestation for sin is to refuse to acknowledge having sinned (ib. a. 1, n. 2). Thus one finds himself in the state of *attrition*, and merits grace by his fitness (*de congruo*, d. 16, q. 2, a. 3, dub. 4). " He has appointed that he will not be lacking to him who does that which is in him, nor will he withhold grace from him who is sufficiently inclined to its reception " (d. 14, q. 2, a. 1, opin. 3). Confession and absolution, then, bring grace, and transform the *attritio* into *contritio*. Despite the variations here in separate points, the general view is the same. Confession and absolution are necessary in order that attrition be changed to contrition, and that sin be blotted out. Thus, the difficulty which cumbered the theory of Abelard was removed by the introduction of the *attritio*. Although in theory contrition was always spoken of as the chief thing, in practice it was attrition that carried the day. It is not easy to say which of the two conceptions was the more dangerous : the exercise of penitential grief to which was affixed the reward of forgiveness of sin, or the sorrow for sin which was to be transformed into complete penitence by the solemnities of divine worship.

(*b*) After absolution there yet remain temporal penalties for the sinner. These are met by the satisfaction of works (*satis-*

---

[1] How coolly and rationally, but with what fine-spun theorizing, is not this process conceived : A certain unrest on account of sin is increased by solemn confession and absolution to the point of contrition, and thereby sin is blotted out in a psychological way !

factio operum). Such works, performed for the re-establishment of the divine honor (Thom. suppl. q. 12, a. 3), are, indeed, not an equivalent (*satisfactio aequivalens*), but this does not prevent their being sufficient (a *sufficiens fieri*) before God (ib. q. 13, a. 1). They consist in our denying ourselves something for the honor of God. But we possess goods of soul, of body, and of fortune. The renunciation of these leads to prayer, fasting, and almsgiving respectively. According to Duns, the sinner may decline to accept the temporal penalty (iv. d. 19, § 27 f.).[1] The failure to perform the good works imposed at confession brings, however, suffering during this life and in purgatory.

(*c*) Very important becomes, therefore, the office of Indulgences. They are justified as follows : "It is conceded by all that indulgences have some efficacy, because it would be impious to say that the church did anything in vain " (ib. q. 25, a. 2)! The attempt was made to draw an argument in their favor from the unity of the church. The merits of Christ, as also of the saints, were greater than necessary. Thus arose the spiritual treasury (*thesaurus*) of the church, which consists of these " works of supererogation (*supererogationes*) of the members of Christ," and of the Lord himself (Alex. iv. q. 23, m. 3, a. 1. Albert, iv. d. 20, a. 16). But, since the body of Christ is one, these deeds of some members redound to the benefit of the rest (Thom. suppl. q. 25, a. 2). Inasmuch, further, as the dead who enter purgatory are still upon their journey heavenward, and as they are yet, on account of their sins, before the forum of the church, they also may secure a share in these treasures of grace (vid. especially Biel, expos. can. miss. lect. 57). It is understood, of course, that the church expects in return a work of piety and of profit to the church (*opus pium et utile ecclesiae*) (ib.). Whilst indulgences are granted to the living, however, by the pope " by the way of judiciary authority," they avail for the dead " by the way of supplication " (*per modum suffragii*); "indulgences profit them by the way of supplication, *i. e.*, on account of some work done by another and applied to them by the way of supplication" (ib. L. Cf. Alex. iv. q. 23, a. 2, m. 5. Bonav. iv. d. 20, p. 2, a. 1, q. 5). By indulgences even the entire penalties of purgatory may be averted (Heinr. quodl. viii. q. 19). Authority over indulgences belongs to the pope alone, but he may at will permit the bishops to share it with him

---

[1] Cf. Duns, iv. d. 15, q. 1. 12. Biel, iv. d. 16, q. 2, a. 1. In this connection Biel presents a thorough discussion of a number of important ethical questions, following in this Duns, dist. 15. In general, it may be said, there is at this point a mine of ethical suggestions in the dogmatics of the Middle Ages.

(Thom. suppl. q. 26, a. 1, 3). This is the doctrine taught also by Eugene IV., though not in precisely the same words: "Acts of penitence are, as it were, the material (*materia*) part of the sacrament." Then follows an enumeration of the usual three parts. Of *confession* it is said : "To which it pertains, that the sinner confess entirely to his priest all the sins of which he has recollection." *Satisfaction* "is rendered chiefly through prayer, fasting, and alms." The *form* of the sacrament consists of the words of absolution ; its *effect* is absolution from sins. Thus was completed the construction of the sacrament of repentance. The elements composing it remained the same, but they were placed in varying relations to one another. The emphasis was at first laid upon the satisfaction ; later, upon the contrition ; and then upon the confession, and by this means, in order to impress the necessity of the latter, upon the attrition.[1] But whenever one element is thus emphasized, questions and doubts arise as to the propriety and significance of the others. The Scholastics established the propriety of confession, and thereby provoked a new inquiry, *i. e.:* If absolution brings grace, what is then the need of subsequent works and of indulgences? At this point was aimed the criticism of the closing period of the Middle Ages.

6. The sacrament of Extreme Unction received no additional development in this period. As to its effect, opinion wavered, some attributing to it a removal of venial sins (Bonav. brevil. 6. 11. Duns, report. iv. d. 23, q. 1, 4); others the blotting out of the dregs of sin remaining after the observance of the other sacraments (Albert, sent. iv. d. 23, a. 1. Thom. sent. iv. d. 23, q. 1, a. 2). To this must be added also, when it follows (*quando expedit*), bodily relief or healing. The doctrine of the Scholastics is clearly summarized by Eugene IV.: "The *material* is the oil of the olive, blessed by a bishop." The ointment is applied "to the eyes, the ears, the nose, the mouth, the hands, the feet, the loins." The *form* is : "Through this sacred anointing and his most pious mercy may the Lord pardon (*indulgeat*)[2] to thee whatever through the sight, etc., and likewise in other members," etc. . . . "But the effect is the healing of the soul (*mentis*), and, so far as it succeeds, even of the body itself."

---

[1] Durand directly denies that contrition and satisfaction are constituent parts of the sacrament, maintaining that everything depends upon confession and absolution, and that the sacrament should of right be called the "sacrament of confession" (iv. d. 16, q. 1, and d. 14, q. 1).

[2] Instead of this deprecative form, the indicative form was in use in some churches, Thom. summ. suppl. q. 29, a. 8.

7. The sacrament of Ordination was more accurately defined. Its necessity appears from the need of an order of men who may make application of the *medicamenta* of the sacraments (Bonav. brevil. 6. 12). The *material* is seen in the symbols, or the vessels used in ordination ; while the accompanying words are the *form* (Thom. iii. suppl. q. 34, a. 5. Duns, iv. d. 24, q. 1. 8). Ordination embraces the seven orders (*ordines*), vid. p. 84. Everyone ordained receives thereby the spiritual character (Thom. q. 35, a. 2). In addition, there is granted to him by his ordination the grace making acceptable (*gratia gratum faciens*) in view of the administration of the sacraments entrusted to him (Thom. 35, a. 1).[1] The question here arose whether the episcopacy is an order by itself, or coincides with the presbyterial office. Thomas and Bonaventura declare that, since the eucharist is the highest sacrament, and priest and bishop have the same authority for its administration, the episcopacy is no separate order in the proper sense of that term. Only when the term, *ordo*, is used in a peculiar sense, to indicate a " certain office with respect to certain sacred acts," or as a " distinction of dignities and offices," can the episcopacy—speaking loosely—be described as a special order. Hence : " Beyond the priesthood, there is no degree of rank " (*gradus ordinis*), and : " The episcopate, in so far as it concerns the order of the priesthood, might well be called an order ; but, in so far as it is discriminated from the priesthood, it expresses a certain added dignity, or office, of the bishop " (Bonav. iv. d. 24, p. 2, a. 2, q. 3. Thom. q. 40, a. 5). Duns gives a different turn to the thought. He, too, in view of the high character of the act (*nobilitas actus*) in the administration of the eucharist, regards the priesthood as the highest rank (*supremus gradus*, sent. iv. d. 24, q. 1. 7), but, nevertheless, that order (*ordo*) which has the authority to elevate to this lofty position stands upon a yet higher plane. " But if to simply administer the eucharist (*conficere*) be not the most excellent act in the church, but to be able to appoint anyone to the lofty position which befits such act, then there are not only seven orders, but eight, because the episcopate is then a special grade and order in the church, whose province it is to confer all orders, and, consequently, to establish all in

---

[1] All the orders have a relation nearer or more remote to the eucharist. The priest consecrates ; the deacon is permitted to distribute the blood ; the sub-deacon may bring the material to be consecrated. The others are engaged in preparing for the reception of the sacrament : the acolyte illuminating for worship, the lector bringing the knowledge, the doorkeeper keeping away the unworthy, the exorcist warding off demons (vid. Duns, iv. d. 24, q. 1. 7).

such lofty position'' (report. iv. d. 24, q. 1. 9). This separation of the episcopacy from the ordinary priesthood found advocates in the later Middle Ages.[1] The administration of the sacrament of ordination belongs only to the bishop. Heretics can,
indeed, validly administer this, as the other sacraments,[2] but in
that case it does not bring the *gratia gratum faciens*, on account
of the sin of those who receive the sacraments from them against
the prohibition of the church (Thom. q. 38, a. 2). In this
way it was possible to remain orthodox and yet appropriately
discredit the sacraments administered by heretics. Eugene IV.
designates as the *material* of ordination : '' That through the delivering of which the order is conferred, just as the priesthood is
conferred through the handing of a cup with wine and a plate with
bread,'' etc. . . . The *form* of the priesthood is : '' Receive
authority for the offering of sacrifice in the church for the living
and the dead in the name of the Father,'' etc. . . . The *effect*
is an increase of grace, so that one may be a suitable minister.

8. Marriage consists in the union for life of man and woman
for the purpose of begetting and rearing children. An additional purpose since the fall is the prevention of fornication
(Thom. suppl. q. 48, a. 2). It accordingly embraces a con-
tract (*contractus*) in respect to '' the mutual giving of the bodies
for carnal copulation '' (Duns, iv. d. 30, q. 2. 4; d. 26. 8.
Thom. q. 58, a. 1). To its contraction belongs therefore
mutual consent (*mutuus consensus*) to the latter (Thom. q.
45, a. 1, 2; q. 48, a. 1). The public profession of this
consent constitutes the establishment of marriage (*matrimonium ratum*), and by it is given the right to demand the
conjugal debt (*debitum conjugale*). It is only the actual
copula carnalis which constitutes the *matrimonium consumma-
tum*. Before this consummation, marriage may be annulled by a
previous solemn vow of continence (Thom. q. 53, a. 2) or by
entering an order (q. 61, a. 2). Marriage once consummated
is indissoluble and monogamistic.[3] It is forbidden to the holy
order (*ordo sacer*).[4] Marriage, as a type of the union of Christ

---

[1] *E. g.*, Durand in sent. iv. d. 24, q. 6. 7.

[2] Only penance is excepted (Bonav. iv. d. 25, a. 1, q. 2. Durand, iv. d.
25, q. 1, ad 2), because the validity of absolution always depends upon the
regularity of the priestly jurisdiction, and this is wanting in the case of heretics and schismatics ; as in their administration of all sacraments. Cf. Duns,
report. iv. d. 25, q. 1, 16.

[3] According to Thomas (q. 65, a. 1), polygamy contradicts natural law.
Duns denies this, and considers it possible that after depopulating wars or pes-
tilences polygamy may be revealed by God to the church as allowable (iv. d.
33, q. 1. 6).

[4] Because those established in sacred orders handle the sacred vessels and

with the church, is a sacrament. Its *form* consists of the words of consent, "but not the benediction of the priest, which is sacramental in character " (*quoddam sacramentale*). This sacrament is, therefore, administered by him who uses it (q. 42, a. 1). In the *consensus*, there is an accompanying divine agency which hallows the married life (q. 45, a. 1).[1] Duns expresses himself most accurately, representing as the sacramental effect of marriage the gracious union of souls (*gratiosa conjunctio animarum*, iv. d. 26, § 15, 17). Inasmuch as the two persons desire to belong to each other, God establishes an inner relation between them. As separate effects are mentioned marital fidelity, the repression of lust during the act of copulation, and the turning of its energy toward a useful union (*copula utilis*, Bonav. iv. d. 26, a. 2, q. 2), *i. e.*, the living together of the married pair and their co-operation in the rearing of children (Albert, iv. d. 26, a. 14). To these is to be added what Christian marriage has in in common with the natural ordinance, *i. e.*, that the copulative act, which is in itself unwortny of man, because for the time being depriving him of reason, is in marriage legitimized and excused in view of the blessings which it brings (Thom. q. 49, a. 1). These blessings are progeny and fidelity, to which Christianity adds the sacrament (thus Lombard, iv. d. 31 A, following Augustine, De genesi ad litt. ix. 7. 12). We need not enter upon a discussion of the hindrances of marriage, which were considered at length by the Scholastics.[2] Eugene IV. describes as the *efficient cause* of marriage, the " mutual consent expressed through words concerning the person present." As the *blessings* of marriage, he enumerates : " Children to be received and educated ; fidelity, which each of the married pair ought to observe toward the other," and "the indivisibility of marriage on account of the fact that it signifies the indivisible union of Christ and the church." It is very evident that this last of the sacraments attained but a loose and unfinished form. Neither is there a distinct definition of its material, nor is it clear how or

---

sacraments, and it is, therefore, becoming (*decens*) that they by continence preserve bodily purity (iv. q. 53, a. 3).

[1] Bonaventura (iv. d. 26, a. 2, q. 3): "Matrimony receives a reason of spirituality and grace when consent is joined with the benediction, where its significance is explained ; and sanctification is obtained through the benediction, and thus in the sacerdotal benediction consists chiefly the spiritual reason." It is remarkable that this idea is not, following the example of the sacrament of penance, crystallized in the formula, that the priestly benediction is the *form*, and the consent of the parties the *material*, of the sacrament. This was done only in sporadic instances during the Middle Ages, though more frequently at a later period. Vid. Kirchenlex. iv., ed. 2, 145 f.

[2] Briefly presented in the Versus memoriales in Bonav. brevil. 6. 13.

whence the consent of the contracting parties has a sacramental character.[1]

9. Such is the Catholic doctrine of the sacraments, as it was afterward adopted substantially unchanged by the Council of Trent. Two elements concurred from the beginning in its construction, the materializing of grace and the hierarchical conception of the church (vid. Augustine). The sacraments infuse grace, but the priests make the sacraments. We have been considering the conception of grace involved, and it remains for us to glance briefly at the conception of the church, where we will find that no advance has been made upon the utterances of Hugo.

(*a*) "The Church is the same thing as the assembly (*congregatio*) of the faithful, and every Christian is, therefore, a member of the church." This definition (Thomas, exposit. symbol. opp. xvii. 69) asserts nothing more than that the Christian community is the church. Thomas employs also, instead of this, the term *communio fidelium* (summ. suppl. q. 23, a. 1).[2] In the church, as in Noah's ark, there is salvation. That is to say, in the "communion of saints" is transmitted, *i. e.*, participation in the sacraments, for this is Thomas's conception of the term.[3]

---

[1] It is true that, for those who express such consent, the creative benediction becomes effective. It may be said, in case they are Christians, that the blessing of the kingdom of Christ is also theirs; but can we think of a display of grace here which would not be identical with that personally experienced? The objection commonly urged by Protestants that, although marriage is acknowledged as a sacrament, virginity is regarded as a higher state, has no force, as a parallel to this is furnished in the case of repentance.

[2] This is the current definition of the church. Vid., *e. g.*, Duns, report. iv. d. 24, q. 1. 5 : *universitas fidelium*. In sent. iv. d. 19, § 15 : *communio fidelium.* The meaning is peculiarly clear in De perfec. statuum 34. 9 : the church is the *congregatio* of all believers, *i. e.*, the Saracens, for example, do not belong to it. Occam, dial. Goldast, monarchia, ii. pp. 402, 503, 471, 481, 498, 788, 799 : *congregatio fidelium*, or *communitas fidelium* or *christianorum*, ib. p. 788 ff., 806 f., 810, 814, 923. Marsil. Defensor pac. ii. 2, p. 193; 6, p. 209, in Goldast, monarch. ii. Biel, expos. can. miss. lect. 22 D. Thomas Motter, doctrinale, ii. 9 ff.

[3] The term, *communio sanctorum*, is very differently interpreted : of the *sacraments*, *e. g.*, Abelard (Mi. 178, p. 629), Ivo of Chartres (Mi. 162, 606), Thom. l. c.; of the *saints*, *e. g.*, *Bruno* of Würzburg (Mi. 142, 500), in Schönbach's Altd. Predigten, i. 42 f. 46; of the *angels*, *e. g.*, Alexander (summ. iv. q. 37, § 9); of the *church triumphant* (Gerson, opp. i. 240); of the *saints and the sacraments*, *e. g.*, Bonav. centiloq., p. 3, § 38—worthy of note is the remark of Joslenus of Soissons (Mi. 186, 1488), in which the two are thus combined : "I believe the truth of the sacraments, in which the saints took part, so that I believe what they, too, believed in regard to baptism and the Lord's Supper;" cf. Richard, iii. d. 25, princ. 1, q. 2. Thom. Motter, doctrinale, v. 95 ; of *fellowship of the saints and the spiritual blessings secured by them* (vid. Hasack, Der chr. Glaube d. deutschen Volkes, etc.,

But the sacraments bring us grace. They lead us, further, to the ministers (*ministri*) who have received from the apostles authority for the forgiveness of sins (expos. p. 70). Thus the definition of the church as the congregation of believers fits in exactly with the conception of it as a body politic (*congregatio politica*, Thom. suppl. q. 26, a. 1), consisting of rulers (*rectores*) and subjects (*subditi*).

(*b*) But since the church is an organized state (*politia ordinata*), there is in it a gradation of rulers (Duns, iv. d. 24, § 3). In addition to the lawgivers, there must be some whose office it shall be to adapt the laws to circumstances (Thom. suppl. q. 20, a. 1). All priests are authorized to administer the eucharist, but some sacraments are reserved for the bishop. In regard to the power of the keys, a distinction is made between the key of the order (*clavis ordinis*) and the key of jurisdiction (*jurisdictionis*). The former, which grants forgiveness, belongs to the priesthood. The latter belongs to the bishop alone, and is his power of spiritual dominion, the plenary authority (*potestas plena*) to grant or refuse the sacraments, and also the jurisdiction in the administration of justice (*in foro causarum*). The bishop alone can grant to the priest the right to use the key which belongs to the latter (Thom. sent. iv. d. 18, q. 1, a. 1), in doing which he reserves special cases for his own decision (Thom. suppl. q. 20, a. 2). Hence: "The bishop alone is properly called a prelate (*praelatus*) of the church, and, therefore, he alone has plenary power in the dispensing of the sacraments and jurisdiction in the administration of justice, . . . but others, on account of that which is committed to them by him. But the priests who are set over the people are not simply prelates, but, as it were, assistants" (ib. q. 26, a. 1).

(*c*) But the church is One Body. In harmony with this is the solitary power of the pope (ib. q. 40, a. 6). "The supreme pontiff is the head of the whole church" (Thom. summ. ii. ii. q. 1, a. 10). He possesses "plenitude of power over ecclesiastical affairs" (ib. q. 89, a. 9). He rules in the church as a king in his kingdom, and the other bishops are admitted by him to a share in his care over the church (*in partem sollicitudinis*, Thom. sent. iv. d. 20, q. 1, a. 4). How then is the episcopal related to the papal power? The bishops, too, have by divine right the *plenitudo potestatis* in their own territories, but they have it together with the pope and in subjection to him. Accordingly, the pope has direct jurisdiction (*regimen immediatum*) over all

1868, p. 90); finally, of the *fellowship of the pious of all times and places*, Wessel, opp. p. 809. Erasm. opp. v. 1174.

10

souls, and can assert for himself episcopal rights in every territory.   This was of great importance for the mendicant orders
in their preaching and confessionals (Thom. sent. iv. d. 17, q.
3, a. 3.   Bonav., Quare fratres minores praedicent ? opp. vii.
340 ff. and Explicat. regul. ib. 324 f.).   To the pope belongs
law-giving and government in the church.   He is to decide what
is correct faith, to publish upon occasion a new symbol of faith,
and to summon general councils (Thom. summ. ii. ii. q. 1, a.
10).[1]   He proclaims indulgences (ib. suppl. q. 38, a. 1).   He
stands above all princes as the vicar of Christ.   If they rebel
against him, he may punish them by removal from office and by
releasing their subjects from the oath of allegiance to them (ib.
ii. ii. q. 67, a. 1 ; q. 12, a. 2 ; sent. iv. d. 44, q. 2).   The
church attains its summit in the pope.   With Aristotle, it was
held : "But the best government of a multitude is that it be
ruled by one" (c. gentil. iv. 76).

As compared with the leaders of the Gregorian age, the later
writers carried out many ideas to a further extent, and supported
their views by more painstaking argument, but they furnish
scarcely anything essentially new.   The Second Council of
Lyons (A. D. 1274) accepted this view of the Romish primacy
(vid. Hefele, vi. 139 f., 141).

10. We stand now at the close of our period.   It had inherited an abundance of suggestive thoughts from its predecessor,
which were all accepted and applied.   Hence the wealth of
views and ideas in this century.   As in the days of Origen and
Augustine, all contradictions seemed blended into a higher harmony.   Reason and faith have entered into covenant, ideal and
reality, religion and science, contemplation and speculation, have
joined hands, and the body serves the regnant spirit.   More than
this, the world appeared to be at length rendering due obedience
to the kingdom of God.   The lord of the church is lord of the
world.   Augustine and Aristotle, Anselm and Bernard, Hugo
and Abelard, Gregory VII. and Francis of Assizi—all the results
of their thought and efforts appeared melted into unity in the
writings of Thomas of Aquino.   It was then that Otto of Frei-
sing wrote : "The kingdom (*civitas*) of Christ appears to have
received already in the present almost all things promised to it
except immortality " (Mon. Germ. scr. xx. 198).   And yet,
shortly after the year 1300, premonitions of the coming crisis
began to appear.   Of this our next chapter will treat.

---

[1] Upon infallibility, vid., further, quodlib. ix. a. 16 ; contra errores Graecor.
Also Albert, sent. iv. d. 20, a. 17.

CHAPTER III.

THE GRADUAL DISSOLUTION OF THE SCHOLASTIC THEOLOGY. THE RELIGIOUS AND ECCLESIASTICAL CRISIS AT THE CLOSE OF THE MIDDLE AGES.

§ 59. *The Theology of Duns Scotus and Its Significance for the History of Doctrines.*

J. DUNS SCOTI, opp. ed. Wadding, 13 vols., 1639. Reprinted in the new Paris edition in Vivès, 1891 ff., 26 vols. We are chiefly interested in the Commentary upon the Sentences known as the Opus Oxoniense (which we quote as "sent."), and the abbreviated copy of it in the Reportata Parisiensia (which we quote as "report."). Cf. WERNER, Duns Scotus, 1881. PLEZANSKI, Essai sur la philosophie de Duns Scot., 1887. SEEBERG, Die Theologie des Duns Scotus, 1900, and in PRE. v., ed. 3, 62 ff. RITTER, Gesch. d. Philos. viii. 354 ff. PRANTL, Gesch. d. Logik, iii. 202 f. ERDMANN, Gesch. d. Philos. i., ed. 4, 446 ff. STÖCKL, Gesch. d. Philos. d. MA. ii. 778 ff. BAUR, Lehre v. d. Dreieinigkeit, ii. 448 ff., 589 ff., 621 ff., 642 ff., 673 ff., 690 ff., 727 ff., 759 ff., 823 ff., 861 ff. RITSCHL, Rechtf. u. Vers. i. 73 ff KAHL, Primat des Willens in Aug., Duns Scot., u. Descartes, 1886, p. 76 ff SIEBECK, Die Anfänge der neueren Psychol. in d. Scholast., Ztschr. f. Philos. u. phil. Krit., vol. 94, p. 161 ff.; 95, p. 245 ff.

1. The history of the dogmatic movements at the close of the Middle Ages must begin with a study of Duns Scotus († 1308). For, however true it may be that the masterly skill of this man in dialectics and his acuteness carried the scholastic method to its point of highest development, yet it is equally true upon the other hand—and this must determine his historical position— that the theological method which he pursued became the controlling influence leading to the dissolution of the scholastic theories and the crisis in theology.

We must first briefly note the leading positions in the general conception of the universe entertained by Duns. Upon the question of Universals he stood upon the basis of a modified Realism (vid. p. 104). The universal he held to be as well *before* as *in* and *after* an object. Everything which exists, exists also, since everything comes from God, as an eternal original image in the mind of God (sent. i. d. 35, q. 1, § 12). Here comes to light an important variation from the view of Thomas, as Duns lays the emphasis upon the singular, and no longer upon the universal. The individual being, the *individuitas* or *haecceitas* is, according to his view, the real goal of nature, and is therefore, as compared with the universal, the higher form of existence (rep. i. d. 36, q. 4. 14). There is an ultimate reality of being (*ultima realitas entis*) which makes the particular object to

be just what it is.   From this results the emphasis laid upon experience as a ground of knowledge (*e. g.*, de anim. q. 15).   In
the theory of knowledge, Duns adopts, in a general way, the
prevailing Aristotelian formulas.   The intellect apprehends the
intelligible form (*species intelligibilis*) which is presented to it
in the sensible object, and thus begets the conception.   He
does not, like Thomas, interject the "intelligible form" between the sensuous perception and the intellect, but it is already
present in the perception and given with it.   Hence, upon the
Scotist theory of knowledge, the individual object is as such perceptible (de anim. q. 22. 4).   But he very strongly emphasizes
also the spontaneity of the spirit in the act of perception.   The
object does not beget the conception in the (passive) spirit, but
the intellect is the organ which apprehends the object and imprints the conception.   But here the will asserts itself.   It impels
to thought, or restrains from it ; it constrains to or prohibits agreement with the conception received (sent. ii. d. 42, q. 4. 5, 10 f.).[1]
Thinking in itself occurs as a necessary and natural process (sent.
i. d. 32, q. 1. 14 ; ii. d. 42, q. 4. 5).   It is only through its
connection with the will, which is free, as perception is not, from
the necessity of the causal process, that it receives a personal
and free character.   From this originates one of the leading
thoughts of Duns, *i. e.*, the doctrine of the *primacy of the will.*   The
entire inner and outer man, with all his thoughts, words, works,
and impulses, is subject to the will.   It is the will alone which
makes human conduct good or bad (sent. ii. d. 42, q. 4).   The
will, and not the thought, is the organ for the appropriation of the
highest objects and values.   Faith does not arise without the consent of the will (iii. d. 25, q. 1. 11).   Love is realized in the will,
and blessedness is experienced by it (ii. d. 25, § 13 f., 19 ;
iv. d. 49, quaest. ex latere, § 10 ff.).   According to Thomas,
blessedness consists in the intellectual contemplation of the
supreme end, from which contemplation results the joy of the
pacified will (Thom. summ. ii. 1, q. 2-5).   According to Duns,
it consists in the apprehension of God, as the present supreme
good, in the voluntary act of love, which brings with it the supreme satisfaction of man's longings.   But this joy is only an
accompanying experience, while the real blessedness consists in
the apprehension of God (iv. d. 49, q. 4. 7, 8).   The will is
free, for as touching the same object the will has the choice of
a *velle* or a *nolle* (ii. d. 25, § 6).   Not in the object therefore
lies the determining ground of the will, nor in the perception,

---

[1] Except when the conception carries its own absolute evidence, Quaest.
subtiliss. in metaphys. 9.

which always but reflects the object, but in the will itself. " Nothing else than the will is the cause of the entire volition in the will " (ii. d. 25, § 22). Only upon the premise of freedom is the possibility of meritorious conduct intelligible (ib.). A strict proof of the freedom of the will, *i. e.*, the existence of a contingent course of action, cannot, indeed, be produced, but it is attested by immediate experience. If anyone were to cast doubt upon contingent conduct and events, he ought to be flogged until he should acknowledge the possibility of not being flogged (i. d. 39, § 13).

This brief summary must here suffice. The interest of Duns centres, not in the universal, but in the singular and in the individual. And in his conception of man, the chief thing is that man himself freely wills. These are ideas which foreshadow a new conception of the universe. The emphasis is laid, not upon ideas nor the perception of them, but as, on the one hand, man himself is nothing more than his individual free will, so the final end, or goal, of the world is to be seen in the concrete separate objects which it contains.

2. What then is the task of Theology? It presupposes revelation. The latter instructs man as to the end which his will should pursue and the means for attaining it (sent. prol. q. 1. 6 ff.). These truths necessary to salvation are presented by the Holy Scriptures. The credibility of the latter is exhaustively proved. The resultant may be stated in two propositions : " That the doctrine of the canon is true," and "that the Sacred Scriptures sufficiently contain the doctrine necessary to the prilgrim " (ib. q. 2. 14). Duns, like Thomas, maintains that this truth is summarized in the Apostles' Creed, or, also, in the three symbols of the ancient catholic church (iii. d. 25, q. 1. 4 ; i. d. 26, § 25 ; iv. d. 43, q. 1. 11). He, however, placed beside the authority of the Scriptures and these symbols, as of equal value, the teaching of " the authentic Fathers " and of the " Romish church " (i. d. 26, § 26). " Nothing is to be held as of the substance of the faith except that which can be expressly derived (*expresse haberi*) from Scripture, or which is expressly declared by the church, or which follows evidently from something plainly contained in Scripture or plainly determined by the church " (iv. d. 11, q. 3. 5). As the church has decided which books belong to the canon, the requirement of subjection to the Scriptures is equivalent to subjection to the church, which "approves and authorizes " the books of Scripture (iii. d. 23, q. 1. 4 ; i. d. 5, q. 1. 8). In the last resort, the Romish church is the only authority. Her utterance decides what is or is not heretical. Even if a doctrine be deprived of all other authority

and all arguments drawn from reason, it must be accepted solely upon the authority of the Romish church (iv. d. 6, q. 9. 14, 16, 17). This is the churchly positivism of the later Scholasticism. The ecclesiastical doctrines are employed as so many legal precepts, and orthodoxy receives a juristic flavor. But, as at a later period, so already in Duns, this positivism is only a counterpoise to an unlimited criticism of the traditional doctrines. He criticizes not only the contemporary theologians, but even Augustine and Aristotle (especially Thomas and Heinrich). In regard to many a traditional dogma, impossibility of proof and aimlessness are openly acknowledged (transubstantiation, habitus), or the possibility of the contrary opinion granted. The decision, however, is always in favor of the Romish doctrine, although under the formal endorsement may lurk many a bold perversion of the sense.

The complex of positive and practical truths[1] of which theology treats is apprehended in faith. Duns acknowledged the possibility of explaining faith in a perfectly natural way, as assent to tradition (*fides acquisita*, vid. iii. d. 23, § 1, 4 ff.). But the "authority of Scripture and the saints" demands the recognition of a supernatural habitus, the *fides infusa* (ib. § 14). This is a habitus infused into the intellect, as the habitus of love is infused into the will. To speak more exactly, it is a *habitus inclinans*, which impels, but does not compel, the intellect to assent. There is thus retained even here some liberty of action for the will (§ 11). This *assensus*, as infused, has a permanence and certainty which does not characterize acquired faith (§ 15 f.). In regard to *implicit* faith, his position agreed with that of Thomas (supra, p. 103).

3. In his discussion of separate doctrines, we will find almost everywhere in Duns suggestions which assumed great importance for later ages. We note first his conception of God. He endeavors from the principles of causality, finality, and eminence to establish the necessity of an Infinite Being, which has its cause or end in nothing else, and which can be outranked by nothing (i. d. 2, q. 2. 10 ff.). But, as in this scheme God is viewed under the aspects of the First Cause (*primum efficiens*) and the Self-acting (*per se agens*), there result a number of valuable

---

[1] Duns strongly emphasized the positive character of theology (sent. prol. q. 2, lateral.). It has an independent sphere, and, as a number of contingent facts are embraced in it, other principles than those of metaphysics (l. c., § 29). He maintains likewise the practical nature of the propositions of theology; for even such doctrines as those of the Trinity or the conception of the Son are of a practical nature, since their aim is to awaken love for the object presented (l. c. § 32).

positive ideas. First of all, "That the first cause is intelligent and volitional" (*intelligens et volens*) (§ 20). This is proved as follows : There is in the world contingent causality. Since now every second cause causes "in so far as it is moved by the first," the First Cause must also act contingently, *i. e.*, it is free will (ib.). "Therefore either nothing happens contingently, *i. e.*, is evitably caused, or the First Cause thus causes immediately what it would be able also not to cause" (§ 21). It is utterly impossible to derive contingency, with Aristotle, from *second causes*, for the necessity of the all-embracing activity of the First Cause would necessitate also the actions of the second causes (i. d. 39, § 12). God is, accordingly, to be represented as free will. This involves, further, that there can be found no reason for his willing or not willing, since all willing is absolutely without ground or reason : " And, therefore, there is no reason (*causa*) why his will willed this, except that his will is will" (i. d. 8, q. 5. 24). God, then, wills this or that, because he wills it. Good is, therefore, good because God wills it to be so ; he does not will it because it is good (iii. d. 19, § 7). All things, considered in themselves, may be said to be possible to the omnipotence of the divine will. This *potentia absoluta* of God has only one limit, *i. e.*, the logically impossible (iv. d. 10, q. 2, 5, 11). God can, therefore, according to his absolute power, save the already lost Judas ; but he cannot give eternal blessedness to a stone, nor make undone what has been done. But by the side of this absolute power stands the ordained power (*potentia ordinata*) of God, *i. e.*, the manifestations of divine power upon the ground and within the bounds of laws and ordinances fixed—arbitrarily—by God himself. God commonly works according to his ordained power, but it is also conceivable that he may, upon occasion, by virtue of his absolute power, vary from the course of the former, or entirely abolish it. For example, the rule that no one shall receive glory who has not accepted grace might be abrogated (i. d. 44, § 1-4). Duns conducts this whole discussion under the heading of the conception of God as the absolute Being ; but it affords evidence that he held ideas of God far transcending the limits of such a scheme. This is proved especially by his important theory, that the sum total of the relations of God to the world is to be described as Love. This idea he develops as follows : God wills, or loves, himself. As now all being originates in God, it is subject to God as its final end, and has, therefore, a share in the love which God exercises toward himself (iii. d. 32, § 2). This love embraces, accordingly, the whole creation, its present and its future. But the creation is a composite with a gradation of its parts according to their relations to the final end. This relationship decides in every separate case the measure of the divine love to be bestowed. This produces the following scheme : (*a*) God loves himself. (*b*) He, therefore, loves that which has immediate relation to himself as its final end, or elect men, *i. e.*, God wills that there shall be men who, with himself, love him, and this loving will is predestination. (*c*) The divine love then directs itself upon the means for the realizing of this predestination, *i. e.*, the ordinances of grace. (*d*) Finally, God, for the sake of the elect, wills the more remote means, *i. e.*, the visible world (l. c., § 6).[1]

The doctrine of the Trinity need not long detain us. Duns, in the traditional way, deduces the Son from the divine thought, and the Spirit from the divine will (i. d. 2, q. 7, 3).

But it is not at this point that the historical significance of Duns' conception of God is to be seen, but in the fact that God is here, more clearly and distinctly than in the writings of Thomas, conceived as a thinking and willing personality, and that love is recognized as the content of the divine activity in the world. But since Duns made the arbitrary will of God the source of all things, faith in the traditional formulas concerning the harmony and order of the universe was shattered. It was, accordingly,

---

[1] Some further remarks upon the views of Duns upon predestination are needful. Although he did not attach much practical importance to the doctrine, he yet applied it theoretically with great zeal. The question, whether a predestinated person can be lost, he answers in the affirmative, since God might have willed the one as well as the other (i. d. 40, § 1, 2). God can, therefore, predestinate any person, or he can fail to predestinate him. Duns answers the objection, that predestination leads to immortality, by asserting that the will of God cannot be limited from without (§ 3). The current conception, that predestination depends upon prescience, he refutes by observing that God always foresees all contingent events in their dependence upon the divine will, and, therefore, the good deeds of men appear as determined by the divine will (i. d. 41, § 10). Besides, this would not apply to children dying in infancy, who are, without any deeds of theirs, either elected or reprobated. Duns himself teaches that predestination has no ground whatever upon man's part ; for the divine will that any creature be saved exists before faith or good works, and hence the latter cannot under any circumstances constitute the ground of the former (ib. § 11). In reprobation, it is true, it appears necessary to grant such a ground in man, the foreseen final sin, since otherwise the justice of the sentence cannot well be conceived (ib.). The difficulties thus remaining were not overlooked by Duns. He suggests, further, that it be supposed that God, while predestinating Peter to glory and then to grace, in regard to Judas, determined nothing at all, but, on the contrary, willed that both belong to the "mass of perdition." Inasmuch as the first-named act of the divine will had relation to Peter, he receives grace and eternal life, while Judas is simply left to perdition (§ 12). The discussion closes with a warning against prying into such matters, and an exhortation that everyone be allowed to hold his own opinion, only so that the divine freedom be guarded against any charge of unrighteousness (§ 13).

no longer eternal ideas and laws, but the positive activity of God, which constituted the material of religious knowledge. On the other hand, a powerful weapon was, by this new conception of God, placed in the hands of the critics of the traditional teachings of the church. If the illogical is to be acknowledged as frequently true, may not the logical also be false? And when once the idea of absolute power has been admitted, may not anything be regarded as conceivable, as possible, or as allowable?

4. The sinlessness of man in paradise was, in and of itself, only potential, since the will as such always involves the possibility of sinning. The actual innocence of the first pair can, therefore, be explained only by their possession of their additional endowment, the *donum superadditum* (ii. d. 23, § 6, 7). There is in man by nature, in consequence of the existence of the sensuous impulses together with the reason and will, an inward rebellion. Only the imparted supernatural *habitus* of grace is able to subject the lower forces to the higher (ii. d. 29, § 4). If, therefore, concupiscence, or the rebellion of the sensuous nature against the spirit, belongs to the original human nature, original sin cannot possibly consist in concupiscence. Original Sin, on the contrary, is to be described as only a want (*carentia*) of original righteousness (d. 30, q. 2. 3). It has as its material concupiscence, but this gains control and becomes sin only through the loss of the restraining rein (*frenum cohibens*, d. 32, § 7). This view presents the question of the propagation of sin in a new light. Duns opposes the theory of physical inheritance. If sin is in the will, how can the latter make the whole body sick? And if this were the case, why should the seed only, and not the spittle and blood as well, be infected? Or again, how should the inherited physical condition transform the will? (d. 32, § 4 f.). The solution must be reached from another direction. Since the original righteousness was bestowed upon Adam for himself and his posterity, it is a righteousness which they now owe, a *justitia debita*. "By virtue of such a gift, the will of every child of his becomes a debtor" (ib. § 8-12).[1] Conception demands attention in the case only as being that which makes man a child of Adam. Only as descended from Adam, is he a debtor to the righteousness granted to the latter (§ 17). It is evident that the Augustinian theory of original sin is here

---

[1] It does not harmonize with this, that Duns asserts that our first parents could not have transmitted their righteousness to their posterity (ii. d. 20, q. 1, 3). He maintains, therefore, in this passage that had Adam not fallen, God would by co-operation have regularly imparted grace to the children of the race. This is, however, nothing more than a postulate—to account in some way for the inheritance of sin—in the doctrinal system of Duns.

surrendered in its fundamental principle.   In place of the physical propagation of the original concupiscence, is posited the
ideal obligation of every child of Adam to the supernatural righteousness once granted to Adam.[1]

The teaching of Duns in regard to Actual Sin is in keeping with
this theory of original sin.   The former is a defect in the will.
Instead of loving the supreme good, or God, the will of man
rests content with an earthly end as its supreme good.   He thus
offends also against the divine law revealed to him (d. 37, q. 1,
6 f.).

5. We may, perhaps, venture the opinion that the Christology
of Duns displays a higher appreciation of the human life of
Christ than is manifested by the other great Scholastics.   This
is noticeable especially in his discussions of the impartation of
grace to the soul of Jesus (iii. d. 13, q. 1. 3), and of the knowledge of Jesus (iii. d. 14), in which he maintains that the soul of
Jesus by its union with the Logos possessed at least an inherent (*habituale*) knowledge of all universals, but that it was
subject to the necessity of gaining a progressive knowledge of the
individual and the contingent, so that Lk. ii. 40 is to be understood of a real progress (l. c., q. 2. 16, 20; q. 3. 6 ff.).   It is
granted also that pain could penetrate to the higher part of the
soul of Jesus (ib. q. 15).   Merit likewise is attributed to the
human nature of Christ.   He merited the favor of God, because
he did not yield to his sensuous desires.   He could merit by
fasting, watching, and prayer (iii. d. 18, § 4-6).   But all of this
does not extend to the experiences and visions of the person of
Jesus which occur so abundantly in the devotional literature of
the Middle Ages (supra, p. 89 f.).   This is to be acounted for by
the fact that Duns clings unalterably to the christological scheme
of the ancient church, which he, like the other Scholastics, interprets after the manner of Abelard.   The union is a relation
of subordination (*relatio ordinis*), a relation of dependence of
the human upon the divine nature, a relation which may be compared to that between attribute and substance (iii. d. 1, q. 1. 3).
The divine nature is in no wise limited by its relation to the human.   The latter, in the moment of its genesis, subordinates
itself to the divine nature and receives at once and thereby from

---

[1] Duns abolished the conception of original sin, or substituted for it that of
original debt.   But the substitution, although aiming to maintain the idea of
guilt, or debt, cannot be regarded as satisfactory, for it fails to afford that
which it is the province of the theory of original sin to furnish, *i. e.*, to explain the universality and depth of the conviction of guilt.   If God withdrew
righteousness from Adam, and this could be bestowed upon his descendants
only by a special divine act, it is not easy to see how the sense of guilt can be
traced to the concupiscence originally inhering in human nature.

the latter its personality (ib. § 9 ; d. 2, q. 2. 12). A human personality, or separate existence, of Jesus is in no wise to be maintained (d. 5, q. 2. 4). It has not even an independent existence (*esse*). It has its existence from the divine Logosperson, as my foot exists only by virtue of my existence (d. 6, q. 1. 2 ff.). The proposition : God became man, is not an accurate statement. The becoming was only an experience of the man, not of the Logos. To speak properly, we should say : " the human nature is united personally with the Word " (d. 7, q. 2. 5 ff.). There is a unity of the two natures, which consists in the union, *i. e.*, in the relation of the one to the other (iii. d. 1, q. 2. 10).[1] These conceptions do not indicate an advance in the knowledge of the subject. The doctrine of Duns is certainly orthodox, but it is, in consequence, not clear. Shall it really be thought possible for us to think of that human nature which resists the allurements of sensuality in order to merit the divine favor as absolutely impersonal—as something which, with no existence of its own, has been united as an attribute to the infinite divinity of the Logos? The two currents of medieval Christology—as represented in Abelard and Bernard—here meet, and it is evident that they will not unite—not, at least, in the channel of the traditional formulas. The rational Christology of Abelard discriminated sharply between the finite and the infinite, in order to insure the independence of the finite ; while the pious reflection of Bernard beheld in the human words and deeds of the finite Jesus the revelation of the love of the infinite God. Abelard was mainly concerned for the humanity of Jesus, but he in reality promoted the undue emphasizing of his divinity. Bernard sought the ever-present heavenly Son of God, and he awakened and deepened appreciation for the humanity of Jesus. Abelard's ideas adapted themselves to the traditional formulas, found a place in the dogmatic system of the Middle Ages, and have endured beyond that period. Bernard's ideas were not accepted by the dogmatic system of the Middle Ages, but they influenced the life of the age, and thus frequently made inroads upon the logical consistency of the dogmatic formulas. An illustration of this may be seen in the portraiture by Duns of the man Jesus as acting meritoriously.

6. Duns confessedly owed something of his repute to his championship of the Immaculate Conception of the Virgin

---

[1] During his stay in Hades, Christ was not a man, as, *e. g.*, the Lombard teaches. For in his state of death the various parts of the human nature were not really united with the divinity of Christ, although they may have still existed. Vid. iii. d. 22, § 18 ff. Christ was, hence, in Hades only according to his divinity.

Mary. He casts doubt upon the then current opinion that, since Mary was born of sinful seed, it was necessary for Christ to be her Saviour as well as her Son. The argument drawn from the sinfulness of the seed had no force for Duns. On the other hand, it would appear fitting that Christ should merit salvation for the person most nearly related to him in an absolutely perfect way, *i. e.*, in such a way that she should remain free from original sin.

As God blots out original sin in baptism, so can he also do in the moment of conception. Christ's passion was then accepted in advance by God as the means of her salvation (iii. d. 3, q. 1. 3 f., 9, 14, 17). Mary, therefore, remained entirely untainted by sin. Her descent from Adam does not of itself involve sinfulness. Even if we should hold that the soul originates through generation in the moment of conception, it would not be necessary to regard Mary as sinful, since God could infuse grace into the soul in the very moment when it comes into being (ib. § 17, 20). Measured by the doctrine of Duns upon original sin, the advantage enjoyed by Mary is none too marked. The whole subject in Duns is treated rather as a theological hypothesis, not at all as a doctrine of any special importance.

7. We turn now to the work of Redemption. Duns denies the infinity of the merit of Christ. The merit of Christ is a matter of his human will ; it is the obedience which he rendered (iii. d. 19, § 4 ; iv. d. 2, q. 1. 7). Hence, as the human will of Christ is finite, so is also the merit which he gains through its exercise (iii. d. 19, § 5). This merit of Christ was foreseen by God as the means of human redemption. The divine predestination embraces that merit as the means of realizing its purpose. The passion of Christ was therefore foreordained from eternity by God as the means for the salvation of the predestinated. To it belongs a peculiar value and a special efficacy, not in and of itself, but by virtue of the foreordination of the divine will, which foreordained this means and *will accept it* as effectual (l. c., § 6). The merit of Christ is not of itself good, nor is it of itself a means of salvation, but it is the divine will alone that makes it the one or the other (§ 7). It might, indeed, of itself avail for all men, but it was God's will that its efficiency should be limited to the predestinated (§ 14).

But was the precise form of Christ's sufferings, or any rendering of satisfaction, necessary to man's salvation ? Duns raises this question in a criticism of Anselm's theory. He disputes, first of all, the necessity of a satisfaction, which he holds to have been necessary only because God so willed. But it was not necessary that God should will it, just as the salvation of men is itself not a necessary, but a contingent, act of God (iii. d. 20, § 7). But even granting the necessity of satisfaction, it would still by no means follow that the one rendering it must be God. It is not correct to say that something greater than the whole creation must be offered up to God. Any pious act of Adam would have sufficed to atone for his first sin (ib. § 8). Just as little can the demand that satisfaction must proceed from a man be strictly proved. The value (of the sacrifice) does not lie in the offered object as such, but in the acceptance by the divine will. But it is perfectly conceivable that God might will to accept the deed of an angel, or of a sinless man, as a sufficient atonement. Yea, it would even be conceivable that every sinful man might have rendered satisfaction for himself, if God should, by imparting the primary grace (*gratia prima*), qualify him for meritorious action and accept this as a satisfaction (§ 9). In this criticism it is plainly to be seen that the conception of God entertained by Duns excludes all necessity for the occurrence of the events connected with the passion of Christ. That which came to pass, came to pass according to God's free will ; and entirely different occurrences were in themselves conceivable. That which has actually occurred is, God has willed ; but who will prescribe to him that he has been compelled so to will? This idea is a gain as compared with the rationalistic speculation of Anselm.

Duns gave but a brief positive response to the above question. Christ suffered " for the sake of righteousness." He beheld the sins of the Jews and their perverted adherence to the law. Christ willed " to recall them from that error through his works and discourses." He declared to them the truth, and died for righteousness. To this is to be added, that since he offered his passion in our behalf to the Father, he bound us to himself, and thus to God, with fetters of gratitude. " Therefore he did this chiefly, as I believe, to allure us to his love, and because he wished man to be more securely bound to God " (§ 10). This theory of satisfaction follows most closely the type of Abelard, although Duns declares it possible to make use of Anselm's ideas, if " divine ordination be presupposed " (§ 10). From another passage we may gather how Duns conceived the objective side of the atonement. God will not forgive the sins of the transgressor unless something be offered to him which pleases him more than the sins of mankind displease him. This could only be the obedience of a person more fervently loved by God than mankind would have been loved by him had they not sinned. This was the person of Christ, who in his obedience offered the highest love in enduring death for righteousness' sake (iv. d. 2, q. 1. 7).

For the sake of the obedience and the love of Christ, God bestows grace upon mankind. There is thus attested in the activity of Christ, as in the divine act of deliverance, the combined action of mercy and righteousness (ib. § 8).

The theory of redemption held by Duns embraces thus two leading thoughts: (1) The pious obedience, or the love, of Jesus is, according to the will of God, acknowledged as meritorious and employed as the means of bestowing grace upon man. (2) This activity of Christ, sealed by his death, has conquered mankind and incited them to love and gratitude. The obedience and love of Jesus thus became the occasion, on the one hand, for the bestowal of grace by God, and, on the other, for the renewal of mankind.[1]

8. The essential result of the work of Christ is, therefore, that he merited for us the impartation of Grace. This leads us to examine the conception of grace. By this term, as *gratia creata* (supra, p. 118 f.), Duns understands the habitus of love, created in man, which inclines the will to meritorious works (ii. d. 27, § 3). This habitus equips man with a worthiness (*dignitas*), "which consists in a correspondence of merit to reward," by virtue of which man becomes dear to God (§ 4). Grace is a co-operating

---

[1] Duns himself did not effect a combination of these two lines of thought, having treated the questions involved but briefly. This may be attempted in various ways. It may be said, for example, that the love of Christ transformed the character of men, and that this became the ground of God's display of grace toward them. If we would gain a proper understanding of the view of Duns, we must bear in mind that he conceived the entire work of salvation and grace under the scheme of means and end (supra, p. 152). In the will of God, priority is given to the glorification and gracious acceptance of the elect above the mission of Christ as the means of effecting grace and of consequent glory. If we now apply this scheme, further, to the two aspects of the work of Christ in the writings of Duns, the logical priority must be given to the manward aspect, since the object of the work of Christ is to win the elect. From this we might derive the thought : that, in order to be able to awaken love and gratitude in men, Christ used his influence with the Father to secure the bestowal of grace. But I doubt whether this was the idea of Duns, for he does not by a single word suggest that the granting of grace is the condition upon which alone the love and example of Christ can become effectual. On the contrary, Christ exerted the latter influence upon the Jews—before grace had been bestowed. If, on the other hand, we seek to combine the two aspects in the activity of Christ in the way first suggested, thus making the influence exerted upon God dependent upon the result secured in man, we come into direct conflict with the fundamental tenor of the discussion. It follows that the two conceptions are not to be subordinated the one to the other, but to be co-ordinated—perhaps somewhat as follows : Christ lived among men and prepared them for the grace which he secured from the Father, or, Christ secured grace from the Father for the men whom he by his life won for the Father. Thus, too, would the relation of Christ and his work to the human race become intelligible. The important thought, that Christ is the head of the race, which we find in Thomas, is lacking in Duns.

principle (*principium co-operans*) beside the will (ii. d. 7, § 15).
Meritorius conduct results therefore from the working together of
the will-power and the habitus (i. d. 17, q. 2. 8). Since the will
without the habitus can produce an act, but not the habitus without the will, the leading part in this co-operation appears to belong to the will. The habitus simply complements the act (ib.
§ 9), or it stimulates to its performance (§ 12). The habitus
is, therefore, a certain supernatural influence which gives to the
will an *inclinatio* to action and secures the performance of the
action " with delight, promptly and expeditiously " (ib.). It
appears, however, since action without the habitus is perfectly
conceivable, that the former has no need of the latter. But
then man would act meritoriously by his natural powers alone
(*ex solis naturalibus*), which would be a Pelagian doctrine.
There must therefore be a supernatural form, which shall imprint
its character upon man's actions without limiting his own activity,
and thus also his merit ! (ib. q. 3. 18, 19).

But it may be urged against the doctrine of the Habitus, that
experience does not attest it, since the moral acts referred to
may very readily be realized without it (q. 3. 21). Duns silently
acknowledges this. But it is not only our separate acts, he holds,
which are acceptable to God, but our whole nature, and the
ground of this is to be found in the habitus (ib. § 22). Of the
habitus it is to be said : " That this habitus, beyond that which is
decorous, is a spiritual (power) inclining to determinate actions "
(§ 23). The acceptance of an act, on the other hand, as meritorious is entirely a matter of the divine will (iv. d. 22, qu. un. § 9).
We may, therefore, discriminate in an act between its substance and
its meritorious quality. In the former aspect, the will occupies the
place of prominence ; in the latter, the habitus has greater influence, since an act appears more worthy of reward when begotten
of love than when begotten of free will (§ 27). The act receives its value in the sight of God—according to divine appointment—from the fact that grace co-operates in its production.
The habitus is the rider, the will the steed. As the steed can
have value for anyone only in so far as it carries the rider to a
definite goal, so the act, produced in the first instance by the will,
is made valuable in the sight of God only through its connection
with the habitus (§ 28).[1] It can hardly be said that this con-

---

[1] Very interesting are the remarks of Duns, l. c., § 28 : As every intellectual capacity necessarily bears within itself the intelligible object, so must
also the moral habituality, to a certain extent, bear in itself the lovable good.
When now this habitus incites to activity, the resulting action will be directed
toward the good embraced in the habitus. Since the habitus receives its
power essentially from the object toward which it is directed, its influence may

ception of the supernatural habitus has been made perfectly plain,
still less that its necessity has been clearly demonstrated !   Duns
retained the traditional physical conception of grace, but he sub-
limated it as far as possible.   Grace is for him not the *material*
of Christian acts, but really only a something which gives to man
a new direction, an inclination toward God, and a value in his
sight.   Duns recognized the fact that there was really no need
of the *gratia creata*, and we can easily understand why he was
unable to make use of it in his expositions of the moral life.
Thus the will remained, after all, as the chief cause of human conduct.   But was not Duns, nevertheless, nearer in his views to the
proper evangelical conception of the matter than Thomas, or even
than Augustine himself?

And what was his conception of Justification ?   He discusses
it in connection with the sacrament of repentance.[1]   We select
the doctrine of the *attritio* as our starting-point.   This is supposed to establish a merit of fitness (*de congruo*), as a preparation
for the achievement of justification.   This half-penitence is,
therefore, meritorious, and through it man merits justification
(iv. d. 14, q. 2. 14, 15 ; cf. d. 19, § 32).   But it must be
borne in mind that the final cause is not really the human merit
as such, but the will of God which has appointed this relationship.   Duns discriminates in justification between the infusion of
grace and the forgiveness of sins (iv. d. 16, q. 1. 4).   The
former is an actual change (*mutatio realis*), for before grace is
infused it has no existence.   The forgiveness of sins, on the contrary, is only an ideal change, since it calls into existence nothing essentially new in man (ib. § 6), and the guilt of man is no
real entity, but only the ideal relationship to the desert of punishment (§ 7).   Even in God, the forgiveness of sins is no separate act, but God never wills that any man be punished without
also willing that—under certain definite conditions—he be no more
punished, and he, likewise, never wills that any man be not punished without willing also that, under certain conditions, punishment be meted out to him (ib. § 12).   If the forgiveness of sins thus
denotes only the ideal and conditional change, that the one liable to punishment (*puniendus*) becomes no longer liable to punishment (*non puniendus*), the infusion of grace is, on the contrary, a real change.   It is the factor which really effects justifi-

---

be ascribed essentially to the activity of the said object.   But that is merely to
say, that the direction of man's activity toward God gives to his conduct its
value and character.

[1] This is, therefore, the appropriate connection in which the conception of
justification stands. Cf., *e. g.*, Carthusian. iv. d. 17, q. 1, 2. This corresponds
with the practical situation of the day.

cation. And, as the infusion of grace is more intimately related to the object, *i. e.*, to the glorification and gracious acceptance of man, than is the forgiveness of sins, the former has the priority in the divine will; but in the actual execution of that will in time, the order is reversed, and stands: first, forgiveness of sins, then infusion of grace (§ 19. Cf. i. d. 17, q. 3. 19: "that God naturally remits an offense before he gives grace to him," *i. e.*, the offender).[1] Here, too, Thomas taught differently (supra, p. 121). Duns denies a causal connection of the two processes, since neither can be logically deduced from the other (§ 19).

Such is the doctrine of grace according to Duns. By attrition man secures the merit of fitness. He is thereby prepared for the reception of justification, or the infusion of grace, particularly in the sacrament of repentance; and this enables him to do meritorious works. These are ideas which became controlling forces in the Scholasticism of the later Middle Ages. But along with them we note, as also characteristic, the separation of forgiveness of sin and infusion of grace, and the spiritualizing of the conception of grace. The ideas of Duns served as a support for the superficial praxis of the church, but, considered in their entire connection, they were nearly always directed against the Augustinian foundations underlying this praxis. In illustration, we recall the statement, that there is really no such thing as "merit" in itself considered, but that God accepts certain definite acts as merits; and, on the other hand, the challenge: If everything depends upon the divine acceptance, to what end then the gradation of merits?

9. At this point the doctrine of the Sacraments finds its place, for it is through the latter that grace is infused into man. As we have already considered them in § 58, we here recall only the chief principle involved. The sacraments are symbols, which signify the working of grace, and which, by virtue of a divine covenant, produce in the soul a creative act of God concurrent with their reception. We may describe the sacrament as, to a certain extent, a cause of grace (*causa gratiae*), inasmuch as it, as it were, compels the accompanying presence of grace (sent. iv. d. 1, q. 5. 12). The critical ability of Duns is here also displayed (criticism of the "character"), as well as a certain inclination to differently interpret and refine the traditional conceptions (repentance and the Lord's Supper).

---

[1] In this order, Duns follows, as far as I can see, the course of ROBERT GROSSETESTE in the tractate, De gratia et justificatione hominis (in Brown, Fascicul. rer. expetendarum et fugiendarum, 1690, append. 282. Cf. Wiclif, De dominio divin. iii. 5, p. 246 f., ed. Poole). So also WILHELM V. PARIS, opp. ii. f., 48 v. Cf. also CARTHUSIAN. iv. d. 17, q. 2.

11

10. It remains for us to characterize the position of Duns in the History of Doctrines. It is hardly saying too much to designate his theology as the key to the dogmatic history of the fourteenth and fifteenth centuries. This is true primarily in a formal sense. The refinement of dialectic art to the point of hair-splitting, the tingling delight in logical proof and disproof, the complicating of linguistic expression—he wrestles with language, and, instead of creating new forms for new ideas, the old forms are split into shreds,—this was learned by latter theologians from Duns. But they also learned from him to apply dialectics ruthlessly and earnestly to even the deepest mysteries of religion. There are no mysteries before which reason must halt. Almost everything is for him open to scrutiny,[1] and the more fully the miraculous can be eliminated the better. "I concede that, even in the things believed, nothing more should be posited without necessity, nor more miracles than necessary" (sent. iv. d. 11, q. 3. 14). All this tended, on the one hand, to hasten the dissolution and downfall of medieval thought ; but it was not only in view of this that it was "timely." It provided for theology, at the proper moment, the forms which assured and directed to it the interest of the age.

As to the material influence of the Scotist dogmatics, its method appears to be only the direct continuation of that of Thomas, *i. e.*, the authorities and reason are to be brought into harmony. But with how much greater enthusiasm and fervency did not Thomas address himself to the task ! For him, dogma and philosophy really coalesced to form one great system of religious philosophy embracing heaven and earth. Thomas yet believed, not only in the absolute truth of the church's dogma, but also in its agreement with scientific knowledge. This second conviction has, in Duns, receded far into the background. Theology and metaphysics are sharply discriminated. It is not the province of theology to construct a universally applicable philosophical system, but a complex structure of practical truths, *i. e.*, truths bearing upon the conduct. Nor is it by any means to be taken for granted that these truths can always be made clear to reason. The criticism of Duns has a keener edge and loftier aim than that of Thomas. In regard to many a leading Romish doctrine he declares, that its suitability for attaining the end in view cannot be proved, and that not much is to be said against the oppo-

---

[1] How much light it casts upon the position and tendency of Duns to observe that he develops his theory of knowledge when treating of the doctrine of angels ; that he presents his psychology under the heading of eschatology ; and that the discussion of the sacrament of repentance gives him opportunity to expound his theory of political economy !

site opinion. Duns is, indeed, particularly fond of throwing out
hints of this nature, and yet in the end working out some sort of
arguments in support of the proposition in question. But the at-
tentive reader will observe, what is elsewhere openly declared,
that the authority of the Romish church is, after all, the decisive consideration. Even the propositions incomprehensible to
reason and incapable of proof are true—because Rome teaches
them. Duns no longer believes in the agreement of dogma and
philosophy ; but he believes in the authority of Rome. Like
Thomas, and yet how different ! For, inasmuch as in Thomas
these two principles coalesce, his faith in Rome retains a religious
character. But since, in Duns, even the incomprehensible and
unreasonable becomes truth through the authority of Rome, this
authority begins to assume the aspect of positive law. Both the
criticism of accepted dogmas and this ecclesiastical positivism
exercised a controlling influence upon the theology of the future.

But Duns is not to be counted among the leaders of thought
who accomplish only negative results. He wrought also out of
the materials of his age positive results for its advancement. And
it was this fact that lent such force to his criticisms. His chief
contribution of this character was his view of the will as the central function of the spirit, which dominates alike his anthropology
and his theology. It is not the world in which man lives, nor
the ideas which he derives from it, which explains his conduct
and his aspirations—but his will. The will is the innermost
faculty in man, the absolutely individual part of his nature. He
no longer views with merely theoretic interest the divine pano-
rama of the world's history, but he has himself become a co-
operating factor in the shifting scenes. In volition he experiences the highest satisfaction. Man can be understood only by
appreciating this will, free in itself and determined by nothing
outside of itself. His worth depends upon it. It is the modern
man[1] whose features are thus drawn in outline. The estimate of
a man according to his own character and deeds, personal responsibility and self-determination,—these are ideas which are
involved, at least implicitly, in the psychology of Duns, however
imperfect and incomplete the latter may be in particular points.
But this theory became even more significant when applied to
God. Since God is conceived as the absolutely free Will, many
of the categories of the traditional logic are dissolved, and the
ground is swept from beneath all the speculations as to what God
must do, and what must come to pass (cf. the criticism of

[1] Vid. also the elaboration of the doctrine of states of the mind by Duns,
in SIEBECK, l. c., vol. 95, p. 251 ff.

Anselm). If the absolutely free, and even wanton Will is the ground of all things, then the truth can be learned only by the careful observation of objects and events. This explains the importance attached to the concrete and the empirical, and the appeal to experience, and, at the same time, the unrestrained liberty of thought as over against traditional theories, as well as a certain skepticism, which time and again leads the thoughtful student to rest content with a " probable " or " more probable." This definition of God betokens, however, a really deeper conception of the divine nature. The God of Duns is no longer the " absolute Substance," but a free, living Spirit. He did not venture even here, it is true, to cast aside the ancient formulas, but he conceived the large thought of God as the Loving-Will, the sum total of whose relations to the world is to be regarded from this point of view. Everything occurring in the world, as well as all divine activity, is—in religious reflection—to be viewed from the view-point of predestination. At this point Augustinian predilections exert their influence (cf. also Thomas, supra, p. 107), the Oxford circle from which Duns came being as distinctly Augustinian in temper as they were inclined to empirical investigation.[1] Nevertheless, Duns was no Augustinian. It was upon the basis of the predestination pervading all things and the divine freedom ordering all things that the theory of merit and good works first began to flourish. The ecclesiastical system is not in itself necessary, but it is—and this is more—positively determined upon and ordained by God. Thus the apparently Augustinian premise is transformed into the popular Catholicism of the close of the Middle Ages.

Finally, we can but point to the separate doctrines in which the theology of Duns scored an advance, i. e., a change as compared with the system of Thomas. In nearly all these instances, the later theologians followed in the steps of Duns. We have noted the divergencies in the question of first principles (skepticism and ecclesiastical positivism); the revision of the conception of

---

[1] A history of theology would find it needful at this point to discuss especially the work of the great bishop of Lincoln, ROBERT GROSSETESTE († A. D. 1253), who paved the way for the ideals of the mendicant orders in England and directed toward its goal the awakened scientific impulse (religion in the sense of Augustine, and empiricism in methods). It is to be regretted that we possess as yet neither a comprehensive biography of this great man, nor even an edition of his more important writings. Some material is furnished in BROWN, Fasciculus, etc., appendix, London, 1690. LUARD edited his letters (London, 1861). Vid. his introduction, and LECHLER, Wiclif, i. 177 ff. Also, supra, p. 161 n., and FELTON, Rob. Grosset., 1887. As to his theological position, see SEEBERG, Duns Scot., p. 11 ff. KROPATSCHECK, Das Schriftprincip der luth. Kirche, i. (1904), 359 ff.

God ; the emphasis upon the will in psychology ; the doctrine of the original state and the minimizing, *i. e.*, elimination, of original sin ; the theory of redemption, with the co-ordination of the subjective and objective aspects of the atonement ; the criticism of the Augustinian definition of grace, *i. e.*, the new definition of the habitus ; the significance of the *meritum de congruo ;* the Pelagianism in the order of salvation ; the logical apprehension of the relation between God and man under the scheme of the *meritum ;* the symbolical interpretation of the sacraments, with the severance of sign and substance ; and the criticism of transubstantiation.

Such is the theology of Duns Scotus. It proclaims the approaching downfall of the cosmology of the Middle Ages. Dogma and reason, church and world, threaten to part company. And yet—Thomas looks backward, Duns faces the future.

§ 60. *Criticism of Hierarchical Conception of the Church.*

1. We must here assume the familiarity of the reader with the outward history of the papacy from the days of Benedict XI., the successor of Boniface VIII. The papacy at Avignon reiterated, indeed, with lofty assumption the ancient claims of supremacy. But its dependence upon the course of French politics—the bull *Unam sanctam* was annulled, so far as France was concerned, and Boniface VIII. barely escaped condemnation for infidelity and frivolity— robbed its claims of all force or sacredness. The great contest against Louis of Bavaria (A. D. 1314-47), despite many humiliations inflicted upon the emperor, set loose a storm of criticism of the papacy, its legality and its claims, which penetrated to its very foundations. The Electoral Union at Rense declared (A. D. 1338) that the electors elect the emperor, and that this election confers upon him the right of government in the empire without any nomination, approbation, or confirmation on the part of the Curia. The papacy, when again transferred to Rome, was rent by the great schism (A. D. 1378). The moral delinquencies of many members of the hierarchy were well known, but, above all, the avarice of the Romish Curia. The trade in spiritual offices, the indulgences, the papal taxes, etc., all served but one end, to procure money and much of it. The unnatural character of the papal dominion made this a necessity ; it was a civil government without the regular sources of revenue. With murmurings against the draining of national resources by the papacy were combined bitter complaints of the immorality and dissipation of the higher as well as the lower clergy.[1] The widespread discontent

[1] A striking portraiture of the times is given in the work of NICHOLAS OF

awakened by these abuses led to a constantly growing demand
for a reformation of the church, which led to the so-called " Reform Councils " at Pisa, A. D. 1409, at Constance, A. D. 1414-17,
and at Basel, 1431-47. The exaltation of the church universal
above the papacy was here asserted[1] and utterance given to many
pious laments and hopes touching the " necessity of a reformation of the church in head and in members."[2] But there was
neither the power nor the courage requisite for a thoroughgoing
reformation. And every politic compromise indicated a victory
for the old order of things. Thus the popes always grasped
again the sceptre, and, despite all the complaints of clergy and
laity, the reformation still remained only a pious wish. In the
bull, " *Pastor aeternus*," Pope Leo X. announced to the world :
" Since also that only the Roman pontiff (in office) for the time
being, as having authority over all councils, has the full right and
power of summoning, transferring, and dissolving councils, is
evident not only from the testimony of the Holy Scriptures, the
sayings of the holy fathers, and of the other Roman pontiffs, . . .
and the decrees of the holy canons, but even from the very confession of the councils themselves " (Binius, Concil. general. ix.
151). And yet the great spiritual agitation, which disturbed
the minds of multitudes for almost two hundred years, was not
in vain. The mistrust of Rome and the hierarchy, the critical
attitude toward the church and her laws, and, combined with
this, the conviction that there is a church of God which is more
and better than the hierarchical system of Rome—these ideas
were engraven more and more deeply upon the general consciousness. And, just in proportion as the sense of national independence gained in strength and the value of earthly possessions increased, must these critical ideas become more extended
in their scope and the unreasonableness of the Romish system

CLEMANGES, De ruina ecclesiae (in VON D. HARDT, Constant. concil. i. 3).
He writes, p. 21 : Everywhere they search for. money (*quaestum*); they are
greatly concerned about money ; they think money is piety. They do nothing at all unless they believe that, upon their doing it, money may be voted for
the increase of their gain. For this they dispute, fight, swear, go to law ;
they would bear with much greater equanimity the casting away of ten millions
of souls than of ten or twelve solidi. Vid. also the other writings collected in this volume—from D'AILLI, GERSON, etc.; also DIETRICH V. NIEM,
De scismate, ll. 3 ed. Erler, 1890.

[1] This council, assembled legitimately in the Holy Spirit, representing the
Catholic church, has authority immediately from Christ, to which everyone of
whatsoever rank or dignity, even the papal, he may be, is bound to render
obedience in those things which pertain to the faith, . . . and to the general
reformation of the said church in head and in members (Constanz sess. 5,
vid. Mansi, xxvii. 590 ; Basel sess. 2, vid. Mansi, xxix. 21).

[2] Title of a document in HARDT, i. 7, p. 277.

become more evident. Cf. HEFELE, CG. vi. vii. SCHWAB, Gerson, 1858. TSCHACKERT, Peter v. Ailli, 1877. ERLER, Dietrich v. Niem, 1887.

2. The criticism of the hierarchical system in the new period found its fullest expression in the literature which was produced during the conflicts of Louis of Bavaria with the pope. Especially MARSILIUS OF PADUA and WILLIAM OCCAM developed ideas which tapped the very roots of the dominant system (vid. Mars., Defensor pacis. Occam, Octo quaestiones ; Compendium errorum papae ; Dialogus ; Opus XC dierum,—all to be found in GOLDAST, Monarchia ii. Frankf. 1614). The most characteristic feature of these publications is the distinct separation of state and church, politics and religion.   As all laws are to be traced back to the people, so the sovereign power lies also with them.   They choose their princes and give them their authority ; they, therefore, may recall it again and remove the princes from office (Mars. i. 12, p. 169 ff.; 9, p. 168 ; 18, p. 184 f.).   There is no necessity for a papal confirmation of the election, nor for an investiture by the pope, any more than the pope has authority to remove the emperor. The election gives the emperor his power ; he stands directly under God (Occ. 8, quaest. 2. 7, 8 ; 4. 8, 9).   As concerns the pope, further, it is held that he is subject to the emperor in all secular affairs, as even Christ allowed himself to be condemned by secular judges, and neither he nor anyone of the apostles ever laid claim to earthly dominion or any kind of coöperative jurisdiction (*jurisdictio coactiva*) whatever, even though the emperor had of his own free-will granted the Donation of Constantine (Mars. ii. 4, p. 195 ff. Occ. 8, quaest. 3. 3, 4 ; dial., p. 750 f., 785, 959, 956).   According to Jerome, the bishops were originally the same as the priests, and it was only at a later day that one of the latter was selected to be, as it were, a superintendent.   There can hence be no thought of any such thing as a divine authority of bishops or popes (Mars. ii. 15).   The papacy, as such, can by no means be described as an institution absolutely necessary for the church. No more cogent arguments can be adduced for a monarchical than for an aristocratic form of civil government.   And even though the monarchy be preferable in civil life, it can scarcely be so in the world-embracing government of the church.   Here Christ reigns as the only supreme Head (Occ. dial., p. 818 f.). Thus the question of the papal primacy is treated entirely from the view-point of the natural reason ; it has for our author no positively religious aspect.   The discussion is regulated by the transfer of the idea of popular sovereignty to the church. The Scriptures, Occam holds, do not teach us that Christ

appointed Peter as the prince of the apostles. All the apostles
received the Spirit in the same way. Paul does not consider
himself subordinate to Peter, and the latter does not preside at
the first council. The injunction to feed the lambs is given
to him only as the representative of the other apostles. Even
in Matt. 16, Peter is only " in a certain way " designated as a
foundation. The real and absolutely necessary foundation of
the church is Christ. It is only as an incidental historical
foundation that Peter comes into view (dial., p. 846-863. Mars.
ii. 22, p. 264). According to Marsilius, it yet remained to be
proved from the Scriptures that Peter was ever at Rome ; and,
in any event, Paul was certainly there before him (ii. 16).
Accordingly, the papacy is to be regarded as an institution
worthy of commendation upon practical considerations, but by
no means as one enjoined by religious precept.

The duties of the pope, as of the clergy in general, are purely
spiritual. Christ bestowed upon Peter, as upon the other
apostles, the keys of the kingdom of heaven and the power to
bind and loose. They were commissioned to spread the teaching and the moral principles of Jesus, and to baptize believers.
But the plenitude of power (*plenitudo potestatis*) consists really in
the exercise of the priestly functions of the sacrament of repentance. But, inasmuch as the forgiveness of sins and the imparting
of grace are matters for God alone, the priestly absolution has
merely a declarative signification. Beyond this, the pope—or
any other priest—may allow the substitution of a temporal satisfaction for the pains of purgatory. It seems of doubtful
propriety, on the other hand, to allow the clergy to administer
the great excommunication. An unjust excommunication, it is
true, does the victim no spiritual harm (" can do no harm for
the state of the future world, because God does not always follow
the church, *i. e.*, the decision of the priests, when, *e. g.*, they
condemn anyone unjustly "); but it is hurtful for the present
life through the accompanying disgrace. It seems, therefore,
prudent to commit the duty of casting out from the church to the
church itself, or to a council, as suggested in Matt. 18. 17.
Finally, to the clergy belongs the power of administering (*con-
ficiendi*) the sacrament of the eucharist (vid. Mars. ii. 6, p.
205-209). The right of the pope in spiritual things consists,
therefore, in the authority to issue precepts and prohibitions in
the church as required by the common good (*utilitas communis*).
In temporal affairs, he has only the right to proper sustenance :
"the right of asking for temporal things for his support and for the
execution of his office " (Occ. dial., p. 786). These sentiments
indicate an immense revolution of thought. The canon law,

the jurisdiction of the church, exemption of the church from taxation, and the holdings of the church in property, are all here surrendered, and there remains no intelligible reason why the state should not hold the prebends and the congregations themselves elect and remove their pastors.[1]   The pope ceases to be a dogmatic entity ; he is an administrator of the devotional services of the church, and is bound to the positive instructions of the New Testament.   He is fallible, as are all other men.   He cannot therefore establish any new articles of faith.   His declaration does not make any opinion her tical, but the crucial question in regard to every doctrine is, whether it can be deduced from the Scriptures (Occ. dial., p. 420).   It would be altogether irrational to suspend one's recognition of the truth until a papal declaration could be secured.   Our faith would thus be made subject to the opinion of a man, whereas Paul in the second chapter of 1st Corinthians instructs us not to let our faith rest upon the wisdom of a man, but upon the power of God (compend. error., p. 976).   Here, for the first time, the infallible Scriptures are set over against the fallible pope : " Holy Scripture cannot err " (*errare non potest*); but, " the pope . . . can err " (ib. p. 843).[2]   But if a pope should stubbornly fall into error, *i. e.*, become a heretic, he may, according to both law and reason, be deposed (p. 464 ff., 568 ff.).

God has indeed promised to lead his church into all truth ; but this promise by no means applies to the pope (for popes have become heretics, ib., p. 464, 468 ff., 958, 976, 994), nor to the college of cardinals—not even to the Romish church nor a general council, for in case every member of such a council were to fall into error before his arrival, how should his fallibility be removed by his arrival at a certain locality or place (p. 495 f.) ?   It is very possible that God may at certain times so order it that the truth may be preserved among the laity alone :

---

[1] Vid. especially Mars. ii. 9, 17, 13.

[2] Let it be observed, that it is the same juristic, abstract infallibility which had been ascribed to the pope, which is here transferred to the Scriptures.   It is based upon a strict theory of inspiration, and falls short of the evangelical view of the Scriptures.   But it is yet important to observe that it was practical considerations which determined the attitude of Occam.   His religion drove him to the Scriptures.   But his religion was epitomized in the doctrine of poverty.   When popes and cardinals denied this doctrine, which Occam believed to be found in the Scriptures, it was evident to him that their teaching was erroneous, and he was compelled to assert the authority of the Scriptures against that of the hierarchy.   The same considerations impelled him to free the civil government from the dominion of the hierarchical power.   Thus inner motives led him to the Scriptures.   It would be instructive to compare his experience at this point with that of Luther.   Vid. SEEBERG upon Occam in PRE., ed. 3.

"He is able to give the poor, simple, illiterate, and rustic for the edification of the orthodox church" (p. 498). This dare by no means be limited to the clergy. The clergy have indeed, in the canon law, limited the term *ecclesia* onesidedly to the *clerici*, but the Scriptures understand by it the whole number (*congregatio*) of Christian believers. It may therefore be said that "laymen and women are ecclesiastics (*personae ecclesiasticae*) as truly as the clergy, because they are as truly of the church (*de ecclesia*) as are the clergy" (ib. p. 502). A new conception of the church breathes in these words. The truth surrendered by the hierarchy may be preserved among the women of the church, and if not among them, among the children. The laity have the full rights of membership in the church. Kings and laymen should be admitted even to the councils (p. 603 f., 605 ; cf. Mars. ii. 20). The papal tyranny must not control the church, for the gospel is a law of liberty (p. 776 f.). Plain laymen, guided by the Scriptures, may soar beyond the knowledge of the ecclesiastical authorities. "Let it be granted, that the simple are not legally (*regulariter*) bound to believe anything explicitly except those things which have been by the clergy declared necessary to be believed. Yet the simple, nevertheless, in reading the divine Scriptures with acuteness of reason, in which even the simple are not altogether lacking, observe that something which the pope and cardinals have not declared follows evidently from the divine Scriptures—this they can and ought to in that case believe explicitly, and they are not bound to consult the pope and cardinals, because the sacred Scripture is to be preferred to the pope and cardinals." Further : "The pope and cardinals are not the rule of our faith" (p. 770).

The transformation in the conception of the church which is foreshadowed in this movement consists in the following points : (1) The state is independent of the church. (2) The sphere of the spiritual (clerical) office is not lordship, but doctrine and the administration of the sacraments. (3) The hierarchical organization of the church has become historic, but is not a religious necessity. (4) Not the pope, but Scripture, is the infallible authority in the church. (5) Pope and clergy may err, and are liable to deposition. (6) In secular affairs, the clergy are subject to the secular jurisdiction. (7) The laity are independent members, and the compeers of the clergy, in the church.

3. But these ideas and their critical motive must, in order to be fully understood, be viewed in a wider connection. Very early in the Middle Ages the Old Germanic idea of a purely legal state was so far modified, after the pattern of the church and the

ancient theory of the state, that the state was no longer regarded as existing only by virtue of the law and for its execution, but as having in view the further object of promoting the common weal, and as based upon natural motives. A compromise of the contradiction between the Germanic idea, that the state exists for the law, and the ancient idea of the subordination of the law to the common weal—both of which ideas existed side by side—was attempted by the combination of the *positive* and the *natural* law. The statutes of the positive law, it was maintained, whether expressions of the will of the ruler or of that of the sovereign people, have their norm in the law of nature. Nothing which contravenes the law of nature can be regarded as authoritative. This primacy of the natural law was, indeed, limited by the condition, that its execution must always be guided by the concrete circumstances in any case. As the idea of popular sovereignty furnished, on the one hand, the controlling thought in the struggles of the councils against the popes, so, on the other hand, the criterion of the natural law was relentlessly applied in criticism of the positive ordinances of the church. The ancient juristic ecclesiastical conception of the primacy of natural law,[1] which had hitherto been employed by the church in criticism of secular laws, was now turned against the church herself. But the application of this weapon was here, no less than in the secular use of it, subject to serious limitation by the positive forms of the church life. Criticism was applied with a keen relish and carried ruthlessly to its logical conclusions ; but no one thought of abolishing the papacy, the hierarchy, the canonical law, or the accepted dogmas of the church. Even the boldest agitators sought no more than a correction of the existing system within its own limits.

What is then the content of natural law?[2] Natural law is the law of reason, and it is the divine law : " Employing the natural dictate (*dictamen*) of reason, this is employing natural law ;" or, " natural reason (*ratio*) is natural law " (Occ. dial., p. 629, 568). It is, therefore, man's innate ideas of law and order in the world (p. 932).[3] Now, the same God who implanted these

---

[1] Vid., *e. g.*, Isidor, etymol. v. 4 f. Gratian, decret., pars 1, dist. 5. Cf. Greg. VII.

[2] I do not enter further upon the differentiation of the *jus naturale, lex dei,* and *commune jus gentium.* Vid. GIERKE, J. Althusius, p. 273.

[3] The latest offshoot of this theory of infallible moral ideas innate in man is in the modern definition of conscience as the voice of God. Its origin is to be sought in the idea entertained by the Apologetes—of the Logos-sharing upon man's part. According to Thomas, natural law is the content of the conscience. Vid. supra, p. 114 n. Also SEEBERG, Gewissen u. Gewissensbildung, 1896, pp. 6 ff., 69 f.

ideas in man, has imparted them likewise through inspiration in
the Holy Scriptures. The law of God is, therefore, identical
with the law of nature (*lex dei et jus naturae*, ib. pp. 772, 778,
783, 786, 934). From this is derived the idea of the absolute
authority of the law of reason and nature—and of the Scriptures :
" Human laws founded in divine and natural law " (ib. p. 587).
" No just positive law can be contrary to natural law " (p. 629).
" There can be no law which is repugnant to the higher law or
to plain reason." Hence, whatever civil law is repugnant to the
divine law, or to plain reason, is no law. In the same way, the
words of the canonical or civil law, in any case in which they are
repugnant to the divine law, *i. e.*, the Holy Scripture or right
reason, are not to be observed " (p. 630). But all of these
declarations are but repetitions of definite ideas of the canonical
law (vid. Gratian, decret., pars i., dist. 1-9). This was, therefore, the path which led to the establishment of the authority of the
Scriptures. Scripture and reason are identical. The Scriptures
present not positive revelation, but the universal truth of reason.
It is quite evident that in this way the Scriptures should come to
be regarded more and more from the view-point of the law. And
it is further beyond question, that this entire legal way of apprehending the church and religion could not possibly lead to a
spiritual conception of the nature of the church. On the contrary, it was just in this age of reform councils and of conflicts
with the Curia that the church came to be almost universally regarded as a polity, based upon juristic principles.

RIEZLER, Die litt. Widersacher d. Päpste, pp. 194 ff., 243 ff. A. DORNER,
Staat u. K. nach Occ. Stud. u. Krit., 1886, p. 672 ff. FRIEDBERG, Die
mittelalt. Lebren üb. d. Verhältn. zw. Staat u. K., 1874. K. MÜLLER, Der
Kampf Ludw. d. Bay. mit. d. Curie, 1879 f. GIERKE, J. Althusius u. die
Entwicklg. der naturrechtl. Staatstheòrien, 1880, p. 77 ff., 123 ff., 264 ff. VON
BEZOLD, Hist. Ztschr., vol. 36, p. 330 ff. KROPATSCHECK, Occam und
Luther (Beiträge zur Förderung christl. Theol. iv.), 1900.

§ 61. *Sketch of Church Life and Religious Agitations at the Close
of the Middle Ages.*

LITERATURE. JANNSEN, Gesch. d. deutsch. Volkes seit Ausg. d. MA. i.
14 A., 1887, and in connection, KAWERAU, Ztschr. f. K. Wiss., 1882, p. 142 ff.,
263 ff., 313 ff., 362 ff. MOLL, Die vorref. KG. d. Niederlande, deutsch. Von
Zuppke, ii. (1895), pp. 396-406, 554-565, 579-768. MÖLLER, KG. ii.,
481 ff., 531 ff. LAMPRECHT, Deutsche Gesch., vol. v. 1, 1894. VON BEZOLD,
Gesch. d. deutsch. Ref. (Oncken Allg. Gesch.). GOTHEIN, Polit. u. rel.
Volksbewegg. vor. d. Ref., 1878. BERGER, Die Kulturaufgaben d. Ref.,
1895. GEFFCKEN, Der Bilderkatechism. d. 15, Jarh., 1855. Joh. Nider's
Formicarius, and in connection, SCHIELER, Mag. J. Nider, 1885, pp. 195-
248. HASACK, D. chr. Gl. d. deutsch. Volkes b. Schluss d. MA., 1868.
LECHLER, J. v. Wicl. u. d. Vorgesch. d. Ref., 2 vols., 1873. BRATKE,

Luther's 95 Thesen u. ihre dogmenhist. Voraussetzungen, 1884. Vid. KRO-
PATSCHECK, Das Schriftprincip der luth. Kirche, vol. i. (Mittelalter), 1904.
BRIEGER, Das Wesen des Ablasses vor Ausgang des MA. Leipziger Pro-
gramm, 1897.

1. Every great revolution in the history of religion is preceded
by a crisis period.   Traditional forms and aspirations no longer
satisfy the world.   Some blame the old order of things, and long
for a new order which they know not how to secure.   Others
glorify the old order.   The new requirements of the age, which
even they must recognize, are to be met by the diligent and
thorough use of the old means.   Harsh criticism of the traditional positions and customs and abnormal devotion to them are
here closely associated.   It is still hoped that the stones may be
made bread.   The crisis through which Luther passed in the cloister
had been hovering over the church in the fifteenth century.   The
individuality of the modern man and the deepening of religious
experience crave a personal assurance of faith and inner certainty.   The church offers instead the rule of faith and the
power of the sacraments.   The heart seeks life through the forgiveness of sins ; the church points to confession and absolution.
The consciousness of the independence of the world and its
interests is crushed beneath the ancient claims of the hierarchy ;
the increasing prosperity of the world and the new business en-
terprises are in conflict with the ideal of "poverty."   New
necessities and old methods, with the zealous attempt to draw
from old forms the satisfaction of new requirements—this constituted the crisis.   It was naturally first felt among the cultured
classes ; but it penetrated also the masses.   All the phenomena in
the religious life of this period—the ecclesiastical institutions, the
brotherhoods,[1] the indulgences, the pilgrimages, the increasing
adoration of relics, of Mary and the saints, the spread and exaggerated terrors of the faith in devils and demons,[2] the craze upon the
subject of celibacy,[3] the mysticism, the revolutionary Christian-
social plans, the contempt for the clergy and the monks, are all
closely connected with the crisis.   So loud were the complaints
that eyes were turned to the future in expectation of a new era of
"prophecy" and the "introduction of a new religion."[4]

    We must observe (a) the means by which the church at-

---

[1] Vid. LEA, A hist. of conf. and indulg. iii., 470 ff.   MOLL, KG. ii., 646 ff.
[2] Vid. esp. the bull of Innocent VIII., Summis desiderantes affectibus, the
Malleus maleficarum, and Joh. Nider's Formicarius, lib. v.   Cf. ROSKOFF,
Gesch. d. Teufels, ii. (1869), p. 206 ff., 226 f.
[3] Vid. Examples in SCHIELER, Nider, p. 203 ff.
[4] Vid. Trithemius chronolog. myst. 18 fin.   Cf. SCHNEEGANS, Trithemius,
p. 183 f.

tempted the culture of piety, (*b*) the way of salvation as conceived by the "Friends of God," and (*c*) the scope of the
reformatory ideas of the age.

2. The means by which the church sought to influence the
multitudes remained the same as of old, except that there was—
as required by the demands of the age—an increased zeal in the
use of them. The duty of preaching is insisted upon with
greater emphasis. It is required that all members of the church
be acquainted with the Creed, the Lord's Prayer, the Ave
Maria, and the teachings of the church concerning mortal
sins and the sacraments. Louis of Bavaria, *e. g.*, proved his
orthodoxy by repeating the Lord's Prayer, the greeting of the
angels, and the Apostles' Creed (R. MÜLLER, Der Kampf Lud-
wigs mit der Curie, ii. 75). This knowledge is to be tested at
the confessional, which thus becomes a religious examination.[1]
The Ten Commandments were frequently here used as the
criterion.[2] In preaching, the moral element still predominates ;
but with it are combined quite rigid doctrinal discussions,
miraculous narratives, and commendations of indulgences and
the grace accompanying them. If it cannot be said that the
church shirked the new task assigned her, she certainly discovered no new means to apply in the performance of it. The
sacraments bring grace, as the power enabling their recipients
to perform meritorious works (HASACK, p. 419, 133, 262 f.).

But Repentance appears as really the chief sacrament.[3] The
religious unrest of the age and the financial schemes of the Curia

---

[1] *E. g.*, HEFELE, vi. 608, 696, 706, 721, 944. MOLL, KG. ii. 396 ff., 653 f.
GEFFCKEN, Bilderkatech., p. 24 ff., and suppl., p. 191 f.; Beichtanweisung
aus d. 15 Jarh., ed. Wagner, Ztschr. f. KG. ix. 445, 462. The "Christian
faith" consists, as before, of the twelve or fourteen articles of the Apostles'
Creed (as to the number, vid. HEFELE, vi. ed. 2, 220 a.); its content is especially the doctrine of the Trinity and Christology, *e. g.*, Gabr. Biel, De festi-
vitat. serm. 21, fol. 214 r, and HASACK, l. c., p. 138 ff. All are required to
believe "what the holy church commands to believe" (Ztschr. f. KG. ix.
462). As examples of open heresy, Occam adduces the denial of the unity
and trinity of God and of the birth of Christ from the Virgin (dial., p. 631).
[2] *E. g.*, HASACK, l. c., p. 191 ff., 227 f. GEFFCKEN, l. c., Ztschr. f. KG.
ix. 445 ff., 462 ff.
[3] The Augustinian, JOHN OF PALTZ, has in his Coelifodina (Lips. 1510)
undertaken to uncover the mine of grace—for the guidance of preachers. Of
what does he treat ? First, there is a detailed exposition and application of the
passion history ; then, sins in thought are discussed, and death ; then the sacraments are explained, with all the emphasis upon repentance and indulgences.
In the Supplementum Coelifodinae (Lips. 1516), indulgences are defended at
length and the doctrine of the sacraments again presented. Vid. also the many
manuals of confession at the close of the Middle Ages, *e. g.*, in HASACK, l. c.
As to the biography of Paltz, vid. KOLDE, Die deutsche Augustinercongrega-
tion, 1879, p. 174 ff.

here joined hands.   The whole religious life of the times finds its centre in the ordinance of repentance.   Here faith is confessed and sins are forgiven : here meritorious works are assigned and men thus *justified;*[1] but here, too, may release from them be purchased.   The dominant conception of confession and abso-lution is in thorough conformity with the scholastic theories (supra, p. 135).   As the logic of the theory led by necessity to the recognition of attrition as the starting point of repentance (p. 136), so in praxis the latter came to be regarded as entirely sufficient.   JOHN OF PALTZ considers the advantage of the new covenant over the old to consist precisely in the fact, that it does not require contrition, as does the old, but is content with attrition, which is then by absolution transformed into con-trition, this contrition being the destruction of sin.[2]   To do this, however, is a matter for the priest (Coelifodina, Cc. 1 v). " Under the new law, the mode of repenting and of salvation is easier " (ib. Q. 5 v).   Paltz gives an excellent definition of attrition.   " And such attrition cannot be better defined in common   speech   than   as   ' gallows-penitence '   (*galgenrew*),[3] because the attrite mourns that he has sinned—on account of the infernal gallows " (ib. Q. 6 v).   It has for its basis servile fear and the fear of death, whereas contrition springs from filial fear and the love of God (ib. Q. 6 r).   Very few get beyond the former: " About all of our people who confess in Lent do not have true contrition, nor do they have attrition in the first grade, because they would then do entirely what they can to attain true contrition ; but they often have attrition in the second grade, doing in some measure what they can, and such are assisted by the priests in the sacramental absolution " (ib. R. 1 v).   It is therefore sufficient if there be within the heart a certain discontent with self and fear of hell, begotten by the con-templation of the commandments (supra, p. 174).   This will be sufficient to secure the forgiveness, *i. e.*, the destruction, of sin.   There was a recognition of the fact, that in the days of the first love there had been no need of indulgences : " But now, love having grown cold in these last times, neither are satisfac-

---

[1] Vid., *e. g.*, in HASACK, p. 137 : " Grace justifies man : whatever infirmity (Bresten) clings to man, it punishes this, and changes it, and cleanses it with repentance."

[2] Attrition is transformed into contrition by other means also, *i. e.*, through extreme unction (coelifod. T. 2 v), the eucharist (Z 6 v), the mass and preaching (Aa 3 r).   The last-named especially confirms the pyschological interpretation of this Scotist formula (vid. supra, p. 138).   Cf. also Tetzel's theses, n. 49 : " attrite and through confession contrite " (Luther, opp. var. arg. i. 300).

[3] So also Luther, Weim. ed. i. 99.

tions commensurately imposed, nor when moderately imposed are they performed : therefore there is a much more necessary and copious use of indulgences, so that what is lacking through indolence (*acedia*) may be supplemented through the prayers of others (Biel, expos. can. miss. lect. 57, fol. 154 v). It is doubtless true that it was always presupposed, whether expressly so stated or not, that, in order to secure the benefit of the indulgence, the purchaser must have experienced and confessed sorrow for sin : " He who remains in sin, and is neither contrite nor attrite nor has confessed, can by no means secure indulgences (Paltz, Aa 3 r). Just as the sacrament of repentance has respect directly to sin (*culpa*), so the benefit of indulgence has respect to penalty," and that the temporal penalty (ib. X 1 r). This is true even of the so-called jubilee-indulgence, whether so stated in the bull proclaiming the latter or not (ib. Z 6 r). But, on the other hand, attention may be drawn to the formula employed in the proclamation of such indulgences : " I absolve thee from punishment and from guilt " (*a poena et a culpa*). Paltz replies : " But a jubilee is something more than a bare indulgence, because it includes the authority of confessing and absolving, and, with this, the indulgence of remitting penalty, and thus it includes the sacrament of repentance and, with this, indulgence properly so called. . . . Commonly, when the pope gives a jubilee, he gives not a bare indulgence, but he gives also authority of confessing and absolving from all sins, even so far as their guilt. And thus guilt is remitted by reason of the sacrament of repentance which is there introduced ; and penalty, by reason of the indulgence which is there employed " (ib. X 1 r). Paltz, therefore, understands the remission of sin as involved in the authority granted by the jubilee-indulgence to select for one's self a confessor, who shall be authorized to absolve in all cases not reserved to the pope himself (Aa 4 r). Even the latter cases were often included in the authority thus given.[1] The jubilee-indulgence thus indeed embraced in itself the sacrament of repentance. The sacrament must not of necessity be administered by the properly appointed confessor, but sacramental functions may also be discharged by the papal commissary. Thus the papal power intruded upon the province of the pastoral cure of souls, and thus, although the forgiveness of sins

---

[1] *E. g.*, LEA, Hist. of conf. and indulg., iii. 70 n. Cf. HASACK, p. 434 : " Indulgence from penalty and guilt . . . is to be thus understood : Indulgence from penalty is a remitting of the penalty which one ought to suffer for his sin. Indulgence from guilt is complete authority to absolve and release from all sins, even those sins which are to be reserved for the holy Roman chair."

was not itself directly secured by the payment of money, yet the especial administration of the sacraments which carried with it the forgiveness of sins was thus purchased. Under these circumstances, the popular perversions upon the subject may be easily understood. The above formula was in the highest degree open to misunderstanding.[1] Popes expressly rejected it,[2] and theologians pronounced against it. Nevertheless, it was permitted still to play its part of deception and confusion of thought in the church (cf. LEA, hist. of conf. and indulg. iii., p. 57-78. MOLL, ii. 728).[3] Matters were made worse, as the theory of the validity of indulgences for the souls in purgatory (*supra*, p. 139) also found endorsement in praxis.[4] Cf., *e. g.*, Paltz, Cc 1 r, Dd 5 v, etc.[5] The idea that, "as soon as the money rings in the chest, the soul leaps out of purgatory," was only a perfectly intelligible inference.[6]

Such was the course of penitential praxis at the close of the Middle Ages. The frightful danger attending it can be understood only when attrition and indulgences are viewed in their combination, and when the misleading glorification of the latter is considered.[7] A little "gallows-penitence" and the confessional, and then a little money, and the sinner is freed from the fear of hell and purgatory, and even from the performance of works of penance. Money was immediately the means of releasing from purgatory, and mediately of securing the forgiveness of sins.

[1] BRATKE prepared the way for this understanding of the jubilee-indulgences. BRIEGER produced convincing evidence of it (Das Wesen des Ablasses (Leipzig, 1899).

[2] Boniface IX., vid. LEA, l. c., iii. 66 f., the papal plan of reformation at Constance, vid. HEFELE, vii. 341. Benedict XIV., vid. WILDT, Kirchenlex. i. ed. 2, 95.

[3] Cf. already the complaints of Berthold of Regensburg, touching the "penny-preachers." When thou standest up and forgivest one all the sin which he has ever done for a single helbeline or a few pennies, then he imagines that he has atoned and at once refuses to atone any more. Thou murderer of God and the world and many Christian souls, which thou murderest with thy false comfort, so that he can never be saved (Pred. i. 117). He claims that he has power from the pope, to take from thee all thy sin for a few helbelincs or for a heller (ib. i. 208). The Reformat. Sigismunds, p. 163, edited by Boehm, also speaks of paying dearly for indulgence of sins. Cf. Wessel, De poenit., opp., p. 798 f.

[4] According to LEA, iii. 345 ff., not before Sixtus IV., A. D. 1476. Vid. also BIEL, expos. can. miss. lect. 57 K.

[5] Indulgences may bring even to the lost a mitigation of punishment, PALTZ, Ff. 4 v.

[6] Vid. KAWERAU, Sobald das Geld, etc., 1889, p. 9, 11 f., 17 ff.

[7] A contrite person may, even before confessing, receive an indulgence (Durand, sent. iv. d. 20, q. 4, a. 2. Paltz holds otherwise, Aa 3). How easily may he be deceived as to his condition, or postpone the subsequent confession!

But along with this externalizing of religion—which the church herself promoted—were heard also some voices emphasizing the seriousness of repentance and its works.   The whole Christian life is a " doing penance : " " That the whole life of a Christian man is nothing else than a cross " (Hasack, p. 443). But this thought is completed by the additional idea, that we " are obligated to the imitation of the crucified life " of Christ, " since the passion of Christ has not been an entire, but a partial, cause of our salvation " (ib., also p. 477).   The " imitation of Christ " is, therefore, a supplementing of the redeeming work of Christ by effort upon our part !

3. The so-called German Mysticism, dogmatically considered, furnishes scarcely anything further than a popular rendering of the scholastic, *i. e.*, Thomistic ideas.   But these ideas are applied to the relation of the soul to God.   The practical aspect of the way to God is the controlling one for these writers.   The ideas of the dogmaticians become, under their hands, practical religious truths, which were employed for edification by the widespread circles of the " Friends of God."   The use of the mother tongue deepened the experience and enriched the religious apprehension.   Little as it belongs to the sphere of the History of Doctrines to follow the speculations of the Mystics, it is important, in tracing the transition from the Middle Ages to the Reformation era, to understand the way of salvation as pursued by the pious at the close of the medieval period.   In endeavoring to trace this briefly, we follow chiefly the following :

Master ECKHART († 1327, vid. Pfeiffer, Deutsche Mystiker, ii., 1857.   Excerpts from his Latin writings in Denifle, Archiv f. Litt. u. KG. d. MA. ii. 553 ff.), JOHANN TAULER († 1361.   Sermons, Basel, 1521), HEINRICH SEUSE (Suso, † 1366, ed. Denifle, MÜNCH., 1880), JOHANN VON RUUSBROEC († 1381. WW. 6 vols., Gent, 1858 ff.), the THEOLOGIA DEUTSCH (ed. Pfeiffer, reprint 3, 1875), the BUCH VON GEISTL. ARMUT (ed. Denifle, 1877), THOMAS A KEMPIS, De imitatione Christi (ed. Hirsche, 1874).

The spiritual life pursues the course : Purification, Illumination, Unification (Theol. D., p. 50).[1]   " A devoted man must be unfashioned from the creature, fashioned with Christ and refashioned in the divine nature " (*entbildet, gebildet, überbildet,* Seuse, p. 248).   He is first a servant, then a friend, and finally a son of God (Ruusbr. vi. 208 ff.).   (*a*) The first step, therefore, is to turn away from the creature and turn toward God. The sacrament and the word of God then exert an influence (Tauler, fol. 65 v); especially repentance and the Lord's Supper are recommended.   These are re-enforced by prayer and the

---

[1] Cf. Dionys. Areop., Hierarch. eccl. 6. 3. 5.

contemplation of the love of God (Eckh., p. 557). Thus man feels himself impelled to a pious and virtuous life, to continuous and earnest self-examination, and penitence. " Purification belongs to the beginning or repenting man, and takes place in three ways, with sorrow and mourning on account of sin, with complete confession, and with perfect penitence " (Theol. D., p. 50). This is the first stage, repentance and its exercises ; the struggle for the overcoming of sensuality (*Sinnlichkeit*) is its essential characteristic. (*b*) In the second stage, the *Imitatio Christi* holds the place of prominence. "Thou must break through my suffering human nature, if thou art really to come to my unveiled divine nature " (Seuse, p. 52. Tauler, f. 117 v, 156 r. Theol. D., p. 220).[1] Here the principal thing is thoroughgoing meditations upon the passion of Christ : " Not with a hasty going over it as one has time and place ; but it must be with a fervent love and with a mournful review " (Seuse, p. 396). The life of Seuse testifies with what dramatic vividness and with what barbarous ascetic exercises these meditations were practiced. The aim is sympathy and imitation.[2] But, apart from these, God himself sends sufferings and crosses of various kinds upon man, in order to make him a true follower of Christ. "The swiftest beast that bears you to perfection is suffering " (Eckh., p. 492). "No one so cordially feels the passion of Christ as he to whom it happens to suffer similar things " (Thom. a Kemp. ii. 121). True, there is in these circles a deep conviction that Christ's passion is our "perfect righteousness " (Seuse, p. 393). "And thus has he redeemed us, not with our works but with his works, and with his merits has he made us free and redeemed us " (Ruusbr. iii. 140). "All my comfort and my confidence rests wholly upon thy passion, thine atonement, and thy merits " (Seuse, p. 427 f.).[3] But Seuse writes also : "And yet every man draws to himself only so much of the atonement as he with sympathy makes himself like me," *i. e.*, Christ (Seuse, p. 398).[4] What is this but saying, as this school bluntly puts it, that Christ is only the partial cause of ours alvation ? The *Imitatio Christi* (vid. Thom. a K. i. 1. 1 ; 25. 3 ; ii. 1. 2) is the religion of these mystics : "Give to me to imitate thee with contempt of the world " (ib. iii. 56. 2). They plunged into asceticism—which

---

[1] Cf. Augustine, serm. 261. 7 : "Through the man Christ thou attainest to the God Christ ;" also the passages cited in Vol. I., p. 262. Already in Origen, c. Celsus, vi. 68.

[2] Vid. Seuse, p. 52 ff., 321 ff., and SEEBERG, Leben Seuse, p. 28 ff.

[3] Particularly the dying are often urged to pray : "Upon thy mercy and goodness will I die, and not upon my good works " (HASACK, p. 437).

[4] Cf. Thom. in sentent. iii. d. 49, a. 2, 3). Thom. a Kemp. i. 24. 1 : satisfactional and purifying sorrow (*dolor satisfactorius et purgativus*).

they regarded as meritorious and entitling to reward (*lonbar*, Seuse, p. 385, 383), but they nevertheless kept alive a love for Jesus and appreciation of his life—as the counterpart to the view which regarded him as a stern celestial judge, before whom Mary and the saints must appear to intercede for us. "As the lodestone draws to it the iron, so does Jesus draw to himself all hearts that are touched by him" (Tauler, f. 43 v). Though all this remains perfectly Catholic, yet these ideas just as truly betoken a "pre-reformation" element.[1] This is the way. Man must return to nothingness (*entwerden*, "unbecome"), for only out of a nothing (*niht*) does God make an it (*iht*), (Eckh., p. 189. Taul. f. 146 v).

(*c*) The goal, finally, is unification with God in the depths of the soul ; and this, too, with God in the inner unity of his nature. "The essence of the soul is united with Nothingness, and the powers of the soul with the works of Nothingness.[2] In this state of absolute passivity God causes his Son to be born in our soul "a hundred thousand times more quickly than the twinkling of an eye" (Tauler, f. 60 r).[3] This state can be experienced in two psychological forms : either in such a way that man in the intellectual process experiences the "vision" (*Schauung*) of the essence of God, or in such a way that "the created will is merged into the eternal Will and therein dissolved and reduced to nothingness, so that the eternal Will alone here wills, acts, and fails to act" (Theol. D., p. 104). The former harmonizes with the Thomistic, the latter with the Scotist theology (RITCHL, Gesch. d. Pietismus, i. 470), although the two forms were not sharply discriminated.[4] The moments of extreme ecstatic exaltation were of brief duration. Lukewarmness and lassitude followed (Seuse, p. 360, 355, 358, 448). The words of the Scriptures —Christ's sweet love-letter, and his presence in the Lord's

---

[1] But it must be ever borne in mind that this conception of the "Following of Christ," which may be traced back to the Apostolic Fathers, is but a mutilated and dislocated presentation of biblical ideas. The following of Jesus means, in the Gospels, that he who attaches himself to Jesus walks with him and finds in him God and the Son of the living God. The result of following him is announced in Matt. 16. 16 and Jn. 6. 67 f.

[2] This is the Areopagite conception of the nature of the Godhead. Cf. my remarks, Thomas. DG. ii., ed. 2, p. 305, A. 2.

[3] Cf. my exposition, Thomas. DG. ii., ed. 2, p. 307 ff.

[4] Cf. my remarks, l. c., p. 310 f. Also Dante, Parad. 28. 109 ff.: "Through vision, therefore, is blessedness attained. Not through love, for this follows only when it has sprung from vision as its source." With Staupitz (ed. Knaake, i. 106), Luther accepted the latter form, vid. Glosses upon Tauler, Weim. ed. ix. 102 : "The whole of salvation is resignation of the will in all things." Also, Thom. a K., iii. 15. 2 ; 56. 1. Goch, dialog. 9. 10 (Walch, Monim. Med. aev. i. 4, p. 129, 132).

Supper—console the pious (ib. 355, 621 f., 450 f. Thom. a Kemp. iv. 11. 4). They should be always ready to turn aside from the highest religious transport to prepare a plate of soup for a pauper (Eckh., p. 553. Taul. f. 128 r, 95 r, 121 r).[1] " He to whom inwardness becomes outwardness, to him the inwardness becomes more inward than to him to whom inwardness becomes inwardness " (Seuse, p. 246).

We cannot overlook the medieval mould—ascetism and ecstacy —in which the controlling ideas here are cast. But, inasmuch as the entire body of the traditional teaching and culture of the church is concentrated upon the religious life of the individual soul, which is to grow by the contemplation of Jesus and by that intercourse of the soul with him[2] in which blessedness consists,[3] these men were, nevertheless, "schoolmasters leading to Christ."[4]

LITERATURE. GREITH, Die deutsche Mystik im Predigerorden, 1861. BÖHRINGER, Die deutschen Mystiker, 1855. PREGER, Gesch. d. deutschen Mystik, 3 vols., 1874, 1881, 1893; cf. DENIFLE, Hist. polit. Blätter, vol. 75, 679 ff., 771 ff., 903 ff., and Archiv f. Litt. u. KG. d. MA. ii. 417 ff. DENIFLE, Das geistl. Leben, 3 A., 1880.

Upon separate topics : LASSON, M. Eckh., 1868. R. SEEBERG, Ein Kampf um jenseitiges Leben (Biogr. Seuses), Dorpat, 1889. C. SCHMIDT, J. Tauler, 1841, and DENIFLE, Taul. Bekehrung, 1879. Upon the Buch v. geistl. Armut, RITSCHL, Ztschr. f. KG. iv. 337 ff. STRAUCH, Marg. Ebner u. Heinr. v. Nördl., 1882, and "Offenbarungen d. Adelheid Langmann," 1875. Upon the Brethren of the Common Life, HIRSCHE, PRE. ii. 678-760. Particularly SEEBERG in Thomas. DG. ii., ed. 2, 290-315.

4. Not least among the influences leading to the crisis at the close of the Middle Ages was the change in the conditions of the business world. (Cf. INAMA-STERNEGG, Deutsche Wirtschaftsgesch. iii. 2, 1901.) The traffic in money emphasized the contrast between the rich and the poor. In the cities there was an accumulation of capital in the hands of individuals, which proved in the highest degree detrimental to the general social advancement, as both the nobles and the peasants realized in sad experience. The Romish canon law was rigidly enforced, and proved, as always, the ally of the financially stronger party. The heaviest burden fell, in the last instance,

---

[1] Cf. Thom. summ. ii. ii. q. 182, a. 1, ad 3.

[2] Thom. a Kemp. ii. 8. 1 : "It is a great art to know how to walk (conversari) with Jesus."

[3] Ib. iii. 59. 1 : "Where thou, there heaven," ii. 12. 3 : "Thou hast found paradise on earth."

[4] Note also the value attached to practical deeds of love. The monastic idea of forsaking the world is often painfully prominent (e. g., Thom. a K. i. 10. 1 ; 20. 1); but see also the splendid sermons of Tauler upon the earthly calling (fol. 117 r f., fol. 94 v f.). Cf. UHLHORN, Die christl. Liebestätigkeit, ii. (1884), p. 350 ff.

upon the peasantry. The impoverishment of the latter, the development of the feudal system, and the pressure exerted by the nobles, gave birth to the "social question" of the fifteenth century. As the only social power of the Middle Ages was the church, it was inevitable that these social problems should assume a religious form. The ethics of the medieval church had not risen to the demands of the new economic conditions. The friendly interest with which the most truly religious spirits of the day regarded the suffering peasants did not alleviate their misery. The terrible strain of mind found vent in forecasts and prophecies. Not only the hierarchy, which had become utterly secularized and was ever thirsting for gold, but all the high and mighty of the world as well, were to be destroyed. All secular ordinances and laws were declared null and void, and only the divine law must rule. The pious shall conquer. Wealth will cease to be ; evangelical poverty will become universal, and with it communism will prevail. All are to be equal, made free by "evangelical liberty." God will bring it to pass. The time would soon be ripe, it was thought, to lay hand to the work. This was the *Christian Socialism* of the day, which, in league with "evangelical liberty," pressed on to revolution.[1] Far beyond the circles of those actually engaged in these movements extended the stimulating and disturbing influence of these ideas. What strange contrasts are here blended—ideas as full of contra-

---

[1] Vid. especially "The Vision and Creed of Piers Ploughman" (ed. Wright, Lond., 1856). Die Reformation Sigismunds (ed. Böhm, 1875). Cf. Gesch. des Hans Böheim (BARACK, Arch. d. hist. Vereins f. Unterfranken, xiv. 3, pp. 1-8). The "new" or "divine" order which the Reformation of Sigismund had in view (p. 241, 242, 170) embraces, in addition to all manner of ecclesiastical and social improvements, the demand of "liberty." The latter is deduced, however, from the redemption achieved by Christ : "Christ suffered for us" that he might free us and release us from all bonds, and herein no one is exalted above the other, for we are in the same condition in redemption and liberty, whether noble or peasant, rich or poor, great or small (p. 221, 214, 245, 246 f.). In the name of this liberty, feudal serfdom is to be abolished, and woods, pasture, and water (Wald, Weide, Wasser) are to be free to all (p. 222 f.). The imperial and papal codes of law are slumbering, but the "Little Ones" are wakeful (p. 225). This liberty which Christ is said to have brought, constitutes one root of the conception of "evangelical liberty." The other is found in the (evangelical) idea of natural law, *i. e.*, that by nature all are free, and all things common to all (vid. sub). To this must be added the great emphasis laid upon evangelical liberty and the evangelical law in pre-reformation circles (vid. especially Goch, dialog. c. 7, 18, 19). I would thus answer the inquiry raised by Von Nathusius (die christl. soz. Ideen d. Ref.-zeit u. ihre Herkunft, 1897, p. 48 ff.), but, in my judgment, not satisfactorily answered by him, as to the medieval origin of the conception under discussion. As to the eschatological framing of these ideas, vid. WADSTEIN, Die eschat. Ideengruppe, 1896, p. 183 ff., 171 ff. KROPATSCHECK, Das Schriftprincip der luth. Kirche, i. 247 ff.

dictions as was the closing period of the Middle Ages itself! Hatred of the church and love for evangelical law, longing for more secure possession of property and enthusiasm for holy poverty, individualistic and socialistic tendencies, practical demands of the present age and lofty apocalyptic expectations (cf. Joachim v. Floris), the gospel and natural law,—here meet. The result was in keeping with it all—revolution in the name of the gospel.

But even here it was theological ideas which lay in the background, *i. e.*, the evangelical, or natural, law as the criterion for criticism of all existing institutions, and the perfect life to be found in the observance of this law. But by natural or divine law was understood : "all possession of all things in common, and there is one liberty of all" (Occam, dial., p. 932. Cf. op. 90, dier. p. 1143).[1] But above all influential here were the ideas of the great Hussite-Wickliffe movement, or the views of WICKLIFFE († 1384), whom Huss and his adherents interpreted for their countrymen.[2] Wickliffe's work, *De civili dominio* (i., ed. Poole, 1885), demands attention.[3] All human rights, it claims, must rest upon divine right. Accordingly, the unpardoned sinner holds unrightfully what he possesses (i., p. 2 f., 28, 8). In the sight of God his possessions would belong to the righteous, and he, therefore, steals them (p. 34): "for by the very fact that anyone takes another's goods unjustly, their owner being unwilling or ignorant (of the act), he commits theft or robbery. Since, therefore, every unrighteous man unjustly takes the goods of his body and goods of fortune, which all belong to every righteous person, . . . he in this way seizes or steals whatever goods (he possesses)." But the righteous are, in Wickliffe's view, the predestinated (vid. sub). These, accordingly, as the adopted sons of God, have rightful claims to dominion over the whole world : "he has a right to the whole kingdom, . . . therefore everyone thus righteous rules the whole visible world" (p. 47 f.). They are, therefore, kings, like Christ ; but also bishops, since they must proclaim the holy doctrine.[4] It is, of

---

[1] Occam borrows this verbally from Isidor, Etymol. v. 4. Gratian also accepts Communism as guaranteed by natural law, with appeal to Acts iv. 32, Plato and Augustine (Decr. pars i., dist. 8). Roman law allows, as included in natural rights, only the union of man and wife, the education of children, and the liberty of all. Vid., *e. g.*, Digest. i. 1.

[2] As to the relation of Huss to Wickliffe, and the controlling influence of the latter upon the Bohemian agitation, vid. LOSERTH, H. u. W., 1884. The influence of this English theologian upon the continent may, perhaps, be in this respect compared with that of Carlyle in the nineteenth century.

[3] It was widely read in Bohemia. LOSERTH, pp. 242, III.

[4] How similar is this to Luther's "Liberty of a Christian Man," and yet how different !

course, not meant by this that the righteous are at once to appropriate to themselves the possessions which others have wrong-
fully seized. On the contrary, the positive duties of life are
contained in the "evangelical law," which term best expresses
comprehensively the practical reformatory demands of Wickliffe.
The Holy Scriptures, or the "law of Christ" (p. 397), is in
and of itself sufficient for the regulation of the entire life of the
Christian world (*Ipsa pure per se sufficit regere totum populum
christianum*, p. 395).[1] There is really no need of any law beyond the Scriptures for the Christian world (opus evangelic. i., p.
200, ed. Loserth). Civil laws are righteous only in so far as they
have the Biblical spirit (civ. dom., p. 400, 139). Only in so
far can they claim acknowledgment at the hand of believers (op.
ev. i. 367). But the requirements of the evangelical law are
met by humility, love, and poverty in the imitation of Jesus :
"But humility, love, and poverty are the doctrine of Christ.
Therefore, whoever shall not hate those things by imitating
Christ as an eagle, knows that he is not of his church" (de eccl.,
p. 63, ed. Loserth). The life of Christ is the commentary upon
his law (trialog., p. 300, ed. Lechler). Ascetic imitation of
Christ is, therefore, in the true Franciscan fashion, depicted as the
duty of the Christian. "It behooves everyone who is to be
saved to follow him either in suffering or in mode of life" (*moribus*) (sermones ii., p. 15, ed. Loserth ; also iii. 491 f.; op.
evang. i., p. 105). "We ought to imitate the life of Christ and
his apostles as far as we are able" (trialog., p. 456 ; op. ev. i.
469 f.; ii. 140). These are the ideas found in Wickliffe. The
predestinated and the pious are the lords of the world, the property of the wicked being robbery and their codes of justice injustice. But, on the other hand, they ought to be imitators of Christ,
poor, humble servants of the divine law. These ideas stand side by
side. Either of them alone, or both combined, may be capable
of arousing a storm of criticism that may shake the world.
Either the evangelical law or the rights of nature may be invoked in deadly assault upon all property and law, upon every
rank and every ordinance of society.[2] The pious may assert
their rights against the ungodly in the name of the gospel. The
rights of nature and the imitation of Christ are woven together,

---

[1] Evangelical law and natural law fall naturally into one, since both are inspired by God, *e. g.*, De civ. domin., p. 1, 22, 37, 28 ; p. 125 : "Divine
created right is divinely inspired right ; human right is right devised by occasion of the sin of humanity."

[2] Wickliffe feels this when he restricts the thought, that civil laws are valid
only in so far as they agree with God's law, by the caution : "Therefore the
things thus said here are not to be proclaimed too freely to the whole populace"
(opp. ev. i. 367).

and the resultant is the holy revolution. Hussitism first put the ideas into practical execution.

Cf. WIEGAND, De eccl. notione quid Wicl. docuerit, Lips., 1891, p. 58 ff. Von BEZOLD, Zur Gesch. d. Husitentums, 1874 ; ib. Die "armen Leute," Hist. Ztschr., 1879, 1 ff.

§ 62. *Review of History of Theology in the Fourteenth and Fifteenth Centuries. Nominalism and Augustinianism.*

LITERATURE. WERNER, Die nachscot. Scholastik, 1883 ; Der Augustinism. in d. Schol. d. spät. MA., 1883 ; Der Endausgang der mittelalt. Schol., 1887. RITTER, Gesch. d. Philos. viii. (1845), p. 547 ff. PRANTL, Gesch. d. Logik, iii. (1867), p. 327 ff. SIEBECK, Occ. Erk.-lehre, Archiv f. Gesch. d. Philos., 1897, p. 317 ff. ULLMAN, Reformatoren vor der Ref., 1841-42. RITSCHL, Rechtf. u. Vers. i., ed. 2, 129 ff. KOLDE, Die deutsche Augustinercongregat. u. Staupitz, 1879. CLEMEN, Joh. Pupper v. Goch, 1896. KROPATSCHECK, Der Schriftprincip der luth. Kirche, i., 1904.

1. As at the beginning of the twelfth century a keen critical mind furnished the occasion, both positively and negatively, for the great theological agitation of the twelfth and thirteenth centuries, so again, at the beginning of the fourteenth century, a critical thinker directed theological ideas into new paths. The former movement conducted to the culminating point of Scholasticism ; the latter, to its fall. Thus far we may find a parallel between Abelard and Duns Scotus. The method of Duns controls his opponents as well as his adherents. Nothing is too lofty nor too sacred, too firmly settled nor too well attested, to be called in question. This method, which stands in intimate relation with the conception of God as the absolute, unregulated Will, became the lever for the critical unsettling of dogma, employed particularly and in a far-reaching way by the so-called Nominalists. The Lombard brought the materials together ; Thomas framed definitions ; Duns built up and demolished arguments ; Occam advocated the positively valid, though not without robbing it of the nimbus of rationality.

(*a*) Although Duns was not yet a Nominalist, the way was prepared for the transition to Nominalism by his emphasizing of the singular and the individual (p. 147). The work was completed by his greatest pupil, WILLIAM OF OCCAM († ca. 1350).

Vid. esp. super quatuor libr. sent. and Centilogium theologic., Lyon, 1495. Quodlibeta, Strassburg, 1491. De sacr. altaris, Strassburg, 1491. Summ. totius logicae, Bologna, 1498. Major summ. log., Venet. 1508. Exposit. aurea super totam artem veterem, Bol. 1496. The writings upon church polity, vid. supra, p. 167. In these and the following citations of literature, I have been guided by no bibliographical interest (for which see Werner), but merely cite the editions which I have used.

Following Abelard, Thomas and Duns, Occam is the fourth

typical figure among the Scholastics. An intellectual acumen
that moved with ease amid the finest subtleties of thought,
a devotion to abstraction and rational criticism of the strictest
type, are his striking characteristics. He is keenly interested in
politics; but in politics, as in theology, he is a fanatical champion
of logic. One looks to him in vain for warmth of feeling or
devotional language. His logic is keen, but its edge is turned
when it meets the authority of the Romish church. The reader
cannot escape a painful impression, when the talented author
apologizes for his bold conclusions as harmless intellectual exercises, or quotes a large number of opinions without stating clearly
which of them accords with his own judgment (octo quaest., p.
391, 398 ; dial., p. 504, 546, 771 ; de sacr. alt. c. 6, fin.)!
His Nominalistic theory of knowledge (vid. sub) as well as
his critical skepticism (upon both, vid. sub, 2 and 3) spread
rapidly in all directions (esp. ADAM GODDAM, ROBERT HOLKOT,
JOH. BURIDAN, MARSILIUS OF INGHEN, PETER D'AILLI. Quaestiones super libr. sent., Strassburg, 1490). But it is scarcely
correct to consider his theological standpoint as merely a consequence of his Nominalism.[1]   His critical radicalism is rather to
be explained as, on the one hand, a direct application of the
Scotist method ; and this method led him, on the other hand, to
the position of external ecclesiastical positivism. The last
important representative of this tendency was GABRIEL BIEL
(† 1495, vid. Collectorium sive epitoma in Sentent. ll. iv. Tüb.,
1501, with the Expositio canonis missae, Basel, 1510. Cf. also
Sermones de tempore u. de festivitatibus, Hagenau, 1515. Cf.
LINSENMANN, Theol. Quartalschrift, 1865, 195 ff., 449 ff.,
601 ff. WERNER, Endausgang, p. 262 ff.). At the same time,
however, pure Scotism still found adherents (e. g., VORILLON
and FRANZ LYCHETUS, who wrote a commentary upon the Opus
Oxoniense).

(b) Parallel with the Nominalist tendency, was still preserved
a line of Thomist theologians (e. g., HERVAEUS NATALIS, † 1323 ;
cf. Seeberg, PRE. vii., ed. 3, 771 ff. PETRUS DE PALUDE,
† 1342); but even such Dominicans as DURANDUS DE ST.
PORTIANO († 1334, vid. in iv. libros mag. sentent., Paris, 1508
et pas.) departed from the doctrine of the great teacher of their
order. The most energetic defender of Thomism against the
Scotist theology was the General of the Thomists, JOH. CAP-
REOLUS († 1444. Defensionum theologiae divi doctoris Thomae,
ll. iv., Venet. 1483. Cf. Werner, D. h. Thom. v. Aq. iii. 151

---

[1] E. g., BAUR, Dreieinigkeit ii. 872 f. Thomas, ii., ed. 2, 92 f. WAGEN-
MANN, PRE. x., ed. 2, 691.

ff.). DIONYSIUS RICKEL (Carthusianus) († 1471, vid. in sent. Venet. 1584) deserves mention in this connection, as he attached himself in essential points to Thomas, although giving, in his eclectic fashion, an excellent summary of the theories of the various scholastic teachers (cf. Werner, Endausgang, p. 134 ff., 206 ff.). The commentaries written by THOMAS SEL VIO (Cajetan) upon the *Summa* of Thomas and by Sylvester Ferrariensis upon the *Summa contra gentiles* (cf. Werner, l. c., p. 305 ff.) extend into the Reformation period.

(*c*) Side by side with these two tendencies, we note a third, which sought to combine certain mystical notions with Averroistic ideas.[1] Its prominent representatives are PETRUS AUREOLUS († ca. 1345, Sentence-comm. and Quodlibet, Rome, 1596), JOH. V. BACONTHORP († 1346, Quaest. in iv. libros sent. and Quodlibet, Cremona, 1618), and JOH. DE JANDUNO (ca. 1320). The last-named especially maintained that the Averroistic ideas of the eternal world and of the one intellect common to all men are rationally necessary truths, *i. e.*, he did not adopt the Thomistic interpretation of Aristotle, but held that of Averroes as the more correct because it made a fundamental distinction between theology and secular philosophy. But, since the Christian conception of salvation can be maintained intact only on the basis of the faith of the church, it was necessary to cling to the ecclesiastical dogmas (Werner, Nachscot. Theol., p. 5 f.). This tendency, with its extreme Realism, was dominant in the theological school of Padua (*e. g.*, URBAN of Bologna, † 1403; PAUL of Venice, † 1429; AUGUSTIN NIPHUS of Suessa, † ca. 1550, etc. Vid. Werner, Endausgang, p. 142 ff.). This view, which prevailed in northern Italy, and outlasted Nominalism by about a hundred years, requires no further notice in the History of Doctrines.

(*d*) Neither can the school of Augustinian Eremites be compared in importance or completeness of thought with the two tendencies first named. At their head stood AEGIDIUS OF COLONNA (also called Romanus, † 1316. The best edition of his Comm. upon the first three books of the Sentences, Cordova, 1707, Kirchenlex. iii. 669). Among his adherents were JACOB CAPOCCI, † 1308; GERHARD OF SIENA, PROSPER OF REGGIO, ALBERT OF PADUA, SIMON BARINGUNDUS, THOMAS OF STRASSBURG († 1357, vid. ll. iv. in mag. sentent., Strassburg, 1490 and passim). But despite the aim of this school to maintain Augustinianism, their theory of sin and grace is by no means

---

[1] Cf. RENAN, Averroès et l'Averroïsme, 3 A. 1866; and briefly, ERDMANN, Gesch. d. Philos. i., ed. 4, 339 ff.

that of Augustine (vid. Werner, Der Augustinismus, p. 171 ff., 181 ff.). The resolution adopted A. D. 1287, to make the theology of Aegidius the doctrine of the order (vid. Ossinger, Bibl. Augustiniana, 1786, p. 237), had comparatively slight effect. Gregory of Rimini († 1358, Lectura in l. i. and ii. Sent., Paris, 1482) advocated variant views, accepting Nominalism, on the one hand, and then demanding strict adherence to Augustinianism, which he held is to be freed from the wrappings of Peripateticism. He was therefore honored with the title, *Doctor Authenticus.* He strongly insisted that man was created in a state of grace, and that concupiscence is the material of original sin. Sin is transmitted through the sensuous concupiscence of the generating act.[1] That in other points the popular theology of the Augustinians before the Reformation did not overstep the bounds of the common Catholicism, may be seen, *e. g.,* in the Coelifodina of Johann of Paltz (supra, p. 175).

(*e*) The tendency which crops out in men like Gregory had from the middle of the fourteenth century been influencing the minds of many theologians, *i. e.,* the desire for a return to the genuine Augustine, or to the simple teaching of the ancient church. In A. D. 1400 Joh. Gerson wrote : " A reformation seems to be necessary in the faculty of theology. . . . First, that useless doctrines without fruit or solidity may not be so commonly discussed, since through these the doctrines necessary to salvation and useful are deserted. . . . Second, that those who are (not) scholars are misled through these (teachings), because they think that those persons are chiefly to be regarded as scholars who give themselves to such things, despising the Bible and the doctors. . . . Through these teachings, theologians are ridiculed by the other faculties : for they are, on this account, called Phantastics, and are said to know nothing concerning solid truth and morals and books. . . . Through these (teachings) the church and the faith are edified neither internally nor externally."[2] A remedy is to be found by lecturing not only, as was customary, upon the first book of the Sentences, but upon the last three, and lectures should be presented in a simple way, and with practical reference to the religious and moral conditions of the age (Gers. opp. ed. Dupin

---

[1] Both Aegidius and Gregory taught the maculate conception of Mary. *Thomas of Strassburg* championed the immaculate conception. Werner, p. 176 f.

[2] In the later commentaries upon the Sentences (already in Hervaeus, and especially since Occam), the metaphysical questions of the First Book really claim the first place in importance and in the space devoted to them. Theology is lost in metaphysics or canonical casuistry.

i. 122 ff.).   The faults here noted are manifest in the scholastic literature of the age.   When criticism found itself limited by the dogmas of the church, it became empty and fruitless.   And a theology which created a thousand difficulties and suggested a thousand possibilities, only to return at last to the formulas so laboriously criticized, became, together with its advocates, ridiculous.   Demand was made for a practical and churchly theology, and gradually the beginnings of such a theology began to appear.   Side by side with the commentaries upon the Sentences, we find treatises and brochures upon popular theology, expositions of the Creed, directions for confessing, "patterns of virtue," etc.[1]   A simple outline of dogmatics is presented, *e. g.*, in the *Compendium theologiae* found among the works of Gerson.[2] If works of this character led back to the simple forms of the earlier theology, there was at the same time a return to Augustine.   Many influences contributed to this movement.   Against the rising tide of Pelagianism, THOMAS OF BRADWARDINA († 1349) lifted the standard of Augustinian doctrine, not however without first refining it into a system of Determinism (vid. De causa dei c. Pelagium et de virtute causarum, London, 1618. Cf. R. Seeberg, PRE. iii., ed. 3, 350 ff.).   In the mind of Wickliffe the conception of the Supreme will of God was associated inseparably with that of predestination, and thus became a critical weapon against the church and the clergy.   His chief opponent, THOMAS NETTER († 1431.   Doctrinale antiquitatum fid. cath.), endeavored to expound the Catholic doctrine from the Scriptures as in opposition to the views of Wickliffe, and with an avoidance of the scholastic forms.   He thus helped to prepare the way for the final statement of the church's doctrine in the Confession of Trent (vid. SEEBERG, PRE. xiii., ed. 3, 749 ff.). The more profound piety of the Mystics produced a certain congeniality in temper and thought with Augustine.   And wherever the deeper religious needs came into collision with the externalized church, they found in him both religious nutriment and

---

[1] The libraries furnish a mass of such material in manuscript.   These documents are partly in refutation of the charges ventilated at the Reform Councils. But cf. in connection with them the mystical tractates, which also present outlines of popular theology.   Wickliffe as a theologian followed strictly the scholastic method ; but, as he always contrived to give to his monographs a practical and reformatory bearing, even he strengthened the union of theology and the church.

[2] This book first expounds the Creed ; then the Decalogue.   It then treats of the seven sacraments, of the three theological and the four cardinal virtues, of the seven gifts of the Spirit, of the eight Beatitudes, of the various sins— and, finally, the definitions of pyschology are discussed, with constant reference to sin.   As to the question of its authorship, see SCHWAB, Gerson, p. 780.

weapons for the conflict. This is true of all the men who are commonly spoken of as the Forerunners of the Reformation, such as JOH. PUPPER OF GOCH († after 1475), JOH. RUCHRATH OF WESEL († 1481), JOH. WESSEL († 1489). But Augustine could give to no one more than he possessed himself ; and hence these men, in the decisive question concerning grace and justification, still held to the Catholic conception of infused grace (vid. sub). They had no more real grasp than the later Scholastics upon the principle of the sole authority of Scripture in matters of faith. It follows, that the term "Forerunners of the Reformation" is a misleading one[1] (vid. Ritschl, Rechtf. u. Vers. i., ed. 2, 129 ff.).

This hasty review is sufficient to reveal the activity and versatility of the intellectual life of the fourteenth and fifteenth centuries.[2] But the progressive impulse in this play of forces came practically from the Nominalistic and Augustinian circles, and to them we must now turn our attention.

2. We first view the positions of Nominalism, as presented in Occam (cf. SEEBERG, PRE. xiv., ed. 3). Man's knowledge has to do with propositions, not with things. Nature produces only the individual object (sent. i. d. 2, q. 4 X). The Universal does not objectively exist, but only in the subjective understanding (ib. q. 8 E). In order that knowledge may come into existence, there is needed only the intellect (*intellectus*) and the thing perceived (*res cognita*); the mediating intelligible forms (*species sensibiles et intelligibiles*) are superfluous (contrary to Duns, supra, p. 147), "because in vain is that accomplished through more stages, which can be accomplished through fewer"[3] (sent. ii. q. 15 O). Objects beget in us a sensuous impression. From this, the intellect is able to beget in the mind a picture (*fictum*), a copy (*simulacra, idola, phantasmata, imagines*), of the actual object (ib. q. 17 S, i. d. 13, q. 1 J), which is of course only a representatively (*objectively*), and not a really (*subjectively*) existent copy (ii. q. 15 SS). "The intellect, seeing anything outside of the soul, constructs a corresponding thing in the

---

[1] This is notably true of SAVONAROLA († 1498), who was in theology a Thomist, and whose reformatory labors pursued strictly the line of the medieval conception of the relations of church and state, and the ascetic ideal of Christian life.

[2] Regarded separately, with almost every name mentioned in the above review is associated a wealth of historical questions of biographical, literary, dogmatic, and philosophic interest. Protestant theology will find it increasingly necessary to devote far more attention and industry to this field of investigation than has been customary.

[3] A favorite principle with Occam, as it had been with Duns, derived originally from Aristotle.

mind" (ib. i. q. 8 E).   This copy corresponds exactly with the object copied.   Over against these results of first intention (*termini primae intentionis*) originating directly from the actual individual object, stand the results of second intention (*termini secundaeintentiones*), which are naturally (*naturalitur*) constructed by the thought from the former.[1]   These are the abstract conceptions, which assert something as common to the separate objects, *i. e.*, the Universals (ib. ii. q. 25 O).   There is no objective existence corresponding to them.   They are simply a result of the inability of the human mind to apprehend a single object without at the same time thinking of it as having a general character.   For example, when one sees a white object, or several white objects, he is compelled to think of the abstract property of whiteness—or, we cannot look upon a thing as having bulk, or as related to other things, or as continuing to exist, without thinking of quantity, or relation, or duration.   It is easy to see from this why knowledge, or science, should be concerned only with conceptions and definitions, not with real objects. But according to Occam, conceptions of both the classes named are truly real entities (*vere entia realia*), *i. e.*, as "qualities subjectively existing in the mind" (quodlib. iv. 19 ; v. 13), and they correspond to existing reality.   It is utterly unjust to accuse Occam of robbing concepts of their content and seeing in them only figments of the imagination.   He writes : "The universal is not such a figment, to which nothing similar in the subjective[2] being corresponds, as if it were only imagined to be in the objective being (sent. ii. q. 8 H).   Intoning, as he does so strongly, the activity of the soul in the act of perception, and shattering so completely the illusive dreams of Realism, Occam is the real originator of the modern theory of knowledge.

3.   This more precise theory as to the nature of perceptions was enlisted in the service of the critical assaults upon the traditional dogmatics.   (*a*) Dogma, it was held, cannot be scientifically proved.   With equal right entirely other views might then be advocated.   In his *Centilogium*, Occam presents a number of examples : If God assumes any other nature than his own, the propositions : "God is an ass, God is a stone," are also possible (concl. 7).   If the Son became the son of Mary, so might

---

[1] Here belong also intelligible processes, such as acts of the thought or will, desire, sorrow, etc., which man experiences within himself and which can become the direct objects of thought, *i. e.*, which furnish an *intentio prima*, or a directly-formed conception (sent. i. prol. q. 1 HH).

[2] *Subjective*—substantively, or objectively : *objective*—imaginatively.   The meaning of the terms is now just the reverse.

also the Father (8) or the Holy Ghost (9). From the doctrine of the *communicatio idiomatum* might be drawn such propositions as, "God is the foot of Christ," or, "the foot is the hand." (13). The Trinity is undemonstrable, and can be known only through infused faith (*fides infusa*) (55). Differences of ethical merit cannot lead to corresponding differences of reward, since the latter is infinite (92). In a similar way, transubstantiation is criticized; the proofs for the unity of God surrendered (Biel, sent. i. d. 2, q. 10); it is declared probable that God created the world in eternity (ib. ii. d. 1, q. 3 A); or taught that God could have forgiven sin without the repentance of the sinner (Occ. sent. iv. q. 8 M); or, that God might have just as well have commanded as prohibited hatred against himself, theft, murder, etc. (sent. ii. q. 19). (*b*) But it by no means follows that the dogmas of the church are to be surrendered, nor their acceptance made a matter of indifference. On the contrary, it is declared : " This is my faith, since it is the Catholic faith ; for whatever the Roman church believes, this alone and not anything else do I believe, either explictly or implicitly " (Occ. de sacr. alt. 1. 16; quodlib. iv. 35). The authority of the church's doctrine is supported by that of the Scriptures. But this is done—theoretically at least—in a different way from that adopted by Thomas or Duns (supra, p. 101 f., 149). Only those truths are Catholic which the Holy Scriptures teach : " Therefore the Christian is not by the necessity of salvation bound to believe ; nor is he to believe what is neither contained in the Bible, nor can be inferred by necessary and manifest consequence alone from the things contained in the Bible " (Occ. dial., p. 411, 769 f., Goldast). " An assertion of the canonical Scripture is of greater authority than an assertion of the Christian church " (D'Ailli in Tschackert, Petr. v. Ailli, append., p. 10). But these doctrines are true because inspired by God, whether as natural and innate in all men, or as revealed for recording in Scripture. The pope or the church can by their declarations alter absolutely nothing in these truths (Occ. ib., p. 419). " Human authority is by no means to be relied upon in those things which pertain to the faith, because our faith is above the human intellect " (p. 432). The truths of the faith are binding simply on account of their conformity to the Scriptures (Biel, sent. iii. d. 25, q. un. dub. 3 ; d. 24, q. un. dub. 3). The credibility of the Scriptures is acknowledged " because there it has been written and asserted by suggestion (*instinctu*) of the Holy Spirit (Occ., p. 822, 834). God immediately infused the knowledge here contained into the minds of the Biblical writers as the most perfect certainty or evidence (Biel, iii. d. 24, q. un. concl.

7).[1] Should anyone, therefore, call the Scriptures in question he would have to be regarded as a heretic : "Whoever says that any part of the New or of the Old Testament asserts anything false, or is not to be received by Catholics, is to be regarded as heretical and stubborn " (Occ. ib., p. 449). D'Ailli, indeed, placed the authority of the New Testament above that of the Old, and could even ascribe to some of the writings of the New Testament an "authority greater" than that of others (Tschackert, append., p. 9); but this had no practical significance. As, now, "all things to be believed are contained in the canonical Scriptures," there can be no quantitative enlargement of the body of truth. The three ancient symbols merely summarize the biblical ideas, or explain them as against the heresies which have arisen (Biel, iii. d. 25, q. un., a. 1 ; a. 3, dub. 2. Durand. iii. d. 26, q. 2, a. 2). " It is evident that the church, or the pope, by ordaining or making a new symbol, . . . does not make new Catholic truths or articles, but declares anew that certain truths have been and are Catholic " (Biel, ib. a. 3, dub. 3 fin.; cf. expos. can. miss. lect. 41 L). But, plainly as the principle of the exclusive authority of the Scriptures is here theoretically expressed, our authors did not undertake to make practical application of it. The teachings of the Scriptures and of the church are unconsciously placed upon the same level (e. g., Occ. l. c., p. 434, 459, 475 ; sent. i. d. 2, q. 1 F).[2] Occam, e. g., declares that he will hold to transubstantiation on account of the authority of the Romish church, although he knows of another view which explains everything better and is not contrary to the Bible, which does not expressly teach transubstantiation (quodlib. iv. 35 ; de sacr. alt. 3). He would not support the usual theory of original sin, unless there were " authorities of the saints " in its favor (sent. ii. d. 26 U). It appears to be safer to submit to ancient authority.[3] " To the apostolic sanctions

---

[1] Biel says (sermon. de temp. fol. 157 r): "But the canonical Scriptures of both Testaments are believed to have been written, the Holy Spirit dictating and inspiring." Paul is the " celestial secretary" (D'Ailli, sermones, Strassb. 1490, form Y 5 v). Durand. sent. prol. q. 1 L : " We assent to them (the articles of faith) alone or chiefly upon the authority of the Scriptures, which we believe to be inspired by God." D'Ailli : " All the canonical Scriptures have been revealed by the same infallible author," i. e., God (Tschackert, Petr. v. Ailli, append., p. 9). Vid. also Duns, sent. iv. d. 14, q. 3. 5. Wickliffe, de civil. dom. i. p. 418, 439 : " Scripture divinely inspired." Other citations may be found in Holzhey, Die Inspirat. d. h. Schr., 1895, pp. 94-119.

[2] Occam (de sacr. alt. 3) even says : " This (transubstantiation) is believed to have been divinely revealed to the holy fathers."

[3] Ritschl's comments upon Occam (Fides implicita, 1890, p. 28 ff.) are unreliable, as he was unacquainted with the thorough discussion of the questions

13

and decrees which are not certainly contrary to the divine and natural law of Holy Scripture, although there should be some doubt of this, assent and obedience are to be rendered " (Biel, serm. de temp. fol. 157 r).[1] It is remarkable that the same men who apply reason so sharply in criticism of the dogmas of the church and subordinate them to the sole authority of the Scriptures, are yet always ready in any given instance to submit to the " Romish " doctrine. But we should not on this account wonder at their studied irony, nor doubt either their honesty or their courage. If I understand the matter rightly, this wavering stands in intimate connection with the juristic conception of the church. Just as in civil life the law of nature holds primacy and yet finds application only in a form adapted to the precepts of positive law (supra, p. 171 f.), so it is also in the church.   Here, the accepted dogma, or the Roman doctrine, is the positive law ; the Scriptures (and reason) correspond to the law of nature (supra, p. 171 f.).[2] The application of the latter criterion produces a radical criticism of dogma and church ; but this criticism is shattered—very much as in the political world—upon actual concrete conditions—upon the positive legal status of the Romish church. Neither in church nor in state has the criticism based on the law of nature abolished the existing positive law, although logical consistency might require that it should do so.   But, since all attempt to prove the teachings of the church to be conformed to reason has been abandoned upon principle, ecclesiastical positivism asserts itself in the naked form : I believe what the Romish church believes !   This position could, of course, not be permanently maintained.   The longer criticism pursued its way, the more intolerable became the positivism of the church, and the longer the latter held sway in the church, the more improper must the bold criticisms appear.[3]

---

at issue in Occam's writings upon church polity.   On p. 30, the *Dialog.* is referred to as " not printed," but see G. HOFFMANN, Die Lehre der fides implicita, 1903, p. 153 ff.

[1] Such a man as D'Ailli could, upon occasion, write of the books of the Bible : " We thus receive the canonical or divine Scriptures on account of the authority of the Catholic church, which so receives and approves them " (Tschackert, append., p. 11).

[2] It is, of course, not implied that the entire contents of the Scriptures fall under the heading of the law of nature ; but, regarded as a whole, they claim the same primacy over the positive ecclesiastical principles devised by man, as the law of nature given to man by God holds over positive human laws.

[3] These theologians, on the one hand, identified the law of reason with the teachings of the Scriptures, and, on the other, regarded the latter as in conformity with the teachings of the church.   Both ideas are equally perverted, and both errors combined in preventing them from seriously applying their view of the authority of the Bible.   Hence, they never established the authority of

4. The truths of Scripture are apprehended in Faith. (*a*) "Faith is a certain adherent (*adhaesiva*) and firm knowledge (*notitia*) of truth pertaining to religion, received through revelation" (Biel, iii. d. 23, q. 2, a. 1 D). In its essential nature, faith is intellectual assent (*assensus*): "To believe is an act of the intellect assenting to the truth, proceeding from a command of the will" (ib. C). But revelation embraces only to a small extent truths which are necessary, or evident to reason ; the majority of its teachings are contingent truths, for which it would be impossible to present a scientific demonstration (Occ., sent. prol. q. 1 N ; q. 7 ; quodlib. ii. 3. Biel, iii. d. 25, q. un., a. 1, n. 3), or which may even directly contradict reason. "Whoever is a Catholic and believing Christian can easily believe anything to which he could by no means by his natural powers assent." Here God comes to his aid : "God, out of his grace, infuses into him a *habitus*, through the medium of which (*quo mediante*) he is able to assent to any article of faith whatsoever" (Occ., centilog. 60). This is the *fides infusa*, without which no act of faith would be possible.[1] It is a "quality (*qualitas*) produced by God in the soul," which inclines the understanding to the act of faith." This habitus is infused in baptism (Biel, iii. d. 23, q. 2, a. 1 G. Occ., quodlib. iii. 7). But, in order that acts of faith may be actually performed, there is always further needed an acquired faith (*fides acquisita*). No child can come to faith, despite the faith infused into it, unless it secure also, through instruction or the reading of the Bible, the concrete faith directed upon particular, separate truths (Occ., sent. iii. q. 8 LM). (*b*) However untenable the conception of the "infused faith" may be, yet our Dogmaticians, in employing it, are guided by a certain presentiment of a real truth. It was their great aim to gain a special sphere for the religious life. The pious reader of the Bible, Biel explains, enlarges not so much his knowledge as his faith, since he is through the infused faith inwardly bound to the authority of Scripture (iii. d. 24, q. un., a. 2, concl. 5). But again, in so far as the material furnished by revelation for faith is not accessible to reason as such, theology is not in the usual sense of the term a science (Occ., sent. prol. q. 1. Biel, sent. prol. q. 7). (*c*) Occam thus defines the *fides implicita :* "To believe implicitly

---

the Scriptures upon any secure basis. It was not establishing it to take from the pope his infallible authority and transfer it to the Bible ! But this is the basis of Occam's regard for the Bible. Vid. supra, p. 169, n. 2.

[1] But Occam in Quodlib., iii. 7, has introduced this conception as required neither by reason nor by experience . . . nor by inference but solely by authority. Cf. Duns, supra, p. 150.

is to firmly assent to some Universal from which many things follow, and not to pertinaciously cling to anything contrary to it" (dial., p. 434). Faith in the doctrine of the Scriptures is thus also included in the category of implicit faith. It is the idea, already familiar to us (supra, p. 103), that we accept everything taught by the Scriptures, *i. e.*, by the church, as taught by these authorities: "Everything contained in the canonical Scriptures is true" (Biel, iii. d. 25, q. 1, a. 1, n. 2; expos. can. miss. lect. 12 B: "I believe as the church believes"). The technical formulas of the doctrine of the Trinity and of Christology fall, for the laity, under the "implicit faith"[1] (ib. a. 2, concl. 5), as well as the facts of biblical history, which cannot be experienced (ib. a. 1, n. 2). Even if a layman, in thus obeying his prelate, should believe what is false, "such a one would not only not sin, but he would even, by thus believing what is false, merit" (words of Innocent III. in Biel, l. c., a. 1, n. 2). But every believer must unconditionally possess *explicit* faith in Christ as the Redeemer (ib. a. 2, concl. 3; further, concl. 5). It is therefore the specific Catholic conception of faith which here again meets us. Faith is knowledge, (*notitia*) and assent (*assensus*) in regard to the biblical revelation. Faith is the same in all persons; but some believe explicitly, others implicitly (ib. concl. 4).

5. Such are the principles of Nominalistic Scholasticism. Within the old forms a new ferment is stirring; but the new wine has not yet burst the old bottles. The Scriptures are the sole authority in the church. It is felt that they constitute a canon of criticism; but yet no dogma is overthrown, nor is any *right* of the hierarchy molested. Reason calls in question the bold systems of the past. Theologians surrender the systems, but allow the definitions to stand. Or, they doubt the separate doctrines, but believe the whole. Skepticism forms a league with the positivism of the church—doubt with implicit faith—and they counterbalance each other. There is an undefined sense of a really positive theology within reach; but what is actually cultivated is a fruitless criticism, a "negative theology." But, amidst all the murkiness of thought, two ideas are never lost sight of, *i. e.*, the authority of the Scriptures as over against the church and her dogmas, and the feeling that the Christian religion is no ordinary human system of religious philosophy, but a special, positive, and clearly marked whole— the historical revelation given by God, which only faith can

---

[2] But Occam claimed also for himself the right of cherishing *implicit* faith in the doctrine of transubstantiation (!) (De sacr. alt. 1, supra, p. 192). Cf. also account in Moll, KG. d. Niederl. ii. 562.

apprehend. The league between the gospel and speculative thought, which held sway in the church from the days of Origen, was glorified by the Scholastics also ; but it was finally shattered, too, at their hands. Duns and the Nominalists proved it untenable. It is this service chiefly which establishes their position among the forces preparing the way for the coming Reformation. It would be a serious error to criticize their separate teachings and ignore the chief service rendered by them.

The separate doctrines are here of interest to us only because of their significance in the historical development. In the closing period of Scholasticism, as we have already treated of the sacraments in § 58, and of repentance in particular in § 61, 2, we shall need to examine only the views held upon sin, redemption, grace, and the appropriation of salvation, together with the modifications in the doctrine of the Lord's Supper. We have, likewise, no occasion to attempt a presentation of the Augustinian tendency in all its details ;[1] and shall therefore confine ourselves to a few remarks touching the doctrine of grace and to criticism of the conception of the church and of the theory of indulgences.

§ 63. *Labors of the Later Middle Ages Upon Separate Dogmas and Doctrines.*

1. As the conception of God held by Duns regulated the theistic speculations of the Nominalists, so in nearly all doctrines they attached themselves more or less closely to the *Doctor Subtilis.* This is evident in their views of Sin and Liberty. The rebellion of the sensuous nature against the spirit is natural. The *donum superadditum* removed it, and in consequence merits became possible (Biel, ii. d. 30, q. 1, a. 1-3). Original sin "consists in a privation of the original righteousness owed" (Biel, ib. q. 2, a. 2, concl. 3.   Occ., sent. ii. q. 26 U ; cf. Durand, ii. d. 30, q. 3). Yet an infection of children through the generating act is also maintained (Biel, ib. q. 2, a. 1, concl. 1. Duns differs, *supra*, p. 153). But, despite sin, the natural freedom of the will remains perfectly intact. "The integrity of his natural will, *i. e.*, its freedom, is not corrupted by sin ; for that is really the will itself, and not separable from it" (Biel, ii. d. 30, q. 1, a. 3, dub. 4). "Through mortal sin nothing is corrupted nor destroyed in the soul" (Occ., sent. iv. q. 8 and 9 D). That these assertions are irreconcilable with the Augus-

---

[1] Of how little interest for the History of Doctrines such a discussion would be may be seen in CLEMEN'S work upon Goch.

tinian doctrine of original sin is very evident.[1] Vid. also Biel,
De festivit. serm. 33.

2. The doctrine of the Atonement and Redemption is treated
entirely in the spirit of Thomas and Duns. The subjective aspect is the more prominent, but the objective is not wanting.
The relation of the two to one another remains, as heretofore,
without clear definition.

(*a*) AUREOLUS, BACONTHORP, DURANDUS, and CAPREOLUS follow in the tracks of Thomas. The merit of Christ is of infinite
value, and is capable of affecting atonement for all (Aur. iii. d.
20, q. 1, a. 1.   Bac. iii. d. 32, a. 1.   Capr. iii. d. 18, a. 3.
Dur. iii. d. 19, q. 1, a. 2: "The passion of Christ was a sufficient
and superabundant satisfaction for the sin of the whole human
race. . . . Christ, by suffering out of love and obedience,
offered to God something more acceptable than the recompens-
ing of the sin of the whole human race required""). Anselm's
idea of the necessity of satisfaction is rejected (Aur. l. c., q. 2.
Dur. d. 20, q. 1). But redemption through the passion of
Christ is, nevertheless, the most suitable way, since man is in this
way assured of the magnitude of the divine love and incited to
a responsive affection, and receives also the example of Christ to
stimulate him to the practice of every virtue (Dur. ib.). The
redemption wrought by Christ is realized only in the case of
those "who are joined to him as members to the Head," or
"through real imitation, *i. e.*, when we suffer after the similitude
of Christ" (Dur. d. 19, q. 1, a. 2).[2]

(*b*) GABRIEL BIEL, on the other hand, follows Duns more closely.
Christ, from the time of his conception onward, by his obedience
merited for us grace and glory : "for he was in the very moment
of his conception a man perfect in every grace and virtue and
meritorious work" (iii. d. 18, a. 2, concl. 2). This merit becomes efficacious through the *acceptio divina* (d. 19, a. 2, concl.
1), but only for the predestinated: "Only for the predestinated
did he merit final grace and glory," for "no one finally obtains
salvation unless he was predestinated from eternity." Here also
Biel follows Duns (supra, p. 152).[3] Salvation rests upon the divine

---

[1] As to the views of this period upon the immaculate conception of Mary,
see Esp. Occam, quodlib. iii. 9. 10, and cf. WERNER, Nachscot. Scholast.,
p. 347.

[2] Wicliffe argues the necessity of a satisfaction upon the ground that man
must perform an act of humility, which, in contrast with Adam's presumption,
shall lower him beneath himself (trialog., p. 215 f., ed. Lechler).

[3] The idea of predestination occurs very frequently in his writings. The
eucharistic sacrifice brings "remission of sin ; not, indeed, to all, but to the
predestinated" (Biel, sermon. defestiv. fol. 279 r). The church is the "multitude of the predestinated" (expos. can. miss. lect. 22 E.; vid. also sent. d.

predestination, and the passion of Christ is only a means for its realization : "If Christ had not suffered, the elect would nevertheless have been saved, because before the passion of Christ God foresaw that the elect would be saved " (ib. concl. 4). By the side of this conclusion stands the other, that, although the passion of Christ primarily (*principaliter*) secures salvation for us, yet our own working (*operatio*) coöperates. For, when anyone becomes a recipient of grace, he needs, upon his part, a certain disposition of the will, such as *attritio ;* and this implies a merit of fitness (*de congruo*). In the case of the baptized child, a substitute for this is found in the merit of the sponsors. The person thus equipped with grace performs works having merit of worthiness (*de condigno*), and these become a ground for the increase of grace. It is concluded therefore : "That, granting that the passion of Christ is the principal merit on account of which are conferred grace, the opening of the kingdom and glory, yet it is never the sole and entire meritorious cause. This is evident, because with the merit of Christ always concurs some work, such as the merit of fitness or of worthiness of the one receiving the grace or glory " (concl. 5). Thus the merit of Christ finds its necessary complement in our merit. This final conclusion is here—not illogically—derived from the idea of merit ; but it is essentially an outgrowth of the Thomistic idea, that we became partakers of the results of the work of Christ only in so far as we are in life conformed to his image (supra, p. 178 f., 179 f., n. 4).[1] This merit of the obedience of Christ, as thus more sharply defined, God accepts as a satisfaction for the sins of all who believe on Christ (d. 20, a. 3, dub. 1). This course of divine dealing cannot; of course, be described as necessary (ib. a. 2, concl. 1); and Anselm is thus refuted with the weapons of Duns (ib. a. 1).[2] On the other hand, the plan of salvation may be shown to be most admirably adapted to the end in view, since it binds us to God and stimulates us to love him

---

27, a. 3, dub. 4). WERNER (Endausgang, p. 285) interprets the above-cited passage from the Sentences as teaching "the universal efficacy of Christ's redemptive act for all the descendants of Adam."

[1] This relationship between Biel and Thomas is, with justice, maintained by an ascetic document dating from the beginning of the sixteenth century, which reproduces the thoughts of Biel (in HASACK, p. 477), where we find also the declaration (p. 443): "Since the passion of Christ was not an entire, but a partial, cause of our salvation." In general, this formula represents admirably the religious conception of the day. But we find, on the contrary, in Duns, iii. d. 19, § 8 : "Christ, as the entire cause (*totalis causa*), merited for us the opening of the gates of paradise."

[2] Yet Biel, like Duns (supra, p. 157), is not indisposed to accept the arguments as valid, "divine ordination being presupposed " (q. 20, a. 1, n. 1 B).

in return (ib. a. 3, dub. 2), and also because God chose this plan and no other (ib. a. 2, concl. 2).

(*c*) It is not correct to say that "the fundamental ideas of Anselm's theory were nevertheless generally accepted" (THOMASIUS, Christi Person u. Werk, ii., ed. 3, 165). Anselm's theory is accepted by no one. On the contrary, we constantly meet the fundamental ideas of Abelard, almost always indeed combined with the older thought of the merit of Christ which avails before God as the ground of divine grace. This combination appears also in the popular treatises of the day, particularly in the mystical literature.[1] The passion of Christ is here treated in the spirit, and often in the very language, of Bernard. Its purpose is to reveal to us God's love and incite us to responsive love and imitation.[2] On the other hand, salvation and eternal blessedness are with the greatest earnestness made dependent upon the objective merit of Christ and the satisfaction rendered by him, the contemplation of which is especially commended to the dying.[3] It is a favorite thought (Anselm, supra, p. 70) that in the redemptive work of God justice and mercy concur (*e. g.*, Biel, sermon. de festiv. fol. 225 v). Exceedingly instructive is a sermon by Biel (De circumcis. domini). Here Anselm's doctrine is first presented in bold outlines, and from it deduced the concurrence of the justice and mercy of God (l. c., fol. 197 v). But this work of Christ has for its purpose the efficacy of the sacraments: "The sacraments . . . by which man is directly disposed to the reception of grace, which is the health and life of the soul; for these he merited efficacy by the shedding of his blood" (fol. 198 r). "Christ, as true God and man, instituted the sacraments, primarily (*principaliter*) according to his divine nature, meritoriously according to his human nature" (ib.). This medicine gives grace, "by which they are able to merit eternal blessedness" (199 v). But even this institution of the sacraments is a work of the grace which grants the means of salvation

---

[1] The numerous sermons and meditations upon the Passion in the Incunabula-literature of before and after A. D. 1500 are especially instructive. Space forbids the citation of these separately. See both views also in WESSEL, De causis incarnat. 6 (opp. p. 424 f.), and GOCH, vid. Clemen, Goch, p. 131 ff.).

[2] *E. g.*, WESSEL, De caus. incarn. 1, p. 414: "Nothing is so effectual for turning the minds of men to good as pious exercise in the life and passion of the Lord." G. Biel, passionis dominic. serm. (Hagenau, 1515), form A 3; expos. can. miss. lect. 85 XY.

[3] Cf. supra, p. 179, n. 3. Upon Christ as atoning sacrifice, *e. g.*, in WESSEL, De caus. incarn. 19, p. 455; de magnitud. passion. 39, p. 539; 40, p. 541; 44, p. 549. Cf. in HASACK, p. 155 f., 143: "Thou wilt to-day interpose between thy wrath and my transgression the most dear and acceptable sacrifice, Christ." Vid. also MOLL, KG. d. Niederl. ii. 657 f.

to its enemy, as well as of the justice which rewards in accordance with the work of Christ, *i. e.*, through the institution of
the sacraments (sent. iv. d. 2, q. 1, a. 3, dub. 1 ; cf. Duns, iv.
d. 2, q. 2. 8). The so-called objective aspect of salvation may,
accordingly, be reduced to the proposition, that Christ has
secured for us the medicine of the sacraments (cf. Duns Scotus).

3. It has already been remarked (p. 174), that the religious
life is moulded under the influence of the sacrament of repentance. It is accordingly under this heading that the development of personal piety is treated.[1] The problem is the conversion of the sinner. (*a*) It is for the sinner—as is repeated
until it becomes wearisome—to do what in him lies (*quod in se
est*), and God will then not suffer grace to be lacking (*e. g.*,
Biel, sent. ii. d. 27, q. un.). The sinner acts from himself up
to the point of attrition. But, according to Paltz, even this is
to be traced back to the influence of a grace gratuitously given
(suppl. R 2 r ; 4 r). "Nevertheless, if we do what is in us,
so that we have attrition, he changes for us that attrition into
contrition—sometimes of his own motion (*per se*) before the
reception of the sacraments, sometimes in the reception of the
sacraments, which is more certain" (ib.). The sacraments,
and even divine worship before their reception, effect this
transformation (see citation, p. 175), in connection with which
man receives simultaneously the peculiar grace (*gratia gratum
faciens*) infused by the sacraments. By contrition mortal sin
in him is destroyed, and by the sacrament the power of doing
good is infused. (*b*) This is the Justification of the sinner. The
ultimate disposition being fixed by an act of the free will, grace,
which is the form of justification, is immediately infused by God
(Durand, iv d. 17, q. 1, a. 3). There is need of faith in connection with this process only in so far as the disposition to
accept the grace which is the prerequisite of the process, *i. e.*,
faith, is necessary. "Therefore for the reception of justification
in the adult there is required a motion of the free will, according to which it consents to grace. And, because the first motion
through which he consents to grace is a motion of faith, therefore that motion itself is a motion of faith. Thus Romans,
chapter 5, justifies through faith" (Paltz, R 2 r). Justification
may, like generation, be understood in two senses : as the
gradual movement toward righteousness, or as a change without
movement (*mutatio sine motu*). In the former sense, it occurs
gradually (*successive*); in the other, "justification is effected in

---

[1] Cf., in addition to Biel's Book of Sentences, also JOH. OF PALTZ, who, in
the supplement of his *Coelifodina*, treats of conversion and justification in connection with a discussion of the sacrament of repentance.

an instant '' (ib. R 5 r). When the sinner thus becomes righteous through the infusion of grace, he receives at the same time
the forgiveness of sins.[1] (c) But the infusion of grace is also the
basis of meritorious works,[2] which are accordingly imposed in the
confessional. By this means the entire process is brought under
the view-point of merit (supra, p. 122). The dominant terminology is derived from Duns (p. 160). The general definition
is : "A meritorious act is an act called forth (elicitus) by free
will, accepted for the repaying of some recompense (ad retri-
buendum aliquod praemium), (Biel, ii. d. 27, a. 1, n. 2 ; cf. iii.
d. 18, q. un.). The initiatory steps, which man is able to take
in his own strength, e. g., the attritio, produce the merit of
fitness (de congruo). "The soul is able, by the removal of an
obstacle and by a good movement toward God elicited by free
will, to merit the first grace by fitness,'' since it is just for God to
reward this merit by imparting grace (ib. concl. 4 ; cf. iv. d.
14, q. 1, a. 2, concl. 5 : meritum de congruo ad justificationem ;
d. 16, q. 2, a. 3, prop. 4 ; Durand, i. d. 17, q. 2, a. 2). But
through the infusion of grace the works become merits of
worthiness. "A merit of worthiness (condigni or de condigno)
is an act elicited by free will for a recompense (praemium) of
someone according to a debt to be repaid to justice.''   An
"equality'' and "proportion of merit to reward '' is here required
(ib. ii. d. 27, a. 1, n. 3).[3] By means of these merits, man
secures for himself both an increase of grace and eternal glory
(vid. also Paltz, coelifod. Bb 3 r and suppl. R 4 r).[4] (d) The
possibility of being sure of the possession of grace was denied by
Biel, though asserted by Duns (ii. d. 27, a. 3, dub. 5).   The
unworldly ideal of life, and the dualism between the religious and
the secular life, were perpetuated (cf. the Mystic literature).
But here also, the views of the church were in conflict with
modern advancement and its ideals.[5]

---

[1] Some follow Thomas (p. 120), and conceive of it as the logical consequent
of the infusion of grace, e. g., Paltz, R 5 r : "Grace is infused before guilt is
remitted, because through grace the guilt is remitted;'' Biel, iv. d. 14, q. 1, a.
2, concl. 5. Others, with Duns, reverse the process (p. 161), e. g., Occ.,
iv. q. 8 and 9 L : "Yet in fact and as a rule, the expulsion of guilt is
previous to the infusion of grace.'' Vid. also supra, p. 161, n.

[2] Cf. HASACK, p. 133 : "It (grace) moves the free will to do well and to
think well, to live well and to work well, and it gives power for all praiseworthy undertakings. . . . Grace makes all work meritorious. . . . But
grace is given, that man may with (the assistance of) grace perform all things
appointed.''

[3] Yet Durand asserts, that, in the strictest sense, man can secure this merit
with men only, and not with God (i. d. 17, q. 2, a. 2).

[4] Cf. HASACK, p. 262 f.

[5] Yet such a man as Biel had a certain comprehension of the economic con-

Our review makes it very evident that in the theology of the Schoolmen only the sacramental and Pelagian tendencies made progress.   The free will and the sacraments are the two forces which mould the Christian life.

4. In regard to the Lord's Supper, mention must be made of a theory which found many adherents.[1]   (*a*) It is the view mentioned already, and not without sympathy, by Duns, *i. e.*, that, even after the creation of the body of Christ, the substance of the bread is retained, and not merely the accidents (supra, p. 131 n.).   Occam calls attention to the fact, that the Scriptures do not contain the theory of transubstantiation (de sacr. alt. 3), and he plainly intimates that the view, that the substance of the bread and wine remain, is " very reasonable :" " Neither is the contrary to this contained in the canonical Bible, nor does it any more include any contradiction, that the body of Christ coëxists with the substance of the bread, than (that it coëxists with) its accidents, nor is it repugnant to reason " (quodl. iv. 35 ; cf. centilog. 39 C).   Nevertheless, out of regard for the Roman church, he will continue to hold transubstantiation (sacr. alt. 1, 5).   But the entire tenor of his discussion (vid. sub) testifies that he is not serious in his submission.[2]   DURAND also acknowledges the possibility of the retention of the earthly sub-

ditions of the age, and when treating of repentance made excellent comments upon it, *e. g.*, against the communism based on the law of nature (iv. d. 15, q. 2, a. 1, n. 1), upon war (ib. q. 4), upon the method of taxation (ib. q. 5, a. 2, concl. 3), upon the wild-game abuses (ib. concl. 5), upon trading and prices (ib. q. 10, a. 1, n. 2), upon the question of coinage and interest (ib. q. 9, 11), etc.   Cf. also ROSCHER, Gesch. der Nationaloekonomik, p. 22 ff.

[1] The high regard for the mass continues (vid. supra, p. 134).   Cf. Luther, Weim., ed. vi. 375 : "That they made of it a sort of magic ! Some have masses held, that they may become rich and that it may go well with them in their business ; some, because they think that if they hear mass in the morning, they are safe for the day from all distress and danger ; some for their sickness ; some for things even more foolish and even sinful,—and yet find priests so stupid as to take money and do their will.   And, further, they have now made one mass better than the others, and esteem one as useful for this purpose, another for that. . . . Here everyone keeps silent and (they) let the people go on for the sake of the accursed, shameful penny."   In connection with the idea that the Lord's Supper blots out venial sins, stands the view that, as Christ atoned for original sin, so the eucharistic sacrifice atones for daily sins, *e. g.*, Pseudo-Thomas, Opusc. 58, c. 1 (opp, ii. 42).   Cf. Confes. Augsb. 24.

[2] A contemporary of Duns, the Dominican JOHN OF PARIS (ca. 1300), declared in favor of the retention of the substance of the bread, which however combines with the body of Christ to form one "subsistence," so that there are indeed two corporeities (*Corporeitäten*), but only one body. Vid. his work : Determinatio de modo existendi Corpus Christi in sacr. alt. alio quam sit ille quem tenet eccl., ed. Alix, London, 1686.   Cf. Kirchenlex. vi., ed. 2, 621 f. ARGENTRE, Collectio indiciorum, i. 264 ff.

stances (iv. d. 11, q. 1, a. 3) ; likewise BIEL (expos. can. miss.
lect., 41 J); THOMAS OF STRASSB. (iv. d. 11, p. 1, a. 2 ; cf.
also Dionys. Carthus. iv. d. 11, q. 1), and JOH. V. WESEL
(vid. ULLMANN, Reform. vor d. Ref. i. 330, 390). D'AILLI
zealously supports this view, " because it is altogether possible
that the substance of the bread coëxists with the substance
of the body. This mode is possible ; it is repugnant to neither
reason nor the authority of the Bible ; it is far easier to
be understood and more reasonable" (in sent. iv. q. 6 E).[1]
WESSEL also holds to both the presence of the body of Christ
(de eucharist. c. 8, 16 ; opp. 1614, p. 673, 688 f.), and the continued existence of the bread, " which truly vivifies and refines
alone by signifying (*significatione*) and by pious commemoration" (c. 13, p. 683). The chief thing is that Christ " desired
to be corporally near (*cominus*) to those longing for him " (c. 23,
p. 695 ; 24, p. 697), and that spirit and life are thereby brought
to us (c. 8, 9, 10). (*b*) For the completion of this theory, we
must bear in mind the conception then held of the presence of
Christ's body in the Supper (cf. supra, p. 116). We follow here
chiefly Occam. According to the Nominalistic view, quantity has no
independent existence, but it is the " how much " of a thing ; it
is not separate from the substance or the qualities of an object
(sacr. alt., form B 2 r and c. 17). The quantity of a thing
may be increased or diminished, as by compression or by extension, without the thing becoming thereby a different thing. Accordingly, a thing may become, like a mathematical point, without quantity, without thereby changing its substance (ib. c. 37 ;
sent. iv. q. 4 H ; cf. Biel, Sent. iv. d. 10, a. 1, n. 2). In this
way the body of Christ exists in the Lord's Supper : The body
of Christ is not quantitatively (*quantum*) in the sacrament of the
altar (sacr. alt., form B 6 r and c. 31, 41). The bodily presence of a thing may be of two kinds : " To be *circumscriptively*
in a place is for anything to be in a place, a part of which
is in a part of the place and the whole of it in the whole place ;
but to be *definitively* in a place is when a whole thing is in
a whole place and not beyond it, and the whole of it is in every
part of that place " (quodl. i. 4).[2] Examples of the latter are
seen in the angels and in the human soul, which are present
entire in every part of the space which they occupy as well as in
the entire space. Thus also the whole Christ is present in the
hostia, just as he is equally in all its parts (sacr. alt. c. 6). If
now the body of Christ exists at the same time with the bread in

---

[1] To this Luther appealed in his De captiv. Babyl., Weim. ed. vi., 508.
[2] Biel added the further category, *repletive* (sent. i. d. 37, q. un. a. 1).

the *hostia*, two questions arise : (1) How the same body can be present at the same time in different places, and (2) How its parts can coëxist in one place.   The former is answered by a reference to the simultaneous presence of the soul in all parts of the body.   In reply to the second question, it is to be said, that the body of Christ is not in the Supper quantitatively, and therefore we are not to think of a correspondence between separate parts of the space with parts of the body.   There is hence no necessity to inquire whether the body present is the glorified or the natural body (sent. iv. q. 4 J K O).   While the body of Christ is at one place in heaven in extended form and quantitatively, it is also present everywhere as a whole in the host (cf. Biel, iv. d. 10, a. 2, concl. 2, and expos. can. miss. lect. 43).[1]   But this presence is not confined to the host : "The body of Christ is present to everyone, is present to himself immediately, and consequently that form of bread, *i. e.*, the host, has nothing to do with (*nihil facit*) the presence of the body " (Occ., ib. N).   Thus regarded, it may be said that the body of Christ can be everywhere (*ubique*) just as God is everywhere (centiloq. 25, 28).[2]   This way of apprehending the matter, which had an influence on Luther, suggests the following comments : (1) The abstract logical method of considering the subject, and the references to the institution of the Supper, and even to the act of worship involved, are not clear.   (2) The eucharistic body of Christ stands in boldest contrast with his actual body— it is a certain omnipresent Something.   (3) As Occam weaves in the problem, How two bodies can be at one place, he betrays the fact that transubstantiation is not in his mind.   (4) Transubstantiation maintained its place in the canons of the church, but the theology of the closing era of the Middle Ages took no delight in it.[3]   Cf. RETTBERG, Occ. und Luther, Stud. u. Krit. 1839, 69 ff.

---

[1] Vid. also Durand, iv. d. 11, q. 1, a. 1, 2.

[2] Cf. also (concl. 23), the view that a stone fallen from heaven might cleave through the body of Christ without dividing it or meeting with any opposition in its course.

[3] We must not overlook at this point the teaching of FABER STAPULENSIS, † 1536 (cf. GRAF, Ztschr. f. hist. Theol. 1852, 3 ff., 165 ff.), since the attempt has been made to trace to him Luther's doctrine of the Lord's Supper (Hospinian, Calixtus).   At the first Supper Christ was present both sensibly and also concealed, sacramentally and impassibly, beneath the outward signs. The result was a union (*unitio*) between him and the participants, which brought to the latter immortality (Comm. upon the Fourth Gospel, Basel, 1523, fol. 115).   Thus he is again present at every subsequent celebration of the Supper.   "For, always remaining in heaven, he, existing everywhere, descends *immobilely* into every believer, whom he vivifies and nourishes."   He gives immortality and life (ib. fol. 318 f.).   But in this his presence is a

(c) In this connection we must recall the very bold and cutting criticism which was during the Middle Ages directed against
the doctrine of transubstantiation.   It originated with Wickliffe
(vid. his work of A. D. 1382-83, De eucharistia, ed. Loserth,
1892 ; cf. Fasciculus zizaniorum, Mag. Joh. Wiclif, ed. Shirley,
1858, p. 115 f.) and was spread by Huss (vid. De corpore
Christi) and the Hussites (cf. LOSERTH, in the introduction to
De euchar., p. xliv ff.).   Transubstantiation is to Wickliffe's
mind worse than heathenism : "They believe worse than the
pagans, that that consecrated host is their God" (p. 13 f.). It
is a new doctrine, against which the Scriptures and reason protest (p. 71).   It has against it the testimony of the eyes (p. 57),
and involves in all manner of contradictions. Will God then destroy
a portion of the entire substance of the body (p. 129), or will he
cause the body to grow at every celebration of the ordinance?
(p. 193).   According to Wickliffe's own view, we must discriminate sharply between the *sign*, or *sacrament*, and the *body*
(p. 18, 38, 112 ; trial., p. 248).   The words of institution are
to be understood *tropice*, or *figurative*.   Their effect is that they
to the bare natural existence (*nudum esse naturale*) of the bread
add a superadded sacramental character (*superadditum esse
sacramentale*) (p. 153, 35, 83, 291).   The bread signifies the
body of Christ, upon which we should spiritually direct our
attention and remembrance.   "That change does not destroy
the nature of the bread, nor alter the nature of the body . . . but
it effects the presence of the body of Christ and destroys the pre-
eminence of the bread, so that the whole attention of the worshiper
is concentrated upon the body of Christ" (p. 100).   "Not
that the bread is destroyed, but that it *signifies* the body of the
Lord there present in the sacrament" (p. 101, 121).   But this
presence of Christ is a spiritual one, mediated through the
symbol : "That the body of Christ is there virtually and in the
sign—not the body of Christ as it is in heaven, but the vicarious
sign of it" (p. 303, 271, 83 f.).   Then, as to the eating :
"We do not tear the body of Christ with the teeth, but

bodily one : "Who is divinely everywhere, and also *corporeally wherever he
will*" (ib. fol. 402 v).   But only the believing recipient obtains this blessed
presence (fol. 318 r).   Faber here lays special emphasis upon the *personal*
presence of Christ (*praesentia salvatoris*).   The punishments inflicted upon
unworthy participants are educational (according to 1 Cor. ii. 29, ff.).
Vid. Epp. div. Pauli, Paris, 1512, fol. 97 v.   This important composition is
distinguished by its independence of tradition.   Faber pays no attention to the
Scholastic problems.   He sought to draw directly from the sources, and insists
upon the personal and bodily presence of Christ, without concerning himself
about the how.   This does indeed remind us of Luther's original position, but
without any evidence of historical connection between the two.

we receive it spiritually " (p. 13). It is eaten, not corporeally, but spiritually, by the believer, since his mind is fed from the memory of the body of Christ (p. 308, 17). This is the doctrine of the Scriptures, which the teachers of the first thousand years—when Satan was bound (Rev. 20. 2)—also advocated (p. 286). It commends itself particularly by its simplicity, as the yoke of the New Testament law is always light (p. 119). This is essentially a reproduction of Augustine, with his view polemically developed and directed against the Catholic doctrine.

5. We are thus already brought into contact with the labors of the Augustinian school upon the doctrines of the church. First of all, we note the resuscitation of the Augustinian doctrine of grace. The latter embraces predestination, which now becomes its leading thought. If predestination was with Augustine an auxiliary line of thought, it now becomes the first principle. With him it was anthropologically developed ; here, in a strictly theological way. The conception is further undesignedly combined with the Scotist conception of God : the absolute Lord of the world rules absolutely as he will, and hence the inexplicable predestination.

(a) BRADWARDINA was especially severe in his arraignment of the age upon the charge of Pelagianism. Free will, man's own strength, merit—is everything, and thus predestination is earned (vid. de causa dei,[1] i. 31, p. 602, ed. Savil.). Thus, he maintains, do his contemporaries teach. On the contrary, he has learned by experience that not merit, but grace alone, saves us (i. 35). Everything which exists and happens is made and brought to pass by God (i. 3, 32 ; ii. 29 f.). Divine foresight (*providentia*) is in reality fore-determination of the divine will (*praevolentia voluntatis*) (i. 27, p. 261). All that happens rests upon the immutable " antecedent necessity " of the divine determination (i. 25). No one can pray better than by saying : Thy will be done. This being the case, all merits fall to the ground (i. 39). Here predestination finds its place. It is " a pre-ordination of the divine will concerning a rational creature ;" and there is a two-fold (*gemina*) predestination (i. 45). All the gifts of grace are grounded upon it : " The effects of predestination are the conferring of grace in the present, justification from sin, good merits, final perseverance " (ib., p. 422). Grace is a " habitus of the soul gratuitously infused by God " (i. 23). The determinism into which this theory leads (*e. g.*, iii. 27,

---

[1] The very numerous manuscripts in which this work has been preserved, even upon the continent, attest its wide distribution.

p. 704)[1] Bradwardina rejects, maintaining free-will (ii. 1, 2 ; iii. 1). Cf. SEEBERG, PRE. iii., ed. 3, 350 ff.

(*b*) WICKLIFFE also exalts predestination to the central place in his theology. God alone is the cause that some are predestinated and others only foreknown (*praesciti*). "God necessitates individual active creatures to whatever action he desires (*ad quemlibet actum suum*), and thus some are predestinated, *i. e.*, ordained to glory after labor, and some are foreknown, *i. e.*, ordained to everlasting punishment after a miserable life " (trialog., p. 122). But human freedom is not thereby excluded : "But God cannot determine that I shall merit or demerit, unless I also determine " (de dom. div., p. 149). The predestinating grace is the deepest ground for the bestowal of grace upon the sinner. Grace is both, as *gratia increata*, the " divine volition, by which God determines to do good to a creature," and, as *gratia creata*, the infused " good quality, by which the creature is formally acceptable to God" (ib., p. 236 f.). But this quality is the condition of the " *acceptatio*, by which God accepts a man " (trial., p. 152 f.; de dom. div., p. 238). Since this divine acceptance is taken into the account, the personal nature of grace comes to some extent into view. But it is the imparting of grace which first capacitates man for meritorious conduct (dom. div., p. 241). Since God " preveniently (*praeveniendo*) incites and necessitates to meriting . . . the freedom of the will being preserved," it follows, that every creature merit is, as such, only a merit of fitness (ib., p. 226 f., 242, 249). It is evident that the Catholic conception of grace underlies also the theory of Wickliffe, but the *gratia increata*, or the free loving will of God, receives at his hands through predestination and acceptance an actual importance which does not attach to it in the popular teaching. It is the old conception, but there is yet in it an element which points the way to a new apprehension of the subject. The divine loving will is the chief thing, and the infused quality is only a means for its realization. Should it be inconceivable that other means might also be found for the accomplishment of the divine purpose?

(*c*) The Catholic doctrine of grace was not repudiated even by the more popularistic theologians of this school, such as GOCH. He combats the Pelagianism of his day, and maintains the necessity of grace for salvation, since faith and love are supernatural acts, which man cannot render without the aid (*auxilium*) of grace (dialog. c. 5, Walch, monimenta med. aev. i. 4, p. 91,

---

[1] Cf. Wickliffe's critique, De dominio div. i. 136 f., 148 ff.

94-97). The *infusio gratiae* consists in this : that God begets in us " a supernatural faculty (*facultas*) for doing supernatural acts " (c. 14, p. 162). The acts thus performed are meritorious (c. 19, p. 192 f.). The *fides formata* makes the soul acceptable to God (c. 4, p. 86). According to WESEL, the forgiveness of sins is the infusion of the *gratia gratum faciens* (adv. indulg. 18, in Walch, monim. med. aev. ii. 1, p. 126). Likewise WESSEL : " Concerning justification it is evident enough, because that sins be taken away is nothing else than to have justifying love, which he who does not have remains in sin. In order, therefore, that he may take away sin, it is necessary to infuse righteousness " (de magnitud. passionis, c. 7, opp. Groning, 1614, p. 466). God accepts the sinner on account of faith, faith being regarded as including love : " And since faith is the source of love, therefore it is also accepted on account of its offspring " (c. 45, p. 550). That is, God will bestow upon the believer the righteousness secured through the satisfaction rendered by Christ (ib. p. 551). " Therefore neither our faith . . . nor the sacrifice of Christ, but the determination of God accepting the sacrifice of Christ, and through Christ accepting the sacrifices of Christians, is our righteousness " (c. 44, p. 549). These are all medieval ideas. As long as they are not abandoned, all the admirable attempts to overthrow the monastic ideal which are found, *e. g.*, in Goch, and the idea of evangelical liberty (which grace does not destroy, but completes) which is not to be resigned in favor of any vow, as though without the latter there can be no " perfection of Christian life " (dial. c. 7, p. 109 ff.; 11, p. 144 ; 12, p. 155 ; 9, p. 125 ff.)—are but a beating of the air. The same must be said of the emphasis laid upon the rights of property : " The proprietorship of law may consist with the highest evangelical perfection ; the proprietorship of love is simply inadmissible and forbidden to all Christians through the precept of love (c. 22, p. 234). But in these thoughts there breathes the atmosphere of a new era. The Holy Scriptures, which in these circles, as in the church in general, are recognized as the highest authority (vid. esp. Goch, Epistola apologetica, in Walch, monim. med. aev. ii. 1, p. 4 ff., 10, 11) begin to be employed as a critical standard, by which not only the laws of the state (p. 183 f.), but the ordinances and ideals of the church as well, are measured.

6. This leads us a step further, to the criticism of the Sacrament of Repentance and Indulgences. " There are two principal sacraments, in which the church is being ruined, viz., the sacrament of the eucharist and the sacrament of repentance " (Wickliffe, De euch. et poenit., in Loserth's edition of De

14

eccl., p. 329). Wickliffe denies the necessity of the sacramental confession, which does not harmonize with the " liberty of the law of the Lord " (ib., p. 331 ff., 341). He combats indulgences most vigorously as a scandalous traffic and blasphemous presumption of the pope (ib., p. 340 ; trialog. iv. 32, p. 357 ff. Cf. Huss, Quaestio disputata . . . de indulgentiis, opp. Norimb. 1558, i. 174 ff.). WESEL teaches that God alone forgives the eternal penalties of sin, which he does by the infusion of grace. To the priest belongs only a sacramental ministration (*ministerium*). There exists a " covenant established with priests " (adv. indulg. 23, 26, 27, 28 ; in Walch, monim. med. aev. ii. 1). Since now God himself imposes temporal penalties for sin in this life, it is clear that indulgences have no ground to rest upon. They would do away with purgatory altogether (ib. 47). The pope can remit only the penalties which men have imposed (34). The doctrine of indulgences has the Scriptures arrayed against it ; they are only " pious frauds upon believers " (50). WESSEL is still more severe. Under his hand, the whole sacrament of repentance falls to pieces. The pope can only outwardly separate any person from the church ; and when he does so, his action has no direct significance for the inner life (de sacr. poenit., opp. p. 772 f., 776, 781). This sacrament has really nothing to do with the matter. God grants the spirit of love, and with it contrition. This is already a work of infused grace : " The contrite (is) righteous before the sacrament " (p. 790).[1] " Repentance, if it be a sacrament, does not need contrition " (ib.). Similarly, it is God alone who forgives sin ; the priest has no judicial power in administering absolution (p. 794 f.). Should God, who remits the eternal penalties, not forgive also the temporal (p. 798)? And if he does not do so, he is but exercising the educational discipline of a father (ib.). Thus the satisfaction to be rendered by good works also falls to the ground. Grace gives peace. What is the benefit of the dismissal " in peace " and the assurance of the forgiveness of sins, if the sinner still remains subject to the severest penalties (p. 800)? It is not a question of a contrite body, but of a contrite heart (p. 801). Satisfaction, strictly interpreted, ends in a blasphemy ; for Christ did his work completely. We receive forgiveness from grace alone, and do not have to contribute anything by works of satisfaction (p. 802).[2] Indulgences can accordingly be understood only as remitting ecclesiastical

---

[1] Cf. my remarks, supra, p. 135 f.

[2] Vid., on the other hand, the view discussed, supra, p. 199.

penalties (p. 781).[1]   The whole theory is overthrown ; but the infused grace still remains.

7. Finally, we must notice the conception of the Church, especially in WICKLIFFE (De eccl., ed. Loserth) and HUSS (De eccl., opp. i. Norimb. 1558).   (*a*) In harmony with the idea of predestination, the church is here defined as the *congregatio omnium predestinatorum*, whether the latter belong to the past, the present, or the future—whether they be men or angels, or even Jews and heathen (Wickliffe, p. 2 f., 5, 70, 409.   Huss, fol. 196 v, 201 r).   The foreknown (*praesciti*) do not belong to the church as thus conceived.   They are not *of* the church, although they are empirically *in* the church : they no more belong to the church than filth and foul humors belong to the body (Huss, fol. 199 v).   Whether anyone really belongs to the church, *i. e.*, is predestinated, can only be judged with probability from his life (Wickliffe, trial., p. 325.   Huss, fol. 198 v).   In the sense of the assembly of the predestinated, the church is an object of faith, since it may be thus brought under the category of Heb. 11. 1 (Wickliffe, eccl., p. 409.   Huss, fol. 204 v, 206 v).   In proportion as Wickliffe's opposition to the accepted doctrines spread, this conception of the church, combined with the emphasizing of the exclusive authority of the "law of Christ," became the critical canon.   The pope errs, when he has the Scriptures against him (eccl., p. 563 f.).   So far from being the head of the church, it is even open to question whether he is a member of the church (p. 464.)   Therefore, no man's salvation can depend upon him (p. 33); and his excommunication can exclude no one from the true church (p. 72).   (*b*) WESEL and WESSEL base their criticism upon other grounds.   Wesel declares that the hierarchical order of the church is "derived from paganism and forbidden by the word of Christ" (adv. indulg. 42).   In the church universal the *church of Christ* exists as a part; and only the latter is holy and spotless (ib. 52 f.).   According to Wessel, the spiritual authority rests upon a compact (de potest. ecclesiastica, opp., p. 752).   But Christians, as rational beings, must criticize their leaders, and not blindly follow them (p. 753).   The latter are "not therefore to be heard simply on account of their pastoral authority" (p. 755).   "A currupt prelate desires the obedience of his subjects, in order that he may rule them at will" (p. 757).   False teachers are not to be followed (p. 762 f.).   If the prelates violate the compact, not observing the law

---

[1] Vid. also the discussion of the sacrament of repentance in MARSILIUS, Defensor pacis, ii. 6, p. 205 f.   Goldast.

as it applies to them, then is the other party, *i. e.*, the subjects, free from every obligation. Such prelates must be deposed. If they are still tolerated, it is only as abandoned women are tolerated in the cities for fear of other evils (p. 765 f.). It is not the clerical office which establishes the unity of the church, but its one Head, the one divine truth,[1] and the faith and love of its members (767, de poenit., p. 778-781). In this communion the spirit of love is infused (cf. supra, p. 209). This is the "*communio sanctorum:*" "All saints have fellowship (*communicant*) in true, essential unity: as many as cling to Christ with one faith, one love; under whatsoever prelates they live; however the latter may ambitiously contend or dissent or err, even though they be heretics; in whatever localities in space; separated by whatever intervals of years; and this is that *communio*, of which we speak in the Creed: I believe in the communion of saints" (de comm. sanct., p. 809). From this spiritual communion no declaration of the church can sever (de poenit., p. 782). The criticism of these men does not extend any further than that of Marsilius and Occam (p. 167); but it attests the wide distribution of the critical temper. It was aided by the fact that the church was coming to be regarded ever more clearly and positively as a spiritual body. The *communio sanctorum*, the *congregatio predestinatorum*,—such is its essential character. The place for its discussion is under the Creed, not under canon law. The forms of the latter are either to be repudiated, or are of temporary value, in the course of historical development. Cf. SEEBERG, Begr. d. Kirche, i. 65-77. GOTTSCHICK, Ztschr. f. KG. viii. 357 ff. BUDDENSIEG, Joh. Wiclif, 1885, p. 157 ff. WIEGAND, Quid de eccl. notione Wicl. docuerit? 1891, p. 11 ff., 92 ff.

§ 64. *The Renaissance and Humanism in Their Significance for the History of Doctrines.*

LITERATURE. J. BURCKHARDT, Die Kultur der Renaiss. in Ital. 4. A., 1885. GEIGER, Renaiss. u. Humanism., 1882. VOIGT, Die Wiederbelebung des klass. Altertums, 2 vols., 2 A, 1880 f. VAHLEN, Lorenzo Valla, 1870. GEIGER, Reuchlin, 1871. VON BEZOLD, K. Celtis in Hist. Ztschr., 1883, 1 ff., 193 ff. DREWS, Pirkheimer's Stellung z. Ref., 1887. STICHART, Erasmus, seine Stellung z. Kirche, etc., 1870. SEEBOHM, The Oxford Reformers, ed. 2, 1869. LEZIUS, Zur Char. d. rel. Standpunktes d. Erasm., 1895. KAMPSCHULTE, Die Univ. Erfurt in ihrem Verh. z. Humanism. u. z. Ref., 2 vols., 1858. MAURENBRECHER, Gesch. d. Kath. Ref. i. 119 ff., 349 ff.

---

[1] " For we believe in God—not in the Catholic church, not in a Latin council, not in the pope," p. 779. " Since therefore it is not obligatory to believe man, neither will it be obligatory to believe the pope," p. 780.

DILTHEY, Archiv. f. Gesch. d. Philos., 1891, 604 ff.; 1892, 337 ff. K. MÜLLER, KG. ii. 167 ff. p. 228 A. Z. 1 v.

1. The spiritual unrest of the fourteenth and fifteenth centuries constituted the starting-point for a revolution in the whole conception of the universe and in the civilization of the world. The latter was accomplished beneath the banner of Individualism. The circle of interest extended beyond the limits of the church and her dogmas. The individual emerges. A man is something more than a member of the ecclesiastical or civil corporation, for he is himself a separate something. The world is looked upon with other eyes—it is not lying in wickedness. Nature and history, man in himself and in his association with his fellows, the state and society at large—are seen in a new light. New criteria are applied: the independence of the spiritual and political spheres, individual character, personal responsibility and honor. In proportion as this spirit was propagated must ensue alienation from the existing order and criticism of it; or, at least, the best men had neither time nor inclination to pursue that which was officially regarded as the best. The reformation of St. Francis, the spread of the Mystic type of piety, the criticism indulged in by Duns and the Nominalists, the revived interest in literature and art (Dante, Petrarch, Boccaccio), and the political and social conditions, combined to create a new spiritual atmosphere. But the most powerful factor in this combination was antiquity. The treasures of the ancient world were brought to light and comprehended. In cultivated circles, especially in Italy, antiquity assumed the leadership and, for not a few, took the place of the church. Its treasures were studied with an indescribable enthusiasm.[1] The ancient world appeared to furnish the ideal of life and culture.

2. Such a profound movement could not but prove highly significant for the History of Doctrines. This is true in a general way, in consequence of the enlarging of the intellectual horizon, the increased study of languages, the introduction of the historic method, and of historico-philological criticism—the evidence adduced by LORENZO VALLA of the spurious character of the Areopagite, the non-apostolic[2] composition of the Creed, and the forging of the *Donatio Constantini*, suggesting what might be expected from the last-named source. To these influences must be added especially the new method of discussion modeled after the ancient patterns. The method of questions, with the *pro*

---

[1] Cf. the account of the body of a young girl of ancient Rome found in 1485 : "She was beautiful beyond all that can be said or written."

[2] Cf. THIEME, Aus d. Gesch. d. apostolicums, 1893, p. 4 ff.

and *contra*, followed by the "resolutions," yields to the simple presentation required by " reason and sound sense." The technical Latin of the Middle Ages makes way for the toilfully-won language of the classic authors, *i. e.*, the Latin is becoming a dead language. The Italians, for the most part, avoided theology ; but Humanistic circles in England (Colet, † 1519, and Thomas More, † 1535) and Germany (especially Reuchlin, † 1522, and Erasmus, † 1536) showed a different disposition. The traditional theology of the Scholastics at least was rejected, although some thoughtful minds still recognized its value : " Scotus and his like are useful for study (*ad rerum cognitionem*), but useless for speech " (*dicendum*) (Erasm., ratio concionandi. ii. opp. Ludg. Bat. 1704, v. 857). The *scholastica dogmata* are not articles of faith (Erasm., ratio verae theol., opp. v. 90). The Scriptures and the Church Fathers are the true authorities. " We may therefore philosophize upon the sacred writings in so far as our industry leads us to the conclusions which Paul has recorded. But those who have not fixed for themselves this limit, but choose this profession in order that they may bring forth any kind of paradoxes or novelties by which they may win the admiration of the populace, who are always ready to admire insipid things, are vanity-mongers (*mataeologi*), not theologians. . . . Now into the sacred assemblies themselves this ostentation has penetrated. . . . I see the simple multitude panting and hanging eagerly upon the lips of the orator, expecting food for their souls, desiring to learn how they may return better to their homes, and there some theologaster . . . ventilates some frigid and perplexing question from Scotus or Occam " (ib. v. 135 f.). " I had rather be a pious theologian with Chrysostom than an invincible one with Scotus " (ib. 137). " Scotus seems to have given these men such great confidence that, without having even read the sacred writings, they yet think themselves unlimited theologians" (enchiridion, 2, opp. v. 8). Erasmus, therefore, published not only the New Testament in Greek (A. D. 1516), but also the works of Jerome, Cyprian,[1] Hilary, Irenæus, Ambrose, Augustine, Chrysostom, and Origen. It was the aim to liberate theology from dogmatics, and introduce a practical, ethical—undogmatic—Christianity. We cannot fail to note here a certain flavor of Augustinian piety, however unwilling the leaders of the movement were to reproduce the entire Augustine. At this point the efforts of the theologians of a practical turn, whether Augustinians or Mystics, and those of the pious Humanists

---

[1] Cf. Lezius, Der Verf. d. pseudocypr. Traktates de duplici martyrio, Neue Jarbb. f. deutsche Theol., 1894.

coalesced.   In this sense, Humanism possesses a "pre-reformatory" character.   But, earnestly as the Humanists desired to
reform the church, they yet shrunk with terror from the Reformation and the "tumult" it occasioned.   Erasmus frequently
thus expressed himself as the movement assumed a serious
form.   The tragedy of his life is thus explained.   He was
prevented by internal and external motives from pressing forward as the new and great agitation surged about him, and he
could not retreat.[1]   It was his fate, like Moses, to die in the land
of Moab.[2]

3.   Consequently, no positively influential ideas emanated from
Humanistic circles.   Despite all their criticism of the church and
its doctrines,   despite their exaltation of worldly delights—
which too often, especially in Italy, led to brutal egotism and
sordid self-indulgence—the old religious ideas maintained their
sway, and in times of distress, in life or in death, the heart turned
to them for comfort.   This was seen in the case of the leaders
of the movement themselves.   "Lived like heathens and died
like Christians—was applicable to very many of the representatives of the new classical culture" (Bezold, l. c., p. 212).   We
may study the same phenomenon in Erasmus.   There was very
much of the "modern man" about him, but yet he remained,
in his unmarried and unsettled life, a monk of the higher order.
And even his religious ideas, particularly in the pre-reformation
period, do not rise beyond the religious conceptions of the Middle
Ages.   It is, to state it briefly, the piety of the *Imitatio Christi*
which he commends.   "Let this be thy . . . rule : set Christ
before thee as the sole centre (*scopus*) of thy whole life, to whom
alone thou mayest bring all thy studies, all thine efforts, all thy
leisure and thy business.   But I think Christ to be not an empty
word, but nothing else than love, simplicity, patience, purity, in
short, everything which he taught. . . . To Christ tends everyone who is lifted to virtue alone " (enchir. 4, p. 25).   But the
History of Doctrines has no occasion to attempt a portrayal of
the theology of Erasmus,[3] nor that of his friend, COLET, who so

---

[1] Cf. esp. the attractive sketch of LEZIUS, Zur Char. . . . d. Erasm., p. 46 ff.
[2] Vid. Luther's opinion of him in Köstlin, Luther, i., ed. 4, 688 f.
[3] Upon particular points Erasmus furnishes much that is of importance; *e. g.*,
his remark as to the gradations of authority in the books of the New Testament (opp. v. 92, 1049); the Bible written under dictation of the Holy Spirit
(v. 274); his criticism of the *homousios* (v. 1090) and of the sacrament of
repentance (ib. 167, 944, 1046); his legal conception of Sabbath observance
(v. 1190 f.); his symbolic view of the Lord's Supper (iii. 521 f., 892 ff., 1028,
1891 ; v. 1019); his definition of faith as *fiduciam, collocare in deo* (v. 105,
777, 798, 1079, 1147, 1166 et passim).   We do not yet possess a detailed
presentation of his views.   Vid. STICHART, and esp. LEZIUS.

earnestly sought to understand the writings of St. Paul.[1] The fundamental ideas are always the same. Christ came down from heaven in order to teach us to despise the world and its possessions, and practice peace, love, and harmony, and to confirm this teaching by his example. "For his life is a doctrine excelling all human (doctrine)" (*Beatus Rhenanus* upon Zwingli, opp. vii. 58). But to this is to be added faith in the *evangelical doctrine*, which is laid down in the Scriptures, the Apostles' Creed, and the Fathers (Erasm. v. 8, 1162, 162 ; i. 653).

Such is the dogmatic history of the Middle Ages. At the first glance it may be thought that doctrinal development was carried backward by more than a thousand years. The declarations of Scripture, the Apostles' Creed, the Fathers, and the dogmas of the ancient church, appear to be all that remain in the shiftings of history. There were extended circles in which this was felt to be the case. But history never simply turns backward. Other forces were in the field, and they, too, were alive, and have perpetuated their vitality to the present day. There was a complicated play of forces ; even the ancient and despised was still a force to be reckoned with. We must differentiate three groups in the closing period of the Middle Ages, which were capable of various combinations. (1) The Popular Catholicism, the official ecclesiasticism. It does not scorn the help of the "Moderns" (*i. e.*, Nominalists), but it begins to rely upon the "old theology" of the thirteenth century. (2) The "negative," critical theology of the Nominalists. They preserved their claim to recognition by their theory of the *fides implicita*. (3) The Mystic, Augustinian, and Humanistic tendencies. To them the future seemed assured, for they sought to serve the cause of reform and progress. Which of these ten-

---

[1] His Opuscula theologica, ed. Lupton, London, 1876, lies before me. Particularly in his commentary upon Romans, his effort to be Pauline is noticeable. He strongly emphasizes the *justitia fidei sola* (p. 209). "By this sole faith of Christ one enters the kingdom of heaven ; believers are righteous ; the faith of Christ is righteousness" (p. 230), and this gratuitously : "through grace men believe, and through grace believers are justified " (p. 251). The divine will alone is the ground of justification (p. 254). But faith is to be more precisely defined as : "The faith of Christ with imitation and representation of him " (p. 241, 272), or "Justifying faith imports in its signification imitation of Christ and co-operation with him " (p. 248). In harmony with this must be understood the declaration : "By this (*i. e.*, faith) believers are justified, so that they may do well in love. . . . Believers, if they imitate Christ Jesus, God will crown this righteousness" (p. 261 f.; cf. p. 186: "made righteous (*facti justi*) by God, that we may live righteously "). Colet thus taught essentially as did Thomas (supra, p. 120). God infuses grace into the sinner, which produces : first, faith, and then love and good works. Further than this, he, like Erasmus, did not attach himself to any particular scholastic theory.

dencies—and with what combinations and concessions—would have gained the victory, if no new element had been introduced? It will not be without profit to reflect upon the problem. The future did actually produce the humanistic Nominalism of the Socinians, the Augustinianism of the Jansenists, the Thomism of the Moderns. But a fourth spiritual power appeared amid the play of forces—the Gospel, or the Reformation. This introduced a new element. Old problems were pushed aside, and the questions pressing for solution assumed a different form.

BOOK III.

FURTHER DEVELOPMENT OF DOCTRINE THROUGH THE REFORMATION AND FIXATION OF THE DOCTRINES OF CATHOLICISM.

BOOK III.

PART I.

GENESIS OF PROTESTANT DOCTRINE.

CHAPTER I.

THE VIEWS OF LUTHER.

§ 65. *Luther's Place in the History of Doctrines.*

LITERATURE. The works of Luther are cited in the following pages from the Weimar edition (= W) and from the first issue of the Erlangen edition (German Works = E); de W. = De Wette, Luther's Briefe, 6 vols., 1825 ff.; opp. ex. = Opera Exegetica and var. arg. = Varii Argumenti—both of the Erlangen edition; Gal. = the large Commentary upon Galatians in the same edition. Cf. KÖSTLIN, M. Luther, 2 vols., 5th edition by Kawerau, 1903. KOLDE, M. L., 2 vols., 1883 ff. KÖSTLIN, Luther's Theologie, 2 vols., 1863, 2d ed., 1901. TH. HARNACK, Luther's Theologie, 1862-86, 2d issue, 1901. LOMMATSCH, Luther's Lehre v. eth. rel. Standp. aus, 1879. LUTHARDT, Die Ethik Luther's, 2d edition, 1875. PLITT, Einleitung in d. Augustana, i., 1868. MÖLLER-KAWERAU, KG. iii., 1894. RITSCHL, Rechtf. u. Vers. i. 141 ff. THOMASIUS, DG. ii., ed. 2, 330 ff. LOOFS, DG., ed. 3, 345 ff. HARNACK, DG. iii., ed. 3, 726 ff.; cf. KÜBEL, Neue kirchl. Ztschr., 1891, 13 ff. HERING, Die Mystik Luther's im Zusammenhang s. Theol., 1879. LIPSIUS, Luther's Lehre v. d. Busse, 1892. THIEME, Die sittl. Triebkraft des Glaubens, 1895. SCHÄFER, L. als Kirchenhistoriker, 1897.

1. In the crisis periods of history there is commonly no lack of vigorous thought and great possibilities. There were now many possibilities in view. But which of these, if achieved, could have solved the problems of the great crisis now threatening the doctrinal structure of the church, as well as the moral and social life of the world? Altogether, they did not extend in scope beyond the horizon of medieval piety. But in the midst of the sultry calm and dark forebodings of those days appeared a man who had something practical to propose in the face of all the vague possibilities. He trod like a giant through his age, tramping to earth what a thousand years had held in veneration; but everywhere new life blossomed in his footsteps. It was the wonder-worker of modern times, MARTIN LUTHER (b. A. D. 1483). He was a genius without parallel, and yet his was a "simple soul." He possessed the wonderful faculty of realizing in the clear depths of his own experience all the emotions and needs of his age. "Yet he possessed" also, "in his

religious genius, a unique and peculiar energy which carried his contemporaries along, at least for some distance, in his path as by a power beyond and higher than their own.   He was born to deal with men and govern them " (DILTHEY, Archiv f. Gesch. d. Philos. v. 356 f.).   His power lay in his faith, which he dis-covered amid the stress of dark and terrifying spiritual struggles. The firm assurance of evangelical faith which he had himself won, he proclaimed to his age with the amazing vividness which only personal experience can give, with the force and versatility of a true religious genius, and with the holy passion of a prophet. Looking back upon his life, he himself declares : " God led me on like a horse whose eyes have been blind-folded that he may not see those who are rushing toward him," and " that a good work should seldom be undertaken or accomplished through wisdom or foresight—everything must be accomplished in the midst of error or ignorance " (E. 57, 31 f.).   Men listened to him.   He led them back from scholastic speculations to the firm ground of historical revelation, from dogma. to faith.   The Reformation, so longed talked of, here became a reality, and in a way which no one had anticipated.   And only gradually has the Christian world learned to understand clearly its controlling principles, to draw the inevitable conclusions and estimate it correctly from a critical point of view, casting aside the peculiar and sometimes incongruous wrappings that have partly concealed its true character.   It would be idle to wish that the great age of the Reformers might itself have wrought out to a logical conclusion all that was involved in the new principles.

2. It is very significant, that the peculiar religious experiences of Luther in the cloister fall within the sphere of the sacrament of repentance and the overvaluation of the monastic life.   The controlling element in the penitential praxis was not for him attrition, but contrition.[1] Luther sought to force himself to con-trition by meditating upon his sins.   He was thus led to " bung-ling work and doll-sins " indeed ; but he also discovered, as the chief source of trouble, sin in the sense of sinfulness.   As his own contrition never reached the required depth, so, on the other hand, absolution—the formula for which makes forgive-ness dependent upon the " contrition of the heart, the good works which thou hast done from love of Christ " (KÖSTLIN, M. Luth. i. 5, 64)—brought him no certainty of the forgiveness of his sins.   The—genuinely Catholic—suggestion, that it was his

[1] In theory, contrition alone was generally spoken of, but in practice attri-tion alone was usually thought of, as the " beginning of penitence " (E. 25, 130).   But this lightening of the burden permitted by the dogmatics of the age, Luther would not allow to himself.

duty to believe the forgiveness of sins, pointed him in a new
direction. He learned that not separate acts, but love to
righteousness and to God, constitute the criterion of true
repentance (Staupitz). From this time onward, Luther fell
more and more under the influence of Augustine and Mysticism.
It is perhaps the greatest work of Augustine, that he prepared
the way in following which this, his greatest son, found Paul.
Gradually Luther is led in his inmost experience into the very
heart of scriptural ideas, and such terms as *grace* and *righteousness* receive a new meaning.

3. There meets us, hence, in the very first connected utterances
of Luther (§ 66), an entirely new apprehension of religious truth.
The differences between the "first form" and the later forms
of Luther's theology are commonly very much exaggerated.   If
we consider the technical terminology, there is indeed a manifest difference ; but if we have in view the actual content and
logical results of his ideas, we can scarcely reach any other conclusion than that Luther had before A. D. 1517 already grasped
the conceptions and attained the points of view which gave
character to his life-work.   This can be traced, as will be done
in the following pages, in the peculiar construction of nearly all
the theological definitions of the later Luther.   But it is most
important of all to observe that he, at the very beginning of his
career, makes practical application of his new idea of faith ; for
the leverage of Luther's reformatory principle lies, not in justification, nor in a new theory of grace, but in the conviction that
faith is the *form* of true religion.   "He who believes, has"
(*e. g.*, E. 27, 180).   But this central conviction dominates his
very first writings, and it is instructive to observe what a transforming influence it exerted upon the theological views there
presented (vid. sub).   It will be advisable, nevertheless, to
present separately the first utterances of his new thoughts, as
their historical relations can thus be more clearly seen.

4. Luther, it is well known, had pursued a thorough course of
Scholastic study, making himself familiar particularly with the
Lombard, Occam, D'Ailli, and Biel.   This schooling is often
apparent in the earlier period (*e. g.*, W. 1. 367 ff.).   But the influence of these studies was a permanent one.   He had imbibed the
outline and organization of the theological ideas of Scholasticism,
and they remained as the points of connection in his theological
thinking.   In the most of his definitions, the form of construction can be understood only if we bear this fact in mind.[1]   Yet

---

[1] Luther was accurately acquainted with the separate Scholastic writers, as
may be seen from his writings during the indulgence controversy—*e. g.*, his
opinion of Duns, W. 2. 403, and of Occam, 6. 183.   E. 24. 347 : "Occam,

Luther was confessedly a passionate opponent of Scholasticism, as well as of Aristotle. "Thomas wrote many heretical things, and is the cause of the dominance of Aristotle, the devastator of pious doctrine" (W. 8. 127). But the motive which impelled him in this opposition was different from that which inspired the hounding of the Scholastics by the Humanists. His criticism was not directed primarily against the formal defects of the system. He regards the teachings of Biel as good, except upon the topics of grace, love, hope, faith, and virtue (De W. 1. 34); at a later date, he speaks approvingly of the Lombard, with the exception that what he has said of faith and justification is "too thin and weak" (E. 25. 258).[1] This is the ground of Luther's opposition: "That carnalizer of consciences, *theologistria*," with its doctrines of free-will, merit, righteousness, and works, directs to a false way of salvation, which leads only to doubt and despair: "I lost Christ there; now I have found him in Paul" (W.·2. 401, 414, 503, 447). It destroys the gospel (W. 2. 416, 465) and opposes "sacred theology" (ib. 416). It mixes Scripture and philosophy (E. 63. 162).[2] "Scholastic theology is nothing else than ignorance of the truth and scandal placed side by side with Scripture" (W. 8. 127).[3] Many have assailed the formalism of Scholasticism; Luther attacked its substance, and he overthrew it.

5. Luther's decisive religious experiences were gained in connection with the sacrament of repentance, under the stress of a false conception of repentance for which he struggled to find a substitute. This was the starting-point from which his fundamental religious ideas were developed. The latter may, therefore, be comprehended under the conception of *Evangelical Repentance, constituting a Substitute for the observance of the Sacrament of Repentance.* This is the point of view from which the work of Luther must be considered in the History of Doctrines.

---

my dear Master;" Scotus and Occam are "the best two." He himself counts himself among the *Moderni*, or Nominalists, W. 9. 9; cf. 1. 226 and op. var. arg. 5. 137 : *sum Occanicae factionis.* As to his studies, see Glosses upon the Lombard, W. 9. 28 ff.; and in the Mystics, upon Tauler, ib. 97 ff.

[1] W. 1. 391 : "Not that I entirely condemn them (the Scholastics), for they have done their part." Cf. especially the remarkable contrasting of the problems of the Scholastic and the Evangelical theology, E. 24. 372 ff.

[2] " . . . Origen, who soured and spoiled the Scriptures by philosophy and reason, as with us the universities have hitherto done."

[3] With this agrees Luther's opinion of Aristotle : "the constructor of words, the deluder of minds" (W. i. 612). In addition to his Moralism, he charges upon him, that his God does not act mightily in the government of the world, but "governs the world blinkingly, as a woman rocks her child in the dark" (E. 10. 321 ; 7. 239 ; W. 6. 457 f.). Vid. NITZSCH, Luth. and Arist., Kiel, 1893.

All his ideas in regard to penitence and faith, faith and works, sin and grace, law and gospel, together with his new ideal of life, constitute a complex of religious conceptions which were developed under the pressure of and in opposition to the sacrament of repentance.[1] This brings his work, however, into the very centre of the current of religious development in the West. The controlling thought in the latter is always the salvation of souls (*salus animarum*) (Vol. I., p. 192 f., 199). Repentance, forgiveness, new life were, hence, the inspiration of all conflicts and schisms from the days of Calixtus to the Fanatics of the Reformation era. One ideal runs through all these movements : the congregation of *saints*. The great church thought of the holiness of her ordinances, the *opus operatum*. To this her critics had nothing to oppose, in the last analysis, but human works, the *opera operantis*—not holiness and righteousness. In the conception of the righteousness of faith, Luther found the solution of the problem. Everything comes to the sinner from God ; but it becomes his only when it begets in him a powerful, glowing, vital experience. Yet the heart does not place its confidence in this experience in so far as it is its own ; but only in so far as it comes from God. This is now both entirely objective and entirely subjective. It is broad enough to embrace all that was right in the position of the church as against the schismatics, and all that was right in the contentions of the latter against the church.[2]

6. We cannot here attempt a review of the reformatory work of Luther. A few observations must suffice. The question of the authority of the church forced itself upon his attention already in the indulgence controversy.[3] The Leipzig Disputation (A. D. 1519) brings Luther to the conviction that the pope and

---

[1] Melanchthon recognizes this in Corp. Ref., xi, 728 : Luther makes evident the true and necessary doctrine ; for that there was densest darkness upon the doctrine of repentance is manifest. Discussing these things, he shows what is true repentance. Cf. v. 568 ; vi. 90 f.; i. 350 ff.; viii. 311.

[2] Regarded from the viewpoint of the medieval church, the Reformation may be considered as the last of the schisms in the Western church. But it must, in that case, be freely acknowledged that it is profoundly and entirely different from all schismatic movements.

[3] Vid., besides, the 95 Theses : Disputat. pro declarat. virtutis indulgent.; Ein sermon v. ablass u. gnade, 1517 ; Asterisci ; Sermo de poenit. Eine freiheit des sermons päpstl. ablass u. gnaden belangend ; Resolutiones disputationum de indulg. virtute ; sermo de virtute excommunicat. (these in W. 1). Eine kurze unterweisung, wie man beichten soll, 1518. Unterricht auf. etl. artikel ; sermo de duplici justitia ; Ein sermon vom sakr. d. busse, 1519 (W. 2). Confitendi ratio, 1520 (W. 3). Cf. esp. for this period the Disputat. c. scholast. theol., 1517. The Heidelberg Theses, 1517 (W. 1), the small commentary upon Galatians, 1519 (W. 2). Responsio ad libr. Ambros. Catharini, 1519 (opp. v. a. 5).

15

councils may err, and that the Scriptures are the only authorized authority in the church.[1] The outward barriers which had hitherto restrained Luther's spirit are thereby broken down. The eyes of men of culture and of all friends of reform are now turned upon him. He is recognized as a prophet. His cause is no longer a theological tournament ; it is the cause of the people. Thus, stimulated and sustained by the longings and hopes of his people, he enters the greatest year of his life, 1520. With wonderful energy he wields the sword and plies the trowel. The old theory of the sacraments is demolished ; there is a new conception of the church ; the new ideal of Christian life appears ; good works are understood in the evangelical sense ; and the program of practical reformation is clearly indicated.[2] Then follows the fiery trial at Worms, the test of sincerity at the Wartburg and in face of the fanaticism[3] at Wittenberg. Political circumstances then open the way for the development of evangelical church life[4] and the spread of the gospel. But to this period of development belong also separations (1524-25). The powerful movement for reform had quickened into new life the other reformatory tendencies of the age, and it seemed as though they might be combined in one current with it. Humanists, Mystics, and social reformers stretch out their hands to Luther. And he recognizes the " other spirit " in them and repels them.[5] It is among the greatest acts of his life. He thereby lost his unparalleled popularity. He, whom nothing had hitherto been able to withstand, was now compelled to realize the inexorable limitations which beset all human efforts. To this was added the alarming revela-

---

[1] Ad dialog. Silv. Prierat. de potest. papae, 1518 (W. 1). Acta Augustana, 1518. Disputat. et excusat. adv. criminationes Ioh. Eck. Resolut. Lutheriana super proposit. sua XIII.; the proceedings of the Disputation at Leipzig (W. 2).

[2] Von den guten Werken ; vom Papstt. z. Rom wider den hochberümten Romanisten z. Lpz.; Ein sermon v. N. T. d. i. von der h. Messe ; an den christl. Adel deutscher Nation von des christl. Standes Besserung ; De captivit. babyl.; Wider die Bulle des Endchristes (W. 6). Also Von der Freiheit eines Christenmenschen (E. 27 and op. v. a.), all in 1520. In 1519 : Ein sermon v. d. hochw. Sakr. der Taufe ; Ein sermon v. d. hochw. Sakr. des h. hochw. Leichnams Christi (W. 2). Vid. also Themata de votis ; Vom Misbrauch der Messe ; De votis monasticis, 1521 (W. 8); An die Herren deutschen Ordens, 1523 E. 29).

[3] Vid. the Eight Sermons, 1523 (E. 28).

[4] E. g., Ordnung eines gemeinen Kastens ; Von d. Ordnung des Gottesdienstes, Taufbüchlein, 1523. Deutsche Messe, 1526 (E. 22). Traubüchlein (E. 23); the two catechisms, 1529, etc.

[5] De servo arbitrio, 1525 (op. v. a. 7); Wider d. himml. Propheten, 1524-25 (E. 29). Ermanung zum Frieden ; Wider d. mörderischen u. räuberischen Rotten der Bauern ; Ein Sendbrief v. dem harten Büchlein wider die Bauern, 1525 (E. 24).

tions of the church visitations. From this time forward a certain austerity of temper is noticeable in the Reformer. Severe utterances touching the "coarse, common man" and "the full and foolish Germans" now belong to his constant repertoire.[1] There is a lowering also of his ecclesiastical ideals.[2] But he remains true to himself and the gospel, even against Zwingli.[3] The evangelical views are now summarized in the Augsburg Confession.

The most wonderful thing in Luther was that his opponents could never confuse him nor force any concessions from him. On the contrary, every obstacle which he met but served to open up new treasures from the deep mine of his fundamental religious idea ; as, in opposition to the Fanatics, he defined more accurately the significance of the means of grace, and against Erasmus maintained salvation by grace alone.

We have thus indicated the points of view from which the reformatory ideas of Luther will be presented in the following pages. One of the most important tasks of the History of Doctrines is thus set before us. For whether we regard Luther as the destroyer of the foundations of the old dogma, or as the originator of new dogmas, it is evident that either opinion can be sustained only by a thoroughgoing study of his teachings. Above all is it the duty of those who extend the scope of the History of Doctrines into the age of Protestantism to furnish a complete portraiture of Luther. It is astonishing to find in some Protestant works upon the subject lengthy discussions of Augustine, Thomas, etc., but only a short sketch of Luther.[4] This is out of all due proportion, whether we regard the matter from the standpoint of medieval doctrinal development or in the light of the Protestant Confessions.

§ 66. *Doctrinal Views of Luther Before the Period of His Reformatory Activity.*

LITERATURE. Expositions of the Psalms, with work upon the Penitential Psalms, lectures upon Judges, sermons and tracts to A. D. 1517 in Weimar edition, vols. i., iii., iv. Cf. DIECKHOFF, L. Lehre in ihrer ersten Gestalt, 1887.

[1] Cf., *e. g.*, E. 24. 305, 309; 22. 255, 181, 194 ; 4. 405 ; also the complaints of the great change of sentiment, 14. 225 f., 233 ; 47. 14 f., 210 ff.; 48. 375.
[2] Cf. KOLDE, Ztschr. f. Kirchengesch. xiii. 552 ff.
[3] Wider die himml. Propheten u. Bildern u. Sakr. 1524-25 (E. 29); letter to the Strassburgers, 1524 (De W. 2. 574 ff.); Vorwort z. Syngramma suevicum, 1526 (E. 65. 180 ff.); sermon v. Sakr., 1526 (E. 29); Das diese Worte, Das ist mein Leib ; noch feste stehen, 1527 ; Bekenntnis v. Abendmal Christi, 1528 (E. 30); Kurzes Bekenntnis v. h. Sakr. 1545 (E. 32).
[4] A praiseworthy exception is found in the Leitfaden of LOOFS.

1. The high regard for the Scriptures, which is already so evident in Luther, is scarcely more pronounced than was usual in the writers of the later Middle Ages (*e. g.*, W. 3. 517; 4. 531; 1. 52). But a new path was opened by his conception of Christ as the real content of the Scriptures (1. 219). Highly significant, too, was his view of the difference between the Law and the Gospel. The external word of the preacher reaches only the ear of the hearer; "but God speaks (*sonat*) and teaches inwardly to the heart" (3. 124, 514). Human speech effects nothing "without the co-operation and inward infusion (Ps. 38. 2) of God." There is an "inward whispering: Thy sins are forgiven thee" (1. 175, 190, 201).[1] This is the Augustinian view. (Vol I., p. 321). The word falls into the two categories of law and gospel. These terms are often synonymous with the Old and the New Testament, *e. g.*: "The law teaches the knowledge of self; but the gospel, or the New Testament, teaches the knowl- of God" (4. 565, 567). In this sense, the law is the rude vestibule to the gospel (3. 249). It conceals the New Testament ideas (4. 251, 305), such as evangelical grace and the righteousness of faith (3. 560). It is unable to give to anyone a good will, or love (4. 250). But, since it can call forth only outward works, it makes men in the end hypocrites (4. 566). It makes men sinners, but the gospel comforts and saves them (4. 566). But Luther finds law also in the New Testament, since the latter teaches the spiritual understanding (*intelligentia*) of the law: "But this understanding of the law spiritually much rather slays, because it makes the law impossible to fulfill, and thereby makes man despairing of his own strength and humiliated" (1. 105). This is, however, a foreign, and not the peculiar, office of the gospel (1. 113; 4. 87.) Its own mission is to comfort and lift up all who have been smitten and humbled by the law. "Therefore, as much as the gospel has caused grief by interpreting the law, so much and more does it cause rejoicing by proclaiming grace" (1. 105, 106, 108, 113). The gospel humiliates, not only by its interpretation of the law, but also by manifesting the works and the glory of God and thereby revealing the sin and shame of man (1. 111 f.). Finally, the gospel imposes a cross and chastisement upon man, since it subjugates the old man (4. 253; 3. 462). The gospel may therefore be called a compound (*mixtum*): "because the gospel imposes cross and life, peace and war, good and evil, poverty and riches. And this is most truly a salutary mixture so

---

[1] It is the word of the gospel, vocal or written, *i. e.*, the Holy Scriptures (3. 404).

long as this life lasts " (3. 516). If it is therefore the chief office of the gospel to proclaim grace and consolation, it yet deepens also the understanding of the law and humiliates and chastens the sinner.[1] We shall treat the doctrinal points resulting from this general view in the order : sin, freedom of the will, Christ, grace, faith, righteousness.

2. Luther did not suffer while in the cloister from outbreaks of any particular sin. He was oppressed by the sense of sinfulness, or Original Sin. He recalls attention to it : " No one is longer solicitous for the mortification of the tinder (*fomes*) and the root-sin, but they are concerned only for the cutting off (*amputandis*) of actual sins by contrition, confession, and satisfaction " (1. 67). But original sin (*peccatum originale*,[2] *Erbsund*, 1. 197) is the concupiscence filling the whole man (1. 126, 225), which is the root of all *peccata actualia*. " It is an abiding sin in this present time " (1. 168, 86), "a very corruption (*corruptio*) of nature " (1. 121), since the memory, the understanding, and the will are weakened by it (3. 453). This is the old man, "which absolutely does not love God, nor fervently hunger and thirst (for him), but thinks to find full satisfaction for mind and spirit in created things " (1. 146). It has a horror, not a fear, of God ; " but horror is the seed-bed of hate " (1. 39).[3] The " nature and essence " of man is, from his birth, an evil tree and a child of wrath (1. 188).[4] Just as little, therefore, as the will is free to do good (1. 148, 224), is man able to prepare himself in worthiness (*de condigno*) or in fitness (*de congruo*) for the reception of grace (1. 147, 148, 70).

3. In Christology, certain definite fundamental conceptions of Luther are already quite prominent. The doctrine of the two natures of Christ (3. 467) is, for example, presented in its practical religious aspect. We recognize the divinity of Christ,

---

[1] Cf. the frequently recurring declarations, that man must become nothing, must be judged and crucified, before God can work in him, *e. g.:* 1. 183 f., 112, 113, 119, 227, 186, 189, 201 f., 214 ; 3. 513, 288 f., 291, 466 ; 4. 376 f., 412. Vid. also the view of the Mystics, supra, p. 180.

[2] Definition, 4. 690 ; cf. 9. 73, 75.

[3] Luther retains the Scholastic idea of the Synteresis (supra, p. 114 f.): "Therefore, just as the synteresis of the understanding (*rationis*) is also conformed to the wisdom of God, although the entire understanding may be totally non-conformed to it, so the synteresis of the will is conformed to the will of God " (1. 36, 558 ; 3. 238).

[4] The wrath of God is attributed to the creature, without having a real existence in God : "God does not, properly speaking, afflict by approaching, but by departing and leaving in the hand of creatures." This is the biblical idea, that God is angry when he forsakes. Luther's conceptions at this time harmonize with Creationism (4. 342).

since we attribute all our blessings to him and expect salvation wholly from him, as well as render him obedience : " To confess that Christ is God is to restore and refer to him all good things received from him, . . . to hope for all good things from him, and to put our trust in no creature " (1. 123, 140). His divinity is "a gracious will to pity and help " (1. 203). "That he pities, proves him to be God and distinguishes him from others, who cannot pity (*misereri*) since they are themselves objects of pity (*miseri*). Therefore he who pities and is good, is God " (4. 248.) But Christ concealed his divinity in his humanity, so that it remained in the Father (*divinitatem suam abscondi ab eis in patre*, 3. 502 f., 124). He put away from him his power : " He banished (*subtraxit*) all his power by which he would have been able to resist them (his enemies) and in every way subjected himself to infirmity " (3. 121). Thus, even his divine works were concealed in the humiliation of his passion (3. 547).[1] Thus God came to us. " Since God pitied us, he also adapted himself to our infirmity, so that he came to us as a man, concealing his divinity and thereby removing all terror " (4. 647; 1. 201). There is, therefore, no knowledge of God, save only in the humanity of Jesus. " All ascent to the knowledge of God is perilous except that which is made through the humility of Christ, because this is Jacob's ladder. . . . Wherefore he who, of himself, makes haste to know God, is hastening to the abyss of despair. . . . In other works God is recognized according to the greatness of his power, wisdom, and justice, and there his works appear to be exceedingly terrible ; but here is seen his most gentle pity and love, so that thus his works of power and wisdom may be contemplated with confidence " (4. 647, 648). God has come to us in Jesus, as the Temple of God (1. 203), through the incarnation. In him alone is God to be known (202).

This is the great revelation of God to us : his love and righteousness are revealed in Christ (1. 140). This, to speak precisely, embraces two ideas : Christ dwells in us (4. 328, 3, 8), as a "counsel of example," and, through his sacraments, an "aid of grace " (1. 77). In the former aspect, his zeal for our salvation inspires our zeal for the same.[2] He still lives in his followers, and incites them to all good. The kingdom in which Christ reigns is the church (4. 85). "And thus

---

[1] It harmonizes with the emphasis thus laid upon the humanity of Jesus that Luther even held it permissible to speak of him as exercising faith (4. 267).

[2] This idea appears to be related to that of Biel, that Christ is only the partial cause of our salvation (4. 596, 645).

it truly comes to pass, that the life of Christ does not lie quiet
in his believing follower, because it has never lain quiet, but
always lives and acts. . . .   We do not live, speak and act, but
Christ lives, acts and speaks in us ; because what we do and say
is accomplished by his acting within us and impelling us "
(4. 646).   No law is able to transform the will and make it
good ; but the life of Christ effects this, moving our will to
imitation (4. 646 ; 1. 121).   The Christ in us is not idle, but
most active (1. 140).   But it is only one aspect of the work of
Christ that is thus described.   The same Christ has also fulfilled
the law for us, endured for us the wrath of God and death, and
overcome the devil (1. 35, 59 ; 4. 609).   He is our righteousness (1. 171, 140 ; 3. 174), and his merits are imputed to us
by God (1. 140).   " Thou, Lord Jesus, art my righteousness,
but I am thy sin ; thou hast assumed mine and given thine to
me ; thou hast assumed what thou wast not. . . .   Therefore
not except in him, by sincere despair of thyself and thy works,
canst thou find peace " (De W., 1. 17).   Christ's blood cleanses
us (1. 189, 121).   He is the hen, under whose wings we find
rest and peace (1. 31, 35, 117).   " Now henceforth our God
is no more the exactor of righteousness and the judge, but he is
through his pity a saving (power) within us " (4. 609).   He
does not simply causally work our righteousness, " for that is
dead, yea it is never given, unless Christ himself is also present "
(1. 219).

These are the permanent, fundamental features of Luther's
Christology and Soteriology.   The historical Jesus is the revelation of God.   In the love of Christ his divinity is revealed ; but
the power of the latter he conceals.   The Christian experiences
Christ as a present and active reality in his life.   Christ hereby
becomes an active force within him, both as the law and pattern
of goodness setting him free to do good and making him capable
of doing it, and as the righteousness transferred from him to us.
Christ's fellowship with us brings us both a new life and the forgiveness of sins ; it makes us good both in the real and in the
ideal sense of the word.   This leads us to consider the conception of grace and the subjective forms of the blessings it
confers.

4. According to the traditional dogmatics, the activity of
grace is two-fold, embracing the infusion of new powers and the
forgiveness of sins.   This must be borne in mind if we would
understand Luther correctly.   When guilt has been removed,
sickness must be replaced by health (3. 453 ; i. 65, 68, 43, 84 :
justificante et imputante).   The infusion of grace is not a momentary act, so that at once all grace is given and all sin blotted

out. That idea leads to despair, as Luther had learned in his
own experience (1. 43). "The *infusio* is an interior illumination of the mind and inflammation of the will . . . this is necessary for the extirpation of concupiscence, until it shall be perfectly
extirpated" (1. 66). It brings the "good-will directed straight
toward God, seeking God alone" (1. 191), and it infuses love
(1. 115; 4. 250). As Christ was conceived by the Holy Ghost, so
every Christian is through love born anew and justified by the Holy
Ghost (3. 468). It purifies us : "But that purification (*purgatio*)
is a work of God and an infusion of grace, a justification without us" (*sine nobis*, 1. 118). It washes and purifies us continually (1. 186, 189). The essential factor in the righteousness
infused by grace is *faith*. "Faith is righteousness" (1. 118,
84). It is from God, who gives the true, fundamentally good
righteousness, which is the faith of Christ (1. 213). To pray
for faith is the same as to pray for life or righteousness (4. 325).
When God, therefore, graciously "begets and creates" the
new man, *i. e.*, works righteousness in him (1. 215 ; 3. 154)
through the Holy Spirit (1. 218), this righteousness consists not
so much in works, as in hope, love, and especially faith (1. 84). So
little does this appear to depend upon the inward state, that Luther
traces it to a divine covenant : "Faith and grace, by which we
are to-day justified, would not of themselves justify us unless a
covenant of God caused them to do so" (3. 289),[1] *i. e.*, that
he who believes and is baptized shall be saved (Mk. 16. 16).

This presentation of the subject runs entirely within the lines
of medieval theology. But Luther's new definition of faith
leads us further. What is faith, and how does it originate? We
recall the fact that the accepted dogmatic scheme found place for
an *acquired faith* in addition to the *infused faith*, and that the
later Scholasticism laid special stress upon the former (supra, p.
150, 195).[2] "When thou hearest that he suffered for thee,
and believest, there springs up already confidence toward him and
tender love, and thus perishes all love of (other) things as useless, and there arises a passionate regard for Christ alone as the

---

[1] This is a Scotist idea. Thus Luther occasionally declares of every human
preparation for receiving grace, that the latter is given, not through such preparation, but by virtue of a divine covenant (4. 329).

[2] The Scotist criticism prepared the way for this (p. 150, 159 f.). We can
understand the advance of Luther from the position held by Duns, although
Luther rejected the self-acquired faith as a work of man himself in favor of the
infused faith (vid. ¿ 67, 5)! And, similarly, the new conception of grace may
be explained by the fact that the *gratia creata* first recedes behind the *gratia
increata* (p. 118 f.), and then makes way for the latter. It follows that the
imputed grace crowds the infused from the field. Here, too, Duns performed
some preparatory work (p. 160).

One Thing necessary, and there remains to thee nothing save Jesus only, he alone enough and sufficient for thee, so that despairing of all things thou hast this Only One, in whom thou hopest for all things, and, therefore, lovest him above all things. But Jesus is the one true and only God whom when thou hast, thou hast no strange God" (1. 399 f.). This is a faith wrought by God, but yet inwardly acquired and experienced —a faith alive and practical, the experience (*experimentum*) of despairing of self in order to allow one's self to be led by God alone (1. 88).[1] This faith, as it springs from the contemplation and experiencing of Christ, "consists more in taking from God than in giving, more in longing than in having, more in becoming than in being pious" (1. 212). But since the Christian recognizes that all his blessings come from God, he gains confidence in him (1. 74 ff.). "His whole life is a trusting, depending, waiting, hoping, in God" (1. 210). "And hence faith takes away from us ourselves and the things that are ours, referring all things to God with praise and gratitude" (1. 123). Faith is a "possession of things hoped for" (4. 271). This faith is, therefore, upon the one hand, the entreating, struggling faith of Augustine (Vol. I., p. 347); but it is, on the other hand, something more, *i. e.*, the apprehending of God in Christ and trust in God. Its essential content is Christ (1. 219); what is his, becomes ours; there is between us and him a *perfectum matrimonium* (1. 104). This leads to the *new conception of grace.* The actions resulting from the infused love find a filling out of their imperfection in the fullness of Christ, "because the fullness of Christ is accepted instead of it, until it is also made perfect" (1. 115): not only thus, however, but in the comprehensive sense, that without any regard to any beginnings of subjective righteousness, the righteousness of Christ alone is our righteousness : "That the Father in his mercy imputes to us the righteousness of his Son" (1. 140). Thus sin is no more imputed to us, but forgiven (1. 86). Lust remains in us. "It is here, but God in grace does not impute it to us" (1. 168). "For to such an one he does not impute sin, because he imputes righteousness to him" (3. 175). But this righteousness is mine only in so far as I accept it. "For his mercy is my righteousness. . . . For what is mercy, if I do not accept it? . . . But my righteousness signifies that I am accepted by the One showing mercy" (3. 43). But this comes to pass through faith.

This is Luther's Soteriology in its first form. Two lines of

---

[1] This does not conflict with the fact that outward perception and recognition of this faith are still excluded (he does not see nor experience it, 1. 102).

thought pervade it. God infuses grace, *i. e.*, faith and love; he makes us righteous. But since faith is regarded as a confidence in the revelation of God inwardly acquired, it may also be said, that faith lays hold on Christ and thereby also upon the righteousness, or forgiveness of sins, which exists in him and is imputed to us. The *gratia infusa* is here supplanted by the Christ living and acting within us. It is no longer the sacraments—Luther very seldom mentions them in this connection— but the word concerning Christ which produces the result. But this Christ is " most active " within us (1. 140); and, although the righteousness of faith is not given to us on account of our works, yet it is given to enable us to perform works (*ad opera*, 1. 119). It may be said : " For righteousness is from God, since, when we are righteous, it is because God justifies and imputes " (1. 84).

5. The religious processes above traced are actualized in experience in connection with the observance of the Sacrament of Repentance. Let us glance at Luther's view of that sacrament. Contrition springs from meditation upon the blessings conferred by God and upon our ingratitude as revealed by our sins : " All these things reflected upon and compared with our own sins wonderfully stir up hatred and detestation of ourselves, but love and praise of God." But this penitence arises from love to God and to righteousness (1. 99; cf. supra, 136 n. 3, 175). " This contrition must be so brought about (*paranda*) that it may proceed, not so much from hatred as from love " (1. 446). But neither the completeness of this contrition nor confession following it imparts the certainty of forgiveness, which comes to us only through *faith :* " Simply believe the word which the priest utters in absolution, that the absolution may be based upon neither his merit nor thine own " (1. 131). The true satisfaction is that required in Lk. 3. 8 : it is a " service of the whole Christian life." Where private confession and satisfaction are taught in the Bible, Luther does not know (1. 98). Through them we cannot secure any righteousness, but only through faith (1. 102). He regards indulgences with suspicion. If no one can be sure of the contrition of another person, it is mere trifling to maintain that a soul escapes from purgatory through indulgences ; for if the individual concerned had not true contrition, the indulgence would not secure his pardon (1. 66). Moreover, the grace imparted impels us to perseverance in the self-mortifications of repentance, so that the true Christian does not desire any indulgence (1. 68).

6. It is to be observed, finally, that upon other points Luther is during this period very conservative. The worship

of Mary and the saints,[1] the seven sacraments, transubstantiation, the mass, and the infallibility of the church are
still maintained.   He has no idea of assailing them (vid. Köstlin, L. Theol. i. 221 ff., Engl. transl. i. 200 f.); but it may
be observed that the elements of his later conception of the
church may be found already in his writings.   The church is the
City of God.   "It is built, not by human teachings or works,
but by the word and grace of God alone" (1. 202 ; 4. 400).
It is the summary of the works of God, or the new creation
(3. 154).[2]   But since the church is thus the work of God, or of
his word, its essence is invisible and perceptible only by faith :
"Because the church is a labor and construction (*opera et
factura*) of Christ, it does not outwardly appear to be anything,
but its whole structure is internal, invisible before God; and
thus they are known, not to the carnal eyes, but to the spiritual
in the mind and in faith " (4. 81 ; 3. 154, 367).

7. Everywhere, beneath the old forms the new life was swell-
ing.   Let us once more recall the leading features of the latter :
The recognition of man's moral bondage ; the new apprehension
of the humanity of Jesus as the absolute revelation of God ; the
conception of faith as a laying hold upon Christ, together with
trust in God ; the thought of Christ working in us ; the idea of the
righteousness of Christ and the forgiveness of sins graciously
attributed to us.   It is a new understanding of religion which
finds expression in these views, however all the elements of the
past—the ancient dogmas, the Augustinian apprehension of sin
and grace, the criticism of the scholastic and pre-reformation
eras, the mystic attempts to mount from the man Jesus to God,
with their doctrine of the indwelling of Christ—may have prepared the way before it.

§ 67. *Criticism of the Sacrament of Repentance and Exposition
   of Evangelical Repentance.   Faith, Sin, Grace, Justification, Atonement.*

1. ."The right way and the proper manner, than which no
other is to be found, is the most worthy, gracious, holy sacrament
of repentance " (W. 2. 715).   "But I, a poor brother, have
kindled a new fire, and have bitten a great hole in the pope's
pocket, by attacking confession " (W. 8. 340).   The central
point in Luther's work lay in the abolition of the sacrament of re-

---

[1] *E. g.*, 4. 694 : " And thus the divine Virgin holds the medium between
Christ and other men," with reference to her conception.
[2] The *communio sanctorum et bonorum* (4. 401) is to be interpreted in
the neuter gender.

pentance and the substitution for it of the new conception of faith
and justification. This must also be our starting-point. In the 95
Theses (A.D. 1517) we find the traditional view of the sacrament
of repentance, as well as some echo of the criticism of the preceding period and of Luther's own evangelical views. (*a*) Luther
does not here assail indulgences as such. They are to be highly
esteemed (Th. 69, 38, 7, 71), and he proposes to combat only
the abuses connected with them (72). The pardoning power of
the pope can extend only to the canonical penalties imposed by
himself, and not to every penalty (5, 20, 21, 34). As regards
the dead, they are valid only in the way of supplication (26).
The forgiveness of sins has in his view only a declarative force
(38, 76, 6). The *thesaurus* of the church is not to be found in
the merits of Christ and of the saints, as these are effectual without the pope (58); but "the keys of the church bestowed through
the merit of Christ" constitute it. (*b*) But this is not in
the present day the character of indulgences. The indulgence-
preachers are in many ways responsible for the abuses, as if souls
were freed from purgatory as soon as the money rattles in
the chest (27, 28, 86), and as though the certainty of salvation
may be purchased (52, 30-32). Good works appear to be no
longer necessary. It might be asked why the pope does not
employ his power to empty purgatory (82, 84), and why
he does not spend his own money to build St. Peter's (86).
The church is being exposed to ridicule (90). (*c*) Our Lord
and Master Jesus Christ, by saying : Repent, intended that the
whole life of believers should be repentance (1). This is not
said, of course, with reference to the sacramental acts, but to the
mortifications of the flesh and the hatred of self (2-4). In this
sense, the penalty (*poena*) of sin remains as long as we live on
earth (4). But if this self-mortification is a duty, then the true
penitent will prefer the penalties, *i. e.*, the works of love,
to indulgences (40, 41, 43, 44). But he cannot by these means
gain a consciousness of forgiveness. "Every truly contrite
Christian has plenary remission of penalty and guilt due him,
even without letters of pardon (36); and he has this through his
participation in Christ and the treasurers of the church (37).
The hierarchy cannot pardon the least sin as to its guilt (76);
there belongs to it only the declaration of that which God does
(38). Therefore, God alone forgives the guilt of sin ; but the
penitent exercises himself in good works. Indulgences are not
necessary. They are indeed dangerous, in so far as they may by
outward means make the sinner feel secure, and in so far as they
give to him something which is altogether uncertain. If scarcely
anyone is certain of his *contritio*, how much less of the attain-

ment of *plenaria remissio?* (30-32). He who has not money in superabundance need pay out nothing for indulgences (46).

Such are the Theses. They are less energetic than many criticisms of earlier date (supra, p. 210). But yet—carried to their logical conclusions—they leave very little remaining of the sacrament of repentance. The contrite sinner secures forgiveness —it is taught with Augustine—to what end does he then need confession and absolution? Works are moral exercises : then indulgences, and works of satisfaction as well, have no ground to stand upon. As indicated in the first Thesis, the repentance which fills the whole life occupies for Luther the central place, and no longer the sacrament of repentance.[1] Cf. DIECKHOFF, Der Ablass-streit, 1886. BRATKE, L.'s 95 Thesen, 1884. BRIEGER, Das Wesen d. Ablasses . . . mit Rücksicht auf L.'s Thesen (Lpz. Progr. 1897).

2. Luther's utterances in the following years develop these ideas in both their positive and their negative aspects. The essence of repentance consists in *Contritio*. (*a*) But true contrition is secured by the contemplation of righteousness, which begets in us love for the good, and, through this, sorrow for our sins (W. 1. 319). "But this contrition is to be produced in such a way that it may proceed, not so much from hatred as from love. But it proceeds from love, . . . if a man reflects with himself upon the benefits of God conferred upon him throughout his whole life. . . . All these things, reflected upon and compared with our own sins, wonderfully stir up hatred and detestation of ourselves, but love and praise of God" (W. 1. 466). The opposite course is most vigorously rejected. He who determines to attain sorrow for sin simply by the contemplation of it, becomes a hypocrite, and is sorry only from fear of punishment. He really gets no further than attrition (ib. 319, also W. 2. 160 f., 421, 363, 368 ; 6. 160, 610. Cf. E. 31. 182, 183 ; 18 6).[2] An actual penitent frame of mind can thus, according to Luther, be induced only upon the basis of positive love for the good,

---

[1] In this consists the historical significance of the first Thesis : all depends, not upon the sacramental acts, but upon the penitent disposition of the heart. This introduction follows the example of the medieval discussions of the subject, which open with a presentation of the virtue of repentance. Particularly in Duns, the sacramental acts are really only means for promoting repentance as a self-mortification dominating the whole Christian life. Vid. my discussion of Duns' doctrine of repentance in Abhandl. f. Alex. v. Oettingen, p. 172 ff.

[2] The last two passages prove that Luther in writings of the years 1530 and 1537 could advocate exactly the same views as in his tract, *De poenitentia*, of the year 1518. But it is of the greatest importance, that he here denies entirely the possibility of begetting contrition before the reception of grace. His own conflicts in the cloister therefore fall under the head of attrition.

which measures its own conduct by the good, and not by the presentation of duties and penalties. But it is important to scrutinize the theological connection of this thought. It was clearly expressed by Luther at the Leipzig disputation (1519): All the Scholastics, he maintains, agree with him, "since they all agree that contrition ought to be produced (*fieri*) in love, . . . that contrition is produced, love impelling and enjoining" (W. 2. 263, 364, 371, 422).[1] This is, in fact, correct, for contrition is an act "formed" by love (p. 135).[2] But it must be said at the same time : (1) That this love presupposes faith—for such is the traditional relation—and (2) That Luther is not here thinking primarily of the empirical beginning of conversion. It is not to be denied, however, that Luther, during the years of the indulgence controversy, not infrequently made even the initial penitence of the Christian life dependent upon faith and love : "The great thing is a heart contrite from nothing else than faith ardently regarding the divine promise and threatening, which, beholding the immutable truth of God, alarms, terrifies, and thus makes contrite the conscience—again exalts and consoles and keeps it contrite, so that the truth of the threatening is the cause of the contrition, and the truth of the promise the cause of the consolation if it is believed, and by this faith man merits the forgiveness of sins" (W. 6. 545 ; 1. 542, 364). Thus faith produces contrition and maintains it. Not fear, but the gentle goodness of God allures the sinner to repentance (W. 2. 362, 363, 370). In the moment when we hear that Christ suffered for us, faith and love arise (W. 1. 399). Contemplation of the sufferings of Christ transforms man, and in them we recognize the magnitude of our sin (W. 1. 137): "This contemplating essentially transforms man and, very nearly like baptism, regenerates him" (ib. 139). "This faith justifies thee, will make Christ to dwell, live, and reign in thee" (ib. 458). Thus as we contemplate the goodness of God in Christ, true contrition appears, while at the same time man is preserved from despair." "When true contrition is about to arise from the goodness and benefits of God, especially from the wounds of Christ, so that man first comes to (a sense of) his ingratitude from the contemplation of the divine goodness, and from that to hatred of himself and love of the

---

[1] Eck acknowledged that this is the higher position, but that it is one which, on account of frailty, cannot be attained (W. 2. 361). Luther was brought to his view through Staupitz, De W. 1. 116.

[2] If, then, grace produces this condition, Luther has a right to say : "It is, therefore, expressly Pelagian heresy to say that repentance begins before love of righteousness ; but love of righteousness is from God, and not from nature" (W. 2. 421, 362).

goodness of God, then tears flow, and he will heartily hate himself, but without despair, since he will hate his sin, not on account of its penalty, but on account of his view of the goodness of God which, being beheld, preserves him that he may not despair, and may hate himself ardently, even with delight " (1. 576).[1] Thus God crushes the sinner's heart by showing him favor.[2] But in that perturbation (*conturbatione*) begins salvation (540). But "the grace of contrition is given to no one, but at the same time the merits of Christ are given to him " (612). This great unrest is the beginning of grace (595). Contrition lasts—as *habitualis poenitentia*—through the whole life (322, 652), being experienced daily (W. 2. 160, 408, 409 f. E. 29. 357). Repentance in this sense can certainly not be identified with the temporal acts of the sacrament of repentance (W. 1. 531 ; 8. 109). "Because this is at length to exercise living and true repentance, to separate the heart from vices for God's sake, and to keep it separated and to separate it the more. But thou who dost practice only that sacramental repentance and initial repentance before the eyes of men, whose fervor and tumult cannot last without a miracle, thou hast devised an impossibility " (1. 649 f.). The meaning is here, that love of the good springs up simultaneously with faith in the heart. The divine benefits, together with the good now ardently desired, beget in us shame and grief on account of the sins yet clinging to us. To this is now added the law, which, as the standard of the good, " cooperates in giving a knowledge of sin, but in no way effects penitence." " I concede that the law, the recounting of sins, the contemplation of penalties, can terrify the sinner ; but they never make him penitent " (W. 2. 362). The Commentary on Galatians already lays very great stress upon this influence of the law. It is said to teach man to know his weakness and his wrong, to show us the good. It can, indeed, never awaken in us a desire for the good, but only increase the desire for evil (2. 526 f.); but it even in this way drives us to Christ (528).[3] This is the

---

[1] The endurance of the pains of hell (W. 1. 557. Cf. E. 12. 387 ; De W. 2. 125) is thus excluded as an abnormal experience ; cf. Gottschick, Ztschr. f. Theol. u. K., 1891, 255 ff.

[2] Ib. "But then (at the infusion of grace) the man is so ignorant of his justification that he thinks himself to be very near to damnation, and does not think this to be an infusion of grace, but an infusion of wrath."

[3] Hence the law makes no one pious, but teaches only the outward piety of hypocrisy, W. 6. 353 f. W. 2. 720 suggests a further use of the law : "But the hard-hearted, who do not yet desire comfort of the conscience, and who have not experienced the same torture, to them the sacrament (of repentance) is of no benefit. They must first be made tender and timid, that they may also long for and seek this comfort of the sacrament." The method of threatening must thus, after all, be employed in dealing with such as are still impenitent.

true childlike fear of God, even though something of servile
fear (*timor servilis*) may yet ever cleave to it throughout life on
earth (W. 1. 321 f.). "Love being possessed, man is at the same
time moved to the fear of God, and thus repentance begins from
fear in love" (W. 2. 364, 369, 396). There thus arises an exultant hatred of sin (1. 543), faith meanwhile restraining from
despair (632). Thus repentance, both as a state of life and as
the beginning of life, is a fruit of faith and love, however much
the law may contribute to its production.

This repentance now begets in the heart a positive desire to
perform good works. The man is willing to bear the penalties
(W. 1. 597); impelled by the Spirit and the Christ dwelling
within, he brings forth fruits of repentance (1. 532, 649, 364;
2. 424).[1] (*b*) Luther at an early period recognized the impossibility of confessing all mortal sins (W. 1. 322; 2. 60; 6.
162, 545). The thought then soon occurred to him, that we
are really under obligation to confess our sins only to God (W.
6. 158 f.), and that the confession required by the church is only
a human ordinance (8. 152 f.). Hence we can confess to whomsoever we will; we are even free to omit confession to man altogether, if we but confess to God (8. 161, 182, 175, 181.   E.
28. 248, 308; 29. 353; 10. 401; 23. 86 f.). From this position Luther never wavered, although he always warmly commended voluntary private confession (8. 168, 173, 176, 178;
6. 546.   E. 23. 26 f.; 28. 249, 250, 308).[2] Absolution is
to be received in faith. In so far as we, in receiving it, believe
the divine promise, it is effectual (W. 1. 595). "Thy sins are
forgiven, if thou believest them forgiven" (ib. 631, 542). It
is faith in the institution of absolution by Christ which is here
meant (W. 2. 14, 59). Everything depends upon this faith:
"It depends not upon the priest, not on thy doing, but entirely
upon thy faith; as much as thou believest, so much thou hast"
(2. 719, 715). Luther still, indeed, at first understands this in
the Catholic way: Grace and faith are infused (1. 364), and
forgiveness results from the infusion: "Remission of guilt
occurs through the infusion of grace before the remission of the
priest" (1. 541).[3] But the essential thing is, after all, only that

---

[1] In view of this connection, Luther laments that works no longer, as of old,
precede absolution, since the sincerity of the contrition would thus be tested,
W. 1. 551, 661.

[2] In A. D. 1519 he demands that, together with the "testing" of the
penitence, faith be also tested (W. 2. 720; cf. the severe arraignment of the
confessional manuals, 6. 163, and E. 15. 469 f.; 22. 3), and similarly in 1526
(E. 29. 358; cf. 11. 185. Conf. Aug. 24. 6: "But none are admitted unless
they have previously been examined").

[3] Cf. W. 1. 542: Remission effects (*operatur*) the grace of God; 543:

the word be believed; and to this end there is no need of the ecclesiastical machinery.

(*c*) Satisfaction cannot be shown to be commanded by God (W. 1. 324, 383; 6. 610). The same is to be said of Indulgences (1. 384 ff.).[1] The *thesaurus indulgentiarum* is rejected (2. 161). Luther for a time adheres to the idea of Purgatory, despite some suspicions (1. 555, 563; 2. 161, 423, 323 f., 332, 324 f.; 2. 70; 6. 17, 370), but at a later period recognizes it as an invention (*e. g.*, 11. 362). Of the penalties of "satisfaction" there yet remain only moral works and readiness to bear the cross. "God changes eternal into temporal penalty, viz., that of cross-bearing" (W. 2. 161).

Luther appears to have preserved almost the entire structure of the sacrament of repentance. But this is only in appearance. Every separate part of it is recast and the structure as a whole demolished. Into the place of attrition, or contrition, has come that repentance which has not to do "piece-meal" with some particular works, but extends "over the whole person with all its life and conduct" (E. 11. 282), and which springs, not from slavish fear, but from love. Instead of the sacramental confession, it is required : "This confession is now so highly necessary, that it should not be omitted for a moment, but should be precisely the whole life of a Christian" (E. 11. 154). Accordingly, every sermon becomes an absolution (11. 267). But by the side of repentance stands *Faith*. This element is now woven into the penitential process by Luther.[2] Satisfaction was replaced by the good works which spring from faith. The sacrament of repentance as a whole is therefore disintegrated. It is only "invented folly" (E. 9. 299; 279 f.; smalc. art. iii., 3. 313 ff.). Into its place comes the moral and religious state of evangelical repentance, consisting of penitence, faith, and good works (E. 10. 401),[3] and embracing justification and the forgiveness of sins. Luther began with criticism of the sacra-

---

"Remission of sin and donation of grace, to justify and to heal;" 428 : "God showing mercy and infusing."

[1] Luther often (W. 1. 587 f.) declared, according to the popular understanding of the matter, "that they sold indulgences for the divine grace which forgives sin" (E. 24. 337; 26. 18). Theologically, he thus expresses himself : "In all indulgence bulls he (the pope) promises forgiveness of the sins of all who have mourned (*bereuet*) and confessed (*gebeichtet*)" (E. 28. 175; 31. 141), who have "mourned and confessed and give money" (25. 132). Eck well expresses the doctrine as understood by the masses (W. 2. 352 f., 359).

[2] A partial anticipation of this is seen in the testing of faith at the confessional toward the close of the Middle Ages. Supra, p. 174.

[3] Only penitence and faith are commonly spoken of as elements of repentance (*e. g.*, E. 6. 340; 3. 76 f.; 11. 293, 296; 17. 125; 19. 64; 23. 39), but it is clear that works fall under the same heading.

16

ment of repentance, and he substituted for it evangelical repentance.   Of a change in his views concerning the initial penitence,
we shall speak in another connection.

We have thus outlined the views of Luther at this period upon
the topics of repentance, faith, works, and the pardon of sin.
We have yet to trace his teachings concerning sin, the relation
of law and gospel, and the work of Christ.

3. In regard to Sin and the moral Bondage of the Will, he maintained the same positions which he had taken in the earliest period
(supra, p. 229).   (a) Before the fall, Adam was inclined only
to good (E. 15. 46).   Since the fall, he and all his descendants
are subject to sin.   The human race is a *massa perditionis* (W.
1. 427 ; 2. 526. E. 28. 206).   Every individual of the race is
full of sins (W. 1. 427), his nature full of lust (W. 2. 412 f.).
Human works may appear outwardly beautiful, and yet be mortal
sins (W. 1. 353).   Every sin is a mortal sin (W. 2. 416, 419).
"And there is therefore included briefly and barely in this
word, Sin, what one lives and does without and outside of faith
in Christ " (E. 12. 111).   Sin constitutes a kingdom of the
devil (W. 2. 96).   Especial emphasis is laid by Luther upon
original sin.[1]   He proposes to defend Augustine's conception of
it against the Pelagianism of Rome (W. 1. 272, 649. E. 11.
281).   The Scholastics of all schools, with the single exception
of Gregory of Rimini (supra, p. 188), were Pelagians (W. 2.
295 f., 303, 394 f., 308).[2]   The danger of that tendency lies
in the fact that it leads to work righteousness (E. 14. 245 ; 30.
365).   This opposition forms the central nerve in Luther's
presentation of the subject.   Through the act of generation,
which is performed in evil lust, sin passes from parents to their
children.   It is inherited sin, or nature-sin (E. 19. 15), as being
the real chief sin (10. 305 ; 15. 49).   As the formative
material in father and mother is corrupt, it remains so in the
children (E. 11. 246 ; 19. 15. W. 2. 167).   From Adam
down, the nature and essence of man is corrupt (E. 10. 304 ;
46. 67).   Human nature is " an evilly disposed nature " (E. 7.
289), a " corrupted nature " (E. 9. 234 ; 15. 187 ; 20. 155),
a flesh poisoned by sin (15. 47 ; 20. 157, 297), in which evil
lust reigns (15. 48 ; 18. 73).   In his doctrine of the "old
man," Luther however strongly emphasizes the spiritual, moral

---

[1] The Scotist definition : Want of original righteousness (E. 15. 46) does
not influence his conception.   The contrast to original sin is the *wirkliche
Sünde* (E. 10. 306), which is simply a translation of *peccatum actuale*.   Vid.
also W. 9. 73, 74 f., 78.

[2] But Pelagianism is the "chief heresy," E. 19, 184.   Upon Gregory, see
STANGE, Neue kirchliche Ztschr., 1900, 574 ff. ; 1902, 721 ff.

side of sin.   Its essence consists in "blindness and wickedness"
(9. 288), "the despising of God, inborn inward impurity of
heart, the disobeying of God's will" (12. 111), "unbelief, the
despising of God, disobedience" (9. 15), but, above all, in
unbelief, as the "real chief sin" (12. 110 ; 50. 57 ; 63. 16)
and "cause of all sin and crime" (13. 158 ; 47. 54).   "The
chief righteousness is faith ; again, the chief wickedness is
unbelief" (12. 178).[1]   It is just the distinguishing feature of
the "natural man," that he has not the Spirit.   Strongly
as Luther emphasizes the natural depravity of man, he just as
positively recognizes also the ability of the natural man.   "The
natural light" sustains the striving after good, without indeed
knowing the good (10. 182 ; 35. 68).   It may protect against
the lusts, but not against lust (14. 151).   In secular affairs, in
law and order, reason judges very correctly (12. 90 f., 109),[2]
although in spiritual matters it appears as the "devil's strumpet"
(29. 241).

(*b*) The consequence of natural depravity is the Bondage of the
Will.   Free-will is for the non-Christian only a word (W. 1. 354.
E. 29. 353).[3]   His will is free only to do evil, but not to repent
(W. 1. 359 ; 2. 362, 702. E. 7. 239, 302).   But it is maintained, on the other hand, that no compulsion to either good or
evil is exerted upon the will (W. 1. 365 ; 2. 370).   The significance which the absolute bondage of the sinner holds in
Luther's circle of thought from the beginning explains his bitter
assault upon the *De libero arbitrio* of Erasmus.   Luther's work,
De servo arbitrio (1525, opp. var. arg. 7), reveals a fundamental difference from the Semipelagianism of the cultured circles of
his day.[4]   This is not saying, however, that his theoretical system was an expression of his fundamental religious position.   To

---

[1] E. 9. 313 gives a classification of sins : If we gather all sins upon
one heap, they fall into two classes, which are the devil's own work, namely,
lies and murder.

[2] The term Conscience (*Gewissen*) is very often used by Luther in the
general sense of the moral consciousness.   As to its nature, see W. 8. 606 :
"For conscience is not a power (*virtus*) of working, but a *power of judging*,
which judges concerning works.   Its proper work is to accuse or excuse, to
make either guilty or acquitted, fearful or secure.   Wherefore its office is not
to do, but to dictate *concerning things done and to be done*, which make either
guilty or saved, in the sight of God."   Similarly in E. 47. 23, 59 ; 18. 58, 22 :
"If we sin greatly, our conscience gnaws us, leaves us no rest ; my heart
passes the judgment : I shall be punished for this."   The medieval conception
is reproduced in E. 29. 156 : "The *natural law*, written upon every man's
heart."   Cf. supra, p. 171.

[3] But see W. 6. 27 : "wounded in (his) free will."

[4] But Erasmus' statement of the question : "Either free will or physical
unfreedom" had an undue influence upon Luther.

the theory of man as free and determining his own destiny he opposes the almighty, all-working will of God. He, not man himself, effects salvation. But this thought is enlarged to a metaphysical determinism: "That God works all things in all things."[1] Hence everything that happens, happens by absolute necessity. This thought is, however, combined with the Scotist idea of the absolute independence of God's will and appointments: "Because he wills, therefore what happens must be right" (p. 260). God is also working in the wicked, but it is their fault that they do evil. It is as when a carpenter cuts badly with a sharp hatchet (p. 255 f.). Everything is the work of God, even the fall of Cain, although Luther does not enter upon the question of the genesis of evil in the world. From this follows, as a logical consequence, the absolute double *predestination* and the subjugation of the free will: "With this thunderbolt he hurls down and crushes the free will to its foundations" (*penitus*, p. 132). What we so name is in reality only the particular form of man's activity, which requires a peculiar divine energy operating upon him. The will is not coerced, but acts according to its own inclination and desire ; but it attains to the doing of good only through the divine action upon it. Man is passive in his relation to God ; God alone has a free will (p. 158). Man is, as Luther, adopting an old metaphor, says, like a steed. He wills what God or the devil wills, just in so far as he is guided by God or the devil (157). But why God converts some and leaves others to destruction we do not know. That is a matter of his secret will, in regard to which we dare ask no questions. It is for us to be guided by his revealed will. In this way Luther attained the end which he had in view, *i. e.*, he proved that free will was inconceivable, and that grace was the sole agency in conversion. This was the essential thing for Luther. The Scotist and Deterministic[2] ideas were only means for reaching this end. We can understand, therefore, why he did not employ them more frequently, but, on the contrary, with all his emphasizing of the moral bondage of the natural man, appealed constantly to God's earnest will, revealed in the word, to save all men (E. 54. 22 ; 55. 162 ; opp. lat. 2. 170). Christ

---

[1] Cf., *e. g.*, E. 11. 110: "All created things are masks and disguises of God, which he chooses to permit to work with him and help him do all manner of things;" or 35. 252, according to which praying and working "are merely a pure sham-battle." But, on the other hand, we find the queries : "Who can coerce the will of a man ?" (E. 24. 310). "Who can control his heart ?" (ib. 311).

[2] This is the conception of predestination found in Bradwardina and Wickliffe. Luther appears to derive it directly from Augustine. See also LOOFS, DG. 376 n.

bore the sins of *all* men ; if all believed, all—and not alone the predestinated—would be saved (46. 107 f.).   The method of the *De servo arbitrio* presents therefore nothing more than theoretical lines of thought employed as auxiliary to the main purpose. But, as is well known, Luther always maintained the correctness of the conclusions here drawn ; vid. Comm. in Gen.   Cf. LUTHARDT, Lehre v. freien Willen, p. 91 ff.   LÜTKENS, L. Praedest.-lehre, Dorpat, 1858.   KATTENBUSCH, L.'s Lehre v. unfr. Willen, Gött., 1875.

(*c*) Luther's views concerning the Wrath of God must be considered in this connection.   Upon the sinner is visited the wrath of God, which "condemns (him) in advance to death, that we must be eternally *separated* from God" (14. 117).   "God cannot deny his nature, *i. e.*, he is not able not to hate sin and sinners, . . . otherwise he would be unjust and would love sin" (Gal. 1. 338).   This relationship to God we have inherited from Adam (46. 67).   But, since God punishes sin, it is clear that sin is our fault : "For since there is wrath here, there must also be guilt, which merits such wrath" (E. 14. 117 ; 19. 213 ; 8. 177). "The word sin embraces the eternal wrath of God and the whole kingdom of Satan" (Gal. 1. 54).   "Death is the eternal penalty of God's wrath" (E. 20. 161).   To feel one's self *forsaken of God* is to experience the wrath of God (39. 44, 46).   Even children dying unbaptized are lost (W. 6. 26).   The sinner, when he is "separated" from God regards "him alone as a stern judge" (17. 37).   The unbeliever remains under wrath (46. 29; 47. 25, 31).   The Christian, on the other hand, recognizes God as *nothing but love.*   He is no longer to think of him as a wrathful judge (47. 21 f., 342).   "For God alone is the Man who ceases not to do only good to the world" (E. 19. 364 f., 377, 366).   If the Christian has now learned to know that *his nature is nothing but love*, he knows then "that, so far as we are concerned, even his works of wrath must be nothing but love," since they serve for the subjugation of our foes and to our "testing" (47. 21).   "There is, therefore, with God no wrath nor disfavor, and his heart and thoughts are nothing but pure love, as may be seen in all his works before our very eyes" (E. 19. 369, 370).   Thus, whoever is "separated" from God experiences his wrath ; the Christian knows him as "nothing but love."[1]

---

[1] The believing Christian cannot and dare not by any means represent God to himself as angered and placated (*iratum et placatum*), as the sacrifice of the mass requires (W. 8. 441).   Cf. 47. 342 : "For he who thinks of God and believes that he is a wrathful God, will also find him such ; for as one holds, believes, and imagines concerning God, so is he also, and one finds him also so, namely, a wrathful God."

He who considers the death of Christ recognizes "how im-measurably great and terrible is the wrath of God against sin, and again how unutterable, yea, how unsearchable, is the mercy and grace of God toward us condemned men" (E. 3. 100).[1]

4. In his understanding of the relation between the Law and the Gospel, Luther also continued within the lines originally drawn by him (supra, p. 228). No one attains salvation, except as the law performs its work upon him before the gospel. Law and gospel are the word of God, but each in a peculiar sense (E. 19. 235). Not to have recognized this difference, is the greatest fault of the Romish theology. Luther never wearied of urging this distinction in ever-new applications. "This difference between the law and the gospel is the highest art in Christianity, which each and everyone who boasts or accepts the name of Christian should know and understand" (E. 19. 235).

(a) The Law is a divine requirement, rule, and mirror. It tells what man ought to do and has not done. "It reveals what man is, what he has been, and what he shall again become" (E. 14. 151). What it says to the heart is confirmed by the conscience (14. 153). But what is here to be understood by the "Law?" The Mosaic law, in so far as it "made particular laws and ordinances," i. e., was a positive system of laws, is only a "Jewish-Saxony code." But in so far as it coincides with inborn *natural right*, it is a permanent requirement valid for all times, which has received a peculiarly excellent ex-pression in the Mosaic law. "Where now the law of Moses and the law of nature are one thing, there the law remains and is not outwardly abolished, only spiritually through faith. . . . There-fore image-making and Sabbath and everything which Moses

---

[1] Luther shared the vivid faith in devils and demons which characterized the close of the Middle Ages. But it must not be overlooked that he repre-sented the central processes of the religious life without making any essential use of these views. Large sections of his sermons may be searched in vain for any reference to the devil. His conceptions here also were more spiritual than those of the Middle Ages. He added, so to speak, a hellish majesty to the devil, and the comic aspects of the popular belief disappear entirely. Touching the work of the devil, he says: "When impurity abounds, the devil fills the arteries and bones as full of such evil lust as man permits" (E. 17. 3). "A Christian must know this, that he is sitting in the midst of devils, and that the devil is nearer to him than his coat or shirt, yea, nearer than his own skin, that he is round about us, and that we are always at dag-ger's points with him" (17. 178, 180 ff. See also 11. 269 ff.). The devils are very shrewd (17. 182, 195). They exist in great numbers (17. 191): "How many devils do you suppose were there . . . at the Diet of Augsburg? Every bishop had brought with him so many devils—as many as a dog has fleas on it about St. John's Day" (ib. 210). Upon the fall of the devil, see 46. 3 f.; upon angels and the protection rendered by them, 17. 177 ff., 182 f., 189, 202, 216, 219; 10. 151.

appointed more than and beyond the natural law, since it has no natural law, is free, void, and done away with " (E. 29. 156 f.; 46. 84, 87; 47. 25). God's law, or love, is natural law (E. 20. 125; 22. 104, 202). These written laws are to be included under the category of the reason, since they have flowed from it as from a fountain of law (E. 20. 106).[1] As Luther shared the medieval conception of an inherited natural law (supra, p. 171 f.), he therefore recognized the "Law" only in so far as it agreed with the latter. In connection with it, he thought of other means of convincing us of our sins. From this point of view, the sufferings of Christ became also a preaching of the law (E. 13. 116 f.; 11. 147). The entire law, however, including the decalogue, together with the laws of the church (Gal. 1. 181. W. 2. 527), does not give life, but slays (W. 2. 468; 6. 353). It has not the power to move or renew man inwardly, but remains an inflexible, tormenting requirement (46. 75). Thus it calls forth the hatred of the sinner against itself (W. 2. 498, 532). The works which he performs without being inwardly conquered by the good, merely upon the requirement of the law, are done from fear of punishment (W. 2. 532), and are in the last analysis therefore hypocritical (2. 513; 6. 354). A "servile spirit" arises in man's heart (E. 7. 247). The law makes him really worse (W. 2. 525, 527), however far outward integrity may be secured by it (E. 7. 283, 284). The righteousness of works which it produces is no righteousness at all : "That righteousness of works is most truly nothing else than to love sin, to hate righteousness, to detest God with his law, and to adore the greatest wickedness" (Gal. 2. 103). Since the law thus presses upon man and he cannot inwardly and actually meet its demands, there seizes him, on the one hand, a terror at the thought of God and desire to escape from him (E. 9. 179); he becomes an enemy of God, without being able to escape from him (E. 18. 73). But, on the other hand, a great longing fills his heart to be free from this pressure. This impels him toward Christ and the gospel (W. 2. 528, 532. E.

---

[1] This passage is very instructive in showing Luther's conception of the Old Testament law. It is indeed a divine revelation ; but it is universally valid only in so far as in harmony with the moral ideas inborn in man. We may here detect a remnant of the natural theology of the Middle Ages. The conclusions which might be drawn from this position—denial of the total depravity of the natural man, the superfluity of the preaching of the law—Luther did not realize. From this point of view we may understand also his interpretation of the Third Commandment and his naturalistic and rationalizing way of regarding the observance of Sunday. See esp. the Larger Catechism, Symbol. Bücher (Müller), p. 401 f. In his works as early as 1518 : W. 1. 436 f. Cf. G. HILLNER, L. Stellung in d. Sonntagsfrage in Mitteil. u. Nachr. f. die ev. K. in Russl., 1888, Sept.-Oct.

7. 289). It awakens displeasure with himself, the resolution to amend the life (6. 390, 339), and a thirst for the grace of God (E. 7. 251).

(*b*) Preachers should begin with this preaching of the law, and never cease (E. 10. 123 f.); for the world surely needs it (10. 283 ; 48. 210). The knowledge of sin must first be preached ; the consciences of men must be terrified by the divine wrath ; the sinner must feel that he, with his sinful lust, belongs to the devil and is lost (E. 14. 15). Only then, after he recognizes his sin, can Christ and grace begin their work (E. 11. 328 ; 13. 295 ; 51. 270). Only after the preaching of the law has had its effect, follows the consolation of the gospel, according to Lk. 24. 47 (E. 29. 139 f.; 11. 327 f.; 27. 124. Gal. 1. 186 f.; 2. 115). Then should be preached, along with repentance, the forgiveness of sins (3. 354). "That is all a preaching of the law, however or whenever it is done, which preaches of our sins and God's wrath. Again, the gospel is such a preaching, which shows and gives nothing else than grace and forgiveness in Christ. . . . Yea, where is there a more earnest and terrible announcement and preaching of God's wrath against sin than the sufferings and death of Christ ? . . . But so long as all this preaches God's wrath and terrifies man, it is not yet the real preaching of the gospel nor of Christ, but a preaching of Moses and the law against the impenitent" (E. 13. 116). "The law is that which displays what we must do ; the gospel, where we are to get the power to do it. . . . The law reveals the sickness ; the gospel gives the medicine" (14. 14 ; cf. 19. 239 f.; 48. 200). "The law has its goal, *i. e.*, how far it is to go and what it is to accomplish, namely, to terrify the impenitent with God's disfavor and wrath and (to lead up) to Christ" (19. 236). He who rests under the law, is without grace and without the Holy Spirit (12. 112). If he is not to fall into despair, the gospel must soon come to his aid (E. 12. 372). With the gospel comes the Spirit ; Moses must now withdraw, and the law is robbed of its power (12. 251 ; 9. 251 ; 19. 246). The gospel proclaims the goodness of God and the forgiveness of sins (7. 156, 327 ; 10. 89). With it, the Spirit enters and quickens the man inwardly, bringing with him Christ, who reigns in us. By this means faith, desire and love for the good, and a new pious life are produced in man (9. 240, 278 ; 13. 234, 265 ; 51. 302). The gospel effects the new birth (12. 323). The law inwardly transforms no one ; it is only the Holy Ghost who does this (52. 296).[1] But the new man needs no law. "Just as

---

[1] The Holy Spirit does not therefore come through the preaching of the law,

three and seven—not ought to be, but are ten, nor is any law or rule to be sought for making them ten . . . so a righteous man—not ought to, but does live well, nor does he need a law which may teach him to live well " (W. 2. 596.   E. 22. 66 f.). The Christian has nothing to do with the law (E. 13. 35, 37, 39).   " It is therefore the highest art and wisdom of Christians not to know the law " (Gal. 1. 16).   Christ has abolished it (W. 6. 354).   Neither the Mosaic law nor the law of nature can longer require anything, since there is no longer need of any requirement.

(c) The law is designed, therefore, to awaken the repentance which is involved in conversion.   To this end it is to be preached.   But it is to be preached also for the maintenance of order among the rude and coarse populace, and to be taught to children (E. 13. 51 ; 19. 246).   The influence of the civil law lies in the same direction.   The same fundamental principle finds expression in all codes of laws.   Finally, even converted Christians, being yet flesh, have need of admonition and the presentation to them of the divine will (13. 118).   " Thus must Moses without Christ do his work, that it may drive those who are not Christians, or, in other words, the old man.   For he does not thereby make Christians pious ; but this indeed he does, he shows them what their calling is, which they according to the Spirit willingly observe—not that the flesh either will or can so readily follow that they do not on its account still need to be put on their guard and admonished " (13. 41).

(d) We cannot fail to observe the difference between this view of the subject and that presented above (under 2 a).   In the large Commentary upon Galatians (A. D. 1535), Luther writes: " But man, being humiliated through the law and brought to the knowledge of himself, *then he is made truly penitent,* for true penitence begins from fear and the judgment of God " (Gal. 1. 193).   But in his publication, *Von den Schlüsseln* (A. D. 1530), we meet again the other position :

but comes afterward, since it is only through the gospel that he acts : " Now the Holy Ghost is not the law, nor the reverse.   Where the law is, there the Holy Ghost is not. . . .   The law is not intended to and cannot make pious, but the Holy Ghost makes pious before God " (E. 52. 297 ; 47. 359).   Parallel with this way of apprehending the process, we find another, which traces penitence directly to the *preaching of Christ,* which awakens terror before the wrath of God and the purpose of amendment.   " But such penitence man cannot himself awaken ; it is the *work of the Holy Ghost* which he begins in us through the word of God, which first reveals sin and at the same time announces the penalty of sins, eternal death."   Here penitence is represented as awakened by the Holy Spirit, whereas faith does not appear to come until afterward (E. 6. 339 f., 389 f., 356).   See also 63. 127 : " The wrath of God is revealed through the gospel " (A. D. 1522).

" In order that repentance also may be begun from desire and love " (E. 31. 183).   And in a sermon of A. D. 1537, he declares :   " Hypocrisy indeed comes from the law, but true repentance follows only from the name of Jesus Christ " (18. 6). One thing is here clear.   In the first passage, " repentance" designates the transitory penitence of the yet unconverted, wrought by the law.[1]   In the other two passages, it is the evangelical repentance, springing from faith and love, and filling the whole life.   Apart, however, from this difference in the use of the term, two things are historically certain.   (1) Luther, from the beginning to the end of his activity, urged the preaching of the law, since it is its office to humiliate, awaken an initial penitence, and point to Christ.   (2) He also, from the beginning to the end of his activity as a reformer, urged a repentance which, springing from faith and love through the agency of the gospel and of the Holy Ghost, indicates a conflict with evil filling the whole Christian life.[2]   And we note also (3) as an episode in the controversy concerning confession, the view that the religious process in the Christian's heart begins with faith and love, and that only as a result of these does repentance ensue.   If I am correct, the last-named view is to be attributed to the effort to retain in the life of the believer only a complete penitence and to avoid everything analogous to the traditional *attrition* (supra, p. 237).   But as early as A. D. 1524, upon the occasion of a controversy upon the question, whether the law must of necessity precede the gospel, he maintained, with appeal to Lk. 24. 47, that law and gospel are to be preached, since the latter comforts only those who have through the former learned to know their sin.   The law is also to be used for the outward disciplining of the rude and ungodly (E. 53. 250).[3]   Cf. KAWERAU in Beitr. z. Ref.-gesch., dedicated to Köstlin, p. 61 ff.   Melanchthon's utterances in the " Unterricht an d. Visitatoren," 1528, follow the same line.   Through the preaching of the law, the people are to be stirred up to penitence and fear.   " For along with this it is

---

[1] This is still the dominant use of the term in the praxis of the church. Using it in this sense, how could we understand Luther's first Thesis ? Cf. E. 6. 151 : " Ceasing from evil, regret, and sorrow for it—he calls repenting (*Busse thun*); believing on Christ he calls being converted to God (zu Gott sich bekehren)," and 27. 194 : " Penitence (*die Reu*) flows from the commandments, faith through the promise of God."

[2] The law here comes under consideration only as a directive and confirming agency.

[3] Under these circumstances Luther could write : " And, in fine, it is more necessary to preach and urge the law of God than the gospel, because there are many wicked who must be restrained through the compulsion of the law, but the pious who understand the gospel are few and known to God " (53. 249).

useful to preach of faith.'' The law is to be proclaimed also in order to incite the justified to good works (C. R. xxvi. 51 ff.). It cannot be said that this is a change from Luther's position. Yet so early as A. D. 1527 Melanchthon was violently assailed for holding this opinion by Joh. Agricola, who deduced penitence from love of righteousness. Luther succeeded in allaying this conflict (cf. Kawerau in Stud. u Krit., 1880, p. 24 ff.), but ten years later Agricola renewed his assault, maintaining that repentance should be taught as produced, not by the law, but by the gospel. There is no need whatever, he held, for the preaching of the law. ''The decalogue belongs to the hall of justice, not the pulpit.'' Man is overpowered by the kindness of God, and thereupon renounces his former life and shrinks from incurring the displeasure of his heavenly Father (Luth. opp. var. arg. iv. 420 ff. FÖRSTEMANN, Neues Urkunden-buch, i. 304. KAWERAU in Beitr. z. Ref.-Gesch., etc., p. 65 ff.). Luther opposes him in the six disputations against the Antinomians, arguing anew in defense of the position which he later, as is well known, maintained. The right to appeal to the earlier Luther can be only to a limited extent granted to Agricola, for Luther had always attributed an influence of some kind to the law, and, in view of the practical demands of the years 1527-28, it was an extreme of folly to speak as did Agricola.

(*e*) Law and gospel represent for Luther two opposing conceptions of the universe. The natural man's view of God and the world is always legalistic (*e. g.*, 46. 87 ; 48. 148). The gospel opposes this ; the mercy of Christ lays hold upon man's heart and transforms him. He allows Christ to lay hold of him, and he lays hold of Christ. This is the source of all good in him. But only he will allow himself to be transformed by Christ who has—according to the appointment of God and under his guidance (the law)—seriously struggled with the legalistic view of the world and has, in his own sin, experienced its insufficiency.[1]

---

[1] But the problem is not thus solved. It is not evident how the law (which is from God, but does not exert the specific divine energy of the Holy Ghost, p. 248 n.) produces contrition. How can the good control us, before we have been inwardly laid hold of by it and have recognized it as good? Luther silently assumes such a recognition, presupposes it upon the basis of the ''law of nature,'' or even of a certain general faith in Christianity, but yet discriminates between the application of the law to the *justificandi* and to the ''wild'' and ''rude.'' But is there not thus presupposed a certain initial faith before the working of the law ? However distinctly this may differ from the specific saving faith—Agricola in his first controversy spoke of a faith in the threatenings of the law (*fides minarum*), see KAWERAU, Stud. u Krit., 1880, 43—which, as Luther shows, cannot arise before there is a full consciousness of guilt, yet it just as distinctly differs from it as being its beginning.

"How is it possible to preach about the forgiveness of sins, where sin is not first present?" (32. 73, 70). In history, the revelation of law preceded the revelation of grace : "This occurs to-day individually and spiritually in every Christian in whom is found a season of law and a season of grace following in turn" (Gal. 2. 109).

Cf. TH. HARNACK, L. Theol. i. 479 ff. HERRMANN, Die Busse des ev. Christen, Ztschr. f. Theol. u. K., 1891, p. 28 ff. LIPSIUS, L. Lehre v. d. Busse, 1892. GALLEY, Die Busslehre Luther's (Beiträge zur Förderung christl. Theol. iv. 2, 1900).

5. The definition of the gospel leads us to consider Luther's conception of faith. (*a*) Christian faith has, in his view, for its object simply the peculiar, positive revelations of God in the words and works of Christ. Christ says : "Come to me, I will refresh (*tränken*) you, *i. e.*, in me and through me you shall find the word and doctrine, which will comfort and strengthen your heart" (E. 48. 199 ; 13. 55, 172 ; 14. 1). Only in the man Jesus is God actually to be found ; here he wishes therefore to be sought, found, and called upon (E. 10. 181 ; 7. 68 ; 41. 385 ; 47. 179, 296, 344, 348 ff.; 48. 334 ; 49. 92, 183 f.; 49. 83 f.; 50. 197). Christ is the "true epistle," "the golden book" in which the gracious will of God is revealed (W. 8. 274 f., 276. E. 10. 187 ; 12. 381). God is "hidden in the despised man, Christ" (W. 8. 381). Just in the Crucified do we discover the

Such a "part of faith" (*Stück des Glaubens*) Luther himself recognizes in the disciples before the resurrection (12. 171). But in positing this legal penitence before true repentance, Luther really establishes a pendant to attrition. It was the same considerations which led him to the acknowledgment of such a legal penitence, and the Scholastics to their theory of attrition (p. 135 f.). It is also with him, in the last analysis, a doing by man of "what is in him" (W. 4. 261), although there remains the immense difference, that he did not allow to this initial penitence in any sense a *meritorious* character ! It may, perhaps, be said, that Luther, both in his pre-reformatory period and again in his later years, regarded his experiences beneath the pressure of "the law" in the cloister as normal, and only during that episode felt them to be simply the result of erroneous views. But even thus, there still remains the vast difference between his position and that of his opponents, that the law and the actual gospel are to be proclaimed together ; and also his contention, that "repentance" is not a sacramental act, but the very substance of the moral development of the Christian. I remark, finally, that both the lines of thought thus traceable in Luther are borrowed from the representations of the law in the New Testament. It is abolished and powerless, as the rule of conduct which is to make righteous (Paul : Rom. 6. 14 ; 10.4); and it remains, as the expression of the divine will (Jesus : Matt. 5. 17). But with the latter thought as a point of departure, and in view of the positive confirmation of the law in the discourses of Jesus, might not Luther have secured some more important place in his theory for the authority of the Old Testament law?

loving-will of God. From the kind heart of Jesus[1] we mount up to the heart of God (W. 2. 140 f., 84 ; 1. 362, 614. E. 9. 17 f., 247 ; 12. 297, 381). Christ should, therefore, not be preached as " a history and narrative from chronicles," but in such a way as to tell us " why Christ came, how we are to use and enjoy him, what he has brought and given to me " (27. 187). This is the right way to find God, and not the opposite course of beginning to speculate from the basis of the divine majesty and government of the world (E. 19. 50 f.; 20. 132, 138). In Christ we may gain a conception of God as he is, so " that we do not place instead of him in our hearts a horrible bugaboo or scarecrow, but long for him rightly, as he wishes to be and has represented himself " (E. 16. 206). If we do not hold to the revelation given us, we will picture him to ourselves " as the painters paint the devil, with long horns and horrible fiery eyes " (ib. 203. 208). In Christ we have the good gathered up as into one word (W. 1. 341), and in him we have the very nature of God. That nature is " merciful will, kind will " (E. 7. 68, 72, 74, 76 ; 12. 230, 246, 260, 311, 325, 373 ; 11. 96 ; 14. 193); " nothing but love " (14. 49) ; " divine nature is nothing else than pure benevolence " (*eitel Wohlthätigkeit*, 7. 159);[2] " an eternal power and divine energy " (3. 302 ; 10. 188). Christ is free, since he is the deliverer (21. 99).

In these ideas are manifest two steps in advance, *i. e.*, the Christian religion, and hence also theology, is understood as a positive entity (in contrast with all innate religion of reason or nature); and the nature of God, which is to be apprehended by faith, is defined as an eternal and almighty loving-will. By either of these conceptions the religious character of Christianity is assured.[3]

[1] Cf. his combating of the popular belief, which looked upon Christ as a " tyrant " and " judge " (*e. g.*, E. 13. 49 ; 15. 485 ; 16. 144 ; 19. 222 ; 20. 151 ; 47. 23.)

[2] In all these explanations, the divinity of Christ is assumed by Luther as a fixed premise (vid. sub), but his ideas carry him also beyond the ancient Greek doctrines of the Logos. In opposition to the view that the " Word of God . . . is a light which shines naturally and has always shone in the reason of men, even of the heathen," he says : " These are all still human, Platonic, and philosophical ideas, which lead us out of Christ into ourselves. The Evangelist, on the other hand, desires to lead us out of ourselves into Christ ; for he does not desire to deal with nor speak of the divine, almighty, eternal Word of God except as in the flesh and blood which walked upon the earth. He does not wish to scatter us out among the creatures which were created by him, that we may there run after him, seek him, and speculate about him as do the Platonists ; but he wishes to recall us from those high-flying and widely-wandering thoughts of Christ " (E. 10. 181).

[3] In both, however, Luther follows impulses which passed from Duns into the life of the later Middle Ages (cf. supra, p. 164, 150 n.).

(*b*) When God thus through the gospel, which is always accompanied by an influence of the Spirit, reveals to men his love in Christ, faith arises (W. 2. 140. E. 7. 164, 76, 109; 28. 417). The love of God overpowers our hearts. "Thus God has nothing but the best, and this he shares with us, nourishes us, supports us, waits upon us through his Son. Thus our heart is converted to follow Christ" (W. 1. 275). "But when thou hearest that he suffered for thee, and believest, there arises already confidence toward him and tender love" (ib. 399; 6. 216. E. 47. 341, 346). The first thing that is to be said of this faith is therefore, that is a *taking* and a *receiving*. "But that such bestowed righteousness should be in us . . . this comes to pass alone through faith, for it must always be received and accepted by us. Now it cannot be grasped by us otherwise than with the heart" (E. 12. 118). Faith lays hold upon the benefits of God (W. 8. 35; E. 12. 118), the works of Christ (E. 14. 286; 10. 101: "Therefore, in order that thy faith may remain pure, do nothing but hold still; let it receive good, accept the work of Christ, and let Christ exert his love upon it"), atonement and salvation, with all gifts from above (7. 178, 227, 272, 304). It is God, therefore, who begets faith in man when the latter accepts the divine revelation. With this, as Luther said at an earlier period, God infuses faith into men. But this does not mean that a *quality* is thereby imparted to them, as the Scholastics taught, but that the heart is penetrated by the word of God, and the dominion of Christ is inwardly experienced: "The heart is imbued with the same truth of the word and through the word is convinced of the truth" (W. 6. 94).[1] Christ is in the soul by faith as king; the will as servant (W. 1. 283). Faith is therefore a having (W. 1. 595. E. 12. 169; 27. 180). God, accordingly, through the revelation in Christ, leads us to accept that revelation. If now the content of the revelation be the unchanging purpose of God to save us, the acceptance of it must take the psychological forms of obedience, confidence, or trust.[2]

---

[1] Luther most vigorously rejects the *fides acquisita* of the Scholastics (supra, p. 150, 195 f.), for this is supposed to be secured by man's own efforts, whereas it is in fact only through a divine influence that we can attain faith. He therefore advocates the *fides infusa*—this it is which justifies (W. 2. 566, 146; 6. 85, 89, 95; 8. 323). No one can apprehend an article of faith "without grace and the giving of God" (E. 18. 111). This leads us back to Occam (supra, p. 150). If the medieval conception of grace be abandoned, no importance then attaches to the figure of an "infusing." Despite of it, in fact, it may be said that it is the *fides acquisita*, which constitutes a prelude to Luther's psychological conception of faith, rather than the idea of an "infused faith."

[2] This remark finds confirmation in the fact that Luther at an earlier period discriminated between *fides* and *fiducia*, by the former designating the accept-

"If faith be genuine, it is a certain sure confidence of the heart
and firm assent, by which Christ is apprehended" (Gal. 1. 191).
Faith is "confidence in God's mercy" (W. 6. 209.   E. 7. 66 ;
11. 50, 116 ; 14. 41 ; 18. 46), the assurance that God, and he
alone, will make it well with us (E. 22. 15, 16, 135).   Faith is
therefore not a theoretical belief of certain things (E. 7. 242),[1]
but it is the practical confidence, that we are ourselves through
the work of Christ in favor with God (12. 97, 149, 164, 174,
333 ; 13. 203 ; 27. 187), and that we and our works will be
pleasing in his sight (W. 6. 206, 209).   In the light of this, we
can understand the declaration : " Faith is never concerned with
things past, but always with future things " (W. 8. 323).

But this confidence in the grace of God is based upon the contemplation of a historical revelation : and it is in particular historical facts that the latter has been given.   Hence, this confidence
with regard to the future embraces also the conviction of the reality and potency of definite facts of the past.   " It is not enough
to believe that Christ has come, but also that he has come as St. Paul
here relates, namely, that he was sent from God and is God's
Son ; likewise, that he is true man ; likewise, that his mother is
a virgin ; likewise, that he alone fulfilled the law ; likewise, that
he did this not for himself, but for our good and grace " (E. 7.
261; 23. 18).[2]   Rome, on the contrary, knows only the outward
fides historica[3] (47. 12 ff.) " To believe the resurrection of Christ
is nothing else than to believe that we have a reconciler before
God" (12. 171 ; 20. 141). The same inner relationship of ideas
prevails also in the exposition of the Apostles' Creed in the catechism.   The connection of thought is therefore as follows : The
revelation of God in Christ influences us to its own acceptance,
which occurs when we place our trust in the love of God as recognized by us and are convinced of the reality of the historical
events in which God was revealed to us.[4]

ance as true, and by the latter the personal application to one's self (W. 1.
593 ; 2. 458).
[1] It is no contradiction of this statement, that Luther upon occasion says :
" Faith means properly the holding to be true . . . what the gospel says
about Christ and all the articles of faith " (E. 12. 204 f.) ; for the context
shows that even here we are to think of a practical religious insight.
[2] To make a universal application of this idea lay far from the thought of
Luther and from the needs of the age.   The birth of Christ from a virgin he
supported from the necessity that the Saviour should be sinless, which would
not be tenable if he had been sexually generated (*e. g.*, E. 7. 263 ; 10. 131, 306 ;
11. 246 ; 14. 161 ; 15. 52 ; 20. 155 ; 29. 49, 52).   Even though this argument be not convincing, it is instructive to observe the attempt of Luther to
find a religious basis for the doctrine.
[3] Cf. his strictures upon " milk-faith " (E. 46. 219).
[4] Faith originates in the reason, but extends also to the will : " For wher-

(*c*) This saving faith, or the trust awakened in us through the revelation of Christ, is, further, the beginning of an absolutely new state of life.   Faith is no natural human work, but something new which God effects in man, the directing of the life toward God.   With faith comes the new birth of the man. " Now the divine birth is nothing else than faith " (E. 10. 206 ; 11. 311).   Faith "renews man " (13. 236).   It is "a living, real thing, makes man entirely new, transforms his disposition, and converts him wholly.   It goes down to the foundations and there occurs a renewing of the whole man " (ib. 267).   It is in harmony with this, that the principle of the new birth, or the Holy Ghost, becomes with faith, according to Luther, effectual in man to his regeneration and renewal (8. 223, 308, 307 ; 7. 240 ; 12. 112 ; 11. 314 ; 14. 149).   The usual representation is that the Holy Ghost through the gospel effects regeneration and renewal, whose first and essential element is faith (W. 1. 632. E. 4. 184 ; 8. 223 ; 7. 171 ; 10. 206 ; 12. 324, 404; 24. 325 ; 46. 269 f., 275 ; 61. 125 ; 63. 124).   But, inasmuch as the renewal effected by the Spirit does not develop into activity until after the entrance of faith, it may also be said that the effectual workings of the Spirit follow faith (W. 6. 206, 356). At all events, the first activity which the gospel begets in man is faith.   And he who believes has begun an entirely new life. " Your faith is not a dream and fancy, but it is life and deed " (W. 8. 385.   E. 24. 325).   It is a life with Christ and from Christ, for he lives and reigns in us (W. 1. 455, 458 ; 8. 608). "Out of a dry block" God makes "a new flourishing tree " (E. 7. 170).   Thus the believer, since his life takes the new direction toward God, is a new man, who now endeavors to love God and be obedient to him (W. 8. 357, 363.   E. 12. 90 ; 10. 289 f., 184 ; 12. 324).

(*d*) Having seen that faith is a work of God, and that its essential nature is trust, as the beginning of a new state of life, there yet remain to be noted, according to Luther, some accompanying phenomena.   First of all, we may observe that faith is intimately associated with a Feeling and Experience of divine grace.   Luther says indeed : " Feeling is against faith, faith against feeling;" but his meaning here is only that faith

ever reason goes, there the will follows after ; wherever the will goes, there follow love and desire" (E. 10. 207 ; 11. 200 ; 22. 135; cf. W. 1. 66; vid. the polemics against Eck's assertion : "The will is in the soul as a king in his kingdom") (W. 1. 283).   According to this, Luther does not accept the Scotist idea of the primacy of the will.   With regard to the relationship of the reason and the will in faith he thus agrees to a certain extent with Thomas (supra, p. 103), Duns (p. 150), Biel (p. 195); but he places a higher estimate upon the share of the will in faith than any of the medieval theologians.

reaches out beyond "what we can apprehend by reason and the senses." It has, according to Heb. 11. 1, nothing whatever to do with "the things which are seen" (E. 11. 198; 12. 165, 89, 341; 14. 55, 62, 231; 46. 276. W. 1. 541). "But when feeling and thinking fail, then comes another light, another feeling" (E. 11. 200). The believer feels directly that he has a gracious God (W. 8. 106). He has and feels Christ and the workings of grace in his heart (E. 9. 278 f.; 7. 170; 48. 333). He feels that Christ has power, and "is man enough for the devil" (E. 20. 148). He feels the Holy Ghost, as well as sin, within him (8. 311; 49. 179). The immediate inner observation of these things effects an experience, not uncertain opinions (*persuasiones*, 50. 28 f.). "For a Christian life consists entirely in the exercise and experience of those things which we daily hear and read from the word of God" (9. 95). The Christian experiences the care of God (W. 6. 125). The "experience of faith" "feels" the presence of Christ (E. 29. 334 f.). In order that the faith that is in us may be steadfast, experience must enter. "Although I should preach of God for a hundred years, that he is so kind, sweet, and merciful, and helps men—and have yet not tasted this by experience, it yet all amounts to nothing, and no one thereby learns to trust God aright" (E. 13. 155). Creation and redemption are not realities for us, "if we do not also experience and feel them to be so" (E. 23. 249). Without such personal experience, Christ is not our Saviour (E. 18. 7 f., 45 f., 47). Only where this feeling and this experience are present, do we become "sure of (our) faith" (E. 14. 220. W. 2. 458), "sure of salvation"[1] (E. 7. 275), and only there is the truth of the gospel and of the doctrine confirmed (E. 12. 362, 386; 13. 118; 23. 250, 267). The immediate (direct) feeling and the abiding experience of the living object of faith are therefore the final evidence of its reality (E. 13. 183 ff.). Only thus is an inner certainty possible, according to Luther; not through trust in one's own works, which are always uncertain (E. 58. 375 f.). This experience is not of itself identical with the act of faith. The feeling may at times be wanting, so that faith must depend solely upon the word (E. 12. 309; 18. 47; 14. 45: "before we experience or feel it." W. 2. 117); but, as a rule, it accompanies every act of faith, as indeed the entire Christian life. "And there comes to him unsought and undesired the feeling and experience, precisely in and through such thinking (*vormuthen*) or believing (W. 8.

---

[1] Luther, on the other hand, most vigorously denounced the false "security" of the impenitent, *e. g.*, W. 2. 737. E. 18. 8; 9. 185, 187.

17

357, 379).[1] And if thou dost not experience it, then hast thou not faith, but the word hangs upon thine ears and floats upon thy tongue like foam upon the water " (E. 13. 184 ; 28. 298).

The believer experiences a light and joyful heart (W. 2. 714). With faith is intimately associated the feeling of present blessedness. " Thou must have heaven and be already saved before thou doest good works." The Christian life is a waiting for the blessedness which we already have (E. 7. 165 ff.; 11. 3, 196 ; 12. 329, 331; 14. 120; 16. 116, 138; 47. 367; 48. 24 f.; 46. 26). The Christian therefore leads a life of peace, joy, and liberty (E. 11. 321 ; 7. 272). He has a " courageous, bold, and unterrified heart" (W. 6. 275 ; 1. 273. E. 63. 125). In all affairs of his outward life also he consoles himself with the thought of the providence of God (W. 8. 215 f. E. 9. 138 ; 10. 241, 244 ; 12. 332 ; 13. 175, 252 ; 47. 183).[2] Faith impels to prayer ; yea, it is itself prayer (14. 47). It makes us thankful (9. 49) and capable of decision in spiritual things (12. 90), etc.

6. But the most important phenomena resulting from faith are Good Works. Christ dwells in the believer and moves him to imitate the works which he himself has done (W. 1. 364, 649). " But he lives in us, not speculatively, but really, most intimately, and efficaciously (Gal. 2. 134). Further, if faith is the new attitude of man toward God, it in consequence works in him as a " leaven " (W. 8. 106); it is the beginning of the pious life from which proceed all good works. The works which the believer performs are hence, in so far as they proceed directly from faith, sinless and good[3] (E. 12. 160 ; 7. 229; 10. 4). Faith (the Spirit) gives power to fulfill the law (12. 113; 9. 259), and that willingly and with delight (7. 290, 296 ; 10. 88). The good is written upon the heart as a law of the Spirit, as a " living will and an experimental life " (W. 2. 499). The energy of faith finds expression in good works.[4] " For, as faith brings to thee blessedness and eternal

---

[1] There are elements here—and they are intimately connected with Luther's conception of faith—which present him in the light of a pioneer of the views which have been prevalent among us since the days of Schleiermacher. The method of detecting the agent in the effect is very common in Luther, *e. g.*: Where faith is, there also grace and the Holy Ghost (E. 7. 164 ; 12. 99, 267 f.); where works, there faith (13. 228).

[2] Luther can even say, that faith makes man a god, since all things are now possible to him (E. 10. 311 ; 11. 52).

[3] With this, indeed, we meet concurrently the thought, that imputed righteousness also makes the works good.

[4] So far as faith is exercised by ourselves, it may also be considered as a " work "—yea, it is the " chief work " (W. 6. 204, 206, 210).

life, so does it also bring with it good works and is unrestrained. For just as a living man cannot refrain, but must exert himself, eat and drink and find something to do, and as it is not possible that such works should fail to appear as long as he lives, and as he does not need to be commended and driven to do such works, but, if he is only alive, does them—so nothing more is needed in order that we may do good works than that it be said : ' Only believe,' and thou wilt do everything of thyself " (E. 12. 16 f., 399 ; 47. 20). The Holy Spirit brings it to pass " that the commandment of God now begins also to live in the heart of man, for he now comes to have desire and love for it, and begins to fulfill it, and thus eternal life begins on earth " (9. 248). It is a pleasure for the believer to serve God ; for this reason he does good, not for the sake of laying up " merits " for himself (W. 6. 207). The heaven within us, which faith has brought us, does these works "without any seeking after merit " (E. 7. 165). Gratitude prompts us to fulfill the will of God and to practice upon our brethren in turn the love which we experience (E. 27. 189 ff.). In such connections, Luther not infrequently maintains that works attest the presence of faith (E. 13. 66, 228, 237 f., 266. Gal. 2. 165). This does not, of course, mean that the works make the man pious. The contrary is true—the man must first be good, then will good works follow, as only the good tree is able to bring good fruits (W. 2. 71, 492. E. 7. 249 ; 27. 191 ff.). The doctrine of Christ is not " about doing and not doing, but about becoming ; so that it may be said : not new work done, but first become new ; not lived otherwise, but born otherwise " (E. 12. 399). Only those works therefore are good which are done by him who has through faith become a good man. But whether these works come from faith or from the Holy Spirit, it is clear that they have nothing to do with the law. They are done in the " liberty of faith " (e. g., W. 2. 425, 479, 485, 560, 497 ; 8. 372, 594 f. E. 7. 268, 270; 29. 140 f.). But since these works are effected in the heart of man by the Spirit, they naturally are in harmony with the works of actual morality as enjoined by the law (W. 6. 204, 225).[1] Thus the Christian performs, indeed, the works of the law, but with free delight in them, and not because they have been commanded. To summarize : The Holy Spirit works faith as the beginning of regeneration. By this means man becomes actually good Faith

---

[1] Cf. Müller, Symbol. Books, 444 : That outside of the Ten Commandments no work nor thing can be good and pleasing to God, let it be as great and precious as it may in the eyes of the world.

becomes the beginning of a new and pious life.   Cf. Thieme,
Die sittl. Triebkraft des Glaubens, 1895.[1]

7. Only now are we in position to examine Luther's doctrine of
Justification.   Here, too, the ground originally taken by him was
maintained (p. 231 f.).   But we must bear constantly in mind that
the theological tradition of the age discriminated in the process of
justification between the infusion of grace and the forgiveness of
sins, the former being a real and the latter an ideal change in the
sinner (p. 120 f., 160 f., 201 f.).   Luther, in harmony with
this conception, regards the matter—viewed in the first aspect—
as follows: The faith which God awakens in man effects a real
inward righteousness (*justitia interior, intus justificatur peccator.*
W. 1. 118, 632 ; 6. 98).   Faith is the inward righteousness
which heals the malady of the soul of man and makes him righteous (*rechtfertig*) (W. 8. 106, 111; 2. 13, 14, 424.   E. 22. 138,
248 ; 12. 89; 13. 238), for Christ and the Holy Spirit dwell in
their power in the heart of the believer (W. 2. 458, 490, 749.
Gal. 1. 245).   Thereby man is made really righteous (E. 12.
89. W. 8. 605).   This righteousness is, however, by its very
nature subject to a process of development, which is never completed in this life.   " Everyone who believes in Christ is righteous, not yet fully in reality, but in hope.   For he has begun to
be justified and healed. . . .   But meanwhile, while he is being
justified and healed, what remains of sin in the flesh is not imputed to him for the sake of Christ, who, although he is without
any sin, has now become one with his follower and intercedes for
him with the Father (W. 2. 495).

Here appears, it will be observed, a new line of thought.
While the process of making righteousness is being carried forward, the sins yet cleaving to him who believes on Christ are *not
imputed* to him.   The sins of him who is undergoing the process
of justification are forgiven, on the one hand, because he is beginning to be righteous—which is God's doing—and, on the other
hand, because he is living in fellowship with Christ.   " Thus,
because through faith righteousness and the fulfilling of the law
have been begun, therefore for the sake of Christ in whom they
believe, what remains of sin and of the law yet unfulfilled is not
imputed.   For faith itself, where it has been born, has this as
its office, to purge the remains of sin from the flesh " (ib. 497).

---

[1] The superficial charge brought against Lutheranism by its opponents of all
ages and all parties, that in Luther's circuit of thought good works and
morality are not sufficiently provided for, is utterly refuted in Thieme's work.
It may be said, on the contrary, that in no other of the Reformers does the
moral principle penetrate so deeply and directly to the very centre of the religious life.

"Sin remains there, but, because it has begun to be driven out (*expurgari*), it is not imputed to him who is driving it out" (ib. 414). In precise harmony with these utterances of A. D. 1519, it is said in 1522, that, although there are still many sins in us, "Yet grace does so much, that we are accounted altogether and fully righteous before God . . . takes us completely under its protection for the sake of Christ, our advocate and mediator, *and* on account of the fact that (its) gifts have been begun in us" (E. 63. 124).[1] The idea is : Inasmuch as sin has been in principle shattered in the believer, and God looks upon him in Christ, sin is forgiven and not imputed. The Smalcald Articles (A. D. 1537) follow the same line of thought : "That we, through faith, secure another and new heart, and God, for Christ, our mediator's sake, will and does consider us as entirely righteous and holy. Although sin in the flesh is not yet entirely banished nor dead, yet he will not impute nor recognize it. And upon such faith, renewal, and forgiveness of sin then follow good works. And what in these is yet sinful or defective, just for Christ's sake shall not be reckoned as sin or defect, but the man shall both in person and in his works be called and be entirely righteous and holy, out of pure grace and mercy shed abroad and poured out upon us in Christ" (E. 25. 142.   Cf. 11. 171 ; 46. 260). The only difference observable in this exposition is that the declaration of man's righteousness by God is no longer based expressly upon the beginning of righteousness within man *and* the work of Christ, but only upon the latter. But the difference is only apparent, and Luther is right when he claims to have thus taught "hitherto and always" (ib.); for in the very first years of his reformatory activity he finds the ground of our comfort and confidence only in the mercy of God (A. D. 1519, W. 2. 100).[2] Christ is our righteousness, since he, as the bridegroom to the bride, gives what he has to us and bears our sin (W. 2. 146. De W. 1.17. E. 27. 182 f.). Thus he teaches also at later periods. In so far as we hide ourselves in Christ, who has made full atonement for our sin, and like chickens seek protection under the wings of this hen, we are righteous before God.   "For our

---

[1] Cf. W. 8. 92 (A. D. 1521) : Because they believe, and are living under the kingdom of mercy, and sin in them is condemned and assiduously mortified, therefore it is not imputed to them. Also ib. 109, 111. E. 8. 255 ; 9. 310 ; 7. 226 ; 12. 97, 100, 103 ; 13. 239, 267 ; 14. 17.

[2] Cf. W. 6. 133 (A. D. 1520) : "We rest, I say, in the righteousness of Christ, by which he is righteous, because we cling to this, through which he is acceptable to God and intercedes as our advocate for us and makes himself entirely ours . . . as impossible as it is therefore that Christ in his righteousness should not be acceptable, so impossible is it that we by our faith, by which we cling to his righteousness, should not be acceptable."

faith and all that we may have from God is not sufficient, yea it
is not genuine, unless it seeks refuge under the wings of this hen
and believes firmly that not we but Christ can render and has
rendered satisfaction for us to the righteousness of God, and that
grace and salvation are granted to us, not for the sake of our
faith, but for Christ's sake" (E. 7. 178; 3. 424; 10. 226; 15.
381, 485; 28. 417; 46. 71. W. 8. 111 f.). If we look upon
the faith which we have, it is only a beginning of righteousness
(Gal. 2. 312; cf. E. 16. 256); but if we look upon Christ, who
is embraced by this faith as a precious stone in a ring, it may be
said: "God regards him as righteous" (Gal. 1. 195, 322, 339).
The true, abiding righteousness is wrought in us by the gracious
forgiveness of sins guaranteed us through the work of Christ and
through his "return to the Father" (E. 25. 76; 50. 60 f.; 7.
299. Opp. ex. 19. 43. Opp. var. arg. 5. 438). "Sin is indeed
still present, but it is forgiven" (E. 5. 251). It is another's (*eine
fremde*) righteousness which is transferred to us (E. 14. 12.
Opp. ex. 5. 269): "That we may become righteous and delivered from sin through forgiveness of sins" (E. 5. 247). And yet
it remains true, in Luther's mind, that abiding righteousness before God belongs to him alone in whom actual righteousness has
through faith begun to exist,[1] not indeed because this faith as a
human activity constitutes the subjective beginning of actual
righteousness, and thus embraces in itself also love (per contra,
Gal. 1. 137), but because it, as a work of the Christ *most actively
working in us*, and by virtue of the power of Christ, furnishes
the guarantee for the continuance of the process of advancing
actual righteousness. Not for the sake of man's faith, but because Christ, the Redeemer, constitutes the substance and power
of this faith, does God, through the forgiveness of sins, pronounce the believer righteous. "Therefore it is not our righteousness, but Christ's righteousness—yea, this righteousness is
Christ himself, and yet becomes my righteousness if I believe"
(E. 3. 435; 50. 61. Opp. ex. 18. 189 f.).

[1] Very instructive is his development of the parallel between the influences
flowing from Adam and from Christ (E. 13. 120) : "As sin has been inherited
by us from Adam, and has now become our own, so must also Christ's righteousness and life become our own, in such a way that the same power of righteousness and life may work in us, just as though they had also been inherited
by us from him. For there is in him not a merely personal, but an actual and
powerful righteousness and life—yea, a fountain which gushes and flows forth
into all who become partakers of himself, just as from Adam sin and death have
flowed into man's whole nature. And it is therefore now declared that men
become righteous and alive from sin and death, not from themselves or through
themselves, but through the alien righteousness and life of this Lord Christ,
namely, when he touches them with his hand and imparts to them through the
word his work and power to blot out sin and death, and they believe the same."

Whoever will be at pains to compare with this the utterances of Luther at the beginning of his career must confess that he has steadfastly kept within the lines which he then marked out : (1) Christ, or the Holy Spirit, works faith.   In the believer (the regenerated) Christ is efficaciously present, together with the Holy Spirit, through and in his faith.   Man is thereby renewed (*verneuert*), made "actually" righteous.   "Justification is, in fact, a certain regeneration into newness (of life) " (Jen. 1. 540 v).   (2) But this fermentative energy of faith is a progressive and not seldom interrupted process.   The sinner can hence find secure comfort only through the fact that God, by virtue of the union between Christ and the believer effected and made effectual in faith, imputes to him the righteousness which Christ has secured for him, *i. e.*, forgives him his sins.   This is the "personal" righteousness which avails for the whole man and makes him, despite his sins, acceptable to God.   In this are firmly rooted the consolation of the believing conscience and the assurance of salvation.[1]

If we now review these delineations of the process involved in the justification of the sinner, it must, it appears to me, be evident to all that the deepest motives of the Pauline and Johannine cycles of thought find expression in them ; but, none the less, that they are moulded formally upon the pattern of the medieval idea of justification.   But, in place of the infused grace of the earlier theology, is now the Christ working effectually in us.   And the powerless forgiveness of sins, which was in one way or another merely a pendant to the *gratia infusa*, is replaced by the energizing consciousness, inseparably connected with the contemplation of the life and work of Jesus,[2] that his redemptive work means for us the forgiveness of our sins.[3]

8. This leads us to Luther's conception of Grace.   It must be

---

[1] Cf. Opp. ex. 19. 48 (A. D. 1532) : " These are the *two parts of justification*.   The former is the grace revealed through Christ, that through Christ we have a God appeased, so that sin is no longer able to accuse us, but the confidence of conscience in the mercy of God is reduced to certainty.   The latter is the bestowal of the Spirit with his gifts, who illuminates against the pollutions of the spirit and the flesh."   So also, E. 12. 285.   It is no more than a dividing of this second element of righteousness, when Luther in other connections discriminates between an "inward " and an "outward" righteousness, describing the former as " righteousness in the heart" and the latter as the "fruit, result, and proof" of the former. *E. g.*, E. 13. 238, 269. W. 2. 146.

[2] Here, as in connection with the above remarks upon the " workings " of Christ, must be borne in mind, what Luther has said (see supra, pp. 230 f., 252 f.) touching the contemplation of Christ and the continued activity of the exalted Saviour.

[3] If this doctrine of justification shall appear " unlutheran " to any, they must explain to their own satisfaction the fact that it comes from Luther !

said here, first of all, that Luther never wearied of assailing
every form of work-righteousness and all claims to human merit.
This is a leading point in his reformatory ideas. As he who now
performs good works does not aim thereby to gain merits, since
God is, in the last instance, the original source of the works
(E. 7. 165. Cf. above under 6),[1] so also by the conception
of the forgiveness of sins all meriting or atoning is excluded
(E. 15. 385; 9. 257 f.; 24. 98; 46. 106). By his own merit
can no one become righteous or be saved (46. 69; 43. 362);
nor can anyone even act meritoriously before the reception of grace (43. 360). " When we are speaking of that
which concerns the Christian life . . . how we may become
pious before God and secure forgiveness of sin and eternal life,
then *all our merit is absolutely excluded* (*rein abgeschnitten*)
and we should not hear nor know anything of it " (E. 43. 359.
Gal. 1. 185 f., 193 f.). Thus is this idea, which had since the
days of Tertullian exerted its fateful influence in the Western
church, finally ejected from the Christian conception of religion.[2]
But this was made possible by the new understanding of grace ;
for so long as the conception of the latter as a substantial endowment prevailed, the legalistic view of the relation between God
and man, together with the associated notions of merit, constituted a counter-weight to it, preserving the personal element in
the relation of man to God.

The dominant idea in the medieval doctrine of grace is the
gratia creata, as a quality created in man (*e. g.*, Biel, p. 195).
Against this idea Luther's criticism is directed. " I accept
grace here properly as meaning the *favor of God*, not a quality
of the soul as our more recent writers have taught " (W. 8. 106,
92 f.   E. 7. 170).   God's favor, his merciful will, as it is revealed and proclaimed by Christ, is grace (W. 6. 209.   E. 7.
128 f.; 10. 90, cf. 50. 61 ; 46. 69).   Hence it follows that
God—just because he is love—forgives sin. The effect of this
grace is not a quality "attached" to the soul, but forgiveness
and salvation (E. 5. 246 f.).   From the grace of God thus understood must be discriminated the gift bestowed upon its
recipient.   "Grace and gift differ in this, that grace properly
means the favor, or regard, which he in himself cherishes toward
us, by which he is disposed to pour upon us Christ and the Spirit
with his gifts " (E. 63. 123 ; 12. 285). This is by no means to
be understood as equivalent to the gifts of the *gratia creata ;* for

---

[1] We may therefore understand also the declaration, that works are unsuited,
yea, even offensive, and a hindrance to justification.   (E. 10. 161.)

[2] Upon the popular use of the idea—drawn from the Scriptures—see E. 43.
364 ff.

grace in the sense of gift is most clearly discriminated from the
"quality" of the old theory.   "It is a very great, strong,
powerful, and active thing—this grace of God.   It does not lie,
as the dream-preachers falsely teach, in the souls of men and
sleep and allow itself to be carried by them as a painted board
carries its color.   Nay, not so!   It carries, it leads, it drives,
it begets, it transforms, it works all things in man, and makes
itself felt and experienced."   This is the grace which "transforms and renews" man (E. 7. 170 f., 30. 368).[1]   It is the
same thing to which Luther applies the term, Gift.   The two
elements in the definition are therefore related as follows: (1)
Grace expresses the favor, or the loving-will, of God, as revealed
in his not imputing sin.   (2) The word "grace," or "gift,"
designates the peculiar workings of this loving-will within the
heart of man.   With these two aspects of grace naturally correspond the two meanings of the term, Justification (p. 263).   The
old conception of grace, as wrought out by Augustine (Vol. I.,
p. 350 f.) is here overthrown.   From the time of Duns, the irre-
sistibly-working natural power of grace had been but a respect-
able phrase (see note, i. e., on this page).   The Augustinianism
of the closing Middle Ages (supra, p. 207) then sought to repris-
tinate Augustine's doctrine of grace.   Luther replaced and surpassed it with the idea of the personal loving-will of God, which
is omnipresently and omnipotently accomplishing its work in the
hearts of men.   It is in this only that we discover the deepest religious motives underlying Luther's *De servo arbitrio* (p. 244 f.).
Luther's God is the Almighty Loving-Will—almighty power,
present in all that exists and shall exist (30. 58), almighty
energy also in the outworking of love.[2]   The grace of this God
is a working force, not a quiescent quality in the soul.

9. Faith in the grace of God embraces the conviction that the
forgiveness of sins is 'granted "not for nothing, nor *without
satisfaction of his righteousness* (justice).   For there can be no
room for mercy and grace to work upon us and in us . . . satisfaction must first be rendered most completely to righteousness,

---

[1] The "Sophists," Thomas and Scotus, say of it, "that it adorns and helps
to produce the works" (ib.); cf. supra, p. 158, 119.   Luther rejected the
gratia infusa, as an empty notion.   At this point the criticisms of Duns prepared the way, as the *gratia infusa* was for him little more than a phrase
(p. 159 f.).   Luther rejected the "infused grace" not because it attributed
too much to God, but because it attributed *too little* to him.

[2] But Luther never, when unfolding his religious ideas, especially in his
sermons, permitted these principles to lead him to determinism or predestination.   For him there exists between God and man a personal and ethical
relation.   It must not be forgotten, that the power of love of which he thinks
is, in the last analysis, the spiritual power of the person of Christ.

Matt. 5. 18." (E. 7. 175). This compels us here to consider the "Work of Christ."[1] (*a*) It is Luther's firm conviction that justification does not rest upon an arbitrary imputation by God, as the passion of Christ would otherwise have been unnecessary (E. 7. 298). In this, he takes up arms against the Scotist theory of an arbitrary divine will.[2] "But if the wrath of God is to be taken from me and I am to obtain grace and forgiveness, then must it be merited (*abverdienet*) from him by someone ; for God cannot be favorable nor gracious toward sins, nor remove penalty and wrath, unless payment be made and satisfaction rendered for them" (11. 290; 9. 381 f. W. 2. 137). But Christ, in obedience to the Father, serving our race in love, has offered this satisfaction or payment to God through his life and death (E. 8. 177 ; 15. 57 f. W. 1. 270 ; 2. 146). The purpose which inspired him in so doing was to obtain for himself the human race as a kingdom and to become their Lord (W. 2. 97. E. 22. 66). All his acts and his endurance were subordinated to this purpose, to become the Lord, that is, "a helpful power to his subjects." His government is forgiveness of sins, peace and righteousness (E. 20. 146 f.; 48. 265 f.; 50. 61). He rules through the gospel of the forgiveness of sins (E. 14. 251 ; 7. 55; 8. 229; 40. 88). "For we should regard Christ's kingdom as a great and beautiful dome or roof, everywhere stretched out above us, which covers us and protects us from the wrath of God ; yea, as a great wide heaven where nothing but grace and forgiveness shine and fill the world and all things, so that all sins are in comparison scarcely as a spark to the great wide ocean" (14. 181 f.). But, as his reign brings to men the forgiveness of sins, so does it bring also the fullness of all virtue, faith, love, purity, happiness, and obedient service. "This flows over upon the Christian world from its Lord, who is a head and beginning of all grace and virtue" (W. 6. 13 f.). The purpose of the work of Christ is therefore the establishment of the kingdom of God, *i. e.*, he becomes Lord, in that he forgives sins and inspires to a new life.

(*b*) The Acts and Sufferings of Christ are subordinate to this purpose.[3] Luther presented the so-called objective aspect

---

[1] Luther uses this term, E. 7. 109; 14. 115. Upon the atonement as a reconciliation of love and righteousness, cf. supra, p. 67, 112, 156 f., 200. Vol. I., p. 295, 361.

[2] But he does not, like Anselm, postulate the necessity of the atonement upon general grounds, but deduces it as an inference from the actual fact of the passion of Christ. On the contrary, see the Scotist ideas, supra, p. 151 : "God is not pious because he does this work, but the work is right, good, holy, and well done, because he himself does it " (E. 35. 168).

[3] Let it be observed, further, that Christ here appears everywhere as the

of the atonement with energy and with variety of form. The sinful race was under the wrath of God, under debt to him, fallen under the power of the devil, under obligation to the law, subject to penalties for the transgression of the law, or to eternal death (E. 15. 57). But Christ has entered the race, and in such a way that he bore for us the lot which had become ours through sin : "But now has he stepped into our place and for our sakes suffered law, sin, and death to fall upon him" (51. 272). He pays and makes good for our debt, so that we are released from it (6. 371 f.). He is sacrifice and payment for the sin of the world (12. 246, 118 ; 18. 49 ; 2. 249 ; 3. 100 ; 47. 46 ; 48. 97 ; 50. 246). Christ "as himself guilty" has "stepped into the place of our sinful nature, heaped upon himself and vanquished all the wrath of God which we had merited" (7. 302 ; 11. 290). He was compelled "to feel in his tender, innocent heart the wrath and judgment of God against sin, to taste for us eternal death and perdition, and, in short, to suffer everything which a condemned sinner has deserved and must eternally suffer" (39. 48).[1] But all this he endured, "that the wrath of God might be placated, in order that we might stand in grace and have forgiveness" (W. 8. 442. E. 10. 418; 11. 290; 12. 283; 311; 14. 119; 20. 161). He likewise fulfilled in our stead and for our benefit the law, which affected only sinners, and endured the penalties prescribed for its violation (E. 15. 260 f.; 1. 310 ff.; 14. 154 f.; 161). He thereby "rendered satisfaction to the law" (15. 17; 11. 314), i. e., the law has, since he has satisfied its demands, no right and no further claim to men (15. 57 f., 262).[2] He also robs the devil of his "right and

God-man. His divinity is recognized in his works, e. g., from his mediatorial activity (E. 18. 225 ; 16. 211); or from the infinite nature of the atonement and his appeasing of the wrath of God (11. 290; 49. 139; 46. 366; 45. 315 f.; 46. 46); or from his exercising of the sovereignty of God in the world (10. 345 ; 40. 50. Opp. ex. 23. 308 ; 18. 85); or from his power to save (47. 6, 198); or from the fact that we can believe only on God (47. 44).

[1] Luther can, of course, not mean to say that Christ was eternally dead and accursed, for the latter could not be the case, if for no other reason, because the former was not true. He means that Christ endured, as all other consequences of sin, also an abandonment by God which corresponded with that awaiting the lost. See W. 2. 260: "was forsaken by God, as one who is eternally accursed." Cf. 20. 161 ; 46. 191.

[2] That is, since the law laid hold upon Christ, the sinless One, Christ robbed it of its power over the race. It is made powerless. This is explained in a thoroughly mythological way (cf. the outwitting of death and the devil, 45. 318; 46. 370); e. g., E. 15. 261 ; 18. 176 f. But in the last citation above appears the expression, "to satisfy the law." In order to understand this, we must clearly keep in mind the fact that the relation established by the law between man and God is to be regarded as one, not of private, but of public obligation. This is of the very highest importance, for it reveals the

power " over men, because he "slew Christ without any guilt "
(49. 250; 33. 107).

Christ therefore became a sacrifice for our debt ; he endured
the wrath of God, took upon himself the works and penalties of
the law, suffered the assaults of the devil and of death.   All this
carries us back to the will of God, who would not forgive before
satisfaction had been rendered to his justice.   "God, nevertheless (*i. e.*, despite his mercy) required that satisfaction be made
for sin, and that his honor and law be recompensed."   His
mercy sent forth Christ, "who merited it for us and in our
stead" (15. 385.   Cf. 12. 266).   The death of Christ was the
payment, or satisfaction, for our sins (19. 74, 211 f.; 11. 290 ;
28. 240).   Thus God requires also that positive satisfaction be
rendered to his law, which is accomplished by Christ's perfect
meeting of its demands.   What he did in this respect is as
though we had ourselves done it (7. 177 f.; 11. 314 ; 1. 312).
Luther's idea is thus: The ordinance of the law, established by
God for the sinful race of men, has been with its penalties abolished by Christ, in that he fulfilled the law and endured its
penalties—and that in such a way that the sufferings of Christ
prevent the execution of the penalties of the law, while his active
fulfillment of the law's requirements deprives the whole ordinance
of the law of its force.   Thus Christ passed through the whole
course of human existence from conception to the state of the
dead, and thereby "consecrated and hallowed it " (20. 156 ff.,
150).   "In him and through him" we become free from death
and all misfortune (ib. 172).   He who holds to him in faith is
for his sake free as well from the works as from the penalties of
the law.   Christ bestows upon us his piety and his sufferings
(12. 230).[1] His obedience, innocence, and holiness are our consolation (1. 311; 7. 178.   W. 1. 593).

entirely different meanings attached by Luther and Anselm to the "satisfaction " rendered by Christ.   In Anselm, the satisfaction is brought to God personally, as to an offended private man ; according to Luther, it consists in the
fulfilling of the divinely given system of laws by our representative, Christ.
Since satisfaction is rendered to this moral order of the world and it is thus
recognized and actually honored, the wrath of God is appeased, and the law
made powerless.   There is thus presented a really ethical view, capable of the
most profound interpretation, in contrast with the objectionable anthropo-
morphism of Anselm.   Here again Duns prepared the way for Luther.   Sent.
iv. d. 14, q. 1, 7.

[1] For ethical purposes, Luther stripped the conception of "Satisfaction " of
its validity, as he had already (supra, p. 264) done with that of merit (11. 296,
280 : " Therefore let this word, Satisfaction, henceforth be nothing and dead in
our churches and our theology, be committed to the judges and to the schools
of the jurists, where it belongs and whence the papists derived it ; " vid. Tertul.,
Vol. I., p. 133).   Yet in the doctrine of Redemption both conceptions play

(*c*) Christ has, according to the will of the Father, appeased wrath, satisfied the law, and effected the forgiveness of sins. Grace is now maintained through his continuous intercession in heaven.   We need no sacrifice, since his blood atones eternally (E. 8. 154; 9. 236; 28. 240) and he "without ceasing offers before God" (W. 6. 369; cf. 1. 703.   E. 7. 109; 12. 118; 47. 23).

These thoughts are for Luther of great practical importance. Since sin at all times yet clings to the believer, he experiences also the divine wrath directed against him.   To counteract this, he lays hold of the thought that Christ intercedes for him before the Father.   He who now by faith is united to Christ becomes certain that, for the sake of Christ's intercession, God forgives him his sin (Gal. 1. 338 f.), for that intercession silences the demands of the law upon us, since he has fulfilled it; and he frees us from sin, death, and the devil, since he has vanquished them.   But this avails for us only in so far as we "creep beneath his mantle and wings," *i. e.*, believe (E. 14. 154 ff., 159, 156; 48. 275).   Since Christ intercedes for us, and his work is well pleasing to the Father, we are sure of being in favor with God (E. 15. 237 ff.).   "But we are very certain that Christ is pleasing to God. . . .   In so far, therefore, as Christ is pleasing and we cling to him, in so far we also are pleasing to God . . . and although sin clings in the flesh . . . nevertheless grace is more abundant and more powerful than sin. . . . Wherefore sin is not able to terrify us nor make us doubtful concerning the grace of God in us.   For Christ, the most mighty giant, has borne the law, condemned sin, abolished death and all evils.   So long as he is at the right hand of God interceding for us, we cannot on account of ourselves doubt concerning the grace of God" (Gal. 2. 164 f.).

(*d*) But Christ is not only our representative before God; he also represents God among us.   This comes to pass in that he reveals to us the love of God and thereby awakens in us faith and love.   According to this, a further element must be included in the Work of Christ.   Christ not only secures the revelation of the grace of God, but he also imparts it to us.   "It was necessary for him to appear before God for us and be our veil, shield, and hen, beneath whom we have forgiveness of sin and salvation from the wrath of God and from hell.   And *not only this*, but he in addition gives the Holy Spirit, that we may also follow him

a leading rôle in Luther—and until the present day ! (Upon the term merit, see also E. 7. 179, 194, 195; 15. 385; 28. 417.   W. 1. 309, 428, etc.) But this is with Luther no inconsistency, for both conceptions fall within the lines of the relation between man and God as fixed by the law.

and here begin to quench and crucify sin'' (E. 14. 161 f.). As the intercession of Christ applies both to his earthly life and to his present existence, so also does his revealing agency. Christ once on earth revealed God, and he now does so again, in that his word is preached, the Spirit sent by him, and thereby a new life begotten within us (e. g., 14. 155).[1] He is the ground of the forgiveness of sins, and is at the same time the source of faith and of personal righteousness (Opp. ex. 18. 189. E. 14. 119 f., supra, p. 260 ff.). "Therefore has God given us, in the first place, a man who should make complete satisfaction for us to the divine justice. In the second place, he through the same Man pours out grace and rich blessing." This occurs through regeneration (7. 177). "This is grace upon grace, that we are pleasing also to the Father for the sake of the Lord Christ, and that we also through Christ receive the Holy Ghost and become righteous'' (46.68). From Christ, as the Second Adam and head of the new race, streams into us new life and righteousness, for he dwells and reigns in us (E. 13. 225 f. W. 2. 531, 502, 529). It is only a varied application of this thought, when it is said that the love of Christ begets a responsive love in our hearts (W. 2. 523 ; 6. 117. E. 12. 258 f., 312), or when he is represented as our pattern, or, in the earlier writings, as a "divine legislator" (W. 1. 533).[2] But in the discussions of Christ as our pattern, we observe a connection between this subjective aspect of redemption and its objective side. To regard Christ merely as an example is papistic and fanatical error (E. 8. 235 f., 248 ; 9. 244 f.; 15. 388 ; 29. 278).[3] "Imitation does not make sons, but sonship makes imitators'' (W. 2. 518. E. 29. 211). We must first accept Christ in faith "as a sacrifice and portion'' and thereby become blessed and righteous, and only then follows "the example and imitation'' (E. 7. 303 f.; 8. 3).[4]

---

[1] Luther thus ascribes to Christ a representative agency toward men similar to that which he exercises in behalf of men before God. But it must be remembered that the revelation of Christ through the Holy Spirit, being limited to the Word, cannot go essentially beyond the historical revelation made during his earthly life. E. 12. 300, and cf. ₵ 69, 2.

[2] Luther afterward expressly rejects this term, e. g., E. 7. 298 ; 47. 302.

[3] How striking is this remark in view of the history of the *Imitatio Christi*, e. g., supra, p. 178, 179.

[4] Luther often speaks of the *Following of Christ* in the sense of the imitation of him as our pattern, e. g., W. 1. 338, 364, 320, 613, 697 ; 2. 138, 141, 147 f., 151, 501, 747 ; 6. 275 ; 8. 367, 420. E. 29. 11 ; 8. 157, 234, 247, 251 ; 9. 51 ; 11. 52, 171 ; 14. 46 ; 15. 175, 425, 462 ; 17. 41. Only seldom, so far as I can recall, did he designate the " Following " in the original sense (supra, p. 180, n. 1, cf. E. 48. 276) expressly as faith (W. 1. 275); but this idea lies at the foundation of his entire conception of the faith obtained in the contemplation of the historical Christ.

(c) Reviewing now the work of Christ as thus portrayed, it is evident that, as in the medieval presentations of the subject, the features of that work having relation to man are to be discriminated from those relating to God. Christ reconciled the Father, and he revealed God to us. In the first aspect of his work, all the conceptions of the traditional teaching are preserved, *i. e.*, satisfaction, merit, sacrifice, deliverance from sin, death, hell, devil, etc.[1] Yet it is important to observe that there is here, after all, a certain modification of the thought. Luther's fundamental idea of the subject is as follows: On account of sin, God has placed the race under the law, with its demands and penalties. The relation of man to God is accordingly not to be apprehended in the light of private obligation (law), but in that of public law (supra, p. 267, n. 2). The legal ordinances thus expressing the will of God have not been observed, but their penalties could be borne only by those who were guilty of their violation. To this divine ordinance Christ rendered satisfaction in our stead through his fulfillment of the law and through the endurance of its penalties. Thereby it became possible for God to abrogate the legal ordinance, since his love has now been revealed to men in Christ, renewing them and filling them with the consciousness that they now enjoy his favor (grace).

It is very clear from this that, in Luther's conception, the reconciliation of the Father by Christ precedes the bestowal of grace as its basis. But it is equally true, that there is lacking here, as distinctly as in Thomas or Duns (p. 114 n. 1, 141 n.), any clear explanation of the inner relationship of the two ideas. This could be secured only by showing the reconciliation of the Father to be a necessary means for securing the end in view, *i. e.*, the bestowal of grace. But this Luther never attempts to do. Since the nature of God is love, the revelation of his righteousness (justice) does not abrogate his mercy. The mission of Christ is to be traced back to the divine compassion. But in what connection does the selection of the particular form of Christ's work stand with the end in view? Why does not love directly abolish the ancient ordinance? To this Luther responds: Because God willed that satisfaction must first be rendered to the latter. The mercy of God sends Christ to bring to us the forgiveness of sins, but God wills that it shall first be earned, or merited (*abverdient*), from him through the satisfaction to be rendered by Christ (15. 385 ; 12. 266 ; 7. 299 f.).[2] It is therefore

---

[1] The "Sermon von der Betrachtung des heil. Leidens Christi," A. D. 1519, W. 2. 136 ff., is peculiarly instructive as displaying the variety of aspects under which Luther could present the sufferings of Christ.

[2] The last of these citations summarizes Luther's view in a classical form:

the will of God—and nothing more can be said—that the bestowal of grace, or the introduction of a new ordinance, shall
follow only upon the ground of the allaying of his wrath through
the satisfaction of the old ordinance.[1]   The connection existing
between this two-fold character of the work of Christ and the
duplex nature which we have traced in grace, justification, faith
and sin, is self-evident.

Cf. HELD, De opere Jesu Chr. salutari (Gött., 1860). VON HOFFMAN,
Schutzschriften, ii. 23 ff.   TH. HARNACK, L. Theol. 288 ff.   GOTTSCHICK,
Propter Christum, Ztschr. f. Theol. u. K., 1897, p. 352 ff.; 1898, 406 ff.

10. The entire Christian life is a repentance.   But contrition
is no longer a fruitless self-torture, for it stands in league with
faith.   And works are no more attempts to render satisfaction,
for God performs them through faith.   This repentance is to fill
the entire life.   It takes the place of the discipline once exacted
through the sacrament of repentance.   Luther's central ideas
can be understood, as we have shown, only when regarded from
this point of view.

Our study of the new conception of moral works leads us, further, to consider Luther's ideal of life ; and the examination of
his conception of the work of Christ leads to the doctrine of the
Word and Sacraments, and also to that of the Church.

"Although now purely out of grace our sin is non-imputed to us by God, yet
he would nevertheless not do this, unless satisfaction should first be fully and
superfluously rendered to his law and his justice.   It was required that such.
gracious imputation should first be purchased and secured for us from his justice.   Therefore, since this was impossible for us, he appointed One for us in
our stead, who should take upon himself all the punishment which we had
merited, and fulfill for us the law, and thus avert from us God's judgment and
reconcile his wrath."   It will be observed how strictly the discussion is here
held to the ideas of law, with its fulfillment and penalties.   The firm relationship here established marks a step in advance which is intimately connected
with Luther's general doctrinal position.   The idea of "superfluous" satisfaction is derived from the Thomistic theology (p. 112, 198).

[1] The influence of Scotist ideas is here unmistakable.   That Christ reconciled the Father was simply because God willed that he should do so.   Only
in this sense could Luther speak of a necessity, and a "must" in connection
with the atonement (see previous note), just as in Duns and Biel.   But in
other aspects also, if I am correct, Luther's way of regarding the matter is formally parallel with the conceptions of Duns and Biel (vid. supra, p. 157,
200), since in them also the purpose to effectually bestow grace upon men
(through the institution and agency of the sacraments) was associated with the
arbitrarily ordained condition of a previous reconciliation of God through the
merit of Christ.   This historical parallel will explain the peculiar lack of connection between the two aspects of the work of Christ.   To speak of an "absolute necessity" of the atonement as maintained by Luther (Th. Harnack, L.'s
Theol. ii. 304 ff.) is therefore in my opinion misleading.   A solution of the
problem thus stated it is the province of Dogmatics to seek with the most careful study of the Scriptural ideas involved.   The History of Doctrines can only
state the fact, that it is not to be found in the writings of Luther.

§ 68. *The Evangelical Ideal of Life.*

LITERATURE. Cf. RITSCHL, Gesch. d. Pietismus, i. (A. D. 1880), 36 ff. LUTHARDT, Gesch. d. chr. Ethik, ii. (1893), 25 ff. UHLHORN, Die chr. Liebestätigkeit, iii. (1890), 3 ff. EGER, Die Anschauungen Luther's von Beruf., Giessen, 1900. SEEBERG, Luther's Stellung zu den sittlichen und sozialen Nöten seiner Zeit., Leipzig, 1902.

1. The crisis at the close of the Middle Ages was occasioned, not only by the dissolution and practical insufficiency of the "dogma" of the church, but by the conflict between practical life and the church's ideal of what life should be (cf. supra, p. 173, 181 f.). The Reformation achieved by Luther was, accordingly, not a reconstruction of doctrine, but the vigorous enforcement of a new ideal of life. Ritschl has rendered good service in emphasizing this. For the medieval Christian, faith was subjection to the canon law of the church. Sin was located chiefly in the sensual impulses of nature. The natural was essentially evil. Hence, the natural order of human life in the state was the direct contrast to the kingdom of God, or the church. At this point the ideas of Luther entered a mighty protest. He drew the conclusion from the entire previous course of development ; or, more properly speaking, he substituted vigorous Christian ideas for the negations and skepticism, the longings and anticipations of the past. The fourteenth and fifteenth centuries had, it is true, prepared the way for him. But in his spirit criticism became assertion, the unchurchly and secular became churchly and biblical. His criticism did not end in the helpless pusillanimity of Occam, nor in the worldly frivolity or secret qualms of conscience which marked so many of the Humanists. He recognized the right of every man to gain for himself religious conviction, without constraint, and pointed to Christ as the way to its attainment. He taught that, since God created man, his natural impulses and ordinances are in accordance with the will of God. No one need be ashamed of them.[1] He recognized the lawfulness of the natural life and of the civil organism, beholding in them ordinances of God which are not sinful. The natural forms of existing things are not essentially evil, but according to God's will, however men, as Luther never forgets, may continually pollute them.

2. From this point of view we may understand his demolition of the medieval ideals both in the sphere of individual life and

---

[1] *E. g.*, E. 10. 440: Dear lad, be not ashamed that you long for a maid, and the maid longs for a lad. Only let it lead to marriage and not to wantonness, and it is then no disgrace to you, just as little as eating and drinking are a disgrace. Cf. 29. 39 ; 28. 199, but also E. 22. 205.

18

in that of the state. The ethics of the desensualizing theory beheld the " state of perfection " in the life of the *religiosi, i. e.*, the monks (p. 124). Luther saw therein only a self-chosen and, in the deepest sense, ungodly sanctity (E. 28. 231). This is not Christian perfection (W. 8. 328. E. 9. 287; 7. 321; 8. 13; 12. 227). Good works, as they are performed either in accordance with the so-called " evangelical counsels " (*consilia evangelica*), which come from the devil (W. 8. 585. E. 22. 65), or in pursuance of the sacrament of repentance (W. 6. 207, 208, 209, 210 f., 212; 8. 366, 378. E. 7. 245; 10. 234, 273; 13. 208, 217 f.), are not good works pleasing to God; for they neither result from the free inner impulse of the heart, nor do they benefit anyone. " It is most shamefully repugnant and contrary, not only to the word of God, faith, Christian liberty, and the precepts of God, but to thee thyself " (W. 8. 639, 605, 616. E. 10. 425 ; 29. 39). The marks of really good works (p. 259) are wanting in these, *i. e.*, the impulse from within, or freedom ; the divine commandment ; and usefulness. It is better to rear one's children well than to make pilgrimages or build churches (W. 2. 169 f.). And since these works are unnatural, the pursuit of them bears bitter fruit, as may be seen in all those who have taken the (monastic) vows ; for example, in the " unchaste chastity " of the monks (E. 29. 17, 327 ; 10. 426). This is one objection which Luther constantly presents against the Romish ideal of life : its works are unnatural and purely legalistic. And just because they are so, they are regarded as " meritorious," which forms his second ground of objection to them. But, as these works are rejected, there remains no place for the " saints." Whatever in them was good, was wrought by God (W. 1. 420). They have had no power to render satisfaction even for themselves (ib. 606). There are no superfluous (*überlängliche*) works (*opera supererogationis*, E. 14. 35).

3. In the sphere of civil life, also, the rightfulness of the natural order is to be recognized as in accordance with the will of God. " The secular law and sword " exist in accordance with the divine ordinance (E. 22. 63, 76), for they are necessary for the world (73). Hence the Christian may with a good conscience hold a civil office (73, 80), provided he can thus benefit his neighbor (78).[1] This is especially true of the " Christian prince." " Service " is his calling (94 ff.). But, essentially,

---

[1] This is true even of war : " What else is war than a punishing of wrong and evil ? Why does anyone go to war, except because he desires to have peace and obedience ? " (23. 249. Cf. 16. 195). From this we may understand Luther's attitude toward the " thieving and murderous peasants."

the civil government has to do only with the outward conduct of men (87), whereas Christ reigns only in the hearts of men by his Spirit (E. 22. 70). In the duty resting upon the government is included a solicitude for culture and education (schools), as well as for social conditions. But "the secular government has laws which do not extend further than over body and property and what is outward in the world. For over the souls of men God cannot and will not allow anyone but himself alone to rule. Therefore in matters which have to do with the salvation of souls, nothing but God's word must be taught or accepted (22. 82, 83, 86; 45. 115). Thus the boundary line of the civil authority and the rights of liberty of conscience are preserved.[1] (Cf. LEZIUS, Gleichheit u. Ungleichheit, in Greifswalder Studien, 1895, p. 287 ff. WARD, Darstellung . . . der Ansichten Luther's vom Staat u. seinen wirtschaftlichen Aufgaben, 1898.)

4. The State of Perfection (*status perfectionis*) is to be (possessed) of a living faith, a despiser of death, of life, of glory, and of the whole world, a servant of all in fervent love (W. 8. 584). Faith and love (or works) are the content of the Christian life. "Now faith and love are the whole life of a Christian man. . . . *Faith receives, love gives*" (W. 8. 355, 362, 366, 385 f.   E. 7. 159, 161; 8. 40, 71, 75; 9. 280 f., 137; 10. 20; 46. 254). "Thus faith remains the doer and love remains the deed" (E. 8. 63). "Faith brings man to God; love brings God to men. Through faith man allows God to do him good; through love God does good to men (E. 14. 40). But all this is not to be required by compulsion or law. The Christian life is a life of freedom, since the good is wrought in the heart by God and is done with delight. Hence no commandments have validity here. This is "evangelical," or "Christian liberty," or "the liberty of faith."[2] The law is valid only for the outward man (vid. supra, 3), where it is necessary, particularly for the rude "Lord Omnes" (E. 24. 140 f.). These ideas are grandly developed in the tract, *Von der Freiheit eines Christenmenschen*. Through faith the Christian becomes a free lord of all things. In faith he lays hold upon the man

---

[1] But Luther places the law of nature (cf., p. 171) above the "written law or the counsels of the jurists:" "The highest law and master of all laws remains the reason" (E. 22. 95, 257). "Such free judgment does love pronounce, and natural law, of which all reason is full" (ib. 104).

[2] *E. g.*, W. 1. 530, 647, 675; 2. 486; 8. 327, 330, 334.   E. 10. 425; 12. 363 f.; 29. 188 f., etc.   The pope and the fanatics, according to Luther, destroy this liberty; the former by commandments, the latter by prohibitions (29. 189). Against Carlstadt he formulated the practical canon, "that everything should be free which God does not in clear language forbid in the New Testament" (29. 188).

Christ, and the righteousness of the bridegroom becomes a property also of the bride, the soul (E. 27. 183). Again, the soul through faith is filled with all goodness (181), so that it needs no law nor commandment. Hereby the Christian is made free. Since he does good with inward heartfelt delight, because the word of Christ dwells in his soul, he does not require the demands of the law. Is God now his in faith, there is thereby given to him the certainty that all things must work together for his good (185), as he has now, on the other hand, to appear before God in intercession for others. Thus the Christian is a king and a priest. "Through his kingship, he has power over all things; through his priesthood, he has power over God" (186). But the Christian must also "govern his own body and associate with his fellow-men." This requires a disciplining and exercising of the body, that it may become obedient and conformable to the inner man.[1] But faith is an inward appreciation of the benefits of God, and hence begets the inner impulse to do what will please God, i. e., to serve one's neighbor. "There thus flow from faith, love and desire toward God; and from love, a free, willing, joyous life of service of one's neighbor" (196). These are the true good works, as they flow forth freely from the heart and bring good to others. "For whatever work is not designed to serve another . . . is not a good Christian work" (198). Thus the Christian is through faith a free lord, and through love a ministering servant.

These remained controlling principles with Luther. Faith is the acceptance (*Hinnahme*) of God and his benefits. These so overpower our hearts that—and also through the Holy Spirit (E. 19. 376)—there follows a self-surrender (*Hingabe*) to God, as a "great fervent love" to him (E. 14. 4). But this love leads us with inward desire to subject ourselves to the will of God (E. 7. 161). And thus out of love to God arises love to our neighbor (W. 8. 386. E. 14. 34, 46; 28. 207; 9. 284). Love is accordingly defined as the will to do good : "Love is nothing but simply to do good and to be useful to all men, friends and foes" (W. 8. 362). "But to love is from the heart to wish good to another" (W. 2. 604).[2] Thus all love is *service*, and the Christian's whole life is a service for God and his brethren (W. 2. 148; 8. 360 f., 367). We know that we were created

---

[1] These ideas produce a complete transformation as to the province of ascetic exercises. These are not a self-mortification nor a meritorious work, but the disciplining and exercise of the natural powers, which they thus make fit agencies for the accomplishment of good in the Christian sense. See R. SEEBERG, Askese, PRE. ii., ed. 3, 138 f.

[2] With this definition compare p. 107.

for the sake of others (E. 8. 263), and that we are instruments in the hand of Christ (12. 365). But such service can be rendered only by really good works, such as we may learn from the Ten Commandments, and not by the self-chosen Romish works (E. 9. 287 ; 10. 411 f.; 11. 318 ; 13. 159). These are the works which belong to the natural course of life, in which we should manifest toward our fellow-men "love, humility, patience, gentleness" (E. 9. 287, 289 f.). This we should do, furthermore, each in his own particular calling : "serve God in his calling and thank him that he uses him also in his position in life as an instrument" (9. 290). The moral equality of all callings, even the lowest, is continually assumed (e. g., E. 7. 228 ; 10. 233 ff.; 8. 259 f.; 16. 137 ; 17. 258 ; 18. 85 ; 19. 337, 352 f.; 30. 367 ; 48. 273). To serve God in the forms of the natural life and calling by the humble service of love toward the brethren —such is the appointed task of the Christian's life. But the power for such service springs from faith, or from God.

But this is also the path to a realization of the Kingdom of God. This term has in Luther a two-fold significance. On the one hand, it indicates the dominion which Christ exercises in begetting faith and life through the word and granting the forgiveness of sins (E. 14. 181 f., cf. supra, p. 266; 21. 115 ; 14. 238 f , 240, 251 ; 18. 234 ; 39. 34 f.; 15. 21 f.; 12. 2 f.; 51. 181 ; 34. 26 : "Christ's kingdom must on earth rule in our hearts"). On the other hand, it signifies the sphere in which this dominion is exercised, or mankind, in so far as they place all that they do or can do at the service of God (W. 2. 97 ; 22. 166). Hence, all virtues in their fullness are combined in this kingdom : "The kingdom of God is nothing else than to be pious, orderly, pure, kind, gentle, benevolent and full of all virtue and graces ; also, that God have his being within us and that he alone be, live, and reign in us. This we should first of all and most earnestly desire" (W. 2. 98). Since Christ exercises his dominion upon us, we become and grow to be members of his kingdom.[1]

This is what is meant by true evangelical perfection in the sense of Luther. But it is not to be thought of as a completed attainment, but as a continual striving. This is true of faith, which maintains itself amid all manner of assaults, so that it be-

---

[1] The term "kingdom" in Luther, as in the New Testament, very often (e. g., E. 4. 356 ; 23. 311 ; 18. 233 ; 15. 21 ; 29. 295) signifies "dominion." He always, as do the Scriptures, thinks of it as in close association with its Ruler (e. g., 2. 95). It is the result of the work of Christ in the world. In this sense, it is a purely religious conception ; but, since men strive with all their power for its realization, it is also the supreme ethical ideal.

comes "tried and experienced faith" (W. 8. 378. E. 14. 52).
The same is to be said also of the entire scope of the inner life :
"It is and remains upon earth only a beginning and increasing,
which will be completed in yonder world" (E. 27. 188). This
ideal of life eradicates the ancient disposition, imbibed from
Hellenism, to flee from the world. It makes possible a life of
active interest in the duties of the natural life and secular vocation, yet in perfect consistency with the most profound religious
experience.

5. The recognition of the validity and independence of the
natural life awakened in Luther the desire to see civil and social
affairs regulated by the principles properly underlying them.
The dispute between the peasants and the nobility had to do, it
appeared to him, with purely secular affairs (E. 24. 283, 277 f.).
The gospel neither advocates communism (ib. 291), nor does it
abolish feudal service (281). The peasants may be never so
clearly in the right, yet let them not press their legal claims in
the Christian name (273). "In the name of the gospel" they
act against the gospel (275). The social question of the age
was accordingly in his view not an ecclesiastical, but a natural
and civil one.[1] But it by no means follows that the church has
nothing to do with this question and its solution. How little
such an idea would harmonize with Luther's meaning[2] is evident
from his broad program of reform, as seen in his Address to the
Nobility, and in his energetic discussion of social problems,
as in his "*Zinskauf*" and "*Kaufhandlung und Wucher.*" But
as the Address is dedicated, not to the church, but to the nobility,
so for himself Luther declined to assume responsibility for the
solution of the technical questions involved.[3] The church calls
attention to the abuses, demands that they be corrected, and
gives her counsel and encouragement to that end ;[4] but to the
state, *i. e.*, to the social organization, belongs the execution of
the task. This is, briefly stated, Luther's attitude upon such
questions.

---

[1] The peasants claimed to be "a Christian mob or union," "Christian
brothers" (24. 265, 290), and on that ground claim for themselves "divine
right" (265) and "evangelical liberty" (270). These terms had for them the
genuine medieval significance, supra, p. 171, 182.

[2] We must here let the "whole Luther" be heard, which will at least not
be "unlutheran."

[3] *E. g.*, W. 6. 6 : "But it is no part of my work to announce whether five,
four, or six per cent. is to be paid. I leave it to the decision of the laws, so
that where the ground is so good and rich, six per cent. may be taken."

[4] DILTHEY, Arch. f. Gesch. d. Philos. v. 366, rightly says : In the name
of the new Christian spirit, Luther demands a reorganization of German society
in its secular and ecclesiastical ordinances.

Cf. SCHMOLLER, Zur. Gesch. d. nat.-ök. Ansichten in d. Ref.-zeit, in Ztschr. f. d. ges. Staatswiss, 1860, 461 ff. ERHARDT, Die nat.-ök. Ansichten d. Ref., in Stud. u. Krit., 1880, 672 ff. Also, BRAASCH, L. Stellung z. Sozialism., 1897. W. KÖHLER, Die Quellen z. L. Schrift an den Adel., 1895. SEEBERG, Luther's Stellung z. u. den sittlichen u. sozialen Nöten s. Zeit., 1902.

§ 69. *Word and Sacrament.*

1. In the religious processes depicted in § 67, a personal influence is exerted by God upon the human heart. It is in keeping with a true conception of the nature of man in its sensuous and social features, that Luther does not conceive of such influence as mystical and direct.[1] In order to win the hearts of men, God makes use of elements of this world and its history ; of Christ and the word which testifies of him ; as also of the sacraments instituted by him. Only through Word and Sacrament[2] does the Spirit, operating upon the heart (*intus operans*), come to us (W. 1. 632 ; 2. 112. E. 29. 208 ; 9. 210 ; 11. 223).[3] Through these are mediated the great chief miracles, which Christ performs upon the soul, and which are far greater than the bodily miracles which he wrought (E. 16. 190 ; cf. 58. 95 ; 59. 3). This view was confirmed and deepened, particularly in the conflict with the "fanatics."

2. But before the outbreak of the fanatical movement, Luther's doctrine was firmly established in its essential features. In the word alone does God work in the hearts of men : "The word alone is the vehicle of grace." Therefore man should hear the word and meditate upon what he has heard (W. 2. 509, 95, 112, 453 ; 1. 698). Only in this form can we apprehend Christ : "He is of no benefit to thee and thou canst not know anything about him, unless *God put him into words*, that thou mayst hear and thus learn to know him " (W. 2. 213). Luther discriminates here, however, between the "inward" and the "outward" word. Yet the two are closely associated : "But when the outward goes rightly, the inward does not fail to appear ; for God never suffers his word to go forth without (bringing) fruit. He is with it, and himself teaches inwardly

---

[1] The mystical way in which Augustine rings the changes upon the theme : "God and the soul," is not characteristic of Luther. His praise is given to faith : "For the two belong together, faith and God" (Müller, Symb. Book, 386, 388. E. 49. 20). But this faith is wrought by the Word, and its content is the God revealed in Christ.

[2] See the association of the two in Augustine, Vol. I., p. 320 f.

[3] Word and sacrament, according to Luther, differ in the fact, that the former is addressed to the church at large, the latter specifically to the individual (E. 29. 345 ; 11. 157 f.).

what he gives outwardly through the priest " (ib. 112). The words of the priest are, accordingly, accompanied with an inner working of God upon the heart.

From the beginning of the third decade of the sixteenth century, there was an energetic effort in both Germany and Switzerland to carry forward and complete the evangelical reformation by exalting mystic and ascetic ideals. The promoters of the movement were representatives of the mystical piety of the closing Middle Ages, with which they not infrequently combined apocalyptic visions or socialistic principles. The " Imitation of Christ " with a " sensible tasting of his sufferings," the " divesting self of material things," the " becoming naked and barren of all created things," the " righteousness of dying to the world," " the righteousness of the Spirit," the " inward call," the " heavenly voice," the " inner word," the " tedium," and the " reformation " of the Christian world into a " congregation of saints,"—such are the watchwords of this party. But, above all, they held that no importance attached to an external ecclesiasticism, or to the outward word and sacraments. The " Spirit " does everything, and has no need of infant baptism or the " bodily " word.[1]   This agitation has importance for the History of Doctrines, because it gave occasion (Zwickau prophets, Carlstadt, Münzer) to Luther to verify and deepen his doctrine touching the word.

In opposition to the idea of a direct operation of the Spirit, Luther maintains: "Since now God has sent forth his holy gospel, he deals with us in two ways: first, outwardly, and secondly, inwardly. He deals with us outwardly through the spoken word of the gospel and through bodily signs, such as baptism and sacrament. Inwardly, he deals with us through the Holy Spirit and faith, together with other gifts; but all this in

---

[1] Luther describes these religious theories very thoroughly in his publication, *Wider die himmlischen Propheten, e. g.,* 29. 138, 146, 152, 173, 177, 180, 168, 160, 278, 285, 295, 177, 209 f.   Cf. H. LÜDEMANN, Reformation and Taüfertum, Bern, 1896. . . .   The " inner word " may be thought of as accompanying the outer word (thus Augustine, and at first Luther).   It may also be conceived as a direct speaking of God to the soul, which was the idea of the Fanatics (*e. g.,* DENK, Stud. u. Krit., 1851, 177, 184, cf. 131. SEB. FRANCK, in Hegler, Geist u. Schrift in S. F., 1892, p. 83 ff.).   It may be understood therefore as the innate intuition of reason, or as the Conscience : " The conscience, which is the Godhead and Christ himself, who now dwells in our hearts, understands and decides what is evil and what is good " (TH. THAMER, vid. Neander, Thamer, 1842, p. 27, 24 f., 26 f., 28, 29, 38 f., cf. 47).   It is interesting to observe that Seb. Franck regards the idea of communism as a part of man's inherited moral endowment (HEGLER, p. 92).   Cf. supra, p. 183.   Upon the entire question, vid. R. GRUTZMACHER, Wort und Geist, 1902.

the manner and order, that the *outward part shall and must pre-cede, and the inward come afterward and through the outward*, so that he has *determined* to give the inward part to no man except through the outward part" (E. 29. 208; 47. 391; 49. 86). "In the same word comes the Spirit and gives faith where and to whom he will" (29. 212). From this time, Luther never ceased to lay emphasis upon this point. Where the word is, there are Christ and the Spirit (9. 275, 229, 236; 11. 35; 14. 326; 47. 57, 198, 221 f.). The Spirit himself "speaks to the heart" and "impresses" the word upon the heart of the hearers. He "touches and moves the heart" (9. 232, 274; 13. 184, 286; 8. 308; 11. 206; 28. 298: 47. 353 f.).

The relation of the outward word to the divine operation accompanying it is explained by Luther in various ways. The Spirit enlightens "with and through the word" (14. 188). The power of God is "with it and under it" (11. 131). Of the Spirit it is to be said, that he is given "through the word and with the word external and preceding" (Smalc. Art., Müller, 321), and that he "comes with and through the word, and goes no further than so far as the word goes" (12. 300). The Holy Spirit therefore teaches nothing else and nothing more than what the words "which pass out of the mouth of Christ from one mouth to another" contain (ib.). He does not enlarge the sphere of revelation, but he with divine power adapts the revelation made to the individual and his needs. Luther discriminates therefore the purely human operation of the word from the resultant operation of the Holy Spirit "in," "with and through," "with and under" the word,[1] but in such a way that the latter occurs absolutely only through the former.[2]

---

[1] E. 18. 38 : "Along with this preaching office, God is present, and through the spoken word touches to-day this heart, to-morrow that heart. All preachers are nothing more than the hand which points out the way, which does no more than stand still and allow (us) to follow or not to follow the right path. . . . They are not the persons whose duty it is to make anyone pious. God alone does that."

[2] These formulas display an interesting parallel to those upon the Lord's Supper. Viewed in detail, the matter is not perfectly clear. Luther began with Augustinian differentiation of the outward and the inward word, but he modified it by positing a fixed connection between the two. For this the Scot-ist theory of the sacraments appears to have originally furnished the suggestion. God has "determined" (29. 208) that wherever the word goes, a divine influence shall accompany it. Vid. also 45. 215 f.: "No one can rightly *understand God according to the Word of God* unless he receives it [*i. e.*, this ability] immediately from the Holy Spirit. But no one can have it from the Holy Spirit, unless he experiences it, tries it, and feels it (*er erfahr es, vorsuchs una empfinds denn*); and in this experience the Holy Spirit teaches as in his own school, outside of which nothing is taught but appearances, words, and idle prattle."

Medieval theology constructed the doctrine of the sacraments. Luther was the first to frame a doctrine of the Word of God.[1] Of the Bible, we shall speak in another connection.[2]   Cf. R. Grutzmacher, Wort und Geist, 1902, 9. 8 ff.

3. As to the general conception of the nature of the sacraments, it is to be observed, that Luther started with the Scotist idea, that the sacraments are efficacious signs (*efficacia signa*) of grace (W. 1. 595). But this is modified by placing them in the most intimate association with faith. Their effectual operation depends upon faith (ib.). They are " signs which help and incite to faith . . . without which faith, they are of no benefit " (W. 2. 686, 693). " And it depends altogether upon faith, which alone brings it to pass that the sacraments effect what they signify" (2. 715; 6. 24). The sacraments are symbols which awaken faith, and thus promise grace to all, but confer it only upon believers (6. 86). The sacrament is a sign: "That is, it is external, and yet has and signifies something spiritual, in order that we may through the external be drawn to the spiritual " (6. 359). In this, Luther has fallen back upon the Augustinian conception. The sacrament is a symbolic transaction, which brings to the believer that which it outwardly signifies. This idea meets us also later, but with the modifications, that the sacrament gives something also to the unbeliever, and that great stress is laid upon the fact that there is a real influence exerted. But, in and of itself, it is, even at later periods, spoken of as an " outward sign," as a " seal or signet ring " (E. 12. 178 f.; 16. 48, 50, 52). In the tract, *De captivitate Babylonica* (A. D. 1520), Luther sharply criticises the Romish doctrine of the sacraments. Of four of the seven sacraments, he asserts that the Scriptures know nothing at all. There remain only three (baptism, the Lord's Supper, and repentance), although, strictly speaking, even repentance dare not be described as a sacrament (W. 6. 549, 572).[3] It therefore gradually became customary—repentance having now entirely lost its sacramental

---

[1] The " Word of God " is for Luther primarily the oral proclamation, since through this God operates upon the heart. But this operation occurs only when such proclamation is in content a presentation of the biblical revelation; *E. g.*, W. 1. 391. E. 9. 230; 36. 197; 46. 240; 65. 170; 3. 347.

[2] Due attention should be given at this point to the ideas formulated at about this time; that the reformation is to be effected not by violent means, but through the proclamation of the word (E. 28. 217 f., 219, 221, 227 f., 308, 310); that outward customs may be retained (28. 237); and that in such matters the rabble (Pofel) is not to have the deciding voice (29. 160, 162 f., 166 f., 206, 226).

[3] In A. D. 1519, he already calls them the two chief (*furnemliche*) sacraments, W. 2. 754.

·character—to count only two sacraments (E. 28. 418 ; 29. 208 ; 12. 179).

But the general definition is here of little importance. As, from the time of Duns, the theory of the Lord's Supper did not fit into the general definition of a sacrament, but was carried along independently (supra, p. 131 n.), so was it likewise with Luther, particularly in the case of the Lord's Supper, but also noticeably in the case of baptism. We must therefore treat directly of the two sacraments in turn.

4. Luther presents a connected view of his theory of baptism in the *Sermon von dem heiligen, hochwürdigen Sakrament der Taufe* (A. D. 1519). The sign is to be distinguished from the signification (*Bedeutung*) of baptism. The latter consists in (1) The duty of dying to sin ; for by baptism a sentence of death is pronounced upon the natural man : " Therefore drown thyself in the name of God." Thus a blessed dying begins with baptism (W. 2. 728). (2) The "spiritual birth." This, like the "increase of grace and righteousness," "begins in baptism, but continues also until death " (ib.)—on the ground that God through baptism contracts a covenant with man, from which result both regeneration and the forgiveness of sins, so that both are continuous : " and begins from that hour to renew thee, pours into thee his grace and Holy Spirit, who begins to crucify the nature and sin " (730). Sin yet remains in man (728) ; but, since God considers it as in principle shattered, he does not thereafter impute it to the sinner : " will not look upon it nor condemn thee for it, is satisfied in regard to it, and is pleased that thou art thyself continually desiring and attempting to slay it." (731). In this fact, that God has "bound " himself no longer to impute sin to the baptized, lies the peculiar consolation of baptism (732, 733). It is here evident that the theory of baptism harmonizes precisely with the original view of justification through the word : regeneration and, in connection with it, the forgiveness of sins (cf. p. 260 f.).

This remained essentially the view of Luther, except that, at a later period, just as in the case of justification, forgiveness is no longer so closely associated with the—divinely wrought—renewal. In baptism, the triune God is present ; the Holy Spirit being particularly operative (E. 19. 76). The word and will of God make it what it is, so that it is not merely a "sign " (Large Catechism, Müller, Symb. Bb. 495, 487 f., 489. " Baptism is united with and confirmed by the divine word and appointment)." [1] It thus secures an "admission to all divine blessings " (E. 22. 165. W. 2. 746).

---

[1] But, on the other hand, baptism is still " nothing more than an outward

This involves two things. (*a*) The Holy Spirit through baptism effects regeneration. It is "a spiritually-rich water, in which the Holy Spirit is, and in which he works; yea, the entire holy Trinity is present, and the man who is baptized is then called regenerated" (E. 46. 266; 16. 69, 74; 29. 341).[1] Thus the heart is washed clean (8. 226), the whole nature transformed (7. 169), the Spirit granted (Cat. 493), grace "infused" (12. 387. W. 2. 168). But since baptism is an act but once performed, it assures of the continuous readiness of God to renew the sinner : "Therefore baptism also remains always, and thou canst not be so far nor so deeply fallen from it but that thou couldst and shouldst again hold fast to it" (E. 16. 99). With this continual renewal, proceeding from God, are given also the impulse and the obligation to constantly renew ourselves. The slaying of the old Adam and the arising of the new man is the duty of the baptized, " so that Christian life is nothing else than a kind of daily baptism" (Cat. 495, 496, 498. E. 16. 103). In baptism is involved the duty of making the whole Christian life a repentance (Cat. 496 f.).[2]

This is one aspect of baptism. But, despite the renewal thus effected, our life remains sinful, and original sin is still operative.

(*b*) The second blessing which the baptismal covenant carries with it is the certainty that God is ever ready to *forgive us our sins*. "They are all forgiven through grace, but not yet all healed through the gift" (W. 8. 107, 57, 88, 93; 2. 160, 415. E. 15. 50; 16. 141). God has in baptism embraced us and laid us upon his bosom (E. 13. 38); all sins are now and shall be forgiven us. Hence, the sinner should ever anew "creep to (his) baptism" (E. 16. 119. Cat. 492). This sign has been given us by God, to assure us that he will through Christ be gracious to us (E. 12. 163, 205), and that we are really admitted to a place beneath his sway and "incorporated" into his kingdom (12. 212). This means, in the sense of Luther, nothing else than that we, by virtue of our fellowship with Christ, al-

sign, that is to admonish us of the divine promise. If we can have it, it is well. . . . But if anyone could not have it, or if it were denied to him, he is nevertheless not lost, if he only believes the gospel. . . . Therefore he who has the sign, which we call sacrament, and not faith, has a bare seal attached to a letter without any writing in it" (E. 12. 179).

[1] "At an earlier period the Scotist foundation underlying the conception of the sacrament was more evident : That the priest pours upon the child, signifies the holy, divine, and eternal grace which is together with this (*do neben*) poured into the soul" (W. 2. 168).

[2] "Thus *resipiscentia*, or repentance, is nothing else than a sort of retracing of the steps and return to baptism, so that that is again sought and practiced which was indeed before begun and yet through negligence intermitted" (Cat. 497).

ways experience the forgiveness of sins and renewal to a better life.

In Luther's view, baptism has thus a double blessing, or effect. God enters into a covenant relationship with the baptized, which signifies: (1) That the Holy Spirit is always present and operative for his renewal.[1] (2) That he always finds God ready to forgive him his sins for Christ's sake. Baptism therefore brings: "namely, victory over death and the devil, remission of sins, the grace of God, Christ with his works, and the Holy Spirit with all his gifts" (Cat. 491). But, since only the believer is capable of enjoying such experiences, it is to be believed that God in some way endows infants brought for baptism with faith, on account of the believing presentation of them and the prayer offered in their behalf by their sponsors (e. g., De W. 2. 126, 202. W. 6. 538. E. 28. 416; 11. 62 ff.; 26. 255 ff. Cat. 494).[2]

These are the leading principles of Luther's doctrine of baptism. We meet in them precisely the same ideas already found in the discussions of grace and justification. In a certain sense, his doctrine of baptism is therefore a complement to his doctrine of the grace operative in the word. Baptism both begets a disposition to yield to the influences exerted by the word, and it accompanies and individualizes those influences.

5. Luther's doctrine of the Lord's Supper, in the form which it assumed through the conflict with Zwingli, will require attention hereafter. We have now to do with his view of the sacrament before the outbreak of the controversy. We take as a starting-point the tract: *Ein Sermon von der hochw. Sacrament des Leichnams Christi u. von den Bruderschaften* (A. D. 1519). The "meaning or work" of the sacrament is here said to be "com-

---

[1] Of the highest importance upon this point is the remark, E. 12. 215 f.: "Where the word goes and is heard and baptism is desired, there it is commanded to administer baptism to both old and young. For where the word as the chief part goes right, there everything else goes right also; where the word or teaching is not right, there is the other also in vain, for neither faith nor Christ is there."

[2] Luther accordingly does not think here of a "vicarious faith" of the sponsors. "The faith of the sponsors and the church implores and obtains for them personal faith, in which they are baptized and believe for themselves" (11. 63). The lack of reason in the child does not, to Luther's mind, make against the possibility, that they may have faith, as it is just reason "which chiefly resists faith and the word of God" (11. 65 f.). But is such faith in any way psychologically conceivable? See KÖSTLIN, L. Theol. ii., ed. 2, 237 ff., where my view is inaccurately stated. With respect to infants dying unbaptized, Luther afterward said that they are "without doubt admitted to grace by him" (God) on account of the intercession of parents and sponsors (E. 3. 166; 23. 340).

munio.'' It establishes a fellowship with Christ and all saints in heaven and on earth, so that all blessings, sufferings, and sins become common to all. Accordingly, the communicant may console himself with the merit of Christ, and his representation of and intercession for the saints above and the church on earth (W. 2. 743, 744): "That we here lay aside from us all misery and distress upon the church (*gemeyn*), and particularly upon Christ " (745). But we are ourselves also obligated by this *communio* to render to others the service which we here enjoy : " Thou must . . . learn, as this sacrament is a sacrament of love, and as love and help have come to thee, to show love and help in return to Christ in his needy followers. For here must thou grieve for all the dishonor of Christ in his holy word, all the misery of the church, all unjust sufferings of the innocent . . . here must thou protect, act, and pray, and if thou canst do no more, have pity. . . . Behold, thus thou bearest them all, and thus do they all bear thee again, and all things are common—good and evil " (745, 747). The fellowship thus effected by the Lord's Supper is symbolized in the bread and wine, composed of many grains and separate grapes, and in the fact that we eat and drink the bread and wine and thus transform them within our bodies that they become one thing with us. It is taught, further, that this sign is a " perfect " one, viz.: " his true natural flesh *in the bread*," since " the bread is changed (*verwandelt*) into his true natural body, and the wine into his natural true blood " (749). In reply to the question, " where the bread remains, when it is changed into the body of Christ," Luther warns against " subtlety." " It is enough that thou knowest that it is a divine sign, in which Christ's flesh and blood are truly present—how and where, commit to him " (750).[1]

But Luther's interest centres in this bodily presence of Christ only in view of the conviction that " Christ has given his body, in order that the meaning of the sacrament, *i. e.*, fellowship and the interchange of love, might be practiced, and he esteems less highly his own natural body than his spiritual body," *i. e.*, the fellowship of his saints. Hence the communicant should fix his mind more upon the spiritual body of Christ than upon the natural body, for the latter without the former would be of no benefit (751). The presence of the body of Christ in the Lord's Supper is therefore designed to remind us that he surrendered this body in order that a fellowship of love might be established. We shall meet this idea again.

---

[1] Literally, transubstantiation is here retained (cf. W. 8. 435), but really Luther is only concerned to hold fast the idea that the body is "in" the bread.

The presence of the body of Christ in the Lord's Supper was thus the fixed belief of Luther from the first. Its denial he regarded as a Hussite heresy (W. 6. 80). But from A. D. 1520, he expressly rejected transubstantiation. It is a Thomistic fiction, that only the accidents of the bread and wine are preserved, but not the substance. It is refuted by eyesight. Luther now, appealing to D'Ailli (supra, p. 204), adopts the view prevalent in theology since Duns and Occam (p. 131 n., 203), that the substance of the bread remains, and with it the body of Christ is at the same time given (W. 6. 508. E. 28. 366 ff.).[1] Bread and wine are signs, "under which is truly Christ's flesh and blood" (W. 6. 365, cf. *sub pane et vino*, W. 8. 440; *im Brot*, E. 29. 336). The significance of this presence of the body of Christ consists in the fact, that it is "a powerful and most noble seal and sign" (W. 6. 359. E. 28. 412; 29. 350; 22. 40): That is, the presence of the body of Christ attests and confirms the grace of God, for it was this body which was offered up to obtain grace for us. "In order that this divine promise might be for us the most certain of all and might render our faith most secure, he appended the most faithful and most precious pledge and seal of all, viz., the very price of the promise itself, his own body and blood with the bread and wine, by which he has merited that the blessings of the promise be given to us, which he paid also in order that we might receive the promise" (W. 8. 440; 6. 230, 358. E. 22. 40; 29. 350). Luther's meaning is: The body of Christ, as it is symbolized by the bread and really present in it, is by its presence the clearest evidence of the grace of God toward us. It does not occur to him to doubt the bodily presence,[2] but its significance consists alone in deepening the impression of the word. This is the important thing, and the believer may even do without the sacrament (W. 6. 355 f., 362, 363. E. 22. 39 f.). As the sacrament can be received with benefit only by him who believes in the atonement and intercession of Christ (E. 28. 240), its blessing consists in the fact, that we therein "remember" Christ and are thereby "strengthened in faith" and "made ardent in love" (W. 6. 358; 8. 437. E. 22. 40; 28. 240). This strengthening of faith, together with the gift of the body of Christ will-

---

[1] His condemnation of transubstantiation is here a mild one, provided that doctrine be not made an article of faith (W. 6. 508). "No great importance attaches to this error, if only the body and blood of Christ are left, together with the word." (A. D. 1523. E. 28. 402.)

[2] The idea of a purely symbolical interpretation occurred to him indeed: "because I saw well that I could thereby have given the pope the greatest thump." De W. 2. 577.

ingly given to death for our sins, assures us of the forgiveness of sins (E. 29. 347 f.). Nothing is here made to depend upon the *eating* of the body. The consciousness of the bodily presence[1] of the Lord increases within us faith in (the offered) grace, and thus produces the assurance of the forgiveness of sins. On the other hand, the fellowship into which he here enters with us is for us the most powerful incentive to serve him and our brethren in love (E. 29. 351). "You have two fruits of the holy sacrament: one is, that it makes us brethren and fellow-heirs of the Lord Christ, so that from him and us one loaf results; the other, that we also become common and one with all other believers . . . and are also one loaf" (E. 11. 186. Vid. also W. 19. 96, 99).

This is Luther's original doctrine of the Lord's Supper.[2] The most profound impulses of his religious consciousness contributed to its formulation, *i. e.*, the Christ in us, who becomes ours only by virtue of the apprehension of his historical character, and the summing up of all the results of his activity in the forgiveness of sins, faith, and love.

It was not until A. D. 1522 that Luther was confronted with a new problem. He learned from certain Bohemian Brethren, that they regarded the bread and wine as bare symbols (cf. Wickliffe, supra, p. 206). At the same time, HONIUS of Holland laid before him by letter the interpretation of the *Est* in the words of institution, as equivalent to *significat*. Then appeared CARLSTADT with his strange idea, that the "This" of the words of institution relates to the body of Christ, while the "Take" and the "Eat in remembrance of me" refer to the bread. These suggestions opened up new questions for Luther. The relation of the body to the elements, and the exegesis of the words of institution, claim the chief attention. From this time forward, he calls for a simple adherence to the words of Scripture (E. 28. 412 f.; 29. 329, 321, 216, 331); when the Bible says "is," we dare not interpret it as meaning "signifies" (28. 393, 396, 398). But the bodily omnipresence of the Lord is not to be disputed, as he does not travel up and down between heaven and earth (29. 289, 293 f.).

Luther, as we have seen, never denied the real presence of the body of Christ in the Lord's Supper. But as the question of the

---

[1] E. 11. 187 : "If I believe that his body and blood are mine, then I have the Lord Christ entire, and everything that he is able to accomplish." According to this and the above, a *personal* presence and fellowship of Christ is also to be maintained. On the other hand, Luther rejected (28. 412) speculation upon the concomitance of the divine nature (supra, p. 132), and discriminated between the presence of the body and that "of the entire Christ, *i. e.*, of his kingdom (lordship)" (29. 295).

[2] What practical applications may be made of these ideas !

" How " of that presence now comes to the front, he is led to ascribe to it a greater and independent significance. Whereas the body was originally only a means of realizing the sacramental gift, it afterward comes to be regarded as being the gift itself, as we shall have further occasion to observe.

6. We note, finally, that, from A. D. 1520, Luther expressed himself clearly and positively in favor of the reception of the Lord's Supper in both elements (W. 6. 502 ff., 78 f. E. 28. 296; 11. 161) and against the sacrifice of the mass. The Scriptures do not teach the latter (W. 8. 421).[1] Neither would it be possible for us to bring a sacrifice (W. 6. 367), nor is it necessary for us to appease God (W. 8. 441 f.). He denounced the abuses which have made of the mass simply a magical jugglery (W. 6. 375, supra, p. 203, n. 1). We should offer to God nothing but prayer, thanksgiving, and praise (6. 368), together with the faith " that Christ in heaven is our priest, offers himself for us without ceasing, presents and makes acceptable us, our prayers and our praises " (6. 369 f.).

§ 70. *The Reformatory Conception of the Church.*

LITERATURE. KÖSTLIN, L.'s Lehre v. d. Kirche, 1853, and L.'s Theol., i. 248 ff., Engl. Tr. i. 289 ff. KOLDE, L.'s Stellung z. Concil. u. Kirche, 1876. SEEBERG, Begriff d. Kirche, i. 85 ff. GOTTSCHICK, Ztschr. f. KG. viii. 543 ff. SOHM, Kirchenrecht, i. 460 ff.

1. The chief elements of Luther's conception of the Church may also be traced in his writings of the pre-reformation period (p. 235 f.) ;[2] but they were made powerless by his bondage to the canonical ideas upon the subject. The pope, as such, is still regarded as an authority (W. 1. 582, 670, 683 ; 2. 30), and he yet looks to councils for new articles of faith (W. 1. 582 ff., 681 ; 2 36 f). This wavering and confusing attitude terminated with the controversy with Eck and the Leipzig Disputation (A. D. 1519). Luther had asserted that the primacy of the Romish church over all others had not been exercised in the days of Gregory I., at least not over the Greek church (W. 2. 161), and that, according to the Fathers, the pope was only a *co-episcopus*

---

[1] See the interesting discussion of the origin of the mass, W. 6. 365 f.

[2] GOTTSCHICK has rightly, in opposition to Ritschl, myself, and others, proved Luther's independence of Huss. At the time of the Leipzig Disputation, Luther was not acquainted with Huss's book upon the Church (E. 24. 22, cf. ENDERS, L.'s Briefe, ii. 196) and he had only a slight knowledge of his sermons, gained while at Erfurt (E. 65. 81). Since the formula, *congregatio praedestinatorum*, does not affect Luther's conception of the church, we cannot think of the acts of the Council of Constance as the source of his views upon that topic. His conception of the church is based upon Augustine and the current medieval definition, *communio fidelium* (supra, p. 144, n. 2).

19

with the other bishops (2. 20, 229). At this point the controversy began. Luther maintained his position (2. 185). Peter does not, according to the Scriptures, stand above the other apostles (ib. 235 f.). The Council of Nice did not attribute primacy to the Roman bishop (238, 265, 397, 672). The duty of obedience to the pope is not called in question, but it is like that which is due to any government, even that of the Turk (186). The papacy is based, not upon divine, but only upon human right; for such passages as Matt. 16. 18 f. have nothing to do with the pope (187, 189 ff., 194). The papal decretals, upon which the claims of the papacy are based, are mere human laws (201). On the other hand, it is the divine law, according to 2 Pet. 2. 13, that the pope, together with all his subordinates, should be subject to the emperor (220 f.). As Peter exercised no secular authority, the ecclesiastical jurisdiction is not of divine right (223). And Luther finally comes to doubt whether, after all, "any other head of the whole church has been appointed upon earth except Christ" (239). Luther now, at Leipzig and elsewhere, defends the proposition, that Huss was right in calling the church the general assembly of the predestinated (*predestinatorum universitas*). But as this definition was condemned at Constance, Luther found himself driven to the further assertion : "*Nor can a Christian believer be forced beyond the sacred Scriptures, which are properly the divine law,* unless some new and proved revelation should be added ; for we are forbidden by divine law to believe except what is proved either through the divine Scriptures or through manifest revelation" (W. 2. 279). A principle of immense scope is thus established, that in all questions affecting doctrine the Scriptures are, as the divine law, the only decisive authority. This idea is not new. It lay at the basis of the medieval criticisms of the papacy (supra, p. 169, 172), and Luther himself had made use of it at an early period.[1] But the establishing of it as a fundamental principle and the energetic concrete application of it were new. The new canon is directed against the councils in general, especially the venerated Council of Constance, and against the pope as well (W. 2. 283 ff., 313, 404, 314, 397). "A council cannot make divine right out of that which is not by nature divine right" (308). To establish the Romish papacy by divine right is a "new dogma," which is not binding. The church needs no head (313 f.). The hierarchical system is not biblical, nor of divine right (379, 433 f.). The canon law begins to totter (423).

---

[1] Cf. UNDRITZ, Neue kirchl. Ztschr., 1897, 579 ff. As the idea was widely current in the later Middle Ages, no importance attaches to its use by Carlstadt, A. D. 1518 (KOLDE, L.'s Stellung z. Concil., p 34).

The great significance of the Leipzig Disputation and the conflicts which preceded and followed it lies in the fact, that Luther
was thus led to break fundamentally and permanently with the
Romish conception of the church and the authorities upon which
it depended (canons, pope, councils, ecclesiastical authority). In
place of the latter, was now acknowledged the *sole authority of the
Holy Scriptures.* The way was thus open to carry out and
apply the ideas of reform, the old barriers being broken down.
Criticism presses forward with rapid pace against Rome (*e. g.*,
W. 6. 287 ff., 290 ff. E. 31. 257, 310), the pope as antichrist (De W. 1. 239. W. 6. 289, 331, 598, 603; 8.
470, 183; 9. 701 ff. E. 28. 224; 17. 25, etc.), the councils (W. 6. 79, 138, 258; 8. 150. E. 22. 143 f.), and
the tradition of the Fathers (E. 31. 205; 11. 10 ff.; 12. 138;
14. 330).

2. But we turn to view the new conception of the Church,
as Luther first develops it in detail in the tract, *Von dem
Papsttum zu Rom* (A. D. 1520). The church is "an assemblage (*vorsamlunge*) of all Christian believers on earth"
(W. 6. 292), and, furthermore, "an assemblage of hearts in one
faith," or "a community (*gemein*) of saints" (293). Since
this assemblage is represented as a spiritual fellowship, the
principle of its unity is not to be seen in an accidental historical body, such as Rome or the papacy, but in Christ
(294 f.), for it is he who so operates upon the members of the
community (*Gemeinde*) that they are thereby united into one community. As the Head, he infuses his "disposition, temper,
and will" into the community (298). The church is therefore the spiritual association of those who believe on Christ,
established and sustained by him. But by the word "church"
is also understood the organized association of those who believe on Christ, "an outward thing with outward actions,"
and the order of the clergy (296). This "outward bodily
church" (*Christenheit*) and the "inner spiritual church"
(Christenheit) are to be carefully discriminated, but not separated. They are related to one another as body and soul in
man (297). It is, of course, of chief importance that we belong to the spiritual church, but this membership stands in
close connection with membership in the external church. At
this point appears the new element in Luther's theory. By
the introduction of the word and sacraments, he prevented the
dissolution of the conception of the church as held by Augustine and the reformers of pre-reformation days. The word
and sacraments, as externally and sensibly set forth, call
into existence the inner spiritual church. "For where baptism

and the gospel are, there let no one doubt that there are also saints, even though it should be only children in their cradles'' (301). The church is therefore, in one aspect, an external, visible association. But this is not " the true (*rechte*) church which is believed." Since, however, the word and sacraments are here operative, faith concludes that here in the external association may be found a community of saints. Thus the church is an object of faith, and not visible, " for what is believed is not bodily nor visible " (300, 301).

3. In this simple combination, the way is pointed out for the solution of the problem of the nature of the church. Luther held without wavering to these principles, not indeed without adapting them to the practical needs of his time. Two things here demanded his attention, *i. e.*, the establishment of an evangelical church order, and defense against the theories of the Anabaptists. If the former task compelled him to a fundamental discussion of the form to be assumed by the external church, in order that it may be an appropriate agency for the production of the *communio sanctorum*, the conflict with Anabaptism emphasized the necessity of such an ecclesiastical system (supra, p. 280 f.). In opposition to Rome, he asserted : Only the word and the sacraments are necessary to the existence of the church ; and against the Anabaptists : Without the word and sacraments no church ! We must note a few features brought into prominence in the further development of the doctrine concerning the church.

(*a*) The spiritual nature of the church is maintained without abridgment of any kind. The church is the *communio sanctorum* (W. 6. 606, 131. Op. ex. 15. 357), for these words are " nothing else than a gloss, or interpretation, by which someone wished to indicate what the Christian church is " (Large Cat. 457). It is the "assembly (*Versammlung*) of all believers " (W. 8. 163), the " holy Christian nation " (E. 25. 355), the regenerated (46. 258). It is holy, because the Holy Spirit reigns in it (W. 8. 163). Those who belong to it are all priests in the spiritual sense (ib. 247 f., 251 f., 254, 382, 415, 417, 470). Thus considered, the church is the " new creation of God " (W. 6. 130), the product and sphere of the redemptive work of Christ (E. 46. 154); or it is the "kingdom of God," in which Christ reigns through the Spirit and faith (E. 29. 3;[1] cf. p. 277).

[1] Upon the relationship of the kingdom and the church, see E. 5. 231 : "Such kingdom of heaven begins on earth below and is called by another name, the Christian church, here on earth, within which God reigns through his word and his Spirit.'' The church is therefore the kingdom of God in its temporal, historical course of development.

The church in this sense is an object of faith, and may therefore, upon the basis of the definition, Heb. 11. 1, be described as *spiritual* and *invisible* (see citations, supra, p. 235, and also Op. var. arg. 5. 295. W. 6. 300; 8. 419, cf. the exposition of the kingdom of Christ as "invisible." E. 12. 96, 127; 17. 236, cf. 63. 168; 19. 26).[1] (*b*) The agency of Christ which incorporates individuals into the church is, however, bound to the chosen means, the word and sacraments; for through them God gathers the community, and they bring the Spirit (E. 9. 124; 12. 406; 22. 142; 49. 220; 50. 75 ff., 48. 68, 346). Hence the peculiar character of the act of faith by which the existence of the church is recognized. Wherever the means of grace are, there faith assumes the presence of a—perhaps very small—community of saints (25. 358, 360; 22. 142). (*c*) By this course of reasoning the necessity for an outward ecclesiastical association is maintained. The church must, further, always exist as an empirical historical entity. Thus considered, it is "the number or multitude of the baptized and believing who belong to a priest or bishop, whether in a city, or in a whole land, or in the whole world" (E. 31. 123). It is evident, also, that membership in the church is necessary to salvation, "for outside of the Christian church is no truth, no Christ, no salvation" (E. 10. 162, 444; 12. 414; 22. 20; 9. 292; 48. 218 f.). (*d*) All this may be said of the church, because the word and sacraments are absolutely essential to its existence. It follows, also, that all the members of the church are called to bear a part in the proclamation of the word, and that the congregation should do all in its power for its own edification (*e. g.*, E. 12. 222, 278). But since the congregation can no longer expect charismatically-endowed preachers, and since the preaching of the word dare not be discontinued, provision must be made for an office to administer the word and sacraments, without allowing this office to interfere with the duty of every individual to bear testimony to the truth (E. 17. 250; 22. 146 ff.). The "keys," *i. e.*, teaching and preaching (15. 395), belong really to all Christians (W. 8. 173), but the public official exercise of this duty, as is

---

[1] Already in the middle of the third decade of the century, the Evangelical party in Franconia assert against the Romanists: "This church is *spiritual* and *invisible*, not that we do not see the persons, but that no one knows which really belong to the Christian church" (in ENGELHARDT, Ehrengedächtnis der Ref. in Franken, p. 97, 123). This is no longer the original method of establishing the point. Luther meant to indicate by the term, *invisible*, only that the nature of the church is spiritual, and hence invisible and an object of faith; and did not apply it as discriminating among the members of the visible church. Cf. Wickliffe and Huss, supra, p. 211). The term was, as appears from the above, first used by Luther, and afterward by Zwingli.

strongly emphasized in opposition to the Anabaptist propaganda, should be restricted to officials regularly called (E. 31. 218, 214 ff.; 48. 298 f.). The object of every divine service is the preaching of the word (22. 153, 155, 235). Whatever is essentially an affair of the congregation is to be actually administered by an office, viz., the preaching of the word, with the administration of the sacraments and the care of souls (E. 22. 113; 31. 315). "Therefore upon whomsoever the office of preaching is laid, upon him is laid the highest office in the church" (E. 22. 151; 9. 220; 19. 205). The office of the pastor can therefore not be outranked by a higher ecclesiastical office, as that of a bishop (28. 181; 47. 16) and the hierarchy; for, according to the analogy of Christ's rulership, no outward government dare be exercised in the church, such as that of the pope, but only "to rule souls through the word of God." There is no ecclesiastical government which has authority to impose laws without the permission and will of the congregation, " but their reigning is nothing else than to use the word of God, and thereby guide Christians and vanquish heresy" (E. 22. 6, 93 f.; 46. 183 ff. Thus the relationship of the word and the Spirit requires an ecclesiastical office.[1]

(e) But since the church must, according to this definition, always be an external association, it is evident that there must belong to it empirically a great number of inchoate, imperfect, and even hypocritical members, who can have no share in its spiritual exercises (E. 9. 303; 14. 211; 16. 247; 2. 53, 61 f.; 25. 363; 65. 66. Gal. 3. 151 f.). Regarded empirically, therefore, the church is like a field in which tares are growing among the wheat.[2] (f) This must be borne in mind when speaking of the evangelical church of the New Testament. If the question be raised, which of the two churches, the Romish and the Evangelical, is the "true" (rechte) one, the answer cannot be given on the basis of their comparative morality. But, since the object of the outward organization of the church is to bring Christ to men through the word, therefore it can lay claim to the title, "true church," just in proportion as its preaching of the word is in harmony with this purpose, i. e., is truly evangelical.[3] The mark of the true church is, accordingly, that in

---

[1] The purely secular character which every form of church government has and must have, in Luther's view, is evident from the above, cf. SOHM, 517 ff.

[2] This affects the conception of the character of public worship, and explains Luther's reference to sinful assemblies of more mature Christians in his *Deutsche Messe*, W. 19, 73, 75, 112.

[3] Cf. E. 26. 42; 31. 389: I have, thank God, reformed more with my gospel than they could perhaps have done with five councils.

it the gospel is purely preached (E. 31. 366), that it has the "teaching, faith, and confession of Christ" (12. 245, 249; 48. 224 ff.; 49. 230; 50. 10 ff.). This can be known from the agreement of its doctrine with the "word of Christ" (12. 289): "That the true church holds with me to God's word" (28. 279; 9. 230). Our doctrine is "the Scriptures and the clear word of God" (13. 219, 223). The "pure doctrine" is therefore of the highest importance, since every corruption of it must immediately influence the life (15. 358; 16. 101; 26. 35 f.). Hence, the church dare not tolerate false teachers (E. 26. 37 f.). As, therefore, the inner unity of the church is established through Christ as its head, so its external unity is secured through the pure doctrine of the gospel.[1] "Therefore this unity of the church is not said to be, and is not, the having and holding of any one form of outward government, law, or ordinance, and church customs, as the pope and his crowd profess and wish to have all excluded from the church who will not in this be obedient to him. . . . It is called one holy catholic or Christian church, because there is here one pure and uncorrupted doctrine of the gospel and outward confession of the same" (9. 293). Where this old, true doctrine[2] has free course, i. e., where the Apostles' Creed is confessed, there the conditions are present for the existence of the *communio sanctorum,* and hence there is the true church.[3] There has been a change in the

---

[1] We dare not here, if we would not lose the spirit of Luther, overlook the practical aim of the "doctrine." Even the theoretical construction of the doctrinal system is, to his mind, subordinate to the great aim of interpreting and appropriating the gospel. (*E. g.,* W. 2. 469.) This is attested by his according to all Christians the right to pass judgment upon the doctrine and preaching of the church (22. 145; 12. 367; 13. 182 ff.; 46. 232 f.; 47. 354). But this assumes an inner experience secured through the hearing of the gospel, which may be used as a criterion.   "If thou knowest God, then hast thou already the level, measure, and yard-stick, by which thou canst judge all the doctrine of the Fathers. . . . Who teaches you this?   Thy faith in thy heart, which believes only this (13. 185). Thou must thyself decide. It means for thee thy neck—it means thy life. Therefore God must say to thee in thy heart, 'This is God's word;' otherwise it is undecided" (ib. 183). There was, accordingly, in Luther's mind no thought of a doctrinal hierarchy.

[2] The papal teachings are a "new" doctrine (*e. g.,* E. 17. 142, cf. 51. 103, where "Scripture and experience" are represented as "two touch-stones of the true doctrine"). The Evangelical party have the "old doctrine" and are therefore "the old, true church."   "For whoever thinks alike and holds alike with the old church, he belongs to the old church" (E. 26. 14).

[3] Although Luther declares the Romish church to be a "devil's church," because it confesses "untrue articles," he yet holds that in it the Lord through baptism and the word "nevertheless retains the young children . . . and some adults, but very few, who have turned to Christ again at their death" (E. 26. 28, 281; 4. 59 ff.). Strictly speaking, the false church has no right to the property of the church (26. 39, 59).

meaning of this term.   Once it signified the " true church, which
is believed " (W. 6. 301); it is now the church of pure doctrine
(E. 12. 245, 249; 26. 43; 28. 379; 48. 359 f.).   Once it
was a purely religious, now it is an empirical conception.[1]   The
doctrinaire tendency which may attach itself to the watchword,
"pure doctrine" (*reine Lehre*), is entirely foreign to Luther.
The doctrine of the church embraces the gospel, and the latter is
a power which lays hold upon the entire life, begetting faith,
love, and works, and binding Christians together in inward and
outward fellowship.[2]

§ 71. *Luther's Attitude Toward the Traditional Standards of
Doctrine, viz., the Scriptures and the Dogmas of the Church.*

LITERATURE.   ROMBERG, L.'s Lehre v. d. heil. Schrift, Wittenberg, 1868.
THIMME, L.'s Stellung z. heil. Schrift, Neue kirchl. Ztschr., 1896, 644 ff.
KATTENBUSCH, L.'s Stellung zu den ökumen. Symbolen, Giessen, 1883.   H.
PREUSS, Die Entwicklung des Schriftprincips bei L. bis zur leipziger Disput.,
1901.   SCHEEL, Luther's Stellung zur heil. Schrift, 1902.   W. WALTHER, Das
Erbe der Reform. i., 1903.   THIEME, Luther's Testament wider Rom, 1900.

1. In the preceding paragraphs we have traced the leading
features of Luther's teaching in so far as it has affected the History of Doctrines.   It may be said that here all is new.   Luther
knew how to present the Gospel in all its heights and depths as
no man had done since the days of Paul and John.   We may
best understand how he was led to this profound knowledge of
the truth by noting, first of all, his new conception of Faith—
not the intellectual acceptance of a dogma, nor the theoretical
conviction of the correctness of a formula, but the heartfelt experience of the omnipotence of love revealed to us in Christ.
This experience makes of me a new man, and inspires me with
the powers and impulses of another world.   But this experience
involves also the assurance that I enjoy the favor of God, although sinful impulses are yet felt within.   There now springs up a
new life, which is full of true evangelical repentance.   The dominion of the sacrament of repentance is abolished by true repentance ; the works once demanded by the former being replaced
by the works of my earthly calling and the introduction of a new
ideal of the Christian life.   But even more than this may be truly

---

[1] It is scarcely necessary to guard here against the misunderstanding of this
change as involving a limitation of the religious character of the church.   The
church of the pure doctrine has value or significance only in so far as it is a
means for the establishment of the *communio sanctorum.*
[2] I still maintain the positions taken in my *Kirchenbegriff, 1. 88,* as to the
social-ethical tendency of Luther's conception of the church, despite the criticisms of K. MÜLLER (Symbolik, p. 326 f.).

said.   As Luther interprets Christianity, with all its facts and
doctrines, from the view-point of faith, all his utterances have
the direct impress of religious experience.[1]   What he sought to
tell of all things was, what influence they might have upon the
believing heart and how the latter might secure such influence.
In this way he fell upon simpler, yet at the same time more profound, formulas than many of those which tradition had handed
down.   He held to Augustine's doctrine of original sin, or, to
speak more accurately, restored it ; but for him the essence of
sin lay no longer in sensuous desire, but in unbelief.   He often
reproduced the theological and Christological formulas of the
ancient church ; but the God of his experience was not the infinite
"Subsistence" (Vol. I., p. 340 n.), but the omnipotent Loving-
will.   He spoke of grace and its gift to us, even of "infused
grace ;" but he meant by it not a "quality glued in," but the
efficient power of love which transforms our hearts.

The re-discovered gospel bore within itself the hidden impulse
for the construction of new theological formulas, and with lavish
hand, and almost recklessly, Luther dashed them from his pen.
But the reformation of the theology which he effected was not
directed by any thought of a complete revision of the traditional
dogmatic system.   It was Luther's aim to obtain a secure and
permanent place for the newly-won conceptions touching the religious life (faith, justification, grace, works, the enslaved will, the
gospel, the law).[2]   He never wearies of seeking to impress them
upon his hearers and readers.[3]   Under the guidance of this cen-

---

[1] Cf. 58. 398 f.: "There is only one article and rule in theology ; he who
does not know and have this is no theologian, viz., true faith, or trust in Christ.
All the other articles continually flow into this one and out again, and the
others are nothing without this."   Similarly in Gal. i. 3.

[2] From this fact, as exemplified particularly in Luther's writings and the
Epistle to the Romans, it may be understood that Melanchthon should have
failed to treat of the Trinity and Christology in his first edition of the Loci.

[3] There may be found in Luther a very great variety of propositions, each
of which is declared to be the "chief article," or "the sum of the gospel."
In reality, they all amount in the end to the same thing.   I cite a few groups :
Justification and the forgiveness of sins, e. g., E. 31. 250 : "The word of
grace and forgiveness of sins, and that we become righteous and are saved
alone through Christ without merit : for this is the chief article, out of which
all our doctrine has flowed, which was held and confessed at Augsburg before
the emperor, as it is based upon the Scriptures."   Cf. Müller, Symb. Bb., 300.
De W. 4. 151.   E. 8. 184, 236 ; 11. 157 ; 14. 188.   *Repentance and forgiveness*, 11, 279.   *Grace, forgiveness, liberty*, 13. 30 ; 40. 324.   *Christ,
the God-man, who delivers us*, 13. 49, 56, 204 ; 15. 155 ; 16. 254 ; 9. 213 ;
10. 346 ; 12. 246 f. ; 18. 24 ; 19. 390 ; 47. 45, 58 ; 48. 98.   But not our free
will, 10. 218 ; 14. 33.   *Grace and love*, 14. 73 ; 22. 233 ; 25. 76.   Gal. 1.
322.   *Faith and baptism*, 12. 204.   *Faith and works*, 16. 140.   *The Trinity*,
9. 1, especially the contents of the Creed, 28. 413 f., 346 f. ; 13. 221 f. ; 49. 5,
and the symbolical writings.

tral idea, he moulded anew all doctrines that came within his range. Whatever stood in its way, he rejected, as, *e. g.*, the medieval Semi-pelagianism and doctrine of grace, the whole theory of the sacraments, the hierarchical system, work-right-eousness, and the doctrine of merits. And just as readily did the fanatical notions of an immediate operation of the Spirit fall beneath the weight of the reformatory principle. Other doctrines, on the contrary, which did not collide with his religious principle, he conserved. If he had been entrusted with the construction of the doctrines of the Trinity or of Christology, he would certainly have framed formulas different from those of Nice or Chalcedon. This does not imply connivance, nor calculation of consequences[1] — not even a lack of logical consistency. With a genuine historic sense, he allowed the formulas in question to stand, for the sake of the important truths imbedded in them. Here arises for us a new question : What was Luther's attitude toward dogma?

2. Before attempting an answer to this query, we must have a clear understanding upon another point. We have seen that Luther, impelled by his central reformatory principle, was led by an inner necessity to abandon the theories of the medieval church and replace them with new doctrinal statements. Faith, with its independent assurance, its " feeling " and " experience " (p. 257. E. 13. 185, 183, supra, p. 295, n. 1, 2.), here became at once the critical and the constructive norm. (*a*) But, in the decisive hour at Worms, Luther appealed not only to his religious experience, but also to the authority of the *Holy Scriptures*. In this he established a further canon for the reformation of doctrine. He habitually appealed to it—very naturally—in controversy with his opponents, and was controlled by it in his own religious life.[2] Its importance became clear to him at the Leipzig Disputation (p. 289 f.). Only the "divine law" (*das göttliche Recht*), or the Scriptures, dare rule in the church : "What is asserted without the Scriptures or proved revelation may be held as an opinion, but is not necessary to be believed" (W. 6. 508 ; 2. 297, 279, 309, 315). No water dare be mingled with this wine (W. 8. 141 f.; 143 f.) ; no lantern held up against this sunlight (ib. 235). The word of God, not the

---

[1] For the legal status of the Reformation, the retention of the Trinitarian and Christological formulas was of the highest importance.

[2] E. 28. 350 : " Now I handled the abomination (indulgences) at first almost tenderly and gently and handsomely, and would very gladly have allowed the papacy to stand and have helped it be something ; *but the Scriptures* I was determined to have uncorrupted, pure and certain : I did not yet know that it (the papacy) was contrary to the Scriptures, but only considered it to be *without Scripture*, as other worldly government set up by men."

teachings of men—Christ, not philosphy, must rule the people of
God (ib. 144, 146, 149, 345. E. 9. 232 ; 11. 7 ; 28. 298).
The servants of Christ must teach only his word (E. 7. 82). The
word itself is to be taught ; it is not to be bound by the interpretation of it, as does Rome (W. 2. 339. E. 11. 31), nor be
robbed of its meaning by neglect of the context (W. 2. 361,
425 ; 8. 348). This principle became the more firmly established for Luther in proportion as the necessity of an authoritative norm became apparent among his own following. He
thus withstood Iconoclasts and Fanatics, and upon this basis
constructed the new evangelical organization of the church. It
was henceforth a maxim: "Thou must plant thyself upon a
clear, transparent, strong statement of the Scriptures, whereby
thou canst then hold thy ground " (E. 28. 223). From this
may be understood his insistence upon the *est* in the formula of
the Lord's Supper. But there is nothing essentially evangelical
as yet in all this reverence for the Scriptures, for it had been
quite common in the Middle Ages (supra, p. 101, 149, 192 ff.).
The strict view of inspiration which Luther sometimes expresses
("the writing of the Holy Spirit," "the Spirit's own writing."
Op. ex. 7. 313; 1. 4. E. 27. 244 ; 11. 248 ; 45. 301 ; 52.
321, 333)[1] was also current in the later Middle Ages (p. 193 n.).
But for Luther the Scriptures were something more than the
"divine right," or law inspired by God, as Occam and Biel
regarded them.

(*b*) This is proved by a number of considerations which point
to another conception of the Scriptures. (1) At the close of
the Middle Ages the natural law (*naturrecht*) innate in the
reason was represented as equivalent to the divine law (*göttliches
Recht*) of the Scriptures (supra, p. 171 f., 192 f., 184 n). Since
Luther denies this (E. 11. 30 ; 19. 266),[2] revelation is not for
him equivalent to the general dictates of reason, but has positive
and peculiar content. (2) This content is Christ and the revelation given through him. "If I know what I believe, then I
know what stands in the Scriptures, because the Scriptures contain nothing more than Christ and Christian faith " (W. 8.
236). The Holy Spirit, operative in the New Testament authors,
merely carried out what Christ said : "As the evangelist John

---

[1] See many more instances in ROHNERT, Die Inspirat. d. h. Schr., 1889,
p. 144 ff.

[2] This is not contradicted by the fact that Luther would at first accept only
"what the holy father proves with Scripture or with reason " (E. 27. 21),
nor his readiness at Worms to be convinced "by proofs of Scripture or by
clear reasons " (KÖSTLIN, L.'s Leben, i. 452). Luther here means citations
from Scriptures or evident inferences from such citations. Cf. Occam, supra,
p. 192.

wrote many more things than Christ said just at this time, but yet always keeps to this one purpose, to most thoroughly present the article concerning the person, office, and kingdom of Christ, of which Christ also himself speaks'' (E. 12. 135 f., 138, 141). Thus is for Luther the specific content of all Holy Scriptures defined. That which is valuable in them, and which determines their character, is their relation to Christ. "This is also the proper touch-stone for the criticism of all books, if we observe whether they treat of Christ or not, since *all Scripture testifies of Christ* (Rom. 3. 21), and St. Paul will know nothing but Christ (1 Cor. 2. 2). That which does not teach Christ is not apostolic, even though St. Peter or St. Paul should teach it. On the other hand, whatever preaches Christ would be apostolic, even if Judas, Hannas, Pilate, and Herod should do it '' (E. 63. 157). (3) In this connection, Luther's critical opinions concerning the Scriptures are very significant. Thus, he asserts that the text of the prophecies has often fallen into confusion ; the discourses were presumably not committed to writing until afterward, and then by redactors (63. 57, 74; 62. 123). The prophets were often in error (*fehlten*), when they prophesied of worldly events (*von weltlichen Läuften*) (E. 8. 23). The books of the Kings are more trustworthy than the Chronicles (62. 132). By whom Genesis was composed, is a matter of indifference (57. 35). It would be better if the book of Esther were not in the canon (op. ex. 7. 195. E. 62. 131). The composition of Ecclesiastes by Solomon is doubted (E. 62. 128). The reports of the synoptic gospels are not of uniform value (30. 314, 331 ; 14. 319). The Epistle of Jude is derived from the Second Epistle of Peter (63. 158). The Epistle of Hebrews errs, in denying a second repentance (ib. 155), "and is apparently composed of many parts.'' James wrote "a right strawy epistle . . . for it has certainly no evangelical character about it '' (ib. 115), *i. e.*, "he teaches nothing '' about Christ, and connects righteousness with works (156 f.). He even says : "James talks wildly'' (*delirat*) (op. ex. 4. 328. W. 2. 425). Luther did not originally regard the Apocalypse as a prophetic or apostolic book, "because Christ is neither taught nor known in it '' (63. 169 f.). He remained in doubt as to its authorship (159).[1] Great emphasis was laid by him upon the testimony borne to the various books by the ancient church.[2] On this ground, Hebrews, James,

---

[1] Luther attaches very little value to prophecies touching outward events, but places the Apocalypse in this respect upon a level with Joachim of Floris and the Lichtenberg prophet ! (E. 8. 22).

[2] Already, A. D. 1519, at Leipzig, he rejected Macc. II. as not canonical (W. 2. 325, 329, 339). As to the Apocrypha in general, see 63. 91 ff.

Jude, and the Apocalypse are distinguished in the Prefaces of
A. D. 1522 from the "real certain chief books" (63. 154).
But the inner canon is for him yet more important. The Gospel
of John and Paul's epistles, especially Romans and First Peter,
are "the real kernel and marrow among all the books. . . .
For in these thou findest not much description of the work and
miracles of Christ ; but thou findest here portrayed in the most
masterly way how faith in Christ overcomes sin, death, and hell
and gives life, righteousness, and salvation—which is the real
character of the gospel" (63. 144 f.; 51. 327). In consistency
with this view of the Scriptures, historical oversights and errors
in the sacred writings disturbed Luther but little (e. g., E. 14.
319; 46. 174; 50. 308 f.; 62. 132. Walch, Luth. WW. xiv.,
1208, 1293 f.).[1] They did not affect the real grounds of his
confidence.[2] (4) It is again in perfect consistency with the
above, that Luther's acknowledgment of the authority of the
Scriptures is not based upon their official recognition by the
church,[3] but upon the *experience* of their truth : "Everyone
must believe only because it is God's Word and because he is
satisfied in his heart (*inwendig befinde*) that it is truth (E. 28.
340 ; 47. 356), *i. e.*, a reality and not a mere 'idea' "
(48. 29).

(*c*) The principles thus avowed indicate a conception of the
character of the Holy Scriptures entirely different from that underlying the medieval formulas employed by Luther as cited in
paragraph (*a*) above. We must not be too ready therefore to
regard such declarations as the hasty utterances of superabundant
enthusiasm, and magnanimously absolve the Reformer from responsibility for them. This is forbidden, not only by the fact
that they occur for the most part in carefully composed passages,
such as the prefaces to his publications, but especially by the important consideration that they stand in very intimate connection
with his reformatory conception of faith. There thus results an
entirely new conception of the authority and inspiration of the
Scriptures. Their specific content, in both the Old and the New

---

[1] It is thus seen that Luther employed "criticism" in the widest variety of
forms. Almost all the criteria employed at the present day were applied by
him in his own way.

[2] In the sense of Occam or Biel, Luther's position is simply *heretical*, since
the Christian is under obligation to accept all the books of the Bible and believe
everything found in them (supra, p. 192). It is very remarkable that the opponents of Luther did not make more capital out of his bold utterances in this
direction. It is true, indeed, that similar views were held by such men as
Erasmus and Cajetan (cf. KUNZE, Glaubensregel, heil. Schrift u. Taufbekenntniss, 1899, p. 516 ff.).

[3] D'Ailli still taught differently, supra, p. 191, n. 1.

Testaments, is Christ, with his office and kingdom. It is this content in which faith is interested, and which faith verifies by inner experience. This is therefore the important thing in the Scriptures. It must accordingly be the impelling motive in the special divine agency which gave the Scriptures their peculiar character. In other words, the testimony of the Holy Spirit in the Scriptures is the testimony to the great facts of salvation and redemption. This is the purpose of their inspiration, and in proportion as they fulfill it do they substantiate their claim to be regarded as an authority in matters of religion.[1] This makes them the criterion and touch-stone, by which all the teaching of the church must be attested as evangelical truth (*e. g.*, E. 9. 207, 372 ; 12. 289 ; 13. 208 ; 15. 144 ; 18. 22 ; 48. 69, 92 ; 46. 231, 240). This places the above-cited passages touching the authority of the Scriptures in a new light. The Scriptures were for Luther an absolute authority. But although he could in controversy employ them as " divine law " in contrast with " ecclesiastical law," yet they were an actual authority for him only as the primitive and original testimony to Christ and his salvation. This determines their nature and their form.[2]

But, when thus regarded, the Scriptures dare not be co-ordinated with justifying faith as the second principle of Protestantism. The controlling principle is faith ; and, since only the believer can understand the Scriptures, and they exist only to minister to faith, they are subordinate to it. This view produced a new and profounder conception of the authority of the Scriptures. The ancient problems : wherein the authority of the Scriptures really consists, how is it to be proved, and what its relation to that of other writings—were fundamentally solved by Luther, since he recognized this authority as based upon religious grounds —a statement which is not invalidated by the fact that Luther did not always in praxis adhere strictly to his own principle.

3. We are now in position to understand Luther's attitude toward the Dogmas of the Ancient Church. We have seen that

---

[1] Cf. the remarkably characteristic declaration, E. 11. 248 : " Thus I would take Moses, the Psalter, Isaiah, and also the same Spirit, and make just as good a New Testament as the apostles wrote ; but since we do not have the Spirit so fully and powerfully, we must learn from them and drink out of their well."

[2] The doctrine of the Scriptures in the dogmatic system of the present day must be framed with due regard to the principles of Luther as above deduced, although the latter were not reduced by the Reformer himself to a complete doctrinal form. How, for instance, could a verbal inspiration be sustained in view of Luther's derogatory remarks upon particular passages in the canonical books, his recognition of redactors, who have collected the materials of many of the books, and his acknowledgment of errors ?

he rejected as unbiblical the medieval doctrine of the sacraments, and denied the infallibility of the pope and the councils. But what was his attitude toward the ancient dogmas? (cf. esp. his tract, *Von den Conciliis und Kirchen*, 1539, the three Symbols of 1538, and the other symbolical writings). It is very clear, in the first place, that Luther acknowledged and frequently reproduced the Nicene doctrine of the Trinity and the Chalcedonian Christology. Also, that he treated the symbols of the ancient church with great respect, especially the Apostles' Creed, which, he declared, contains all the principal articles of faith (28. 413 f., 346 f.; 9. 29 ff.; 13. 221 f.; 20. 297 f.).[1] But this is not to be understood as implying that he believes these symbols or councils as such, and thus subjects himself to an earthly authority. His liberty in this respect is manifest from his criticism of the ancient terminology. "That if my soul loathes the word, *homousion*, and I am unwilling to use it, I am not a heretic; for who will compel me to use it, provided I hold the thing which is defined from the Scriptures by the council" (W. 8. 117 f.).[2] He objected to the word "*Trinity*" (E. 6. 230), declaring that it "sounds cold," and was "discovered and invented" by men (E. 12. 378); although he afterward admitted that the form of expression is not important, as "original sin," for example, is not found in the Scriptures (E. 25. 291 f.; 28. 382; 29. 183 f.). And in his tract, *Von den Conciliis*, etc., he "with masterly historical criticism"[3] denies all binding authority to the ancient councils. The highest council was that of the apostles, and it enjoined refraining from blood, an injunction which no one now observes. "If we want to be guided by councils, we must recognize this one above all others; if we do not, then we need not recognize any of the other councils, and *are therefore free from all councils*" (25. 240). Just as little are all the decrees of Nice observed (244, 251 f.). And no council has set forth "the whole Christian doctrine" (261). The decrees of councils are not on their own account true, but because they repeat the old truth, as given to the apostles by the Holy Spirit (266 f., 295, 328, 331). Councils likewise have "no power to form new articles of faith, but should indeed smother and condemn new articles, in accord-

---

[1] E. 20. 155: "I have a little book which is called the CREDO. . . . This is my Bible, which has stood so long and still stands unshaken, to this I hold fast, to this I was baptized, upon this I live and die." E. 9. 29: "Thus this Symbol has been excellently and briefly composed out of the books of the holy prophets and apostles for children and plain Christians, so that it is fitly called the Apostles' creed, or faith."

[2] Eck, on the other hand, at Leipzig highly lauded the ecclesiastical definition of the homousia. W. 2. 335. Erasmus already criticises it. Opp. v. 1090.

[3] *E. g.*, his investigations concerning Nestorius, 25. 304 ff.

ance with the Holy Scripture and the ancient faith." Thus, at
Nice, Constantinople, Ephesus, and Chalcedon, the "new articles" of Arius, Macedonius, Nestorius, and Eutyches were rejected (333, 345). Luther's idea is, that the dogmas are true only
in so far as they agree with the Scriptures; they have no authority in themselves. But the truth of the Scriptures is inwardly
attested. Hence it may be said, in harmony with Luther's idea,
that the Holy Spirit begets in us an experience of the truth of
the doctrine (of the Creed) (E. 23, 249, 267; 20. 148); for in
no other way can we be led to faith than by being practically
and inwardly convinced of that which has been taught (20.
141, 136, 144 f.; 22. 15 f.).[1] The doctrine of the two natures
in Christ is in itself of no interest to the Christian; it is only
from the work of Christ that he learns to understand it (35. 208).

We have thus before us the criteria and rules which Luther
applied in the criticism of religious utterances of all kinds. A
thing is true, if it is attested by faith, by his own experience,
and by the Scriptures. The outward and legalistic testing of
religious views by the standard of the ancient dogmas has been
abolished; the ancient canon of VINCENT OF LERIUS shattered.
But, beyond this, the legalistic use of the Scriptures is itself upon
principle abandoned. Luther's attitude toward the Bible was
thus very different from that of Occam. The problems which
in every age arise in this field of study, in consequence of advancing historical knowledge, may all be adjusted to the principles of
Luther and thus find their solution. That his praxis was not
always consistent or worthy of imitation can be here merely
suggested.

4. In conclusion, we may at least touch upon a further question: Was not Luther's peculiar apprehension of religious truth
limited or restrained by the recognition and acceptance of the
Trinitarian and Christological dogmas? The reader of his discussions of the knowledge of God in Christ (supra, p. 252 f.) receives at first the impression that the Father was revealed in the
words and works of Jesus, and that a separate divinity of the Son
is therefore not in the author's mind. But, on the other hand,
Luther emphasizes most vigorously the idea that the divinity of
the Son is revealed in his own life. He is true God and true

---

[1] Hence the papists have, in Luther's opinion, the whole second article of
the Creed only "with the mouth"—"in the heart they deny it," since they
hold that "man is not so utterly lost," and credit him with "free will" (E.
20. 142; 46. 87; 63. 154). It is evident that everything is made to depend,
not upon the acceptance of the traditional formula, but upon a practical experience, upon the basis of which alone can the formula be really comprehended.
Critical objections to any one of the facts asserted in the Creed had never
fallen under Luther's observation.

man, two natures and one person (E. 7. 185 f., 196). His
human life, with its deprivations, sufferings, and temptations, is
depicted in the most animated and vivid way (E. 13. 307 ; 10.
131 f., 299 ff.) This man was entirely under the guidance of
the divine nature. It was "personally present" in him (7.
185). His human nature does not see and feel everything, but
what the divine nature permits it to feel and know—hence Jesus
does not know when the day of judgment shall be (ib.). Thus
it becomes, since the Spirit more and more profoundly and constantly controls it, the "instrument and dwelling place of the
divine nature" (10. 300). Yet, in his passion and death, the
divine nature "lay entirely hidden and quiet within him, and
did not assert itself nor shine forth" (3. 302 ; 39. 47 f.,
supra, § 66, 3), as, upon the other hand, Jesus restrained his
omnipotence and, as it were, concealed it (37. 33 ; 39. 55 ;
40. 49). The intimate conjoining of the divine and human
natures, as the emphasis laid upon the reality and genuineness of
the human life of Jesus, is by no means a product of the sacramental controversy, but is closely connected with the most profound tendencies of Luther's thought : in the words and works
of Jesus, God is revealed. But, in the first line of thought, it
seemed necessary to think of the Father ; in the latter, only
directly of the Son (cf. 8. 156 ff.; 40. 109).[1] The difficulty
cannot be overcome by assuming a Modalistic conception of the
Trinity,[2] for Luther reproduces the orthodox doctrine in its
regular form (e. g., Smalc. Art., Müller, 299 ; 9. 2 ff. 22,
32, 116, 231 ; 10. 166, 171 f.; 12. 378 ff.; 16. 79, 108 f.;
18. 23 ; 30. 363 f.; 45. 294 f.; 308 f.).[3] It is true, that even in
so doing he manifested a Western feeling. The term "Trinity"
(*Dreifaltigkeit*, three-foldness) does not please him, because

---

[1] Upon the Christology of Luther, cf. TH. HARNACK, L.'s Theol. ii.
126 ff. THOMASIUS, DG. ii., ed. 2, 573 ff. H. SCHULTZ, Gottl. Christi,
182 ff. LEZIUS, Die Anbetung Jesu neben d. Vater, Dorpat, 1892.

[2] Cf. LOOFS, DG. 358. A. HARNACK, DG. iii., ed. 3, 752 f. This position
is not justified, but it is true that Luther had a strong consciousness of the one
personal God.

[3] Cf. 28. 136 : God is "not only one person ;" but, on the other hand, see
30. 227, 217. Christ is "one undivided person with God ;" cf. also the remark, 7. 189 : "The Holy Spirit is easily believed," "if a man is brought
so far as to regard two persons as One God." The Holy Spirit is a separate
person (49. 149); his divine nature is recognized in his working (49. 391);
in word and sacrament he works (49. 220 ; 50. 75, etc.) faith and everything
good in man. He is a comfort against the Evil Spirit in the world (49. 382).
The place in which he is revealed is the church : "Learn . . . how and where
thou shouldst seek the Spirit : not up above the clouds . . . but here on
earth below is he, just as the church is on earth . . . so that we may draw
him into the office and government of the church, the word and sacrament"
(49. 223 f.).

20

God is "the supreme Unity." Simply *Dreiheit* (threeness) "sounds entirely too ironical." The comparison with three angels or men will not do, for there are not "three Gods." "There is indeed in the Godhead *ein Gedrittes* (a tripartate reality) but this same *Gedrittes* consists of persons of the One only Godhead (6. 230).[1]   Luther was therefore not a Monarchian.   But he had a vigorous consciousness of the absolute unity of God, and this enabled him to see in each trinitarian person the entire Godhead.   God is therefore fully revealed through Christ (30. 62 ; 45. 295; 47. 180 ; 49. 93), just as through the Holy Spirit, with his sway in the hearts of men (16. 214). Father and Son are "one nature, one will," "one heart and will" (47. 305 f.; 49. 144).   Where one part is, "there is certainly the entire Godhead" (50. 94).   There is therefore no contradiction between the expressions referred to and Luther's consciousness of the Trinity—all the less since Luther did not conceive the nature of the Godhead as "Subsistence," but as omnipotent Loving-will.   He was able to combine this idea in his own mind with the traditional content of the doctrine concerning God.   The theoretical problems which arise in this connection never presented themselves to his mind.[2]

CHAPTER II.

DOCTRINE OF ZWINGLI.   OPPOSITION OF LUTHER AND ZWINGLI UPON THE DOCTRINE OF THE LORD'S SUPPER.

§ 72. *The Reformatory Principles of Zwingli.*

SOURCES.   Zwingli's Works, edited by Schuler and Schulthess, 8 vols., 1828 ff.   Among the writings of Z., the following are the most important for our purpose : Von klarheit und gewüsse des worts gottes, 1522; Uslegen und

---

[1] Cf. Augustine : *deus ter*, not *dii tres*.   Vol. I., p. 240.
[2] If the divine nature is to be conceived as Loving-will, how must we then represent to our thought the trinitarian life of the Godhead, particularly the divinity of Christ?   The divinity of Christ consists chiefly in this, "that the Father has just the will which I have" (47. 306, 308, 315).   "This will of the Father thou canst not miss, if thou keepest thyself to the man Christ, but meetest him in this man" (ib. 318 ; 48. 142).   Luther represents to himself the trinitarian life as a conversation in God (45. 300 ff.; 50. 82).   These are problems which Luther has left to Protestant dogmatic theology.   DILTHEY also recognizes that Luther's faith does not touch "the material of the ancient Christian dogma"—Arch. f. Gesch. d. Philos. v. 358 ff.

gruud der schlussreden, 1523; Ynleitung, 1525 ; Von göttl. und menschl.
gerechtigkeit, 1523 (vol. i.). Archeteles, 1522 ; De vera et falsa relig.,
1525 (vol. iii.). De provident., 1530; fidei ratio, 1530·; fid. exposit., 1531
(vol. iv.). Cf. MÖRIKOFER, Huldr. Zw., 2 vols., 1867-9. R. STÄHELIN,
Huldr. Zw., 2 vols., 1895-7, cf. PRE. xvii. 584 ff. HUNDESHAGEN, Beiträge
zur Kirchenverfassungsgesch., etc., i. 1864, 136 ff. MÖLLER-KAWERAU,
KG. iii. 44 ff. ZELLER, Das theol. Syst. Zw., 1853. SIGWART, U. Zw., 1855.
SPÖRRI, Zwinglistudien, 1866. A. BAUR, Zw. Theol., 2 vols., 1885-9.
USTERI, Initia Zwinglii, Stud. u. Krit., 1885, 607 ff., 1886, 95 ff. RITSCHL,
Rechtf. u. Vers. i. 165 ff. SEEBERG, Zur Charakteristik der ref. Grundge-
danken Zw. in Mitteilgn. u. Nachr., etc., 1889, 1 ff., and Thomasius, DG. ii.,
ed. 2, 395 ff. LOOFS, DG., ed. 3, 381 ff. NAGEL, Zw. Stellung z. Schrift, 1896.

1. At the close of A. D. 1506, while Luther was seeking "a
gracious God" in the cloister, ULRICH ZWINGLI (b. A. D.
1484), became pastor at Glarus. His pastorate was a stormy
and eventful one. When Luther in 1517 began the great conflict, Zwingli was at "Einsiedeln in the Dark Forest," searching
in the Scriptures for the true "philosophy of Christ." The
former stepped forth from the loneliness of inner struggles into
the great conflict of the church ; the latter had learned to know
men and human life before devoting himself in solitude to his
studies. Luther was impelled by the religious needs of his own
heart, the personal experience of faith making him a reformer.
Zwingli followed the counsel of Erasmus and the humanistic tendency of the age, in turning to the "very purest sources." His
point of departure was different from that of Luther, i. e.,
the humanistic, critical temper of the age, as differentiated from
the church and its teachings—a return to the sources, or the conviction that only the doctrine of the Bible is the truth. These
were ideas which Erasmus advocated, and which the majority of
the cultured classes applauded. It was under these circumstances
that Zwingli began his study of the Scriptures. The scope of his
reformatory activity was in consequence, from the first, wider
than that of Luther, and he was more conscious of a definite purpose. The idea of a reformation, which only gradually dawned
upon Luther, was the controlling motive with Zwingli from the
beginning. From A. D. 1519 he labored in Zurich, preaching
the Scriptures, taking up one book after another. Reformatory
ideas, in the proper sense of the term, were at first foreign to
him (USTERI, Stud. u. Krit., 1886, 122 ff.). As the religious
lever of his work as a reformer was undoubtedly found in
the idea of justification through Christ and by faith, it is natural
to inquire from what source he derived this idea ; and there can
be no doubt that he derived it, as well as his fundamental
reformatory views, from Luther. This is manifest, not only
in view of his known acquaintance with the writings of Luther
(USTERI, l. c., 141 ff.), but as well from the form of his doctrinal

writings, as they are found in his "Schlussreden" and "Usle-
gung."[1] Zwingli started with the Erasmian ideas of a reformation. This led him to the Scriptures; but it was Luther's range
of ideas that continually guided him in their interpretation. At
the central point of his apprehension of religious truth, Zwingli
is dependent upon Luther. But, as the more comprehensive aims
of the school from which he sprung fitted him, on the one hand,
for more varied application and a more speedy realization of the
reformatory ideas; so, on the other hand, he retained some elements which were not up to the evangelical standard, and which
betray their origin from the medieval conceptions of the
humanistic party.[2] This explains his agreement with Luther in
the central doctrines, as well as the divergence of their theological
and ecclesiastical views.

2. In endeavoring to depict the reformatory ideas of Zwingli,
we must begin with the emphasis laid by him upon the Authority
of the Holy Scriptures. Here the will of God is revealed to us
(i. 54. 207), and here the Holy Spirit teaches us "all that we
should know of God" (176). All doctrine is to be based upon
the inspired word (i. 81. 177; iii. 51. 359). The proclamation of the latter and obedience to it are the essential tasks of
the Reformation (i. 36. 38; iii. 70). This was the point of
departure which regulated all his thinking: "Is it proper to
conform to (*obtemperare*) divine things or human?" (iii. 67).
This went, indeed, beyond the attitude of the medieval reformers
toward the Scriptures; for with Zwingli they were more than a
book of external laws. His obedience to them was a result of
inner religious experience (i. 79). But he never attained in

---

[1] Zwingli's dependence upon Luther may without hesitation be asserted as
a settled historical fact. USTERI, l. c., and STÄHELIN, Zw. i. 164 ff., 175 f.,
furnish the material to substantiate this, although their own judgment upon it
is limited to a "perhaps." We can understand their hesitancy from the fact
that Zwingli himself denies all such dependence (i. 253 ff.; iii. 489, 543; vii.
144; ii. 2. 20 ff.). But we can understand also the sad self-deception to
which he has here fallen a victim. The study of the Scriptures was and
remained for him the source of his doctrinal views; and he found Luther's
ideas in the Scriptures—after he had learned them from Luther. It is somewhat similar to this, when he disputes Luther's claim to having brought forth
the Scriptures from their obscurity by pointing to Erasmus and Reuchlin
(ii. 2. 21). Cf. also KAWERAU (Möller, KG. iii. 46).

[2] In Luther, the general demands for reformation, in so far as he joined in
them, were thoroughly subordinated to the religious principle; for it was not
those demands which had awakened his energy and directed his course. With
Zwingli, they occupied an independent position side by side with the religious
principle; or, rather, the latter stood related to them as means to an end.
Those who embraced the Erasmian conception of reform, unless they gained
also the religious experience of Luther, found what they sought in Zwingli
rather than in Luther. Of this, history furnishes many illustrations.

his relation to them the lofty religious freedom of Luther.[1] Zwingli holds the humanistic view, that the Scriptures are the original source of primitive Christianity ; yet he also applies the medieval, juristic conception, that they constitute the divine law which is to regulate public life.

3. In order to understand Zwingli's conception of Justification, we must familiarize ourselves with his doctrine of Sin. Adam was created free, but died through his sin, and with him the whole human race. " There he and all his race in him died as dead as stone " (i. 183, 196). Sin, as original sin, is " the infirmity and defect (*Bresten und Mangel*) of shattered nature." In this invalided nature, the flesh is more powerful than the spirit. From this disease of original sin grow individual sins like branches from a tree (i. 190, 264, 60 ; iii. 203). " Sin, then, is when, the law of the Creator being neglected, man prefers to follow himself rather than the banners of his leader and Lord " (iii. 169). Sin is disobedience toward God. The sinner cannot obey the law of God (i. 184 f.), because his nature has been " shattered " (*zerbrochen*). But original sin in itself is only "a defect which one derives from birth without his own fault " (ii. 1. 287; i. 309 ; iii. 203 f.). The longing for eternal life is likewise innate (i. 59, 58), since the " natural law," or an internal illuminating and drawing agency of the Spirit of God, still remains to all men, even the heathen : "although I think that few of them have understood it " (i. 326, 360 f.). Accordingly, all truth in the natural man is inspired by God (iv. 36, 93, 95 ; iii. 156). But, however this may be, for practical purposes we must regard sin as a shattering force which excludes all possibility of self-deliverance.

4. Christ is the Deliverer. In the work of deliverance (salvation), the divine Mercy finds exercise, and at the same time satisfaction is rendered to the divine Justice (i. 186 ; iii. 180 ; iv. 475). (*a*) Christ has by his innocent sufferings made payment to the divine justice (i. 186, 387 ; ii. 2. 7 ; iii. 194, 187, 198, 498). He suffered for us, bought us, reconciled us with God (*ut iratus placetur*, iii. 181), became a sacrifice for us, and delivered us (i. 76, 179, 233 f., 236 ; iii. 189, 197, 209, 194). There is therefore no need of the sacrifice of the mass (i. 237), nor of other mediators, such as the saints (i. 268 ff.). His payment of the debt covers not only original sin, but all sins (i. 264 ; ii. 198 ; supra, p. 203, n. 1). He, the Innocent and Just, fulfilled the law for us (i. 213, 263, 309). The latter he

---

[1] Zwingli holds the Humanistic view, that the Scriptures are the original source of primitive Christianity ; yet he also applies the medieval, juristic conception, that they constitute the divine law which is to regulate public life.

did as God, since his will was the divine will ; the former, as a
pure man, who could render a spotless sacrifice (i. 264). By
thus effecting our deliverance, God " by this example of justice
removed from us our languor and torpor and displayed himself
to us as he was—just, good, and merciful " (iii. 180).[1] (*b*) This
last idea leads further. Christ is also by his works the
Revealer of God. He has made known to us the will
of God (i. 179). This, strictly speaking, carries beyond
the mere fact of deliverance : " is come not alone to deliver
us, but also to teach true love of God and works which God
requires of us " (180). He thus becomes our leader (195) and
pattern (313), whom we should follow (iii. 194, 211). Thus
the agency of Christ is two-fold : " For Christ everywhere in-
culcates these two things, viz.: redemption through him, and
that those who have been redeemed by him ought now to live
according to his example " (iii. 324). (*c*) Christ's redemptive
act now becomes ours through his relation to us as our Head,
and in the way appointed, *i. e.*, through our believing in him.
" But Christ is righteous and our Head, and we are his members ; therefore we the members come to God through the
righteousness of the Head " (i. 310), and : " If we believe upon
the Lord Christ Jesus, that he is our propitiation, etc., then is
he our entire perfection before God, our salvation, our payment
and atonement " (i. 186). He who believes on Christ is counted
by God as righteous (iii. 164) and has the forgiveness of sins
(i. 296, 393 ; iii. 230); so far, that is, as he follows Christ.
" Whence also his righteousness is our righteousness, if only we
walk, not according to the flesh, but according to the Spirit "
(iii. 209 f.). These are clear and thoroughly evangelical ideas.
Christ has endured for us the penalty of unrighteousness and performed the works of righteousness. Because we believe on him
and hold to him, God for his sake regards us as righteous.

　　5. Here arises the further question : How about Faith and its
origin ? The revelation of the love of God in Christ overcomes
us : " So that . . . at length the great humility of his mind
and his deeds of mercy . . . compel us to hold him in love and
to anticipate all good things from him " (i. 186, 311 ; iii. 205).
Faith is thus confidence in the grace of God. " For faith is
that by which we rest immovably, firmly, and undistractedly
upon the mercy of God " (iii. 231). But it is not to be understood in the sense of the *fides acquisita* (iii. 174. Cf. Luther, supra,
p. 254, n. 1), but it is wrought by the Spirit of God (iii. 223).

---

[1] But Zwingli adds : " or, that we may not presume to say too little about
his counsels, because it thus pleased him." Cf. Luther, supra, p. 271.

The Spirit makes man's spirit (*Gemüth*) "to understand his word" (i. 389) and gives man's spirit to understand that the word "comes from God" (i. 81). As one reads the Scriptures, comes the consciousness: " I have experienced that" (79). Hence, because the Spirit of God incites, we understand and comprehend the teachings of the Scriptures as the word of God. Thereby we are overpowered with a sense of satisfaction and inward health : "For Christian faith is something which is felt in the soul of believers, as health in the body" (iii. 198). To state the matter briefly in the sense of Zwingli, we may say : The Holy Spirit so moves man, that he feels the Scriptures to be the truth, and thereby attains confidence in the grace of God. This is faith. The Scriptures, as doctrine, have thus for him a significance different from that which they have for Luther, whose faith arose directly from the experience of the efficacious working of Christ (supra, p. 252 f.).

6. The movement begun in us by the Holy Spirit continues in such a way that good works follow faith (i. 278, 311). Since God thus works in us, we are his "fellow-workmen," *i. e.*, "tools in his hand" (406). Although the "infirmity" (*Bresten*) still clings to us and we sin in many ways, yet God continually "moves" us again, so that we return to him. And thus our very sin compels us to take refuge anew in God (i. 191 f.). Since now the Spirit of God works in believers that which is good, they no longer really need the law, "for the Spirit is above the law ; and where it is, there one no longer needs the law" (i. 212, 214).[1] The example of Christ takes the place of the law. "Therefore there is need of no law, for *Christ is his law ;* upon him alone he looks, yea, Christ guides and leads him alone, so that he needs no other leader, for Christ is the end of the law" (i. 213). As the example of Christ here replaces the old law as an outward rule of conduct, it may also be said that all who are born of God obey his word (iii. 178). In this sense, the law remains, and is even a part of the gospel. "The gospel thus understood, namely as the will of God revealed to men and required of them, contains in itself . . . commandment, prohibition, precept, and obedience ; so that all commandment and prohibition of God must remain in force forever" (i. 209 ff., 308).[2] The believer is to fulfill his commandments, except the tinsel-work of the ceremonial law (i.

---

[1] Cf. also the freedom from the law of Sabbath-observance, which recalls Luther's position, i. 317.

[2] Cf. also in i. 308, 554, the complaint concerning those who speak insolently (*unbescheidenlich*) of the law, representing that it makes us despair and hate God (referring to Luther).

311, 586), *i. e.*, the commandments, in so far as they coïncide with the "law of nature" (i. 359, 361). The law is therefore the permanent moral rule of conduct (i. 359, 325 ; iv. 102). But it can be fulfilled only as God works in us the necessary power. "The believer does it not of his own power, but God works in him the love, the counsel, and the work, as much as he does" (i. 311). But when we, warmed by the fire of love within us, fulfill the law, we do it freely, not under compulsion (iii. 205). Herein is a further modification as compared with Luther— Zwingli does not realize that "the law" is the expression of an entirely different conception of life, and he unconsciously makes the gospel a "new law" (i. 311). God impels us, but he impels us to the fulfilling of his commandments. Luther laid more stress upon the negative than upon the positive character of the law ; Zwingli, on the contrary, put the chief emphasis upon the latter.

7. In seeking to discover Zwingli's Ideal of the Christian Life, we shall find especially instructive his tract entitled : *Quo pacto ingenui adolescentes formandi sint* (iv. 149 ff.). Faith here stands first. Christ is our attorney, surety, and advocate ; he has opened for us the way to the Father. He who believes on him, to him are his sins forgiven. But faith is also the principle of a life of ceaseless striving after the good : "Only believers experience how Christ gives them no ease and how cheerfully and joyfully they address themselves to his business" (p. 152). Among the means of preserving the spirit in this exalted state, the study of the word stands first, but the example of Christ is also particularly mentioned. As Christ gave himself for us, so should we also not live unto ourselves, but seek to become all things to all (155 f.). At the same time, we should be always humble as was Christ. "He will therefore be perfect (*absolutus*) who resolves to emulate Christ alone" (157). A life in the assurance of faith and in the steadfastness of love in the imitation of Christ—this is the ideal. The Christianity of Zwingli is thoroughly practical. "It is the duty of a Christian man, not to talk magnificently about doctrines, but to be always doing great and difficult things with God" (158). Only when life is conducted in obedience to God and his word, in true doctrine and right living, is justice done to the glory of God (*e. g.*, i. 237, 322, 392, 398. Cf. iii. 165, 132, 48 f.).[1]

8. These are the fundamental reformatory principles of Zwingli. Their essential agreement with Luther's ideas must be evident to all. With these fundamental ideas were, however, combined a

[1] Cf. also the discourse of Schmidt of Küssnacht, i. 536 f.

number of subordinate convictions which help to explain the
new form assumed by his teaching in opposition to the medieval
views. In opposition to the Romish doctrine of *merit* and works,
he developed his theory of predestination. God is " an eternally
existent Working and Knowing" (i. 276); "the eternal
Power of all good, and an unchangeable Working" (277) ; and
"the first moving Cause" (278). Yea, he is, properly speaking, Causality itself, since all second causes are only figuratively
speaking causes (iv. 96). God rules in the world, as the soul
in the body. Nothing can transpire which is contrary to his
will (iii. 283). Everything which occurs may be traced back
to his power. The believer recognizes that his works are really
works of God, and that he " is only an instrument and tool by
which God works" (1. 276). This is divine providence.
" Providence is the perpetual and immutable government and
administration of the affairs of the universe" (iv. 84). This
leads to the denial of all accidental occurrences as well as of all
free actions (iv. 93). Everything, even evil, is based upon the
will of God (iv. 112 ff.). This determinism involves the doctrine of *Predestination* (iii. 283) : " He elects one, to be fitted
for his work and use ; another, he does not desire" (i. 276). " So
that thus election is attributed only to those who are to be saved ;
but those who are to be lost are not said to be elected, although
the divine will has determined also concerning them, but for the
repelling, rejecting, and repudiating of them, by which they
may become examples of justice " (iv. 115). It is in accordance with the sole agency of God, that when some are saved and
others lost, the fate of both is ascribed to the divine will. Everything depends upon the eternal election of God. Only in the
elect is faith wrought ; it follows election, and is a sign of its
presence (iv. 121 ; vi. 1. 215, 340 ; vi. 2. 106, 105, 155). He
who believes is elect. But even the elect who die before attaining faith will be saved. " For it is election which saves (*beatos
facit*)" (iv. 122, 123). Only in a figurative sense can faith be
traced to the preaching of the word. God uses the latter only
as an instrument: " He implants faith, as with an instrument,
but his own hand being also very near. This inward drawing
is (the work) of the Spirit directly operating" (iv. 125).
Election alone saves ; it works everything good in man.
Only upon the ground of fixed election can man be sure
of salvation (iv. 140). One thing is clear—and this was what
concerned Zwingli—that this doctrine excludes all insistence
upon works and merits. " By the providence of God therefore
are abolished at once both free will and merit, for since it determines all these things, what are our parts, that we should be able

to think anything done by ourselves? But since all works are from him, how shall we merit anything?" (iii. 283; iv. 116; i. 275 f., 278). The Synergism of the Middle Ages is thus shattered by the doctrine of the sole agency of grace. Zwingli in this entered upon the path pursued by Luther in his *De servo arbitrio*. But there is still an essential difference between the two. While Luther never allowed his speculative determinism to effect his Soteriology, it assumed great importance in Zwingli's religious thought. He constantly recurs to it. While Luther once broaches the idea, Zwingli lays a constantly-increasing stress upon it, particularly in the controversy with Anabaptism. His ideas were doubtless moulded by Thomas of Aquino and the Stoic conception of God.[1] In fact, the parallel to Thomas' doctrine of grace is very striking. As the latter, for example, reduces grace finally to the idea of the Prime Mover (p. 118), so also does Zwingli (vid. supra). Whereas Luther conceived of God as Almighty Love revealed in Christ, Zwingli did not make this positive limitation of the earlier conception. God is to be known before Christ : "The knowledge of God by its very nature precedes the knowledge of Christ" (iii. 180).[2] It is certainly a perversion to describe the determinism of Zwingli as the "fundamental principle" of his theology, since his doctrine of justification had other sources and motives. But neither is it correct to regard it as a passing episode. It is a foreign, but permanent, intrusion—otherwise than in the case of Luther—into the warp and woof of his religious thought.[3] This foreign element robs

---

[1] IV. 139: "To be of the universe is therefore to be of God;" cf. 90: "What he (Pliny) calls nature, we call God." Seneca, p. 95, 93, the doctrine of ideas : "These patterns of all things God has within himself." He studied Thomas, iv. 113. And shall we see no connection between the division of his material in the *Comm. de ver. et fals. religione* (God, to whom religion tends, and man, who by religion tends to God) and the arrangement in the *Summa* of Thomas? (cf. supra, p. 98).

[2] The whole passage—which combats a fundamental thought of Luther's—reads : "That therefore our rivals shall here say, that we have hitherto discoursed of piety in such a way as to have made no mention of salvation through Christ and of grace, they caw in vain : first, because whatever we have said concerning the fellowship of the soul and God has been thus said also of Christ just as of God (for Christ is God and man) ; second, because the knowledge of God by its very nature precedes the knowledge of Christ."

[3] I cannot therefore agree with K. MÜLLER (Symbolik, 450), when he pronounces it just as improper to bring the charge of a metaphysical determinism against Zwingli as against Luther. He has failed to take account of the *increasing* significance of the theory for Zwingli. Cf. also DILTHEY's opinion as to the "pantheism" of Zwingli (Archiv. f. Gesch. d. Philos. v. 370). The close-drawn lines of the whole document, *De providentia dei*, attest both the humanistic and philosophical trend of Zwingli and the lingering influence of Thomistic metaphysics upon him.

man indeed of the freedom of the will, but it also inspires his will—as an instrument of the almighty divine agency—to the most strenuous activity. "A long list of stern, heroic spirits down to Cromwell stands beneath the influence of this attitude of will (DILTHEY, Arch. f. Gesch. d. Philos. v. 369).

9. Another consequent of Zwingli's reformatory views is seen in his conception of the Church. The hierarchical view disappears entirely. Christ alone is the foundation of the church. All disciples, "all believers and teachers," receive the keys, *i. e.*, the authority to preach the gospel (i. 386, 387 f., iii. 215, 221). The prelates are not the church, but it is "the entire congregation of all those who are founded and built up in one faith upon the Lord Jesus Christ." With this congregation at large is contrasted the individual congregation, or *kilchhöre* (i. 197 ff, 656; iii. 125 ff.). The church, as the communion of saints, that is, of all believers (iii. 131), is not visible, since its members are scattered throughout the whole world (i. 201). It is composed of believers, who place their confidence in Christ alone, and obey, not human ordinances, but the authority of the divine word (i. 201 f.). That is the true church, which never errs, which clings to the word of God, and follows only the shepherds who bring that word (iii. 129). These simple conceptions were afterward modified by the introduction of the idea of predestination. The invisible church now becomes the totality of the elect and believing of all ages (vi. 1. 337, 447). Whereas, in the earlier writings of Zwingli, the conceptions of the true church universal and the *communio sanctorum* are not kept distinctly separate, this is now done. The separate congregations, or *Kilchhören*, form in combination the universal *ecclesia sensibilis*, or *visibilis* (iii. 574, 576 ff., 580, 586; vi. 432; viii. 380), in which the *ecclesia spiritualis invisibilis*, or *electa* is contained (iv. 8 f, 58). The source of the latter's existence is to be found solely in predestination. Therefore may children, even though baptism effects no real change in them, be fully qualified members of the church. It was, in part, the effort to maintain his theory of baptism against the Anabaptists and yet preserve the membership of children in the church, which led to this application of predestination to the conception of the church (cf. GOTT-SCHICK, Ztschr. f. KG. viii. 604 ff.). But the church thus falls asunder into two unconnected parts: the elect of all ages and places, including noble heathen whom we shall meet in heaven—[1] in short, all whom the Spirit shall have transformed by the exer-

---

[1] *E. g.*, Hercules, Theseus, Socrates, Aristides, Antigonus, Numa, Camillus, the Catos and Scipios, iv. 65; vi. 1. 242; 2. 69; viii. 179; vii. 550.

tion of his omnipotence—and the historical fellowship of believers
in Christ.   There exists no necessary connection between the
two, for "a conductor (*dux*) or vehicle of the Spirit is not
necessary" (iv. 10).   See SEEBERG, Begr. d. Kirche, i. 78 ff.

10. This brings us to the conception of the Sacraments.
Zwingli here adopts the Augustinian, purely symbolical view,
which was also advocated by Erasmus.   The sacraments are
nothing more than "a sure sign, or seal" (1. 239).   They, on
the one hand, remind the believer in a symbolic form of salvation and its blessings, and are, on the other hand, a means by
which he testifies his membership in the church of Christ.   There
resides in them no kind of purifying or sanctifying power ; they
are simply signs in the sense indicated (iii. 229, 231 ; iv. 117).
We dare not attribute to the symbols the "things which belong
to the divine power alone " (iv. 119).   Only two signs of this
kind were instituted by Christ ; the other five sacraments are to
be abolished as not being commanded by him.[1]   Baptism also
falls under this symbolical point of view.   Through it we engage
ourselves to Christ (is "either a candidate or a soldier of
Christ"), and we receive a symbol, "that we are to conform our
life to the rule of Christ" (iii. 231, 643).   It is an "initiative
sign," an engagement, as when a member of a confederacy wears
a white cross as a badge of his membership (ii. 1. 242, 249).
If Zwingli himself at first entertained doubts as to the propriety
of infant baptism (ii. 1. 245 ; vii. 365), he distinctly advocated
it after the Anabaptists began to make it a prominent object of
their assaults (A. D. 1525.   See esp. Von Tauf, Von Wieder-
tauf, and Von Kindertauf).   But while Luther in these conflicts
was led to value more highly the historical and positive ordinances,
Zwingli thought that he could best sweep away the foundations
of the Anabaptist party by making baptism a bare symbol, and,
particularly, by insisting upon it as an obligatory symbol.   By
the greater stress laid upon predestination and the purely external character of baptism, it appeared that the great importance
attached to baptism by the opposing party might be best shown
to be unjustifiable ; while by insisting upon the obligatory character of the ordinance its administration to children was made to
appear necessary.   It was in combating the Anabaptists that
the speculative and philosophical element became more promi-

---

[1] See criticisms in the "*Uslegen*," etc.: confirmation, 1. 240 f.; unction,
241 ; against confession to men (*lyselbicht*), with slight criticisms of Luther,
393 f., 400, cf. iii. 543, 562 ; ii. 2. 22 ; confession to be made only to Christ,
396 f.; the priest is only to be asked for advice, 394 ; works of penance, 397 ;
indulgences, 398 ff.; purgatory, 402 ff.   Against the priestly character of the
clergy—the priesthood an " office," not a rank, 414 f.

nent in Zwingli's teaching.   His determinism, having served
him as a weapon against the Romish work-righteousness, was
turned also against the mystical dreams of a visible congregation
of saints.   Upon Zwingli's doctrine of the Lord's Supper, see
§ 73.   Cf. STÄHELIN, i. 484 ff.   USTERI, Darstellung d. Tauflehre Zw., in Stud. u. Krit., 1882, 205 ff.

11. Zwingli proclaimed the truth of the gospel, and drew the
doctrinal inferences which seemed involved in it.   The source
upon which he depended was primarily the Holy Scriptures.
But he felt himself also in full accord with the doctrine of God
and the Christology found in the ancient symbols (i. 57 ;
iv. 3 ff.).   He presented no original ideas in these connections.
He conceived of God as the all-working Power, and at the same
time accepted the orthodox formulas, without attempting to harmonize the two conceptions.   His Christology has the Nestorian
tendency of the Scholastics (see below).   His interpretation of
original sin harmonizes with that of the later Middle Ages.   His
theory of the sacraments follows the symbolic view not infrequently held in the Middle Ages.   He mingles philosophical
theories with his presentations of the gospel, lacking Luther's
sense of the positive character of revelation—Duns and the Nominalists having here prepared the way.   Thus Christianity became
a kind of philosophy deduced from the Bible.   In view of these
characteristics of his teaching, it may be said that the undeniable
difference between Zwingli and Luther—despite their common
understanding of the gospel—is to be explained by the fact, that
Zwingli received his impulse originally from the Erasmian illuministic tendency, and that, in consequence, the medieval ideas
continued to exert a greater influence upon him than upon Luther.

As in the particulars already noted, so also in his practical
operations in the church, Zwingli betrays his dependence upon
the medieval ideals.   But the theocratic ideal which he pursued
allows to neither church nor state its proper position.   On the
one hand, the secular government conducts the discipline of the
church in such a way that the doctrine of the latter becomes directly the law of the state ; while, on the other hand, the secular
government is absolutely subject to the authority of the Scriptures,
its laws and ordinances being valid only in so far as they are scriptural.   If the government acts in a way contrary to the Scriptures,
it is to be abrogated.   The subjection of the church to the state is
only apparent, for the laws of the state are, after all, valid only
in so far as they conform to the law of the church, or the Bible.
This is a genuinely medieval idea.[1]   The carrying out of his re-

---

[1] Supra (p. 172, 183 f.).   Cf. Zw. i. 524 : " My lords should also prescribe
no law otherwise than out of the holy undeceptive Scripture of God.   If they

formatory work embraced both a new system of doctrine and a new
order of social and practical life, which must be enforced
by the agency of the state.   Christianity is an affair of the
state, but the state is the organ of the church.   Like Savonarola, Zwingli sought to reform his city according to the divine
law of the Bible, with the help of the secular power.   It was
also in accord with the example of Savonarola, that Zwingli's
political ambition was not satisfied with the direction of his
native city, but associated his direct reformatory labors with
political combinations of the widest and most daring character
(cf. LENZ, Zw. u. Landgraf Philipp, in Ztschr. f. KG. iii.
28 ff., 220 ff., 429 ff.).   Thus, in every sphere of his doctrinal
and practical activity, we are impressed with the medieval and
humanistic limitations of Zwingli, and that, too, in such forms as
to emphasize the contrast between his ideas and those of Luther.[1]

§ 73. The Controversy Upon the Lord's Supper.

LITERATURE.   DIECKHOFF, Die ev. Abendmalsl. im Ref.-ztalter, i. 1854.
THOMASIUS-SEEBERG, DG., ii. 522 ff., 571 ff.   BAUR, Zw's Theol. ii. 292 ff.
STÄHELIN, Zwingli, ii. 213 ff.   KÖSTLIN, Luther, ii., ed. 4, 66 ff.   W.
WALTHER, Reformirte Taktik im Sakr.-streit der Ref., in Neue kirchl.
Ztschr., 1896, 794 ff., 917 ff.   KAWERAU (Möller, KG. iii.), 74 ff.   KÜBEL,
PRE. xvi., ed. 2, 121 ff.   JÄGER, Luthers relig. Interesse an der Lehre von
der Realpräsenz, 1900.

1. The difference in the views of Zwingli and Luther found
expression in the controversy upon the Lord's Supper.   But
Zwingli had already, before the outbreak of the controversy,
developed his view of the Lord's Supper to a certain degree of
maturity.   The theory of transubstantiation he had from the
beginning regarded with suspicion (WW. vii. 391).   He received
the impulse to the construction of a positive theory, as he
reported to Melanchthon, from Erasmus (C. R. iv. 970).   The
purely symbolical view was in harmony, as well with the critical
humanistic school of thought, to which he originally belonged,
as with his general conception of the sacraments and the separation of the immediate divine operations from all earthly media,

should become negligent at this point and recognize anything else, as I hope
(they may) not, I would none the less stiffly preach against them with the
word of God."   See also "Schlussreden," 42: "But should they (the government) become untrustworthy and act beyond the rule of Christ, may they
be deposed by God."   Zwingli here has in mind by no means simply the form
of the republican constitution.   On the basis of his conception of popular sovereignty, it is his view that "the mass of the people," or the "greater part,"
are authorized to "cast out" ungodly kings (see Vol. I., p. 318).
[1] I do not, of course, forget that Luther also had medieval limitations.

to which he advanced. It therefore fits logically into the framework of his theological ideas, although it cannot be regarded as a criterion of his fundamental reformatory principles. For as, one the one hand, he derived his ideas upon the subject from a foreign source, so also in the illuminated circles of the day the symbolical theory was in the very air. His ideas were brought to a definite conclusion only in consequence of the correspondence of Honius with Luther (p. 288), in which the former interpreted the *est* as equivalent to *significat*.[1] The publication of Zwingli upon the subject seems not to have become known until the latter part of A. D. 1523 (Loofs, DG. 387 n.). Thenceforth he is clear in his mind. Basing his argument upon Jn. 6 ("the flesh profiteth nothing"), he, in harmony with Augustine and the older Scholastics (Vol. I., p. 323; supra, p. 133 f.), conceives of the existence of the body of Christ in heaven as local, and accordingly rejects the presence of the body in the Lord's Supper, being thus, of course, compelled to interpret the words of institution in a purely symbolical way. He was from the first conscious of the deviation of his ideas from those of Luther, which explains in part the zealous assertions of his (supposed) independence of the Saxon reformer (supra, p. 308). If he at first, indeed, represented this difference as a merely formal one, though emphasizing the idea of a repeated memorial (Wiedergedächtniss, i. 257), yet he very soon resolved to assail the theory of Luther, and from the year 1525 built up a carefully planned and vigorous propaganda for the purpose of winning the Southern Germans to his view, at first through the fictitious letter to Alberus (iii. 591 ff.).[2] Like-minded friends rallied around him with advice and aid (Oecolampadius,[3] Bucer, Capito), and means of doubtful character were employed (the corruptions in Bugenhagen's commentary upon the Psalms, and the notes in the translation of Luther's Church Postils). There was a feeling of strong confidence that Luther's view could be explained

---

[1] The formula, *significat*, has a point of attachment in the general sacramental theory of the later Middle Ages (supra, p. 127). What was relatively new was really only the application of the formula to the Lord's Supper, which held an exceptional position in relation to the medieval sacramental theory. But see already Wickliffe, supra, p. 206.

[2] The following among Zwingli's writings have a bearing at this point : the Comm. de ver et fals. relig., 1525 (iii. 239 ff.); Subsidium sive coronis de eucharist, 1525 (iii. 326 ff.); Ad Io. Bugenhagen, 1525 (iii. 604 ff.); Underrichtung vom Nachtmal, 1526 (ii. 1. 426 ff.); Amica exegesis, 1527 (iii. 459 ff.); fründlich verglimpfung, 1527 (ii. 2. 1 ff.); Dass dise worte Christi . . . ewiglich den alten einigen sinn haben werdend, 1527 (ii. 2. 16 ff.); Uiber Luther's buch bekenntniss genannt, 1527 (ii. 2. 94 ff.).

[3] Oecolampadius entered the controversy with his tract, De genuina verborum Christi . . . expositione liber, 1525.

away as simply the product of hypocrisy and timidity (*e. g.*, vii. 390 f.). Zwingli and his friends were impatient in their desire to measure swords with Luther and undermine his authority, and counseled against the use of prudent or pious tactics in dealing with him. (See proofs adduced in WALTHER, l. c., p. 815 ff., 916 ff.)[1] And they actually succeeded in stirring up a serious agitation against Luther's doctrine in Southern Germany, although their efforts met with some determined opposition upon that territory (Osiander, Brenz, the Syngramma, Pirckheimer).[2] These facts must be kept in view if we would understand the severity of Luther when he finally broke his silence and entered the fray.[3]

2. Zwingli's theory is a simple one. Bread and wine are signs of the body and blood offered up in sacrifice for us. These signs signify the body and blood thus offered, and thus remind us of the redemptive act (*e. g.*, iii. 599). The *est* of the words of institution is therefore equivalent to *significat* (ii. 2. 41 ff., 61; iii. 257, 336, 553, 606). Only faith can apprehend and appropriate salvation; but faith has to do only with spiritual entities. Hence the eating of the body of Christ can signify only the believing appropriation of the salvation secured for us by the sacrifice of that body. Christ is present in the Supper only "by the contemplation of faith" (*contemplatione fidei*), but not "in essence and really" (*per essentiam et realiter*). Faith in Christ

---

[1] Bucer writes very characteristically to Zwingli: "O Flesh! O Satan! what work hast thou made for us! It shall be destroyed by us for the promotion of the glory of God, and we shall see this arrogance vanish" (Zw. opp. vii. 521). Luther expresses his opinion of the conflict from the moral point of view with unsurpassable clearness (E. 30. 266): "My free, open, simple snapping at the devil is to my notion much better than their poisonous, plotting assassination, which they practice against the upright under the pretense of peace and love." As to the method of his opponents, see also 30, 24, 38, 61, 98, 139, 148 ff., 160, 205. It is more important to set forth clearly the spirit of these opponents and the historic basis of it, than to shudder at the thought of Luther's coarseness in dealing with them.

[2] See Bilibaldi Pirckheimeri de vera Christi carne et vero ejus sanguine ad Io. Oecolamp. respons. Norimb. 1526, and B. Pirckh. de vera Chr., etc., respons. secunda, Norimb. 1527. The argumentation of these documents touches the positions of Luther at many points (*e. g.*, the clearness of the words of institution—see the first response, form B, 7 r, E 4, and in the conclusion, upon the definition of a *tropus*, E 5 v; against the *significat*, F. 2 r and the two resp. F. 8 r); even in the conception of the ubiquity: "And it would not indeed be impossible with God . . . that one body, most highly clarified, should be in many places" (1st resp. F. 5 v). But STÄHELIN (Zw. ii. 269 f.) is in error when he represents Pirckheimer as having "first" introduced the idea of the ubiquity into the controversy, as Luther had already done so in 1525 (E. 29. 288 f., 294). Pirckheimer had read Luther (*e. g.*, resp. 1 F. 3 v, 6 v; H. 1 r, 2).

[3] See Luther's writings during the controversy. Cf. supra, p. 227, n. 3.

is really the eating of his body.   " The body of Christ is then eaten, when his death (*caesum*) for us is believed " (iii. 243 f., 595, 331; iv. 53, 118).   If we would take the eating of the body of Christ seriously, we would come into conflict, on the one hand, with the maxim, that the flesh profiteth nothing (Jn. 6. 63 f.; ii. 2. 85 ff., 184 ff.); and, on the other hand, collide with the limitation of Christ's body to locality (ii. 2. 81 ; iii. 332, 338, 512).   Moreover, at the time of the institution of the Lord's Supper, the blood of Christ had not yet been shed (iii. 333 f.).

The Christology of Zwingli is at this point called into service. While Luther interprets the traditional dogma from the viewpoint of personal unity, Zwingli always premises the abstract difference of the two natures.   God "assumed human nature " —the incarnation signifies nothing more than this (ii. 2. 69 f.). As in the history of Christ's earthly life his two natures are to be carefully discriminated (so that, for example, he according to his human nature does not know the day of his second coming, yet according to his divine nature knows all things, iii. 537 f.; ii. 2. 67), so also his divine nature fills heaven and earth, while at the same time his human nature is limited to a particular place in heaven (for, as created, it is " not infinite ") and is a type of our resurrection (ii. 2. 71, 72, 81 : " willst also never be able to maintain that the human nature of Jesus Christ is in more than one place ").   If now in the Scriptures that is ascribed to the one nature which belongs to the other, or attributes of the one nature are attributed to the entire person, this is to be explained through the figure of speech known as *Alloeosis*, or " interchange," *i. e.*, it is a rhetorical " exchange by which, when speaking of the one nature of Christ, we use the terms belonging to the other" (iii. 525 ; ii. 2. 68 f.).   Thus, if it is said of Christ that he is at the right hand of God, this, strictly interpreted, applies only to his divine nature (ii. 2. 71).   Zwingli's ideas as to the divine and human natures of Christ and his personal unity are here orthodox (*e. g.*, ii. 2. 66 ff., 82 ; ii. 1. 449).   But for the great thought in Luther's theology—that even the human words and works of Christ are a revelation of God—he has no comprehension.[1]   His Christology remains absolutely upon the plane of the medieval conception.   The divine and human natures are assigned to the opposite categories of finite and infinite nature.   The consequences of this

---

[1] STÄHELIN is not entirely correct, when he (Zw. ii. 175) describes, as the reformatory factor, in Zwingli as in Luther, " the overwhelming impression of the vision of Christ upon the sensibilities of the soul burdened by sin."   Cf. supra, p. 314, but also p. 310.

position came to light in the controversy upon the Lord's Supper.

The Lord's Supper is thus, according to Zwingli, on the one hand, a memorial celebration designed to remind us of the redemption wrought by the death of Christ; and, on the other hand, a profession of adherence to Christ in the presence of the congregation, and thus the assuming of an obligation to lead a Christian life (iii. 601).[1]

3. We found, as the result of our study of Luther's doctrine of the Lord's Supper (supra, p. 288), that he from the beginning taught the presence of the body of Christ in the Supper, and in such a way that the body, as a seal of the forgiveness of sins wrought by it and by the word appropriated by faith, strengthens and confirms the communicant in his faith. The theories of Carlstadt, who misinterpreted the τοῦτο; of Zwingli, who interpreted the *est* as meaning *significat;* of Oecolampadius, who explained the σῶμα as a sign of the body,—all fell beyond the lines of his thought. It was just at this time, moreover, that Luther became thoroughly convinced of the indissoluble connection between the empirical word and the exertion of the Spirit's agency. Here appeared to be another attempt, similar to that of the Anabaptists, to tear the two asunder (E. 30. 136, 353). Finally, he felt the new theory to be unspiritual and unchurchly, and he was convinced that it was unscriptural as well. The words of the institution appeared to him simple and plain. What need for interpretations of such plain terms as bread, wine, body, blood, eat, drink, is (29. 329, 331; 30. 33 ff., 154, 293, 355)? And as the words point to reality, this is confirmed by the circumstance that the traditional preservation of them is in all the sources in the same simple form (30. 311), and by the consideration that symbols are characteristic of the Old Testament, not of the New (ib. 338). Accordingly, he inferred that we truly eat the body of Christ in the Lord's Supper (29. 338; 30. 30, 103). " But how this occurs, or how he is in the bread, we do not know, and are not to know. We should believe the word of God, and not dictate ways and means to him" (30. 30). The

---

[1] Zwingli thus summarizes the errors of Luther: (1) That the body of Christ, naturally eaten in this sacrament, confirms faith. (2) That the body of Christ, naturally eaten, forgives sins. (3) That the body of Christ is naturally brought in the vehicle of the words spoken. (4) "That when I offer the body of Christ to be naturally eaten, I bring the gospel very near to him to whom I offer this, and to whom I give the body and blood " (iii. 561). Also, ii. 2. 93: "That the flesh of Christ is an entirely spiritual flesh ; that the body of Christ is, like the divine nature, omnipresent, . . . that the body of Christ, bodily eaten, preserves our body for the resurrection, . . . gives and increases faith."

exegetical difficulties of the words of institution never troubled
Luther, and he denied the application of Jn. 6 to the Lord's
Supper (30. 79 ff.). Nor did the manner of the union of the
body and bread disturb him. There was another problem,
however, which awakened his most profound concern. His opponents asserted the impossibility of the bodily presence at many
places. If Luther meant to maintain his position, it was, therefore, incumbent upon him to prove that the ubiquity of the body
of Christ was conceivable (30. 49, 56, 58, 70, 201, 206, 282).

4. In order to follow the arguments employed by Luther in
support of this position, we must bear two things constantly in
mind. In the first place, for Luther, as a scholastically trained
theologian, the problem was not an uncongenial one ;[1] and, in
the second place, his Christology furnished the materials to be
used in its solution. He had from the beginning thought of the
two natures of Christ as so united that the man Jesus was, in all
his words and works, the expression and organ of his divine nature. He knew no God except the One revealed in the man
Jesus. God "is present and substantial" (*gegenwärtig* und *wes-
enlich*) in all created things, but he "dwells" in Christ bodily,
so that one person is man and God (30. 63). When these ideas
are considered in the light of the formula of the doctrine of
the two natures, the inference is, that the two natures are
"one single person" (30. 63, 206 f., 211, 222), in absolutely inseparable union, so that where the one is the other
must also be (211 f.). There subsists between the two a relation like that between body and soul (204); and the flesh of
Christ is, therefore, being permeated by God, "nothing but
spirit, nothing but holiness, nothing but purity" (231). It is
"a divine flesh, a spirit-flesh." "It is in God and God in it"
(30. 125 ; 48. 26, 58). God has become completely man, so
that all human attributes, such as suffering and dying, have also
become his (25. 310, 312, 314). "Out of the infinite God has
been made a finite and definable man" (47. 182). The *communicatio idiomatum* is thus taken in its full meaning (25. 309). All
the activity and suffering of the man is also the activity and suffering of God (30. 62, 67 ; 46. 332 f.). "Whatsoever I behold in Christ is at the same time both human and divine" (47.
361 f.). "Wherever thou canst say, Here is God, there must
thou also say, Therefore Christ the man is also here. And if
thou shouldst point out a place where God was and not the man,

---

[1] Supra, p. 133, 204. Luther had the feeling of superiority of a dogmatically (scholastically) trained theologian as compared with Zwingli. The
latter was for him "a self-grown doctor ; they generally turn out so" (30.
267).

then would the person be already divided, since I might then say with truth, Here is God, who is not man, and never yet became man. But nothing of that God for me ! . . . Nay, friend, wherever thou placest God for me, there must thou also place for me the human nature. They cannot be separated and divided from each other. There has come to be One person " (30. 211).[1] The divine nature gives its peculiarity (attributes) to the human nature, and the human nature also in return its peculiarity to the divine nature (30. 204 ; 47. 177). It is no more wonderful that God dies, than that he became man (25. 312). Hence Luther could see in the *Alloeosis* only " the devil's mask " (30. 203, 205, 225), for this separation of the works of the two natures no longer permits us to see in the human nature the full revelation of God. It misleads us, after the fashion of the Scholastics, to take refuge in the divine nature and cling to this, looking away from the man Jesus (47. 361 f.). It robs the atoning work of Christ of its specific divine value (25. 312 f.; 30. 203 ; 18. 225). It is, therefore, by no means a product of polemical necessity which we behold in Luther's Christology, as developed in the controversy with Zwingli. It is the same Christology which he had advocated from the beginning. And this doctrine marks an advance in the development of the traditional Christology—effected by evolution from within. The divine nature no longer swallows up the human nature, but the latter is the organ and bearer of the former. It is precisely the unqualified preservation of the human nature which makes Jesus capable of really becoming the God revealed among us. Luther's most profound ideas concerning the knowledge of God and faith may be understood in the light of these principles (supra, p. 252 f.). But historical fidelity requires the recognition of the fact, that Luther in the controversy upon the Lord's Supper extended his Christology by including an inference not previously drawn. The practical identity of the divine and human natures in the earthly life of Jesus is deliberately transferred to the state of exaltation. If the words and deeds of Jesus on earth were the words and deeds of God, then are the works of the Lord in heaven also the works of the man Jesus. And this means that the man Jesus is at the same time the omnipotent and omnipresent Lord of the world. If he is present in the Lord's Supper, he is there also the man Jesus ; and since he arose from the dead bodily, his body is also present in the sacrament. Thus the theory of the Ubiquity is,

---

[1] Luther does not yet employ the term, Person, in the modern sense. It corresponds precisely with the ancient " Hypostasis," *e. g.*, 30. 204 : " Because body and soul is one person." Luther elsewhere speaks of Christ as "one person " with God (30. 216, 227).

in Luther's understanding of it, only a logical inference from his Christology.[1]

5. Luther opens the discussion with a definition of the term : the Right Hand of God. This cannot be conceived of as a "golden chair" beside the Father (30. 56 f.). We must here recall Luther's conception of God as the "omnipotent Power." If now God is the all-permeating and all-moving Will, then his Right Hand is simply everywhere. If God is "substantial and present at all places," in "the smallest leaf upon the trees," in "the most inward" and "most outward" things (58),[2] then his Right Hand is also "everywhere in all things" (64). Accordingly, Christ is also omnipresent, and that, too, in his body, *i. e.*, he reigns and has power over all things. "If he is to have power and reign, he must certainly also be there present and substantial" (65). This must, of course, be applicable in a general sense, even apart from all thought of the Lord's Supper.[3] The body of Christ is in every stone, in fire and water. But we can really find and apprehend him only where he has in his word directed us to seek him (29. 338). "But he is then present for thee when he adds his word, and thereby binds himself, and says : Here shalt thou find me." He is omnipresent, but in his divine mode of presence incomprehensible : "He has now also become incomprehensible, and thou wilt not seize upon him, although he is in thy bread, unless it be that he may bind himself to thee and assign thee to a particular table by a word, and point out to thee the very bread by his word" (30. 69 f.). As the divine nature, so also is Christ in his body near to all, "and it is only a question of his revealing himself" (30. 67); but this takes place in the words of institution, which instruct us to seek and find in a particular loaf him who is essentially present in

---

[1] A peculiarity of Luther's Christology is the lack of a sharp discrimination between the states of humiliation and exaltation. This may be understood, when we remember that his practical religious mode of apprehension saw in the man Jesus the full and real revelation of God. If we recall his definition of the divinity of Christ as the omnipotent Loving-will (p. 253), the question arises : How, in the light of this, shall the Ubiquity be conceived in harmony with Luther? We might, perhaps, reply : The omnipotent Redeeming-will, which became one with the man Jesus, is present with the man Jesus in the Lord's Supper, in order by this presence to assure us of the reality of redemption. But Luther did not draw these inferences.

[2] "Therefore must he be himself present in every creature in its most inward and most outward (parts), around and about, through and through, beneath and above, before and behind, so that nothing can be more truly nor profoundly present in all creatures than God himself with his power."

[3] Even the earthly body of Christ was "present everywhere," 30. 67 ; upon the glorification of his body Luther lays but little stress, 30. 98 ff.; cf. Occam, supra, p. 205.

every loaf. The presence of the glorified body is to be conceived of in the same manner as the divine presence in the world in general. God is not " such an outspread, long, broad, thick, high, deep Being," filling the world as straw fills a sack (ib. 221); as though God were such a great outspread Object, reaching through and out beyond every created thing " (213, 216). We are not, therefore, to think of any local, sensible presence. There are, says Luther, "three ways of being in a place : *locally* or *circumscriptively, definitively*, and *repletively* (207). The first indicates a purely spacial relation, as of wine in a cask. Anything is *definitively*, or " incomprehensibly," at a place when it does not correspond with the portions of space in the latter ; as an angel may be in a whole house, in one room, or even in a nutshell (208). The mode of presence is *repletive*, or supernatural, " when anything is at the same time in its entirety at all places and fills all places, and is yet measured and contained by no place " (209).[1] This repletive existence is now attributed also to the body of Christ (211). All things are " as related to the body of Christ, present and penetrable " (210, 216). His body was present *circumscriptively* during his earthly life, " since it took and gave space according to its size " (216). The *definitive* form of presence is to be attributed to the body which passed out of the closed grave and through the locked doors, and to the body present in the bread (216). As the soul is present at the same time in the whole body just as in every separate part ; as vision or sound reaches over great distances ; as sound passes through air, water, boards, and walls, and enters many ears at once, in such a way are we to conceive also of Christ's presence in the Lord's Supper (29. 333 f.; 30. 216, 218 f.). We are, hence, to represent to ourselves the presence of Christ in the sense in which God as the Omnipotent Will dwells in all things, or in which the soul permeates the body, and not in the " crude, fat, and thick ideas " of the circumscriptive mode of existence (215). The word " in " is not to be understood in the sense in which "straw is in a sack and bread in a basket " (223). Not in this external, local way is Christ's body in the Lord's Supper, but in some such way as color and light are in the eye (66. 189 f.). A " sacramental unity " (*Einigkeit*) exists between the body and the bread (297, 300). But the body, which is here spoken of, is the veritable body of Christ which was born of the Virgin (89).

If we compare with this Occam's doctrine of Ubiquity, p.

---

[1] This classification is of scholastic origin. The first two modes are derived from Occam (supra, p. 204). The three-fold classification (adding the *repletive* mode) was taken from Biel (Sent. i. d. 37 qu.).

204 f.),[1] it is clear that Luther was influenced by Occam.   Both
the classification of the modes of spacial existence, and the super-
spacial existence of the body of Christ in the Lord's Supper and
in all existing things, point unmistakably to that source.   But
a profound difference is here traceable.   While Occam, in addition to this bodily presence everywhere, thinks of the real body
of Christ as in one place in heaven ; for Luther the body of
Christ is, by virtue of the *communicatio idiomatum*, absolutely
omnipresent.   Occam appends to the current medieval doctrine
a speculative inference, postulating a certain Something which
may figure as the body of Christ in the Lord's Supper.   Luther
defends the religious idea, that, just as we apprehend Christ only
in the positive forms of his human life, so he is present in the
Holy Supper also as the man Jesus with the human nature (including his body) by which he effects our salvation.   What he is
most earnestly striving for will be evident if we compare his original conception of the Lord's Supper : " The same Christ who
has secured for us grace and the forgiveness of sins is present in
the Lord's Supper in order to assure us of his redeeming act."[2]
Here lies the nerve of his opposition to Zwingli and Oecolampadius.   The sacrament is not " a sign of a future or absent thing ; "
but a " form of the thing present and yet invisible."   Under
the visible form of bread and wine are " his invisible body and
blood present " (105).   The important thing, for which he con-
tends, is that Christ, and Christ the historical Redeemer, is himself present, and that we are not merely to think of him as
present by an effort of our imagination.   The scholastic material by which he seeks to establish this position is regarded as
means to the end in view.[3]

   6. With this view harmonize also the utterances of Luther
concerning the Reception and Fruits of the Sacrament.   We do
really eat and chew the body of Christ, and the pope was therefore justified in requiring this confession from Berenger (supra, p.
76).   But the bread is the body, as the dove is the Holy Spirit ;
for " no one sees, grasps, eats, or chews the body of Christ, as
we visibly see and chew other flesh.   For whatever we do to
the bread is well and properly applied to the body of Christ, on
account of the sacramental unity " (297, cf. 57. 75 f.).   The
bread is therefore really eaten, but with it at the same time the

---

[1] See already Alger, supra, p. 77, and Gerhoh, p. 66.
[2] Cf. 29. 348 ; 48. 23 ; 30. 85, 134, 137 : " What is the difference now ?
Yea, how is it any better for them to eat flesh and bone with the soul, than
that we should eat it with the mouth ? "
[3] Luther himself wished these explanations to be regarded only as possibilities, which do not exclude other explanations, 30. 200, 202, 210, 217.

spiritual body of Christ ; bread and body are at the same time and together present (300). There results "a substantial (*natürlich*) unification of the body of Christ with us, and not alone a spiritual, subsisting in the mind and will" (202). But despite this *manducatio oralis*, our reception of this gift must be spiritual, *i. e.*, the heart must believe the presence of Christ in the bread, which the word proclaims (90 f., 93, 185).[1] Only faith apprehends life and salvation in the present body of the Lord (130). This is the spiritual eating, which must accompany the bodily eating (86, 185). The body of Christ is therefore present in the Lord's Supper, but only the believer understands and grasps this and has in consequence the blessing which the body brings : "That which is given therein and therewith, the body cannot grasp nor take to itself; but this is done by the faith of the heart which discerns this treasure and desires it" (Large Cat., Müller, p. 504).[2]

From this we may understand Luther's view of the Benefit of the Sacrament. The body of Jesus, whose presence in the bread faith apprehends, strengthens faith (135) and gives to it the assurance of the forgiveness of sins (136). The presence of the body and blood of Christ brings us the salvation which he has secured by means of this body and blood. The new testament is here and brings us "the forgiveness of sins, the Spirit, grace, life, and all blessedness" (338). Thus the word, combined with the Redeemer offered by it and bodily present in the sacrament, effects a strengthening of faith, the sense of forgiveness, life, and salvation.[3] To this spiritual effect produced by the

---

[1] But unbelievers also receive the body (*manducatio infidelium*), although to their own hurt, 29. 346 ; 30. 369, 86, 343). Cat. 509. But those who do not at all believe the words of institution, such as the Fanatics, receive nothing but bread and wine (30. 132. Cat. 504).

[2] The presence of the body and blood, as Luther always maintained, involves the personal presence of Christ, by virtue of the personal unity (29. 295 ; 30. 130 ff.). On the other hand, the idea that the older German linguistic usage, in which *Leib* (body) is equivalent to "person" (*e. g.*, in Luther, 45. 13 f.: "In the German language we do not call a dead man a 'body,' but a living man who has body and soul"), influenced Luther's conception of the "body" of Christ, is, so far as I can see, without any foundation.

[3] 30. 338 f.: "The words are the first thing, for without the words the cup and bread would be nothing. Further, without the bread and cup, there would be no body and blood of Christ. Without the body and blood of Christ, there would be no new testament. Without the new testament, there would be no forgiveness of sins. Without forgiveness of sins, there would be no life and salvation. Thus the words, in the first place, embrace the bread and the cup (to constitute) the sacrament. The bread and cup embrace the body and blood of Christ. The body and blood of Christ embrace the new testament. The new testament embraces the forgiveness of sins. The forgiveness of sins embraces eternal life and salvation. Behold, all this do the words of the Lord's Supper offer and give to us, and we grasp it by faith."

Lord's Supper is added further, in harmony with the representations of the ancient church (Irenæus, ib. 116 ff.), an effect upon the body of the recipient.   The body of Christ is a pledge which gives to our body the assurance that it shall, by virtue of the " eternal food " thus received by us, also live forever (72). This " spiritual food " transforms the poor " moth-sack," so " that it also becomes spiritual, that is, eternally alive and blessed " (101 f. 132, 135).   But this second train of thought, which was of course particularly adapted for use against Zwingli, had but a secondary importance for Luther.   He could omit it altogether in his exposition of the subject on the Large Catechism,[1] where the whole benefit of the sacrament is made to consist in the strengthening of faith, or in the consciousness of the forgiveness of sins, and that, too, in a way thoroughly in keeping with Luther's original conceptions, viz.:   The word proclaims forgiveness; the Christ present confirms and seals it, as it is he himself who secured it for us.   " Therefore we come to the sacrament in order that we may there receive such a treasure, through which and in which we obtain remission of sins. Wherefore this ?   Because the words are here and give these things to us.   If therefore I am commanded by Christ to eat and drink, in order that he may be mine and may confer a benefit upon me, it is, as it were, a certain pledge and surety, or rather the very thing itself which he has presented and pledged for my sins, death, and all evils " (Müller, 502).[2]   In view of this resultant, the divergence of Luther's later from his earlier view of the Lord's Supper must not be overestimated.   The bodily presence of the Saviour in the bread and wine for the sealing of the words of institution, for the strengthening of faith, and for giving assurance of the forgiveness of sins, was beyond question his leading thought.   The only addition made to this was the adoption of certain definite ideas as to the mode of presence of the heavenly body, to which he was led by the course of controversy upon the subject.   These were, in the first instance, only auxiliary ideas, but they gradually assumed the character of permanent elements in the dogma of the Lord's Supper.[3]

[1] Or at least set it in new relations, p. 509 :   The sacrament is " nothing but a wholesome and comforting medicine, which may help thee and give thee life in both body and soul.   For where the soul is restored, there help is given also to the body."

[2] Cf. the discussions as to " worthy" and " unworthy " communicants (504 ff.).   Faith, together with the sense of unworthiness, makes worthy (504, 509 f.).   " Therefore we call those alone unworthy who do not feel their faults nor are willing to be (regarded as) sinners " (510), i. e., " who are insolent and wild," 508.   Under no conditions dare we think of the sacrament as " though it were a poison, in which we should eat death " (509).

[3] Luther from this time most vigorously rejected the position of those who

7. The Colloquy at Marburg could not, under the circumstances, lead to harmony, although Zwingli, impelled by political considerations (" *Burgrecht* ")[1] made as large concessions as possible to the Lutherans. Agreement was indeed reached upon fourteen articles of faith, modeled upon formulas drawn by Luther (Trinity, Christ, original sin, faith, justification, word, baptism, works, civil government). In regard to the Lord's Supper, there was agreement in the demand for " both forms according to the institution of Christ," in the condemnation of the mass, and in the assertion that " the spiritual partaking of this body and blood " is " especially necessary for every Christian." But there remained the difference that they "have at this time not agreed whether the true body and blood of Christ are bodily in the bread and wine " (art. 15). Luther, although he had not hesitated to express to the Strassburgers his conviction that they had " another spirit," yet hoped for a " good-natured friendly harmony, that they may in a friendly spirit seek among us for that which they lack " (E. 36. 322). Zwingli wrote : " Luther, impudent and contumacious, was vanquished . . . although he meanwhile declared that he was unconquered " (opp. viii. 370). Upon the return journey to Wittenberg, the Saxon theologians drew up the Schwabach Articles, which assert of the Lord's Supper : " That in the bread and wine the true body and blood of Christ are truly present, according to the word of Christ" (art. 10). This doctrine belongs with others to the faith of the true church : " Such church is nothing else than believers in Christ, who believe and teach the above-named articles and parts" (art. 12). And they really reproduced the doctrine of the Lutherans. The fault lay, not in this exaltation to the position of a " dogma," but in the fact that a peculiar theological method of establishing the doctrine very soon began to be included in the " pure doctrine " itself.

Cf. KOLDE, Luther, ii. 308 ff., and Der Tag v. Schleiz, in Abh. f. Köstl., 1896, p. 94 ff. STÄHELIN, Zwingli, ii. 395 ff. The text of the Marburg and Schwabach Articles in KOLDE, Die Augsb. Conf., 1896, p. 119 ff., 123 ff.

held that there is here no article of faith, and we should therefore not quarrel about it, but each one should be allowed here to believe as he wishes (32. 406; 30. 43). This is the opinion of some laymen, such as Henry of Kronberg : "My understanding is not competent to reach an opinion " (see BOGLER, H. v. Kr., Schriften des Vereins f. Ref.-gesch., 57, p. 14). See also Luther's opinion upon Schwenkfeld's doctrine of the Lord's Supper, 30. 285 ff., 305, 354 ; 32. 397, 404 ff. Also KADELBACH, Ausfürl. Gesch. K. v. Sch., 1860, p. 104 ff.

[1] Considerations of the same character—the possibility of reconciling the Emperor—influenced the opposition of Melanchthon, whom the Strassburgers regarded as their real and most dangerous opponent.

8. Nor did the *Wittenberg Concord* (A. D. 1536) produce an actual and permanent agreement. From the time of the Diet of Augsburg, Bucer labored unweariedly to bring about an agreement between the Saxons and the theologians of Southern Germany. His formula was: "That the true body and the true blood of Jesus Christ are truly present in the Lord's Supper and are offered with the words of the Lord and the sacrament." [1] Both Luther and Melanchthon hoped that an understanding might be reached upon this basis.[2] But Luther did not change his own opinion. Although he was willing to refrain from laying special stress upon the assertion, that the body of Christ is present also for the unbelieving, yet the formula finally adopted expresses his view : " that with the bread and wine are truly and substantially present, offered, and received (*vere et substantialiter adesse, exhiberi et sumi*) the body and blood of Christ." Just on this account the Wittenberg Concord failed to attain the desired result. Cf. KOLDE, PRE. xvii., ed. 2, 222 ff. BAUM, Capito u. Butzer, 1860, p. 498 ff.

---

[1] As in general, so in the doctrine of the Lord's Supper, Bucer found his point of departure in Luther (see the summary of his preaching, Strassburg, 1523), form g 3 v. During the sacramental controversy, he was on Zwingli's side. His view at this time is given in Ennarrationum in evang. Matthaei, l. ii. (Argentorati, 1527), p. 329 ff.: As food strengthens the body, so the recollection of the deliverance and forgiveness of sins wrought by Christ strengthens faith. Thus the body is truly eaten, p. 329 r. To this end Christ instituted the Supper, p. 330 r. The transition to his later position was made possible by the strongly emphasized assertion, that we at least with our spirit eat the body of Christ (p. 330 v, 336 v, 333 v), and through the misinterpretation of Luther's doctrine : " They contend that the body of Christ is really . . . transported into the bread by the word, *i. e.*, that the body of Christ is really present in the bread " (p. 331 r, 338 r). But influential, above all, were political considerations and the feeling that " what ought to be for us the symbol of the warmest love, some evilly disposed men have made the occasion of the most violent hatred and of the separation of brethren and of the rending of churches" (l. c., p. 329 v).

[2] Cf. the formula of compromise agreed upon at about this time between Blaurer and Schnepf for Wittenberg : " That the body and blood of Christ are truly, *i. e.*, substantially and essentially (*substanzlich und wesentlich*), but not quantitatively, nor qualitatively, nor locally, present and offered."

CHAPTER III.

THE NEW DOGMA.

§ 74. *The Augsburg Confession.*

LITERATURE. PLITT, Einleitung in d. Augustana, vol. ii. 1868. PLITT, Die Apol. d. August., 1873. ZÖCKLER, Die Augsb. Conf., 1870. KOLDE, Die Augsb. Conf., 1896 (together with the Marburg, Schwabach, and Torgau Articles, the Confutation, and the Augustana variata). TSCHACKERT, Die unänderte Augsb. Konf. nach den besten Handschriften, 1901. FICKER, Die Confut. d. Augsb. Bek. in ihrer ersten Gestalt, 1891. KNAAKE, Luther's Anteil an der Augsb. Conf., 1863. VIRCK, Melanchthons polit. Stellung auf d. Reichstag zu Augsb. 1530, Ztschr. f. KG. ix. 67 ff., 293 ff. THOMASIUS-SEEBERG, DG. ii., ed. 2, 364 ff. LOOFS, DG. 397 ff. MÖLLER-KAWERAU, KG. iii. 94 ff. J. W. RICHARD, Luther and the Augsburg Confession, in the Lutheran Quarterly, 1899 and 1900.

☞ In the references in this section, a. indicates an article in the Augsburg Confession; p. refers to a page in Müller's Symbolische Bücher; the second figure following, to a paragraph upon the same page. The excellent English translation in JACOBS, Book of Concord, may be used, as Müller's paging is there carried in the margin.

1. The adherents of the Lutheran doctrine gave confessional expression to their religious convictions at Augsburg in 1530. It was not their aim to establish a "new dogma," but they on the contrary desired only, as they professed adherence to the ecumenical symbols, to furnish the proof that they really held the genuine old Catholic faith. But the doctrine which they presented in the Confession became nevertheless the fixed dogma of the new church. It formed originally the charter of the Smalcald League, and gradually became the recognized standard of pure doctrine for the universities as well as for the congregations (as proved in Möller-Kawerau, iii. 98 f.). The same may be said of the Apology. But it was the Religious Peace of Augsburg, A. D. 1555, which first officially and plainly designated the Augsburg Confession as the standard, by which new associations in the church were to be tested in order to secure recognition from the empire. While we must leave to Symbolics the more precise treatment of this subject, it is necessary for us to consider the question, in what forms the new doctrine attained recognition as the official teaching of the church. The dogmas of the ancient church received a canonical character from the fact that they were the decrees of general councils which were "accepted" by the church at large. These decrees were recognized and given legal force by the state, or by an ecclesiastical authority—the Roman bishop—recognized by the state. The former was the case with the dogmas of the Greek church; the

latter, with the decrees promulgated during the Pelagian and Semipelagian controversies. The council did not itself possess binding authority ; for when the acceptance, *i. e.*, the civil recognition, was withdrawn because another council had adopted new and contrary decrees, the decrees of the former were annulled. This is plainly illustrated in the conflicts within the Greek church. The medieval conception of the church changed the formal basis of accepted dogma and led to the establishment of the rule, that the decrees of ecumenical councils, or the doctrine of the Romish church, or the formal proclamation of a pope, received *eo ipso* dogmatic authority in the church. Dogma became simply the formal statement made by official teachers of the church. But the authority which these were supposed to possess was shattered in its very foundations by the Reformation. The congregations were looked to for the reformation of doctrine and life, as to them belonged the right of passing judgment upon doctrine (supra, p. 295 n.). Practically, however, the princes were regarded as the agency possessing the necessary power for the carrying out of reform. Luther had voiced this sentiment in his "Address to the Nobility," and this led to the unique fiction of "emergency bishops" (*Notbischöfe*). The princes were utilized for these ecclesiastical purposes, not as being the bearers of the specific civil authority, but as representatives of "Christianity," *i. e.*, of the congregation at large, and particularly as "prominent" (*praecipua*) members of it (thus expressed first by Melanchthon, Schmalk. Art., Müller, p. 339, 54. C. R. iii. 244). When the new church fellowship had taken tangible shape through the carrying out of the ideas of the Reformation by the secular authorities, the princes and magistrates were at once recognized as its official representatives. Negotiations were entered into with them, and they became the public defenders of the new doctrine. The theologians formulated the latter, but they attained a legal character only when adopted by the secular government ; and this applies to their inner contents as well as to the outward form. This principle was first openly recognized in the decree of the Diet of Spires in 1526, although indeed the real force of the latter was only the postponement of an imperial decision. It then became the guiding principle for the organization of the new church, and received the legal sanction of the empire through the Religious Peace of Augsburg. The teachings of the Evangelical church— in Reformed as well as in Lutheran districts—thus became the fixed doctrine of the church, or dogma, when the doctrinal statements formulated by the theologians were "accepted" by the secular government in the name of the church. There was in this a certain analogy with the genesis of the dogmas of the ancient church. As a result, the dogmas of the church were no longer, as in the Middle Ages, the creation of merely ecclesiastical, *i. e.*, hierarchical procedure. Nor does there lie behind them the mystical authority of general councils. They are propositions which the theologians hold to be biblical, and to which the church at large, *i. e.*, the state, gives assent. But it is not, as in Greek Christianity, the civil authority as such which expresses this assent, but the state as the representative of the church at large. The latter idea is a genuinely medieval one. The state is not yet recognized as the organism of secular jurisprudence nor sharply discriminated from the church. From this combination resulted all the weaknesses of territorialism. But the latter were associated with the concrete application of the theory, and not with the principle itself. The principle is expressed in the simple axiom : The doctrine of the church, or dogma, is biblical truth, discovered by theologians, but recognized and accepted by the Christian congregation as such. This was Luther's meaning when he clearly and distinctly granted to the congregation the right to pass judgment upon doctrine.[1] Cf. as to the bearings upon ecclesiastical jurisprudence, SOHM, Kirchenrecht, i. 322 ff., 330 ff., 560 ff., 658 f.

2. The Augsburg Confession was composed by Melanchthon, but it reproduces, though as a "gentle-stepper" (*Leisetreterin*), the thought of Luther.[2] The "timidity" and "philosophy" of Melanchthon, and his attempts to moderate and compromise, do not belong to the History of Doctrines. But it is important to bear in mind the circumstances under which the Augsburg Confession was prepared. It was the Emperor's chief desire to discover whether the Protestant doctrine was in harmony with the twelve articles of the Christian faith (KAWERAU, Agricola, p. 100. C. R. ii. 179). Eck had in 404 theses charged almost all heresies upon the Protestants. These considerations required of the Reformers a distinct emphasizing of their agreement with the doctrine of the ancient church and a clear rejection of all heresies. It appeared to be important, likewise, to avoid all fellowship with Zwingli, whose political aims made him an object of suspicion (C. R. ii. 25 ; i. 1099, 1106). In all these particulars Melanchthon's personal inclinations were in accord with the

---

[1] This does not exclude a recognition of the fact, that Luther always maintained his demand for the general recognition of a harmonious pure doctrine, *e. g.*, 32. 406.

[2] Melanchthon had before him, when composing the Augsburg Confession. on the dogmatic side the Schwabach Articles, and on the practical reformatory side the so-called Torgau Articles. Upon the latter, see BRIEGER in the Kirchen-geschichtl. Studien f. Reuter, 1888.

demands of ecclesiastical policy. But all this was only the out-ward framework for the real task, *i. e.*, to present the fundamen-tal ideas of the evangelical party, and to show clearly that they demolish the monastic ideal of life and the external legality of the Romish church, but that they have no connection with the revolutionary tendencies of the Anabaptists. The Confession, therefore, undertakes to present the evangelical doctrine as the genuine ancient doctrine, which is supported by the Scriptures as well as by the better Fathers, *e. g.* (p. 91 f., 29). "Only those things are recited," it is said in the Epilogue, "which seemed to be necessary to be said, in order that it might be known that nothing is received among us in doctrine and ceremonies con-trary to the Scriptures or to the Catholic church; because it is manifest that we have been most diligently on our guard lest any new and impious doctrines should creep into our churches." Not all evangelical convictions found expression under such a rule (*e. g.*, C. R. ii. 184, 182 f. Luther, Briefe, De W. iv. 110, 52); but, on the other hand, nothing was asserted which had not been included in the faith of the evangelical party.

3. Articles I.-III. reproduce the results of the dogmatic labors of the ancient church: "One divine essence . . . three per-sons of the same essence and power" (a. 1). Original sin consists in the inheritance of sin : "Without the fear of God, without trust in him, and with concupiscence." This marks the connection of Luther's thought with that of Augustine (cf. Apol., p. 79. 7 ff.; 81. 23). The main practical point of the doctrine is seen in the condemnation of the idea, that a "man may by the powers of his own reason be justified before God" (a. 2 ; cf. a. 20. 9, 10 ; p. 88. 9 f.). In respect to the power of "working (*efficienda*) the righteousness of God," man, without the influ-ence of the word or of the Spirit, is not free, although he has "some power to work a civil righteousness and to choose the things subject to reason" (a. 18 and p. 219. 73). Sin is con-centrated in a historical kingdom of the Evil One. "The his-tory of the world shows how great is the power of the devil." Hence, "it will not be possible to recognize the benefits of Christ unless we understand our evils" (p. 86. 50). This is the religious point of view from which sin is regarded. Of Christ it is said : "two natures, . . . inseparably joined together in unity of person." The object of his work was, "that he might reconcile the Father to us and might be a sacrifice, not only for original guilt, but also for all actual sins of men:"[1] The result

---

[1] Also, a. 24. 21, where the blotting out of daily sins is represented as wrought by the sacrifice of the mass. Cf. Zöckler upon this passage, and supra, p. 203, n. 1; also Zwingli, opp. iii. 198.

of his resurrection and ascension is his dominion over his followers and their sanctification through the Holy Spirit (a. 3 ; cf. p.
94. 40). Further, "Christ does not cease to be Mediator, after
we have been renewed." He remains such, "in order that for
his sake we may have a reconciled God, even though we are unworthy." For his sake, who is always interceding for us before
the Father, we have the forgiveness of sins (p. 116 f., 42, 44).

These are the initial principles, which the new church held in
common with the old. Yet they are not absolutely identical.
The Confutators were, from their point of view, right in object-
ing to the " born without the fear of God, without trust in him,"
as a definition of original sin (Ficker, p. 8). They quote
Luther's remark in regard to the *homousios*, and call attention to
the fact, that the trinitarian formulas as such are not found in the
Scriptures (ib. p. 4 f.). The deliberate hostility of the critics
should not blind us to the fact, that a difference in point of view
is here revealed.

4. Article V. marks the transition to the evangelical principle :
"Through the word and sacraments, as through instruments, is
given the Holy Spirit, who worketh faith where and when it
pleaseth God in those who hear the gospel, namely, that God,
not for our merits' sake but for Christ's sake, justifieth[1] those who
believe that they are for Christ's sake received into favor." The
word and the sacraments are the means through which the Spirit
begets faith. But faith "doth not only signify a knowledge
of the history," . . "which believeth not only the history,
but also the effect of the history, namely, this article, the remission of sins" (a. 20. 23 ; p. 96. 51). "But this is to believe,
to trust in the merits of Christ, that for his sake God wisheth to
be reconciled to us" (p. 99. 69); "to *desire and accept* the
offered promise of remission of sins and justification" (p. 95.
48 ; p. 94 f., 44 ff.; 139. 183). This is evangelical saving faith,
as the trusting acceptance of the grace of forgiveness which has
been revealed through the work of Christ. In this light may be
understood the central thought of Justification: "That men
cannot be justified before God by their own powers, merits, or
works ; but they are justified freely (*gratis*) for Christ's sake
through faith, when they believe that they are received into favor,
and that their sins are forgiven for the sake of Christ, who hath by
his death made satisfaction for our sins. This faith doth God impute for righteousness before him" (a. 4 ; cf. 24. 28 ; p. 123.
93; 105. 97). Here the whole Romish system is excluded :

[1] The German translation of the *Editio princeps* is important : "Are accounted righteous before God for Christ's sake." Cf. KOLDE. Augsb. Conf.,
p. 28.

" they teach only that men treat with God through works and merits " (p. 97. 60). The relationship between God and man is not to be thought of in accordance with the scheme of merits : " as though Christ had come for the purpose of delivering certain laws, through which we might merit the remission of sins " (p. 89. 15). But neither is it as though the " knowledge of the history concerning Christ," together with the infusion of a " habitus inclining us the more readily to love God," would suffice (p. 89. 15, 17). In all of this human merit still remains. Nor does the distinction drawn between the merits of fitness (*congrui*) and of worthiness (*condigni*) help matters ; for if God must of necessity reward the *meritum congrui* by the bestowal of grace, it is in reality a *meritum condigni* (p. 90. 19).[1] Only faith justifies. It does this, however, not as being in itself a worthy work, nor as being the beginning and source of good works, but solely because it apprehends the grace revealed and promised in Christ, and applies and appropriates this to itself (p. 96. 56 ; 102. 84, 86 ; 100. 77 ; 113. 27 ; 115. 40 ; 99. 71). Man therefore becomes righteous through an " *imputation of another's righteousness.*" This is Christ's righteousness.[2] But since faith is the only appropriate organ for the apprehension of this righteousness, it is our righteousness. " Faith is righteousness in us imputatively, *i. e.*, it is that by which we are made accepted before God on account of the imputation and ordination of God " (p. 139. 186).[3] The leading elements in the conception of justification are here brought into conjunction. The law terrifies the heart with the wrath of God ;[4] the gospel awakens in it trust in Christ, or the assurance that God for Christ's sake forgives us our sins and regards us as righteous (p. 101. 79 ff.).

Faith is thus represented as the reception of the grace revealed in Christ, and justification as the forensic declaration that the person involved is righteous. But faith is also at the same time the beginning of a new life. " This faith, encouraging and consoling in these fears, receives the remission of sins, justifies and quickens ; for this consolation is a new and spiritual life." The Holy Spirit, who works faith through the word, works in and with faith a new life (p. 98, 63 ff., p. 177, 60). Only it

---

[1] These terms are here used in the sense attached to them from the time of Duns Scotus. Cf. supra, p. 161, 202.

[2] And Christ alone, not " partly our works," p. 130. Cf. Biel, supra, p. 199).

[3] Cf. p. 99. 69 : " For how will Christ be Mediator if we do not believe (*sentimus*) that for his sake we are accounted righteous ? " p. 99. 62 : " this forgiveness, reconciliation, and righteousness are received through faith."

[4] The same influence is also ascribed to the gospel, p. 98. 62.

22

must be borne in mind that justification in the above sense does not depend upon faith in so far as the latter is considered as the beginning of a new life. But faith is also the beginning of the regeneration of man, or of the process of making him actually righteous. Inasmuch as faith sets free from the sense of guilt, the heart becomes animated, peace and joy enter, and also eternal life "which begins here in this life" (p. 105. 100).[1] The Holy Spirit has begotten faith, and faith brings with it the Spirit, thereby renewing the man (p. 108. 115). Hence we might more appropriately designate faith than love as the grace making acceptable (*gratia gratum faciens*, p. 108. 116). But, as faith is a new life, it also produces "new movements and works in man" (p. 130. 129). The Apology itself summarizes its view of justification as follows : "Thus far we have shown with sufficient fullness and from testimonies of Scripture, that by faith alone we obtain the remission of sins for Christ's sake, and that by faith alone we are, justified, *i. e.*, from unrighteous men are made rightous, or regenerated" (p. 108. 117). Therefore, faith, which is begotten by the Holy Ghost, is (1) the organ for the apprehension of grace, and (2) the beginning of a new life. In the former sense, it receives the imputed righteousness of Christ ; in the latter, it is the beginning of ethical rightness in character and conduct. But the former is the fundamental element (p. 100. 75). From it, *i. e.*, from the sense of the forgiveness of sin, the Apology psychologically deduces the inward renewal ; for he who has become sure of the forgiveness of his sins, becomes at heart free and joyful (supra).[2] This portraiture of justification and sanctification in the Apology corresponds exactly with the conceptions of Luther, except that he laid still more stress upon the actual righteousness wrought by faith (supra, p. 260 ff.).[3] Upon the doctrine of justification in the Apology, compare the treatment

---

[1] Upon the idea of eternal life as begun by faith on earth, see also p. 215. 54 ; 287. 10 ; 110. 111 ; 216. 58 ; 146. 231.

[2] Melanchthon, p. 101. 79, assails the Scotist separation of forgiveness and infusion (Duns, iv. d. 16, q. 2. 6, cf. supra, p. 160).

[3] The terminology of p. 100. 72 ff. presents difficulties : "And because to be justified means from unrighteous men to be made righteous, or to be regenerated, it signifies also to be pronounced or accounted righteous, for the Scriptures speak in both ways." That is, the general sense of *justificari* includes "also" the particular form of justification indicated by the term *justum pronuntiari*. Upon the basis of this is constructed the following syllogism : 1. Since the chief thing in justification is forgiveness, we may say : "To obtain remission of sins is to be justified, Ps. 32. 1. 2. By faith alone, and not on account of love or works, we obtain remission of sins, although love follows faith. 3. Therefore, by faith alone we are justified," and that in the sense that "from unrighteous men we are made righteous, or regenerated" (p. 100. 75-78). The conclusiveness of this deduction may be doubted.

of the subject by Loofs, Stud. u. Krit., 1884, 613 ff. Eich-
horn, ib. 1887, 415 ff. Frank, Neue kirchl. Ztschr., 1892,
846 ff. Stange, ib., 1899, 169 ff.

5. Faith is followed by Good Works as its fruits. "For
good works are to be done on account of God's command ; likewise, for the exercise of faith ; likewise, on account of confession
and giving of thanks" (p. 120. 68, a. 6. 1 f.). They spring from
the Holy Ghost, or from regeneration and justification (a. 20.
29, p. 109. 4) [1]—both the "spiritual movements" and the
"external good works" (p. 110. 15). But works are in no
way the ground of justification (a. 20. 9, 27). Good works are
accordingly such as spring from the agency of the Holy Spirit
and the impulse of faith, and as are performed according to the
will of God (a. 20. 27); and hence, such as are in accord with
the commandments of God, and not with the self-made ideals of
the Catholic church (a. 27. 57). By virtue of their origin in
the inward man, these works are performed in Christian liberty
(a. 28. 51). These four criteria determine the character of
good works in the evangelical sense. Accordingly, all civil and
secular occupations are, contrary to the view of the Anabaptists,
good works (a. 16 ; a. 26. 10). Marriage likewise assumes a
new dignity (a. 23). On the other hand, the works of monastic
observances and of an external ecclesiasticism are not good
works (a. 26. 8 ff.). It follows, further, that ascetic exercises
are not in themselves good works, but are undertaken for the
purpose of preparing ourselves to do good works : "Not in
order that through this discipline he might merit remission of
sins, but in order that he might have a body apt and fit
for spiritual things and for doing his duty according to his
calling" (a. 26. 38). Finally, this conception of good works
gives birth to a new Ideal of Life. In contrast with the perfection of the monastic vows, evangelical perfection embraces
the Christian life in its religious central impulse, and, as well, in
its discharge of the duties connected with the secular calling.
"Christian perfection is to reverently fear God, and again to conceive great faith and confidence that we have a reconciled God ;
to ask and certainly look for aid from God in doing all things in
connection with our calling ; and meanwhile outwardly to diligently perform good works and attend to our vocation" (a. 27.
49, cf. p. 216. 61 f.; 281. 48 ff.). But this perfection exists
only in the form of earnest effort : "For they ought to strive
after perfection as long as this life endures, and always grow in

---

[1] It is only upon the ground of the personal experience of the divine mercy
that God becomes for us an object of affection (*objectum amabile*), p. 110. 8.

the fear of God, in faith, in love toward their neighbor and the like spiritual gifts '' (p. 279. 37).

6. Articles VII. and VIII. present the evangelical conception of the church.   There will always be a holy church.   '' But the church is the congregation of the saints, in which the gospel is rightly taught and the sacraments rightly administered '' (a. 7). Since the word and the sacraments constitute the church, it may be said : '' And unto the true unity of the church it is sufficient to agree concerning the doctrine of the gospel and the administration of the sacraments,'' but it is not necessary that ceremonies and traditions be everywhere the same (ib., cf. Torgau Art., i.).   This church, which holds the pure doctrine and *in which* the preaching is in harmony with this doctrine, cannot possibly, as is the common belief, be the church as an object of faith, or as the so-called '' invisible church.''   Melanchthon, on the contrary, in the note to Article XII. of the Schwabach Articles (supra, p. 294 f.; cf. Luther's conception of the '' true, *rechten*, church,'' supra, p. 294), expresses the opinion, that there has always been and always will be a true church, *i. e.*, men who hold essentially the pure evangelical doctrine (cf. C. R. xii. 481 f., 483, 433), and that this church requires for its continued existence only the word and the sacraments.   Since in this congregation assembled around the word there will always be a '' fellowship of faith and of the Holy Spirit in the hearts '' of men (p. 152 f., 5, 8), it is called *congregatio sanctorum ;* [1] but since it exists in an empirical earthly form, there are always '' many hypocrites and wicked men mingled in it '' (a. 8, p. 157. 28).   These ideas are in the end practically the same as Luther had expressed.   But the definition of the church is constructed by Melanchthon from a somewhat different point of departure from that of Luther.   Luther started with the idea, that the presence of the word guarantees to faith the existence of believing Christians, or the (invisible) church.   The differences in the proclamation of the word led him afterward to discriminate between the true and the false (visible) church. Melanchthon begins with the idea, that there has always been and always will be a true (visible) church, but shows, further, that it can never exist without a commixture of wicked men and hypocrites.   In the church, which is in its essential nature the *congregatio sanctorum*, there are found a kingdom of Christ and a kingdom of the devil ; but only members of the former are really members of the church (p. 154 f., 16 ff.). [2]   There has

---

[1] For the '' saints,'' and they only, are properly the church.

[2] This different point of departure explains also the later construction of Melanchthon's definition of the church (vid. sub).   He always starts

always been, Melanchthon means to say, a congregation (of professing Christians), which possessed the gospel, as did the association of evangelical believers existing at that time. In this congregation—not outwardly corresponding with it in dimensions—is the kingdom of Christ, *i. e.*, the church as an article of faith. The marks which prove the existence of the former, and therefore enable us to infer the existence of the latter, are the " pure doctrine of the gospel[1] and an administration of the sacraments in harmony with the gospel of Christ " (p. 152. 5).

From this definition of the church were drawn a number of inferences. (1) That the bishops do not have the right " to ordain anything contrary to the gospel" (a. 28. 34). (2) That the peculiar power and authority of the church is the preaching of the gospel, and therefore: " The preaching office is the highest office in the church" (p. 213; p. 215. 54; a. 28. 5, 8, 10). (3) That all other ordinances in the church are of purely human origin and must prove their legitimacy by the gospel (a. 26. 28). (4) That the church has no right to claim or exercise any kind of secular authority (a. 28. 2 ff.). The " power of the sword " (*potestas gladii*) must not be confused with the ecclesiastical power (*potestas ecclesiastica*), which includes only the " power of the keys," or the " commandment of God to preach the gospel, remit and retain sins, and administer the sacraments " (a. 28. 2-5, 10 f.). Hence the gospel cannot come in conflict with civil and social ordinances, but, on the contrary, confirms them (p. 215. 56 f.).

7. This brings us to the evangelical doctrine of the Sacraments, which is treated in Articles IX.-XIII. Of Baptism it is taught, that it is necessary to salvation, and that through it " the grace of God is offered ; " that children also, who are to be baptized, are received into the favor of God " (a. 9). Sin is forgiven, not annihilated (p. 83. 36). Of the Lord's Supper, it is said : " That the body and blood of Christ are truly present

---

with the visible church. The (later) heading of Art. vii., *De Ecclesia*, should rather have been *De perpetuitate ecclesiae.* Cf. Apol., p. 153. 7, 9. C. R. xii. 524, 432, 482 ; xxv. 688, and my comments in Neue kirch. Ztschr., 1897, 143 f., n.

[1] This expression points beyond question (cf. a. 28. 70 and *doctrina fidei*, p. 101. 81) to the specific evangelical conception of salvation and grace ; for this was, in Melanchthon's view, all that was lacking in wide circles of the ancient church ; but it does not exclude—on the contrary includes—the acceptance of the ancient dogmas (cf. C. R. xxiii. 600). To the marks of the true church belongs also beyond question, according to Melanchthon, as the following words attest, the Lutheran conception of the sacraments. It was Luther's main argument in support of his doctrine of the Lord's Supper, that it was " in harmony with the gospel of Christ."

and distributed in the Lord's Supper (a. 10); that they are "truly and substantially" present, and "we speak of the presence of the living Christ" (p. 164. 57).[1] Melanchthon *intended* to reproduce in the language of the Augsburg Confession the doctrine of Luther (C. R. ii. 142). The Confutators interpreted Article X. in the sense of transubstantiation (Ficker, p. 40),[2] and Melanchthon, so far from contradicting them, even introduced into the Apology a citation containing the expression "changed (*mutari*) into flesh" (p. 164. 55).[3] Private absolution is recognized, but not in the sense that the preceding confession is an "enumeration of all faults" (a. 11 ; also a. 25). Repentance is open to everyone who turns from his sins, and the church must grant him absolution. Repentance consists of two parts. One is *contrition*, or terrors stricken into the conscience through the knowledge of sin ; the other is *faith*, which is conceived by the gospel, or absolution. . . . Then ought to follow good works, which are fruits of repentance (a. 12). These two, or three (p. 171. 28 ; cf. supra, p. 241, n. 3), parts therefore constitute evangelical repentance. Here again it is very evident that the general evangelical conception of salvation furnishes the direct contrast to the theory of the sacrament of repentance, and presents a substitute for it ; for the ideas we have just cited simply summarize what has been already presented in the discussion of faith, justification, and works. This is still more distinctly brought to light in the extended discussions of the Apology. The law and the gospel are the substance of the Scriptures (p. 175. 53). The law, as also the gospel (according to Lk. 24. 47), first exercises its office of rebuke upon man and begets contrition. "We say that contrition is the true terrors of conscience, which feels that God is angry with sin, and grieves that it has sinned. And this contrition thus occurs when sins are censured from the word of God, because this is the sum of the

---

[1] This language is chosen in view of the charge of the Confutators, that by Luther's view there is present in the bread "a body alone, without the accompaniment of soul and blood," and that thus he "offers a dead body of Christ," Ficker, p. 41.

[2] As did also later Catholic writers (*e. g.*, HEPPE, Gesch. d. Prot. iv. 371 f. This interpretation of the German text : "That . . . body and blood . . . are present under the form (*Gestalt*) of the bread and wine," is not an impossible one, since the form (*species*) of the bread, according to the Catholic theory, remains despite the transubstantiation.

[3] Strictly speaking, Melanchthon cites Vulgarius (Theophylact) only to prove that the Greeks also teach the presence of the body of Christ. He by no means thereby commits himself to their *mutari*, and did not, therefore, "drag in" this term (as LOOFS asserts, DG. 399). But we dare not deny a fatal diplomacy in the choice of the citation. Upon the entire question, see CALINICH, Ztschr. f. wiss. Theol., 1873, 541 ff.

preaching of the gospel, viz., to convict of sin and to offer remission of sins and righteousness for Christ's sake, . . . and
that, as regenerate men, we should do good works" (p. 171.
29).[1] But, since the preaching of the gospel accompanies that of
the law, contrition is followed by " special faith : this faith follows terrors in such a way as to overcome them and render the
conscience pacified. To this faith we ascribe that it justifies
and regenerates, since it frees from terrors and brings forth in
the heart peace, joy, and a new life" (p. 177. 60). Hence
the gospel, or absolution, as the better Scholastics also recognized (supra, p. 137), constitutes the real substance of the sacrament of repentance (p. 173. 41). The proclamation of the
gospel is, therefore, the real power of the keys (a. 25. 3 f.).

As the Confession places Article XIII., on the use of the Sacraments, after the discussion of baptism, the Lord's Supper and
repentance, it is evident that it recognizes three sacraments
(cf. Apol., p. 202. 4).[2] The general conception of the sacraments is not merely that they are marks of profession (as in
Zwingli), " but rather that they are signs and testimonies of the
will of God toward us, for the purpose of awakening and confirming faith in those who use them " (a. 13. 1). They are
"rites" (*Riten*) instituted by God, which, in connection with
the word (of institution), move the heart, since they reach us
through the eye as does the word through the ear. " Wherefore
the effect of both is the same " (p. 202. 5). Now, as God has
affixed definite promises to these rites, faith is necessary as the
prerequisite for their proper reception (a. 13. 2 ; p. 204, 19 ff.).
The sacraments are, therefore, to be evangelically defined as
signs, through the observance of which God gives that which the
words employed in their institution promise. As their substantial result is the strengthening of faith, so faith is also the prerequisite for their profitable reception. The Apology rejects the
Scholastic doctrine, that they bestow grace by virtue of the mere
administration of them (*ex opere operato*, p. 204. 18).[3] The
religious character of the sacramental acts is here in an admirable
way preserved.

8. The remaining articles of the Confession, especially those
directed against the prevailing abuses, have already been referred
to as far as they have important bearing upon the History of

[1] The question, when contrition springs from love and when from fear, is
waived aside as profitless scholastic disputation, p. 171. 29.

[2] But the Smalcald Articles enumerate two sacraments, p. 485. 1.

[3] The corresponding words of the Augsburg Confession (a. 13. 3) were not
in the original document, as the Confutators (Ficker, p. 48) do not mention
them.

Doctrines. We mention here only the articles upon the saints, who are not to be regarded as mediators in addition to Christ, nor to be worshiped (a. 21. Upon Mary, see p. 227); upon the marriage of priests (a. 23), the prohibition of which is contrary to the law of nature (p. 236 f.); upon the mass (a. 24); upon confession (a. 25); upon discrimination of meats (a. 26); upon monastic vows (a. 27); upon episcopal authority (a. 26); and of Christ's return to judgment (a. 17).

Reviewing the entire document, it may be said that the Augsburg Confession affords a clear, compact, and thorough presentation of the views of Luther in their fundamental features.

§ 75. *The Earlier Reformed Confessions.*

LITERATURE. NIEMEYER, Collectio confessionum in ecclesiis reformatis publicatarum, 1840. K. MÜLLER, Die Bekenntnisschriften der reformirten Kirche, 1903. THOMASIUS-SEEBERG, ii., ed. 2, 417 ff. K. MÜLLER, Symbolik, 398 ff.

1. The original documents which here demand our attention (Tetrapolitana, 1530. Basileensis prior, 1534. Helvetica prior, 1536) are only in a general way in accord with the views of Zwingli. The influence of Bucer's irenic efforts is already traceable in them (vid. sub).

2. It must be distinctly noted, first of all, that these confessions also give clear expression to the doctrine of justification by faith alone. This is " the highest and most prominent chief article . . . that we are preserved and saved alone through the simple mercy of God and through the merit of Christ. . . . Such high and great benefits of divine grace and the true sanctifying of the Spirit of God we receive not from our merits and powers, but through faith, which is a pure gift and bestowal of God " (Helv. 12. Tetr. 3. Bas. 83).[1] The sole authority of the Scriptures is also maintained. Only that is to be preached which is found in them, or deduced from them (Tetr. 1. Helv. 1).

The fundamental reformatory principle excludes the meritorious character of works and justification by means of them (Bas. 83). But as faith is, in one aspect, the receptive organ by which all the gracious gifts of God are appropriated, it is also, in another aspect, the fundamental principle of a new moral life. " This faith is a sure, firm, yea, an undoubted foundation and apprehension of all things which we hope for from God, who

---

[1] These figures indicate articles of the confessions, except in the case of the Basileensis, where they refer to the marginal numbers in Niemeyer.

causes love, and hence all virtues, to grow from it. . . This faith, which does not rely upon its own work, although it performs innumerable good works, but upon the mercy of God, is the real true service, by means of which we please God " (Helv. 13).

The spiritual nature of the Church is here also plainly asserted (Helv. 14. Bas. 81. Tetr. 15). In the doctrine of the sacraments, there is a general agreement with Zwingli. The sacraments serve " for the begetting of faith and brotherly love " (Bas. 81) ; but yet they are—according to the Helvetica—not only symbols (*symbola*), but they " consist of signs and at the same time realities " (*signis simul et rebus*). Thus in baptism, water is the sign, and regeneration and adoption the reality ; in the Lord's Supper, bread and wine constitute the sign, while the reality is " the imparting (*communicatio*) of the body of the Lord, the procuring of salvation, and the remission of sins." This is however upon the condition, that an inner reception by the heart accompanies that of the outward symbols (21. 16). The chief attention is naturally given to the Lord's Supper. Christ is the food of believing souls. Our souls are through faith refreshed by his flesh and blood (Bas. 81 f.). Christ left his body to his disciples as food for the soul (Tetr. 18). The difference from Luther's view here remains evident, however carefully it is kept in the background. A carnal presence (*carnalis praesentia*) is expressly denied. The Supper brings a commemoration of the Crucified One, and thus refreshes our hearts (Helv. 23). Zwingli could certainly have subscribed these statements in detail ; but we can nevertheless discern here, as elsewhere in the Confessions, a certain modification of his ideas. There is here an effort to associate the spiritual influence as closely as possible with the bodily reception of the sacraments.[1]

---

[1] This softening down of Zwingli's ideas is manifest also in the theory of original sin (Bas. 80. Helv. 8). Predestination is not discussed, but the characteristic separation of the divine influence from the earthly means remains as the fixed premise to the doctrine of the means of grace.

PART II.

THE FURTHER DEVELOPMENT AND (PROVISIONAL) COMPLETION OF PROTESTANT DOCTRINE.

CHAPTER I.

LUTHERAN DOCTRINE TO THE ADOPTION OF THE FORMULA OF CONCORD.

§ 76. *Theology of Melanchthon and its Significance for the History of Doctrine.*

LITERATURE. SCHMIDT, Ph. Mel., 1860. HARTFELDER, Mel. als Präceptor Germ. (= Mon. paed. vii.), 1889. HERRLINGER, Die Theol. Mel., 1870. TRÖLTSCH, Vernunft u. Offenb. bei J. Gerh. u. Mel., 1890. RITSCHL, Die Entstehung d. luth. Kirche, Ztschr. f. KG. i. 51 ff.; ii. 366 ff. LOOFS, DG., ed. 3, 408 ff. SEEBERG, Mel. Stellung in d. Gesch. d. Dogmas, Neue kirchl. Ztschr., 1897, 126 ff.[1] HAUSSLEITER, Aus d. Schule Mel. (Greifswalder Festschr.), 1897. SELL, Mel. u. die deutsche Ref. bis 1531 (Schriften des Vereins für Ref.-Gesch., 56), etc. DILTHEY, in Archiv. f. Gesch. d. Philos. vi. 226 ff., 347 ff.

1. In the first period of Protestant doctrinal history, we have familiarized ourselves with the genesis of the Lutheran and Reformed Doctrines. We studied first of all the religious ideas of Luther in their peculiar character and force, and sought to understand them in the light of the circumstances attending their development. We then followed the course of Zwingli, and the influence of his teachings.

The second period is marked by the development and provisional[2] completion of doctrinal construction in the Protestant church. If in the first period ideas were produced and new ideals created, the second period addressed itself to the task of constructing forms and formulas for their permanent embodiment. The former was an essentially religious, this an essentially

---

[1] A part of this article is reproduced in the present section.

[2] The completion of dogmatic statement thus attained is described as merely "provisional," partly upon general historical principles, for we can of course not tell in advance to what modifications, additions, and omissions the Protestant doctrines may yet be subjected in the church. But the word has also a special significance, as guarding against the error of regarding the present forms of statement as final, which would be an unauthorized dogmatic opinion.

theological era.   Melanchthon and Calvin are the leaders in the
toil of the second period.   The historical transition from the first
to the second stage of development may be easily understood.
Luther had restored the gospel to the church ; but his religious
instinct preserved him from the attempt to simply reproduce the
thought of the apostolic age, ignoring the entire historical development which intervened.   Upon the contrary, many ideas and
elements derived from the past became coëfficients in the shaping
of his religious views.[1]   This was at first quite unavoidable in the
sphere of external historical forms.   Continuity of life demands
points of attachment to the forms of the past.   But as, in this
case, a great literary and scientific revolution preceded the religious movement, the direct dependence of Protestant theology
upon the scholastic materials of the preceding epoch was less
marked than might otherwise have been expected.

2.   It was Melanchthon who, on Lutheran territory, rendered
the important service of providing a system of doctrine for the
youthful Protestant church.   His universal culture, which fitted
him, by the publication of many text-books, to become the instructor of his age in the spheres of general philosophy and phil-
ology, his delicate sense, so averse to all extremes and disturb-
ances, and his wonderful talent for formulating, fitted him to become the *Praeceptor Germaniae* also in the sphere of theology.
As early as A. D. 1521 appeared the first draft of his *Loci* (ed.
Plitt-Kolde, 1890).   There is here presented in brief and compact form an excellent epitome of Luther's views touching the
plan of salvation.   The Scriptures alone, it is held, furnish the
"form of Christianity" (*forma christianismi*) ; they alone establish articles of faith (p. 59, 139).   The doctrines immediately
connected with Soteriology are presented, but no attention is
devoted to the doctrine of the Trinity or to Christology.[2]   Sharp
protest is entered against the injection of philosophical speculations into religion.[3]   A fuller description of the work would be
apart from our present purpose (see my review in Neue kirchl.

---

[1] In this sense the entire period from the time of Augustine may be described
as pre-reformatory.   We can in the light of this understand also the simple
retention of the dogmas of the ancient church.

[2] Melanchthon accepts the Nicene doctrine (p. 139 f.), but he thought that
a "compendium of Christian doctrine" might be given — following the example of the Epistle to the Romans—without detailed theories in regard to
God and Christ (p. 64, 61) ; cf. C. R. 1. 305 : "for I condemn metaphysical
theories, because I think it a great peril to subject celestial mysteries to the
methods of our reason."

[3] See his fine remark, p. 37 : "For just as in these modern times of the
church we have embraced Aristotle instead of Christ, so, immediately after the
beginning of the church, Christian doctrine was weakened through Platonic
philosophy."

Ztschr., 1897, 129 ff.), although we shall have occasion to ex-
·amine the later theological views of Melanchthon. His aim is
here very distinctly to present the teachings of Luther. But we
notice a characteristic materializing and leveling down of the
ideas of Luther, while upon certain points the author knowingly
advocates positions differing from his. Both these tendencies
became most highly significant in their influence upon the devel-
ment of doctrine, although the former is to be regarded as the
more important in its results. We begin with the deliberate doctrinal divergences.

3. There were two doctrines upon which Melanchthon consciously differed from Luther, viz., free will and the Lord's
Supper. That he wavered from his original deterministic position is perhaps to be attributed to the influence of the polemical
writings of Erasmus against Luther (cf., *e. g.*, C. R. i. 688).
As early as 1527, in his exposition of the Epistle to the Colos-
sians, he recognizes human freedom in the sphere of the outward
life, although no one can fear and love God except he be impelled by the Holy Spirit (cf. LUTHARDT, Die Lehre vom fr.
Willen, p. 162 ff.). Similarly, in the *Unterricht der Visitatoren*, xxvi. 78. In the Augsburg Confession, he purposely
avoids questions concerning predestination (ii. 547). And upon
the occasion of a disputation at Wittenberg in 1534, he pointed
out that neither religion nor morality could be harmonized with
the Stoic doctrine of the necessity of all events (x. 70 f., 785 ff.).
Already in the *Loci* of 1535, Melanchthon attributed to the
human will an active, although small, part in producing conversion. He there recognizes three causes of conversion : the word,
the Holy Spirit, and the human will. He explains, further, that
the will either determines to accept or determines not to accept
the grace of God (xxi. 376 f., 332). He expresses himself most
plainly upon this point in the third revision of the *Loci* (A. D.
1543). His inner motive is opposition to the Stoic ἀνάγχη. Man
yet retains freedom as a power of applying himself to grace (*facultas applicandi se ad gratiam*) (xxi. 652, 659 f.). Accordingly,
in conversion God stirs the heart through the word read or heard,
and the heart then, by virtue of a certain freedom yet left to it,
decides for or against God. "God anticipates (*antevertit*) us,
calls, moves, aids ; but we must see to it that we do not resist "
(658).[1]

---

[1] In order to rightly judge this view of Melanchthon's, we must bear in
mind (1) That he holds strictly to the doctrine of original sin, and therefore
excludes every form of salvation by man's own efforts (xx. 1. 669), and (2)
That he sought, in opposition to the doctrine of predestination, which he understood as magical, morally untenable, and deterministic, to retain the personal

4. In a similar way, Melanchthon gradually lost confidence in Luther's doctrine of the Lord's Supper.   He at first shared the symbolic conception of Augustine, as advocated by Erasmus.   He then fully adopted the view of Luther (*e. g.*, C. R. i. 760, 823, 830, 1109 f.).   Zwingli's theory appeared to him at this time and afterward as profane (ib. i. 1067, 1077).   In Marburg, he assisted Luther in making a collection of citations from the Fathers in confirmation of the latter's position.   With his growing respect for the consensus of the ancient church, he was very profoundly impressed by the dialogue of Oecolampadius, which produced evidence that, in a closer study of the Church Fathers, the symbolical view might also be found in their writings.   He confessed this to Luther (ii. 217); yet he still clung to the Lutheran conception (ii. 212, 222 f., 226; i. 1109 f.).   This is also the position taken in the tenth article of the Augsburg Confession (ii. 142).   The formula of Bucer (supra, p. 331), appeared to him to prepare the way for a union of the divergent parties (ii. 498 f.). But he still distinctly maintains the bodily presence of Christ (ii. 311, 315, 787, 801).   He was able, indeed, to accept the formula which Luther now framed, *i. e.*, that the body of Christ is "crushed with the teeth" (E. 55. 75 f.), only as "the spokesman of another's opinion" (*nuntius alienae sententiae*, ii. 822). But, in view of the testimonies of the ancient church, he could find no rest.   "I affirm the true presence of Christ in the Supper.   I am not willing to be the author nor defender of a new doctrine in the church" (ii. 824; cf. xxi. 479; ix. 785).   At heart, he inclined more and more to the view of the theologians of Southern Germany (ii. 824, 837, 841 f.; iii. 292).   Melanchthon always held to the presence of the Lord in the Supper, but he became less and less satisfied with Luther's conception of that presence.   At a later period, he never wearied—at least in his private correspondence— of inveighing against bread-worship (ἀρτολατρεία), as against the "Stoic necessity" (*e. g.*, viii. 362, 791, 660). He fell back whenever possible upon the thought, that there is in the Lord's Supper a "communion of the body and blood of Christ."   He denied the bodily ubiquity of Christ (vii. 780, 884; viii. 385; ix. 387, 962, 963), and emphasized in contrast the spiritual presence of Christ : "The Son of God lives and reigns, and wishes to be present in the sacrament instituted for this purpose, and joins us as members to himself" (xv. 1112).[1]   In this sense is the tenth article of the Augustana

and moral element in conversion.   But he did not succeed in the solution of the problem.

[1] Cf. iii. 514 (A. D. 1538): "Not to depart very far from the ancients, I have affirmed a sacramental presence in the celebration (*in usu*) and have said

Variata (A. D. 1540) also to be understood : " Concerning the Lord's Supper they teach, that with the bread and wine the body and blood of Christ are truly offered to those eating in the Lord's Supper.[1] The "damnant" is here also wanting. Cf. HERR-LINGER, Theol. Mel., p. 124 ff.

5. The *Loci* of Melanchthon, after the second revision, fell more and more into the track of the traditional doctrinal statements. Refraining from the attempt to trace the development of his theological views, we present a general summary of them based upon the third redaction of the *Loci*. The pedagogical character of the work has become increasingly prominent as it has been popularized in the manner so characteristic of the author.[2] The simplicity of form and the desire to secure practical usefulness exclude the discussion of the more profound problems and extended logical proof of the positions taken.[3] Although, even in the last revision of the *Loci*, Melanchthon followed no methodical plan beyond the enumeration of the separate doctrines, yet the study of his later writings makes it manifest that the Reformer had at least grouped his theological ideas around certain definite fundamental principles. These were (1) the combination of ideas involved in justification and the new conception of repentance, and (2) the conception of the church (cf. xxviii. 371 f.). These ideas constantly recur. They lay nearer to his heart than all else. To make them plain to all, and to impress them upon all hearts, appeared to him his chief duty. They may be designated as the two focal points in the theology of Melanchthon.

We take as our starting-point the question as to the Sources and Standards of Christian truth, which Melanchthon of course answers by pointing to the Holy Scriptures. Therefore let us regard it as a great blessing of God, that he has given and pre-

---

that with these elements *Christ is truly present and efficacious. This surely is enough.* Nor have I added such an inclusion or conjunction by which the body would be joined to the bread. . . . Sacraments are pledges that something else is present with the things received."

[1] The formula of Bucer and the Wittenberg Concord (supra, p. 331) here exerted a controlling influence, but the possibility of an interpretation favoring transubstantiation is excluded. But it is significant that the *vere et substantialiter adesse* of the Wittenberg formula is omitted. Luther himself originally intended to express himself in a way similar to this in the Smalcald Articles : " That under bread and wine the true body and blood are present," etc., but wrote instead : " The bread and wine in the Lord's Supper are the true body and blood of Christ." (See KOLDE, Stud. u. Krit., 1893, p. 159.) However true it may be that the formula of the Augustana Variata may be interpreted in a Lutheran sense, it is equally true that it was in reality designed to favor the divergent conception of Melanchthon.

[2] " With every new issue, paper and tradition exerted greater influence" (DILTHEY, l. c., vi. 230).

[3] Cf. the remark of Erasmus, C. R. iii. 87.

served to the church a certain book, and binds the church to it.
That company of people alone is the church, which embraces this
book, hears it, teaches it, and retains its true sense in the worship of God and in the regulating of conduct (xxi. 801).[1] As no
parallels can be found in the writings of Melanchthon to the free
utterances often made by Luther in regard to the letter of the
Scriptures (supra, p. 300 f.), so also his conception of the authority of the Scriptures receives a different coloring from his endorsement of their teachings as being the same as embraced the
three ancient symbols of the church (xii. 399, 568, 608; v.
582).[2] Their doctrine he approves as being genuinely Catholic.
" This is a Catholic association (*coetus*), which embraces the
common consensus of prophetic and apostolic doctrine, together
with the belief (*sententia*), of the true church.   Thus in our Confession we profess to embrace the whole doctrine of the word of
God, to which the church bears testimony, and that in the sense
which the symbols show" (xxiv. 398; xxi. 349).[3] He condemns whatever varies from the *symbola accepta* (iii. 826, 985;
ix. 366).   He will not extend his hand to any "new dogma"
(i. 823, 901, 1048), nor alter anything in the ecclesiastical
formulas, for " often a change of words begets also new beliefs"
(xxiv. 427).   This high valuation of the ancient symbols is very
different indeed from the attitude of Luther toward them.   Whilst
Luther most clearly declares that they have value for him only because, and in so far as, they agree with the Scriptures (supra, p.
304), Melanchthon makes no express limitation of this kind in
his endorsement of them.   Thus again, the ideas of Luther
are contracted and materialized.   To the symbols of the ancient
church was added, as we have seen, the Augustana.   But this is
not sufficiently explicit.[4] The genuine, true doctrine is that of
Luther.   Melanchthon was the first to understand the relation of
Luther to the historical development of the world, and he ex-

---

[1] Cf., *e. g.*, xxiv. 718; xii. 479, 646 f., 649, 698; xxiii. 603; xi. 42; v.
580: "has revealed in certain testimonies, and given a particular doctrine and
word."   Here are the germs of the later theory of inspiration.
[2] Osiander assailed the subscription of the three ancient symbols and the
Augsburg Confession under oath, which was customary at Wittenberg (xii.
6, 7).   Upon the daily devotional use of the Apostles' Creed, see xxv. 449;
xxiv. 394, 581.
[3] Cf.: " With true faith I embrace the whole doctrine handed down in the
books of the prophets and apostles, and comprehended in the Apostolic, Nicene, and Athanasian symbols" (Thesis of A. D. 1551, in HAUSSLEITER, l. c.,
p. 95).
[4] III. 286, 298, 1000, 827, 929: "Confessio u. Apologia," v. 581; ix.
386; viii. 284; xxxiii. p. xxxviii. names, besides the three ancient symbols,
"Catechismus u. Bekenntnis Lutheri u. Confessio," ix. 319, 366, 618,
213 f.   Also Smalcald Articles.

pressed it with classical lucidity. He counts him among the mighty heroes of the church and her faith: Isaiah, John the Baptist, Paul, Augustine, and Luther. "Luther brought to light the true and necessary doctrine" (xi. 728; cf. vi. 57, 72, 73, 92; vii. 398; xi. 272). We must hold fast to the pure doctrine, namely, the *confessio Lutheri* (xi. 272 f.; viii. 49).[1] It is the doctrine of the Church and of the University of Wittenberg (xi. 327, 600; xxi. 602; iii. 1106). But the truth of the church's doctrine is attested also by the experience (*experientia*) of the pious (xxi. 420; xii. 426; cf. Luther, supra, p. 256 ff.).

6. This, therefore, is the truth: The teachings of the Bible, as understood and summarized by the ancient doctrinal standards, Luther and the Wittenberg theology. To the understanding and presentation of this truth all other sciences minister as "handmaids" of theology (xi. 394), not only by pedagogically sharpening the intellect for the apprehension of Scriptural truth, but also by furnishing the necessary preliminary scientific knowledge. Without scientific education, the theologian could produce only unconnected and confused statements, which would beget innumerable errors and a "cyclopian" monster (xi. 280). Hence the church needs, not only grammar and dialectics, but also physics and philosophy. "Not only for the sake of method . . . is philosophy necessary, but also many things must be taken (*assumenda*) by the theologian from physics." Thus the theologian derives his physiological, psychological, and logical definitions from the sphere of the arts and sciences (*orbis artium*) (ib. 281, 934). It is, in other words, the popularized philosophy of Aristotle, which theology requires as a prerequisite and support. To this naturally-acquired knowledge it adds that derived from the Scriptures. The light of reason (*lumen naturale*, xii. 514, 577, 648) furnishes every man with a number of innate moral and religious ideas. It plays as important a rôle in Melanchthon's line of thought as the "law of nature" in the later Middle Ages. In the application of this principle, he follows largely the example of Cicero. There is a natural religion, a natural morality, and a natural law. Although sin may have beclouded this light, it yet remains as an endowment of human nature. It cannot be denied that a dangerous tendency is thus inaugurated. Theology appears to be the product of a combination of the cosmology of the ancient world and the "articles of faith" derived from the Scriptures.[2] Cf. DILTHEY,

---

[1] The co-ordination of "Gottes Wort und Luther's Lehr" is perfectly in accord with Melanchthon's feeling. See already Anton Otto, C. R. viii. 460: "the faith (*sententia*) of Luther, that is, of Christ."

[2] This combination reminds us of Thomas (supra, p. 100 f.), but DILTHEY

23

Archiv., etc., vi. 236 ff. TRÖLTSCH, l. c. HARTFELDER, Mel., p. 161 f., 181 f., 240.

7. In this last period of Melanchthon's labors, he emphasizes with great energy the idea, that those who confess the correct faith are the true church—thus following Luther also in the conception of the Church (p. 294 f.). He recognizes the altered conditions—there being now an evangelical church organization, having as its distinguishing mark the possession of the true doctrine—in most clearly from this time onward designating the visible assembly of the called (*coetus vocatorum*) as the church. "The visible church is the assembly of those embracing the gospel of Christ and rightly using the sacraments, in which God through the ministry of the gospel is efficacious and regenerates many to eternal life, in which assembly, nevertheless, are many unregenerated, but assenting to the true doctrine" (xxi. 826, and constantly. See Neue kirchl. Ztschr., 1897, 154, n. 1). This definition and the connection of thought in which it is found very clearly reveal the general conception of Melanchthon. The true church under any circumstances exists only where the true doctrine is found. Thus Zacharias, Anna, Elizabeth, the shepherds, etc., since they did not accept the official teaching of their age, but remained steadfast in the true doctrine, constituted the true church in that age. God provides that there shall always be some servants of his word, like Zacharias, as faithful representatives of this true doctrine. Only in this true church, in which are gathered the really called, may believers and the elect be found,[1] as only there is the church, in which God is known, confessed and worshiped, as "he has revealed himself" (xxi. 834).[2] In the Middle Ages the church existed only where the doctrines of an Augustine and Bernard, a Tauler and Wessel, were taught (xxi. 837; xxiv. 309; xxv. 862 f.). They only, according to the Scriptures, are churches, "which hold the pure doctrine and are in harmony with it" (*in ea consentiunt*, xi. 273). Only in this church are to be found the forgiveness of sins and justifica-

(p. 238) very properly points out the difference—that Melanchthon does not, like Thomas, unite faith and philosophy in the construction of a system of metaphysics, but only makes the natural consciousness his point of departure. Nevertheless, this Melanchthonian combination led historically to the orthodoxy of the seventeenth, as well as to the illumination of the eighteenth century.

[1] This is the "church of the elect," xxi. 913; xii. 678: the "church of the regenerate;" xii. 589, 431; xxiii., p. xxxv.: the "eternal church;" xi. 760: the "elect" alone in this "army of the called;" xii. 567. On the other hand, the term, true church (*ecclesia vera*), is used to designate the church which holds the true doctrine; but only in this are the "true members of the church," *i. e.*, the "saints"—see xxiii. 599.

[2] Cf. xi. 273; xii. 567; ix. 557; xxv. 220 f., 325, 640; xxiii. 597 f.

tion (xi. 400). But those who, like the Romish church, do not
hold the central principle of the true doctrine, but persecute the
real church, do not belong to the true church.[1] Yet Melanchthon also maintains the conception of the church as an *object
of faith*, since it is only by faith that we can be assured that there
is really in this visibly assembly (*coetus*) a number of elect persons (xii. 368 f.; xxiv. 365, 368, 400, 405 ; xxv. 148 f., 221,
677 ; viii. 284). The marks which attest the existence of the
" true visible church," and at the same time assure to faith the
presence of a " church of the regenerate " within the former,
are therefore the true evangelical doctrine and the proper administration of the sacraments—to which Melanchthon afterward
habitually added—reverence (*reverentia*), or obedience, to the
ministry (*obedientia ministerii*).[2]

Such is the church. In it the divine purpose is being accomplished in the world. It is the realization of the aim of the
work of Christ.[3] But this it is, because in it alone the truth of
God is apprehended by men and becomes effectual through them.
To maintain this doctrine in its simplicity and purity is the task
of theology, as well as of every branch of science. This end is
to be served by universities, princes, and states (xi. 272, 326 f.;
iii. 198 ; viii. 401; vii. 666. HARTFELDER, p. 437). It may be
said that the maintenance and spread of " pure doctrine " is the
great motive which inspired Melanchthon's life-work, as a Reformer of the church and of the universities, as a theologian, phil-
ologian, and teacher.[4] This involved again, as compared with
Luther, a narrowing of the horizon, resulting not merely from
the great importance attached to the " pure doctrine," but from
the fact that the life-giving energy of the church was attributed

[1] XII. 526, 628 ; xxiii.; p. xxxvii.; xxiv. 781, 855 : " There is the church
where are the fountains of Israel. . . . The Turks are not the church, neither
are the Papists."

[2] XII. 599, 433, 602, 655 ; xxiv. 367, 401, 502 ; xxv. 129, 685, etc. The
peculiar importance attached to the clerical office (see also xxv. 692) marks
one of the materializing features of Melanchthon's later writings. The
church, he holds, is neither a tyranny nor a democracy, but an honorable
aristocracy (*honesta aristocratia*), xii. 367, 496; cf. also ii. 274, 284, 334,
376 ; iii. 942.

[3] XXI. 345 ; xxiv. 307 ; xii. 520 : " To this end he established the human
race, that there might be a church obeying God and worshiping him," 566 ;
xiii. 199 ; xxiii. 198 ; xii. 339, 539, 616, 634, etc.

[4] This explains his severity toward heretics (*e. g.*, Servetus), ii. 18 ; iii.
197 f., 199, 241 f.; viii. 520 ff.; iv. 739 ; xii. 696 ; xxiv. 375, 501. On the
other hand, we may thus also understand his fatal attitude toward the Interim,
vii. 382 f., 322 f., and toward Calvin and his party ; for, aside from the devi-
ations which had separated himself as well from Luther, he believed himself
to be in doctrinal accord with Calvin—and everything to his mind depended
upon doctrine.

directly to the latter. It cannot be denied that in these views of Melanchthon are to be found the germs of the errors of the orthodoxy of the seventeenth century.[1] Melanchthon even defined faith, as, in the first instance, an "assent," with which intellectual act, the voluntary act of trust is necessarily associated (xxi. 790). But this is only a passing remark, trust still remaining for him the first and controlling element of faith. "This consolation is trust, by which the will acquiesces in the promise of mercy granted for the sake of the Mediator. But trust in the mercy embraces also a knowledge of the history, because it looks upon Christ, whom it is necessary to know as the eternal Son, crucified, arisen, etc., for us. And the history must be brought into relation with the promise, or effect, which is presented in the article : ' I believe in the forgiveness of sins ' " (ib. p. 743 ; vi. 910). None of these passages must, of course, be interpreted as making the salvation of the individual dependent upon the possession of the pure doctrine. "Although the true church . . . preserves the articles of faith, nevertheless that true church may itself hold the articles of faith with obscurity on account of erroneous conceptions of them." If very much in the teaching even of the Fathers is overlooked, if they have only held fast to the fundamental truth, how much more must be forgiven weakness and errors found among the laity (ib. p. 837 f.; cf. xii. 433 f.; xxiii. 599, 601, 207). The important matter is only that the proper foundation be laid in the acceptance of the chief doctrine. He does not regard all separate doctrinal statements as of equal importance, but expressly recognizes a gradation of doctrines. "But this faith embraces all the articles of the Creed, and refers the others to this one : ' I believe in the forgiveness of sins ' " (xii. 406, 540 ; xxi. 422). There are chief articles, which are important above everything else. The chief article is that concerning the blessings of Christ, or justification.[2] In this lies the whole practical comfort of the Christian religion, and it is in their relationship to it that all the

---

[1] This remark is not a novel one. See G. Arnold, Kirchen u. Ketzerhistorie, ii. Bk. 16, c. 9, 4 ff. Zierold, Einleitung zur Kirchenhistorie (Leipzig u. Stargard, 1700), i. 387 ff., 384 ; recently Ritschl, Die Entstehung der luth. Kirche, in Ztschr. f. Kirchengesch. i.

[2] Cf., e. g., xxiii. 600, 280; v. 582 (original sin, grace, faith, works, sacraments); vi. 116; vii. 117 f., 532, 433; xxv. 863. Cf. also similar lists in Luther (supra, p. 297, n. 3). But note also, in a disputation held under Melanchthon, the remark in reference to the Athanasian Creed : "When they say, ' This is the Catholic faith ' (*fides*), they do not mean this trust (*fiducia*). But nevertheless the principal good work and destruction of the kingdom of Satan is to think rightly (*recte sentire*) concerning God, to confess God," etc. (in Haussleiter, p. 51).

other doctrines receive their position and significance. It may, perhaps, be correctly said, that Melanchthon in this really means to say no more than that spiritual life can be aroused and flourish only when the gospel is actually preached. But it would be an error, in view of such a remark concerning Melanchthon's personal sentiment in the matter, to minimize the historical results traceable to the form in which he expressed that sentiment. And it will scarcely suffice to interpret him as holding merely that the church has in the pure doctrine a substantial means for the effectual proclamation of the gospel. This was certainly essentially what Melanchthon meant.[1] But he *said* more than this. Only they are members of the church who preserve "the doctrine uncorrupted," *i. e.*, the foundation, namely, *all* the articles of faith and the teachings of the decalogue.[2] And it is just in the uncompromising one-sidedness of this position that its power and significance lie. It was in the sphere of doctrine, as including the ideal of practical life, that the issue had been joined with Rome. Under the circumstances of the age, it could have occurred in no other sphere. The "pure doctrine" was the only legal title to existence held by the youthful evangelical church. This was a controlling factor in her political fortunes ; it opened the nations to the new church. Hence the duty of proclaiming the pure doctrine must be constantly impressed upon her preachers,[3] for the age was full of echoes of the scholastic teachings and superstitions of the past. There was still a strong tendency to disputations upon doctrine and its forms, and it was needful to decline many a hand outstretched to the Reformers with proffers of assistance or of sworn alliance. The practical conditions of the

---

[1] See the fundamental definition, supra, p. 354; "those embracing the gospel" and the "true doctrine." We may, perhaps, say, that when Melanchthon speaks of the evangelical doctrine, he thinks primarily of saving truth in the narrower sense of the term (cf. xxiii. 600). As in his first edition of the Loci, the Trinity and Christology were regarded rather as matters for reverent contemplation than for teaching, so it is known that shortly before his death he still hoped to gain clear ideas in regard to these objects of faith only in a higher world.

[2] XII. 433 : "It is necessary that those who receive the uncorrupted doctrine of the gospel . . . retain the foundation, all the articles of faith, and the doctrine of the decalogue." The text of the C. R. places the "and," not after faith, but as follows : *et omnes articulos fidei doctrinam decalogi,* which can hardly be correct, as it is said in almost immediate connection : "By the term *consensus in fundamento* is required agreement in the articles of faith and in the decalogue."

[3] Cf. the catalogue of doctrines in the "Examen ordinandorum," and the remark : "that they upon opportunity present these questions in an orderly way in their sermons, so that the people may among themselves reflect and meditate upon a clear and fundamental outline of the Christian doctrine which is necessary . . . to (lead them to) conversion and to faith," xxiii., p. xl.

age gave birth to the formula of Melanchthon, and it in turn reacted upon the age. We may to-day recognize its one-sidedness without calling in question its historical justification. It undoubtedly fixed upon the Lutheran church for a long time to follow something of the character of a school ; but it was also the legal title upon which that church based, maintained, and justified its existence. Cf. SEEBERG, Begriff d. Kirche, i. 104 ff.

8. The Church of the Pure Doctrine—this is the one focal point in the intellectual horizon of the later Melanchthon. The other is Justification, or—which is the same thing (supra, p. 235 ff.)— the substitute for the sacrament of repentance. It appears at first but an illustration of the lack of strict systematic order in Melanchthon, that the terms discussed under the heading of repentance, such as faith, works, justification, etc., have all been already exhaustively treated in an earlier portion of the Loci. But it is also an evidence that these religious processes are not to his mind limited to the praxis of confession, but that the latter praxis merely includes also these processes.[1]

Melanchthon's starting-point is the Law. The law is the immutable wisdom of God, a rule for discrimination between good and evil. It teaches men that there is a God, and what is his character, that he has placed all men beneath this rule of life and will punish all who do not live in accordance with it (xii. 614, 658 f.; xxi. 421, 685, 741, 885). Since now all men are from their birth guilty and subject to condemnation, the law brings primarily to all men judgment and condemnation ; it leads us to recognize that we are under the wrath of God (xxi. 692 f.; xxv. 777). But since even the regenerate still commit sin, the law awakens in them also a sense of the wrath of God. To this are to be added reflections upon the misery of life in this world, future punishments, and the necessity for the atoning death of Christ (xxi. 876, 883 f.). The result of this—faithfully prosecuted—preaching of the law is *contrition*. The latter, however, would but drive man to despair, if preaching of the law were not at once accompanied with the proclamation of the gospel. The gospel, as the announcement of the forgiveness of sins, teaches us to know Christ and the blessings which he bestows (xii. 605).[2]

---

[1] We cannot fail to note here a formal approach to the Romish model, especially when we remember the importance again attaching to the confessional in the latter half of the century. Cf. Von ZEZSCHWITZ, Katechetik, i. 570 : " Thereby (*i. e.*, through the combination of private confession and examination upon doctrinal points) the Lutheran Church substantially readopted the pedagogical system of the Middle Ages in a purified form. Cf. also RITSCHL, Gesch. d. Pietismus, ii. 201 f., 539 f.

[2] Parallel with this narrower definition of the Gospel, Melanchthon recog-

At this point the doctrine of the Atonement is considered. If we are to speak of mercy to the sinner who is alarmed at thought of the divine justice, so there must be some means of accounting for this change of the divine attitude toward him. This requirement Melanchthon meets by substantially reproducing the satisfaction theory of Anselm, to whom he expressly refers, thus exhibiting both the divine and the human natures of Christ in their connection with human salvation. In this alone lies the significance of Christ's redeeming work : " Christ has a ministry of teaching, but this is not his principal office. He was sent chiefly to be the victim for the human race, to be their Redeemer, to free us from the curse of the law." [1] The tempering of justice with mercy was brought about by Christ's bearing the punishment for us, or bringing a sacrifice and an " equivalent price," and thereby satisfying the justice of God. As such service could be rendered only by a man, so, on the other hand, only God could offer a " price equivalent " for the " infinite wickedness " of the race (xxiv. 78 f., 569, 579; xxv. 171, 776; xii. 577 593, 446 f.; 616, 424, 428 ; xxi. 733, 743, 904). The obedience of Christ was the price rendered for us (xii. 424, 607 ; xxiii. 451). [2] Christ is now standing before the Father and interceding (*interpellirt*) for us, for the whole church, as for everyone who prays to him. " We are righteous on account of Christ, his righteousness which he discharged in doing and bearing being imputed to us " (xxiv. 216). His " merit " and " intercession " are the foundation of the Christian faith (xii. 426). The effect of this redeeming work is the forgiveness of sins and the imputation of the righteousness of Christ, the impartation of the Holy Spirit of love and righteousness and of the new eternal life (xxiv. 80. 216, 654 f., 656, 748, 775, 798, 873, 864, 875; xxiii. 452 ; xv. 895). [3]

Faith lays hold upon the consolation which the gospel pro-

---

nizes also a broader conception, according to which it is " the preaching of repentance and the promise " (following Lk. 24. 47); xii. 589, 640; xxi. 732 f.

[1] XXV. 171 f.; xxiv. 78 : " The final cause of the incarnation of the Son is that he may be a victim, the placator of the wrath of God." But in xxiv. 694, the object of the sending of Christ is said to have been the gathering, preservation, and sanctification of the church. In xv. 133, teaching and atonement are co-ordinated.

[2] According to xxiv. 242 ; xxv. 175, the fulfilling of the law by Christ had also a vicarious significance.

[3] " Eternal life," as Melanchthon often insists, begins in the present life, xxiv. 625 : " The beginning of eternal life is in this life, *i. e.*, by faith to know this eternal God who has sent his Son, and it is to know him to be reconciled through the Son, and to call upon him, to ask and expect consolation in all tribulations. This faith and consolation in genuine griefs is a taste of eternal life."

claims, *i. e.*, it appropriates justification, or the forgiveness of sins. But with justification there is at the same time given the Holy Spirit, who begets a new life. Thus upon *contritio* and *fides* follows *justificatio*, and together with the latter is effected *regeneratio*, or *renovatio* (xxi. 427 f.). "And when God remits sins, he at the same time gives to us the Holy Spirit, who begins new powers (*virtutes*) in the pious " (742). Justification is conceived strictly as a forensic act, and hence clearly discriminated from renewal. *Justificatio* is a " forensic term," and indicates the "remission of sins " and " reconciliation or personal acceptance" (*acceptatio personae*, 742). In this consists the essential work of grace. "Let this therefore be the definition of grace. Grace is the remission of sins, or mercy promised for Christ's sake, or gratuitous acceptance, which the gift of the Holy Spirit necessarily accompanies." Even here, in the doctrine of justification, Melanchthon's conception varies from Luther's form of presentation. According to Luther, the Spirit works faith through the word. Faith is both the principle of a new life and the organ for apprehending the forgiveness of sins. To justification belongs the begetting of faith and the new life, as well as the forgiveness of sins (supra, p. 260 f.). This was also the position taken by Melanchthon in the Augsburg Confession and the Apology (supra, p. 336). *Now* faith seems to arise before the bestowal of the Spirit and before regeneration.[1] Faith apprehends the purely forensic decree of justification. And because this occurs, the Spirit is also granted to the individual for his regeneration. The inseparable connection which is in Luther always maintained between regeneration, justification, and sanctification is thus broken. These are the ideas which underlie the thoroughgoing revision of the Articles IV. and V. in the Variata Edition of the Augsburg Confession.[2] Whether the complete separation ("*reinliche Scheidung*") of justification and sanctification is to be regarded as a step in advance or not, can only be decided by dogmatical and exegetical study. We here merely call attention to the fact, that Melanchthon, under this new grouping of the conception referred to, was

[1] There is here a peculiar lack of clearness in Melanchthon, since faith is for him on the one hand a product of the Holy Spirit working through the word (xii. 607, 426 f.), and yet, on the other hand, is supposed to precede the bestowal of the Spirit. Faith is accordingly a prerequisite of justification and begotten by the Holy Spirit, and yet, according to the recognized formula, the Holy Spirit is imparted only as a consequence of justification, *e. g.*, xxi. 742, 421, 427. Cf. HERRLINGER, p. 54.

[2] If the Augsburg Confession is to be interpreted in accordance with the Apology, then the prevalent formula of the Lutheran doctrine of justification finds its symbolical support in the Variata !

not able to make the ethical motive power of faith as manifest as in Luther's theory. Faith is now for him essentially nothing more than the organ, by which the forgiveness of sins is apprehended. It is not, indeed, merely a historical knowledge, but the repose of the will in the proffered gracious acceptance—confidence in the grace of God. From this practical experience (faith as confidence, *fiducia*, applying this benefit to ourselves) of the effects of the history and the doctrine, may be understood the intellectual conviction of both the history and the doctrine (xxi. 422, 743, 746, 785, 886 ; xii. 431). "Faith signifies to *assent* to the promise of God (which is in the *intellect*), and with this assent is necessarily connected *confidence* (which is in the will), willing and accepting the promised reconciliation and acquiescing in the Mediator set forth" (xxi. 790).[1] Since the sinner now desires above everything else the forgiveness of sins, justification takes place (xxi. 742). But, as the impartation of the Spirit renews the man, reconciliation must necessarily be followed by good works and a righteousness of a good conscience. Upon a detailed examination of the nature of good works as represented by Melanchthon we need not enter. They are necessary, since without them faith would be lost (for it is not compatible with sinful thoughts or deeds), and, further, since they have been commanded by God and are in keeping with the dignity of the Christian calling (xxi. 429, 762, 775 ff.). They are works which are really good on account of the faith which prompts them, and which may also be spoken of as "meritorious," but not in the sense that they merit the forgiveness of sins. They, however, merit other spiritual and material blessings (xii. 448, 454).

It will be observed that we have here a combination in a fixed order of all the elements which are of prime importance, in the view of Melanchthon, for the development of the religious life. But it is just as evident also that this entire general theory finds its closest parallel in the Reformer's doctrine of repentance. Contrition, faith, and new obedience are for him the constituent elements of *poenitentia*,[2] to which he adds confession and absolution.[3] There can be nothing suspicious in this, unless re-

---

[1] XXI. 759 enumerates : *notitia, assensus, fiducia ;* but the last two terms are used as equivalents (see also HAUSSLEITER, p. 22) : "Faith is to assent to every word of God given to us and in this promise of the gospel, and it is confidence acquiescing in the Mediator."

[2] XXI. 877 ; xxv. 62 ; xxiv. 426. Melanchthon at first enumerated only *contritio* and *fides.* C. A. 12 ; Apol. 12, 28 ff.; xii. 506 f., 510 ; Erl. 23. 39.

[3] From the contrition which precedes faith must be discriminated the *contritio cum fide,* which awakens, not like the former a servile, but a filial fear (*timor*), and which has a purer sorrow for sin (*purior. dolor*). It does not

pentance and justification were again limited to the confessional, and the first Thesis of Luther thereby discredited. Of itself, it is ground for neither criticism nor surprise that the doctrine whose definition started the whole reformatory movement should furnish the frame-work for the systematic construction of the entire compass of religious truth won by the Reformation.

It would be an error to infer from Melanchthon's method of arranging his doctrinal views in separate "*Loci*," that he has transmitted his religious ideas in a confused and unconnected form. On the contrary, he summarized all the results of his religious study under two headings: the Church and Justification by Grace. The former of these is most intimately associated with the conception of "pure doctrine," and the latter with that of the law and the gospel. This double complex of ideas presents, in the theology of Melanchthon, a substitute both for the conception of the church which dominated the ecclesiastical life and for the sacrament of repentance which regulated the practical piety of the Middle Ages. This furnishing of new guiding principles for both ecclesiastical and individual religious life is a matter of such immense historical significance as to abundantly atone for any defect in his method of presentation. In formulating his definition of the empirical church, he fixed a goal, toward which not only all the gracious dealings of God were seen to tend, but toward which, as well, all human effort might be directed. As no one might hope for salvation outside of this church, all the moral and scientific energies of the age were pressed into the service of this supreme aim. This conception impressed a uniquely ecclesiastical character upon the intellectual and practical life of more than two centuries. But the conception of the "pure doctrine" was the boundary-line within which the self-consciousness of this church was developed and confirmed. Although modern theologians may deem the limits thus affixed too narrow—there were historical reasons for allowing them no wider scope—it cannot be denied that the consciousness of having in possession the pure doctrine became one of the most powerful coëfficients in the expansion and preservation of the church thus endowed.

§ 77. *The Theological Controversies in the Lutheran Church from the Death of Luther to the Adoption of the Formula of Concord.*

Literature. Schlüsselburg, Haereticorum catalogus, 13 parts, 1597 ff.

flee from God, but seeks him and his forgiveness with the acknowledgment of its sin (xxi. 886 f.).

WALCH, Einleitung in d. Religionsstreitigkeiten innerh. u. ausserh. d. Luth. Kirche, 10 parts, 1730 ff.   PLANCK, Gesch. d. prot. Lehrbegriffes, 6 vols., 1781 ff. (1-3 in ed. 2, 1791 ff.).   HEPPE, Gesch. des deutschen Protestant-ism. 1555-81, 4 vols., 1852 ff.   FRANK, Theol. der CF., 4 vols., 1858 ff. THOMASIUS-SEEBERG, DG. ii., ed. 2, 425 ff.   LOOFS, DG., 438 ff., 422 ff.

1. The significance of Melanchthon for the History of Doc-trines may, in accordance with the foregoing review, be sum-marized in three particulars : (1) He gave permanent form to the ideas of Luther, thus laying the foundation for the theology of the following period and determining the direction of its progress.   Luther created a new church ; Melanchthon estab-lished a theology in harmony with it.   (2) He laid down the lines within which the spiritual life of the ensuing centuries was to be developed, obtaining a secure position for secular learning and the natural sciences by setting them in an auxiliary relation to the church of the " pure doctrine."   Thus the maintaining and the proclamation of the pure doctrine became more and more the essential and constituent function of the church.   Doctrine threatened to swallow up life.[1]   (3) He advocated a number of theological doctrines of his own, at variance more or less with those of Luther.   Although he proceeded cautiously in this direction during Luther's life-time, it is important to observe that the latter allowed these divergences of his associate to pass unchallenged.   They assume importance, although supported by very many of Melanchthon's disciples, only in view of the strict definition of " pure doctrine " and of the authority of Luther, which had been, by the efforts of Melanchthon himself, carried to the highest point and stamped as dogmatic.   The practical application of these principles and views led to the lamentable doctrinal controversies in the period from the death of Luther to that of Melanchthon.   Both the unfortunate waver-ing of Melanchthon in connection with the Interim—when the doctrine appeared to him to be sufficiently guarded—and the bitter assaults made upon him by the so-called Gnesio-Luth-erans for his lack of firmness upon that occasion and for his doctrinal divergences find explanation in the one-sided character of his later conceptions of the church and of doctrine.[2]

The great prophetic age of Protestantism was followed by a didactic age.   We can understand the necessity for the tran-

[1] But it is unfair to ascribe this onesidedness entirely to the influence of Melanchthon (Arnold, Ritschl, and others), for (1) The same thoughts are found not seldom in the writings of Luther, and (2) Melanchthon only gave expression to a tendency which dominated the period and characterized its particular stage of cultural development.

[2] With the above compare also my article, Die Stellung Mel. in d. Gesch. der Kirche u. der Wiss., ed. 2, Erlang., 1897.

sition ; but it proved a retrogression similar to that from the days
of the old prophets of Israel to the great Synagogue ! We must
glance briefly at the leading controversies of the period.

2. THE INTERIM AND THE ADIAPHORISTIC CONTROVERSY.
Melanchthon and the Wittenberg theologians announced themselves prepared (see BIECK, Das dreifache Interim, Leipz., 1721,
p. 361 ff.) to accept the so-called Leipzig Interim, A. D. 1547.
In this document, justification was modified and made to signify
"that man is renewed by the Holy Spirit, and can fulfill righteousness with his works (*Gerechtigkeit mit dem werk vollbringen
kann*), and that God will for his Son's sake accept in believers
this weak beginning of obedience in this miserable frail nature"
(BIECK, 372).[1] In addition to this, the episcopal jurisdiction was
restored, and almost all the Romish ceremonies were to be again
introduced (p. 377 f., 380 ff.). It is not surprising that on every
hand a most bitter conflict was precipitated. Melanchthon by
his course on this occasion forfeited the confidence of wide
circles of his former friends. The controversy is known as the
Adiaphoristic, because the chief question at issue was, whether it
is morally permissible to yield in unessential external matters,
provided the chief matter, *i. e.*, pure doctrine, be conserved.
To this the Wittenbergers answered in the affirmative. Their
opponents (esp. FLACIUS, vid. PREGER, Flac. i. 142 ff.) applied
the principle : "Nothing is indifferent (ἀδιάφορον) in a matter
of confession and abuse (*in casu confessionis et scandali*)."

3. THE MAJORISTIC CONTROVERSY. Luther was accustomed,
upon occasion, to employ the paradox, that good works are a hindrance to justification (supra, p. 264, n.1). Melanththon, on the
contrary, declared them to be necessary. (*a*) George Major
(A. D. 1552), following the latter suggestion, maintained that
good works are necessary to salvation, since no one is saved by
wicked works and no one without good works. He then further
explains, that they are necessary for retaining salvation (*ad
retinendam salutem*). JUSTUS MENIUS, after A. D. 1554 (vid.
Thomasius, ii. 473 ff.), held a similar view. These ideas were
by no means meant to be understood in a Catholic sense, but
were simply designed to establish the profound connection
between faith and a new life, and were therefore genuinely
Lutheran in their tendency. But AMSDORF and FLACIUS raised a
vigorous opposition. The former declared, that anyone who
would defend the statement that good works are necessary to
salvation was a "Pelagian, a Mameluke, and denier of Christ"

---

[1] Free will is treated in harmony with Melanchthon's views (p. 362 f.). It
is asserted that "God does not deal with man as with a log, but draws him in
such a way that his own will also co-operates."

(SCHLÜSSELBURG, Catal. vii. 210). The latter argued, that, if faith alone justifies and saves, this cannot be said in any sense of works (Wider den Evangelisten des h. Chorrocks, 1553, form C.). And in the same way the preservation of the state of grace can be based only upon faith. In the whole course of the Christian life, faith must maintain its dominant position and dare not share the latter with good works (vid. Schlüsselb. vii. 162 ff., 534 ff., 572 ff.). This criticism did not indeed apply to the tendency of Major and Menius. Melanchthon wished to rest in the proposition : "New obedience is necessary," and advised that the qualifying words, " to salvation," on account of the possibility of interpreting them as involving the idea of merit, be used only in connection with faith (C. R. ix. 498 f., 405 ff., 474 ; viii. 410 ff.). (*b*) But the opposing party now went further. They asserted that the gift of the Holy Spirit is only "an appendage, consequence, and supplement of grace" (Synod at Eisenach, A. D. 1556, in Flacius, *De voce et re fidei*, p. 199) or, " Renewal is an entirely separate thing from justi-fication" (Flac., *De justif.*, 182). This position was really only a logical inference from the Melanchthonian conception of the doctrine of justification (supra, p. 360). But while Melanchthon himself had, in his theory of the ethical necessity of good works, a certain corrective for the severance of justification and renewal, Amsdorf pressed on to the bold assertion, that " good works are injurious to salvation," and in other declara-tions threatened to carry out the idea of freedom from the law to the extreme statement : " God does not care for works " (cf. C. R. viii. 411). But not only Melanchthon and his school opposed these excesses in doctrinal statement ("in the divine order man owes obedience," C. R. ix. 370, 474 ; cf. den Endlichen Bericht vnd Erklerung der Theologen beider Vniversiteten Leipzig u. Wittemberg, 1570), but Gnesio-Lutherans also recognized the necessity of the new obedience as proceeding from the inward impulses of the new heart (vid. Schlüsselb. vii. 572 ff., 603, 615, 617 ff.).

4. THE ANTINOMISTIC CONTROVERSY is most intimately con-nected with the foregoing. At the Synod at Eisenach, Amsdorf had proposed the thesis : " Good works are, even in the forum of the law and in the abstract (*de idea*), not necessary to salvation (SALIG, Gesch. d. Augsb. Conf. iii. 56 f.). In en-dorsing this, ANDREAS POACH maintained, that it is the office of the law only to accuse and condemn, and that the gospel alone leads to the doing of good : " After grace has been obtained and remission of sins and salvation accepted, we cease to do evil and begin to obey God " (SALIG, iii. 58 f. Schlüsselb. iv. 265 ff.,

338 ff., 342, 344). ANTON OTTO advanced to crass Antinomi-
anism, affirming that there is no "third use of the law;" that
the new obedience belongs not to the kingdom of Christ, but to
the world, as to Moses and the supremacy of the pope; that the
Christian is "above all obedience." We should pray God that
we may remain steadfast to our end in faith without any works
(cf. PLANCK, v. 1. 62 f.). It was the old ideas of Agricola
which were thus continually reäppearing, although Luther had
refused to countenance them (supra, p. 251).

5. THE EUCHARISTIC CONTROVERSY. Calvin's doctrine of the
Lord's Supper (vid. sub) was enabled for some time to prosecute a silent propaganda in Germany, as Melanchthon and his
followers maintained a friendly attitude toward it. In A. D.
1552, JOACHIM WESTPHAL, the Hamburg pastor, raised his voice
against it. He pointed out that Calvin's view of the Lord's
Supper was not that held by Luther. Immediately there was
great excitement. Wild conflicts were waged in Bremen (Hardenberg and Timann), in Heidelberg (Tilmann, Hesshusen, and
Klebitz), in the Palatinate (cf. SCHMID, Der Kampf d. luth.
Kirche um Luther's Lehre v. Abendmal, 1868, p. 151-225).
Under the leadership of BRENZ, the church of Würtemburg
(Synod at Stuttgart, 1559) pronounced in favor of the Lutheran
doctrine. Melanchthon anxiously avoided a public deliverance.[1]
He died in 1560. The Wittenbergers, at the request of their
Electors, temporized, condemning Zwingli and defending themselves against "Flacian innovations." The atmosphere was clarified by the "Exegesis perspicua et ferme integra de sacra coena,"
1574, written by JOH. CUREUS in Glogau (ed. Scheffer, Marburg,
1853). In this document the doctrine of the ubiquity of the
body was controverted, with keen polemic against the Lutheran
conception of the communicatio idiomatum.[2] Christ is present
for believers only according to his divine nature and personally.
"The substance of this Supper is communion (κοινωνία) with
Christ. As now this ingrafting (insertio) cannot be effected, as
we have often declared, without faith, so the sacraments have
been instituted for believers, and not for the ungodly" (p. 24 f.).
The book thus summarizes the author's view: "Believers are,

[1] "I beg of you," he wrote to Hardenberg, "dissimulate much (multa
dissimules)" (C. R. viii. 736; cf. ix. 15 ff., 960: "To answer is not difficult, but dangerous." Against Brenz, ib. 1034 f.).
[2] This, it was held, destroys the true corporeality of Christ and is Eutychian (e. g., p. 41). "The body of Christ is, as it were, abducted from us;
therefore no part of his substance (substantiae) is infused into us" (p. 11).
"We think, indeed, of no magical nor physical binding of Christ to the word
or sacraments, but we say that he is, according to his covenant, most freely
efficacious in believers through the word and sacraments" (p. 10).

in the use of the bread and wine, made by faith true and living members of the body of Christ, who is present and efficacious through these symbols, as through a ceremonial agency (*ministe-rium*), inflaming and renovating our hearts by his Holy Spirit. But unbelievers are not made participants or communicants (κοινωνοί), but are guilty of the body of Christ on account of their contempt" (p. 26). This document became the occasion for a severe condemnation of the Saxon *Crypto-Calvinism,* and the express rejection of Calvin's doctrine of the Lord's Supper. Melanchthon's doctrine was pronounced in harmony with that of Luther, but the doctrine of the ubiquity was disapproved (Torgau, A. D. 1574).[1] Cf. HEPPE, Gesch. d. deutschen Prot. ii. 431 ff.

6. THE SYNERGISTIC CONTROVERSY. (*a*) PFEFFINGER in Leipzig had in A. D. 1555, following Melanchthon (supra, p. 349), taught in his *Quaestiones de libertate voluntatis humanae,* that man is in conversion not "purely passive," as a statue, but must also do his part. The ability to give *assensio* must in him be called into exercise for the actualizing of conversion. Against this AMS-DORF and FLACIUS protested. Two startling events then surprised the church. VICTORIN STRIGEL, at the very seat of Gnesio-Lutheranism, suddenly announced himself as a Synergist (A. D. 1559), and FLACIUS, the fanatical champion of the pure doctrine, in combating him, fell into the grossest of all heresies. In A. D. 1560, a disputation was held at Weimar between Strigel and Flacius (see Disput. de originali peccato et lib. arb. inter M. Flac. Ill. et Vict. Strigel, 1562. Also, SALIG, Gesch. d. Augsb. Conf. iii. 587 ff.). (*b*) Strigel taught : No man can be converted to God by his own power without the Holy Spirit. But neither can conversion occur by magic nor by compulsion. God takes into consideration, among other things, the nature of man, as a creature endowed with a will. The natural difference existing between a free agent (*liberum agens*) and a natural agent (*naturaliter agens*) (Disput., p. 22, 210) is the ground of a special divine agency adapted to the peculiar character of man. "The will cannot be coerced, . . . if the will could be coerced it would not be will, but rather non-will" (*voluntas,* p. 82, 25, 73, 176). Sin has not abolished and de-

---

[1] We may mention also the superstitious conception of the *consecration* taught by JOH. SALIGER and FREDELAND in Lübeck and carried by the former to Rostock : The body is present in the Lord's Supper immediately after the consecration and before the distribution (A. D. 1568-69). Similiar superstitions spring up elsewhere (hair of the beard upon which a little of the wine has hung is plucked out ; stones upon which it falls are crushed and the powder gathered up and preserved ; the upsetting of the cup is regarded as a serious offense). See HEPPE, Gesch. des Prot. ii. 385 ff.

stroyed free-will, but depraved it[1] (p. 49). Nor does grace
move this will in a mechanical or natural way. "The conversion of man differs from a violent and natural movement (of an
object). And the will acts in its own way in conversion, and is
not a statue or a log in conversion" (p. 73). Strigel means,
therefore, that even in conversion man's peculiar "mode of
action" must be preserved, *i. e.*, that no inward transformation
can be real except the will has also given its assent. But he
combined with this mode of action also features of a material
freedom of will. He conceives of the natural man as only bound,
wounded, and hindered by sin, and hence teaches a material co-
operation of the will in conversion. Although it be but weakly,
yet the will of man co-operates ; its attitude toward grace is not
simply passive, but only "more passive than active" (p. 232). At
this point, Flacius parts company with him. A co-operation of
the will is acknowledged also by the latter, but only as beginning
after the actual moment of conversion. This was with him the
only question : "I ask whether you say that the will co-operates
before the bestowal of faith, or after faith has been received?
Whether you say, that it co-operates by its natural powers, or in
so far as (the power) to will well has been granted to it by the
renewal of the Holy Spirit?" (p. 43, 71, 100, 178, 233). But
to this clear-cut question Strigel did not give a precise answer.[2]

(*c*) According to Flacius, the sinner is completely dead to
good impulses. His attitude in the (momentary) act of conversion is "merely passive ; " yea, before, in, and after conversion, his attitude is purely one of resistance (ib., p. 131).[3]
Thus he asserts, that "man is converted (while) willing and re-
sisting (*volentem, repugnantem*);" and that he "is converted,
not only when his natural free will co-operates, but even when it
raves and howls" (p. 131 and thesis 4). "God alone converts
man—he does not exclude the will, but every efficacy or operation of it" (p. 118). As Flacius, reversing Strigel's method,
starts with the material bondage of the will, he loses sight of its

---

[1] Strigel is here evidently thinking of the formal freedom of the will.

[2] What he had in view is evident from the following illustration : "A child
cannot seek nourishment from its mother unless the mother gives it to him.
She must even turn his mouth in the proper direction. But the child must itself draw the milk from the mother's breast" (p. 131 f.). The fundamental
mistake of Strigel was that, while he had a proper sense of the personal character of conversion, he failed to give proper expression to his conviction, because the natural, formal freedom of choice was transformed under his hand
into a material and ethical freedom. He was, accordingly, unable to ascribe
the ground and beginning of conversion absolutely to God.

[3] Cf. Amsdorf : "God deals with willing and knowing men just in the
same way as with all other created things, a stone or a log, through his own
sole willing and decreeing (*velle et dicere*)." See Schlüsselburg, v. 547.

formal freedom.   Conversion thus becomes, in the end, a transformation of man's nature.   From this point Flacius went a
step further, and maintained that sin is not an attribute (*acci-
dentia*), but of the essential substance of man.   He was guided
by the Aristotelian definition of an attribute : "That which is
present or wanting without destruction of the subject."   According to this, original sin, regarded as an attribute, would appear
to be only an accidental trait.   But in the view of Flacius, the
essential nature of man has been itself transformed by sin.
Although Flacius may have used the term, substance (*substanz*),
rather in the sense of formal nature (*essentia formalis*), or substantial form (*forma substantialis*), there yet remained the idea
of a transformation of man's nature by sin.   A "horrible
metamorphosis" has taken place ; the image of God has been
replaced by the "true and living image of the devil."   Man's
nature has been distorted into a diabolic nature, and every point
of attachment for divine influences has been lost.   For the
advocacy of these ideas Flacius sacrificed his position and the
fortunes of his life (see esp. Theil. ii. of the Clavis, p. 651 ff.,
and "De essentia justitiae originalis et injustitiae," 1568).
(*d*) The Lutherans persisted in their external and mechanical
conception of conversion, and the Philippists also maintained
their position.   To the latter, the conceptions of the purely
passive attitude of man in conversion, his resistance to it, and
the illustrations of the animating of a stone or log, appeared
overdrawn and enthusiastic (see the Endl. Bericht, 1570).
They were anxious, on the other hand, to retain in some way
the personal and psychological element in the process of conversion.   But it is of the greatest significance that they clearly
and plainly deny "any kind of ability or a free will for their
own conversion" in the unregenerate.   Man can, they held, do
nothing whatever toward his own conversion (Endl. Bericht,
form Ii, 1 b ; 4 b ; 4 a).   This acknowledgment opened the
way for a possible understanding with the theologians of the
former group.   The controversy therefore effected a positive
clearing of the atmosphere.

7. THE OSIANDRIAN CONTROVERSY.   (*a*) In A. D. 1850 and
the following years attention was drawn to a new theory of justification taught by ANDREAS OSIANDER (Disput. de justificatione,
1550 ; Von dem einigen Mitler Jhesu Christo vnd Rechtfertigung des Glaubens, 1551 ; Widerlegung der vngegrundten vn
dienstlichen Antwort Phil. Melanthonis, 1552).   "They teach
(doctrines) colder than ice, that we are accounted righteous
only on account of the remission of sins, and not also on account
of the righteousness of the Christ dwelling in us by faith.   God

24

is not indeed so unjust as to regard him as righteous in whom there is really nothing of true righteousness " (De justif. thes., 73 f.). This citation reveals his aim. Justification as connected solely with imputation is to his mind an irreligious conception. Justification is more than a mere declaring the sinner to be righteous. But the talented man now placed these ideas in a wider setting. To understand him, we must briefly reproduce his entire scheme of thought. Man was created in the image of God. This image of God is in the Son, and in the Son, furthermore, as from eternity appointed to become incarnate. Accordingly, the appointed goal of human nature can be realized only by the indwelling of God in it. This was actualized in the case of Adam, as in him the Son of God already dwelt before the fall.[1] Through this indwelling he became righteous. Through sin this " original righteousness " was lost. The renewal of the race is now effected by Christ's entering it in the incarnation. But Christ is brought to the individual soul through the word. He is himself the " inner word " (according to Jn. i.); but the latter enters the human soul in and through "the outer word." The words of Jesus and his apostles are thus the vehicle through which the Logos takes up his abode within us (Von d. Mitler, C. 1). It is, therefore, through this indwelling that man becomes righteous. Righteousness is " no work, no act, no endurance ; " "but it is the character (*die Art*) which makes him who receives and possesses it righteous and moves him to act and endure aright" (ib. H. 4). It is the piety (*Frommbkeit*) which makes the man absolutely a new man. Thus the righteousness of man is a condition, but a condition which is and will be effected by God himself. This righteousness is God himself. As the humanity of Christ became righteous through its union with God as the essential righteousness, so we also become righteous by virtue of such a union with Christ (H. 3 b).

But this union depends upon Christ's mediatorial work as its prerequisite. The latter has two aspects: *redemptio* and *justificatio*. Redemption embraces two things. The sinner is under obligation to bear the eternal penalty of his sin, or the wrath of God, and also to fulfill the law. By his innocent sufferings, Christ endured the wrath of God and obtained for us the forgiveness of sins. And since we, even after regeneration, are unable to fulfill the law perfectly, he, in order that the law might not further accuse us, " fulfilled it purely and perfectly for us and for our benefit, in order that it might

---

[1] See already Methodius, supra, Vol. I., p. 174.

not be imputed to us, nor we be accursed because we do not in this life perfectly fulfill the law" (ib. A. 3 b; 4 a). By both of these aspects of redemption[1] our objective salvation is effected. Everyone who belongs to the church of Christ is by it—without regard to his subjective attitude—objectively saved.[2] But this reconciliation, or forgiveness of sins, is not yet by any means our righteousness. The relation of justification to redemption is to be conceived óf as that of a consequent: "That righteousness is granted because sin has been before forgiven" (Widerleg. J. 4 a). We are righteous only in so far as we become alive; but we become alive, or righteous, only through the indwelling of Christ. Justification is therefore not to be conceived forensically, but as a making-righteous (B. 2 a). *Justificare* is "from an ungodly to make a righteous man, *i.e.*, to recall the dead to life" (De justif., thes. 3). This indwelling of the divine nature of Christ, with which at the same time the Triune God dwells in us, is our righteousness before God. Still more precisely, "his divine nature is our righteousness" (Widerleg. L. 2 a; Von d. Mitler, B. 1 b). It is therefore perfectly clear, that justification is the renewal of man wrought by the presence of Christ, or at least that it embraces this as its chief element. If the Scriptures make righteousness dependent upon faith, faith is thus mentioned by them because its content is Christ (J. 1 b), *i. e.*, "Jesus Christ, true God and man, who dwells in our hearts by faith" (J. 2 b). In this connection, Osiander acknowledges, after all, a certain imputation. When we are united with Christ by faith, we are "overwhelmed and filled" with divine righteousness. And although sin indeed still clings to us, yet it is only as an impure drop compared with a whole pure ocean, and, on account of Christ's righteousness which is within us, God will not regard

---

[1] *I. e.*, the *passive* and the *active obedience* of Christ, cf. Luther supra, p. 268. This discrimination became, as a result of the present controversy, a permanent feature of the accepted doctrine of the church. See, *e. g.*, Flacius, Von d. Gerechtigk. D 2: "The essential righteousness of God . . . demands two kinds of righteousness: the first is, that we make full satisfaction for the transgression and sin which we have committed; the other, that we thereafter be also perfectly obedient to his law in heart and works." Cf. THOMASIUS, Das Bek. d. Luth. Kirche v. d. Versönung, 1857, p. 56 ff. Osiander also gave a peculiar coloring to this double obedience of Christ by representing the active obedience as filling out the deficiencies in the incipient righteousness. The original idea associated by Luther with the two terms was, that by the sufferings of Christ the penalties of the law were nullified, and by his active fulfilling of the law the whole economy of law (which as the "law of nature" held sway over all men) was abrogated for us. See citations, supra, p. 271 f.

[2] But, despite this, man remains under the wrath of God until repentance and justification take place (Von d. Mitler, B. 4 a; 2 b).

it (X. 4 b). " When he dwells in us by faith, he brings with him into us his righteousness, which is his divine nature, and this is then also *imputed* to us, as though it were our own " (Q. 3 a). The theory of Osiander is thus, briefly stated, as follows : Christ through his sufferings appeased the wrath of God, and through his fulfillment of the law made satisfaction for our continuing disobedience. We are thereby objectively redeemed. Salvation becomes ours subjectively in this way : In the preached word the Logos enters us, and he, embraced by faith, begets in us a new life. Thus is our righteousness really begun, and yet it is righteousness only because Christ's abiding presence in us maintains it and leads God to regard our beginning of righteousness in the light of his (Christ's) perfection. This theory is evidently not Roman Catholic ; for it neither takes any account of merit upon our part, nor does it really base justification upon our new life, the ground of the latter being, on the contrary, the power of Christ.[1] Penetrating to the heart of Osiander's contention, it cannot be denied that he was endeavoring to reproduce the early Protestant doctrine of justification, and in this he had a right to make appeal to Luther. Like the latter, he intoned with unwearying energy the indwelling of Christ within us, and, like him, he saw the believer's righteousness and goodness in faith because of its content, *i. e.*, Christ (supra, p. 260). And yet, if we compare with him the entire Luther, we will observe a distinct difference. Osiander was distinctively a scholar— dominated by thoughts, and not by experience—and he wrote also under the stimulus of a visible opposition. This made him one-sided. He was not able by his train of connected ideas to combine, as did Luther, the legality and the consolation of the imputed righteousness. The accent is differently placed by the two men. According to Luther, the Christ for us is our consolation and is the effectual power of the Christ in us ; while according to Osiander, the former is but the logical prerequisite for the latter. The practical result of the forgiveness of sins is for Luther above all else faith ; for Osiander, the power of doing the good. But we should not on this account minimize the service which Osiander rendered by advocating ideas embraced in original Lutheranism as against Melanchthonianism.[2]

---

[1] The connection between *redemptio* and *justificatio*, the objective and subjective aspects of the work of salvation, remains for Osiander thoroughly beclouded. His most serious fault is his placing of the forgiveness of sins in the background. In this, he reminds us somewhat of Duns.

[2] A broad systematic instinct permeates the discussions of Osiander. He had a connected general theory of Christianity, such as no other among the theologians succeeding Luther possessed until Calvin appeared. Among the men of second rank in the Reformation period, he was perhaps the

Cf. MÖLLER, A. Os., 1870. THOMASIUS, ii. ed. 2, 437 ff. FRANK, Theol.
d. CF. ii. 5 ff. RITSCHL, Rechtf. u. Vers. i., ed. 2, 235 ff. LOOFS, DG. 423 ff.[1]

(*b*) Both Philippists and Lutherans at once arose with one
accord against the theory of Osiander. There was no appreciation of the relative (historical) justification of his contention.[2]
His charge, that under the doctrinal formulas sufficient emphasis
was not laid upon man's renewal, was indignantly resented
(Mel. C. R. vii. 895). The chief objections to his theory
were the following. He depreciated, it was said, the forgiveness of sins, by separating it from justification, and laid the
emphasis, not upon the revealed gracious disposition of God
toward us, but upon the "gift" (*donum*) of grace (Mel. C. R.
vii. 899. Menius, Von d. Gerechtigk., E. 4 a). He thus
reverses the proper order, regarding renewal as the ground instead of the result of justification. But this, it was further said,
was connected with his second chief error, namely, that he tears
asunder redemption and justification. The obedience of Christ,
by virtue of which he both made atonement for our sins and fulfilled the law in our stead, is at the same time our righteousness
and our redemption (see esp. the Censur of the theologians of
Electoral Saxony, B. 4 b, C. 2 b, and Flacius, Von d. Gerechtigk. wider Os., Magdeb., 1552, D. 4 a). "In such a way that
this obedience of the Mediator, Jesus Christ, at the same time
delivers and justifies the poor sinner and reconciles God who has
been angry" (Menius, l. c., E. 2. Flac., l. c., D. 3 a). As
we lay hold upon this righteousness of Christ in faith, it becomes
ours, and the objective certainty of this righteousness secures us
the comfort of the assurance of salvation. Osiander, on the
contrary, bases our righteousness and salvation upon our own
state, or condition, and thus the assurance of salvation is stolen
from "poor distressed consciences" (Lauterwald, Fünf. Schlus-
sprüche wider Os., 1552, A. 3 b. C. R. viii. 583. Flacius,
Verlegung Os., J. 3 a). These objections were certainly well

greatest. Viewed historically, his attempt constitutes the contemporaneous
counterpoise to the doctrine of justification taught by the later Melanchthon.
Both men gave one-sided interpretations of ideas of Luther's; the latter,
through undue emphasis, upon the imputed, the former by exalting out of
proper proportion the effective, righteousness of faith. But it must, after all,
be accounted a blessing, that the Melanchthonian and not the Osiandrian
scheme met the approval of the church.

[1] My estimate of Osiander agrees, so far as I can see—up to a certain
point—with that of LOOFS.

[2] Brenz opposed an express condemnation of Osiander at Worms in 1557
(see G. WOLF, Gesch. d. deutsch. Protestanten, 1555-9, 1888, p. 334, 339,
363). Calvin also most vigorously combated his views (Institut. iii. 11. 5 ff.;
cf. ii. 12. 5 f.; i. 15. 3).

taken.   Osiander's method of presenting the doctrines involved
was in fact liable to the serious peril of making the redemption
wrought by the historical Christ but a comparatively unimportant precursor of the effective agency of the Logos, and of
confusedly mingling our righteousness and that of Christ.   But
was not the Melanchthonian doctrine also liable to the perilous
misconception, that man may by simply giving intellectual
assent to the theory of satisfaction become sure of his salvation?

(*c*) In opposition to Osiander, FRANZ STANCAR, appealing to
the Lombard, for whom he entertained an exceedingly warm regard, maintained :[1] " Christ is (our) righteousness only according to his human nature " (sent. iii. dist. 19. 7).   Since it was the
mission of the Mediator to reconcile men to God and to die for
them, his works, because mediatorial, were human (*e. g.*,
SCHLÜSSELBURG, ix. 244).   And the human voluntary acts of
the Mediator cannot be attributed to the immutable God (ib.
277).   He thus moved in the direction of Nestorianism.

8. The Christological conflicts belong to a later period.   (*a*)
The Heidelberg theologians assailed the Lutheran Christology
(see esp. Gründl. Bericht, v. h. Abendm., 1566) by denying
the *ubiquitas* and the *communicatio idiomatum* (Thomasius, ii.,
ed. 3, 603), and the Würtembergers, especially BRENZ (De per-
sonali unione duarum naturum, 1561 ; De divina majestate domini nostr. Ies. Chr., 1562), appeared in its defense.   According
to Brenz, the entire fullness of the divine attributes was at the
moment of the incarnation infused into the human nature of
Christ.   And Christ, even during his life on earth, actually exercised these divine attributes, although secretly.   Whilst he
lay dead in the tomb, he was filling and ruling heaven and earth ;
whilst he was, at the time of the death of Lazarus, outwardly far
from Bethany, he was according to his divine nature present at
his death-bed.[2]   Cf. THOMASIUS, Christologie, ii., ed. 2, 384 ff.
H. SCHULTZ, Gottheit Christi, p. 216 ff.

(*b*) A similar conflict of views was developed in Saxony.
The Crypto-Calvinists, P. Eber, G. Major, Krell) also rejected
the *communicatio idiomatum* (Von der Person vnd Menschwerdung vnseres HEerrn J. Christi, der waren christl. Kirchen
Grundfest, 1571).   The " great and high gifts and glories "

---

[1] Thus already Augustine (Vol. I., pp. 260, 361 n.) as well as Thomas
and the other Scholastics.

[2] Brenz based his theory upon ideas developed by Luther in the controversy upon the Lord's Supper.   The interests of Christology are for him entirely wrapped up in the *communicatio idiomatum* ; but, measured by the historical career of Christ, his theory, framed entirely in conformity with the
ubiquity idea, proves insufficient.

which the humanity of Christ received are " not eternal, infinite attributes of the divine nature " (l. c., 23, 25). Each of the two natures retains its own peculiar attributes and energies unmingled with those of the other nature. Against this, MARTIN CHEMNITZ directs his treatise, *De duabus naturis in Christo,* 1571.[1] If we compare the ideas here presented with those of Brenz, we are favorably impressed with his strict adherence to the scriptural terms,[2] his familiarity with the historical development of doctrine and his dogmatic carefulness; but he lacks the broad, pacific temper which impresses the reader so favorably in the works of Brenz. He holds that the human nature of Christ receives infused gifts, qualities, and habitus (*dona, qualititates, habitus,* p. 253 ff., 267, 40) from the divine nature. It receives these in the fullest measure possible to a finite nature,[3] and its susceptibility is thereby increased, so that it is enabled by virtue of the hypostatic union to receive the essentially divine attributes (c. 20 f.). This leads to a real manifestation of divine attributes in the human nature. The human nature is permeated by the divine as iron by fire (c. 23, 6). An interpenetration (περιχώρησις) takes place. But—and this is a significant thought —Chemnitz very frequently conceives of this relationship as an exertion of the energy of the divine will in the human nature and its natural powers. The divine will with its energy constitutes the divine nature in Christ; the human nature is the appropriate Organ for the actualizing of its *operationes.* " He wished to assume as an organ our nature, taken up into the communion of his divine energies (*operationes*), particularly in the work of the Messiah," p. 323. The human nature is the intelligent and self-determining Organ through which Christ accomplishes his redeeming work. There is a co-operation, since the powers of the human nature have an *organon co-operans* in the divine nature, and *vice versa* (p. 224, 363, 261). The will of the Logos guides the human will, and the latter willingly accepts the leadership. The human will in Christ desires, craves, wills, and approves what Christ performs in his offices by his divine power (p. 224). " For this soul (*anima*) of Christ willed those things which the divine will of the Logos willed that it should will " (p. 473). As, according to this, the divine nature of Christ consists, in the last analysis, in the omnipotent Loving-will which is revealed in the works of Jesus; the whole character of the

---

[1] The citations are from the Leipzig edition of 1578.

[2] P. 328: " For concerning God we should neither think nor speak otherwise than as he has in the very word (employed) revealed himself in the Scriptures."

[3] He sees a parallel in the indwelling and operating of God in the believer.

life and sufferings of Jesus must be traced to the will of the
Logos (p. 39, 72, 227, 46). With this connection of ideas the
Ubiquity appears in a new light. It is now the power of the
God-man to determine to be bodily present where he will (multivolipresence): "That the Son of God is by virtue of the hypostatic union able to be present with his assumed nature wherever, whenever, and in whatsoever way he will, *i. e.*, wherever
he has in a positive word taught and promised that he desires to
be present with it" (p. 517, 477, 479, 480, 496). Upon this
basis, Chemnitz secures more room for the human development of
Jesus and for discriminating between the states of humility and
exaltation. The divine nature refrains from exercising its energy
upon the human nature (*paullisper retrahens et retinens*), although
the latter has from the moment of the conception really possessed
and had at command the fullness of the divine nature.[1] Thus the
sufferings and death of Christ became possible, and we can thus
understand also that the divine nature should, during the state
of humiliation, deliberately refrain to a certain extent from the
exercise and revelation of its full glory, in order to again bring
into action the fullness of its divine glory in the state of exaltation. But as Jesus, from the commencement of his human existence, really possessed the whole compass of the divine attributes, or the divine nature itself, this refraining was also a concealing. The human nature therefore possessed the fullness of the
divine nature (*plenitudo divinitatis*), but "did not always
exercise and apply it" (p. 57). This is the meaning of the
term *exinanition :* "He concealed and withdrew and made
quiescent the employment and display of his divine glory and
power in the flesh and through the flesh" (p. 353). Chemnitz
further declares: "He, as it were, restrained and withdrew
the rays of the indwelling fullness of the divine nature, not
only in order that they might not shine forth from him, but
that they might not always be fully and perfectly cast even
upon the nature assumed, . . . but slowly and gradually,"
making a growth possible (p. 553). As the exercise of the
divine glory was thus restricted in the state of humiliation, so in
his state of exaltation should the plenary and manifest possession and employment of his majesty be reässumed (p. 58, 295,

---

[1] Chemnitz was, therefore, by no means a Kenotist in the modern sense of
the term. Every form of alteration in the divine nature in the sense of diminution or accretion is excluded (p. 163, 250, 252). On the other hand, all
the attributes of the divine nature, as *essentialia*, are inseparable from the divine
essentia, or nature (p. 253 ff., 267, 14, 23, 279 f., 328). Christ, therefore,
as God, retained the full possession of these attributes and placed a voluntary
limitation only upon their employment and manifestation.

346). These ideas are all combined in the exposition of the *communicatio idiomatum*. Chemnitz discriminates three forms of the latter, a classification which had an important influence in the shaping of Lutheran dogmatics: (1) Each of the two natures imparts its attributes to the One person (p. 161 f.). (2) The action of the two natures is always a combined action ; the person effects salvation "according to both natures. The Son of God did not wish to operate in one nature alone, but in both, with both, and through both " (p. 162). (3) The human nature, since it cannot of itself perform all the works necessary to our salvation, is illuminated in every part by the divine light, and is the Bearer and Organ of the operations of the Logos (p. 163 f.).[1] Inasmuch as this mode of presenting the subject does not deal merely with quiescent " substances," but sets forth the two natures of Christ as actively engaged (in the work of redemption), it proved successful in preserving some important elements in Luther's conceptions of Christology.[2]   Cf. THOMASIUS, Christol. ii., ed. 2, 383 ff.   H. SCHULTZ, Gotth. Christi, 223 ff.

But the Würtemberg theologians also gradually learned to think more specifically than formerly of the state of humiliation. Christ as a child "did not know, did not see, did not hear, did not do all things, although the power of God, of which he became partaker through the personal union, is infinite and uncircumscribed." His condition while his body lay in the sepulchre is to be compared with that of a sleeping person. As the union of body and soul continues during sleep, although the sleeper does not see, hear, nor do anything, so the soul of Christ was also in the state of death without detriment to its union with the divine nature (Würtemberg Theologen, Bekenntn. v. d. Majestät des Menschen Christi, 1585, p. 37 ff.   Cf. THOMASIUS, Christol. ii., ed. 2, 365 ff.).[3]

---

[1] The later dogmatics discriminated the *genus idiomaticum, majestaticum,* and *apotelesmaticum,* see SCHMID, Dogmatik d. luth. Kirche, ed. 7, p. 226 ff.; English Transl., Hay and Jacobs, ed. 3, p. 312 ff.

[2] But the concentration of the divine and human life under the category of the *will* is, after all, less energetic than might have been expected.   Contrast with Luther, supra, p. 253.

[3] Mention may be here made of the controversy upon the *Descensus ad inferos,* started by JOHANN AEPINUS (from A. D. 1549). In his view, 1 Pet. 3. 18 refers, not to a preaching after the descent of the soul of Christ into Hades, but to a proclamation made by Christ in his divine nature before the Incarnation.   The Descensus, as a part of the obedience rendered by Christ, must be considered as the final act of his humiliation.   The soul of Christ descended into Hades while his body lay in the grave ; but, although the obedience thus rendered by Christ certainly vanquished hell, this was not a manifestation of the power of the Risen Saviour.   Cf. FRANK, Theol. d. C. F. iii. 398 ff., 434 ff.

9. A CONTROVERSY UPON PREDESTINATION arose in Strassburg, A. D. 1561, between HIERONIMUS ZANCHI and JOHANN MARBACH, HESSHUSEN having already in 1560 assailed the Calvinistic view of that doctrine. The controversy was precipitated by the request of the Lutheran, Marbach, that his Calvinistic colleague should base the certainty of election not *a priori* upon the eternal counsel of God, but upon the will of God as revealed in the word. It was not until later that Marbach attacked the doctrine, that God grants faith but once to the elect and that they, by virtue of the "gift of perseverance," cannot lose it (LÖSCHER, Hist. motuum, iii. 30). The way was opened for a settlement of the conflict by the adoption of a formula of compromise in 1563 (vid. Löscher, ii. 286 ff.). According to this, everyone who believes on Christ obtains grace. The promises are universal, and everyone may therefore lay claim to them. Why the divine call does not work faith in all, or why God does grant faith to all, is a mystery. Into this mystery we should not seek to pry, but confine our attention to the gracious will of God as revealed in Christ. These explanations lay along the line of the Lutheran development. Cf. SCHWEIZER, Die prot. Centraldogmen, i. 418 ff.

§ 78. *The Formula of Concord.*

LITERATURE.   PLANCK, Gesch. des protest. Lehrbegriffs, vol. vi. FRANK-SEEBERG, PRE. x., ed. 3, 732 ff.   FRANK, Die Theolg. der C. F., 4 parts, 1858 ff.   THOMASIUS, Das Bek. d. ev. luth. Kirche in der Consequenz s. Princips., 1848, and DG. ii., ed 2, 425 ff.   HEPPE, Gesch. d. deutsch. Prot., vol. iii., 1857 ; Die Entstehung u. Fortbildung d. Luthertums u. die kirchl. Bek.-schriften desselben, 1548, 1576, 1863.   G. WOLF, Zur Gesch. d. deutschen Protestanten, 1555-59, 1888.   K. MÜLLER, Die Symbole des Luthertums in Preuss. Jarbb., vol. 63, 129 ff.   MÖLLER-KAWERAU, KG. iii., 265 ff.

1. The pernicious principle, that religious differences prohibit even political combination, gave a double importance to the embittered controversies above reviewed. When the Gnesio-Lutherans at the Religious Colloquy at Worms, in 1557, denied to the Philippists the right to claim adherence to the Augsburg Confession, thus excluding them also from the benefits of the Religious Peace secured at Augsburg in 1555, the Protestant princes felt themselves compelled to place all possible restraint upon the theological conflicts which were dominating all other interests. The passion displayed and the worship of formulas reminded of the worst periods of the dogmatic struggles upon Byzantine territory. As then, the attempt was made to restore peace either by prohibiting contention, or by constructing

formulas upon which all could agree. The movement originated indeed among the theologians, but its direction and the fixation of definite ideas as legally-authorized dogmas was, as heretofore, taken in hand by the princes, and political considerations also influenced the course of thought. The first attempt to restore peace was made in the Frankfort Recess of 1558 (C. R. ix. 489 ff.). The princes, "as a Christian, pious civil government, to which has been solemnly committed and commanded the protection and secure establishment of divinely-revealed truth,"[1] here affirm that they desire always to support the "pure true doctrine" as contained in the Scriptures "and also in the three chief symbols and likewise in the Augsburg Confession, together with its Apology" (494). It is then asserted in detail: that righteousness consists in "the forgiveness of sins and imputed righteousness" (495); that new obedience and good works are indeed necessary for the begetting of faith, but that no one should place his trust in them (498); that Christ "is true, living, substantial, and present" in the Lord's Supper, or that "the bread is communion (*die Gemeinschaft*) with the body of Christ" (499 f.).[2] Non-essential (*mittelmässige*) ceremonies are to be conducted in so far as possible in harmony with the word of God, and local differences in their celebration are to be tolerated without quarreling (501). In cases of "conflicting opinions," the counsel of the learned, "gently and kindly" given, as will readily be done by the consistories and superintendents, should be followed. No "writing nor booklet in religious matters" should be printed "which has not first been examined by the constituted authorities and found in accord with the true confession of our faith" (502). This document—which is instructive as showing the spirit of the incipient secular ecclesiasticism—accomplished nothing. The strict Lutherans published in response to it in 1559 the *Weimar Confutation*, which vigorously condemned the Philippists. The conflict in regard to the *Invariata* and *Variata* editions of the Augsburg Confession[3] first appeared at the Imperial Diet of Naumburg, in 1561, leading at that time to no results. It was the controver-

---

[1] P. 492. This is the conception of the "Christian government" (p. 495), when just upon the verge of transformation into the secular "ecclesiastical government."

[2] Here, as in what precedes, the Melanchthonian basis is traceable, cf. C. R. ix. 407, 409 f.

[3] It was the edition of 1531 which was subscribed. Of the editions of 1540 and 1542 it is said, that they "reproduce the above-named Confession in a somewhat more becoming and detailed form; also, explained and enlarged upon the basis of the Holy Scriptures." It is the "Amended (*verbesserte*) Confession," *i. e.*, an exposition and development of the Invariata.

sies upon the Lord's Supper (p. 366) which now proved the chief obstacle in the way of conciliatory movements. The authority of Luther was here arrayed too distinctly against Melanchthon. So long as the Philippists would not agree to reject the Melanchthonian view of the Lord's Supper, there could be no thought of reconciliation. On the other hand, some progress was made toward a comparative unity of doctrine in the separate territorial churches by the introduction of Bodies of Doctrine (*corpora doctrinae*). The first of these, the so-called "Corpus Philippicum," or "Misnicum," was a private undertaking of the book-dealer, Vögelein, in Leipzig, who in 1560, shortly after the death of Melanchthon, edited a collection of the latter's doctrinal writings, which contained, in addition to the three ancient symbols, the Augsburg Confession, the Apology, the Confessio Saxonica, the Loci (ed. 1556), the Examen ordinandorum, and the Responsiones ad impios articul. Bavaric. inquisitionis. This collection was not only introduced into Electoral Saxony, but was received with favor in other regions (*e. g.*, in Hesse and Pomerania). There at once appeared in opposition to it a number of strictly Lutheran *Corpora doctrinae*. There were commonly found in these—besides the three ancient symbols, the Augsburg Confession and the Apology—only writings of Luther, such as the two catechisms, the Smalcald Articles, various smaller publications, and extracts from controversial works.[1]

2. A fixed doctrine was thus secured for the separate territorial churches. The plan of uniting the various churches by a common confession seemed now more feasible. The efforts to promote concord which JACOB ANDREAE had been making since A. D. 1569 (see JOHANNSEN in Ztschr. f. hist. Theol. 1853, 344 ff.) were at first fruitless. But the times were constantly becoming more auspicious. A new generation had succeeded the earlier leaders of the Gnesio-Lutherans, less deeply involved in the old doctrinal controversies, and hence able to pass calmer judgment upon their merits. In the general apprehension of evangelical doctrine, as well as upon many separate points, the Melanchthonian views prevailed. But the only reformatory authority was Luther, as Melanchthon had himself maintained. Wherever they openly differed, the views of Luther were accepted. The specific Lutheranism of this circle really consisted, there-

---

[1] *E. g.*, the city of Brunswick, 1563 ; Prussia, 1567 ; Brunswick-Wolfenbüttel, 1569 ; also the so-called *Corpus Julium*, 1576 ; the dukedom of Saxony, 1570 ; Brandenburg, 1572 ; Lüneburg, 1576. Vid. the first collection of the documents in the Book of Concord of 1580, in the *Corpus* of Brunswick-Wolfenbüttel, which was also composed by Chemnitz and Andreae.

fore, only of the doctrine of the Lord's Supper, in connection with the *communicatio idiomatum*, and in the rejection of Synergism.[1] On the other hand, the specific Philippism was dying out. There were no conspicuous leaders to carry forward the work of Melanchthon. The great Reformer had two souls, one of which was orthodox Lutheran and the other Humanistic. The heirs of his Humanism had since A. D. 1574 (cf. p. 367) been branded as Crypto-Calvinists and regarded with suspicion, and they were also the supporters of the positions in which Melanchthon differed from Luther. Some of them—influenced in part by the adoption of the Formula of Concord—went over to Calvinism.[2] The peculiar characteristics which marked German Calvinism in many particulars may be at least partly accounted for by this commingling of Humanistic-Melanchthonian and of Calvinistic elements.[3] Other followers of Melanchthon, drifting away from the peculiar teachings of their master, became Lutherans from conviction (*e. g.*, Chemnitz, Selnecker, Chytraeus). They were at heart in harmony with the new group of Lutherans, although always characterized by the dogmatic caution of their great teacher (cf. Chemnitz, supra, p. 375). It was not accidental that two such men as Chemnitz, an original Melanchthonian, and the Würtemburger Andreae, who came from a church which had attested its Lutheranism especially by its fidelity upon the doctrine of the Lord's Supper (Brenz, supra, p. 366), were found to lead in the interest of concord. The consensus aimed at was, in its essential aspects, here already actualized—a Melanchthonian Lutheranism.[4]

The movement for concord must, in view of the circumstances, address itself to a two-fold task. It must (1) Construct a Body of Doctrine which should find acceptance with all Lutherans,

---

[1] This course of historic events explains the fact that the general estimate of Lutheranism has been more and more restricted to these two points.

[2] Cf., *e. g.*, the biographies of Widebram, Pezel, Hyperius, Fink, Ursinus, and the younger Cruciger.

[3] This furnishes HEPPE and others the point of attachment for their construction of history, in which a great general reformatory movement, embracing Melanchthonianism, a humanistic undercurrent, and Calvinistic elements, is represented as crushed out by the domineering spirit of the Gnesio-Lutherans.

[4] It furnishes an instructive illustration of the confusion which existed in regard to the divergences between the teachings of Luther and Melanchthon—apart from their views of the Lord's Supper—that at the colloquy at ALTENBURG in 1569, the Lutherans charged the Melanchthonians with holding "that we become righteous before God alike by *imputatio* and by *inchoatio*, *i. e.*, from imputed righteousness and obedience begun" (HEPPE, Gesch. des Prot. ii. 217). They were here thinking of the Interim (vid. supra, p. 364). They thus seized in an entirely superficial way upon Melanchthon's formula of good works, although this very error might have been charged upon Luther instead, at least with an appearance of justice (supra, p. 260).

and (2) Formulate its consensus with due regard to the controversies of the preceding decennium ; for only thus could there be any hope of finally disposing of them (see Pref. Form. Conc.). The former of these requirements was met by including in the Book of Concord a collection of the normative documents (the three ancient symbols, the Augsburg Confession, the Apology, the Smalcald Articles, and Luther's Catechisms); the latter, by the second portion of the work, viz.: the Formula of Concord. The Formula of Concord thus at once assumed a position among the regulative symbols of Lutheranism.   It would lead us too far from our purpose to attempt in this connection a history of the genesis of this important composition.[1]   It was published officially at Dresden, June 25, 1580. Fifty-one princes, counts, and barons, thirty-five cities, and more than eight thousand theologians had subscribed to it.   The book was not accepted by Brunswick-Wolfenbüttel (because of hostility to Chemnitz), Schleswig-Holstein, Hesse, Pomerania, Anhalt, Pfalz-Zweibrücken, Nassau, Bentheim, Tecklenburg, Solms, Magdeburg, Nordhausen, Bremen, Dantzic, Frankfort, Worms, Strassburg, Spires, Nuremberg, Weissenburg, Windsheim.[2]

In forming our estimate of the Formula of Concord, it must be borne in mind that it is based upon the fundamental symbols of the Lutheran Church ; that the problems with which it deals were dividing the church in that age ; that it actually gave expression to a consensus already inaugurated ; and that it consequently succeeded in gradually restoring the peace of the church. The detailed theological definitions of the pure doctrine which it presented were in keeping with the spirit that had prevailed in the church it represented for about a century and a half.[3]   We

---

[1] The process of its development is regulated by the following documents : Six controversial sermons of Andreae (in HEPPE, iii., suppl. 3 ff.); the Tübingen Book, or Schwäbian Concord, 1574 (Ztschr. f. hist. Theol. 36. 234 ff.); the Schwäbian Saxon Concord (in HEPPE, suppl. 75 ff.); the Maulbronn Formula, 1576 (Jarbb. f. deutsche Theol. 11. 640 ff.); the Torgau Book, 1576 ; the Bergen Book, 1577 (see HEPPE, Der Text d. Bergischen C. F. verglichen mit dem Text der Schwäb. Conc., der Schwäb. sächs. Conc. u. des Torgauer Buches, 1857).   The original plan of having the work adopted by a great assembly of the churches—such as was often spoken of—was afterward abandoned. Such an assembly, modeled after those of the ancient church, had been desired by the Jena theologians as early as 1560 (HEPPE, i., suppl. 124).   The Formula of Concord is composed of the *Epitome* and the *Solida declaratio.* The latter is the Bergen Book ; the former a summary of the Torgau Book, prepared by Andreae and revised at Bergen.

[2] Silesia took no part in the proceedings.   Strassburg accepted the Formula in 1597.   Pomerania in 1593 added to an edition of the Corpus Philippicum, enlarged by a volume of Luther's writings, some parts of the Formula of Concord.

[3] I cannot agree with the opinion of KAWERAU (Möller, KG. iii.), p. 268,

can, therefore, as little ignore the historical necessity of the enterprise, as we can fail to be impressed with the tactful and energetic literary labor which it reveals. The Formula of Concord did indeed make final the breach between the Lutheran-Melanchthonian and the Calvinistic-Melanchthonian types in the evangelical church of Germany; but this breach was, under the existing circumstances, unavoidable. No reproach can be cast upon a confession for giving expression to a condition of affairs already existing.

We must note the leading doctrinal statements of the Formula.

3. Articles I. and II. are devoted to Original Sin and Free Will. (*a*) The Formula opposes Flacius' theory of original sin and every view which does not acknowledge that man is "utterly corrupted and dead toward good" (p. 589. 7). There yet remains, indeed, in the natural man a certain knowledge of God and the capacity of "civil righteousness" (589. 9). This makes him capable of experiencing conversion (593. 22). (*b*) Accordingly, God does not deal with man as with a log or a stone (603. 61). He does not coërce man (602 f.), although the latter does not possess the "power of applying himself to grace" (590, 594). In this respect, it may be said that "not even a spark of spiritual strength remains" (589. 7), and "no more than a stone, log, or lump of clay;" even "in this particular he is worse than a block, because he is rebellious and hostile to the divine will" (578. 23; 591 ff.; 599. 46). (*c*) The only cause of conversion is therefore the Holy Spirit, who through the word lays hold upon the heart and works faith, "new spiritual emotions, regeneration. and renovation, and new obedience." Man is "merely passive" in conversion (530. 22). But this dare not be so represented as when "a seal is impressed upon wax," but in such a way that, in the very moment of the beginning of the divine operation within us ("until the Holy Spirit has first . . . begun in us . . . his work of regeneration"), the will,

---

that the Formula of Concord abandons Luther's conception of faith. He appeals in its support to the passage : "The gospel is properly the doctrine which teaches . . . what that most miserable sinner ought to believe in order that he may obtain the forgiveness of sins before God" (Müller, p. 637. 20). This sentence is certainly unfortunately framed, but the context shows clearly what is meant: "For whatever consoles fearful minds, whatever offers the favor and grace of God to transgressors of the law, this is, properly and correctly speaking, the gospel, *i. e.*, the most joyful announcement that the Lord God does not wish to punish our sins, but for Christ's sake to forgive them. Wherefore penitent sinners ought to believe, that is, they should place their entire confidence in Christ alone, *i. e.*, because he was offered up on account of our sins," etc. (ib. § 21 f.). We are here told what evangelical faith is. The "rightly-believing" are those "who have true and living faith in Christ" (p. 534. 39). Similarly also Luther (supra, p. 225, n. 1).

impelled by God, engages according to its own nature in active
Synergy (" we are able, and ought, to coöperate " (604. 65).
Hence it is said : The man who is of himself absolutely unfree
for the doing of good is by the Spirit of God made free
(*liberatum arbitrium*, 604. 67), and, in the moment of the
effectual touch of the Spirit, the will is able to co-operate
actively in the work of renewal.

4. Article III. treats of Justification.   (*a*) It is asserted, in
opposition to Osiander and Stancar, that our righteousness
depends exclusively upon neither the divine nor the human
nature of Christ, but : " in his whole person, who, as both God
and man, is alone in his entire and most perfect obedience
our righteousness " (622. 55 ; 629).   The personally rendered obedience is thus the point of view under which the
work of Christ is regarded.   This obedience was manifested
"in doing and suffering " (612. 14, 15).   It was a " most perfect obedience, by which he fulfilled the law for us."   It constitutes the merit of Christ, which God imputes to us for righteousness (618. 30).   That man now receives grace, is based
upon the fact that Christ by his double obedience has first nullified both the penalties and the demands of the law (supra, p.
371, n. 1).   (*b*) Justification consists in this imputation of the
righteousness (*i. e.*, the obedience) of Christ (611. 4 ; 612. 15 ;
613. 17).   The result of this imputation is forgiveness of sins,
reconciliation with God, adoption, and the inheritance of
eternal life (615. 25 ; 613. 16).   But this justification is apprehended by faith, not because the latter is the beginning of
a new life, but because it is the receptive organ for the appropriation of the merit of Christ (612. 13 ; 616. 31).   The
genesis of faith is expressly traced to the operation of the Holy
Spirit in the gospel (619. 41).   (*c*) Faith and Justification are
therefore the central acts.   They must be preceded by " true
and not simulated contrition," for only thus can faith exist
(614 f., 23, 26).[1]   The Holy Spirit now works faith.   " And
this apprehends the grace of God in Christ, by which the person
is justified."   But the believer is also " renewed and sanctified
by the Holy Spirit, which renewal and sanctification are then
followed by good works."   But this "inaugurated righteous-

---

[1] 615. 36: "Contrition precedes, and justifying faith exists in those who
truly, not fictitiously, exercise repentance."   The last term here has a
narrower signification (= *contrition*, penitence) than in the earlier confessions,
cf. also the remark, p. 634. 7 ff.   This may be explained by the fact that the
original parallel with the sacrament of penance was gradually fading from
memory and in its stead such passages as Mk. 1. 15 regulated the usage of the
term.

ness of the new obedience'' dare never be taken into consideration as influencing justification itself, since no one can stand before God upon the ground of this yet ''incomplete and impure'' righteousness. Justification has to do only with the ''righteousness of the obedience, sufferings, and death of Christ, which is imputed to faith'' (617. 32; cf. 620. 44 ff.). By means of this exposition, the Melanchthonian construction of justification secured definite ascendancy.[1]

5. Article IV. discusses Good Works. (*a*) There was here a general agreement upon the following points : That, according to the will of God, believers should perform good works; that good works are not such as are self-chosen, but such as are commanded by God ; that works are pleasing to God in so far as the person of the one performing them is acceptable to him ; that faith is the ''mother and original source of good works'' (625 f.). (*b*) It was pointed out how dangerous and liable to misunderstanding was the position assumed by Amsdorf (supra, p. 364). Against Major it was argued (supra, p. 364), that works dare in no wise be introduced into the ''article of justification and salvation,'' as otherwise ''assailed and distressed consciences will be robbed of the consolation of the gospel '' (629. 23). The thesis of Major concerning the necessity of works to salvation is therefore untenable (632. 37). (*c*) The doctrine, positively stated, is that faith brings with it good works, as the determination to persevere in evil-doing is inconceivable as cherished along with faith (627. 15);[2] and that these works are voluntarily performed (628. 18).

6. Articles V. and VI. treat of the Law and the Gospel. (*a*) The law is the '' divine doctrine, in which is revealed the most just and immutable will of God, as to what manner of person man ought to be,'' together with the threatening of temporal and eternal penalties (636. 17). The gospel, in the ''proper understanding'' of it, is the preaching of the grace of God (634. 6; 637. 21). The law teaches us to recognize our sin and the wrath of God. But, in order that man may not fall into despair, the preaching of the gospel must follow (635. 9 f.).[3]

---

[1] Yet the presentation of the Formula is to be preferred for lucidity and well-considered statement to that of Melanchthon. A number of problems were allowed to remain unsolved, *e. g.*, the genesis of contrition, the relation of the operations of the Holy Spirit in the begetting of faith and works, etc.

[2] Many erroneously hold a dead faith, or a certain empty persuasion, which is without repentance and good works, in place of true faith.

[3] It is therefore not only the office of the Holy Spirit to administer comfort, but he also, as a ''strange work,'' administers rebuke (635. 11). This is analogous to Christ's taking the law into his own hands and interpreting it spiritually (ib. 10).

25

This works faith, and through it righteousness (637 f.). (*b*) If the law is thus necessary at the beginning of the Christian life, it is none the less so during its progress : First, because sin and infirmity still cling to the regenerate, and they therefore still require "instruction and admonition, warning and threatening" (641 f.); secondly, in order "that they do not fall into a holiness and worship of their own," and may be preserved from imagining that their "work and life are entirely pure and perfect" (644. 20 f.). Yet it must ever be borne in mind that the Christian "fulfills the will of God, in so far as he is regenerate, from a free and joyous spirit" (643. 17).

7. Article VII. discusses the Lord's Supper. (*a*) The view of Zwingli is rejected (646. 4), as well as that of Calvin, the latter of which acknowledges indeed in words a " presence of the body of Christ," but means by this only a "spiritual presence " and that of the divine nature (647. 5 f.). Upon the basis of the words of institution, the bodily presence of Christ in the Lord's Supper is taught (646 ff., 656 f., cf. supra, p. 14 f.)—in harmony with the Augsburg Confession, the Apology, the Wittenberg Concord, the Smalcald Articles (by which "all evasions and loopholes are stopped up " against the sacramentarianizing interpretations of the Wittenberg Concord), and the catechisms. Thus it is said : "that in the Lord's Supper the body and blood of Christ are truly and substantially present, and that they are together with the bread and wine truly distributed and taken " (539). From this follows the "oral manducation," which does not mean the Capernaitic eating of the body of Christ, but which takes place, although " with the mouth " (*ore*), yet in a spiritual way (*modus spiritualus*) (543. 661). The reception by the unworthy (*manducatio indignorum*) also follows as a logical conclusion (666. 89). (*b*) It is therefore to be confessed, that "under the bread, with the bread, in the bread is present and offered the body of Christ " (654. 35). Between the substance of the bread and the substance of the body of Christ there is a union, which may be compared to the union of the two natures in Christ. Yet this union is not a *unio personalis*, but a *unio sacramentalis* (654. 36 f.). The possibility of this union is based upon the Ubiquity, which is defined in the sense of Chemnitz (supra, p. 376): "that, namely, even according to that assumed nature and with it, he can be present, and is indeed present, wherever he wishes to be " (692. 78). (*c*) This furnishes also the point of view from which may be understood the effect of the reception of the Supper. The Formula, with a fine tact, brings out the leading ideas of Luther. The Lord's Supper testifies that Christ desires to be continuously operative in believers according to his human

nature (622. 79). It is a seal, assuring us that the blessings which Christ obtained for us in his body are through it present for us (cf. supra, p. 287, 329). " And the pious, indeed, receive the body and blood of Christ as an infallible pledge and assurance that their sins are surely forgiven them, and that Christ dwells in them and wishes to be efficacious in them (661. 63 ; 655. 44). Thus the forgiveness of sins is recognized as the substantial result of participation in the Lord's Supper (661. 63).[1] (*d*) " Christians who are weak in faith, timid, and distressed, who are terrified at heart on account of the magnitudé and multitude of their sins and think they are in this their great uncleanness not worthy of this noble treasure and the benefits of Christ . . . these are the truly *worthy* guests, for whom this sacrament was principally instituted and appointed" (662. 69). (*e*) But it is only as a *transaction* that the Lord's Supper is a sacrament : the mere consecration makes no sacrament, if distribution and reception do not follow (665. 83 f.). But where this transaction occurs, there Christ is himself present as the real transacting personage (663. 75). These definitions, which follow essentially in the line of Luther's views, form one of the chief dogmatic contributions of the Formula.

8. Christology is presented in Article VIII. (*a*) The Formulas of Chalcedon furnish the point of departure. *The communicatio idiomatum*[2] is based upon the personal unity constituted by the combination of the two natures (676. 11). The entire glory of God has entered into the human nature and manifests this glory in and through it, " whenever and however it seems good to itself." But a full and continuous revelation of the divine glory occurs only after the laying aside of the " form of a servant," in heaven (688 f., 679). The God-man, as it were, concealed the glory dwelling in him : " he held it secretly, . . . employed it as often as seemed good to him " (680. 26). These ideas may be traced to Chemnitz (supra, p. 376). (*b*) The union of the two natures and their attributes is, here also, presented under the view-point of coöperation (689. 66 ; 685. 51 f.). But in this combined operation, the relations of the two natures are not strictly mutual, since the divine nature can be subject to no addition nor diminution (684. 49). (*c*) As to the Ubiquity of Christ, in addition to the *Multivolipresence* mentioned in paragraph 7, he is said to be " present in all created things " (547. 16 ; cf. 682 ff., 667 ff.). The presentation of this topic, regarded as a whole,

---

[1] The Formula is silent—and certainly rightly so—in regard to Luther's occasional references to effects of the Lord's Supper upon the body (p. 329).
[2] It presupposes that human nature is capable of receiving the divine, 685. 52 f.; 549. 14.

leaves the impression of incompleteness.   It is hampered by the
differences of opinion existing between Brenz and Chemnitz.
The ideas of Luther are really presented in a connected way only
in the discussion of the Lord's Supper.   The influence of Chemnitz, on the other hand, is everywhere felt.

9. In regard to the Descent into Hell, it is said in Article IX.
" that the entire person and man descended after the burial into
hell, vanquished the devil, and destroyed the power of hell "
(696).   Yet we should lay aside "lofty and precise thoughts "
as to the manner in which this occurred.

10. Article X., discussing *Adiaphora*, asserts that the church
has the authority at any time to change ceremonies and church
customs (698. 9), but that when the church is in the state of
confession (*in statu confessionis*), it must not yield to its opponents even in such matters.

11. The topic of Article XI. is Predestination.   (*a*) As contrasted with foreknowledge (*prescientia*), which relates to both
the good and the evil, predestination is the ordaining to salvation (705. 5).   Prescience has no causative character, but the
cause (*Ursache*) of the salvation of the elect is the divine election (554. 36).   But prescience includes the fact, that God has
" set bound and measure " to those whose wickedness he has
foreseen (705. 6).   It is, of course, to be understood that God,
before the beginning of the world, foresaw who of the called
should believe and persevere in faith, and when his call should
reach each individual and nation, and when it should be withdrawn from them (716. 54 ff.; 708. 23).   (*b*) But the Christian
should confine his attention to the gracious revealed will of God
and avoid all speculation in this field (717 f.; 719. 70; 715.
52 ff.; 706. 9 ff.; 707. 13 f.).   He should further remember that
the " promise of the gospel " is really "universal," *i. e.*, it
" pertains to all men " (709. 28); that the call (*vocatio*) is therefore always sincere (710. 29; 257. 18); and that the Holy
Spirit is always operative in the word as heard (712. 39).   It is
not the divine foreknowledge, but the human will, which is to
blame if the word does not attain its end (713. 41).   The divine
will aims at the salvation of all, and does not desire that any
should perish (555. 12; 722. 83 f.).   (*c*) There is, therefore,
an "eternal predestination " (717. 65).   It is the active will
of God, that all men who believe on Christ shall be saved through
the gospel.   This will is based upon the merit of Christ, not upon
our works (720. 75; 723. 88).   Upon the ground of this eternal will, we may be certain of our salvation; for it rests in the
hands of God (724. 90), and is based " upon his eternal purpose, which cannot fail nor be overthrown " (714. 45).   There

is thus "completely and fully given to God his glory," since
salvation is traced alone to his gracious will (556. 15 ; 723. 87).

Of these propositions, it must likewise be said, that they do not
furnish a conclusion in all respects satisfactory.   Yet their logical consistency is not so obscure as is often thought.   God, by
virtue of his foreknowledge, knows everything which shall ever
happen.   This foreknowledge enables him to set measure and
bound to that which is to happen.   We must distinguish from
this the gracious will of God to save through Christ all who shall
believe.   If this aim be not achieved, the fault lies with man.
This view can, indeed, scarcely be designated predestination in
the strict sense of the term.[1]

12. Article XII. speaks " of Other Factions and Sects," and
recounts the " erroneous articles" of the Anabaptists, the
Schwenkfeldians, and the " new Antitrinitarians."   Here again,
the breach, now put upon record, had long been complete.

13. Such are the doctrinal articles of the Formula of Concord.   They record the conception entertained of Lutheran doctrine in the second generation of the Reformation period, or the
form of Lutheranism which became the basis for the development of Lutheran theology.   Historical investigation can only
record, that the Formula accomplished the purpose which it had
in view.   It presented the fixed results of doctrinal development,
and exhibited in connected form the ideas of Luther and Melanchthon which were influential in that generation.   But, when
compared with the entire scope of Luther's religious and theological ideas, the decision must be, that the Formula of Concord
was not in a position to rescue from neglect and recoin all the
valuable truth—the whole historical material—which Luther had
given to the church.   The contribution which Luther brought to
the church still furnishes material for earnest study.   Evangelical theology must continue to seek, and seeking shall yet find, in

---

[1] 708. 23 : " And God, indeed, by this his counsel, purpose, and ordination
(*i. e.*, that all who believe on Christ shall be saved, vid. ¿ 18), not only pro-
cured the salvation of his own in general, but also mercifully foresaw, all and
each, the persons of the elect who should be saved through Christ, elected
them to salvation, and decreed that . . . he wished through his grace . . . to
make them partakers of eternal salvation . . . to strengthen and preserve
them."   Even this passage does not lead to strict predestination ; for, in the
context in which it is found, it can scarcely mean more than the following :
God, by virtue of his prescience, knows in advance what particular result will
be accomplished by his gracious will, which is in itself considered universal
in its application.   And, just as his prescience in general guides him in the
ordering and directing of all things (vid. supra), so also in this particular
instance, since God takes a particular interest in the guidance and protection
of those whom he foresees as believers.   The connection of this article with
the Strassburg Concord should not be overlooked (supra, p. 378).

the marvelous intuitions of the Reformer's ideas view-points, inspiration, energy, and a renewal of her strength.

CHAPTER II.

COMPLETION OF DOCTRINAL CONSTRUCTION IN THE REFORMED CHURCH.

§ 79. *The Theology of Calvin and its Influence Upon the History of Doctrines.*

SOURCES. CALVIN, Opp. ed. Baum, Cunitz, Reuss (= Corp. Ref. xxix. ff.). We shall have occasion to refer especially to vols. xxix. and xxx. (Institutio religionis christianae), vol. xxxiii. (the catechism), vol. xxxvi. (theol. discussions), vol. xxxviii. (ordonnances écclesiastiques). Upon the life of Calvin, see HENRY, 3 vols., 1835 ff. E. STÄHELIN, 2 vols., 1863. KAMPSCHULTE, J. Calvin, seine Kirche u. sein Staat in Genf., vol. i., 1869. A. LANG, De Bekehrung Joh. Calv., 1897 (Studien z. Gesch. d. Theol. u. Kirche, ed. Bonwetsch u. Seeberg, ii. 1). Upon his theology, vid. KÖSTLIN, Calv. Institutio, in Stud. u. Krit., 1868, 7 ff., 410 ff. RITSCHL, Rechtf. u. Vers. i., ed. 2, 203, 227 ff. SEEBERG (Thomasius, DG. ii., ed. 2), p. 638 ff. LOOFS, DG., ed. 3, 427 ff. A. LANG, Die ältesten theol. Arbeiten Calv., in Neue Jarbb. f. deutsche Theol. ii. 273 ff. SCHWEITZER, Centraldogmen, i. 150 ff. MULLER, De Godsleer von Calvijn, 1881. SCHEIBE, Calv. Praedest.-lehre, 1897. USTERI, Calv. Sakraments u. Tauflehre, Stud. u. Krit., 1884, 417 ff. SEEBERG, Begriff d. Kirche, i. 119 ff. LOBSTEIN, Die Ethik Calvins, 1877. DILTHEY, in Archiv. f. Gesch. d. Philos. vi. 528 ff. ELSTER, Calv. als Staatsmann, Gesetzgeber u. Nationalökonom, in Jarbb. für Nationalökonom, vol. 31. 163 ff.

1. As Zwingli's political plans were frustrated by his death, so the direct influence of his theology also, within a comparatively short time, ceased to be felt. Even men who stood so near to him as BULLINGER accepted his doctrinal views only in their general outline, and proceeded to "deepen" and develop them (see PESTALOZZI, H. Bull., 1858, and cf. USTERI, in Stud. u. Krit., 1883, p. 730 ff.). In the circles in Southwestern Germany in which Zwingli's influence had been particularly felt arose a new theological type, which, with a close adherence to the principles of Luther, combined a certain leaning toward ideas of Zwingli. The most important and active representative of this group was the great compromise theologian, MARTIN BUCER († 1551). Its characteristic features were the following : "The fundamental ideas of the Reformation upon sin, grace, justification, and sanctification were reproduced in harmony with

Luther and Melanchthon. The relation to Luther is incomparably more intimate and evident than was Zwingli's.[1] The assurance of salvation was commonly based upon predestination, or the " gift of perseverance." In the doctrine of the sacraments, and especially of the Lord's Supper, the attempt was made to find a median ground between the views of Luther and Zwingli. The men of this group very earnestly insisted upon referring everything to the Scriptures in a somewhat legalistic way, the statements of the latter being regarded as fixed formulas of doctrine and of ecclesiastical life. With this tendency is closely associated the marked biblical character of the theology in question, as well as the effort by the fuller application of biblical ideas to carry out the principles of the Reformation more completely than had been done upon more strictly Lutheran territory. Standing upon the historic ground of the earlier ideas of reform, and inspired by Erasmian ideals, it was sought to realize the practical ideas of reform by a strict discipline and by benevolent operations and careful church organization, in so far as this appeared possible and desirable within the scope of the evangelical reformation. The church was regarded as the " kingdom of Christ," in which there exists a new covenant (*foedus*) with God. Living under the sovereignty of God, it is proper for us to minister to his glory. As, on the one hand, the entire Christian life became, in the light of this conception, one of active service, so, too, it was thought that the glory of God demands that he alone—and not our works nor any agency other than divine—be recognized as effecting the salvation and life of the church.[2] Hence their advocacy of predestination. Not, indeed, in the form of a connected theological system, but as a practically influential combination of opinions and sentiments, this tendency secured adherents and became a recognized power in the church.

It may be studied most readily in the writings of Bucer. His last publication treats of the Kingdom of Christ, *De regno Christi* (vid. in Scripta Anglicana, Basil, 1577, p. 3-173). This kingdom is an *administratio populi* (p. 3). " The kingdom of our Servitor, Jesus Christ, is an administration and procuring

---

[1] This is plainly seen in Bucer's first publications. The *Summary* of his sermons of 1523 presents in its positive explanations an excellent outline of the fundamental religious conceptions of Luther.

[2] In Bucer, as in Zwingli (supra, p. 312), the thought of the glory of God constantly recurs. How practically pervasive was this idea is indicated, *e. g.*, in the subscription appended by the citizens of Strassburg to a petition, A. D. 1527, for the complete abolition of the mass : " The obedient citizens of your Excellencies, who desire the advancement of the glory of God and of the kingdom of Christ" (in BAUM, Capito u. Butzer, p. 393).

of the eternal salvation of the elect of God, by which he himself,
our Lord and the King of heaven, by his doctrine and discipline
administered through special ministers appointed for that purpose,
. . . gathers his elect to himself and incorporates them in himself
and his church, and in it so governs them that, daily purged more
fully from their sins, they may live well and blessedly" (p. 31).
The elect allow themselves to be guided and governed by the
"ministry regularly constituted (p. 34). The ministry teach, con-
fining themselves strictly to the Holy Scriptures (p. 36).[1] The
first marks of the true church are scripturalness of doctrine and of
the administration of the sacraments ; the third is discipline (p.
40 ff.), to which is added care for the poor (p. 50). The second
Book contains a fully detailed plan for the introduction of the
Kingdom into England.[2] In the Introduction to the exposition of the Epistle to the Romans is found a brief statement of
Bucer's Soteriology.[3] He here also presents at length his view
of predestination (vid. excurs., p. 358 ff.). This is, in the
proper sense, an election to salvation. The practical importance of the doctrine lies in its making known to us " this
certain and immovable will of God concerning our salvation,
which no creature is able to prevent" (p. 358 a, 360 b).
If salvation is based upon the eternal counsel of God, we
may then be sure of it. Predestination leads to the measures
for attaining its end, *i. e.*, vocation, justification, and glorification. He to whom the call is given may, therefore, be
sure of his election (p. 359 b). In a wider sense, predestination in general is traced to the divine pre-determination (*prae-
finitio*); in which sense we may also speak of a " predestination
of the wicked." They, too, have an appointed place in the
divine plan of the world. God knows in advance for what purpose he will use them : " He then ordained and destined them
to these ends, *ad ea* " (p. 358 b). " God foresaw and destined
even these to this lot before he created them. For he does all
things by predeterminate and infallible counsel" (p. 359 a). Predestination is thus utilized in a purely practical way as a means

---

[1] Cf. in the Einleitung zur Enarratio ep. ad Roman. (Argentorat. 1536), p.
19 a : " To this republic the Scriptures are instead of law, for they set forth
and appoint the will of its head concerning all the duties of life."

[2] See also the interesting suggestions for the advancement of farming, industry, and commerce in England, p. 136-140.

[3] *Justificare = absolvere.* We are assured of this pardon of sins, secured
through Christ, by the Holy Spirit, who begets faith in us, but at the same
time subdues evil lust and calls into being a new will (vid. Enar. in ep. ad
Rom., p. 11 ff.). Faith is a "*persuasio* (= πίστις, p. 22 a) of the mercy of
God toward us," p. 14 b, or an *assensus*, not only with the intellect, but also
with the will, p. 15 f. See also briefly in the Epitome doctr. eccles. Argentorat., in Scripta anglicana, p. 173 ff.

in establishing the certainty of salvation. Zwingli's speculative method of theorizing on the subject is foreign to Bucer, nor does he follow Luther's deductions as to the enslavement of the will. As to his doctrine of the Lord's Supper, vid. supra, p. 331, n. 1.[1] These excerpts from Bucer may serve to illustrate the above-noted characteristics. The theological type which they represent—which may be briefly styled Bucerism—is the contemporaneous pendant of Melanchthonian Lutheranism. The ideas of Luther were by Bucer, as by Melanchthon, recast in the forms demanded by his practical aims. The parallel may readily be carried out in detail. In neither of these men, with the tendencies which they represented, was the process developed without omissions and displacements in the Lutheran complex of ideas.[2] But, while it was the fortune of Melanchthon to construct formulas which should dominate the thought of two centuries, Bucerism became but the stepping-stone to Calvinism. Bucer's mediating theology was almost everywhere merged in Calvinism. This did not involve any violence to the former, but was but the transition from a lower to a higher form. Calvin, like Bucer, drew his first inspiration from Luther. Luther's ideas moulded him in a general way as a theologian, and also in his views of particular doctrines.[3] Yet he was a Lutheran only in the same sense as Bucer. Or, we may say, the impulses which made Calvin a theologian and churchman proceed, not only from the influence of Luther, but also from that conception of religion and of the church and her duty which prevailed at Strassburg and which pervades the writings of Bucer. Not only his ethical apprehension of the work of reformation, but his views upon a number of important doctrines—as of the sacraments, particularly the Lord's Supper, of predestination, and of faith—point distinctly to this source. Calvin starts therefore, not with Zwingli, but with Luther,[4] and promotes that conception of the work of the Refor-

---

[1] For the biography of Bucer, see BAUM, Capito u. Butzer, 1860. A worthy presentation of his theology has recently been published by A. LANG. Vid. Das Evangelienkommentar M. Butzers, u. die Grundzüge seiner Theologie (Bonwetsch-Seeberg, Studien zur Gesch. der Theol. u. der Kirche, ii. 2), 1900.

[2] In the doctrine of the Lord's Supper, Melanchthon and his school draw from Bucer.

[3] See LANG, Bekehrung Calvins, p. 47 ff., and the same author's collection of utterances of Calvin concerning Luther in Deutsch-Evang. Blätter, 1896, 322 ff.

[4] Zwingli's significance for the History of Doctrines really consists therefore only in the fact, that he by his energetic opposition prevented the complete dominance of the Lutheran doctrine of the Lord's Supper. The statement of DILTHEY (Archiv. vi., 529, 531), that Calvin drew his inspiration from Zwingli's "freely breathing religious animation" and from his spiritual wealth (*Seelenfülle*), is historically untenable.

mation which originated—not indeed without Zwingiian influences
—in Southwestern Germany, particularly at Strassburg. These historical facts explain the divergence of view from that of the
Wittenbergers upon methods of practical reform (supra, p. 391),
and also the phenomenon, that a Calvinistic church should arise
upon German soil, and, as is acknowledged, win the allegiance
of a number of Melanchthonian Lutherans.[1] As the Calvinistic
type became the dominant one in the Reformed church, it falls
to the province of the History of Doctrines to present an outline
of his teachings. As to their historical relations, the above must
for the present suffice.

2. It is of the first importance, for a proper appreciation
of Calvin, to remember that he is a man of the second generation of this great period. He received his ideas and program
of action by tradition in an essentially complete form. It was
his task, in the church as in theology, to complete and organize—
and for this his special talents also fitted him. Calvin was not
a genius like Luther, nor did he possess the happy balance
of endowment which distinguished Zwingli. Neither was he a
scholar unskilled in the ways of the world, like Melanchthon.
He possessed the wonderful talent of comprehending any given
body of religious ideas in its most delicate refinements and
giving appropriate expression to the results of his investigations.
This made him the greatest exegete of the Reformation period,
and enabled him to accomplish a remarkable work in organizing
the dogmatic materials within reach. As a dogmatician, he
furnished no new ideas, but he with most delicate sense of perception arranged the dogmatic ideas at hand in accordance with
their essential character and their historical development. If
we compare Melanchthon and Calvin, for example, in their views
upon the appropriation of salvation, we shall observe that the former
constructs tenable formulas, while the latter traces the inner relations of spiritual experience. His was a keen and delicate, but not
a creative mind.[2] With these intellectual gifts was combined the
will of a nature born for organizing—the tenacious, imperial
spirit and govermental skill of the ancient Roman. But this was
held in check and guided by the obedience which dedicates the
life to the glory of God, without regard to the demands of the
world.[3] Thus Calvin was just the man to represent most

---

[1] At this point must begin the study of the interesting question of the
genesis of the Reformed Church in Germany.

[2] We may compare Melanchthon and Calvin as dogmaticians, separately and
in their mutual relationship, with the Lombard and Thomas Aquinas.

[3] Cf. C. R. xliii. 738 : "I am not ignorant of what is pleasing or offensive
to the world, but nothing is of more concern to me than to follow the rule
prescribed by the Master."

worthily and effectively the second type of reformatory character which sprung from Luther's prolific principles. That its peculiar characteristics were due in measure to the influence of earlier ideals of reform, has been already observed (p. 391).

3. Our study of the theology of Calvin must be confined to the points bearing particularly upon the history of doctrinal development.[1] Beginning with the source of Christian truth, we find this to be the Holy Scriptures, and they alone. "For the Scriptures are a school of the Holy Spirit, in which, as nothing necessary or useful to know is omitted, so nothing is taught except what it is profitable to know" (iii. 21. 3).[2] God has deposited in them the "oracle" of his truth, and, since they come from heaven, they are endowed with full authority (*plena autoritas*) among men (i. 7. 1). "Belief (*fides*) of the doctrine is not established until we have been indubitably persuaded that *God is its author* " (ib. 4). God first revealed the law, "then followed the prophets, through whom God published, as it were, new oracles." By divine command, the prophets recorded the latter, all of which served for the explanation of the law. "With these came at the same time the histories, which are themselves also productions from the pens of the prophets, but composed under the dictation of the Holy Spirit" (*dictante spiritu sancto*, iv. 8. 6). Then followed the New Testament (ib. 8). Of the authors of these writings, it is said : "They were infallible and authentic amanuenses of the Holy Spirit, and therefore their writings are to be held to be oracles of God" (ib. 9). The truthfulness of these scriptural oracles is therefore established from the fact, that they, together with the historical narratives, were dictated and inspired by the Spirit of God (cf. i. 18. 3).[3] This conviction as to the origin of the Scriptures is confirmed by the testimony of the Holy Spirit, which is effectually given through them, and through the divine majesty which characterizes them (i. 7. 4). Through this unique testimony we become certain of the character of the word (i. 8. 1 ; 9. 3). Thus Calvin establishes the authority of the Scriptures partly upon their divine dictation, and partly upon the testimony of the Holy Spirit working through them. His-

---

[1] We depend, in so doing, chiefly upon the last revision of the *Institutio religionis Christianae*, A. D. 1559. We shall occasionally quote, for the purpose of comparison, from the first edition, A. D. 1536, and from other doctrinal writings of Calvin.

[2] These and similar references indicate books, chapters, and paragraphs of the last edition of the *Institutio*.

[3] HEPPE'S remark in referring to Calvin (Die Dogmatik d. ev.-ref. Kirche, 1861, p. 16 f.): "He is not speaking of any real inspiration in the recording," is not well founded.

torically considered, he thereby combines the later medieval
conception of inspiration (supra, p. 192) with the theory of
Luther.   Calvin is therefore the author of the so-called inspiration theory of the older dogmaticians.[1]   Of the ancient symbols
and decrees of the councils, Calvin says, that they formulated
Biblical truth more exactly in opposition to the heretics (i. 13.
3 f.): "For they contain nothing but pure and native interpretation of the Scriptures" (iv. 9. 8).   He set a high value
upon pure doctrine for the church[2] (ii. 2. 7), but acknowledged
also that no one should forsake his church for the sake of "any
little differences of opinion" (iv. 1. 12).

4. In the doctrine concerning God, the Reformation conception of the Divine Being as omnipotent Will is the controlling
thought.   The divine omnipotence is not to be represented as
alternating between action and non-action, but as in "continual
action."   It is manifested in the divine providence which rules
all things (i. 16. 3).   Calvin meets the charge of Stoic fatalism
by pointing out that the latter rests upon the inviolability of the
natural order of cause and effect, while Christian faith, on the
contrary, refers all events to the determination of the divine
will: "We acknowledge God as the arbiter and director of all
things, who, according to his wisdom, decreed from the most remote eternity what he would do, and now by his power performs
what he has decreed" (ib. 8).   Accordingly, the totality of all
events, as well the course of nature as all that men endure or do,
is referred back to the eternal counsel of God.   In other words,
everything that happens, happens as it does because God so wills.

---

[1] It is just this combination which constitutes the theory in question:
Because there proceeds from the Scriptures an influence of the Holy Spirit
which attests their contents to the heart as truth, their origin must be traced to
the Holy Spirit.   This combination, in itself considered, is open to no
objection.   But, since the inspiration is conceived of as a dictation of the entire
historical material, the proof of it from religious experience cannot be sustained, because this experience can by no means attest all the separate words of
Scripture.   We need not here refer to the objections raised against the theory
by historical criticism.   Calvin writes: "I know how some obscure men
clamor in their little corners to show the keenness of their talents in assailing
the truth of God.   For they inquire, Who will make us very sure that these
things which are read under the names of Moses and the prophets were
written by them?   For they even dare to raise the question whether there ever
was any Moses?   But if anyone should raise a doubt as to whether there ever
was any Plato or Aristotle or Cicero, who would not say that he deserved to
be thrashed with cuffs or lashes?" (i. 8. 9).

[2] This is attested by the sworn confession of faith, based on his catechism,
to be required of the citizens of Geneva (C. R. xxxiii. 355-362).   This contains
in a nutshell a system of dogmatics in a plain and practical form.   No attempt
is made to present the doctrines of the Trinity or Christology in a scholarly
way.

What transpires in the world serves the interest of man, of the church, and of salvation (ib. 6 ; i. 17. 1); but its final purpose is the revelation of the glory and honor of God (i. 16. 1ff.): " That our salvation was a matter of concern to God in such a way that, not forgetful of himself, he kept his glory primarily in view, and therefore created the whole world to this end, that it might be the theatre of his glory " (C. R. xxxvi. 294). The purpose of God therefore extends beyond the salvation of the human race. It follows from the above that even the actions of the wicked must be referred to the divine will. Calvin rejects as frivolous the explanation of these as due to divine *permissio* (i. 18. 2). It is to be said, on the contrary, that the will of God "not only exerts its power in the elect, who are controlled by the Holy Spirit, but also compels the reprobate to obedience " (ib.). The application of these principles in the sphere of the religious life leads to the theory of a double election (vid. sub), namely, that the divine will leads the elect to the goal by caus- ing duly appointed means to work upon them in a determinative way. The elect, accordingly, do not die until they have been regenerated and sanctified (iv. 16. 18). We have thus here, as in Thomas or Zwingli, a religious determinism carried out to its logical conclusions. The cosmic system has been established by God as a complex of means inwardly adapted to the realiza- tion of the end in view. Thus regarded, the adoption of the particular means employed may be maintained as being a rational necessity. Or, where there is an election, the redemption through Christ, the church, and her means of grace are involved in it as necessary means for its realization. This explains the energy of the adherents of these views in prosecuting the work of the church, with her means of grace and her morality ; for these are the means requisite to the carrying out of the divine purpose, which can only thus be realized. But now, as in Luther's treatise upon the Enslaved Will, this logical structure is apparently buttressed, but really broken down, by the introduc- tion of the Scotist idea of the irresponsibility of the divine will. The reason for the introduction of this idea is, as in Luther, easily discovered. By the association of the divine will with a system of earthly means, its absolute freedom and its exalted majesty appear to be endangered. Hence the inner necessity of these means is called in question, and their employment looked upon as a fixed rule indeed, but their selection regarded as accidental, and the original possibility of the adoption of other means or of the abolition of all means asserted : " which means he cer- tainly employs in the calling of many, upon whom he be- stows a true knowledge of himself by the illumination of the

Spirit in an internal way without the intervention of preaching "
(iv. 16. 19 ; 1. 5 in.).   Even of Christ's work it must accordingly be said : " not except by the good pleasure of God could
it merit anything " (ii. 17. 1).[1] The aim of Calvin is clear
from such passages as iii. 23. 2 : " For so truly is the will of God
the highest rule of right, that whatever he wills is, just because
he wills it, to be accounted right. Therefore when it is asked,
why the Lord did thus, the response must be, Because he wished
to do so." God is not, indeed, to be considered lawless (*exlex*),
for his will is the " law of all laws ; " but all seeking for the
ground of any divine appointment is forbidden. Its ground lies
simply in the will of God, as otherwise we would have to acknowledge som thing superior to the divine will (ib., cf. § 5, C.
R. xxxvi. 115). Hence, the election of some men and rejection of others must be traced simply to the unrestrained will of
God[2] (iii. 22. 1). But just at this point this second line of
thought falls into the first. The will of God is alone the ground
of all events. As the ultimate end of all things is fixed by this
Will, so also the means by which that end is to be attained ; but
a rational necessity for the latter cannot from our point of view
be proved or maintained. This conclusion confirms our view of
the relation existing between the two lines of thought,[3] a point
to which we shall recur (¶ 7 e).

5. The Sin of Adam consisted in disobedience (ii. 1. 4). His
sinful character was handed down to his posterity : " From a
corrupt root have sprung corrupt branches." But no good end
can be served by brooding over specific possibilities. It
is the divine appointment, that the sin of Adam should
become the sin of his posterity : " The cause of the contagion lies neither in the substance of the flesh, nor in that of
the soul ; but because it has been thus ordained by God, that
man should hold or lose at the same time both for himself and
for his posterity whatever gifts God had at first conferred upon

---

[1] This passage taken alone is not sufficient to appear in evidence, as we
must grant to SCHEIBE (Calv. Präd.-lehre, p. 110 f.), for it merely asserts
that Christ was " foreordained to the end that he might appease the wrath of
God by his sacrifice." But it must be studied in the light of Calvin's general
apprehension of the subject (vid. ii. 12. 1) and the parallels in Luther's
writings have weight in deciding upon its proper interpretation (vid. supra,
p. 271).

[2] Calvin rejects in this connection the " profane " idea of " absolute
power." But what have we in the above-cited passage, iv. 16. 19, but an
application of this idea that goes even beyond the position of Duns ?

[3] This doctrinal conception of God is inferior to that of Luther in animation and consistent force, if for no other reason, because Calvin assumes a
two-fold source of our knowledge of God, *i. e.*, in the course of nature and
in Christ (i. 2. 1 ; v. 1 f.).

him " (ii. 1. 7).[1] Original sin is defined as " the hereditary depravity and corruption of our nature . . . which first makes us subject to the wrath of God, then also produces in us works which the Scriptures call works of the flesh " (ib. 8). Thus the entire man is depraved : " From the crown of the head to the sole of the foot, not a spark of good can be found " (iii. 14. 1). The natural freedom of the will yet remains, but not as though it had an equally free choice of good and evil, but because it commits evil by free-will and not from coërcion " (ii. 2. 7). There still remain the natural talents, which are requisite for the prosecution of political affairs, science, and art, although they have also become depraved (ii. 2. 12. ff.).[2]

6. The consideration of this our natural condition, combined with the stress of the law (ii. 7. 2 f., 6 ff.), awakens in man the sense of helplessness (ii. 2. 11). Grace alone saves us, through Christ. The purpose of God is the " first cause " of our salvation. He appoints his only-begotten Son to be a "fountain of grace" (ii. 17. 1). Since now it was to be the mission of Christ, both to convince men of the gracious disposition of God toward them, making them his children, and to render satisfaction to the Father in our stead, it was necessary that the Son of God should become man, since for both the purposes indicated both divine and human nature would be required in him (ii. 12. 1-3 ; iii. 11. 9). Yet we cannot speak here of an "absolute necessity," but only of the divine decree by which this was made the method of our salvation (ii. 12. 1).[3] With this general premise, Calvin presents the mediatorial work of Christ under the three aspects of the prophetic, royal, and high-priestly offices (ii. 15). According to Hebr. 1. 1, Christ is the last and perfect revelation of God (ii. 15. 1, 2). Endowed by God with eternal power, he exercises spiritual and eternal dominion over the church. " Such is the character of his government, that he

---

[1] Even here we can trace the influence of the Scotist element in Calvin's conception of God ; but he rejects as insufficient the Scotist definition of original sin, and frames his positive statement of the subject upon Augustinian lines.

[2] But conscience remains to man as the organ of innate natural law : " It is affirmed that the law of God, which we call the moral law, is nothing else than the testimony of the natural law and the inner sense (*conscientiae*) of it which has been inscribed by God upon the hearts of men " (iv. 20. 16. Cf. Luther, supra, p. 247, 243, n. 2). Similarly (ii. 8. 1), where its operation is thus described : " it sets before us the discernment between good and evil, and thus accuses us when we depart from duty."

[3] Calvin warns against " vain speculations," as to whether Christ would have become man if there had been no need of redemption, since the Scriptures present the incarnation as subordinate to the purpose, " that he should, as a victim, make satisfaction to the Father for us " (ii. 12. 4).

may share with us whatever he has received from the Father"
(ib. 4). As priest, finally, he procures for us the grace of God
by making atonement for us through his sacrifice and appeasing
the wrath of the Father (ii. 12. 3 ; 15. 6, *ad placandam iram
dei*). "He poured out his sacred blood as the price of redemption, by which was extinguished the wrath (*furor*) of God
burning against us, and our iniquities also were purged" (C. R.
xxxiii. 339). But this result was achieved by the obedience
covering his entire earthly life (according to Rom. 5. 19). The
latter was manifested both in his sufferings and death, and
(according to Phil. 2. 7) in "the other part of obedience which
he rendered in this life" (ii. 16. 5). In the course of this
obedience, he became an atoning sacrifice (*victima satisfactoria*),
the condemnation merited by our sins being visited upon him
(ib. 6. 5).[1] The enduring of the wrath of God included also
the struggle with eternal death and condemnation : "Whence it
was necessary for him to wrestle, as it were, hand to hand with
the powers of hell and with the horror of eternal death"
(ib. 10). Not alone his body was the price of our deliverance,
"but there was another greater and more excellent price, that
he endured in his soul the dire agonies of condemned and lost
man" (ib.). Discrimination is made between the effects of the
death and of the resurrection of Christ. By the former, "sin
is abolished and death destroyed," while by the latter "righteousness is restored (*reparata*) and life established" (ib. 13).
The ascended Lord ministers in heaven as our *advocatus et
intercessor*, attracting the eye of the Father from our sins upon
his righteousness. He also sanctifies us from heaven by his
Spirit (ib. 16).

If we disregard the three-fold division of the work of Christ,
which, in Calvin's discussions as elsewhere, does not prove
helpful in elucidating the subject, we may trace a clear line of
thought. The human race was, as sinful, subject to the wrath
and curse of God. The God-man endured this wrath and curse
in obedience to the divine will, without perishing beneath the
burden. He thereby secured the forgiveness of sins and abolition of all penalties, as well as the positive bestowal of grace
upon man, which he now, as the Ascended Lord, administers
through the Spirit. This leaves only the question of the existence
of wrath and love together in God. It is, says Calvin, a pedagogical mode of speech, when the Scriptures represent God as the

---

[1] The dominant idea in this connection is that of *satisfaction*. It is only
incidentally that he introduces, in ii. 17, the idea of *merit*, without at all
designing thereby to change the general conception of the subject. Cf.
RITSCHL, Rechtf. u. Vers. ii., ed. 2, 228.

enemy of the sinner (ii. 16. 2). It is however fully justified ; for as God is righteousness, he cannot love sin. As sinners, we rest under his wrath. Yet even thus we are still his creatures, and his love therefore goes out toward us, so that his love became the motive (Eph. i. 4) for the mission of Christ (ii. 16. 3, 4).[1] Love is accordingly the fundamental attitude of God toward the elect of the race. On account of sin, wrath is also awakened, but this is dissipated by the work of Christ which was planned and executed by love (ii. 17. 2). It might here easily have occurred to Calvin to make this work of Christ also the principle of the effectual renewal of the race, but he does not broach this idea.[2] On the contrary, it was clearly his conception, that "God, to whom we were odious on account of sin, was reconciled by the death of his Son, so that he is propitious toward us" (ii. 17. 3). Thus the objective reconciliation of God is the ground of the effectual bestowal of grace. This type of doctrine forms an average presentation of the ideas upon the atonement in the Reformation period.[3]

7. From the work of Christ, Calvin turns to the Application of Redemption to the individual soul. As he describes the course of man's renewal and, in this connection, develops the idea of justification, he not only brings into play his great systematic talent, but reveals especially his profound appreciation of the original aims of Luther. Christ is the Head of the human race. What he by his sufferings and works secured from the Father becomes ours by virtue of fellowship with him (iii. 1. 1). This occurs, however, through the imparting of his Holy Spirit to us: "by the grace and virtue of his Spirit we are made members of him, so that he holds us in union with himself (*sub se*), and we in turn possess him" (ib. 3). (*a*) The essential thing which the Spirit works in us is Faith (ib. 4). By faith we apprehend Christ and his kingdom (iii. 2. 1, 6): "Faith itself is a certain infallible and secure *possession* of those things which have been promised us by God" (ib. 41 ; cf. iii. 3. 1). It is not "a certain assent to the evangelical history," but the apprehending of God revealed in Christ (ib. 1); not the regarding as true that

---

[1] Calvin here follows Augustine. See in Joh. tract., 110. 6.

[2] Cf. the rejection of the idea, that Christ's righteousness is given to us only as an example for imitation, ii. 1. 6.

[3] The theological difficulties connected with this conception are not overcome by Calvin. This will be the more evident, if we remember that here too the idea of the irresponsibility of the divine action appears as a disturbing feature, and if we have in mind the complications inevitably attending the conception of a predestination according to which the work of Christ is available only for the elect.

which the church instructs us to believe,[1] but the recognition of
the fact that God is through Christ gracious to us (ib. 2),
together with the repose of the heart in this assurance (7). We
believe, not only with the understanding, but from the bottom of
our hearts (36). Faith is a "knowledge of the divine will
toward us," united with a firm conviction of the truth of revelation. "But the foundation of this (knowledge) is a presumed
conviction concerning the truth of God" (*praesumta de veritate
dei persuasio*) (6. 14, 15). Thus is derived the definition of
faith : "We may say that it is a firm and certain knowledge
(*cognitio*) of the divine benevolence toward us, which, the truth
of the free promise in Christ having been established, is through
the Holy Spirit revealed to our minds and sealed to our hearts"
(7). Faith is the firm conviction of the grace of God, together
with the sense of repose and security begotten of such conviction. "In short, no one is truly a believer unless, assured
by firm conviction that God is to him a propitious and benevolent Father, he promises to himself all things from the divine
goodness" (16).[2] Upon the ground of this, "it is a firm and
solid confidence (*fiducia*) of the heart, by which we *securely
acquiesce* in the mercy of God promised to us through the
gospel" (C. R. xxxiii. **333** f.). Since this faith is the appropriation of Christ, it not only assures to man the forgiveness of
sins, but also constitutes the beginning of a new life in him.
"Christ cannot be known except in connection with the sanctification of his Spirit. It follows, that faith can by no means be
separated from pious affection" (iii. 2. 8). Thus by faith we are
united to Christ and become partakers of all his gifts and
blessings (ib. 35). It follows, that faith essentially lays hold of
the promises of God ; but it also "obediently accepts his commandments" (29). It is noticeable, further, that Calvin lays
more stress than Luther upon the intellectual element of faith.

(*b*) Faith leads to Repentance (iii. 3. 1), *i. e.*, with faith a
new moral condition is inaugurated (ib. 2).[3] But repentance is
conversion and regeneration extending through the whole life of
the believer. "Thus repentance might be defined to be the

---

[1] This excludes *implicit faith* in the Catholic sense. Yet Calvin acknowledges a kind of implicit faith, in that there may be, as in the case of the disciples, some belief before full enlightenment, though of course only as a *fidei
praeparatio*, or *initium*. See l. c., § 4 f.

[2] The term *persuasio* (conviction) is characteristic of Calvin's expositions of
faith—and was so from the beginning—see C. R. xxix. 56; xxxiii. 334. It
appears to have been derived from Bucer (supra, p. 392 n. 3).

[3] We are therefore not to insert a "space of time" between faith and
repentance. Nor is repentance to be confused with the *timor initialis* which
often precedes the reception of grace, II. 3. 2.

true conversion of our life to God, proceeding from a sincere and serious fear of God, and consisting in the mortification of our flesh and of the old man, and in vivification by the Spirit" (iii. 3. 5). "I interpret repentance therefore with one word . . . regeneration, whose scope is nothing else than that the image of God . . . be re-formed in us" (ib. 9). Repentance is therefore the state of regeneration, and one of its essential elements is faith. Without faith, there can be no repentance (ib. 5). This repentance consists in mortification, or anguish of soul, in view of recognized sin, together with the crucifying of the old man, and vivification, or the "effort to live holily and piously" (ib. 3. 8). Both are results flowing from fellowship with Christ (9). Both penitence and the new moral striving in repentance are wrought through Christ and the blessings of his kingdom (19). The antecedent fear (*timor initialis*) which frequently precedes this state is not to be included under repentance (2). These statements lead us in the path which Luther followed during the controversy upon confession and absolution (supra, p. 238 f.).[1] There is no thought in this connection of the influence of the law.[2] But the Christian possesses this new life only in a constant conflict of self-preservation (ib. 10.). The goal toward which he strives is the actual manifestation of the filial character bestowed upon him (iii. 8. 1). As an external means to the attainment of his goal, the law is mentioned (ii. 7. 12 f.; iii. 19. 2), as also the example of Christ. "He adds, that Christ has been set before us as an example, whose image we should express in our lives" (iii. 8. 3). But the goal of "evangelical perfection" Christians cannot attain in this life; yet it is their duty to strive earnestly to advance upon the road which leads toward it (ib. 5) and, in this way, in obedience to the divine will, to promote the glory of God (iii. 7. 1, 2).[3]

(*c*) Now only does Calvin treat of Justification. This arrangement of topics does not, however, by any means imply that justification is to be understood, as in the Roman Catholic system, as

---

[1] Differently conceived in the first edition of the *Institutio*, where Calvin limits repentance to "mortification of the flesh," denying, however, that the latter can exist without faith (xxx. 149).

[2] In Calvin's doctrine of the law, we are taught that the law fills the sinner with a sense of his unrighteousness, in order that he may feel his need of grace (iii. 7. 6, 8). Since this influence of the law is exerted upon such as yet lack faith (ib. 11. 12), there is always in Calvin's mind a stage of conscious condemnation under the law as an experience preparatory to evangelical repentance—a stage which finds a parallel in the Catholic attrition (cf. supra, p. 251 n.).

[3] In this connection, Calvin treats of evangelical asceticism, iii. 3. 16; iii. 8, cf. iv. 12. 15. See also his critique of Stoic ethics, iii. 8. 9.

a result of effectual grace.   The meaning is, that the fellowship
with Christ which we secure in faith brings to us a *double grace.*
First, on account of his innocence we are reconciled to God ;
and, secondly, " that, sanctified by his Spirit, we may practice
innocence and purity of life " (iii. 11. 1).   In thus understanding justification as intimately connected with the new life springing from faith, Calvin falls back into the original channel of
early Reformation thought.   Justification and sanctification cannot be separated *de facto :* " for, since God really renews for the
practice of righteousness those whom he graciously regards as
righteous, he combines that gift of regeneration with this gracious acceptance."   But it does not follow from this that the two
conceptions dare be confounded, as was done by Osiander (ib.
6 ; cf. iii. 11. 10 ; 16. 1).   Justification is God's regarding of
the sinner for Christ's sake as righteous.   " He is justified by
faith who, shut out from the righteousness of works, apprehends
by faith the righteousness of Christ, clothed in which he appears
in the sight of God, not as a sinner, but as righteous."   It is the
" acceptance by which God regards us, having been received into
his grace as righteous."   It consists, accordingly, in the " remission of sins " and in the " imputation of the righteousness of
Christ " (ib. 2).   The consciousness of righteousness does not,
therefore, at all rest upon the beginnings of the new life or its
works (3. 2), but solely upon the gracious imputation of the
obedience of Christ.   " What else is it to locate our righteousness in the obedience of Christ, than to assert that we are for his
sake alone accounted righteous, because the obedience of Christ
is said to be accepted for us as though it were our own ? " (23).
Although it is thus perfectly clear that the assurance of salvation depends solely upon divine grace, yet it dare not be forgotten that
this assurance can never arise nor be preserved unless there is first
a living fellowship with Christ.   " We may distinguish between
them, yet Christ contains them both (justification and sanctification) in himself.   Dost thou desire therefore to attain righteousness in Christ ?   It is necessary for thee first to possess Christ.
But thou canst not possess (him) unless thou becomest a partaker of
his sanctification, because he cannot be rent asunder and made of
no effect. . . .   It is hence clear how it is true that we are not justified without works, nor yet by works, since in the fellowship (*par-
ticipatio*) of Christ, by which we are justified, is contained sanctification no less than justification " (iii. 16. 1 ; xxxiii. 335).   As
thus with faith the new life is effected in man by the Spirit, there
is at the same time implanted in him an active, ethical principle,
as the organ with which, despite all the imperfections and defects
of the incipient new life, to apprehend the pardoning grace of

God. Believers attain assurance and confidence in God not through the "gift of regeneration—which, as it is always mutilated in this flesh, so also contains in itself mutiform material to awake doubt"—but, "because they are implanted in the body of Christ, they are freely accounted righteous. For, so far as justification is concerned, faith is a merely passive thing, contributing nothing to our conciliating of the grace of God, but receiving from Christ what is lacking in us" (iii. 13. 5 ; cf. 11. 11 ; 14. 9 ff.). This way of regarding the matter is said to give the glory to God, as well as to actually assure rest and peace to us (iii. 13. 1 ff.).[1] It is just as evidently in harmony with the profoundest impulses of the teaching of the Reformation as it surpasses the formulas of the later Melanchthonian doctrine.

(d) For a proper understanding of the evangelical doctrine of justification, it is further necessary to note the significance of Christian liberty, which, for Calvin, implies three things : (1) That from our conception of justification we exclude all thought of legal righteousness (iii. 19.2). (2) That we obey God, not under the pressure of the law, but willingly (ib. 4 ; cf. ii. 7. 14). (3) That we do not allow the religious life to be bound or determined by any external things or *adiaphora* whatsoever (ib. 7); although the law teaches us to recognize really good works (ii. 8. 5).

(e) Calvin concludes this presentation of the order of salvation[2] with a discussion of Election. The place thus assigned in itself reveals the practical interest which he felt in this doctrine. Man can be certain of his salvation only if the latter is founded upon the eternal will of God ; and this certainty is but increased by the fact, "that he does not choose all for the hope of salvation, but gives to some what he denies to others" (iii. 21. 1). But with this is combined another thought, arising from the conception of the divine nature. According to the doctrine of Determinism, all things that occur must be understood as caused by the divine determination. But the call to salvation fails entirely to reach some, and with others it is ineffectual. In both cases, the cause must be located in the divine will (ib. 1 init.). This explains the importance attached by Calvin to the doctrine of predestination. He defines the term as follows : "We call the eternal decree of God by which he has determined with him-

---

[1] The *efficient* cause of salvation is, therefore, the mercy of God ; the *material* cause, Christ with his obedience ; the *formal* or *instrumental* cause, faith, iii. 14. 17.

[2] Prayer is treated of (iii. 20), between Liberty and Election, as the principal exercise of faith " and as the daily means for the reception of divine blessings.

self what he wishes to have come to pass concerning every man, predestination. For not all are created under the same condition (*condicio*), but to some eternal life is foreordained, and to some eternal damnation. Therefore, accordingly as anyone has been formed for one or the other end, we say that he has been predestinated to life or to death " (ib. 5). When, therefore, God wins for himself particular men by calling, justification, and sanctification, this achievement accomplished in time is an expression of his eternal will. But it is just as truly an expression of his will, when this does not occur in the case of others, but in its place a devoting to destruction (*exitio devovere*) (ib. 7). But it is impossible to refer the election and not the reprobation to a positive act of the divine will (iii. 23. 1 ; ib. 8 : "Why do we say 'permit' unless because he wills?"), which is evident enough in view of the determinism of the system. Just as God has chosen some, he has also rejected all those whom he has seen fit (C. R. xxxvi. 109). On the other hand, the Scotist element in the conception of God (supra, p. 397) here asserts itself, since the only reason which can be assigned for the election of some and the reprobation of others is the purely arbitrary will of God (ib. 2. 5). But if God thus foreordains the final destiny, together with the means which bring it about, then must the first occasion for this evil destiny of man have also been foreordained by him, *i. e.:* "God not only foresaw the fall of the first man and the ruin of his posterity in him, but appointed it by his own will." In general, it is his special prerogative " to rule and govern all things by his hand" (ib. 7). His will is "the necessity of things." He willed that Adam should fall, and that all the misery of sin should descend upon his posterity. Why he so wills we know not. This does not, however, in Calvin's view, exclude the opinion that man of himself found occasion for the fall, and by it became guilty : " Therefore man fell, the providence of God so ordaining ; but he fell by his own fault " (8 ; cf. xxxvi. 110). All attempts to cast reproach upon God in view of this double election must fail, because no one has authority to coërce the divine will, and because no wrong is done to sinners by their reprobation. The justice of God is made manifest in them, as his mercy in the elect (11 f.).

Calvin's theory of predestination goes beyond that of Bucer in that it lays special stress upon the double predestination. His view embraces chiefly the following points : (1) The idea that everything which occurs on earth is a direct result of divine causality. Hence the divine call with its results is but the carrying out of predestination (iii. 24. 1, 10). Only the elect attain to real faith (iii. 2. 11); and they alone receive the gift of perseverance and gain the assurance of salvation (iii. 24. 6).[1] In this way the sole sovereignty of God and his glory and honor are displayed in all earthly events (vid. citations in SCHEIBE, C's Praedestinationslehre, p. 115 ff.). (2) Thus our salvation, being based upon the eternal will of God, is absolutely assured. (3) Predestination embraces a double election : that in some men only the divine justice, while in others his mercy also is made manifest, has no other ground than the will of God. At this point we observe a Scotist influence moulding the thought.[2]

If we now seek to estimate the significance of this doctrine in the Calvinistic theology, it is not correct either to see in it his "central dogma" (SCHWEIZER, Centraldogmen, i. 57), or to pronounce it an "appendage" attached to the doctrine out of regard for the authority of Paul (RITSCHL, Jarbb. f. deutsche Theol., 1868, 108). It is not the former, as the doctrines of redemption and justification are not deduced from it ;[3] nor the latter, as exegetical considerations have but a subordinate place in this connection. It is, however, true that this doctrine has for Calvin an entirely different significance than for Luther. For both it is a subsidiary conception. Calvin bases upon it the certainty of salvation ; Luther, the sinner's lack of liberty.[4] But this conception found in Calvin an important point of attachment in his idea of God as the Almighty Lord, who works all things, and to whose glory all things minister. The God of Luther is the Almighty Loving-will revealed in Christ. As Calvin's thought was not controlled by Luther's vivid sense of Christ, so, in his conception of God, sovereignty and omnipotence assumed the place of prominence rather than love. It was to him not an intolerable thought, that God, for the display of his justice, never felt any love whatsoever for a portion of the human race. From this, it may be readily understood that predestination should have con-

---

[1] At this point is seen the injustice of the charge brought against Calvin, that this doctrine leads to moral indifference ; for God is represented as working effectually in the predestinated to the end of the sanctification, so that predestination is the most powerful stimulus to the new life, iii. 23. 12.

[2] This is the case when Calvin appeals only to the divine *will* as such (iii. 23. 2); but he also at times pointed to the inscrutability of the divine purposes to the human intelligence (*e. g.*, iii. 21. 1 ; C. R. xxxvi. 10). This is evidently another thought. In the former case, the course of events, being determined by the will of God, is without cause and incomprehensible : here, being divine, it is inscrutable by the finite reason. In the one instance, Calvin may be said to be Scotist in conception ; in the other, Thomistic or Augustinian.

[3] Let it be observed, *e. g.*, that predestination is not in itself justification, but the latter becomes a reality only in those who believe.

[4] Luther used predestination chiefly as an argument against the Pelagian doctrine of sin ; Calvin, against the Pelagian doctrine of grace.

tinually grown in importance for him, and that the theologians
who attached themselves to him should have made it the first principle of their theology.[1] Compare SCHEIBE, C's Praedestinationslehre, p. 117 f.

8. The doctrine of the Church logically follows the discussion
of the redemption wrought by Christ and its attainment through
the Holy Spirit. (*a*) The Church is the totality of all the predestinated (iv. 1. 2, 7 : "it comprehends, not only the sanctified who dwell upon earth, but all the elect who have existed
from the beginning of the world"), as well as also the totality
of all those who have been led by the Holy Spirit to fellowship
with Christ (ib. 3 fin., 7). This coördination of the elect and
the sanctified may be understood when we remember that election is realized in the individual through sanctification. The
elect have now a desire to influence one another. In this way
the church becomes also a communion : "in order that they
may mutually distribute among themselves whatever blessings
God confers upon them" (ib. 3). This takes place through
external means, *i. e.*, word and sacrament, which human weakness requires and which God has therefore bestowed upon the
church (ib. 1) : "God inspires faith in us, but by the agency
(*organo*) of his gospel." In harmony with this, the development of the believer is secured only "by the tuition of the
church" (5). Thus the entire empirical activity of the church is
brought into the relation of a means to the work of salvation implied in predestination. (*b*) The church, as the totality of the *elect*,
is invisible and an object of faith.   But, inasmuch as the elect are
found in an empirical communion, which has its marks in the profession of faith in God and the true doctrine, in a common participation in baptism, the Lord's Supper, and works of love, as
well as in the maintenance of the office of the ministry, we are
to acknowledge also a visible church, which includes hypocrites
among its members. We are to believe in the former; of the
latter, it is said : "we are commanded to respect it, and to cultivate its communion" (7). Since this attitude toward the visible
church is required on account of its recognized aim, the title
"church" in the creed may also be applied with some reservation (*aliquatenus*) to the visible church (3 init.). Further, we
may always from the presence of word and sacrament infer the
presence of an actual church, as the former can never remain fruitless (ib. 9, 10). Severance from the (visible) church is, therefore, also a denial of God and Christ (10). This view of the

---

[1] This point requires further elucidation through historical research;
Ritschl's investigations are here not satisfactory.

church approaches that of Luther, as the attempt is here also made to deduce from the presence of the means of grace the assurance that the true church is likewise present. But there remains the difference, that for Luther grace is always effectually present with the means of grace, whereas Calvin—influenced by his conception of God—regards the external means of grace as, after all, merely symbols of a possibly accompanying divine influence (ib. 6; iv. 14. 8; 16. 19). Since there is, accordingly, such a thing as a proclamation of the word without an accompanying influence of the Holy Spirit, the motto: "Where the word, there the church," has not the profound basis for Calvin which it finds in the teaching of Luther.

(*c*) But Calvin always antagonized with the greatest energy the conclusion which sectarian leaders might easily deduce from his premises, that the external organization of the church is of small importance. He emphasized the necessity of ecclesiastical forms and ordinances more strongly than Melanchthon himself. The administration of the means of grace and the preservation of pure doctrine necessitated the divine appointment of definite ecclesiastical offices. "For this reason it has seemed good that the spiritual government, such as our Saviour has indicated and appointed by his word, should be reduced to good form. . . . First, there are four orders, or kinds of offices, which our Saviour has appointed for the government of his church: namely, pastors; then teachers; after that, elders; fourthly, deacons" (xxxviii. a. 92 f.; cf. 15 ff.). Christ has, therefore, instituted "a ministry of men . . . as it were a vicarious work" (iv. 3. 1); "he has shown the human ministry which God employs for the governing of the church to be the chief nerve by which believers are held together in one body" (iv. 3. 2). It is not an ideal plan of organization, resulting with historical necessity from the nature of the tasks assigned, which here confronts us, but a divine commandment, *i. e.*, a precept of the old divinely-ordained ecclesiastical law. It must be remembered, further, that these officers have not only the duty of preaching, teaching, and the care of the poor; but, above all, the duty of exercising Christian discipline. "Just as the saving doctrine of Christ is the soul of the church, so this discipline stands for its strength (*pro nervis*)." Discipline restrains the opponents of Christian doctrine; it is the goad for the indolent and the rod for the erring (iv. 12. 1). The consistorium, composed of spiritual and lay-elders, or the "assembly of the elders," exercises the disciplinary power, which includes that of excommunication (ib. 2). Upon the particulars of this authority it is not the province of the History of Doctrines to enter.

But it is important to recognize clearly the fact, that Calvin believed in a divinely-appointed form of church government. Cf. SOHM, Kirchenrecht, i. 648 ff. CORNELIUS, in Abhandl. d. bayr. Akad. der Wiss. Hist. Cl., vol. xx., 1893, 251 ff.

(*d*) Since the church has, in this way, a form of government given by God himself and therefore immutable, the sphere of her independence of the state is a wider one than upon the territory of the Saxon reformation. But even in Geneva the idea of Calvin was but imperfectly carried out,[1] since the state retained in its hand as well the regulation of the ecclesiastical judicatory as the confirmation of the election of clergymen; and further-more, the extension of moral discipline required an enlarged co-operation of the state in the sphere of religion and morals. Calvin, therefore, found it possible to carry out his ideas of re-form only by regarding the civil authority as the agency for the exercise of Christian discipline, or by ascribing to the state the duty, in its service of God, of putting into execution the ideals of the church even by worldly means.[2] "And it is the duty of the chief magistrates to consider whom they serve in their office, and not to permit any harm to the ministers and vicars of God. But their whole care should properly lie in this, that they may preserve the public form of religion unpolluted, that they may mould the life of the people by the best laws, and that they may secure the prosperity and tranquillity of their realms both publicly and privately" (C. R. xxxiii. 354; cf. iv. 20. 3, 2). The state is therefore under obligation to punish every uprising against the recognized religion, and to be solicitous for the observance of the commandments, not only of the second table of the decalogue, but of the first table as well. This is attested not only by the history of the Israelites, but even by the view of heathen nations, which makes the guarding of piety the first duty of the state (iv. 20. 3, 9). Of course, in so doing the state dare make no change in the divine law (ib. 3). In reality, it will therefore only be required to carry out what is prescribed by the incumbents of the spiritual offices. From this point of view we can understand the personal attitude assumed by Calvin in Geneva, as well as the drastic rigor of the government and its administration under his leadership. Since every sin is an act

---

[1] "The consistent application of Calvin's ideas of church government first became possible in those Reformed churches which were compelled to develop their polity in opposition to the authority of the State." SOHM, KR. i. 655 f.; cf. WEBER, Geschichtl. Darstellung d. Calvinism. im Verhältnis zum Staat, 1836.

[2] It must here be borne in mind that Calvin most strenuously discriminated *in principle* between the "spiritual kingdom of Christ" and the "civil government."

of rebellion against the divine majesty, it is also to be visited
with the severest civil penalties (cf. ELSTER, Jarbb. f. National-
ökon., vol. 31, p. 182 ff., 207 ff.).[1] Hence, Calvin's reformation was conducted after the manner of the theocracy. God is
the Lord, whose worship the church desires and the state compels. But, inasmuch as this attitude of the civil government
toward the church in the end coincides with the ecclesiastical
office endued with divine authority, the coincidence of Calvin's
ideal of the church with the conceptions of the Middle Ages is
yet far more evident than in the case of Zwingli.[2] And in this
parallel we are confirmed by observing the narrow spirit, hostile
to all natural enjoyment and social pleasure, which marked the
civil administration of Calvin (vid., *e. g.*, the laws concerning
luxury in Gaberel, hist. de l'église de Genève, i., 1858, p.
339 ff.). It is manifest, therefore, that the enlarging of the
reformatory aims of Luther was accomplished only by re-adopt-
ing the ideals of the Middle Ages.

9. We are led to consider, finally, the doctrine of the Sacraments. Calvin defines a sacrament as an " external symbol by
which the Lord seals to our consciences the promises of his benevolence toward us, and we, in turn, . . . testify our piety toward him " (iv. 14. 1). The sacrament itself is thus a symbolic
confirmation of the grace announced in the words of institution (ib. 4). But it is more—a sure pledge of his grace (7).
It confirms to us what the word has taught us (8). But the
sacrament in itself is just as little accompanied by the Spirit of
God as is the word. The Spirit follows the word and sacrament, and only where this inner teacher (*interior magister*) inwardly opens, moves, and enlightens the heart, do they bring
grace to man (ib. 8-12 ; cf. Consens. Tigur. 16). Hence, for
the unbelieving, they are merely signs without content (15).
Here again the idea of predestination asserts itself—only the pre
destinated receive anything through the sacrament. In them
God works immediately, just as all things are only means

---

[1] C. R. xli. 76 : "The great and enormous corruptions which I see everywhere constrain me to beseech you to have solicitude that men may be kept in
strict and honest discipline. Above all, the honor of God is maintained in
punishing the crimes of which men have not been accustomed to take much
account. I say it, since larcenies, fightings, and extortions will sometimes be
severely punished, because men are injured. Yet they will suffer lewdness,
adultery, drunkenness, and blasphemy of the name of God, either as lawful
things or as of very little importance. Now we see, on the contrary, in what
esteem God holds them. He declares how precious his name is to him. It
is not possible then that he should allow such wrongs to be unpunished."

[2] Although, of course, even in Calvin's view this office has no authority to do
more than maintain and execute the commandments of the Bible. But this
does not essentially transcend the limits of the theory of the Middle Ages.

through which his agency is exerted.   Not to them, but to God alone, belongs the glory (12).

(b) Baptism is "like some sealed diploma " and testifies to us the forgiveness of sins (iv. 15. 1).   The recollection of his baptism serves the believer therefore as a standing testimonial, that God will forgive us our sins (3).   It thus takes the place of the Romish sacrament of repentance (4).   Baptism, further, introduces us into fellowship with Christ, with his death and resurrection, for our *mortification* and *vivification* (5).   Through it we become partakers of all the blessings of Christ (6).   As in his general view of the sacraments, so also here in his doctrine of baptism, which is in thorough harmony with the former, Calvin goes further than Zwingli.   While the latter regarded the sacraments as purely symbolical, there was, in the view of Calvin, a real divine energy connected with the administration of these symbols.[1]   But this energy is not involved in the mere external ceremony, but accompanies it—only, however, in the case of the predestinated.   This view thus becomes in form analogous to the Scotist theory of the sacraments (see p. 127),[2] except that with Calvin the accompanying divine energy is limited to the elect.

(c) We find that in Calvin also, as so frequently in other cases, the doctrine of the Lord's Supper oversteps to a certain extent the limits of the general definition of the sacraments.   In this sacrament we receive the body of Christ, "in order that, as we see ourselves made partakers of it, we may assuredly believe that the virtue of his vivifying death shall become efficacious in us." It is, as it were, a reminder of the covenant established through the blood of Christ (iv. 17. 1).   As bread and wine become one with us and nourish our bodily life, so the Lord's Supper effects a real spiritual fellowship with Christ, which nourishes our soul (ib. 3. 5).   As we receive the body of Christ, we experience the continuous efficacy of his sacrifice, and his blood as a "perpetual drink."   There is, therefore, here a real presence of Christ, even a presence of his corporeal nature (*Leiblichkeit*):

---

[1] An evidence of this is seen in Calvin's idea, that, in the case of children, regeneration is effected in an initial way by baptism without the word : "We confess that the word of the Lord is the one and only seed of regeneration ; but we deny that it is to be inferred from this that infants cannot be regenerated by the power of God, which is to him as easy and plain as it is to us incomprehensible and wonderful" (iv. 16. 18).   Why should not God, since he can awaken faith even without the word, bestow also upon children "some share of his grace," or a certain knowledge of God, "the full abundance of which they are soon after to enjoy ? " (ib. 19).   Cf. Luther, supra, p. 285, n. 2.

[2] As Duns denies that God binds his power to the sacraments (p. 127), so Calvin says : "No power is by us located in created things " (iv. 14. 12).

"I declare that in the mystery of the Supper through the symbols of bread and wine *Christ is truly offered to us*, even as to his body and blood" (11). It is not sufficient to speak merely of a spiritual fellowship with Christ, since he has designated his flesh and his blood as veritable food (7). Christ, coming from heaven, has infused into his flesh his life-giving energy, "in order that thence the communication of life might extend to us" (8). From his flesh, life flows into us as from a gushing fountain (9). But the body of Christ is now far removed from us in space: how then can his flesh come to us and serve us as food? This occurs through the "secret power of the Holy Spirit: therefore what our mind does not comprehend, faith accepts, *i. e.*, that the Spirit truly unites things which are separated in localities." We must, therefore, believe that where the visible symbols are offered to us, "the body itself is also certainly given to us" (10; cf. C. R. xxxvii. 72). The reception of the body takes place therefore by means of faith (5, 11, 32).

Accordingly, Calvin teaches a real presence of Christ,[1] which is mediated through the symbols of the bread and wine—he even speaks of a presence and energy of the body of Christ. But it is, according to 1 Cor. x. 16, a κοινωνία of the body of Christ: "but a communication is something different from the body itself" (22). We do not receive the body of Christ, "but all the blessings which Christ has offered to us in his body" (C. R. xxix. 123). If we would understand this view, as contrasted with that of Luther, we must bear three things in mind: (1) That the "substance" of the sacrament is "Christ, with his death and resurrection." (2) That the "prodigious ubiquity" is unconditionally excluded. If we do not wish to volatilize the body of Christ into a phantasm, we must firmly maintain his circumscribed local existence in heaven (12, 26, 29, 30). (3) That, in strict consistency with the above, the presence of the body of Christ is to be represented as a presence mediated by the Spirit to faith, yet in such a way that "the flesh itself of Christ does not enter into us" (10, 32). Calvin's view is, therefore, clear. Christ is present in the Supper as he who in his body and through it has accomplished our salvation: his power (*potentia*) and efficacy (*virtus*) as Redeemer is present. "He is always present with his own, breathing into them his life; he lives in them, sustains them, confirms them, quickens them, keeps them safe, *not otherwise than* if he were present in body: finally, indeed, he feeds them with his very body, the commu-

---

[1] He expressly guards himself against the misunderstanding: "As though, when I say that Christ is received by faith, I should wish to be understood as meaning only by the mind and the imagination" (ib. 11).

nion of which he infuses into them by the power of his Spirit. In this way the body and blood of Christ are offered to us in the sacrament'' (18). The difference between this doctrine and that of Luther is manifest. However emphatically Calvin maintains the earlier position of Luther, that the significance of the body of Christ consists in the presence, as a pledge to us, of him who has suffered for us (supra, p. 287 f.), yet the difference is always equally manifest—Calvin having in mind the spiritual influence, and Luther the real bodily presence. When the question is raised, whether Calvin's doctrine of the Lord's Supper is nearer to that of Luther or to that of Zwingli, the decision is usually, under confessional bias, given in favor of the latter opinion.[1] But when it is remembered that, in contrast with Zwingli's purely subjective commemorative view, Calvin maintains both a special '' presence of the living Christ'' (Apol., vid. supra, p. 342) and the religious influences exerted by it, quite in the spirit of Luther,[2] the conclusion may, nevertheless, be reached, with due account of the differences above noted, that in his religious conception of the sacrament Calvin stands nearer to Luther than to Zwingli.[3] Calvin himself pronounced Zwingli's theory of the sacraments profane (C. R. xxxix. 438). The words of institution are, according to Calvin, to be understood as a metonomy, somewhat as circumcision is called a covenant ; the Rock, Christ ; the Old Testament sacrifices, atonements. But '' it does not only represent, as a bare and empty token, but also truly offers'' (ib. 21). Such is Calvin's doctrine of the Lord's Supper. It affords additional evidence of his dependence upon Luther in his apprehension of religious truth.

10. The significance of Calvin for the History of Doctrines lies in the fact, that his view of Christianity and the church expresses in classical completeness the conception of the Reformation which prevailed in Switzerland and Southwestern Germany. To the wide acceptance which this type of doctrine gradually

---

[1] SCHWEIZER, Glaubenslehre d. ev.-ref. Kirche, ii. 656. HAGENBACH, DG., ed. 6, 556. THOMASIUS, DG. ii., ed. 2, 550, 554 f.

[2] The sacrament not only brings the fullness of the gifts of Christ and fills us with the assurance of eternal life, '' but it even makes us secure in regard to the immortality of our flesh '' (ib. 32); it also lays upon us the duty of brotherly love (44).

[3] This also throws light upon the relation of Bucer's theory and the later teaching of Melanchthon to Luther. For Luther's mild judgment of Calvin and his doctrine of the Lord's Supper, vid. STÄHELIN, C. Leben, i. 226 f. Luther firmly maintained his own position to the last, notwithstanding the well-known utterance said to have been made to Melanchthon. See KÖSTLIN, Luther, ii., ed. 4, 627 f., and Stud. u. Krit., 1875, 373 ff., as also DIESTELMANN, Die letzte Unterredung Luther's mit Mel. üb. d. Abendmalsstreit, and especially HAUSSLEITER, Neue kirchl. Ztschr., 1898, 831 ff.

attained, we can here merely refer in passing.[1] The close connection between Calvin's conception of the central ideas of Christianity and Luther's underlying thoughts need not be further
emphasized.   We must not allow the confessional conflict of the
following century to obscure for us the important fact, that the
two types of Reformation doctrine which gained ascendancy in
Protestantism, *i. e.*, the type of Luther and Melanchthon and
that of Bucer and Calvin, are in essential accord in their understanding of faith and works, of justification and atonement, of
repentance and sanctification, in their recognition of the dogmas
of the ancient church, as well as in their rejection of the Roman
Catholic Pelagianism and hierarchism.   At the same time, the
differences must not be overlooked.   But it is not correct, so
far as I am able to judge, to attribute these differences to a
religious conception begotten upon the territory of the church as
remoulded by the Reformation.   Rather are they sufficiently
explained—when studied from the purely historical point of
view—as the preservation and propagation, upon the territory of
the so-called Reformed Church, of ideals and doctrines of the
pre-reformation period.   This is true, for example, (1) of the
aim and scope of the assumed task of practical reform, which included a reformation of the moral life, to be enforced with
stringency and finding its justification in positive biblical ordinances, and also a thorough revision and revolution of the
ecclesiastical system.   (2) In this undertaking, the ecclesiastical
offices ordained of God come into prominence; a covenant
must be formed between the civil authority and the church,
which involves a subordination of the former to the ordinances
of the latter.   (3) The prevalent ideal of a practical life frequently betrays a relationship with the medieval renunciation of
the world and of the natural impulses.   (4) The Scriptures, as the
source of authority for the conduct of the reformation sought,
are verbally inspired ; both ideas being, as we have seen (supra,
p. 169 172, 192, ff.), embraced in the theory of the later
Middle Ages.   (5) The conception of the sacraments is related
to the ideas of Erasmas, and reminds us of the Scotist-Nominalist
theory.   (6) The difference in the doctrine of the Lord's
Supper rests chiefly upon the adherence to the Augustinian and

---

[1] The influence of Calvin as a theologian upon his church exceeds that
exerted by Melanchthon, and even by Luther, in a similar respect upon their
followers ; for it may be said, that *his theology has become the accepted doctrine of the Reformed Church.*   Nearly all the later confessions reproduce his
formulas, and we may hence pass them by with slight notice.   Calvin did not
leave behind him questionable coins, as did Melanchthon ; nor, on the other
hand, like Luther, uncoined gold.

Scholastic idea of the corporeal nature of Christ as transported to a heavenly place. (7) Even the determinism, which is a natural outcome of the conception of God, is no new discovery, but is the common factor in a number of reformatory movements appearing in the Western church since the days of Augustine. We need but briefly point to the Thomistic and Scotist elements which appear concurrently.

It is precisely in this conception of the nature of God—more in the practical, unwritten conception than in the theoretical formulas—that we find the basis of the peculiar character of the Reformed view, and at this point accordingly begins the divergence from the Lutheran view. God is, to pious minds in the Reformed church, the Lord who rules omnipotently.[1] The development of the universe is the product of his sovereign will ; its goal his honor or glory. But the sovereignty of God is displayed above all through the "Law," which controls all life and all its ramifications. All that is and is done in the world, everything personal and natural, must subserve this end. Obedience is the whole content of life. Natural inclinations are bent and crushed beneath the pressure of the "law ;" the state and society at large are agencies for its enforcement. There is something "unmodern" in this magniloquent portrayal of the energy of obedience and the fanaticism of submission. We always, when we allow the system as a whole to make appeal to us, receive an impression of a piety in keeping with that of Augustine and the Middle Ages. This impression is often confirmed in a startling way by the history of the Reformed Church. This history rests upon a foundation-wall of holy zeal, and a cloud of strong-willed witnesses overshadows it. But the gospel, as it appears in Paul and John, we find in clearer and brighter form in Luther than in Calvin. The God of Calvin is the omnipotent Will, ruling throughout the world ; the God of Luther is the omnipotent energy of Love manifest in Christ. In the one case, we have acts of compulsion even in the heart, subjection, law, service ; in the other, inward conquest by the power of love, free self-surrender, filial love without compulsion. The one does not necessarily exclude the other ; but the tone and emphasis give rise to the differences which undeniably exist. From the practical energy of the Reformed ideals—with which praxis has not always been able to keep pace—the Lutheran church may learn a valuable lesson. But when, in any age of

---

[1] *E. g.*, Heidelb. Cat., Niemeyer, p. 398 : What dost thou understand by the providence of God ? The almighty and ever-present power of God, by which he still upholds and also governs heaven and earth, together with all created things, as with his hand.

evangelical Christianity, faith grows dim, and love grows cold, and it seems as though the gospel were no longer sufficient to satisfy the advanced spirit of the "modern" world, then will deliverance be found, not in the views of Calvin, but in return to the gospel and the faith of Luther.[1] Evangelical Christianity has yet much to learn from her Luther.

§ 80. *The Triumph of Calvin's Doctrine of the Lord's Supper.*

LITERATURE. NIEMEYER, Collect. confessionum in ecclesiis reformatis, 1840. HUNDESHAGEN, Conflikte des Zwinglianismus, Luthertums u. Calvinismus in d. bern. Landeskirche, 1842. PESTALOZZI, Bullinger, 1858, p. 229 ff., 373 ff. STÄHELIN, Calvin, ii. 91 ff.

1. Luther's severe condemnation of Zwingli in his "Kurz. Bekenntnis vom h. Sakr.," 1545, induced Bullinger to revive the Zwinglian doctrine of the Lord's Supper in the baldest form ("Warhaftes Bekenntnis der Diener der Kirche zu Zurich"). At about the same time, a series of conflicts arose in the church at Berne in consequence of the demand of the Council that all pastors should accept the Zurich doctrine of the Lord's Supper. Calvin took a hand in the controversy, as he had a large number of adherents in the territory of Berne. Under his influence, the CONSENSUS TIGURINUS appeared in A. D. 1549, setting forth the doctrine as agreed upon between Bullinger and Calvin.[2]

2. The Consensus, while bringing the doctrine in outward form nearer to the position held by Zwingli, is in substance Calvinistic. The sacraments are signs of recognition and commemoration (art. 7). Yet these signs are not empty, but accompanied by God with special exertions of his energy. With the sacramental signs the believer also really receives Christ with all spiritual gifts (9). More precisely speaking, this is true only in the case of the elect (16, 17). A bodily presence of Christ is to be rejected (21, 24). The words of institution are to be understood figuratively (*figurate*, 22).

3. The Reformed Confessions did not here depart from the

---

[1] I cannot therefore agree with K. MÜLLER (Symbolik, 540), who regards it as "certain" that in the evangelical church of the future "the spirit of the general Evangelical Reformed Church will be in the ascendancy," since Luther's contributions to the church "were substantially already adopted in the sixteenth century." Müller has moreover acknowledged that in a certain sense the Reformed Church stands nearer to Roman Catholicism than does the Lutheran (p. 387 A.).

[2] This document is pronounced by E. Stähelin (Calv. ii. 121): "the solemn act by which the Zwinglian and Calvinistic reformations were joined in everlasting wedlock as the one great Reformed church.

27

teachings of Calvin. The sacraments are efficacious signs (*effi-cacia signa*) of grace (39, art. 35). Accordingly, with the recep-tion of the bread and wine, there is an impartation of grace, not only in that we are thereby enabled to realize the sacrifice of Christ upon the cross, but also : " that he himself feeds and re-freshes my soul to eternal life with his crucified body and shed blood as certainly as I receive . . . the bread from the hand of the administrator" (Heidelb. Cat., Niemeyer, p. 409). Be-lievers " through the Holy Spirit receive also the flesh and blood of the Lord, and are by these nourished (*pascuntur*) unto eter-nal life" (Conf. Helv. poster. a. 21). The body and blood of Christ are thus really received, but by the soul in faith, their presence being secured by an operation of the Holy Spirit. When, *e. g.*, the Gallican Confession (a. 36) teaches : "nourishes and vivifies us with the substance (*substantia*) of his body and blood," this is at once (a. 37) explained to mean that the body and blood are food and drink of the soul, as the bread and wine of the body (cf. Westminster Conf. c. 29. 7 ; 39 a. 28. Conf. Belg., Scot. i., Niemeyer, p. 386, 352). This is the Cal-vinistic doctrine.

§ 81. *Fundamental Evangelical Principles in the Later Confes-sions of the Reformed Church.*

Sources. Cf. Niemeyer, l. c. K. Müller, Symbolik, 1896, p. 415 ff., 445 ff.

1. The later Reformed Confessions all distinctly display the controlling influence of the spirit of Calvin (cf. Conf. Gallicana, 1559. Conf. Czengerina, 1557. Conf. Belgica, 1566. The 39 Articles, 1562. Conf. Scoticana prior, 1560. Conf. Helve-tica posterior, 1566. Heidelberg Catech., 1563. Westminster Conf., 1646. Declaratio Thoruniensis, 1645). Of these vari-ous confessions, the Heidelberg Catechism, the Westminster Con-fession, and the Later Helvetic Confession attained the greatest authority.

2. The fundamental evangelical ideas find clear expression in these writings. For the sake of the satisfaction and obedience of Christ, God forgives the sins of those who believe on Christ and regards them as righteous : " God, without any merit of mine, out of pure grace, bestows upon and imputes to me the perfect satisfaction, righteousness, and holiness of Christ, as though I had never committed any sin and had myself rendered all the obedience which Christ has rendered for me, if I only accept such benefit with a believing heart" (Heidelb. Cat., p. 405 f.;

cf. Helv. 15, 16.   West. Conf. 8. 5 ; 11. 1, 3).[1]   God works
faith through the Holy Spirit in the elect " by means of the
preaching of the gospel and the prayer of the believer " (Helv.
post. 16.   Westm. Conf. 14. 1).   Faith is "not only a sure
knowledge by means of which I regard as true everything which
God has revealed to us in his word, but also a heartfelt confidence " (Heid. Cat. 396).   It is an assured acknowledgment of
the divine truth " presented (*proposita*) in the Scriptures and the
Apostles' Creed " (Helv. 16).   Since faith accepts the contents
of the Scriptures as true " on account of the authority of God
himself speaking therein," it embraces obedience to the commandments, as well as the acceptance of the promises and repose
in Christ (Westm. Conf. 14. 2).   These, too, are Calvinistic
ideas, which deviate from the view of Luther.   Faith is not only
acceptance of Christ, but also the obedient subjection to God and
the reception of the doctrines revealed by him.[2]   The emphasis
laid upon penitential discipline is also to be traced to Calvin
(Heid. Cat. 412.   Westm. Conf. 15).   The Helvetic Confession defines repentance as follows : "a change of mind in man
the sinner, incited by the word of the gospel and the Holy Spirit,
and accepted by true faith."   It is "conversion" to God and
to all good, and "aversion" from the devil and evil (a. 14.
Heid. Cat. 413 f.).

3. The recognition of the spiritual nature of the church is
epitomized in the formula :   The church is the fellowship of the
predestinated (*e. g.*, Westm. Conf. 25. 1.   Heid. Cat. 404).
This definition stands by the side of a strong emphasizing of the
visible church, with its offices, and discipline, and the obligation
to submit to the latter and diligently use the means of grace

[1] Upon Original Sin and the Enslaved Will, vid. Helv. 8.   Gal. 10, 11.
Scot. 3.   Heid. Cat. 393.   Belg. 15, 39, art. 9, 10.   Westm. Conf. c. 6 and 9.

[2] We in this connection naturally recall the strong emphasis upon the inspiration of the Scriptures and the enumeration of the books of the canon in
the Reformed confessions, *e. g.*, Helv. 1 : " We believe, therefore, that from
these Scriptures are to be sought true wisdom and piety ; also, the reformation
and government of churches, and the institution of all the duties of piety."
The West. Conf., I. 1 and 2, after enumerating the canonical books, says :
" Which have all been given by divine inspiration as the rule of faith and life."
In 4 : " The authority of the Holy Scriptures . . . depends . . . alone upon their
author, God."   In 5 : " A full persuasion and certitude, as well of their infallible truth, as of their divine authority, is not otherwise begotten than by
an internal operation of the Holy Spirit, testifying through the word and with
the word in our hearts."   Thus the Small Catechism of the Puritans, in
Niem., p. 98 : " There are two things which the Scriptures teach first of all :
what man should believe concerning God, and what duty God demands of
man."   Gal. 2-5.   Belg. 3-7 ; 39 art. 6 (8 : the three symbols, the Nicene,
Athanasian, and what is commonly called the Apostles', are to be entirely received and believed).

(*e. g.*, Heid. 407.   Helv. I. 17, 18.   Westm. Conf. 25. 2 f.).
It is precisely the predestinarian determinism and the representation of God as the Lord who does all things that are done,
which afford the explanation of the strictness and severity of
Reformed church life.   All that is done by the church and its
members is but the carrying out of the divine Will.   Through
vocatio and *justificatio* predestination is realized (Westm. 10. 1 ;
11. 1).[1]   Thus God alone works, and all human action serves
his ends.   These ideas find utterance in the term, "the divine
glory" (cf. supra, pp. 312, 391, 416, and Müller, Symbolik, p.
445 ff.).   We are thus brought to the doctrine of predestination.

§ 82.   *Triumph of the Doctrine of Predestination.*

LITERATURE.   SCHWEIZER, Centraldogmen, 2 vols., 1854-6.   SEEBERG-
THOMAS., ed. 2, 660 ff.   LINSENMANN, A. Pighius u. sein theol. Standpunkt,
in Tüb. Quartalschr., 1866, 571 ff.   Upon Bolsec, vid. C. R. xxxvi. 145 ff.

1. In harmony with his fundamental religious temper, and in
opposition to foolish opposers, Calvin developed the doctrine of
predestination with constantly increasing clearness and distinctness.   ALBERT PIGHIUS had in A. D.   1542 made a vigorous
assault upon this doctrine in his publication, *De libero arbitrio
et divina gratia*, ll. 10.   To this Calvin replied in his *De libero
arbitrio* (C. R. xxxiv. 233 ff.).   He here develops the ideas
grown familiar to us : that God alone works salvation, but to a
certain extent includes his working in the church's means of
grace (252 ff.); that the sinner himself is to blame (256 f.);
that the doctrine of predestination is not equivalent to Stoic
fatalism (257).   If Pighius had employed against the doctrine
the common arguments, that it leaves no room for morality and
human responsibility, nor for merits, etc., JEROME BOLSEC,
who came to Geneva in A. D.   1551, endeavored to find the
source of faith in grace alone, but with the exclusion of election.
God, he held, works faith through efficacious grace (*gratia
efficax*).   That it is not always produced, is to be attributed to
rebellio in man, and not to the decree of God (C. R. xxxvi.
217, 213).   But he taught also "that man has not been
entirely deprived of free-will . . . but his will remains, wounded
and corrupt" (ib. 218).   Though Bolsec by no means questioned
salvation by grace, he strongly opposed the idea of a pretemporal
election (vid. also l. c., p. 179 f.).

---

[1] Vid. esp. 3, 6 : "But, just as God has destined the elect to glory, so he
has foreordained all the means by which they shall attain it.   Wherefore the
elect, after they had fallen in Adam, have been redeemed by Christ, are by
the Holy Spirit efficaciously called to faith in Christ, justified, sanctified, and
by his power kept through faith unto salvation."

An appeal issued from Geneva to the other Swiss theologians awakened but a lukewarm response, instead of the clear and incisive testimony in favor of the double predestination which the Genevans expected (cf. SCHWEIZER, i. 218 ff.). The CONSENSUS GENEVENSIS, *De aeterna dei praedestinatione*, in which Calvin, in A. D. 1552, again presented his view (C. R. xxxvi. 249 ff., in Niemeyer, Coll. conf., 218 ff.), was hence officially accepted only in the Genevan church.

2. The doctrine is treated in the most of the Reformed confessions in a very moderate way. God elects some in Christ and leaves others to perdition (Belg. 16 ; Gal. 12). The Heid. Cat. passes over the subject of predestination entirely (but see 404 : the elect church, *ausserwelte gemein*). The Helv. recognizes it, indeed, but warns : "Nevertheless we should hope well for all, nor is anyone to be rashly counted among the reprobates," and also : "It is to be considered as beyond doubt, if thou believest and art in Christ, that thou art elect" (a. 10 ; cf. SCHWEIZER, i. 290 f.).[1] The definitions of the Westm. Conf. are more positive ; but even there the doctrine of predestination serves only to enforce the certainty of salvation, since it is the basis underlying the entire soteriological activity of God (3. 8, 6, also 1 : "Neither is liberty, or the contingency of second causes, taken away, but rather more firmly established"). But, in contrast with this moderation, in the theology of the leaders of the second generation (Beza, Peter Martyr, Musculus, Zanchi) the doctrine of predestination is advocated in its most extreme supralapsarian form. This emphasis upon predestination became but the more pronounced in the course of the development, and thus this doctrine, *i. e.*, of the divine decrees, gradually became the starting-point of Reformed dogmatics.

3. The growing prominence of this doctrine is reflected in the decrees of the Synod of Dort, A. D. 1618-9, which was devoted to its consideration (cf. Acta synodi Dortrechti habitae Lugd. Bat., 1620, Niemeyer, 690 ff. GRAF, Beiträge zur Kenntnis d. Synode v. D., 1825. SCHWEIZER, ii. 141 ff.). The occasion for the holding of this Synod was the Arminian controversy. JACOB ARMINIUS, from A. D. 1603 professor at Leyden, was brought, in consequence of his freer views upon the subject, into conflict with his colleague, FRANCIS GOMARUS, who held to the strict doctrine of predestination. His death occurring A. D. 1609, JAMES UYTENBOGAART and SIMON EPISCOPIUS became the

---

[1] In the *Confessio Sigismundi* (A. D. 1614), salvation is indeed traced to the pretemporal election, but it is, on the other hand, denied "that he (God) does not desire to have all saved" (Niemeyer, p. 650).

leading champions of the modified position. In A. D. 1610, the Arminian leaders, branded as heretics by their opponents, united in a protest, the REMONSTRANTIA (Schaff., The Creeds of Christendom, iii. 545 ff.), whose positions are the following : God determined, before the foundation of the world, to save through Christ those of the fallen human race who should believe on him. Man does not by the power of his free will attain saving faith, but he is born and renewed to such faith by Christ through his Holy Spirit. As the beginning, so also the progress and completion of good in man, is dependent upon grace, but grace does not work irresistibly. Those who have received the Spirit and faith are able, through the assistance of grace, to struggle against all temptations and come off victorious. The question, whether the regenerated can fall from grace, is left undecided.

The Remonstrants were at once confronted by the Contra-remonstrants. The agitation increased, and it was decided to settle the dispute by a synod, to which nearly all the Reformed national churches were invited. It was held at Dort, lasting from November 13, 1618, till May 9, 1619. Delegates were present from the Palatinate, Hesse, Nassau, East Friesland, Bremen, Emden, England, Scotland, Geneva, and German Switzerland. It was a council which has no parallel in the history of Protestantism. In view of the overwhelming majority of the Contra-remonstrants, the result could not be doubtful,[1] and it is not surprising that the Remonstrants were from the first placed in the position of defendants. The canons of the synod cast a strong light upon the significance of the doctrine of pre-destination for the later Reformed church. We reproduce the leading thoughts : The fact that only some of the race of sinful men come to faith must be attributed to the eternal counsel of God. God elected a definite number of men in Christ to salvation, whilst in his justice leaving the others to perdition. But the election is realized in the mission of Christ, the effectual call, the bestowal of faith, justification, sanctification, and glori-fication (c. 1. 6, 7). Hence man is assured of his election by its infallible fruits. Faith, the fear of God, sorrow for sin, hunger and thirst after righteousness, constitute thus the basis of our recognition of predestination ; or, the latter is the real basis of the entire new life (1. 12). The activity of God in the in-terest of human salvation is therefore regarded as, in its entire scope, nothing more than the actualizing of predestination.

---

[1] The assembly decided for the infralapsarian view of the doctrine, only Gomarus still adhering to the supralapsarian formula.

Consequently, the sacrifice of Christ, or the satisfaction rendered by him, which is in itself considered of infinite value and abundantly sufficient for the salvation of all men, effects only the salvation of the elect (2. 3, 8). Hence, God accompanies the calling through the word with illumination through the Holy Spirit and the agency of regenerating grace: "He infuses new qualities into the will and makes it from dead, living; from evil, good; from unwilling, willing" (3. 10, 11).[1] This regeneration is a creative act of God, like the recalling of the dead to life. It is not accomplished by means of moral persuasion, and it does not impart to man the mere possibility of conversion; but it is a wonderful work of divine agency: "In order that all those in whose hearts God operates in this wonderful way may *certainly*, *infallibly* and *efficaciously be regenerated* and *actually believe*" (3. 12). In the case of the elect, therefore, the call certainly produces regeneration; but, on the other hand, it is also held that "as many as are called through the gospel are seriously (*serio*) called," so that it is to be ascribed only to their unwillingness if they are not converted (3. 8, 9). As this latter position is evidently out of accord with the former, so, if strictly interpreted, it carries us entirely beyond the bounds of the determinism which otherwise pervades the document.[2]

The certainty of the salvation of the elect is secured finally by the Perseverance of the Saints. Although the elect may fall into grave sins, and thereby lose for a time the consciousness of grace (5. 1-5), yet God so preserves his Holy Spirit in them that they can never fall entirely out of the state of grace nor commit the sin against the Holy Ghost (5. 7). The unchangeableness of the divine decree excludes the possibility that they should entirely fall away or be lost (5. 8).

4. In this document, the later Reformed view attained adequate expression.[3] Predestination was exalted to the position of a dogma, and its opponents defeated. But the decrees of Dort

---

[1] It is necessary merely to contrast with this the prudent remarks of the Formula of Concord (supra, p. 383) in order to understand the benefit of the Philippistic ideas.

[2] For, according to the leading principles here maintained, the call is an effectual expression of the divine will only in the case of the elect. Upon these it *must* have its effect; upon others it cannot have any inward efficacy at all. The idea expressed above is hence a concession, similar to the other one already noted, *i. e.*, that the death of Christ was sufficient to effect the salvation of all men, although it is intended to actually benefit only some.

[3] The decrees of Dort were officially recognized by the Netherlands; but they were received largely also in Switzerland, France, and the Palatinate, as well as by the Puritans.

—as also the Westminster Confession (supra, p. 419)—indicate
a displacement of the original order of thought in the sphere of
soteriology. Predestination was once a support for the assurance
of salvation ; now it has itself been made the fundamental conception. The course was once from below upward, *i. e.*, from
justification to predestination ; now it is from above downward,
i. e., from predestination to justification.[1] This transformation
indicates something different from a victory for the theoretical
idea of Calvin ; for the *Institutio* did not observe the order followed in the later statements of the doctrine, and, on the other
hand, the Confession of Dort did not fully reproduce the rigor
of the Calvinistic ideas. It was rather that practical conception
of God which marks the writings of Calvin—God, the all-working Lord, who rules all things for his own glory—which was here
victorious. This practical point of view must be kept in view in
order to understand the later form and relationship of the doctrine of predestination.

But the definitions of Dort are also, in another direction, of
the greatest historical significance, since they mark the breach
between ecclesiastical Calvinism and its humanistically-inclined
followers. Among the adherents and forerunners of the Reformation in the spirit of Zwingli and Calvin were not infrequently
found representatives of the Erasmian ideals of reform. Practical ethical reforms, a large-hearted undogmatic Christianity, and
scholarly tastes were often combined in these circles. It was
among them especially that the Arminians found recruits. Their
opposition by no means signified merely dissent from a single
doctrine, but it was rather a protest against the enlargement of
the sphere of dogma and against the limitation of exegetical
freedom by dogmatic formulas. This is proved by the further
history of Arminianism. As against this tendency, the Synod
of Dort marks the victory of strict orthodoxy within the Reformed church.

5. This may be seen, as well as the important place occupied
by the doctrine of predestination in the theological thought of
the age, in the discussions called forth by the modifications of
this doctrine, in themselves of no great moment, suggested by
Moses Amyraldus in Saumur (vid. Traité de la predestination
et de ses principes, 1634; cf. Schweizer, ii. 280 ff.). He
maintains firmly the Reformed doctrine of predestination, that
God has elected some to salvation, but has purposed to leave
others to perdition. He, however, modified this position at two

---

[1] The original view may be expressed in the formula : Because there is
justification, there is predestination ; the later view reverses this : Because
there is predestination, there is justification.

points in a way which was out of harmony with the prevalent view.   In the first place, he held, upon the ground that the will always follows the intellect, that the irresistible working of God upon the will of man is effected through the illumination of the intellect.[1] The process of conversion, he claimed, was thus made psychologically more intelligible.[2] Secondly, he introduced the idea of the so-called *hypothetical universalism* of grace. In order to throw some light upon the rejection of the reprobate —acknowledging, as he did, the absolute inscrutability of the grounds upon which the divine election is based—he conceives that there is in nature and history, independent of the gospel message, a certain dim revelation of the grace of God.   Both forms of revelation have been made possible, however, only because satisfaction has been rendered to the divine justice by the sacrifice of Christ.   But neither this general revelation, nor the preaching of the gospel in itself, can bring salvation to the sinner.   This depends upon the divine election.   Yet since, upon this theory, a certain announcement of the grace of God has in some way reached all men, the destruction of such multitudes is more easily accounted for, since all have been guilty of rejecting either the general or the special offer of grace.

Whether Amyraldus succeeded in establishing his positions, may well be doubted.   But he was certainly justified in defending his position as within the bounds of orthodoxy.   A French national synod, at Alencon, in A. D. 1637, certified to this, and simply advised him to avoid such unusual and startling forms of expression.   Another synod in A. D. 1645 (vid. Aymon, Tous les synodes nationaux des églises reformées de France, 1710, vol. ii. 571 ff., 663), pronounced the same judgment.   But the Swiss theologians were also greatly disturbed by the teachings of Amyraldus.   They feared that they might thus become "the sport of the exultant Papists, Luthoromanites, and Arminians, to whose doctrines the windows were thus opened," and they felt themselves under obligation to construct a new symbol in the interest of orthodoxy.   Thus originated, after many conferences and conflicts, the FORMULA CONSENSUS HELVETICA, composed by Heidegger, and adopted as a symbol, A. D. 1675 (Niemeyer, p. 729 ff.).   This document rejects the view of Amyraldus (c. 6), teaches the strictest particularism in the election (4), and maintains with emphasis, that Christ died only for the elect and recon-

---

[1] Just as sin began in the intellect and passed thence into the will.   Amyraldus in this follows JOHN CAMERO in Montauban († A. D. 1625); vid. SCHWEIZER, ii. 235 ff.

[2] Cf., on the other hand, the severe formulas of Dort upon the transformation of the will, supra, p. 423.

ciled them alone to God (13). Only the elect come through the *external call*, which is serious and sincere (*seria et sincera*), to faith. "But that, by the will of God, in the call thus universally announced, only the elect are led to faith, but the reprobate are hardened—this proceeds from the discriminating grace of God alone" (19). The theory of predestination in its strict form is thus formally proclaimed as the doctrine of the church.[1]

In view of the above, we cannot avoid the conclusion that the theology of Calvin has become, in its essential points, the doctrine of the Reformed church. What has been said in Section 79, 10 is, therefore, here equally applicable.

---

[1] It is here also, in view of the controversy of L. Capella with Buxtorf, declared, that the Hebrew text of the Old Testament "is inspired (θεόπνευστος) both as to the consonants and as to the very vowels or points, or as to the force and power of the points, and both as to the subject-matter and as to the words" (2).

PART III.

COMPLETION OF DOCTRINAL CONSTRUCTION IN THE ROMAN CATHOLIC CHURCH.

§ 83. *Establishment of Medieval Theology as the Doctrine of the Church by the Council of Trent.*

SOURCES. Canones et decreta Conc. Trid., ed. RICHTER ET SCHULTE, 1853. Doctrinal formulas also in STREITWOLF ET KLENER, Libri symbol. eccl. Rom. i., and in DENZINGER'S Enchiridion, in Mirbt, Quellen z. Gesch. d. Papstt., 124 ff. A. THEINER, Acta genuina conc. Trid., 2 vols., 1874. LE PLAT,. Monum. ad histor. conc. Trid., 7 vols., 1781 ff. V. DÖLLINGER, Ungedruckte Berichte u. Tagebb. z. Gesch. d. Conc. v. Tr., 1872. Concilium Tridentinum, diariorum, epistolarum tractatuum novacollectio,vol. i., ed. Merkle, Freiburg, vol. 1., 1901 ff. This work when completed will include the protocols and a comprehensive collection of all other original documents bearing upon the work of the Council ; vid. SEEBERG, in Theol. Litt.-bl., 1903, 6 ff. PAOLI SARPI, Istoria del conc. Trid., 1619, Germ. translation by Rambach, 6 vols., 1761 ff. SFORZA PALLAVICINI, Istoria del conc. di Trid., 1656, Latin translation, Antwerp, 1673, cf. RANKE, WW., vol. 39, append., p. 25 ff. SALIG, Vollst. Hist. d. trid. Conc., 3 parts, 1741 ff. MENDHAM, Memoirs of the Counc. of Trent, 1834. RANKE, vol. 37, 129 ff. MAURENBRECHER, in Hist. Taschenbuch, 1886, 147 ff.; 1888, 305 ff. MÖLLER-KAWERAU, KG. iii. 215 ff. Upon the doctrines, vid. CHEMNITZ, Exam. conc. Trid., 1566. SEEBERG, Beitr. z. Entstehungsgesch. d. Lehrdekrete v. Tr., in Ztschr. f. k. Wiss., 1889, p. 546 ff., 604 ff., 643 ff., and in THOMASIUS ii., ed. 2, 688 ff.

1. The Reformation made astonishing progress during its first decades. The intellectual activity of the closing Middle Ages had prepared the way before it both positively and negatively. The old church was incapable of damming the current. This can be plainly seen in the course of the early antagonists of the new movement. In the general consternation, the Catholic theologians accepted the challenge of their opponents,[1] defended with half-heartedness the worst outgrowths of medieval Chris-

---

[1] *E. g.*, the defense of indulgences by Tetzel and Eck. DIETENBERGER'S publication, "Der leye, ob der gelaub allein selig mache." BERTHOLD of Chiemsee, Tewtsche Theologey (ed. Reithmeyer, 1852). SCHATZGEIER'S works (1543). A review of the positions maintained in this pre-Trentine theology is given by LÄMMER, Die vortrid. kath. Theologie, 1858. Our space forbids a fuller delineation, but a further study of this literature—from a wider historical point of view than LÄMMER (Schul- und Ordens-Theologie)—would yield valuable results.

tianity assailed by the latter, fell back upon the "authority" of the church, and relied for protection and victory in the great intellectual conflict upon politics and measures of external force. It was, indeed, a difficult task to defend the ancient positions at large. The theologians were soon divided into a number of hostile groups. In every important point of doctrine, the differences of the ancient schools of theology came to light. The Thomistic, and the Scotist, or Nominalist, views were still zealously advocated. The confusion was increased by the fact that the age looked with misconception and contempt upon the technicalities and methods of theology. Finally, it must not be overlooked that in their own camp, the champions of Roman Catholicism were compelled to hear clamorous demands for reform (Spain, Italy, the Oratorium, the Theatines, etc.). And yet all these tendencies—advocates of reform and strict adherents of the curia, mystics and dogmaticians of every class—constituted from one point of view, *i. e.*, their common opposition to Protestantism, a compact unity. The will was present, and a way was found. We can understand therefore how it came to pass that the internal differences were reconciled, and that, in the compromise, the ruder and coarser ideas and tendencies held the ascendant.

It is not our task to trace the reforms in the ecclesiastical life which were forced upon the Romish church by the Reformation. We are concerned only for the theological development. The Thomistic theology again assumed the lead in this post-reformation age. There had at an earlier period been a disposition to regard it as the specifically ecclesiastical doctrine. It now became a necessary equipment of the church. It was free from the foreign skepticism and critical temper of Duns Scotus, and it was simpler—a compacted system. Authority and dogma were here securely fixed and rationally established, and curialism found here a valiant champion. This theology was the destruction of the ideals and the faith which prevailed in the thirteenth century, at the time of the church's greatest power. We are not surprised that appeal should be constantly made to this earlier period. But in every attempted repristination of the former doctrines, the original accurate adaptation to actual circumstances has vanished, and the ideas are in consequence eviscerated and vulgarized. The system of Thomas, once a lofty conception of ecclesiastical idealism, was forced into the narrow limits of ecclesiastical positivism as fixed by Duns. There was no use in this age for the keen criticism of the Nominalists, their impertinent skepticism, and their remorseless dialectics— and they became a thing of the past. But there was need now

of *implicit faith* and subjection to formulas—and these were retained. That which was great and imposing in Thomas and
Duns must be eliminated from them, and the dregs—their
formulas—remain.

2. But if medieval theology had been shattered by its contact
with the spirit and the religious needs of the modern man, then
no victory could be permanent which should fail to take due
account of this spirit. Here the Jesuits found their field (cf.
GOTHEIN, Ignat. v. Loyola u. die Gegenreformation, 1895).
They required obedience and subjection to the church as strictly
as had ever been done in the Middle Ages; but they were
shrewd enough to adapt the form of this requirement to the
spirit and temper of the modern man. The old theology was
adopted, but it was adorned with the embellishments of modern
humanistic learning. The authors wrote in elegant style, and
exegetical and historical studies were pursued with diligence.
But it was in the Sacrament of Repentance that the force of the
movement was most distinctly felt. It was here that the Jesuit
praxis gained its greatest triumph—it constructed the modern
Roman Catholic sacrament of repentance. The penitential discipline, which in the closing period of the Middle Ages had
been so often utterly neglected (vid. DÖLLINGER and REUSCH,
Gesch. d. Moralstreitigkeiten in d. röm.-kath. K., 1889, i.,
p. 20 n.), was revived and enlarged (ib. i. 19 ff., 61 ff. GOTHEIN,
l. c., p. 324 ff.). It became again, with its attrition and
probabilism, its intentionalism, and mental reservations, the
dominant force in the church, forming the historical counterpart
to justification by faith and the new life of faith among Protestants. And it was at this point that the worst elements in the
theology of Duns and the Nominalists poured in a great flood
upon the church, viz.: the minimizing of sin and the fondling of
the sinner; the dialectic trifling with the intentions, the will, and
the sensuous impulses; the juggling with the authorities (cf.
LUTHARDT, Gesch. d. chr. Ethik, ii. 120 ff.). But it was just
in this way that the chasm between the church and the world
was spanned. In the confessional was learned the art of living
in the world, continuing to cherish the spirit of the world, and
yet being sure of salvation. This was the "*dévotion aisée,*"
the compact of the church with the world. Dogmas no longer
formed the theme of the pulpit—that remained dangerous
ground—but preachers discoursed eloquently upon the beauty
of virtue and the repulsiveness of vice. Thus the minds of men
were diverted from the burning questions of the day.[1] But a

[1] Cf. GOTHEIN, p. 319 ff., who very correctly says: "The preaching of the

compromise was effected also in the sphere of dogma. A new definition of faith was framed. Even the old faith of assent seemed to require too much—and it had no really practical object. It was therefore replaced by the faith of silent obedience. It is sufficient that one do not publicly oppose the formula of the church. Thus the dogma appeared to be saved, and faith made possible to everyone. In this way, the freest modern spirits could submit to the rule of the church. Everyone now became churchly again. As the art of the confessor met the wants of the great masses, so the change in the ascetic method was carried out in a way to suit the modern man. The age of merely sensuous discipline was past, as was that of simple obedience to authority. Ignatius accordingly attached little importance to outward asceticism. In its place came the inwardly transforming meditations of spiritual exercises (*exercitia spiritualia*). Ascetic exercises in the outward form were but means to an end (cf. GOTHEIN, p. 227 ff., 240, 416 ff.). In accordance with this, the aim of obedience is to be seen, not only in the outward subjection which it manifests, but in the regulation of the life according to one's own convictions.[1]   And even though this aim should in separate instances not be attained, yet it would still have a suggestive influence upon the inward disposition. The deed thus prompted was done from obedience; but it was done by the man himself, and was done to further the glory of God.[2]

Such are some of the ideas which stirred Roman Catholicism after the Reformation. First of all, the return to Thomas, the ancient dogma and curialism, together with the rejection of all critical and skeptical elements in theology. In the sphere of dogma and ecclesiastical politics, Thomism appeared to gain a

---

Jesuits, dealing with things near and comprehensible, was well calculated to wean the Catholic masses from their anxiety about the dogmas; it was for them a soothing potion'' (p. 321).   This method has become characteristic of the preaching of the Roman Catholic church.

[1] Upon this obedience, vid. DÖLLINGER AND REUSCH, Moralstreitigkeiten i. 623 ff. GOTHEIN (p. 332) finds a contradiction between the emphasizing of the will and the will-less obedience. This is scarcely justified, since the obedience is supposed to be rendered with delight and devotion (vid. ib. 455) as a voluntary personal act.   On the contrary, it is just in this refined adaptation of all requirements to the temper and spirit of the modern man that the power of the Jesuits lies.

[2] Ignatius, too, speaks frequently of the relation of obedience to the " glory of God" (vid. GOTHEIN, p. 334, 426, 452, 455). If we would find upon the so widely different territory of Protestantism a parallel to this remarkable man, we must look for it not in Luther, despite the inner struggles which constitute a feature of similarity—but in Calvin, the fellow-student of Loyola at Paris.

decisive victory. But as its energy was lost under the pressure of the positivism of Duns, so in the sphere of practical Christianity, the emasculating of the conceptions of sin and grace and the refinement of the dialectics that excuses all things and makes all things possible—for which Duns was also responsible—gained ascendancy in the church. Much was borrowed from the two great leaders of medieval theology, but no way was found to make use of that which was best in either. The legacy which they had left was deftly woven into the texture of the practical church politics of the Jesuits. In a word, it was Jesuitism—the history of its spread being the history of the counter-reformation—which accomplished the great task of making the traditions of the Roman Catholic Middle Ages acceptable to the Spirit of the modern age. In this consists its historic significance, and in this way it became the counterpart of the Reformation.

3. The COUNCIL OF TRENT (A. D. 1545-63) discharged the difficult task of marking out a median course between the conflicting views of scholastic theology, which was then proclaimed as the official doctrine of the church. Only with great difficulty was the result attained. The contradictory principles of the opposing schools came into prominence in the discussion of nearly every question. It was possible to preserve an outward unity only by the employment of the most studied diplomatic arts. The points of controversy were either avoided altogether or carefully veiled. Thus, to the student familiar with the history of the formation of the doctrinal definitions of the council, the latter but too often appear as the deliberate productions of church politics and diplomatic refinements. The decrees do not present to us a vigorous and joyous confession of sincere faith, but formulas of compromise artfully welded together, bent to this side or that with great labor and pains, and then finally filed into proper dimensions.

4. Turning now to the doctrinal decrees of the Council of Trent, we must first observe their attitude toward the Scriptures and Tradition (session 4). We note at the outset the complete co-ordination of the two. The council receives the Holy Scriptures and the traditions of the church "with equal feeling of reverence" (*pari pietatis affectu*). The former have God for their author; the latter have been "dictated by Christ or by the Holy Spirit." The opposition to this co-ordination of tradition with Scripture was in vain. The council distinctly recognized the ecclesiastical traditions, being inspired as truly as the Scriptures, as of equal dignity. It carefully avoided, however, any designation of the particular traditions to which this

principle was to be applied. " We receive those which we wish, but reject altogether those which displease us " (acta, i. 71 b) —these naïve words of a bishop betray the general attitude. The Vulgate is, with appeal to tradition, established as the authentic translation. The apocryphal books of the Old Testament are also acknowledged. The attempt to co-ordinate Scripture and tradition here, as always, results in the actual subordination of the former to the latter. But it might now be rightly claimed that the church had gone half-way in the right direction.[1]

5. The 5th session established the doctrine of Original Sin. Here, too, the contrary principles of the opposing schools were manifest, the one party wishing to locate original sin in concupiscence, while the other regarded it as merely the lack of righteousness. The subject was at once complicated by the question as to the relation of the Virgin Mary to original sin (acta, i. 145 f.). The doctrine finally adopted is, in brief, as follows : (a) The first man, through his own fault, lost the righteousness and holiness into which he had been inducted (constitutus)[2] in paradise, and thereby fell under the wrath of God and the power of the devil. There was, in consequence, a deterioration of the whole man. " The whole Adam was by that offense of transgression changed for the worse according to body and soul." Yet this is true only in the sense : "Although free-will had by no means been extinguished in them, yet it was weakened in its power and perverted " (ses. 6, c. 1). (b) The sin and guilt of Adam passed over upon the whole human race. (c) Since the sin of Adam passed over upon his descendants " by propagation, not by imitation," human means are not able to release from it. (d) Even children can be purified from their inherited condition only by the regeneration of baptism. (e) Not only is original sin forgiven by imputation through baptism, but the latter actually renews the sinner. There remains in him, however, concupiscence (concupiscentia) or the tinder of

---

[1] Cf. the *Profess. fid. Trid.*: " I most firmly acknowledge and embrace the apostolic and ecclesiastical traditions and other observances and appointments of the same church. Also the Holy Scripture, according to that sense which the holy mother, the church, has held and holds, whose (part) I acknowledge it to be to judge concerning the true sense and interpretation of the Holy Scriptures, nor will I ever accept and interpret them except in accordance with the unanimous consensus of the Fathers." In these declarations the Scriptures are not only assigned a place second to tradition, but they are also bound and gagged. At the same time all attempts to attain a profounder religious or scientific knowledge of the Scriptures were excluded.

[2] Instead of *constitutus*, the original draft of the decree had *creatus* (acta, i. 130 b). The words occurring in the original draft : " no part of the soul remaining uninjured," were also stricken out. The first-mentioned change was required by the doctrine of the *donum superadditum* (supra, p. 115).

evil (*fomes*).   Concupiscence is, indeed, sometimes spoken of
by the apostle as sin, but this must not, according to the doctrine
of the church, be understood in the sense "that it is in the regenerate truly and really sin, but because it comes from sin and
inclines to sin."   (*f*) These definitions do not apply in the case
of the Virgin Mary.

6. The 6th session undertook to treat of Justification.   Upon
this topic much time and labor were expended.   Sarpi relates
that at least a hundred sessions were devoted to it, and that the
second president of the council, Cervino, made emendations of
the decree daily in order to meet all demands and make it acceptable to all parties.   This may be readily understood.   On
the one hand, the opposition of the Protestants made a precise
definition necessary ; on the other hand—and in this, as Cervino
pointed out, lay the difficulty—the scholastic tradition afforded no
material,[1] as in it justification was treated only, and that but briefly,
as an element in the sacrament of repentance.   The specific doctrine of justification, as it was now framed, was forced from the
Roman Catholic church by the pressure of Protestantism. It was
modeled upon the pattern found in Thomas.   The doctrine was
at the council divided originally into three sections : (1) How
one may attain justification ; what part God has to do in it, and
what part man ; what is the significance of faith in relation to it.
(2) How one may preserve the justification attained.   (3)
How one may again secure justification when it has been lost.
The first was the decisive section.   Agreement was, indeed, soon
reached upon certain definite fundamental points, *i. e.*, (1)
That the call comes through the law and the gospel, to the preaching of which man gives assent through faith.   (2) That grace is
a new disposition of the soul, which is attested by good works.
(3) Accordingly, there are everywhere traces of a certain synergism, and faith is the condition of justification, because the latter
presupposes the acceptance of the teachings of the church.   But
within the lines of these fundamental Roman Catholic ideas,
which all held in common, there were not lacking marked differences.   The Thomistic tradition made the forgiveness of sins
dependent upon the previous effectual equipment with grace
(supra, pp. 121, 201); the Scotist view, on the contrary,
placed forgiveness first, to be followed by the infusion of grace
(supra, pp. 161, 201).   Under the influence of the Protestant, or Pauline, doctrine of justification, the latter way of
viewing the subject had come to have a significance which by no

---

[1] Note also the obscurity in the decree upon justification (c. 1), according
to which all men are "servants of sin, although free-will had by no means
been extinguished in them, yet it was weakened in its power and perverted."

28

means attached to it when understood in the sense of its greatest medieval advocate.[1] Both points of view were advocated at the council. The one party maintained : " The imputation of Christ effects in us that sins are not imputed, yet it does not justify ; but, after the remission of sins, God justifies us ; and justification is not remission of sins, because remission occurs before justification " (acta i. 176 a); the other party held that " God first infuses grace, then remits sins " (ib. 180 b). Finally, we meet in some of the fathers of the council a certain sympathy for the evangelical view.[2] Another difference appears in the fact, that one party (e. g., acta i. 179 b, 176 b, 180 a) would ascribe a meritorious character, disposing to the reception of grace, to works done under the general influence of the grace of the call (gratia vocationis),[3] whereas others would attach importance only to the works wrought through grace (ib. 181 a ; cf. Sarpi, ii. 366 ff.). There were divergent opinions also as to the measure of the divine influence and of human liberty in the bestowal and reception of grace.

As to the second section in the statement of the doctrine, the use of the sacrament, prayer, and good works were mentioned as the means by which justification once secured was to be retained. He who is in a state of grace can secure for himself by worthiness (de condigno) eternal life (acta i. 195). The restoration of the state of justification, when lost—treated of in the third section of the doctrinal statement—is accomplished through the sacrament of repentance, just as that condition was in the first instance attained through baptism. There is, however, this difference in the two transactions, that if, in the latter case, the lapsed one has not lost his faith, there is no necessity for the re-

---

[1] We are reminded here of PIGHIUS and GROPPER, both of whom represent the imputed righteousness of Christ as preceding the infused righteousness and place the emphasis, for the practical religious consciousness, upon the former. Cf. LINSENMANN, Tüb. Quart.-schr., 1866, 641 ff. BRIEGER, in Ersch. and Gruber's Encycl., sect. i., vol. 92, p. 135. DITTRICH, Gasp. Contarini, p. 660 ff. If I am not mistaken, this view, which was advocated also by Seripando at Trent (SEEBERG, Ztschr. f. kirchl. Wiss., 1889, 671 ff.), points back to the Scotist scheme. I have proved the Thomistic and unevangelical character of Cardinal Contarini's theory of justification, l. c., 657 ff.; cf. 676 f. In this KAWERAU agrees with me (MÖLLER, KG. iii. 129).

[2] Here may be mentioned JUL. CONTARINI (nephew of the well-known cardinal), THOMAS SANFELICE, Bishop of Cava, and the Augustinian General SERIPANDO. We must be on our guard, however, against the error of pronouncing the opinions of these men—without large reservation—as " evangelical." Vid. SEEBERG, l. c., 652 ff.; also the Archbishop BANDINI of Siena (Pallavicini, viii. 4. 7).

[3] Upon this term, vid. supra, p. 122.

establishment of this (ib. 188 b).[1] Furthermore, the lapsed one must himself satisfy the temporal penalties of sin by works of penance, since the sacrament of repentance releases him only from the eternal penalties ; whereas by baptism both the temporal and the eternal penalties are removed.

The first draft of the decree was rejected (i. 203 ff.). While a new formula was being prepared, a number of questions arose for discussion, upon which no agreement could be reached : for example, whether the inherent "righteousness" imparted to man is sufficient, through the works which it produces, to merit eternal life, or whether there is needed in addition the imputation of grace for the completing of the human works. Very many prelates maintained the former view, e. g., i. 258 b : "The justified man, if he shall have retained his inherent righteousness and done good works, is able with this to appear before the tribunal of God without any other imputation of righteousness." Similarly, in regard to the assurance of salvation, some held it to be unattainable without a special revelation, while others maintained that one may, by virtue of his reception of the sacraments and fulfillment of the commandments, be sure of his salvation. The former is a Thomistic, the latter a Scotist theory (supra, pp. 121, 202). The discussions upon Justification by Faith are especially instructive. Both the *fide* and the *sine operibus* gave rise to difficulties. There were not wanting some who desired to strike out the last words from the decree (1. 340 f.); and they were finally suppressed. Faith was conceived as a completed faith (*fides formata*), or as another designation of the Christian religion (*religio christiana*), or as an inclination (*dispositio*) toward justification. Cf. my studies in Ztschr. f. k. Wiss., 1889, 649-700.

We now turn our attention upon the finally accepted Decree. We note traces of the original three-fold division of the material, both in the positive statement of the decree and in the canons condemning the contrary teachings (cap. 1-9, 10-13, 14-16, and can. 1-22, 23-26, 27-33). (*a*) Of justification, it is said : "That it is a translation from that state in which man is born a son of the first Adam into the state of grace" (c. 4). The order of salvation begins, in the case of adults, with prevenient grace (*gratia praeveniens*), *i. e.*, with the call and the awakening (*excitans*) and assisting (*adjuvans*) grace which accompanies it. Man himself now, by consenting to the work of God and working with him (*eidem gratiae libere assentiendo et co-operando*) prepares himself for justification (c. 5). There is thus, on the

[1] At this point the utterly unevangelical conception of faith, which pervades the whole discussion, is clearly revealed.

one hand, a recognition of a coöperation preceding justification, and an acknowledgment that the works preceding justification are not altogether sinful (can. 7); while, on the other hand, the call comes before any merit exists (*nullis eorum existentibus meritis*). With this both the Thomists and the advocates of the *meritum de congruo* could be satisfied. The preparation for justification produced by this general influence of grace embraces, first of all, faith : " Receiving faith by hearing, they of free-will draw near to God, believing those things to be true which have been divinely revealed and promised," above all, that God out of grace will justify the sinner in Christ.[1] From fear of the divine justice, they rise in faith to the contemplation of the mercy of God: " believing that God will for Christ's sake be propitious." Now begins love to Christ as being the source of righteousness, " and afterward they are impelled against sins by a certain hatred and detestation," and this is followed by the resolution to lead a new life (c. 6). Thus faith, the beginnings of love to God and abhorence of sin, and the resolution to obey the commandments of God—are all wrought by the word before the actual infusion of grace.

(*b*) Upon this inclination (*dispositio*), or preparation, now follows justification itself: " which is not the bare remission of sins, but also sanctification and renewal of the inner man through the voluntary reception of grace and of gifts, whence the man from unrighteous becomes righteous " (c. 7). The opinion is expressly condemned : "that men are justified by the bare imputation of the righteousness of Christ, or by the bare remission of sins, the grace and love being excluded which are shed abroad in their hearts by the Holy Spirit and abide in them ; or, that the grace by which we are justified is only the favor of God " (can. 11). Justification consists in the renewal of the inner man, which occurs through baptism. By this, faith, hope, and love are imparted to man at the same time as the forgiveness of sins. This impartation is granted in such measure as seems good to the Holy Spirit, and "according to the peculiar inclination and coöperation of each individual" (c. 7).[2] The decree differs from Paul so widely as to understand by the term, " by faith " (*per fidem*), only that faith is " the basis and root of all justification," and by the term " freely " (*gratis*), that the faith and works

---

[1] Even here the expression is not clear : "Christ died for the sins of the whole world, for all ; but only they receive the benefit of his death to whom the merit of his passion is communicated " (*communicatur*, c. 2, 3).

[2] Here again all is designedly left in uncertainty. It is not clear whether the infusion precedes forgiveness or follows it. Similarly, the free imparting of grace is at once corrected by this " coöperation."

preceding justification do not merit grace. As to the term, "without works" (*sine operibus*), nothing is said (c. 8). Just as artfully is the question as to the assurance of salvation evaded, while at the same time a thrust is made "against the empty confidence of the heretics." Certainly sins are forgiven through grace, but if any man boasts of the certainty of this forgiveness, or trusts in it alone, his sins are not forgiven ! It is not desirable that all who are justified should be sure of their justification. We dare not, of course, have any doubts as to the efficacy of Christ and the sacraments; but everyone "may" have some fear as to "his grace" in view of his own weakness (c. 9).[1] This basal section of the document is a combination of two lines of thought : (1) The word is accompanied by a general preparatory influence of grace, which, in a psychological way, begets faith and a striving after the good. (2) The power to pursue the good—faith, hope, and love—is infused into man by the sacrament of baptism. He here receives justification as an impartation of grace, together with the forgiveness of sins. Although the former of these ideas appears to approximate the Protestant position, yet the difference is very evident, since the influence here accorded to the word does not embrace the gracious acceptance of the individual, and since the emphasis in the discussion is laid, not upon the word and faith, but upon the sacrament and the inherent grace.[2]

(*c*) The gift of justification is preserved by obeying the commandments and by good works. By this means there is effected also an increase of the justification : "Through the keeping of the commandments of God and of the church, faith coöperating by good works, they grow in that righteousness itself received through the grace of Christ, and are *more justified*" (c. 10). Justification, as a creative act of God, is, indeed, a momentary act (vid. Thomas, supra, p. 121); but, since it also establishes a moral condition, an advance in it is yet possible, as is indicated by the above citation. Man ought to and can obey the divine commandments, since God gave them to him for that purpose. If the justified man, in seeking to render this obedience, fall into venial sin, he does not on that account cease to be righteous, or justified (c. 11). No one dare be secure in view of his supposed predestination (c. 12; can. 15, 16). The fundamental spirit of

---

[1] This chapter is a laboriously-constructed composition. The decision of points at issue is avoided, but it inclines more toward the Thomists, since the opposition of the Protestant position—which is horribly caricatured—drove its authors in that direction.

[2] How the process is realized in the case of those baptized in infancy is not explained.

the Christian life is fear, which can never do enough to satisfy itself in the works of the prescribed devotion in the Roman Catholic church : " With fear and trembling let them work out their salvation in labors, in vigils, in alms, in prayers and oblations, in fasting and chastity ; for they ought to fear, knowing that they have been regenerated to the hope of glory and not yet to glory " (c. 13). To one reading these declarations in a central position in the formal statement of the church's doctrine, it must appear as though there had never been an Augustine in the Western church. The decree, in its practical aspects, moves in the circuit of Cyprian's ideal of piety, with its legal observances and its servile fear (Vol. I., p. 194 ff., 308). The moral life is dominated by this idea of *merit*. Whoever doubts this, falls under the anathema (can. 26). It is insisted, indeed, that these *merita*, being wrought in the members by the power of Christ, the Head of the church, and being a product of the *inherent righteousness*, are gifts of God (c. 16). But " the good works of a justified man " are also " merits of the justified himself " and, as such, merit eternal life (can. 32). It is evident enough—the old positions must be preserved unchanged !

(*d*) But the grace of justification may be lost, not only through unbelief, but by any mortal sin (c. 15). Those who have mortally sinned may again be justified (*rursus justificari poterunt*), *i. e.*, by the sacrament of repentance, and not, as some fancy, by faith alone ('can. 29). But to secure this, there is need, not only for *contrition*, but also for *confession*, at least in pledge and to be made at the appropriate time, together with *absolution* and the works of *satisfaction*. The eternal penalties, as well as the guilt, are removed by absolution, but for the canceling of the temporal penalties (*poena temporalis*) there must be works of satisfaction (c. 14). The practical experience of justification can be realized, accordingly, only within the limits of the sacrament of repentance.

This is doctrinally but a reproduction of the average scholastic views (cf. Chemnitz, Examen conc. Trid., i. 369). But the reception of this teaching is now the necessary antecedent of justification ; " which (*i. e.*, the Roman Catholic doctrine of justification) unless anyone shall faithfully and firmly accept he cannot be justified " (c. 16 fin.). In the apprehension of the Christian life here set forth, it is no longer a matter of the adoption of theological views, but of the acceptance of the fixed doctrines of the church, which are absolutely necessary to salvation.

7. The 7th session was devoted to the doctrine of the Sacraments. The scholastic conflict was here also at once renewed—

the one party maintaining that the sacraments include in themselves grace, the other regarding them as signs, which God, in view of his covenant, accompanies with his own energy (vid. supra, p. 126 f.). This question was not solved, nor was that of the "indelible character."[1] There was essential agreement in the general doctrine of the sacraments, and as the discussion of the differences might have led to the revival of profounder points of opposition between Thomists and Scotists,[2] it was decided to frame no decree upon the subject, but merely to condemn the teaching of the adversaries by appropriate canons. It is possible, however, to gather from the discussions the positive views which found general acceptance. They were essentially as follows : The seven sacraments were instituted by Christ (can. 1). They are necessary to salvation, since without them the *gratia justificationis* cannot be secured (4). They do not merely serve for the nourishment of faith (5), nor are they only external signs and badges of discipleship ; but they contain grace (6).[3] They work *ex opere operato*, and they—and not only faith—bring grace (8). Three of them impress a *character* upon the soul, "that is, a certain spiritual and indelible mark (signum)" (9).

8. In regard to Baptism also, the council contented itself with the framing of canons. The baptism of heretics is valid, provided it is administered "with the intention of doing what the church does" (4). Baptism does not release from the obligation to obey the law of Christ and all the commandments of the church (7, 8). Sins committed after baptism are "not forgiven simply by the remembrance and the faith of the baptism," *i. e.*, are not venial (10). Finally, the Anabaptists are condemned (12-14).

9. In the discussion of Confirmation, anathemas are pronounced upon the views : that it is not a true sacrament ; that it "was formerly nothing more than instruction" (1); that it may be administered by a "simple priest," and not only by a bishop (3).

10. It was not until the 13th session, that dogmatic utterances were again attempted. The doctrine of the Lord's Supper was now the topic of discussion. (*a*) Here again we meet the conflicting scholastic principles (SARPI, iii. 240 ff.). The positive

---

[1] This theory never recovered from the shattering criticisms of Duns (vid. supra, p. 128).

[2] Cf. PALLAVICINI, ix. 7. 1, and SARPI, ii. 597 ff.

[3] *Continere gratiam*—is the ancient formula (vid. supra, p. 126). Here Zwingli is rejected, but at the same time the way is paved for the Scotist theory.

dogma is as follows : Under the form (*species*) of the elements, Christ, the God-man, is really and substantially (*realiter et substantialiter*) present. He is, indeed, seated at the right hand of God "according to the natural mode of existing," which does not, however, exclude a "way of existing" (*existendi ratio*) which we cannot indeed express, but which we can recognize as possible, in accordance with which Christ, "sacramentally present in many other places, may be in his substance (*sua substantia*) present with us" (c. 1). By means of the consecration, there is a "conversion (*conversio*) of the entire substance of the bread into the substance of the body of Christ " (c. 4). The entire Christ (*totus et integer Christus*) is present under the form of the bread and in every portion of it (c. 3). Whereas in all other sacraments the sanctifying power (*vis sanctificandi*) enters only in the moment of the administration, in the eucharist the body of Christ is present already before the reception of the elements by the communicant, since the Lord called his body bread before the disciples had received it (c. 3). These views naturally led to the defense of "the worship of adoration (*latriae cultus*) which is due to the true God," for the host, and to the advocacy of the festival of Corpus Christi (c. 5). The blessing of the sacrament consists in the forgiveness of venial sins and in preservation from mortal sins. The sacrament is, further, a pledge of future blessedness and glory, and a symbol of the unity of Christ's body (c. 2).

The following, among other positions, are condemned : That the substance of the bread remains the same after consecration (can. 2); that Christ is present in the celebration, while it is being received (*in usu, dum sumitur*), but not before nor after (4); that the forgiveness of sins is the chief, or even the only, fruit of the eucharist (5); the rejection of self-communion by the priest (10); the characterizing of faith as a "sufficient preparation " for the reception of the sacrament (11).[1]

(*b*) It was not until the 21st session (A. D. 1562), that action was taken upon the demand for the granting of the cup to the laity, although this had been often urged upon the attention of the council. It was then decided, that the institution of the Supper does not require that all believers must receive it in both forms (c. 1.), and that the church has authority to introduce changes "in the administration (*dispensatione*) of the sacraments, their substance being preserved." This was done when it, "led by weighty and just reasons," ex-

---

[1] In the original draft of the canons, the demand of the cup for the laity is also anathematized (8. 10 ; act. i. 520 b). But political considerations led to the postponement of a decision upon this point (act. i. 503 a, 521 b, 528 b).

cluded the laity from the cup (c. 2). And there is the less occasion for objection to this upon internal grounds, since the entire Christ is present under each of the two forms, and hence no one is robbed of a blessing by the withdrawal of the cup (c. 3). Those are accordingly condemned who doubt that the church for just reasons withdrew the cup from the laity (can. 2). Finally, consideration of the question, whether the church must always exclude the laity from the cup, or whether "under any conditions" it might grant the cup to a particular nation or kingdom, was postponed. It was afterward decided that the matter should "be referred to our most holy lord" (*ad sanctissimum dominum nostrum*, act. ii. 96 ff.). No decision was given.

(*c*) In this connection we naturally consider the Mass, which was the subject treated at the 22d session. Christ, the Melchizedekian High-priest, in order that his sacrifice might not be obliterated, instituted in the Lord's Supper a sacrifice to be repeated by his disciples, "by which that bloody (one) once offered on the cross should be represented" (*repraesentaretur*). The repetition of the sacrifice is commanded by the words: "This do in remembrance of me" (c. 1). Whoever questions this exegesis, is anathematized (can. 2).[1] The same Christ who offered himself up upon the cross is here in the mass sacrificed in an unbloody way. The anathema is pronounced upon everyone who questions the reality of this sacrifice (can. 1). By this offering God is reconciled, and grants grace and the gift of repentance, and forgives even great sins (*peccata etiam ingentia*).[2] This sacrifice avails also for the dead. Its efficacy is due to the fact that it is in content identical with the sacrifice upon the cross, "only the method of offering being different" (c. 2). The entire Romish praxis in connection with the mass is thus dogmatically stated: Masses "in honor and memory of the saints" and private masses (*missae privatae*) (c. 36); the mixing of water with the wine (c. 7); the canon of the mass (c. 4); the cere-

---

[1] This theory involves a complete confusion of thought. The sacrifice of the mass is said to be merely a copy, or representation, of the offering upon the cross ; but yet it is to preserve the priesthood of Christ in the world and to repeat the sacrifice made upon the cross. We may easily understand what difficulties this must have occasioned in the debates. If the Lord's Supper— already in the first celebration—is the sacrifice of Christ, for what purpose then the subsequent death upon the cross ? (*e. g.*, act. ii. 78 b, 82 b, 81 a, 83. DÖLLINGER, Berichte u. Tagebücher, ii. 81).

[2] Here, too, the decree is full of contradictions. According to this passage (c. 2), the mass, as a sacrifice of Christ, blots out all sins—even mortal ; but in c. 1 it is said : "the virtue of this is applied for the remission of those sins which are daily committed by us." In view of these diffiulties, we can understand the origin of the theory mentioned *supra*, p. 203, n. 1 ; cf. p. 335.

monies and garments; the alternation of the "lowered and elevated voice" (c. 5). Anathemas are pronounced upon all variations from these positions (c. 5-9). There was thus again adopted a feature of the popular Christianity of the Middle Ages, with all its murkiness and fallacies. The work of Christ was committed to the hands of the church, *i. e.*, the priests,[1] which was in perfect keeping with the entire tendency of the medieval doctrine of the sacraments.

11. The 14th session treats exhaustively of the Sacrament of Repentance. This is said to have been instituted by Christ (Jn. 20. 22 f.) for the forgiveness of the sins of those who have lost the grace of their baptism (c. 1, 2). Its essence consists in the priestly absolution (cf. supra, p. 136, 140 n.). It embraces *contrition, confession,* and *satisfaction*. It works reconciliation with God, which is at times followed in the case of the pious by peace of conscience and the comfort of the Holy Spirit[2] (c. 3). The opinion that repentance consists in " terrors of conscience " and faith is condemned (ib.). The decree then treats of Contrition (c. 4). This embraces sorrow for past sins and the determination to sin no more. It obligates itself to the right reception of the sacrament, " with confidence in the divine mercy and with a vow to perform the things remaining." Even when the contrition, being combined with love, is perfect, it does not itself work reconciliation, but does so only by virtue of the " vow of the sacrament " connected with it.[3] " Imperfect contrition," which is called attrition, not only does not make man a hypocrite, but is a gift of the Holy Spirit, by the help of which the sinner " prepares for himself a way to righteousness." It is not indeed able *per se* to lead the sinner to justification, but

[1] Observe also the crass conception of the effect of the sacrifice of Christ which was perpetuated by the sacrifice of the mass (vid. already Gregory, supra, p. 24). It would be a profitable exercise to trace historically the mutual influences of the theory of satisfaction and the doctrine of the sacrifice of the mass. The ecclesiastical sacrifice was not seldom the counterpart of the sacrifice of Christ.

[2] The language is instructive : " Reconciliation with God, which sometimes (*interdum*), in pious men and those receiving this sacrament devoutly, peace of conscience and serenity, with great consolation of spirit, are accustomed to follow." The *opus operatum* is of itself sufficient, and its " objective " result, the peace of repentance, is an accessory which sometimes in the case of the " pious " follows !   Luther's comment was, that this " objective " result was not sufficient, but that a way should be sought by which the " *interdum* " might become the rule.   The 5th canon pays its respects to this proposed search by condemning the view, that a man will by simply recounting his sins become a hypocrite.

[3] This requirement, in itself considered, removes a difficulty of the medieval system, but it is no more consistent with the connection in which it is found than was the position of Thomas. Vid. supra, p. 136.

it "disposes" him toward the sacrament. This is essentially the popular medieval doctrine. But it is now further asserted with emphasis, that no impartation of grace is granted " without a good motive of the recipients," and that the Ninevites advanced from the imperfect penitence of one beneficially alarmed (*utiliter concussus*) to " repentance full of terrors." Thus contrition again appears to be necessary, but it will be observed upon careful examination that even this presentation of the matter does not indicate any real advance upon the popular medieval view, as the latter also required a transformation of the attrition into contrition—by means, it is true, of the sacrament (vid. supra, p. 137, 175).[1]

Upon contrition follows Confession, in which all mortal sins which can be remembered—and that not only in general (*in genere*), but in particular (*in specie*)—must be confessed, together with a detailing of all the circumstances which may be essential to a correct judgment of the offense. Only thus can the priest form a correct opinion and find the appropriate penalty (c. 5). The priest has not merely the "ministry . . . of declaring that sins are forgiven; but after the manner of a judicial act, in which sentence is pronounced by him as by a judge" (c. 6). Sins of particular gravity are " reserved " for the decision of the higher authorities (bishop, pope) (c. 7).

Works of Satisfaction are designed, first of all, as a pedagogic measure, to restrain the sinner from future sins : " As by a kind of rein, these satisfactorial penalties make penitents more cautious and vigilant in the future." In the second place, they make the sinner like Christ, "since in making satisfaction we suffer for our sins." This determines, thirdly, their atoning, satisfactorial character, in which connection, however, emphasis is laid upon the fact, that it is only from the satisfaction rendered by Christ that " all our sufficiency comes." Of the design of satisfaction, it is said : " It is not only for the guarding of the new life and a medicine for infirmity, but also for a punishment and castigation of past sins " (c. 8). Finally, it is observed, that

---

[1] But the matter is not clear. The original draft of the decretal said of attrition : " but it suffices for the constitution of this sacrament" (act. i. 584 a). These words were indeed afterward stricken out, but the other statements in regard to attrition were allowed to stand (vid. PALLAVICINI, x. 12. 25, 26). But DÖLLINGER-REUSCH, Moralstreitigkeiten, i. 72, go too far in their attempt to acquit the Tridentine Confession of the charge of attritionism. Here, too, there was doubtless a deliberate avoidance of clear definition. The Constitution designates Pius VI. as the " Promoter of the faith " (*auctor fidei*) and describes the " fear of Gehenna " as a *donum supernaturale* and as a " way (*modus*) inspired by God, preparing for the love of righteousness" (DENZINGER, Enchirid. n. 1388).

there is a satisfactorial significance, not only in the penalties imposed by the priest, but also in the patient endurance of the temporal chastisements which are appointed by God (c. 9). But as to the relation of the latter penalties to the former—a point often assailed by the later criticism (vid. supra, p. 210)— nothing is said.

The canons condemn the Protestant doctrine, *e. g.*, that baptism contains the sacrament of repentance (2); that repentance consists of only penitence (*terrores*) and faith (4); that contrition alone leads to hypocrisy (5); that the sacramental confession and the extension of its scope to cover " all and separate mortal sins, which can be held in memory by due and diligent premeditation, even those which are secret "—are not "of divine right " (6, 7); that the priestly absolution is not a "judicial act " (9); that Matt. 16. 19 and Jn. 20. 23 give to all Christians the authority to pronounce absolution (10); that bishops do not have the " right of reserving cases to themselves" (11); that satisfaction is nothing more than faith in forgiveness (12); that satisfactions are merely human traditions (14); that it is a " fiction," that, after the removal of the eternal penalties, temporal penalties often remain to be discharged (15).[1]

Indulgences were considered at the 25th session (Dec. 4, 1563). The impatient haste with which all business was transacted toward the close of the council did not admit of a thorough discussion of this subject (act. ii. 676 b. Sarpi, vi. 368 f.). But in order not to pass over the topic entirely, a sketch was prepared in the last night (act. ii. 680 a). Since Christ, it is held, gave indulgences to the church, this " practice very salutary for the people " is to be retained. Those who pronounce indulgences useless, or challenge the right of the church to grant them, are condemned. But in the granting of them moderation should be exercised, in accordance with the ancient and approved custom of the church, in order not to weaken ecclesiastical discipline. The abuses which have attached themselves to the system of indulgences and have given to the heretics an occasion for blasphemy against "this noble name of indulgences," are to be corrected—especially " all unworthy (*pravos*) gains in return for the securing of these, whence has come the greatest cause of abuses among the Christian populace, are to be entirely abolished."[2] Furthermore, the bishops are to take notice of the abuses and make report of them to Rome. The pope would then see to it, " that thus the favor

---

[1] As to public repentance, vid. sess. 24, De reformat. c. 8.
[2] Here, too, in the last minute it may be said, there was an alteration which

(*munus*) of the holy indulgences may be sacredly and without corruption dispensed to all believers.'' Even here, it will be observed, there was no surrender of any part of the traditional dogmatic position.[1]

Purgatory was also here discussed (ses. 25). The decretal drawn up in great haste (vid. ses. 6, can. 30) affirms that help may be given to souls in purgatory by the intercession of the saints and the sacrifice of the mass. This doctrine is to be preached without entering into discussion of the difficult questions connected with it. Masses, prayers, alms, and '' other pious works'' should be ''piously and devoutly'' rendered in behalf of the dead.

12. Extreme Unction (ses. 14) is said to remove the remains of sin in the dying and to lighten and confirm the heart (c. 2)— again, it will be observed, a reäffirmation of traditional doctrine.

13. The sacrament of Ordination, it is affirmed (ses. 23), was instituted in connection with the New Testament sacrifice. It was, therefore, instituted by Christ, who thereby committed to the apostles and their followers the ''power of offering and administering his body and blood both for the remitting and for the retaining of sins'' (c. 1). In view of the sacredness of the matter, it was appropriate that there should be in the church '' more and diverse orders of ministers.''' The Scriptures attest the priesthood and the diaconate, and the other ranks have been appointed from time to time since the early days of the church (c. 2). But since, according to the Scriptures, apostolic tradition, and the harmonious consensus of the Fathers, grace is conferred in ordination by words and outward signs, it is without doubt to be counted among the sacraments of the church (c. 3). Whoever denies this, or that the '' character '' is impressed by ordination, falls under the anathema (can. 4). The universal priesthood of believers is directly rejected. Not all have the same spiritual power (*spiritualis potestas*). Priests are discriminated from the laity not only by a '' temporary power.'' All these opinions are refuted by Eph. 4. 11 and 1 Cor. 12. 28 ff. The hierarchical government of the church is of divine appointment (*divina ordinatione*) (can. 6). Bishops are superior to presbyters (*presbyteris superiores*); to them are reserved confirmation and ordi-

---

was not in the interest of lucidity. '' Nevertheless, in this there were then stricken out certain words, which expressly forbade that certain large sums be impo·ed for the securing of indulgences '' (act. ii. 680 b); vid. PALLAVICINI, xxiv. 8. 1.

[1] Cf. the condemnation of the theses of the Synod of Pistoja in the Constitution, '' Auctorem fidei '' (1794), where the doctrine, that indulgences effect the forgiveness of temporal penalty, is presupposed (DENZINGER, Enchirid. n. 1403).

nation "and many other things." Ordination thus confers the spiritual office. The approval of the civil government, its call and authority, are not required in the sense "that without this ordination would be invalid."[1] On the other hand, all who are called and inducted into office only by the people or the civil authority are, like those who arrogate a spiritual office to themselves, "thieves and robbers" (Jn. 10. 1) (c. 4).[2]

14. The discussion of Marriage (ses. 24) is in very general terms, treating of its nature and the grace which Christ has won for it. As by the latter, Christian marriage is made superior to that of earlier times, it must now be reckoned among the sacraments. The canons discuss a number of canonical questions, forbid marriage to clerics and monks (can. 9), and condemn the view, that "it is not better nor more blessed to remain in virginity, or celibacy, than to be joined in marriage" (can. 10). Thus the medieval ideal of life is transported into modern times, which, aside from the practical ecclesiastical situation of the period, constitutes the historical significance of these canons.

15. Although the defenders of the old church placed the definition of the church at the centre of discussion—and rightly so —it was yet deemed prudent at Trent to refrain from a full discussion of this topic.[3] The debates occasioned by the presentation of the section upon ordination reveal the grounds for this caution. The highest officials desired a recognition of the papal system; but a great number of the bishops were thoroughly episcopal in their ideas. The original draft of the decretal upon ordination gave quite open expression to papalistic premises, the hierarchical organism being described as standing "under one supreme hierarch, the vicar of Christ on earth;" or (according to the second draft) the bishops standing under the pope being said to be "called to participation in care (*in partem sollicitudinis*), but not to plenitude of power" (*in plenitudinem potestatis*) (act. ii. 152 a, 155 b, with can. 7, 156 a). It was but logically consistent, when in the subsequent proceedings it was maintained, that all ecclesiastical authority belongs primarily to the pope, who can appoint and endow bishops at his will—he the sun, they the rays. The pope is, accordingly, the "vicar of Christ" in an absolute sense (*e. g.*, act. ii. 158 b, 175 a, 168 a : "Bishops are, therefore, not directly from Christ, but from the pontifex").

---

[1] Observe the prudent selection of language which would permit in praxis many interpretations. The entire conception is only a deduction from the sacramental character of ordination.

[2] The 8th canon also deserves mention : "If anyone shall say that bishops appointed by the authority of the Roman pontiff are not legitimate and true bishops, but a Roman figment, let him be anathema." Cf. act. ii. 155 f.

[3] Eck's Loci, *e. g.*, begin with a section, *De ecclesia*.

In opposition to this it was, however, maintained by many, that the pope is only "the chief vicar (*summus vicarius*) of Christ" (act. ii. 157 a, 165 a, 170 a, 193 b, et pas.). The apostles received their power, not from Peter, but from Christ. Not Peter, but Christ, selected the substitute for Judas. Thus the bishops also receive the "power for ruling and for governing the church of Christ" directly from Christ, and not from the pope (ib. ii. 188 f.). Primacy is ascribed to the pope only for the sake of earthly order : "Therefore the bishops have (their) power originally from God, but from the pope as a second cause" (ii. 165). The episcopal power (*potestas*) comes from Christ; the specific earthly territory within which it is to be exercised is assigned by the pope (ii. 168 f., 191 b, 192 f., etc.). Hence the constantly-recurring controversy as to the introductory clause of the decretals, *i. e.*, whether to the word *synodus* should be added the words *universalem ecclesiam representans*. Under these circumstances, it was certainly the most practical course to follow the counsel of those who advised an avoidance of this point of the controversy. The final draft of the decretal presents, therefore, in an almost unrecognizable form the original curialistic conception.

This clashing of views is historically intelligible ; but it appeared impossible in the situation then existing to find any way of harmonizing the antagonistic parties. Both agreed in acknowledging a double tradition. To the bishops belongs, by virtue of the apostolic succession, a peculiar power over the church, and—the popes, as the successors of Peter, are the rulers of the church. The episcopal party reasoned : If the bishops have apostolic power by *divine right*, then the papal primacy must have reference only to the external economy of the church. But no one ventured to draw the further inference, that the papacy must then exist only *by human right* (cf. supra, p. 167 f.), since the primacy of Peter was also instituted by God. Here lies the fault of the system. At this point the logic of the Curialists is brought to bear, the actual conditions in the church constituting an argument in their favor. If the papal primacy exits *jure divino*, then the pope is the lord of the church ; to him belongs all power in the church ; and the bishops are only called by him to a share in his practical oversight (*in partem sollicitudinis*). They possess the apostolic succession only in the form—illustrated in the apostolic age—of dependence upon Peter. But, in this case, can the power of the bishops be described as of divine right?[1] Does it not fall merely under

---

[1] Cf. the definition of the "divine right" by the Jesuit Salmeron : "That is of divine right which God himself does directly through himself" (LE PLAT, Monument. v. 524).

the category of canon law, or *jus humanum?* This neither party could or would acknowledge. There was at this point a very patent failure of logical consistency. The apostolic succession bound the hands of the Curialists, while Peter stood in the path of the Episcopalists; and neither of these obstacles could be cast aside.

That which the council could not do was accomplished at a later day by the CATECHISMUS ROMANUS. The doctrine of the church is here treated on the basis of Thomas (cf. supra, p. 144 f.). The church is the assembly of believers (*congregatio fidelium*, i. c. 10). Pious and wicked live in it side by side, possessing in common "the profession of faith and the communion of the sacraments." The pious are united to one another "by the spirit of grace and the bond of love " (ib. quaest. 6). But in this fellowship there must prevail obedience to that rank which is not only entrusted with the proclamation of the gospel, but is also judge and physician for the sinful (c. 7, q. 2, 28). But all this power is concentrated in the pope. · "For there is indeed one ruler and governor of it (the church), the invisible Christ; but also that visible (one) who occupies the Roman chair as the legitimate successor of Peter, the chief of the apostles" (c. 10, q. 10; cf. 7, q. 24). Christ, who rules the church, "appointed a man as vicar and minister of his power ; for, since the visible church needs a visible head, therefore our Saviour established Peter as the head and pastor of the whole race of believers " (c. 10, q. 11). The papalistic theory here finds a positive recognition which it could not have secured at the council.

The PROFESSIO FIDEI TRIDENTINA contains, as a component part of the Catholic faith—"outside of which no one can be saved "—the assertion : " I promise and swear true obedience to the Roman pontiff, successor of the blessed Peter, the chief. of the apostles, and the vicar of Jesus Christ."

16. The council preserved intact the Christianity of the Middle Ages. Nothing of importance in it was overlooked. Even the worship of saints and the veneration of images and relics are commended (ses. 25). Medieval theology was exalted to the position of ecclesiastical dogma. In this lies the chief significance of the Confession of Trent. We cannot but regard with amazement the great work which was here accomplished. Out of the innumerable array of contradictory formulas and theories, a reduction was made which, in a most masterly way, presents the fundamental principles of the Scholastic theology. True, many things are passed over or concealed, and others are expressed ambiguously ; but, viewed as a whole, the result was a self-

consistent system of doctrine such as the Roman Catholic church had not hitherto possessed. By this means the medieval theology was made independent of the shifting favor or disfavor of the schools. The Tridentine Confession rescued the Scholastic theology from the Scholastics, by placing it upon an elevation beyond their reach. But, comprehensive as was this doctrinal scheme in general, in particular points it was just as noticeably capable of indefinite expansion and modification. Many variant tendencies and shades of opinion might be gathered beneath it, and interpret their views into its language. In fact, Thomists and Scotists, Augustinian mystics and Jesuits immersed in practical politics, did just this, and did it without rebuke. It is only the gospel, as understood by Protestantism, to which there is no bridge from the Tridentine theology. In this direction only its declarations are clear, sharp, unyielding, and enclosed in a hedge of innumerable anathemas. The supremacy of tradition, the sacramental infusion of grace, faith as an assent or subjection to formulas, the hierarchy as the almoner of supernatural powers and gate-keeper of the celestial world, the ascetic ideal of life—upon these points there is no wavering and no uncertain sound. It is here, therefore, that the ways part. The anathemas of the Tridentine canons branded as heresy the Protestant teaching in its entire compass, as the decretals elevated the Roman Catholic theories to the position of dogmas. This constitutes the two-fold significance of the Council of Trent.

§ 84. *Revival of the Augustinian Doctrine of Grace and Its Ecclesiastical Rejection.*

LITERATURE. LINSENMANN, Mich. Bajus, 1867. MÖLLER-SEEBERG, PRE. ii., ed. 3, 363 ff. SAINTE-BEUVE, Port Royal, ed. 3, 6 vols., Paris, 1867. REUCHLIN, Gesch. v. Port-Royal, 2 vols., 1839-44. SCHNEEMANN, Entstehung u. Entwicklg. d. thomist.-molinist. Controverse, 2 parts, 1879-80. SCHRÖCKH, KG. seit der Reformat. iv. 310 ff. HENKE, Neuere KG., ii. 98 ff. RANKE, Französ. Gesch., vols. iii. and iv. SCHILL, Die Constitution Unigenitus, 1876. REUSCH, Index der verbotenen Bücher, ii. 457 ff., 539 ff., 552 ff., 724 ff. THOMASIUS-SEEBERG, DG. ii., ed. 2, 717 ff. HARNACK, DG. iii., ed. 3, 647 ff.

1. The Augustinian doctrine of grace found recognition at Trent in but a mutilated form. More emphasis was laid upon it in the Romish Catechism, as the latter was influenced by Thomas. But the ethics and dogmatics of the Jesuits soon banished this doctrine entirely from the regnant theology. There were not lacking, indeed, some theologians of Augustinian tendencies to oppose this growing Pelagianism. They

asserted themselves in Belgium and France, being influenced also
by humanistic predilections. Their distinguishing characteristic was merely the advocacy of the Augustinian doctrine, their
orthodoxy being unassailable in all other points. More important, therefore, than their views is the papal condemnation which
was visited upon them, as this falls with all its force upon
Augustine himself. They were accordingly in the right who, in
A. D. 1563, laid before the pope the complaint : "Under a
mask, they condemn the doctrine of Augustine," or : "O
grief ! Augustine is condemned under the name of the Jansenists " (REUSCH, Index ii. 469).   We must trace the course
of the controversies induced by Baius, Jansen, and Quesnel.

2. MICHAEL BAIUS (De Bay, A. D. 1513-89), a professor in
Louvain, advocated the Augustinian doctrine of grace. Original
righteousness, as the subjection of the sensuous nature to the spirit
united with God, is not to be designated as an added endowment
(*donum superadditum*). If man was created good by God, then
concupiscence, as the rebellion of the flesh against the spiritual
nature, is really sin. Man is utterly depraved by sin : "free-
will without the assistance of God avails for nothing except for
sin." As the entire man, so also the entire race has become
subject to sin. The justification of the sinner takes place through
the transformation of his will by God : "Our evil will is transformed into a good (will)." This new will man now employs
in good works : "Righteousness is properly obedience to the
law." [1] But since this righteousness wrought in man upon earth
by grace can never be flawless, God here grants as supplementary
the forgiveness of sins. "Justification is nothing else than a
certain continuous progression both in the practice of virtues and
in the remission of sins." This whole structure of thought is
thoroughly Catholic.[2] Nevertheless, the 79 theses of Baius were
condemned by Pope Pius V. in the bull, *Ex omnibus afflictioni-
bus*. Thus genuinely Augustinian ideas were rejected, *e. g. :*
That the will without grace can only sin ; that even the con-

---

[1] This is a definition strongly emphasized by Bajus, *e. g.*, in his theses condemned by the pope, n. 42 : "Righteousness, by which the man is justified
by faith, consists formally in obedience to the commandments ;" 69 : "The
justification of the wicked man occurs formally through obedience to the law,
but not through a secret communication and inspiration of grace which causes
those who are justified to fulfill the law through it."

[2] The independent role here attributed to the forgiveness of sins—which is
not, as in Thomas, the recognition of an act of making righteousness already
accomplished—reminds us of PIGHIUS and GROPPER (supra, p. 434, n. 1). Let
it not be overlooked, however, that forgiveness removes only the guilt
(*reatus*) of sin, whereas grace in the proper sense atones for or transforms the
act itself.

cupiscence that is contrary to the will is sin ; that the sinner is moved and animated by God alone, and not by the ministrations of the priest ; that merits are bestowed upon men gratuitously.[1] Bajus recalled his assertions.

3. The controversy associated with the name of the Jesuit, LUDWIG MOLINA († A. D. 1600), ran its course without producing any permanent result. In his work, *Liberi arbitrii cum gratiae donis, div. praescientia, providentia, praedestinatione et reprobatione concordia* (A. D. 1588), an acute attempt is made to reconcile Pelagianism, Semipelagianism, and Augustinianism. Man is even in his sinful state free to perform, not only natural, but also surpernatural works, the coöperation of grace being presupposed. Grace elevates and stimulates the soul, making it capable of supernatural works ; but the real act of decision is not wrought in the will by grace, but is made by the will itself, the will being, however, in union with grace. Thus, as the free decision of the will and the capacitating of the soul for the supernatural (grace) in their coöperation mark the beginning of the state of acceptance with God (*Heilsstand*),[2] so both combined in simultaneous combination (*concursu simultaneo*) produce the supernatural acts. They work together like two men who tug a vessel with one rope. Now the thoroughgoing coöperation thus attained becomes a mere illusion if all the free acts of created beings are really recognized, as among the Thomists, as willed

---

[1] A few of the important theses (vid. the Bull in DENZINGER, Enchiridion, 881 ff.) are as follows : 20. " No sin is by its nature venial, but every venial sin merits eternal punishment." 25. "All works of unbelievers are sins, and the virtues of the philosophers are vices." 27. "Free-will without the assistance of the grace of God avails only for sin." 28. "It is a Pelagian error to say that free-will avails for the avoiding of sin." 35. "Everything which the sinner, or servant of sin, does is sin." 51. "Concupiscence, or the law of the members and its depraved desires, which men now willingly feel, is a real disobedience of the law." 73. "No one except Christ is without original sin ; hence the blessed virgin is mortal on account of sin contracted from Adam, and all her afflictions in this life, just as those also of other righteous persons, were avengings of actual or original sin." 58. "The penitent sinner is not vivified by the ministration of the absolving priest, but by God alone, who, suggesting and inspiring (his) repentance, vivifies and resuscitates him ; but by the ministration of the priest guilt alone is removed." 8. "In those redeemed by the grace of Christ, no good merit can be found which is not conferred gratuitously upon the unworthy." 77. "Temporal satisfactions do not avail to expiate *de condigno* temporal punishment remaining after sin has been pardoned." 10. "The remitting of the temporal punishment, which often remains after sin has been pardoned, and the resurrection of the body, are properly to be ascribed to nothing but the merits of Christ."

[2] Molina gains a place for *prevenient grace* by maintaining that, in the first act (*actus primus*), before the advent of the second act (*actus secundus*) of the will, *i. e.*, in the habituality of the will while not as yet realized in acts, grace alone acts. The coöperation is posited only of the *actus secundi*.

by God himself of his own original motion. At this point, Molina's theory of a "median knowledge" (*scientia media*) is introduced. God, he maintains, foresees what his free creatures under any given circumstances will do or not do. The *scientia media* is, therefore, a knowledge of the contingent future. By means of it God beholds the entire future, and he orders the course of the world in accordance with the knowledge thus in his possession. In contrast with the theory of a causal connection of events strictly determined by divine decree, there is here retained a place for human freedom. Upon the metaphysical questions which are thus left unanswered, it is not needful for us to enter. The aim of Molina is clear. Grace and human freedom are to be combined with one another in a peaceful union. The ancient problems are to be thus solved in a very simple way. Predestination and reprobation may be readily accounted for by the *scientia media*, by virtue of which God foresaw which men would coöperate with grace, and which of them would not do so. But this foreseen free activity of man is to be regarded only as a means, and not as a cause, of predestination, as the latter idea would be Semipelagian.

It is true, a critical eye will readily discover that the combination thus assumed is only apparent, and that the Augustinian-Thomistic conception of grace is here torn out by the roots. It is not the all-working power of the divine will which effects salvation ; but the hands of God and man work together as coördinate factors. Synergism in its boldest form is the confessed first principle of this theology. But the opposition to it inaugurated by the Dominicans was crippled by the championship of the Jesuits, who adopted this theory of grace as the official doctrine of their order. The popes did not dare to give decision against the powerful order, and hence the whole matter was buried in the sessions of the commission of the *congregatio de auxiliis gratiae* without the promised papal declaration. As a result, the Jesuits were allowed to propagate their doctrine without opposition from the church. Cf. SCHNEEMANN, l. c. MORGOTT, in Kirchenlex. viii., ed. 2, 1737 ff., and iii., ed. 2, 897 ff.

4. The most powerful reaction against the lax and Pelagianizing moral principles of the Jesuits came from circles which centred about the abbey Port Royal, situated not far from Paris. The medieval form of piety was indeed preserved in these circles, but they drew their inspiration from Augustinian Mysticism, and in this they believed themselves to possess the means of rescuing all serious-minded persons from the nets of the Jesuits. Hence it was that this party could find its program in a work which professed to be, and really was, nothing else than a revived Augustine. This was

the publication of the Bishop of Ypres, CORNELIUS JANSENIUS († A. D. 1638): *Augustinus seu doctrina Augustini de humanae naturae sanitate, aegritudine, medicina adv. Pelagianos et Massilienses.* It was published in A. D. 1640, Jansen having completed it shortly before his death. As Bradwardina had done at an earlier day, Jansen holds up as a mirror before his age, sunken in Pelagianism, the genuine teachings of Augustine. This is done with historic fidelity, and not, as was the case with the English theologian, in order to establish a deterministic system. Original sin, he taught, has filled the entire human race with lust and ignorance. The sinner is now free in the domain of sin. Justification by grace is by no means to be identified with the forgiveness of sins, as is done by the Protestants. Christ brings the "medicinal aid of the Saviour." Irresistible grace, and this alone, works the good in men : it "makes them will" (*facit ut velint*). Grace consists essentially in the inspiration of good concupiscence, or love. Grace aims at love as its goal, and love is crowned with the forgiveness of sins. These ideas are marshaled within the lines of the Augustinian doctrine of predestination.

The Augustinian character of Jansen's teaching cannot be called in question. He in reality simply reproduced Augustine. Yet this book precipitated a bitter conflict, which convulsed all France for more than a century. Upon the suggestion of the Jesuits, Pope Urban VIII. in A. D. 1642 in the bull, *In Eminenti*, called attention to the condemnation of the doctrine of Bajus, of which it declares the teaching of Jansen to be a revival. This was the signal for the strife. Protests were uttered against the moral principles of the Jesuits, the secularized Christianity of the age, and the smothering of liberty by the church. The contestants strove with flaming words and glittering irony, not only for dogmatic formulas, but for the genuine Christian religion—for the rights of the inner life and personal conviction (*e. g.*, ANTON ARNAULD, BLAISE PASCAL). Nevertheless, they thought it still possible to remain good Catholics, and no attempt was made to assail the infallibility of papal deliverances. Outwardly less untrammeled, and with a fuller inward apprehension of the truth, than the representatives of the great reformatory movement upon the same territory in the fifteenth century, the Jansenists were at one with their predecessors in the idealism which thought it possible to mend and make available for practical purposes the old garment by sewing upon it the great patch of a reform conducted upon the ancient ecclesiastical and national basis. When this attempt at the restoration of the church without tearing down any part of her structure collapsed, Jansenism fell with it ; not, indeed, without contributing its share to induce the great calamity which overwhelmed its adversary in the Revolution.

But the doctrine of Augustine never again gained the ascendency. Five theses selected from Jansen's book by the Sorbonne were condemned by Innocent X. in the bull, *Cum occasione* (A. D. 1663). They were as follows : 1. "Some commandments of God are impossible to righteous men willing and striving according to the present powers which they have : there is lacking also to these the grace by which they would be made possible." 2. "Resistance is never offered to inward grace in the state of fallen nature." 3. "For meriting or demeriting in the state of fallen nature, there is not required in man freedom from necessity, but freedom from coërcion suffices." 4. "The Semipelagians admitted the necessity of prevenient inward grace for single acts, even for the beginning of faith, and they were heretics because they maintained that this grace was of such a nature that the human will was able either to resist it or to conform to it." 5. "It is Semipelagian to say that Christ died, or shed his blood, for all men whatsoever."[1]

Inasmuch as the Jansenists did not wish to call in question the papal authority, they attempted to extricate themselves from their embarrassing position by discriminating between the "question of fact" and "the question of right," maintaining that, as a matter of fact, Jansen had not advocated the theses which the pope thus—and rightly—condemned. The compromising position of the Jansenists soon brought them into further difficulty, as Pope Alexander VII. plainly declared, that the five theses had been condemned "in the sense intended by the same Cornelius Jansen" (Constitut. *Ad sanct. Petri sedem*, A. D. 1665) ! The five theses remained therefore under condemnation, and even the "obsequious silence" observed by Clement IX. (A. D. 1668) was declared insufficient by Clement XI. (1705). Port Royal was destroyed, A. D. 1710. The particulars must be referred to Church History.

5. Yet once again the embers of the strife were rekindled. The occasion was the publication by the Oratorian, PASCHASIUS QUESNEL († A. D. 1719), of his Meditations upon the New Testament (*Le nouveau test. en français avec des reflexions*

---

[1] These theses, although torn from their context and therefore difficult to fully comprehend, no doubt reproduce the doctrine of Jansen. The first thesis means to maintain, that for each separate good work there is necessary a reception of efficacious grace (*gracia efficax*). It must be borne in mind also that beneath them all lies as a premise the predestinarian *gratia irresistibilis.* Cf. HENKE, ii. 103 f. REUCHLIN, Port-Roy. i. 761, 778 f.

morales sur chaque verset).   At the instigation of the Jesuits, the notorious constitution, *Unigenitus*, condemned no fewer than 101 theses of this biblical commentary.   With terrific directness, not only the Augustinian theology, but the entire structure of Augustinian Christianity was here condemned.   It is heretical to teach : that the natural man is only sinful ; that faith is a gift of God ; that grace is given only through faith ; that faith is the first grace, and the first grace is the forgiveness of sins ; that grace is needed for all good works ; that grace works in us what God has commanded.[1]   But, in reality, this condemnation strikes at a higher authority than Augustine.   It is directed, in the last instance, against Paul, who had occasioned the Council of Trent so many laborious hours (cf. supra, p. 436); for Quesnel was influenced not only by Augustine, but also by Paul (*e. g.*, thesis 26).   Intense excitement was awakened (the Appellants *versus* the Acceptants), but it subsided without result when compelled to face the firm alliance of the papal infallibility (to which the Appellants could at best submit

---

[1] We cite a few of the most important theses : 38. " The sinner is not free, except toward evil, without the grace of the Redeemer." 62. " He who does not abstain from evil except from fear of punishment, commits it in his heart, and is already guilty before God." 48. " What else can we be than darkness, than error, than sin—without the light of faith, without Christ, and without his love ? " 39. " The will which grace has not anticipated (prae-venit) has no light (lamp) except for erring," etc.   29. " Outside of the church no grace is granted." 73. " What is the church, except the assembly of the sons of God, abiding in his bosom ? " 74. " The church, or the entire body, has Christ the incarnate Word as its head, but all the saints as its members." 76. " Nothing is broader than the church of God, since all the elect and righteous of all ages compose it." 79. " It is useful and necessary for every age, every place, and every class of persons to study and know the spirit, piety, and mysteries of the Holy Scriptures." 80. " The reading of the Holy Scriptures is for all." 82. " The Lord's day ought to be sanctified by Christians by readings of piety and, above all, of the Holy Scriptures." 85. " To forbid to Christians the reading of the Holy Scriptures, especially of the gospel, is to forbid to the children of light the use of the lamp, and to make them suffer a kind of excommunication." 69. " Faith, the practice, increase and reward of faith—all is a gift of the pure generosity of God." 26. " No graces are given except through faith." 27. " Faith is the first grace and the fountain of all others." 28. " The first grace which God grants to the sinner is the remission of sins." 51. " Faith justifies when it works, but it does not work except through love." 2. " The grace of Jesus Christ, the efficacious source of every kind of good, is necessary for every good work ; without it, not only is nothing done, but neither can anything be done." 3. " In vain, O Lord, dost thou command, unless thou thyself dost also give what thou commandest." 11. " Grace is nothing else than the will of the omnipotent God, commanding and effecting what it commands."   Are not these almost literally Augustinian propositions ?   And how remarkable is the condemnation of the 29th thesis !   To the naturalistic Pelagianism of this bull, even Cyprian appears dangerous !

only against the protest of their consciences) with the influence of the court and the Jesuit interpretation of the gospel.   Benedict XIV. finally decided, that the Constitution, *Unigenitus*, must be regarded as legally valid, but that no one was to be persecuted who did not publicly assail it (A. D. 1756). We note here the intrusion of that worst of all the externalizations of faith effected by the Jesuits, viz.: the theory that assent to dogma is not necessary, but silent submission is sufficient.   Within the whole range of the History of Doctrines, there is no official document which so richly merits condemnation as scandalous as does this.   And yet it has not only been confirmed by a great number of popes, but accepted by several French councils and " by the entire Catholic world " (vid. DENZINGER, ante n. 1216). It marks the definite expulsion of Augustinian piety from the official Roman Catholic church.

6. Here may be mentioned the dogmatization of the doctrine of the Immaculate Conception of the Virgin by Pius IX. in the Constitution, *Ineffabilis deus* (8. dec., 1854).   In proportion as the strict logical consistency of the Augustinian doctrine of sin and grace was impaired, did it become possible to give to the doctrine of the immaculate conception dogmatic authority, especially as the masses of the populace had long regarded Mary as miraculously endowed and holy.   The pope now proclaimed :

" We declare, pronounce, and define, that the doctrine which holds that the most blessed Virgin Mary was in the first moment of her conception, by the peculiar grace and privilege of the omnipotent God, in view of the merits of Christ Jesus the Saviour of the human race, preserved immune from all pollution of original sin, has been revealed by God, and is therefore to be firmly and constantly believed by all the faithful," etc.   Thus, here too, a doctrine of the Scotist and Jesuistic theology triumphed.

§ 85. *Completion of the Romish Dogma of the Church.   The Vatican Council.*

SOURCES. PLANCK, Neueste Religionsgesch., vol. i. 2, 1787 ff. V. MÜNCH, Vollst. Sammlg. aller älteren u. neueren Konkordate, 2 vols., 1830 f.; ib., Gesch. des Emser Kongresses u. seiner Punktate, 1840. NIPPOLD, Handb. d. neuesten KG., ed. 3, vols. i. and ii. MEIER, Zur Gesch. d. röm.-deutschen Frage, 2 vols., 1871-3 ; ib., Febronius, ed. 2, 1885. H. SCHMID, Gesch. d. Kath. Kirche Deutschlands, 1874. HENKE, Neuere KG., vol. iii. NIELSEN, Gesch. d. Papstt. im 19 Jarh. i., ed. 2, 1880 ; ib., Aus dem inneren Leben d. kath. Kirche im 19 Jarh. i., 1882. FRIEDBERG, Sammlg. von Aktenstücken zum Vat. Conc., 1872. Die Constitutiones d. Conc., also in DENZINGER, Enchirid. n., 1630 ff., and MIRBT, Quellen, p. 255 ff. FRIEDRICH, Gesch. d. Vat. Conc., 3 vols., 1877, 1883, 1889. QUIRINUS, Röm.

Briefe v. Conc., 1870. ACTON, Zur Gesch. d. Vat. Conc., 1871. FROMMANN, Gesch. u. Krit. d. Vat. Conc., 1872. JANUS, Der Papst u. d. Conc., 1871.

1. The ancient struggle between the curial and the episcopal systems was, as we have seen, not brought to a conclusion at the Council of Trent. The episcopal view subsequently asserted itself with great energy in both France and Germany. The inconsistencies, which had always been involved in this view (vid. supra, p. 446), were even now not eliminated. Despite the resort to rationalistic and illuministic principles in support of it, the advocates of the episcopacy did not yet venture to draw the final conclusions to which their theory logically pointed. In the nineteenth century, it was definitely vanquished.

In France, under Louis XIV., the *Declaration du clergé de France* had plainly asserted the liberties of the Gallican church. It contains the following propositions: 1. "The power of Peter and his successors extends only to spiritual, but not to secular and temporal things, so that in matters of the latter kind princes are in no way subject to the spiritual government." 2. The "full power (*plena potestas*) of spiritual things" inheres in the popes in such a way that at the same time the decrees of tne Council of Constance, "upon the authority of the general councils," recognized by the popes and the entire church, also remain in force. 3. The papal power is, therefore, to be circumscribed: "The rules, customs, and institutions adopted by the Gallican kingdom and church are also valid." 4. "In questions of faith also, the chief parts belong to the supreme pontiff, and his decrees pertain to all churches and every church; nevertheless, his decision is not irreversible (*irreformabile*) unless the consensus of the church shall have been added to it" (in MIRBT, 209 f.).

These articles were at various times condemned at the instigation of Rome. Louis XIV. did not dare to maintain them without modifications. It was Napoleon I. who, in A. D. 1810, made them a part of the civil law. But since he, without regard to the French episcopate, in the Concordat of A. D. 1801, combined with the pope in regulating the affairs of the French church, he in reality brought the latter again under the dominion of the pope. The despot used the pope for the furtherance of his own plans ("if there had not been a pope, we would have had to invent one"), but he incidentally increased the latter's power.

2. In Germany, the suffragan, NICHOLAS OF HONTHEIM, in Treves, impressively advocated the episcopalistic theory in his work published under the pseudonym, FEBRONIUS, *De statu ecclesiae et legitima potestate Romani pontificis, . . . Bullioni, 1763."* All the apostles, he maintained, were on an equality, and all were entrusted with the same power of the keys. The

bishops have their authority directly from Christ. The papal primacy dare not claim to exceed that of Peter himself. The papacy is designed only to serve for the promotion of church order. It is not the pope, but the general council, which represents the church. The pope is subordinate to the whole council, and is merely on a parity with its separate members. These principles, it was held, must be carried out with all energy.

Occasion was given for the practical application of these ideas by the controversy in regard to the nunciatures. A part of the episcopal functions had been unlawfully assigned to the papal nuncios.[1] When the Elector of Bavaria now applied for a nuncio, the archbishops of Cologne, Mayence, Treves, and Salzburg attempted to break the curial system. Their representatives prepared at Ems the so-called "Punctation of Ems" (vid. Von Münch, Emser Kongr., 103 ff.). In this it is acknowledged that the pope is "the chief-overseer and primate of the whole church— the central point of her unity, and endowed by God with the jursidiction requisite to this end." But, on the other hand, the bishops are the immediate successors of the apostles, and hold directly from Christ the power to bind and loose and te make laws, as well as to grant dispensations from the latter (e. g., in regard to hindrances to marriage). Romish bulls and breviaries are therefore valid only in so far as they are acknowledged by the bishops. By these principles, the ground is torn from beneath the nunciatures.

But Bavaria persevered in her request, and the pope in his claims. The attempt to exalt the episcopacy based upon divine right above the primacy based only upon human appointment was met by Rome with the exaltation of faith in the divine right of the papacy : "And that this is the power of primacy, which he holds by divine right in order that he may outrank other bishops, not only in the degree of honor, but also in the fullness of supreme power." The theory, that Christ gave to all the apostles equal authority, and that all bishops have the same claim as the pope to participation in the government of the church, is rejected as folly (vid. the brief, *Super soliditate*, 1786, in Denzinger, n. 1363).[2] The old title of Peter as the rock did good service also in this modern age.

3. It must be noticed, finally, that at the Synod of Pistoja (A. D. 1786), under the leadership of Recci, a reform program

---

[1] Vid. Meier, Die Propaganda, ihre Provinzen und ihr Recht, ii. 180 ff. The Nunciatures are the incorporated claims of the curial system, in which the latter, against law and order, seeks to encroach upon the episcopal jurisdiction.

[2] The brief condemns the book of *Eybel*, "Was ist der Papst?" 1782. Cf. Kirchenlex. iv., ed. 2, 1152 f.

was prepared, which also included a recognition of episcopal principles. But the constitution, *Auctorem fidei* (A. D. 1794), condemned, in connection with the whole program, particularly the theses : " That the Roman pontifex is the ministerial head ; " " that the bishop has received from Christ all necessary rights for the good government of his diocese ; " " that the rights of the bishop, received from Jesus Christ for the governing of the church, can neither be altered nor impeded " (Denzinger, n. 1366, 1369, 1371). The French Revolution at this point distracted the growing interest in these plans, associated as they were with the general movement of the Illumination.

4. On the other hand, the conditions prevailing in the age of the Restoration were as favorable as possible for the papacy. Talented advocates arose for its defense, who skillfully directed the thought of the age, impressed, as it now was, with its need of authority, toward Christianity, identifying Christianity at the same time indissolubly with the papacy. The kingdom of the devil must be destroyed and the old order of things restored. Two citations may serve to exhibit the spirit in which this program was carried out : " If it were permitted to establish degrees of importance among the things of divine institution, I would place the hierarchy before the dogma, so much is it indispensable to the maintenance of the faith " (de Maistre). " The company of the devil cannot but recoil before the company of Jesus " (Bonald). With the open and sinister reactionary ecclesiastical tendencies was combined a romantic enthusiasm for the rock of Peter, which had defied the storms of the Reformation and the floods of the Illumination, and a deep interest in the political reaction. It was imagined that these drifts of sentiment might now be encouraged without danger, since the Illumination had ensured absolute security against all Romish attempts. This was a sad mistake. At scarcely any period since the great days of the Middle Ages has the Curia ever displayed such a susceptibility to the whole course of events, such a ready adaptation in tactics and in speech, such zeal in well-considered action—as in the past century. The results are clearly manifest. The concordats, for which Napoleon had set the example, and which were from A. D. 1816 concluded with many states, subjected the church to the pope as her lord. Their significance consisted less in that which they contained than in the fact that they were concluded, and that, too, with the pope directly, without any recognition of the bishops. The course of action deliberately chosen by the curia with a view to the achievement of the end in view was acquiesced in by the states and nations. No more is henceforth to be heard of the episcopalistic ideas of reform which

agitated so many minds before the Revolution. Curialism has triumphed.

5. The VATICAN COUNCIL (1869-70) really did no more than give dogmatic form to the conquest thus long before achieved. There was at the outset laid before the council an outline of the faith (*Schema de fide*). This was approved April 24th, 1870 (vid. MIRBT, Papsturkunden, p. 255 ff. Denzinger, n. 1630 ff.). This summary contains nothing new. In opposition to Rationalism and Naturalism, the pope declares with the assent of the bishops,[1] "relying upon the word of God written and handed down," what is the true doctrine. First of all, God—"an entirely simple and unchangeable spiritual subsistence"—is acknowledged as the Creator and Ruler of the world (ses. 3, c. 1). Secondly, it is taught, that God has revealed himself. This revelation "is contained in written books and traditions without writing." The latter come from Christ or the apostles ; the former embrace the books approved at the Council of Trent, which are to be found in the Vulgata. These books are canonical, not because they contain the revelation without error, "but for this reason, that, written by inspiration of the Holy Spirit, they have God as their author, and, as such, they have been handed down to the church." The church establishes the meaning of the Scriptures : "That is to be considered as the true sense of the Sacred Scriptures, which the holy Mother, the church, whose office it is to judge concerning the true sense and interpretation of the Holy Scriptures, has held and holds" (c. 2).[2] To this revelation we are to render obedience in faith : "We are under obligation to render obedience of intellect and will in faith." Faith consists in this : "that we, the grace of God inspiring and assisting, believe the things revealed by him to be true." This "assensus" pertains to all things "which are contained in the written or handed-down word of God, and which are by the church, either by solemn decision or in her ordinary and universal ministrations, pronounced worthy to be believed as divinely revealed" (c. 3).

6. But these were merely incidental matters. More and more plainly the real object had in view by the curia and a considerable number of the members of the council was revealed. The

---

[1] Ses. 3, c. 1 : "The bishops of the whole world, assembled to this ecumenical synod by our authority in the Holy Spirit, sitting and judging with us"—these words, as indeed the very superscription of the "Constitution :" "Bishop Pius, servant of the servants of God, the holy council approving," assume as granted the curial conception.

[2] Vid. this view of inspiration and the interpretation of Scripture also in the apostolic circular letter of Leo XIII. (A. D. 1894), in MIRBT, Quellen, p. 280.

pope was, in a formal address, requested to present a paper upon
the Infallible Authority of the Pope.   A smaller party made
some opposition, expressing themselves no opinion upon the
subject, but pronouncing the definition of the new dogma as
inopportune and ill-timed.   The pope "felt" his infallibility.[1]
An appendix upon the infallibility was added to the outline
previously presented to the delegates (in FRIEDBERG, Aktenstücke, p. 572).   What difference did it make, that the public
opinion of Europe arose in amazement against the new dogma :
that the anti-infallibilists assailed the document before them with
well-grounded arguments ; that they besought the pope to withdraw or modify the passages in question in the new paper laid
before the Council on May 10th ?   The pope held to his opinion.   The Infallibilists produced a mass of arguments—some
of them most astonishing—for their theory.[2]   Many of its opponents left the city.   On July 18th, the vote was taken, of the 535
bishops present only two voting "Non placet."

The constitution, *Pastor aeternus*, defines the new dogma.   In
order that there might be one episcopate, and that the multitude
of believers might by it be held together in harmony, Christ
placed Peter above the other apostles : "In him he established
both a perpetual source of unity and a visible foundation upon
whose stability should be constructed the eternal temple"
(Pref.).   The "primacy of jurisdiction over the universal
church of Christ" was imparted by Christ directly and immediately to Peter and to Peter alone.   It conflicts with the teachings of the Scriptures to say that "this same primacy was conferred, not immediately and directly upon the blessed Peter himself, but upon the church, and through it upon him as a minister
of this church" (c. 1).   This power has passed from Peter
upon his successors : "Whence whoever succeeds in this chair
of Peter, he, according to the institution of Christ himself,
obtains the primacy over the universal church" (c. 2).   According to this doctrine, which is demanded by the Scriptures and
tradition, the pope—as the Florentine decretal has taught—is to be
recognized. as the successor of the prince of the Apostles, "the

---

[1] Cf. his declarations : "As for infallibility, being the priest Mastai, I
always believed it ; now, being the pope Mastai, I feel it ;" and with this,
his pendant to the well-known saying of Louis XIV.: "The tradition I am"
(Quirinus, p. 107, 555).
[2] Among the "proofs" were the passages, Lk. 22. 32 ; Iren. iii. 3 ; the
title, Vicar of Christ ; the fact that Peter was crucified with his head downward, his head thus bearing the burden of his body ; that Peter himself
in Sicily claimed for himself infallibility ; and that Mary, being asked,
declared that Christ had indeed granted this plenary authority to Peter.   Vid.
QUIRINUS, p. 412 ff.

true vicar of Christ and head of the whole church and father
and teacher (*pater et doctor*) of all Christians." To him belongs
the actual "power of jurisdiction" (*potestas jurisdictionis*).
This power is "ordinary" and "immediate," and extends to
every single believer, *i. e.*, the pope exercises such power, not
only in special cases as a last resort, but he can employ it at all
times and under all circumstances. It is a "truly episcopal"
power, inasmuch as the pope is authorized to perform all episcopal functions in all places. Every individual is therefore bound
to render direct obedience to the ordinances of the pope in all
things affecting faith and life, or the discipline and government
of the church: "This is the doctrine of Catholic truth, from
which no one can deviate without forfeiting faith and salvation."
The pope is the supreme judge of believers (the faithful). It is
an error to desire to appeal from his decision to a council as a
higher authority (c. 3). The popes have always been acknowledged as the supreme authority in matters of faith. A "char-
ism of never-failing truth and faith" has been bestowed upon
Peter and his followers, in order that the church may remain
free from error and the pure doctrine be preserved in power.
Since in our time many oppose this authority, the new dogma
is, for the glory of God and the salvation of the nations, formulated as follows :

"Therefore we . . . the holy council approving, teach and
declare to be divinely revealed the dogma : That the Roman
pontiff, when he speaks from the chair (*ex cathedra*), that is, when
he, exercising the office of pastor and teacher of all Christians
by virtue of his supreme apostolic authority, defines the doctrine
concerning faith or morals (*fide vel moribus*) which is to be held by
the universal church, he acts, through the divine assistance promised to the blessed Peter himself, with that infallibility by which
the divine Redeemer wished his church to be instructed in the
defining of doctrine concerning faith and morals ; and therefore
the definitions of such Roman pontiff are *of themselves, but not
by virtue of the consent of the church*,[1] beyond revision (*irre-
formabiles*). If anyone (which may God prevent) shall presume
to contradict this our definition, let him be anathema" (c. 4).

7. The excitement caused by the Vatican Council subsided
within a remarkably short period. A small party of pious Idealists
protested vigorously, but few listened to them. There was no opportunity for a popular demonstration upon the part of Old Cath-

---

[1] The words : "*non autem ex consensu ecclesiae*," which in as crass a
form as possible express the personal infallibility, were not placed before the
council until July 15th (FRIEDRICH, Documenta ad illustr. conc. Vat. ii.
318).

olicism.   The unexampled rapidity with which the aims of the council were secured may be understood when we remember that the whole world had long since become accustomed to think of the pope as the legitimate lord of the Roman Catholic church, and that the very ancient claims of the popes to be the bearers of divine truth had ever since the days of the Counter-reformation been constantly gaining a firmer foothold in Catholic circles. That which in the days of the reform-councils would have appeared inconceivable could become a reality in the Nineteenth Century—the acknowledgment of the infallibility of the pope as over against and superior to that of the council.   The Vatican Council caused but little excitement in the church because it produced nothing new.   But there was also another reason.   The influence of Jesuitical teaching had long since dissipated the interest of the Catholic masses in doctrine as such.   Their attitude toward the dogmas of the church was very largely the same as toward the Scriptures—they have them as though they had them not.   Obedient submission to the formulas, *i. e.*, refraining from criticism of them, is sufficient.   Or, the dogmas might be used for an ascetic disparagement of the "reason."   But the real sources of religious life do not, for the Roman Catholic masses, lie in the realm of doctrine.   Sacraments and good works, relics and scapularies, the sacrifice of the mass and all kinds of holy water, the mother of God with her appearances and her adoration, the worship of the heart of Jesus and that of the Virgin,[1] etc.—bring grace and regulate the intercourse of the soul with God.   The most of these customs could not well stand the test of dogmatic authorization.   But there was no need of this as long as the dogma and the church but left room for them. It must not be forgotten that it was only at the Council of Trent —and then only under the pressure of the opposition of the Protestant church and its Augustana—that Roman Catholicism secured any consistent system of ecclesiastical doctrine.   It is, therefore, not difficult to understand that, now that the strain of the conflict has been moderated by time, the church should gradually sink back into the medieval forms, although a somewhat different shading may be given by the influence of Jesuit skill upon the character and temper of the modern church life.   In the Oriental churches, dogma has become a mystery and a relic (supra, Vol. I., p. 306); the mystagogy of worship is to produce life. In the West, it has become chiefly a means for discipline and an incentive to obedience ; but—at least in the present age—it ap-

---

[1] Vid. esp. REUSCH, Die deutschen Bischöfe u. der Aberglaube, 1879. For Italy material is furnished in TREDE, Das Heidentum in der kath.-Kirche, 1889 ff.

pears to represent as little vital influence in the church as in the
Middle Ages.   And yet the Roman Catholic church has of late
again—not without some effort—urged the study of Thomas and
prescribed it as a panacea.. Truly it is possible to adorn the
graves of the prophets without catching their spirit!   But no
one can deny that, even in Catholic theology, the spirit of serious
labor and earnest effort has not died out.   Are there still lurking here the elements which are yet to infuse into Roman Catholicism the "principle of progress" (Schell)?   Shall scientific
culture—as Thomas understood it—or shall the ecclesiasticism of
the Ultramontanes assume the spiritual leadership in the further
doctrinal development of Roman Catholism ?

Be that as it may, the Protestant student of the History of
Doctrines cannot turn from the subject without calling attention
to the different conception of Dogma which prevails in his own
church as contrasted with the positions which the churches of the
East and of Rome have finally assigned to their dogmatic utterances.   It was the church of the "pure doctrine" which made
Dogma again a vital and powerful factor in history.   Luther put new
life into the ancient dogma.   It had become a toy of theology ;
he made it a sword of the Spirit.   The ideas embodied in divine
revelation, not mysticism nor magic, are to give birth and guidance to the church of the gospel.   "Doctrine" and "dogma"
have their source in the ideas grasped by faith.   The evangelical
church as such cannot sink into "undogmatic Christianity"—
there is always in the individual soul an eternal "undogmatic"
life—without losing its very life.   But while the church clings
steadfastly to her doctrine, she does it, and must ever do it, in
the spirit of Luther.   This will mean : (1) That the dogma
which she proclaims, and which regulates her preaching, must be
the *evangelical doctrine of salvation.*   Her doctrines must find
their source in the redemption which is in Christ, and their goal
must be faith in Christ.   They must be from faith and for faith.
The significance of this may be most clearly seen in the teachings of Luther himself, above all in the manifest relation of his
interpretation of the Creed to the Creed itself.   (2) That the
evangelical church must always continue to labor upon her dogmatic statements, always ready—not only in principle and in word
—to prove and improve them upon the basis of the divine revelation given in the Scriptures.   From this it follows, (3) That the
evangelical church highly values a free theology, in the assured
conviction that such a theology has a vital function to perform in

the church of the pure doctrine.   The immense accumulations of dogmatic tradition will otherwise rest heavily upon her, as upon the Romish and the Oriental churches.   She cannot pass around this mountain by any arts of interpretation or of silence, but must surmount it.   It is true, life itself will here silently and unobserved accomplish much.   The course of the ages alters the accentuation placed upon various parts of the traditional doctrinal structure.   Some members of the organism become rudimentary and others attain fuller development.   But all of this will not suffice.   If evangelical theology is not to become merely an episode of the "History of Religion," if it is to remain an ecclesiastical science—and who will seriously doubt that it shall so remain?—then must it in the future, as in the past, recognize its calling to study the treasures of tradition with all the means which God has given to man, with all the watchfulness and keen criticism which the importance of the subject demands (biblical and historical theology), and, upon the basis of this earnest and conscientious study, seek the forms and formulas which the age may require for a proper comprehension of the gospel (systematic theology).   The "ancient truth" remains; the method of presenting it will change, as it has constantly changed in the past.   From this may be readily understood the entirely different attitude which the Protestant—Luther himself being an illustrious example—assumes toward the dogma of the church from that which the Roman Catholic must hold.   Even the thought of a "new dogma" has for him—however fully he may realize the immense historical difficulties which such a proposition would have to face, since all the forms of the church's life are attached to the ancient dogma[1]—nothing repulsive in principle, so long and in so far as this should be a true expression of the divine revelation in the Scriptures.

But against one stupendous error must the spirit of the Protestant world be ever scrupulously upon its guard, viz.: the delusion so readily embraced by the ecclesiastical politician, that sufficient honor has been accorded to the dogma of the church when it is publicly confessed and silence maintained as to the points in which it contradicts the convictions personally held.   We may in our day hear voices openly raised in defense even of the ancient delusion of "implicit faith."   The principles above stated protest with united voice against this thoroughly unevangelical position, and the protest is abundantly confirmed by the History of Doctrines.[2]   What we Protestants need is a living and life-

[1] Cf., e. g., LASSON, Zur Theorie des Dogmas, 1897, p. 18 ff., 100 f., 112, 120.

[2] The demand might at this point be made, that the History of Doctrines

producing, an intelligible and convincing system of doctrine
(dogma)—not a relic of the past nor a manual of ascetic practices (supra, 463, 430). Such a system of doctrine the evangelical church possesses in the ancient symbols and the Confession of the Reformation. To comprehend and give proper expression to the religious depth and the wealth of practical suggestion of these inherited treasures, with unhesitating return, if
need be, to the ideas of the original sources of evangelical truth
—the *ritornar al segno*—is the task of the Protestant theology
of the present, and, in a measure also, of the History of Doctrines.

should trace the development of Christian teaching down to the present time
(cf. the works of BAUR and HAGENBACH upon the subject, and KRÜGER :
Was heisst and zu welchem Zweck studirt man DG. ? 1895). But, although
the possibility of thus extending the scope of the History of Doctrines must be
granted, yet we must maintain also the scientific propriety of the presentation
of the publicly acknowledged and binding statements of the church's official
doctrine. It is a historical fact, to be recognized by the historian—whether or
not it be in accord with his own preferences—that the church of the present
knows and acknowledges such a public doctrine (*doctrine publica*). Our
position is confirmed by the consideration, that in any such "History of
Modern Theology" there would be lacking the organic principle of the proper
History of Doctrines, viz.: the relation of the views therein delineated to the
Dogma of the future ; for who shall to-day venture to say which of the negations and affirmations, which of the buttressing arguments and destructive
criticisms, which of the omissions and supplements registered in the progressive history of theology, shall lead to the completer Dogma of the future ? The
history of theology may be represented as the history of the varying experiences
of Dogma ; but to attempt to treat it as "Prolegomena to any and every
future" dogma is a most indefinite and uncertain task. The writing of a history of modern theology—when one considers the state of the investigations
which must necessarily precede such delineation—is in itself an undertaking
sufficiently great, without the complication of keeping ever in mind the relation
of the theological views of the present to the yet unknown official statements of
the future.

Finally, even a history of the Union (cf. LOOFS, DG. 462 f.) does not, in
my opinion, strictly speaking, lie within the province of the History of Doctrines ; for the Union, as known to history, did not effect any transformation
or reconstruction of the dogmas of the church. The original aim to accomplish
something of this character spent its force in a comparatively short time. Cf.
the decree of the Cabinet, February 28, 1834 : "The Union indicates and
effects no surrender of the previous confession of faith, nor is the authority
which has been hitherto enjoyed by the confessional writings of the two evangelical confessions destroyed by it. Adherence to it is merely an exhibition
of the spirit of moderation and mildness," etc. The details of the movement lie within the sphere of Symbolics.

INDEX.

A.

Abelard, estimate of, 56, 57 f., 62, 64, 96, 98, 100 n., 185 ; opposition to, 60 ; on reason, fai+h, tradition, Scriptures, 58 ; Trinity, 58 f.; sacraments, 59, 7ᶜ, 79 ; knowledge, 60 ; person of Christ, 64, 155 ; atonement, 70, 110 ; love, 71 ; Lord's Supper, 77 n.; repentance, 81 f.; contrition, forgiveness, 81 ; confession, 81, 92 n.; purgatory, 81 ; satisfaction, 82 ; communion of saints, 144.

Ability, human. In Gregory, 21 f.; Semi-Augustinians, 32 f.; Thomas, 118 f.; Bonaventura, 120 ; Biel, 138 ; Duns, 159 ; Bradwardina, 207 ; Luther, 243 f., 256 ; Zwingli, 313 ; Augsburg Confession, 335 ; Melanchthon, 349 ; Synergistic controversy, 367 f.; Formula of Concord, 383 ; Calvin, 399 ; Arminius, 421 ; Remonstrants, 422 ; Amyraldus, 425 ; Council of Trent, 433 f.; Quesnel, 455 n.

Absolution. In Gregory, 24 ; Early Middle Ages, 44 ; Hugo, 82, 92 ; Pullus, 83 ; Lombard, 83, 92 ; Gratian, 92 ; Council of Treves, 92 n.; Thomas, Duns, 137 f.; Bonaventura, 137 f., 142 n.; Durand, 142 n.; John of Paltz, 176 ; Wessel, 210 ; Luther, 234, 240 ; Augsburg Confession, 342 ; Council of Trent, 438, 442, 444.

Acceptants. In Unigenitus controversy, 455.

Adiaphora, 388.

Adiaphoristic controversy, 364.

Adoptionist controversy, 27 f.

Advent, Second, 344.

Aegidius of Colonna, works of, 187 ; on sin and grace, 187 ; immaculate conception, 188 n.

Aepinus. On descent into hell, 377.

Agobard, works of, 27 ; on Scriptures, 101 n.

Agricola. On law and gospel, 251, 366.

Alanus ab Insulis. On attrition, contrition, 136 f.; preaching, 92 n.

Albert, The Great. Works of, 96, 98 ; philosophy of, 99, 105 ; influence of, 99 ; on original state, 114 ; infused grace, 115 ; sacraments, 128 ; confirmation, 130 ; Lord's Supper, 134 ; extreme unction, 140 ; marriage, 143.

Albert of Padua, philosophy of, 187.

Alberus, Zwingli's letter to, 319.

Alcuin, works of, 27, 29 ; on Adoptionism, 28 ; Lord's Supper, 35.

Alexander III. On Nihilianism, 65 ; and Jansenists, 454.

Alexander of Hales, estimate of, 98 f.; on person and work of Christ, 110 f.; original state, synteresis, 114 ; original sin, 116 ; indelible character, 128 ; sacraments, 125 f., 126 n.; Lord's Supper, 131 f., 133 ; repentance, 135 f.; attrition, contrition, 136 f.

Alger. On Lord's Supper, 76 f.

Alloeosis. In Zwingli, 321 ; Luther, 324.

31

Christ, 65 ; Lord's Supper, 77;
sacraments, 79; repentance, contrition, confirmation, ordination,
purgatory, 81.

Roman Catholic Church before the
Reformation, 146 ; reformation
within, 428 ; modern condition of,
463 f.; Luther on, 289, 294 ; Melanchthon on, 355.

Roman Catholic Theology, sources
for, 427 ; estimate of, 427 f., 430,
431 ; Thomistic character of, 428 ;
influence of Duns upon, 428, 431 ;
and Paul, 455 ; and opposing
schools, 428, 431, 432, 433, 438,
439.

Romans, Epistles to, Luther on, 301.

Rome, councils at, 29, 76.

Roscellin, philosophy of, 56 ; on
Trinity, 56.

Rupert. On Lord's Supper, 78 n.

S.

Sabbath. In Erasmus, 215 n.; Luther, 246, 247 n.; Zwingli, 311,
n. 1.

Sacraments. In Abelard, 59, 72, 79 ;
Hugo, 61, 79, 80; Lombard, 63,80;
Anselm, 72; Bernard, Roland, Pullus,Omnebene, St.Florian,79; Berthold, 93 ; Later Middle Ages, 98,
124 f.; Eugene IV., 125 ; Thomas,
Bonaventura, 125 f.; Alexander,
125, 126 n.; Duns, 127 f., 161 ;
Albert, 128 ; Biel, 187, 200 ;
Luther, 235, 279, 282 ; Zwingli,
316 ; Augsburg Confession, 341 f.;
Apology, 343 ; Calvin, 411 ff.;
Reformed theology, 415, 418 ;
Consensus Tigurinus, 417 ; Reformed Confessions, 345 ; Council
of Trent, 438 f.; definition of, 79,
80, 93, 125, 411 ; number of,
37 n., 63, 79, 80, 93, 125, 135,

282, 316, 439 ; place of, in dogmatic system, 59 ; validity of, 94 ;
matter and form of, 126 ; intention in, 125 ; as symbols, 126,
127 f., 282, 316, 411, 417, 439 ;
as pledges, 411 ; and word, 78,
123 n., 285 f., 411 ; administered
by heretics, 50, 51, 142 ; benefits
of, 80, 93, 127, 345.

Saints, communion of, 144 f., 212,
235, 286 f., 291 ff., 408.

Saints, intercession of. In Early
Middle Ages, 44, 91 ; Waldenses,
94 ; Thomas, 124 ; Later Middle
Ages, 173 ; Augsburg Confession,
344 ; Council of Trent, 445.

Saliger. On Lord's Supper, 367 n.

Salmeron. On divine right, 447 n.

Salvation, causes of, 405, n. 1 ; of
souls, 94, 225.

Sanctification, in Apology, 338 ; Luther, Melanchthon, 360 ; Southwestern Germany, 390 ; Calvin,
402, 404 (see Life, New).

Sanfelice, evangelical views of, 434,
n. 2.

Satisfaction. In Early Middle Ages,
43, 47 ; Anselm, 67 f.; Roland,
81 ; Abelard, Hugo, 82 ; Lombard, 83, 92 ; council at Aachen,
84 ; Thomas, Duns, 139 ; Eugene
IV., 140 ; Wessel, 210 ; Luther,
234, 241, 265 f., 267, n. 2, 268,
n. 1 ; Council of Trent, 435, 438,
443, 444 ; Bajus, 451 n.

Savonarola. On asceticism, church
and state, 198 n.; politics, 318.

Scepticism, Abelard, 58 ; thirteenth
century, 60 ; Frederick II., 91.

Scholasticism, estimate of, 54 ff., 57,
105, 146, 196, 214 ; in Luther,
223 ; Luther on, 224.

Schnepf. On Lord's Supper, 331 n.

Schwabach Articles, 330,

Schwabian Concord, 382 n.

Duns, 153 ; Biel, 197 ; Council of
Trent, 432 n.; Bajus, 450.
States of Christ, 325 n., 376 f., 387.
Stephen of Paris, philosophy of, 98.
Strigel. In Synergistic controversy,
367 f.
Stuttgart, synod at, 366.
Subjective vs. objective, 191.
Sufferings of Christ. In Gregory, 19,
53 ; Anselm, 69 ; Thomas, 112 f.;
Duns, 156 f.; Luther, 266 f. (see
Atonement, Work of Christ).
Supererogation, works of, 23, 124,
139.
Superstition, 49.
Symbols, estimate of, 466 ; the an-
cient, in Gregory, 18 ; Thomas,
Bonaventura, Anselm, Alexander,
Richard, Durand, 102 ; Duns,
149 ; Luther, 303 ; Zwingli, 317 ;
Melanchthon, 348, 352 ; Calvin,
396 ; later Reformed theology,
419 n.
Synergism, controversy upon, 267 ff. ;
in Formula of Concord, 384; Coun-
cil of Trent, 433, 435 f.; Molina,
451 f.
Syngramma, 320.
Synod, at Alençon, 425 ; Dort, 421 ;
Eisenach, 365 ; France, 425 ;
Pistoja, 445 n. 1, 458 ; Stuttgart,
366 ; Torgau, 367 (see Council).

T.

Tauler, works of, 178 ; on word and
sacraments, 128 ; imitation of
Christ, 178 f.
Tetrapolitan Confession, 344 f.
Theodulf. On filioque, 30.
Theology, Systematic. In Abelard,
59 ; Honorius, Hugo, 61 ; John
of Damascus, Lombard, 63 ; Mid-
dle Ages, 96, 189, 214; Albert,
Thomas, 99 ; Gerson, 189 ; Me-

lanchthon, 348, 362, 363 ; nature
of, 104 n., 149, 150 n.; German,
178.
Thomas of Aquino, estimate of, 96,
97, 98, 99, 100, 146, 185, 224 ;
method of, 99 ; on God, 100, 107;
revelation, 100 f.; Scriptures, 101 ;
faith, 103, 121 ; will, 103 ; universals, 104 ; Trinity, 100, 109 ;
communicatio idiomatum, 110 ;
person of Christ, 110 f.; work of
Christ, 111 f.; intercession of
Christ, 113 ; fruits of redemption,
113 ; synteresis, 114 ; original
state, 114 f.; infused grace, 115,
119 ; original sin, 116 ; forgiveness, 112 f., 121 ; free-will, 119 f.;
justification, 120 f.; faith, 103,
120 ; guilt, 117 ; grace, 115, 118 ;
good works, 116, 121 ; human
merit, 116, 121 f., 124 ; merit of
Christ, 113 ; monastic life, 124 ;
sacraments, 125 f.; indelible character, 128 ; baptism, 130 ; Lord's
Supper, 133 ; repentance, 134 f.;
contrition, 136 f.; confession, absolution, 137 f.; indulgences, satisfaction, 139 ; extreme unction, 140;
ordination, 141 ; marriage, 142 ;
church, 144 f.; pope, 102, 145 f.;
blessedness, 148.
Thomas of Bradwardina. On person
of Christ, 110 ; predestination,
189, 207.
Thomas of Strassburg, philosophy of,
187 ; on immaculate conception,
188 n.; Lord's Supper, 204.
Thomas sel Vio (see Cajetan).
Tilmann. On Eucharistic controversy, 366.
Timann. On Eucharistic controversy
366.
Torgau, synod at, 367.
Torgau Book, 382 n.
Toucy, council at, 33.